D0890266

4th EDITION

health psychology

To the love of my life, Martha Ahrendt. You exemplify all the research showing just how valuable having a strong source of social support is. Thank you.

4th EDITION

health psychology

WELL-BEING *in a* DIVERSE WORLD

Regan A. R. Gurung

University of Wisconsin–Green Bay

Los Angeles | London | New Delhi
Singapore | Washington DC | Melbourne

FOR INFORMATION:

SAGE Publications, Inc.
2455 Teller Road
Thousand Oaks, California 91320
E-mail: order@sagepub.com

SAGE Publications Ltd.
1 Oliver's Yard
55 City Road
London EC1Y 1SP
United Kingdom

SAGE Publications India Pvt. Ltd.
B 1/I 1 Mohan Cooperative Industrial Area
Mathura Road, New Delhi 110 044
India

SAGE Publications Asia-Pacific Pte. Ltd.
3 Church Street
#10-04 Samsung Hub
Singapore 049483

Printed in Canada

ISBN 978-1-5063-9236-3

Acquisitions Editor: Lara Parra
Content Development Editor: Emma Newsom
Editorial Assistant: Zachary Valladon
Production Editor: Olivia Weber-Stenis
Copy Editor: Alison Hope
Typesetter: C&M Digitals (P) Ltd.
Proofreader: Theresa Kay
Indexer: Mary Harper
Cover Designer: Gail Buschman
Marketing Manager: Katherine Hepburn

This book is printed on acid-free paper.

18 19 20 21 22 10 9 8 7 6 5 4 3 2 1

BRIEF CONTENTS

iStockphoto.com/ maodesign

DETAILED CONTENTS

iStockphoto.com/ RoBeDeRo

andresr/ E+/ Getty Images

iStockphoto.com/ imtmphoto

Steve Debenport/ E+ / Getty Images

iStockphoto.com/ Allkindza

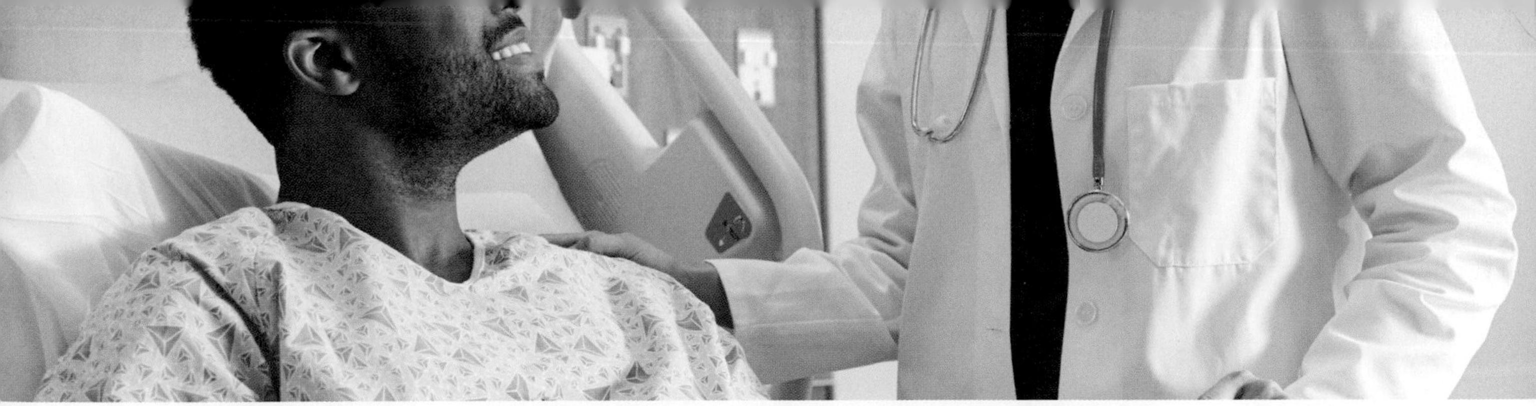
iStockphoto.com/ monkeybusinessimages

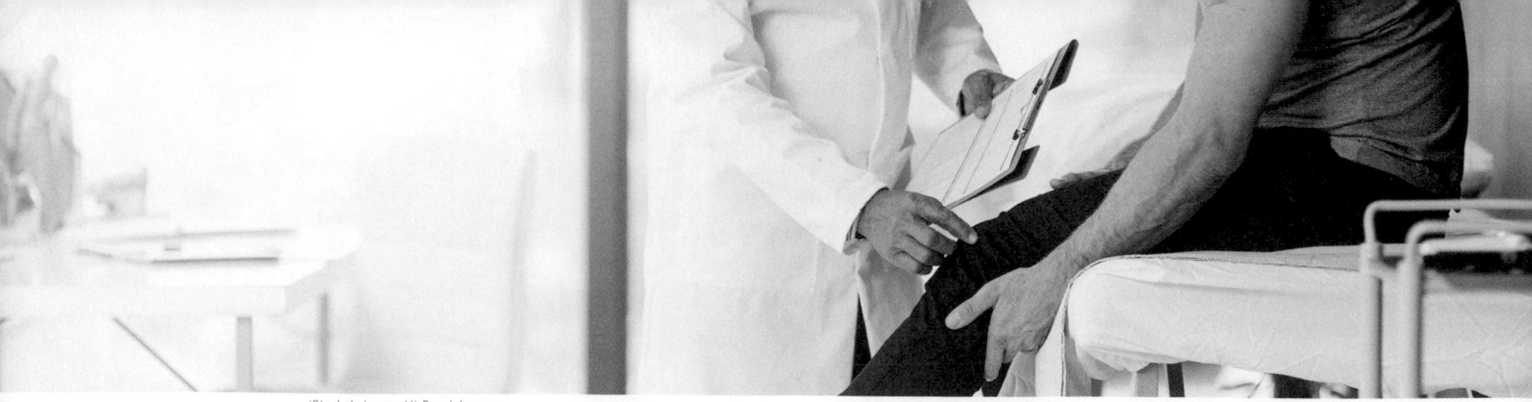
iStockphoto.com/ it:PeopleImages

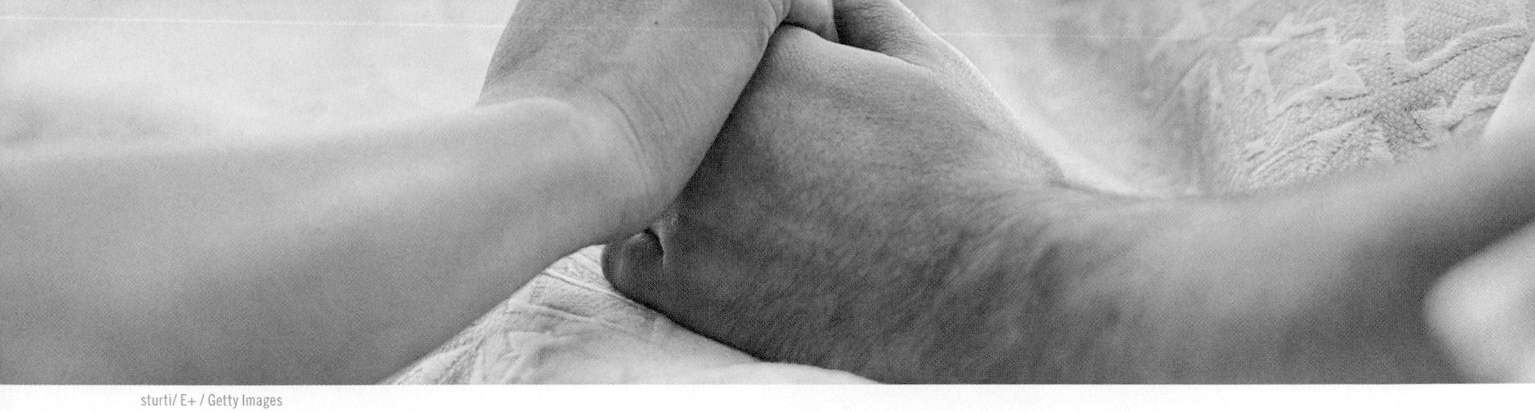

sturti/ E+ / Getty Images

iStockphoto.com/ KatarzynaBialasiewicz

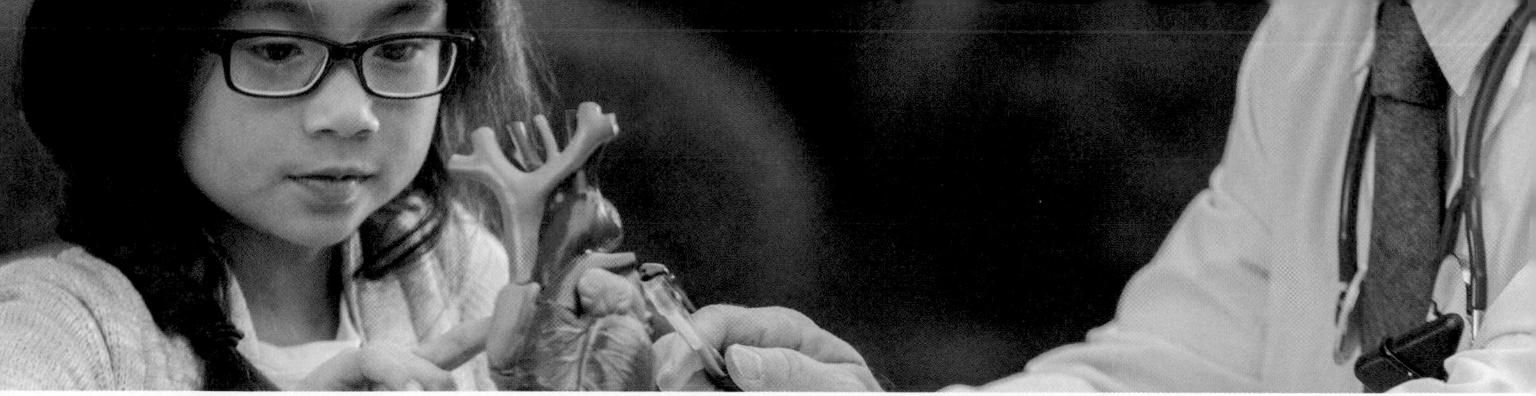

Steve Debenport/ E+/ Getty Images

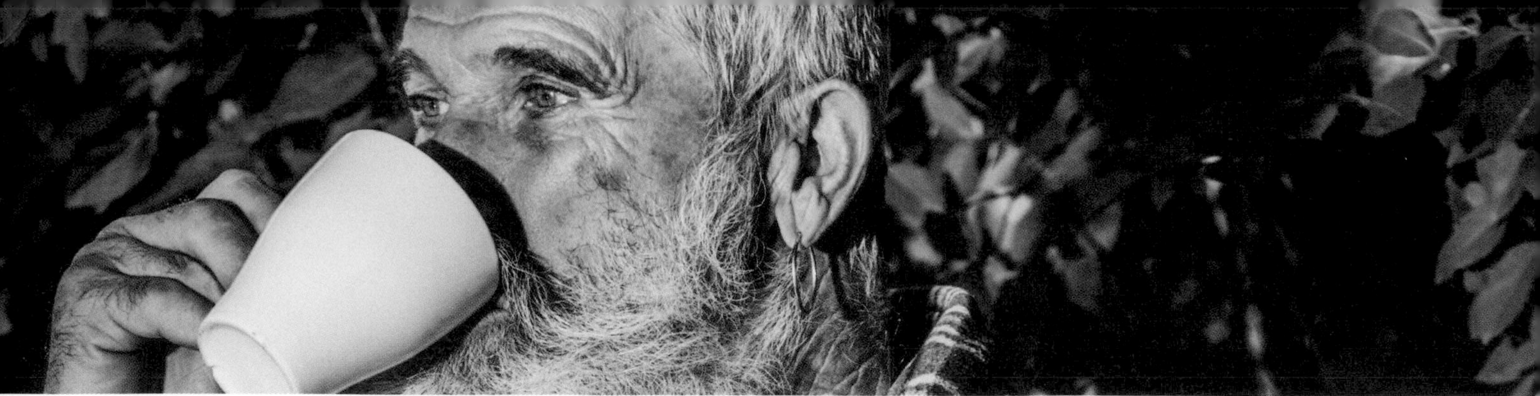
iStockphoto.com/ CasarsaGuru

PREFACE

PHILOSOPHY

I knew culture and diversity were important when I first pitched this book more than 15 years ago. They are even more important today. In 2018 there are great health disparities in America and a cultural discomfort that most college-aged students have never lived through before. There continue to be significant differences in health behaviors and the incidence of illnesses such as coronary heart disease and cancer across ethnic groups. It is crucial for researchers to acknowledge these cultural differences. The limited attention to diversity catalyzed me to present an introduction to health psychology with a cultural approach. In this fourth edition, I have further fine-tuned the cultural focus and explained more thoroughly how culture is an important predictor of health. I have aimed to focus more on well-being in general and to enhance the discussion of diversity. I even changed my subtitle to reflect this focus. I also took the opportunity to use a more applied approach to make the material even more relevant to readers' everyday lives. With the multitude of new and exciting research in the field published monthly, this fourth edition offers an opportunity to update you on new developments in diversity and health.

THIS EDITION

The goals of this fourth edition are to examine how you can study the areas of health, illness, and medicine from a psychological and cultural perspective and to introduce the main topics and issues in the area of health psychology. This is in combination with providing training to judge the scientific quality of research on psychology and medicine. I begin by describing what health psychology is all about, emphasizing the importance of cultural competence. In a new chapter for this edition I highlight research methods in health psychology and provide a primer to navigating research in scholarly publications. I build on these basics with a revealing chapter on cultural variations in health beliefs and behaviors (how do shamans, acupuncture, yoga, and sweat lodges fit into health?). Our physiology is an important determinant of health. Chapter 4 describes essential physiological systems and processes that will aid your understanding of the different topics discussed later in the book. I then unravel the mysteries of stress and the ways to cope. In Chapters 5 and 6, I discuss the theories explaining stress and the many practical ways to alleviate it. Armed with tools to make everyday life stress-free, I turn to another common aspect of life: health behaviors that many of us do (or try to do more often) and those we try not to do. Chapter 7 describes some of the ways we can change health behaviors, and Chapter 8 describes some of the behaviors in detail. The second half of the book turns to topics relating to sickness, such as factors that surround illness (such as adherence and patient–practitioner interactions; Chapter 9), pain (Chapter 10), and chronic illnesses, terminal illness, and death (Chapter 11), before examining some of the major health concerns and illnesses plaguing society today (such as HIV, cancer, and cardiovascular disease; Chapters 12 to 14). Finally, I identify the major challenges faced by those in the field of health psychology (and provide some avenues for future exploration and training in this area).

Each chapter first lets you measure yourself. In a new pedagogical addition, I have added Measuring Up sections. Each features an actual published scale that lets you see where you stand. I then provide you with three major questions in a new Ponder This section. There is an outline of the topics covered as well as a clear preamble to the main topics of the chapter to orient your reading. Every chapter ends with a summary to help you review the major points and a list of the key terms, concepts, and people. Sections called "Synthesize, Evaluate, Apply" serve to break up the chapters into easy, manageable segments and allow you to test your knowledge. In addition, each chapter ends with ten multiple-choice questions to help further your comprehension. Finally,

I have provided a short list of *absolute must-reads*—a selection of essential readings comprising classic articles in the field or contemporary research studies regarding some of the material most cited by health psychologists. These are essentially the articles that are most likely to be used in any writing on the topic. You will get insights into the field and feel a better part of it if you read them.

If you think I have missed something, if you have a suggestion for how this book can be improved, if you want to share a way that your culture has influenced your health, or even if you want to share that you really enjoyed learning about health psychology using this book (that's my goal), you may contact me by email at gurungr@uwgb.edu.

WHAT ELSE IS NEW?

A lot. As luck would have it, I just finished a major editing project. I am coeditor of a new edition of the *Handbook of Health Psychology* and got to read 40 chapters written by experts in the field. This reading shaped this revision, enabling me to make sure you have the latest on the field of health psychology. This edition covers all the major subdisciplines of health psychology. I also coauthored a paper reporting on a national survey of professors of health psychology courses, conducted with the cooperation of the Society for Health Psychology (Division 38 of the American Psychological Association). This study again helped me revise the text with an eye to what teachers want and need (Panjwani, Gurung, & Revenson, 2017).

Nothing saved me from reading a lot of published literature. To ensure you get to read the most updated information, this new edition is based on more than 1,000 new research articles cited. Additionally, as a testament to my commitment to providing you with a robust scientific introduction to the field, I enforce the chapter discussions with relevant and interesting citations.

There are some major changes to this edition. In every chapter I have provided more information on how the topics discussed are measured by health psychologists in the field. Interested in coping? The relevant chapter has the most recent coping measures and the most used ones. This emphasis on measurement reflects the field's greater focus on the same. Speaking of measurement, I now have an entirely new chapter on research methods. Having it as part of the first chapter in the first three editions was acceptable, but research is the foundation of psychological science. The stand-alone chapter on methods now is a testament to this.

I have shortened many chapters and rearranged some topics to allow for better reading. For example, I moved some information on culture from the first chapter to the third. I also noted that the chapter on health behaviors (e.g., smoking and exercise) was very unwieldy. It is now divided into two parts to make the material easier to digest.

I have completely overhauled the artwork program with the help of some great editorial assistance. There are new photographs, reworked figures and graphs, and current examples related to recent events in the news.

ACKNOWLEDGMENTS

Together with those who fueled my passion for health psychology (acknowledged in my first edition, but Shelley Taylor, Christine Dunkel-Schetter, and Margaret Kemeny in particular) and those who first helped me get this project off the ground (especially Michele Sordi), I am grateful to the friends I have made in the field over the last ten years. Tracey Revenson in particular, with her passion for diversity and expertise in health psychology, has been a great muse and kept me honest with this new addition. I salute the wonderful students I have had the pleasure to teach using this book. They have helped me make this fourth edition even stronger. The many colleagues who used this book have also been wonderful resources, providing useful suggestions for improvement. I am also grateful to the increased efforts of community organizations in my home city of Green Bay, Wisconsin (shout out to Wello) for working to increase well-being and address the diverse approaches to health.

Lara Parra, my editor at SAGE, has been a joy to work with helping me transition between publishers. Emma Newsom provided valuable suggestions to improve this revision and did a lot of the heavy lifting through production. I would also like to thank all the SAGE staff who worked behind the scenes in bringing this book to life and to Zachary Valladon in particular for his help in finding photographs that fit. He is one chill dude. Speaking of chill, a special thank you to Roz Stoa, UW–Green Bay psychology major par excellence. She was particularly instrumental in my finding the most up-to-date research papers.

A number of dedicated reviewers read draft chapters and the first edition and suggested insightful improvements. In particular the following people provided invaluable comments:

Karen Linville Baker, University of Memphis Lambuth

Erin M. Fekete, University of Indianapolis

Joel A. Hagaman, University of the Ozarks

Michael Lindsey, Dedman College of Humanities and Science

Angie MacKewn, The University of Tennessee at Martin

Erin Wood, Catawba College

I am particularly grateful to my wife, Martha Ahrendt, for her patience during the entire process. She not only tolerated the times I needed to be focused on this revision, but also read drafts and shared her own expertise. A special shout out to my son and daughter who always listened with rapt attention to the latest research I shared with them almost daily.

ABOUT THE AUTHOR

REGAN A. R. GURUNG is the Ben J. and Joyce Rosenberg Professor of Human Development Psychology at the University of Wisconsin–Green Bay.

Born and raised in Bombay, India, Dr. Gurung received a Bachelor of Arts in psychology at Carleton College (Minnesota) and Master of Science (MS) and doctoral (PhD) degrees in social and personality psychology at the University of Washington (Washington State). He followed with 3 years at the University of California, Los Angeles, as a National Institute of Mental Health (NIMH) research fellow.

His early work focused on social support and close relationships; he studied how perceptions of support from close others influence relationship satisfaction. His later work investigated cultural differences in coping with stressors such as HIV infection, pregnancy, and smoking cessation. He continues to explore cultural differences in health and is heavily involved in pedagogical research directed toward improving teaching and student learning.

He has received numerous local, state, and national grants for his research in health psychology and social psychology regarding cultural differences in stress, social support, smoking cessation, body image, and impression formation. He has published articles in a variety of scholarly journals, including the *American Psychologist, Psychological Review,* and *Personality and Social Psychology Bulletin,* and is a frequent presenter at national and international conferences. He is the author, coauthor, or editor of fourteen other books including the *Handbook of Health Psychology* (2019, with Tracey Revenson), a two-volume *Multicultural Approaches to Health and Wellness in America* (2014), *Easyguide to APA* [American Psychological Association] *Style* (2017, with Eric Landrum and Beth Schwartz), *Culture & Mental Health: Sociocultural Influences on Mental Health* (2009, with Sussie Eshun), *Getting Culture: Incorporating Diversity across the Curriculum* (2009, with Loreto Prieto), and *Exploring Signature Pedagogies: Approaches to Teaching Disciplinary Habits of Mind* (2009, with Nancy Chick and Aeron Haynie). Dr. Gurung is also a dedicated teacher and has interests in enhancing faculty development and student understanding. He is codirector of the University of Wisconsin (UW) System Teaching Scholars Program, has been a UW–Green Bay teaching fellow and a UW System teaching scholar. In 2017 he won the American Psychological Foundation's prestigious Charles L. Brewer Award for Distinguished Teaching in Psychology. He also has won the Carnegie Association's Wisconsin Professor of the Year (2010), the UW System Regent's Teaching Award (2011), the UW–Green Bay Founder's Award for Excellence in Teaching Excellence in Scholarship, and the UW Teaching at Its Best, Creative Teaching, and Featured Faculty awards. He has organized statewide and national teaching conferences and is an active member and past president of the Society for the Teaching of Psychology (American Psychological Association [APA]-Division 2). He is an elected fellow of the American Psychological Association and Association for Psychological Science and will be the president of the Psi Chi International Honor Society in Psychology in 2019.

When not reading, writing, or helping people stay calm, Regan enjoys culinary explorations, travel, and immersing himself in his son's and daughter's latest pursuits.

FOUNDATIONS OF HEALTH PSYCHOLOGY

CHAPTER 1

WHAT IS HEALTH?

Cultural and Historical Roots

iStockphoto.com/ maodesign

Chapter 1 Outline

MEASURING UP

HOW HEALTHY ARE YOU?

1. In general, would you say your health is
   a. Excellent
   b. Very good
   c. Good
   d. Fair
   e. Poor

2. How TRUE or FALSE is **each** of the following statements for you?

	Definitely true	Mostly true	Don't know	Mostly false	Definitely false
I seem to get sick a little easier than other people	1	2	3	4	5
I am as healthy as anybody I know	1	2	3	4	5
I expect my health to get worse	1	2	3	4	5
My health is excellent	1	2	3	4	5

3. During the **past 4 weeks**, how much of the time has **your physical health or emotional problems** interfered with your social activities (like visiting with friends, relatives, etc.)?
   a. All of the time
   b. Most of the time
   c. Some of the time
   d. A little of the time
   e. None of the time

WHAT IS THIS? WHY DOES IT MATTER?

These are items from the general health subscale of the 36-Item Short Form Health Survey (SF-36). RAND developed this scale as part of the Medical Outcomes Study (MOS), a multiyear, multisite study to explain variations in patient outcomes. This is a very common measure of self-rated health (Benyamini, 2016).

▼ Ponder This

> How do you define health, and what signifies being healthy?
>
> Could how you think about life be as important as the way your brain is wired?
>
> If you like health and helping people can health psychology be the career for you?

Are you healthy? Sounds like a simple question to answer, right? Take a moment to consider it. What is your answer? If you are like most people, you probably think that you are reasonably healthy. Even if you do not think you are like most people, you may be more like most people than you know. Be warned, most people do not think that they are like most other people and this has health consequences, as you will see later. How did you arrive at your answer? Did you quickly drop down on the floor and see how many push-ups or sit-ups you could perform and how fatigued the exercises made you? Did you put down this book (or e-reader) and time how long it took you to sprint to the corner and back? Maybe you put a finger on your wrist and took your pulse. More than likely, if you do not presently have a cold or other illness, if you have not recently stumbled and twisted an ankle, or if you do not have any other physical ailment, you probably answered the opening question with a statement like, "Yes, pretty healthy, I guess."

RESEARCHER SPOTLIGHT

> Dr. Yael Benyamini has a PhD in health and social psychology and teaches assessment at Tel Aviv University in Israel. She has a great chapter on self-rated health assessment (Benyamini, 2016; see Essential Readings).

For most people living in the United States, basic indicators of good health include the absence of disease, injury, or illness; a slow pulse; the ability to perform many physical exercises; or the ability to run fast. The self-report health measure the chapter opens with is one simple way to measure your health (Benyamini, 2016). You may be surprised to learn that these all represent only one general way of being healthy, the one supported by Western medicine and as seen on multiple shows on Netflix, Hulu, and Amazon Prime, not to mention on the big screen. The definition of what is healthy varies from person to person and is strongly influenced by his or her way of thinking and his or her upbringing. For some, being happy signifies good health. For others, being spiritually satisfied signifies good health. Are some people right and others wrong? What are the best ways to measure health and what are the different factors that influence how healthy we will be? In particular, what are the psychological and sociocultural factors that influence health?

The United States is a diverse nation with approximately 321 million citizens (U.S. Census Bureau, 2017). Not all Americans are similarly healthy (Arcaya & Figueroa, 2017; Gurung, 2014). For example, death rates for African Americans are significantly higher than those of Americans overall due to heart disease, cancer, diabetes, HIV, and homicide (Edwards et al., 2019; Noonan, Velasco-Mondragon, & Wagner, 2016). Corresponding to such differences, the U.S. health-care system has been making active attempts to broaden approaches toward health care in order to fulfill the needs of the diverse population (Schooler & Baum, 2000) and advance knowledge about different cultures or cultural competence (see below, Purnell & Pontious, 2014). Unfortunately, the differences between cultural groups is getting worse due to several trends such as changing health-care technologies, health-care access and reform policies (e.g., Affordable Care Act), widening gaps in income and education, and environmental hazards (Arcaya & Figueroa, 2017). There are critical cultural variations in the conceptualization, perception, health-seeking behaviors, assessment, diagnosis, and treatment of abnormal behaviors and physical sickness.

Many Americans also have different answers to questions about health. For example, ask a child what being healthy is, and it is almost certain that his or her answer will be different from that of an older person. Someone earning less than $13,000 a year will probably answer differently than someone making more than $100,000 a year. A Catholic will probably answer differently than a Buddhist or a Hindu or a Muslim (Von Dras, 2017). Essentially, a person's cultural background, ethnicity, age, gender, and educational level make substantial differences in how he or she answers. Furthermore, our many different actions influence our health—things that often vary by culture as well. The amount of sweetened carbonated beverages that you drink can make a difference; younger people tend to drink more of these types of beverages than older people do.

What you eat, including the amount of fast food you eat, makes a difference too. As with beverage consumption, some ethnic groups tend to eat more fast food than other groups.

In fact, the answer to the simple question, "Are you healthy?" can vary according to where you live, how old you are, what your parents and friends think constitutes health, what your religious or ethnic background is, and what a variety of other factors indicate about you (Gurung, 2012). If you live in California, where the sun shines most of the time, your health habits are probably different than they would be if you live in Wisconsin, where it is often overcast (Nelson et al., 2002). Though both states are leading producers of dairy products in the United States, statistically, Wisconsinites tend to weigh significantly more than Californians. (Is it too much cheese? Is it the lack of sun?) Factors such as where you live, your age, or your ethnicity interact with others to influence what you do and how healthy you will be. "**Culture**" is the term that adequately captures all these different elements that influence health. Thus, the focus of this book is on how our cultural backgrounds influence our health, shape healthy behaviors, prevent illness, and enhance our health and well-being. The schematic diagram in Figure 1.1 provides a map for the route we will take in this book.

▲ **Different Pictures of Health.** These individuals may seem healthy to the naked eye. It is important to also look beyond mere physiological health and the lack of disease and consider mental, spiritual, and emotional health.

▼ FIGURE 1.1

Health and Its Correlates

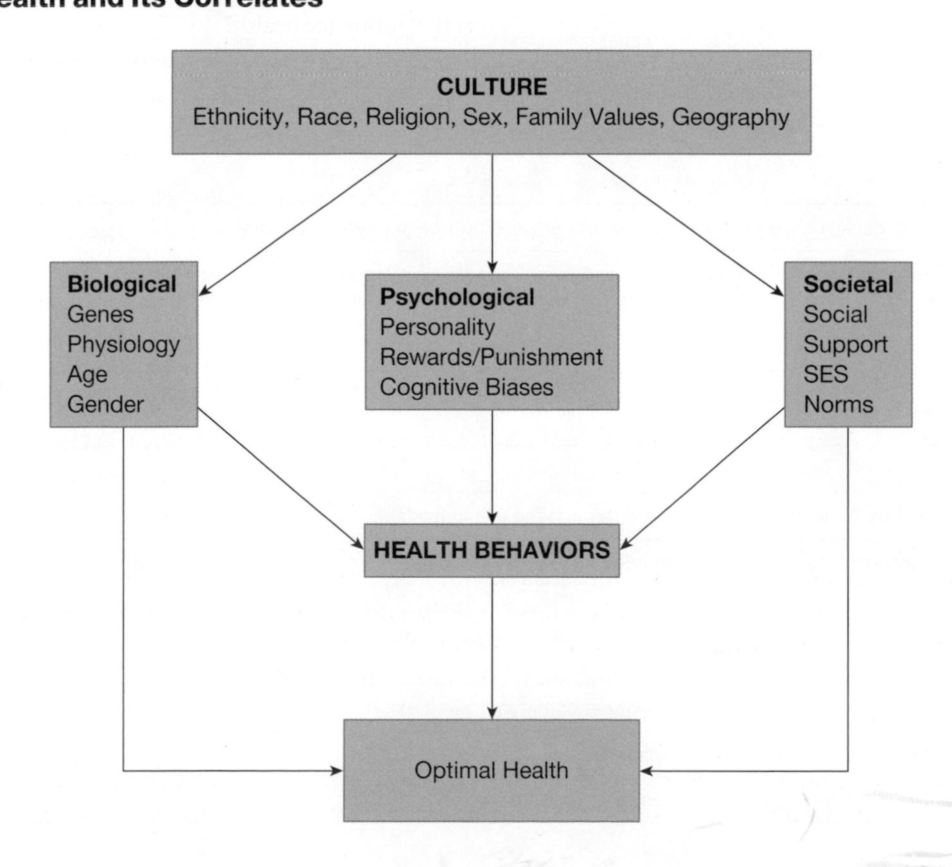

Notice (Figure 1.1) how many different pathways can determine health and how culture is often the basis of biological, psychological, and societal differences. In fact, many of the health disparities, "differences in health that are not only unnecessary and avoidable, but in addition, are considered unfair and unjust" (Whitehead, 1992, p. 433), are due to cultural factors (Centers for Disease Control and Prevention [CDC], 2015; Office of Disease Prevention and Health Promotion, 2014). There are many examples of disparities: for example, African Americans' heart disease death rates are more than 40% higher than European Americans' death rates (Edwards, 2018). The suicide rate among American Indians is 2.2 times higher than the national average, and those living below the poverty level are significantly more depressed that those higher in **socioeconomic status** (SES; Harris, 2017; King, 2017). In general, health care, mental health, and disease **incidence rates** vary significantly across cultural groups (Abradio-Lanza, 2018; Ruiz, Steffen, Doyle, Flores, & Price, 2019). The Institute of Medicine (IOM) performed an assessment on the differences in the kinds and quality of health care received by American racial and ethnic minorities and nonminorities and recommended specific actions (American Medical Association, 2012). See Table 1.1 for the full recommendations. Consequently, this book takes a cultural approach to discussing health psychology.

To begin, I discuss the dissimilar ways we define and measure health and culture. Next, the discussion introduces you to the field of health psychology and provides an overview of what

▼ TABLE 1.1

Institute of Medicine (IOM) recommendations to reduce differences in the kinds and quality of health care received by U.S. racial and ethnic minorities and nonminorities.

RECOMMENDATIONS
General Recommendations
Recommendation 2-1: Increase awareness of racial and ethnic disparities in health care among the public as well as key stakeholders.
Recommendation 2-2: Increase health-care providers' awareness of disparities.
Legal, Regulatory, and Policy Interventions
Recommendation 5-1: Avoid fragmentation of health plans along socioeconomic lines.
Recommendation 5-2: Strengthen the stability of patient–provider relationships in publicly funded health plans.
Recommendation 5-3: Increase the proportion of underrepresented U.S. racial and ethnic minorities among health professionals.
Recommendation 5-4: Apply the same managed care protections to publicly funded HMO enrolees that apply to private HMO enrolees.
Recommendation 5-5: Provide greater resources to the U.S. Department of Health and Human Services (DHHS) Office for Civil Rights to enforce civil rights laws.
Health Systems Interventions
Recommendation 5-6: Promote the consistency and equity of care through the use of evidence-based guidelines.
Recommendation 5-7: Structure payment systems to ensure an adequate supply of services to minority patients, and limit provider incentives that could promote disparities.
Recommendation 5-8: Enhance patient-provided communication and trust by providing financial incentives for practices that reduce barriers and encourage evidence-based practice.
Recommendation 5-9: Support the use of interpretation services where community need exists.
Recommendation 5-10: Support the use of community health workers.
Recommendation 5-11: Implement multidisciplinary treatment and preventive care teams.

RECOMMENDATIONS
Patient Education and Empowerment
Recommendation 5-12: Implement patient education programs to increase patients' knowledge of how to best access care and participate in treatment decisions.
Cross-Cultural Education in the Health Professions
Recommendation 6-1: Integrate cross-cultural education into the training of all current and future health professionals.
Data Collection and Monitoring
Recommendation 7-1: Collect and report data on health-care access and use by patients' race, ethnicity, SES, and, where possible, by their primary language.
Recommendation 7-2: Include measures of racial and ethnic disparities in performance measurement.
Recommendation 7-3: Monitor progress toward the elimination of health-care disparities.
Recommendation 7-4: Report racial and ethnic data by Office of Management and Budget (OMB) categories but use subpopulation groups where possible.
Research Needs
Recommendation 8-1: Conduct further research to identify sources of racial and ethnic disparities and assess promising intervention strategies.
Recommendation 8-2: Conduct research on ethical issues and other barriers to eliminating disparities.

Source: Reprinted with permission from "Unequal Treatment: Confronting Racial and Ethnic Disparities in Health Care, 2003", by the National Academy of Sciences, Courtesy of the National Academic Press, Washington, DC.

health psychology covers. Finally, the chapter concludes with career and graduate training information related to health psychology. We look at how each of us is multicultural, especially focusing on differences in family structure, and how sociodemographic variables such as gender and income level are critical aspects of culture.

iStock.com/ monkeybusinessimages

▲ **Key Health Behaviors.** Getting six to eight hours of sleep, being physically active, eating a nutritional meal, and not smoking are all important health behaviors that can prolong life. Even stretching frequently is a good thing.

WHAT IS HEALTH?

Social media shares and newspaper headlines scream the latest health findings almost every day. Eat a big breakfast (Kahleova, Lloren, Mashchak, Hill, & Fraser, 2017), sugar causes most of society's health issues (Taubes, 2017), running barefoot might be better for you than running in shoes (Daoud et al., 2012), and diets are not the answer to the obesity crisis (Mann et al., 2007). Not only do news agencies report on countless research efforts every day, but much of the information presented is contradictory. Much of the media blitz capitalizes on the fact that people, in general, seem to be paying more attention to getting and staying healthy. Supermarket shelves overflow with supplements to enhance quality of life, and bookstores brim with recommendations on how to live better. The answer to the question, "What is health?" depends on who you ask. Let's start with the **WHO (World Health Organization)**. This organization defines **health** as a state of complete physical, mental, and social well-being (WHO, 1948/2017).

▲ **Key Health Behaviors.** Getting a good night's sleep is one of the best health behaviors to practice.

As you can see, this is a general definition and encompasses almost every aspect of life. One aspect that could be added is the word "spiritual." Definitions such as this one are relatively common when we look at books or magazines that cover health in a nonspecific way. One way to see health is as a continuum with optimal health (broadly defined) at one end and poor health at the other, sitting on two ends of a great big teeter-totter (Figure 1.2). The number of healthy things we do in life determines our relative position (closer to optimal health or closer to death) at a particular moment. The healthy things we do (e.g., eat and sleep well, exercise, and take time to relax) make the optimal health side of the teeter-totter heavier. The unhealthy things we do (e.g., get stressed, smoke, and drink excessively) make us tilt toward the poor health side of the balance.

This imagery also captures how we sometimes rationalize some unhealthy behaviors by practicing some healthy behaviors to ensure the teeter-totter is leaning in the right direction and we are moving toward the optimal end of the spectrum. Of course, this analogy can only go so far: If you have smoked for 20 or 30 years, it will be quite difficult to compensate the balance. Furthermore, it is difficult to compare the extent to which different behaviors translate into longevity. Just because you do not smoke does not mean that you can drink excessively. Just because you exercise a lot does not mean you can afford to avoid a nutritional diet. Keeping your life tilted toward optimal health is a daily challenge and a dynamic process.

CROSS-CULTURAL DEFINITIONS OF HEALTH

In Western medical circles, you are healthy if disease is absent. Of course, this definition focuses primarily on the physical or biological aspect of life; this approach taken by Western medicine is often referred to as the **biomedical approach** to health. Non-Western societies have a different understanding of health. For example, in **Traditional Chinese Medicine** (TCM), health is the balance of yin and yang, the two complementary forces in the universe (Kaptchuk, 2000;

▼ FIGURE 1.2

Health Is a Continuum

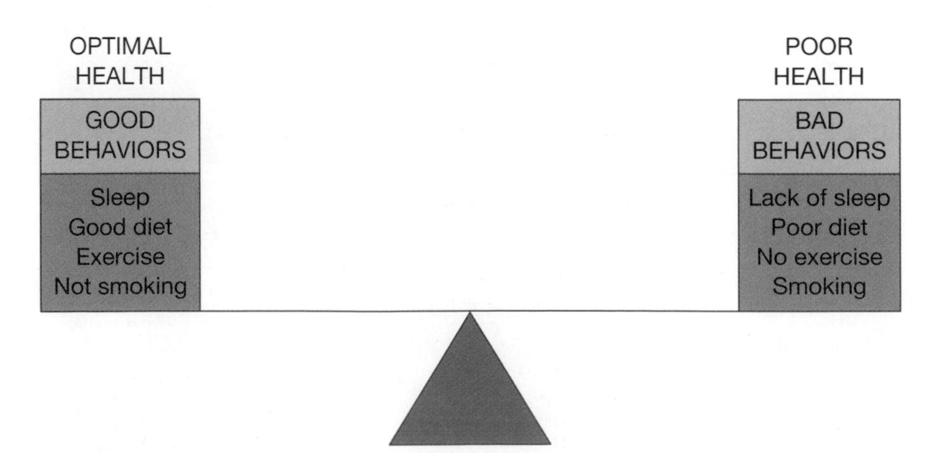

Santee, 2017). Yin and yang are often translated into hot and cold (two clear opposites), referring to qualities and not temperatures. For optimal health you should eat and drink and live your life with equal amounts of hot qualities and cold qualities. Balancing hot and cold is a critical element of many different cultures (e.g., Chinese, Indian, and even Mexican), although some of the foods that constitute each vary across cultures. Some hot foods include beef, garlic, ginger, and alcohol. Some cold foods include honey, most greens, potatoes, and some fruits (e.g., melons, pears). Chapter 3 in this book covers a complete description of diverse approaches to health.

▼ TABLE 1.2

Some Cross-Cultural Definitions of Health

Culture	Definition
Western	Absence of disease
Chinese	Balance of yin and yang Balance of hot and cold
Indian	Balance of mind, body, and spirit
Mexican	Balance of body types and energies
American Indian	Spiritual, mental, and physical harmony Harmony with nature
Hmong	Prevention of soul loss
Ethiopian	Prevention of spirit possession

Other cultures also believe that health is the balance of different qualities (Table 1.2) (Galanti, 2014). Similarly, ancient Indian scholars and doctors defined health as the state in which "the three main biological units—enzymes, tissues, and excretory functions—are in harmonious condition and when the mind and senses are cheerful" (Agnihotri & Agnihotri, 2017, p. 31). Referred to as **Ayurveda**, which means knowledge of life, this ancient system of medicine focuses on the body, the sense organs, the mind, and the soul (Svoboda, 2004). Another way of looking at health is the approach of Mexican Americans, the largest non-European ethnic group in the United States. Mexican Americans believe that there are both natural biological causes for illness (similar to Western biomedicine) and spiritual causes (Tovar, 2017). Though Mexican American patients might go to a Western doctor to cure a biological problem, they trust only *curanderos,* or healers, to cure spiritual problems (Arellano & Sosa, 2018).

American Indians do not draw distinctions between physical, spiritual, and social entities or between religion and medicine (Peters, Green, & Gauthier, 2014). Instead, most tribes (especially the Navajo) strive to achieve a balance between human beings and the spiritual world (Alvord & Van Pelt, 2000). The trees, the animals, the earth, the sky, and the winds are all players in the same game of life. Most of the world's cultures use a more global and widespread approach to assessing health instead of just looking at whether or not disease is absent to determine health (as the biomedical model and most Western approaches do). We will discuss each of these different approaches to health in more detail in the Chapter 3.

Synthesize, Evaluate, Apply

- How has our view of the mind–body connection changed over time?
- What is the best way to view health? What do you feel is the best definition?
- How do different cultures vary in their definition of health?

WHY IS CULTURE IMPORTANT?

One easy answer to the question, "Why is culture important?" is to explain why there are significant differences in the health of European Americans and non–European Americans. However, the cultural differences predict and relate to more than health differences.

What do your mother, your best friend, and your religion have in common? They each constitute a way that you learn about acceptable behaviors. Take parents, for example. Whether we do something because they told us to (e.g., "Eat your greens!") or exactly because they told us not to (e.g., "Don't smoke!"), they have a strong influence on us. If our friends exercise, we will be more likely to exercise. Similarly, religions have different prescriptions for what individuals should and should not do. Muslims should not eat pork or drink alcohol (Amer, 2017). Hindus are prohibited from eating beef (Agnihotri & Agnihotri, 2017). Even where we live can determine our habits and can help predict the diseases we might die from as studied in detail by the area of health geography (Greenhough, 2011). Parents, peers, religion, and geography are a few of the key determinants of our behaviors and are examples of what makes up our culture.

Dimensions of Culture

If you think that there are many ways to describe health, then prepare for the challenge of defining culture. At first, it does not seem too difficult, but both trained psychologists and laypeople often mean different things when they discuss culture. Many use the words "culture," "ethnicity," and "race" interchangeably (see Figure 1.3). Beyond these specific examples, people also think culture represents a set of ideals or beliefs or sometimes a set of behaviors. Behaviors and beliefs are other accurate components of what culture is and are often amplified in cultural stereotypes. In the cable show *Silicon Valley,* Gavin the stressed-out devious head of Hooli, a major technology firm, has an Indian (East Asian) spiritual guide to keep him calm. The guru is a stereotypical Indian mystic complete with loose robes, beads, and calming mantras. Going back to the time of the Beatles, Westerners flocked to India to meditate and follow the teaching of holy men, and this stereotype makes it into many American shows. Many non-White actors such as as Kal Penn (of *Harold and Kumar* fame) play on these stereotypes to comic effect. The idea is that members of certain cultures share the beliefs and values of others in that culture.

Although we rarely acknowledge it, culture has many dimensions. Many of us limit discussions of culture to race or ethnicity. Look at what happens if you ask someone what she thinks the dominant culture around her is. In most cases, she will identify an ethnic category. Someone in Miami might respond that the dominant culture in her area is Cuban. Someone in Minnesota might say it is Scandinavian. When we pose the question in Green Bay, Wisconsin, people often say it is Hispanic or Hmong (people from Laos, near Vietnam). Or they sometimes say American Indian because they think we asked which ethnic group is most visible in town. In reality, culture can be a variety of things. The dominant culture in Green Bay is Catholic, but people rarely realize that religion constitutes a form of culture as well. You could also say being a Packers fan is the dominant culture Green Bay? Is there an American culture? What do you think?

Defining Culture

Culture can be defined as "a unique meaning and information system, shared by a group and transmitted across generations, that allows the group to meet basic needs of survival, by coordinating social behavior to achieve a viable existence, to transmit successful social behaviors, to pursue happiness and well-being, and to derive meaning from life" (Matsumoto & Juang, 2017, p. 4). Culture can also include similar physical characteristics (e.g., skin color), psychological characteristics (e.g., levels of hostility), and common superficial features (e.g., hairstyle and clothing). Culture is dynamic because

▼ FIGURE 1.3

Defining Culture

Our race, ethnicity, and nationality are all interconnected and part of our "culture."

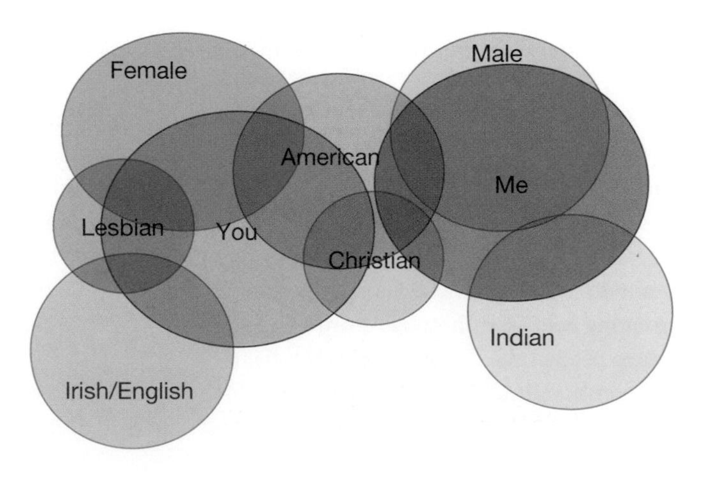

some of the beliefs held by members in a culture can change with time. However, the general level of culture maintains stability because the individuals change together. The beliefs and attitudes can be implicit, learned by observation, and passed on by word of mouth; or they can be explicit, written down as laws or rules for the group to follow. The most commonly described objective cultural groups consist of grouping by ethnicity, race, sex, and age. Look at Figure 1.4 for a summary of the different types of cultures and characteristics. There are more subjective aspects of culture that we cannot see or easily link to physical characteristics. For example, nationality, sex/gender, religion, and geography also constitute different cultural groups, each with its own set of prescriptions for behavior.

A broader discussion and definition of culture is important for a full understanding of the precedents of health behaviors and health. Culture includes ethnicity, race, religion, age, sex, family values, geography (the region of the country), and many other features. High school adolescents belong to a different culture than do college students. Even in college, there are different cultures. Some students live in dorms, and some live in off-campus apartments. On campus, also, there are athletes and musicians, among many others; each group provides different prescriptions for what is correct behavior. For instance, it is normal for the athletes to exercise a lot. Aspects of the specific culture we belong to correspondingly influence each of our health behaviors. Understanding the dynamic interplay of cultural forces acting on us can greatly enhance how we face the world and how we optimize our way of life. This book will describe how such cultural backgrounds influence the different behaviors we follow that can influence our health.

There are probably as many different definitions for culture as there are for health. For example, Soudijn, Hutschemaekers, and Van de Vijver (1990) analyzed 128 definitions. A good way to comprehend the breadth of culture is to see if you know what your own is. For the next 30 seconds, think of all the ways that you would answer the question, Who am I? Write down or just think of every response that comes to mind in the space provided in Figure 1.5.

You will notice that you use many labels for yourself. Social psychologists call this the "Who am I?" test (not a very inventive name, obviously). They use it to measure how people describe themselves. You probably generated a number of different descriptors for yourself, and your responses provide a number of different clues about yourself and your culture. Your answers may have included your religious background (e.g., I am Lutheran), your sex (e.g., I am male), or your major roles (e.g., I am a student, a daughter, or a friend). You might have even mentioned your nationality (e.g., I am American), your race (e.g., I am Black), or your ethnicity (e.g., I am Asian American). Therefore, if you really took the 30 seconds suggested, you should be staggering

▼ FIGURE 1.4

The Variety of Cultures

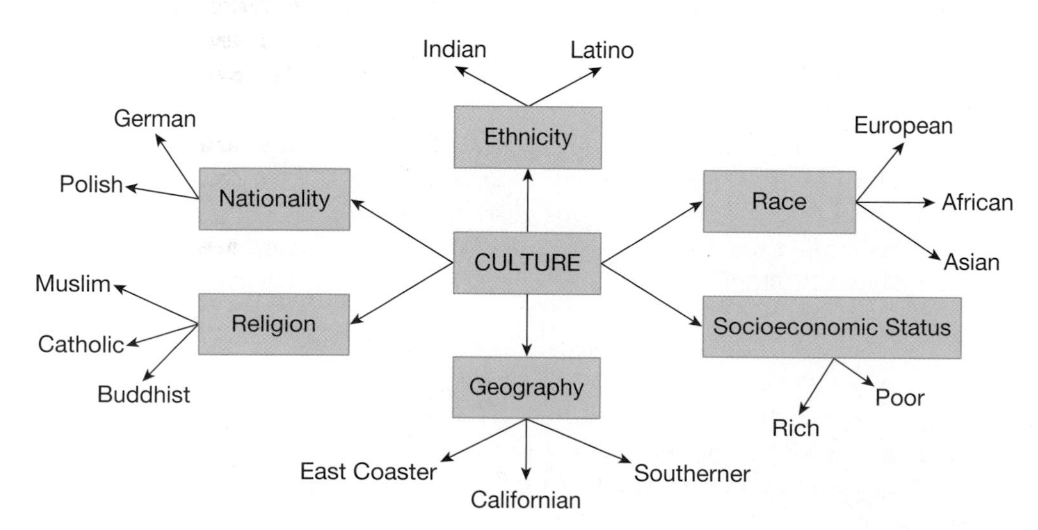

▼ FIGURE 1.5

Who are you? Jot down the words you use to describe yourself in the space below.

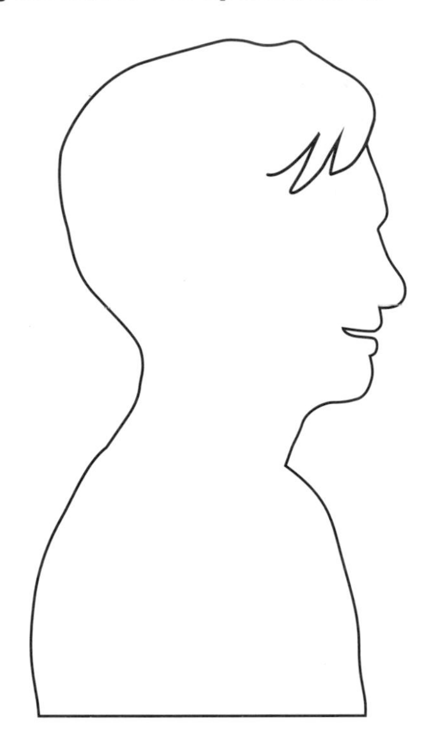

under the realization that you actually have a lot more culture than you previously thought. Before doing these listing exercises, many European Americans have said things like, "I do not have any culture. I'm just White." Part of the exciting thing about life is that every one of us has different experiences and backgrounds, and we will keep these backgrounds at center stage as we discuss health behaviors and health.

Profile of a Multicultural America

What does it mean to be American? The presidential race of 2016 brought race and **sex,** two of the most salient and visible forms of cultural diversity, to the fore. For the first time in the history of the United States, a woman, Hillary Rodham Clinton, was a candidate for president. For 8 years prior, Barack Hussein Obama served as the first African American president. The months of campaigning were often accompanied by discussions of not just positions and platforms but also gender, sexual orientation, and race and ethnicity. Pollsters paid close attention to how women, Latinos, or LGBTQ (lesbian, gay, bisexual, transgender, and queer or questioning) Americans would vote. For the first time in many years people had to confront the fact that for all of America's history presidents have been White men. Is that profile what it means to be American? Does being American mean being White? Of course, it does not, just as being male is not a component of American. American citizens have many different skin colors, religions, and styles of dressing, and that is only the beginning of our country's diversity. America consists of a variety of cultural groups; it is critical to remind ourselves that not only is the country multicultural, but we ourselves are also multicultural.

The most recent census data lists the population of the United States at approximately 321 million. That number can be broken down along different cultural lines. An example of a cultural group that most people tend to think of first is ethnicity. Of that 321 million population, approximately 13% are African American or Black, approximately 4% are Asian American (including Americans of different Asian backgrounds such as Chinese, Japanese, Korean, and Indian), and approximately 1% are American Indians or Native Americans. The remaining 82% of the population are considered European American or White and include people of Latin American and Spanish ancestry. Commonly referred to as Latinos, the preferred term, or Hispanic (a term applied to this ethnic group by the U.S. government in the 1980 Census), the truth is that people in this same group have their own names for their groups depending on which part of the United States they live in and their specific country of origin (Arellano & Sosa, 2017). For example, Texans and those in the Southeast prefer the word "Hispanic," New Yorkers use both "Hispanic" and "Latino," and Chicagoans prefer "Latino" (Shorris, 1992). Even the term "Mexican American," part of the general classification Hispanic, includes people of Cuban descent, those from Puerto Rico, and Central or South America (Tovar, 2017). Ethnicity is just one way to divide cultural lines (see Figure 1.6).

A second type of culture is religion. When you look at our planet, the majority of humans are Christians (Pew Research Center, 2017), accounting for 31.2%. Muslims comprise 24.1%. Surprisingly, 16% are unaffiliated. Hindus comprise 15.1%. In the United States, 71% are Christian and 22.8% are unaffiliated. Importantly, some well-known religious groups are not present in large numbers: Only about 2% of Americans are Jewish. Testifying to the fact that we as human beings tend to overestimate the actual occurrence of something just based on the extent to which we hear about it (referred to as the **availability heuristic**),

Muslims only constitute a minute part of the U.S. population (0.9%). Because of political events (e.g., trouble in the Middle East and the wars in Afghanistan and Iraq, areas whose populations are predominantly Muslim), many Americans believe that there are many Muslims in the United States (and unfortunately have prejudices against them), when in fact they are a very small minority.

We can also think about culture in terms of ethnicity, different age groups, socioeconomic status (SES), or different geographical regions. People living in different parts of the country have different health behaviors (e.g., the Southeastern states such as Kentucky and Virginia show some of the highest levels of smoking). Different age groups—children, adolescents, teenagers, young adults, or older adults—experience different stressors. When you break down the U.S. population along different lines, you realize that there are many such groups and that each has its own specific health issues. The numbers in each of these groups also change over time. For example, the population of Americans over age 65 is projected to double from 36 million in 2003 to 72 million in 2030, and to increase from 12% to 20% of the population in the same time frame (He, Sengupta, Velkoff, & DeBarros, 2005). This difference in the age profile can have implications for each different group's health care.

Two Key Areas of Diversity

Two of the most important aspects that define cultural groups, often discussed as diversity, are **socioeconomic status** (SES) and sex. SES, often measured by combining income and education level (e.g., Tackett, Herzoff, Smack, Reardon, & Adam, 2017), is becoming one of the most important and widely studied constructs in health psychology (Ruiz et al., 2019). Almost any study done on this topic shows that poverty and illness tend to go together, often linked by factors such as access to health care and insurance. SES can also influence and underlie relationships among other factors such as race, parenting, and cardiovascular health. For examples, Black men exposed to positive parenting during adolescence had more ideal cardiovascular health based on American Heart Association guidelines (Matthews et al., 2017). SES also relates to body mass index (BMI) in young adults (Bradshaw, Kent, Henderson, & Setar, 2017).

▼ FIGURE 1.6

Culture and Ethnicity

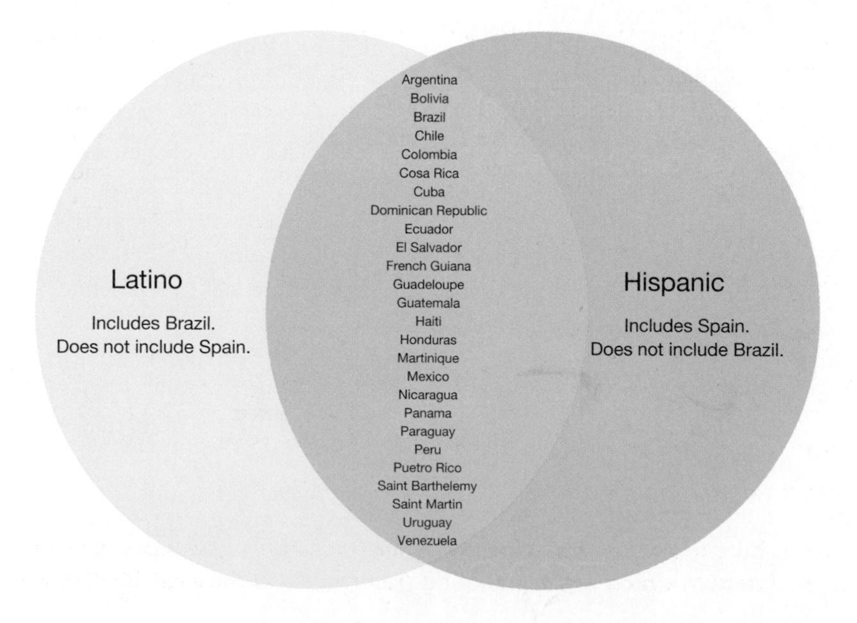

The poor (currently those with a yearly income equal to or less than $23,050 for a family of four, U.S. Department of Health and Human Services [DHHS], 2017) make up a large percentage of Americans without health insurance. If you have money, you can afford healthy food and higher-quality health services. Of particular importance to taking a cultural approach to health is that the cultural make-up of those considered poor is changing. For example, Indiana's Manchester University and Massachusetts's Bentley University examined poverty rates and income levels from 1995 to 2006 for several U.S. population groups. They found that the disparity in poverty rates between European Americans and other ethnic groups had decreased 7 of the past 11 years, dropping 23% overall since 1995. Whereas European American poverty is remaining relatively stable (8.2% in 2006 vs. 8.5% in 1995), the poverty rates for African Americans dropped from 29.3% to 24.2%, for Hispanics from 30.2% to 20.6%, and for Asian/Pacific Islanders from 14.6% to 10.1% (Wollman, Yoder, Brumbaugh-Smith, & Haynes, 2007). Such changes can influence usage of health services and consequently a number of other factors that health psychologists study.

Socioeconomic status is related to a higher occurrence of most chronic and infectious disorders and to higher rates of nearly all major causes of mortality and morbidity (Ruiz et al., 2019). In one study SES differences accounted for 60% of the racial differences in death rates (Thorpe et al., 2012). Even the neighborhood in which you live can be important (Yao & Robert, 2011). Neighborhood SES has been associated with poorer health practices (Petridou et al., 1997) and a variety of other health conditions such as coronary heart disease (Walsemann, Goosby, & Farr, 2016). The relationship between SES and health is also direct: usually, the more money you have, the better your health. This relationship is seen in children and in older adults alike. Several ways of measuring SES have been proposed, but most include some quantification of family income, parental education, and occupational status. One common measure, the Hollingshead Four-Factor Index of Socioeconomic Status, uses parents' education level and occupational status (e.g., Matthews et al., 2017). Research shows that SES is associated with a wide array of health, cognitive, and socioemotional outcomes with effects beginning before birth and continuing into adulthood (Gottfried, Gottfried, Bathurst, Guerin, & Parramore, 2003). Even perceptions of how well-off your family is (i.e., subjective perceptions of familial SES) have been found to influence health (Goodman, Huang, Schafer-Kalkhoff, & Adler, 2007).

Many differences in health are due to sex, which is an innate, biological characteristic (Rosenthal & Gronich, 2019). For instance, men are more likely to die after intracerebral hemorrhages, a type of stroke (Marini et al., 2017), older women are more likely to benefit from exercise than are older men (Barha, Davis, Falck, Nagamatsu, & Liu-Ambrose, 2017), men and women react differently to hospitalization (Shlomi Polachek et al., 2017), in their need for health information (Stewart, Abbey, Shnek, Irvine, & Grace, 2004), and to illness in general (Westbrook & Viney, 1983). Sex often interacts with other elements of culture such as race and ethnicity (Zissimopoulos, Barthold, Brinton, & Joyce, 2017). For example, many Korean American males believe heavy drinking is associated with Korean traditions such as Poke-Tang because they encourage men but not women to drink alcohol (Sung Hyun & Wansoo, 2008). In the Latino community there are sex differences in relation to health seeking behavior, especially substance use (Abradio-Lanza, 2018).

Although women live longer than men (Murphy, Xu, & Kochanek, 2012), they report symptoms of illness more frequently and use health services to a greater extent (Waldron, 1991). The once-common belief that women have poorer health in general than men has been challenged (Macintyre, Hunt, & Sweeting, 1996). There are both pros and cons to being female. The female sex hormone estrogen has a protective effect against cardiovascular illness in women younger than age 50 (Orth-Gomer, Chesney, & Wegner, 1998). On the other hand, women are more likely to be victims of violence and sexual assault (U.S. Department of Justice, 2015) and have body image, eating, and diet problems (Harrison, Taylor, & Marske, 2006). It is interesting to note that although body dissatisfaction is higher in girls than boys, the negative impact of body dissatisfaction on adolescents' quality of life does not differ by sex (Griffiths et al., 2017).

Boys and men are not always better off (Mitchison et al., 2017). Boys have body image issues as well, often spurred on by the media in general and some media (e.g., video gaming magazines) in particular (Harrison & Bond, 2007). Sometimes these differences are due to gender, which includes behaviors determined by socialization, and learning of social roles. For example, sociological factors related to gender include the extra demands of balancing different roles (e.g., being the primary caregiver for children and working outside the home). Most studies acknowledge these differences by statistically controlling for sex and implicitly (and sometimes explicitly) treating biological sex as a proxy for gender. Remember that sex and gender are not identical constructs, although the two are often treated interchangeably (Pryzgoda & Chrisler, 2000). In fact, biological sex is also different from sexual orientation. Figure 1.7 shows the differences between these terms.

ADVANCING CULTURAL COMPETENCE

There are many different cultural approaches to health, as you will see in Chapter 3. It is of great importance for health psychologists, health-care workers, and the administrations that support them to be culturally aware. Table 1.3 provides a summary of key recommendations for health-care administrators (Gurung, 2012). Not all clinicians and health-care workers have received the necessary instruction to be culturally competent, but there are some easy

▼ FIGURE 1.7

The Genderbread Person

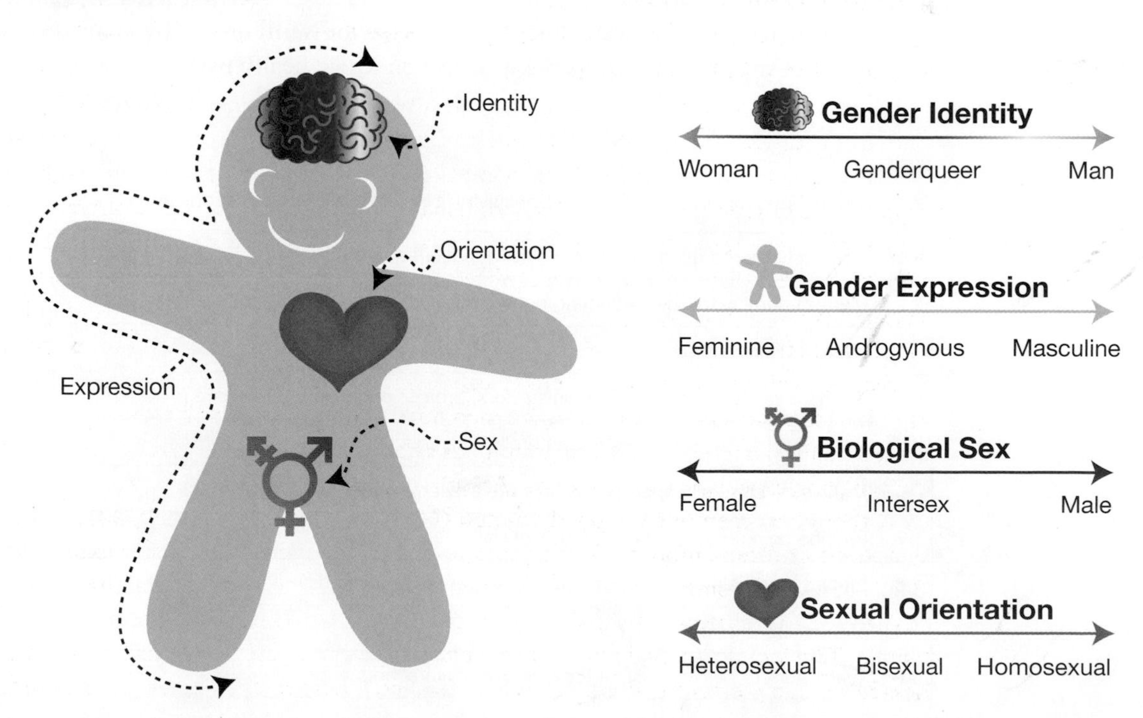

ways to be prepared. Perhaps the most helpful model of cultural competence is the Purnell Model of cultural competence (Purnell, 2009). The model posits 12 main cultural domains that a clinician should be aware of and should attempt to learn about for each client. Chapter 3 illustrates the main domains and provides sample questions for the clinician to use to gain cultural competence.

It is important to acknowledge that many cultural variations exist within ethnic communities. Knowing how different cultural groups approach health and having a better understanding of how factors such as acculturation are important can help clinicians, health-care workers, and others with an interest in how lifestyle decisions are made to be more culturally competent. The efforts to increase cultural competency in the treatment of mental and physical health are promising, but the wider health-care arena needs to pay attention to the causes of health disparities and the role played by multicultural approaches to health (Purnell et al., 2011). We need a better connection between health care and the community so individuals can seek out treatments that best fit their cultural needs (Rogers, 2010); in so doing we can reduce the manifold health disparities.

A person's culture has a major impact on behaviors that influence health. Culture influences some explicit health behaviors. For example, how much do we exercise? Do we drink or smoke? Do we eat well? Culture also influences a whole range of behaviors that indirectly influence our health. For example, how do we form relationships? How many close friends do we have and do we call on them when we are under stress or in need?

HEALTH PSYCHOLOGY'S BIOPSYCHOSOCIAL APPROACH

An understanding of the different definitions of culture becomes a useful aid to study health and to examine why we do or do not do things that are good for us. Most behaviors that influence health—whether healthy behaviors such as physical activity and eating nutritionally balanced diets or unhealthy ones such as smoking or drinking excessively—depend heavily on the culture in which we grew up. If both of your parents exercised, there is a high probability that you will exercise as well. The fact that behavior is influenced by many different factors outside of the individual is a critical aspect on which health psychologists focus. We will

▼ TABLE 1.3

Recommendations for Fostering Cultural Sensitivity in Health-Care Organizations and Clinics

1.	Post pictures representing the diversity of patient and staff throughout the organization.
2.	Make cultural resources reflecting patient population available to staff.
3.	Recruit bilingual staff.
4.	Initiate diversity classes for administrators, professionals, and other care providers.
5.	Initiate mentoring programs for culturally diverse staff.
6.	Make sure culturally appropriate toys are available in pediatric settings.
7.	Provide pain scales in the language of patients.
8.	Ensure food selections are available to match cultural needs.
9.	Make cultural references readily available.
10.	Teach staff to be responsible for their own cultural education.

Source: Adapted from Purnell et al. (2011).

discuss the exact ways that culture influences our development and health behaviors in more detail throughout this book.

How does the culture that we come from and surround ourselves with influence our health and behaviors? Answering this question with a concerted look at sources of influence outside a person (i.e., not just his or her biology or psychology) is a distinctive feature of the approach taken by health psychologists in studying health. In contrast to the biomedical approach of Western medicine described previously, health psychologists use a **biopsychosocial approach** (Revenson & Gurung, 2019; Suls & Rothman, 2004). Most terms used in psychology reflect common sense, and this term is no exception. This type of approach focuses on the biology or physiology underlying health; the psychology or thoughts, feelings, and behaviors influencing health; and the ways that society and culture influence health. The term "biopsychosocial" nicely reminds us that different components go together. For example, there is an association between depression, a mental health issue, and cardiovascular disease, a physical health issue (Carney & Freedland, 2017). The biopsychosocial approach goes beyond defining health as simply the absence of disease and instead forces us to focus on the broader range of the critical determinants of health (Suls & Rothman, 2004).

Synthesize, Evaluate, Apply

- What are the components of a good definition of culture?
- What aspects of life are influenced by culture? How is culture transferred?
- What factors can influence responses to the "Who am I?" test?
- Why are cultural differences important in the context of health?

Smoking provides a good example of how the biopsychosocial model is useful. People might start smoking for psychological reasons such as thinking it makes them less stressed or because of personality traits (extroverts are more likely to smoke). People might also start to smoke due to pressure from their social networks or because of perceived cultural norms. Finally, addictions have a strong biological component in terms of their heritability.

The Evolution of Health Psychology

Health psychology is conceptualized as a discipline encompassed by the general field of behavioral medicine together with medicine and an array of public health sciences and services (Freedland, 2017). In the recent past, health psychology emerged when humans starting dying more due to chronic diseases than due to famines, infections, and communicable diseases (epidemiologic transition; Omran, 2005). Going back even farther, the first two components of the biopsychosocial approach—focusing on biology and psychology—represent a current resolution to an ancient debate.

For centuries researchers, thinkers, and philosophers have questioned if and how the mind (and psychology) and the body (and our biology) are related and whether this relationship influences health. Is the mind connected to the body? Does it reside in the body? Where is the soul? Philosophers and scientists alike have debated these questions for millennia. Modern health psychology has roots in philosophy, 19th-century scientific discovery, medical and clinical psychology, epidemiology and public health, medical sociology and anthropology, and psychosomatic medicine (Friedman & Adler, 2007; Taylor, 2010).

The earliest evidence, such as oral traditions and pictorial evidence from early civilizations, suggests that the mind and body were originally considered to be one (Ellenberger, 1981). Spirits invading the body were thought to cause illness, and gruesome solutions such as trephination—the drilling of holes in the skull to release spirits—were practiced to make people healthy. This was not a highly successful method (nor was it likely to have been extremely popular with people developing illnesses).

Many of the world's early philosophies seemed to share the view that the mind and the body were intimately connected; about 5,000 years ago both the ancient Chinese Taoist sages and the ancient Indian practitioners of Ayurveda wrote about various ways the mind could calm the body and vice versa (Agnihotri & Agnihotri, 2017; Santee, 2017). It is also certain that the rich traditions of medical practice in Egypt and the Middle East around 2000 B.C. (e.g., Mesopotamia, present-day Iraq) also focused on this connection (Amer, 2017; Udwadia, 2000). Greek philosophers around 300 to 400 B.C. challenged this notion and proposed that the mind and the body were separate. Greeks valued reason and rational thought—basic components of the Greek approach to life—more than the biology of the body, but hypothesized that basic bodily substances caused different diseases. For example, the Greek philosopher **Hippocrates**'s rational explanation of why people get sick concerned the balance of four major bodily fluids (something that he borrowed from Alcmaeon of Crete). He argued that people got sick or showed different symptoms if the amount of one fluid exceeded that of the others. If you had a lot of blood, you would be cheerful; if you had a lot of black bile, you would be sad or melancholic. History considers Hippocrates, who made many other contributions to the biological study of illness, the father of Western biomedicine. In fact, most doctors take an oath before they practice medicine, one of which is the Hippocratic Oath (Table 1.4).

Many centuries after Hippocrates the French philosopher **Rene Descartes** (1596–1650), famous for his argument, "I think therefore I am"— "je pense, donc se suis" in Descartes's original French, or "cogito ergo sum" in Latin —strengthened the Greek idea about the separation of the mind from the body. The hundreds of years that people believed that the mind was separate from the body helped medical science develop as scientists dissected dead bodies and increased our knowledge of human anatomy. The Greek **Galen** first pioneered the examination of the dead to find the cause of disease, working primarily on animals. Centuries later, the study of human anatomy was fine-tuned by Andreas Vesalius (1514–1564) and the Italian artist (and the prototypical Renaissance man) Leonardo da Vinci (1452–1519). Both drew detailed diagrams of the construction of the human body. Dissections came to a halt when the

▼ TABLE 1.4

The Modern Physician's Oath

I swear to fulfill, to the best of my ability and judgment, this covenant:
I will respect the hard-won scientific gains of those physicians in whose steps I walk, and gladly share such knowledge as is mine with those who are to follow;
I will apply, for the benefit of the sick, **all measures which are required**, avoiding those twin traps of overtreatment and therapeutic nihilism.
I will remember that there is art to medicine as well as science, and that warmth, sympathy and understanding may outweigh the surgeon's knife or the chemist's drug.
I will not be ashamed to say "I know not," nor will I fail to call in my colleagues when the skills of another are needed for a patient's recovery.
I will **respect the privacy** of my patients, for their problems are not disclosed to me that the world may know. Most especially must I tread with care in matters of life and death. If it is given me to save a life, all thanks. But **it may also be within my power to take a life; this awesome responsibility must be faced with great humbleness** and awareness of my own frailty. Above all, I must not play at God.
I will remember that I do not treat a fever chart, a cancerous growth, but a sick human being, whose illness may affect the person's family and economic stability. My responsibility includes these related problems, if I am to care adequately for the sick.
I will prevent disease whenever I can, for prevention is preferable to cure.
I will remember that I remain a member of society, with special obligations to all my fellow human beings, those sound of mind and body, as well as the infirm.
If I do not violate this oath, may I enjoy life and art, respected while I live and remembered with affection hereafter. May I always act so as to preserve the finest traditions of my calling and may I long experience the joy of healing those who seek my help.

Source: Thttp://www.aapsonline.org/ethics/oaths.htm#lasagna.

iStock.com/ monkeybusinessimages

Roman Catholic Church explicitly banned dissections, which it deemed unholy. Finally, Descartes brokered a deal with the Church resulting from a complex set of sociopolitical factors. Active antagonism had existed between the Church and science, but the declining power of the Church and the draining of Church resources due to the Inquisition made it easier for Descartes to convince the Holy Father to allow dissections. Descartes essentially argued that because the mind and body were separate, the mind and soul of a person left the body when the person died. Hence, only the biological body was left behind, and it was unimportant. The Church accepted this explanation, and human dissections began in earnest.

▲ **Cultural Influences on Behavior.** Our own health behaviors are largely dependent on the health behaviors of other individuals who share our cultural group.

In the early 20th century psychology started to play a part in the examination of health. Part of the reason this involvement came so late is that psychology was not a field of study in its own right until then. If you think back to your introductory psychology class, you probably will remember that the German William Wundt founded the first psychology laboratory in 1879. The first book in psychology, *Principles of Psychology* by Harvard University psychologist **William James**, was published in 1897. In a precursor of sorts to the biopsychosocial model, James also wrote *Varieties of Religious Experience* (1902) that referred to spirituality, health, and psychology. Also in the late 1890s, **Sigmund Freud** first generated his ideas about the structure of the human mind. When one mentions Freud's name, people quickly think of couches, bearded psychologists, and other stereotypical Freudian artifacts. Yes, Freud did have clients lie on his couch while he sat behind them and listened to them speak. Yes, we often see pictures of him in a beard and most movie psychoanalysts are similarly bearded (e.g., *Analyze This*, *Girl on the Train*). These tidbits aside, Freud was one of the earliest health psychologists, though few would call him such (Karademas, Benyamini, & Johnston, 2016).

iStock.com/ efenzi

▲ **Cultural Influences on Behavior.** If many of your friends smoke and drink, you are more likely to do the same.

How did Freud revolutionize the way we look at illness? Freud was the first to draw attention to the possibility that illness could have psychological causes. Trained as a neuroscientist, Freud had a strong biological background. He was perplexed by clients who reported strong symptoms of illness but who lacked physical evidence of illness. He also noticed the work of Pierre Janet and of Franz Anton Mesmer, who cured cases of hysteria with hypnosis. In talking to his clients, Freud discovered that many of their physical illnesses were due to psychological issues. Once these psychological issues were resolved, the physical symptoms disappeared. This focus on the workings of the mind in disease was continued later in the 20th century by the psychoanalysts

▲ **Galen.** A key figure in the history of medicine who was one of the first to dissect bodies.

Franz Alexander and **Helen Flanders Dunbar.** Together they established the first formal gathering of individuals interested in studying the influences of the mind on health. This movement within the mainstream medical establishment was coined **psychosomatic medicine**.

The new field of psychosomatic medicine had many supporters, which led to the formation of the first society specifically dedicated to the study of mind and body connections. The American Psychosomatic Society was formed to "promote and advance the scientific understanding and multidisciplinary integration of biological, psychological, behavioral and social factors in human health and disease, and to foster the dissemination and application of this understanding in education and health care" (American Psychosomatic Society, 2018). In 1936 the New York Academy of Medicine's joint committee on religion and medicine headed by Dunbar assembled a collection of the psychosomatic medical literature, together with publications examining the relationship of religion to health. Dunbar's early collection of articles led her to organize the publishing in 1939 of the first journal for this field, *Psychosomatic Medicine,* which still publishes research today. Although the early movement faltered and received mixed attention because it was based heavily on Freudian ideas and case study methods of research, the American Psychosomatic Society survives and is still active.

Another movement within the field of medicine, **behavioral medicine**, looks at nonbiological influences on health. Doctors and health-care specialists within the medical community were probably always aware that changes in behavior and lifestyle improve health, prevent illness, and reduce symptoms of illness, although they did not focus on this fact. The Society of Behavioral Medicine, a multidisciplinary, nonprofit organization founded in 1978, is dedicated to studying the influences of behavior on health and well-being. This organization brings together different disciplines—nursing, psychology, medicine, and public health—to form an interdisciplinary team. The society's explicit mission is "promoting the study of the interactions of behavior with biology and the environment, and the application of that knowledge to improve the health and well being of individuals, families, communities and populations" (Society of Behavioral Medicine, 2018). Similar to *Psychosomatic Medicine* for the APS, the SBM also has its own journal, the *Annals of Behavioral Medicine.* Another important resource for health psychology and clinical health psychologists in particular is the *International Classification of Diseases,* 9th revision (ICD-9), a classification of diseases and disorders. The connection between health psychology and medicine is strong. Even today, health psychology and clinical health psychologists play an important role in the practice of medicine and management of disease (Nicholas & Stern, 2011).

▲ **Descartes.** A key figure who advocated for the separation of the concept of the mind from the concept of the body.

Other groups of individuals also began to draw attention to the fact that health issues needed to be addressed by a broader approach than the point of view taken by the medical establishment. Individuals in the field of **medical anthropology** are committed to improving public health in societies in economically poor nations. Based on the biological and sociocultural roots of anthropology, medical anthropologists have long considered health and medical care within the context of cultural systems, although not necessarily using the tools or theoretical approaches of psychologists. Similarly, medical sociologists are individuals working within the framework of the medical model, focusing on the role of culture and a person's environment in health and illness.

There are many fascinating studies of health and behavior conducted within these different fields that we will refer to in this book. These fields and health psychology share common interests and terms. For example, health psychology and medical sociology both are influenced by the field of **epidemiology**—a branch of medicine that studies the frequency, distribution, and causes of different diseases with an emphasis on the role of the physical and social environments. We will also be paying close attention to clear-cut outcome measures used by epidemiologists. For example, we shall look at how different biopsychosocial factors relate to the number of cases of a disease that exist at a given point in time, or **morbidity**, and to the number of deaths related to a specific cause, or **mortality**.

Even within mainstream psychology, researchers in social psychology, personality psychology, cognitive psychology, and clinical psychology realize that the basic theories that they derived to describe and predict behavior easily could be applied in the study of health and well-being (Taylor, 2010, 2011). Beyond simply explaining what many laypeople (especially senators in Congress who begrudge the use of government money to fund psychological studies) considered commonsensical and mundane issues, psychological theorizing can actually save lives! As we will soon discover, social psychological theories form one of the core foundations of health psychological research (Taylor, 2011), and many social phenomena can explain why we do what we do. Are children likely to start smoking? What makes a person more or less likely to exercise or eat well? The answers to each of these questions come from theories derived from basic social psychological research.

▲ **Freud.** A key figure who first explored the role of the mind in physical health.

WHAT IS HEALTH PSYCHOLOGY?

Health psychology is defined as an interdisciplinary subspecialty of psychology dedicated to promoting and maintaining health and preventing and treating illness (Leventhal, Weinman, Leventhal, & Phillips, 2008; Matarazzo, 1982; Taylor, 1990). Health psychologists pay close attention to the way that thoughts, feelings, behavior, and biological processes all interact with each other to influence health and illnesses ranging from chronic heart disease and cancer to diabetes and obesity (Freedland, 2017). In many ways, health psychology is greater than a subfield within the discipline of psychology, as it is built on theoretical ideas and research findings from many other areas in psychology. For example, many of the ways to understand the causes of stress and how we cope come from social and personality psychology. As previously discussed, in the evolution of psychology, even clinical psychologists such as Freud, Alexander, and Dunbar contributed to the development of the field. The biological bases of health have been studied by physiological psychologists. As we discuss in later chapters the ways in which health psychologists try to change behaviors, the influence of behaviorists such as Skinner and Watson will become apparent. Applying basic behaviorist theories (e.g., classical and operant conditioning) can help someone to stop smoking or help them to eat better or exercise more.

▲ **Early Cures for Illness.** Many bizarre remedies for illness, such as bloodletting, were used prior to the discoveries of modern medicine.

Whenever I refer to Health Psychology (with the capital letters) I refer to the subdivision of the American Psychological Association (**APA Division 38** now referred to as the **Society for Health Psychology**) that is dedicated to four issues:

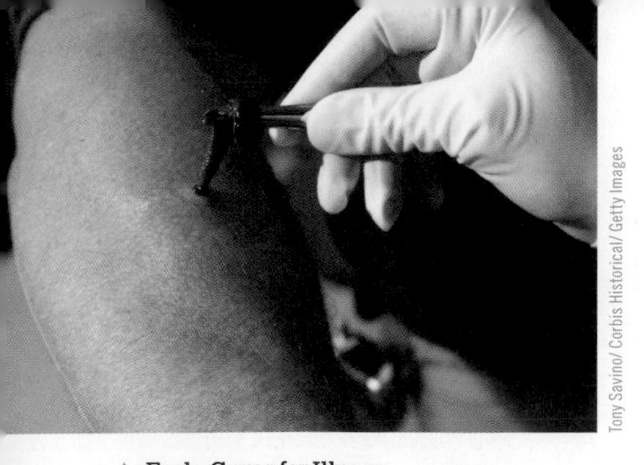

Tony Savino/ Corbis Historical/ Getty Images

▲ **Early Cures for Illness.** Using leeches to cure.

1. Advancing the contributions of psychology to the understanding of health and illness through basic and clinical research
2. Encouraging the integration of biomedical information about health and illness with current psychological knowledge
3. Promoting education and services in the psychology of health and illness
4. Informing the psychological and biomedical community and the general public about the results of current research and service activities in this area (APA, 2012)

Unlike the Society of Behavioral Medicine or the American Psychosomatic Society, whose members are overwhelmingly physicians, APA's Division 38, the Society for Health Psychology is a group specifically for psychologists. That fact aside, it is also open to (and is driven to foster collaborations with) members of the other health-care professions who are interested in the psychological aspects of physical and mental health. The Division's main goals are to (1) understand the etiology and promotion and maintenance of health; (2) prevent, diagnose, treat, and rehabilitate physical and mental illness; (3) study psychological, social, emotional, and behavioral factors in physical and mental illness; and (4) improve the health-care system and formulation of health policy.

Main Areas in Health Psychology

The field of health psychology, as well as the contents of this book, is naturally segmented into three areas: (1) stress and coping, (2) health behaviors, and (3) issues in health care. One major area under the umbrella of health psychology is **clinical health psychology**, a broad specialty in professional psychology that spans the three main segments and in which clinical practitioners work (Belar, 2008). Many health psychologists are clinicians and, although we will discuss clinical issues throughout this book, especially **evidence-based treatments** (Davidson, Trudeau, & Smith, 2006; Phillips, 2012), our focus is on the wider field of health psychology.

At the psychological roots of this area of study, the first part of this book will examine the biopsychosocial determinants of stress and then investigate how these same factors can influence coping style. The next part of the book will primarily describe the main health psychological theories relating to why we act in various healthy ways using different health behaviors as examples. We will look at the good (e.g., physical activity), the bad (e.g., eating too much fast food), and the ugly (e.g., seeing what smoking can do to a person's teeth and lungs). The last part of the book will focus on different factors relating to health care. These include the complexities of dealing with chronic and terminal illnesses and the different psychological factors influencing the quality of interactions between doctors and patients. We will begin by looking at how health psychologists do research, followed by an overview of some critical biological systems and discussing how different theories of human development and cultural variations can help us understand our health-related behaviors and our health. As you continue in the book, you will also learn about some of the fascinating ways that different cultures approach health and illness.

Synthesize, Evaluate, Apply

- What are the different areas of knowledge/psychology that play a role in health psychology?
- A 9-year study (Berkman & Syme, 1979) showed that people who practiced healthier behaviors lived longer but examined men and women over the age of 45 only. What aspect of this finding is a challenge for health psychologists (as we try to change the behaviors of younger adults)?
- How are the three main organizations for health psychology different from each other?
- Contrast the two approaches used by medicine and health psychology. What are components of each?

APPLICATION SHOWCASE

CAREERS AND GRADUATE TRAINING IN HEALTH PSYCHOLOGY

Health psychology enjoys growing popularity in colleges and universities (Panjwani et al., 2017). In one study, 177 out of 374 (48%) undergraduate psychology programs surveyed offered the course in 2005 (Stoloff et al., 2010) compared to only 112 of 400 programs surveyed (less than 26%) in a study conducted just 10 years previously (Perlman & McCann, 1999). After reading this book you may want to consider working in this fascinating field.

Most health psychologists work in either basic research settings or in applied settings. The former are academic psychologists who could be affiliated with a university or research center. The latter are clinicians who might be affiliated with hospitals or clinics. Researchers aim to determine the biopsychosocial factors involved in the many areas discussed in this book such as stress, cardiovascular diseases, cancer, and HIV. Clinical activities include conducting a variety of tests such as cognitive and behavioral assessments, psychophysiological assessments, clinical interviews, demographic surveys, objective and projective personality assessments, and various other clinical and research-oriented protocols. Health clinicians also implement interventions to change health behaviors, reduce stress, help people cope with chronic illnesses, and increase adherence to treatment. Many psychologists work in health-care settings and many HMOs include psychologists as well. Health psychologists have also been employed in governmental agencies, rehabilitation centers, medical schools, and pain centers (Belar & Deardorff, 2009). Table 1.5 shows the main types of levels of clinical health psychologists.

Although few undergraduate institutions offer specialized programs in health psychology, a growing number of graduate programs offer a degree or at least an emphasis in health psychology. The best preparation at the undergraduate level is a psychology major with many supporting courses in biology, statistics, and research methods. Many schools around the country are also adding an introductory health psychology course to the curriculum, but similar material may be covered in courses with titles such as behavioral health care, behavioral medicine, health behavior change, and health promotion. Because the biopsychosocial mode incorporates many different subject areas, you can cultivate your interest in health psychology by working in a variety of related fields. Many social workers, occupational and physical therapists, nutrition and exercise physiologists, dieticians, and other health-care workers also use the health psychological approach even if not the explicit label. Many county, state, and national organizations also hire students with backgrounds and interests in health psychology to work with related departments. Even within the field of psychology many social, personality, clinical, and counseling psychologists (some of the classic and traditional areas of psychology) sometimes also take a strong health psychological approach in their work.

After an undergraduate degree, most health psychologists enroll in graduate school and work toward a master of science (MS) or doctoral degree (PhD). A master's degree can take 2 to 3 years, and a doctoral degree can take 5 or more years; the content of the coursework will vary with the institution. Some graduate schools will focus more on the psychological aspects of the biopsychosocial model, including a greater number of advanced courses in psychology. Others will lean more heavily on the biological side of the model, with more courses that are specialized in biology and medicine. If you use the most traditional way to look for graduate schools—the American Psychological Association's guide to graduate study—here is something to look for. There are a small (although growing) number of health psychology PhD programs, but a larger number of clinical psychology programs that offer health psychology tracks. There are also many schools that have a health psychology emphasis within their social psychology doctoral programs (e.g., the University of California, Los Angeles [UCLA]). There are also schools with behavioral neuroscience or behavioral medicine programs whose curriculum is very close to that of health psychology programs. For one of the most up-to-date sources for programs with health psychology training, check the Society of Behavioral Medicine's health psychology education and training websites (Society of Behavioral Medicine, n.d.a, n.d.b).

Applied health psychologists have a doctoral or master's degree and are licensed for the independent practice of psychology in areas such as clinical and counseling psychology. Applicants have access to board certification in health psychology through the American Board of Professional Psychology. Clinical and counseling doctoral students are required to complete a 1-year internship before obtaining their doctorates, and many of these programs offer some training in health psychology. After graduate school, a number of individuals choose to specialize in a particular area of the field and take on postdoctoral positions. Although these positions rarely pay much, they are excellent opportunities to work closely with experienced researchers in the field and learn much more about specific topics.

If this brief exposure of what is available to you has whetted your appetite for more information about being

(Continued)

(Continued)

a health psychologist, the best place to look is the Society for Health Psychology's (APA Division 38) education and training website (https://societyforhealthpsychology.org/training/training-resources/#) or a similar site hosted by the Society for Behavioral Medicine (http://www.sbm.org/). At both sites you will find a listing of doctoral programs in health psychology, a guide to internships in health psychology, and a listing of postdoctoral programs in health psychology. Commercial job searching sites carry health psychology jobs as well, but be careful of the search terms you use. This is an expanding, exciting field with a tremendous potential to change how long and how well we live. I hope you are eager to learn more about it in the pages ahead, and consider becoming a health psychologist, too.

▼ TABLE 1.5

Levels of Clinical Health Psychologists

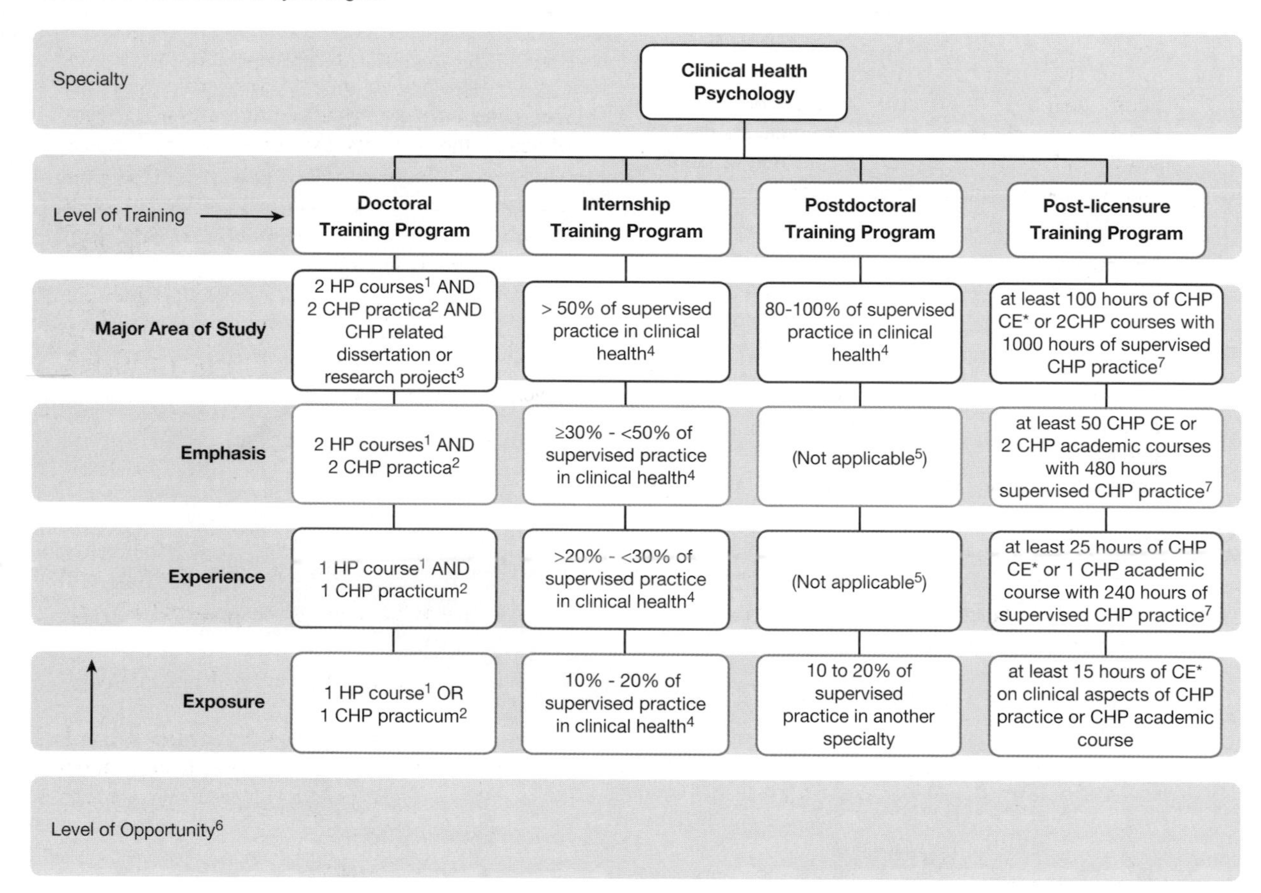

Specialty	Clinical Health Psychology			
Level of Training →	**Doctoral Training Program**	**Internship Training Program**	**Postdoctoral Training Program**	**Post-licensure Training Program**
Major Area of Study	2 HP courses[1] AND 2 CHP practica[2] AND CHP related dissertation or research project[3]	> 50% of supervised practice in clinical health[4]	80-100% of supervised practice in clinical health[4]	at least 100 hours of CHP CE* or 2CHP courses with 1000 hours of supervised CHP practice[7]
Emphasis	2 HP courses[1] AND 2 CHP practica[2]	≥30% - <50% of supervised practice in clinical health[4]	(Not applicable[5])	at least 50 CHP CE or 2 CHP academic courses with 480 hours supervised CHP practice[7]
Experience	1 HP course[1] AND 1 CHP practicum[2]	>20% - <30% of supervised practice in clinical health[4]	(Not applicable[5])	at least 25 hours of CHP CE* or 1 CHP academic course with 240 hours of supervised CHP practice[7]
↑ **Exposure**	1 HP course[1] OR 1 CHP practicum[2]	10% - 20% of supervised practice in clinical health[4]	10 to 20% of supervised practice in another specialty	at least 15 hours of CE* on clinical aspects of CHP practice or CHP academic course
Level of Opportunity[6]				

[1]Clinical Health Psychology (CHP) and Health Psychology (HP) Courses and Training -- Must have content congruent with *Clinical Health Psychology Education and Training and Guidelines and Post-doc-CRSPP 2011* (available on Council of Specialities in Professional Psychology website http://cospp.org/guidelines). Doctoral programs may be on quarter or semester academic calenders and a course in either system is considered equivalent. 2 semesters/3 quarters constitute one academic year.

[2]Clinical Health Psychology Practicum (CHP)—one academic year (approx. 9 months) of supervised training, at least 8 hours per week, or its equivalent (e.g., total clock hours 240 hours) with at least 50% of clinical service delivery with *health-related issues* of patient, family members, and/or *interprofessional* care teams.

[3]Clinical Health Psychology dissertation or research, project -- empirical research, extended case studies, literature critiques and analyses, or capstone projects.

[4]Clinical Health supervised practice: must include >50% of clinical service delivery to clinical health psychology patients, family members, and/or interprofessional care teams (e.g., assessment, treatment, consultation). The remainder of supervised experience can include seminar attendance, readings, research, provision of clinical supervision, teaching, program development and evaluation, and administration.

[5]Not applicable: By definition, postdoctoral education and training in clinical health psychology is a major area of study requiring 80% or more of time spent in this specialty area, but does allow for an exposure to other specialty areas.

[6]The term "focus" should be used to describe opportunities in non-specialty areas of training. Training programs should strive to provide explicit explanations of the type of training provided in these non-specialty areas.

[7]Supervised practice is expected with either the CE or CHP course(s) and defined as >50% of clinical service delivery to clinical health psychology patients, family members, and/or interprofessional care teams (e.g., assessment, treatment, consultation)

*CE course = must be organized CE program, APA sponsor of psychology continuing education.

Source: Reprinted with permission of the Society for Health Psychology.

CHAPTER REVIEW

SUMMARY

- There are many different definitions of health, each varying in its culture of origin. Western medicine sees health more as the absence of disease whereas other cultures see health more as a balance of opposing forces or spiritual harmony. The most common definition is that used by the World Health Organization: health is a state of complete physical, mental, and social well-being.
- Culture is broadly defined and includes ethnicity, sex, religion, gender, and nationality. Various dimensions of culture shape our health behaviors and our general health. Individualism and collectivism are examples of basic cultural dimensions. Socioeconomic status and sex are two of the most important cultural variables, each leading to a variety of health differences.
- Health psychology uses a biopsychosocial approach. This approach focuses on the biological, psychological, and sociocultural factors that influence health and health behaviors.
- Theorizing about the extent to which the mind and the body are connected has varied over time and across cultures. The ancient Chinese and Indians saw the two as connected, but the Greeks and other Europeans saw the mind and body as separate. Today we recognize that the two are clearly interconnected, and this connection is critical to understanding health and illness.
- Freud was the first psychologist to link the mind and body and to hypothesize psychological bases for physiological problems. His early views led to the formation of the first organization of behavioral medicine in the late 1930s, followed by further growth in the late 1960s.
- Health psychology as a unique area of psychology came to the forefront in the 1970s and has since grown. Its main goals are the prevention of illness, the promotion of health, the understanding of the biopsychosocial aspects of physical and mental illness, and the improvement of the health-care system. The main areas of health psychology are stress and coping, health behaviors, and issues in health care.
- Three major organizations cater to those using the biopsychosocial model: the Society of Behavioral Medicine, Society for Health Psychology, and American Psychosomatic Society.

TEST YOURSELF

Check your understanding of the topics in this chapter by answering the following questions.

1. The most comprehensive definition of health is provided by the
   a. Biomedical model.
   b. Hippocratic model.
   c. World Health Organization.
   d. Population Health model.
   e. International Classification of Functioning.

2. Which of the following is the primary focus of health psychology?
   a. health promotion, maintenance, and recovery
   b. etiology and correlates of health and illness
   c. revising the health-care system
   d. finding the cure for diseases like HIV and cancer
   e. studying patient–practitioner interactions

3. ________ refers to the number of cases of a disease that exist at some given point in time. __________ refers to the number of deaths due to particular causes.
   a. Morbidity; Mortality
   b. Mortality; Morbidity
   c. Epidemiology; Pathogenesis
   d. Etiology; Epidemiology
   e. Morbidity; Etiology

4. The Greek physician best known for dissections and providing us with anatomy data was
   a. Plato.
   b. Galen.

c. Hippocrates.
d. Descartes.
e. Aginostophenes.

5. The most common definition of health across cultures is health as
   a. the absence of disease.
   b. spiritual happiness.
   c. communion with God.
   d. a state of balance.

6. One of the first organizations to combine medicine with psychology, started by Dunbar and Alexander, was the
   a. Society for Health Psychology.
   b. Society for Behavioral Medicine.
   c. American Psychosomatic Society.
   d. Mind–Body Institute.
   e. National Institute of Mental Health (NIMH).

7. Culture is best defined as
   a. a set of beliefs shared by a group.
   b. race and ethnicity.
   c. religion, family values, and race.
   d. the values of our parents and family members.

8. One of the most powerful predictors of health disparities in North America is
   a. sex.
   b. socioeconomic status.
   c. race.
   d. ethnicity.

9. In studying about cultural differences in health, we should remember that
   a. in-group differences are often larger than between-group differences.
   b. between-group differences are often larger than in-group differences.
   c. racial differences outweigh all other cultural differences.
   d. most cultural differences are insignificant from a global level.

10. Studies where one group gets an experimental drug and another gets a placebo are called
    a. randomized clinical trials.
    b. correlational studies.
    c. quasi-experimental studies.
    d. longitudinal studies.

KEY TERMS, CONCEPTS, AND PEOPLE ▶▶

ESSENTIAL READINGS ▶▶

Benyamini, Y. (2016). Self-rated health. In Y. Benyamini, M. Johnston, & E. C. Karademas (Eds.), *Assessment in health psychology* (pp.118–30). Boston, MA: Hogrefe.

Freedland, K. E. (2017). A new era for health psychology. *Health Psychology, 36*(1), 1–4. doi:10.1037/hea0000463

Revenson, T. A., & Gurung, R. A. R. (2019). Health psychology: The biopsychosocial model today. In T. A. Revenson & R. A. R. Gurung (Eds.), *Handbook of health psychology* 3e. New York, NY: Routledge.

iStockphoto.com/ maodesign

CHAPTER 2

DOING HEALTH PSYCHOLOGY

Research Methods

iStockphoto.com/ gorodenkoff

Chapter 2 Outline

MEASURING UP

IS PSYCHOLOGY A SCIENCE?

Listed below are a number of statements. Read each statement carefully and indicate the extent to which you agree or disagree by writing the appropriate number by each statement on a scale from 1 (*strongly disagree*) to 7 (*strongly agree*).

1. An undergraduate degree in psychology should be a bachelor of science rather than a bachelor of arts degree. _______
2. It's just as important for psychology students to do experiments as it is for students in chemistry and biology. _______
3. Research conducted in controlled laboratory settings is essential for understanding everyday behavior. _______
4. Even though each person is unique, it is possible for science to find general laws explaining human behavior. _______
5. Carefully controlled research is not likely to be useful in solving psychological problems. _______
6. Our ability as humans to behave in any way we choose makes our attempts to predict behavior ineffective. _______
7. Psychological advice given in popular books and magazines is often as useful as claims that are more research based. _______
8. Government funding of experimentation is as necessary for expanding what we know about psychology as it is for gaining knowledge in areas like chemistry and physics. _______
9. The study of psychology should be seen primarily as a science. _______
10. Courses in psychology place too much emphasis on research and experimentation. _______
11. Psychological research can enable us to anticipate people's behavior with a high degree of accuracy. _______
12. Psychologists working as counseling professionals don't need to be so concerned with research findings. _______
13. Psychological theories presented in the media should not be trusted unless they are supported by experiments. _______
14. Psychology will never be a true science because its predictions of individual behavior are seldom exact or certain. _______
15. Students get little benefit from learning about procedures for conducting psychology experiments. _______

Source: "The Psychology as a Science Questionnaire" (Friedrich, 1996).

▼ Ponder This

> Before you share a research study on Facebook, Twitter, or other social media, what should you be looking for in order to know it is valid?
>
> What are the different ways to design research?
>
> Does a startling research finding need to be shown again (replicate) before you believe it? Why or why not?

"Coffee is good for you." "Coffee is bad for you." "Eating chocolate leads to longer life." "Cell phone usage may cause cancer." "Daily mindfulness interventions lead to happiness." You have probably seen social media blaring similar headlines. Our Facebook and Twitter feeds are often flooded with the latest "Research shows . . . " type shares. Often, the advice is contradictory. Sometimes what is good for us in one year is bad for us in another year. Whereas it is easy to think nothing is true and that health is too complex to fully predict, the reality is that the media do not always do a good job of reporting research. We textbook authors aim to do a much better job but you will be a better consumer of information (both in life and in understanding health psychology) if you have a working understanding of the basic elements of research, the major designs used, and some common statistical analyses (and their interpretation). Scientific knowledge and research has a toolkit and a common methodology. This textbook is based on peer-reviewed journal articles—research published in academic journals that have passed the tests of independent review. How is that research done? What are the major designs used? In this chapter I will give you the tools to enable you to open up any research journal and be able to better understand the findings discussed within. By chapter's end we get to a major question for all scientific research—Do the findings replicate?

Common Rubrics for Health

Regardless of which definition of health we consider, each definition of health is broad and ambiguous. How can we measure mental, spiritual, and social health? Does simply the absence of physical problems or disease equate to health? Can anyone even measure a balanced yin and yang? The answer is no, not really, or at least not by any measure that we know of or use in the United States or in the scientific community, and not in a way on which we can all agree. To understand what keeps us healthy, it is important to start with a good measurement of health. As you learn about the field of health psychology, you will see that although most researchers will use a common understanding and relatively broad definition of health to guide their general thinking (e.g., a general state of well-being), every researcher uses a different specific measure of health to help understand what makes us healthy.

Take a quick look at the major research journals that report on health psychological research, and you will see that different studies use slightly different measures. This is the first major element to watch for when reading articles. The main categories of measures vary with each journal. For example, *Health Psychology* is the leading journal in the field and publishes the results of studies on the topic of health psychology. This journal features many studies that define health in terms of the extent to which health-improving behaviors are practiced (e.g., how much did the participants in the study exercise in a week?) or in terms of psychological well-being (e.g., what were the participants' scores on the Profile of Mood States, a common measure of mood?). You will also see many studies that assess the extent to which health-diminishing behaviors are practiced. For example, how much does a person smoke? What predicts the amount of alcohol consumed?

Other journals, such as the *Annals of the Society for Behavioral Medicine* and *Psychosomatic Medicine,* measure many specific physiological outcomes. For example, what are the levels of immune cells in the blood? Figure 2.1 shows sample contents from the three major journals. The bottom line is that we determine if people are healthy by measuring a variety of aspects. You will see measures of basic physiological levels of bodies' various systems (e.g., blood pressure, heart rate, or cholesterol level). You will see measures of how much people practice healthy behaviors (e.g., exercising). You will also see many measures of psychological well-being (e.g., levels of depression or optimism) and how well people practice healthy psychological ways (e.g., good coping skills). There are so many different ways to measure the key elements of health, an entire book focuses on the different measures used in health psychology (Benyamini, Johnston, & Karademas, 2016).

▼ FIGURE 2.1

Journal Covers

Sources: Applied Psychological Measurement, 42(3); *Cross-Cultural Research, 52*(2); *Clinical Case Studies, 17*(2).

A RESEARCH PRIMER

Health psychology relies firmly on the scientific method. The key elements of a science are (1) that it is empirical (relying on sense observations and data) and (2) that it is theory driven. The data or empirical evidence is collected in ethical, rigorously controlled, and standardized ways whether you are identifying causes of stress or testing the psychological effects of an intervention to reduce smoking. The research enterprise is a fascinating one; to get a good feel for the results of research (discussed throughout this book), you should have a good idea of the main research designs and data collection methods. Because the bulk of our knowledge comes from research, courses in experimental methods and statistics are great companions or foundations for the health psychology course. This chapter should be a good refresher for those of you who have taken such courses or provide the rest of you with enough to really enjoy reading research journals.

Understanding the common research methods used by health psychologists and knowing how to interpret common statistical results will also enable you to make better sense of peer-reviewed journal articles, the source of the information used in writing this book. Even if you learn of results of research on the radio, television, or via the Internet, it is always good practice to go to the original published article to substantiate the results. You will be surprised how often media outlets spin a finding to amplify the possible implications. Reading the original sources for yourself (and understanding them) will make you a better consumer of science. You may want to head over to PsycInfo (or a related database) right now and look up the latest issue of *Health Psychology*. Then go back to it after you read the rest of this chapter and feel the thrill of being research savvy.

Watch for different ways studies are set up. There are a wide variety of research designs in health psychology (Lovejoy & Fowler, 2019). As discussed in Chapter 1, Health Psychologists may be trained as clinicians, experimentalists, developmentalists, or social psychologists. Health psychology research is also conducted in different health-related disciplines such as nursing, medicine, and public health. Each of these different areas favors different research designs. Someone with a public health degree may favor population-wide measurement of bike path usage.

Dr. Regan A. R. Gurung

▲ **Research Presentations.** We often hear about research from conference presentations or even listening to TED talks. Listen to mine on how to Chill, Drill, and Build for healthy living. Remember, neither go through the same level of peer review as do scholarly journals.

Developmental psychologists may prefer studies conducted over a period of time. Social psychologists may prefer experimental tests of different treatments. Each design has its pros and cons, as you will see in the pages ahead.

Key Steps to Doing Research

The steps for conducting research on health mirror most of the steps used to conduct research on any topic. First, the researcher identifies a question of interest and then reviews what has been published on the topic. Next, the researcher ascertains what is left to be discovered or needed to be researched and then decides how to conduct that research. One common approach to this sort of research is to measure basic relevant health behaviors or states of health whether psychological or physiological. There are a variety of specific scales or questionnaires one can use to measure, assess, or evaluate health (Luszczynska, Kruk, & Boberska, 2019). *Measurement* focuses on describing characteristics of an individual (e.g., self-efficacy). *Assessment* relates to obtaining information according to a goal (e.g., how much did exercise increase after an intervention). *Evaluation* "accounts for the individual in a specific situation and the goals or criteria which were externally set resulting in a normative judgment" (Luszczynska et al., 2019). In health psychology these terms are often used interchangeably.

Similar to conducting psychological science in general, health researchers can start with descriptive studies (e.g., How much are people exercising?), move on to correlational designs (e.g., What is exercising associated with?), and then design interventions (e.g., If I introduce a new way of talking about exercise, will amount of exercise change?). In designing interventions, researchers can choose from a wide variety of models. Lovejoy and Fowler (2019) present a fuller description of different research designs and particular adaptations for health psychological interventions.

RESEARCHER SPOTLIGHT

Dr. Krista Ranby earned her PhD in social psychology from Arizona State University, Tempe. She currently teaches at the University of Colorado, Denver, and is skilled at research design. See her chapter in Essential Readings (Ranby, 2019).

Good news. The basic process of doing research is common across the board and a recent chapter in the *Handbook of Health Psychology* (Revenson & Gurung, 2019) provides us with a major research designs in health psychology (Ranby, 2019). I summarize the main steps in Table 2.1. As you can see, most map nicely onto what you have read about in your research methods class. There are some nuances, of course. In health psychology research you tend to have to spend more time and energy collecting data and are more likely to be measuring sensitive topics. You have to pay particular attention to selecting your measurement tools, as well. Let's first overview the major types of research designs used in health psychology. We can then focus in on measurement.

Major Research Designs

Descriptive Studies The most basic form of research describes what is going on: How many people smoke? How prevalent is a certain disease or disorder? If you receive an electronic survey over email asking you about your behaviors you are probably being recruited for a descriptive study. This basic form of design is exploratory and aims to establish baselines for behaviors. You are most likely to see descriptive studies in the field of epidemiology and public health. Epidemiological studies often report **prevalence rates**, the proportion of the population that has a particular disease at a particular time (commonly reported as cases per 1,000 or 100,000 people), and **incidence rates**, the frequency of new cases of the disease during a year.

▼ TABLE 2.1

Major Steps in Research Design

1. Plan Your Study a. Consider a program of research that plans, in advance, for different studies to answer the key questions. b. Clarify the study's main purpose. c. Identify a target population. d. Consider if important subgroups exist in the population. e. Predict or hypothesize the effect you expect.
2. Pick a Design a. Descriptive b. Correlational c. Experimental d. Longitudinal
3. Recruit Participants
4. Conduct study
5. Analyze Data
6. Replicate and Report

We see descriptive studies all around us. Take this headline: "Too many older patients get cancer screenings" (Szabo, 2017). This particular *New York Times* article reports on a study published in the *American Journal of Public Health* (Mehta, Fung, Kistler, Chang, & Walter, 2017) showing that nearly one in five older women are getting regular mammograms when they should not. The issue is that mammograms are not recommended for people with limited life expectancy. The study does not tell you why or if there is a downside, but just reports on the numbers of individuals doing the certain behavior. Make sure you do not draw conclusions beyond what is measured in the study. Well-written research articles do not go beyond the data but we cannot expect the same from media reports of those same articles. The more research savvy you are the less likely you are to waste time and energy on false conclusions.

Correlational Studies The most basic form of research design describes relationships between variables. Are heavier people at more risk for cardiovascular disease? Do poorer people smoke more? A **correlation coefficient** is the statistical measure of the association represent with a lower-case *r*. Correlations range from −1.00 to +1.00 with values closer to 1 (regardless of sign) signifying stronger associations. This is a key point because $r = -.54$ is stronger than $r = .38$. Many novices see the negative sign and assume it is not good. Wrong. The sign refers to the direction of the relationship. Positive correlations indicate variables that change in the same direction (e.g., higher weight correlates with higher risk of cardiovascular disease). Negative correlations indicate variables that change in opposite directions (e.g., lower **socioeconomic status** correlates with higher smoking rates).

▲ **Correlations.** The correlation is one of the most misunderstood statistics (and research designs, yes it is both) in psychology.

As you read journal articles, do not be surprised to see emphasis about correlations around the .2 to .3 level. If 1.00 is the highest, .2 and .3 seem low. They are, but given that there are many factors accounting for any behavior or result, a *statistically significant* correlation in the .2 to .3 range between any two variables suggests a worthy relationship. Make sure you also pay attention to statistical significance. The results section of a journal article will report the significance level of any findings. Statistical analyses with p-values (probability values) less than .05, .01, or .001 (reported as $p < .05$, $p < .01$, or $p < .001$) are significant. All results tables will indicate statistically significant differences with an asterisk (*) so you can be on the lookout for these asterisks. The more asterisks you see, the higher the statistical significance (and unlike correlations, the *lower* the p value, the better). A probability value of less than 0.05 suggests that the probability of getting the same result by chance is less than 5 in 100. You can see why $p < 0.001$ is a significant level. The p value is influenced by sample size; given that many studies in health psychology have very large samples, you will note that even small correlations could be statistically significant.

Many journal articles in health psychology will report correlations between variables although I have noticed that more-complex statistics (such as odds ratios) are replacing this simple statistical. Speaking of simple, when only the relationship between two variables is tested (e.g., distress correlated with coping style) you call it a zero-order or **direct correlation.** Yes, this is helpful and illustrates a relationship, but quite honestly it is somewhat misleading. There is often more than one variable influencing another; to statistically control for multiple associations, researchers use a **partial correlation**. When you calculate a partial correlation or control for another variable, the relationship between two variables is tested while controlling for a third variable (or more). For example, researchers often statistically control for a research participant's age when assessing correlations, which essentially acknowledges that the association between the variables of interest (e.g., distress and coping style) could vary for people of different ages.

When you read a journal article, do not be intimidated by the large mass of numbers you see. Even correlational tables may seem like a mess of numbers, but take your time to orient yourself to what you are seeing. Take a look at the correlational table presented in Table 2.2. In this

▼ TABLE 2.2

Means, Standard Deviations, and Correlations Among Study Variables for Sample ($N = 204$)

Study variables	1	2	3	4	5	6	7	8	9	10	11	12
1. W1 age	—											
2. W1 nativity[a]	.06	—										
3. W4 economic hardship	–.05	.18**	—									
4. W4 ethnic discrimination	–.01	.13	.24***	—								
5. W4 family support	.07	–.06	–.19**	–.19**	—							
6. W4 friend support	.03	–.03	–.14*	–.16*	.37***	—						
7. W4 risky behaviors	–.04	.16*	.18**	.27***	–.19**	–.11	—					
8. W5 family support	.05	–.09	–.19**	–.22**	.64***	.25***	–.19**	—				
9. W5 family support	.18**	.04	–.20**	–.14*	.28***	.63***	–.08	.40***	—			
10. W5 risky behaviors	.01	.13	.20**	.28***	–.30***	–.06	.06***	–.36***	–.05	—		
11. W6 body mass index	–.10	.06	.10	–.13	–.03	.00	.11	–.04	–.02	.13	—	
12. W2 to W6 pregnancy status[b]	–.08	–.04	.08	.09	–.09	–.15*	–.10	–.04	–.17*	–.06	–.01	—
Mean	16.81	.64	.01	1.32	5.90	5.50	1.24	5.92	5.53	1.24	26.71	.55
Standard Deviation	.99	.48	2.37	.42	1.17	1.34	.30	1.21	1.27	.28	5.26	.50

Note: W = Wave. Means and Standard deviations reported here were calculated prior to centering. W4 economic hardship is calculated as a weighted summed score.
[a]Nativity coded as: 0 = Mexico born; 1 = U.S. born. [b]Pregnancy status was coded as 0 = *not pregnant after W1* or 1 = *pregnant at least once between W2 to W6.*
*p < .05. **p < .01. ***p < .001.

Source: Bravo, Derlan, Umaña-Taylor, Updegraff, & Jahromi, 2017.

study, researchers wanted to test the link between factors such as ethnic discrimination and risky behaviors (Bravo, Derlan, Umaña-Taylor, Updegraff, & Jahromi, 2017). All the participants were Mexican-origin adolescents. Although there are a lot of numbers, orient yourself to the basic elements of the American Psychological Association style table.

iStock.com/filadendron

▲ **What type of food is best for you?** Research on carbs, proteins, and fats is heavily debated, an especially good reason to know what makes good research.

The main variables are listed in the column down the left (e.g., 1. Age, 2. Nativity). The same variables are referred to along the top, and, conveniently, the labels (e.g., Age) do not have to be rewritten. Each dash (–) represents the association of a variable with itself. Given that one variable will be perfectly (i.e., 1) correlated with itself, the numeral 1 is not used. All the numbers with asterisks represent the statistically significant correlations. The more *s, the higher the statistical significance. Note that body mass index, the major medical measure used to assess obesity, is not related to any other measures. None of the numbers in row 11 have any asterisks. You can see negative correlations (e.g., nativity and economic hardship). The U.S.-born participants were less likely to have economic hardship. There are some positive correlations too. The more economic hardship reported by participants, the more ethnic discrimination they report ($r = .24$). Once your eyes orient to the numbers there is a lot of information to pull from this one table.

There are many examples of **correlational studies** around. Something that the lay public often ignores is that many of the studies on issues they care about are correlational studies. A common interest? What to eat. Most food studies, especially those with large sample sizes, are correlational. For example, Dehghan et al. (2017) conducted a large epidemiological study in 18 countries. They measured the diets of 134,335 individuals and followed them over a 10-year period. At the end of that time, the researcher measured how many people were alive, and how many had had heart attacks. In the latter group, they looked to see if the deaths were linked to their diets. Higher-carbohydrate intake was linked to higher deaths but not with risk for heart attacks. [A geeky aside: I cannot help but share that this article had more than 400 authors. Probably the best use of the et al. citation style ever. Lucky Mahshid Dehghan who was first author and the only one you see unless you go to the references at the end of the book.]

Correlational designs do not allow us to draw causal conclusions. In the study above can we conclude eating carbs kills? Is this reason enough to start piling on the bacon? Not exactly. This does not stop the casual reader or the uninformed, and can sometimes lead to mild panic where none is warranted. For example, another study found that oral sex was correlated with incidences of mouth cancer (Kreimer et al., 2004). Does this mean that practicing oral sex causes mouth cancer? If the study was correlational, it does not. In fact, the study also showed that oral sex was highly correlated with smoking and drinking, two behaviors more likely to cause mouth cancer.

Experimental and Quasi-Experimental Designs **Experimental designs** help us determine causality. All health psychology interventions are, by definition, experiments. If we really want to know if something caused something else we need to introduce that something and see if it has an effect. If carbohydrates are bad for health, we need to design a study that measures health first, then introduces carbohydrates, and then measures health afterwards, controlling for other factors. If health changes after the carbohydrates are introduced and nothing else changes, then we can conclude carbohydrates cause poor health. In experiments, the researcher manipulates the variable that is believed to be important—the **independent variable**—and measures how changes in this variable influence another variable—the **dependent variable**.

Experiments have two or more groups, each of which experiences different levels of the independent variable. If the participants are randomly sampled (everyone in the population has an equal chance of being in the study) and extraneous variables (other variables that may influence the outcome of interest such as socioeconomic status or other health behaviors) are controlled for, then one can be fairly certain that changes in the dependent variable are due to changes in the independent variable. Cause can be determined. Many of the studies in this book are experiments.

To test whether exercise is good for concentration, you can have one group of people exercise (the independent variable) three times a week and the other not exercise. You can then see if the two groups vary in concentration (the dependent variable). In health psychological research, it is often impractical and unethical to manipulate key variables of interest (e.g., making people smoke or have oral sex) so groups that naturally vary in the variable of interest are used instead (e.g., compare groups of people who vary in how much they smoke or have oral sex). Because using naturally occurring groups is not a perfect experiment, such designs are referred to as **quasi-experimental designs**, and the independent variables are called subject variables. Examples of common subject variables are age, sex, ethnicity, personality type, occupation, socioeconomic status, and disease state (level or presence of).

Whereas in correlations you look at how close to 1 the *r* value is and whether it is statistically significant, in experiments you look at whether the test for group differences is statistically significant. The main statistics you look for a *F tests* or *t tests* (more on this later in this chapter).

Randomized Control Trials In the health psychology world, experiments more often take the form of **randomized, controlled, or clinical trials (RCTs)**, in which one group gets an experimental drug or intervention treatment and a second group unknowingly gets a **placebo** (an inactive substance that appears similar to the experimental drug) or nothing (the control group). A large number of evidence-based treatment reviews and clinical interventions use RCTs.

Most RCTs are to test interventions and use clinical trials that begin with controlled study designs, have restricted patient samples, and include well-trained researchers to maximize internal validity. Internal validity essentially means ensuring that the active intervention, and not other factors, caused observed changes in the outcome (Lovejoy & Fowler, 2019). These trials are referred to as clinical *efficacy* (or Phase III) trials. There are also clinical *effectiveness* (or Phase IV) trials where an intervention is delivered with the goal of testing how well it will generalize to a large sample (i.e., building external validity).

A useful heuristic for developing health psychology interventions for chronic diseases was recently proposed by the Obesity-Related Behavioral Intervention Trials (ORBIT) consortium, in conjunction with National Institute of Health (NIH) representatives and other experts in health-related behavioral treatments (Czajkowski et al., 2015). According to the ORBIT model, the process begins with identification of a key clinical problem that is catalyzed or perpetuated by a behavioral, psychological, and/or social factor, and that could thus be remediated with a health psychology intervention. In the subsequent design phase, researchers conduct systematic reviews, meta-analyses, epidemiologic research, small-sample experimental studies, and qualitative research to establish evidence for the pathway between a behavioral, psychological, or social risk factor and a meaningful clinical or biological outcome (Lovejoy & Fowler, 2019). Preliminary testing follows the design phase.

Perhaps one of the best examples of an RCT is the Women's Health Initiative study that was launched in 1991 and in which more than 161,000 healthy postmenopausal women were given hormone replacement pills or a placebo. Researchers stopped the study before completion because the results indicated that women taking the pills were actually more at risk for heart disease (Manson et al., 2003). To make matters worse, recent results suggest that even after stopping the study, women who received the hormone replacement pills still had a higher risk of heart disease (Heiss et al., 2008). The data set is so rich and detailed that researchers continue to mine it to answer questions about a range of illnesses and predictors of mortality (Chen, Brody, & Miller, 2017; Jones et al., 2017).

Cross-Sectional and Longitudinal Designs Research can also be **cross-sectional**, conducted at one point in time, or **longitudinal**, conducted over a period of time and often involving many measures of the key variables. Cross-sectional studies often sample a large number of people and examine different cultural groups in the sample comparing men and women, and people of different ethnicities.

Research can be **prospective**, following disease-free participants over a period to determine whether certain variables (e.g., eating too much fast food) predict disease, or **retrospective**, studying participants with a disease and tracing their histories of health behaviors to determine what caused the disease.

There are a number of well-known prospective studies. One study is the Women's Health Initiative described previously. Another study that you will see many references to in the media and in health psychology research is the Nurses' Health Study (NHS). Started in 1976, the NHS and the NHS II are among the largest prospective studies of the risk factors for major chronic diseases in women (e.g., Tamimi et al., 2005). Approximately 122,000 registered nurses in 11 states were followed over time; findings shed light on a variety of health issues ranging from preventing premenopausal colorectal cancer and breast cancer, to the impact of weight on cancer risk (Dworetzky, Townsend, Pennell, & Kang, 2012).

Synthesize, Evaluate, Apply

- What are the pros and cons of different research designs?
- What are some constraints you might experience doing health psychology research?

Ensuring Strong Measurement

Regardless of your research design, you need to have robust measurement. If your measurements are inaccurate or not precise, your results are not valid. There are number of key factors to keep in mind. Health psychology measurement involves five major steps (Luszczynska et al., 2019). These steps involve (1) the choice of a general framework, considering purpose and domains of measurement, (2) characteristics of the target population, (3) the type of measurement, (4) psychometric characteristics, and (5) issues of implementation of an instrument.

It is particularly important to have a general framework that influences either the purpose of the measurement or the domains measured (Karademas et al., 2016). Frameworks relating to the purpose of measurement distinguish between measurement conducted to reach a clinical decision, describe a target population, or clarify health-related processes that predict psychosocial outcomes. Frameworks organizing measurement by the domains in health psychology include domains of health and prevention, stress and health, and illness and care (Luszczynska et al., 2019).

When considering who you want to study, researchers need to plan differently for different age groups as well as different cultural groups in the population. Many measures were created in English but may need to be translated for use with non-English-speaking participants. The cultural adaptation of measures is an important endeavor when one takes a cultural approach to health (Lopez-Roig & Pastor, 2016). Fortunately, there are many guidelines, methods, and procedures for translating measures and working with different cultural populations.

Once you are ready to measure you can pick from one of a variety of measures. Most common are self-reports (diaries, surveys, questionnaires). You can also use biomarker-based measurement (e.g., cortisol in the blood) and one of a wide variety of biological and physiological measures (Segerstrom, Out, Granger, & Smith, 2016). With advances in technological innovation you can

iStock.com/ DisobeyArt

▲ **Data Collection.** New models of data collection involve the use of smartphones.

also use wearable cameras, accelerometers for motion, or sensor-based measurement (e.g., medication events monitoring systems, or MEMS). MEMS include adherence monitoring devices such as electronic pill containers that register and code information about when each pill is taken (Lam & Fresco, 2015).

Need a blast from your (research methods class) past? When we talk about measurement we need to keep in mind the main qualities of measurement. Key psychometric properties include the reliability of the instrument (e.g., its internal consistency, inter-rater reliability, test-retest reliability), its validity (e.g., construct, criterion, concurrent, predictive, or convergent validity), and sensitivity, that is the extent to which the instrument may detect small changes occurring over time (cf. Johnson, Benyamini, & Karademas, 2016).

Finally, one needs to measure implementation. How acceptable is your measurement? To what extent were your measurement tools adopted by those who are using them? Besides assessment of implementation of the actions of health psychologists, the other issue refers to the implementation of any measurement instruments, conducted by health psychologists. Would using a certain measure make participants less likely to take part in the study or perhaps to drop out at a later stage? Measurement in health psychology research is not as straightforward as one may think (Luszczynska et al., 2019).

GETTING STATISTICALLY SAVVY

Together with looking at correlational coefficients (reported using the italicized letter *r*) and tests of group differences (reported using the italicized letters *F* or *t*), there are a number of statistical elements to watch for that can make journal article reading palatable.

Be aware: Not all associations or changes may be statistically significant. Furthermore, not all statistically significant change may be *meaningful* change. We can launch a philosophical debate around the topic of what constitutes meaningful change in weight or happiness. However, there is one simple answer that is hard to negate: statistically significant changes that could not have taken place by chance are important. That said, there are some simple factors that can artificially create statistical significance. The most critical to consider is the number of participants being studied (or the sample size). Researchers perform many health psychological studies on hundreds or thousands of participants. Increasing the sample size can make previously insignificant changes significant.

There are some safeguards and limiting factors. For example, only phenomena that have a large *effect size* will be significant when the sample size increases. If the psychological intervention or the drug tested or a cognitive behavioral change was not effectual (a simple paraphrase of effect size that adequately conveys its intended meaning), many more participants may not make results significant. Most journal articles report effect size, something that is now required if you are writing in American Psychological Association (APA) style. Look for it as one of many Greek letters representing a variety of effect size calculations, most commonly reported using ηp^2 and read as "partial eta squared."

Common Statistical Tests

There a number of major statistical tests you will encounter over and over again. The first time you run into them they may sound like gibberish, but once you walk through it you will see that they are actually quite simple. Let's look at three of them: **analyses of variance (ANOVAs)**, **multivariate analyses of variance (MANOVAs)**, and **regression analyses**.

Both ANOVAs and MANOVAs test for differences between group means. Is the weight loss in one group different from the weight loss in another group (ANOVAs)? If you want to test for differences between a number of variables that are related to each other, you would use a MANOVA (hence, the multivariate). Are the ratings of quality and taste of one type of food better than another (MANOVA)? The good news is that just like for a correlation, you are paying attention to the *p*-value of the statistical test. Look for if it is significant. If the *p* value of the *F* test, the test used for ANOVA, is less than .05 the means you are comparing are significantly different. When I teach this class I have all my students complete a short set of questions about their health behaviors and their health. The students then get the data (with names removed, of course) and calculate some simple analyses themselves. They often find some interesting findings. Recently, my class compared the body mass index (BMI) scores of men and women using an ANOVA and found a statistically significant difference where the average BMI scores of women were higher than that for men, $F(1,44) = 5.34, p = .023$.

Regression Analyses Regressions are used to predict the likelihood of an outcome from a list of variables. In regressions, you can actually get a sense of how much of the variance in the dependent variable your predictor variables account for. Variance in the dependent variable equals how the dependent variable is different for different people. If there is no variance all people have the same score. If there is a lot of variance, different people have very different scores. How do we predict why different people have different scores?

In a recent study, researchers wanted to predict how good health formed (Fournier et al., 2017). Forty-eight students took part and attempted to practice a certain stretch (psoas-iliac stretch). The students practiced the stretch in the morning or the evening (one variable referred to as condition) consequently had different intentions to stretch (a second variable) and were men and women (a third variable). The researchers wanted to predict how these three variables predicted the students' levels of cortisol, a chemical that plays a role in habit formation. They conducted a regression analysis and their results table is reproduced in Table 2.3.

Once more, you see a lot of numbers. Once more you pay the most attention to the *p* values. There were three separate regression analyses represented by the three blocks of numbers. For our purposes, look at the first block of numbers. The variable that significantly predicted cortisol was the model with condition in it showing a **direct effect** of time of day on levels of cortisol. The other two models, the second and third blocks, show that neither sex nor intentions are significant variables (again look down the column beneath *p*).

Odds Ratios One other statistical test that is relatively common in health psychology articles is the **logistic regression**. This analysis predicts the probability of the occurrence of an event. Articles will often report an **odds ratio**, which is the ratio of the odds of an event occurring in one group to the odds of it occurring in another group. Are men more likely to have a heart attack than women? (See Chapter 14 for the answer.) An odds ratio of 1 suggests the phenomenon (e.g., a heart attack) is equally likely in both groups. An odds ratio greater than 1 suggests the phenomenon is more likely to occur in the first group. Being comfortable with some commonly used statistics and analyses will make you a much better consumer of health psychology research and ultimately a better health psychologist. (See Field, 2018, for a good introduction to statistics and for more details on the terms discussed above.)

For a great example of how odds ratios look, here's an almost sad example. You know how many restaurants include so-called healthy options on their menu? Do you wonder if those options are presented in any different way than the regular items? Turnwald, Jurafsky, Conner, and Crum (2017) took menus from 100 top-selling U.S. chain restaurants. They collected

▼ TABLE 2.3

Regression Models Used to Determine the Mediating Role of Cortisol in the Effect of the Condition on the Time Taken to Form a Behavioral Habit

					95% CI	
Model and variable	Coefficient	*SE*	*t*	*p*	LL	UL
Model predicting cortisol: R^2 = .28, *F*(1, 40) = 14.89, *p* = .0004						
Constant	1.627	.138	11.831	.000	1.349	1.905
Condition	.531	.138	3.859	.001	.252	.809
Model predicting $x_{.95}$ without inclusion of the mediator: R^2 = .20, *F*(3, 38) = 2.34, *p* = .09						
Constant	288.495	172.121	1.671	.102	−59.950	636.941
Condition	−26.601	10.169	−2.616	.013	−47.187	−6.015
Intention	−30.528	35.453	−.861	.395	−102.299	41.244
Sex	−25.043	20.269	−1.236	.224	−66.075	15.990
Model predicting $x_{.95}$ with inclusion of the mediator: R^2 = .29, *F*(4, 37) = 2.58, *p* = .053						
Constant	290.459	150.281	1.933	.061	−14.044	594.962
Cortisol	−22.413	10.779	−2.079	.045	−44.254	−.572
Condition	−14.218	11.213	−1.268	.213	−36.937	8.502
Intention	−23.578	31.366	−.752	.457	−87.133	39.976
Sex	−22.316	19.782	−1.128	.267	−62.398	17.767

Note: CI = confidence interval; LL = lower limit; ULCI = upper limit

Source: Fournier et al., 2017.

262 healthy menu items with 5,873 words and 2,286 standard menu items with 38,343 words and measured if the type of words used in each type of menu was different. Table 2.4 reproduces a results table from their article and shows the use of odds ratios. As you see, restaurants described healthy items in less-appealing ways. Look at the odds ratio column and you see the words more likely to occur in a standard menu were words such as "Exciting" OR = 3.26 and "Provocative" OR = 1.89. Words more likely to occur in a healthy menu were words such as "Simple" OR = 3.27 and, no surprise, "Nutritious" OR = 164.61. So healthy food choices are clearly portrayed differently and in a less appealing way. Perhaps this could be associated with those items being picked less.

The statistic that is now overtaking the journals in health psychology is the **hazard ratio**. Both the odds ratio and the hazard ratio relate to relative risk. The probability of seeing a certain event in some group is called risk (Stare & Maucort-Boulch, 2016). The odds ratio is the odds of the probability of an event occurring in one group, divided by the probability of it not occurring. The hazard ratio is the comparison between the probability of events taking place in a treatment group compared to the probability of the events taking place in a control group. The hazard ratio essentially provides a statistical test of the efficacy of a treatment (Spruance, Reid, Grace, & Samore, 2004). Almost every other health psychology journal article now seems to be reporting hazard ratios so be on the lookout for them.

Other important terms to watch for in the reporting of health psychological research are **relative risk**, the ratio of incidence or prevalence of a disease in an exposed group to the incidence or

▼ TABLE 2.4

Results of Healthy Menu Item Versus Standard Item Descriptions

Theme	Odds ratio [95% CI]	Log likelihood	Frequency in healthy menu (% of words)	Frequency in standard menu (% of words)
Words more likely to occur in standard menu				
Exciting	3.26 [1.73, 6.15]	19.26***	0.17	0.55
Fun and engaging	2.04 [1.56, 2.66]	33.11***	1.00	2.03
Traditional	1.96 [1.56, 2.47]	38.85***	1.35	2.61
American regional	1.96 [1.31, 2.92]	13.4***	0.44	0.86
Texture	1.95 [1.50, 2.54]	29.31***	1.02	1.98
Provocative	1.89 [.96, 3.73]	4.04*	0.15	0.29
Spicy hot	1.64 [1.12, 2.40]	7.29**	0.49	0.81
Artisan	1.63 [1.07, 2.48]	5.96*	0.41	0.67
Taste	1.52 [1.11, 2.08]	7.71**	0.75	1.13
Indulgent	1.37 [1.14, 1.65]	12.04***	2.21	3.01
No difference in healthy menu vs. standard menu				
Size	1.32 [.92,1.88]	2.46	0.58	0.76
Vague positive	1.27 [.77, 2.10]	.93	0.29	0.37
Choice	1.13[.81, 1.57]	.54	0.68	0.77
Farm	1.20 [.87, 1.66]	1.15	0.73	0.61
Social	2.72 [.96, 7.72]	3.01	0.09	0.03
Words more likely to occur in healthy menu				
Foreign	1.27 [1.02, 1.58]	4.26*	1.62	1.28
Fresh	1.38 [1.09, 1.75]	6.39*	1.41	1.03
Simple	3.27 [1.68, 6.37]	10.25**	0.22	0.07
Macronutrients	8.76 [5.57, 13.77]	81.89***	0.75	0.09
Thinness	10.72 [7.22, 15.91]	134.28***	1.11	0.10
Deprivation	17.70 [8.56, 36.59]	68.68***	0.46	0.03
Nutritious	164.61 [40.04, 676.7]	185.49***	0.85	0.01

Note: *p < .05; **p < .01; ***p < .001.

Source: Turnwald, Jurafsky, Conner, and Crum (2017).

prevalence of the disease in an unexposed group, and **absolute risk**, a person's chance of developing a disease independent of any risk that other people may have.

Structural Equation Modeling With an increase in technological sophistication, statistical tools allowed researchers to model multiple relationships simultaneously. A far cry for the zero-order correlation that maps the association of two variables, there are now analyses that can map out the relationships between an array of factors at the same time. One of the most popular is called structural equation modeling. As the name implies, you can draw a structure

Synthesize, Evaluate, Apply

- How do the conclusions from a correlational test vary from those drawn from an experiment?
- Which statistical test would be best to test whether a new intervention to increase healthy eating on campus worked?
- What are the advantages of structural equation modeling over regression analyses or correlational tests?

of variables and hypothesize how they are related. The statistical program then fits your model onto the data and generates an index to tell you how well your model fits the data. Not a great fit? Then, like trying on another piece of clothing, you can redraw your structure and try again.

Figure 2.2 shows you two structural equation models examining the relationships between trauma, resilience, and depressive symptoms on biological outcomes in African American smokers and nonsmokers (Berg et al., 2017). The solid black lines show the statistically significant associations and the gray lines show nonsignificant associations.

You now have all the key tips to make journal reading a much more pleasurable experience, not to mention a more educational one. Before diving into a broad discussion of how cultures vary in their approaches to health (Chapter 3), there are two more important discussions that will help you understand and interpret research better.

CONTEXT AND LEVEL OF ANALYSIS

In Chapter 1 I had you answer the "Who am I?" test. If you (did what few readers do and actually) followed the question prompt, you would have a list of thoughts about who you were. The order in which the different descriptors came to your mind gives you a good idea of the aspects of yourself that are most important to you right now. It also alerts us to two critical factors to consider in this conversation of research design and measurement.

First, the order in which we use words to describe ourselves often depends on the **context** or the environment in which we are. If you are male and are answering the "Who am I?" question sitting in a room full of women, the answer, I am a man, is likely to be near the top of your list. Even if you did not answer with, I am American, your nationality probably would be one of the first descriptors that would come to mind if you were on a holiday abroad, say checking out the Tower of London surrounded by tourists from many different countries.

Even though the context can influence our ordering, it does not mean it changes the content of our self-views. This is where the **level of analysis** is important. This means that our views of ourselves reside at different levels of conscious awareness. Although you may think of yourself as a runner, this description may be far down on the list you generated and correspondingly we would have to go to a deeper level of analysis to uncover it. If we really want to get a good sense of a person and his or her culture, we have to remember that many different levels could be important and that the context in which we make our assessment can make a world of difference. Look at the example shown in Figure 2.3 and notice how the order of ways Manish describes himself varies depending on the context in which he is.

Having culture can offer a person many things. Think about what you may get from being part of a certain culture. Like someone in an army or someone on an athletic team (both cultures of their own), the culture in which you live influences ideas about what to do, what to wear, how to behave, and even how to feel. These prescriptions of how to be form the basis of the way the scientific literature defines culture.

MODERATORS VERSUS MEDIATORS

Earlier in this chapter I introduced you to the difference between zero-order correlations and partial correlations. The former looks at only two variables, the latter factors in or controls for others. I also introduced you to ANOVAs and MANOVAs. Even in those tests of group differences in variables you can also control for third variables. The resulting analyses

▼ FIGURE 2.2

Two Structural Equation Models

a. Ever Smokers

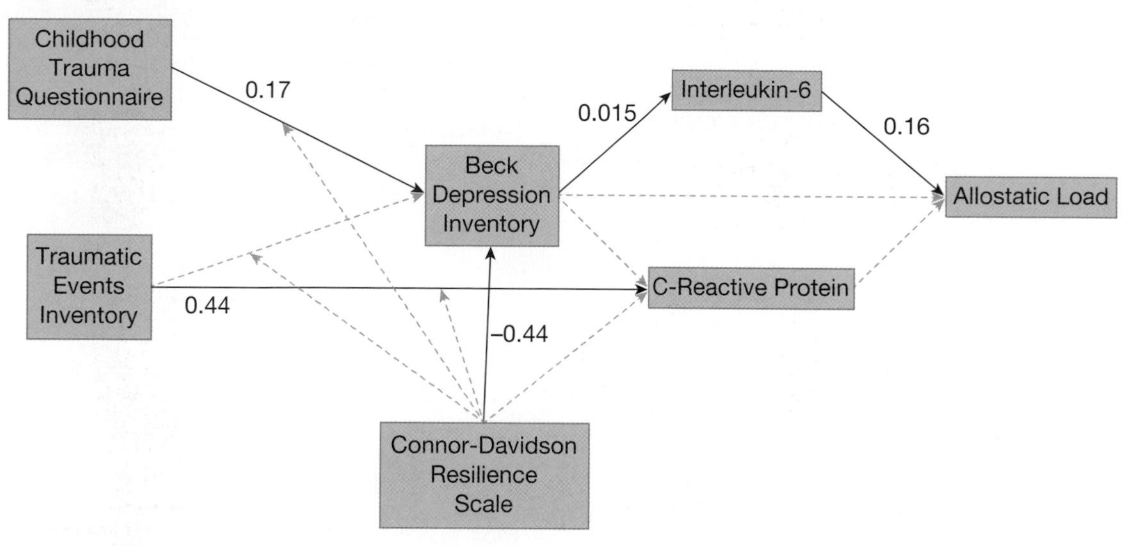

b. Never Smokers

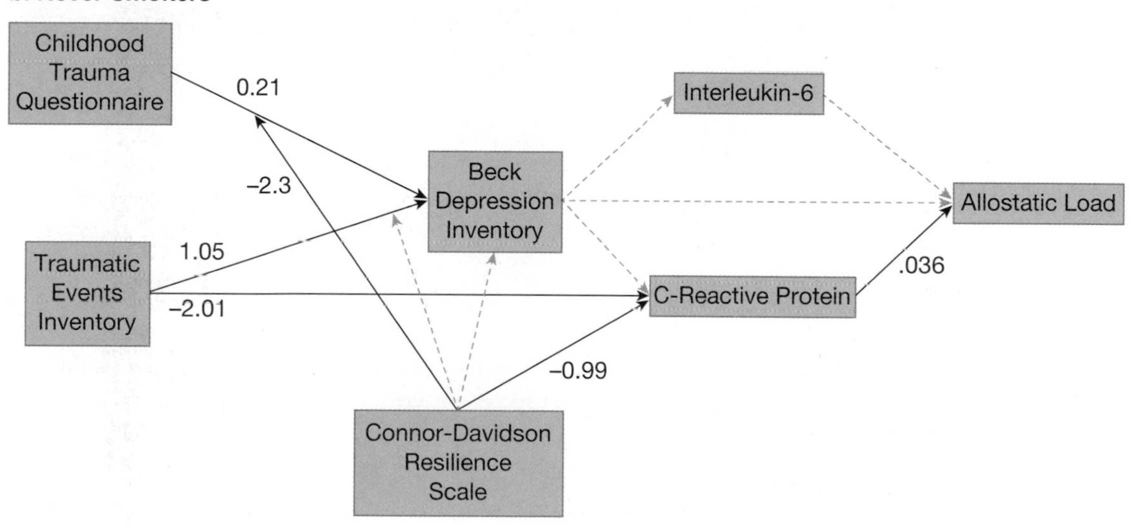

Source: Berg et al., 2017.

are called ANCOVAs and MANCOVAs, where the "C" stands for covariance. Beyond just controlling for variables, health psychological research aims to test for the different ways that third variables can influence relationships between two other variables. If you have a large sample and the statistical chops, you can use structural equation modeling that maps out different relationships simultaneously. Before you do so, it is important to get comfortable with two types of roles variables can play. Welcome to the terms "mediation" and "moderation." You will see many mediators and moderators in health psychology research.

Let's take the example of coping. There are many different ways coping can influence a health outcome. Although health psychologists originally focused on studying the direct relationships between stressors (e.g., public speaking) and outcomes (e.g., blood pressure), today researchers are paying more attention to underlying processes by which biopsychosocial factors influence health (Aldwin, 2018). Asking questions about specific effects (e.g., how, when, for whom, under what conditions, does public speaking lead to increased blood

▼ FIGURE 2.3

Levels of Analysis and Context

The context we are in can influence the things that first come to mind when we are asked to describe ourselves. If Manish were awakened from a nap and asked to describe himself, the order of things that would come up would be very different from those if he had an accident and were taken to the hospital. The context (the hospital) would bring different things to the level of consciousness. Being Hindu in a Western hospital may make those aspects of his self-concept more salient.

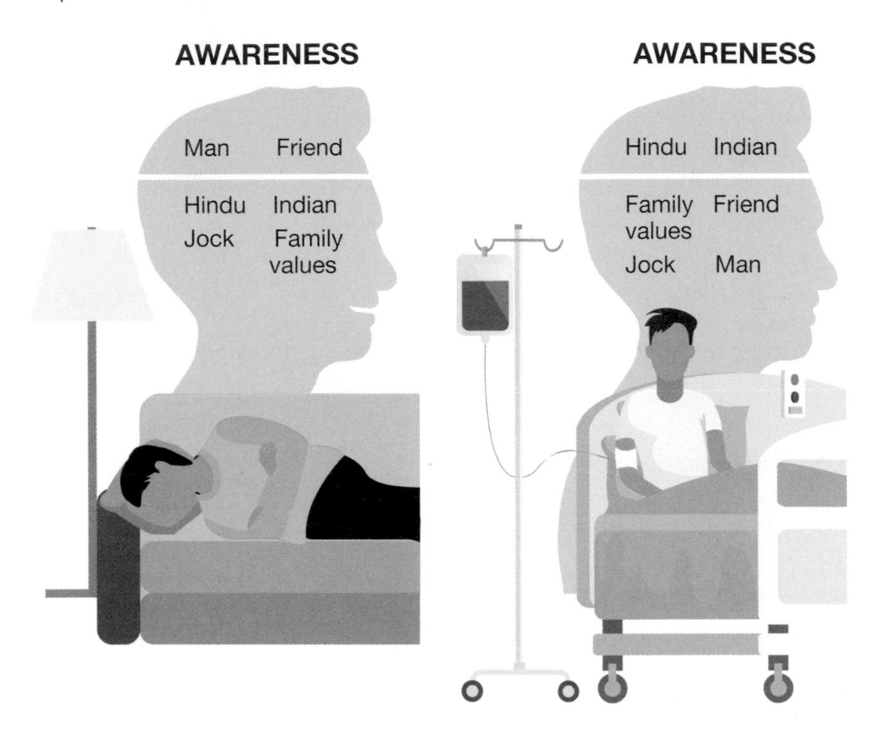

pressure?) requires moving beyond the examination of direct relationships to focus on additional factors that can explain how two variables are related. *Mediation* and *moderation* are two common examples of the type of processes now studied in detail across the field of health psychology (Talebi, Matheson, & Anisman, 2016).

In life you will see that people who have a lot of a certain characteristic (or are high on that variable) tend to behave and react differently than people who have a little of that characteristic (or are low on that variable). The rich tend to be healthier than the poor. Older people tend to be more health conscious than younger people. People high in social support tend to cope better than people low in social support. In each of these cases the variable—income, age, and social support—are called moderators. A **moderator** is a variable that changes the *magnitude* (and sometimes the direction) of the relationship between an antecedent variable and an outcome variable (Aiken & West, 1991). This is easier to understand in a picture. Look at Figure 2.4.

In the example of social support, the number of stressors can be the antecedent variable and well-being is the outcome. A simple **direct effect** would be that people with more stressors are unhappier (a positive correlation). However, things are more complex than that. In any group of people, some individuals will have more social support than others. Let's measure social support and divide the people into a high support and a low support group. We would find that people with more support are happier than people with less social support. Social support has moderated or buffered the relationship between stress and well-being. Such moderating effects of support are now well established and can be seen in a variety of life examples. For example, social

▼ FIGURE 2.4

Moderation

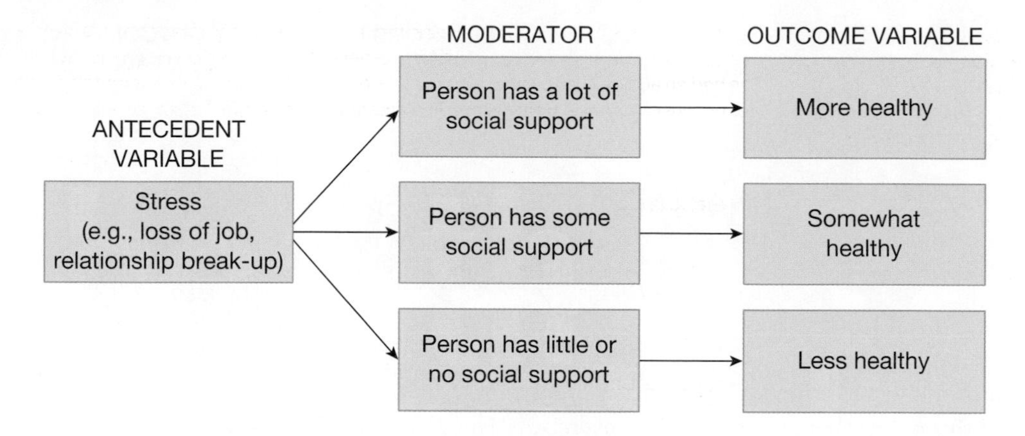

support moderated the relationship between stress, mood, and alcohol use in a study of U.S. Navy personnel (Kelley et al., 2017). Being high or low on some factor often moderates how we react to stress.

Coping is often what you do when you are stressed. What you do can either help or hurt. The response to a stressor and the factors that follow a stressor influence what the outcome is going to be. These responses and factors between the stressor and the outcome are called mediators. A **mediator** is the intervening process (variable) through which an antecedent variable influences an outcome variable. Mediation can be described as a relationship where an independent variable changes a mediating variable, which then changes a dependent variable (MacKinnon, 2008). Coping behaviors in general and specific health behaviors are common mediators. Look at Figure 2.5. Instead of stress directly making you feel good or bad, it may influence your health behaviors (e.g., you drink alcohol or eat more) that *in turn* influence whether you feel good or bad. Here, health behaviors have mediated the relationship. Different cultures have different coping behaviors that can mediate the relationship between stress and well-being (Kuo, Soucie, Huang, & Laith, 2017). In one study of Chinese nurses, coping styles mediated the relationship between factors such as hope, optimism, resilience, and distress (Zhou et al., 2017).

A large body of literature in health psychology concerns interventions aimed at improving well-being by enhancing coping, based on the assumption that effective coping is a mediator (Coyne & Racioppo, 2000). There are a number of statistical procedures to test for mediation (Field, 2018). It is easy to see whether mediation is taking place by comparing the correlation between the antecedent and outcome variables before and after the potential mediator is entered into the statistical analysis. Stay with me here. If the variable you are studying is a mediator, the relationship between the antecedent and outcome variable significantly changes (gets lower) once the mediator is in the analysis. If you are stressed and you take a nap, you will probably wake up feeling better. If you are stressed and you do not take a nap, you may feel worse. In this example, sleep is said to mediate the relationship between your stress level and how you feel. This chapter will discuss many other mediators and moderators.

Think about the different biopsychosocial variables we discussed so far and see whether you can tell the difference between moderators and mediators. Most variables that health psychologists study (e.g., coping styles and social support) can be both mediators and moderators. The role of the variable depends on the study (e.g., a cross-sectional study vs. a prospective study), the statistical analyses used to test the variable, the situation, or the variable under study. As a rule, mediators are changed by the stressor and correspondingly change the outcome. If more stress leads to you asking for more social support, which leads to you feeling better, social

▼ FIGURE 2.5
Mediation

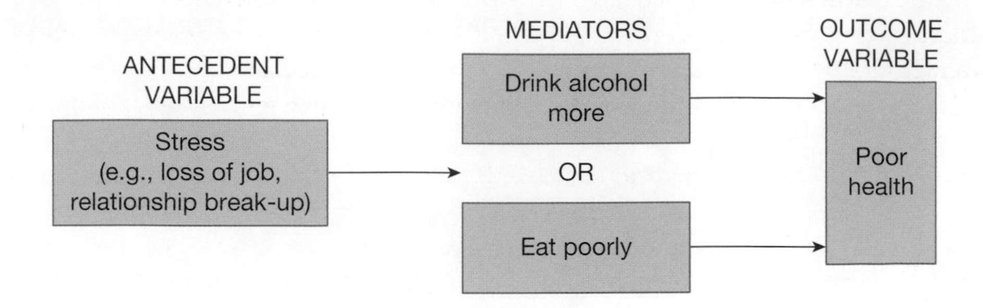

support is a mediator. If a longitudinal study shows that those with more stress exercise more and this makes them feel better, then exercise is a mediator. If a correlational study shows that the group of people who exercise more are less distressed than a similar group of stressed individuals who exercise less, then exercise is a moderator. In the first case (mediation), exercise follows the stressor, changing in level (e.g., increasing) and influencing the outcome. In the second case (moderation), we are looking at two separate groups of exercisers. The only variables that cannot be both mediators and moderators are those that cannot change as a function of the stressor or antecedent variable. Age, ethnicity, and race are examples of moderators that cannot be mediators (e.g., being more stressed cannot change your age even though some of us parents complain our kids' behavior age us faster).

SOME FINAL WARNINGS

A key goal of this book is to present health psychology using a cultural approach. When we talk about culture, we often tend to emphasize cultural differences. To some extent, this is a natural human phenomenon. Even if people who are similar in age, ethnicity, and intelligence were to be randomly separated into two groups and forced to compete with each other, members of each group would tend to believe that they are better than those of the other group (e.g., the minimal subgroup paradigm, an important social psychological effect considered in later chapters). Even if we are not competing for resources we still emphasize how we are different from other people.

There are two major problems here. First, this emphasis on differences often leads us to treat some groups better than others (factors such as prejudice are discussed later in this book). For example, we may be more likely to help people who look like us. We may be less likely to give information to someone who is not from a social group to which we belong. Second, whenever we deal with an individual from a culture with which we are not familiar, we are likely to use the key ways that he or she is different and generalize from that one person to the entire culture (this book later discusses the dangers of stereotyping as well). By focusing on major group differences, we often forget that differences exist within a group as often as between groups. Let's review an example.

Look at the two bell-shaped curves in Figure 2.6. The horizontal *x*-axis represents the number of push-ups a person can do, and the vertical *y*-axis represents the number of people who can do each number of push-ups. Now suppose we walk around town for a few days, and we ask every man and woman we see to get down on the pavement and do as many push-ups as he or she can in one minute. We continue this odd request until we have spoken to 100 men and 100 women. Each curve you see represents one of the two sexes. Therefore, the point of the curve for women above the number 10 means that of all the women we talked to (and who agreed to our strange request), 15 could do 10 push-ups. Now you will probably notice that the two curves are slightly set apart from each other. If we were to ask one of the most commonly asked questions in much of psychology, "Are there significant sex differences?" it is easy to see that the answer is yes. The average number of push-ups men can do is significantly higher than the average number of push-ups women can do. You can also see that there are more men who can do 30 or more push-ups than women, and more women than men who can only do 10 or fewer push-ups in one minute.

There are two critical things to notice about those two overlapping curves. First, even though there are men who can do more push-ups than any woman, and women who can do fewer push-ups than any man, notice how many men and women can do the same number of push-ups. The entire center portions of each curve overlap (the shaded part). At the heart of all this, we are all much more similar than we are dissimilar. Excluding unfortunate and unpredictable circumstances, we all have two eyes, two legs, a nose, and two ears. We all look pretty much the same. We all need to eat, drink, and sleep to live. So why then do we often look at either end of the curves or focus on group differences only? We do so because differences are more noticeable and provide a way to distinguish groups.

Even though we all need to eat, drink, and sleep to live we vary in how we accomplish each of these activities, and how much food, drink, or sleep we need. These variations often make the difference between illness and health. This book will draw your attention to these variations. All humans have about 20,000 genes (compared with the fruit fly with 18,000 or the common earthworm at 12,000), but a variety of environmental and cultural factors can influence the kind of organisms those genes transcribe onto (Mukherjee, 2016). Humans share 99.8% of their genes, but that 0.2% of a difference is very important. In short, even though we should always remember that there are more similarities than differences, sometimes we can learn much from the differences.

There is something else to notice in Figure 2.6. Look at each curve by itself. Notice that there is a lot of diversity in push-up ability *even within each sex*. The average number of push-ups

▼ FIGURE 2.6

People within Cultures Vary, Too

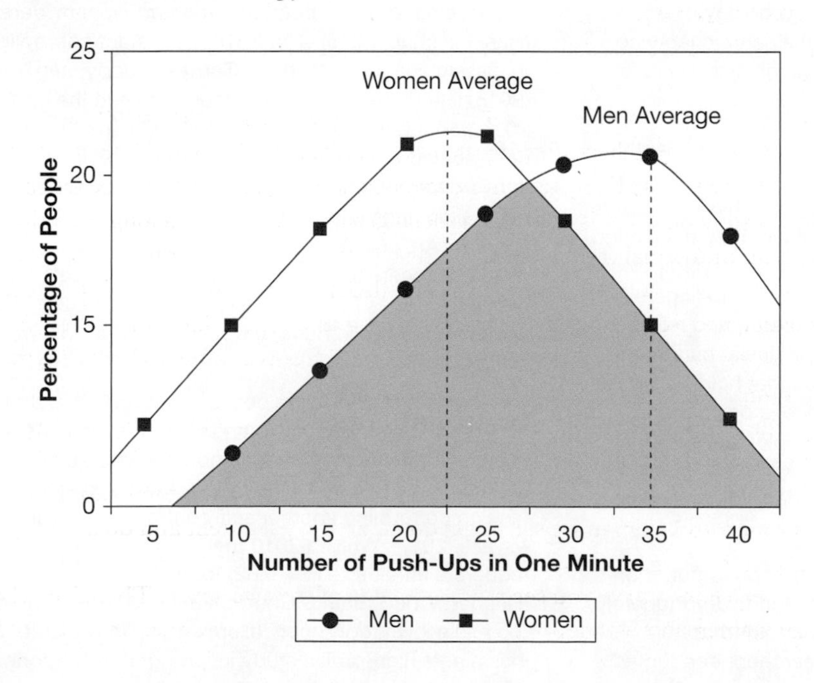

Synthesize, Evaluate, Apply

- How can the discussion of context and level of analyses influence how you design research?
- How can context and level of analysis play a role in describing culture?
- Relate the discussion of moderators and mediators to statistical analyses that control for third variables.
- The overlapping bell curves reminds you to watch how you interpret averages. Provide an example to demonstrate how this can be important.

women can do provides a sense of general ability but notice the number of women at different stages of ability level. A lot of diversity is seen among women. This is a critical observation to hold on to as we discuss the many different topics in this book. No matter how many significant group differences we see, we must also remember that there are many differences within each culture as well. This basic understanding of the differences *within* versus *between* cultures applies to every culture we discuss. We can be talking about men and women as in the lighter push-up example above, or we can be comparing young and old, rich and poor, or Mexican American and African American. To make it easier to understand the different aspects of health psychology, this book will highlight how groups differ. Every time it does, keep these two overlapping curves at the back of your mind and always remember that these are average group differences only.

APPLICATION SHOWCASE

THE REPLICATION CRISIS IN PSYCHOLOGY

It has been a great few years for Wonder Woman. Movies featuring her have exceeded expectations at the box office, raking in millions. You may know of one way Wonder Woman is related to psychology. Her creator, William Moulton Marston, the same chap who invented the lie detector, was a psychologist. There is another way she is linked.

In 2010 Carney, Cuddy, and Yap published a paper that got people to sit up and take notice. Yes, both sit up and take notice. They demonstrated that our physical postures can influence a range of factors. In their study they found that participants who assumed a pose conveying power, sitting back in a chair with feet on a desk and fingers laced behind their neck, actually felt better and released different hormones. One finding in particular caught the public's attention. The study claimed that holding a pose that expresses power and dominance, a power pose, before a meeting can influence psychological and physiological processes, as well as decision making. The classic analogy is standing like Wonder Woman with legs slightly apart and arms on hips.

The pose, and Amy Cuddy, went on to be featured on TED talks and in media around the world. Unfortunately, the findings of the 2010 study do not stand up to replication. In 2015 a group of researchers conducted a conceptual replication study using the same methodology as Carney et al. (2010) but using a much larger sample (200 vs. 42). They also strengthened their research design so the experimenter was blind, or unaware as to which condition the participants were in (Ranehill et al., 2015). The 2010 results did not replicate. In classic academic fashion, Carney, Cuddy, and Yap (2015) listed the many differences between the original 2010 paper and the 2015 failure to replicate that might have served as possible moderators. In 2017 11 studies in two different journals failed to provide evidence of the original findings (Cesario, Jonas, & Carney, 2017). Along the way, Amy Cuddy was much maligned by her academic peers, a disturbing story well illustrated in a *New York Times Magazine* feature (Dominus, 2017) and with much of the intrigue and mayhem of a Hollywood box office hit.

The problem is not power poses. The problem is that a number of psychological findings fail to replicate. Another example involves the phenomenon known as *ego depletion,* the negative effect of performing a self-control task on performing another self-control task (Lurquin & Miyake, 2017). While a 2010 meta-analysis reported a moderate effect size (d = 0.62) for this phenomenon (Hagger, Wood, Stiff, & Chatzisarantis, 2010), this finding too has shown replication failures (Lurquin et al., 2016), including a high-profile study involving 23 laboratories (Hagger et al., 2016).

The big exposé happened in 2015. Members of the Open Science Collaborative, more than 200 researchers led by Brian Nosek at Harvard, conducted replications of 100 experimental and correlational studies published in three psychology journals using high-powered designs and original materials when available. They checked for reproducibility using *p* values and effect sizes. Here is the shocker: Whereas 97% of original studies had significant results, only 36% of replications had significant results (Open Science Collaborative, 2015).

This issue, termed the replication crisis, also influences how we view health psychology research. It may be even more of an issue. For example, much public health research considers interventions that influence and are influenced by both individuals' health and the society around them. These complex systems necessitate explanation alongside statistical inference in light of the replication crisis (Grant & Hood, 2017).

Given the failures of replication, many people now look at the results of psychological research with caution. Some do not trust research. There are several statistical issues we should consider. One type of bias, known as **p-hacking**, occurs when researchers collect or select data or statistical analyses until nonsignificant results become significant. What the casual reader (or even the casual academic) fails to remember is that designing, collecting, analyzing, and reporting of psychological studies entail many arbitrary choices. Referred to as researcher degrees of freedom, these choices are problematic because they can influence the results. Wicherts et al. (2016) present an extensive list of 34 degrees of freedom that researchers have in formulating hypotheses, a great checklist.

There are other statistical issues as well. Researchers planning replication studies often use the original study sample effect size as the basis for sample size planning. However, this strategy ignores uncertainty and publication bias in estimated effect sizes, resulting in overly optimistic calculations. Anderson and Maxwell (2017) show that even if original studies reflect actual phenomena and are conducted in the absence of questionable research practices, popular approaches to designing replication studies may result in a low success rate, especially if the original study is underpowered.

I hope you are wondering if the different classic findings were false positives. Perhaps the replications showed that the emperor has no clothes and correctly indicates that there is truly no effect after all. One approach suggests failures to replicate may not be failures at all, but rather are the result of low statistical power in single replication studies. Statistical power, the likelihood that a study will detect an effect when there is an effect there to be detected, is another topic not discussed as much. Maxwell, Lau, and Howard (2015) provide examples of these power problems and suggest some solutions using Bayesian statistics and meta-analysis.

Measurement error adds noise to predictions and makes it more difficult to discover new phenomena. While our eyes always go to the *p* value, it is important to remember statistical significance conveys very little information when measurements are noisy. This problem and related misunderstandings are key components in a feedback loop that perpetuates the replication crisis in science (Loken & Gelman, 2017).

A lesson to the wise. Recognize the pressures that may implicitly drive p-hacking, measurement issues, and failures to replicate. The growing emphasis on external funding as an expectation for faculty promotion may pose a large hazard for psychological science, including (a) incentives for engaging in questionable research practices, (b) a single-minded focus on programmatic research, (c) intellectual hyperspecialization, (d) disincentives for conducting direct replications, (e) stifling of creativity and intellectual risk taking, (f) researchers promising more than they can deliver, and (g) diminished time for thinking deeply (Lilienfeld, 2017).

Forewarned is forearmed. We live in an age when beyond not trusting social media shares of research studies, we need to focus on the statistical robustness of the studies as well.

CHAPTER REVIEW

SUMMARY ▶▶

- Health psychology uses the scientific method to design and plan research.
- There are many different types of research design and data collection methods. Research is primarily correlational or experimental in nature. Correlations are the assessment of association between variables. In experiments, researchers manipulate key variables (independent variables) to see the effects on others (dependent variables).
- The most common research design in health psychology is the randomized clinical trial. A special case of experiment, care is taken to select the target population and to ensure strong measurement.

- Common statistical tests include correlational analyses that assess the association between variables but can also control for third variables (partial correlations).
- ANOVAs and MANOVAs test for group differences while regression analyses predict variance in an outcome variable from a number of predictor variables.
- One of the most commonly seen analyses in health psychology today are odds ratio and hazard ratio analyses created using logistic regressions. Hazard ratios provide the likelihood or risk of a certain outcome in an intervention group as compared to a comparison group.
- Structural equation modeling allows one to simultaneously map the relationship between numerous variables and to ascertain the fit of a hypothesized set of relationships between variables with data collected.
- The context surrounding us can influence what we think about and how we see ourselves. Similarly, the deeper we analyze someone the more we learn about him or her.
- Although most research results, especially those discussing group differences, discuss averages, remember there can be a lot of difference across individuals within a group.

TEST YOURSELF ▶▶

Check your understanding of the topics in this chapter by answering the following questions.

1. The research journal of the Society for Health Psychology is called
   a. *Health Psychology.*
   b. *Annals of Behavioral Medicine.*
   c. *Psychosomatic Medicine.*
   d. *Biopsychosocial Research.*
2. Which of the following is *not* a key element of science?
   a. Empirical
   b. Replicatable
   c. Theory driven
   d. Independent
3. What is defined as obtaining information according to a goal?
   a. Measurement
   b. Assessment
   c. Evaluation
   d. Observation
4. Which of the following correlations is strongest?
   a. −.62
   b. .44
   c. −.23
   d. .57
5. Researchers measure the extent to which men and women exercise at a local university. They conclude that women exercise more. The research design used is
   a. case study.
   b. correlation.
   c. quasi-experimental.
   d. experimental.
6. Studies where one group gets an experimental drug and another gets a placebo are called
   a. randomized clinical trials.
   b. correlational studies.
   c. quasi-experimental studies.
   d. longitudinal studies.
7. The Nurses' Health Study (NHS) followed 122,000 registered nurses for many years to identify factors that could prevent cancer. This type of study is called
   a. prospective.
   b. retrospective.
   c. cross-sectional.
   d. experimental.
8. Many health psychology studies use very large samples. A major problem with a study with a large sample is that
   a. it is expensive.
   b. large differences are insignificant.
   c. small differences are significant.
   d. statistically significant differences are hard to find.
9. When you read research articles, one of the most important parts of the results section to look at is the
   a. analysis of variance.
   b. statistical tests employed.
   c. degrees of freedom.
   d. effect size.

10. One of the best ways to understand the relationships between a number of different variables simultaneously is to use a statistical analysis called
    a. structural equation modeling.
    b. analysis of variance.
    c. hazard ratios.
    d. moderation.

KEY TERMS, CONCEPTS, AND PEOPLE ▶▶

absolute risk, **41**
analyses of variance (ANOVAs), **39**
context, **42**
correlation coefficient, **33**
correlational studies, **35**
cross-sectional, **37**
dependent variable, **36**
direct correlations, **34**
direct effect, **39**
experimental designs, **35**
hazard ratio, **40**
incidence rates, **32**
independent variable, **36**
level of analysis, **42**
logistic regression, **39**
longitudinal, **37**
mediator, **45**
moderator, **44**
multivariate analyses of variance (MANOVAs), **39**
odds ratio, **39**
p-hacking, **49**
partial correlation, **34**
placebo, **36**
prevalence rates, **32**
prospective, **37**
quasi-experimental designs, **36**
randomized, controlled, or clinical trials (RCTs), **36**
regression analyses, **39**
relative risk, **40**
retrospective, **37**
socioeconomic status, **33**

ESSENTIAL READINGS ▶▶

Benyamini, Y., Johnston, M., & Karademas, E. C. (Eds.). (2019). *Assessment in health psychology.* Boston, MA: Hogrefe.

Luszczynska, A., Kruk, M., & Boberska, M. (2019). Measurement in health psychology research. In T. A. Revenson & R. A. R. Gurung (Eds.), *Handbook of health psychology* (3e). New York, NY: Routledge.

Randby, K. (2019). Major research designs in health psychology. In T. A. Revenson & R. A. R. Gurung (Eds.), *Handbook of health psychology* (3e). New York, NY: Routledge.

CHAPTER 3

CULTURAL APPROACHES TO HEALTH

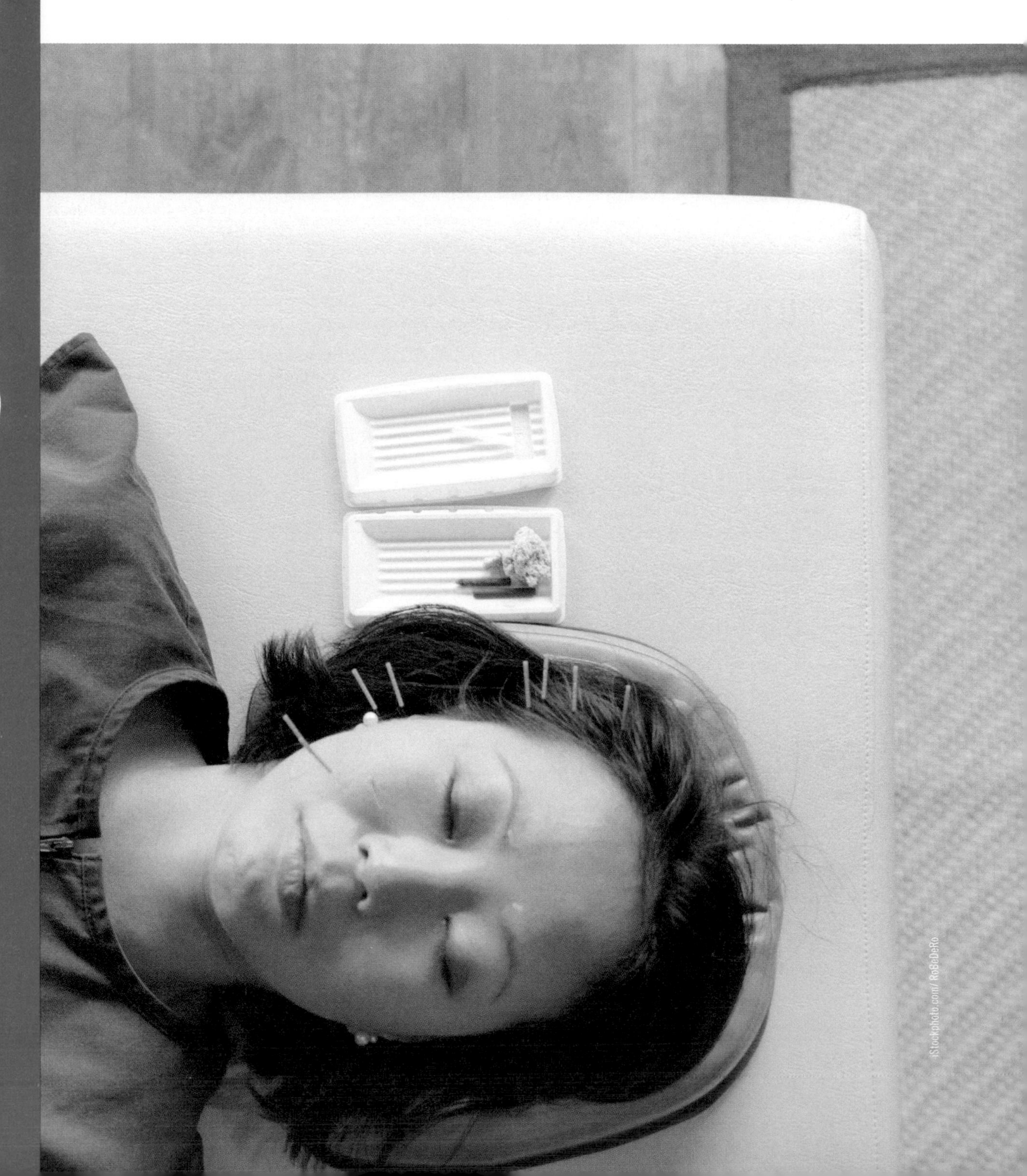

iStockphoto.com/ RoBeDeRo

Chapter 3 Outline

MEASURING UP

ARE YOU CULTURALLY COMPETENT?

See how many of the answers to these questions you know. Ask your family for information you are missing.

a.	What is your ancestry?
b.	How many years have you lived in the United States?
c.	Do you mind being touched by health care workers?
d.	Do you find it difficult to share thoughts with health care workers?
e.	Are there extended family members who live in your household?
f.	What are the duties of men and women in the family?
g.	What difficulty do you have working with people whose religion, sexual orientation, race, or ethnicity is different from yours?
h.	What do you do when you do not know something related to your job?
i.	What are major diseases in your family?
j.	With what race do you identify?
k.	How many cigarettes do you smoke a day?
l.	How much do you drink each day?
m.	What foods do you avoid when you are ill?
n.	What foods do you eat on particular holidays?
o.	What does it mean to you and your family when you are pregnant?

(Continued)

(Continued)

p.	What do you want with you when you deliver your baby?
q.	What special activities need to be performed to prepare for death?
r.	How do men and women grieve?
s.	How many times a day do you pray?
t.	What gives strength and meaning to your life?
u.	In what prevention activities do you engage to maintain your health?
v.	What traditional health-care practices do you use?
w.	Do you prefer same-sex health-care providers for routine health problems?
x.	For what conditions do you use healers?

Source: Adapted from Purnell & Pontious (2014). Why is this important? These are key Cultural Domains from the Purnell Model of Cultural Competence with sample questions to ask to determine each (first introduced in Chapter 1).

▼ Ponder This

Are causes of illness the same the world over?

Could blocked energy channels through your body influence health?

What role does yoga play in well-being?

You are probably not aware of the number of things that you take for granted. There are many facts that you probably accept easily: The earth is round. It revolves around the sun. These facts you know. You also may believe you know why some things happen the way they do. If you stay outside in the cold rain without a raincoat, you believe you will catch a cold (at least that is what your mom always told you). If you eat too much fatty food, you know you will put on weight. Every culture has its own beliefs. Many Southeast Asian mothers place a black spot on their babies' heads to ward away the evil eye that could harm their babies. Kabbalah-following celebrities, such as Madonna, wear red bracelets for the same reason. Some religious groups, such as the Christian Scientists, believe suffering and pain have no objective reality and so are wary of using doctors and medication. All of us grow up with understandings of how various illnesses are caused. These understandings come from the cultural groups of which we are a part. However, we are not always aware that our understandings of the causes of our good health and of the treatment of sicknesses are culturally dependent. If we believe a virus or bacteria caused an infection, we will be willing to use antibiotic medications to treat it. What if you believed that an infection was caused by the looks of a jealous neighbor or because you had angered the spirits of the wind?

In most of the countries around the globe, health is understood using either the Western evidence-based medical approach or traditional indigenous approaches (Prasadarao, 2014). In traditional systems, wide ranges of practitioners provide help. For example, the Maori of New Zealand have different priests who help heal the mind, the spirit, or family ties (*tohungas*) (Manatū Hauora, 2012). Similarly, in sub-Saharan Africa, there are four types of traditional healers, both men and women, who provide health care: traditional birth attendants (TBAs), faith healers, diviners and spiritualists, and herbalists. Not surprisingly, one's religiosity has been a major focus of health psychologists (Park & Carney, 2018).

Even in the United States health beliefs and health behaviors vary by cultural groups (Landrine & Klonoff, 2001; Von Dras, 2017). The majority of the population of the United States is of European origin, with the largest ancestral roots traceable to Germany (15%), Ireland (11%), the United Kingdom (9%), and Italy (6%). Major racial and national minority groups include Hispanics, African American (either of U.S., African, or Caribbean parentage),

Chinese, Filipinos, and Japanese (U.S. Census Bureau, 2017). The U.S. Census Bureau estimates that European Americans comprise 72.4% of the population; Hispanics comprise 16.3%, African Americans comprise 12.6%, Asian and Pacific Islanders comprise 5.7%, and Native Americans (American Indians, Eskimos, and Aleuts) comprise 0.9% (U.S. Census Bureau, 2017). Italian Americans in New York may have different traditional ways of approaching illness than do Polish Americans in Milwaukee. Women in New Mexico and men in Chicago may have the same physical problem, but their doctors must take into account the existing differences in their patients' social systems (differences in culture, beliefs, family structure, and economic class) and their patients' expectations of health care and health-care workers to cure them.

This chapter describes the major philosophical approaches followed by Americans of different cultural backgrounds. These different approaches can explain variances in health behaviors. Remember that an effective health psychologist has to be ready to deal with diverse beliefs, and so be well versed in different approaches to health and diverse values and attitudes. Essentially, we all need to be knowledgeable about different cultures or *culturally competent* (Purnell & Pontious, 2014). To help a person stay healthy and recover when sick, you must understand what his or her specific understanding of health and sickness is. Once you understand, you can use variations on the basic tools and theories to intervene and help. I will describe some of America's diverse ethnic and religious beliefs as they relate to health, focusing on contemporary views of the Chinese Taoist and East Indian Ayurvedic approaches to health, Latino folk medicine (*curanderismo*), and American Indian spiritualism. Be aware that the majority of the beliefs and practices we will discuss have not passed the critical eye of Western scientific inquiry (e.g., that spirits cause illness). However, as all good psychologists know, if someone believes something strongly enough, then those beliefs can influence that person's behavior and reactions. Thus, it is important to know what different people believe. Even if you do not believe it yourself, shared understanding facilitates communication and successful health and healing.

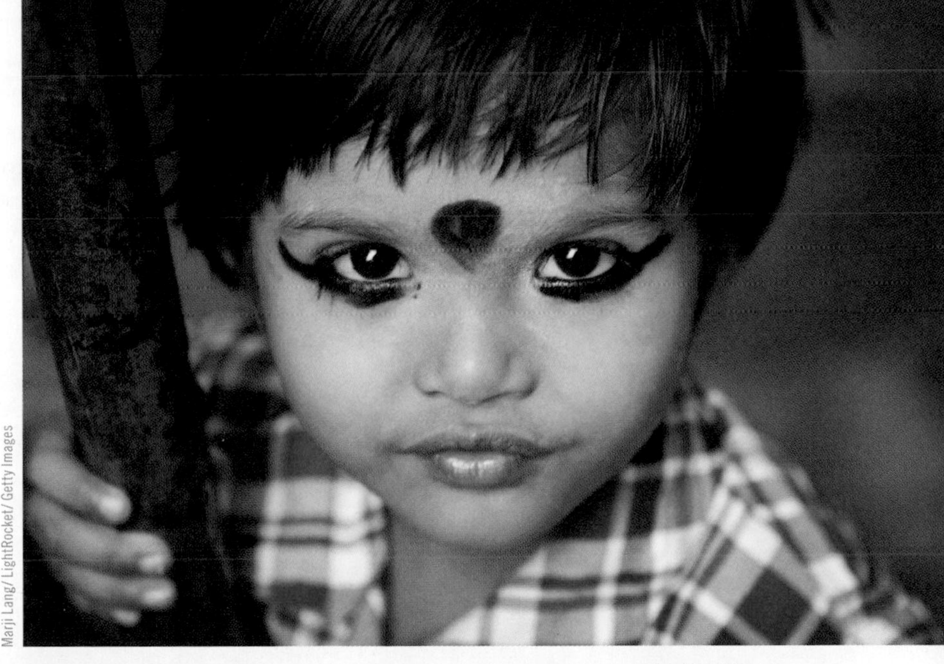

Marji Lang/ LightRocket/ Getty Images

▲ **The Evil Eye.** In cultures around the world, the evil eye is the name for a sickness transmitted — usually without intention — by someone who is envious, jealous, or covetous. Many Latino and Asian Indian mothers try to make sure their children do not get the "evil eye" by placing large black dots on their children's foreheads.

VARIETIES OF WORLD MEDICINE

Different cultures have different definitions of health. Each culture evolves with a unique understanding of the creation of human beings and our purpose in life. According to archaeological evidence, our ancestors probably believed that our bodies worked because of magic. Potions, rings, charms, and bracelets were devised to rid the body of the harmful demons and spirits that brought illness and suffering (Offit, 2013). Some of these ancient beliefs often find their way into popular literature and underlie our enchantment with heady fare such as the *Lord of the Rings* and the *Hunger Games* trilogies, the *Chronicles of Narnia,* and even the fanciful *Harry Potter* series. A person's eyes in particular were believed to be the sites of power and magic, whereas animal eyes routinely were used in a range of treatments (Monte, 1993).

Globally, health beliefs and practices are closely tied to religion and nationality, which are components of culture not given much attention in Western medicine. In fact, Western culture sometimes even tries to suppress non-Western beliefs. In the early 20th century the predominantly White New Zealand parliament passed a law banning Maori *tohungas* from practicing (Moon, 2011). In non-Western countries, predominantly Hindu countries such as India, for example, modern medical practitioners are complemented by traditional healers who offer treatment for physical and mental illness in rural villages (Agnihotri & Agnihotri, 2017).

There are many examples around the world of how religious beliefs vary and play a role in how health is perceived. In addition to the five major approaches discussed in this chapter, there are others that you may be interested in exploring as well. Many Japanese practice Shinto and Shamanism (Olson, 2017). In Muslim countries such as Pakistan and Bangladesh, traditional healers include *khalifs, gadinashins,* imams, *hakims,* and others who practice magic and sorcery (Amer, 2017). Farooqi (2006) studied the nature of traditional healing consultation in 87 Muslim psychiatric patients treated at public hospitals in Pakistan. This study revealed that 55% to 73% of patients with various psychiatric disorders sought help from one or more traditional healers. Islamic populations are a growing part of American society, but not as much is known about this population's view of health (Swaroop, DeLoach, & Sheikh, 2014).

Beyond Islamic practices of Muslims (Amer, 2017), different sects of Islam, such as Sufism, have unique beliefs about health as well (Bozorgzadeh, Bahadorani, & Sadoghi, 2017). Lesser-known spiritual approaches such as Bahá'í, Rastafari, and Zoroastrianism also have numerous adherents (Nelson-Becker, Atwell, & Russo, 2017). Even nonbelievers—agnostics, atheists, and the nonreligious—have distinct health orientations (Hwang & Cragun, 2017).

Although still changing, our understanding of the body crystallized about 5,000 years ago when the Chinese, Indians, Greeks, and Egyptians began to study the body extensively. Table 3.1 shows the evolution of different medical systems. The medical traditions and different approaches to health held by most Americans today derive from these early systems.

Synthesize, Evaluate, Apply

- What are your main beliefs about the causes and cures of illnesses?
- From where do your spiritual beliefs come? How do they tie to your health?
- What evidence do you need to support your beliefs?

▼ TABLE 3.1

Many of these key figures and events are mentioned in this chapter and throughout the text. However, the history of health psychology is rich, and you may find it worthwhile to research other key figures and events on your own. See the notes at the end of the chapter for suggested readings.

Western Medicine	Traditional Chinese Medicine	American Indian	Mexican/Mexican American *Curanderismo*	Other World Cultures and Medicine
Hippocrates (400 B.C.) Galen (100 B.C.) Avicenna (A.D. 1000) da Vinci (1500s) Vesalius (1600s) Harvey (1600s) Pasteur (1800s) Roentgen (1800s) Fleming (Penicillin) (1928)	The Yellow Emperor's Classic of Internal Medicine (approximately 100 B.C.)	Folk medicine passed on orally for centuries Europeans first witness native rituals and traditions (approximately A.D. 1500)	Aztec, Mayan influences (dates unknown) Spanish-Moorish medicine (15th century) Folk medicine passed on orally for centuries	Mesopotamia (4000 B.C.) Indian Ayurveda (4000 B.C.) Egypt (3000 B.C.) Iti (2500 B.C.) Imhotep (2700 B.C.) Unani (A.D. 900)

WESTERN BIOMEDICINE

The most common approach to medicine, **Western biomedicine,** is derived from the work of Greek physicians, such as Hippocrates and Galen. Most Americans support the practice of Western biomedicine, and it is also used around the world, even in very non-Western countries such as China and Korea (Han, 2011). American medical schools, hospitals, and emergency rooms all use this Western approach.

Also referred to as modern medicine, conventional medicine, or **allopathy**, Western biomedicine is one of the most dominant forms of health care in the world today. Hallmarks of this approach are an increasing reliance on technology and the use of complex scientific procedures for the diagnosis and treatment of illness. Treatments using this approach are designed to cause the opposite effect as that created by the disease. If you have a fever, you are prescribed medication to reduce the temperature. Western biomedicine views the body as a biochemical machine with distinct parts. Often called **reductionist**, Western biomedicine searches for the single smallest unit responsible for the illness. Western doctors try to localize the cause of an illness to the parts directly surrounding the original point of the problem.

Greek Roots

Western biomedicine often claims the 4th-century B.C. Greek, **Hippocrates**, as its father, primarily because he was the first to separate medicine from religion and myth and to bring scientific and analytical reasoning to health care. There were physicians before Hippocrates. In the third millennium B.C., physicians in ancient Mesopotamia (modern-day Iraq) developed an official medical system based on a diagnostic framework that derived from sources as varied as omens and divination techniques and the inspection of livers of sacrificed animals (Porter, 2002). A lead physician coordinated treatments and combined religious rites and empirical treatments such as the use of drugs and the practice of surgery. Similarly, in Egypt the pharaohs also had a line of physicians. There was Iri, called the Keeper of the Royal Rectum (the pharaoh's enema expert), and the most famous, Imhotep, chief physician to the Pharaoh Zozer, both of whom used large amounts of religious rituals to aid their curing (Udwadia, 2000). Essentially, medicine not bound directly to one specific religion only appeared in the Greek-speaking world as practiced by the 5th-century B.C. Hippocratic doctors (Bynum, 2008).

Personality psychologists often recount Hippocrates's humoral theory of what made people different. He argued that our personalities were a function of the level of certain bodily fluids or humors. If you had a lot of black bile, you would be sad or melancholic. If you had a lot of blood, you would be cheerful or sanguine. Because there were very few explicit cures back then, the etiology of disease had not yet been sufficiently mapped out; one of the main roles of the physician was to provide support. Beyond this supportive element of the medical practitioner, biomedical doctors use few of Hippocrates's healing methods today. A few centuries later, **Galen**, the so-called emperor of medicine during the Roman Empire, and much later the Italian artist **Leonardo da Vinci** (in the 15th to 16th centuries) and the Flemish physician **Andreas Vesalius** (16th century), greatly advanced Western biomedicine with their studies of human anatomy. **William Harvey**, an English physician, first described the circulation of blood and the functioning of the heart to the Western world in 1628. The Chinese are said to have discovered blood circulation about 3,000 years earlier (Hsu, 2010). Biomedicine had its first major boost with the discovery of the high-power microscope. The Dutch naturalist **Antonius van Leeuwenhoek** ground lenses to magnify objects 300 times. Compare this magnification to that of the electron microscope, invented in 1932, that magnifies specimens to a power of 5 million. Here is a *trivia question:* What was one of the first specimens observed under the lens? (Answer: Human sperm. Leeuwenhoek was careful to establish that the specimen was a "residue after conjugal coitus" and not a product of "sinfully defiling" himself; Leeuwenhoek, 1677, in Roach, 2006, p. 62.)

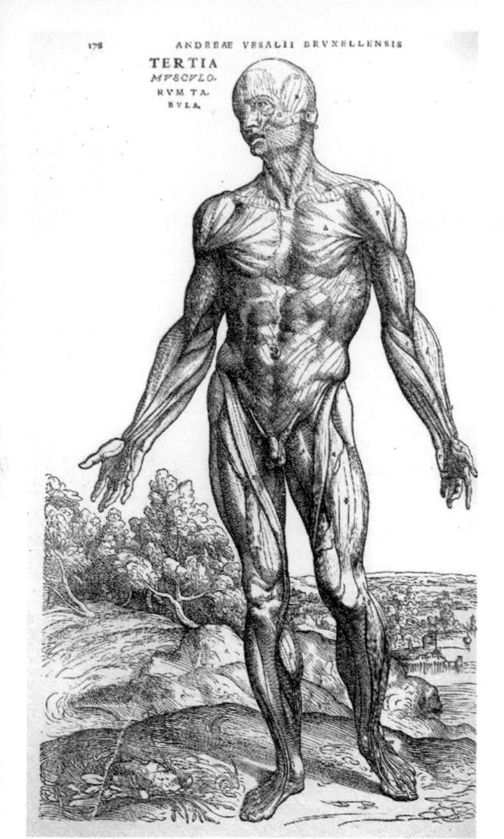

▲ **Early Drawings of Anatomy.** Some of the earliest drawings of anatomy were done by the Flemish physician Andreas Vesalius.

Technological Innovations

Western biomedicine has strong ties to technology. Once the microscope became widely used, blood, saliva, and other bodily fluids were closely examined, leading to a better understanding of the structures and functions of a wide variety of cells. **Louis Pasteur** really took the next big leap for medicine. In one of the most significant events of the 19th century, Pasteur proved that viruses and bacteria could cause disease. In 1878 Pasteur presented his germ theory to the French Academy of Medicine (Udwadia, 2000). To be fair, I must salute the Hungarian doctor Ignaz Semmelweis, who in 1847, 30 years before Pasteur's discovery, tried to get doctors to wash their hands before examining women. This simple act when practiced finally saved many lives (Markel, 2015).

In 1885 the German scientist Wilhelm Roentgen discovered X-rays. Roentgen discovered that passing highly charged waves of energy through the body and then onto a sensitive photographic plate created accurate images of the body's interior. This technological advance enabled doctors to look into the body to see what was causing illnesses or problems and together with the microscope took the diagnosis of illness to new heights. More advances in the 20th century, such as magnetic resonance imaging (MRI) and computerized axial tomography (CAT) scans, led to closer examinations of the body and bodily functions, especially the brain. Technology, by introducing the study of the cellular level, fueled the drive of Western medicine to find the answers to the causes of illnesses and death. Similar to the behavioral psychologist, Western medicinal practitioners primarily focus on what can be observed. The presence of observable factors (e.g., cancerous cells or bacteria) thereby explains any move away from positive health.

Cures and treatment, especially modern pharmacology, developed to attack ailments in the body. Medicines, using a biomedical approach, can be defined as essentially concentrated purified chemical substances that target a particular aspect of the disease process. The chemical composition of some drugs (e.g., **opioids**) mirrors that of naturally occurring substances (e.g., **opiates**). For example, morphine, an opioid that was first extracted in 1805, is identical to chemicals produced by opiates in our body, because there are receptors that accept morphine in our brains. Other milestones in the development of drugs include the discovery of antibacterial sulfonamides in 1935 and the production of antibiotics such as penicillin in the 1940s (although it was first discovered in 1928). Many thousands of different drugs are available today for nearly every ache, pain, or irritation you may have.

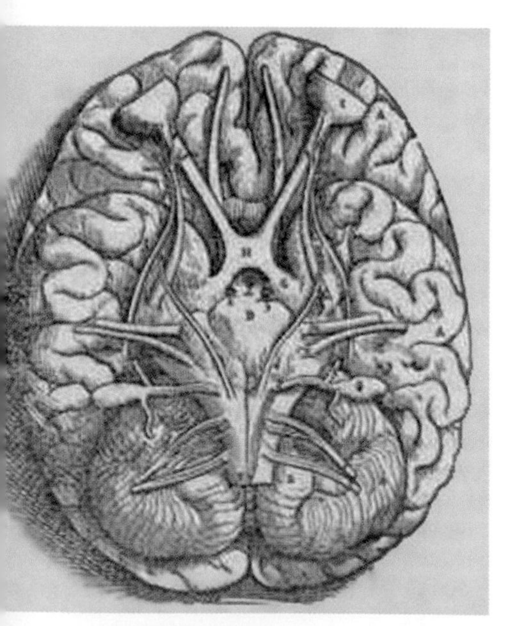

▲ **Early Drawings of Anatomy.** Vesalius' drawing of a brain.

The other main element of Western biomedicine is surgery. First practiced by early Egyptians and Aztecs 6,000 years ago, surgery has evolved into an art. If an X-ray reveals a problem or a miniscule camera detects an issue in a vein, artery, or one of the many ducts and tubes that we have (e.g., gastric tract or pulmonary tract), skilled surgeons open up the body and attempt to remedy it. The first coronary bypass was performed in 1951 and the first heart transplant was performed in 1967. While major surgical milestones are relatively recent, today there are few operations still deemed medically impossible. The reliance on technology and the evolution of pharmacology and surgery signal the main approach of Western biomedicine to healing. If you visit a medical doctor with a problem, the routine is straightforward. Your answers to the doctor's questions guide what tests, X-ray studies, or scans you will need. Subsequent test results help the doctor identify the disease-causing agents and medicines or surgical method needed to cure the problem. Health, according to this model, is the absence of disease. The Western doctor starts with a symptom, searches for the underlying mechanisms or causes, and attempts to fight the disease with drugs or surgery. Most Americans believe that germs cause disease and expect to take some sort of pill to treat the disease. This main belief of Western medicine is very different from the beliefs and approaches of other cultural groups.

TRADITIONAL CHINESE MEDICINE

Traditional Chinese Medicine (TCM) is probably used to treat more people than any other form of medicine (largely because China is the most populous country in the world). However, even in North America there are a large number of TCM schools and practitioners (Lam & Lim, 2014). In fact, acupuncture, one form of TCM, is covered by most health insurance policies. Acupuncture will be discussed in the Focus section at the end of this chapter. Feng shui is not a part of TCM, but if you have heard of this Chinese art of arranging your living space to optimize energy flow, you will have some feel for this very different approach to life. In fact, you will see that you may have been exposed to many aspects of the beliefs underlying TCM.

> **Synthesize, Evaluate, Apply**
>
> - Identify the two most significant events in Western medical history. Rationalize your choice.
> - Would you be willing to participate in a medical trial?
> - Why would medical inventions and innovation make folk medicine use less likely?

In TCM, the body is treated as a whole. Each part of the body is intrinsically connected to other parts of the body and to what is happening around the person (Hsu, 2010). Critical elements of a healthy life include a person's food choices, relationships, and emotional life. In TCM, everyone is a part of a larger creation and lives and flourishes in unison with it. In stark contrast to reductionist Western biomedicine that focuses on a cellular microscopic level of diagnosis, TCM is macroscopic. In TCM, humankind is viewed in relation to nature and the physical laws that govern it. Some interesting paradoxes are seen when we compare Western medicine with TCM. Although TCM does not have the concept of a nervous system nor does it recognize the endocrine system, TCM still treats problems the West calls endocrine and neurological disorders. TCM also uses terminology that may appear bizarre to a Westerner. For example, diseases are thought to be caused by imbalances in yin and yang or by too much heat or wind.

Sources of Illness

Two main systems categorize the forces identified in TCM that influence health and well-being: yin and yang (Figure 3.1) and the five phases. According to one Chinese philosophy, all life and the entire universe originated from a single unified source called **Tao** (pronounced "dow"). The main ideas about the Tao are encompassed in a 5,000-word poem called the *Tao Te Ching* written about 2,500 years ago that describes a way of life from the reign of the Yellow Emperor Huang Ti (Santee, 2017). In fact, Chinese medicine is based on *The Yellow Emperor's Classic of Internal Medicine* (approximately 100 B.C.). The Tao is an integrated and undifferentiated whole with two opposing forces—the *yin* and the *yang*—that combine to create everything in the universe.

Yin and yang are mutually interdependent, constantly interactive, and potentially interchangeable forces. As you can see in Figure 3.1, each yin and yang contains the seed of the other (the little dot in the center of each comma-shaped component). The circle represents the supreme source, or Tao. Yin translates to "shady side of a hill" whereas yang translates to "sunny side of the hill." Yin is traditionally thought of as darkness, the moon, cold, and female; yang is thought of as light, the sun, hot, and male. In TCM, 10 vital organs are divided into five pairs, each consisting of one solid yin organ and one hollow yang organ. TCM practitioners believe that the yin organs—the heart, liver, pancreas, kidney, and lungs—are more vital than the yang organs, and dysfunctions of yin organs cause the greatest health problems. The paired yang organs are the gallbladder, small intestine, large intestine, and bladder. A healthy individual has a balanced amount of yin and yang. If a person is sick, his or her forces are out of balance. Specific symptoms relate to an excess of either yin or yang. For example, if you are flushed, have a fever, are constipated, and have high blood pressure, you have too much yang.

The five phases or elemental activities refer to specific active forces and illustrate the intricate associations that the ancient Chinese saw between human beings and nature (Figure 3.2). Energy, or **qi** (pronounced "chee"), another critical aspect of TCM, moves within the body in the same pattern as it does in nature with each season and with different foods helping to optimize energy flow within the body. The five elements of wood, fire,

▼ FIGURE 3.1

The Chinese Symbol for Yin and Yang

earth, metal, and water each link to a season of the year, a specific organ, and a specific food (Table 3.2). Each element has specific characteristics, is generated by one of the other forces, and is suppressed by another. For example, you can burn wood to generate fire, which in turn reduces things to earth, which in turn forms metals. The heart is ruled by fire, the liver by wood, and the kidneys by water. Fire provides qi to the heart and then passes on qi to the earth element and correspondingly to the stomach, the spleen, and the pancreas. Table 3.2 illustrates how the different elements, seasons, organs, and foods interact.

Figure 3.3 also illustrates how one system depends on another. TCM doctors use such diagrams to treat patients. Let's say that a person eats too much salt, which causes kidney disorders. The kidney and bladder (the water element) control the heart and small intestine (fire). Consequently, kidney disorders cause heart disorders and high blood pressure. To treat the condition, the TCM doctor treats the controlling element, water, by reducing the intake of salt, oils, and fats (which influences body water levels) and increasing mild aerobic exercise (fire).

Treatment

In TCM, optimal health consists of balancing yin and yang and optimizing the smooth flow of qi through the body by the coordination of the five elements (Lam & Lim, 2014). Qi flows through the body in 12 precise, orderly patterns called meridians. Meridians translate from the Chinese term *jing-luo*, meaning to go through something that connects or attaches. In Chinese meridian theory, meridian channels are unseen but embody a form of informational network (Kaptchuk, 2000). The 12 meridians are associated with organs in the body. Two additional meridians unify different systems (Figure 3.4). Blocked meridians can cause illness by bringing about hyperactivity of certain organs and underactivity of others. Without the right amount of qi, the organs, tissues, and cells no longer eliminate waste and therefore, with the accumulation of such toxins, harbor more disease. Thus, many symptoms of diseases are interpreted as the body's efforts to cure itself. The runny nose and sweating of a cold and fever are the body's ways of eliminating the underlying conditions that cause the disease. The meridians can be cleared and qi recharged with acupuncture and specific diets.

▼ FIGURE 3.2

The Five Chinese Elements with Related Numerals and Animals

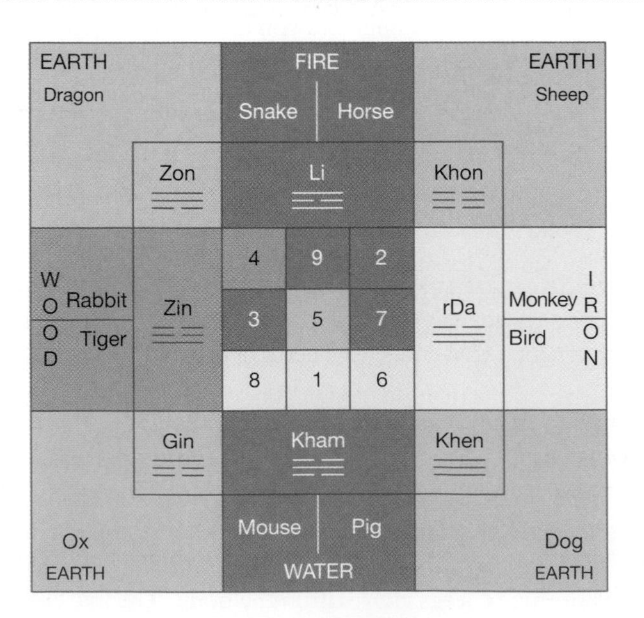

▼ TABLE 3.2

The Chinese Elements and Associations

Elements	Wood	Fire	Earth	Metal	Water
Colors	Blue/green	Red	Yellow	White	Black
Symbols	Dragon	Phoenix	Caldron	Tiger	Tortoise
Seasons	Spring	Summer	Between	Autumn	Winter
Months	1–2	4–5	3, 6, 9, 12	7–8	10–11
Conditions	Rain	Heat	Wind	Clear	Cold
Directions	East	South	Center	West	North
Planets	Jupiter	Mars	Saturn	Venus	Mercury
Days	Thursday	Tuesday	Saturday	Friday	Wednesday
Animals	Scaled	Winged	Naked	Furred	Shelled
Actions	Countenance	Sight	Thought	Speech	Listening
Senses	Sight	Taste	Touch	Smell	Hearing
Sounds	Calling	Laughing	Singing	Lamenting	Moaning
Tastes	Sour	Bitter	Sweet	Acrid/spicy	Salty
Smells	Goatish	Burning	Fragrant	Rank	Rotten
Organs	Liver	Heart	Spleen	Lungs	Kidneys

The trained TCM physician focuses on both the physiology and the psychology of the individual. Yes, this is similar to the way health psychologists function, but with different tools and underlying assumptions. All relevant information, including the symptoms and patients' general life characteristics, such as whether they are happy with their jobs and what they are eating, are all woven together into a pattern of disharmony. Instead of asking what is *causing* what, the doctor asks what is *related to* what. The aim of treatment is to settle the imbalance. The TCM practitioner prescribes massage, acupuncture or acupressure, herbs, dietary changes, and exercises such as *qi gong* as primary treatments. *Qi gong* combines movement, meditation, and the regulation of breathing to enhance the flow of qi in the body to improve circulation and to promote immune function.

For some North Americans, the preceding sections may read like Greek (or Chinese!). Meridians? Qi? Yin? Yang? Does any of this work? The answer may depend on where the work was done and who interprets the results. Many Western scientists see TCM as being no better that a placebo (Offit, 2013). TCM has been the subject of considerable study for more than 50 years (Liao, 2011). The Chinese have performed many experimental analyses of traditional medicine, and the results have been positive enough to give TCM and Western biomedicine equal places in modern Chinese hospitals. Not only do many doctors in China provide patients with a prescription for pharmacological drugs as they would receive here in America, but they also provide a prescription for TCM cures (e.g., herbs or ointments). In many Chinese hospitals, the two dispensaries sit side by side. Most patients in China as well as in America have the choice of which method to use. Western medicine is used more often for acute problems (by Chinese and Chinese Americans), and TCM is used more often for chronic problems.

There is a growing body of research being conducted on different TCMs. Some empirical studies suggest that TCMs are no more effective than Western medicines. For example, 620 cocaine-dependent patients took part in a randomized clinical trial where one third of the participants received acupuncture. The acupuncture group did not show significant reduction in

▼ FIGURE 3.3

Balance between Seasons and Organs

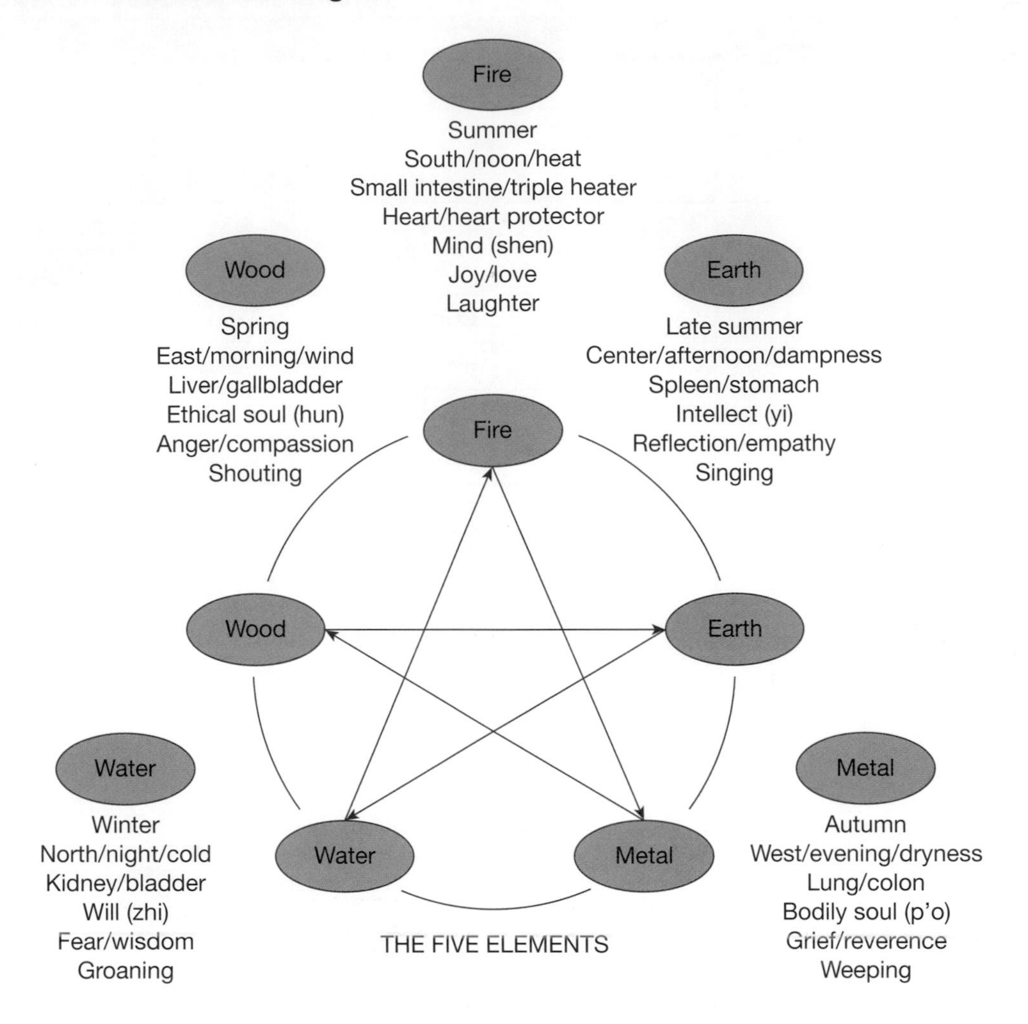

drug use (Margolin et al., 2002). Some of the research validating TCM was done without the use of robust Western scientific methodology; however, there is a larger body of work supporting TCMs (Santee, 2017).

Part of the problem is that testing TCMs presents special challenges (Bausell, 2007; Nahin & Straus, 2001). How do you provide a comparative control condition or placebo when you are testing acupuncture? If the basis of the underlying mechanisms for change (e.g., meridians) cannot be demonstrated in methodically sound, randomized controlled trials, then for all practical purposes Western science deems the approach invalid (Colquhoun & Novella, 2013). Comparative alternatives to having fine needles being inserted into your skin are difficult to find. There are special standards to report randomized controlled trials: CONSORT, which means consolidated standards of reporting trials. A draft of the CONSORT for TCM was published in both Chinese and English in 2007, but researchers raised concerns about which items should be included in the CONSORT for TCM such as the rationale of the trial design, intervention, outcome assessment, and adverse events (Bian et al., 2011). Once these standards are set and used it may be easier for Western doctors and scientists to accept the majority of the Chinese findings.

The Chinese are beginning to use better research methodologies, and research results have begun to satisfy Western doctors. For example, a Western medical examination showed patients to have peptic ulcers, and a Chinese examination of the same patients yielded a diagnosis based on the

▼ FIGURE 3.4
Meridians

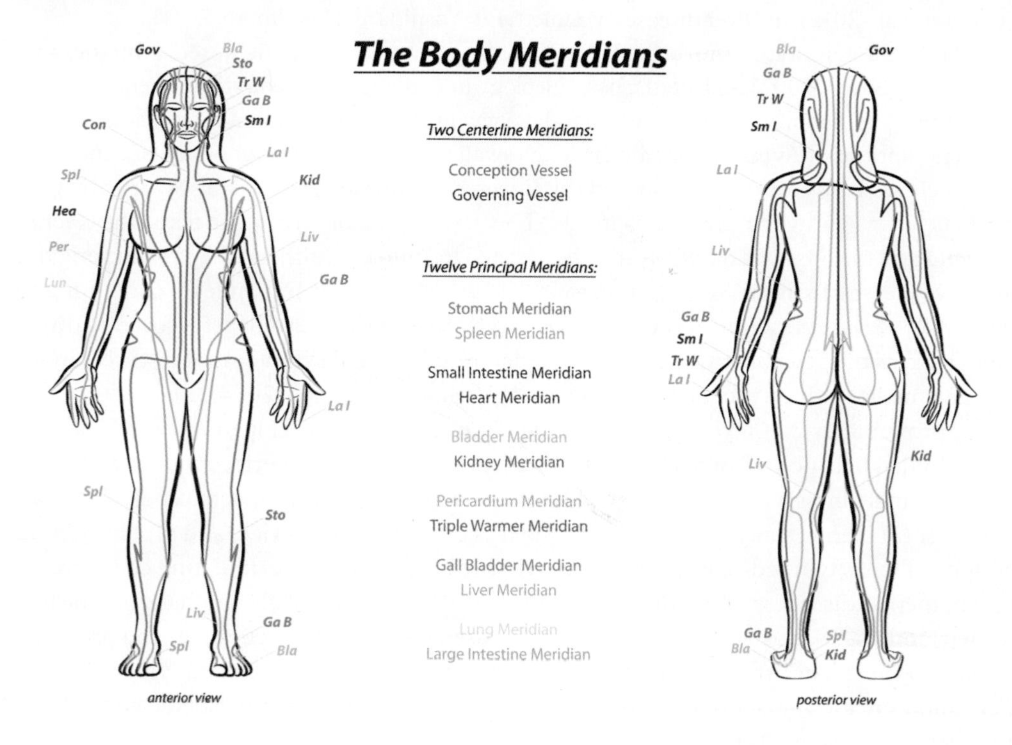

Source: Peter Hermes Furian/ Alamy Stock Photo

five elements previously described. Doctors treated these patients with herbs based on TCM, and the patients showed significant recovery 2 months later (Zhou, Hu, & Pi, 1991). Treatment of patients with heart disease provides similar success stories (Zhang, Liang, & Ye, 1995). In some cases, TCM treatments are less invasive, as in the case of sleep-disordered breathing (SDB). Compared to current treatment options of SDB, TCM was found to be a safe and effective treatment option (Wu, Wei, Tai, Chen, & Li, 2012). Much of the research conducted on TCM in America analyzes the constituents of herbs used in treatment, and many such studies show that the active ingredients of the herbs facilitate cures (Chang, Chang, Kuo, & Chang, 1997; Hon et al, 2007; Li, Lin, & Zuo, 2009; Liu et al., 2012; Stickel, Egerer, & Seitz, 2002; Way & Chen, 1999). The growing evidence notwithstanding, it will be some time before TCM is accepted widely, but its time may come sooner than we think.

Dr. Sonia Suchday has a PhD in clinical psychology and is associate director for the Center for Public Health Science at the Albert Einstein College of Medicine in New York. She is an expert on Ayurvedic medicine and how practices such as yoga aid health (Suchday et al., 2014).

AYURVEDA: TRADITIONAL INDIAN MEDICINE

You may be more familiar with **Ayurveda**, or traditional Indian medicine, than you realize. This is not American Indian medicine (which will be discussed later) but the approach to health that came from the Indian subcontinent. Yoga is a part of Ayurvedic practices. Many herbal supplements in use today came into prominence because of ancient Ayurvedic writings, and various health-care products on the market that tout natural bases (e.g., Aveda products) have roots in Ayurveda (Suchday et al., 2014). Although you do not see as much explicit evidence of this form of medicine in North America (i.e., you may not find Ayurveda shops in the Little India sections of American cities, but certainly may find Chinese herb shops in American Chinatowns), many Americans practice forms of Ayurveda. Ayurveda is also actively researched (Bagla,

2011), and some components such as yoga have a strong scientific basis (Broad, 2012). A range of Ayurveda-derived herbs are used to treat a variety of disorders such as rheumatoid arthritis (Chopra et al., 2012) and liver disease (Tremlett, Fu, Yoshida, & Hashimoto, 2011).

Ayurveda originated more than 6,000 years ago and was considered a medicine of the masses (Singh, 2007). In fact, the basic ideology underlying Ayurveda still influences how the more than 1 billion inhabitants of India today view health. Many Indian Americans even use the prescriptions of Ayurveda in daily life (e.g., swallowing raw garlic is good for you and chewing on cloves helps toothaches), and many European Americans are using Ayurvedic practices such as yoga and natural supplements. The first two major Ayurvedic texts, the *Charaka Samhita* and the *Sushruta Samhita*, have been dated to 1000 B.C., although Ayurvedic practices are also referred to in the Vedas (3000 to 2000 B.C.), the ancient Indian texts containing the wisdom of sages and sacrificial rituals. The *Charaka Samhita* has 120 chapters covering diverse areas such as the general principles of Ayurveda, the causes and symptoms of disease, physiology and medical ethics, prognosis, therapy, and pharmacy (Svoboda, 2004).

Approximately 2,000 years ago, Charaka, an Indian sage, developed Ayurveda, a traditional Indian holistic system of medicine (Singh, 2007). Charaka described four causative factors in mental illness: (1) diet (incompatible or unclean food); (2) disrespect to gods, elders, and teachers; (3) mental shock due to emotions such as excessive fear and joy; and (4) faulty bodily activity. Thus, Ayurveda considers a biopsychosocial approach in formulating causative factors in mental disorders (Prasadarao & Sudhir, 2001). Charaka, while emphasizing the need for harmony between body, mind, and soul, focused on preventive, curative, and promotive aspects of mental health. Ancient Indian court physicians further developed Ayurvedic practices and were given vast resources because the health of the king was considered equivalent to the health of the state (Agnihotri & Agnihotri, 2017).

Ayurvedic medicine was well developed by the time of the Buddha (500 B.C.) and the rise of Buddhism. Jivaka, the royal physician to the Buddha, was so well known that people actually became Buddhists so he could treat them. When Alexander the Great invaded India in 326 B.C., Ayurvedic physicians returned to Greece with him—one of the first times people of the two cultures were exposed to each other. The use of Ayurveda flourished until A.D. 900 when Muslim invaders came into India and created a new form of medicine called Unani, a combination of Greek and Ayurvedic medicine with Arabic medicine (Udwadia, 2000). Ayurveda continued in different forms even after European forces invaded India around A.D. 1500, bringing Western medicine with them.

The basic core of Ayurvedic medicine parallels the way members of most Asian American cultures view life. A healthy system is made up of healthy units working together in a symbiotic relationship with the well-being of the individual being indivisible from the well-being of the community, the land, the supernatural world, or the universe. This collectivistic orientation automatically influences perceptions of social support, as well as how people react when they are sick or stressed. This book elaborates on this subject in later chapters.

Sources of Illness

TCM and Ayurveda share many similarities. Ayurvedic science also uses the notion of basic elements: five great elements form the basis of the universe. Earth represents the solid state, water the liquid state, air the gaseous state, fire the power to change the state of any substance, and ether, simultaneously the source of all matter and the space in which it exists (Agnihotri & Agnihotri, 2017). Each of these elements can nourish the body; balance the body, serving to heal; or imbalance the body, serving as a poison. Achieving the right balance of these elements in the body is critical to maintaining a healthy state. These elements also combine to form three major forces that influence physiological functions critical to healthy living. Ether and air combine to form the *Vata dosha,* fire and water combine to form the *Pitta dosha,* and water and earth elements combine to form the *Kapha dosha. Vata* directs nerve impulses, circulation, respiration, and elimination. *Pitta* is responsible for metabolism in the organ and tissue systems as well as cellular metabolism. *Kapha* is responsible

▼ TABLE 3.3

The Major Constitutions of the Body in Ayurvedic Medicine

Characteristic	Vata	Pitta	Kapha
Body frame	Thin, irregular	Medium	Heavy
Weight	Easy to lose Hard to gain	Easy to lose Easy to gain	Hard to lose Easy to gain
Skin	Dark, tans deeply	Light, burns easily	Medium
Sweat	Scanty	Profuse	Moderate
Hair	Dry, coarse, curly Often dark	Fine, straight Light	Oily, thick brown
Appetite	Variable	Intense	Regular
Climate	Prefers warm	Prefers cool	Prefers change of season
Stamina	Poor	Medium	Good
Speech	Talkative	Purposeful	Cautious
Sex drive	Variable	Intense	Steady
Emotion	Fearful	Angry	Avoids confrontation
Memory	Learns quickly Forgets quickly	Learns quickly Forgets slowly	Learns slowly Forgets slowly

Source: Svoboda (2004).

for growth and protection. We are all made up of unique proportions of *Vata, Pitta,* and *Kapha* that cause disease when they go out of balance. These three *doshas* are also referred to as humors or bodily fluids and correspond to the Greek humors of phlegm (*Kapha*) and choler (*Pitta*). There is no equivalent to the Greek humor blood, nor is *Vata* or wind represented in the Greek system (Udwadia, 2000). Similar to the meridians in TCM, the existence of these forces is demonstrated more by inference and results of their hypothesized effects than by physical observation. *Vata, Pitta,* and *Kapha* are also associated with specific body type characteristics, as shown in Table 3.3.

In addition to diseases caused by the imbalances of the *doshas,* Ayurveda identifies diseases as having six other key causes. Some diseases are recognized as being due to natural changes in the body, genetic predispositions, trauma, gods or demons, the season, or deformities present at birth. Again, similar to the Chinese, Ayurvedic sages evoke the importance of balancing hot and cold. Heat, even the fever of desire for certain foods, is also thought to be an important source of illness.

In general, Ayurvedic practitioners believe that health is a natural state maintained by keeping the body clear of toxins and the mind relaxed and stress-free (Agnihotri & Agnihotri, 2017). The accumulation of toxins can occur when we are stressed and when waste is not effectively eliminated from the body. Consequently, some of the major Ayurvedic treatments involve detoxification and effective waste removal.

Treatment

The Ayurvedic physician uses different methods to diagnose a disease. First, there is a complete inspection of the patient. This involves looking for abnormalities in the body (e.g., discoloration of the skin), listening for abnormal sounds (e.g., irregular breathing), and even smelling the patient, because imbalances in diet and the body are thought to result in characteristic odors (especially in the urine). The physician also palpates the body to feel for problems and often thoroughly interrogates the patient to assess for any changes in lifestyle or routine. After a diagnosis is made, a number of treatments are prescribed.

There are many forms of treatment in the Ayurvedic system of medicine, and many of them have made inroads into the Western consciousness. Some of these treatments exist on the fringe of Western biomedicine as complementary therapies (these are discussed in more detail later in this chapter). Others, such as yoga, are now common in even the smaller American cities and towns (see the box at end of Chapter 11). New age spiritualists, who probably encountered treatments having origins in Ayurveda on travels through Southeast Asia, also practice many of them. Because imbalance is a source of illness, Ayurvedic medicine employs a number of techniques to reestablish balance. These include purification, surgery, drugs, diet, herbs, minerals, massage, color and gem therapy, homeopathy, acupressure, music, yoga, aromatherapy, and meditation. These treatments can be divided into therapies involving dietary changes and changes of activities at the level of the physical body and in tune with the seasons and climate, therapies aimed to clear the mind, and therapies involving spiritual rituals. Although not labeled Ayurvedic, you will encounter many of these (especially the last few) in health clinics around North America today.

Perhaps one of the most commonly seen forms of Ayurvedic treatments in North America (in alternative medicine circles, spas, and clinics nationwide and especially in California, New Mexico, and New York) is the Panchakarma (meaning five actions). Similar to ancient Egyptian methods to purify the body, Ayurvedic medicine recommends five ways that the body should be purged of toxins: vomiting, laxatives, enemas, nasal medication, and bloodletting. Some of these may sound primitive and you should definitely not try any of them at home, but each is considered critical in a return to health. Other distinctive treatments involve the ingestion of oily and fatty foods as a form of internal purification and making the patient sweat, the latter being a therapy also common to American Indian medicine, as we will discuss shortly.

The use of plants and herbal remedies plays a major part in Ayurvedic medicine and is also gaining attention in Western medical circles (Agnihotri & Agnihotri, 2017; Aranha, Clement, & Venkatesh, 2012). About 600 different medicinal plants are mentioned in the core Ayurvedic texts. A note of caution: Just knowing the name of the plant is not enough. The texts even prescribe how the plant should be grown (e.g., type of soil and water) and where it should be grown. The use of plants to cure is perhaps one of the key areas in which you will see Ayurveda used in North America. Western drug companies have used a number of plants originally used in India to cure diseases. For example, psyllium seed is used for bowel problems, and other plants are used to reduce blood pressure, control diarrhea, and lessen the risk of liver or heart problems. A substance called forskolin, isolated from the *Coleus forskohlii* plant, has been used in Ayurveda for treating heart disease, and its use has been empirically validated by Western biomedicine (Ding & Staudinger, 2005). Ayurvedic herbal medicines now also attract attention as potential sources of anticancer agents (Kumar, Jawaid, & Dubey, 2011).

CURANDERISMO AND SPIRITUALISM

The year 2003 signaled a major change in the cultural face of the United States of America. For the first time in its history, Americans of Latino descent became the largest minority group, narrowly edging out African Americans, a finding that holds today (U.S. Census Bureau, 2017). Latinos are present in every state in the United States, with large concentrations in California, Texas, and Arizona. Latinos are a diverse group of people. There are Latinos from Mexico, Puerto Rico, Cuba, and the Dominican Republic (Arrelano & Sosa, 2018). The health beliefs of this large part of the North American population correspondingly become important to consider. We will focus on the beliefs of the largest subgroup of Latinos, Mexican Americans.

Curanderismo is the Mexican American folk healing system that often coexists side by side with Western biomedicine (Valdez, 2014). Coming from the Spanish verb *curar* meaning to heal, *curanderos* are full-time healers. The *curandero*'s office is in the community, often in the healer's own home. There are no appointments, forms, or fees, and you pay whatever you believe the healer deserves. This form of healing relies heavily on the patient's faith and belief systems and uses everyday herbs, fruits, eggs, and oils. In studies beginning as early as 1959, researchers (Clark, 1959; Torrey, 1969) first focused on Mexican American cultural illnesses such as *mal de ojo* (sickness from admiring another too much). Later work (Trotter & Chavira, 1997) focused on the healers themselves, their beliefs, training processes, and processes for treatment, and now work is documenting the manifestation of *curanderismo* in different parts of North America (Ross, Maupin, & Timura, 2011; Valdez, 2014). Surveys of Mexican Americans show that even among highly assimilated Mexican Americans, traditional and indigenous practices persist (Arellano-Morales & Sosa, 2018; Tovar, 2017).

AP Photo/ Melanie Dabovich

▲ ***Curanderismo.*** *Curandera* Maria de Lourdez Gonzales Avila of Mexico City, left, performs an incense cleansing ritual on her students during a *curanderismo*, or Mexican folk healing, workshop at the University of New Mexico in Albuquerque, N.M. *Curanderismo* is a holistic, spiritual approach to medicine and is in high demand in the United States.

Sources of Illness

Traditionally, this Mexican American cultural framework acknowledges the existence of two sources of illness, one natural and one supernatural. When the natural and supernatural worlds are in harmony, optimal health is achieved. Disharmony between these realms breeds illness (Madsen, 1968). Beyond this supernatural balance component, the *curandero*'s concept of the cause of illness parallels that of Western biomedicine (Valdez, 2014). Like biomedical practitioners, *curanderos* believe that germs and other natural factors can cause illness. However, *curanderos* also believe that there are supernatural causes to illness in addition to natural factors. If an evil spirit, a witch, or a sorcerer causes an illness, then only a supernatural solution will be sufficient for a cure. Illness can also be caused if a person's energy field is weakened or disrupted. Whether diabetes, alcoholism, or cancer, if a spirit caused it, supernatural intervention is the only thing that can cure it. Although *curanderos* seem to give the devil his due, they often are realistic in their searches for a cause. Trotter and Chavira (1997) conducted extensive interviews with *curanderos* and reported that some identify more supernatural causes than others do. For example, a student once asked Trotter and Chivara to take him to a *curandero*. The student, let's call him Hector, felt hexed by a former girlfriend, who he admitted he had treated badly. Now Hector was feeling sick and exhausted and was performing badly in school. The *curandero* examined Hector and then asked him a series of questions concerning his health behaviors and habits. He determined that instead of a hex, Hector's symptoms developed from too much partying, too much drinking, and not enough studying! Though Hector could have received similar advice from a traditional doctor, he trusted the advice of the *curandero* more based on his cultural context.

Unlike Western biomedicine and TCM, the practices of *curanderismo* are based on Judeo-Christian beliefs and customs. The Bible has influenced *curanderismo* through references made to the specific healing properties of natural substances such as plants (see Luke 10:34). *Curanderos'* healing and cures are influenced by the Bible's proclamation that belief in God can and does heal directly and that people with a gift from God can heal in his name. The concept of the soul, central to Christianity, also provides support for the existence of saints (good souls) and devils (bad souls). The bad souls can cause illness, and the good souls, harnessed by the shamanism and sorcery of the *curanderismo,* can cure.

Treatment

Curanderos use three levels of treatment depending on the source of the illness: material, spiritual, and mental (Trotter & Chavira, 1997). Working on the material level, *curanderos* use things found in any house (eggs, lemons, garlic, and ribbons) and religious symbols (a crucifix, water, oils, and incense). These material things often are designed to either emit or absorb vibrating energy that repairs the energy field around a person. Ceremonies include prayers, ritual sweepings, or cleansings (Torres & Sawyer, 2005). The spiritual level of treatment often includes the *curandero* entering a trance, leaving his or her body, and playing the role of a medium. This spiritual treatment allows a spirit to commandeer the *curandero*'s body, facilitating a cure in the patient. On some occasions, the spirit will prescribe simple herbal remedies (via the *curandero*). On other occasions, the spirit will perform further rituals. The mental level of treatment relies on the power held by the individual *curandero* rather than on spirits or materials. Some illnesses (e.g., physical) often are treated by herbs alone (DeStefano, 2001), and psychological problems may be treated by a combination of all these types of treatments.

In a manner akin to that of health psychologists, *curanderos* explicitly focus on social, psychological, and biological problems (Trotter & Chavira, 1997). The difference is that they add a focus on spiritual problems as well. From a social perspective, the community where the *curanderos* work recognizes and accepts what the *curandero* is trying to achieve. The social world is important to the *curanderos* who evaluate the patient's direct and extended support system. The patient's moods and feelings are weighed together with any physical symptoms. Finally, there is always a ritual petition to God and other spiritual beings to help with the healing process.

Curanderos each have his or her own set of specializations. For example, midwives (*parteras*) help with births, masseuses (*sobaderos*) treat muscle sprains, and herbalists (*yerberos*) prescribe different plants (Avila & Parker, 2000). For most Mexican Americans, the choice between *curanderismo* and Western biomedicine is an either/or proposition. Some individuals use both systems, and some stay completely away from Western hospitals as much as they can, sometimes because they do not have enough money to use them. Acculturated and Mexican Americans from a higher social class tend to rely exclusively on Western biomedicine. The existence of this strong cultural and historical folk medicine and the large numbers of its adherents make this approach to illness an important alternative style for us to consider in our study of the psychology of health.

There are limited empirical studies of the effects of *curanderismo,* though there are many different accounts of the practices available in health and medical journals (Healy, 2000; Trotter, 2001). There is evidence that Mexican Americans who work at preserving their cultural values are more likely to consult a *curandero* (Davis, Peterson, Rothschild, & Resnicow, 2011). More and more medical journals are publishing articles on this form of healing (e.g., Bearison, Minian, & Granowetter, 2002, on asthma; Miller, Safranski, & Heur, 2004, on the treatment of diabetes; Ortiz & Torres, 2007, on the treatment of alcoholism) but little has been found in mainstream health psychology. The uses of *curanderismo* have been associated with negative health outcomes that are more often seen in the news. For example, DeBollonia et al. (2008) report a case of a young child who had to be hospitalized for isopropyl alcohol toxicity due to the use of a *curanderismo* treatment of *espanto* (evil spirits).

AMERICAN INDIAN MEDICINE

Many elements of the American Indian belief system and the approach to health are somewhat consistent with elements of *curanderismo* and TCM and provide a strong contrast to Western biomedicine (Hajdu & Hohmann, 2012). American Indians comprise about 1% of the population of the United States today. In many ways, the historical trauma faced by this group at the hands of invaders from Columbus onwards has led to contemporary Native Americans mistrusting Western medicine (King, 2017; Peters et al., 2014). Although approximately 500 nations of American Indians live in the United States, a set of core beliefs appear consistent across the groups. I will provide a generalized introduction in this section; note, though, that different tribes have different variations on the basic beliefs (e.g., Crow, 2001, for the Muskogee; Harris, 2017, for the Eastern Cherokee; Howard & Willie, 1984, for the Oklahoma Seminoles; Lewis, 1990, for the Oglala Sioux; Looks for Buffalo Hand, 1998, for Oglala Lakota practices; Mayes & Lacy, 1989, for the Navajo). Four practices are common to most (Cohen, 2003; Kavasch & Baar, 1999): the use of herbal remedies, the employment of ritual purification or purging, the use of symbolic rituals and ceremonies, and the involvement of healers, also referred to as medicine men, medicine women, or **shamans** (though the latter is primarily used for the healers of northern Europe; Eliade, 1964). Native Americans have used and benefited from these practices for at least 10,000 years and possibly much longer.

A brief aside: You may wonder what the politically correct way to refer to American Indians, Native Americans, or First Nations Peoples is. Today, as was the case historically, First Nations People identify themselves by family, community (or band), clan, and nation. The terms "nation" and "tribe" are often used interchangeably, though the term "nation" is generally more appropriate (Cohen, 2003). If you are not going to use the family-band-clan-nation nomenclature, First Nations People, Native American, or American Indian are also appropriate.

Sources of Illness

Similar to the ancient Chinese, American Indians believed that human beings and the natural world are closely intertwined. The fate of humankind and the fate of the trees, the mountains, the sky, and the oceans are all linked (King, 2017). The Navajos call this walking in beauty, a worldview in which everything in life is connected and influences everything else. In this system, sickness is a result of things falling out of balance and of losing one's way in the path of beauty (Alvord & Van Pelt, 2000). Animals are sacred, the winds are sacred, and trees and plants, bugs, and rocks are sacred. Each human and each object corresponds to a presence in the spirit world, and these spirits promote health or cause illness. Spiritual rejuvenation and the achievement of a general sense of physical, emotional, and communal harmony are at the heart of American Indian medicine. Shamans coordinate American Indian medicine and inherit the ability to communicate with spirits in much the same way that Mexican American *curanderos* do. Shamans spend much of their day listening to their patients, asking about their family and their behaviors and beliefs, and making connections between the patient's life and his or her illness (Harris, 2017). Shamans do not treat spirits as metaphors or prayers as a way to trick a body into healing. Shamans treat spirits as real entities, respecting them as they would any other intelligent being or living person.

Bob Chamberlin/Los Angeles Times/ Getty Images

▲ **Blessing Ceremony.** Sac & Fox Nation Hereditary Chief Saginaw Grant performs a blessing ceremony during a national day of prayer to protest slaughter of buffalo in Yellowstone National Park.

Treatment

Ritual and ceremony play a major role in American Indian medicine. One of the most potent and frequent ceremonies is the sweat lodge (Garrett et al., 2011). Medicine men hold lodges or sweats for different reasons. Sometimes a sweat purifies the people present; at other times, a sweat is dedicated to someone with cancer or another terminal illness. Before each sweat, attendees tie prayer strings and pouches, which are little bags of red, black, yellow, or white cloth (Cohen 2003). Each color represents a direction and type of spirit, and the choice of color depends on the ceremony to be performed. Each pouch contains sacred tobacco, the burning of which is believed to please the spirits. The sweat leader, often a shaman, decides on the number of prayer bags depending on why the sweat is needed. The ceremony takes place in a sweat lodge, which looks like a half dome of rocks and sticks covered with blankets and furs to keep the air locked in and the light out. The lodge symbolizes the world and the womb of Mother Earth.

▲ **An American Indian Sweat Lodge.** Navajo Tribal Park, Oljato-Monument Valley, Utah.

Even though the structure is only a half dome, participants believe that the rest of the sphere continues down inside the earth below it. Heated rocks are placed in a pit in the middle of the half dome. A short distance away from the lodge, a firekeeper heats rocks in a wood fire, often for hours before the event. The rocks are called *elders* because the rocks of the earth are seen as ancient observers. The number of rocks used also depends on the type of ceremony and is decided on by the lodge leader. The firekeeper builds a fire, prays over it and with it, and then places the stones in the fire, building the wood up around the rocks. He then keeps the rocks covered until it is time for them to be brought into the lodge (carried in with a pitchfork or shovel). Participants in the sweat sing sacred songs in separate rounds during the ceremony. After each round, the firekeeper brings in another set of hot rocks, and more songs are sung or prayers said. The sequence of prayers, chants, and singing following the addition of hot rocks continues until all the rocks are brought in. The hot stones raise the temperature inside the lodge, leading to profuse perspiration, which is thought to detoxify the body. Because of the darkness and the heat, participants often experience hallucinations that connect to spirit guides or provide insight into personal conditions (Mehl-Medrona, 1998).

Other ceremonies are also used. For example, the Lakota and Navajo use the medicine wheel, the sacred hoop, and the *sing,* which is a community healing ceremony lasting from 2 to 9 days and guided by a highly skilled specialist called a *singer.* Many healers also employ dancing, sand painting, chanting, drumming (which places a person's spirit into alignment with the heartbeat of Mother Earth), and feathers and rattles to remove blockages and stagnations of energy that may be contributing to ill health. Sometimes sacred stones are rubbed over the part of the person's body suspected to be diseased.

Although many American Indians prefer to consult a conventional medical doctor for conditions that require antibiotics or surgery, herbal remedies continue to play a substantial role in treatment of various physical, emotional, and spiritual ailments. The herbs prescribed vary from tribe to tribe, depending on the ailment and what herbs are available in a particular area. Some shamans suggest that the herbs be eaten directly. Others suggest taking them mixed with water (like an herbal tea) or even with food. Healers burn herbs such as sage, sweet grass, or cedar (called a smudge) in almost every ceremony and let the restorative smoke drift over the patient.

Today most American Indians use a blend of Western biomedicine and American Indian spiritualism. Most reservations usually have both spiritual healers and Western doctors, but traditional American Indians are often wary of the doctors and first seek out medicine men.

AFRICAN AMERICAN BELIEFS

In addition to these four basic approaches to health, there is also a wealth of other belief systems to learn such as those of different religious groups, including Islamic (Amer, 2017), Judaic (Korbman, Appel, & Rosmarin, 2017), Sufi (Bozorgzadeh, Bahadorani, & Sadoghi, 2017), Buddhist (Colgan, Hidalgo, & Priester, 2017), Santeria (a creole religion; Martinez, Taylor, Calvert, Hirsch, & Webster, 2014), and agnostics (Hwang & Cragun, 2017). A full description of all of the different folk medicines existing in the world today is beyond the scope of this book, but remember that there are additional belief systems both in Northern America and around the globe that remain for your further explorations.

One example is the African American culture. For many members of this cultural group, health beliefs may reflect cultural roots that include elements of African healing, medicine of the Civil War South, European medical and anatomical folklore, West Indies voodoo religion, fundamentalist Christianity, and other belief systems (Wendorf & Bellegrade-Smith, 2014). African Americans who use complementary and alternative medicine (CAM) in general are more likely to use folk medicine in particular (Barner, Bohman, Brown, & Richards, 2010).

African American communities are very diverse, often populated by people descended from Haiti, other Caribbean countries, and Africa. Similar to the American Indians, many people of African descent also hold a strong connection to nature and rely on *inyangas* (traditional herbalists). Even today in parts of Africa, hospitals and modern medicines are the last resort in illness. Traditionally in tribal Africa, people sought relief in the herbal lore of the ancestors and consults the *inyanga,* who is in charge of the physical health of the people (Bradford, 2005). When bewitchment is suspected, which happens frequently among the traditional people of Africa, or when there is a personal family crisis or love or financial problem, the patient is taken to a *sangoma* (spiritual diviner or spiritual/traditional healer), who is believed to have spiritual powers and is able to work with the ancestral spirits or spirit guides (Wendorf & Bellegrade-Smith, 2014). The *sangoma* uses various methods such as throwing the bones (*amathambo,* also known by other names depending on the cultural group) or going into a spiritual trance to consult the ancestral spirits or spirit guides to find the diagnosis or cure for the problem, be it bewitchment, love, or another problem. Depending on the response from the higher source, a decision will be made on what herbs and mixes (*intelezis*) should be used and in what manner (e.g., orally, burning). If more powerful medicine is needed, numerous magical rites can or will be performed according to rituals handed down from *sangoma* to *sangoma* (Wendorf & Bellegrade-Smith, 2014). In South Africa there are more than 70,000 *sangomas* or spiritual healers who dispense herbal medicines and even issue medical certificates to employees for purposes of sick leave (Bradford, 2005).

Even though you may have had some awareness of the Greek roots of Western medicine (e.g., the Hippocratic Oath taken by doctors) or Chinese medicine (e.g., acupuncture) or even Indian traditional medicine (e.g., the Ayurvedic practice of yoga), other cultural ways of healing such as the *sangoma* are not as well-known and, worse, are often ridiculed by the mass media. For example, many visitors to the city of New Orleans take voodoo tours around the city and joke about sticking pins in dolls made up to look like their bosses or enemies. The story is that a pin in the arm of the doll should cause pain in the arm of the person it is meant to represent. There is a rich history and tradition of voodoo that goes well beyond such parodied anecdotes. Many African Americans believe in a form of folk medicine that incorporates and mirrors aspects of voodoo (really spelled vodou), which is a type of religion derived from some of the world's oldest known religions that have been present in Africa since the beginning of human civilization (Wendorf & Bellegrade-Smith, 2014).

When Africans were brought to the Americas (historians estimate that approximately 1.25 million enslaved Africans were transported), religious persecution forced them to practice voodoo in secret. To allow voodoo to survive, its followers adopted many elements of Christianity. Today, voodoo is a legitimate religion in a number of areas of the world, including Brazil, where it is called Candomble, and the English-speaking Caribbean, where it is called Obeah. In most of the United States, however, White slavers were successful in stripping slaves of their voodoo traditions and beliefs (Heaven & Booth, 2003). In some parts of the United States, the remnants are stronger than in others. Some African American communities in isolated areas such as the coast and islands of North Carolina survived intact well into the 20th century. Here, Gullah culture, involving the belief in herbalism, spiritualism, and black magic, thrived (Pinckney, 2003). What was called voodoo in other parts of the country was called the root (meaning charm). A number of other cultures, such as the American Indians described earlier and Hmong Americans, still believe that shamans and medicine men can influence health. Although shamanistic rituals and voodoo rites may

Synthesize, Evaluate, Apply

- What are the main causes of illness in Traditional Chinese Medicine? To American Indians? In *curanderismo*?
- Compare and contrast the different treatments used in the different approaches.
- How can the field of health psychology best use information about diverse approaches to health?
- Identify the critical biopsychosocial factors underlying each diverse approach to health.

seem to be ineffectual ways to cure according to Western science, the rituals have meaning to those who believe in them and should not be ignored or ridiculed.

ARE COMPLEMENTARY AND ALTERNATIVE APPROACHES VALID?

Most of the non-Western approaches to medicine described in this chapter are commonly referred to as complementary and alternative medicine (CAM). Table 3.4 describes the main CAMs. Voodoo and shamanistic rites do not fall under the CAM umbrella; however, the term "**complementary and alternative medicine**" generally describes any healing philosophies and therapies that mainstream Western (conventional) medicine does not commonly use. A Western focus often tends to influence views of CAMs. One definition of CAMs sees them as "therapies practiced in the absence of both scientific evidence proving their effectiveness and a plausible biological explanation for why they should be effective" (Bausell, 2007, p. 21). Other authors have gone so far to refer to this entire category of non-Western medicine as "snake oil science" (Bausell, 2007, p. 1), no different from magic and generally nonsense (Offit, 2013). Are these opinions justified? As you can see from the sections above, many of these alternatives to Western science have different levels of scientific testing; it cannot be denied that many who

▼ TABLE 3.4

Integrative Medical Approaches

Integrative Medical Approaches
Acupuncture is a method of healing developed in China at least 2,000 years ago. Procedures involve stimulation of anatomical points on the body by a variety of techniques.
Aromatherapy involves the use of essential oils (extracts or essences) from flowers, herbs, and trees to promote health and well-being.
Ayurveda is a medical system that has been practiced primarily in the Indian subcontinent for 5,000 years. Ayurveda includes diet and herbal remedies and emphasizes the use of body, mind, and spirit in disease prevention and treatment.
Chiropractic focuses on the relationship between bodily structure (primarily that of the spine) and function, and how that relationship affects the preservation and restoration of health. Chiropractors use manipulative therapy as an integral treatment tool.
Dietary supplements are products (other than tobacco) taken by mouth that contain a dietary ingredient intended to supplement the diet. Dietary ingredients may include vitamins, minerals, herbs or other botanicals, amino acids, and substances such as enzymes, organ tissues, and metabolites.
Electromagnetic fields (EMFs; also called electric and magnetic fields) are invisible lines of force that surround all electrical devices. Earth also produces EMFs: electric fields are produced when there is thunderstorm activity, and it is believed that magnetic fields are produced by electric currents flowing at the earth's core.
Homeopathic medicine is an alternative medical system. In homeopathic medicine, there is a belief that like cures like, meaning that small, highly diluted quantities of medicinal substances are given to cure symptoms, when the same substances given at higher or more concentrated doses would actually cause those symptoms.
Massage therapists manipulate muscle and connective tissue to enhance the function of those tissues and promote relaxation and well-being.
Naturopathic medicine proposes that there is a healing power in the body that establishes, maintains, and restores health. Practitioners work with the patient with a goal of supporting this power, through treatments such as nutrition and lifestyle counseling, dietary supplements, medicinal plants, exercise, homeopathy, and treatments from Traditional Chinese Medicine.
Qi gong is a component of Traditional Chinese Medicine that combines movement, meditation, and regulation of breathing to enhance the flow of *qi* in the body, improve blood circulation, and enhance immune function.
Reiki is a Japanese word representing universal life energy. Reiki is a technique based on the belief that when spiritual energy is channeled through a reiki practitioner, the patient's spirit is healed, which in turn heals the physical body.
Therapeutic touch is derived from an ancient technique called laying on of hands. It is based on the premise that the healing force of the therapist affects the patient's recovery; healing is promoted when the body's energies are in balance. By passing their hands over the patient, healers can identify energy imbalances.

Source: National Center for Complementary and Integrative Health (2018).

practice CAMs feel better. Based on rigorous scientific testing CAMs are not always distinguishable from placebos in randomized control trials (see Chapter 2) but many practitioners do not need scientific proof (Offit, 2013). Let's explore CAM origins a bit more.

Earlier, we described how Western medicine started. Spurred on by technological innovations and inquiring minds, Western biomedicine became what we know today. How did different non-Western people discover their methods? The most plausible answer and one supported by contemporary adherents of non-Western treatments is that the methods were discovered by trial and error. When a person was sick, he or she ate the bark or leaves of a number of different herbs. Most of the herbs may not have had any effect, and the person either suffered or died. Some herbs may have produced an immediate cure. Automatically then, that herb would be known to help with that certain ailment. Of course, many practitioners of traditional medicine do not offer the trial and error explanation. The ancient Chinese text, *The Yellow Emperor's Classic of Internal Medicine*, which is the basis for Traditional Chinese Medicine, suggests that communications with the heavens account for traditional medical practices (Santee, 2017). Similarly, American Indian shamans and Latino *curanderos* derive their healing powers from communications with spirits (Trotter & Chavira, 1997). The different origins of traditional beliefs notwithstanding, the fact is that many different cultures (ethnic, racial, religious, and others) have different beliefs about health and illness. Are these valid beliefs? Do the different methods work? This is a question that modern science is beginning to tackle. Given the growing diversity in the composition of North America, a major way to increase the use of health services is to learn more about the different cultural approaches to health. The major treatments used by each are summarized in Table 3.5.

If you are not already surprised by the different aspects of Chinese medicine, *curanderismo,* and American Indian spiritualism, you may be when you look at what some other peoples in North America actually do to cure themselves. You may have heard of special diets (e.g., Paleo, Mediterranean, Zone, Atkins, Weightwatchers), but there is also a category of treatments called orthomolecular therapies in which patients eat substances such as magnesium, melatonin, and megadoses of vitamins. Some biological therapies use laetrile (iron and aluminum oxide), shark cartilage, and bee pollen to treat autoimmune and inflammatory diseases. In other CAMs, the body is manipulated. For example, chiropractors and osteopathic manipulators work with the musculoskeletal system. There are separate categories of energy therapies, such as reiki. Practitioners channel energy from their spirit to heal the patient's body. Other energy treatments use magnetic and electrical fields to alleviate pain and cure sickness.

There is a wide spectrum of therapeutic modalities covered by the CAM umbrella (Jones, 2005). Approximately 38% of people in North America use some form of complementary medicine, according to the National Center for Complementary and Alternative Medicine (Arias, 2004; Barnes, Powell-Griner, McFann, & Nahin, 2004; NCCAM, 2012). When prayer and the use of megavitamins are included, that number climbs to 62%, and the findings are relatively consistent across ethnic groups. People of all backgrounds use CAMs, but some people are more

▼ TABLE 3.5

Treatment Differences Summarized

Medical Tradition	Major Treatments
Western biomedicine	Medication, surgery
Traditional Chinese medicine	Herbs, acupuncture, *qi gong*
Ayurveda	Herbs, yoga, *panchakarma* (purification), meditation, aromatherapy, massage
Curanderismo	Material, spiritual, and mental
American Indian medicine	Sweat lodges, prayer, herbs, medicine wheel
African American beliefs	Herbs, magical rites

▼ TABLE 3.6

Trends in the use of selected complementary health approaches during the past 12 months, by type of approach: United States

Complementary health approach	2002		2007		2012	
	Number (in thousands)	Age-adjusted percent[1] (standard error)	Number (in thousands)	Age-adjusted percent[1] (standard error)	Number (in thousands)	Age-adjusted percent[2] (standard error)
Nonvitamin, nonmineral dietary supplements	38,183	18.9 (0.28)	38,797	17.7 (0.37)	40,579	17.7 (0.37)
Deep-breathing exercises[2]	23,457	11.6 (0.24)	27,794	12.7 (0.30)	24,218	10.9 (0.26)
Yoga, tai chi, and qi gong	11,766	5.8 (0.17)	14,436	6.7 (0.22)	22,281	10.1 (0.25)
Chiropractic or osteopathic manipulation[3]	15,226	7.5 (0.19)	18,740	8.6 (0.27)	19,369	8.4 (0.22)
Meditation[4]	15,336	7.6 (0.20)	20,541	9.4 (0.27)	17,948	8.0 (0.21)
Massage therapy	10,052	5.0 (0.16)	18,068	8.3 (0.23)	15,411	6.9 (0.15)
Special diets[5]	6,765	3.3 (0.12)	6,040	2.8 (0.14)	6,853	3.0 (0.13)
Homeopathic treatment[6]	3,433	1.7 (0.09)	3,909	1.8 (0.11)	5,046	2.2 (0.11)
Progressive relaxation	6,185	3.0 (0.12)	6,454	2.9 (0.15)	4,766	2.1 (0.10)
Guided imagery	4,194	2.1 (0.10)	4,866	2.2 (0.16)	3,846	1.7 (0.10)
Acupuncture	2,136	1.1 (0.07)	3,141	1.4 (0.10)	3,484	1.5 (0.08)
Energy healing therapy	1,080	0.5 (0.05)	1,216	0.5 (0.06)	1,077	0.5 (0.06)
Naturopathy	496	0.2 (0.03)	729	0.3 (0.04)	957	0.4 (0.04)
Hypnosis	505	0.2 (0.03)	561	0.2 (0.04)	347	0.1 (0.03)
Biofeedback	278	0.1 (0.02)	362	0.2 (0.04)	281	0.1 (0.02)
Ayurveda	154	†0.1 (0.02)	214	†0.1 (0.03)	241	0.1 (0.02)

† Estimates are considered unreliable. Data have a relative standard error greater than 30% and less than or equal to 50% and should be used with caution.
†† Direct comparisons are not available.
§ Difference between both years is statistically significant at $p < 0.05$.
0.0 Quantity more than zero but less than 0.05.
* Significance of the chi-squared statistics is < 0.001.
** Significance of the chi-squared statistics is < 0.01.
*** Significance of the chi-squared statistics is < 0.05.
[1]The denominator used in the calculation of percentages was all sample adults.
[2]In 2012, deep-breathing exercises included deep-breathing exercises as part of hypnosis; biofeedback; Mantra meditation (including Transcendental Meditation, Relaxation Response, and Clinically Standardized Meditation); mindfulness meditation (including Vipassana, Zen Buddhist meditation, mindfulness-based stress reduction, and mindfulness-based cognitive therapy); spiritual meditation (including centering prayer and contemplative meditation); guided imagery; progressive relaxation; yoga; tai chi; or qi gong. In 2002 and 2007, the use of deep-breathing exercises was asked broadly and not if used as part of other complementary health approaches. No trend analyses were conducted on the use of deep-breathing exercises.
[3]In 2002, the use of chiropractic care was asked broadly, and osteopathic approach was not specified on the survey. No trend analyses were conducted on the use of chiropractic or osteopathic manipulation.
[4]In 2012, meditation included Mantra meditation (including Transcendental Meditation, Relaxation Response, and Clinically Standardized Meditation); mindfulness meditation (including Vipassana, Zen Buddhist meditation, mindfulness-based stress reduction, and mindfulness-based cognitive therapy); spiritual meditation (including centering prayer and contemplative meditation); and meditation used as a part of other practices (including yoga, tai chi, and qi gong). In 2002 and 2007, the use of meditation was asked broadly and not if practiced as part of other complementary health approaches.
[5]Respondents used one or more named special diets for 2 weeks or more in the past 12 months. Special diets included vegetarian (including vegan), macrobiotic, Atkins, Pritikin, and Ornish diets.
[6]No distinction was made between persons who sought treatment from a homeopathic practitioner and those who self-medicated.
NOTES: Estimates were age-adjusted using the projected 2000 U.S. population as the standard population and using four age groups: 18–24, 25–44, 45–64, and 65 and over. The denominators for statistics shown exclude persons with unknown complementary and alternative medicine information. Estimates are based on household interviews of a sample of the civilian noninstitutionalized population.

Source: CDC/NCHS, National Health Interview Survey, 2002, 2007, and 2012.

Lou Linwei / Alamy Stock Photo

▲ **Chinese Herbalist.** A Chinese herbalist weighs herbal medicine using a traditional scale in Beijing, China.

likely than others to use them. Overall, CAM use is greater by women, people with higher educational levels, people who have been hospitalized in the past year, and former smokers, compared with current smokers or those who have never smoked. U.S. health-care workers use CAMs significantly more than the general public (Johnson, Ward, Knutson, & Sendelbach, 2012). A recent meta-analysis showed satisfactory clinical evidence for the use of a number of herbal remedies and treatments such as flaxseed for hypertension, and St. John's Wort for relieving some symptoms of menopause, while also highlighting the potential for negative herb–drug interaction effects (Izzo, Hoon-Kim, Radhakrishman, & Williamson, 2016).

Given the growing exposure of the Western world to non-Western medicines, it is important to ask whether the different approaches meet the rigorous tests of the scientific method before adopting alternative styles of behavior or different cures. The U.S. government recognizes the importance of different approaches to health. In 1998 Congress established the National Center for Complementary and Alternative Medicine (NCCAM) to stimulate, develop, and support research on CAMs for public benefit. In addition to the techniques used by the main approaches described earlier, the NCCAM also studies the effectiveness of other CAMs such as aromatherapy, meditation, acupuncture/acupressure, hypnosis, dance, music and art therapy, and even prayer.

The critical point to realize about these varying beliefs is that health psychologists must be aware of a person's beliefs in order to treat the person comprehensively. Followers of Western medicine arrive at their beliefs about the values of Western medicine in the same way that the believers of other cultures come to their beliefs about their medical practices. People learn their beliefs from their parents or other people around them. Your mother telling you that your cold is due to a virus establishes a belief system just as someone else's mother telling him that his cold is due to the evil looks of a neighbor also establishes a belief system. In both cases, the listening child may believe the story. What people believe influences what they do to remedy the situation. Giving antibiotics to someone who believes her cold is due to evil eyes may not yield the same effects as giving antibiotics to someone who believes her cold is due to a germ. Belief is a strong tool in the arsenal of the healer and an important element for the health psychologist to consider when attempting to maintain health and prevent illness (Table 3.6).

Often people educated in the West will express contempt for non-Western ways of looking at health. What do you mean spirits and evil eyes can cause illness? How can the weather and winds make a difference? Why do you have to keep the spirits happy to be healthy? Ideas such as these make some snicker and others roll their eyes in disbelief. Although many non-Western beliefs have not been tested by the scientific method, for many of their practitioners, there is no need to have this proof. A long tradition of believing in a medical practice is enough for many who hold non-Western beliefs. To some extent, this is comparable to Christians who have faith in the words of the Bible or Hindus who believe in the Upanishads or the Bhagavad Gita (ancient Hindu scriptures). Scientific evidence is not needed when you have faith. To successfully treat and influence people with different beliefs, we have to know first what they believe.

Synthesize, Evaluate, Apply

- What do the different approaches to health have in common?
- Using an empirical scientific approach, evaluate each different approach to health.
- What are the psychological processes by which a health belief can influence recovery?
- Compare and contrast the different philosophical approaches to health.

APPLICATION SHOWCASE

ACUPUNCTURE

"Needles, needles, big long needles, poking into me. A human pin cushion." This is a common response when people are asked what the word acupuncture brings to mind. Yes, needles are involved. Yes, they are poked into the patient. Yes, the patient often looks like a pincushion. However, you should also know that the needles are minute, thin, flexible wires, barely a few millimeters thick. The procedure is so painless that if you close your eyes when the needles are being placed, you will not even feel them. (Believe me. I have tried it many times.)

Acupuncture is one of the most scientifically validated forms of alternative medicine and is gaining popularity in hospitals nationwide, although portions of Western biomedicine heavily mistrust it (Bausell, 2007; Offit, 2013). In 1993 the Food and Drug Administration estimated that Americans made nearly 12 million visits per year to acupuncture practitioners, spending more than $500 million. The 2007 National Health Interview Survey estimated that more than 10 million Americans had used acupuncture and 3.1 million had used it the previous year (Barnes, Bloom, & Nahin, 2008). The practice of acupuncture in North America began only in the 1970s. (As stated earlier, acupuncture has been a part of Chinese traditional medicine for thousands of years.) When President Nixon first opened the door to the Far East, journalists who accompanied him on his tour of China witnessed surgeries performed on animals and humans without anesthesia used. Instead, Chinese surgeons used acupuncture with slender needles piercing into predetermined points of the body.

Practitioners of Traditional Chinese Medicine determined that there are as many as 2,000 acupuncture points on the human body connected by 20 pathways (12 main and 8 secondary), called meridians. These meridians conduct energy, or qi, between the surface of the body and its internal organs. Each acupuncture point has a different effect on the qi that passes through it. Acupuncture keeps the balance between yin and yang, thus allowing for the normal flow of qi throughout the body and restoring health to the mind and body.

Several theories have been presented to explain exactly how acupuncture works. One theory suggests that pain impulses are blocked from reaching the spinal cord or brain at various gates to these areas. Because a majority of acupuncture points are either connected to (or are located near) neural structures, it is possible that acupuncture stimulates the nervous system. Another theory hypothesizes that acupuncture stimulates the body to produce endorphins, which reduce pain. Other studies have found that opioids (also pain relievers) may be released into the body during acupuncture treatment.

In the late 1970s the World Health Organization recognized the ability of acupuncture and Traditional Chinese Medicine to treat nearly four dozen common ailments, including neuro-musculoskeletal conditions (e.g., arthritis, neuralgia, insomnia, dizziness, and neck/shoulder pain); emotional and psychological disorders (e.g., depression and anxiety); circulatory disorders (e.g., hypertension, angina pectoris, arteriosclerosis, and anemia); addictions to alcohol, nicotine, and other drugs; respiratory disorders (e.g., emphysema, sinusitis, allergies, and bronchitis); and gastrointestinal conditions (e.g., food allergies, ulcers, chronic diarrhea, constipation, indigestion, intestinal weakness, anorexia, and gastritis). A summary statement released by the National Institutes of Health (1997) declared that acupuncture could be useful by itself or in combination with other therapies to treat addiction, headaches, menstrual cramps, tennis elbow, fibromyalgia, myofascial pain, osteoarthritis, lower back pain, carpal tunnel syndrome, and asthma. Other studies have demonstrated that acupuncture may help in the rehabilitation of stroke patients and can relieve nausea in patients recovering from surgery.

Many Western medicine practitioners in North America are actively incorporating acupuncture into mainstream medicine. Some doctors belong to the American Academy of Medical Acupuncture, an organization founded in 1987 by a group of physicians who graduated from an acupuncture training program at the University of California, Los Angeles (UCLA) School of Medicine. Schools for acupuncture training also have been established all across America. Several councils provide structure for the various training schools (e.g., the Council of Colleges of Acupuncture and Oriental Medicine), and accreditation boards (e.g., the Accreditation Commission for Acupuncture and Oriental Medicine [ACAOM]) have brought more acceptance and oversight to the practice of acupuncture in the United States.

CHAPTER REVIEW

SUMMARY ▶▶

- Different cultures have varied ideas about what constitutes being healthy and what behaviors are healthy. Such beliefs vary by sex, religion, ethnicity, and nationality, to name a few. Writings about health and illness go as far back as 3000 B.C. to the times of the Mesopotamians and ancient Egyptians.
- Western medicine has its roots in the writings of the Greek physicians Hippocrates and Galen. Also called allopathy, this approach focuses on causing the opposite effect from that created by the disease and is driven to rid the body of illness. Clear ideas of anatomy and circulation were some of the early contributions of Greek research to health.
- Western medicine advanced with improvements in technology, specifically the discovery of the microscope and the X-ray and innovations in surgery. Pasteur's work on germ theory showing that germs and bacteria caused illness greatly solidified the focus of Western medicine on physical sources of illness.
- *Curanderismo* is the Mexican American folk healing system that often coexists with Western medicine. This healing system uses herbs, fruits, eggs, and oils, and places emphasis on spiritual causes of illness. An imbalance between the spiritual and natural world is seen to be the cause of illness.
- *Curanderos* treat patients on material, spiritual, and mental levels, depending on where the illness is thought to have begun. Spiritual treatments may involve the healer going into a trance and playing the role of a medium. Material treatments involve household items and religious symbols, and mental treatments rely on the power held by the healer.
- Traditional Chinese medicine (TCM) treats the body as a whole in which every single part is intrinsically linked to other parts and to what is happening around the person. According to TCM, food, relationships, and spiritual harmony are all conducive to health. Diseases are thought to be caused by imbalances in yin and yang.
- Yin and yang are mutually interdependent, interchangeable forces that make up the entire universe. The Tao, or energy force, of the universe is influenced by the balance of yin and yang and needs to be fostered for optimal health. Main treatments include acupuncture and herbal therapy.
- American Indian medicine also focuses on spiritual balance and living in harmony with nature. The most common practices involve the use of herbal remedies, ritual purification or purging, symbolic rituals and ceremonies, and the involvement of shamans.
- Acupuncture could be useful by itself or in combination with other therapies to treat a number of issues such as addiction, headaches, menstrual cramps, pain, carpal tunnel syndrome, and asthma.

TEST YOURSELF ▶▶

Check your understanding of the topics in this chapter by answering the following questions.

1. Complementary and alternative medicine is the name given to a category of medical treatments
   a. designed to add to Western medicine.
   b. practiced by Chinese and Indians.
   c. that are non-Western in origin.
   d. that do not involve biomedical drugs or procedures.
2. Western biomedicine is also referred to as
   a. allopathy.
   b. homeopathy.
   c. Hellenistic.
   d. physiopathy.
3. The earliest known diagnostic system of medicine involving physicians and combining religious rites and empirical treatments was seen in
   a. Mesopotamia.
   b. Greece.
   c. Pakistan.
   d. Japan.
4. Each of the following directly contributed to our knowledge of human anatomy except
   a. William Harvey.
   b. Galen.
   c. Leonardo da Vinci.
   d. Andreas Vesalius.

5. According to the most recent census data, the largest minority group in the United States is
   a. African American.
   b. Latino.
   c. Asian American.
   d. American Indian.
6. The Mexican American folk healing system is referred to as
   a. *mal de ojo*.
   b. machismo.
   c. *curanderismo.*
   d. *el chupacabra*.
7. Which of the following cultural belief systems of medicine is heavily based on Christian beliefs and practices?
   a. Western biomedicine
   b. *curanderismo*
   c. Traditional Chinese Medicine
   d. American Indian medicine
8. One folk remedy common to American Indian, Mexican American, and Traditional Chinese Medicine is
   a. plants.
   b. needles.
   c. saunas.
   d. prayer.
9. Which of the following assumptions of Traditional Chinese Medicine is *not* correct?
   a. Meridian channels guide energy through the body.
   b. The nervous system is linked to the meridian system.
   c. Health is a balance of mind and body.
   d. Health is best dealt with in a macroscopic fashion.
10. Which of the following is *not* something a shaman would do?
    a. Listen to patients and ask about family, behaviors, and beliefs
    b. Treat spirits as metaphors
    c. Chant and pray in a trance
    d. Attempt to connect illness to a patient's life

KEY TERMS, CONCEPTS, AND PEOPLE ▶▶

allopathy, **57**
Ayurveda, **63**
complementary and alternative medicine, **72**
curanderismo, **66**
da Vinci, Leonardo, **57**
Galen, **57**
Harvey, William, **57**
Hippocrates, **57**
opiates, **58**
opioids, **58**
Pasteur, Louis, **58**
qi, **60**
reductionist, **57**
shamans, **69**
Tao, **59**
Traditional Chinese Medicine, **59**
van Leeuwenhoek, Antonius, **57**
Vesalius, Andreas, **57**
Western biomedicine, **57**

ESSENTIAL READINGS ▶▶

Cohen, K. (2003). *Honoring the medicine: The essential guide to Native American healing.* New York, NY: Ballantine Books.

Kaptchuk, T. J. (2000). *The web that has no weaver: Understanding Chinese medicine.* Chicago, IL: Contemporary Books.

Suchday, S., Ramanayake, N. P., Benkhoukha, A., Santoro, A. F., Marquez, C., & Nakao, G. (2014). Ayurveda: An alternative in the Unites States. In R. A. R. Gurung (Ed.), *Multicultural approaches to health and wellness in America* (pp. 152–169). Santa Barbara, CA: ABC-CLIO.

Trotter, R. T., & Chavira, J. A. (1997). *Curanderismo: Mexican American folk healing.* Athens, GA: University of Georgia Press.

iStockphoto.com/ RoBeDeRo

CHAPTER 4

ESSENTIAL PHYSIOLOGY

Chapter 4 Outline

MEASURING UP

KNOW YOUR VITAL STATS

There are some key physiological pieces of information and some lifestyle factors that can predict how long you are expected to live. Complete the questions below to provide a sense of what all can influence your longevity. For your personal prediction, check out a lifespan calculator online.

Current year (4 digits):	
Your age:	
Age you plan to retire at (or current age if already retired):	
Sex:	○ Female ○ Male
I live in urban area with over 2 million people	○ Yes ○ No
One of my grandparents lived to age 85 or over	○ Yes ○ No
All four grandparents lived to age 80 or over	○ Yes ○ No
A parent died of a stroke or heart attack before 50	○ Yes ○ No
A parent, brother or sister under age 50 has (or had) cancer or a heart condition, or has diabetes	○ Yes ○ No
I personally earn over $60,000 a year	○ Yes ○ No
I finished college	○ Yes ○ No
I have a graduate or professional degree	○ Yes ○ No
I am still working	○ Yes ○ No
I live with a spouse or friend	○ Yes ○ No
Number of 10-year periods I have lived alone since age 25	
I work behind a desk	○ Yes ○ No
My work requires heavy physical labor	○ Yes ○ No
I exercise strenuously (tennis, running, etc.) at least 1/2 hour . . .	○ 5x/wk ○ 3x/wk ○ 0x/wk
I sleep more than 10 hours each night	○ Yes ○ No
I am intense, aggressive and/or easily angered	○ Yes ○ No

(Continued)

(Continued)

I am easy-going and relaxed	○ Yes ○ No
I am generally . . .	○ Happy ○ Unhappy ○ In between
I have had a speeding ticket in the last year	○ Yes ○ No
Number of packs of cigarettes I smoke per day	○ 2+ ○ 1-2 ○ 1/2-1 ○ 0

I drink the equivalent of two drinks of hard liquor a day	○ Yes ○ No
Number of pounds I am overweight by	○ 50+ ○ 30-50 ○ 10-30 ○ < 10

▾ Ponder This

How does your brain help you think, feel, and behave?

What are the major chemicals that make you tick?

Can playing video games influence your physiology and health?

Our biology determines our longevity and how comfortably we live. Even more importantly, when it comes to understanding health and behavior, a growing opinion is that it "makes no sense" to distinguish between elements of behavior that are "biological" and those that are "psychological" or "cultural." They are "utterly intertwined" (Sapolsky, 2017, p. 5). As much as I will emphasize how we can use our psychology (e.g., our thinking, personality styles) to change our health and behaviors, remember that all that psychology comes from our biology. Our thoughts, emotions, and feelings are constructed by our brains based on the context, our past history, and a range of other factors (Dennett, 2017; Feldman Barrett, 2017). It pays to know your biology.

Our biological systems—our brain, heart, lungs, nervous system, circulatory system—keep us alive, but can be damaged or compromised when we are sick or when we practice unhealthy behaviors. Smoking and drinking can clog arteries just as much as a poor diet can, and sometimes even more. A premise of health psychology is that our minds (e.g., how we think), our personalities, and our behaviors influence our bodies and our biology. Thus, a firm understanding of the basic physiological systems is critical to comprehending how the different components of the biopsychosocial model come together and influence behavior (Robles, Mercado, Nooteboom, Price, & Romney, 2019).

For some readers of this book, reading a chapter dedicated to biology is onerous. Maybe you took a psychology course hoping to get away from biology and thought that the biology chapter in your introductory psychology textbook was peculiar. The good news is that understanding biology often makes many psychological phenomena clearer. For example, why do we have trouble remembering facts we have studied when we are stressed during an exam? Answer: Because the memory part of the brain (the hippocampus) and the emotion part (the amygdala) are right next to each other. If one is activated, it can activate the other. To comprehend health psychology, it is critical to first understand basic physiology (and it is worth the extra effort to do so). This chapter covers the pertinent material; many more biological details exist that are relevant to health.

RESEARCHER SPOTLIGHT

Theodore (Ted) Robles earned his PhD from the Ohio State University in health psychology, with clinical psychology as a secondary area. He is currently at the University of California, Los Angeles (UCLA). Robles is an expert on biological processes of health (Robles, Mercado, Nooteboom, Price, & Romney, 2019; see Essential Readings).

This chapter details the most essential components that are important in understanding the biopsychosocial model and the health psychological research, theories, and processes described in this book. Health psychologists also employ a wide range of biological and physical measures for each of these systems; that material is not covered here, but a great review is available (Segerstrom et al., 2016).

Each of the following sections corresponds to different chapters in the book (e.g., the nervous system is necessary to understanding stress processes described in

Chapter 5). You can choose to read each corresponding section as needed or read all of the following and get the whole biological story up front right now.

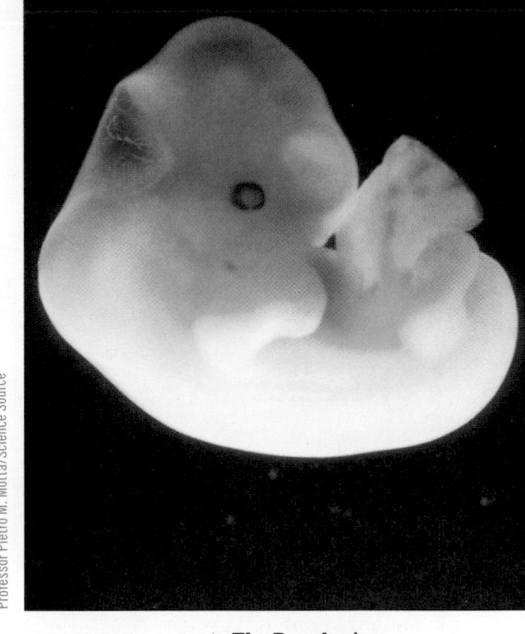

▲ **The Developing Human Being: Different Stages of Prenatal Growth.** A five week old human embryo.

BIOLOGICAL DEVELOPMENT

Our first challenge is to understand how our bodies develop. This sets the stage for us to discuss how our psychology and society can influence this biological development and subsequently our health (and the field of health psychology).

The Prenatal Period

The infant is born with predispositions and a genetic inheritance that shape many future developments. For the baby to have a chance to grow and develop, it first has to be born. Although that may sound like an odd thing to say (or at least extremely obvious), not all pregnancies end with a successful labor and delivery (Dunkel-Schetter, Gurung, Lobel, & Wadhwa, 2001). Furthermore, many things can happen in the time *before* a baby is born (the **prenatal period**); the less time that the baby has in the womb, or in utero, the less time it will have to grow and develop normally. In fact, the length of **gestation**, or time in womb, is one of the most important health psychological outcome variables used to study pregnancy. **Preterm births**, those where delivery occurs before 37 weeks of gestation, are the most direct causes of **low-birth-weight** (LBW) babies, who have a higher risk for developmental and mental complications over the first few years of life (Agarwal et al., 2017). Unfortunately, the issue is worse for Black women than White women (Mutambudzi, Meyer, Reisine, & Warren, 2017). Extreme preterm and LBW babies have a substantially higher risk of infant mortality (McCormick, 1985), a finding again worse for Black babies (Gillespie, Christian, Alston, & Salsberry, 2017). Surprisingly, the United States has an exceedingly high rate of LBW babies relative to other industrialized nations (David & Collins, 1997). For example, the percentage of LBW infants born in the United States is estimated to be 8% compared with only 4% for Sweden (WHO, 2004).

As another good example of the usefulness of the biopsychosocial model, the *biological* development of the fetus can be seriously influenced by the psychological state of the mother—her moods, her feelings, and her thoughts (the *psycho* part)—as well as the networks she has and the social situation in which she is living (the *social* part). In fact, the quality of the social environment the mother lives in may prove to be one of the main factors in the influence psychosocial aspects have on healthy biological functioning (Gondwe, White-Traut, Brandon, Pan, & Holditch-Davis, 2017). The biopsychosocial model also provides comprehensive predictions of complications in pregnancy, length of gestation, and fetal growth (St-Laurent et al., 2008).

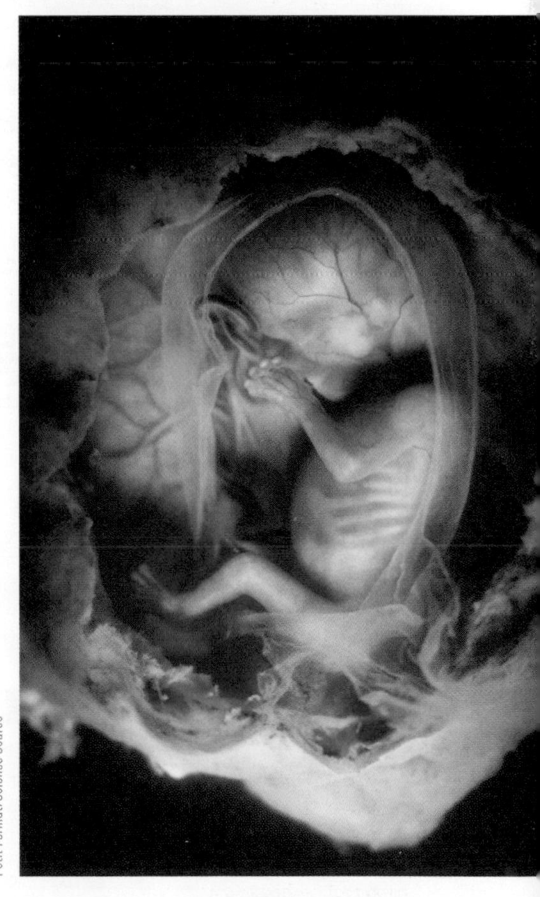

▲ **The Developing Human Being: Different Stages of Prenatal Growth.** A fourteen week old fetus.

During the 9 months before delivery, many clear-cut physiological changes take place. A woman may not even know that she is pregnant until approximately 2 weeks after conception, when she is unlikely to menstruate (although some women do have what looks like a menstrual flow even when pregnant). However, there are clues. Her breasts may swell and become tender, and some women may become nauseated. Once the sperm fertilizes the egg (or ova), the zygote implants itself in the uterine wall and begins to grow, and cells differentiate into various internal structures. By the end of the second week, the organism is called an embryo. At the ninth week of gestation, the embryo is called a fetus, and the time until delivery is called the fetal period.

Of all the senses, only hearing develops before birth, and the fetus shows a preference for the mother's voice. Some mothers believe that playing classical music will improve fetal development.

iStockphoto.com/ DGLimages

▲ **Mother-Infant Bonding.** An infant on her mother's chest takes a nap.

Similarly, you may have heard of the Mozart effect (Rauscher, Shaw, & Ky, 1995), the finding that listening to the first movement allegro con spirito of Mozart's Sonata for Two Pianos in D major (K 448) can improve performance in certain areas (spatial-temporal tasks such as jigsaw puzzles and some forms of reasoning). However, here is some bad news for classical music fans—other than an occasional study here and there (Su, Kao, Hsu, Pan, Cheng, & Huang, 2017), a major meta-analysis shows there is little evidence for the performance-enhancing effect of listening to Mozart (Pietschnig, Voracek, & Formann, 2010).

The developing embryo and fetus are particularly sensitive to teratogens, factors such as environmental toxins, and drugs, which are capable of causing developmental abnormalities (Figure 4.1). A key focus for the health psychologist is to ensure that expectant mothers refrain from the use of alcohol, caffeine, nicotine, and some drugs or medications (Zimmer & Zimmer, 1998). Behaviors such as smoking, bad diet, and not going to the doctor to receive needed treatments all negatively affect fetal growth and infant health (McCormick et al., 1990). Consequently, some argue that universal screening for alcohol and drug use in prenatal care may reduce existing disparities between White versus Black in reporting to Child Protective Services, but this has not borne out (Roberts & Nuru-Jeter, 2011). Black and Hispanic pregnant women are more likely to use both tobacco and marijuana during pregnancy than White women (Coleman-Cowger, Schauer, & Peters, 2017).

The mother's alcohol consumption during pregnancy can continue to influence her child as an adult (Santhanam, Coles, Li, Li, Lynch, & Hu, 2011). Any alcohol misuse can harm the development of the baby's organs. Fetal exposure to teratogens is higher for ethnic minority populations (Dunkel-Schetter et al., 2001). Stress is particularly dangerous to the prenatal infant; and the more stress a mother experiences, the more she risks delivery of a preterm or LBW baby (Nkansah-Amankra, Luchok, Hussey, Watkins, & Xiaofeng, 2010). However, let's not forget about the baby's father. Secondhand smoke from the baby's father, for example, as well as stress in the form of emotional or physical abuse, can also interfere with the baby's and mother's health (Dunkel-Schetter et al., 2001).

▼ FIGURE 4.1

Critical Milestones in Prenatal Development

Embryonic stage
Fetal stage
Full term
Prenatal 3
Week 4
5
6
7
8
9
16
32
38
Central nervous system
Heart
Upper limbs
Eyes
Lower limbs
Teeth
Palate
External genitals
Ears
Most sensitive period for damaging effects
Moderately sensitive period for damaging effects

Two other aspects of pregnancy have strong psychological components: miscarriage and labor/delivery. A miscarriage (medically referred to as a spontaneous abortion) occurs when the zygote, embryo, or fetus detaches from the uterus before it is ready to survive on its own. Although not usually discussed publicly, miscarriages occur often. Between 15% and 20% of pregnancies end in miscarriage (U.S. National Library of Medicine, 2012). Again, a health behavior, smoking, is one of the big culprits.

▼ FIGURE 4.2

Rates of Maternal Deaths in the Developed World

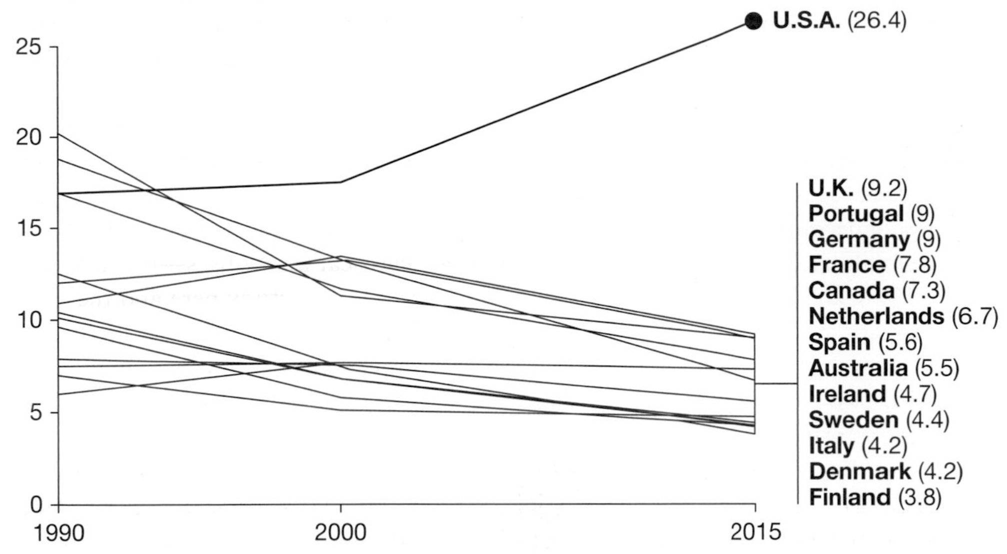

Source: "Global, regional, and national levels of maternal mortality, 1990–2015: A systematic analysis for the Global Burden of Disease Study 2015," *Lancet* (2016); 388: 1775–812.

Smoking is independently associated with an increased risk for recurrent miscarriage (Pineles, Park, & Samet, 2014).

Miscarriage can be a traumatizing experience, and expecting couples often seek counseling and other types of support to better cope with the stress. Some personality types can manage such trauma better than others (more on this in Chapter 5 and Chapter 6), but the amount of social support provided to the couple and the way they process their feelings and cope with this event can have major implications for their mental and physical health (Rowlands & Lee, 2010). Often discussing the problem versus ignoring it eases the emotional pain. Having friends and family express their love and care for the couple at this point is also especially helpful.

Another period when social support can play a major role in pregnancy is during labor and delivery. Childbirth is a stressful event, especially because it involves risk to both the mother's and the infant's lives. Complications arising during this time are the fourth-highest causes of infant mortality in the United States (CDC, 2015) with birth defects being the leading cause. The United States also has the worst rate of maternal deaths in the developed world (see Figure 4.2; Martin & Montagne, 2017). Psychosocial factors (e.g., social support, the mother's personality, or the presence of a companion) play a major role at this point and show great differences among cultural groups (Kashanian, Javadi, & Haghighi, 2010). Social support will prove important over the life span in general.

Close family relationships, especially during childhood, can reduce the extent of health issues across an individual's life span (Chen et al., 2017). Family influences are particularly important for some cultural groups (Campos & Kim, 2017). For example, the family is reportedly the most important source of support for African American mothers (Miller, 1992), followed by Mexican Americans and European Americans (Sagrestano, Feldman, Rini, Woo, & Dunkel-Schetter, 1999).

Infancy and Early Childhood

The growth and development of the newborn is dramatic during the first 2 years of life. Driven by the secretions of the pituitary gland and coordinated by the hypothalamus, hormones pulse through the body, stimulating growth. Based on the work of investigators such as Gesell (1928) and Meredith (1973), we now have a good picture of what normal development for a child should be. As can be seen on charts in the doctors' office or in the parents' home, babies grow irregularly. There are long intervals between growth spikes, and they do not grow in a continuous pattern with the same growth every week (Crandell, Crandell, & Vander Zanden, 2011).

The nervous system develops the most rapidly in the early months. How parents interact with their babies is a key factor in infant development. Greater physical contact between the caregiver and child has always been associated with more successful social and physical development (Stern, 1995), although there is mixed support for this hypothesis. For example, Field (1998) demonstrated that the more a baby is touched and stroked, the faster it develops. However, a review of the research suggests that, although massage for preterm infants influences clinical outcome measures such as medical complications or length of stay and caregiver or parental satisfaction, the evidence of benefits for developmental outcomes is weak (Vickers, Ohlsson, Lacy, & Horsley, 2002). Touch has other important influences, and plays a role in stress and coping, as we shall discuss in the next chapter (Taylor et al., 2000).

During early childhood (ages 2 to 6), the child tends to become more active. Food plays a critical role in muscle growth and the height of the child. This is an important time for parents to watch how much a child eats and when he or she eats. Strength, coordination, and range of motion all continue to increase. Some interesting cultural differences are seen in these early years of development. African American children tend to mature more quickly (as measured by bone growth, percent fat, and number of baby teeth) than European American children (Crandell et al., 2011). Asian American children show some of the slowest rates of physical change (Keats, 2000).

After early childhood, physical growth slows down in general and children become more skilled in controlling their bodies. Middle childhood (age 7 to adolescence) is the stage during which children tend to be the healthiest and experience significant changes in cognitive development.

Adolescence

Adolescence (ages 12 to 17) can be perhaps one of the most turbulent periods in an individual's life. A flurry of biological activity morphs the child into a young adult and sometimes the grown-up exterior surges ahead of the still underdeveloped interior or cognitive development. This mismatch between biological and psychological factors often has dire health consequences. A young girl's developing body may garner attention she is not emotionally ready to cope with.

The key biological milestone in adolescence is **puberty**. At puberty, a genetic timing mechanism activates the pituitary gland and an increasing level of growth hormone is produced in the body. The activation of the pituitary stimulates the manufacture of estrogen and progesterone in girls and testosterone in boys. The increase in sex hormones triggers the growth of secondary sex characteristics, leading to the development of breasts and the beginning of menstruation in women and the deepening of the voice and the growth of facial hair in men. Of direct importance to our study of how different health behaviors may develop is research that shows that boys with higher levels of testosterone are more likely to make risky decisions (Alarcón, Cservenka, & Nagel, 2017).

The age at which puberty occurs has been shifting forward in time, demonstrating the possible interaction between our biology and our psychology and society (Lee & Styne, 2013). For example, at the beginning of the 20th century the average age for the onset of menstruation was 15 or 16. Less than a century later, the average age was just older than 12 (Brumberg, 1997). Why is this the case? The best guesses are increases in stress and higher levels of environmental toxins in contemporary society, but there is no answer yet. Environmental factors combine to make this physiological milestone a great equalizer of ethnic differences. When girls of Jewish, African, Italian, and Japanese descent are raised under the same living conditions, they all begin to menstruate at the same early age (Huffman, 1981). Furthermore, after years of immigration, regardless of ethnicity, girls menstruate earlier in North America than they would have if they had stayed in their countries of origin (Brumberg, 1997). Both boys and girls experience a growth spurt, although this tends to happen for girls almost 2 years before it happens for boys. This spurt continues until around the age of 18. Young adults increase between 7 and 8 inches in height.

Adulthood and Aging

Ages 18 to 21 are often referred to as the young adult years, with adulthood stretching up to at least 65 years of age. After that point, adults are often referred to as older adults (though there are many 67-year-olds who would take offense to this label). Health psychology provides a useful framework for examining the intersection of health with behavioral and psychological functioning among older adults (Emery, Landers, & Shoemake, 2018).

Limited changes in physical development occur after the adolescent years. The body does not appear to have any other specific timed changes occurring for at least another 10 to 30 years after puberty and the adolescent growth spurt. Yet, during this period, our health behaviors are perhaps most important in determining how pain free we live our lives and how long we will live. Some changes do happen. The hair tends to thin and turn gray, and many men experience receding hairlines. The storage of body fat also increases and the distribution of fat changes. For example, our bodies store more fat on our waists, causing an increased waist-to-hip ratio (WHR). Higher WHRs are warning signs for coronary heart disease and a signal of excessive wear and tear on the body (Bishnoi & Kaur, 2010). Overall, our bodies tend to put on weight until our mid-50s. Constant physical activity is necessary to compensate during these years. We then start to lose weight and slowly our height decreases (after approximately age 60). Our bones shrink (from our body using up the calcium stored in them) and the discs between our vertebrae dehydrate and compress.

Some other clear physiological markers of aging are also present. Hearing and vision degrade first, which can have a severe impact on the quality of day-to-day life by interfering with activities such as driving and walking. Other age-related changes including hormonal functioning are seen, most notably in women.

Menopause, or the ending of the menstrual period, typically occurs in the early 50s. Simultaneously, secretion of a number of female sex hormones decreases, and these changes may be associated with a variety of mood problems and even risks for various diseases (Guérin, Goldfield, & Prud'homme, 2017). Psychology can play a role in this as well. Reactions to menopause vary greatly, depending on the expectations that women have (Dasgupta & Ray, 2017), and many women experience few emotional problems (Dennerstein, 1996). Expecting to experience mood swings and depression can make mood swings and depression more likely.

iStockphoto.com/ FatCamera

▲ **Being Mentally and Physically Active Has Few Age Limits.** Although there are some natural physiological changes as we age, the greater cause of loss of muscle tone is not using them enough.

The bigger issue on the table is whether women should start taking hormone pills to replace the natural cycle. Hormone replacement therapy was a common practice for many years. Then, in 2002, the intervention arm of the Women's Health Initiative study testing the effects of hormone replacement was halted because women receiving the drug were found to have a higher risk for certain cancers (Rossouw et al., 2002). Some evidence suggests that some forms of hormone replacement may be safe (Stevenson, Hodis, Pickar, & Lobo, 2011), and researchers now study factors that predict whether women decide to try it (Schaller & Malhotra, 2015). The bottom line is the choice to use it depends on a variety of

> **Synthesize, Evaluate, Apply**
>
> - Given what you know about physical development, what recommendations do you have for expectant parents?
> - What are the psychosocial implications of the different physical milestones of development (e.g., puberty, menstruation, menopause)?
> - What are the different ways that psychosocial factors can hinder prenatal development?

factors and varies with each woman. As they say: Consult your doctor before trying it.

Although we often stereotype older adults as being weak and forgetful, the natural breakdown of muscles and the loss of memory do not start until much later in life. In a longitudinal study begun in 1956, Schaie (1993) demonstrated that the majority of participants showed no significant decline in most mental abilities until the age of 81. The common saying, "Use it or lose it," is very pertinent (Millington, 2012). Maintaining a constant routine of physical activity can prolong good health and activity and ensure that an aging adult can continue to perform comfortably the activities of daily living into their 70s and 80s. Similarly, older adults who have new experiences to occupy their minds, such as solving crossword puzzles, experience less memory loss over time (Pillai et al., 2011). Of note, the much-advertised online brain games that promise to keep the aging brain sharp are not what they are sold to be. In a large review of the use of online games as a means to enhance performance on other tasks, Simons et al. (2016) found no clear evidence of the efficacy of brain games.

THE NERVOUS SYSTEM

Understanding the physiological bases of stress provides us with a better understanding of how psychology can make a difference. The nervous system is the most critical physiological player (Prus, 2018). A focus on the brain in particular is at the heart of the growing field of health neuroscience (Zoccola, Woody, & Bryant, 2018). The brain's functioning also influences the endocrine system, with which it modulates the functioning of the cardiovascular system, the respiratory system, the digestive system, and the reproductive system.

The nervous system can be divided into two main parts: the central nervous system (CNS) (consisting of the brain and spinal cord) and the peripheral nervous system (consisting of all the nervous tissue and cells outside the brain and spinal cord).

The Central Nervous System

The primary function of the central nervous system (CNS) is to process and coordinate information that it receives from the peripheral nervous system. In essence, the CNS is the command center of the body with the brain as the main coordinator. The brain coordinates every aspect of the stress response. In addition, the psychological part of health psychology has its physiological basis in different parts of the brain (Figure 4.3).

The vertebrate brain can be divided into three main parts (Freberg, 2016). The hindbrain or rhombencephalon is located at the back of the brain and consists of the medulla, pons, and cerebellum. The medulla controls life-support functions (e.g., breathing), the pons relays information from the spinal cord to the higher brain areas, and the cerebellum controls motor coordination and movement in response to sensory stimuli. The midbrain or mesencephalon consists of structures that process visual information (superior colliculus) and auditory information (inferior colliculus) and those that play a key role in attention, pain control, and emotions (tegmentum, periaqueductal gray, and substantia nigra). The reticular formation plays a key role in the stress response, handling emergency responses. It is a group of neurons that takes up a large portion of the midbrain but runs from the hindbrain to the forebrain.

The forebrain, or prosencephalon, is the part of the brain that you most likely associate with the word *brain,* that bean-shaped structure with grooves and fissures (Prus, 2018). This is the area where all that makes us human resides. Thinking, consciousnesses, talking, eating, and creating are all functions housed in the forebrain. Best estimates suggest we have 86 billion (yes, with a B) neurons and glia cells, each making thousands of connections with each other (Eagleman, 2011).

▼ FIGURE 4.3

The Human Brain

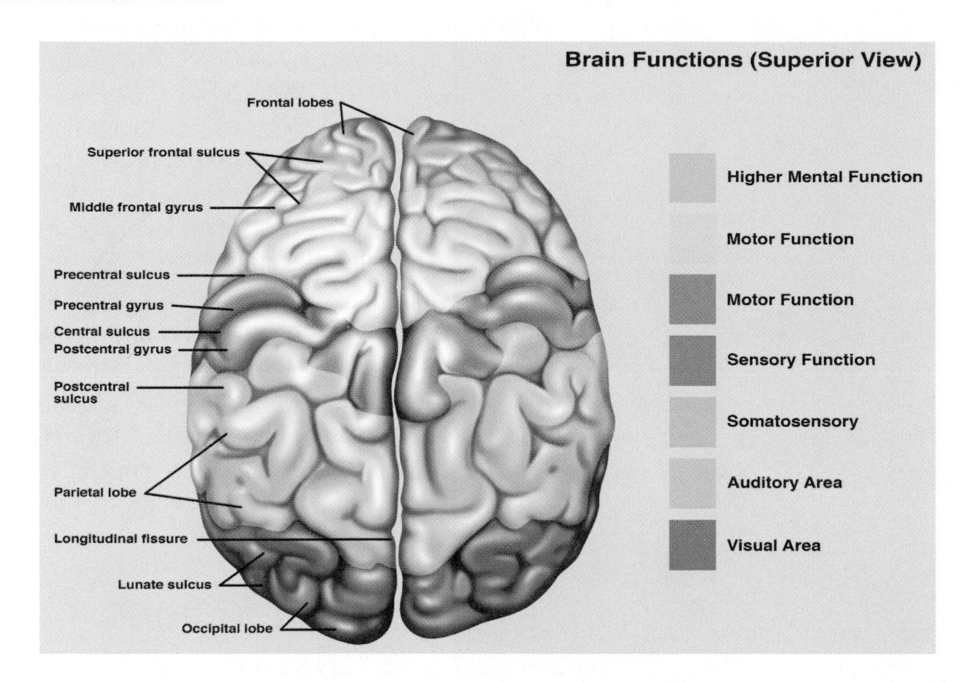

Most of what you see or picture is only the cerebral cortex, the surface lobes of the brain. The cortex consists of four lobes. The frontal lobe contains the motor cortex and key command centers for the body. The parietal lobe processes sensory data from the body. The temporal lobe processes auditory, smell, and taste information. The occipital lobe processes visual information. And watch out: our brains are still developing well into our 20s, which is a key reason excessive alcohol use can damage brain development in the college years (Erblich, 2018).

Under the cerebral cortex are other key forebrain structures (Eagleman & Downar, 2015). Perhaps the single most influential part of the brain is located in the forebrain. The hypothalamus directly controls the activity of the pituitary gland, which releases hormones and correspondingly regulates all of our motivated behaviors. Just above the hypothalamus (*hypo* means *below, hyper* means *above* or *over*—just like a *hyper* friend is *overactive*) lies the thalamus, which relays information from the brain stem to the entire cerebral cortex. The temporal lobe houses the hippocampus and amygdala, two structures making up the limbic system. The hippocampus plays a pivotal role in emotions and memory, and the amygdala produces fear, escape, rage, and aggression. Many of these structures will feature prominently in the first major stress theory we discuss.

The spinal cord extends from the base of the skull to the tailbone, and in cross-section resembles a gray X. The gray matter consists of cell bodies of neurons and is surrounded by bundles of white axons. Bundles of axons are referred to as tracts (in the CNS) and nerves (in the peripheral nervous system). Bundles of cell bodies are referred to as nuclei (in the CNS) and ganglia (in the peripheral nervous system). Sensory information from the peripheral nervous system travels up the tracts in the CNS to the brain.

The Peripheral Nervous System

The peripheral nervous system transmits information to the entire body with 12 pairs of cranial nerves and 31 pairs of spinal nerves (one pair leaving the spinal cord at each of the vertebra in our spines). The two nerves comprising a pair serve each side of the body. The peripheral nervous system has two main divisions, the somatic nervous system and the autonomic nervous system. The somatic nervous system controls the skeletal muscles and is under conscious control. You can decide to move your arm to prop this book up higher, and then you can do it. The autonomic

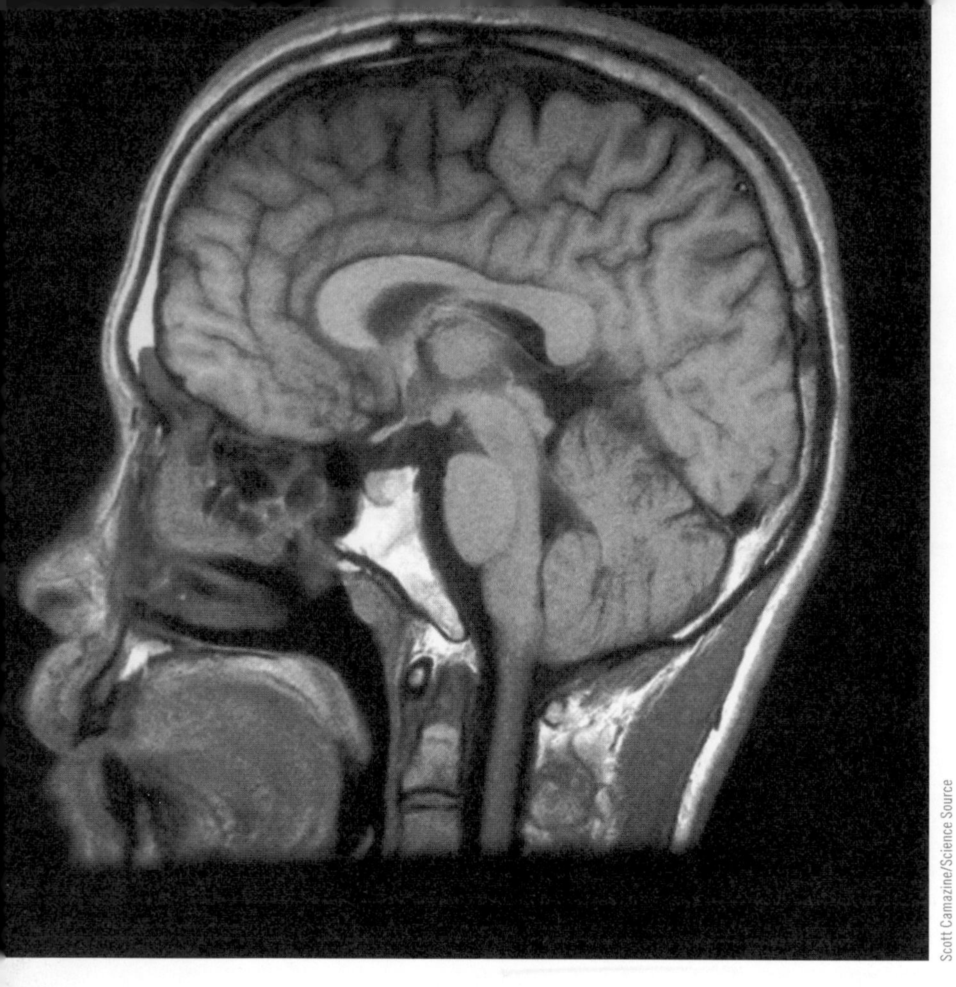

Scott Camazine/Science Source

▲ **Head MRI.** A view inside a real human brain showing the compartments of the skull and brain matter.

nervous system coordinates muscles not under your voluntary control and acts automatically in response to signals from the CNS. Your heart muscles, for example, are under autonomic control. One signal from the hypothalamus can lead to your heart rate jumping up. Another signal can make it slow down. An arm of the autonomic system called the sympathetic nervous system (SNS) produces the speeding up responses. Another arm of the system known as the parasympathetic nervous system (PNS) produces the slowing down responses (Prus, 2018). We discuss further these two arms of the autonomic system in the context of stress in the next chapter.

THE ENDOCRINE SYSTEM

Why should you care about the endocrine system? One word: diabetes. There was a time when type 2 diabetes (the most common form) occurred mainly in the elderly. Today, even children as young as 13 are diagnosed with it (CDC, 2018) and approximately 25.8 million North Americans have diabetes (National Diabetes Information Clearinghouse, NDIC, 2018). Both forms of diabetes (more on this later in this section) are a result of the body's cells not taking in enough **insulin**, a hormone produced in the pancreas that regulates glucose uptake. Insulin and a host of other hormones regulate a number of the body's activities and are secreted by the endocrine glands.

It was originally thought that the nervous system with its network of neurons spreading throughout the body was the main way the body's functions were regulated. In the 1900s researchers studying the triggers of pancreatic juices blocked the action of neurons in the intestines and found that the pancreas was still able to respond. They assumed that the gland itself was secreting an active substance (creatively called *secretin*) that worked on food. This substance was later called a hormone from the Greek *hormon,* meaning to set in motion. Correspondingly, the discovery of a separate system from the nervous system led to its being called the **endocrine system** from the Greek *endon* meaning within, and *krinein* meaning separate (Starr & McMillan, 2016).

Synthesize, Evaluate, Apply

- What are the major parts of the nervous system?
- What different parts of the brain are most active when you are dancing to music?
- Defend the statement, "The nervous system is the most important system of the body."
- What nervous system physiological mechanisms could explain how psychological and societal factors interact with biological mechanisms?

Key Components and Mechanics

The key players in the endocrine system are the hormones and the ductless glands that produce them (which are seen in Figure 4.4). The major glands (with examples of the hormones they secrete) are the pituitary gland (oxytocin), pineal (melatonin), thyroid (thyroxine), parathyroid (parathyroid hormone), thymus (thymosins), pancreas (insulin), adrenal (Cortisol and catecholamines), ovaries (estrogen), and testes (androgens). The ovaries and testes, collectively referred to as the **gonads**, are also our primary reproductive organs.

▼ FIGURE 4.4

The Endocrine System

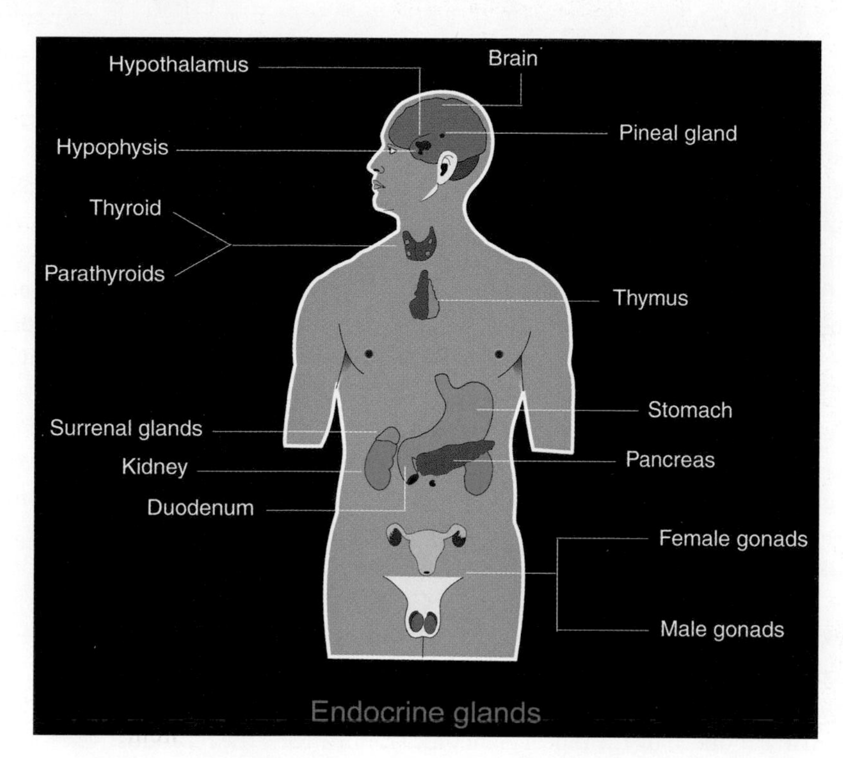

The major functions of each of these hormones are also summarized in Figure 4.4. Hormones often interact and have different functions (Starr & McMillan, 2016). The effect of one hormone can counteract the effect of another (e.g., glucagon and insulin). Sometimes, two hormones are needed to interact to cause an effect (e.g., lactation from prolactin, oxytocin, and estrogen). There is even a warm-up act function: One hormone serves to start a process that is finished by another hormone (e.g., implantation of a fertilized egg after the uterus is exposed to estrogen then progesterone).

The hormones are divided into two major categories: steroids such as estrogens, testosterone, progesterone, aldosterone, and Cortisol; and nonsteroids such as the amines (e.g., norepinephrine and epinephrine), peptides (e.g., oxytocin), proteins (e.g., insulin and prolactin), and glycoproteins (e.g., follicle stimulating hormone). The steroid hormones are synthesized from cholesterol whereas the nonsteroids are derived from amino acids.

The hypothalamus and the pituitary gland (described in the nervous system section) are the major controllers of the different endocrine glands. You will see a specific detailed case of these players in action in Chapter 5 on stress. In general, the hypothalamus and the pituitary gland interact to control secretion of hormones, nicely illustrating the partnership between the nervous and endocrine systems. In fact, the two systems are often referred to as one neuroendocrine system. The glands of the endocrine system secrete hormones directly into the bloodstream by which they are circulated to different parts of the body. Just like the lock-and-key mechanisms of our brain chemicals, **neurotransmitters**, hormones are also specialized to connect to unique receptors on target cells.

In addition to the key role played by the endocrine system in the stress response, the functions of hormones are also directly tied in to the etiology of diabetes, a common chronic illness. When we eat, the pancreas secretes insulin that stimulates the uptake of glucose by muscles and fat cells. Insulin lowers the glucose level in the blood. Between meals our body's cells use up glucose and as the blood glucose decreases, the pancreas secretes *glucagon*, which breaks down amino acids and glycogen to increase the glucose level in the blood. When the body cannot produce enough insulin or when the insulin target cells cannot react to it, **diabetes mellitus** (or diabetes for short) develops.

Diabetes can be of two forms. In type 1 or insulin dependent diabetes (10% of diabetics), insulin-producing cells are destroyed. This form is seen at an early age and is treated with insulin injections (American Diabetes Association, 2018). In type 2 diabetes, insulin levels are close to normal but the receptor cells cannot properly respond to insulin.

Diabetes is a classic example of why the biopsychosocial model in health psychology is so important and shows the relevance of culture. Biology interacts with psychological moods and health behaviors such as eating, which in turn are influenced by societal norms (Sapolsky, 2017). After adjusting for population age differences, compared with non-Hispanic White adults, the risk of diagnosed diabetes was 18% higher among Asian Americans, 66% higher among Hispanics/Latinos, and 77% higher among non-Hispanic Blacks (NDIC, 2011). The age-adjusted prevalence rates for diabetes show that whereas close to 20% of American Indians, 15% of African Americans, and 14% of Hispanic Americans have diabetes, only 8% of European Americans have diabetes.

Though a bad diet is a direct risk factor for diabetes, research now suggests that smoking is a major factor as well (Isaac & Rief, 2017). A literature review of studies including 1.2 million participants showed that, on average, tobacco users have a 44% higher chance of developing type 2 diabetes (Willi, Bodenmann, Ghali, Faris, & Cornuz, 2007). The risk of diabetes was greater for heavy smokers (20 or more cigarettes per day) than for lighter smokers, and lower for former smokers compared with active smokers.

In addition to insulin, another hormone that has implications for mental and physical health is **melatonin**. Produced by the pineal gland, melatonin affects the reproductive cycle and how we sleep. Not receiving enough sunlight can cause seasonal affective disorder (SAD), which can be alleviated by controlling levels of melatonin (Praschak-Rieder, Willeit, Sitte, Meyer, & Kasper, 2011). We shall hear more about diabetes and the risks of trying to get more sun in Chapter 7 on health behaviors.

THE CIRCULATORY SYSTEM

The circulatory system had many people guessing for centuries. Today we understand the mechanisms that provide every cell in our body with life-giving oxygen, but this was not always the case. At first, it was believed that life was maintained not by the constituents of blood, but by a vital spirit, or *pneuma*. The Greek Empedocles of Agrigentum, who lived around 500 to 430 B.C., was the first to postulate that the heart was the center of the circulatory system, although he believed it to be the seat of life-giving pneuma. This pneumatic theory held a long time. Later Greeks added to our knowledge of circulation, but pneumaticism still reigned. For example, Erasistratus (around 300 B.C.) identified the role played by veins and arteries and even traced them down to the limits of his vision, to the fine branches that later came to be called capillaries.

The greatest early contributor to our understanding was Galen (around 150 B.C.; see Chapters 1 and 3) who through his animal dissections clarified the functions of the arteries and veins. His only mistake, apart from also accepting the pneumatic theory, was in believing the heart was a form of heater that warmed the blood instead of recognizing it as a pump. He believed blood flowed because of the pulsing of the arteries and moved back and forth like the tides (not in a circular fashion). It was not until the work of English physician William Harvey in 1628 that we got a complete understanding of the circulatory system. The Italian Marcello Malphighi discovered capillaries in 1689, the only component that Harvey could not see but about which he had correctly hypothesized.

Key Components

The circulatory system is so named because the blood flows in a circle (from the Latin *circus*—the next time the circus is in town notice that it plays in the middle of a big circle as well). The heart, arteries, veins, and capillaries are the key components of the system (Freberg, 2016).

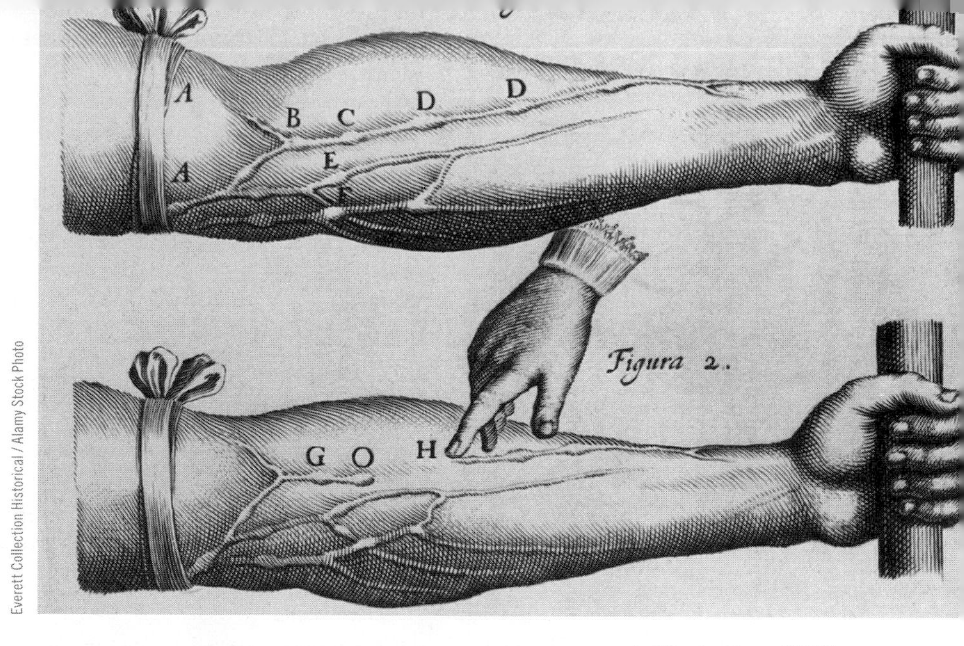

Everett Collection Historical / Alamy Stock Photo

▲ **Illustration of William Harvey's Experiments (1628).** Venal valves had already been discovered, but here Harvey shows that the venal blood flows only toward the heart. He put a ligature on an arm to make the veins and their valves obvious and then pressed blood away from the heart and showed that the vein would remain empty because it was blocked by the valve.

The human heart with its muscular myocardium walls is about the size of a clenched fist, sits just beneath our breastbone, and is protected by a fibrous sac called the pericardium. The heart has two main halves. The right half receives blood low in oxygen from all over the body and pumps it to the lungs. The left half receives blood rich in oxygen from the lungs and pumps it back all over the body. Each half of the heart is further divided into two chambers. The upper and thinner-walled chambers on each side are called the **atria**; the lower, thicker-walled chambers on each side are called **ventricles**.

Blood vessels that carry blood away from the heart are called arteries, and the vessels that carry blood to the heart are called veins. Two large veins, the superior (from the upper parts of the body) and the inferior (from the lower parts of the body) venae cavae, carry deoxygenated blood into the heart. A large artery carries oxygenated blood to the rest of the body. Two other vessels carry blood between the heart and the lungs. The **pulmonary artery** carries deoxygenated blood from the heart to the lungs, and the **pulmonary vein** carries blood from the lungs to the heart. What keeps everything separate? The heart's valves. A system of valves ensures that the blood flows in one direction only (a nice idea that would work great to keep backwash to a minimum when one is sipping from a can or bottle). Each valve consists of flaps of connective tissue; the actual sound of a heartbeat is the sound of the valves closing. The first sound is buh, which is when the valves between the atria and ventricles close. The second sound is bub and is when the valves between the ventricles and the arteries shut. The heart, the valves, and its main vessels and chambers are shown on page 95.

The Mechanics of Circulation

As Harvey first clearly showed, humans have what is called double circuit circulation. Deoxygenated blood from all over the body flows into the heart, from where it is pumped to the lungs. In the lungs, the carbon dioxide in the blood is removed and oxygen flows into the blood in the tissues and air sacs of the lungs. The blood then flows back to the heart and is pumped to the rest of the body. The circuit between the heart and the lungs is called pulmonary circulation (*pulmo* is Latin for lung). The circuit around the rest of the body is called systemic circulation. As the arteries leave the heart, they get narrower and branch out many times into smaller vessels called arterioles. They then narrow into even finer vessels called **capillaries**. Veins similarly branch into smaller vessels, called venules, and into even smaller vessels also called capillaries. Is this the same word? Yes, it is, and the same location too. Because the blood vessels all form one giant circle, they must meet somewhere, and that place is the capillaries. Like a neighborhood recycling center where metal cans are turned in and the material is reused, oxygen slips out of the capillaries and into the surrounding cells and tissues, and carbon dioxide and other cell wastes slip in. The blood then moves from the capillaries into the veins and back to the heart to be rejuvenated.

The main function of the heart is to help put oxygen into the blood and to push the blood around the body to the places where it is needed. When the heart beats, it pumps blood to the arteries.

▼ FIGURE 4.5

The Circulatory System

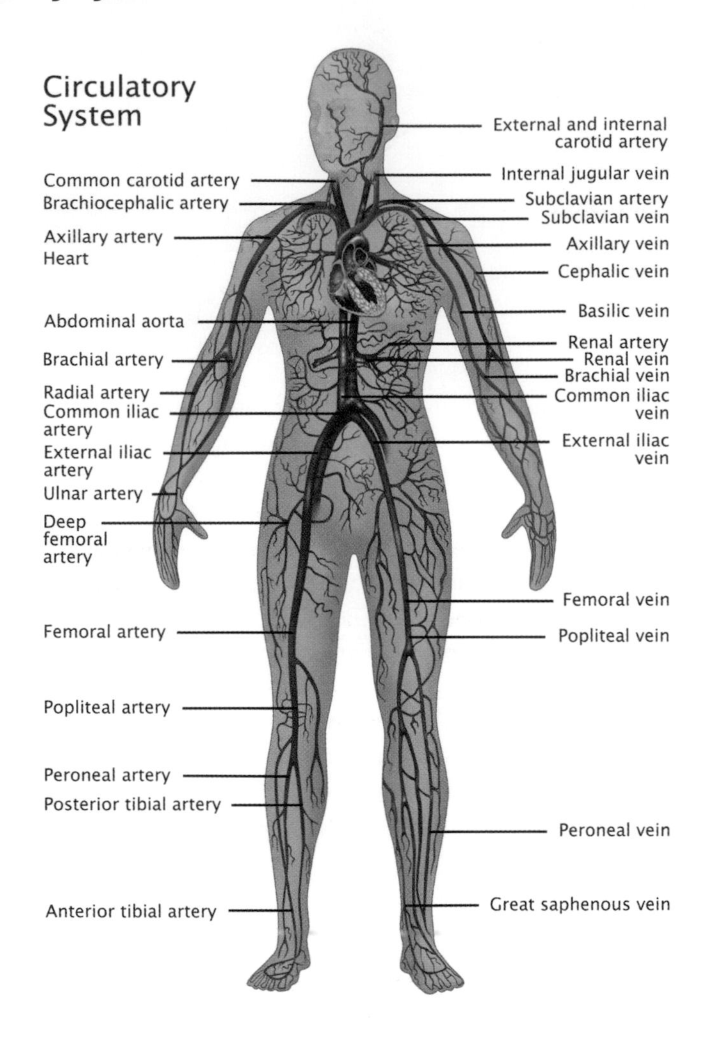

Because the diameters of the vessels near the heart are much larger than the diameters of the arteries that the blood is being pumped into, there is pressure in the arteries. The arteries also influence this blood pressure as they resist the blood flow. Healthy arteries are muscular and elastic. They stretch when your heart pumps blood through them, with more stretching being produced by stronger pumping. The pressure rises with each beat and falls in between beats as the heart muscles relax. The actual process of pumping is a two-stage process consisting of a cycle of contractions by different parts of the heart. In the first stage, the atria contract and the ventricles relax. In the second stage, the reverse takes place.

The heart beats between 55 and 85 times per minute when you are at rest, but the rate of beating can change dramatically with each different move. Break into a run, and the rate will increase to get oxygen to the organs and muscles that need it. Take a nap, and it will slow down. It can even change from minute to minute, depending on what you are thinking. If you are watching a movie and a scary part comes on, your heart will speed up (or even skip a beat, which really reflects an irregular beat and not really a skipped beat). Blood pressure is described using two numbers, the **systolic** pressure (when the heart is beating) and the **diastolic** pressure (when the heart is resting) and is measured in millimeters of mercury (mm Hg), which is the height in millimeters of mercury that the pressure could support. A healthy adult's blood pressure should be less than 120/80 mm Hg.

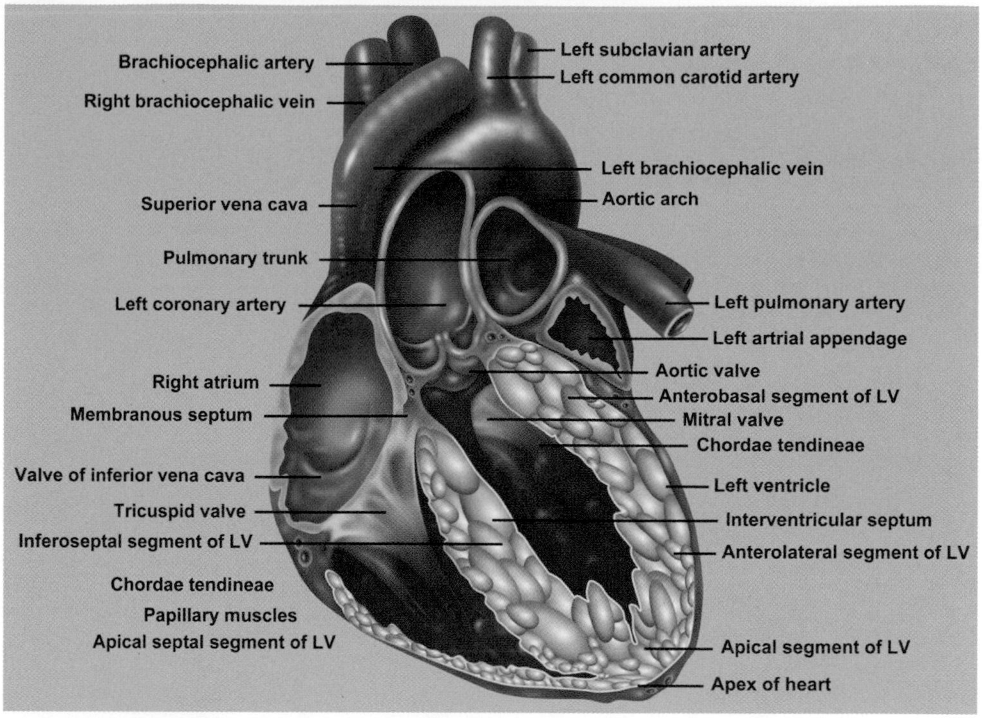

A Biological Primer

You may have noticed that medical journals tend to be filled with a lot of big words. Those of you in premedical programs or in medical school or those working toward degrees in occupational or physical therapy have probably already had your encounters with medical terminology (it pays to know some Latin, doesn't it?). If you are truly term phobic, then skip the next paragraph (and lose the chance to impress your friends with your erudition and M.D.-like medical knowledge). In discussing cardiovascular diseases (CVDs) and reading the medical literature, you will probably encounter many technical terms with which you need to be familiar. **Angina pectoris** (chest pain) is a common symptom of heart attacks, or **myocardial infarctions** (also called cardiac arrest). The myocardium is the medical term for the muscle of the heart. You may also read about **ischemia**, a term for the condition in which blood flow is limited in a certain part of the body. Heart attacks are called myocardial ischemias, although, more specifically, heart attacks result from ischemias to the cardiac region. Many millions of Americans have ischemias without even knowing it; these are called silent ischemias. Because silent ischemias are not accompanied by angina, individuals who have them may also have a heart attack without warning (American Heart Association, 2018).

▲ **A Real Mammalian Heart (Pig).** Notice the thick muscular lining of the walls. These muscles contract and expand to pump blood

THE DIGESTIVE SYSTEM

What you eat can have serious implications for your health (see Chapter 8 for details on what a healthy diet is). Your diet also is linked to your likelihood of being diabetic and developing coronary heart disease and can influence how you cope with cancer (see Chapter 13 and Chapter 14). A diet high in fat and cholesterol is a major contributor to obesity. Therefore, it helps to know a little about the digestive process.

Key Components and Mechanics

The digestive system is essentially a tube with two openings (sorry, facts are facts). We take in food through our mouths and, well, you know how we excrete what is left of it. The entire span from mouth to anus is referred to as the **gastrointestinal tract (GI)**. Food moves from the mouth through the throat and pharynx into the esophagus and then into the stomach. The stomach can stretch to take food in and is often the site of invasive surgery to curb eating (more on this later). From the stomach, the food moves into the small intestines (the duodenum, the jejunum, and the ileum), which totals almost 20 feet in length and is all wound up in our body cavity. The last part of the GI tract is the large intestine, or colon, which terminates in the rectum and anus. A little-known fact: Colon cancer is the third leading form of cancer for both men and women and results from small clumps of cells called **polyps** that turn cancerous (see Chapter 13). Figure 4.6 summarizes the main parts of the digestive system.

Chewing and salivary enzymes begin breaking down food in the mouth. In the stomach, gastric fluids start digesting proteins. Secretions from the liver, gallbladder, and pancreas act on food in the small intestine where nutrients are absorbed. The entire inner length of the small intestine comprises many circular folds that greatly increase its surface area to optimize nutrient absorption. The large intestine stores undigested matter for excretion (Starr & McMillan, 2016).

▼ FIGURE 4.6

Main Parts of the Digestive System

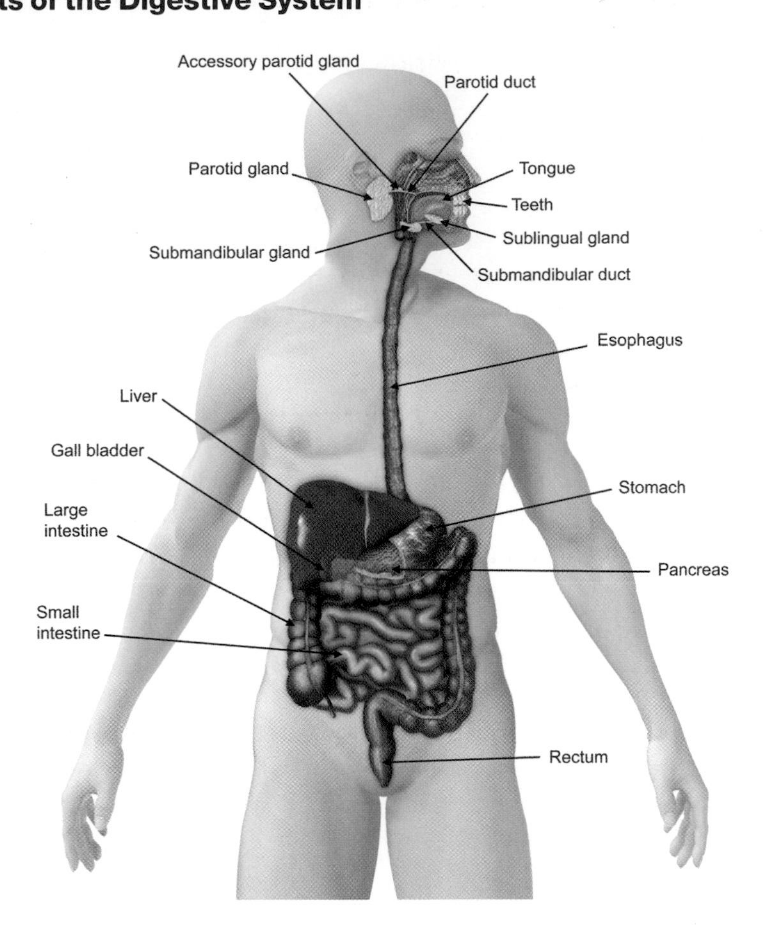

In addition to obesity, other major health problems related to the digestive system are gastroenteritis (an inflammation of the lining of the stomach and small intestine), diarrhea (frequent watery bowel movements), lactose intolerance (inability to digest milk products), hemorrhoids (condition in which the veins around the anus or lower rectum are swollen and inflamed), gallstones (pebble-like substances that develop in the gallbladder that block bile flow), and irritable bowel syndrome (disorder characterized commonly by cramping, abdominal pain, bloating, constipation, and diarrhea). Ulcerative colitis is a disease that causes inflammation and sores, called ulcers, in the lining of the rectum and colon (National Digestive Diseases Information Clearinghouse [NDDIC], 2018). Sixty to 70 million people are affected by digestive diseases (NIH, 2009).

One digestive system health problem that is of special relevance to the study of health behaviors is alcoholism. Alcohol is processed through the liver and excessive alcohol use can damage the liver, which is why alcoholics often develop liver disease. Liver cirrhosis (see Chapter 8 for more detail) is one of the ten leading causes of death in the United States (CDC, 2016).

Regarding health behavior (and in the face of the rise of obesity rates in North America), you may be curious about bariatric, or weight loss, surgery. **Bariatric surgery** is becoming more popular for cases of severe obesity (Chang & Wittert, 2009; Thiara et al., 2017). The most common type is gastric bypass surgery, which is the stapling of the stomach to create a smaller pouch. A section of the small intestine is then cut out. This bypass of sections of the intestine cuts down on how many nutrients are absorbed. Another bariatric technique is Lap-Band surgery, where an adjustable silicone band is attached to the stomach to make it smaller and to cut down on eating. Inflating the band squeezes more of the stomach shut. It is important to note that these techniques are not for everybody. It is only recommended for obese individuals who have severe weight-related medical problems. Even though these procedures are an effective treatment for severe obesity, there is risk of early death following bariatric surgery (Smith et al., 2011).

A Note on the Renal/Urinary System

The digestive system does not handle metabolism and excretion of wastes on its own. Every time you feel your bladder pressure you to search for the nearest bathroom, you are experiencing the effects of the renal or urinary system. Isn't it the worst when it happens during the really good part of a film?

The major components of the renal system are the kidneys, ureters, urinary bladder, and urethra (see Figure 4.7). Each kidney contains blood vessels and tubes called nephrons. The nephrons filter water and substances such as urea and sodium out of the blood and produce urine. Each day more blood flows through your kidneys than through any other organ except the lungs (Starr & McMillan, 2016).

The contents of your urine provide important insights into your health. If you are stressed, your urine will show high levels of cortisol and other stress hormones (Freberg, 2016). The body maintains a balance between acidity and alkalinity with the aid of the renal system. If the blood stream is too acidic, the urine will be acidic. If you are diabetic, your urine will have high levels of glucose. In fact, Greek physicians reportedly tasted their patient's urine to confirm a diagnosis of diabetes (Adler, 2004), and the technical name for diabetes, *diabetes mellitus*, reflects the sweeter urine phenomenon (mellitus means honey).

THE PHYSIOLOGY OF IMMUNITY

The **immune system** is the component of our bodies that protects us from threats, mostly in the form of bacteria and germs. The components of the immune system serve two main functions:

▼ FIGURE 4.7

Main Parts of the Renal System

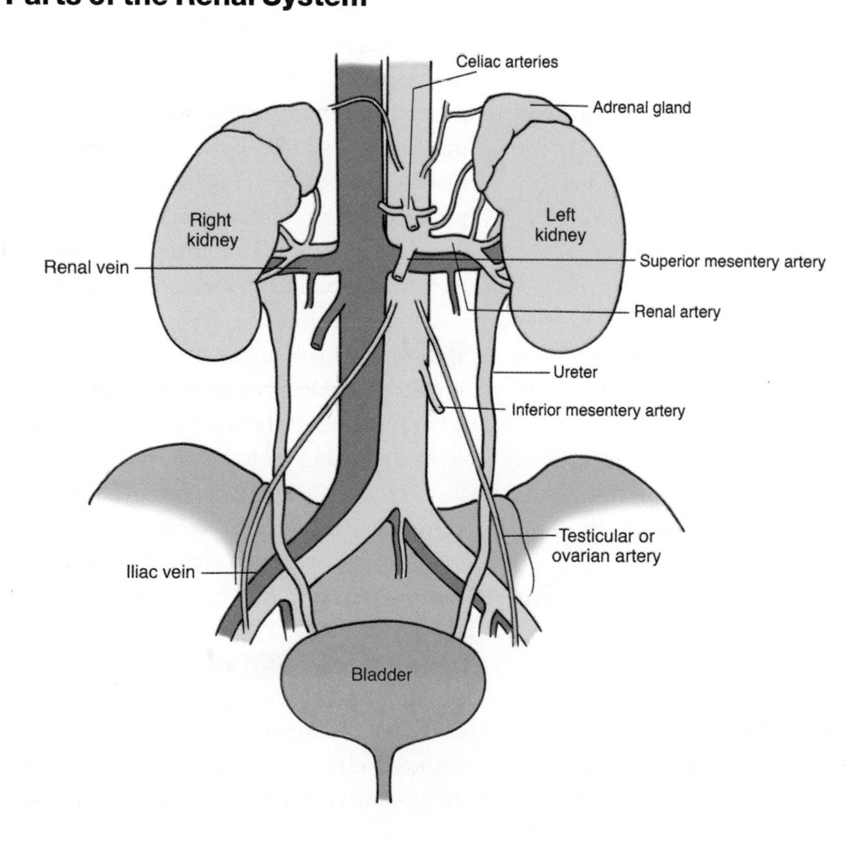

> **Synthesize, Evaluate, Apply**
>
> - What are the ways the digestive, endocrine, and circulatory systems interact?
> - What are the main parts of each system and what function do they serve?
> - How could different health behaviors influence the workings of each of the systems described above?

(1) to discriminate what constitutes our bodies from what are foreign substances, and (2) to destroy and clear those foreign substances and infected cells. A large portion of health psychological research focuses on the interface between psychological factors and the working of the immune system (e.g., Byrne et al., 2017; Robinson et al., 2017). We shall give you first an overview of the main components of the system, and then we will take a closer look at exactly how immunity works.

The immune system is composed of a collection of cells and organs (see Table 4.1). Similar to the circulatory and nervous systems, the immune system has a network of capillaries, the **lymphatic system**, and small oval bodies called lymph nodes (Figure 4.8). The lymphatic capillaries lie along blood vessels and carry a colorless fluid called lymph that is composed of fats, proteins, and water and holds the key cells of the immune system, white blood cells (WBCs), or **leukocytes**. Lymph nodes serve as a filtering system and are packed with leukocytes. Leukocytes filter microorganisms and other particles from the lymph and greatly reduce our risks of infection. There are three main types of leukocytes. The most common (comprising between 50% and 70% of leukocytes) are polymorphonuclear granulocytes. While common, polymorphonuclear granulocytes play a minor role in psychoneuroimmunology and have proven difficult to study. Therefore, we do not discuss them in detail in this book. The most important leukocytes are lymphocytes, which comprise 20% to 40% of leukocytes (Freberg, 2016). These are the true fighters of the immune system.

▼ FIGURE 4.8
The Immune System

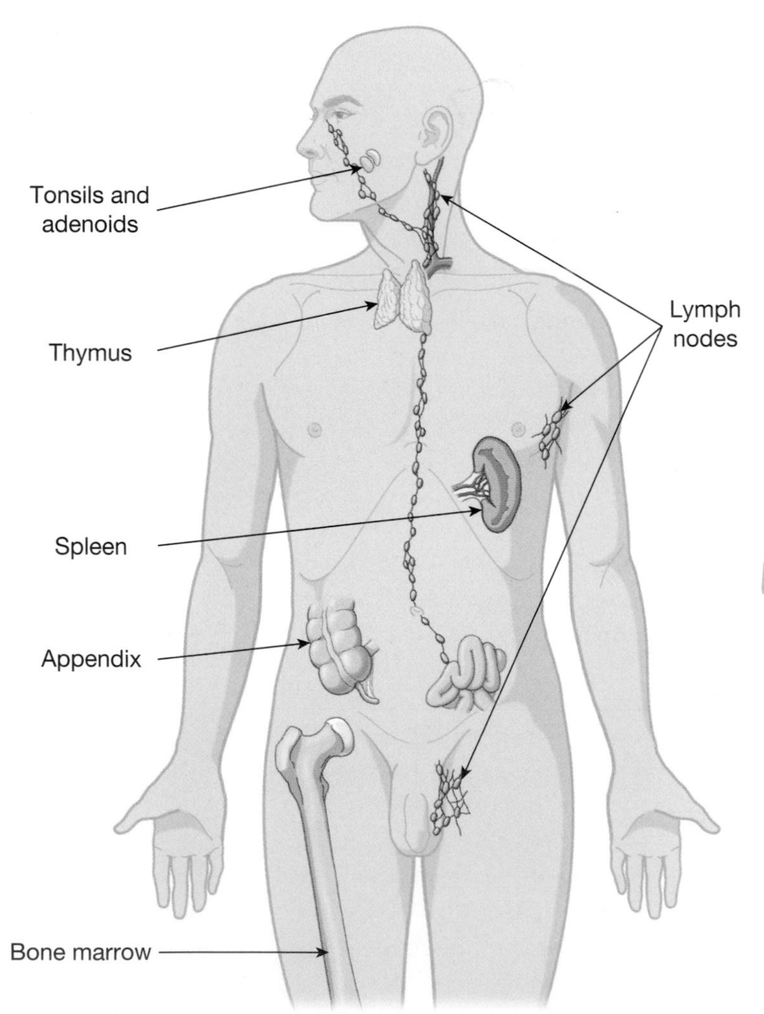

There are three main types of lymphocytes, two of which, **T cells** and **B cells**, are further subdivided into more types. T cells and B cells are both formed in the bone marrow, but each type of cell is conveniently named based on where the cells mature. T cells mature in the thymus gland, an organ situated at the base of the neck. Although you rarely hear much about the thymus (unlike the liver, kidneys, or heart), it is the main site for T-cell development. It is prominent when we are young but shrinks after we reach puberty. There are three main types of T cells. The workhorses are the T cytotoxic cells, or T_c cells. These cells are responsible for killing virally infected cells.

A second kind of T cell is the helper T cell, or T_h cell. These cells enhance the functioning of other T cells and play a role in the maturation of B cells. They serve as sentinels, prowling through our bloodstreams looking for invaders. When they encounter foreign cells, germs, or bacteria, they secrete chemical messengers that draw other types of immune cells to the location and destroy the invaders. T_H cells are some of the most common T cells, comprising 30% to 60% of T cells. The third kind of T cell is the suppressor T cell, or T_s cell. These cells slow down the functioning of the immune system and prevent the body from damaging itself. In particular, once foreign germs have been eliminated, the T_s cells secrete chemicals to turn off the action of T_c and T_H cells.

▼ TABLE 4.1

Main Cells of the Immune System

Key components
1. Bone marrow (origin of white blood cells [WBCs]) or leukocytes (three types)
a. 50% to 70% polymorphonuclear granulocytes (PMNs)—hard to study, minor role in psychoneuroimmunology
b. 20% to 40% lymphocytes
T (mature in thymus)
T cytotoxic (T_C) (CD8): kill virally infected cells
T helper (T_H): enhance functioning; moderate maturation of B cells
(30% to 60% of T cells)
T suppressor (T_S): slow down the immune system
B (mature in bone marrow)
B antigen-producing
B memory
Natural killer (NK)
c. 2% to 8% monocytes (circulating)/macrophages (in tissue). Their chemical messengers are interleukin-1 and -2; interferon.
2. Lymph vessels (lie along blood vessels) and lymph node—filtering system (packed with WBCs)
thymus (T-cell school where T cells differentiate)
spleen (filter for blood)

B cells are both born in and mature in the bone marrow. One type of B cell, the antibody-producing B cell, forms specific substances earmarked for specific germs or **antigens** (*antibody* generators; more on this later). The other form of B cell, the memory B cell, is the one that explains why so many of us are subjected to immunizations and vaccinations during childhood. Memory B cells are cells that form a template or identification for invading antigens. Memory B cells circulate in the body for many years after an antigen has been eliminated, ready to identify it if it were to invade the body again. By having this indicator of the antigen, illness is less likely to recur because the moment we are infected by the antigen, the memory B cells recognize it and activate our bodies' defenses.

The third kind of lymphocyte is the **natural killer (NK) cell**. These cells circulate in the body, playing a role in different immune responses and especially in destroying diseased cells by injecting them with toxic chemicals. Table 4.1 shows a summary of the different components of the immune system.

There are other hard-working immune cells as well. The foot soldiers of the effort, and often those at the forefront of defenses, are monocytes (circulating in the lymphatic system) and macrophages (a type of monocyte found in the tissue). These cells are the first to attack germs or foreign invaders, destroying them by engulfing and devouring them. In fact, if you want to joke with a friend of yours who eats a lot, you can call him a macrophage, because the word translates literally from its Greek origins to mean large eater (yes, this is somewhat nerdy humor). Other important immune system components are the chemical messengers, especially interleukin-1 and -2, and **interferon**, a chemical that prevents viral infections from spreading. Another component of the immune system is the spleen, a ductless organ in the upper left of our abdomen, which serves as a filter for blood. The least common cells are the monocytes and macrophages. Last and perhaps least

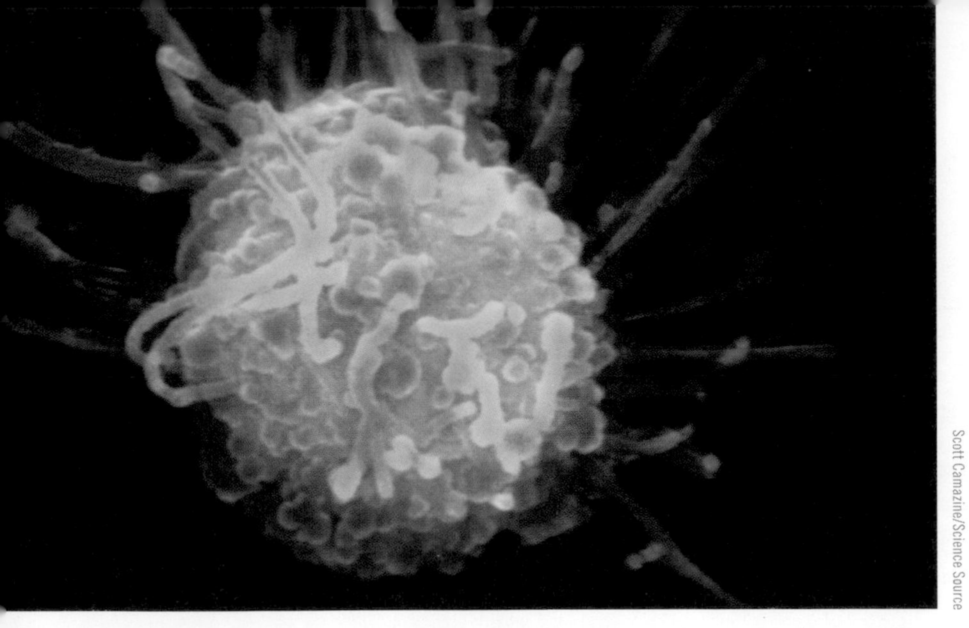
Scott Camazine/Science Source

▲ **A T Cell.** There are three main types of white cells—lymphocytes, leukocytes, and monocytes. Lymphocytes originate in the bone marrow and mature there or in the thymus—hence the names B-lymphocytes and T- lymphocytes. B-cells produce antibodies, chemicals that disable invading microorganisms. Some T-cells attack other cells infected with viruses directly.

important (given that many people have them removed) are the tonsils. The tonsils are oval tissue masses in the mouth (open up and say "ah" and you can see them). Their primary function is the storage of lymphocytes.

THE PROCESS OF DEFENSE

Our primary foes are microorganisms such as bacteria and viruses. As mentioned at the start of this chapter, germs surround us. The doorknobs you touch, the chairs you sit on, and the air that you breathe are all filled with germs. Sometimes germ transmission is more direct; for example, when people with a cold hand something to you after blowing their nose, they are probably passing on the cold virus. Most directly, you can be infected by the bite of another living creature that carries the virus (e.g., an insect, animal, or fellow human being).

The main lines of entry for foreign invaders are the skin and the different openings of the body: the nasal passage and mouth (the upper respiratory system), the walls of the stomach and intestine (the gastrointestinal tract), and the sexual and excretory organs (urogenital tract). We have a number of basic processes that protect us at each of these points. We secrete mucus (e.g., in the lining of the nose) that serves to trap germs and prevent their entry. We cough to get germs out of our lungs. Our skin also has a number of glands that secrete a mild oily substance called sebum that also serves to prevent microorganisms from breaking the skin barrier or from growing on the skin. Most microorganisms do not get past the barrier of the thick pile of cell layers that make up the epidermis. As shown in Figure 4.9, the outer layer consists of nondividing cells, many of which are dead or dying, that protect the dividing skin

▼ FIGURE 4.9

Cross Section of the Skin

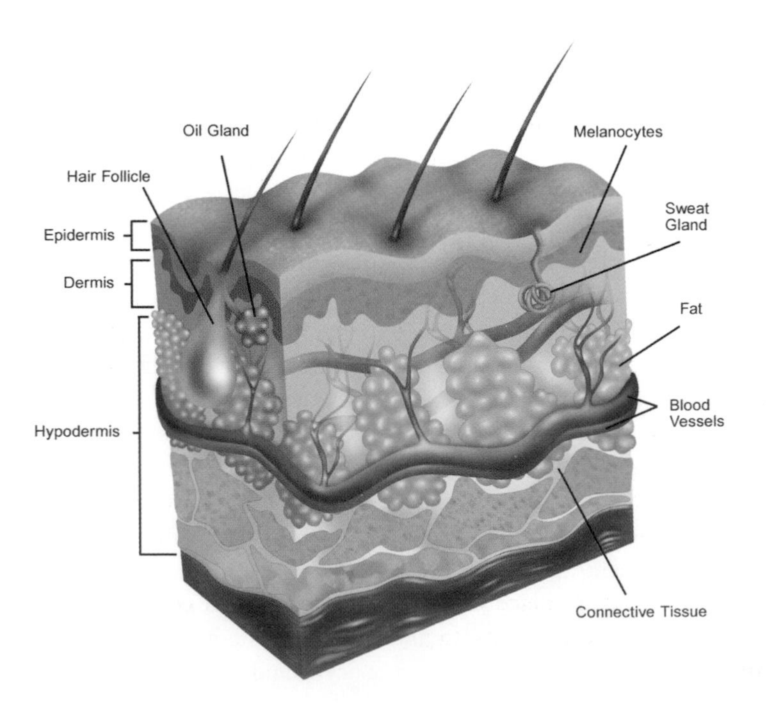

cells beneath. Even when germs do enter the body on particles of food or dust, they usually die due to exposure to lysozyme, an enzyme found in saliva and tears, which digests the cell walls of many microorganisms. These barriers do not rely on the cells of the immune system and are referred to as **nonimmunologic defenses**.

Nonspecific or Natural Immunity

In addition to these defenses on the body's surface, we also have internal processes that similarly do not differentiate between different types of invaders. These **nonspecific immune** defenses work on a wide variety of disease-causing microorganisms. In the body, macrophages, described previously, circulate in the immune system on the lookout for external cells not recognized as being the body's own. When such cells are identified, the body may respond with inflammation and swelling. You may notice this if you fall and skin your knee. The area around the injury swells from an increase in blood flow to the area. The immune cells stream into the damaged site to destroy and inactivate germs potentially present in the dirt or dust you have in the wound. The secretion of chemicals such as **histamine** instigates the swelling or **inflammatory response**. If you have allergies, you are probably familiar with the effect of histamines, which can cause the itching in the eyes, nose, and throat that accompanies the swelling. When the pollen count is too high or you find your allergies being active, your immune system is essentially reacting to all the substances in the air (as taken in through your nasal passage and mouth) and secreting histamine. The inflammation is accompanied often by a fever, indicating that your body is combating the germs (bacteria cannot survive in high temperatures). The actual destruction is accomplished by macrophages that engulf the antigens by **phagocytosis** (the name given to the engulfing process). NK cells and T_c cells may also join the fray. This form of immunity is also referred to as natural or innate immunity.

Acquired Immunity

Do you wonder why we give babies a large number of injections? Those immunizations function as a proactive step to prevent future infection. How does that work? We have another form of immunity, which is referred to as **acquired immunity** and is a form of a specific immune response. This immunity involves the activation of a unique group of cells, the lymphocytes, which are designed to respond to specific microorganisms that the body has encountered before. Acquired immunity is distinguished from nonspecific or natural immunity by five characteristics (Kusnecov, 2002):

1. *Specificity.* Each foreign particle generates only one specific immune response. In this form of immunity, the body is responding only to specific antigens that it has encountered before.
2. *Diversity.* Different immune cells recognize different antigens.
3. *Memory.* Each lymphocyte that bonds to a specific antigen the first time it invades the body will recognize the same antigen if it returns. In subsequent attacks of the same antigen, its matching lymphocyte will be higher in intensity and faster.
4. *Self-limitation.* After an antigen is destroyed, the responding cells will be turned off or suppressed (T_s cells).
5. *Self/Non-self-discrimination.* An essential capability of the lymphocytes of the immune system is their ability to discriminate cells from within our own body from those that originated outside our body.

Acquired immunity takes place either in the blood or in cells. The form of immunity orchestrated by immune cells circulating in the blood is also referred to as **humoral-mediated immunity**.

▼ FIGURE 4.10

Humoral-Mediated Immunity

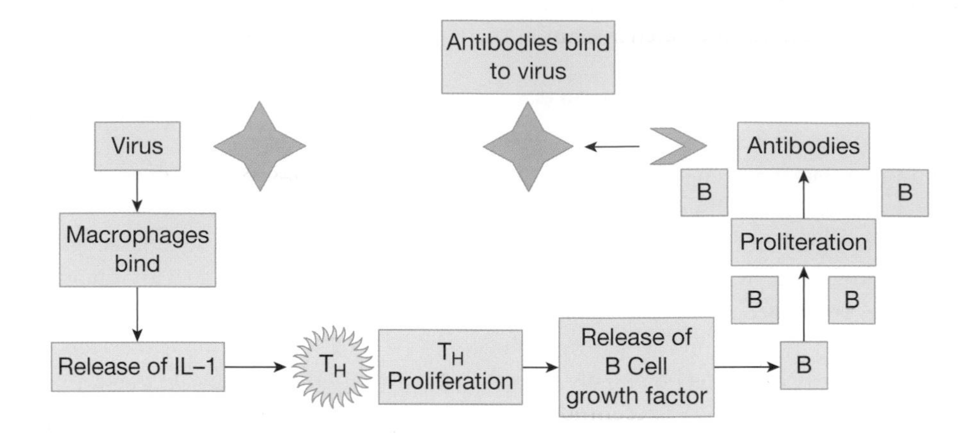

Here is how humoral-mediated immunity works (Figure 4.10). When a bacterial or viral cell enters the bloodstream, the macrophages identify the antigens on the cell's surface and bind to the cell. This bond causes the macrophage to release the chemical transmitter interleukin-1 that alerts T_H cells. The T_H cells proliferate or multiply and release a second chemical messenger, B-cell growth factor. This chemical causes B cells to proliferate. The B cells form structures named antibodies that are designed to bond to the specific invader, hence immobilizing it and targeting it for destruction. Different B cells produce different antibodies, depending on the type of antigen with which they are faced. Every antigen contains one or more **epitopes**, a specific shape and charge distribution recognized by antibodies. Epitopes are small parts of molecules on each antigen, and it is estimated that the immune system can make antibodies to recognize more than 100 million different epitopes (Starr & McMillan, 2016). In addition, memory B cells save a copy of the antibody and remain circulating in the blood after the attack has been completed. These memory B cells have a print, as it were, of the invader and, therefore, are ready to sound the alarm if they encounter the same invader again. When we are immunized as babies, our body produces a large number of memory B cells in response to a small amount of the injected germ (e.g., smallpox), hence protecting us from getting that same sickness later in life. Of course, we also acquire this form of immunity when we actually have (not just been vaccinated for) certain illnesses. For example, if you had chickenpox as a child, you are not likely to get it again because you have circulating memory B cells for chickenpox.

▼ FIGURE 4.11

Cell-Mediated Immunity

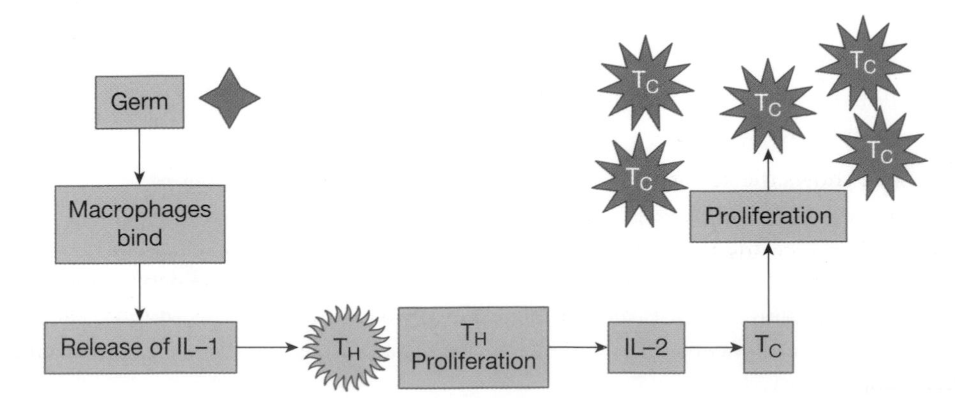

Humoral-mediated immunity is one form of specific immunity. Another form takes place at the level of the cell. **Cell-mediated immunity** involves T cells although the first few stages are similar to the process for humoral-mediated immunity. In this case, the antigen is first recognized by macrophages, which activate T_H cells. T_H cells then release interleukin-1, which stimulates the proliferation of more T_h cells. The multiplying T cells now release interleukin-2, which leads to T_c cell proliferation. The T_c cells then attack and destroy the antigens. Figures 4.10 and 4.11 shows both forms of immune responses.

> **Synthesize, Evaluate, Apply**
>
> - Describe the pros and cons of the body's way of protecting itself from illness.
> - What functions do the various cell differentiations serve?
> - What are the basic nonspecific immune responses?
> - Given what you know about the immune system, what health behaviors would you recommend to maintain optimal health?
> - How are cell and humeral mediated immunity different?
> - Why do people start sniffling during an allergic reaction?

Measures of Immune Response

How do you know how active your immune system is? Well, we could make you sick and see how quickly you recover, but there are easier ways to find out. Researchers measure immunity by using blood or saliva samples. A common technique is that an antigen (germ) is added to the sample and then cell activity is measured. First, you can look for **differentiation**, or how much the immune cells divide into the different types of cells (e.g., T_c or T_H or T_s). You can also look for **proliferation** or the extent to which the immune cells multiply. A strong immune response is characterized by great differentiation and proliferation (Starr & McMillan, 2016). Immune functioning can also be measured by the extent or levels of chemical messengers (e.g., interferon) present in the sample in response to the antigen (Phares, Stohlman, Hwang, Min, Hinton, & Bergmann, 2012). Finally, and perhaps most directly, you can measure **cytotoxicity** or the extent to which the antigens are killed or destroyed. If there are no antigens left in the sample shortly after they are introduced, the person probably has a strong immune system.

Although seemingly straightforward, assessing immune functioning is associated with many problems. First, no single test is available, and it is hard to compare reports from different tests or **assays**. There is also a lot of variability among assays; results vary from laboratory to laboratory, depending on the technician performing the tests and the serum used. The time of the day and the season can also influence results. Paradoxically, it is not always clear what a good direction of immune functioning is. Sometimes a lot of differentiation may suggest strong immunity (the body is reacting); at other times a lot of differentiation may suggest low immunity (the first lines of defense are inadequate). Finally, tests of immunity are available only for blood and not for lymph, making a good measurement difficult.

THE RESPIRATORY SYSTEM

To run, walk, bike, mountain climb, or live in general, you need oxygen, because the cells in our body rely on **aerobic respiration**, a metabolic pathway (means of getting energy) that requires oxygen and produces carbon dioxide. The respiratory system is what facilitates this gas exchange.

Key Components and Mechanics

Figure 4.12 shows the key structures that are part of the respiratory system. You know the basic drill. We breathe in through our nose and mouth and the air moves into the throat, past the larynx, through the trachea, or windpipe, into the lungs. The nose has some first lines of immune defenses: nose hairs that keep out dust and other particulate debris, and mucus, which traps bacteria. The windpipe branches into two airways, one leading into each lung. The lungs are elastic organs protected by the ribcage and separated by our heart. Each soft, spongy lung is covered in a thin membrane.

▼ FIGURE 4.12

Respiratory System

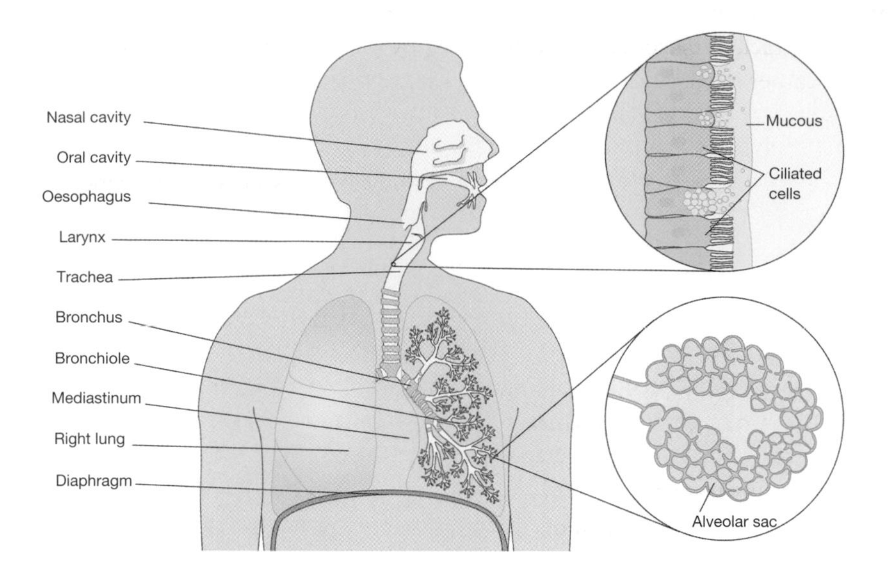

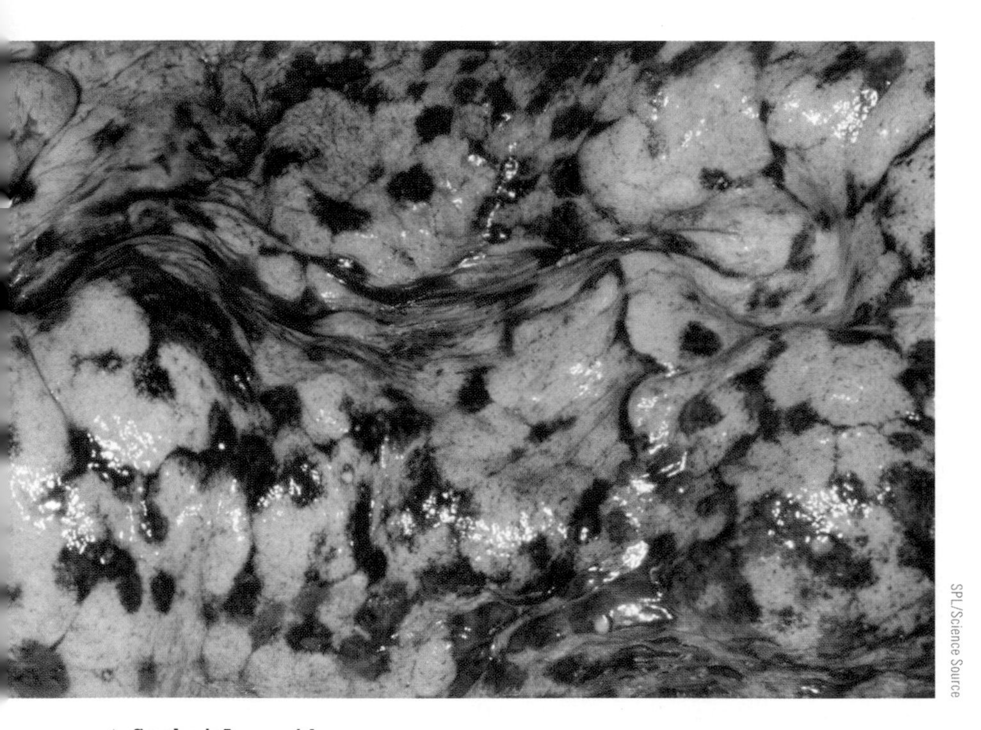

SPL/Science Source

▲ **Smoker's Lung with black spots.** A smoker's lungs show disease. The black areas are tar deposits from cigarette smoke. Cigarette smoking damages the lungs and can cause disorders such as lung cancer, bronchitis, and emphysema.

Inside each lung, the airways (bronchi) branch into smaller and smaller bronchioles. The bronchioles end in little sacs known as **alveoli** clusters. Each lung has approximately 150 million alveoli (Starr & McMillan, 2016). The alveoli are the point at which the cardiovascular system takes over (see Figure 4.12) and where the main gas transfer takes place.

For our purposes, the respiratory system is important in a number of ways. First, poor health behaviors such as smoking wreak havoc on the lungs (see the accompanying photographs of lungs). Second, lung capacity is an important measure of cardiovascular fitness (see Chapter 8). In addition, asthma, one of the most common chronic illnesses, is an incurable respiratory condition.

Asthma is a chronic illness that requires a lot of coping, but it is not always thought of as being in the same category as CVDs, stroke, and diabetes, because it is rarely fatal by itself. Deaths from asthma range from 0.8 per 100,000 for European Americans to 2.5 per 100,000 for African Americans (National Center for Health Statistics, 2012). Asthma affects approximately 19 million Americans, including approximately 7 million children. Asthma may occur at any age, although onset is more common in individuals younger than age 40. The number of people diagnosed with asthma grew by 4.3 million from 2001 to 2009. From 2001 through 2009 asthma rates rose the most among Black children, almost a 50% increase (CDC, 2012).

Asthma is a disease of the airways of the lungs, characterized by tightening of these airways. If you have asthma, you may cough or wheeze (a whistling sort of breathing), feel out of breath, and have chest pains. The tightening of the airways and inflammation, referred to as an asthma attack or episode, can be triggered by tobacco smoke, excessive exercise, allergies, some weather conditions (high humidity or cold air), and even extreme emotional experiences. For example, some people with asthma have been known to have an episode during very exciting movies. However, coping with asthma has not received much attention in health psychology literature because of asthma's significantly lower association with mortality.

WHAT ABOUT CULTURE?

You may have noticed that there has been little discussion of cultural differences in our study of human physiological systems. That is because there are few differences in physiology across cultures. Unlike different humanoid cultures that inhabit diverse worlds in a science fiction film whether *Avatar*, *Aliens*, or *Guardians of the Galaxy*—some with two heads, others who have evolved to not need nostrils—all humans have the same physiological systems. Different cultural groups even have near-identical genetic make-ups (Collins, 2007; Freberg, 2016). The more critical question is whether the different cultural approaches to health (described in Chapter 3) also use knowledge of the physiological systems as Western biomedicine does. Unlike the theoretical meridians of TCM, the existence of the physiological systems is not in doubt, though remember the Chinese do not doubt meridians exist. Not all cultures describe physiological processes in the same way.

TCM recognizes a number of important organs but focus on the activity and functions of the organs instead of on the fixed somatic structure that performs the activity (Hsu, 2010). In this sense, the Chinese do not use a comparable system of anatomy as described in this chapter. Whereas the Chinese recognize organs such as the liver, what is meant by "the liver" is not the same as what Western medicine refers to as "the liver." Similarly, some organs recognized by the Chinese, such as the triple burner, are not recognized by Western medicine. As mentioned in Chapter 3, TCM organizes the organs by yin (heart, lungs, spleen, liver, and kidneys) and yang (gall bladder, stomach, small intestine, large intestine, bladder, and triple burner). Each set has different categories of functions. Instead of focusing on physiology, TCM focuses on symptoms displayed by the patient to arrive at a diagnosis.

Ayurveda, similar to TCM, also describes uniquely human physiology. Unlike TCM, Ayurvedic writings more explicitly detail anatomy, and uses a complex set of terms and descriptions for the different physiological components and processes (see Chapter 3). For example, the substances called *doshas* discussed in the previous chapter enable the spiritual and mental planes of existence to express themselves through the physical body (Agnihotri & Agnihotri, 2017). There are counterparts to the circulation system, such as *srotas* that channel nutrients and waste. There are also structures similar to the nerve plexuses of Western biomedicine (e.g., the solar plexus), the chakras, although again the form and function of these nodes is somewhat different from that described by Western science. According to ayurvedic science, there are six chakras arranged along the spinal cord that serve to channel *prana,* or life-force.

Curanderismo, as a blend of Western biomedicine and spiritualism, uses a similar understanding of the physiological systems as Western science, but uses a wealth of additional alternative treatments to influence the same systems (Valdez, 2014). With American Indian medicine and African American medicine, comparable anatomy and physiological systems are not explicit or integral parts of the understanding and treatment of health and illness.

APPLICATION SHOWCASE

THE GAMES WE PLAY (CAN HAVE PHYSIOLOGICAL IMPLICATIONS)

Every holiday season brings a new gaming console to the market. Those of you who were children in the 1970s and 1980s may remember Atari, Commodore 64, and Donkey Kong. If a Nintendo WiiU or Switch, Playstation, or Xbox Kinect was your first gaming platform, you probably think Atari is a relic from a museum (hey, it was fun and all we had in those good ole days). Video/computer games were once either shoot-em-up or fantasy and involved little more than moving your fingers/thumbs/joystick. We've come a long way, baby! The Wii has onscreen players that mimic your every kinesthetic move (e.g., golf, tennis, or yoga). You swing your arm, your player on the screen swings its arm. Games now come in greater varieties than ever before. Some can be played online with partners across the planet. Graphics are getting better. The action is better. The links to aggression are strong (Anderson et al., 2010; Kepes, Bushman, & Anderson, 2017) although some research nicely identifies problems with putting sole blame on the games (Ferguson, San Miguel, Garza, & Jerabeck, 2012) and shows that playing violent games cooperatively actually reduces the aggression effects (Velez, Greitemeyer, Whitaker, Ewoldsen, & Bushman, 2016). Yes, some video games have been shown to increase violence in the children, adolescents, and adults playing them. This translates into physiological reactivity and the activity of the nervous and endocrine systems. If video games can be used for evil, can they also be used for good? Perhaps.

Important note: There are now new ways that researchers are getting health behavior change techniques to people. One new game is called *Superbetter:* you play the game spending time doing things good for you based on research, to earn points. Early work shows this gamification (i.e., using the rules of game design) of behavior change increases physical and psychological health (McGonigal, 2015). Superbetter is a resilience-building game. Let's focus on a calming one.

There is a product on the market called Wild Divine. It is billed as providing "multimedia solution to promote self-care and wellness" (https://www.unyte.com/). The website has calming imagery and phrases such as "Breathe, meditate, relax" and features well-known names in health and healing such as Dr. Dean Ornish, Dr. Deepak Chopra, and Dr. Andrew Weil. There are a number of packages that feature computer games designed to make you relax using biofeedback. The game comes with little sensors you clasp onto your fingers, which connect you to the computer (Star Trek fans, if any remain, think of Borg). As you relax, images, structures, and forms on the screen change as they are manipulated by your changing heart rate. For example, one exercise involves juggling. The more you relax, the more colored balls on screen (amid a fantastical setting) rise in the air and jump somersaults. However, could what was essentially a video game actually relate to physiological changes in the endocrine and nervous system activity? Roethel and Gurung (2007) decided to find out.

There is little empirical evidence to prove that stress management techniques reduce anxiety and the psychological symptoms of stress. Roethel and Gurung (2007) tested the effectiveness of the guided biofeedback provided by the game by collecting self-reported and physiological measures of stress (see more on the stress response in the next chapter). Salivary cortisol samples were taken pre- and post-intervention in each condition. Subjects obtained the saliva samples themselves by using a disposable pipette, which was inserted below the tongue, and samples were transferred to small plastic vials. The samples were then immediately transferred to a laboratory refrigerator, and soon after transferred to a laboratory freezer. The saliva samples were analyzed using high-sensitivity salivary cortisol enzyme-linked immunosorbent assay (ELISA) assay kits.

Subjects were instructed to refrain from consuming alcohol 6 hours prior to participation in the study, and to refrain from smoking, high-intensity physical activity, eating, and consuming caffeine one hour prior to their appointment to control for error in cortisol levels. Additionally, the experiment was scheduled in the morning hours (9:00–11:00 a.m.) to control for the diurnal rhythm of cortisol. In true biopsychosocial fashion, we measured both physiological and psychological reactions.

Subjects were assigned to one of two conditions to learn and practice a stress management technique in the lab: the game or a control condition. Subjects in the biofeedback condition learned and practiced the Healing Rhythms by the Wild Divine Project, which is marketed as a New Age innovative relaxation technique. In this game, subjects practiced breathing techniques, regulated their heart rate, and increased their level of concentration with devices that recorded the physiological responses to these exercises. The biofeedback sensors detect galvanic skin conductance (GSR), or the activity of the subject's sweat glands, and **heart rate variability (HRV)**, the variation in the beat-to-beat interval of the pumping heart. Subjects were instructed to complete six specified biofeedback challenges, each lasting approximately five minutes. Directions were given for each challenge through the interface with the game. The biofeedback challenges were successfully navigated by controlling physiological responses with respect to proper breathing, concentration, and general level of arousal.

Subjects in the control condition worked on homework for 30 minutes, the same amount of time as in the other conditions, and later were given the opportunity to participate in one of the stress management programs. There were two in-lab training sessions (interventions). The interventions included one-on-one guided training and practice of the assigned stress management technique early in the spring semester, which we expected would be a time of low stress. The participants were also asked to practice the same intervention in the lab just prior to finals week of the same semester, which we expected would be a more stressful time for the students.

Playing the game actually resulted in both physiological and psychological changes. Within the guided biofeedback condition, significant differences in measures of mood states were observed, as well as a decrease in psychological symptoms. Specifically, there were significant decreases in measures of anger and hostility, depression, and fatigue. Analysis of salivary cortisol showed a significant decrease in cortisol, a major stress hormone, for the guided biofeedback condition (Roethal & Gurung, 2007).

Not bad for a video game.

CHAPTER REVIEW

SUMMARY ▶▶

- The prenatal stage of human development is critical to the formation of a healthy physiological system. The health behaviors of the mother, influenced by her culture, can strongly influence the development of the fetus.
- The nervous system is divided into the central and peripheral systems. The central nervous system comprises the brain and spinal cord. The peripheral nervous system comprises the somatic and autonomic nervous systems.
- The nervous and endocrine systems regulate the functioning of the body by secreting different neurotransmitters and hormones.
- The digestive and renal systems are responsible for the metabolic activity in the body and for the excretion of waste. The liver is a major organ debilitated by excessive alcohol consumption. Diabetes is a major chronic illness caused by the body's inability to use insulin.
- The heart is made up of four chambers: two atria and two ventricles. Arteries carry oxygenated blood away from the heart, and veins carry deoxygenated blood to the heart. Blood pressure is described as systolic and diastolic pressures for when the heart is beating and resting, respectively.
- The immune system comprises our body's protection system. The cells and organs of this system filter out bacteria and viruses that infiltrate our bodies and break down infected cells.
- The main components of the immune system are the lymph nodes, lymph fluid, and leukocytes or white blood cells. Lymphocytes are T cells and B cells, the primary defensive cells of the system along with macrophages. There are many types of lymphocytes, each with specific immune functions. The strength of an immune response can be determined by measuring cell differentiation, proliferation, or cytotoxicity.
- Natural immunity is brought about by circulating macrophages and the secretion of histamines, which instigate inflammatory responses. Macrophages engulf antigens or invading germs by phagocytosis. Acquired immunity is the response of lymphocytes to specific microorganisms and takes place in the blood or in the cells and tissue.

TEST YOURSELF ▶▶

Check your understanding of the topics in this chapter by answering the following questions.

1. One of the facts of physical development and aging is that we tend to lose certain functions (e.g., muscle fitness and memory) faster if

   a. our cognitive development is faster.

   b. we misuse them.

   c. we get older faster.

   d. we do not use them.

2. Pregnant mothers should watch out for ________, environmental toxins that can cause developmental abnormalities.
   a. teratogens
   b. cytoclines
   c. carcinoxides
   d. butalamenes

3. The group of neurons that runs from the hindbrain to the forebrain and plays a key role in handling emergency responses during stress is
   a. basal ganglia.
   b. reticular formation.
   c. suprachiasmatic nucleus.
   d. inferior colliculus.

4. The superior colliculus, inferior colliculus, tegmentum, periaqeductal gray, and substania nigra are all structures in the
   a. forebrain.
   b. midbrain.
   c. hindbrain.
   d. hypothalamus.

5. The endocrine hormone most related to the metabolism of food, especially glucose, is
   a. oxytocin.
   b. prolactin.
   c. gastrin.
   d. insulin.

6. Problems due to limited blood flow in certain parts of the body are referred to as
   a. ischemias.
   b. arteriosclerosis.
   c. cardiac arrhythmias.
   d. angina pectoris.

7. Excessive obesity can be cured by________, but it is a risky procedure.
   a. isometric exercise
   b. bariatric surgery
   c. laparoscopic surgery
   d. cardiac surgery

8. One of the main functions of the immune system is to
   a. minimize the pain from illness and infection.
   b. destroy foreign substances and infected cells.
   c. rebuild cells after illness.
   d. reduce stress at the cellular level.

9. The most important cells of the immune system are the
   a. leukocytes.
   b. macrophages.
   c. microphages.
   d. red blood cells.

10. An important organ in the immune system that filters the blood is the
   a. heart.
   b. lungs.
   c. spleen.
   d. kidneys.

KEY TERMS, CONCEPTS, AND PEOPLE

acquired immunity, **101**
adolescence, **86**
aerobic respiration, **103**
alveoli, **104**
angina pectoris, **95**
antigens, **99**
assays, **103**
asthma, **104**
atria, **93**
B cells, **98**
bariatric surgery, **96**
capillaries, **93**
cell-mediated immunity, **103**
cytotoxicity, **103**
diabetes mellitus, **92**
diastolic, **94**
differentiation, **103**
endocrine system, **90**
epitopes, **102**
gastrointestinal tract (GI), **95**
gestation, **83**
gonads, **90**
heart rate variability (HRV), **106**
histamine, **101**
humoral-mediated immunity, **101**
immune system, **97**
inflammatory response, **101**
insulin, **90**
interferon, **99**
ischemia, **95**
leukocytes, **98**
low-birth-weight, **83**

lymphatic system, **98**
melatonin, **92**
menopause, **87**
myocardial infarctions, **95**
natural killer (NK) cell, **99**
neurotransmitters **91**
nonimmunologic defenses, **101**
nonspecific immunity, **101**
phagocytosis, **101**
polyps, **95**
prenatal period, **83**
preterm births, **83**
proliferation, **103**
puberty, **86**
pulmonary artery, **93**
pulmonary vein, **93**
systolic, **94**
T cells, **98**
ventricles, **93**

ESSENTIAL READINGS ▶▶

Robles, T., Mercado, E., Nooteboom, P., Price, J., & Romney, C. (2019). Biological processes of health. In T. A. Revenson & R. A. R. Gurung (Eds.), *Handbook of health psychology* (3e). New York, NY: Routledge.

Sapolsky, R. M. (2017). *Behave: The biology of humans at our best and worst.* New York, NY: Penguin.

Segerstrom, S. C., Out, D., Granger, D. A., & Smith, T. (2016). Biological and physiological measures in health psychology. In Y. Benyamini, M. Johnston, & E. C. Karademas (Eds.), *Assessment in health psychology* (pp. 227–238). Boston, MA: Hogrefe.

andresr/ E+/ Getty Images

STRESS AND COPING

Chapter 5
Diverse Understandings of Stress

Chapter 6
Coping and Social Support

CHAPTER 5

DIVERSE UNDERSTANDINGS OF STRESS

iStockphoto.com/ imtmphoto

Chapter 5 Outline

MEASURING UP

GOT DAILY HASSLES? WHAT'S YOUR STRESS SCORE?

Identify which of the following events you experienced in the past six months.

Event	Points
1. Death of a close family member	100
2. Death of a close friend	73
3. Divorce between parents	65
4. Jail term	63
5. Major personal injury	63
6. Marriage	58
7. Fired from job	50
8. Failed important course	47
9. Change in health of a family member	45
10. Pregnancy	44
11. Sex problems	44
12. Serious argument with family member	40
13. Change in financial status	39
14. Change of major	39
15. Trouble with parents	39
16. New girlfriend or boyfriend	38
17. Increased workload at school	37
18. Outstanding personal achievement	36
19. First semester in college	35
20. Change in living conditions	31
21. Serious argument with instructor	30
22. Lower grades than expected	29
23. Change in sleeping habits	29
24. Change in social habits	29
25. Change in eating habits	28
26. Chronic car trouble	26
27. Change in number of family get-togethers	26
28. Too many missed classes	25
29. Change of college	24
30. Dropped more than one class	23
31. Minor traffic violations	20

On the scale, you can determine your "stress score" by adding up the number of points corresponding to the events that you have experienced in the past six months or expect to experience in the coming six months.

Source: Hales (2018).

▼ Ponder This

How can changing how you think about events change your stress level?

What is going on in your body when you are stressed?

Can your cultural background determine your stress level?

Don't you detest those times when you have to introduce yourself to a large group of strangers? Most of us do. Maybe it is a first day of class, and the instructor has everyone say something about themselves. Maybe it is a meeting where everybody has to share opinions. Your heart starts to beat a little faster as your turn approaches. You review what you want to say in your head, while thoughts about how others will perceive you intrude on your planning ("How will this make me look?"). You barely notice what other people say before your turn. Your palms may become moist, and your face may turn red. The moment arrives when you must speak, and the drumbeat of your heart hammers away in a frenzied crescendo. Suddenly, when you finish, the world is a whole different place, and you can hear the birds singing in the trees again.

Stress is a term that everybody uses freely and that we all seem to understand naturally. "Don't stress out" is often used interchangeably with other soothing advice, such as "Don't freak out," slang phrases related to those dreaded times when everything seems to go wrong or there is too much to do and too little time. There are many such stressful times in life. For example, when you have not started on the large paper that is due the next day, or you reach Sunday night after having wasted the entire weekend when you should have been studying for Monday's test. How about experiencing getting sick, your car breaking down, and learning a close family member had a major accident—all at the same time? Almost everyone can recall a number of times when they felt stressed. The American Psychological Association's yearly *Stress in America* surveys show Americans have high stress levels, rely on unhealthy behaviors to manage stress, and experience physical health consequences of stress (American Psychological Association, 2017). The survey also shows 86% of Americans constantly check their electronic devices, a new form of stress called "telepressure" (Barber & Santuzzi, 2017).

Stress can be a tricky monster. There are many intriguing aspects to stress and how we experience it. Some things that caused you stress at one time (e.g., giving a five-minute presentation) may amuse you today. Some things that are stressful for some people (such as getting up to sing at a karaoke machine) are actually enjoyable for others. At its most extreme, stress can kill, severely hamper health, or drive someone to behave in risky, unhealthy ways.

iStockphoto.com/ MCCAIG

▲ **A Variety of Stressors Are Present in Everyday Life.** From the realities of career and family obligations, to mundane stressors like traffic, life can be overwhelming and stressful at times.

WHAT IS STRESS?

What exactly is stress? Why do different people and cultures experience stress differently? What can we do to reduce stress? These are some of the questions that we will answer in this chapter. We begin by defining the term and looking at how health psychologists study stress. You will notice that causes of stress for people vary historically. Next, we will look at how we can measure stress in an effort to control and manage it. Then we shift our focus to the role of psychological processes, specifically thinking and behavior. We also examine how different types of stress (e.g., prejudice and noise) are associated with different cultures (e.g., SES and ethnicity), reviewing how different cultural beliefs influence the experience of stress.

We can define stress in many different ways. It has been studied using different approaches, and each of us has different notions of what is stressful (Table 5.1). It is important that a definition of stress can be applied to many different people (and animals, too). Not all negative events are stressful, and not all positive events are automatically free from stress. For example, losing your job may sound initially like a stressful event, but it may be a happy event if you hated your job and if this now opens up new opportunities for you. Similarly, although finding a romantic partner after a long period of being single sounds like a very positive event, you may worry about how to make sure the relationship lasts or whether your partner likes you or not. These worries could make this positive event stressful. As you can see, stress is subjective. What then is the best way to measure stress?

▲ **A Variety of Stressors Are Present in Everyday Life.** Balancing work and family can be particularly stressful.

Most researchers argue that the best way to know when a person is stressed is to look at how his or her body responds to a situation (Gruenwald, 2019). If the sympathetic nervous system activates in response to an event, then the person is under stress. This activation results in elevated heart rate, respiration, and circulation (this is a good time to look over the section on the nervous system in Chapter 4). Many early definitions of stress relied heavily on biological activity. **Walter Cannon** (1929) viewed stress as the biological mobilization of the body for action, involving sympathetic activation and endocrine activity. **Hans Selye** (1956) similarly saw stress as the activation of a host of physiological systems. Later theorists added more psychological components to the process of stress (e.g., Lazarus, 1966).

Psychological theories defined stress as the result of perceived demands on the organism that exceed the resources to meet those demands (e.g., Frankenhaeuser et al., 1989). Although these different definitions have all been well supported, the easiest way to define stress is as the upsetting of homeostasis (Cannon, 1929). Each of our bodies has an optimal level of functioning for blood glucose level, body temperature, rate of circulation, and breathing. **Homeostasis** is the ideal level of bodily functions (Prus, 2018). Similar to the thermostat in homes, our body is designed to maintain its optimal level in all areas of functioning. We set our thermostats and if the temperature drops

▼ TABLE 5.1

Definitions of Stress

Definition	Source
A substantial imbalance between environmental demand and the response capability of the focal organism.	McGrath (1970, p. 17)
The response to the actual loss, threat of loss, or lack of gain of resources that all individuals actively seek to gain and maintain.	Hobfoll (1989)
A condition or feeling experienced when a person perceives that demands exceed the personal and social resources the individual is able to mobilize.	Lazarus (1966)
Psychosocial stress reflects the subject's inability to forestall or diminish perception, recall, anticipation, or imagination of disvalued circumstances, those that in reality or fantasy signify great and/or increased distance from desirable (valued) experiential states, and, consequently, evoke a need to approximate the valued states.	Kaplan (1983, p. 196)
A perceptual phenomenon arising from a comparison between the demand on the person and his or her ability to cope. An imbalance in this mechanism, when coping is important, gives rise to the experience of stress, and to the stress response.	Cox (1978)
The upsetting of homeostasis.	Cannon (1929)

below the set level, the furnace starts. In this way, a constant temperature is maintained. The hypothalamus in our brains similarly maintains set levels. Stress to our systems can thus be seen as something that upsets our ideal balance. This simple but effective definition of stress harkens back to the origins of the word "stress."

Physicists have long studied the effects of large forces on solid structures, and stress was originally used to describe the force exerted on a body that results in deformation or strain. Stress has similar effects on our body. A **stressor** is *anything* that disrupts the body's homeostatic balance. The **stress response** is what is done to reestablish the homeostatic balance. This definition allows for subjectivity because stressors can vary among individuals (Guenole, Chernyshenko, Stark, McGregor, & Ganesh, 2008). If an event does not activate your stress response or disrupt your system, it is just another event. If an event disrupts you, it is a stressor. One person's event can be another person's stressor. For example, even if talking in public is not stressful for you, it could be very stressful for someone else.

MEASURING STRESS

A variety of tools can assess the different psychological and physiological aspects of stress (O'Connor & Ferguson, 2016). There are measures of stressfulness of specific events, measures of how we appraise situations, and generic measures. Table 5.2 summarizes some of the main measures of stress.

The easiest way to measure whether someone is stressed is to ask. If your colleague at work seems stressed, a simple question may confirm your observation. To make a valid and reliable measure of stress, health psychologists have devised a number of different forms of measurement.

▼ TABLE 5.2

Some of the Major Measures of Stress

Title of Scale	Author	Number of Items/ Events	Dimensions Assessed
Generic Measures			
Perceived Stress	Cohen, Kamarck, & Mermelstein (1983)	14, 10, & 4	Global perceived stress score
Stress Arousal Checklist	Mackay et al. (1978)	30	Stress scale, arousal scale
Trier Inventory of Chronic Stress	Schulz, Schlotz, & Becker (2011)	57	Work overload, social overload, pressure to perform, work discontent, excessive demands at work, lack of social recognition, social tensions, social isolation, and chronic worrying
Event Measures			
Social Readjustment Rating Scale (SRRS)	Holmes & Rahe (1967)	43	Total life change unit
Life Events and Difficulties Scale	Brown & Harris (1978)	N/A (events elicited via interview)	Ratings of acute (events) and chronic (difficulty) stressors based on expert ratings following detailed interview and assessment
Hassles Scale	Kanner et al. (1981)	117	Work, family, social activities, environment, practical considerations, finances, and health
Hassles and Uplifts Scale	DeLongis, Folkman, & Lazarus (1988)	53	Work, family, social activities, environment, practical considerations, finances, and health
Single-item Visual Analogue Scale/Rating Scale	N/A	1	Perceived stress in relation to single events

Title of Scale	Author	Number of Items/ Events	Dimensions Assessed
Daily Hassles/Stressors — free response format	O'Connor et al. (2008)	N/A	Frequency/intensity of ego-threatening, interpersonal, work-related, and physical
Cognitive appraisal measures			
Stress Appraisal Measure	Peacock & Wong (1990)	28	*Primary appraisals:* Threat, challenge, centrality *Secondary appraisals:* Uncontrollable, controllable-by-others, controllable-by-self
Appraisal of Life Events	Ferguson, Matthews, & Cox (2010)	16	*Primary appraisals:* Threat, challenge, loss
Dimensions of Cognitive Appraisal	Gall & Evans (1987)	19	*Primary appraisals*, undesirability/threat, gain/challenge, need for information, familiarity, need to accept
Emotion	Folkman & Lazarus (1985)	15	Threat, challenge, harm, benefit
Stressor Appraisal Scale	Schneider (2008)	10	*Primary and secondary appraisal*, but no challenge, loss, or control items
Stressor Appraisal Scale, modified	Gartland, O'Connor, & Lawton (2012)	10	*Primary and secondary appraisal*, but no challenge, loss, or control items

Early stress research focused primarily on major events in people's lives, or **life events** (Brown & Harris, 1978; Holmes & Rahe, 1967). For example, the Social Readjustment Rating Scale (SRRS) consists of 43 items, each given a value called a life change unit (Holmes & Rahe, 1967). Although the SRRS is one of the critical landmarks in the measurement of stress, it has been heavily criticized and is not as widely used today. Sometimes the occurrence of an event does not make it stressful.

Most measures take the form of questionnaire checklists containing a number of different events (e.g., getting fired, having a fight with a romantic partner, or getting in trouble with the law). Test subjects are asked to indicate which of the events happened to them in a given period of time (e.g., the past 6 months). Totaling the number of events that the person experienced provides an estimate of the demands placed on the individual and hence the level of stress. Examples of such questionnaires are the Life Experiences Survey (Sarason, Johnson, & Seigel, 1978) and the SRRS (Holmes & Rahe, 1967).

Together with major life events, you probably know that small hassles add up: hearing the noisy neighbor every morning, being stuck in traffic, or having too many things to do. There is a scale to measure even these little things. The Hassles Scale (Kanner, Coyne, Schaefer, & Lazarus, 1981) consists of 117 events. Small hassles have been shown to negatively affect health and aggravate the damage done by major life events (Weinberger, Hiner, & Tierney, 1987; Werner, Frost, Macnee, McCabe, & Rice, 2012).

Shelley E. Taylor is a distinguished professor of psychology at the University of California, Los Angeles. She received her PhD from Yale University and is one of the founders of the modern field of health psychology. In addition, she is the lead author of the *Tend and Befriend* theory of stress (see Taylor et al., 2000 in Essential Readings).

Although many of these measures tap into acute one-time events and daily hassles, other questionnaires assess major chronic stressors (Lepore, 1997). For example, Gurung, Taylor, Kemeny, and Myers (2004) demonstrated how measuring chronic stress could predict depression in an ethnically diverse sample of low-income women (see Table 5.3). Chronic stress or burden and low SES were significant predictors of increased depression for African American women and Latina women, respectively. Gurung et al. (2004) measured chronic burden using a 21-item scale developed

▼ TABLE 5.3

The Chronic Burden Scale

1.	Not having enough money to cover the basic needs of life (food, clothing, housing)
2.	Not having any savings to meet problems that come up
3.	No reliable source of transportation (such as car that works or reliable bus service)
4.	Housing problems (uncertainty about housing, problems with landlord)
5.	Problems arranging child care
6.	Being a caregiver for someone (taking care of someone sick, elderly, or infirm)
7.	Divorce or separation from partner
8.	Long-term unresolved conflict with someone very important (child, parent, lover/partner, sibling, or friend)
9.	Being fired or laid off
10.	Trouble with your employer (in danger of losing job or being suspended/demoted)
11.	Having work hours or responsibilities change for the worse
12.	Partner's work hours or responsibilities change for the worse
13.	Serious accident, injury, or new illness happening to you or a close family member/spouse/partner/close friend
14.	You or a close family member/spouse/partner/friend being the victim of a crime or physical assault
15.	Chronic pain or restriction of movements due to injury or illness
16.	Long-term medical problems
17.	Either you or someone you are close to and depend on having immigration or citizenship problems
18.	You or a close family member/spouse/partner/close friend being arrested or sent to jail
19.	Living in a high-crime area
20.	Losing the help of someone you depend on (person moved, got sick, or otherwise was unavailable)
21.	Being discriminated against because of your race, nationality, gender, or sexual orientation

Source: Gurung, Taylor, Kemeny, and Myers (2004).

from focus groups in which HIV-positive women discussed the life stresses that they faced. The researchers compiled a list of the most commonly mentioned stressors from the focus groups. Then participants in the study indicated whether they had experienced each stressor during the previous 6 months and the extent to which each stressor was a problem for them using a 4-point scale ranging from 1, "Not a problem for me in the past 6 months," to 4, "A major problem for me in the past 6 months." The final list, shown in the Measuring Up section at the start of the chapter, included financial difficulties, transportation problems, housing problems, child-care or caregiving difficulties, difficulties in personal relationships, work-related difficulties, exposure to accident or injury, immigration or citizenship problems, and exposure to crime and discrimination. Another new measure of chronic stress that promises to add to our ability to predict the effects of long-term stressors is the Trier Inventory of Chronic Stress (Schulz, Schlotz, & Becker, 2011).

Most of the measures of stress discussed so far ask whether certain specific events actually took place. Whether hassles or life events, the assumption is that if you experienced one of these, then you are likely to experience stress. A different type of assessment focuses on perceived stress (Uchino, Bowen, Carlisle, & Birmingham, 2012). As the term suggests, this approach relies on what the individual feels. Cohen, Kamarck, and Mermelstein (1983)

▼ TABLE 5.4

Perceived Stress Scale

The Perceived Stress Scale (PSS) is a classic stress assessment instrument. The tool, originally developed in 1983, remains a popular choice for helping us understand how different situations affect our feelings and our perceived stress. The questions in this scale ask about your feelings and thoughts during the past month. In each case, you will be asked to indicate how often you felt or thought a certain way. Although some of the questions are similar, there are differences between them and you should treat each one as a separate question. The best approach is to answer fairly quickly. That is, don't try to count up the number of times you felt a particular way; rather, indicate the alternative that seems like a reasonable estimate.
For each question choose from the following alternatives: **0 - never, 1 - almost never, 2 - sometimes, 3 - fairly often, 4 - very often**
l. In the past month, how often have you been upset because of something that happened unexpectedly?
2. In the past month, how often have you felt that you were unable to control the important things in your life?
3. In the past month, how often have you felt nervous and stressed?
4. In the past month, how often have you felt confident about your ability to handle your personal problems?
5. In the past month, how often have you felt that things were going your way?
6. In the past month, how often have you found that you could not cope with all the things that you had to do?
7. In the past month, how often have you been able to control irritations in your life?
8. In the past month, how often have you felt that you were on top of things?
9. In the past month, how often have you been angered because of things that happened that were outside of your control?
10. In the past month, how often have you felt difficulties were piling up so high that you could not overcome them?

Source: Uchino, Bowen, Carlisle, & Birmingham, 2012.

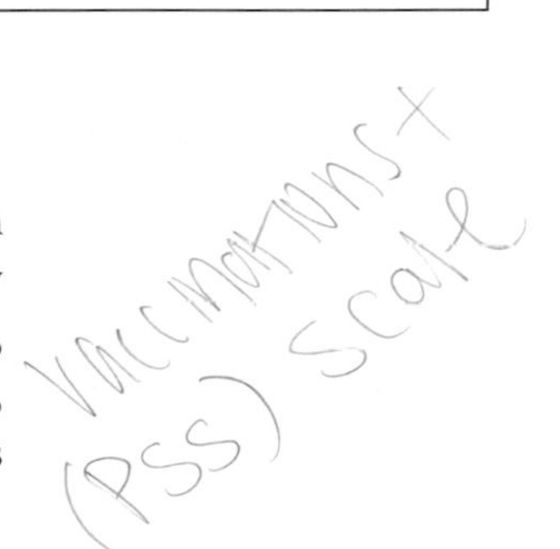

developed the Perceived Stress Scale (PSS) that asks respondents how often they had certain thoughts or feelings in the preceding month. Responses to the perceived stress scale reliably predict a range of health issues such as coronary heart disease (Ghasemipour & Ghorbani, 2010; Strodl, Kenardy, & Aroney, 2003) and immune responses to vaccinations (Burns, Drayson, Ring, & Carroll, 2002). The PSS is one of the most commonly used stress scales today (Gruenwald, 2019). Table 5.4 shows you all the items.

Asking if someone is stressed can be a good indicator of how stressed they really are. However, our perceptions of stress are not always accurate. Sometimes we may not be completely honest about our experiences (both to ourselves or to researchers who want to know). To compensate for these inaccuracies, a vast array of physiological measures can be used. It is difficult to trick your physiology. If you look back to the physiological effects of stress, you can see how you can get a measure of stress without asking questions. You can measure a person's blood pressure (systolic and diastolic), take a person's temperature, or measure a person's heart rate. When we become stressed, sympathetic activation increases all these physiological measures. Most laboratory studies of stress, especially experimental studies in which a person is stressed on purpose, use physiological measures. Some use galvanic skin responses, a measure of how our skin conducts electricity. We sweat more when we get stressed; even a minute increase in perspiration at the skin's surface increases the rate at which our skin conducts electricity. Measuring devices pick up this increase in conductance.

In many studies, blood samples are assessed for the levels of different chemical markers. The levels of stress chemicals in the blood, such as cortisol, epinephrine, and norepinephrine, increase when we are stressed. The number and types of different immune system cells vary when we

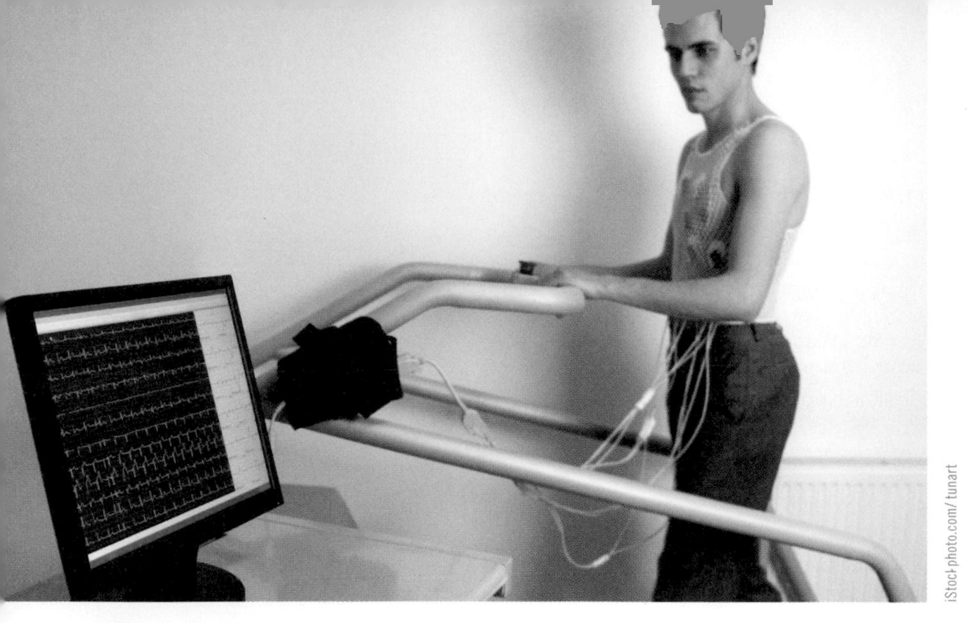
iStock photo.com/ tunart

▲ **Stress Test.** A modern measure of physiological reactions to stress.

become stressed. A small sample of blood, even a few tablespoons, helps researchers assess stress levels. For example, **Janice Kiecolt-Glaser** and colleagues watch married couples fight and then use blood samples from them to assess how stressed the argument made them (Kiecolt-Glaser & Wilson, 2017; more in the relationship stress section below). Note that many other activities besides stressful ones can also instigate some of these physiological responses, so measures need to be interpreted with caution.

Stress over Time

Stressors today differ from what was perceived as stressful in the past. A list of common stressors can be seen in the Daily Hassles Scale (chapter opening). If you review the list you will see that most of the examples are psychological in nature. They are not tangible threats such as impending invasion by a powerful army or being mauled by a wildcat, but instead are things that we worry about or stress over. There is also a range of stressful events that are tangible, such as living in a high-crime neighborhood or a very cold environment (Lowe et al., 2016). In a study of single-parent families living in violent neighborhoods in Philadelphia, parents described high levels of stress and concern for their children's well-being (Jacoby, Tach, Guerra, Wiebe, & Richmond, 2017). The effects of stress can add up. The cumulative effects of stress and living a disadvantaged life influence how young children react to stress (Tackett et al., 2017).

Our current stress response is hypothesized to have developed in response to the stressors faced by primitive humans. Both early theorists such as Walter Cannon (1929) and contemporary researchers such as Robert Sapolsky (2017) suggested that the physiological responses to stress evolved many hundreds, even thousands, of years ago. Consider the early days of human history before we lived in cities and towns. Archaeological evidence suggests that humans as we know them today first flourished on the African continent (see Diamond, 2005, for a review of the archaeological evidence). Many wild animals and predators roamed freely. Most of the early stressors were physical in nature and short term or **acute**. The body had to be able to get ready to mobilize for sudden action in this fashion (e.g., run from an animal). Early stressors were most likely acute physical stressors.

With an acute physical stressor, your stress response either worked—you escaped the beast or defeated the ravaging tribes—or that was the end of your story. Those humans with better stress responses lived to reproduce. As civilization proceeded, humans started to live longer and experience more long-term, or **chronic**, stressors. Once agriculture flourished, humans traded nomadic lifestyles for village and town living, and the types of stressors changed. Sometimes crops failed, and people would go hungry for long periods. At other times, climate conditions such as drought made food scarce. As the domestication of animals increased, their germs probably caused large numbers of illnesses in people. All of these stressors could cause prolonged illnesses, but again the stressors were physical in nature. For much of human history, especially through the Middle Ages when millions died of the plague (e.g., bubonic, septicemic, and others), the main stressors and causes of death were physical in nature. As described in Chapter 1, medicine was not a successful cure of disease until the past hundred years, and diseases such as pneumonia, tuberculosis, and influenza caused great physical stress and death.

Today, stressors are very different. Yes, people still die of diseases due to viruses and bacteria. People who live in countries experiencing political strife or civil war and people living in high-crime neighborhoods also suffer from acute stress due to threats to their physical safety. But the main physical killers in the United States, such as heart disease, are caused and made worse by the slow accumulation of psychological damage (Bishop, 2019). Much of this damage is related to stress. Today, the major stressors in North America are psychological in nature. Our thoughts, and the pressures we apply to ourselves, generate stress (*anticipatory* stress; Sapolsky, 2004/1994). Few physical stressors exist here today. Instead, the bulk of our stress is self-generated and related to the pressures, frustrations, and changes of everyday modern life.

Yet the bottom line is that stress, whether physical or psychological in nature, leads to a variety of poor health outcomes (e.g., Gruenwald, 2019).

MAIN THEORIES OF STRESS

Cannon's Fight-or-Flight Theory

Walter Cannon applied the concept of homeostasis to the study of human interactions with the environment (Cannon, 1914). Specifically, he studied how stressors affect the sympathetic nervous system (SNS). His basic idea is intuitive and can be remembered by a simple example.

▼ FIGURE 5.1

Major Components of the Autonomic Nervous System

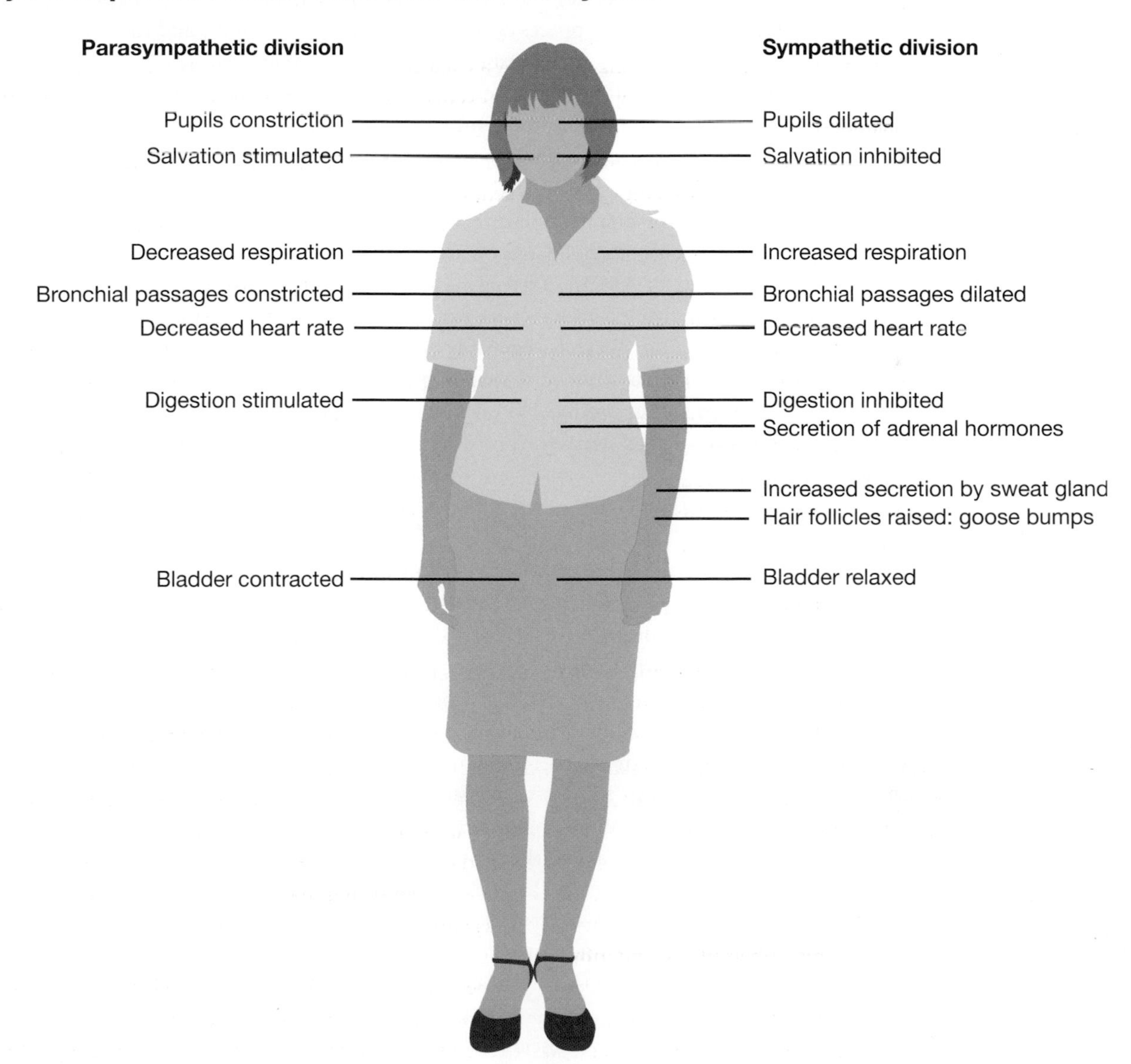

Imagine going to a Saturday night movie. You drove to the cinema by yourself and the only parking spot you found was far away from the theater doors. After the movie, you walk back to your car alone because the friends you met had closer parking spots. As you reach your car, you hear a crunching sound in the dark behind you. You stop. The crunching stops. You start walking faster, and the crunching speeds up. You scramble for your keys and in the reflection of your car window you see a hulking figure draw up behind you. You can probably guess what your body is doing. Your heart pumps faster, your blood pressure rises, you breathe faster, you may be a little flushed, and your palms may be sweaty. All these reactions that prepare our body for action are caused by the SNS, as described in Figure 5.1.

Activation of the SNS increases circulation, respiration, and metabolism, all factors that fuel your body to ready it to either fight or flee. The higher respiration rate gets more oxygen into your lungs, the increased heart rate and blood pressure get the oxygenated blood to the muscles, and the increased metabolism breaks down energy for use by the fighting/fleeing muscles. The SNS also turns off certain systems in response to stress. Faced by a threatening mugger, you are probably not in a mood for two things: food and sex. Your body cannot be wasting resources and energy on these things. The SNS down-regulates (turns down) the digestive system and the reproductive system in times of stress. For example, many female high school cross-country runners have irregular menstrual cycles—to the body running cross-country is a stressor.

The complete reversal of this process (the activating of some systems and the deactivating of others) is what helps your body recover from a stressor and is managed by the parasympathetic nervous system (PNS). The PNS decreases circulation and respiration and increases digestion and reproduction. Correspondingly, most stress management techniques work to activate your PNS and slow down breathing and heart rate. The PNS and SNS are both parts of the autonomic nervous system and are coordinated by higher brain structures such as the hypothalamus.

Cannon (1914) was the first to sketch this pattern of responding to stress and to map out the full level of physiological activation. Cannon argued that, when faced with a stressor, the SNS is activated and in turn it activates the adrenal glands that secrete a class of hormones called **catecholamines**. The two major catecholamines are epinephrine and norepinephrine. Epinephrine is also known as adrenaline. You have probably heard the phrase, "My adrenaline was flowing," to suggest that someone was stressed or ready for action. The inner part of the adrenal glands, an area called the medulla, produces both these hormones. Consequently, Cannon's **fight-or-flight theory** of stress describes stress as leading to **sympathetic-adrenal-medullary (SAM) activation**.

This fight-or-flight system has eight clear-cut effects (Guyton, 1977). Blood pressure, blood flow to large muscles, total energy consumption, blood glucose concentration, energy release in the muscles, muscular strength, mental activity, and the rate of blood coagulation all increase.

An intricate dance of chemical secretions leads to all these events. The hypothalamus orchestrates the SNS via the secretion of corticotropin-releasing factor (CRF). CRF stimulates the secretion of adrenocorticotrophic hormone (ACTH) from the anterior pituitary gland and stimulates the locus coeruleus (located in the pons area of the brain stem) to increase the levels of norepinephrine in the system. Epinephrine is what increases both the heart rate and blood pressure. With prolonged stress, there is a circular reaction, and higher levels of epinephrine increase the secretions of ACTH. Research during the past 60 years has shown that the relative levels of epinephrine and norepinephrine vary with the type of emotion experienced with one being more of a flight chemical and the other being more of a fight chemical. Epinephrine is present in greater amounts when we are scared; norepinephrine is present in greater amounts when we are angry (Ax, 1953; Ward et al., 1983). The different physiological parts of SAM activation are heavily interconnected.

In recent years, the basic fight-or-flight idea has been modified to include the option of freezing. As the term suggests, new work looks at how in the face of something stressful we freeze up and seem unable to do anything. Research is mapping out both the cognitive and physiological associations of freezing in humans (Alban & Pocknell, 2017) as well as ways to measure fight, flight, and freeze tendencies (Maack, Buchanan, & Young, 2015).

Taylor et al.'s Tend-and-Befriend Theory

For years health psychologists assumed Cannon's model was the only major way both sexes reacted to stress. Then a team from UCLA launched a challenge to conventional thinking about stress. **Shelley Taylor** and colleagues suggested that women **tend-and-befriend** in addition to fighting or fleeing (Taylor et al., 2000).

Diverse findings in the stress literature do not fit with the fight-or-flight model. The fight or flight model assumes that men and women faced the same challenges in our evolutionary history. However, this was not true. Due to pregnancy and nursing, women have been the primary caregivers of infants. Men have easily been able to fight or flee, but women often had to look after infants. If women fought and lost they would leave their infant defenseless. If women ran they would either have to leave their infant behind or the weight of the infant would surely slow them down. Instead, Taylor et al. (2000) argued that women developed additional stress responses aimed to protect, calm, and quiet the child, to remove it from harm's way (i.e., tending), and to marshal resources to help. Essentially, women create social networks to provide resources and protection for themselves and their infants (i.e., befriending).

The tend-and-befriend response thus provides more-reasonable stress responses for women than the basic fight-or-flight theory. This relatively new theory builds on the brain's attachment/caregiving system that counteracts the metabolic activity associated with the traditional fight-or-flight stress response—increased heart rate, blood pressure, and cortisol levels—and leads to nurturing and affiliative behavior.

Existing evidence from research with nonhuman animals, neuroendocrine studies, and human-based social psychology supports this new theory (Israel-Cohen & Kaplan, 2016; Taylor & Masters, 2011). Neuroendocrine research shows that although women show the same immediate hormonal and sympathetic nervous system response to acute stress as men, other factors intervene to make fight-or-flight less likely. In terms of the fight response, while male aggression appears to be driven by hormones such as testosterone, female aggression is not. In fact, a major female hormone, oxytocin, actually counteracts the effects of stress chemicals such as cortisol and the catecholamines (Cardoso, Valkanas, Serravalle, & Ellenbogen, 2016; Doom, Doyle, & Gunnar, 2017). Men low on this hormone do not reap its benefits (Berger, Heinrichs, von Dawans, Way, & Chen, 2016). Oxytocin inhibits flight and enhances relaxation, reduces fearfulness, and decreases the other stress responses typical to the fight-or-flight response. Strong evidence suggests oxytocin underlies both the tending and the befriending parts of the theory. Supporting the role of oxytocin in befriending, blocking oxytocin in women actually makes them spend less time with their friends (Jamner, Alberts, Leigh, & Klein, 1998). On the flip side, spraying oxytocin into someone's nose via a nasal spray can improve how accurate people are at recognizing feelings in others, a critical part of befriending (Graustella & MacLeod, 2012), and can modify social perceptions relating to friendship (Hecht, Robins, Gautam, & King, 2017). In fact, research is even exploring the potential of oxytocin nasal spray treatment for specific mental health problems that involve impairments in engaging comfortably with other people (Liu, McErlean, & Dadds, 2012; Mah, 2016). On a related note, oxytocin is also related to trustworthiness (Zak, Kurzban, & Matzer, 2005).

In terms of tending, oxytocin plays a key role in maternal bonding (Szymanska, Schneider, Chateau-Smith, Nezelof, & Vulliez-Coady, 2017). Although extensively studied in animals, the tending role of oxytocin in humans has only recently been illustrated. Feldman, Weller, Zagoory-Sharon, and Levine (2007) measured the oxytocin levels in pregnant women twice during their pregnancy and once after they had given birth. Women with higher levels of oxytocin bonded better with their babies and behaved in ways to form better bonds (e.g., feeding in special ways). More oxytocin in early life is also related to later tending and befriending in both animals (Mandel & Nicol, 2017) and humans (Taylor, 2012).

Tending is observed in animal studies when rat pups are removed from their nest for brief periods—a stressful situation for pups and mothers—and then returned. The mothers immediately move to soothe their pups by licking, grooming, and nursing them (Meaney, 2001). Similar behaviors are seen in sheep (Dwyer, 2008) and many mammals (Anacker & Beery, 2013). In humans, breastfeeding mothers are found to be calmer (Uvnäs-Moberg, 1996), and touch has been shown to soothe both the mother and infant (Uvnäs-Moberg, Handlin, & Petersson, 2015). In clear support of the tend-and-befriend model, Repetti and Wood (1997) showed that after a stressful day on the job, men want to be left alone and often fight with their spouses and kids, while women who felt stressed tended toward spending more time with their kids and having more physical contact with them. A more recent review shows that men exhibit more-negative reactions to work stress than women and a partner's stress can significantly influence how much social support is given in a family (Repetti & Wang, 2017).

One humorous but related aside. You may be surprised by what increases oxytocin. In one study, Internet shoppers received a $10 coupon. These shoppers showed an increase in oxytocin and happiness, compared to a control group of shoppers who did not get the coupon (Alexander, Tripp, & Zak, 2015).

Selye's General Adaptation Syndrome

Hans Selye was a young assistant professor in search of direction when a colleague gave him some ovarian extracts (Sapolsky, 2005). Selye set out to determine the role played by these extracts and, quite by chance, discovered another major explanation for the stress response. In his early experiments, he injected rats with ovarian extract and observed them for changes. After months of study, he found that the rats had developed ulcers. As a good scientist, he decided to replicate his findings. He recreated the study and added a control group—a group of rats who got a placebo injection instead of the extract. Then he found that his control group developed ulcers as well. What did this mean?

Well, Selye was not an established animal handler, and he had a lot of trouble weighing, injecting, and studying his rats. Through different forms of (unintended) mistreatment, he actually stressed both the experimental and control groups, resulting in both groups developing ulcers. The rats also had other physiological problems, such as shrunken adrenal glands and deformed lymph nodes (Selye, 1956). On realizing the actual true cause of the ulcers, Selye exposed rats to a variety of stressors such as extreme heat and cold, sounds, and rain. He found that in every case, the rats developed physiological problems similar to those in his first groups of rats. Selye concluded that organisms must have a general, nonspecific response to a variety of stressful events. Specifically, he hypothesized that no matter what the stressor, the body would react in the same way and theorized that these responses were driven by the **hypothalamic-pituitary-adrenal (HPA) axis**.

The first part of the HPA axis sequence of activation resembles the characteristics of SAM activation. The hypothalamus activates the pituitary gland that then activates the adrenal gland. The difference in Selye's theory is that a different part of the adrenal gland, the cortex, gets activated. The cortex is the outer part of the adrenal gland (the medulla in SAM activation is the inner part) and secretes a class of hormones called corticosteroids. The major hormone in this class is cortisol (hydrocortisone). Cortisol generates energy to deal with the stressor by converting stored glycogen into glucose, a process called gluconeogenesis. Gluconeogenesis aids in breaking down protein, the mobilization of fat, and the stabilization of lysosomes. See Figures 5.2A and 5.2B for a summary of the basic physiological reactions to stress.

Selye argued that organisms have a general way of responding to all stressors, what he called the **general adaptation syndrome** (Figure 5.3). When faced with a stressor, whether a wild animal, a threatening mugger, or intense cold, the body first goes into a state of alarm. HPA axis activation takes place, and the body attempts to cope with the stressor during a period of resistance. Short-term reactions to stress and HPA activation can even be experimentally

▼ FIGURE 5.2A

The Basic Fight-or-Flight Response

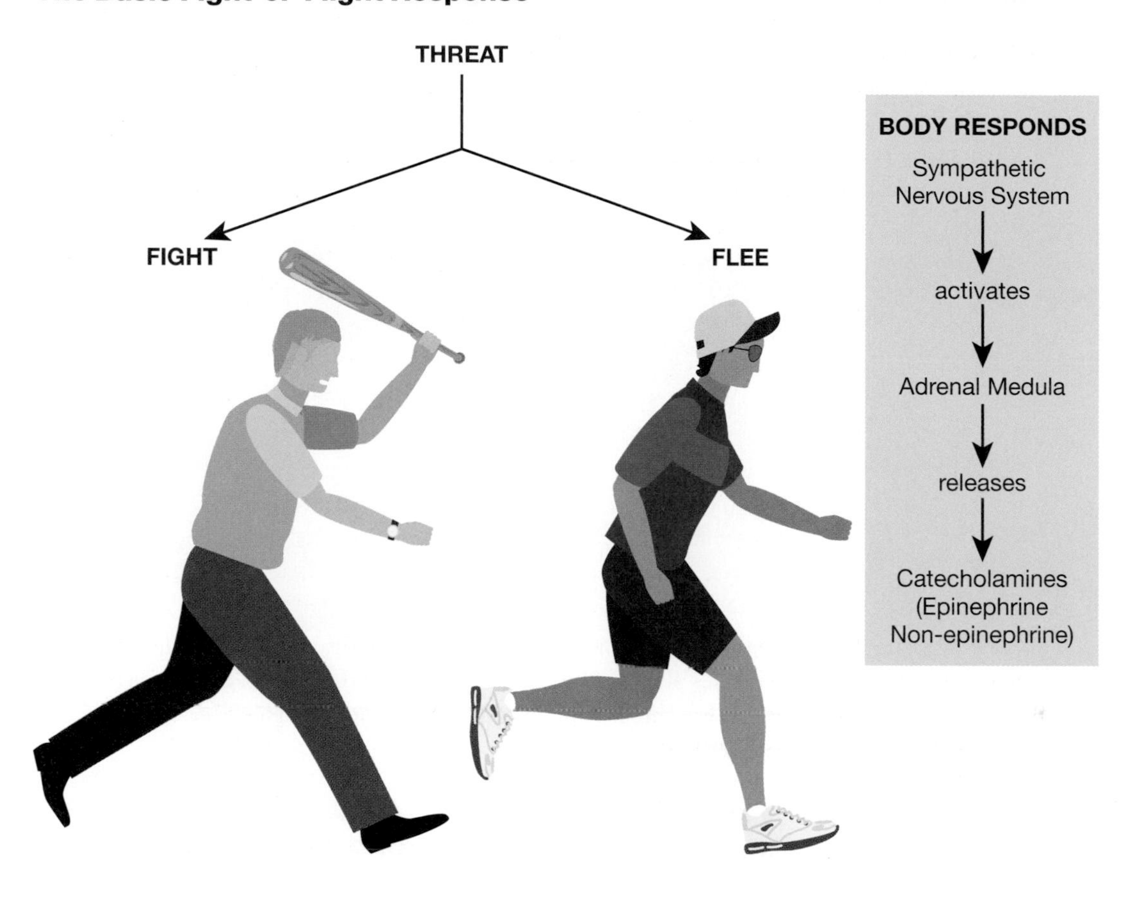

▼ FIGURE 5.2B

The Main Physiological Pathways in Hans Selye's General Adaptation System

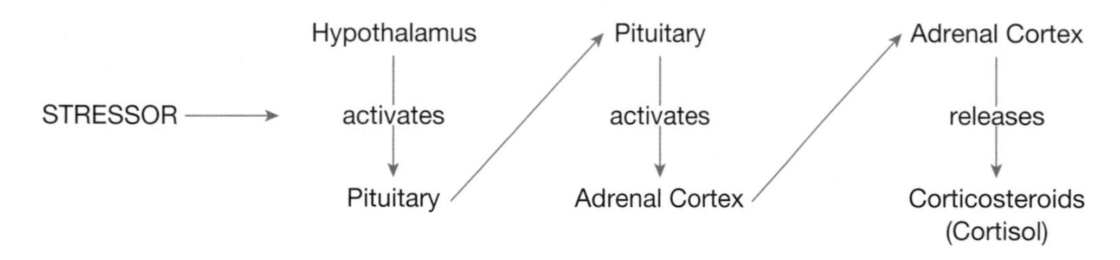

demonstrated (Roos et al., 2017). Many acute or short-term stressors can be successfully dealt with in the resistance stage; however, if the stressor persists for too long, the body breaks down in a state of exhaustion. Chronic stressors can exert true physiological and psychological damage on human bodies. Recent work on the HPA axis looks at how genetic variations and early stress can influence brain functioning (Di Iorio et al., 2017).

Cannon (1914) and Selye (1956) were the earliest theorists to offer physiological bases for stress. In summary, combining their models suggests that our SNS and the hypothalamus coordinate a physiological stress response that involves the pituitary and adrenal glands and the secretion of catecholamines and corticosteroids. Psychological aspects did not play major roles in their theories. Cannon suggested that organisms had threshold levels and that if stressors were below

▼ FIGURE 5.3

Main Stages in Hans Selye's General Adaptation System

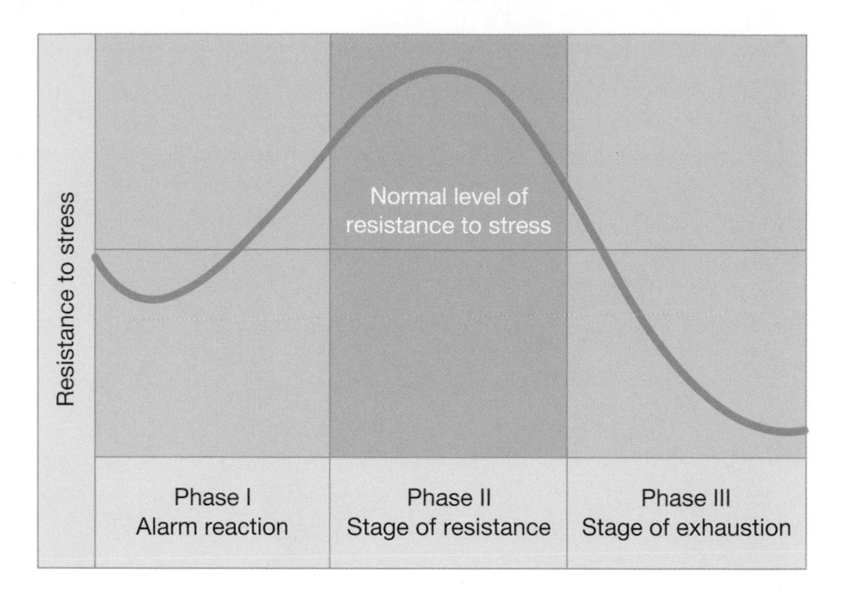

these limits, the fight-or-flight response did not activate. He also discussed emotional stressors, suggesting that mental processes played some role. Likewise, both Cannon and Selye believed that events had to be recognized as threatening to activate the response. However, neither scientist explained how this happened.

Lazarus's Cognitive Appraisal Model

Richard Lazarus (1966) devised the first psychological model of stress, which is still actively used in stress research designs today (Eschleman, Alarcon, Lyons, Stokes, & Schneider, 2012). Lazarus saw stress as the imbalance between the demands placed on the individual and that individual's resources to cope (Figure 5.4). He argued that the experience of stress differed significantly across individuals, depending on how they interpreted the event and the outcome of a specific sequence of thinking patterns called **appraisals**.

▼ FIGURE 5.4

Main Stages of Lazarus' Cognitive Approach

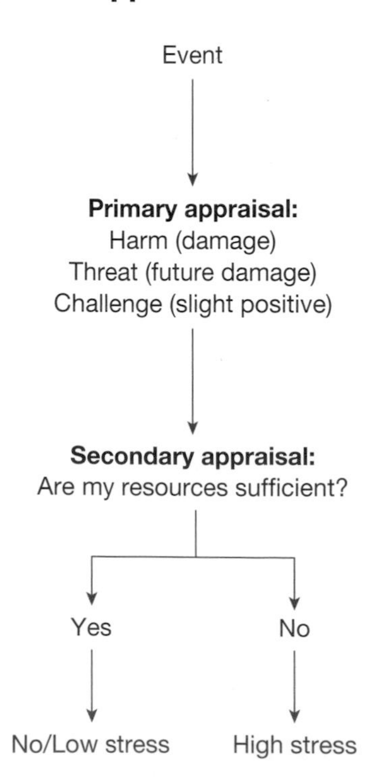

All of us are faced with demands. In school, you have papers to write and exams to take. At work, you have projects and production deadlines to meet or a certain number of sales to make. Even in our personal lives, our family and friends rely on us and expect us to do various things. These different expectations, deadlines, and situations are all potential stressors. However, according to Lazarus, these expectations, deadlines, and situations are just events until we deem them to be stressful. The main cognitive process at work here is making appraisals. On the television show *Antiques Road Show*, people bring in possessions from their homes, attics, and garages to be evaluated. Experts appraise the articles for how much they are worth, sometimes surprising the owners ("Did you know the table you bought at a garage sale for $50.00 is a Colonial collectible worth $15,000?"). When we appraise events, we follow essentially the same process. We set a value or judge the nature or quality of a situation or event.

Lazarus suggested that we make two major types of appraisals when we face any potentially stressful event. During **primary appraisals**, we ascertain whether the event is positive, negative, or neutral; if negative, we ascertain if it is harmful, threatening, or challenging. A harm (or harm–loss) appraisal is made when we expect to lose or actually do lose something of great personal significance. For example, when we break up a close relationship we lose a confidante. The event can involve psychological aspects, such as loss of support from the ex-partner or love of a dying parent, harm to one's self-esteem with the loss of a job, or even physical harm and loss from the diagnosis of a terminal illness.

Threat appraisals are made when we believe the event will be extremely demanding and will put us at risk for damage. If you think that your bad performance on an upcoming project can severely ruin your reputation, or that taking part in a certain race will hurt your body, you are seeing the project or race as a threat. Challenge appraisals occur in situations when we believe that we can grow from dealing with the event and may even look at the positive ways that we can benefit from an event. For example, you can view an exam as harmful to your self-esteem and a threat if you expect to do badly, or as a challenge to your intelligence and how much you have studied. A primary appraisal can be heavily influenced by the stake we have in the outcome of the event (Lazarus, 1991), or how good we are at the challenging task (Liu & Li, 2018). A primary appraisal is also tied to quality of life in caregivers and patients with chronic illnesses (La & Yun, 2017).

After we make a primary appraisal, we assess whether we have the necessary resources to cope with the event. During **secondary appraisal** we essentially determine whether we can deal with the event and how we can cope. We may think about the social support we have, who can help us, and what exactly can be done. We ask ourselves, "Do I have what it takes to cope?" The answer is critical. If the answer is "no," and we appraised the event as being harmful and threatening and determined that we do not have the resources to cope, then the event is a stressor. If we appraised the event as a challenge and feel that we have the resources to deal with it, the event remains just that—an event. Cognitive appraisals can play a significant role in specific situations such as responding to a laboratory stressor (O'Connor, Wilson, & Lawton, 2017) and to our psychological health in general (Gomes, Faria, & Lopes, 2016). All along this process there is often cognitive reappraisal taking place during which we can change how we view the situation. As Shakespeare's Hamlet said, "There is nothing either good or bad, but thinking makes it so."

Synthesize, Evaluate, Apply

- What are the different factors that make it difficult to define stress?
- What are the pros and cons of the different theories of stress?
- How can you merge the different theories of stress?

FACTORS INFLUENCING OUR APPRAISALS

Many factors contribute to appraisals of events (Table 5.5). The duration of an event can play an important role in the process. Acute or short-term events may be appraised differently from chronic or long-term events. For example, you may not worry too much if you know that you will have houseguests for a weekend. You know that even though your routine is going to be disrupted, it will not be for too long. You will have an entirely different reaction if, on the other hand, you hear that your in-laws will be staying with you for 3 months. Similarly, acute physical threats, such as taking a wrong turn and driving through a dangerous part of town, can have very different effects from chronic physical threats, such as living in a high-crime neighborhood (Anderson, Akeeb, Lavela, Chen, & Mellman, 2017).

Events can have either a positive or negative **valence**. This dimension of stress is more straightforward. Some events are automatically more threatening on the surface, such as having

▼ TABLE 5.5

Main Dimensions of Stress

Duration: Acute vs. chronic	**Predictability:** Predictable vs. unpredictable
Valence: Negative vs. positive	**Definition:** Ambiguous vs. clear cut
Control: Having control leads to longevity	**Centrality:** Proximity to cause

to speak in front of 500 people or being the victim of a crime. Others can be positive on the surface, such as getting married. However, positive events can involve a lot of demands on your mind and body such as planning and coordinating the event. The valence of an event often is colored by our emotional memories of similar events. We store emotional memories with other details of the event (Feldman Barrett, 2017), and these can influence future appraisals. A negative experience of public speaking in the past can influence our appraisal of doing it again in the future.

Control is another important feature in stress. When we believe that we have control over a situation, the situation is less likely to be stressful. Knowing that you are capable of changing the event is less stressful than not having any control over it. In a classic study demonstrating the positive effects of control, researchers gave 91 nursing home residents extra control over their day-to-day activities, their menus, and a little plant (they were told that they were completely responsible for the care of the plant). They were told that they were also responsible for themselves and their day-to-day lives. In contrast, a similar group of residents was given a communication emphasizing that staff members were responsible for them and planned their activities. The comparison group had no control over aspects of their lives, such as their menus. After 6 months, the group with control was significantly better off (Langer & Rodin, 1976).

Control can make a difference in how we cope with diseases, such as Type 2 diabetes and coronary heart disease (Thakur et al., 2017). If you monitor what you eat and how much exercise you get, you reduce your chances of having a heart attack or getting diabetes (Ornish et al., 1998). Knowing that you can control the course of these diseases (based on your lifestyle choices) makes the diagnosis of coronary heart disease and diabetes less stressful. Having cognitive control also helps prevent episodes of **post-traumatic stress disorder** (PTSD; Bomyea, Amir, & Lang, 2012).

Predictability is related to control. Think about sitting in a dentist's chair. If the dentist needs to use the drill but you have no idea how long the drilling is going to last, you will be stressed. Being able to predict how long a drill is going to be used reduces stress. Research from the first Gulf War showed that when Israel was targeted, the citizens' ability to predict what the missiles held greatly reduced their stress. When the missiles first rained down, many people were hospitalized *just from the trauma* of not knowing whether the warheads contained chemical weapons (Wolfe & Proctor, 1996). In a similar wartime study, when a signal preceded an oncoming missile attack, this predictability of stress led to a reduction in the number of stress-related problems reported (Rosenhan & Seligman, 1989). Not being able to predict the onset of a stressor can, not surprisingly, also interfere with sleep (Yang, Wellman, Ambrozewicz, & Sanford, 2011).

Not having all the details about an event, not being able to tolerate ambiguity, or not having the mental resources to understand fully what needs to be done in a certain case may make the outcome of an event unpredictable and stressful (Kebelo & Rao, 2012; Tomono, 2010). For example, patients in a veterans' hospital did not perceive scheduled medical examinations to be stressful when information about medical procedures was provided (Mischel, 1984). Hence the **definition** of the event is also important. Ambiguous events are a lot more stressful than are clear-cut ones, an issue that also applies to jobs where the responsibilities are not well defined. In fact, new research is aimed at designing better measures of work role ambiguity (Bowling et al., 2017). More on this later in this chapter.

Synthesize, Evaluate, Apply

- What are the key dimensions in which stress can vary?
- How do you think the dimensions of stress can influence how you cope with stress?
- Does an event have to be consciously experienced to be stressful? Why or why not?

THE ROLE OF CULTURE IN APPRAISAL

Culture influences both the appraisal of stress and the experience of stress. Given the central role of appraisal to the process of stress, anything that influences your appraisals correspondingly can influence how much stress you experience. One major influence on appraisals is culture.

Different cultural groups have different expectations for various aspects of life, and these different expectations can make a low-threat event to one cultural group be a high-threat event to another group. For example, European Americans customarily look one another in the eye when speaking (Galanti, 2015). This same behavior is considered rude among many Asian Americans. This difference between ethnicities is also influenced by cultural gender roles. In some cultures, it is impolite for a woman to look a man directly in the eyes and the converse, or even to have the most basic physical contact. Cultural differences can lead to many stressful situations, especially in the context of health care (Wendorf, Brouwer, & Mosack, 2014). Imagine the stress a male Asian American patient might experience when being examined by a female European American doctor. Interactions such as these between doctors and patients of different cultures and genders can sometimes be strained, as we will discuss in more detail in Chapter 9.

Culture also influences the experience of stress. Not everyone in the United States is treated in the same way. Therefore, members of some cultural groups may experience more stress than others (Van Dyke et al., 2017). Ethnic minority women living with HIV face multiple stigmas that lead to overwhelming levels of stress (Lopez, Antoni, Fekete, & Penedo, 2012). In a different domain, it can be stressful for a female manager to work with a group of male managers (Bourg Carter, 2011). Age often interacts with gender to differentially influence how much stress someone experiences (Rauschenbach & Hertel, 2011). Adolescent girls, for example, experience some of the highest levels of stress among children (Starrs et al., 2017).

Together with age and gender cultural differences, some of the most critical differences in the experience of stress are due to race and ethnicity (Carter, Muchow, & Pieterse, 2017). It may be stressful for a white European American to live in a predominantly African American neighborhood or for an African American to live in a predominantly White European American neighborhood. It is stressful for many Black men and women to live in society in general because they fear mistreatment. In 2016 and 2017 a number of high-profile cases involving the shooting of unarmed Black men by police made many Americans take a closer look at race and crime and policing.

Many minority groups experience high levels of stress because of their ethnicity, race, or religious beliefs. This discomfort is highlighted in the 2018 Academy Award–winning *Get Out* in which a White woman takes her Black boyfriend to stay with her parents who live in an all-White community. His discomfort is captured well and the movie puts a finger on what many African Americans feel. Many cities in North America have ethnic enclaves that may make outsiders feel unwelcome. For example, driving through a Chinatown in New York, Toronto, or San Francisco and not being Chinese or strolling through Little Havana in Miami and not being Cuban or through Little Italy in Boston and not being Italian can be stressful to many. Of course, a large part of the stress may be in the appraisal and the mind of the perceiver, but as we know, real or not, even a perception of stress is bad for our bodies.

Cultural differences in appraisal and in exposure to situations have led to the formulation of multicultural models of the stress process. Hobfoll (2011) directs our attention to how the appraisal process can be biased by a range of conscious and nonconscious processes, such as cultural and familial norms. If your family has raised you to fear a certain group (e.g., White police officers) you are going to be conditioned to fear persons of that group. In a similar vein, Slavin, Rainer, McCreary, and Gowda (1991) expanded Lazarus and Folkman's (1984) **cognitive appraisal model** of stress to include a number of culture-specific dimensions (Figure 5.5).

Slavin et al. (1991) argued that the occurrence of potentially stressful events can vary based on minority status, discrimination, or specific cultural customs. Furthermore, the primary appraisal of the occurring event can be biased by how the culture interprets the event. Similarly, the secondary appraisal, coping efforts, and final outcomes can be modified by the culture of

▼ FIGURE 5.5

A Cultural Model of the Stress Response

Basic model	Major Stressors Minor Stressors →	Primary Appraisal →	Secondary Appraisal →	Coping →	Major Outcomes & Adjustment
Additional Cultural Factors	• Minority status stress • Discrimination • Socio-economic status stress • Specific customs	• Cultural and familial definitions of the event • Fill with cultural frame of understanding	• Culture-specific behavioral options • Ethnic identity and beliefs about group • Cultural variations in family, community, and social support	• Culture specific coping and rituals • Possible sanctions against cultural coping strategies • Roll of acculturation in skill acquisition	• Cultural norms regarding symptom expression • Cultural norms for behavior

the individual. For example, some cultural groups (e.g., Mexican Americans and African Americans) have closer family ties and more-active social support networks that could influence secondary appraisals. These cultural differences can even be seen at the level of the family (influenced by, but not necessarily completely due to, race or ethnicity). Some family cultural environments, based on the way parents raise their children, can be a lot more stressful than others. Families in which both parents are always fighting or that experience low socioeconomic levels that lead to hardships can be stressful (Repetti, Taylor, & Seeman, 2002).

STRESS AND PSYCHOPATHOLOGY: THE DIATHESIS-STRESS MODEL

The relationship between stress and psychopathology has been well documented in adolescents and younger children (Compas et al., 2001) and in adults (Hammen, 2003). Yet, not everyone who experiences stressful life events and chronic stress develops psychological disorders (Gurung & Roethel, 2009).

To explain this, one of the main frameworks in which the etiology of psychopathology is described is through the diathesis-stress model (Tiegel, 2017). This multidimensional model, first described in the context of schizophrenia (Bleuler, 1963), involves a relationship between vulnerable predispositions (diathesis) and stress as contributors to the development of psychopathology. The theory posits that stress may serve as an activator of the diathesis, leading to the development and manifestation of psychopathology (Monroe & Simons, 1991). Individuals with a diathesis (a vulnerability) who are exposed to significant stress may be more likely to develop mental disorders than individuals who do not have similar predispositions (Pruessner, Cullen, Aas, & Walker, 2017).

For individuals suffering from a mental disorder, the occurrence of stressful life events may act to further sensitize the individual to subsequent stressful life events and may initiate future episodes or relapses of the mental disorder, as seen with major depressive disorder (Braet, Van Vlierberghe, Vandevivere, Theuwis, & Bosmans, 2013) and schizophrenia (Pruessner et al., 2017).

CULTURE AS A CRITICAL STRESSOR

Culture may act as a stressor in the diathesis-stress model of psychopathology, activating certain vulnerabilities and predispositions that may lead to the emergence of psychopathology (Krueger, Saint Onge, & Chang, 2011). In a study comparing differences in psychological distress, social stress, and resources in a sample of culturally diverse adolescents, Hispanic and Asian American teens reported higher levels of social stress, were more likely to experience psychological distress, and had lower scores on resources in the context of family, coping, self-esteem, and SES than European American adolescents. Furthermore, compared to European American teens, Hispanic and African American teens had an increased likelihood of experiencing social stress (Choi, Meininger, & Roberts, 2006).

The interactions between physical and mental stressors and mental health issues are clearly seen in studies of specific ethnic groups such as American Indians. American Indians have a high risk of developing mental health disorders and have higher numbers of this population in need of mental health services (Peters et al., 2014). Two major studies document the magnitude of this problem. Data from the National Health Interview Survey indicated that American Indians were significantly more likely to report experiencing recent serious psychological distress and feelings of helplessness compared to all other ethnic groups surveyed (Barnes, Adams, & Powell-Griner, 2005). Data from the Behavioral Risk Factor Surveillance System (BRFSS) regarding health-related quality of life show that during the years 2000 through 2004, American Indians experienced the greatest mean number of mentally unhealthy days per month (4.8). They also experienced the greatest percentage of frequent mental distress, defined as 14 or more unhealthy days in a month (15.1%), compared to all the other ethnic groups in the nationwide sample (CDC, 2005). As a general survey of the mental health prevalence in American Indian populations living on or near a reservation in the Northern Plains and the Southwest area of the United States, Beals et al. (2005) found that diagnoses of alcohol dependence, post-traumatic stress disorder, and depression were the most prevalent *Diagnostic and Statistical Manual of Mental Disorders,* 4th edition (*DSM-IV*; American Psychiatric Association, 1994) diagnoses. American Indians in both tribes studied had a higher prevalence of PTSD, a higher prevalence of substance abuse, and a lower prevalence of depression, compared to a nationally representative survey documenting the prevalence of mental health disorders.

Perceived Discrimination

One of the biggest cultural chronic stressors that has serious implications for the development of poor health is perceived discrimination (Irby-Shasanmi & Leech, 2017). The current emphasis of research in race-based discrimination spans disciplines such as sociology, psychology, and neuroscience. For example, Mays, Cochran, and Barnes (2007) describe and review current perspectives in a comprehensive approach for understanding the mediating and moderating variables in the relationship between race-based discrimination and health disparities. Specifically, these perspectives are social spaces and environments, family environments and development, and physiological approaches.

A nationally representative study of discrimination viewed in the context of major discrimination and day-to-day perceived discrimination found that for all races, major discrimination was significantly correlated with psychological distress and major depression, while day-to-day perceived discrimination was significantly associated with the development of emotional problems and mental disorders such as psychological distress, depression, and generalized anxiety disorder (Kessler, Mickelson, & Williams, 1999). Recently, the study of day-to-day discrimination has expanded to focus on those events that are so subtle that sometimes they are not seen as problems (Mercer, Zeigler-Hil, Wallace, & Hayes, 2011). Such **microaggresions** are defined as everyday insults, indignities, and demeaning messages sent to people of color by well-intentioned White people who are unaware of the hidden messages they are sending (Sue, 2010). Predominantly White environments are prime contexts for producing microaggression fatigue among men and women of non-White ethnicities (Anderson & Finch, 2017).

The link between perceived discrimination and depression is common and has been found in a number of ethnic groups (Chou, 2012). In a study examining the relationship between perceived discrimination and depression and moderating variables of coping, acculturation, and ethnic social support in a sample of Korean immigrants living in Canada, Noh and Kaspar (2003) found a significant association between perceived discrimination and depression. The use of ethnic social support (i.e., support from other Koreans) moderated the relationship between perceived discrimination, emotion-focused coping, and depressive symptoms. (For more on moderation see Chapter 2; for more on coping see Chapter 6.) Individuals who used emotion-focused coping frequently and had more ethnic social support had fewer depressive symptoms, as compared to others who had less ethnic social support (Noh & Kaspar, 2003).

A significant association between perceived discrimination and depressive symptoms was also seen in a sample of immigrants from Mexico and U.S.-born individuals of Mexican descent in California. The immigrants who were highly acculturated were the most likely to have experienced perceived discrimination, followed by less-acculturated immigrants, and U.S.-born individuals of Mexican descent, who were the least likely to have experienced perceived discrimination (Finch, Kolody, & Vega, 2000). Perceived discrimination was also associated with depressive symptoms in a sample of American Indians in the upper Midwest (Whitbeck et al., 2002). However, participation in traditional activities such as powwows, in addition to familiarity with tribal languages (reflecting measures of cultural identification), decreased the association between discrimination and depression (Whitbeck et al., 2002).

There is some evidence that the effects of discrimination stress can have a stronger effect on men of color. Utsey, Payne, Jackson, and Jones (2002) found gender differences in the relationships among race-related stress, quality of life, and life satisfaction in a sample of elderly African Americans. Men in this sample had significantly higher scores than women for race-related stress in the context of institutional racism and collective racism. Data also indicated a significant relationship between institutional racism as a predictor of quality of life and life satisfaction; higher ratings of race-related stress attributed to institutional racism predicted a lower rating of quality of life and life satisfaction.

Perhaps most disturbing is that discrimination can have biological effects at the microscopic level. A recent large study looked at the association between discrimination and leukocyte telomere length, a biological marker of aging. Both African American men and women who experienced high discrimination showed shorter telomeres (Lee, Kim, & Neblett, 2017).

The negative effects of discrimination go beyond the ethnic and racial aspects of culture. Individuals in sexual minority groups may be at increased risk for suffering from mental disorders. Studies have shown that there is a higher prevalence of mental health disorders among lesbian, gay, and bisexual populations. Explanations for the increased prevalence may include sources of minority stress such as prejudice, stigmatization, and discrimination (Meyer, 2003). A study by Greenland and Taulke-Johnson (2017) found that social discrimination was a strong predictor of mental health symptoms and psychological stress in a sample of gay and bisexual men in the workplace. Furthermore, social isolation and low self-esteem were two sources of stress identified that may be viewed in the context of stemming from social discrimination.

Synthesize, Evaluate, Apply

- What are the key ways that culture can influence the experience of stress?
- Why may some cultural differences be more pertinent to the study of stress than others?
- Which of the different varieties of stress are most susceptible to cultural differences?
- What are the sociopolitical benefits and hazards of taking a cultural approach to stress?

STRESS, HORMONES, AND GENES

To a large extent the study of stress did not produce significant innovations for many years. Taylor et al.'s (2000) tend-and-befriend theory spurred a large increase in research, but the newest contributions to our understanding of stress are in the area of genetic mechanisms determining how stress leads to disease (Gruenwald, 2019; Robles, Mercado, Nooteboom, Price, & Romney, 2019).

One important mechanism involves a receptor for glucocorticoids (Sarabdjitsingh, Joëls, & de Kloet, 2012). Glucocorticoids play an important part in the breakdown of glucose and form in the adrenal cortex. A type of steroid hormone, glucocorticoids bind to their receptors, which in turn speeds up the release of anti-inflammatory proteins in the cell. You ran into the most common glucocorticoid in Chapter 4, cortisol, a key outcome of Selye's general adaption syndrome theory of stress discussed previously. In a protypical study, Chen et al. (2017) recently reviewed a large body of work linking harsh family environments to the modification of children's genes. Specifically, a proinflammatory phenotype develops that is signaled by excessive immune responses to bacterial stimuli and resistance to the anti-inflammatory properties of cortisol. Miller and Chen (2010) repeatedly measured psychological stress and immune activity in 135 female adolescents on four occasions over 1.5 years. Those raised in harsh family environments showed the proinflammatory phenotype during the follow-up analyses. The researchers introduced bacteria into blood samples taken from the children and found the exaggerated immune responses and reduction in cortisol's ability to properly regulate inflammatory responses. This reaction could eventually lead to increased sickness over time.

A similar pattern occurs with the serotonin transporter gene (Way & Taylor, 2011) and the oxytocin receptor gene (Kim et al., 2010). Similar to the harsh familial stress study, in stressful situations people with a certain variation of the serotonin transporter gene (a short allele) are more likely to be depressed (Caspi, Hariri, Holmes, Uher, & Moffitt, 2011) and show increased cardiovascular activity (Way & Taylor, 2011).

Are there effects of culture? Kim et al. (2011) examined sensitivity to cultural norms regarding emotion regulation by measuring the expression of the oxytocin receptor gene (OXTR). Given that suppressing emotions is common among East Asian cultures but not in American culture, they predicted an interaction of culture and OXTR in emotional suppression. Korean nationals and American nationals completed measures of emotion regulation and were genotyped for OXTR. Kim et al. found that among Americans, those with one form of the OXTR gene used emotional suppression less than those with another type of gene allele, whereas Koreans showed the opposite pattern.

DIFFERENT VARIETIES OF STRESSORS

Many different areas of life can be stressful. In today's world and in the health psychological literature on stress, we tend to focus on three main areas of stress that encompass the majority of life: relationships, work, and the environment. In addition, a number of physical stressors also are present in today's world. Millions of people around the world do not have enough food to eat or sufficient shelter. Many of us in North America do not experience these stressors but often create our own stressful worlds in our heads as we negotiate our situations of relationships and work.

iStockphoto.com/:AndreyPopov

▲ **Conflict.** Sometimes arguments are unavoidable, but tumultuous relationships can cause wear and tear on the mind and body.

Relationship Stress

At every stage of life, interacting with others can be potentially stressful. The adolescence period in particular is a transitional period during which the importance of the peer group increases as the importance of the family decreases (Larson & Asmussen, 1991). Levels of conflict with parents and hence interpersonal stress rise (Laursen, 1996). The large number of divorces in North America also reflects the level of relationship conflict in adulthood. A number of health psychologists are actively studying the effects of marital conflict and divorce as stressors and their effects on health.

An unhealthy close relationship can be particularly problematic not just for your state of mind but for your physiology as well. Kiecolt-Glaser, Bane, Glaser, and Malarkey (2003) collected physiological measures from 90 couples during their first year of marriage (time 1) and found that these measures related to breakups and marital satisfaction 10 years later (time 2). Compared with those who remained together, the stress hormone levels (e.g., epinephrine) of divorced couples were 34% higher during conflict discussions and 22% higher throughout the day, and both epinephrine and norepinephrine levels were 16% higher at night. Couples whose marriages were troubled at time 2 produced 34% more norepinephrine during conflict, 24% more norepinephrine during the daytime, and 17% more during nighttime hours at time 1 than the couples with untroubled marriages.

The family is another area of focus in the context of stress and relationships. The family cycle has distinct phases—partner selection, marital adjustment, raising and caring for children, having children leave the home, and retirement—each of which can be associated with stressors (Aldwin, 1994; Patterson, 2002). The ways parents deal with stress can serve as critical models for how children deal with stress and can influence the children's own health as well (Hilliard, Monaghan, Cogen, & Streisand, 2011). Events such as the death of a parent, divorce, the departure of a child to college or to the military, the loss of income, hospitalization, a long-term chronic illness of a family member, or imprisonment of a family member can be stressful and need to be adjusted to. A number of stress theories have been devised, especially to focus on family dynamics and stress (e.g., Hill, 1949; Patterson & Garwick, 1994; Santiago, Etter, Wadsworth, & Raviv, 2012), that closely parallel Lazarus' (1991) cognitive appraisal model described above.

Abuse is one family stressor receiving great attention today. There is growing focus on spouse and child abuse (MacKenzie, Kotch, Lee, Augsberger, & Hutto, 2011) and violence during pregnancy (e.g., Arslantaş et al., 2012). In fact, family violence may be a more common problem for pregnant women than some conditions for which they are routinely screened and evaluated.

iStockphoto.com/ gilaxia

▲ **Daily Grind.** Workload can be a major form of stress.

Work Stress

A 2017 APA poll reported that most North Americans felt work was their top stressor (APA, 2017). Job stress can produce physical health problems, psychological distress, and behavioral changes. On a physical level, there are many thousands of deaths on the job every year. Day-to-day stress can make a person more likely to develop physical problems later.

Occupational stress even has an entry in the *DSM-IV* (American Psychiatric Association, 1994), the main tool used to diagnose clinical disorders. Some symptoms of work stress include feelings of frustration, anger, and resentment; lowered self-esteem; boredom; job dissatisfaction; mental fatigue; loss of concentration; loss of spontaneity and creativity; and emotional hyperactivity. Know anyone experiencing any of these? Maybe this person should look at how happy he or she is at work. Psychologically speaking, work stress can arise from a number of factors, many of which interact (Barr, 2017):

1. Cognitive overload: having too much to do
2. Role conflict: being unsure of one's job description
3. Ambiguity: not knowing what one is supposed to be doing
4. Discrimination: job ceilings that prevent one from rising in the ranks
5. Not getting promoted because of sexism, ageism, or other prejudices
6. Poor social networks preventing outlets to process job stress
7. Lack of control over what one is doing and when it is done
8. Multiple roles that need to be balanced
9. Not being challenged enough

At first glance it may seem like the last item should not be a problem. Why would someone not want a comfortable, easy job? Everly and Girdano (1980) described and documented deprivational stress, a form of stress resulting from a job that fails to maintain the worker's interest and attention. The National Institute for Occupational Safety and Health even described assembly-line hysteria, a condition in which workers with boring, repetitive jobs display symptoms of nausea, muscle weakness, headaches, and blurry vision, all without any physical basis. Lacking a physical cause, these symptoms are more likely a psychological consequence of boredom.

If a person is unhappy or stressed at work there are consequences for both the individual and for people close to the individual. Work stress has been shown to spill over into family life and personal interactions (Hamaideh, 2012; Wang et al., 2007). For example, Doumas, Margolin, and John (2003) had 49 husbands and wives separately complete daily diaries addressing questions about work experiences, health-promoting behaviors, and marital interactions over 42 consecutive days. The researchers found that spouses reported more-positive marital interactions on days when they worked less.

Many different theories demonstrate the interconnectedness of the work and home spheres. This interconnectedness is referred to as a **stress contagion effect** (Mo-Yeol & Yun-Chul, 2017; Voydanoff, 2002). Bolger, DeLongis, Kessler, and Wethington (1989) first recognized and defined two specific types of stress contagion: spillover and crossover. **Spillover** refers to the intra-individual transmission of stress, when stress occurring in one domain of an individual's life affects other domains of his or her life (Westman & Etizon, 1995). Often stress from the workplace spills over to influence parenting and spousal relationships (Malinen, Rönkä, Sevón, & Schoebi, 2017). In comparison, **crossover** is the transmission of stress *between* individuals. Crossover occurs when stress or strain experienced by an individual affects the stress or strain of another individual (Westman & Vinokur, 1998). Crossover can occur between workers at a worksite or between an employee and his or her family.

The majority of studies on work stress have been cross-sectional, focusing on the crossover from the husband to the wife. Most studies show positive correlations between occupational stressors and spouse's stress or strain (Jones & Fletcher, 1993; Westman, 2001). Of note, crossover studies examining crossover from wives to husbands have not produced any consistent findings (Westman, 2001), and the literature suggests that a wife tends to be more vulnerable to her husband's stress than a husband is to his wife's stress.

The work stress contagion findings are explained by a combination of ecological theory and role theory. **Ecological theory** (Bronfrenbrenner, 1977) identifies different levels or systems in which the individual acts. Work and home domains are examples of **microsystems**. A microsystem includes the activities and roles the individual takes on in a particular setting. A **mesosystem** contains the relationships and interactions between microsystems at a specific point in time. Bronfenbrenner's concept of **reciprocity** recognizes that systems are not independent of one another but are in constant interaction. Consequently, elements of the work domain affect elements of the home domain, and vice versa.

According to the **role theory** of Kahn, Wolfe, Quinn, Snoek, and Rosenthal (1964), stress contagion from work to home rises as a person gains more roles and as those roles lack definition. A role is the set of behaviors to be performed and is determined by one's own perceptions and the expectations of others. As an individual accumulates roles, the quantity and incompatibility of role demands increase. An individual experiences role strain that results in increased role conflict and ambiguity (Voydanoff, 2002). **Role ambiguity** is the degree to which required information regarding role expectations are available, clear, and communicated to the focal person. When companies establish new positions, the expectation for what someone in that position has to do is often undefined. Someone in this new position or in any position for which the job description is inadequate can experience role ambiguity. **Role conflict** is the incompatibility of expectations for a given role and between different roles. For example, a job may require you to evaluate a member of your own work team, when the resulting evaluation contributes to your raise or bonus. In this case you have a conflict between making an accurate assessment and potentially hurting your own pay.

Environmental Stress

Working and living in a noisy environment can lead to many problems. Noise can even retard learning in children (Bronzaft & McCarthy, 1975). Children living close to an airport where constant roars of jet engines interrupt their daily lives were found to have higher levels of stress and more learning difficulties than students not living close to an airport (Cohen, Evans, Krantz, & Stokols, 1980). In a similar study, Cohen, Glass, and Singer (1973) showed that children living in noisy homes near busy roadways had greater difficulties with reading tasks than did children who lived in quiet homes. In a classic series of studies on the effects of noise, Glass and Singer (1972) had students work on different tasks and then exposed them to bursts of sound. Unpredictable bursts of sound hindered their performance the most, but those students who faced consistent background sounds during early tasks performed badly on later tasks. Noise can play a large role in how stressed we feel and often implicitly influences our well-being.

Just as noise can be a problem, crowding can also be stressful. If you grew up in a city or town with a population of between 30,000 and 100,000 or less, your experiences with crowding are very different from mine. I grew up in Mumbai (previously called Bombay), a city with a population tipping the scales at more than 20 million people. Overcrowding can often produce negative moods for men (Freedman, 1975; not so much for women in support of the tend-and-befriend theory), physiological arousal (e.g., higher blood pressure), increased illness, more aggression, and a host of other stressful outcomes. Even if you do not live in a big city, you can see the effects of crowding at large gatherings. Large rock concerts, state fairs, or amusement parks during holiday weekends can become overcrowded, making people feel stressed and frustrated.

Environmental stressors can be divided into three main categories: background stressors, natural disaster stressors, and techno-political stressors. **Background stressors** include crowding and noise, together with air pollution and chemical pollution (Fisher, Bell, & Baum, 1984). All of these can be long-term stressors and affect a large number of people. A second major category of environmental stressors is **natural disaster stressors**. These are short-term stressors and are often more severe than long-term stressors. For example, natural disasters such as flooding, earthquakes, and hurricanes can kill thousands of people, and survivors often experience severe psychological consequences lasting a lifetime (Leach, 1995; Norris, Byrne, & Diaz, 2002).

Take Hurricane Katrina. It hit New Orleans in 2005 and damaged 80% of the city. Almost the entire city was evacuated, and close to 2,000 died (Brunkard, Namulanda, & Ratard, 2008).

AP Photo/ David J. Phillip

▲ **Environmental Stress.** Natural events are a form of environmental stress. Here, rescue boats float on a flooded street as people are evacuated from rising floodwaters brought on by Tropical Storm Harvey in Houston. The National Hurricane Center's official report on Harvey shows that more than 80 people died, and Harvey caused more than $150 billion in damage.

Not surprisingly, this major disaster had stressful effects resulting in a range of symptoms, including diagnoses of post-traumatic stress disorder (PTSD), a specific form of mental illness related to the experience of severe stress, that impacted thousands (Arcaya et al., 2017; Trivedi, 2019). Two years after Katrina, the rate of PTSD was ten times higher in New Orleans than in the general public. The majority of adults who developed PTSD did not recover within 18–27 months (McLaughlin et al., 2011) and the effects were worse for those with pre-Katrina mental illnesses (Constans et al., 2012).

The third category of stressors can be called **techno-political stressors**. Although these types of stressors can be unpredictable and uncontrollable like natural disasters, they are directly linked to technological or political causes. Some examples are nuclear reactor accidents (e.g., Three Mile Island in Pennsylvania and Chernobyl near the Ukraine border), chemical plant accidents (e.g., the Union Carbide accident in Bhopal, India), and dam-related flooding (e.g., Buffalo Creek in West Virginia). Political tragedies, such as wars and acts of terrorism, are also extremely stressful. A longitudinal study of more than 2,000 adults found that stress responses to the 9/11 attacks predicted increased heart problems even 3 years after the attacks (Holman et al., 2008).

A number of other factors are stressful even though at first they do not appear to be. Many of us wish we had less to do and become stressed trying to complete everything that we have to do. However, not having enough to do can also be stressful. Bexton, Heron, and Scott (1954) paid students to just lie in bed and sleep. This seems pretty easy, right? Well, the twist was that they had to lie in a cubicle with their hands and arms padded and with glasses on that blocked their vision. They could not hear any outside sounds. No subject could do it for more than 3 days, and all reported extreme boredom, restlessness, and growing levels of stress, thus proving that boredom and low levels of sensory stimulation can be stressful too.

CONSEQUENCES OF STRESS

In a nutshell, stress can make a person sick (Gruenwalk, 2018). Stress can have a variety of direct physiological effects on the body: damage to the heart (Johnston, Tuomisto, & Patching, 2008), suppression of the immune system and neuronal damage (Adamo, 2016; Segerstrom, 2007), an increase in GI symptoms (Blanchard et al., 2008), and irritable bowel syndrome (Levenson, 2007). Many different physiological systems interact when we are stressed (Ali, Nitschke, Cooperman, & Pruessner, 2017). Stress can also shape how we respond to challenges (Crum, Akinola, Martin, & Faith, 2017) with direct cognitive and behavioral effects such as increasing risky decision making (Uy & Galvan, 2017) and smoking (Wiggert, Wilhelm, Nakajima, & al'Absi, 2016). Stress can also make one more resilient (Dooley, Slavich, Moreno, & Bower, 2017) and improve memory for emotional aspects of events (Buchanan & Tranel, 2008). Stress also can have secondary effects such as exacerbating illnesses and delaying recovery (see Dougall & Baum, 2002). Figure 5.6 illustrates some stress-related illnesses.

Most of the early major theories of stress (e.g., Selye and Cannon) paid a lot of attention to the physiological changes in the body that accompany the experience of stress. There is a good reason for that. A lot happens in our body when we get stressed. For example, the sympathetic nervous system has connections all over the body (nerves project all over the body from the brain and spinal cord) from sweat gland to muscles and hair follicles, all of which are stimulated to some extent during stress. We have also discussed the two main systems that are activated: the HPA axis releasing corticosteroids and SAM activation releasing norepinephrine and epinephrine. From a practical standpoint, the activation of these systems is important and critical.

▼ FIGURE 5.6

Stress-Induced Illness

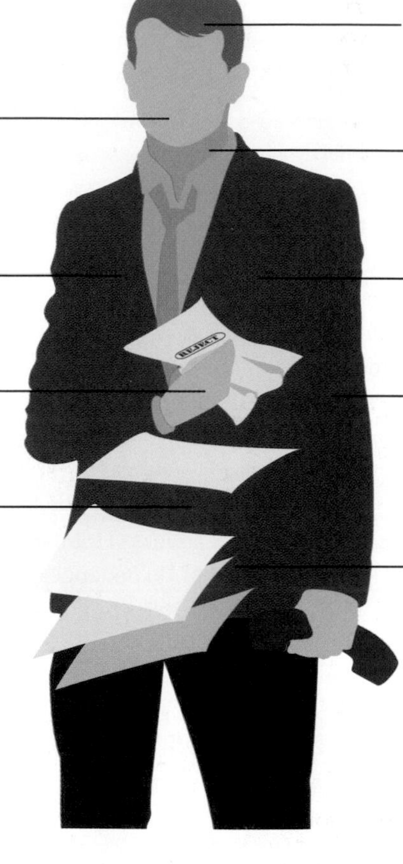

They prepare our bodies to deal with stressors. A problem arises when we experience stress for a long time. Chronic, long-term stressors cause wear and tear on body systems, leading to tissue damage and irregular responding, hypertension, and ulcers (Levenson, 2007). How long is too long? The answer to that question depends on the individual.

Chronic stress can lead to other physiological consequences. Some people develop heart problems or loss of appetite. Others develop sexual dysfunction (e.g., men are unable to achieve or maintain an erection), skin problems (e.g., rashes), or nervous tics (e.g., uncontrollable jerky movements or winking). Chronic stress is a problem for many people and can be either objective (living in a noisy neighborhood) or subjective (overworking week after week and month after month). Health psychologists who focus directly on **allostatic load**, or the effects of chronic stress, have unearthed some disturbing findings (McEwen, 1998).

Allostasis is defined as the ability to achieve stability through change (McEwen & Lasley, 2007). Our environments keep changing, putting our body systems through various fluctuations to adjust to them. The different forces that shake our homeostatic balance stretch our systems to act like rubber bands. It is critical to our survival that our systems go back to their original shape and function like a taut rubber band does when it is released. With chronic stress, wear and tear on the body result from chronic overactivity or underactivity of allostatic systems (i.e., a load). Being under an allostatic load (AL) can have three main consequences.

Look at Figure 5.7. The first line represents normal responses to stress (a). For most acute stressors, our sympathetic system is activated before and during the event (e.g., you have to make an oral presentation), and we adapt afterwards. Even if this acute stressor is repeated a few times (e.g., you have to give a number of talks in a month), the healthy stress response shows an

▼ FIGURE 5.7

Main Effects of Allostatic Load

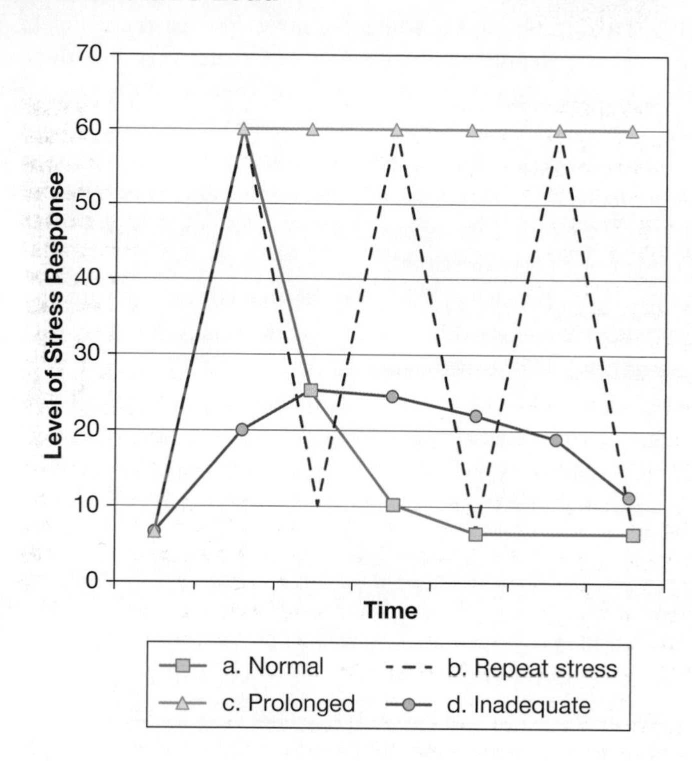

activation followed by a return to baseline functioning. In the case of chronic stress (e.g., living in a high-crime neighborhood where there are frequent stressors), AL is seen when the post-stress adaptation or the normal lessening of the response for repeat stressors is not seen (b). You still respond, but it is a lower activation each time. Correspondingly, there is a prolonged exposure to the different stress hormones. This extra exposure can lead to a host of problems, such as coronary heart disease. Another result of AL takes place when our body is unable to shut off the stress response after the stressor stops. This again leads to extended exposure to stress hormones.

The final case is system malfunctions in the response to stress. One system may not work, and other systems overcompensate. This also leads to extended exposure to stress hormones.

Bruce McEwen and colleagues have identified many markers of AL (McEwen & Wingfield, 2003). Major markers include hypertension (high blood pressure), atherosclerosis (plaque deposits on arteries), fat staying in the system longer, higher waist-to-hip ratios (when the body stores fat at the waist and not at the hips), and sleep disruption. In an example of how these markers are used that also illustrates some cultural differences, Deuster, Su Jong, Remaley, and Poth (2011) summed measures of fitness, body fat, C-reactive protein (CRP), mood, social support, blood pressure, sleep and exercise habits, coping, and insulin responses. They found that African Americans have significantly higher allostatic load scores than European Americans. Significantly more African Americans score greater than 3 (67.9%) than European Americans (48.9%).

Extended stress also interferes with the immune system (more on this in Chapter 13) and with memory. Long-term stress actually destroys neurons in the hippocampus (they grow back if the stress is short term). Long-term stress and allostatic load as well as short-term stressors also have negative effects on our behavior, our thoughts or cognition, and our feelings. Going beyond physiology, stress makes us act, feel, and think differently.

Stress affects one's mood, behavior, problem solving, motivations, and goals and can cause distraction, memory lapses, and a host of other psychological consequences (Dougall & Baum, 2002). You are more likely to get depressed and be fearful when you are stressed, angry, or aggravated. People under stress often lose their tempers and are not as patient as they normally would be. In an interesting study about the effects of stress on memory, Cahill, Prins, Weber, and McGaugh (1994) told two groups of students a story. The experimental group heard about a boy who had an accident that amputated his legs, which were subsequently reattached (a very stressful situation). The control group heard a neutral version of the story in which the boy watched what was happening in a hospital. Half the participants in each group received a drug that blocked the action of norepinephrine, thereby reducing stress; the other half got a placebo. A week later all participants were asked to recall as many elements of the story as they could. The participants in the stress condition who received the placebo (and hence felt the effects of stress) remembered the least amount of information.

Stress also influences our behaviors. When we are stressed, we often are busy thinking about the cause of the stress, which allows our attention to other tasks to suffer. Paying bills on time, remembering appointments, taking medicines, watering plants, or caring for a pet can all be negatively affected (Baba, Jamal, & Tourigny, 1998; Kompier & DiMartino, 1995; McNally, 1997). Obviously, the quality of work and the nature of interactions with friends and colleagues can also suffer. In some cases, people may not be able to sleep and may experience changes in their eating and drinking behavior (Conway, Vickers, Weid, & Rahe, 1981; Mellman, 1997).

POST-TRAUMATIC STRESS DISORDER

Post-traumatic stress disorder (PTSD) is a psychological disorder that is a possible consequence of a major stressful event. The PTSD diagnosis includes a prerequisite traumatic event, three subsets of symptom types (e.g., flashbacks), a requisite duration of symptoms beyond 1 month after the associated event, and a significant decrease in functioning (Helsley, 2008). Major symptoms include migraine headaches or poor respiratory health (Arcaya et al., 2017; Waszczuk et al., 2017). Recently, psychologists have argued that PTSD can occur even if the event is not experienced directly (i.e., the event is seen on television). Evidence surrounding 9/11 supports this perspective (Marshall et al., 2007). There have been many controversies surrounding this disorder such as the recent broadening of the definition of the traumatic event that is required to meet a diagnosis for PTSD and the political climate surrounding its conception (Yeomans & Forman, 2009).

In one of the biggest reviews of studies on PTSD, Ozer, Best, Lipsey, and Weiss (2003) reviewed 2,647 studies of PTSD and found that psychological processes at the time of or around the trauma (i.e., peritraumatic) and not prior characteristics (e.g., family history, prior trauma, and prior adjustment) are the strongest predictors of PTSD. Ozer et al. (2003) also noted that for a long period of time the study of extreme responses to stress centered around war but have since expanded to other stressors such as environmental stress (see above) and sexual assault (Campbell, Greeson, Bybee, & Raja, 2008). Even parents whose children experience severe accidents such as burns can experience PTSD (Egberts, van de Schoot, Geenen, & Van Loey, 2017).

There is considerable cultural variability in PTSD prevalence. For example, differences in traumatic stress across gender have been observed in both the United States and Mexico after landfall of comparable hurricanes (Norris, Perilla, Ibanez, & Murphy, 2001). Al-Saffar, Borga, Edman, and Hallstrom (2003) sampled foreign nationals (from Iran, Turkey, and Saudi Arabia) who had immigrated to Sweden at least 4 years prior to the study. All participants had previous trauma exposure, yet response across ethnic differences was highly variable. The study found the presence of PTSD in 69% of the Iranians, 59% of the Saudis, 53% of the Turks, and only 29% of the Swedes.

A growing number of international epidemiological studies conclude that PTSD is found across cultures, particularly in samples exposed to violence (Marsella & Christopher, 2004; Yeomans & Forman, 2009). Nonetheless, the sole application of the PTSD model may not be the most useful model around which to focus prevention and treatment services across cultures. De Jong (2005), despite having researched PTSD prevalence rates around the globe, articulates the need to put more attention on other mental health issues that remain underinvestigated, such as mood disorders, somatoform disorder, dissociative disorders, and other anxiety disorders. PTSD may not always be the best diagnosis, covering other problems. For example, Laban et al. (2005) found that among Iraqi asylum seekers, postmigration challenges in their daily life were the best predictors of psychopathology, even more so than traumatic events themselves.

Stress has many different causes, can be studied in different ways, and has many different effects. In the next chapter we shall examine the different ways to cope.

Synthesize, Evaluate, Apply

- How can your knowledge of Lazarus's theory reduce relationship stress?
- What strategies and structures can employers use to keep work stress at a minimum?
- How can the results of spillover and contagion studies be applied to improving family life?
- What do you think are the most potent consequences of stress?

APPLICATION SHOWCASE

STRESS REALLY CAN KILL: THE BASKERVILLE EFFECT, CULTURE, AND STRESS

Many crime and mystery buffs regard the classic Sherlock Holmes tale, *The Hound of the Baskervilles,* as one of the best ways to be introduced to author Sir Arthur Conan Doyle's legendary detective. (Spoiler alert: If you have not read it yet but are tempted, skip this section because it will reveal a major plot element.) Perhaps you had your introduction via Benedict Cumberbatch's interpretation of the same character. In the novel, the fictional Charles Baskerville dies as a result of the stress of running into the fierce hound of the book's title. The book has all the elements of a good read: family curses, smart detective work, and rich descriptions of the English moors. Key point: man dies of fright. Does this literary case study have real-life parallels? There are tales of Australian Aborigines dying if they are cursed: healthy people can keel over and die from one day to the next if told they are cursed. The sociologist David Phillips and colleagues provide some provocative data on the Chinese and Japanese (Phillips et al., 2001). Also, the University of California, San Diego, team showed that heart attacks actually increase on psychologically stressful unlucky days.

Phillips et al. (2001) compared the death certificates of more than 200,000 Chinese Americans and Japanese Americans with 47,000 European Americans. The researchers matched deaths by cause, patient status, sex, age, and marital status, and controlled for seasonal differences. The findings were astounding: for the Chinese Americans and Japanese Americans, deaths peaked on the fourth day of the month. On such days, there was a 13% increase in deaths. No such pattern existed for the European Americans.

Many Chinese and Japanese consider the number four to be unlucky. In fact, in Mandarin, Cantonese, and Japanese, the number four (4) is pronounced quite similar to the word "death" (Milne, 2002). Throughout China and Japan, the number is not used in numbering floors or rooms in hospitals. In North America, the number 13 is the one to fear. The bottom line is that superstition can be stressful. If you believe bad things will happen on a certain day, there is a chance they will. This phenomenon, referred to by social psychologists as a **self-fulfilling prophecy** (Merton, 2010; see Chapters 8 and 9), has only recently been found to also result in powerful behavior

(Continued)

(Continued)

changes (see Madon et al., 2008, for self-fulfilling prophecy and drinking behavior). The suggestion from the Phillips et al. (2001) data is that the stress of an unlucky day may be strong enough to cause physiological damage. This takes the self-fulfilling prophecy to a whole new level.

The Baskerville effect, as this special type of self-fulfilling prophecy has come to be called, could not be explained in any other way. The ethnic groups who fear the number 4 seem more likely to die of cardiac arrest on the fourth of the month. This finding has some major implications for health psychologists and health-care practitioners, because it highlights the need to take into account patients' beliefs and superstitions. If an American Indian or Hindu patient comes into a hospital room with a black or red thread tied around his or her wrist and the doctors or nurses have it cut off, the patient's health could be at stake. American Indians (see Chapter 3) and Hindus both use sacred threads. Sometimes the threads are part of healing ceremonies such as sweat lodges. People wearing the thread may believe that their health is dependent on the string and cutting it off may prove to be a psychological affront that could tip the balance between fighting the good fight and throwing in the towel. The Baskerville effect certainly seems to suggest that this may be the case. Different cultural groups are superstitious about or fear different things. Being sensitive to these differences and helping people cope, even with stressors that may seem silly, can clearly be very important to their well-being. Chapter 6 tells the full story of coping and resilience.

CHAPTER REVIEW

SUMMARY ▶▶

- Stress is the physiological and psychological experience of disruption to our homeostatic balance. We are stressed any time excessive demands are placed on our body and mind. Stressors are factors that disrupt our homeostasis. Early stressors were acute and more physical in nature. Today stressors are long term and more psychological in nature.
- Stress activates the nervous system, especially the sympathetic nervous system, which in turn mobilizes the body for action. The parasympathetic system restores the body to rest after the stressor ends. The physiological stress response is characterized by the activation of different physiological pathways and the release of stress hormones.
- There are four major theories of stress. Cannon described the fight-or-flight response, which involves sympathetic adrenal medulla activation and the release of catecholamines. Selye described the general adaptation syndrome involving hypothalamic-pituitary-adrenal axis activation and the release of cortisol. Lazarus described a cognitive appraisal model of stress with primary and secondary appraisals of events as determining stress.
- Many factors influence stress appraisal such as the duration, severity, valence, controllability, predictability, and ambiguity of the stressor.
- Stress can be measured by questionnaire and using physiological measures such as blood pressure and galvanic skin response, and analysis of stress chemicals in saliva and urine.
- Different cultural groups experience different stressors by how they appraise stress and by how they are treated (e.g., low SES individuals experience higher stress levels). Different cultural models of stress exist to incorporate such factors.
- Research is conducted on three main varieties of stressors: work stressors, environmental stressors, and relationship stressors.
- Stress has serious physiological and psychological consequences on the body. Allostatic load, or the effects of chronic stress, can cause heart and memory problems.

TEST YOURSELF ▶▶

Check your understanding of the topics in this chapter by answering the following questions.

1. Stress is best defined as
   a. negative events that tax the body.
   b. challenges to the body systems.
   c. the perception of strain.
   d. upsetting of homeostasis.

2. The earliest theory of stress suggests our current response is a remnant of our evolutionary past and was developed by
   a. Walter Cannon.
   b. Hans Selye.
   c. Richard Lazarus.
   d. Rene Descartes.

3. During the fight-or-flight response, epinephrine does which of the following?
   a. Increases heart rate and blood pressure
   b. Energizes the muscles
   c. Converts fat into energy
   d. Gets oxygen into the bloodstream

4. According to Hans Selye, the__________ phase of the stress response is responsible for the physiological damage related to stress.
   a. alarm
   b. resistance
   c. threat
   d. exhaustion

5. According to Lazarus's cognitive appraisal model, in primary appraisal, people assess whether an event involves each of the following except
   a. fear.
   b. harm.
   c. threat.
   d. challenge.

6. When a close friend is undergoing a lot of stress, we tend to feel stressed as well. We are not as affected by events taking place in far off lands and to strangers. The main dimension of stress varying in this example is
   a. duration.
   b. valence.
   c. definition.
   d. centrality.

7. Not having money to cover basic needs, divorce, living in a high crime area, being fired, having housing problems, and long-term medical problems are all examples of which of the following?
   a. Environmental stressors
   b. Chronic burden
   c. Acute stressors
   d. Unpredictable stressors

8. As someone gets stressed, the heart rate increases along with a slight increase in perspiration. This can be seen best by measuring
   a. galvanic skin response.
   b. temperature.
   c. blood pressure.
   d. electroencephalograms.

9. Workers with boring, repetitive jobs sometimes show symptoms of nausea, headaches, muscle weakness, and blurry vision without any physical basis. This is known as
   a. deprivational stress.
   b. assembly-line hysteria.
   c. cognitive load.
   d. ambiguity disorder.

10. Chronic stress over time can cause wear and tear on the body. This can have serious physical and psychological consequences and is called
    a. exhaustion.
    b. allostasis.
    c. contagion.
    d. fatigue.

KEY TERMS, CONCEPTS, AND PEOPLE ▶▶

acute, **120**
allostasis, **138**
allostatic load, **138**
appraisals, **126**
background stressors, **136**
Cannon, Walter, **115**
catecholamines, **122**
chronic, **120**
cognitive appraisal model, **129**
control, **128**
crossover, **135**

definition, **128**
ecological theory, **135**
fight-or-flight theory, **122**
general adaptation syndrome, **124**
homeostasis, **115**
hypothalamic-pituitary-adrenal (HPA) axis, **124**
Kiecolt-Glaser, Janice, **120**
Lazarus, Richard, **126**
life events, **117**
McEwen, Bruce, **139**
mesosystem, **135**
microaggresions, **131**
microsystems, **135**
natural disaster stressors, **136**
predictability, **128**
primary appraisals, **126**
post-traumatic stress disorder **128**
reciprocity, **136**
role ambiguity, **136**
role conflict, **136**
role theory, **136**
secondary appraisal, **127**
self-fulfilling prophecy, **141**
Selye, Hans, **115**
spillover, **135**
stress, **114**
stress contagion effect, **135**
stress response, **116**
stressor, **116**
sympathetic-adrenal-medullary (SAM) activation, **122**
Taylor, Shelley, **123**
techno-political stressors, **137**
tend-and-befriend, **123**
valence, **127**

ESSENTIAL READINGS ▶▶

Gruenwald, T. (2019). Stress processes. In T. A. Revenson & R. A. R. Gurung (Eds.), *Handbook of health psychology* (3e). New York, NY: Routledge.

Kemeny, M. E. (2003). The psychobiology of stress. *Current Directions in Psychological Science,* 12(4), 124–129.

Taylor, S. E., Klein, L. C, Lewis, B., Gruenewald, T., Gurung, R. A. R., & Updegraff, J. (2000). The female stress response: Tend and befriend not fight or flight. *Psychological Review, 107*, 411–429.

iStockphoto.com/ imtmphoto

CHAPTER 6

COPING AND SOCIAL SUPPORT

Steve Debenport/E+/Getty Images

Chapter 6 Outline

MEASURING UP

HOW DO *YOU* COPE?

Instructions: Think about a *major stressor.* These items ask what you've been doing to cope with this one. Obviously, different people deal with things in different ways, but we are interested in how you've tried to deal with it. Each item says something about a particular way of coping. I want to know to what extent you've been doing what the item says. How much or how frequently. Don't answer on the basis of whether it seems to be working or not—just whether or not you're doing it. Use these response choices. Try to rate each item separately in your mind from the others. Make your answers as true *for you* as you can. The items represent different types of coping discussed in this chapter.

1 = I haven't been doing this at all

2 = I've been doing this a little bit

3 = I've been doing this a medium amount

4 = I've been doing this a lot

1. I've been turning to work or other activities to take my mind off things.
2. I've been concentrating my efforts on doing something about the situation I'm in.
3. I've been saying to myself "this isn't real."
4. I've been using alcohol or other drugs to make myself feel better.
5. I've been getting emotional support from others.
6. I've been giving up trying to deal with it.
7. I've been taking action to try to make the situation better.
8. I've been refusing to believe that it has happened.
9. I've been saying things to let my unpleasant feelings escape.
10. I've been getting help and advice from other people.
11. I've been using alcohol or other drugs to help me get through it.
12. I've been trying to see it in a different light, to make it seem more positive.
13. I've been criticizing myself.
14. I've been trying to come up with a strategy about what to do.
15. I've been getting comfort and understanding from someone.
16. I've been giving up the attempt to cope.
17. I've been looking for something good in what is happening.
18. I've been making jokes about it.

(Continued)

(Continued)

19. I've been doing something to think about it less, such as going to movies, watching TV, reading, daydreaming, sleeping, or shopping.
20. I've been accepting the reality of the fact that it has happened.
21. I've been expressing my negative feelings.
22. I've been trying to find comfort in my religion or spiritual beliefs.
23. I've been trying to get advice or help from other people about what to do.
24. I've been learning to live with it.
25. I've been thinking hard about what steps to take.
26. I've been blaming myself for things that happened.
27. I've been praying or meditating.
28. I've been making fun of the situation.

Source: The Brief COPE —Carver, C. S. (1997). You want to measure coping but your protocol's too long: Consider the Brief COPE. *International Journal of Behavioral Medicine*, 4, 92–100.

▼ Ponder This

Do you have a standard way of coping when you get stressed?

What exactly is mindfulness and why is it great for coping?

How strong are your social support networks? Have you recently told a friend you appreciate him or her?

You do not have to look far for examples of how to cope. Even popular music through the ages provides us with examples of what we should do when we are stressed. The Eagles suggest we "take it easy," The Beatles remind us we can "get by with a little help from our friends," and The Police recommend that "when the world is running down, you make the best of what's still around." In another musical example of good coping, the band REM suggested that even when it may seem like "it's the end of the world as we know it," you can still feel fine. More contemporary musicians have suggestions too: Taylor Swift suggests we "shake it off," echoed by Florence and the Machine ("shake it out"), and Eminem implores us to be "not afraid."

Apart from reflecting life, music also provides a wonderful way to cope with stress. I know many people who listen to specific songs when they feel unhappy or anxious. A warning: Do not listen to sad music because it can make you feel worse (Garrido, Eerola, & McFerran, 2017). Of course, listening to music is just one way to cope, but the songs above illustrate two major categories of coping with stress. First, you can cope by virtue of things you do as an individual that will vary with your personality and coping style (e.g., be optimistic or make the best of the situation). Second, you can cope by drawing on social networks for what you need to help you through the stressful situation (e.g., ask a friend to help you). Whereas research from the 1970s to the late 1990s focused more on the individual, contemporary research focuses heavily on the social contexts in which coping takes place (Revenson & Lepore, 2012).

RESEARCHER SPOTLIGHT

Carolyn Aldwin received her PhD in the Adult Development & Aging Program, University of California, San Francisco. She is the Center for Healthy Aging Jo Anne Leonard Endowed Director at Oregon State University. She is an expert on coping research (Aldwin, 2019, in Essential Readings).

WHAT IS COPING?

In this chapter, we review the major ways to cope. **Coping** was defined as "constantly changing cognitive and behavioral efforts to manage specific external and/or internal demands that are appraised as taxing or exceeding the resources of the person" (Lazarus & Folkman, 1984, p. 141). If stress is a disturbance in homeostasis, coping is whatever we do to reestablish our homeostatic balances. Different factors can influence the severity of a stressor (i.e., moderators and mediators of stress discussed below) and influence coping as well (Aldwin, 2018). I first give you a chance to measure your own coping, then briefly summarize the most common ways to cope and discuss different styles of coping across cultures. Given the central role of **social support**, we will spend some time getting a good feel for this powerful construct, highlighting how it varies across cultures.

Given the physical and psychological consequences of stress (Gruenwald, 2019), finding successful ways to cope is imperative. Also remember that both stress and coping predict both psychological and physical health (Jaser, Patel, Xu, Tamborlane, & Grey, 2017). Unfortunately, finding the best ways to cope is not as easy as it may sound (Gottlieb, 2016). Yes, you can observe people coping with stress and see which people get sick and which people do not. You can see who shows grace under pressure and who cracks. Finally, you can figure out why the successful people did not get sick or did not crack, and you have your answer. Oh, if only it were so simple.

There are two key issues. First, people and situations vary a lot. What may work for one person may not work for another. Similarly, what works in one situation may not work well in another, or be used in every situation, something called a *coping style.* If that is not enough variability, what works for one person in one situation, something called *situational coping,* may not work for another person in the same situation. Second, as human beings we are tempted to look for direct causes of events. For example, we tend to think in very straightforward ways and believe that some factor, say personality, will directly lead to a certain outcome. If you are optimistic, you will cope better and be less stressed. If you do not have a lot of social support, you will be more stressed and cope worse than if you had high social support. Although these statements are true in general, they greatly simplify the actual process of coping. A lot can influence what happens when you are stressed and what the result of your coping with the stressor will be.

To compensate for these two issues—that people and situations vary and that coping is a complex process—health psychologists measure different aspects of the person or organism coping to best account for individual differences in coping. These individual differences and the different factors that influence the process are **moderators** and **mediators** (see Chapter 2). As you will see, coping both moderates and mediates the relationship between stress and how you feel because of it. Getting a good feel for what these terms mean and how they are different from each other can be a challenge (recognize the primary appraisal?), but we know you have the skills to do it (nice secondary appraisal, right?). Go back to Chapter 5 if you do not remember primary and secondary appraisals. (For bonus points, do you remember what this model of stress is called?)

COMMON MEASURES OF COPING

Can specific styles of coping be identified across individuals and settings? Although there are not necessarily a Big Five of coping as there are for personality (see below, this chapter), people cope in some clear-cut ways. Each of the two main styles discussed previously, problem-focused and emotion-focused coping, have many separate subcomponents, each of which can be assessed by questionnaires. Two of the most commonly used measures are the COPE (Carver et al., 1989) and the Revised Ways of Coping Checklist (RWOC) (Vitaliano, Russo, Carr, Maiuro, & Becker, 1985).

The COPE

The **COPE** inventory (Carver et al., 1989) contains 13 subscales with four items each measuring the extent to which you use each type of coping. The main subscales representing different forms of problem-focused and emotion-focused coping are the following:

1. Active Coping (e.g., I do what has to be done, one step at a time)
2. Planning (e.g., I make a plan of action)
3. Suppression of Competing Activities (e.g., I put aside other activities to concentrate on this)

4. Restraint Coping (e.g., I force myself to wait for the right time to do something)
5. Seeking Social Support for Instrumental Reasons (e.g., I talk to someone to find out more about the situation)
6. Seeking Social Support for Emotional Reasons (e.g., I talk to someone about how I feel)
7. Positive Reinterpretation and Growth (e.g., I learn something from the experience)
8. Acceptance (e.g., I learn to live with it)
9. Turning to Religion (e.g., I put my trust in God)
10. Focus and Venting of Emotions (e.g., I let my feelings out)
11. Denial (e.g., I refuse to believe that it has happened)
12. Behavioral Disengagement (e.g., I just give up trying to reach my goal)
13. Mental Disengagement (e.g., I daydream about things other than this)

Later versions included additional items relating to the use of humor and alcohol as coping mechanisms. The COPE has separate subscales for the different types of social support seeking: problem-focused and emotion-focused support seeking.

Other Coping Questionnaires

The Revised Ways of Coping (RWOC) questionnaire consists of 66 items with a 4-point Likert-type response format. This easily available checklist measure is written in a way to allow for comparisons across different types of stressful situations. It lists a number of different ways of coping and measures how much each is used.

Other measures of coping are targeted for special populations, such as the Life Events and Coping Inventory for Children (Dise-Lewis, 1988), the Adolescent Coping Orientation for Problem Experiences Inventory (Patterson & McCubbin, 1987), and the Life Situations Inventory (Feifel & Strack, 1989), which is aimed at assessing coping with real-life circumstances in middle-aged and elderly men. New measures are also aimed at measuring specific coping behaviors (e.g., the Coping Experiences Scale; Friedman-Wheeler, Pederson, Rizzo-Busack, & Haaga, 2016).

Be warned: some researchers lament the overuse of coping instruments (e.g., Coyne & Racioppo, 2000), and others report few consistent positive associations between the use of any particular coping style and positive outcomes (Gottlieb, 2016). The main problem seems to be that some of the questions are too general, and researchers tend to use one standard measure across many different situations, thereby ignoring the unique aspects of different stressors. In addition, the summary scores achieved by adding together the responses to the different questions on the scales dilute and omit important information such as timing, sequencing, and appropriateness of a specific behavior (Coyne & Racioppo, 2000). Finally, many of the coping styles are closely related to personality characteristics and correlate strongly with distress, both variables that serve to confound coping results.

These problems notwithstanding, the coping scales allow health psychologists to study large numbers of people using limited time and money and allow for a quantification of the **coping process** (Lazarus, 2000). To compensate for some of the problems of scale measures, most contemporary coping researchers also include detailed interviews and observations to assess coping (Folkman & Moskowitz, 2000), and research is advancing in new directions primarily due to methodological innovations (Revenson & Lepore, 2012).

New Developments in Coping Research

Three major changes in coping research in recent years hold great promise. First, health psychologists are paying greater attention to the role played by relationships. Paralleling a move away from individualistic measures to measures of the social context, the conceptualization of **relationship-focused coping**, or **relational coping**, recognizes that maintaining relatedness with others is a basic human need and as fundamental to coping as eliminating or minimizing stressors (Revenson & Lepore, 2012). Relational coping includes compromising with others and being open in communication (Manne & Badr, 2010). In a study of couples coping with a diagnosis of cancer, Manne and Badr (2010) showed that couples that enhanced relationship intimacy by disclosing cancer-related concerns facilitated both partners' adjustment to illness.

Second, researchers are changing how they design research studies on coping. One of the biggest problems with past methodology was that studies were primarily cross-sectional and retrospective (see Chapter 2). **Daily process methodology**, also called daily diaries, provides a rich set of information and addresses past concerns. This method involves many different assessments over time and automatically provides a clear picture of the process of coping. Daily process methods assess timing, frequency, emotions, and more details on the spot because participants often carry around an electronic device such as iPads and answer questions at different times of the day (Bolger, Stadler, Paprocki, & DeLongis, 2010). Even newer research is looking into the benefits of using technology to cope (e.g., online coping; van Ingen, Utz, & Toepoel, 2016).

Finally, health psychologists now use statistical techniques that better allow complex data, such as that derived from daily process methodology, to be analyzed. For example, structural equation modeling is useful to examine the structure of coping with national population samples (Meng & D'Arcy, 2016; see Chapter 2).

THE STRUCTURE OF COPING

Coping includes anything people do to manage problems or emotional responses, whether successful or not (Carver & Vargas, 2011). Coping can be separated depending on the level of analysis you use (Gottlieb, 2016). You can study specific ways of coping at the item level (e.g., drug use; Cuttler et al., 2017), coping through roping together similar items (e.g., religious coping strategies for substance use Parenteau, 2017), or coping as a higher-order level, mode, or style (e.g., approach coping in African Americans; Womack & Sloan, 2017).

Coping styles are general predispositions to dealing with stress; they are tools a person tends to use repeatedly. In general, adaptive coping styles are associated with better health (Zeidner, Matthews, & Shemesh, 2016). African Americans using more religious coping styles showed better well-being (Park, Holt, Le, Christie, & Williams, 2017). Coping styles are also common moderators. For example, women high in social support coping showed lower levels of the stress hormone cortisol in a lab study (Sladek, Doane, Jewell, & Luecken, 2017). The two most basic styles are **approach coping** and **avoidant coping**. An individual can approach a stressor and make active efforts to resolve it or can try to avoid the problem (Moos & Schaefer, 1993). Avoidant coping moderates the relationship between stress and depression-related eating in adolescents (Young & Limbers, 2017) and in general is associated with more-negative health outcomes (e.g., more diabetes-related distress in adolescents; Iturralde, Weissberg-Benchell, & Hood, 2017). Studies of these two basic styles use many terms, as shown in Table 6.1.

▼ TABLE 6.1

Coping Styles

Approach	Avoidance	Reference
Monitoring	Blunting	Miller (1987)
Vigilance	Cognitive avoidance	Krohne (1993)
Problem-focused	Emotion-focused + Appraisal-focused	Billings and Moos (1984)

Coping strategies refer to the specific behavioral and psychological efforts that people use to master, tolerate, reduce, or minimize stressful events (Drapeau, Blake, Dobson, & Körner, 2017; Lazarus & Launier, 1978). Even though coping can refer to many different behaviors, it is easy to identify some main types of coping. Either you can do something about the problem or you can ignore it. Researchers have particularly distinguished between problem-focused or emotion-focused coping strategies.

Problem-focused coping involves directly facing the stressful situation and working hard to resolve it. For example, if you have a demanding, aggressive boss at work, you may experience a lot of stress at your job. If you report the issue to your human resources department or have a direct conversation with your boss, you are taking concrete action to deal with the situation and following a problem-focused approach (of course, your boss could retaliate). Problem-focused coping can be a useful strategy. For example, problem-focused coping mediates the impact of partner violence on mental health in Chinese women (Wong et al., 2016). The women who use more of this form of coping in response to partner violence show fewer mental health problems.

Sometimes the first thing you do is deal with the emotions surrounding the stressor. A person finding out that he or she is HIV positive or has test results showing cancer may experience a surge of fear and anxiety and so be driven to cope with these feelings. The person may deny the test results or not want to talk about them for some time. This strategy of coping is referred to as **emotion-focused coping** because you use either mental or behavioral methods to deal with the feelings resulting from the stress. African Americans tend to use more emotion-focused coping strategies than European Americans (Vassillière, Holahan, & Holahan, 2016). Recent work has further divided emotional coping into active emotional and avoidant emotional. For example, undocumented Latino workers tend to use higher levels of active emotional coping styles (e.g., "I get support from someone") than avoidant emotional styles (e.g., "I tell myself it's not real"; Cobb, Xie, & Sanders, 2017).

More often than not, problem-focused and emotion-focused styles are pitted against each other. The problem-focused versus emotion-focused binary separation has been called into question (Folkman, Lazarus, Dunkel-Schetter, DeLongis, & Gruen, 1986; Revenson & Lepore, 2012). Although conceptually distinct, both strategies are interdependent and work together, with one supplementing the other in the overall coping process (Lazarus, 2000). Both styles can be useful as seen in a study of what resilient adolescents use (Lee et al., 2017). Researchers today tend to look toward broader categories of coping. For example, Skinner and colleagues conducted a major review of the coping literature and identified five core categories of coping: support seeking, problem solving, avoidance, distraction, and positive cognitive restructuring (Skinner, Edge, Altman, & Sherwood, 2003). Most measures of coping incorporate these main categories, as I discuss below.

Synthesize, Evaluate, Apply

- What are some biopsychosocial mediators and moderators of stress and coping?
- What are the major drawbacks to current coping research?
- What are the main coping styles? Generate situations in which each would be optimal.
- How do the different ways of coping apply to the different theories of stress?

What Is the Best Way to Cope?

One coping style seems better than the others. In general, people who rely primarily on *problem-solving coping* adapt better to life stressors and experience less-negative affect than those who make use of *avoidant coping* (Aspinwall & Taylor, 1992; Folkman, Lazarus, DeLongis, & Gruen, 1986). A large body of work demonstrates the deleterious emotional impact of avoidant coping in a variety of populations (e.g., Bartone, Johnsen, Eid, Hystad, & Laberg, 2016; Iturralde et al., 2017; Young & Limbers, 2017). Avoiding paying your phone bill or rent can cause more stress as you rush to get in the money at the last moment or face the consequences of losing service or your apartment. Waiting until the last moment to study actually makes those last moments even more stressful. Sure, not thinking about taxes until April 14 or about the exam until the night before may seem like you are gaining some carefree days, but your avoidance has only accentuated your stress.

The benefits from avoidance may be fewer than you think. In some samples, avoidance may increase emotional distress. Ironically, people often become preoccupied with the thoughts that they attempt to suppress, and the inhibition of thoughts, feelings, and behaviors can cause have negative implications for your health (Kaplow, Gipson, Horwitz, Burch, & King, 2014). Also, the use of avoidant coping requires sustained effort to screen out stressor-relevant thoughts. If you do not want to think of the test that you have not studied for or the work assignment that you have not started on, parts of your cognitive processes are making sure that you are not thinking of the troubling aspect. You are using some mental energy just to make sure you do not think about something that troubles you.

Given all that, it sounds like avoidant, emotion-focused coping may not be the best style. There is one more complication. Some coping styles, such as seeking support, can be both problem-focused and emotion-focused (Coyne & Racioppo, 2000; Revenson & Lepore, 2012). For example, wanting your doctor to spend more time with you to tell you about a diagnosis is a form of seeking support that gives you emotional support and information on how to deal with the issue.

So, is there a single best way to cope? The situation is an important consideration. The best coping style to use depends on the severity, duration, controllability, and emotionality of the situation (Aldwin, 2018; Gottlieb, 2016). Even when you consider the type of situation, it is critical to be specific about it. People may want to know the best way to cope with breast cancer or diabetes. Just referring to cancer in general may not be as helpful as discussing coping with different types of cancer or with specific populations such as adolescents. For this reason, researchers developed measures for different forms of stressors. One example is the Mental Adjustment to Cancer scale (Watson & Homewood, 2008). Given an increase in the genetic testing (e.g., the children's movie *Despicable Me 3* was sponsored by a genetic testing company, 23andMe), there is even a scale to measure coping with the stress of genetic testing (Phelps et al., 2010).

It is essentially best to match the type of coping you use with the situation and with your comfort level. For example, if you work in a hospital and you are stressed by how many hours you work and how many patients you see, you have some control over the situation. Finding a way to be scheduled for better hours is a problem-focused way to cope. By way of contrast, avoidant, emotion-focused coping may be beneficial in the short term because this coping style gives your body time to recover from the physiological responses to and shock of the stressor. If you were diagnosed with strep and that made you so anxious that you could not get your work done, it may be better to be emotion-focused and first cope with your emotions and ignore the issue because it stresses you. At some point, however, you must face the problem, get more information about it, and learn what you should do to deal with it.

WHO COPES WELL?

Some people cope with stress by buying and consuming a pint (or a gallon!) of their favorite ice cream. Others go for a fast run. Still others sleep extra hours and do not eat. You may have some friends or coworkers who are not fazed even when everything seems to be going wrong. Other individuals fall apart and get freaked out by the most minor negative events. As you read in Chapter 5, how a person appraises an event can determine the extent to which that person thinks it is stressful. According to Lazarus and Folkman's (1984) framework, cognitive appraisals and coping are two critical mediators of responses to stressful events. A person's subjective perception of stress will depend on the objective features of the situation (e.g., potentially stressful life events) and the way that person appraises the events. Your feeling of stress depends both on how many things you really have due and on how serious or demanding you think the assignments or deadlines are. Even if you do not really have too much to do, just believing that you have too much to do or that what you have to do is very difficult can be stressful.

▲ **Indulgence.** One way of coping is to indulge in something that you know is not great for you. Too much snack food and watching television all night is bad for your health, but it may seem soothing when you are stressed.

A person experiences distress when primary appraisals of threat exceed secondary appraisals of coping ability (Folkman et al., 1986). One's secondary appraisal will depend in large part on the personal resources a person brings to the situation, such as personality factors (e.g., optimism) and perceived resources for coping with the situation. Many factors influence how someone appraises a situation and correspondingly copes with stress. In this section, we will examine some of the factors that influence appraisals and coping and will determine what makes the difference between weathering the storm and falling to pieces.

PERSONALITY AND DIVERSE COPING STYLES

A person's personality characteristics provide some of the best clues as to how he or she will cope with a stressor (Laborde, Guillén, Watson, & Allen, 2017; Park & DeFrank, 2018). You may have been called laid back. Although not a scientific personality trait, being easy-going could help you cope. **Personality** is defined as an individual's unique set of consistent behavioral traits, where traits are durable dispositions to behave in a particular way in a variety of situations. When you described yourself in the "Who am I?" task in Chapter 1, you probably used a number of trait terms to describe yourself (e.g., honest, dependable, funny, or social).

One of the earliest personality psychologists, Gordon Allport (1961), scoured an unabridged dictionary and collected more than 4,500 descriptors used to describe personality. Later personality theorists such as Cattell (1966) used statistical analyses to measure correlations between these different descriptors. Cattell found that all 4,500 descriptors could be encompassed by just 16 terms. It gets better. McCrae and Costa (1987) further narrowed these 16 terms down to a core of only five as part of their five-factor model of personality. A wealth of research has led to the Big Five or the Five Factor Model, suggesting that personality can be sufficiently measured by assessing how conscientious, agreeable, neurotic, open to experience, and extroverted a person is (John & Srivastava, 1999). For an easy way to remember them, we like to use the acronym CANOE, or OCEAN if you live on the coast. Clear definitions and examples of each trait are listed in Table 6.2.

▼ TABLE 6.2

The Big Five/Five Factor Model Personality Traits

Trait	Characteristics
Conscientiousness	Ethical, dependable, productive, purposeful
Agreeableness	Sympathetic, warm, trusting, cooperative
Neuroticism	Anxious, insecure, guilt-prone, self-conscious
Openness to experience	Daring, nonconforming, imaginative
Extroversion	Talkative, sociable, fun-loving, affectionate

In addition to the Big Five traits, a number of other personality characteristics, sometimes grouped into patterns, influence health (Strickhouser, Zell, & Krizan, 2017). For example, you have probably heard about Type A personalities. The Type A behavior pattern was perhaps the first and most controversial aspect of personality that was thought to relate to stress and coping. The cardiologists Friedman and Rosenman (1959, 1974) identified the **Type A coronary-prone behavior pattern** based on their observations of heart patients who showed a sense of time urgency (always doing more than one thing at the same time), competitiveness, and hostility in their interactions with other people. People with this constellation of personality characteristics were found to have a higher risk for coronary heart disease and stress. Early interventions helped such individuals cope better. There were problems replicating Friedman and Rosenman's hypothesized link between cardiovascular disease and Type A personality, and it later became clear that the critical personality risk factors were anger and hostility (Dembrowski, MacDougall, Williams, Haney, & Blumenthal, 1985). Hostility reliably predicts heart attacks and early death (Chida & Steptoe, 2009) and influences family relationships, as well. In a large study of 13,406 children from different ethnicities and geographical boundaries, the hostility of the parents correlated with psychological maladjustment of the children (Khaleque, 2017). Having a sense of time urgency and being competitive is all right, but being hostile is most dangerous to your health. Remember this the next time you feel like snapping at someone or giving in to road rage. Maybe this is a good time to watch Adam Sandler and Jack Nicholson in *Anger Management* or think of what happens to the Hulk in the *Avenger* movies.

Hostility also provides us with another good example of how personality characteristics can be moderators of the relationship between psychological factors and stressful outcomes. Vella, Kamarck, and Shiffman (2008) tested the role of hostility in moderating the effects of positive social interactions on ambulatory blood pressure (ABP). The researchers monitored the ABP of 341 adults for 6 days (readings taken every 45 minutes while participants were awake). Participants also kept a diary and recorded mood and social interactions at the time of each ABP measurement. Sure enough, low-hostile participants experiencing supportive interactions showed reductions in ABP. This was not the case for high-hostile participants (remember moderation = differences between participants high and low on a variable). The researchers concluded that hostile individuals may find offers of support stressful and may fail to benefit from intimacy during everyday life (Vella et al., 2008).

Does it follow then that people with different personalities will use different methods to cope with stress? For the most part this is true. It is probably no surprise that some personality types use different coping styles than others, and empirical tests mostly confirm this assumption. For example, a study of 648 U.S. Army soldiers in Iraq showed how conscientiousness, neuroticism, and extroversion were associated with different coping behaviors (Peng, Riolli, Schaubroeck, & Spain, 2012). Conscientiousness was positively associated with problem-focused coping and negatively with avoidance coping, whereas neuroticism was most positively associated with avoidance coping. Extroversion was positively related to both seeking social support and avoidance coping. In another study, patients with less-adaptive coping strategies (i.e., emotion-focused coping) had less-adaptive personality traits (i.e., neuroticism) and were more depressed. Clearly, personality styles can predict what coping style a person is likely to use, but there is not always a direct relationship.

One thing to keep in mind is that coping styles are not merely reflections of personality but mediate the relationship between personality and well-being (Magnano, Paolillo, Platania, & Santisi, 2017). Yes, having a high level of optimism or a low level of neuroticism is associated with feeling less stressed in general, but people with these personality characteristics are more likely to use more-adaptive coping styles and have different physical reactivity and decrease their stress. A study of adults with diabetes illustrates this process. Researchers exposed 140 people with type 2 diabetes to a stressor in a lab (Puig-Perez, Hackett, Salvador & Steptoe, 2017). Researchers then measured some classic health psychology variables, heart rate, systolic and diastolic blood pressure, and cortisol (see Chapter 2). People high in optimism showed heightened stress reactivity and lower daily cortisol output. People low in optimism showed poorer self-reported physical and mental health, illustrating a protective stress modulating role. Therefore, the personality style led to certain physiological reactions, which then influenced well-being. The personality style did not directly influence the outcome.

Beyond these core aspects of personality, people vary on a number of other characteristics that can influence their coping. For example, health psychologists suggest that we pay close attention to the concepts of optimism, mastery, hardiness, and resilience.

Optimism refers to generalized outcome expectancies that good things, rather than bad things, will happen (Carver & Scheier, 1999; Carver, Scheier, & Weintraub, 1989). Optimists are the people who can always find the positive aspects of any situation and always seem to look on the bright side of life no matter how bad things are. This personality trait is associated with a number of health-related factors and predicts longevity in general (Cherry et al., 2017). Optimists tend to cope better with stress and practice better health behaviors (Anderson, 2017). Optimism is strongly and positively correlated with problem-focused coping strategies and strongly negatively correlated with avoidant coping strategies (Scheier, Weintraub, & Carver, 1986). Optimists show good psychological well-being (Armor & Taylor, 1998), suggesting that optimism may moderate depression (Calandri, Graziano, Borghi, & Bonino, 2016).

Optimism is associated with a range of physiological factors. It predicts slower progression of artery clogs and hence heart attack (Matthews, Raikkonen, Sutton-Tyrell, & Kuller, 2004) and better cardiovascular health (Boehm & Kubzansky, 2012), and relates to the presence of active potent natural killer cells during stress (Segerstrom, Taylor, Kemeny, & Fahey, 1998). Measures of AIDS-related optimism have been related to a slower disease course (Taylor, Kemeny, Reed, Bower, & Gruenewald, 2000). Optimists differ significantly from pessimists in secondary (but not primary) appraisal, coping, and adjustment. In addition, knowing a person's level of optimism adds significantly to predictions of that person's adjustment (Chang, 1998) and also to predictions of his or her likelihood to take risks—gay men optimistic about survival with HIV actually take more risks (Prestage et al., 2012).

Mastery is a relatively stable tendency of an individual and is another variable that can influence the appraisal of stress and help people cope (Gil & Weinberg, 2015). Mastery is defined as the extent to which one regards one's life chances as being under one's own control (Pearlin & Schooler, 1978, p. 5). Someone with a high level of mastery believes that he or she has the capability to succeed at whatever task is at hand. Conceptually similar to perceived control, locus of control, and self-efficacy, mastery has been found to be a moderator in many studies of stress and appraisal (Assari & Lankarani, 2017; Herts, Khaled, & Stanton, 2017). For example, Mausbach et al. (2008) showed that for people high in mastery, negative life events were not related to increases in plasma PAI-1 antigen levels (an antigen related to cardiovascular disease). This was not the case for people low in mastery, demonstrating the moderating effect of mastery.

Mastery is also a mediator. In a study of HIV-negative and HIV-positive midlife and older gay-identified men, mastery mediated the effects of stress on mental health (Wight, LeBlanc, de Vries, & Detels, 2012). For men with increasing stress, a greater sense of personal mastery reduced negative feelings. The effects of mastery also vary by age. Ben-Zur (2002) measured the coping styles and mastery levels of 168 young and old community residents and found that older people with elevated feelings of mastery used more-efficient coping strategies.

Two other personality characteristics that moderate the effects of stress and aid coping are *hardiness* and *resilience*. People who are strongly committed to their lives, enjoy challenges, and have a high level of control over their lives are high on the trait of **hardiness** (Maddi & Kobasa, 1991). In general, being hardy is related to better adjustment to a range of health issues (Figueroa & Zoccola, 2015; Maddi, 2012; Stoppelbein, McRae, & Greening, 2017). This variable is particularly useful for coping with collegiate athletics (Madrigal, Gill, & Willse, 2017) and in competitive situations (Martinent & Nicholas, 2016).

Resilience closely relates to hardiness. If you know a person who has encountered a tremendous number of stressful events but always seems to bounce back into action and still do fine, he or she is said to be **resilient** (Fredrickson, Tugade, Waugh, & Larkin, 2003). Like hardiness, resiliency accompanies adaptive coping strategies that lead to better mental and physical health (Perna et al., 2012). A number of psychological factors are linked to resiliency, such as finding/having a purpose in life (Wang, Lightsey, Pietruszka, Uruk, & Wells, 2007) and depression (Karatzias, Jowett, Yan, Raeside, & Howard, 2017). Although early studies of this concept were conducted with children, there is now a wealth of research on resilience across the life course (see Ryff & Singer, 2003a, 2003b, for reviews).

Resilience can also be studied at a group level (e.g., the family resilience studies of Ortega, Beauchemin, & Kaniskan, 2008) and varies by cultural group (Harvey & Tummala-Narra, 2007). Prominent factors of resilient families include positive outlook, spirituality, family member accord, flexibility, family communication, financial management, family time, shared recreation, routines and rituals, and support networks (Black & Lobo, 2008).

Research exploring the interaction of culture and resilience is growing. In a review of how adversity and resilience influence the development of youth from diverse cultural backgrounds, Clauss-Ehlers (2008) found that cultural factors were related to measures of five aspects of resilience: childhood stressors, global coping, adaptive coping, maladaptive coping, and sociocultural support. Childhood stressors were experienced differentially by individuals from different racial/ethnic and social class status backgrounds, supporting proposals that ecological aspects, notably cultural background and experiences, influence the development of resilience. In another example, African American college students who received racial socialization messages (e.g., messages emphasizing pride in being Black) and perceived that they had social support were more resilient (Brown, 2008).

COPING AND CULTURE

Although culture brings its own unique set of problems to accentuate stress and accordingly mental illness (see Chapter 5; Brondolo, Lackey, & Love, 2012), culture also has its strengths. It is also important to consider cultural variation in coping methods and strategies when individuals are dealing with stress.

Coping styles vary across cultures; in fact, culture can be a factor that mediates specific coping styles and strategies through its influence on vulnerability to stress and the availability of support (Revenson & Lepore, 2012). Culture can also influence which coping responses are appropriate, limiting coping options (e.g., use of emotional expression and anger; Stanton & Revenson, 2011). Terms such as "individualistic" and "collectivistic" are often used to describe the general orientation of other cultures and can be extended to describe individuals' coping styles in these cultures. For example, many East Asian cultures are collectivistic. These cultures emphasize interdependence on others in many roles and functions. The orientation of the United States and European countries, by contrast, is individualistic. They emphasize independence and reliance on the self (Markus & Kitayama, 1991). These cultural orientations, in turn, may influence how individuals in these cultures cope with stress (Chun, Moos, & Cronkite, 2006).

Specific coping methods within the collectivistic orientation included individualistic coping (coping alone through participation in solitary activities); seeking social support from family, members of own ethnic groups, or individuals who had gone through similar loss; forbearance (emotion-based coping); religiosity; and traditional healing practices. Coping strategies typically associated with individualistic cultures are approach-based, while avoidance-based coping strategies are often associated with collectivistic cultures (Chun et al., 2006). In an example of these styles, Yeh, Inman, Kim, and Okubo (2006) found that in a sample of Asian American families who had lost a family member in the 9/11 attacks, the subjects used collectivistic coping methods to deal with the stress caused by their losses.

In another example of how culture moderates coping styles, Wei, Liao, Heppner, Chao, and Ku (2012) examined if using a culturally relevant coping strategy (forbearance coping) is associated with a lower level of psychological distress in a group of Chinese international students. Less-traditional Chinese students' use of forbearance coping positively associated with psychological distress when they were under high stress (not when acculturative stress was lower). For those with a stronger cultural heritage identification, the use of forbearance coping was not significantly associated with psychological distress.

Ethnic Identity

One of the major mediators of the stress-mental health relationship is ethnic identity. Different ethnic groups' experiences with racism and discrimination create stress and reduce coping resources leading to poor coping (Yoon et al., 2017). Ethnic identity can also be a strength. For example, in a study of 395 African American students, those with stronger ethnic identities had better coping skills, allowing them to better navigate discrimination (Swanson, 2016).

Mental health outcomes may be better for immigrants to the United States, as opposed to people from the same cultural group born in the United States. For example, Mexican immigrant women, compared to Mexican Americans born in the United States, report fewer stressful life events and fewer adverse health behaviors (Arellano & Sosa, 2018). Vega et al. (2004) compared 12-month prevalence rates of mood, anxiety, and substance use disorders of Mexican American immigrants and U.S.-born citizens of Mexican descent, finding that the prevalence rates of these disorders were significantly less in the immigrant population than in the U.S.-born population.

Being an immigrant can sometimes make things worse. For example, for immigrants the rates of psychiatric disorders may increase with duration of time living in the United States (Tovar, 2017).

Other studies have looked at the impact of generational status on rates of mental health disorders for immigrants to the United States. Williams et al. (2007) found that in a sample of Black Caribbean immigrants and African Americans, ethnicity, gender, and generational status variables moderated the risk of 12-month prevalence of psychiatric disorders. For instance, Caribbean Black women had lower rates of psychiatric disorders than African American women did, while Caribbean Black men had higher rates of psychiatric disorders than African American men did in the past 12 months. Furthermore, the prevalence of psychiatric disorders varied by generational status, such that third-generation immigrants had the highest rates of psychiatric disorders, while first-generation immigrants had the highest rates of psychiatric disorders in the past 12 months.

Acculturation

Ethnic identity formation is more of an issue for non–European Americans, because they are often made very aware of their not being White. For non-White children, the stress of forming one's ethnic identity is compounded by the fact that often the non-White parents experience their own problems with the White culture that surrounds them (Berrol, 1995). Immigrants, for example, often single-handedly enter a culture different from their own, leaving their families behind in their home cultures. They differ in the extent to which they acculturate, and while some remain steadfast in retaining the values and norms with which they were raised, some subtly adapt to the different world around them. Often these stressors and changes have health consequences (Jang, Park, Chiriboga, & Kim, 2017). Acculturation is correspondingly an important variable.

Being acculturated may mean different things to different people, and there have been many approaches to studying acculturation (Sam & Berry, 2016). Roland (1991), who has studied and compared various cultures, sees the acculturation process as primarily entailing the adoption of one culture at the expense of the other. In contrast, Berry, Trimble, and Olmedo (1986) define four models of acculturation that directly pertain to the issues we have raised here. A strong identification with both groups is indicative of integration or biculturalism; a strong identification with only the dominant culture reflects assimilation; with only the ethnic group, separation; with neither group, marginalization.

Acculturation and ethnic identity formation are both critical aspects of human development that are of much more significance to non-European Americans and can influence health and health behaviors. Attending to acculturation and ethnic identity takes us beyond the basic cultural differences in health and can be seen in both mental and physical health. For example, African Americans have been found to have higher rates of mental disorders compared with European Americans and Mexican Americans, but these findings vary with acculturation level (Tovar, 2017). Acculturation is also a mediator between Latino perceptions of discrimination and levels of distress, influencing coping (Torres, Driscoll, & Voell, 2012). In many cases, greater acculturation is associated with better mental health (e.g., Balls Organista, Organista, & Kurasaki, 2002), although this is not the case for all ethnic groups or with physical health.

The acculturation-physical health link is just as fascinating. In general, recent immigrants are healthier than better-acculturated nonimmigrants (Myers & Rodriguez, 2002). Cancer, diabetes, and risky sexual behavior are higher among most acculturated non-Europeans (Fujimoto, 1992; Harmon, Castro, & Coe, 1996; Hines, Snowden, & Graves, 1998). There are only a few exceptions: acculturation is related to lower rates of diabetes among Mexican Americans (Hazuda, Haffner, Stern, & Eifler, 1988). There are, however, differences between health behaviors within cultural groups. For example, higher acculturation among Arab Americans is more predictive of drinking, whereas lower acculturation is more predictive of smoking (Jadalla & Lee, 2012).

The positive relationship can be seen across many cultural groups, although, as you can guess, the relationship is sometimes very complex when you add sex differences to the mix. More-acculturated Mexican Americans are more likely to have high blood pressure than less-acculturated Mexican Americans (Espino & Maldonado, 1990). Still, whereas less-acculturated Latino American men drink more and are more likely to engage in risky sexual behavior, it is the more acculturated Latina women who drink more (Hines & Caetano, 1998).

Given that culture can be broadly defined as encompassing other factors such as religion, it is important to remember that acculturation may take place when any two or more cultural groups come into contact, and that there is a lot of variance within each cultural group. When a Catholic dates or marries a Lutheran, or someone from the South dates or marries someone from the North, acculturative pressure can influence both relationships, and the children of both couples can have problems forming their identities, which could affect their health and health behaviors.

Synthesize, Evaluate, Apply

- How do different personality styles/traits relate to coping?
- What are the key cultural factors involved in coping?
- How would you evaluate your own coping mechanisms?
- Do you cope in ways not discussed in this chapter?

SOCIAL SUPPORT

How we cope with stress often is influenced by how much support we receive from others around us. Even more importantly, just the perception that support would be available if we need it can greatly enhance our coping strategies and health (e.g., Lett et al., 2007). Not surprisingly then, social support is one of the most important factors in the study of stress and coping (Knoll, 2018; Wills, Bantam, & Ainette, 2016).

The sociologist Durkheim (1951) first provided empirical evidence of the importance of social support and showed that a lack of social relationships increased the probability of a person committing suicide. The connections of social support to health were strengthened by the work of Cassel (1976) and Cobb (1976) who demonstrated that the presence of other members of the same species was a critical ingredient to good health. This social support to health connection was supported later by the now classic 9-year epidemiological study done in Alameda County, California, that found men and women who were socially integrated lived longer (Berkman, 1985; Berkman & Syme, 1979). In fact, the age-adjusted relative risk for mortality for the men and women with weak social

▲ **Support Network.** Our social networks, friends, and colleagues can be a major source of social support.

connections (e.g., marriage, contact with family members and close friends, and memberships in religious and volunteer organizations) was almost twice as high as the risk for the participants with strong social connections.

The evidence showing the usefulness of social support is astounding. Social support, generally defined as emotional, informational, or instrumental assistance from others (Dunkel-Schetter & Bennett, 1990), has been tied to better health, more-rapid recovery from illness, and a lower risk for mortality (House, Umberson, & Landis, 1988; Uchino, 2009). Couples with better social support cope better with the stress of deployment (Blow et al., 2017). Social support also reduces psychological distress during stress (Gallagher, Phillips, Ferraro, Drayson, & Carroll, 2008), promotes better coping with heart problems (Roohafza, Talaei, Pourmoghaddas, Rajabi, & Sadeghi, 2012), and puts one at less risk for depression (Gerlach et al., 2017). Studies of people with HIV infection suggest that social support from peers is critical for emotional well-being and, in periods of crisis, family support may become an especially important determinant of emotional well-being (Cederbaum, Rice, Craddock, Pimentel, & Beaver, 2017).

Types of Social Support

Beware of loose definitions! The statement, "Social support is helpful," is really too general to be practical. Social support undoubtedly is an effective aid to health and coping with stress. However, the majority of research findings available mask an important fact: there are many different types of social support (Wills et al., 2016). Table 6.3 provides an overview of the main ways in which social support can differ. The most basic division is between **network measures** and **functional measures**. The earliest research looked at a person's networks (e.g., Berkman, 1985), asking if the person was married, or asking how many people the person saw on a weekly basis. The measurement of networks also varied. Some researchers just asked for the number of people in a network whereas others also assessed the relationship of the support provider to the support recipient.

▼ TABLE 6.3

Main Forms of Social Support and How It Can Be Measured

Form of Support	Types and Measures
I. Networks	Structure and existence of social relationships. Frequency contacts; composition (who—friend, family, coworker)? *Perceived:* If something happens you will get help (if needed it will be there). Are you loved, valued, and esteemed? *Satisfaction:* Was what you got enough? *Received:* When something happened, how much did you get?
II. Sources	Relationship partner, family, friends, fellow workers, doctors, nurses.
III. Types	*Emotional:* Empathy, caring, concern. *Esteem:* Confidence building, encouragement. *Instrumental/Tangible:* Direct assistance, cash, etc. *Informational:* Advice, directions, feedback.
IV. Specificity	*Global:* For stressor or for source. *Specific:* For this event *or* in this relationship. *Time:* Over past year, past month, past week.

Even greater variety exists in the functional measures of support. Functional support is assessed in two main ways. You can measure the social support the person reports was provided to him or her, called **received support**, or the social support the person believes to be available to him or her, called **perceived support**. These two forms of support vary further in the function that they serve. If you think about when you are stressed, the type of support that you get and that will be helpful will depend largely on the type of stress you are experiencing. If you are stressed because you have a big assignment due at school, but you do not even know how to begin, any information that you obtain about how to do it will be helpful. If you are stressed because your car broke down and you do not know how you will go to work, then someone giving you a ride will best help you cope. If someone close to you passes away or you have trouble in a close relationship, people who show you that you are esteemed, loved, and cared for will be the most supportive. These are the three main types of received support, and each has its counterpart form of perceived support. Received or perceived support can be (1) instrumental (also called tangible or material support, e.g., the loan of the car), (2) informational (or advice, e.g., how to do your assignment), and (3) emotional (e.g., being told that people care for you).

Other distinctions become important in the measurement of support and are essential to maximizing its predictor power. For example, you can measure global support—a person's sense of support from people in general, or specific support—support from a specific person or relationship. The recipient or perceiver's satisfaction with social support can be studied. Finally, you can create categories by focusing on who is providing the support and the source of support (e.g., spouse, family, friends, doctors, or medical staff). These different categories can fit into a hierarchy with the general approach (received or perceived) as the primary dimension (Table 6.3). Within each of these, the source of support can be distinguished, and finally, different types or functions of support can be embedded within each source (Schwarzer, Dunkel-Schetter, & Kemeny, 1994). The most effective and theoretically compelling model combines received and perceived support measures but separates them by source (Wills et al., 2016).

A study of social support provided during pregnancy provides an example of how different forms of social support can be studied. The major comparison is between support transactions at the level of a couple or dyad (e.g., support provided to the baby's mother from the baby's father) versus at the level of a network or group (e.g., support provided by friends and family). Another set of studies focused on the impact of support from professional sources (e.g., nurses and doctors). How do the effects of support from these three different sources compare? In a study designed to answer this question, Gurung, Dunkel-Schetter, Colins, Rini, and Hobel (2005) compared the support a woman received from her baby's father with the support she received from her friends and family. The ethnically diverse sample consisted of 480 women (African American, Latin American, and non-Hispanic European Americans). Various types of support measures were assessed at multiple time points before the birth, together with standard measures of depression and anxiety.

Different sources of support were associated with different outcomes. Specifically, social support from the baby's father predicted significantly less anxiety but not significant differences in depressed mood. Support from the mother's friends and family was a significant predictor of the mother's depressed mood but did not predict her anxiety. Social support from the baby's father predicted maternal changes in anxiety independent of sociodemographic variables such as age, ethnicity, and SES and individual difference measures such as mastery and coping. This difference in support effects by source is consistent with the theory and with some results in the social support literature showing that support is most effective when the type of support a person needs matches the type of support provided (e.g., Merluzzi, Philip, Yang, & Heitzmann, 2016). Others discuss the existence of an optimal support provider for different specific needs (Litwak, 1985).

iStockphoto.com/ Steve Debenport

▲ **Social Support Among Women.** Women often turn to other women for social support and to share their emotions.

CULTURAL VARIABLES IN SOCIAL SUPPORT

Culture shapes beliefs about health and illness and provides the context by which an individual evaluates his or her situation and decides whether he or she needs social support and how much (Lopez, Antoni, Fekete, & Penedo, 2012). Not surprisingly, strong cultural differences exist in social support (Wang & Lau, 2015). Findings from three studies by Taylor et al. (2004) indicate that Asians and Asian Americans were less likely to rely on social support for coping with stress than are European Americans. Additionally, the data indicate that these cultural differences in seeking social support may be due to concerns with violating relationship norms. In the collectivist Asian cultures, the emphasis is to maintain group harmony and cohesion, putting the needs of others before the self. Therefore, relying on others for social support was seen as disrupting this balance (Taylor et al., 2004).

Gender is one of the most robust predictors of use of social support (Taylor et al., 2000; Unger, McAvay, Bruce, Berkman, & Seeman, 1999). Women receive and give more support over the life course, and women experience greater benefits from social network interactions (Bonneville-Roussy, Evans, Verner-Filion, Vallerand, & Bouffard, 2017; Wills et al., 2016). Some studies have shown that, for men, friendships and nonfamily activities decline with age, whereas women's friendships outside the home do not change (Field, 1999).

Strong gender differences exist in social support (Helgeson, 2012). Luckow, Reifman, and Mcintosh (1998) analyzed gender differences in coping and found that the largest difference arose in seeking and using social support. Of the 26 studies that tested for gender differences, one study showed no differences and 25 favored women. None of the studies favored men (Luckow et al., 1998). Indeed, so reliable is this gender effect that, following the early studies on affiliation in response to stress by Schachter (1959), most subsequent research on affiliation under stress used only female participants.

For most of the life cycle, females are more likely to mobilize social support, especially from other females, in times of stress (Taylor et al., 2000). They seek support out more, they receive more support, and they are more satisfied with the support they receive. New research suggests these differences amplify after adolescence but not many differences appear for adolescents. In a large meta-analysis of 273,149 participants, gender differences were mostly absent (Rueger, Malecki, Pyun, Aycock, & Coyle, 2016). Furthermore, although both male and female adolescents may use social support, they use it for different purposes. In one study, boys prioritized support that helped them achieve self-control as a first step toward awareness of their emotional distress, while girls prioritized support that helped them achieve awareness of the problem as a first step toward self-control (Martínez-Hernáez, Carceller-Maicas, DiGiacomo, & Ariste, 2016).

Female college students report having more available helpers and receiving more support than males do (e.g., Ptacek, Smith, & Zanas, 1992). Adult women maintain more same-sex close relationships, mobilize more social support in times of stress, rely less heavily on their spouses for social support, and turn to female friends more often (McDonald & Korabik, 1991). They also report more benefits from contact with their female friends and relatives (although they are also more vulnerable to network events as a cause of psychological distress) and provide more-frequent and more-effective social support to others than men (Taylor et al., 2000). Although females give help to both males and females in their support networks, they are more likely to seek help and social support from other female relatives and female friends than from males (Wethington, McLeod, & Kessler, 1987).

So consistent and strong are these findings that theorists have argued for basic gender differences in orientation toward others, with women maintaining a collectivist orientation (Markus & Kitayama, 1991) or connectedness (Niedenthal & Beike, 1997), and men maintaining a more individualistic orientation (Cross & Madson, 1997). These findings appear to generalize across cultures. In their study of six cultures, Whiting and Whiting (1975) found that women and girls seek more help from others and give more help to others than men do, and Edwards (1993) found similar sex differences across 12 cultures.

Let's go back to social support in pregnancy to highlight some more-specific cultural differences. Studies of ethnic minority groups in the United States show that for some groups (e.g., African Americans and Latinas), the family, particularly female relatives, are a critical source of support during pregnancy (Zuniga, 1992). Mexican American families tend to live in close units with tight bonds to other family units and with the extended family serving as the primary source of support (Tovar, 2017). Similarly, the family is the most important source of support to African Americans (Asiodu, Waters, Dailey, & Lyndon, 2017).

In one of the most cited studies of ethnic differences in support, Norbeck and Anderson (1989) measured life stress, social support, anxiety state, and substance use at mid and late pregnancy in Hispanic, European American, and African American low-income women. This study found that none of the social support measures was a significant predictor of gestational age, birth weight, or gestation and labor complications when the sample was analyzed as a whole. However, for African American women, lack of social support from the woman's partner or mother was a significant predictor of gestational complications and of the likelihood of prolonged labor and Cesarean section complications. For European Americans, social support was significantly related to length of labor and to drug use. None of the support measures was a statistically significant predictor of complications or birth outcomes for the Hispanics. Analyzing ethnic groups separately, none just using ethnicity as a statistical control, has yielded similar differences in social support in a number of other studies (e.g., Gurung et al., 2005).

In a direct test of ethnic differences in social support, Sagrestano, Feldman, Rini, Woo, and Dunkel-Schetter (1999) analyzed data from two multiethnic prospective studies of African American, Latina, and non-Hispanic White pregnant women and found strong ethnic differences in support from family and friends. African American women reported receiving the most support from family. While Latinas and European American women both reported receiving similar support levels, White women reported more family members in their social networks than did Latinas. Furthermore, Latinas reported higher-quality interactions with family. In another study, Campos et al. (2008) examined the association of **familialism**, a cultural value that emphasizes close family relationships, with social support, stress, pregnancy anxiety, and infant birth weight. Latinas scored higher on familialism than European Americans. Familialism was positively correlated with social support and negatively correlated with stress and pregnancy anxiety in the overall sample. The associations of familialism with social support and stress were significantly stronger among Latinas than European Americans. Moreover, higher social support was associated with higher infant birth weight among foreign-born Latinas only.

THEORIES OF SOCIAL SUPPORT CHANGE

How do our social networks change over time? Are you still friends with the people you were friends with when you were in grade school? Do you call the same people for help today as you did 10 years ago? There are two main theories of how our networks change (Gurung & Von Dras, 2007).

The **social convoy model** (Antonucci, 1991) provides a conceptual framework for studying age-related changes in structural and compositional characteristics of social networks (Figure 6.1). This model suggests that people are motivated to maintain their social network sizes as they

▼ FIGURE 6.1

A Social Convoy

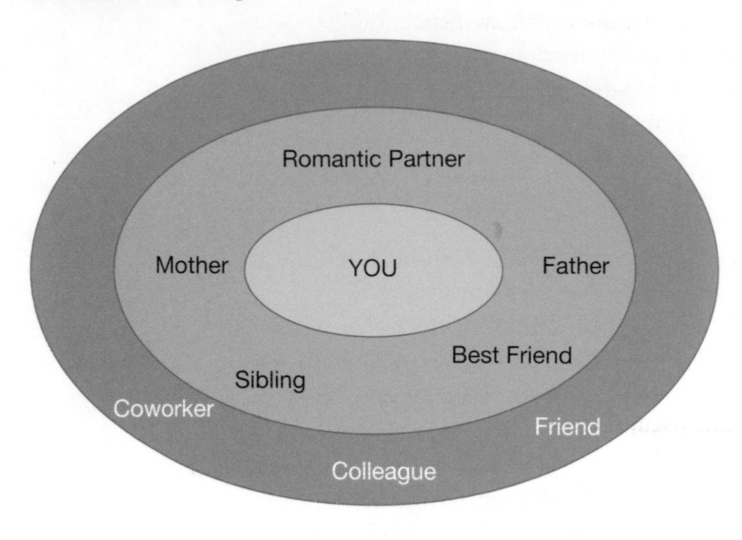

themselves age, despite changes in the composition of the networks. Individuals construct and maintain social relationships while becoming increasingly aware of specific strengths and weaknesses of particular members. This knowledge allows them to select different network members for different functions (e.g., certain people are relied on for emotional support and others for instrumental support) and possibly avoid members who are not supportive. Empirical support for the model (Antonucci, Ajrouch, & Birditt, 2014) clearly identifies the importance of simultaneously looking at different sources when studying changes in age-related social support. Although specific nonsupportive network members may drop out over time, the social convoy model suggests that general levels of support will be constant or even increase, given that social support is coordinated to optimize support receipt. We work to make sure we get the most out of our networks and that our networks contain those who will give us what we need.

Socioemotional selectivity theory (Carstensen, 1987; Carstensen & Fisher, 1991) proposes that people prune their social networks to maintain a desired emotional state depending on the extent to which time is perceived as limited. Basic functions of social interaction, such as maintaining a good mood, differ in respect to their relative importance for determining social preferences across the life span. When we get older, we believe that we have less time and want to maximize the time we have. We do not want to waste time on people or things that are not worth it to us. Emphasis in old age is placed on achieving short-term emotional goals. Correspondingly, whereas older adults' social networks may be smaller than those of younger adults, the numbers of close relationships are comparable (Lang, Staudinger, & Carstensen, 1998). Lang and Carstensen (1994) examined the interrelationships among age, network composition, and social support in a representative sample of 156 community-dwelling and institutionalized adults aged 70 to 104 years. They found that the social networks of older people were only half as large as those of younger people, but the number of very close relationships did not differ across age groups.

Both theories have empirical evidence supporting them (Antonucci et al., 2014; Barber, Opitz, Martins, Sakaki, & Mather, 2016). The evidence indicates that it is not necessarily the size, membership, or particular structure of the network, but the quality of transactions (i.e., perceived and received social support) that is critical to mental and physical health.

Is there clear evidence of whether support increases or decreases in time? Using longitudinal, community-based data from the MacArthur Studies of Successful Aging, Gurung et al. (2003) examined determinants of changes in social support receipt among 439 married older adults. Men and women in the sample were surveyed over a period of 6 years, and support received was assessed at the beginning and end of the study. In general, social support increased over time, especially for those with many preexisting social ties, but those experiencing more psychological distress and cognitive dysfunction reported more negative encounters with others.

One last point on social support. At the start of this chapter, we noticed there are many individual differences in coping. This is true for social support as well. We are active managers of our social networks

Synthesize, Evaluate, Apply

- What are the main types of social support?
- Which dimensions/types are more related to distress?
- What are some factors to bear in mind to provide effective social support?
- What would you rate as the most effective measure of coping?

and play a role in determining how much support we get. In addition to experiencing changes in who we have in our networks due to nonelective events such as death of network members, people differ in their propensity to prune or augment their own networks and in their likelihood of being pruned from or added to others' networks. Referred to in the support literature as evocative qualities, personal characteristics may be critical determinants of whether support transactions increase or decrease over time (Pierce, Lakey, Sarason, & Sarason, 1997).

KEYS TO COPING WITH STRESS

Suggesting you just relax may sound trite, but if you can successfully relax, you can bring about psychological and physiological changes that will help you deal well with stress. Even though it may seem easy, relaxing well requires some practice and some knowledge. Health psychological research has identified two major types of strategies that are useful to help people cope better and relax. The first broad category is called relaxation-based approaches and includes methods such as mindfulness, meditation, yoga, biofeedback, hypnosis, and the relaxation response. The second major category is cognitive-behavioral approaches and includes the use of learning theory (i.e., classical and operant conditioning) and other means designed to help a person label the problem, discuss the emotions associated with it, and find a way to solve it.

Relaxation-Based Approaches

In relaxation-based approaches, the goals are to reduce the cognitive load or number of thoughts a person is experiencing and to activate the parasympathetic nervous system to help the body recover from the activation of the sympathetic system. Most stressors that we experience today are stressors related to thinking. It is our worrying about problems and anticipating threats that cause the most havoc. We can sit around and think ourselves into a frenzy. Right now, you can let your mind wander to how much money you owe, to all the different things that you have to do, to a performance you have to give, to the kids you have to pick up or feed, and so on. The generation and fixation on all these thoughts can activate the stress response (mediated by the specific primary and secondary appraisals we make, of course). Relaxation-based approaches stop or at least reduce our fixation on these different stressful thoughts, thereby automatically lessening the stress response.

iStockphoto.com/ Image Source

▲ **Relaxation.** Here a person reads a magazine and tries to relax.

Most relaxation-based techniques ask a person to focus on a specific thought, word, image, or phrase. By focusing on just one item and giving it complete attention, the person is not thinking about all the things that are stressful. Together with the focus on a single object comes a slowing down of the breathing and a lowering of heart rate, cellular respiration, circulation, and essentially all the functions of the body supervised by the parasympathetic nervous system. Most importantly, the different stress chemicals (catecholamines

▼ FIGURE 6.2

Guided Imagery Instructions

Have a friend read these out to you slowly or if an e-book have Siri or Alexa read it to you. Find a comfortable position and listen to the words and try to picture what is being said.

Picture yourself right now in a log cabin somewhere high up in the mountains . . . It's wintertime, but even though it is very cold outside, you can enjoy the comfort of being in that cabin . . . for inside of the cabin is a large fireplace with a brightly blazing fire providing plenty of heat and warmth . . . and now you can go up to one of the windows and notice the frost on the windowpane . . . You can even put your warm hand on the cold, hard glass of the windowpane feeling the heat from your hand and fingers melting the frost . . . And then to get a view of the outside, you can begin to open the window, feeling it give way against the pressure of your hand; as the window opens, you take a big breath of that pure, fresh, cool mountain air and feel so good Looking outside you can see the snow on the ground and lots of tall evergreen trees You look off in the distance and see a wonderful view . . . perhaps of a valley down below or other mountain peaks far, far in the distance . . . And now you can close the window and walk over to the fire feeling its warmth as you get closer . . . Go ahead and sit back in a comfortable chair facing the fire or if you wish, you can lie down next to the fire on a soft bearskin rug . . . feeling the soothing warmth of the fire against your skin . . . letting your body absorb the warmth bringing deep relaxation and comfort . . . You can also enjoy looking at the fire, seeing the burning logs, hearing the crackling of the logs and hissing sound from the sap encountering the fire . . . smelling the fragrant smoke from the burning logs You can even look around noticing the room as it is illuminated by the light from the fire . . . noticing the flickering shadows on the walls . . . noticing the furniture and any other objects in the room . . . Just look around and take it all in all the sights and sounds and smells . . . feeling so peaceful in this place . . . So calm and completely tranquil And you can be reminded that even though the cold wind is howling outside, you can feel so warm and comfortable inside . . . letting that comfort spread to all parts of your mind And in this place you have absolutely nothing to worry about . . . for all that really matters is that you just allow yourself to enjoy the peacefulness, enjoy the deep comfort of being in this place right now . . . as a relaxed, drowsy feeling comes over you . . . and all the sights and sounds and smells gradually fade far away . . . while you drift . . . and float and dream in that cabin far off in the mountains. [Pause] And now, whenever you are ready, you can bring yourself back to a normal, alert, and wide-awake state by counting slowly from 1 to 3, so that when you reach the number 3 you will open your eyes feeling completely refreshed and comfortable.

and cortisol) are no longer released. Most practices such as mindfulness, meditation, and yoga use this slowing down of the breath and clearing of the thoughts to bring about stress relief. Mindfulness, in particular, involves intentionally bringing one's attention to the internal and external experiences occurring in the present moment and is often taught through a variety of meditation exercises. It has been empirically demonstrated to result in reductions of HIV-associated pain (George, Wongmek, Kaku, Nmashie, & Robinson-Papp, 2017), stress reduction (Wisner, Jones, & Gwin, 2010), and a host of other positive health outcomes (Crane et al., 2017; O'Driscoll, Byrne, Mc Gillicuddy, Lambert, & Sahm, 2017).

Sometimes guided imagery (imagining different peaceful scenarios) or aromatherapy (the use of calming smells and scents) can also aid in relaxation. Figure 6.2 gives you something you can try at home. Similarly, progressive muscle relaxation, in which you focus your attention on specific muscle groups and alternately tighten and relax them, can be beneficial.

Biofeedback involves the use of an electronic monitoring device that tracks physiological processes (e.g., brain activity) and provides feedback regarding changes, often on an app on your phone. For example, for a bit more than $100 you can buy a headband with electrodes that can help you relax (e.g., Muse headband). If you are stressed, your high activity is indicated by either a sound (e.g., pinging) or an image on a screen (e.g., a large circle). The goal is to make your brain activity slow down (hence making the pinging slow or the image on the screen smaller). By trying different methods, such as slowing down your breathing, you see the results directly on the phone or computer. The app reinforces your attempts to calm down by producing less pinging or rewarding you with chirping birds when your brain waves reflect calming. You are more likely to do whatever it was you did to reduce the pinging, and operant conditioning helps you develop a way to cope. Biofeedback is often used in conjunction with cognitive-behavioral therapy to help people cope with stress (Goessl, Curtiss, & Hofmann, 2017); in one head-to-head comparison, biofeedback was more effective than exercise for stress reduction (Meier & Welch, 2016).

Another form of conditioning, classical conditioning, lies between relaxation and behavioral therapy. **Systematic desensitization** is a form of classical conditioning in which stressful thoughts or events are paired with relaxation (e.g., Triscari, Faraci, Catalisano, D'Angelo, & Urso, 2015). According to classical conditioning, whenever two events are linked enough times, responses that came naturally in response to one event now are found to occur in

Will & Deni McIntyre/Science Source

▲ **Biofeedback.** A patient undergoes biofeedback monitoring for stress. The machines are measuring brainwaves, blood pressure, and heart rate, and conveying the data to the patient in real time.

▼ TABLE 6.4

An Anxiety Hierarchy for Systematic Desensitization

Degree of fear	
5	I'm standing on the balcony of the top floor of an apartment tower.
10	I'm standing on a stepladder in the kitchen to change a light bulb.
15	I'm walking on a ridge. The edge is hidden by shrubs and treetops.
20	I'm sitting on the slope of a mountain, looking out over the horizon.
25	I'm crossing a bridge 6 feet above a creek. The bridge consists of an 18-inch-wide board with a handrail on one side.
30	I'm riding a ski lift 8 feet above the ground.
35	I'm crossing a shallow, wide creek on an 18-inch-wide board, 3 feet above the water level.
40	I'm climbing a ladder outside the house to reach a second-story window.
45	I'm pulling myself up a 30-degree wet, slippery slope on a steel cable.
50	I'm scrambling up an 8-foot-high rock.
55	I'm walking 10 feet on a resilient, 18-inch-wide board, which spans an 8-foot-deep gulch.
60	I'm walking on a wide plateau, 2 feet from the edge of a cliff.
65	I'm skiing an intermediate hill. The snow is packed.
70	I'm walking over a railway trestle.
75	I'm walking on the side of an embankment. The path slopes to the outside.
80	I'm riding a chair lift 15 feet above the ground.
85	I'm walking up a long, steep slope.
90	I'm walking up (or down) a 15-degree slope on a 3-foot-wide trail. On one side of the trail the terrain drops down sharply; on the other side is a steep upward slope.
95	I'm walking on a 3-foot-wide ridge. The slopes on both sides are long and more than 25 degrees steep.
100	I'm walking on a 3-foot-wide ridge. The trail slopes on one side. The drop on either side of the trail is more than 25 degrees.

The most stressful event is at the bottom. You pair relaxation with the first event and then move down until you can imagine your most stressful event and be relaxed.

response to the second event. Let's say that you are scared to speak in public. Your first step is to create a hierarchy of the things about public speaking that scare you with the scariest thing at the top of the list (e.g., the moment just before you start and are facing 50 strangers) and the least scary aspect at the bottom (e.g., a month before you have to speak). Then, while thinking about the thing at the bottom of your list you practice relaxing. You do this until you can think about the speech a month away and still feel the conditioned response, relaxation. You now pick the next scary event in your hierarchy and pair that one with relaxation. In this way, you move up your list until you can think about being in front of people and still feel relaxed. Once this link between the thought and the relaxation has been strengthened, the next time you are in front of a group of people you should feel the relaxation that you conditioned (Table 6.4).

Cognitive-Behavioral Approaches

Cognitive-behavioral therapies that treat clinical disorders can easily be adapted to cope with stress. For example, **cognitive restructuring** can be used to replace stress-provoking thoughts (e.g., "Everyone is going to be looking at how I perform") with realistic, unthreatening thoughts (e.g., "Everyone is too busy to see what I am doing"). Similarly, Ellis's (1987) rational-emotional therapy is often used to identify and change irrational beliefs that a person may have that can cause stress. In a similar fashion, Beck's (1976) cognitive therapy involves the identification and change of maladaptive thought patterns that can often be automatic and cause stress (e.g., you always assume that people do not believe you). Another cognitive approach, Meichenbaum and Cameron's (1983) stress-inoculation training, provides people with skills for reducing stress such as having the person (1) learn more about the nature of the stressor and how people react to it, (2) learn and practice things to do when they do get stressed (separately referred to as proactive coping by Aspinwall & Taylor, 1997), and (3) practice the new skills in response to a real or imagined stressor.

Emotional expression is one of the most widely researched forms of cognitive-behavioral therapies in recent history (Niederhoffer & Pennebaker, 2002), as shown in Table 6.5. Although most therapies involve the sharing and discussion of a troubling issue, emotional expression involves disclosure in writing. A number of studies have shown that just writing

▼ TABLE 6.5

Key Examples of Emotional Expression Studies

Author/Date	Sample	Duration	Result
Francis and Pennebaker (1992)	University employees	1/week, 4 weeks	Lower absenteeism
Pennebaker (1991)	College students	3/week	Better grades
Spera et al. (1994)	Unemployed professionals		Quicker reemployment
Pennebaker and Susman (1988)	College students		Improved immune functioning
Langens and Schuler (2007)	College students	Study 1–3 days (20 minutes each), Study 2–4 days (20 minutes each)	Reduction of emotional impact of upsetting event (Study 1) and in physical symptoms (Study 2)
Petrie et al. (2004)	HIV-infected patients	4 days (30 minutes each)	Increased lymphocyte count
Ullrich and Lutgendorf (2002)	College students	1 month	Increased meaning finding
Zakowski et al. (2004)	Cancer patients	3 days (20 minutes each)	Reduced stress

out your feelings can lead to a range of positive outcomes. The basic procedure is simple. Participants write about extremely important emotional issues, exploring their deepest emotions and thoughts. They are asked to include their relationships with others (parents, lovers, and friends); their past, present, and future; and their goals and plans. All their writing remains completely confidential, and they are asked not to worry about spelling or grammar.

iStockphoto.com/AJ_Watt

▲ **Exercising.** Physical activity is a great stress reliever.

The only rule is that once they begin writing they are to continue until the time (often 15 minutes) is up. People following this simple exercise are less likely to get sick (Richards, Pennebaker, & Beall, 1995) and report reduced levels of stress, fewer negative moods, and less depression (Kline, Fekete, & Sears, 2008).

Another way to cope with stress is to increase your physical activity (Chafin, Christenfeld, & Gerin, 2008; Lang et al., 2017). People who exercise on a regular basis tend to be less depressed and less stressed (Cairney, Kwan, Veldhuizen, & Faulkner, 2014), and it even helps coping with pain during times of trauma (Liedl et al., 2011). If you are wondering if this is just a correlation and guessing that people who are less stressed may exercise more (notice how many people skip their workouts when they have a lot of things due?), fear not. Even taking a walk in the park helps cope with job stress (de Bloom et al., 2017).

Synthesize, Evaluate, Apply

- How would you design a stress management program for people at a local company using what you know about coping?
- What are the coping styles inherent to emotional expression interventions?
- How can religion be just another form of social support?
- How are the different physiological components of stress counteracted by the different coping methods?

In addition to correlational studies, a number of experimental manipulations have established that exercise helps individuals cope with stress (Babyak et al., 2000). For example, Johansson et al. (2008) measured anxiety and depression in 59 regular *qi gong* (a traditional Chinese exercise; see Chapter 3) exercisers. Depression, anger, fatigue, and anxiety scores decreased significantly in the *qi gong* group but not in the control group. Exercise helps mainly by influencing the release and metabolism of stress hormones and varying the way that the sympathetic nervous system reacts to stress (Forcier et al., 2006). For example, 53 members of the Austin Fire Department were randomly assigned to an exercise or no exercise condition and then stressed with a fire drill. Before training, the groups did not differ in their cardiovascular response to the fire drill. Significant group differences were observed after training. Exercise-trained participants reacted with significantly lower pulse and mean arterial pressure than their counterparts in the control condition (Throne, Bartholomew, Craig, & Farrar, 2000). The next time you feel stressed with work, it may be worth the effort to exercise even if you only take a quick-paced walk outside.

How do you know when coping works? You feel better; your heart rate, pulse, and breathing are normal; your thinking is clearer; and your general sense of well-being improves. Consistent with the movement in psychology to focus on the positive outcomes in life, referred to as the **positive psychology** movement (Seligman & Csikszentmihalyi, 2000), health psychologists have begun to investigate a wide range of positive outcomes (Goodmon, Middleditch, Childs, & Pietrasiuk, 2016; Slezackova & Sobotkova, 2017).

APPLICATION SHOWCASE

MAY GOD HELP YOU

Millions of people around the world turn in the same direction when they are stressed. It is not a point on the compass; it is toward God. It may not be the same God, but for many people religion and religious institutions provide a major way to cope with stress. After being neglected in the field of psychology for many years, religion and prayer have received a lot of attention in the past decade. Does believing in God cure diseases and help you live longer?

Prior to the 1700s there was no division between church and state and religion guided everyday life (Armstrong, 2016). Then with the rise of secularism, religion moved out of politics. But, as often in our history, world events forced religion back onto center stage. The 9/11 attacks by Islamic terrorists in the United States, the clashes between Palestinians and Israelis in the Middle East and Hindu and Muslims in India, and the sex abuse scandals in the Catholic Church are just some examples. More importantly, religion is a focus of study because most people who are stressed or who face seemingly insurmountable problems pray. In fact, religious beliefs and practices appear to be especially important in stressful situations that push people to the limits of their resources (Von Dras, 2017). Religious coping has been found to help people deal with a range of problems such as coping with hurricanes (Tausch et al., 2011), living in stressful neighborhoods (Krause, 1998), and dealing with lack of sexual gratification (Wallin & Clark, 1964).

Are you religious? To some, the answer is as simple as saying whether they believe in God or not. To others and to the researchers who study it, **religiosity** is measured by looking at the frequency of temple/church/mosque/synagogue attendance, the average frequency of prayer, and the commitment to religious rituals. Many people classify themselves as followers of a certain denomination but rush to add that they are not practicing. Such people may identify themselves as being of a certain religion (e.g., Hindu), but still not stick to prescriptions of that religion (e.g., being vegetarian). No matter what your religious background, you probably use some form of religious coping at some time or the other. Different world religions such as Christianity, Islam, and Hinduism include different beliefs, rituals, practices, and standards, but they all share the idea that entities or higher powers created us and are in some way involved in our lives. Turning to the higher powers in times of stress is as natural as a young child turning to her parent when she is scared or threatened.

An interesting example of the use of religion and faith as a coping mechanism can be seen in a movie called *Signs.* In it, Mel Gibson plays a former priest named Graham Hess who lost his faith after his wife was killed in an accident. Strange crop circles turn up on his Pennsylvania farm and around the world. Suddenly, aliens invade the earth (the circles are the signs of contact). People are terrified. Graham's brother in the movie needs reassurance, and Graham replies that there are two kinds of people. Some people see scary things like the aliens and recognize them as signs from God. These are the people who believe in miracles and have faith. They see these signs as evidence that God exists, trust that God will save them, and are calm. The other kind of people are nonbelievers and, seeing the invasion, realize that they have no one to turn to or no one to watch out for them and are terrified. Which type you are determines how you cope. Although not scientifically tested (this is a Hollywood production, after all), that basic dichotomy is at the heart of the role of religion in coping.

As you read in our discussion of coping styles, the COPE does have a subscale to assess the use of religion, but the study of religious coping has been much more intensive than that. Pargament (1997), in his book on religion and psychology, documents an array of cases in which religion is used as a coping mechanism and notes that our tendency to turn to God intensifies as situations become more critical. More recently, Von Dras (2017) edited a book demonstrating how a variety of spiritual practices can lead to better health.

Of course, people use religion in different ways. You can turn everything over to God (deferring religious coping: "Whatever happens is God's will, what will be will be"), you can engage God's help and work with what God has provided (self-directed religious coping: "God helps those who help themselves"), or you can work with God (collaborative religious coping: "With God on my side, how can I lose?"). Religious coping is actively used in a number of different context such as predicting personal growth (Exline, Hall, Pargament, & Harriott, 2017) and coping with cancer (Bowie et al., 2017).

Pargament, Smith, Koenig, and Perez (1998) identified two major dimensions of religious coping: positive and negative religious coping. Positive religious coping methods (e.g., seeking spiritual support from God and using collaborative coping) have helped a wide range of people including refugees (Ai, Peterson, & Huang, 2003), victims of natural disasters (Smith, Pargament, Brant, & Oliver, 2000), older hospitalized patients (Koenig, Pargament, & Nielsen, 1998), and students (Pargament, Koenig, & Perez, 2000). Negative religious coping methods (e.g., questioning the power of God and expressing anger toward God) have been related to poorer adjustment among many groups such as medical rehabilitation patients (Fitchett, Rybarczyk, DeMarco, & Nicholas, 1999), students (Exline, Yali, & Lobel, 1999), and victims of natural disasters (Pargament et al., 1998).

Religious coping in general can be such a great aid that the lack of it can be problematic for some. For example, Grinstein-Cohen, Katz, and Sarid (2016) found that women coping with the stress of trying to get pregnant significantly benefitted from their religious beliefs and religious observances. Being religious was positively correlated with their problem-solving coping.

CHAPTER REVIEW

SUMMARY

- Coping is defined as individual efforts to manage distressing problems and emotions that affect the physical and psychological outcomes of stress.
- A coping response may be anything we do to reestablish our homeostatic balance.
- Many different cultural factors buffer or moderate and mediate the effects of stress and influence coping. Our age, sex, socioeconomic status, religion, and ethnicity are some of the key cultural buffers.
- The two primary coping styles are problem-focused or approach coping and emotion-focused or avoidant coping. The efficacy of each depends on the nature of the stressor, especially its duration and controllability.
- A variety of personality traits is associated with more-effective coping. People high in self-esteem, who are conscientious, low in neuroticism, optimistic, hardy, and resilient and have a sense of mastery cope better with stress.
- Social support is one of the most important factors influencing coping. Commonly defined as emotional, informational, or instrumental assistance from others, social support has been associated with a variety of positive health outcomes.
- Social support can be received or perceived, global or specific, or vary in function. It can be emotional, informational, or tangible. Support works best when it matches the needs of the individual.
- Some cultural groups have higher levels of support than others, depending on the context. African Americans tend to derive more support from their families than do European Americans. Individuals with strong religious ties perceive having more support than those with weak religious ties. Women also give and receive more social support than men.
- Coping is commonly measured by questionnaire and is divided into many categories. Major types of coping are confrontative, distancing, self-controlling, accepting responsibility, seeking social support, escape avoidance, positive reappraisal, suppression, planning, turning to religion, venting of emotions, denial, and the use of humor.
- Two major categories of coping are relaxation-based (meditation, yoga, biofeedback, hypnosis, guided imagery, and progressive muscle relaxation) and cognitive-behavioral (using learning theory, systematic desensitization, psychoanalysis, and emotional expression).

TEST YOURSELF

Check your understanding of the topics in this chapter by answering the following questions.

1. Coping is best defined as
   a. individual efforts made to manage the outcomes of stress.
   b. processes designed to increase relaxation.
   c. ways to prevent stressful events from occurring.
   d. techniques to reduce the impact of stress.

2. Life is complex and few variables directly influence each other. Moderating variables
   a. are those that directly influence stress and coping.
   b. change the relationship between variables.
   c. are more powerful than mediator variables.
   d. are more important for predicting Western coping styles.

3. Most of the following variables can be mediators and moderators except for
   a. happiness.
   b. optimism.
   c. social support.
   d. sex.

4. The theory of social support change that proposes that people prune their networks to maintain a desired emotional state depending on the extent to which time is perceived as limited is
   a. socioemotional selectivity theory.
   b. gain-loss theory.
   c. social convoy theory.
   d. optimization theory.

5. One of the most commonly studied mediators in health psychology is
   a. sex.
   b. social support.
   c. health behaviors.
   d. stress.

6. The two most basic styles of coping are
   a. positive and negative.
   b. acute and chronic.
   c. approach and avoidant.
   d. primary and secondary.
7. Each of the following is considered one of the Big Five factors in personality except
   a. extroversion.
   b. neuroticism.
   c. agreeableness.
   d. optimism.
8. In contrast to early research on the Type A personality, current views hold that the unhealthiest component of the Type A profile is
   a. being competitive.
   b. showing a sense of time urgency.
   c. being hostile.
   d. being hardy.
9. People who enjoy challenges, have a high level of control, and are committed to their lives are high in
   a. optimism.
   b. hardiness.
   c. extroversion.
   d. mastery.
10. The empirical evidence suggests that the following cultural group receives the most social support from its members during stressors such as pregnancy:
   a. European American.
   b. Chinese American.
   c. Japanese American.
   d. Mexican American.

KEY TERMS, CONCEPTS, AND PEOPLE ▶▶

approach coping, **151**
avoidant coping, **151**
biofeedback, **166**
cognitive restructuring, **168**
COPE, **149**
coping, **148**
coping process, **150**
coping strategies, **152**
coping styles, **151**
daily process methodology, **151**
emotion-focused coping, **152**
familialism, **163**
functional measures, **160**
hardiness, **156**
mastery, **156**
mediators, **149**
moderators, **149**
network measures, **160**
optimism, **156**
perceived support, **161**
personality, **154**
positive psychology, **169**
problem-focused coping, **152**
received support, **161**
relational coping, **151**
relationship-focused coping **151**
religiosity, **170**
resilient, **157**
social convoy model, **163**
social support, **149**
socioemotional selectivity theory, **164**
systematic desensitization, **167**
Type A coronary-prone behavior pattern, **155**

ESSENTIAL READINGS ▶▶

Aldwin, C. (2019). Coping. In T. A. Revenson & R. A. R. Gurung (Eds.), *Handbook of health psychology* (3e). New York, NY: Routledge.

Knoll, N., Scholz, U., & Bitzen, B. (2019). Social support and family processes. In T. A. Revenson & R. A. R. Gurung (Eds.), *Handbook of health psychology* (3e). New York, NY: Routledge.

Skinner, E. A., Edge, K., Altman, J., & Sherwood, H. (2003). Searching for the structure of coping: A review and critique of category systems for classifying ways of coping. *Psychological Bulletin, 129*(2), 216–269.

HEALTH BEHAVIORS

Chapter 7

Why Don't We Do What We Need To?

Models of Behavior Change

Chapter 8

Health Behaviors

Eating, Being Active, Smoking, and Drinking

CHAPTER 7

WHY DON'T WE DO WHAT WE NEED TO?

Models of Behavior Change

iStockPhoto.com/Sompong_tom

Chapter 7 Outline

MEASURING UP

WHAT DO YOU BELIEVE ABOUT EXERCISING?

The following are possible outcomes of not exercising: coronary heart disease, high blood pressure, heart attack, low stamina, poor physical work capacity, obesity, poor muscle tone, poor joint flexibility, stress, cancer, depression, anxiety, tension.

How likely do you think it is that any of these could happen to you?

How severe do you think the consequences of each are or could be?

How much do you worry or care about each of these outcomes?

What are five health behaviors that you could improve on? Do you know the extent to which doing them or not doing them influences your risk of an early death? Most of us know what it takes to live a long and healthy life—at least we think we know. Eat well. Don't drink too much alcohol. Don't smoke. Get some exercise. These are some of the most common actions considered to make someone healthy. You can also hope that you do not inherit any dangerous conditions from your parents. However, it is not that easy. You may want to eat well, but what exactly does eating well mean? You may think you know, but research and the media suggest that the right things to eat are always changing. One day, eating a lot of meat is thought to be bad for you; the next day not eating enough meat is bad. Even if you do figure out what is good for you through all the mixed messages in the media, it is still one thing to know what the good thing to do is, and a completely different thing to actually do it.

▼ Ponder This

What keeps you from doing healthy behaviors you know you should but that you do not?

What are the different thoughts, feelings, and behaviors that can keep someone from physical activity?

Why would diverse groups of people perform healthy behaviors to different extents?

Likewise, you may know that exercise is important, but do you manage to exercise as often as you should? Do you plan on exercising but don't because you are too tired or you do not have enough time? Join the club, and we don't mean the YMCA or your local health club . . . just being a member of a health club does not always mean you will exercise more anyway. Millions of people would like to exercise, and plan on exercising more than they do currently, but just do not manage to do it.

In this chapter, we will look at how Health Psychologists explain why we don't do all that we should and why we do some of what we should not. Even though people know that it is important to get physical activity, why do some people not exercise? If smokers know the risks of tobacco addiction, why do they still smoke? What are the different stages that people go through as they consider changing a behavior and then try to do it? Health Psychologists have devised many theories to explain the performance of health behaviors and ways to institute change (Glanz, Rimer, & Viswanath, 2015). My goal in this chapter is to provide you with information to help you become healthier. I shall review both the psychological research describing the processes of change and the key factors that prevent it, as well as key interventions shown to improve health behaviors.

WHAT ARE HEALTHY BEHAVIORS?

Healthy behaviors are defined as any specific behaviors that maintain and enhance health. These can range from the mundane (e.g., brushing your teeth and flossing) to the critical (e.g., not practicing safe sex). Health behaviors vary on a number of dimensions. Some are episodic (e.g., getting a flu shot) others are long-term/lifestyle (e.g., healthy eating). You may need to restrict behaviors (e.g., stop smoking) or add behaviors (e.g., start exercising). A behavior such as cigarette smoking may need a gradual change (e.g., cutting down on amount smoked) or a rapid change (e.g., going cold turkey).

Many of our daily behaviors influence our health, as well as how long and how happily we live. Do you wear your seat belt when you ride in a car? You should. A majority of road fatalities are due to the drivers or passengers not wearing seat belts (National Highway Traffic Safety Administration, 2017). Wearing a seat belt is a health behavior. Many of the most common health problems that plague us today are worsened, and in some cases even caused, by unhealthy behaviors. For example, the absence of excess body fat, a result of healthy eating and adequate physical activity, lowers the risks of most cancers (Lauby-Secretan et al., 2016). One specific unhealthy behavior, smoking, can be tied to a range of negative health outcomes such as lung cancer and heart disease (National Cancer Institute, 2017).

Before health psychology was a field of study in its own right, health educators stressed the relevance of political, economic, and social factors as determinants of health (Derryberry, 1960; Nyswander, 1966). In the 1970s the emphasis shifted to urging health educators to focus on the institutions and social conditions that impede or facilitate individuals reaching optimal health instead of focusing on just individuals and their families (Griffiths, 1972). Today, health behavior change takes place in schools, communities, work sites, health-care settings, homes, and social media (Glanz et al., 2015). **Health education** attempts to close the gap between what is known about optimal health practices and what is actually done (Griffiths, 1972). The goal of health education is to teach people to limit behaviors detrimental to their health and increase behaviors that are conducive to health (Simonds, 1976). Closely paralleling the biopsychosocial approach, health educators pay attention to a range of factors including the individual, interpersonal relationships, institutions, community, and public policy (Smedley & Syme, 2000). Health psychologists essentially follow the same agenda but with more focus on individual factors such as attitudes, beliefs, and personality traits.

The Healthy People Programs

Different health behaviors are important for different people. Nonsmoking and fit but very overworked nurses may need to change their sleeping habits. On the other hand, healthy college students practicing unsafe sex may have sexual behavior as their key change behavior. The most important health behaviors are outlined as **Leading Health Indicators** established by the U.S. Department of Health and Human Services' (DHHS') **Healthy People 2020** Program. Healthy People 2020 involves 42 topic areas with nearly 600 objectives (DHHS, 2017). A smaller set of Healthy People 2020 objectives, the Leading Health Indicators, communicate high-priority health issues and actions that can be taken to address them. The Leading Health Indicators are listed in Table 7.1. The Healthy People series of programs are science-based, 10-year national objectives for promoting health and preventing disease. The program consists of a statement of national health objectives designed to identify the most significant preventable threats to the health of Americans as well as national goals to reduce these threats. Healthy People 2020 is guiding a national

iStockphoto.com/ Daxus

▲ **Physical Activity.** Being physically active is one of the most beneficial health behaviors you can perform. Many individuals use gyms or clubs to get their workouts, but even paddle boarding, walking, or climbing stairs at work can burn enough energy to keep you healthy.

▼ TABLE 7.1

Healthy People 2020: Objective Topic Areas

Healthy People 2020: Objective Topic Areas
Access to Health Services
Adolescent Health
Arthritis, Osteoporosis, and Chronic Back Conditions
Blood Disorders and Blood Safety
Cancer
Chronic Kidney Disease
Dementias, including Alzheimer's Disease
Diabetes
Disability and Health
Early and Middle Childhood
Educational and Community-Based Programs
Environmental Health
Family Planning
Food Safety
Genomics
Global Health
Health Communication and Health Information Technology

(Continued)

▼ TABLE 7.1 (Continued)

Health-Care–Associated Infections
Health-Related Quality of Life and Well-Being
Hearing and Other Sensory or Communication Disorders
Heart Disease and Stroke
HIV
Immunization and Infectious Diseases
Injury and Violence Prevention
Lesbian, Gay, Bisexual, and Transgender Health
Maternal, Infant, and Child Health
Medical Product Safety
Mental Health and Mental Disorders
Nutrition and Weight Status
Occupational Safety and Health
Older Adults
Oral Health
Physical Activity
Preparedness
Public Health Infrastructure
Respiratory Diseases
Sexually Transmitted Diseases
Sleep Health
Social Determinants of Health
Substance Abuse
Tobacco Use
Vision

Source: HealthPeople.gov, n.d.

improvement effort to increase quality of life and to eliminate health disparities. Planning for Healthy People 2030 is currently under way.

The Healthy People Consortium, an alliance of more than 350 national membership organizations and 250 state health, mental health, substance abuse, and environmental agencies, developed the current Healthy People 2020 program. Additionally, the public commented via a series of nine regional meetings across the country and an interactive website. The American public had a say and provided input from all levels of society. You can add your comments for the next version of this program, HealthyPeople 2030, here: https://www.healthypeople.gov/2020/About-Healthy-People/Development-Healthy-People-2030/Public-Comment. The Leading Health Indicators will be used to measure the health of people in the United States between the years 2010 and 2020.

WHAT DETERMINES HEALTH BEHAVIORS?

Living a healthy life entails more than just doing the right things on a personal level. Many health behaviors necessitate the help of medical institutions and trained professionals. For example, although you control what you buy and eat, whether you exercise or smoke, and how much you drink, it is also important to have medical check-ups. Cancers, such as breast cancer and testicular cancer, begin as tiny lumps. Whereas personal self-examinations catch many lumps in their early stages, it is important for both men and women to schedule regular check-ups for a thorough examination. Scheduled check-ups for prostate or breast cancers are more important for older men and women, respectively, but even young children need to visit medical institutions for vaccinations and immunizations.

▲ **Mammogram Machine.** Women being tested place their breasts between the plates, which then are clamped down to squeeze the breast tissue. Although playing a key role in the prevention of breast cancer, mammograms can be painful and cause discomfort. Tests for testicular cancer do not involve any such machine squeezing.

Our developmental history—comprising both our physiological and psychological make-up—plays a major role in the health behaviors we practice. If you smoke, why? Why don't you get enough exercise? Do you eat well? No single factor or set of factors adequately accounts for why we do what we do (Sallis & Owen, 2015). We need to examine our developmental history and our social, cultural, and economic backgrounds using the biopsychosocial perspective, which can answer all these questions (Figure 7.1).

Biological Factors

Biologically, we are born with many predispositions that can influence the types of health behaviors that we practice. For example, if both your parents are very overweight, there is a good chance that you will be overweight or have a propensity to put on weight. From our parents we inherit metabolic rates, which determine how we break down and process what we eat. We also inherit the type of muscle definition we can have (Andersen, Schjerling, & Saltin, 2000).

▼ FIGURE 7.1

Key Factors Influencing Health Behaviors

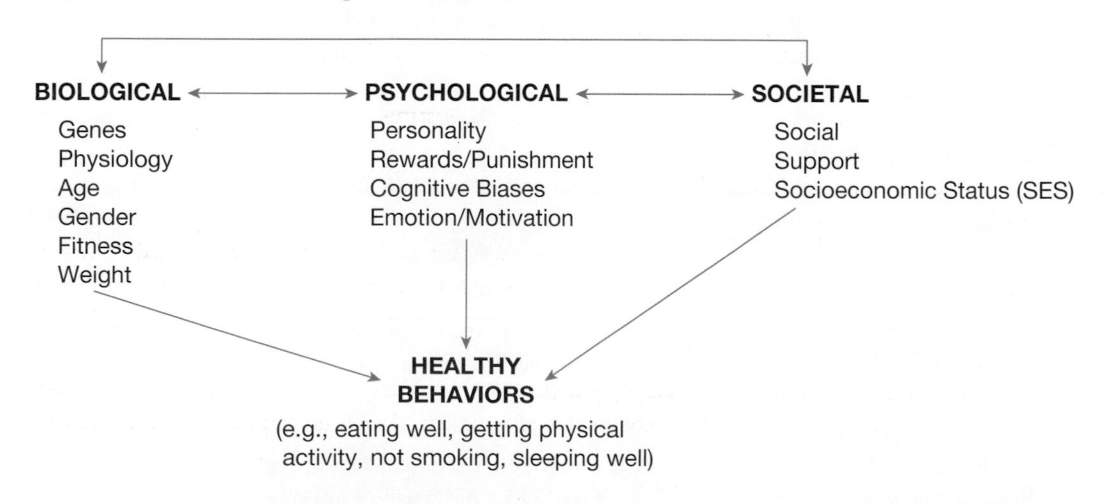

For example, if you have always wanted a flat stomach with each separate muscle block clearly defined (a six-pack), you must watch what you eat and do many sit-ups. Unfortunately, that is not the end of the story. Some of us will not be able to achieve a well-defined six-pack no matter how many sit-ups we do because we may not have the specific muscle type for this. Yes, having the right muscle type in the abdominal region is determined by your biology and genetic inheritance. Similarly, the likelihood of becoming addicted to smoking or drinking has been shown to have a biological basis. For example, the dopamine D_2 receptor gene plays a role in alcoholism. People (and animals) who have more copies of this gene show a higher likelihood of becoming addicted to alcohol. Dopamine is also associated with addiction to gambling and to food addictions (Majuri et al., 2017).

Psychological Factors

In examining the psychological predictors of health behaviors, we see many of the usual suspects again. Similar to our discussion of stress in Chapter 5, personality traits and characteristics play a large role in determining health behaviors (Husson, Denollet, Ezendam, & Mols, 2017). The Big Five personality traits (discussed in Chapter 5) are good indicators of a person's likelihood to practice specific health behaviors such as getting a cervical screening (Hill & Gick, 2011) and can even predict children's health behaviors. Studies of specific behaviors show similar results: boys higher in extroversion are more likely to attempt unsafe cliff jumps and practice unsafe water activities (Moran, Quan, Bennett, & Franklin, 2011). Watch who you swim with.

Conscientiousness and agreeableness are particularly noteworthy predictors of health behaviors and cognitive attitudes and tendencies (Hagger-Johnson & Whiteman, 2007). You can guess who is more likely to watch what they eat. In a study of more than 1,000 older adults, the healthiest eaters were those high in conscientiousness and agreeableness (Mõttus et al., 2013). However, because associations are evident for each of the personality traits, all of the Big Five personality traits should be included in research on health behaviors to investigate their relevance for clinical practice. It is also important to note that positive traits are not always associated with positive health behaviors. For example, extroverts are more likely to participate in risky behaviors such as drinking (Pilatti, Cupani, & Pautassi, 2015) and to start drinking at an earlier age (Nees et al., 2012).

In a demonstration of the long-term impact of personality, Hampson, Goldberg, Vogt, and Dubanoski (2007) studied 1,054 participants in the Hawaii Personality and Health study. This population-based longitudinal study of personality and health spanned 40 years from childhood to midlife. The study found that childhood agreeableness and conscientiousness influenced adult health status mediated by healthy eating habits and smoking. Similarly, Caspi et al. (1997) followed individuals from infancy until the age of 21. Results showed that a constellation of adolescent personality traits (with developmental origins in childhood) did link to different health-risk behaviors at 21. The study also determined that associations between personality and different health-risk behaviors were not seen simply because the same people engaged in different health-risk behaviors. Instead, the associations implicated the same personality type in different but related behaviors. Therefore, in planning campaigns, perhaps health professionals need to design programs that appeal to the unique psychological makeup of persons most at risk for particular behaviors (Caspi et al., 1997).

Social Factors

The social part of the biopsychosocial model is very important as well. Think back to when you were young. Did your parents ever hassle you about what you watched on television, which movies you went to, or (depending on how old you are) which websites you surfed on the Internet? If you complained about the restrictions they placed on what you were exposed to, here is something to think about: The media messages we are exposed to have a strong impact on the types of health behaviors we perform. The culture we live in and what we are surrounded by give us a lot of information about what is acceptable and what is not. As we grow and look out at the communicators of culture (e.g., magazines, movies, or television), what we see can influence what we do. This sounds feasible, right?

To prove this association Meija et al. (2017) studied 2,502 Argentinian students in 33 secondary schools who had never smoked; about 68% of the students completed a follow-up survey 17 months later. Then, the researchers watched a lot of movies. Focusing on the top 100 money makers, they counted how much tobacco use was featured. The students were asked which of the movies they had seen. It was found that watching movies with tobacco use had an effect. At follow-up, 24% of students who had never smoked reported having tried smoking and nearly 10% were regular smokers. In general, exposure to smoking in films increased the likelihood of future smoking.

Psychological and social factors also interact. Jessor, Turbin, and Costa (1998) tested the role of psychosocial factors on a wide range of adolescent health-enhancing behaviors—healthy diet, regular exercise, adequate sleep, good dental hygiene, and seat belt use. The researchers assessed the perceived effects of health-compromising behavior, the presence of parents or friends who model health behavior, involvement in prosocial activities, and church attendance among 1,493 Hispanic, White, and Black high school students in a large, urban school district. Both individual difference factors and social factors (e.g., church attendance and behaviors of social networks) predicted adolescent health behavior. Correspondingly, Health Psychologists incorporate more of a public health perspective that is concerned with individuals as part of a larger community (Glanz, Rimer, & Viswanath, 2015). Newer interventions target not only the individual but also interpersonal, environmental, and organizational factors (Heaney & Viswanath, 2015).

Given how personality traits influence a number of different behaviors, how can you best use knowledge of someone's personality to predict his or her likelihood of performing health behaviors?

Synthesize, Evaluate, Apply

- Pick a healthy behavior that you do not perform sufficiently. Use each of the three main theories of health behavior change to explain why.
- What are the pros and cons of the Healthy People 2020 approach to changing health behaviors? Look at www.healthypeople.gov for more details.
- What are the main biopsychosocial factors determining why you get the physical activity that you do?

CHANGING HEALTH BEHAVIORS

Let's make this personal. Reading this book highlights the importance of health behaviors. There are probably some behaviors you would like to change. How do you do it? Before we review the scientific literature on the mechanisms of behavior change, take a look at what it would take to change your own behavior. As you can see from the preceding section, our health behaviors are a result of a constellation of factors. Your biology, your personality, and societal factors all play an important role. Identifying the critical factors determining the behavior is a good starting point.

Pick a health behavior (e.g., smoking, eating, physical activity) and pick an achievable goal that is specific (e.g., I will drop 10 pounds by semester's end). Write both in the margins right now. A major part of individual-level interventions, goal setting, and behavior contracting involve setting achievable incremental goals, committing to achieving the goals through a behavior contract, monitoring and documenting progress, and reinforcing goal achievements through rewards (Glanz et al., 2015). Key properties of your goal include difficulty (e.g., running 10 miles vs. jogging for 1 mile), the time frame (e.g., lose 1 pound in a week or 20 pounds in a year), and type of goal setting (e.g., self-set, doctor prescribed, or collaborative). The next chapter provides more information on key health behaviors to provide you with some target levels to aim for. If you have not written your behavior and goal out, do it before moving on.

Once you have a specific behavior, take a week or two and closely monitor the behavior that you want to change. If you would like to eat better, write down everything you eat or drink for a week (including times, places, and hunger level). If you want to stop smoking, similarly write down every time you smoke (the urge, the company, and so on). Self-observation or self-monitoring is the first and most important step. Make sure you list all relevant biopsychosocial factors. For example, physical activity is influenced by your weight at the biological level, self-efficacy at the psychological level, and support from family and friends at the societal level.

Next, list the barriers that are preventing you from changing the unhealthy behavior or adding the healthy behavior. These may be practical issues (e.g., no time) or psychological ones (e.g., you do not think you will succeed). For each barrier you need a solution. Using this information, you can develop a plan to change in an organized manner. Use principles of operant conditioning (reinforcement and punishment) to make sure you keep on track and set achievable goals. By paying close attention to the different biopsychosocial correlates of health behaviors discussed here, you should be able to develop the behavioral and cognitive skills to change any behavior you desire. Don't forget to use what you have learned from this chapter and other parts of the book (e.g., Chapter 6 for help to cope with stress, something that thwarts most attempts to stop smoking). Use the area in Table 7.2 to try all the above to really make a difference in your life.

Whereas you can probably follow the above instructions relatively well, your chances of succeeding are low if you do not factor in some key findings from health psychological research. What are the biggest barriers to behavior change? Your attitudes, beliefs, knowledge, and skills are all important factors, but each of these terms (e.g., attitudes) is broad. Furthermore, what can you use to guide your search for factors thwarting your attempts to change or to understand the process of change? The answer is theory.

▼ TABLE 7.2

Planning Your Behavior Change

Pick a specific behavior that you wish to change and set up a plan for changing it.This is a good time to take a break from reading and complete your plan on your computer. Really. Try it.
1. Goal Setting: State the specific behavior you wish to change (well defined). Pick only one behavior, not a set of behaviors, or several different ones to change all at once.
State your goal. What do you plan to achieve in the next 2 weeks? Be specific. How many times a week for how long and doing exactly what?
2. Knowing the Context and Devising Steps: Do you know the context in which this behavior now occurs? Under what conditions are you most likely to engage in the behavior you wish to change? What situational factors tend to increase the behavior? If you know these things, explain them. If you do not know these things, would it be useful to monitor yourself for 2 to 3 days and keep a log of the behavior frequency and circumstances in which it appears? If so, state this as a step. Results of monitoring will improve your plan of behavior change.
Break the goal down into small steps that are more easily attainable. For example, to meditate for 5 minutes 3 times a week might be a good start toward meditating for 30 minutes 5 times a week. In between would be a gradual progression of small steps toward the goal.
What new techniques will you use to increase the likelihood of behavior change? This is a plan of specific ways to combat your normal behavior tendencies, and to initiate new ones. For example, if you drink too much soda, what methods can you devise to decrease this behavior? Perhaps you could pay a friend every time you drink soda?
3. Keeping Track of Progress and Giving Yourself Rewards: Use some kind of record keeping (a log or chart) to keep track of your progress. If no progress is made after the first week, revise the plan. Keep your records to hand in later. Decide on small rewards to give yourself each time you see progress, e.g., listen to music or watch TV or have a special food on each day you practice a new behavior. Decide on bigger rewards for major progress over a longer period of time such as 1 month, or a quarter, e.g., dinner or a movie with a friend; buy a CD or some item for yourself.

The Importance of Theory

Scientific theories guide our search to understand why behaviors are difficult to change and to predict successful change. At the core, theory explains behavior and suggests ways to influence and change behavior. If you want to successfully adopt healthy behaviors, you can rely on explanatory or predictive theories to identify key factors, and theories and models (analogous to theories) of behavior change to help focus on the process. There are many available options, so there is no need to begin from scratch or use personal brainstorming. You can certainly start without reading the next section, but the reality is that theoretically informed health behavior change programs are more effective than those without a theoretical basis (Glanz et al., 2015).

Mind you, not all published research will explicitly use a theory. In one review, only 68% of articles were informed by theory (Painter, Borba, Hynes, Mays, & Glanz, 2008). However, without theory one cannot identify the factors most plausibly related to what we are interested in (Rothman, Hertel, Baldwin, & Bartels, 2008). In the next section I discuss some of the most common theories and models used in health psychology. Watch for the variables that can help you change your own health behaviors.

Key Theories of Health Behavior Change

Health psychologists' approaches to understanding and changing the extent to which health behaviors are practiced nicely illustrate a full-cycle version of the scientific method (Suls, Luger, & Martin, 2010). Observe a real-world problem, generate hypotheses and a theory of why it occurs, design research to test it, and then apply successful theory to help intervene and solve the problem. There have been and continue to be a number of different theories to explain why we practice some behaviors and fail to practice others (Michie, Marques, Norris, & Johnston, 2019). Most theories draw on Social Cognitive Theory (SCT; Bandura, 1986, 1998), a comprehensive theory of behavior change that posits that characteristics of people (i.e., their attitudes and beliefs), their environments, and their health behaviors all interact and determine whether each person performs a health behavior. SCT suggests that the most central determinant of health behavior change is self-efficacy, a concept that is now included in numerous theories of health behavior (Noar, 2005).

In addition to SCT, three theories dominate the literature: the Transtheoretical Model and stages of change, the Health Belief Model, and the Theory of Planned Behavior. These theories all focus on some key predictors of behavior, our attitudes, our intentions, and our readiness to change.

TRANSTHEORETICAL MODEL

Think about New Year's resolutions. Men and women around the nation vow to do more of this or less of that. The media provide tips on how best to make and keep resolutions. We see a similar pattern when summer approaches and we rally to get ready for swimsuits, or for shorts and t-shirts. You often see extensive mention of the **Transtheoretical Model** (TTM) (Prochaska & DiClemente, 1983) of behavior change. Get ready for some major insight into why your past behavior change efforts may not have worked.

TTM was developed to identify common themes across different intervention theories (hence *Trans*theoretical) and notes that we process through different stages as we think about, attempt to, and finally change any specific behavior.

James O. Prochaska is professor of psychology and director of the Cancer Prevention Research Center at the University of Rhode Island. He also developed the transtheoretical model of behavior change. Check out a great chapter by him in Essential Readings (Prochaska, Redding, & Evers, 2015).

Different psychological traditions had different processes to account for why people changed their behaviors: the behaviorists argued that people changed to manipulate the contingency of reward and punishment, the humanists believed that helping relationships spurred change, and the psychodynamic theorists suggested that change came about due to consciousness raising. DiClemente and Prochaska (1982) assessed whether a group of smokers who were trying to quit used any of these processes. The researchers found that smokers used different processes at different times in their quest to quit smoking and first identified that behavior change unfolds in a series of stages. From smoking, the stage model was extended to study a variety of behaviors with health consequences including alcohol and substance abuse, delinquency, eating disorders and obesity, consumption of high-fat diets, unsafe sex with the risk of sexually transmitted diseases, and sun exposure (Prochaska, Redding, & Evers, 2015).

The TTM sees change as a process occurring through a series of six stages. The main stages are summarized in Figure 7.2. If you know what stage a person is in, you will need to tailor your intervention to fit the state of mind that the stage describes. When people are not aware that they are practicing a behavior that is unhealthy or do not intend to take any action to change a behavior (especially not in the next 6 months), they are said to be in the **precontemplation** stage. People could have tried to change before, failed, and become demoralized to change, or they may just be misinformed about the actual consequences of their behavior. Some teenage smokers are so confident about their own health that they do not believe smoking is a problem for them and have no intention of quitting. People in this stage avoid reading, thinking, or talking about their unhealthy behaviors. Health promotion programs are often wasted on them because they either do not know they have a problem or do not really care.

Paramount Pictures/ Moviepix/ Getty Images

▲ **Smoking in the Movies.** One of the major social factors influencing adolescent smoking is the movies. In the early days of filmmaking, actors were often sent cartons of cigarettes so they would smoke on screen. Later, movie companies were paid to show cigarettes on screen.

When people recognize they may be doing something unhealthy and then intend to change (within the next month), they are said to be in the **contemplation** stage. Here they are more aware of the benefits of changing and are also very cognizant of the problems that changing may involve. For the dieter, it may be avoiding the foods that he or she has grown to love. For the smoker, it may mean not spending time with the buddies he or she always used to smoke with. The ambivalence associated with knowing the pros and cons of the behavior change often keeps people in this stage for a long time and calls for unique interventions.

Preparation is the stage in which the person is ready to take action to change the behavior. He or she generates a plan and has specific ideas of how to change. Someone who wants to lose weight may go out and buy new workout clothes and a gym membership. Someone who wants to drink less may give away all the alcohol in the house or have a talk with a doctor to get help. In essence, these people make a commitment to spend time and money on changing their behaviors. As you can guess, this is the stage people should be in if an intervention is going to have any effect.

Once people are actually changing their behavior, they are in the **action** stage. The change has to have taken place over the past 6 months and should involve active efforts to change the behavior. For example, frequent trips to the gym characterize someone who is in the action stage of trying to get in shape. Does any attempt to change behavior no matter how small count as being in the action stage? No, it does not. People must reach a criterion that health professionals can agree is sufficient to reduce the risk for disease (Prochaska et al., 2015), for example, losing enough weight to no longer be classified as obese or abstaining from smoking for a significant period of time. Can you slide back?

Maintenance is the stage in which people try to not fall back into unhealthy behaviors, or to relapse. They may still be changing their behaviors and performing new behaviors, but they are not doing them as often as someone in the action stage. In this stage, the temptation to relapse is reduced, and there is often confidence that the new behavior changes can be continued for a period of time. For example, maintenance of abstinence from smoking can last from 6 months to 5 years (DHHS, 2017).

ullstein bild / ullstein bild/ Getty Images

▲ **Smoking in the Movies.** If you saw characters smoking in a movie, would you be more likely to smoke?

Finally, people may reach a stage in which they are no longer tempted by the unhealthy behavior they have changed. The ex-smoker no longer craves a cigarette, the ex-fast food addict now no longer feels like eating a burger and fries, and the former couch potato is committed to regular physical activity. If a person reaches this point, he or she is in the **termination** stage. Can this stage be achieved? Snow, Prochaska, and Rossi (1992) found that fewer than 20% of former smokers and alcoholics reached this zero-temptation stage. For the most part, this part of the model has been loosely interpreted as representing a lifetime of maintenance, and most interventions aim to get participants to the maintenance stage (Mauriello et al., 2010).

The most helpful contribution of the TTM is that it clearly identifies how interventions can be successful. Interventions need to be tailored according to the stage of change that a person is in. The most common application involves the tailoring of communications to match the needs of the individual. Individuals who are in the precontemplation stage could be given information that would make changing their behavior more of a pro and hence move themselves into the contemplation stage. For example, to get a person in the precontemplation stage to consider getting a flu shot researchers would use strategies to capture attention using narratives of compelling images (Rimer & Kreuter, 2006). Tailored interventions using the TTM now also use the Internet. Puff City was a Web-based program focused on asthma management among urban African American adolescents (Joseph et al., 2011).

You can use the TTM to see how ready you are to change. Another important component is your beliefs relating to the behavior. This is where the Health Belief Model comes in.

▼ FIGURE 7.2

Stages of Change: The Transtheoretical Model

1. Precontemplation —Not aware of behavior, no intention to change
2. Contemplation —Aware that problem exists, thinking about change —Weighing pros and cons
3. Preparation —Intend to change, modified but not committed
4. Action —Modified and commitment to time and energy
5. Maintenance —Working to prevent relapse
6. Termination Phase

THE HEALTH BELIEF MODEL

The **Health Belief Model** (HBM) represents one of the first theoretical approaches to studying why we behave the way that we do (Skinner, Tiro, & Champion, 2015). The basic contention of the HBM is that our beliefs relating to the **effectiveness**, ease, and **consequences** of doing (or not doing) a certain behavior will determine whether we do (or do not do) that behavior. It is one of the most widely used frameworks and has been used for both behavior change and maintenance. It was developed when a group of social psychologists were brought together at the U.S. Public Health Service to try to explain why people did not participate in programs to prevent or detect disease (Hochbaum, 1958; Rosenstock, 1960). The HBM was then extended to explain people's responses to illness symptoms (Kirscht, 1971) and also to explain what influences whether someone will adhere to his or her prescribed treatments (Becker, 1974).

The formulation of the HBM provides a good illustration of how social psychology and cognitive and behaviorist views influenced health psychology. For example, learning theorists such as Skinner (1938) believed that we learned to do a certain behavior if it was followed by a positive outcome (a reinforcement). Therefore, if exercising made us feel healthy we would be more likely to exercise. Cognitive theorists added a focus on the value of an outcome (e.g., health) and the expectation that a particular action (e.g., exercise) will achieve that outcome. The HBM is a value-expectancy theory in which the values and expectations were reformulated from abstract concepts into health-related behaviors and concepts. A big issue in the 1950s was that a large number of eligible adults did not undergo screening for tuberculosis (TB) although TB was a big health problem and the screenings were free. Beginning in 1952, Hochbaum (1958) conducted surveys of more than 1,200 adults to understand why this was the case. He found that 82% of the people who believed they were susceptible and who believed early detection worked had at least one voluntary chest X-ray. Only 21% of the people who had neither belief had an X-ray.

cdc.gov

▲ **College-Based Interventions.** A number of college-based interventions have used the Health Belief Model to increase the use of sunscreen and reduce skin cancer. This poster uses credible, athletic role models to make sun protection more normative.

How does the HBM explain health behavior? The model, built on Hochbaum's surveys, suggests that individuals will perform healthy behaviors if they believe they are susceptible to the health issue, if they believe not performing the behavior will have severe consequences, if they believe that their behavior will be beneficial in reducing the severity or susceptibility, if they believe there are benefits to taking action, and if they believe that the anticipated benefits of the behavior outweigh its costs (or barriers). Individuals must also receive a trigger or cue in order to act (Aiken, Gerend, Jackson, & Ranby, 2012). The main components are described in Figure 7.3.

These components have also made the transition outside research labs. In an examination of 574 magazine articles and 905 images related to skin cancer, McWhirter and Hoffman-Goetz (2016) found susceptibility and severity information was very common in texts (48% and 60%, respectively). Perceived benefits (36%) and barriers (42%) to prevention were fairly mentioned as well.

▼ FIGURE 7.3

Main Components of the Health Belief Model

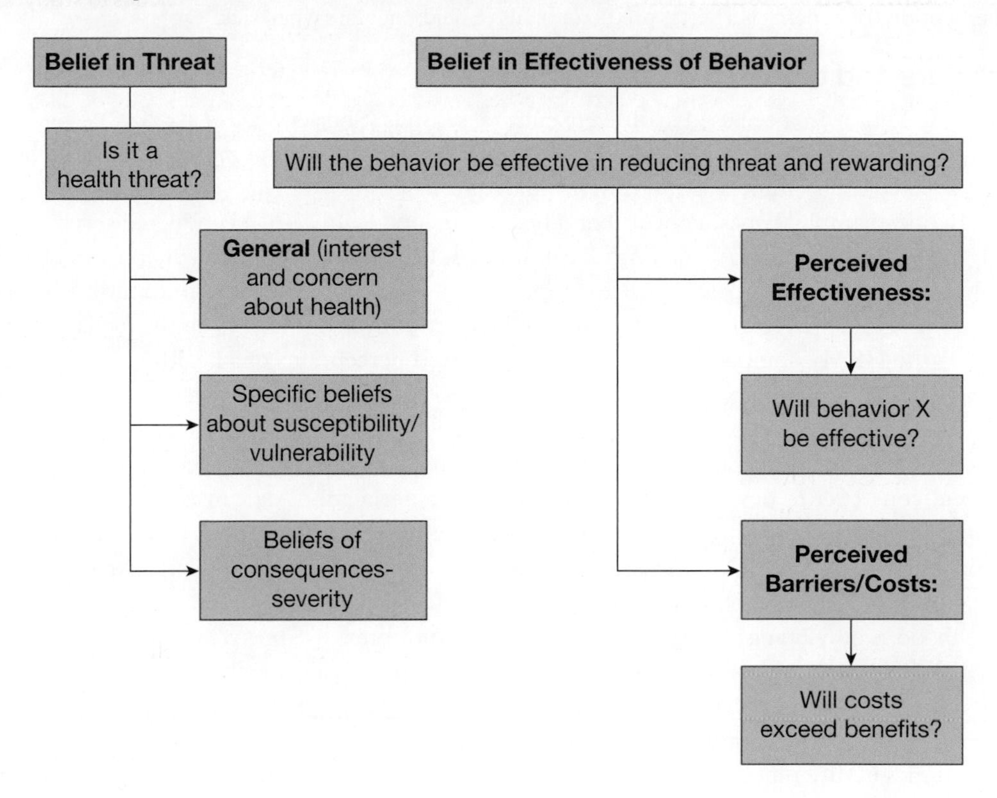

Another factor that was added to the model with great success was the concept of **self-efficacy**. Self-efficacy is defined as the conviction that one can successfully execute the behavior required to produce the outcome (Bandura, 1977) and was added to the HBM by Rosenstock, Strecher, and Becker (1988). This suggests that it is not enough just to know what behaviors *will* efficiently reduce severity and susceptibility, but one has to be confident that one can actually do that behavior.

Is one more component more important than the others, you may ask? There is a problem with answering that question. The measurement of HBM components has been inconsistent, and a majority of studies conducted with it did not use reliable or valid measures of constructs. Part of the reason is that researchers fail to adequately control for the relationship between different components. Another reason is that health beliefs and health behaviors have often been measured simultaneously, contaminating the findings. If I first ask you whether you believe drinking is dangerous and then immediately ask you if you drink, your answers may not be the same as if I asked you each question at a different time.

Here is an example of how you can take a theory and put it into action. Haghighi et al. (2017) decided to use the HBM to reduce work-related accidents from unsafe behaviors in an oil refinery near Tehran. They designed a Safety Culture Promotion Intervention Program using components of the HBM. They randomly assigned 45 employees to the experimental group and another 45 to the control group. The experimental group received a safety culture education program designed to influence components of the HBM such as vulnerability and severity. It worked. Before the intervention there were no differences between the control and experimental group. After the intervention, the groups varied on the HBM components.

In general, a number of empirical studies have established the utility of the HBM (Skinner et al., 2015). Perceived barriers are the most powerful component of the model across studies.

Although perceived susceptibility and benefits are both important, knowing how susceptible one feels is a better predictor of that person's health prevention behavior and knowing the person's perceptions of benefits is a better predictor of his or her behaviors when sick.

Culture and the Health Belief Model

The HBM has also been used in different cultural settings (Shojaeizadeh et al., 2012). Together with scales and interventions being designed for specific cultural groups, numerous studies have investigated the usefulness of the HBM in multicultural settings.

In one example, James, Pobee, Oxindine, Brown, and Joshi (2012) conducted seven focus groups with overweight African American women. Fifty women were recruited from beauty salons, churches, sororities, a college campus, and a low-income housing community. Three community liaisons recruited participants and located convenient venues for the focus groups. Using the HBM components, focus groups discussed perceptions of a healthy weight, overweight, and obesity; perceived consequences of obesity; barriers and motivators to weight loss; information needed to lose weight; and sources of dieting information. The HBM provided a good fit for the data and allowed the researchers to use the themes generated from each theoretical construct to develop weight-management materials for African American women. This study also draws attention to how different cultures view health behaviors differently. Understanding how African American women define concepts such as healthy weight, overweight, and obesity is important because definitions affect perception of weight, body image, and likelihood of developing obesity. The women in this study often used sexy, flirtatious words such as "stacked," "brick house," "curvy," and "big boned" to describe their bodies. Randall (2012) nicely sums it up when she says, "Chemically, in its ability to promote disease, black fat may be the same as white fat. Culturally it is not."

Studies in different cultural groups illustrate similarities and differences across cultures in regard to HBM components. Kim and Zane (2016) decided to explore why Asian Americans underuse mental health services relative to European Americans. They examined perceived severity of symptoms, perceived susceptibility to mental health problems, perceived benefits of treatment, and perceived barriers to treatment influenced intentions to seek help among a sample of 395 Asian American and 261 White American students. Perceived benefits partially accounted for differences in help-seeking intentions. Although Asian Americans perceived greater barriers to help seeking than did White Americans, this did not significantly explain differences in help-seeking intentions. Perceived severity and barriers were related to help-seeking intentions in both groups.

Research has even found differences between age groups within ethnicity (i.e., between young and old Chinese Americans; Tang, Solomon, & McCracken, 2000) and provides us with ways to adopt health-care delivery to best suit different populations. For example, one study found that American Indian women were reluctant to talk openly about their personal health to physicians (a barrier) and so lay health educators presented a screening education program instead (Dignan et al., 1995).

Focusing on beliefs is clearly an effective way to change behavior, so take a good look at yours. Another way to try to predict whether someone is going to do something is to see if he or she *intends* to do something.

THEORY OF PLANNED BEHAVIOR

Let's say we go to dinner together at a restaurant that has great barbeque. If you want to predict whether I am going to get some barbeque, all you have to do is ask. If I intend to get some barbeque, I will probably get some (I love barbeque, and other items at restaurants my editor asked me to not mention in the book). Behavioral intentions play a major role in many models of health behavior change such as the Theory of Reasoned Action (Fishbein & Ajzen, 1975), the Theory

▼ FIGURE 7.4

Major Components of the Theory of Planned Behavior

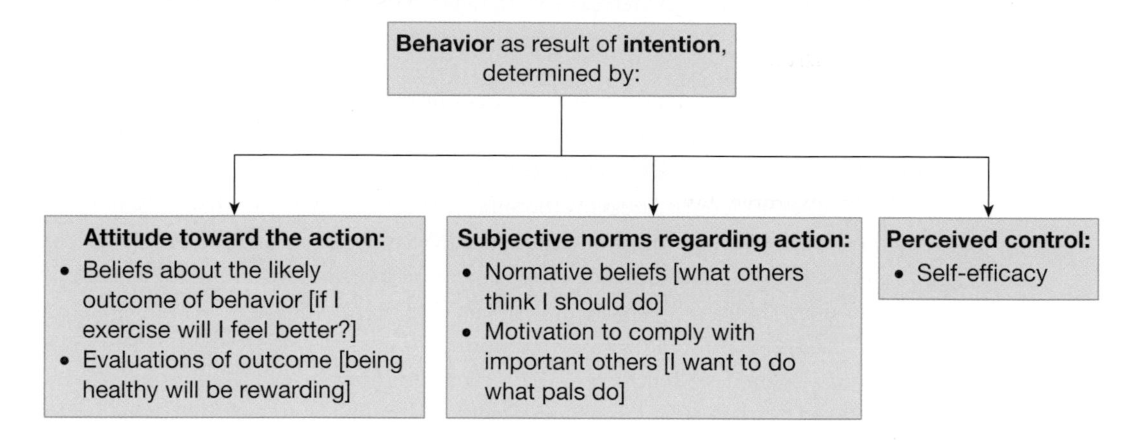

of Planned Behavior (TPB) (Ajzen, 1988), the Protection Motivation Theory (Rogers, 1983), and the previously mentioned concept of self-efficacy (Bandura, 1977).

So what is an **intention**? Fishbein and Ajzen (1975) defined an intention as a person's subjective probability that he or she will perform the behavior in question. It is essentially an estimate of the probability of your doing something. Time for another food example: If you ask me if I want dessert at the start of a meal when I am hungry, the probability that I will say "yes" will be higher than after a meal when I have stuffed myself. Thus, to get a good measure of intentions, they need to be measured with a high degree of specificity regarding the attitude toward the exact action (e.g., eating dessert), the target (e.g., chocolate cake), the context (e.g., on that day), and the time (e.g., right after the meal). The TPB, an extension and updating of the Theory of Reasoned Action, assumes that people decide to behave a certain way on the basis of their intentions, which are dependent on their attitude toward the behavior and their perceptions of the social norms regarding the behavior (Montano & Kasprzyk, 2015).

Similar to the HBM, attitudes toward the behavior are based on what the person believes are the consequences of the behavior and how important these consequences are (both costs and benefits). Will eating dessert make me gain weight? One of the most useful components is the one assessing perceived norms. This assesses what *you* think others think about the behavior or the **normative beliefs**. Do the people you know support eating sweet things? If you believe that everyone around you thinks that eating dessert is acceptable, you are more likely to want to do it. Of course, you also may not care what people around you think. Your **motivation to comply** with others' preferences is also part of the perception of social norms. If you care about the people around you *and* they support dessert eating, you are more likely to eat dessert. Still speaking of eating, the TPB predicts the likelihood to eat novel foods, including insect-based products (Menozzi, Sogari, Veneziani, Simoni, & Mora, 2017), and fruits and vegetables (Kothe, Mullan, & Butow, 2012) among other health behaviors such as alcohol consumption (Gabbiadini, Cristini, Scacchi, & Monaci, 2017) and texting while driving (Tian & Robinson, 2017). It even predicts selfie-posting behavior (Kim, Lee, Sung, & Choi, 2017), social networking (Jafarkarimi, Saadatdoost, Sim, & Hee, 2016), and intentions to graduate (Sutter & Paulson, 2016). The full model with its components is shown in Figure 7.4.

Culture and the Theory of Planned Behavior

The TPB has been used in many different settings and around the world (Saal & Kagee, 2012). In a good demonstration of the theory and a focus on culture, Bai, Wunderlich, and

Fly (2011) explored how mothers of different races and ethnicities make decisions to continue exclusive breastfeeding for 6 months after birth. They recruited 236 participants (93 non-Hispanic African American, 72 non-Hispanic White, and 71 Hispanic/Latina). Each mother completed measures based on TPB and relating to their intention to practice breastfeeding. Intentions to continue exclusive breastfeeding for 6 months were similar across ethnic groups explained by attitudes, subjective norms, and perceived behavioral control. Predictors of intention varied by group. Attitude best predicted intention for White mothers, while subjective norm best predicted intention for African American mothers, and perceived behavioral control best predicted intention for Latina mothers. Beliefs held by family members and the general public contributed to the subjective norm of African American mothers. Perceived behavioral control in Latina mothers was highly correlated with pumping breast milk.

In a study of condom use, Montano, Kasprzyk, von Haeften, and Fishbein (2001) used questionnaire data to identify TPB measures that best predicted condom use among African American, Latina, and European American women. They recruited participants from the Seattle area and interviewed them at two times 3 months apart. Participants were asked about their condom use, their beliefs about the consequences of the condom use, their intentions to use condoms, and their attitudes toward condom use. The researchers also measured the participants' perceptions of the subjective norms about condom use. Specifically, Montano et al. (2001) had participants rate whether 15 different friends and relatives thought they should use condoms. The researchers also assessed the participants' motivation to comply with what their friends said. There was a strong significant correlation between intending to use a condom and actually using one, as measured by self-report. Similarly, in support of the TPB model, subjective norms and attitudes toward condom use and perceived behavioral control were also significant predictors of the behavior.

Although tested in multiethnic samples (Montano et al., 2001), it is clear that models such as the TPB do not apply in the same way across cultural groups. Ethnic differences are seen in the relative effects of peers and parents on adolescents' substance use or in the components of the model that are significant. Peers exert a stronger influence on cigarette use among Whites and Latinos than among African Americans (Gottfredson & Koper, 1996). On the other hand, parents have a greater impact on the use of alcohol among African American children than among White children (Clark, Scarisbrick-Hauser, Gautam, & Wirk, 1999). Thus, although the TPB might predict tobacco use among both African American and White children, the relative contribution of the key components (especially of the subjective norm factor) differs among cultural groups. The TPB and Theory of Reasoned Action have both been used to predict adolescent smoking in other cultures, such as cultures in China (Guo et al., 2007).

Synthesize, Evaluate, Apply

- Compare and contrast each of the main models of health behavior change.
- Are there any factors that need to be added to the models of behavior change?
- How would you use the Transtheoretical Model to refine interventions to decrease smoking?
- Let's say you want to get all your friends to eat better. You have read about the Health Belief Model in class and think that is an interesting model to use. Write down one question that you would ask your friends to assess each component of the model.

ADDITIONAL THEORIES OF HEALTH BEHAVIOR CHANGE

In addition to the three major theories discussed above, there are many theories used to explain and predict health behaviors (Aiken et al., 2012). A host of other theories/models are garnering attention (Table 7.3). For example, similar to the TTM discussed above, the Precaution Adoption Process Model (PAPM) identifies seven stages along the path from lack of awareness to action (Weinstein & Sandman, 1992).

Another theory, Schwarzer's (1992) Health Action Process Approach (HAPA), bears some scrutiny because it rectifies many of the shortcomings of other models. The HAPA

▼ FIGURE 7.5

The Health Action Process Approach

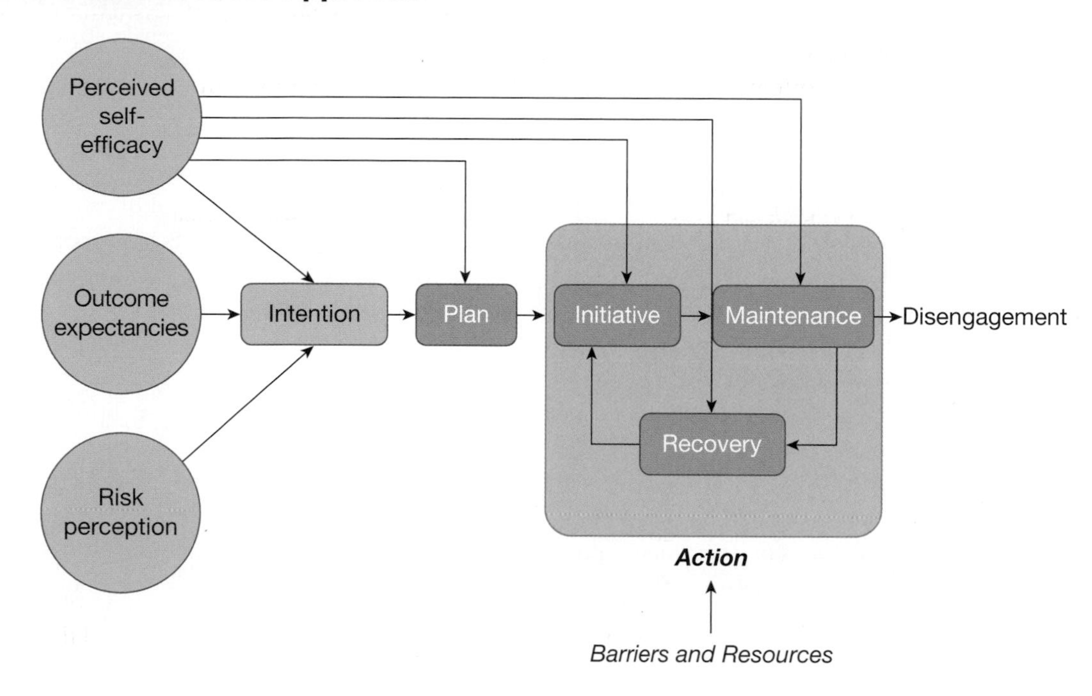

distinguishes between two main phases: when a decision to act is made, and when the action is carried out (Schwarzer, 2008). During the initial phase of the HAPA, people develop an intention to act based on beliefs about the risk and outcomes and their self-efficacy. After a goal has been established within this phase, people enter a volition phase in which they plan the details of action, initiate action, and cope with the difficulties of successfully completing the action. The main components are seen in Figure 7.5. The HAPA has been found to be applicable to a wide variety of health behaviors such as exercise, breast self-exams, seat belt use, dieting, and dental flossing (Schwarzer, 2008).

▼ TABLE 7.3

Major Theories Compared

Theory	Main Components/Ideas
Health Belief Model (HBM)	Beliefs in threat (severity, susceptibility) and effectiveness of health change behaviors.
Theory of Planned Behavior (TPB)	Intention to change; attitudes toward action; subjective norms regarding action; self-efficacy.
Transtheoretical Model (TTM)	Six stages that a person proceeds through: precontemplation, contemplation, preparation, action, maintenance, termination.
Social Cognitive Theory (SCT)	Health behaviors must be understood in the context of reciprocal determinism, or the idea that characteristics of a person, one's environment, and the behavior itself all interact and determine whether a behavior is performed.
Precaution Adoption Process Model (PAPM)	Person moves from being unaware of issue, to unengaged by issue, to deciding not to act, to planning to act but not yet acting, to acting, to maintenance.
Health Action Process Approach (HAPA)	Two main phases: factors influencing intention to act and the processes that take place after the intention leading up to the behavior.

COMPARING THE MODELS AND THEIR LIMITATIONS

The HBM, TPB, and TTM are the most widely cited models of health behavior change in health psychology (Glanz, Rimer, & Viswanath, 2008). They have each received strong support but they (and the studies used to test them) also have some limitations (Ogden, 2003; Schwarzer, 2008; Weinstein, 2007).

In general, the models discussed do not explicitly factor in changes in mindsets over time (Schwarzer, 2008) and do not address how beliefs or intentions are translated into action, or the intention-behavior gap (Sheeran, 2002). There are other limitations. For example, the HBM has not been as rigorously quantified as the TPB, but its components have received considerable empirical support (Mullen, Hersey, & Iverson, 1987). Some of its components still need to be better understood and others, such as beliefs about severity, have low predictive value (Rimer, 2002). Similarly, the TPB and the TTM do not necessarily include all the elements responsible for behavior change and can each be supplemented with additional concepts. The TPB does not recognize emotional elements such as the perceived susceptibility to illness as does the HBM.

The TTM has been criticized for suggesting individuals cannot move back or progress forward without skipping steps (Bandura, 2000). Sutton (2005) argued that the stages are arbitrary subdivisions of a continuous process and hence the TTM is circular and flawed. Furthermore, different studies use different time frames (e.g., 6 months vs. 1 year) in operationally defining a stage. Based on these issues, some researchers call for greater precision in articulating the processes through which theories are refined, in specifying the mediating variables and processes of change, and in describing techniques to change behavior and their links with theory (Michie, Rothman, & Sheeran, 2007).

Few studies have pitted more than one theory against another (c.f., Weinstein, 1993). Noar and Zimmerman (2005) found that of 2,901 articles reviewed, only 16% mentioned more than one theory. Only 19 (1%) were true empirical comparisons of theories. In a notable exception, Garcia and Mann (2003) tested the ability of several social-cognitive models to predict intentions to engage in two different health behaviors (change eating habits and performing a breast self-examination). All constructs from the HBM (with and without self-efficacy), the TPB (with and without perceived behavioral control), and the motivational process of the HAPA (Schwarzer, 1992) were measured simultaneously in two samples. The authors hypothesized that models that included self-efficacy (or the related construct of perceived behavioral control) would be more effective than the models that did not include it. Their results supported this prediction. The HAPA was the best predictor of intentions to engage in both behaviors. In a more recent comparison of theories (HAPA, TPB, and a prototype-willingness model) to explain skin protection, the HAPA was again the best predictor (Matterne, Diepgen, & Weisshaar, 2011). Additional comparative research will continue to provide health psychologists with practical theories.

Stephen Lance Dennee/ Associated Press

▲ **Billboards.** Billboards like these are a form of intervention that reaches many thousands of people.

CHANGING BEHAVIORS: INTERVENTIONS

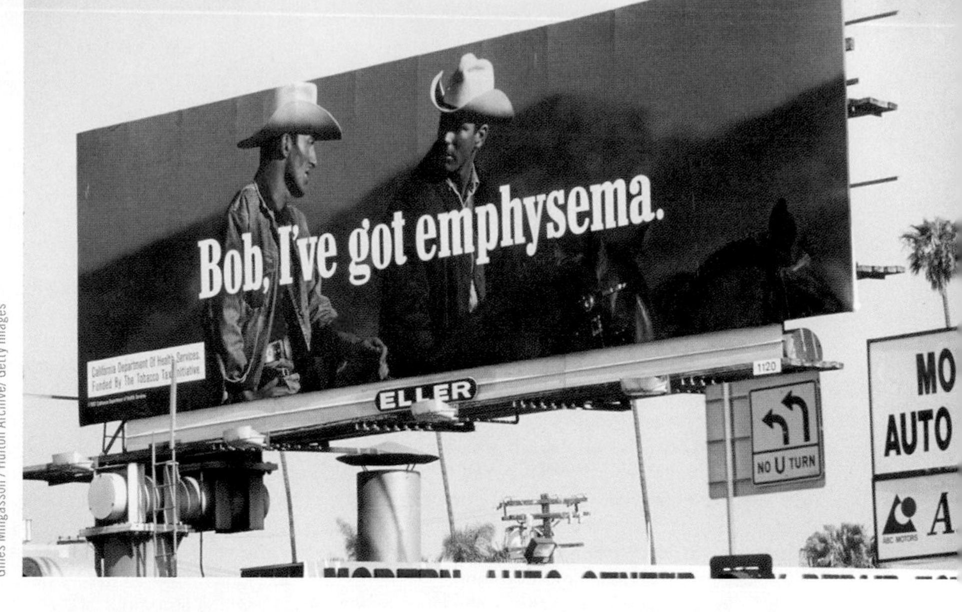

▲ **Billboards.** Note how the classic image of the cowboy is changed here to stress the health risks of smoking.

While you can try to change your own behavior using the information in this chapter, it helps to have professional help. Health psychologists aim to get people to improve personal health behaviors and to remember to get the various check-ups that their cultural demographics (i.e., age, sex, and ethnicity) may require. **Interventions** are specific programs designed to assess levels of behaviors, introduce ways to change them, measure whether change has occurred, and assess the impact of the change. The ultimate goal of health psychological interventions is to decrease the number of deaths due to preventable diseases, delay the time of death, and improve quality of life, especially for the elderly. Health psychologists have tried different techniques to get people to do what is healthy. In the 1950s the most common advertisements to change behavior tried to scare the viewer into changing. Many high schools still use posters of blackened lungs or rotten teeth to get students not to smoke. Today fear appeals are still used via the Internet or multimedia campaigns (Goodall, Sabo, Cline, & Egbert, 2012). Most mass media appeals have the benefit of reaching a large number of people relatively easily. Together with alerting people to health risks, these forms of interventions can have a cumulative effect over time and can also reinforce other change techniques (Table 7.4).

In one example, Goodall et al. (2012) collected all stories about seasonal influenza and influenza A (H1N1, or swine flu) appearing in six national news outlets between April and September 2009. They showed that most stories made reference to the threat of the H1N1 virus, sometimes overemphasizing and sensationalizing virus-related death. Approximately half of the stories mentioned actions that individuals or organizations/communities could take to protect themselves from the virus, but almost none provided evidence that such methods were effective, and some explicitly questioned their effectiveness.

▼ TABLE 7.4

Success Strategies for Interventions

1. Use private enterprise models of product development to increase the dissemination of the intervention to the general public.
2. Initiate interventions by teams committed to a specific problem.
3. Provide investigators with training in management.
4. Establish the acceptability of the program's design features to consumers, providers, and funding agencies before the development and evaluation of the program.
5. Use data from national marketing surveys to tailor intervention designs and delivery formats for different subgroups.
6. Identify essential ingredients of the intervention to facilitate adaptation of the program.
7. Implement the program with a goal to maintain change over extended periods of time.
8. The implementation plan should include program evolution over time, rather than replication with fidelity.
9. The intervention should be branded and certified by a credible agency.

Source: Rotheram-Borus, M. J., & Duan, N. (2003). Next generation of preventive interventions. *Journal of the American Academy of Child and Adolescent Psychiatry, 42*(5), 518–526.

▼ TABLE 7.5

Top Ten Prescriptions for Successful Interventions

1. **Interventions Should Be Based on Theory.** Having a theory is important for many reasons (Suls et al., 2010), but unfortunately not all interventions are theory based (Painter et al., 2008). A theory helps focus attention on the most important factors that need to be addressed for the behavior change at hand. For example, the application of the TPB to change specific behaviors involves identifying underlying beliefs that determine one's attitude, subjective norms, and perceived behavioral control, and having the intervention address these components. Theories also help target special cultural groups (e.g., low socioeconomic status individuals). For example, there is substantial evidence that richer people tend to be in more-advanced stages of change than poorer people are (Adams & White, 2007).

   Far too often researchers try to address as many different aspects of behavior as they can in an intervention. They fill posters with arguments and information that tackle these different aspects. If such interventions do result in changing behavior, it is hard to identify what catalyzed the change because the contents of the intervention were not based on a theory. Thus, it is hard to replicate the findings and difficult to focus on and identify what actually worked. This throw-in-everything-including-the-kitchen-sink approach to interventions can lead to change but more often than not involves the use of money without the promise of successful replication of the behavior or prolonged success. Interventions based on theory have a better chance of being useful over the long run (Noar & Zimmerman 2005). Many interventions also combine a number of theories to be as effective as possible (e.g., increasing physical behavior; Michie, Hardeman, Fanshawe, Prevost, Taylor, & Kinmonth, 2008).

2. **Intervene at the Appropriate Level.** When designing an intervention, the researcher has to choose the best unit of intervention. You can design an advertising campaign to target an entire city, state, or region of the country. You can also decide to target areas of a city or town, neighborhood, or community (Campbell et al., 2007). You can get even more specific and target couples, families, or specific individuals in a family. Research overwhelmingly suggests that if one member of a relationship practices healthy behaviors, the other will be more likely to practice healthy behaviors as well (Meyler, Stimpson, & Peek, 2007).

   The level at which you intervene should be appropriate to the problem at hand. If the issue is something like obesity, and people in specific states are more at risk than others, a statewide campaign may be better. If the issue is something like smoking and only members of a specific cultural group, say high school students, are at risk, then targeting that group is critical. Interventions can also target policy makers; changing the superstructure of government and policies toward specific health behaviors can also result in behavior change. Many state governments have raised the tax on cigarettes and have seen a corresponding drop in cigarette purchases among young adults (Campaign for Tobacco-Free Kids, 2017).

3. **Size Matters.** The size of the intervention closely relates to the extent of behavior change seen in response to it. Size can refer to the duration of the intervention and to the intensity of the intervention. Sustained interventions are more likely to lead to sustained behavior change. Furthermore, in many studies the rates of high-risk behavior increase when interventions are withdrawn. Having an intervention continue over a long period, even if it is not too involved for the participants, can still ensure that the unhealthy behavior is kept at bay. For example, if you want to have a group exercise more, having them complete weekly exercise logs that are turned in (increasing accountability and involvement) is likely to make them be active. More-intense interventions are more likely to result in greater risk reduction. For example, Rotheram-Borus and colleagues (2003) designed a successful intervention called Street Smart for runaway children. Street Smart provided these children with access to health care and condoms and delivered a 10-session skill-focused prevention program based on social cognitive theory. The more sessions were conducted, the better the success rate was. Finally, the effect size of an intervention is another good indicator of success. Effect size is a statistical measure of the power of any experimental manipulation. Even if there is a small sample, looking at the effect size can provide a useful estimate of the effectiveness of the intervention.

4. **Interventions Should Target People at Risk.** When researchers do not take pains to intervene at the appropriate level, large numbers of people are exposed to the intervention with the hope that those who need it are included in the exposed group. This shotgun approach can waste a lot of time and money. In some cases, it may be difficult to find out who is most in need of the intervention, but attempting to do so can lead to better, more-directed interventions. Investigators can find out who is at risk by identifying risk factors. For interventions to increase the use of mammograms, investigators can identify groups of women who have high rates of breast cancer and find measures to identify them. Culture comes in handy here. There may be people in a specific part of the country, a specific ethnic group, a religious group, or an age group who are more likely to perform an unhealthy behavior or be at risk for a specific disease. Identifying that group, finding out where they are located, and going to them are effective ways to intervene. The more an intervention is tailored to fit individuals at risk, the more likely it will work (Noar, Benac, & Harris, 2007).

5. **Interventions Should Be Appropriate for the Risk Group/Risk Factor.** Once a risk group is identified, the intervention should be designed to be appropriate for that group. If you are targeting a specific age group, sex, ethnic group, or member of a specific sexual orientation, format the intervention in a way that appeals to and is understandable by the target group. If you want to target bad eating behaviors of seventh-grade students, the language of the intervention should not be set at the level of college first-year students. If the intervention is to appeal to a certain ethnic or religious group, it should use terminology, images, or styles familiar to that group. In addition, it is important to remember that not everyone speaks English fluently. Interventions aimed to change the behaviors of people from different ethnic groups in which different languages are spoken should be designed in the language of the target population.

6. **Be Sure Your Intervention Does Only What You Want It to Do.** Sometimes an intervention can have unintended effects. Interventions aimed at moving people toward the norm can have the negative effect of leading individuals whose behaviors are healthier than the norm to shift to less healthy behavior (Schultz, Nolan, Cialdini, Goldstein, & Griskevicius, 2007).

   Attempts to curb eating disorders provide a sad example. Many prevention programs for eating disorders attempt to simultaneously prevent new occurrences (primary prevention) and encourage students who already have symptoms to seek early treatment (secondary prevention), even though ideal strategies for these two types of prevention may be incompatible with each other. In a study to assess the effectiveness of such programs, Mann et al. (1997) evaluated an eating disorder prevention program.

In the intervention, classmates who had recovered from eating disorders described their experiences and provided information about eating disorders. Paradoxically, at follow-up, intervention participants had slightly more symptoms of eating disorders than did control subjects, rather than fewer symptoms. Mann et al. hypothesized that the program may have been ineffective in preventing eating disorders because by reducing the stigma of these disorders (to encourage students with problems to seek help), the program may have inadvertently normalized them. Similarly, researchers should be sure that their control group is not receiving anything special. If an intervention consists of providing social support over the phone but the control group also receives phone calls (for information gathering), control group participants may still rate the calls as being supportive.

7. **Preventing Dropouts Should Be a Priority.** Not everyone in a longitudinal research study stays in the study until the end. Similarly, not everyone who enrolls in an intervention study attends all the sessions. Although dropouts are an unpleasant fact for most longitudinal research studies, they can be especially problematic for interventions. First, the participant is not getting the entire treatment. Second, the presence of dropouts hinders a thorough assessment of the intervention. This is akin to having an infection and being prescribed a course of antibiotics only to stop taking the medicine once you start feeling better. Just like serious infections, unhealthy behaviors can return once the intervention/treatment has been stopped. Researchers need to devote resources to preventing attrition and simultaneously collect data to be sure they can assess the effects of attrition.

8. **Be Ethical.** Although interventions are designed to get people to perform healthy behaviors and reduce unhealthy behaviors, these notable ends do not justify unethical means. It is important for the researchers to respect participants' rights and refrain from using deception or making false claims about the ills of unhealthy behaviors or the virtues of healthy ones. There are enough facts about most health behaviors so that researchers should not be tempted to exaggerate details for a stronger effect. In interventions that include a control group and an intervention group, it is critical that members of the control group participate in the intervention after the study is over. This way they too can get the benefits of the intervention. Health professionals should also be thinking of what will happen once the intervention is removed. Will the behavior go back to what it was before the intervention? Will an unhealthy behavior get worse because the intervention is seen as a crutch, the removal of which is detrimental?

9. **Be Culturally Sensitive.** Some models of health behavior change are automatically culturally sensitive, but most theories are designed to apply to any cultural group. Researchers must pay close attention to the symbols and language used because the same symbol may mean different things to different cultures. An example is the swastika, a cross made up of four Ls. For centuries it was a good luck emblem, and is still considered a good luck emblem by Hindus. But its meaning was corrupted when it became the symbol of Hitler's Nazi Germany. Now this symbol is tied to racism and hatred and even linked to homicide. In August 2017 a man plowed his car into counterprotesters at a far-right rally in Charlottesville, Virginia, killing a 32-year-old woman. The swastika is a symbol that will deeply offend many in North America due to what it has come to stand for. Similarly, researchers cannot assume that everyone speaks English, and language differences should be kept in mind. Interventions that apply at the community level often take cultural differences into account. For example, the Community Organization and Development model for health promotion in communities of color involves community-controlled coalitions that undertake their own community assessment and design culturally relevant interventions (Braithewaite, Bianchi, & Taylor, 1994).

   In other cases, general theories are revised for use with culturally diverse populations. Gilliland and colleagues (1998) tweaked Social Cognitive Theory ideas into an intervention especially designed to reduce the incidence of type 2 diabetes among American Indians and native Hawaiians. Their programs use problem-solving approaches and involve family and social networks to fit the different circumstances and values of each cultural group. Such culturally based interventions have increased movement along stages of change for fat intake and physical activity (Mau et al., 2001). Some researchers do not believe that a general, one-size-fits-all-cultures theory is valid and suggest that new culturally sensitive models need to be developed and used (Oomen, Owen, & Suggs, 1999). Given the increase in cultural diversity in North America today, much more research needs to be applied to designing and assessing culturally valid interventions.

   In one example, Fisher, Burnet, Huang, Chin, and Cagney (2007) reviewed culturally sensitive interventions aimed at narrowing racial disparities in health care. They identified 38 interventions of three types: interventions that modified the health behaviors of ethnic minority patients, those that increased access to health care, and those that modified the health-care system to better serve minority patients. Individual-level interventions (see points 2 and 3) typically tapped community members' expertise to shape programs. Access interventions largely involved screening programs, incorporating patient navigators and lay educators. Health-care interventions focused on the roles of nurses, counselors, and community health workers to deliver culturally tailored health information. These interventions increased patients' knowledge for self-care, decreased barriers to access, and improved providers' cultural competence. The researchers concluded that interventions that explicitly factor in culture show tremendous promise in reducing health disparities, but more research is needed to understand their health effects in combination with other interventions.

10. **Prevent Relapse.** Sometimes it is not enough to intervene to change behavior, see the behavior change, and then walk away. One of the biggest problems in health behavior change involves fostering maintenance of the new behavior (Marlatt & George, 1990). Be aware that smoking a single cigarette after quitting, eating one slice of pizza if you are on a diet, or skipping one day of exercise may not constitute relapse. Yet, the person's failure to change can be demoralizing and can sometimes lead to increased levels of the original unhealthy behavior. Relapse occurs when the behavior that was changed reoccurs on a consistent basis. Good interventions should strive to ensure that relapse does not occur by providing participants with the cognitive and behavioral skills to maintain the behavior change.

Different interventions focus on different antecedents of behavior. Some health psychologists choose to change a person's attitudes to change his or her behavior, while others attempt to change the person's beliefs or intentions. The way an intervention is designed can depend on the specific behavior that needs to be changed (e.g., obesity; Stice, Shaw, & Marti, 2006), the funding available for the behavior change, and the number of people that the intervention has to reach. To put all these different factors into order, let's look at some of the basic principles of intervention design. Some additional suggestions from a review summarizing effective interventions (Rotheram-Borus & Duan, 2003) are shown in Table 7.5.

Together with these main points, health professionals designing interventions should strive to compensate for individual differences as much as possible. A smoking intervention that works on one campus may not necessarily work in exactly the same way on another campus even if it is in the same state. People's personalities vary as well, and not everyone in an intervention is going to react in the same way. A good way for you to assess how well you understand the 10 key aspects is to use them. Pick a health issue—e.g., secondhand smoke in the workplace or binge drinking on campus—and see if you can design an intervention using these 10 principles. Fine-tune your intervention according to the demographics of your location. You know your peers best, and your intervention can be as powerful (if not more powerful) as those designed by the experts. In the next chapter I will discuss some of the main health behaviors that interventions attempt to influence and give you some examples of interventions to compare yours with.

Synthesize, Evaluate, Apply

- Can you think of any additional factors to optimize the delivery of interventions?
- What are the major weaknesses of a shotgun approach to interventions?
- Design a study that would incorporate the best aspects of all the models of health behavior change.
- What biopsychosocial factors do you think can predict relapse?

APPLICATION SHOWCASE

YOU KNOW YOU WANT TO . . . : REDUCING SMOKING IN COLLEGE

Interventions to reduce smoking in college students have focused on the use of antismoking advertising campaigns and educational material (Freeman, Hennessy, & Marzullo 2001; Greenberg & Pollack, 1981). Even when the message that smoking is harmful is broadcast loud and clear, many college students still choose to smoke. Some interventions have attempted to change behavior by changing campus smoking policies (Butler, Rayens, Hahn, Adkins, & Staten, 2012). Results indicate that campus-wide policy changes result in both a decrease in the number of cigarettes smoked and changed attitudes toward smoking (Seo, Macy, Torabi, & Middlestadt, 2011).

Research consistently shows that teenagers and college students misperceive and overestimate their peers' use of tobacco (Perkins, Meilman, Leichliter, Cashin, & Presley, 1999). Changing high school and middle school children's misperceptions might be a beneficial strategy (Hansen, 1993; Sussman et al., 1998), though until recently there have been few published studies related to correcting tobacco use misperceptions (see Perkins, 2003, for a review). Here is a case study about how some researchers tried to change misperceptions.

Researchers at the University of Wisconsin, Oshkosh, first studied the different psychological reasons why people smoked. They noticed that one of the biggest reasons students started smoking was that students thought that it was a normal thing to do. Students believed that many of their peers were smoking.

The researchers knew that this was not the case. The researchers realized that if the college could show that this was not really the case, students may decrease their smoking behavior. This approach is called a Social Norms Approach.

Social norming research has shown that people often believe that those engaging in healthy behavior are in the minority when, in fact, they are not (Karasek, Ahern, & Galea, 2012). Health psychologists acknowledge that norms are important predictors of health behaviors. For example, the theory of planned behaviors discussed previously holds that health behaviors directly result from behavioral intentions that are composed of attitudes toward the specific action, perceived behavioral control, and subjective norms regarding the action. If people who smoke believe that smoking is normative, or if they believe that their friends do not believe that not smoking is the norm, they are less likely to change their behavior. An inaccurate perception of the norms could also get nonsmokers to try smoking. If impressionable students believe that most students their age smoke, these distorted perceptions of group behavior and attitudes may lead them to comply with an inaccurate peer pressure (Grube, McGree, & Morgan, 1986).

So what did the research team do? They assessed the actual and perceived behaviors and attitudes of the students and developed a social marketing campaign to modify misperceptions.

The multimedia campaign used posters (as shown), an art car (a car painted with antismoking information), television and radio ads, a mannequin (covered with messages about the dangers of smoking), information tables, varsity sport promotions, and other promotional items (e.g., plastic piggy banks) to convey the message collected from the campus-wide surveys. The primary message was that few students smoked and those who did wanted to quit smoking. The "You know you want to . . ." theme shown in the posters tested well with students and captured the power of positive norming. "You know you want to . . ." promoted cessation services and directed smokers and nonsmokers toward resources to learn more about the health benefits of being smoke free.

▲ **Posters.** Posters are often a cheap way to convey a message, whether in the workplace or across college campuses.

For example, one poster, "You know you want to . . . get out of the cold," included the statistics of quitting and the finding that nearly three out of four students wanted to help a friend quit smoking (and get out from the cold where smokers who cannot smoke indoors have to go). A marketing survey completed 3 months after the introduction of the campaign showed that 91% of students reported seeing the "You know you want to . . ." posters.

Did the Social Norms Approach work? The intervention was a resounding success (Gurung & Abhold, 2004). At the start of the intervention, 34% of students on campus smoked. When the students were surveyed a year after the media campaign, the number of smokers dropped down to 27%. Twisting the old adage—what you don't know can't hurt you—well, what you *think* you know can hurt you, especially when it is inaccurate.

CHAPTER REVIEW

SUMMARY ▶▶

- Health behaviors are specific behaviors that maintain and enhance health. The most important are getting physical activity, limiting the consumption of alcohol, not smoking, and eating well, all described as Leading Health Indicators. Health educators close the gap between what is known as optimal health practices and what is actually done. Interventions are specific programs designed to assess levels of behaviors, introduce ways to change them, measure whether change has occurred, and assess the impact of the change.

- There are biopsychosocial determinants of health behaviors. Biologically we have genetic predispositions that can influence the types of health behaviors we practice and our metabolic rates or risk of addiction. Psychologically, personality traits, self-esteem, and social support are some key factors influencing health behaviors. Social aspects such as the culture we are raised in also predict healthy behaviors.

- Three major theories predict the extent to which we perform health behaviors. The Health Belief Model suggests that our beliefs relating to the effectiveness, ease, and consequences of performing or not performing a behavior will influence whether we do or do not do it. Our perception of susceptibility, the consequences of the illness, and the extent to which we believe behavior change is effective and worthwhile all contribute to the likelihood of performing the behavior.

- The Theory of Planned Behavior suggests that our intentions to perform a behavior are the most important predictors of whether we do it and are influenced by our attitudes toward the behavior and the perceptions of the social norms regarding the behavior.

- The Transtheoretical Model of behavior change suggests that we pass through key phases in regard to a behavior. We move from not thinking about changing or precontemplation to contemplating change, to preparing to change, to changing (action stage), and then to maintenance of the change.

- There are several prescriptions to keep in mind when one is designing interventions to change behavior. Interventions should be based on theory, be at the appropriate level, be at the right level of severity, target people at risk, be appropriate for the risk group, only do what they are designed to do, be ethical, be culturally sensitive, and be designed to minimize dropouts and relapse.

TEST YOURSELF ▶▶

Check your understanding of the topics in this chapter by answering the following questions.

1. According to the demographic factors discussed in class and the text, which of the following individuals is most likely to practice good health behaviors?
   a. Joan, a 45-year-old high school dropout who works two jobs to support her family
   b. Janet, a 30-year-old high school graduate who is a file clerk in a small store and will be married next month
   c. Doug, a divorced 50-year-old corporate attorney
   d. David, a 35-year-old assistant professor who has just celebrated his eighth wedding anniversary

2. The specific field that stresses the relevance of political, economic, and social factors in health is
   a. health psychology.
   b. medical sociology.
   c. epidemiology.
   d. health education.

3. Personality plays a big role in health. For example, people high in the trait of ________report more medical problems and more visits to the doctor.
   a. conscientiousness
   b. open to experience
   c. extroversion
   d. neuroticism

4. According to the Health Belief Model, health behaviors are strongly linked to
   a. beliefs in threat.
   b. stages of change.
   c. social norms.
   d. age and sex.

5. Which of the following is not a major component of the Health Belief Model?
   a. belief in susceptibility
   b. belief in consequences
   c. belief in effectiveness
   d. belief in social norms

6. The theory of planned behavior focuses on a person's
   a. attitudes toward health.
   b. intentions to the behavior.
   c. beliefs about the behavior.
   d. plans to change behavior.

7. It is not enough to only know a person's perceptions of what the social norms are to predict if they will change their health behavior. You must also assess their
   a. motivation to comply.
   b. self-efficacy.
   c. age and sex.
   d. perception of vulnerability.

8. As we think about changing our health behaviors, we progress through different stages. The best health psychological model to get at this is the
   a. Health Belief Model.
   b. Theory of Planned Behavior.
   c. Transtheoretical Model.
   d. Health Action Process Approach.

9. Relapsing, or falling back into unhealthy behaviors, is the biggest problem in which stage of the Transtheoretical Model?
   a. Termination stage
   b. Contemplation stage
   c. Action stage
   d. Maintenance stage

10. To change a behavior, the very first thing a person should do is spend a week or so and use
   a. self-monitoring.
   b. operant conditioning.
   c. classical conditioning.
   d. self-control.

KEY TERMS, CONCEPTS, AND PEOPLE

action, **184**
consequences, **186**
contemplation, **184**
effectiveness, **186**
Health Belief Model, **186**
health education, **176**
healthy behaviors, **176**
Healthy People 2020, **177**
intention, **189**
interventions, **193**
Leading Health Indicators, **177**
maintenance, **185**
motivation to comply, **189**
normative beliefs, **189**
precontemplation, **184**
preparation, **184**
self-efficacy, **187**
termination, **185**
Transtheoretical Model, **183**

ESSENTIAL READINGS

Lovejoy, T., & Fowler, D. (2019). Designing and evaluating health psychology interventions. In T. A. Revenson & R. A. R. Gurung (Eds.), *Handbook of health psychology* (3e). New York, NY: Routledge.

Michie, S., Marques, M. M., Norris, E., & Johnston, M. (2019). Theories of health behavior change. In T. A. Revenson & R. A. R. Gurung (Eds.), *Handbook of health psychology* (3e). New York, NY: Routledge.

Prochaska, J. O., Redding, C. A. & Evers, K. E. (2015). The transtheoretical model and stages of change. In K. Glanz, B. K. Rimer, & K. Viswanath (Eds.), *Health behavior: Theory, research, and practice* (5th ed., pp. 125–148). San Francisco, CA: Jossey-Bass.

CHAPTER 8

HEALTH BEHAVIORS

Eating, Being Active, Smoking, and Drinking

iStockphoto.com/ Allkindza

Chapter 8 Outline

MEASURING UP

ARE YOUR BEHAVIORS HEALTHY?

Instructions: For each of the following health behaviors you do on a regular basis, give yourself 1 point. Definitions of many of these behaviors are in this chapter. (Note: Score a 7 and you are likely to live significantly longer than classmates scoring 0–3.)

- never smoked
- drink fewer than five drinks at one sitting
- sleep 7–8 hours a night
- exercise
- maintain desirable weight for height
- avoid snacks
- eat breakfast regularly

"Eat, drink, and be merry!" sounds like a simple plan for being content. Of course, we need to eat and drink to survive; however, recent studies link happiness to active, longer lives as well (Lathia, Sandstrom, Mascolo, & Renfrow, 2017; Lawrence, Rogers, & Wadsworth, 2015). Unfortunately, being merry is associated too often with eating too much (or eating unhealthy foods), drinking too much, smoking, and a host of other unhealthy activities. The extent to which people perform each of these major health behaviors can vary dramatically. Some people eat too much, while others eat too little. Some people rarely move from the couch, whereas others spend too much time working out. While many people have never smoked a cigarette in their lives (puffing but not inhaling still counts as smoking), 17% of men and 14% of women in the United States smoke regularly (CDC, 2016). Now a number of people vape or use electronic cigarettes, and the jury is still out on how harmful this behavior is (Mermelstein & Brikmanis, 2019).

▼ Ponder This

Are you at a healthy weight? And who or what decides, anyway?

Can doing healthier behaviors compensate for some unhealthy behaviors?

What are the biopsychosocial reasons that cause people to binge drink?

There are even trends and fads within each of these behaviors. At the turn of the 21st century, yoga centers became popular as millions of Americans began trying this form of physical activity. Simultaneously, many thousands of people experimented with specialized diets, such as cutting out all carbohydrates from their diets as suggested in the Paleo, Atkins, and South Beach programs. What is healthy eating? How much physical activity is appropriate? When does substance use become substance *abuse,* leading to unhealthy consequences? In this chapter, we explore the different behaviors that can influence our health.

Every health behavior (particularly what and how much we eat and how much exercise we get) is strongly influenced by a range of sociocultural factors. Health problems relating to poor eating habits and limited exercise are more prevalent in some cultures than in other cultures. For example, many African Americans experience high rates of hypertension (Long, Ponder, & Bernard, 2017), and many American Indians experience high rates of diabetes (Peters et al., 2014). Let's determine why these cultural differences exist and what can be done about them. This chapter focuses on four major behaviors: eating, physical activity, smoking, and drinking. Because that is a lot of material, I have broken it up into two parts: healthy factors and unhealthy factors. We will describe the factors influencing each behavior, how they develop, and how they vary across cultures.

izusek/ E+/ Getty Images

▲ **Behaviors that can influence our health.** Eating can be a lot of fun, but one should not eat too much, too little, or the wrong variety of food. If you eat too much and do not get the physical activity to burn off the same extra calories, you have even more problems. Do you drink alcohol with your meals? Do you smoke? All these behaviors have serious health consequences.

NUTRITION AND WEIGHT

What percentage of your daily diet is carbohydrates? What percentage is protein? Are you eating a balanced diet? What *is* a balanced diet? These are some of the most common questions asked about food and eating. The answers to these questions are decisive in determining your health. However, with new research coming out weekly and the influence that media coverage has on health-related issues and trends, answers seem to change weekly! The following section provides facts relating to all of these questions and issues. It also provides a behavioral background for why we eat what we eat, when we choose to eat, and how much we choose to eat. I shall also touch on health problems that arise when we do not eat well and the most common types of eating disorders.

Eating is something we all must do. However, most of us do not pay enough attention to what and how we eat. Many of us do other activities while we eat such as watch television, read newspapers or magazines, or drive (not a good idea). Assess your consumption. Think about the past few days. How many times did you ingest something yesterday? What did you eat? How much did you eat? What determined what and how much you consumed? Why did you pick what you ate? Use Table 8.1 and list everything that you have eaten in the past 24 hours. Try to identify why you ate what you did. Your list will provide a reference point to think about while reading the remaining material in this chapter.

What Should We Be Eating?

When trade books answer this question, you know food is on a lot of people's minds. To Michael Pollan (2008), the answer is easy: "Eat food, mostly green, not too much." This food journalist draws our attention to the fact that too many of us eat too much processed food (hence the directive to eat real food), and too much. Gary Taubes (2017) makes a strong case against sugar, and addresses why we get fat and what to do about it (Taubes 2011). These are all good reads that get into the science and the politics of food.

iStockphoto.com/ kwanchaichaiudom

▲ **Obesity.** Obesity is one of America's greatest health concerns today. Even children are getting larger, and the health consequences of being overweight are increasing.

Speaking of politics, the U.S. Department of Agriculture's (USDA's) earliest attempts to inform consumers about how much protein, fats, and carbohydrates to consume date back to the early 1900s. The first food guide was published in 1916 and consisted of five major food groups (e.g., fats, sugars; Welsh, Davis, & Shaw, 1993). The economic problems of the Great Depression in the 1930s greatly influenced American families' food purchasing and consumption habits because they were forced to balance price and nutrition. Affordable foods were often low in nutritional value. To alleviate this situation, the USDA released buying guides with 12 food groups in the 1930s (USDA, n.d.).

The USDA changed guides several times over the next several decades with the determined number of food groups fluctuating from seven in the 1940s to five in the 1970s with the introduction of the Hassle-Free Foundation diet. The **Food Guide Pyramid**, which was introduced in 1984 and used six food groups as a guide, was printed on such products as bread packages and cereal boxes and was used until early 2005. This guide was revised once in the early 1990s based on the U.S. Department of Health and Human Services' (DHHS) "Surgeon General's Report on Nutrition and Health" (DHHS, 1988). This report included the recommendations of a panel of nutritional experts selected by the USDA and the DHHS.

The Food Guide Pyramid, while easily recognized, was neither well used nor well understood (Escobar, 1999). In 2005 a new pictorial guide—MyPyramid (DHHS, 2005; Haven, Burns, Britten, & Davis, 2006)—rolled out. A modified version for older adults was released in January 2008 (Lichtenstein, Rasmussen, Yu, Epstein, & Russell, 2008).

Not surprisingly, things changed again. In 2011 yet another new pictorial guide ditched the previously used food pyramid altogether. The new guide is a plate showing you what you should eat (www.choosemyplate.gov). Key changes include clearly showing amounts needed by age and sex, explicitly urging the consumption of more whole grains and a variety of fruits and vegetables and including simple direct recommendations such as ensuring half of the plate (daily food

▼ TABLE 8.1

Eating Habits Survey

Examine the factors that affect your eating habits. Choose one day of the week that is typical of your eating pattern. List all the foods and drinks that you consumed on that day. Then list the other requested information. Use these symbols: taste (T), convenience (C), emotion (E), availability (A), advertising (AD), weight control (WT), hunger (H), family values (FV), peers (P), nutritional value (NV), cost (S), and health (HT) as reasons for choice. You may be surprised by what you see.

Time of Day	Minutes Spent Eating	Meal/Snack	Degree of Hunger (0–5)	Activity While Eating	Food and Quantity	Others Present?	Reason for Food Choice

consumption) is fruits and vegetables. As you can see in Figure 8.1, the plate has different colors to represent the amount of different food groups you should eat. The new plate program is also explicit in that it is only one way to get healthy and focuses solely on eating. You may want to take the food you listed in Table 8.1 and put it on a plate and see how you do with balancing your food!

The food guides suggest the types and amount of foods to eat each day. Four factors were considered in establishing the serving sizes: typical portion sizes from food consumption surveys, ease of use, nutrient content, and traditional uses of foods (Herring, Britten, Davis, & Tuepker, 2000). Did the phrase "traditional uses of food" make you think? Do different cultural groups have different traditional foods? Absolutely they do! To compensate for this, Oldways Preservation and Exchange Trust of Cambridge, Massachusetts, developed food plates for different cultural groups. Mediterranean, Asian, Latino, American Indian, and African Heritage Diet Plates as seen in Figure 8.2 incorporate habits of various cultural groups in the United States. The main difference between these plates and the USDA MyPlate is that the culturally diverse plates feature foods specific to the different cultures. (Don't look at them on an empty stomach because you will get hungry.)

These different guides highlight the fact that what we eat often is deeply tied to our cultural backgrounds. Throughout history, many cultures have ascribed health-promoting powers to certain foods, and many religions have followed specific dietary practices. Chinese herbs of immortality were a popular fad among the ancient Chinese (Hsu, 2010). These herbs have a modern manifestation in Chinese herbs marketed to bodybuilders in health food stores. Different cultures have different beliefs about what foods to consume. As described in Chapters 1 and 3, many cultures, including the Chinese culture, believe that some foods are hot and others are cold. This belief refers to a food's influence on health and well-being, and not to the temperature or spiciness of foods. Cold foods include most vegetables, tropical fruits, dairy products, and inexpensive cuts of meat (e.g., rump roast). Hot foods include chili peppers, garlic, onion, most grains, expensive cuts of meat, oils, and alcohol.

Speaking of China, a major study done in China (among others) suggests a vegetarian diet is better for health (Campbell & Campbell, 2016). The China Study, as it is called, is heavily debated. While it seems to be the exemplar for vegetarianism, some point to flaws in how the data are selected, suggesting the claim for vegetarianism made in the study may not stand on firm footing (Minger, 2013). This is a great example of why knowing about research methods and being research savvy is important (see Chapter 2). Read on for what is the best for our health given the current science.

Just as MyPlate balances nutritional value, cultures such as the Chinese and the ancient Indians suggested eating foods to balance energy levels. Most non-Western cultures believe that the type of food eaten needs to balance the type or condition of the person. For example, pregnancy is considered a hot condition during which many Latinas typically avoid hot foods, believing this will prevent the infant from contracting a hot illness, such as a skin rash. In contrast to the Hispanic beliefs, the Chinese believe that pregnancy is a cold condition during which the expectant mother should consume hot foods to keep in balance and remain healthy.

Development of Food Preferences

Have you wondered why you like certain foods and dislike others? Some of our **food preferences** are biologically programmed into us (Bartoshuk, 1993) although they vary by culture (Sorokowska et al., 2017). The sweet, salty, bitter, sour, and umami (savory) tastes guide the intake of calories, electrolytes, possibly dangerous stimuli, acids and ions, and protein consumption, respectively (Lindemann, 2001). Two of these tastes, sweet and salty, are completely innate. Humans are born preferring sweet and salty tastes and are averse to sour tastes. Beyond this, our experiences and exposure to food determine the bulk of our preferences. If the context in which you were given broccoli was positive, you probably will develop a preference for broccoli. If you always were forced to eat your beans, you probably will develop an aversion to beans.

▼ FIGURE 8.1

The USDA MyPyramid and MyPlate

Some parents try to sneak vegetables into foods but studies show children's preferences for many foods (e.g., broccoli–chocolate chip bread) do not change significantly if they are told the dishes contain vegetables (Pope & Wolf, 2012). Kids do draw the line somewhere. In the previous study, kids preferred the unlabeled chickpea chocolate chip cookies (i.e., when chickpea presence was not known) to the labeled one.

Basic reward and punishment and sociocultural factors also play a large role in the development of our food preferences (Finlayson, King, & Blundell, 2008). Children growing up in families who eat together often develop healthier eating habits—and are healthier adults too (Franko, Thomson, Affenito, Barton, & Striegel-Moore, 2008). Foods used as rewards (e.g., clean your room and you get your ice cream) or paired with fun social events or holidays (e.g., Mom's spice cake at Christmas) automatically become preferred. Attach a toy related to a movie (movie tie-in) and the kids will even prefer healthy meals over unhealthy ones with the tie-in toy (Dixon, Niven, Scully, & Wakefield, 2017).

Culture plays an important role as well. In a study of more than 1,000 children, the ethnicity of the parents and correspondingly ethnic food preferences also influenced what children ate (Bruss, Applegate, Quitugua, Palacios, & Morris, 2007). Sociocultural factors can predict preference for unhealthy foods. In a Mexican study, parents' monthly income, the father's education, and the type of day care 3- and 4-year-olds attended were associated with the food preferences, with high calorific foods being most preferred (De Lira-Garcia, Bacardí-Gascón, & Jiminez-Cruz, 2012). Too, do not take presentation lightly. When researchers asked adults from Italy, Japan, and the United States to assess preferences for various plating arrangements, there were diverging preferences regarding the preferred position of the featured main course, how the items should be organized, and whether they should be casually presented (Zampollo, Wansink, Kniffin, Shimizu, & Omori, 2012). Children have notably different preferences than adults, preferring seven different items and six different colors on their ideal plates (vs. three different colors and three different items for adults; Zampollo, Kniffin, Wansink, & Shimizu, 2012).

Obesity

As of this writing adult obesity rates exceed 35% in five states, 30% in 25 states, and 25% in 46 states (Segal, Rayburn, & Beck, 2017). Just as shocking are the obesity prevalence rates for children. Nationally, 32% of children age 10 to 17 are overweight or obese (Child and Adolescent

▼ FIGURE 8.2

Food Pyramids from Different Cultural Groups

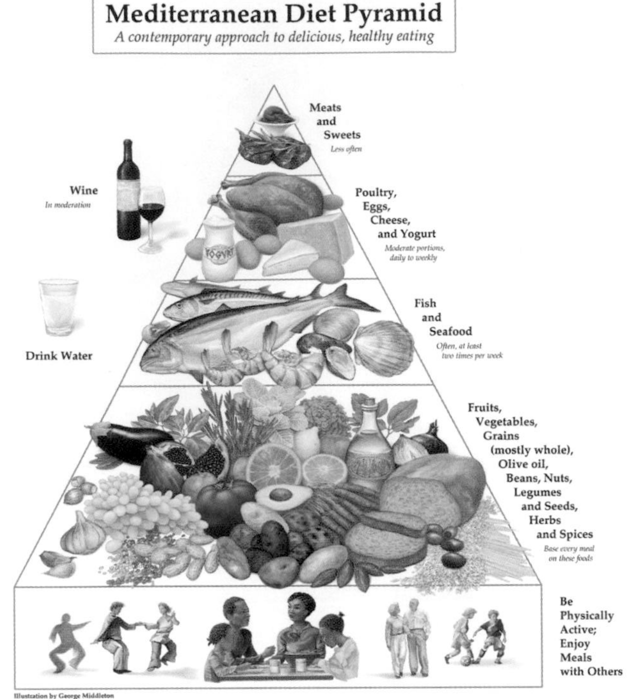

© 2009 Oldways Preservation and Exchange Trust • www.oldwayspt.org

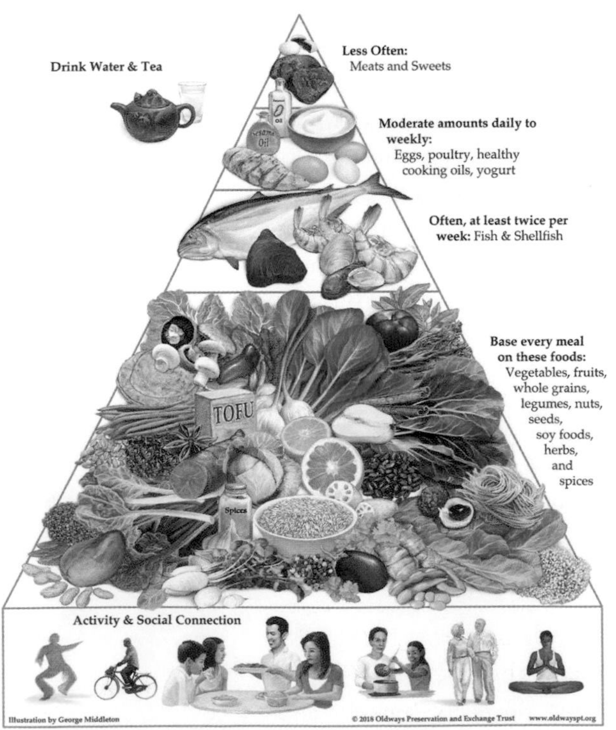

Health Measurement Initiative, 2016). In the 1980s only 13% of adult Americans were considered obese (Ogden, Carroll, & Flegal, 2008). That is a significant difference. It is imperative that we grasp healthy eating behaviors and proper nutrition in order to turn this dangerous trend around.

What exactly do the terms "obese" and "overweight" mean? There are established norms for body weight and different grades of overweight (see below). Research has established the weight range for healthy living for people of different heights. If a person weighs more than his or her normal range, that person is referred to as being overweight. **Obesity** is defined as having a **body mass index (BMI)** of 30 or greater, also called Grade 2 overweight. A BMI of between 25 and 29.9 qualifies a person as overweight. To calculate your BMI, multiply your weight by 703 and divide it by the square of your height measured in inches [BMI = (Wt × 703)/(Ht × Ht)]. OK, who does math anymore right? Go here: https://www.webmd.com/diet/body-bmi-calculator.

Although the BMI score is commonly used, there is an important caveat in its use and it should not be used as the only indicator of a person's healthy weight. It misrepresents weight in different cultural groups (Bates, Acevedo-Garcia, Alegria, & Krieger, 2008). This misrepresentation also helps explain some inconsistencies in the eating behavior literature by demonstrating the impact of statically adjusting for BMI when BMI and eating behaviors are compared in individuals from different racial or ethnic backgrounds. Gluck and Geliebter (2002) demonstrated this in a study of European American, African American, and Asian American women who completed an Eating Habits Questionnaire (EHQ) and other measures of body image and eating. European Americans had greater body dissatisfaction (as measured by a higher difference between current and ideal image) than Asian Americans and higher EHQ scores than both Asian Americans and African Americans. More African American women chose a larger body size as their ideal than the other groups. The caveat with BMI is this: Asian American women had a significantly lower BMI than both other groups. However, after controlling (i.e., statistically adjusting) for BMI, ideal body size differences were minimized. Also, after controlling for BMI, both European Americans and Asian Americans had greater body discrepancy and EHQ scores than African Americans (Gluck & Geliebter, 2002).

The bottom line is that, similar to many of the health behaviors discussed in this chapter, obesity varies significantly by ethnicity and SES (Hill et al., 2017; Wong, Showell, Bleich, Gudzune, & Chan, 2017). In a large national study, Black men have greater odds of obesity

▼ FIGURE 8.3

Percent of People Overweight per Group Increases with Age

As you get older, you are at risk for gaining weight. As the body's metabolic rate slows down, you need to increase your physical activity level and pay more attention to what you eat.

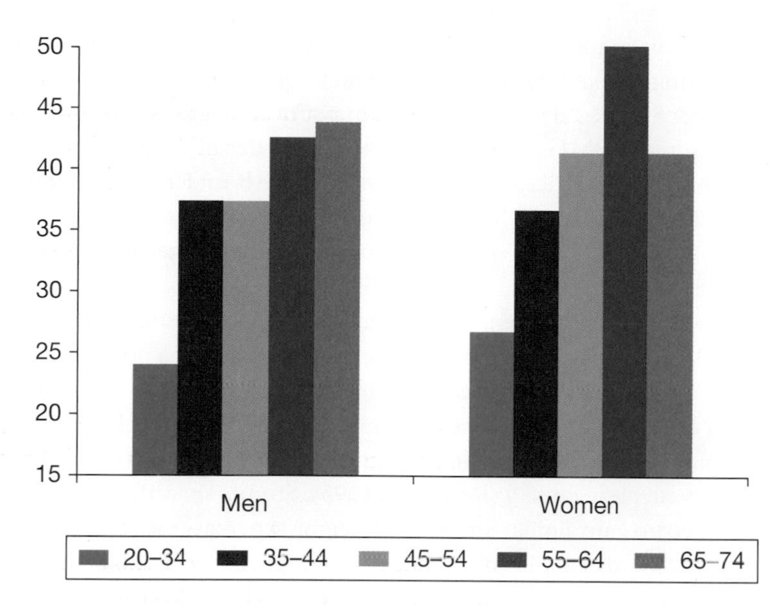

than White men in the South, West, and Midwest. In the South and West, Hispanic men also have greater odds of obesity than White men. In all regions, Asian men have lower odds of obesity than White men (Kelley et al., 2016).

Here is some bad news. Our weight increases (not counting the weight gain with pregnancy) as a natural part of the aging process (Figure 8.3). The weight of infants usually doubles in the first 6 months, and older adults gain weight as their metabolic system naturally slows with age. For important reasons, pregnant women add 30 to 35 pounds of weight on average to sustain a pregnancy. Obesity, however, is more than a normal addition of weight needed for growth or health. The chance of being obese increases with age, and obesity occurs more commonly in women than in men, especially among non-European American women. Approximately 55% to 60% of African American and Mexican American women 40 to 60 years of age are overweight (Wing & Polley, 2002).

Obesity is associated with a number of health issues. Obesity increases the chances of having a chronic disease, exacerbates conditions such as coronary heart disease, and correspondingly shortens life (Song, 2019). This association is well known and interventions focusing only on health risks of *obesity* may provide minimal new information and induce little new weight loss (Finkelstein, Brown, & Evans, 2008). As the number of overweight and obese people increases, the prevalence of problems such as type 2 diabetes, gallbladder disease, coronary heart disease, high blood cholesterol levels, high blood pressure, and osteoarthritis also increases. The chance of having two or more health conditions increases with weight in all racial and ethnic subgroups (DHHS, 2005).

Gaining extra weight in adulthood even increases the risk of heart attacks (Willett & Singer, 1995). In the Second National Health and Nutrition Examination Survey (NHANES II), overweight adults were three times more likely to develop diabetes and high blood pressure (Van Itallie, 1985). In fact, there is almost a direct negative correlation between BMI and mortality. The higher your BMI, the sooner you may die. Being classified as Grade 3 overweight (e.g., BMI of 40 and higher, called morbid obesity) in particular is very unhealthy (Flegal et al., 2005). One study, the Nurses' Health Study, followed 115,000 women ages 30 to 55 for 16 years (Manson et al., 1995). Women with BMIs of 19 to 21 showed the lowest mortality rates. Women with a

BMI of 32 or greater were almost four times more likely to die from cardiovascular disease and twice as likely to die from cancer compared with women who had BMIs less than 19.

It is important to note that there is a growing body of research making health psychologists take a closer look at the relationship between obesity and health. First, there is a controversy regarding the exact levels of BMI that are unhealthy. It is possible that being classified as Grade 1 overweight (e.g., BMI between 25 and 30) may serve a protective function, a relationship called the "obesity paradox" (Lechi, 2017; Saguy & Almeling, 2008, p. 53). Many argue the research supporting the paradox is ignored and that suggesting fat is only unhealthy leads to fat shaming (Konik & Smith, 2015). Second, BMI measure is criticized for obscuring many key relationships. For example, BMI is also correlated with bone density and mass. In case you were wondering, you *can* be too thin! Research also shows that BMIs under 18 put a person at risk for health problems (Flegal et al., 2005). These data combined with the social pressures and prejudices experienced by overweight individuals, especially women, suggest caution in how we talk about obesity (Chrisler, 2018).

Obesity is caused by a complex blend of biology, psychology, and social factors (Berthoud & Morrison, 2008). A person may be obese or have excess body fat for a number of reasons. The significant reason is a combination of bad eating habits (eating too much or too many high-calorie foods) with lack of enough physical activity. In addition, if calorie intake is greater than calorie output, you are going to gain weight. Both genetic and environmental factors also are at work. Clearly, genetics plays a role in obesity (Bouchard, 1995). Studies show that identical twins when overfed are both likely to gain similar amounts of weight, whereas fraternal twins do not show this relationship (Bouchard et al., 1990). There are even specific genes linked to obesity. Seven to ten specific genes contribute to common forms of obesity (Bradfield et al., 2012). The *ob* gene, which codes for the protein leptin, was one of the first genes linked to obesity (Campfield, Smith, & Burn, 1996). Leptin signals satiety, and people with a mutated *ob* gene do not have as much leptin, which possibly leads to overeating. Of course, dramatic increases in obesity are not necessarily due to dramatic mutations of the *ob* gene. A person's environment factors in as well.

Changes in food marketing and availability are the most recent and blatant environmental factors influencing eating (Linn & Novosat, 2008). The fast-food industry has been supersizing its offerings. For a small increase in cost, fast-food chains generate a large profit from the public, many of whom like to get large servings. The influence of larger servings in restaurants is seen as one component of a Western way of life because it tends to be localized to developed countries. As proof of the ills of Western living, Ravussin, Valencia, Esparza, Bennett, and Schulz (1994) compared Pima Indians in the United States with Pima Indians in a rural part of Mexico. The U.S. Pima Indians had mean average BMI of 35.5. The Mexican Pima Indians had an average BMI of 25.1. Similarly, Alvord and Van Pelt (2000) have documented rising cases of gallbladder infection and other diet-related problems in the Navajo Indians of New Mexico.

How much food does a person really need? The actual amount of food in a recommended serving may surprise you (Figure 8.4). Weight gain is associated with frequent consumption of fast foods, sugar-sweetened drinks, food prepared outside the home, alcohol, and large portion sizes (Wing & Phelan, 2012). Most overweight people eat more than normal weight people eat, and often do not even realize the quantities they consume (Lichtman et al., 1992). That said, overweight people do not just eat more of anything. Taste and quality are particularly important. One study suggests that overweight individuals actually prefer (and eat) more fat than normal weight people (Rolls & Shide, 1992). Be warned though, most people eat more if they are given larger servings (Wansink, van Ittersum, & Painter, 2006). Furthermore, a greater variety of foods presented leads to greater quantities consumed by individual eaters (Temple, Giacomelli, Roemmich, & Epstein, 2008). Hetherington and Rolls (1996) showed that if only one type of food is available at a meal, people eat a moderate amount of it. If a second food is then introduced, the amount of the new food eaten will be more than if it was presented by itself. This phenomenon is called **sensory specific satiety**.

▼ FIGURE 8.4

A Handy Guide to Serving Size

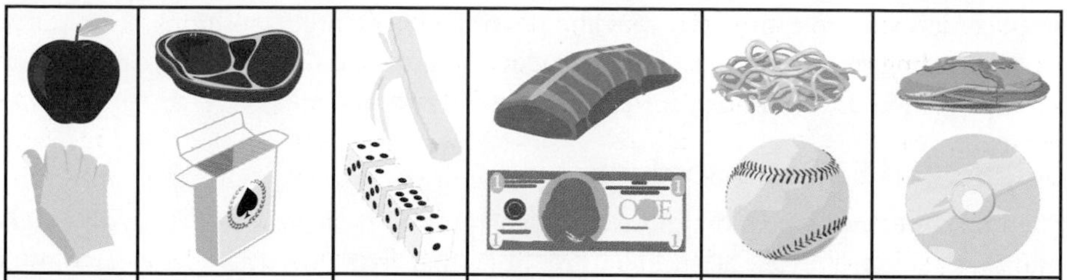

Item:	Fruit	Meat	Cheese	Fish	Pasta	Pancake
Size of:	Fist	Cards	2 pair of dice	Dollar Bill	Baseball	1 CD

Even thinking that there is more variety can make you eat more. Kahn and Wansink (2004) showed that people will eat more jellybeans when they are mixed up (and there seems to be more variety) than when a number of varieties are served separately. Simply changing the cost of foods makes a difference too (Faith, Fontaine, Baskin, & Allison, 2007). The cheaper the food is, the more people will eat, which even applies to healthy items such as fruits (Jeffery, French, Raether, & Baxter, 1994). Therefore, a variety of social and psychological factors influence how much we eat and when we eat it (Stroebe, 2008). For example, we also eat more when we are stressed or hassled (O'Connor, Jones, Conner, McMillan, & Ferguson, 2008).

A review of obesity prevention programs showed that the most successful programs targeted children, adolescents, and females; were relatively brief; solely targeted weight control versus other health behaviors (e.g., smoking); were evaluated in pilot trials; and were trials in which participants must have volunteered to participate (Stice, Shaw, & Marti, 2006). Unfortunately, studies have not found any particular diet to be successful over the long run (Konik & Smith, 2015; Mann, 2015). Not surprisingly given our attachment to technology, weight control interventions are now presented with apps and over the Internet and show significant success in changing nutritional behaviors (LaChausse, 2012).

Eating Disorders

The defining characteristic of all eating disorders is a severe disturbance in eating behaviors (American Psychiatric Association, 2000). Diagnostic criteria are currently provided for two eating disorders: *anorexia nervosa* and *bulimia nervosa*, and a third general category, *eating disorder not otherwise specified*. It is important to note that dieting by itself has not been linked to increased eating disorder symptoms (Williamson et al., 2008).

Many people have psychological problems, such as low self-esteem, that contribute to an unhealthy relationship with food. For others, being overweight leads to disorderly eating. For example, obesity has been associated with binge eating disorder, in which individuals consume large quantities of food and experience a lack of control over their lives (Marcus, 1993). Eating disorders have biological and psychological bases (Monteleone, Tortorella, Castaldo, Di Filippo, & Maj, 2007; Stice, 2002). Problems with low self-esteem coupled with pressures to be like slim models or actresses and actors on television, in the movies, or in magazines, and bad role models often drive some young girls and boys to starve themselves. Young girls, in particular, are at risk for developing anorexia nervosa or bulimia nervosa.

Anorexia involves an intense fear of gaining weight, a disturbed body image, a refusal to maintain normal weight, and extreme measures to lose weight. People with anorexia often exercise 2 to 3 hours a day, take weight-loss pills or appetite suppressants, abuse laxatives, and skip meals. No matter how thin they get, anorexics still feel they need to lose more weight.

This condition can sometimes be fatal. Bulimia involves habitually overeating followed by self-induced vomiting, fasting, and excessive exercise. The eating is usually done in secret and is then accompanied by intense guilt and weight gain concerns. Given the strong psychological and social components to eating disorders and possible genetic predispositions, the biopsychosocial approach of health psychologists to illness can be a great aid in preventing eating disorders and helping individuals who already suffer from one or more of them.

Culture and Eating Disorders

The cross-cultural study, diagnosis, assessment, and treatment of eating disorders is in its infancy, although a review of the literature shows that eating disorders are clearly influenced by culture (Markey, Vander Wal, & Gibbons, 2009).

There are some significant cultural differences in eating disorders and with the body image problems that cause them. Cultures vary in their concepts of ideal body shape, and sociocultural models of body image suggest that the prevalence of eating disorders and body image disturbance in Western countries is partially attributable to cultural ideals of beauty that value thinness. Furthermore, most assessment tools have been validated only on samples of European Americans, lack specificity in defining cultural groups, and show biases in detecting and reporting eating disorders in women of color (Gilbert, 2003).

Eating disorders are not just a European American problem (Becker et al., 2010; Hansen, 2011; Kuba, Harris-Wilson, & O'Toole, 2012). For example, Edman and Yates (2004) found no cultural differences in eating disorder symptoms or self-dissatisfaction or body dissatisfaction scores between Asian American and European American women. Furthermore, eating disorders have been reported in nearly every area of the world (Anderson-Fye & Becker, 2004). Prevalence rates of eating disorders outside North America, especially in Africa, Japan, Korea, the Middle East, and Singapore, have been found to be comparable to those in Western countries.

Rates of eating disorders do vary by ethnicity within the United States, and no ethnic group is completely immune. Some cultural groups may have higher rates of eating disorders than others. Caballero, Sunday, and Halmi (2004) compared Latino and European American patients with anorexia or bulimia on severity and types of preoccupations and rituals related to eating disorders and the motivation to change. Patients were interviewed with the Yale-Brown-Cornell Eating Disorder Scale (YBC-EDS). All YBC-EDS scores were higher for the Latino group, who also had more preoccupations and rituals. Latinos were also more likely to have rituals in many measured categories. Exactly how culture contributes to eating disorders is still unclear, but researchers are beginning to explicitly look at the role of culture in the development of eating behaviors and the formation of body image (Markey, 2004).

When compared with European American women, African American women tend to have lower rates of anorexia nervosa but similar rates of binge eating, and Latinas may have slightly higher rates of eating disorders than both of these ethnic groups (Markey, Vander Wal, & Gibbons, 2009). Asian American women have the lowest rates of eating disorders among the major ethnic groups in the United States, while Native American women have the highest rates.

Having contact with or being influenced by Western culture significantly increases the prevalence of eating disorders, especially in the case of bulimia nervosa (Keel & Klump, 2003). In an unsettling example, Becker, Burwell, Gilman, Herzog, and Hamburg (2002) showed that exposure to Western media (introduction of television) in Fiji was associated with an increase in symptoms of eating disorders and self-induced vomiting to lose weight. Rapid modernization has also

Synthesize, Evaluate, Apply

- How do your physical activity and dietary patterns compare with prescribed levels for good health?
- What are the main reasons for people not eating a balanced diet?
- What are the differences between the cultural food pyramids?
- What are the pros and cons of having different pyramids?
- What are the biggest factors influencing the development of food preferences?
- Apply what you know about food and exercise to develop a plan for optimal health.

been found to result in difficulties with disordered eating and body dissatisfaction in Asian and Caribbean countries (Katzman, Hermans, Van Hoeken, & Hoek, 2004).

iStockphoto.com/ kali9

▲ **Physical Activity.** You do not have to go to a gym to get your daily requirement of physical activity. Even walking can burn energy. A brisk 20-minute daily walk has been found to be enough to prevent weight gain.

PHYSICAL ACTIVITY

Physical activity is any bodily movement produced by contraction of the skeletal muscles that increases energy expenditure above a baseline level (WHO, 2018). The more current term used by public health researchers to describe any physical activity sufficient to enhance health is health-enhancing physical activity (Brassington, Hekler, Cohen, & King, 2012). How physically active are you? Do you work out regularly? Do you take an elevator when you could use the stairs?

Most people know that exercise is good for their health. Unfortunately, few people manage to successfully adopt and maintain an exercise habit (Marcus et al., 2000; Shields et al., 2008). There are many physical and psychological benefits of physical exercise, including lowered blood pressure, weight loss, stress reduction, and increased self-confidence (LaCaille & Hooker, 2019). At the other end of the spectrum, being inactive (e.g., sitting for long periods of time) is independently associated with a wide array of health risks (Missoni, Kern, & Missoni, 2012; van Uffelen et al., 2010).

How much physical activity is needed? A group of scientists appointed by the DHHS focused on studies testing the relationship between physical activity and nine health outcomes (e.g., mortality, cancer, mental health) and developed national physical activity guidelines (WHO, 2018). The guidelines suggest that each of us should take part in at least moderate-intensity physical activity on most days of the week. Children and adolescents (6–17 years) should engage daily in 60 minutes or more of activity and do muscle and bone strengthening activities at least 3 days a week. Adults (18–65) should engage in 150 minutes of moderate-intensity or 75 minutes of high-intensity activity every week. A key aspect to note is that this activity can be a combination of 10-minute episodes spread through the week. The guidelines also suggest muscle strengthening activities for all muscle groups at least twice a week. No time for a long jog? At least you can spare 10 minutes, right?

It is important to remember that there are numerous ways that you can expend energy and be physically active. When people think about the recommendations for physical activity they often picture going to a gym, running, biking, or lifting weights. Additionally, about 50% to 70% of the total amount of energy we burn relates to the working of our different cells and organ systems, referred to as our *basal metabolic rate*. Another 7% to 10% of energy is used to break down the food we eat, called the *thermic effect of food* (Ravussin & Rising, 1992). The rest of the energy we burn through physical activity, including the things we have to do every day, such as bathing, grooming, or moving around the house or campus, and the things that we choose to do, such as playing sports, dancing, or walking as a leisure time activity. The more physical activities we choose to do, the more energy we expend. The amount of energy used in different daily activities is shown in Table 8.2.

Exercise is defined as activity planned with the goal of improving one or more aspects of physical fitness (Caspersen, Powell, & Christenson, 1985). Exercise contributes to our level of fitness, defined as the ability to perform daily tasks with vigor and alertness without undue fatigue, to enjoy leisure time activities, and to meet unforeseen challenges (Phillips, Kiernan, & King, 2002). Are you fit? Several different components can assess whether you are fit. Cardiovascular

▼ TABLE 8.2

Energy Used in Various Physical Activities

	Calories Burned in 5 Minutes (Typically*)	
Activity	Women	Men
Walking fast	20	30
Washing a car	20	30
Having sex	20	30
Doing yard work	20	30
Painting	20	30
Mowing the lawn	25	35
Biking to work	30	40
Walking up stairs	35	45
Running up stairs	75	100

*Calories estimated for a 132-pound woman and a 176-pound man. Adjust proportionally to your weight if needed.

endurance, often referred to as aerobic fitness, refers to the body's capacity to take in, transport, and use oxygen. A common measure of aerobic fitness is the volume of oxygen (VO2) a person uses during different tasks. Muscular strength, muscular endurance, muscular power, speed, flexibility, agility, balance, good reaction times, and a low percentage of body fat are other components used to assess fitness (Phillips et al., 2002). Generally, most national studies of health behaviors use physical activity rather than exercise levels to assess health, although both are important components of a healthy lifestyle (Brassington et al., 2012). The term "exercise" more often refers to specific activities such as running on a treadmill at the gym, whereas the term "physical activity" can be more general and unstructured (e.g., walking around the block).

Most commonly used measures of physical activity assess leisure time activities that require energy use above the level of daily living. An example would be taking a fast walk to the store. This type of measurement works well in countries such as the United States and in the study of other populations with high socioeconomic status (SES) because most jobs in these economic environments do not require expending too much energy. Sitting at a desk or standing in one spot in a production line does not use as much energy as working in a field. In developing countries and among populations with lower SES, a lot more energy is spent on the job (Pereira et al., 1998). In the United States ethnic minority groups have lower levels of leisure time physical activity (LTPA) than do European Americans but it is unclear how much of this is explained by differences in socioeconomic status and health (Xiaoxing & Baker, 2007). Leisure time physical activity was lower for African Americans and Latinos compared with European Americans, and steadily declined with lower levels of education. This may be a function of lower-educated individuals having less money or less time for LTPA.

Cultural Variations in Physical Activity

Ethnic, socioeconomic, age, and sex differences all account for cultural differences in physical activity (Cerin, Vandelanotte, Leslie, & Merom, 2008; Swartz, Strath, Parker, Miller, & Cieslik, 2007). Minority groups in the United States consistently have relatively lower physical activity levels than majority group members (Cassetta, Boden-Albala, Sciacca, & Giardina, 2007). Minority women are among the least active subgroups in American society (Brownson et al.,

2000; Lee, 2005). A cross-sectional study conducted in 1996 and 1997 among 2,912 African American, American Indian, Alaskan Native, Latina, and European American women age 40 years and older showed that physical activity was lowest among African Americans, American Indians, and Alaskan Natives (Brownson et al., 2000). In three national surveys, the **National Health Interview Survey** (**NHIS**, 1991), the **Third National Health and Nutritional Examination Survey** (**NHANES III**, 1988–1991), and the **Surgeon General's Report** (DHHS, 1996), physical activity was found to be lowest among people with low incomes and lower levels of education.

In general, people are more active when they are younger. For example, 64% of students in grades 9 to 12 engaged in vigorous physical activity 3 or more days per week for at least 20 minutes versus only 16% of people age 18 and older (CDC, 2003). Age and ethnicity also have an effect. In a large study comparing physical activity levels by race or ethnicity, age, gender, and weight status, White boys spent three to four fewer minutes per day in vigorous physical activity than Mexican American and African American boys but had lower obesity rates (Belcher et al., 2010). In another study, minority girls also watched television on average 5 hours longer per week than nonminority girls (Wolf et al., 1993). Having a television in your bedroom is even worse. Adolescents with a bedroom television reported more television viewing time, less physical activity, poorer dietary habits, fewer family meals, and poorer school performance (Barr-Anderson, van den Berg, Neumark-Sztainer, & Story, 2008). Sex, ethnicity, socioeconomic status, and age were also associated with the presence of a bedroom television. More TV watching is associated with more sitting, and health psychologists are paying more attention to the negative consequences of sedentary behavior (Lacaille & Hooker, 2019).

Physical Consequences of Physical Activity

Being physically active and exercising daily are good for physical health (Brassington et al., 2012). As mentioned earlier, there is some debate about how much exercise is needed, but no debate about whether it is needed. As early as the mid-20th century, physically active individuals were shown to be less likely to develop coronary heart disease (Kahn, 1963; Morris, Heady, Raffle, Roberts, & Parks, 1953). Physical activity not only reduces mortality from different diseases (Bouchard, 2001) but also increases life expectancy (Blair, Kohl, Gordon, & Paffenbarger, 1992; Lee & Skerrett, 2001) and improves cardiovascular recovery from stress (Chafin, Christenfeld, & Gerin, 2008). In particular, physical activity (controlling for the ill effects of a bad diet or smoking) has been identified as an independent risk factor in development of diseases such as cardiovascular disease (Berlin & Colditz, 1990; Pate, 1995).

Evidence is accumulating that shows connections between physical activity and cancers (Loprinzi, Cardinal, Winters-Stone, Smit, & Loprinzi, 2012; Thune & Furberg, 2001). In general, higher levels of both occupational and leisure time physical activity relate to lower levels of prostate, lung, testicular, colon, rectal, and breast cancers, although evidence in some of these cases is inconsistent. In addition, being physically active relates to lower incidence of type 2 diabetes (Hu et al., 2001; Wannamethee, Shaper, & Alberti, 2000), osteoporosis or loss of bone density (Mussolino, Looker, & Orwoll, 2001), strokes (Wannamethee & Shaper, 1992), and hypertension (Reaven, Barrett-Conner, & Edelstein, 1991). The report of the Physical Activity Guidelines Committee (WHO, 2018) documents an extensive list of the associations between physical activity and physical health outcomes (www.health.gov/paguidelines/default.aspx).

Why does physical activity help with physical health? Evidence suggests the answer is a complex mix of interactions among different body systems (see Chapter 3) ranging from gene expression to organ functioning, immune responses, metabolism, inflammation, and oxidation (Alexander, 2010; Brassington et al., 2012). Physical activity may prevent heart attacks by increasing heart capacity, improving heart cell activity, reducing coronary artery thickening, and decreased inflammation (Handschin & Spiegelman, 2008).

Psychological Consequences of Physical Activity

Being physically active is probably beneficial for psychological health as well. Why only probably? At this point, few methodologically sound longitudinal studies have been performed to test the causal relationship between physical activity and mental health (Morgan, 1997; Phillips et al., 2002). Nevertheless, a strong body of correlation work suggests that there is a link. Furthermore, a growing number of studies support the idea that physical exercise is a lifestyle factor that might lead to increased physical and **mental health** throughout life (Hillman, Erickson, & Kramer, 2008).

In Chapter 5 you read that exercising can be a great stress reliever. This is just one of the many positive associations between physical activity and mental health. Numerous epidemiological studies and reviews of research link higher levels of physical activity with reduced symptoms of depression (Dunn, Trivedi, & O'Neal, 2001; Paffenbarger, Lee, & Leung, 1994). Physical activity is also associated with less anxiety (Moljord, Eriksen, Moksnes, & Espneg, 2011) and increases self-esteem (Haugen, Säfvenbom, & Ommundsen, 2011). Covey and Feltz (1991) highlighted the role of physical activity in development, concluding that physically active high school girls report significantly healthier self-image and coping characteristics than physically inactive girls. Similarly, Wankel and Berger (1990) showed that physical activity is significantly related to personal growth, social integration, and positive social change. However, these associations may not hold for elderly persons (Brown, 1992) and interventions to increase physical activity among the elderly show limited success (Baker et al., 2007). Evidence does exist showing physical exercise may reduce depression in the short term among the elderly (Sjosten & Kivela, 2006).

To some extent, finding links between physical activity and mental health can be frustrating. The link appears to make sense. You may notice that you feel better after a run, walk, or bicycle ride, but robust demonstrations of this association are difficult to find. Physical activity could lead to better mental health because activity increases monoamines such as norepinephrine, epinephrine, dopamine, and serotonin, and it releases endorphins. Depression may be decreased by physical activity's ability to increase the brain chemicals related to neuronal health and growth, and modifying the release of neurochemicals (Sylvia, Ametrano, & Nierenberg, 2010). Unfortunately, evidence for many of these possibilities is spotty (Phillips et al., 2002) and the connections not well understood (Brassington et al., 2012). What can we be sure of? Physical activity prevents excessive weight gain (the dangers of which are described above) and is linked clearly to physical well-being.

Synthesize, Evaluate, Apply

- How would you design an experiment to identify the best exercise for positive psychological effects?
- Describe how eating and physical activity can interact with each other.
- Apply your knowledge to design an intervention to increase physical activity among your peers.

SMOKING AND DRINKING

Both smoking and drinking are commonly considered to be vices. Although tobacco and alcohol are both potentially addictive substances, the body metabolizes alcohol and nicotine differently. Alcohol is a liquid, absorbed in the stomach, and from there it travels to the heart, the lungs, and finally to the brain. The active elements of tobacco, such as nicotine, are usually inhaled, resulting in a rapid transmission to the brain. Smoking has quick effects. Whereas a drinker may consume alcohol several times a week or even several times a day, a pack-a-day smoker experiences about 200 puffs a day, or behavioral reinforcers, in a wide variety of social settings. The majority of regular smokers are addicted, although many people can use alcohol socially and not become addicted (Russell, 1990). This difference in social use and the amount of **behavioral cueing** explains, in part, why the relapse rates for tobacco addiction is higher than those for alcohol **addiction**. Many alcoholics can quit drinking but have more difficulty quitting smoking because smoking seems to have greater biological and psychological interactions with other health behaviors such as drinking. People who always smoke at a bar are tempted to smoke when they are at a bar.

Our society has social and cultural differences in how we treat the use of each substance. In the United States tobacco use is legal for the vast majority of college-age students, whereas alcohol use is illegal for those younger than 21. Alcohol use is also prohibited at most work places and has been relegated to certain social events (except for alcoholics who drink regardless), which usually occur in the evening. Tobacco use, on the other hand, is a more accepted daily behavior and can occur at any time of the day in a variety of settings. Circumstances may make smoking appear more common than it actually is. Because of current indoor air policies, smokers are required to stand outside building entrances, which further increases their visibility and fuels misperceptions of the prevalence of smoking.

TOBACCO USE

In 2016 15 of every 100 U.S. adults admitted to regularly putting a flame to little paper-covered cylinders of dry leaves and sucking the bitter smoke into their lungs (i.e., smoking; CDC, 2018). Tobacco contains roughly 500 chemicals, and tobacco smoke contains about 4,000 chemicals (Dube & Green, 1982). With these statistics and this knowledge of cigarettes containing so many chemicals, not to mention cancer-causing black tar and an addictive substance called nicotine, one may wonder why smokers persist. DeBernardo et al. (1999) found that whereas 98% of smokers understood the harmful effects of smoking, just 39.1% of smokers seriously considered stopping and even 11.5% of nonsmokers intended to start smoking! These data prove that knowledge alone is insufficient to change behavior.

Tobacco use is the leading cause of preventable morbidity and mortality in the United States (Grunberg, Berger, & Starosciak, 2012). Yet, smoking continues in the broader culture as well as on high school and college campuses (Freedman, Nelson, & Feldman, 2012). Indeed, the number of smokers substantially decreased between 1993 and 2010 for all age groups, except those between age 18 and 24 (DHHS, 2012). The percentage of high school students who reported smoking cigarettes in the past month dropped to 19% in 2009 from 36% in 1997. Within the past 10 years, college student smoking prevalence has dropped from nearly 30% (Wechsler, Kelley, Seibring, Kuo, & Rigotti, 2001) to around 16% (Harris, Schwartz, & Thompson, 2008; Williamson et al., 2011).

Cultural Variations in Smoking

When looking at the general population, we see some clear-cut cultural differences in who smokes. Men smoke more than women (DHHS, 2012). People who earn less and who have less education smoke more than people higher on the socioeconomic ladder (Aekplakorn et al., 2008; DHHS, 2007). In fact, people in more deprived neighborhoods that have higher crime rates and less access to health care are more likely to smoke (Duncan, Jones, & Moon, 1999). Studies also show that military people with lower ranks smoke more than higher-ranked officers (Cunradi, Moore, & Ames, 2008). Geography also accounts for differences in smoking rates. In 2010 Kentucky had the highest number of smokers in the United States. Figure 8.5 shows smoking rates for different states, while Table 8.3 shows smoking rates for different countries.

The most pronounced differences in smoking are racial and ethnic (Figure 8.6). The CDC (2012) reports that American Indians have the highest rates of smoking (31%), followed by African Americans (21%), European Americans (21%), and then Asian and Pacific Islanders (9%).

Smoking and culture have some interesting interactions. African Americans who are more traditional are more likely to smoke than African Americans acculturated to mainstream European American ways (Klonoff & Landrine, 2001). In contrast, some Asian Americans and Latinos are less likely to smoke if they are more traditional in their ways (Lafferty, Heaney, & Chen, 1999). When African Americans are exposed to stress (demonstrated in an experimental setting), they show greater changes in the functioning of their blood vessels than in the functioning of their heart muscles (Llabre, Klein, Saab, McCalla, & Schneiderman, 1998). This has implications for the development of cerebrovascular disease for African Americans who are smokers. This finding is particularly interesting in the light of recent data showing that psychological distress was related to smoking status for White but not for Black or Hispanic respondents (Kiviniemi, Orom, & Giovino, 2011). Clearly the differences between physiological responses to stress and cognitive and behavioral coping vary.

Why Do People Smoke?

There are two main subparts to this important question: First, why do people start or initiate smoking? And second, why do they keep smoking? In keeping with the biopsychosocial approach of health psychology, biological, psychological, and social factors contribute to the initiation of smoking (Mermelstein & Brikmanis, 2019). Biologically, nicotine has some pleasing effects

▼ FIGURE 8.5

Cigarette Use Among Adults, 2016

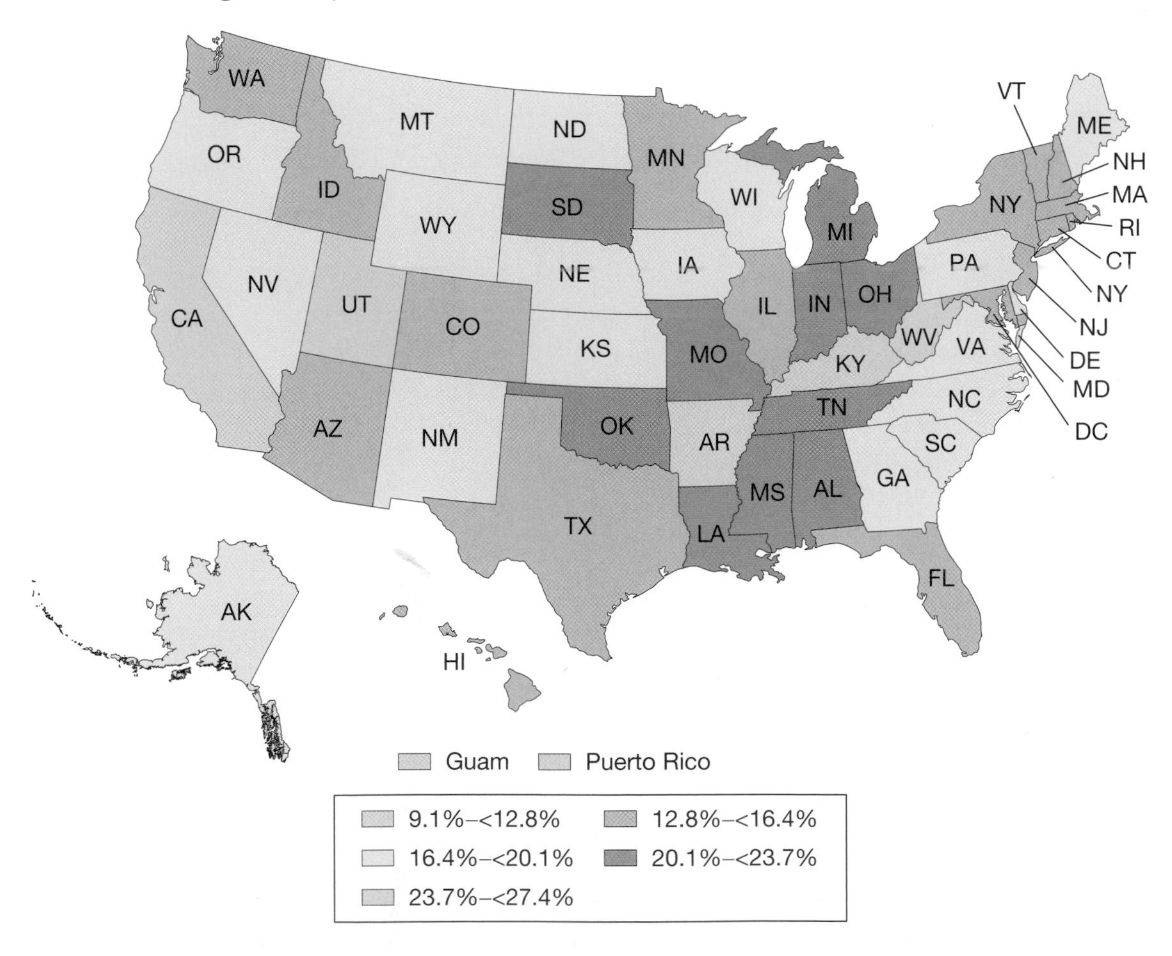

Source: Centers for Disease Control and Prevention (2016).

▼ TABLE 8.3

Percentage Regular Daily Smokers by Country, Adults Aged 15 Years and Over, Latest Year Between 1997 and 2005, Selected European Countries

Source: World Health Organization (2006). European Health for All statistical database, http://www.euro.who.inthfadb. Office for National Statistics (2005). Living in Britain: Results from the 2004 General Household Survey. The Stationary Office: London.

FIGURE 8.6

Percentage of U.S. Adults Who Smoke

There are significant differences in smoking rates across cultural groups.

- Nearly 22 of every 100 non-Hispanic American Indians/Alaska Natives (21.9%)
- More than 20 of every 100 non-Hispanic multiple race individuals (20.2%)
- Nearly 17 of every 100 non-Hispanic Blacks (16.7%)
- More than 16 of every 100 non-Hispanic Whites (16.6%)
- More than 10 of every 100 Hispanics (10.1%)
- 7 of every 100 non-Hispanic Asians (7.0%)

Source: Centers for Disease Control and Prevention (2016). Cigarette Smoking Among Adults—United States, 2005–2015. Morbidity and Mortality Weekly Report 2016;65(44):1205–11

on the brain and body, and it works extremely fast. The moment a smoker puffs a cigarette, the nicotine is absorbed through the fine inner lining of the cheek and reaches the brain within 15 seconds. In general, nicotine causes good moods, reduced feelings of hunger, and increased alertness and attention (Grunberg, Faraday, & Rahman, 2002).

In addition to these biological effects, there are some clear genetic components to smoking (Pomerleau & Kardia, 1999; Tang et al., 2012). If one member of an identical twin set chooses to smoke, the other will probably smoke as well. Is a specific gene involved? Lerman et al. (1999) showed that versions of the dopamine transporter gene SLC6A3 and the dopamine receptor gene DRD2 are associated with the likelihood of smoking. The genotype most related to addictive behavior, *DRD2-A1*, was most commonly found in African Americans, the ethnic group with high smoking rates.

Genes also influence how nicotine is broken down. Tang et al. (2012) investigated how nicotine metabolism and genetic variation in CYP2A6, a gene that mediates nicotine breakdown, influence the neural response to smoking cues. Tang et al. used functional magnetic resonance imaging to scan smokers with variations in the gene and hence high and low in nicotine metabolism. Fast metabolizers, by phenotype or genotype, had significantly greater responses to visual cigarette cues than slow metabolizers in the amygdala, hippocampus, striatum, insula, and cingulate cortex. This finding helps explain why fast metabolizers who smoke have lower cessation rates. Similar brain mapping of smokers with different genes show how variations in the amygdala (responsible for emotion and pleasure) may influence cessation (Jasinska et al., 2012).

Another clue to the physiological reasons for smoking comes from studies showing how people are addicted to nicotine. Smokers may not even be conscious of the extent of their physiological addiction. For example, when unknowing smokers were given cigarettes that had lower levels of nicotine, they automatically puffed longer and took more puffs (Schachter, 1980). Consequently, they smoked more low-nicotine cigarettes to get amounts of the nicotine comparable to those that they were used to.

Psychological Causes of Addiction

People start smoking for many psychological reasons (Grunberg et al., 2012). Some personality types, such as individuals with low self-esteem who can be easily influenced or extroverts who savor the stimulation of nicotine, are more likely to smoke. Extroverts find the nicotine arousal rewarding and smoke to increase this arousal. Some psychological developmental theories also help to explain initiation. For example, Erikson's theory of human social development suggests that the struggle both to overcome feelings of inferiority and establish an identity can make a person more likely to smoke (Erikson, 1968). Others have extended Erikson's theory to explain adolescent deviant behavior. Turbin, Jessor, and Costa (2000) see problem behaviors such as smoking as special cases of the transition process experienced by all adolescents.

Although difficult to measure and not conclusively linked to smoking, some theorists and many advertisers have used psychoanalytical theory to explain smoking. These groups argue that a smoker has experienced difficulties during Freud's theorized psychosocial oral stage. Because the pleasure-causing erogenous zone is the mouth, the smoker derives pleasure from the mouth and the placement of the cigarette in it. Many suggestive advertisements also use Freudian ideas to attract people to smoking.

People start smoking for many social and cultural reasons. Movies can be a strong influence (see Chapter 7). An extensive body of research has shown a strong correlation between the number of people shown smoking in the movies and the number smoking in the population. Many people imitate the heroes and heroines of the big screen. Even cartoons are not off limits to tobacco companies for product placements. Goldstein, Sobel, and Newman (1999) found that more than two-thirds of animated children's films made between 1937 and 1997 by five of the major production companies (e.g., Walt Disney, Universal, and 20th Century Fox) featured tobacco in story plots without clear verbal messages of any negative long-term health effects associated with its use.

Sometimes social pressure leads people to smoke. Rebellious adolescents may smoke to appear more adult or to distinguish themselves from others. Paradoxically, many children start smoking because they want to be like others, and thus they imitate their peers or family members who are smoking. Perhaps the key social factor is advertising (Emery et al.,

▼ FIGURE 8.7

Cigarette Smoking Overall Among Adults in the U.S. Is Down

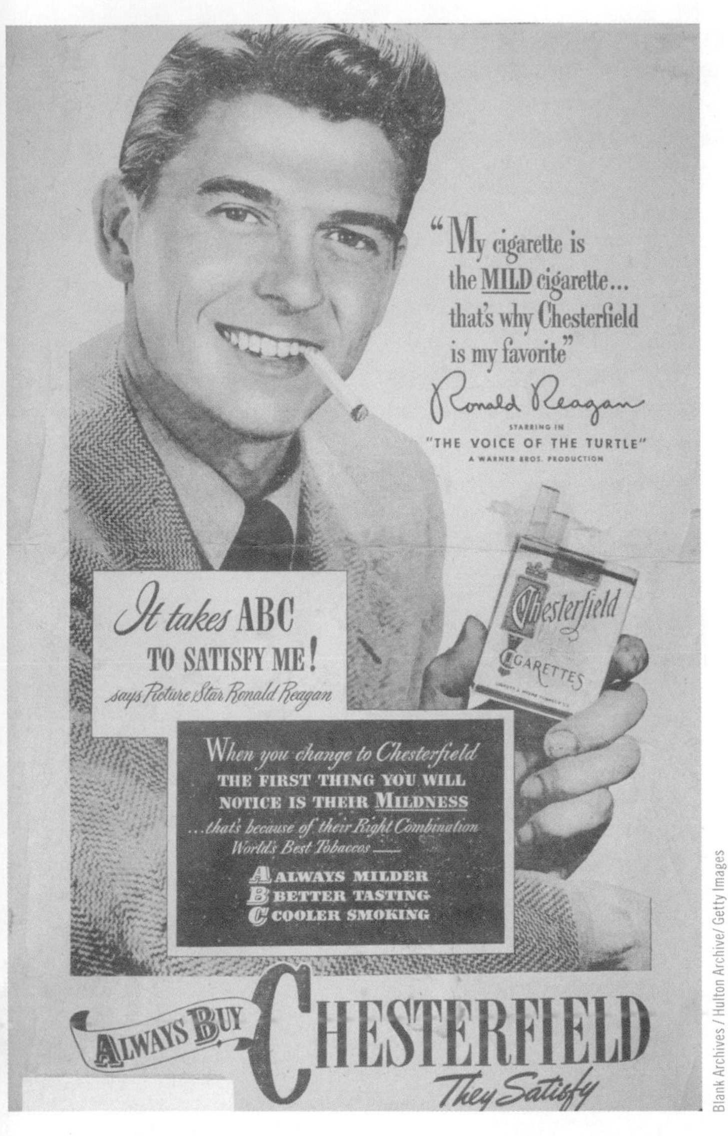

Blank Archives / Hulton Archive/ Getty Images

▲ **Smoking.** Before media advertising was regulated by the Surgeon General, early media campaigns used celebrities to get people to smoke. Here, then actor and later President Reagan appears in ads and press photos with cigarettes lit.

2012). Cigarettes are some of the most heavily advertised products in the media with advertising budgets reaching more than $8.7 billion per year (Federal Trade Commission, 2016). Until recently, younger children were the key targets. Camel cigarettes had a cartoon character named Joe Camel that was recognized second to only Mickey Mouse among North American children (Grunberg, Brown, & Klein, 1997). It is suggested that the use of the cartoon character and the subsequent higher familiarity of the Camel brand accounts for why close to 40% of adolescent smokers began smoking with Camels or Camel Lights.

Physiological Consequences of Smoking

There is no doubt that smoking can kill. A smoker has a significantly greater chance of dying earlier than a nonsmoker, if all other variables are held constant. The chance increases with the amount smoked, the length of time one has smoked, and the tar and nicotine contents of the cigarettes (Grunberg et al., 2012). The longer one smokes, the greater the risk of dying prematurely. The overall risk of dying also increases for smokers who inhale smoke versus those who only puff it in and out. Smokers are most likely to die prematurely from coronary heart disease, related cardiovascular diseases, or a range of cancers of the respiratory tract. Common smoking-related cancers are cancers of the lung, larynx, oral cavity, pancreas, and esophagus. Cigarette smoke is by far the most common cause of emphysema, a progressive lung disease (Carpenter et al., 2007). Thankfully, the rates of smoking are dropping in many groups. Figure 8.7 shows how the rates of smoking are dropping, while highlighting the groups still at risk.

Smoking has a **synergistic effect** on many health issues. Women who use oral contraceptives and who smoke have an increased risk of dying from ovarian, cervical, or uterine cancers (Vessey, Painter, & Yeates, 2003). Teenage girls who smoke have an increased risk of developing breast cancer before they reach menopause (Band, Le, Fang, & Deschamps, 2002). Similarly, people who have coronary heart disease and who smoke are more likely to die from a heart attack than are nonsmokers with coronary heart disease (Goldenberg et al., 2003). Howard et al. (1998) found that cigarette smoking increases plaque formation around arteries by as much as 50% in a 3-year period. This atherosclerosis can increase blood pressure and hasten the occurrence of a stroke or cardiac arrest.

Among women undergoing treatment for early breast cancer, those who smoke are more than twice as likely to die from the cancer as are nonsmoking women. In a study examining the effect of smoking on long-term outcomes of breast cancer patients treated with conservative surgery and radiation, researchers found that women who continue to smoke during therapy are 2.5 times more likely to die from the cancer than are women with no history of smoking (American Cancer Society, 2005). The study examined 1,039 nonsmokers and 861 smokers who underwent conservative therapy for breast cancer from March 1970 to December 2002. In addition, smoking correlates with increased occurrences of numerous diseases: sexual impotence, vision and hearing problems, ovarian cysts, multiple sclerosis, and even the common cold (ACS, 2005).

Secondhand smoke or **environmental tobacco smoke (ETS)** is the tobacco smoke inhaled by nonsmokers who are in the presence of smokers. This passive smoking is linked to lung cancer (Kreuzer, Krauss, Kreienbrock, Jockel, & Wichmann, 2000), cardiovascular disease (He et al., 1999; Kawachi et al., 1997), and smoking addiction in passive smokers (Wang, Ho, Lo, & Lam, 2012). Infants and children are probably most at risk from ETS. In fact, pregnant women should take pains to stay away from smokers and secondhand smoke because passive smoking during pregnancy affects several aspects of the child's neurobehavioral development (Hernández-Martínez, Arija Val, Escribano Subías, & Canals Sans, 2012). Early exposure to ETS has been linked to an increased risk of asthma (Dong et al., 2011). All in all, it is clear that any amount of tobacco use is detrimental to health.

Synthesize, Evaluate, Apply

- What are the different reasons people smoke?
- How would you weigh the physiological and the psychological causes of smoking against each other? Is one category higher for smokers you know?
- What theories from the previous chapter would you use to change the smoking behavior of a friend?

ALCOHOL

When health psychologists refer to drinking as a health behavior, they are referring to alcohol consumption. Drinking water seems to be good for you although the prescription to drink eight glasses of water a day was recently found to have no scientific basis (Negoianu & Goldfarb, 2008; everybody promotes the prescription, but nobody is sure where it came from). In contrast, alcohol consumption is responsible for 100,000 deaths each year, the third-leading cause of death after tobacco use and insufficient physical activity and poor diet (Mokdad et al., 2005). Be aware that whether drinking alcohol is a good thing or a bad thing has probably stimulated more spirited conversations than any other health behavior topic. Smoking is dangerous, no question, but is drinking? The government recommendation is that men can safely consume two drinks per day and that women can safely consume one drink per day (U.S. Department of Agriculture [USDA], 2000). You have also probably had friends justify their drinking by citing research concluding that a drink per day is actually *better* than no drinks at all. Is this true? How much alcohol, if any at all, is healthy? First, let's get familiar with usage.

Movie Poster Image Art / Moviepix/ Getty Images

▲ **Smoking.** Before media advertising was regulated by the Surgeon General, early media campaigns used celebrities to get people to smoke. Here, Hollywood legend James Dean appears in ads and press photos with cigarettes lit.

Who Drinks, How Much, and Why?

Patterns for drinking and causes for initiation of drinking are similar to those for smoking. This chapter outlines some of the major differences. While many sources suggest that some drinking is all right, it is important to distinguish between use and abuse.

Alcohol abuse is characterized by one or more of the following as a result of alcohol use: (1) failure to fulfill major role obligations, (2) recurrent physically hazardous use, (3) recurrent alcohol-related legal problems, or (4) continued use despite persistent alcohol-related social or interpersonal problems (Wood, Vinson, & Sher, 2002). At most colleges, alcohol abuse is evident. Nearly half of college students are **binge drinkers**—men who have consumed five or more drinks in a row and women who have consumed four or more drinks in a row at least once during the previous 2 weeks (Wechler, Moeykens, Davenport, Castillo, & Hansen, 2000). The proportion of current drinkers that binge is highest in the 18- to 20-year-old group (51%) (Naimi et al., 2003).

Alcohol has also been linked to severity of aggression, especially at bars and parties for college students (Tremblay, Graham, & Wells, 2008). In the general population, approximately 13.8 million people abuse alcohol or are dependent on it (Grant et al., 1994). Alcohol abuse is 2.5 to 5 times higher in men than in women, but this sex difference is least pronounced in people age 18 to 24 (Grant et al., 1991). Like smoking, many cultural differences are manifested in drinking, especially across ethnic, SES, religious, and geographical lines. Beer is the most commonly consumed alcoholic beverage (57% of drinkers) followed by hard liquor (e.g., gin, rum, and vodka, 29%) and wine (13%) (Williams, Stinson, Sanchez, & Dufour, 1998).

As with many other health behaviors, it is important to take a biopsychosocial approach to understanding why people drink (Erblich, 2019). Biologically, there are some genetic predictors of alcoholism (Johnson-Greene & Denning, 2008). Alcohol misuse tends to run in families (Merikangas, 1990), and identical twins have a much higher concordance of both alcohol use and misuse than fraternal twins (Ball & Murray, 1994; McGue, 1999). This shows that there are genetic predispositions to starting to drink.

Research has even identified different markers at the genetic level. For example, people with certain genes, such as the beta-subunit of alcohol dehydrogenase, are more sensitive to alcohol (Johnson-Greene & Denning, 2008). The presence of this gene varies across ethnic groups (McGue, 1999; National Institute on Alcohol Abuse and Alcoholism [NIAAA], 1993). Earlier research was misleading. For example, from the early 1990s, researchers were certain that the dopamine DRD2 receptor gene was one of the best markers for severe alcoholism (Blum et al., 1990). Later research showed this was not the case (Gelernter, Goldman, & Risch, 1992). However, there is considerable optimism that we are close to identifying the key genes that place a person at risk for alcoholism (McGue, 1999).

Some significant nongenetic biological markers of vulnerability to alcoholism are known. Children of alcoholics, a vulnerable group, have different brain wave activity (reduced P3 waves) in response to the presentation of alcohol-related stimuli material (Polich, Pollock, & Bloom, 1994). They show also lower activity levels of the enzyme monoamine oxidase (von Knorring, Oreland, & von Knorring, 1987) and are less sensitive to the subjective intoxicating effects of alcohol (Schucklit, 1994). The lower sensitivity to alcohol (i.e., they do not feel as buzzed as a more sensitive person after drinking) may lead them to drink greater amounts.

RESEARCHER SPOTLIGHT

Joel Erblich earned his PhD in clinical psychology from the University of Southern California. He currently teaches at Hunter College in New York. His research focuses on the interactions between emotional, cognitive, behavioral, and genetic factors in addictive behaviors. Read his informative chapter on alcohol (see Essential Readings; Erblich, 2019).

Psychologically, three broad personality characteristics are linked to alcoholism. People who are high in neuroticism, who are impulsive, and who are extroverted are more likely to become alcoholic (Finn & Robinson, 2012; Sher & Trull,

1994). Given the many behaviors with which these traits are associated, they are seen more as mediators or moderating variables within larger psychosocial etiological models of alcoholism (Wood et al., 2002). They are not direct causes of alcoholism. Research has also identified patterns of thinking that could put a person at risk for alcoholism. Maisto, Carey, and Bradizza (1999) reviewed the ways that social learning theories have been applied to alcohol use. This review showed that there are a number of specific beliefs that people have about the behavioral, cognitive, and emotional effects of drinking (alcohol outcome expectancies), which can predict their likelihood of drinking (see also Goldman, DelBoca, & Darkes, 1999). For example, if young adults have a positive alcohol outcome expectancy (they expect good effects from drinking) before the first time they drink, then they are more likely to drink subsequently (Smith, Goldman, Greenbaum, & Christiansen, 1995). More recently, Akins, Smith, and Mosher (2010) found unconditional support for social learning theories when applied to alcohol abuse among Whites but more conditional support when applied to patterns of adult alcohol abuse among Hispanics and Blacks. These results suggest that these three racial/ethnic groups experience somewhat different pathways to alcohol disorder.

Culture Club/ Hulton Archive/ Getty Images

▲ **Drinking and Addiction.** The British painter William Hogarth had some strong opinions of what could happen if people drank too much strong liquor. In *Gin Lane* (1751) he represents the horror of what could happen if people became addicted to gin.

Blending biological and psychological causes of drinking, alcohol also seems to be used to reduce stress (Cappell & Greeley, 1987; Ostafin & Brooks, 2011). The consumption of alcohol serves as a reinforcement: the positive feelings after alcohol consumption increase the behavior of drinking, and drinking is associated with a decrease in stress. For example, students in a study were told that they were taking part in a taste test in order to obscure the true intent of the researchers (which was to test effects of alcohol). These students drank more when they were stressed by the experimenters than when they were not (Statsiewicz & Lisman, 1989). Alcohol, stress, and smoking all go together. In a study of African American women, Webb and Cary (2008) found that the odds of smoking were greater for older women who had less education, lower income, greater perceived stress, and more-frequent heavy alcohol use.

The company you keep can influence how much one drinks. From a psychosocial standpoint, children of alcoholics are more likely to drink (Chassin, Rogosch, & Barrera, 1991), as are people with friends who drink (Wills & Cleary, 1999). Curran, Stice, and Chassin (1997) also showed that drinkers do not just pick friends who drink, but drinkers can make nondrinkers start drinking. Sometimes, just believing that it is normal to drink can make a person drink even if this perceived norm is completely inaccurate. Baer, Stacy, and Larimer (1991) found that college students nearly always perceived that their close friends consumed alcohol more frequently than they did. Accuracy does matter (and not in a way you would expect). At campuses where students have more-accurate perceptions of alcohol use, students are likely to drink on more days throughout the year than at campuses where students have greater misperceptions of alcohol use (Licciardone, 2003).

Finally, as with smoking, the media and advertising also play a large part in getting people to start drinking (Grube & Wallack, 1994; Koordeman, Anschutz, & Engels, 2012). In a study of more than 1,000 sixth, seventh, and eighth graders, researchers found the following:

29% of those who never drank alcohol either owned or wanted to use an alcohol-branded promotional item; 12% of students could name the brand featured in their favorite ad for alcohol; and, 59% were not receptive to alcohol marketing (Henriksen, Feighery, Schleicher, & Fortmann, 2008). During a follow-up study 1 year later, approximately 29% of the adolescents reported having drunk alcohol, and 13% reported drinking at least 1 or 2 days in the past month. Those who had never had alcohol at the time of the initial study, but who had reported high receptivity to alcohol marketing, were 77% more likely to have started drinking by the follow-up study than those who had not been receptive to the alcohol advertising.

Consequences of Alcohol Abuse

Drinking too much has been shown to negatively impact most organ systems and to be a major cause of injuries, many of them fatal (NIAAA, 1997). For many of the injuries, age is a critical factor because consequences of drinking are different across the life span. Prenatal infants often suffer the consequences of alcohol. Of course, they are not doing the drinking. Mothers who drink during pregnancy can influence the development of their fetuses. Fetal alcohol syndrome, a major result of mothers drinking, results in developmental abnormalities (NIAAA, 1997; Streissguth et al., 1994).

Alcohol-related motor accidents are the leading consequence of drinking for underage drinkers. The 21-year age limit may seem like an arbitrary line drawn by the government but that number corresponds to brain development. A report compiling several studies on brain damage and alcohol concluded that underage drinkers face a greater risk of damage to the prefrontal regions of their brains. Double the amount of alcohol is required to do the same damage to someone older than 21. The development of the frontal lobes continues until age 16, after which the brain maintains a high rate of energy expenditure that does not decrease until age 20 (Hoover, 2002). Consequently, underage drinking does retard brain cell growth. As science becomes more sophisticated and technology provides a clearer picture of the inner workings of the body, especially the brain, so does the need for a better understanding of the profound negative effect of alcohol, especially on youth. Some of the most compelling data come from numerous brain studies conducted showing the deterioration of the brain after heavy alcohol use. Previous studies indicated that most brain development occurs between the ages of birth to 3. However, findings from the UCLA Brain Development Study show a significant increase in brain development occurring with hormonal onset—approximately age 12—and continuing into the early to mid-20s (Schuckit et al., 2012).

Liver disease is one of the most common consequences of drinking excessively for older drinkers (Crabb, 1993; Kilbourne, Cummings, & Levine, 2012). Problems range from excess fat in the liver, to a swelling of the liver, or to permanent and progressive scarring, referred to as cirrhosis of the liver. The risks of developing cirrhosis vary by sex; women are more likely to develop the problem (Lieber, 1994). Drinking too much—more than six drinks per day (less for some)—also increases the risk of cardiovascular problems (Richardson, Wodak, Atkinson, Saunders, & Jewitt, 1986) and stroke (NIAAA, 1997). Drinking three to four drinks per day and drinking frequently have both been linked to hypertension (Thadhani et al., 2002). Other health consequences include problems with the pancreas (Steinberg & Tenner, 1994), blackouts (Vinson, 1989), memory loss (Marlon, 2012), and chronic brain disease (Victor, 1993).

Together with its interactions with other health behaviors, alcohol use also relates to many different psychological problems and negative social behaviors. Families in which the parents abuse alcohol are often uncomfortable environments for a child. More fighting and conflict, less cohesion and expressiveness, and more child injuries are reported in alcoholic families (Bijur, Kurzon, Overpeck, & Scheidt, 1992; Sher, 1991). People who abuse alcohol are also more likely to partake in risky sex (Leigh & Stall, 1993), drive dangerously (Yi, Stinson, Williams, & Bertolucci, 1998), and be involved in crimes such as assault (Murdoch, Pihl, & Ross, 1990) and especially sexual assault (Cole, 2006; Roizen, 1997). People who drink too much alcohol or who drink too often are also more at risk for a range of psychological disorders, such as anxiety and mood disorders (Kessler et al., 1997). Note, however, that in many of these cases, it is hard to establish causal links because of the many other factors that may have been involved.

The possibility of the benefits of some alcohol consumption has received a lot of media attention in the past few years. Some reports show evidence of health benefits for small or moderate amounts of alcohol consumption (Friedman, Armstrong, Kipp, & Klatsky, 2003; Van Velden, Kotze, Blackhurst, Marnewick, & Kidd, 2011). In fact, people who consume two standard drinks per day may have a 20% lower risk for coronary heart disease than those who do not drink (Corrao, Bagnardi, Vittadini, & Favilli, 2000). What is a **standard drink**? The medical field agrees that a 12-ounce serving of beer (a standard bottle or can), a 5-ounce glass of wine, or 1.5 ounces of gin, vodka, rum, or scotch is a standard serving.

Some hypothesize moderate alcohol consumption to be the answer to the **French paradox**—the fact that most people in France have a diet that is high in fat, yet still have lower rates of heart disease. For example, Renaud, Gueguen, Siest, and Salamon (1999) studied 36,250 healthy French men between 1978 and 1983 and found that both those who drank beer (28% of the sample) and those who drank wine (61%) had less risk of cardiovascular diseases. The reduction in mortality risk varies depending on what one consumes. People who drink a glass of wine each day show a lower risk for mortality than those who drink spirits or beer (Gronbaek at al., 1995; Renaud et al., 1999). Still, this lowered risk may be due to other positive health behaviors that wine drinkers perform, or to healthy elements in their environment (Mortensen, Jensen, Sanders, & Reinisch, 2001; Wannamethee & Shaper, 1999). For instance, wine drinkers may be better off economically, may eat better, and may exercise more.

Yet, there are actual benefits to moderate alcohol consumption, which are tied to the ability of alcohol to reduce the risk for coronary heart disease by raising the drinker's levels of high-density lipoprotein (HDL) cholesterol. Higher levels of HDL cholesterol help to keep the arteries free of blockage. So should nondrinkers older than 21 now start drinking? The answer is "no," still (Bau, Bau, Rosito, Manfroi, & Fuchs, 2007; Fuchs & Chambless, 2007). There is simply not enough clinical and epidemiological evidence for science to recommend the consumption of alcohol to those who abstain. Remember, other health behaviors can lower the risk of coronary heart disease, and moderate drinkers face the risk of becoming heavy drinkers, which would truly be detrimental to their health. Furthermore, the French eat smaller serving sizes than Americans, which could partially explain the paradox (so wine may not be your answer to overeating).

Synthesize, Evaluate, Apply

- What are the common elements underlying the performance of health behaviors?
- How would high levels of stress influence each of these behaviors and why?
- What are possible causes for the cultural differences seen in the performance of each behavior?
- What should the priorities for future research on health behaviors be?
- What aspects of 21st century society accentuate the performance of unhealthy behaviors?

APPLICATION SHOWCASE

THE TRUTH ABOUT THE FRESHMAN 15

Almost every college first-year student has been warned to watch out for the dreaded freshman 15. Stories of this mythical beast, the supposed 15-pound weight gain that takes place during the first year of college, has echoed around college dorms and hallways for decades. Parents warn their sons and daughters to be careful, and friends and classmates at school are on the lookout for the impending additional pounds. Woman in particular see this gain as inevitable (Smith-Jackson & Reel, 2012). Similar to the eight-glasses-of-water-a-day rule (debunked by Negoianu & Goldfarb, 2008), the facts on this issue are still unclear. Given the severe health consequences of being overweight, and that millions of college students could be at risk if this phenomenon is valid, the freshman 15 is a great topic to explore. The freshman 15 is a good example of how our biology, our psychology, and societal factors interact. Our discussion of the topic also provides us with another opportunity to explore health psychology. Besides, scrutinizing data (if any) of folklore is fun!

The good news is that there is some solid research on the topic (Butler, Black, Blue, Gretebeck, 2004; Holm-Denoma, Joiner, Vohs, & Heatherton, 2008; Morrow et al., 2006). The bad news is that if you only listened to the spin the media put on the research without reading actual articles from the research, you may wind up misinformed or underinformed. It is imperative to do good research and read original research. The articles cited in this book will give you a good start; start by exploring articles about the topics that interest you. For example, even research that does not completely support the freshman 15 idea (e.g., Levitsky, Halbmaier & Mrdjenovic, 2004) is spun to sound like it does. In order for you to better understand this (and how it can be misinterpreted), we will discuss four studies on college student weight gain.

First, it is easy to see why the freshman 15 idea is intuitively believable. You do not need to be a first-year student to know that some students gain weight in school. Professors often notice the difference in students' appearances even from fall to spring sessions! Going to college, away from the routine of home and home-cooked food, can change certain dietary patterns. Most college food is not considered especially low in fat or healthy. College students are continuously exposed to unhealthy food options like low-cost food and fast food. Due to late-night studying, they can experience drastic shifts in sleep–wake cycles and associated snacking, and many skip breakfast and make other unhealthy food-related choices. In 2004 the media exposed a study that seemed to support the freshman 15 idea. Levitsky et al. (2004) studied 60 first-year students at Cornell University recruited from two large introductory courses. The students were weighed at the beginning and end of their first 12 weeks of college. The students, on average, gained about 0.3 pound per week, which is almost 11 times more than the weekly weight gain expected in 17- and 18-year-olds and almost 20 times more than the average weight gain of an American adult. However, the results showed that the mean weight gain of the first-year students was a little more than four pounds. Four pounds. Not 15. The study showed that the two main influences for the weight gain were eating in the all-you-can-eat dining halls and snacking and eating high-fat junk food. More than likely, the media picked up only the statistics that showed some students in the study gaining as much as 18 pounds. However, by reading the original article, you will learn that some of the students even *lost* 13 pounds!

The low mean in the Levitsky et al. (2004) study is not an anomaly. Morrow et al. (2006) studied 137 first-year women students during the 2004 to 2005 academic year. A baseline measurement occurred within the first 6 weeks of the fall semester, with the follow-up visit occurring during the past 6 weeks of the following spring semester. At each visit, the researchers measured height, weight, BMI, waist and hip circumferences, and body fat composition. Morrow et al. (2006) found significant increases on all measures except waist-to-hip ratio. The mean weight gain was only 2.2. pounds.

A different study by Holm-Denoma et al. (2008) used a larger sample size (607 students) with both men and women participating. The study was robust. They studied students during their last year of high school (not first year of college) through the first 9 months of their first college term. They not only recorded the students' weight and height, but measured self-esteem, eating habits, interpersonal relationships, exercise patterns, and disordered eating behaviors throughout the study. The results showed that both men and women gained a significant amount of weight (3.5 and 4.0 pounds, respectively). Weight gain occurred before the end of the fall semester and was maintained as the year progressed. Similar to Levitsky et al. (2004), students in this sample also gained weight at a much higher rate than that of average American adults. For men (and somewhat paradoxically), frequently engaging in exercise predicted weight gain as did (not so paradoxically) having troublesome relationships with parents. For women, having positive relationships with parents predicted weight gain. The final nail in the coffin of this myth? Zagorsky and Smith (2011) used a nationally representative random sample, the National Longitudinal Survey of Youth, and also found average weight gains during the first year of college to be only between 2.5 and 3.5 pounds.

CHAPTER REVIEW

SUMMARY ▶▶

- Obesity is one of America's greatest health threats. Few Americans eat a balanced diet or get a sufficient amount of nutrients. Obesity increases the chances of developing a chronic disease and increases the chances of developing coronary heart disease. Obesity can be caused by both genetic and environmental influences. MyPyramid illustrates the USDA recommendations for a healthy diet and has been modified for different cultural groups.
- Food preferences develop at an early age and are strongly influenced by the ways parents feed infants and children. There are innate preferences, but the majority of our tastes come about because of exposure to various foods as we grow.
- Physical activity is any bodily movement that results in energy expenditure. People should get at least 30 minutes of physical activity five times per week to maintain a healthy lifestyle. Ethnic, socioeconomic, age, and sex differences all account for cultural differences in physical activity. Physically active individuals are less likely to develop coronary heart disease and are more likely to live longer. Physical activity has also been associated with better mental health.
- Smoking is most common among college-aged individuals. Rates of smoking are dropping across most age groups (except the 18- to 24-year-old range). The most pronounced differences are ethnic and racial, followed by SES. Evidence is building to support a genetic component to smoking, whereas a number of different personality traits, such as low self-esteem and extroversion, are associated with increased addiction to smoking. The media and movies are also linked to rates of smoking.
- Smokers are more likely than nonsmokers to die prematurely from coronary heart disease and numerous cancers; there are significant sex differences in rates of cancer due to smoking.
- Alcohol consumption is responsible for more than 100,000 deaths each year although some research suggests that drinking moderate levels of alcohol can actually have health benefits. Like smoking, there are genetic and environmental reasons for alcohol abuse. People who are extroverted, neurotic, and impulsive are most likely to abuse alcohol. Drinking too much has been shown to negatively impact most organ systems and to be a major cause of injuries.

TEST YOURSELF ▶▶

Check your understanding of the topics in this chapter by answering the following questions.

1. The most current guide to eating, MyPyramid, was published in
   a. 1930.
   b. 1984.
   c. 1990.
   d. 2005.
2. According to Chinese and Indian cultures, garlic, onions, most grains, alcohol, and oils are all considered
   a. cold foods.
   b. hot foods.
   c. energy foods.
   d. qi foods.
3. Westernization has often been blamed for problems with obesity. Strong evidence comes from the study of Pima Indians (Ravussin et al., 1994). Which of the following results is correct?
   a. Acculturated Pima Indians had the highest BMIs.
   b. Unacculturated Pima Indians had the highest BMIs.
   c. U.S. Pima Indians had the highest BMIs.
   d. Mexican Pima Indians had the highest BMIs.
4. Having more varieties of food present often leads to the consumption of more food. This phenomenon is referred to as
   a. lipid overload theory.
   b. sensory specific satiety.
   c. hypersatiation.
   d. hypersensory saturation.
5. Which of the following statements about culture and eating disorders is *not true*?
   a. Most body image research has focused on European Americans.
   b. Cultures vary in ideal body shape perceptions.
   c. Eating disorders are primarily a problem associated with European Americans.
   d. Research has found no differences between Asian American and European American women.

6. Which of the following is the primary carcinogenic component of smoking?
   a. nicotine
   b. tar
   c. damage to air sacs/alveoli
   d. higher lung carbon monoxide

7. The standard definition of overweight according to U.S. medical institutions is a BMI rate that is
   a. close to 1.00.
   b. above 20.
   c. between 25 and 29.
   d. above 30.

8. One of the paradoxical synergistic effects of smoking relates to stress. New data show that
   a. stress can actually make a nonsmoker start to smoke.
   b. stress could make someone likely to drink more, and therefore possibly start smoking.
   c. smoking and stress are actually not related at all.
   d. smoking and nicotine addiction could actually make someone more stressed.

9. The ethnic group with the highest smoking rate is
   a. African American.
   b. Asian American.
   c. Latino.
   d. European American.

10. People high in the personality traits of ________ are more at risk of becoming alcoholic.
    a. neuroticism and conscientiousness
    b. neuroticism and extroversion
    c. extroversion and pessimism
    d. pessimism and self-esteem

KEY TERMS, CONCEPTS, AND PEOPLE

addiction, **214**
alcohol abuse, **222**
behavioral cueing, **214**
binge drinkers, **222**
body mass index (BMI), **206**
environmental tobacco smoke (ETS), **221**
exercise, **211**
Food Guide Pyramid, **203**
food preferences, **204**
French paradox, **225**
mental health, **214**
National Health Interview Survey (NHIS), **213**
obesity, **206**
physical activity, **211**
secondhand smoke, **221**
sensory specific satiety, **208**
standard drink, **225**
Surgeon General's Report, **213**
synergistic effect, **220**
Third National Health and Nutritional Examination Survey (NHANES III), **213**

ESSENTIAL READINGS

Erblich, J. (2019). Alcohol use. In T. A. Revenson & R. A. R. Gurung (Eds.), *Handbook of health psychology* (3e). New York, NY: Routledge.

LaCaille, R. A., & Hooker, S. A. (2019). Physical activity. In T. A. Revenson & R. A. R. Gurung (Eds.), *Handbook of health psychology* (3e). New York, NY: Routledge.

Mermelstein, R., & Brikmanis, K. (2019). Nicotine and tobacco use. In T. A. Revenson & R. A. R. Gurung (Eds.), *Handbook of health psychology* (3e). New York, NY: Routledge.

Song, A. (2019). Weight loss and obesity. In T. A. Revenson & R. A. R. Gurung (Eds.), *Handbook of health psychology* (3e). New York, NY: Routledge.

Chapter 9
Illness Cognitions, Adherence, and Patient–Practitioner Interactions

Chapter 10
Diverse Approaches to Pain

Chapter 11
Chronic Illness, Terminal Illness, and Death

CHAPTER 9

ILLNESS COGNITIONS, ADHERENCE, AND PATIENT–PRACTITIONER INTERACTIONS

Chapter 9 Outline

MEASURING UP

HOW DO *YOU* SEE ILLNESS? THE BRIEF ILLNESS PERCEPTION QUESTIONNAIRE

For the following questions, please circle the number that best corresponds to your views:

How much does your illness affect your life?	0 no effect at all	1	2	3	4	5	6	7	8	9	10 severely affects my life
How long do you think your illness will continue?	0 a very short time	1	2	3	4	5	6	7	8	9	10 forever
How much control do you feel you have over your illness?	0 absolutely no control	1	2	3	4	5	6	7	8	9	10 extreme amount of control
How much do you think your treatment can help your illness?	0 not at all	1	2	3	4	5	6	7	8	9	10 extremely helpful

(Continued)

(Continued)

How much do you experience symptoms from your illness?	0 no symptoms at all	1	2	3	4	5	6	7	8	9	10 many severe symptoms
How concerned are you about your illness?	0 not at all concerned	1	2	3	4	5	6	7	8	9	10 extremely concerned
How well do you feel you understand your illness?	0 don't understand at all	1	2	3	4	5	6	7	8	9	10 understand very clearly
How much does your illness affect you emotionally? (e.g., does it make you angry, scared, upset or depressed?)	0 not at all affected emotionally	1	2	3	4	5	6	7	8	9	10 extremely affected emotionally

Please list in rank-order the three most important factors that you believe caused your illness.

The most important causes for me:

1. ______________________________

2. ______________________________

3. ______________________________

▼ Ponder This

When you felt sick growing up, how did your parents react and what remedies did they provide?

What factors do you think influence whether you follow the doctor's orders?

What would you do if your religious beliefs clashed with those of Western medicine?

What do you do if you have a headache? Most of us wait some time to see if it goes away and take a pill if it does not. What if you sprain your ankle or pull a muscle? You may have heard that you first apply a cold pack, then apply a hot pack, and wrap the ankle and rest. However, more-complex remedies may be required for other types of aches or pains. What if you develop a rash or your skin turns different colors? What if you find a lump under your skin? Do you go to your doctor immediately? Do you use a homemade family remedy and see if the problem goes away? Would you have a local shaman sacrifice a chicken for you?

Different cultures have different ways of coping and reacting to symptoms of illness. This chapter describes what we do when we do not feel well. We will focus primarily on physical health and describe what we do if and when we get sick (for a complete description of the role of culture in mental health, see Gurung, 2014). Figure 9.1 shows an overview of the main stages in the process of feeling better and the major accompanying factors. If you are seriously considering a career in the health-care profession, especially as a doctor or nurse, this chapter is especially important for you to read. Likewise, given that many health psychologists work in hospital settings, it is important to understand the factors surrounding illness.

▼ FIGURE 9.1

The Commonsense Model of Illness Behavior

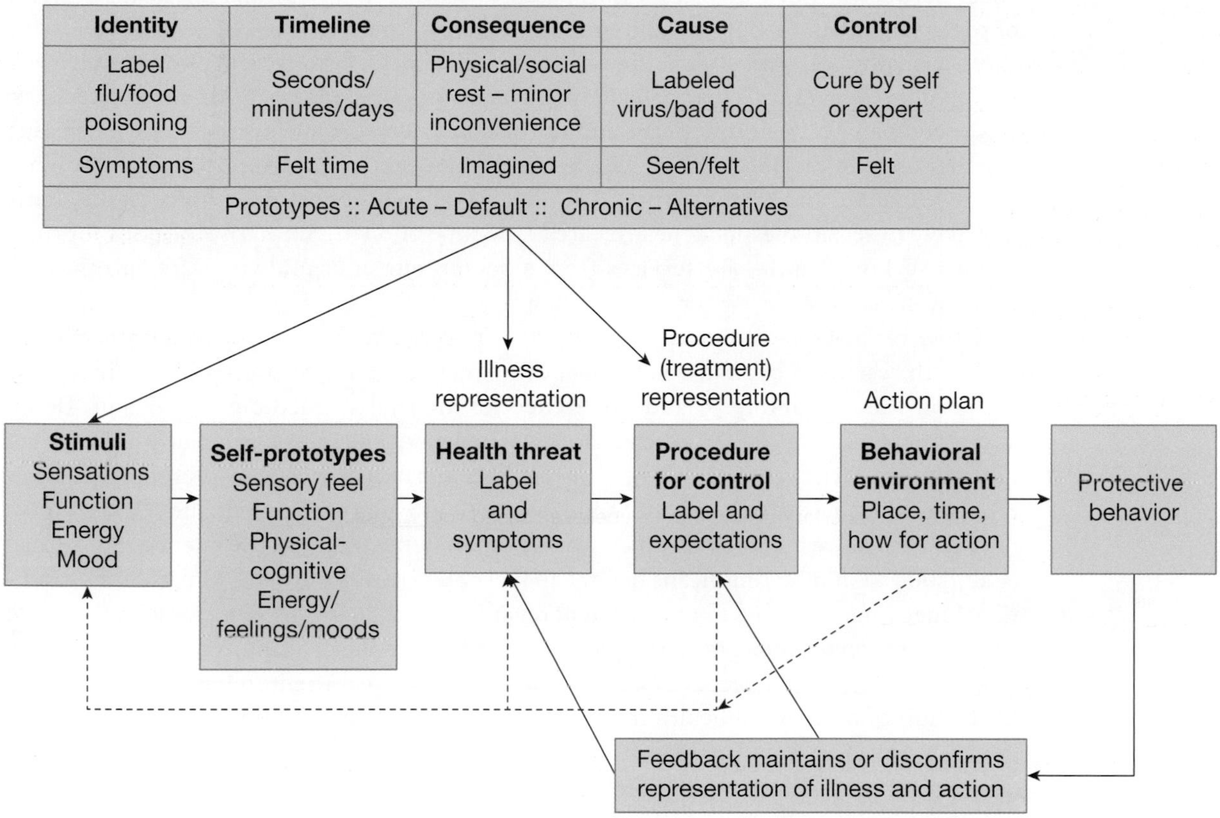

Identity	Timeline	Consequence	Cause	Control
Label flu/food poisoning	Seconds/ minutes/days	Physical/social rest – minor inconvenience	Labeled virus/bad food	Cure by self or expert
Symptoms	Felt time	Imagined	Seen/felt	Felt
Prototypes :: Acute – Default :: Chronic – Alternatives				

Illness representation

Procedure (treatment) representation

Action plan

Stimuli Sensations Function Energy Mood

Self-prototypes Sensory feel Function Physical-cognitive Energy/ feelings/moods

Health threat Label and symptoms

Procedure for control Label and expectations

Behavioral environment Place, time, how for action

Protective behavior

Feedback maintains or disconfirms representation of illness and action

CULTURE AND ILLNESS BEHAVIORS

Many factors surround illness, and culture influences every one of them (Abradio-Lanza, 2019; Suchday, Feher, & Grujicic, 2019). Before we are treated, we have to recognize that we have a problem. We then seek treatment. Once we get a diagnosis, we have to adhere to the course of treatment prescribed for us. Recognition, seeking treatment, and adhering to treatment—collectively referred to as **illness behaviors**—are three main stages influenced by our cultural backgrounds.

Illness behaviors are the varying ways individuals respond to physiological symptoms, monitor internal states, define and interpret symptoms, make attributions, take remedial actions, and use various forms of informal and formal care (Mechanic, 1995). A number of sociodemographic variables such as age, sex, ethnicity, and SES can influence people's illness behaviors. The rising number of medical errors and deaths due to malpractice raises questions about safety and quality issues, resulting in rising public mistrust and patient dissatisfaction (Piper, 2011). This gets even worse for members of different ethnic minorities (Washington, 2006). For example, African Americans' mistrust of the health-care system is often cited as a cause of racial disparities in health (Edwards, 2019). This has even led to the development of a questionnaire measure, the Cultural Mistrust Inventory (Moseley, Freed, Bullard, & Goold, 2007). In addition, Latinos do not use inpatient mental health services as much as other ethnic groups (Arellano & Sosa, 2018).

Even when there may be few superficial differences, a closer analysis reveals some of the complexity of culture. For example, Berkanovic and Telesky (1985) found few differences between African American, European American, and Mexican Americans in terms of reporting illnesses, but they did find that African Americans were less likely to define short-term physical sensations as illnesses and were more likely to consult physicians if it was easy to do so and if they felt a particularly high risk for illness. African Americans were also less likely than Mexican Americans and European Americans to consult others in deciding whether to go to the doctor. Even your age and where you live are important. Chowdhury, Islam, Gulshan, and Chakraborty (2007) found that younger mothers were significantly less likely to seek professional health care at the time of birth. Similarly, the odds for rural women seeking health-care services from a doctor, nurse, or midwife were half those of urban women.

Other variables also influence use of health services: There is a marked underuse of mental health resources by many non-European American groups, suggesting an increased focus on the availability of and preference for alternative medicine (de Haan, Boon, Vermeiren, & de Jong, 2012). Foreign-born Asian Americans show particularly high rates of underuse of services (Ciftci, 2018). Nearly 75% of Asian Americans in a recent large study reported using at least one type of complementary and alternative medicine (CAM) in the past 12 months, which was significantly higher than the national prevalence rate (Hsiao et al., 2006). Chinese Americans had the highest prevalence of any CAM use. Thus, traditional medicine continues to be important regardless of the significant increase in the use of Western medicine among minority patients, and many minority groups report the use of a dual health system (Santee, 2017). Ayurvedic medicine, an ancient Indian tradition rooted in the humoral theory of health in which the proper balance of bodily humors indicates health, is especially popular among Indians (Agnihotri & Agnihotri, 2017).

The Role of Acculturation

Acculturation and ethnic identity (discussed in more detail in Chapter 3) can play an important part in the use of Western mental health resources and health services as well (Ciftci, 2018). For example, African Americans who strongly identified with their ethnicity and who had experienced discrimination reported a lower probability of health-care use in comparison with those with weaker ethnic identities (Richman, Kohn-Wood, & Williams, 2007). Folsom et al. (2007) found that, for Latino Americans, having a provider who spoke the same language as the patient (indicating less acculturation) was a better predictor of mental health service use than having a provider of the same ethnicity. Spanish-speaking Latinos differed from both English-speaking Latinos and Caucasians on most measures of health-care use.

Here is a twist. Acculturation is sometimes linked to more negative health behaviors. For example, in a study of 505 Filipino, 598 Chinese, 518 Vietnamese, and 466 other Asian respondents, Asian American men born in the United States were more likely to report high levels of drug use in the past year (Bersamira, Lin, Park, & Marsh, 2017). Filipinos had the highest rates of drug use.

Whereas this is good to know in itself, the acculturation and ethnic identity of the health providers may be even more important, given the way the American health system is set up (Pacquiao, 2007). Doctors are seen as credible people in powerful positions whose advice can have an important impact on the health behaviors of their patients. This perception suggests that it is important to look at the ethnic identity and acculturation of doctors and, more importantly, at their beliefs and preferences, since these factors may influence their referrals and their prescriptions (Gurung & Mehta, 2001). Minority doctors with strong ethnic identities who are well assimilated or integrated may be more likely to be comfortable prescribing alternative medicine or serving minority patients (Cokley, 2007). Yet evidence suggests that the underuse of medical resources by some ethnic groups, such as Asian Americans, is due to under-referral by their health practitioners (Ahmed et al., 2007).

Dr. Elizabeth Broadbent received her PhD in health psychology from the University of Auckland in New Zealand, where she currently teaches. Her research interests include how stress affects our health, how our body posture affects our mood, interventions to help patients make sense of and cope with illness, and human–robot interaction in health contexts. Check out her chapter on illness cognitions (Broadbent, 2019; in Essential Readings).

Before getting more deeply into how culture intersects with illness behaviors, let's understand some basic processes at work. First, note that health psychologists lump together all thoughts or cognitions about the subjective experience of an illness under the umbrella term **illness representations** (Broadbent, 2018; Cameron, Durazo, & Rus, 2016). Your illness representation will influence your behaviors and experiences whether it is a common cold or inflammatory bowel disease (van Erp et al., 2017). When your illness representation is activated, specifics behaviors may follow. In one study, participants made to think of the common cold actually walked more slowly, fitting their mental schema of how you behave with a cold (Orbell & Henderson, 2016). We will first discuss a comprehensive model that helps to organize the process of coping with an illness and then focus on specific theories that demonstrate how different cultural beliefs can influence the use and utility of health-care services.

THE COMMONSENSE MODEL OF ILLNESS BEHAVIOR

To a lot of the lay public, psychology is just common sense. Nothing can be farther from the truth. It is always easy to say "I told you so" once you see the results of a study, but a lot harder to successfully predict an outcome in advance. If that is not enough, many seemingly commonsensical notions are often proved wrong (Lilienfeld, 2012). Common sense is, however, handy to capture the everyday way people approach illness. Correspondingly, one of the best major frameworks used to understand how people adapt to health threats, whether at home or in hospitals, is called the Commonsense Model (CSM) of illness behavior (Leventhal et al., 2012).

The CSM is based on the parallel processing model (Leventhal, 1970), which itself emerged from a study of fear communications—those attempts to change behavior that used gruesome statistics or pictures to get a person to change their behavior. The parallel processes reflected how we use both thinking and feelings to guide our behavior. The parallel processing model then morphed into a self-regulation model to encompass how our views of ourselves guide our actions. In time, it was clear that thought processes were highly important, so how we think about illness (illness cognitions) became a key focus (Croyle & Barger, 1993), leading to the contemporary iteration named the CSM (Leventhal et al., 2012).

The CSM identifies variables, constructive processes, and behaviors that reflect how people in different settings perceive, understand, react to, and interact with others in managing threats to health (Leventhal et al., 2012). Not only does the CSM explicitly build on social and personality psychology research, but it also includes studies of folk medicine by medical anthropologists such as Kleinman (1980), which makes this model perfect for a cultural approach to health psychology.

CSM has two fundamental elements that make it a useful guide to study illness behavior. First, individuals are seen as active problem solvers trying to make sense of needed changes in their physical states while acting to avoid and control changes perceived as signs of illness. When we notice symptoms that suggest we are ill, we have to make decisions based on our understanding of the potential threat (an illness representation), our options to manage that threat, and our sense of the costs and benefits of the procedures. This should be reminiscent of the Health Belief Model from Chapter 7.

▼ FIGURE 9.2

Overview of the Main Stages of an Illness

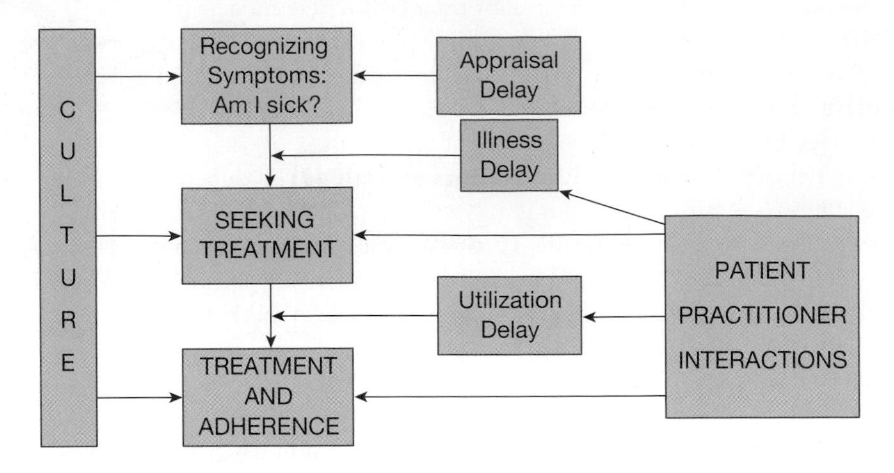

The second element is that individuals' decisions will be based on their beliefs, commonsense perceptions, and available skills at that point in time. Perception is key here. It does not matter what the objective physiological issues are or what the optimal medical procedures are; people's illness representations are a function of their past experiences, cultural backgrounds, and sense of themselves. CSM explicitly assumes that illness representations and how people choose to manage the threats are shaped by the attitudes and beliefs of their sociocultural environments. The environments could include family, friends, doctors, traditional healers, and the media (Leventhal et al., 2012). Figure 9.2 illustrates the content and structure of CSM.

The development of two measures guided by the CSM have driven a lot of research in recent years. The Illness Perception Questionnaire–Revised (IPQ-R; Moss-Morris et al., 2002) has 73 questions divided into three sections. The first tackles symptoms tailored to a specific illness. The second section captures the timeline, consequences, control, and emotional components of the illness. The third section involves the most important causes. The Brief Illness Perception Questionnaire (Brief IPQ; Broadbent, Petrie, Main, & Weinman, 2006) includes a single item for each of nine components of illness (e.g., timeline, consequences; see Measuring Up for the full scale).

In a recent meta-analysis, Hagger, Koch, Chatzisarantis, and Orbell (2017) examined how the dimensions of illness representation, coping strategies, and illness outcomes relate to each other, and tested whether relations between illness representations and outcomes were mediated by coping strategies. They looked at 254 studies and showed the direct effects on health outcomes of illness representations. They also showed that coping strategies were a mediator (see Chapter 2 for a refresher on mediation). Emotional representations and perceived control influenced the use of more or less coping strategies to deal with symptoms or manage treatment that in turn related to illness. Representations signaling threat (consequences, identity) had specific positive and negative indirect effects on outcomes through problem- and emotion-focused coping strategies (i.e., mediation).

Let's take a closer look at some of the key steps in the process of seeking health care.

RECOGNIZING SYMPTOMS

With physical problems, it is often clear when you need to see a doctor. A serious car or bike accident immediately brings medics to the scene. Other physical accidents such as those from sports-related activities (e.g., sprains or breaks) are usually also taken care of immediately. The limited movement caused by a sprain or the pain from a potential broken bone leads people to go to a hospital for an X-ray or to have the injury examined by a doctor. With other injuries, if symptoms at first do not seem to be life threatening, people may ignore them or delay going to a doctor. This may even happen before receiving a diagnosis of a serious illness because patients often ignore symptoms (e.g., colorectal cancer; Rogers, Siminoff, Longo, & Thomson, 2017). Why is this the case? Many psychological factors help us understand some of these reasons.

Columbia TriStar/ Moviepix/ Getty Images

▲ **Misattributions.** Some wounds are hard to misattribute. This knight from *Monty Python and the Holy Grail* will lose both arms and legs. In the movie, however, the knight says, "It's just a flesh wound." We often misattribute certain symptoms and avoid getting medical attention.

The Confirmation Bias

Once we believe something is true, we often change the way we interpret new information and the way we look at the world because of it. We tend to try to confirm our belief and have a bias in how we process information. This is a **confirmation bias**. Social psychologists have shown that if there is any ambiguity in a person's behavior, people are likely to interpret what they see in a way that is consistent with their bias (Olson, Roese, & Zanna, 1996).

If we believe that a change in our bodies is not a symptom of illness, we will probably look for information to support that belief and find it. For example, if you have spent too much time in the sun and have pale skin there is a chance that you may develop some form of skin cancer (Rowan-Robinson, 2017). The first signs are often discolorations of the skin that are round in nature (i.e., without irregular outlines). You could look at one of these developing spots and believe that it is a blemish or a growing pimple or that it was always there. You may now look at your skin and try to draw attention to parts that look great, ignoring the developing skin spots. You confirm your bias that you are right and cancer free by thinking that you have always had those spots off and on and they never meant anything before. You may even think that you have actually been feeling especially great recently, so the spots could not be the beginning of a problem.

This confirmation bias can lead to an accentuation of symptoms that do get attention (Moritz et al., 2017). If you believe that you do not need to go to a doctor to seek treatment for flu-like symptoms or a cold, and you have managed without seeing a doctor on past occasions, or if you see others who do not seem to go when they have symptoms, you may begin to overestimate how successful you can be by not going to a doctor.

We not only find confirmation for what we expect to see, but we also tend to overestimate how often we are right (Kaplan et al., 2016). The belief that our expectations have been correct more often than they actually have been is referred to as an **illusory correlation**. In eating disorders, participants often have an illusory correlation between body size and emotion (Treat, Viken, Kruschke, & McFall, 2010). A partial explanation for why confirmation biases occur is that we ignore disconfirmations of our biases and selectively remember information to support our biases (Fiske, 1998).

Attributions and Misattributions

Another social psychological process that can influence the recognition of symptoms is related to how we determine the cause of events. The cognitive process of assigning meaning to a symptom or behavior is referred to as making **attributions** (Jones et al., 1972).

Many factors influence our attributions (Miller & Diefenbach, 1998). If your stomach hurts, you may attribute the pain to what you just ate. If you have not eaten anything different recently, you are more likely to worry about a stomach pain than if you have just tried something that is very different (spicier or oilier than you are used to). How you attribute a pain in your chest may depend on physical factors such as your age, or psychological factors such as beliefs that you hold about illness in general. A teenager may be likely to think of a chest pain as gas or a cramp of sorts. An older person may worry about a heart attack (Hage, Adegunsoye, Mundkur, & Nanda, 2012). The cause to which you attribute your symptoms can influence whether you seek treatment for them or not (Chan, 2012).

Attributions vary across cultures and are influenced by culture as well (Noël, 2010). Mexican American children may consider hearing voices to be evidence of a religious experience (Padilla & Ruiz, 1973), whereas most European Americans may consider it a sign of mental imbalance. Hmong Americans consider epilepsy the mark of a shaman (Fadiman, 1997). Beliefs about the cause of a disease will directly correspond to how it will be dealt with. If the spirits want you to have a certain pain, then it would be angering them and risking further pain if you tried to do something to alleviate it. A study of the role of cultural context of psychological illness among elder immigrants from the former Soviet Union showed that cultural stigma influenced the attribution of cause, physical expression of symptoms, and attitudes toward seeking professional help (Polyakova & Pacquiao, 2006).

Sometimes, we mistakenly label our physiological experiences based on external factors (Schachter & Singer, 1962). If you feel tired and there are several people at work with colds, you are likely to **misattribute** your tiredness to your developing a cold, when it could be due to you not getting enough sleep. This misattribution can increase your anxiety and, in combination with a confirmation bias (that you have caught a cold), you may soon find yourself accumulating more evidence to support your theory. Your belief that you are getting sick will, in fact, make you sick (a **self-fulfilling prophecy**). Such self-fulfilling prophecies can contribute to the continual use of folk medicines and treatments. If you are biased against Western biomedicine, you will probably not try to get better after a visit to a doctor. If you are biased toward shamanism, you are probably going to feel a lot better after a shamanistic ritual is performed over you (Chapter 3). Sometimes your doctor does not even have to support your attribution to help you feel better. African Americans who believe they had been hexed could be treated effectively by a psychiatrist using hypnosis, even when the psychiatrist did not believe in hexing (Snell, 1962).

Yet physicians can fall prey to misattribution problems as well. Evidence suggests that biases against the mentally ill lead physicians to commonly misattribute physical illness signs and symptoms as being due to concurrent mental disorders (Thornicroft, Rose, & Kassam, 2007). This can lead to underdiagnoses and mistreatment of the physical conditions.

Personality

Perhaps the most common individual factor that influences the recognition of symptoms and the seeking of treatment is personality (Smith, 2019). As described in Chapter 6, personality is what defines each of us. We have a unique and stable set of characteristics that relate to consistent patterns of behavior across situations. In general, different personality characteristics are related to a number of health outcomes, but there are many personality characteristics that relate to seeking treatment.

Studies have shown that people who are relatively high in anxiety tend to report more symptoms of illness than others do (Foster, Sanderman, van der Molen, Mueller, & van Sonderen, 2008). Neuroticism is another key personality trait in this regard. People who are high in neuroticism experience higher levels of anxiety and tend to be high-strung. This characteristic often translates into oversensitivity to symptoms and to more complaining about ill health (Brown & Moskowitz, 1997). In fact, a thorough review of the personality and health literature suggested that people with chronic negative affect show a disease-prone personality (Friedman & Booth-Kewley, 1987).

Some people's personality types make them more attentive to bodily sensations, and they report more symptoms than others (Ferguson, 2000). People who monitor their symptoms to an extreme may be **hypochondriacs**. Hypochondriasis, or hypochondria, is a psychological disorder characterized by excessive preoccupation with one's health and constant worry about developing physical illnesses. Hypochondriacs believe that any minor change in their condition could be a sign of a major problem. They are constantly going to their physicians to be checked. Even when they are told they are all right, they do not believe the diagnosis and may change doctors (Holder-Perkins & Wise, 2001). In a study of symptom reporting among patients with different psychological problems, hypochondriacs reported suffering more often from abdominal pain, and they reported a higher intolerance of bodily complaints (Bleichhardt, Timmer, & Rief, 2005).

Other personality traits such as optimism and self-esteem normally buffer us against stress and illness but may delay us from seeking treatment. For example, look at people with high self-esteem. They believe that they are very healthy and are optimistic in their outlook. They may also believe that their bodies can fight off infections or heal without any specific medical treatment. These people may wait to see if they get better. Low self-esteem individuals have been found to report more health problems (Stinson et al., 2008).

Other specific individual differences influence how patients fare in the health-care process. Patients vary in how much they want to be involved in their treatment and how much information they want. **Behavioral involvement** includes the patient's attitude toward self-care, specifically an active involvement in treatment. **Informational involvement** measures how much the patient wants to know about his or her illness and specific details of its treatment. Each form of involvement has different implications in the health-care setting (Auerbach, 2000). For example, it may be important to match a patient with a certain preference for information (high in informational involvement) with a practitioner who is accepting of such a preference (called a preference-match). A large-scale review of the literature on the preference-match strategy in physician–patient communication showed varying degrees of support for the positive effects of matching patients' preferred levels of information, decisional control, and consultative interpersonal behavior (Kiesler & Auerbach, 2006).

In a college health-care center setting, the degree of match between students' desired and actual level of involvement in their care was associated with greater satisfaction (Campbell, Auerbach, & Kiesler, 2007).

The need for information may vary with social norms as well. In Chapter 6 you encountered the Theory of Planned Behavior. One of its components is social norms. A recent study found that social norms around patient involvement can also play a role in medical decision making. In a study of 974 Dutch patients, researchers found that the more conservative the social norms, the less people are involved in their medical decision making (Brabers, van Dijk, Groenewegen, & de Jong, 2016). Family and peers, a key source of norms for many, can also play a key role in an individual's need for informational involvement (Laidsaar-Powell, Butow, Bu, Fisher, & Juraskova, 2017; O'Kane, Park, Mentis, Blandford, & Chen, 2016).

Some individuals are more sensitive to their health states than others (Graef, Rief, Nestoriuc, & Weise, 2017). Referred to as **private body consciousness**, this increased vigilance over the body may also cause the patient to feel more discomfort than the patient with low vigilance. Differences in vigilance may underlie a major sex difference in symptom reporting. Women both perceive and report more physical symptoms than men do (Goldberg, DePue, Kazura, & Maura, 1998), which could be due to women being higher in private body consciousness. A study designed to investigate how symptom reporting varies by time of day, day of the week, gender, and generation found that women report more symptoms throughout the day (in general, symptoms are reported most in the mornings and evenings; Michel, 2007). Gender differences in help-seeking behaviors have been experimentally tested and established in the lab as well (Juvrud & Rennels, 2017).

Keep in mind that factors influencing symptom reporting (or lack thereof) will vary with the illness. For example, participants in a study of factors influencing delay in reporting symptoms of lung cancer reported lack of symptom experience, lack of knowledge, and fear as key issues (Tod, Craven, & Allmark, 2008). Blame and stigma because of smoking were also prevalent

> **Synthesize, Evaluate, Apply**
>
> - What are the cultural factors that influence your use of health care?
> - What do you think the personality would be of a person most likely to seek treatment at the optimal time?
> - What are the main psychological processes that underlie the recognizing and reporting of symptoms?
> - How could the different approaches to health described in Chapter 2 influence symptom recognition and the health-care process described in this chapter?

influences, as well as cultural factors, irregular patterns of health-care use, and underlying attitudes of indifference. Families played a critical role in overcoming delay. For some illnesses, the previously mentioned sex differences are not seen (for example, post-traumatic stress disorder; Chung & Breslau, 2008).

SEEKING TREATMENT

Once you recognize you have a problem, you have to decide whether to seek treatment. Who do you go to? The answer also depends on your illness representations. The anthropologist Arthur Kleinman developed one form of representation, called an exploratory model, that explicitly applied across cultures. Kleinman (1980) showed that complex systems have three overlapping health-care systems. The popular or lay sector involves culturally based personal and familial beliefs and practices. The folk sector involves cultural traditions and specialists. The professional sector involves legally sanctioned professionals and the Western medical system that is dominant in American society. Most people first turn to their popular sectors.

Kleinman (1980) developed an interview to measure cross-cultural exploratory models. See how you would answer these:

1. What do you think caused your problem?
2. Why do you think it started when it did?
3. What do you think your sickness does to you?
4. How severe is your sickness? Will it have a long or short course?
5. What kind of treatment do you think you should receive?
6. What are the most important results you hope to receive from this treatment?
7. What are the chief problems your sickness has caused for you?
8. What do you fear the most about your sickness?

These eight questions are particularly useful for tapping into the full details of a person's illness representations. You can probably see how individuals of some cultures would answer some of these questions differently. Let's take a closer look at the role of culture.

The Role of Culture

The cultural norms and the values of collectivistic families mean that care of all immediate and extended family members is provided by the family at home (Purnell, 2013). In collectivist cultures, it is absolutely imperative to include the family, and sometimes the community, for effective counseling; otherwise, the treatment plan will not be followed. For many indigenous populations (e.g., American Indian people), the fact that one member of the tribe or clan is ill means that the tribe or clan is sick.

Among many Middle Eastern and other collectivistic cultures, people with a mental or physical disability are hidden from the public because their so-called pollution may mean that other children in the family will not be able to obtain a spouse if the condition is known (Purnell, 2013). For example, people with tuberculosis will be relegated to sleeping on the back porch and not allowed in their home in Haitian American culture. In many Orthodox and conservative Jewish communities, children with weak eyes (vision problems) are not given glasses, so that the child and his or her siblings will attract spouses with strong eyes or from highly valued families. For other impairments, such as ones resulting from HIV, the condition may be kept hidden—not because of confidentiality rights, but for fear that news of the condition will may spread to other family members and the community (Colin & Paperwalla, 2012).

In addition, in many cultures, spiritual healers—*curandero,* root-worker, voodoo priest, medicine man/woman—are typically consulted first for all illnesses but especially for those cultural illnesses such as *susto* (physical suffering from emotional trauma due to witnessing the suffering of others) or those caused by the evil eye, curses, or bad spirits entering a person. The greater the cultural stigma and the more the culture values spiritual or religious healers, the more likely there will be a delay in seeking health care and counseling, resulting in the condition being more severe at the time of treatment (Tovar, 2017). For example, children from the Mexican culture are frequently first taken to the eldest family female, then to a *paterna,* then a *curandera,* then a *pharmacia,* and then finally to a Western medical clinic for asthma, by which time the asthma attack may be severe (see Chapter 3, Arellano-Morales & Sosa, 2018).

Going beyond cultural norms and the role of popular and folk sectors, health psychologists have tried to understand the main reasons why people do not seek treatment. DiMatteo (1991) suggests that (1) people often misinterpret and underestimate the significance of their symptoms, (2) they worry about how they will look if the symptoms turn out to be nothing, (3) they are concerned about troubling their physicians, (4) they do not want to change their social plans by having to see a doctor, and (5) they tend to waste time on unimportant things, such as gathering and packing personal belongings before going to the hospital.

Understanding Delays

A substantial area of health psychology examines why people delay seeking treatment (Broadbent, 2018). There are three main components of delay. People sometimes take a lot of time to recognize they have symptoms; this is **appraisal delay**, and many psychological factors discussed previously can prevent symptom recognition. Appraisal delay can lead to **illness delay**, the time between the recognition that one is ill and the decision to seek care. Finally, there are often **use delays** between the decision to seek care and the actual behaviors to obtain medical health care. Beyond the absence of the main triggers described above, a host of other psychological reasons explains why people delay. Sometimes the delay in seeking treatment results from the symptoms of a problem being misattributed. For example, many heart attack patients do not immediately call 911 for assistance because they believe the pains they are experiencing may be due to other, less-serious problems such as indigestion, which is not potentially fatal (Scherck, 1997). At other times a delay is due to concern over not having health insurance (Liabsuetrakul & Oumudee, 2011).

The different psychosocial barriers to recognizing symptoms and reporting them notwithstanding (Table 9.1), some factors increase the likelihood that a person will seek treatment (Figure 9.3). Health psychologists refer to these as **triggers** (Verbrugge, 1985). There are five triggers that will increase the likelihood that a person will seek treatment (Zola, 1964). First, the degree to which you are frightened by symptoms is critical. If the symptoms are out of view, such as if they are located on your back, or if they do not cause too much pain, they may be easy to ignore. You may tell yourself that you will do something about the problem if it gets worse but not otherwise. If your symptoms do cause a lot of pain or are noticeable or if you believe they may indicate a serious illness, you may worry about them, and your anxiety will increase, possibly prompting you to go to a doctor.

The second trigger is the nature and quality of symptoms. The more symptoms you have and the worse they are, the more likely you are to go to a doctor. Sometimes symptoms get so severe that your interactions with your romantic partner, spouse, friends, and family may

▼ TABLE 9.1

Major Reasons for Delays in Seeking Treatment

Major Reasons for Delays in Seeking Treatment
Misinterpretation of symptoms
Fear of false alarms
Concerns with troubling health-care professionals
Interference with social plans
Packing and rescheduling before going to the hospital

suffer. If you are in too much pain to attend social events or have had low energy for some time and your symptoms interfere with relationships, this interpersonal crisis is likely to trigger a visit to the doctor (the third trigger). This interference with life can go beyond your personal relationships and extend to your job or to plans that you have made. Social interference—when your occupation or vacation is threatened by symptoms—is the fourth trigger. Finally, even if you do not want to seek treatment, your employer could pressure you to get treatment or return to work. Many businesses have noticed that their insurance rates are much higher for smokers. To cut health insurance costs, employees are provided with incentives to get treatment to quit smoking and in many cases face implicit and explicit pressure to quit smoking. **Social sanctioning** such as this can also trigger a visit to the doctor (the fifth trigger).

In addition to the various psychosocial factors influencing treatment seeking, a number of explicit cultural variables play a role. To begin, there are consistent age and sex differences (Mackenzie, Reynolds, Cairney, Streiner, & Sareen, 2012). Women and elderly persons use health services at a significantly higher rate than do men and younger individuals (National Center for Health Statistics, 2017). Part of this difference is because these two groups have specific issues that need care such as pregnancy and childbirth for women, and chronic and terminal illnesses among elderly persons. In addition, women have been shown to be more sensitive to changes in their bodies than men are (Leventhal, Diefenbach, & Leventhal, 1992) and may find it more socially acceptable to report symptoms than men. Men may not report symptoms or pains as much so as not to appear weak ("boys don't cry").

Treatment seeking varies by ethnicity as well (Lee, Lundquist, Ju, Luo, & Townsend, 2011). In one of the most systematic studies of ethnic differences, Suchman (1965) studied ethnic groups in New York and found that many non-European Americans tended to form close, exclusive relationships with friends, family, and members of their ethnic group and to show skepticism of medical care. These groups were more likely to rely on a **lay-referral system**—nonprofessionals such as family, friends, and neighbors—in coping with illness symptoms instead of seeking biomedical treatment. Beyond relying on a lay-referral system, some ethnic groups refrain from seeking treatment from biomedically trained physicians in hospitals, relying instead on folk medicine (as discussed in Chapter 3).

Few recent studies on the treatment-seeking behavior of different ethnic groups exist, but older studies of groups such as Mexican Americans show them as being reluctant to visit physicians (Andersen, Lewis, Giachello, Aday, & Chiu, 1981). Having close-knit networks or having strong religious beliefs does not always prevent someone from seeking treatment. Geertsen, Kane, Klauber, Rindflesh, and Gray (1975) showed that members of the close-knit Mormon community in Salt Lake City were actually more likely to seek treatment than members of loosely knit communities.

▼ FIGURE 9.3

Main Triggers in Seeking Treatment

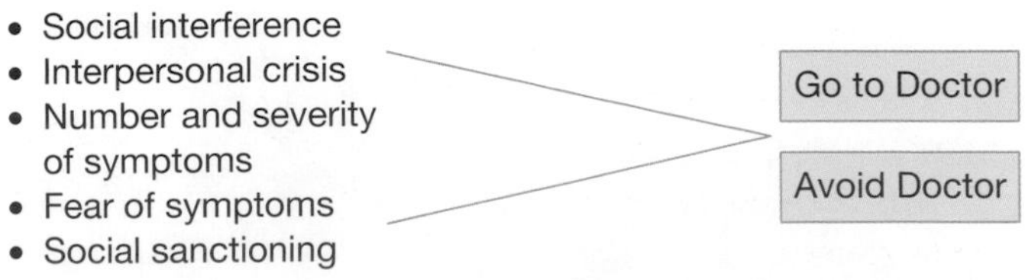

Perhaps the biggest cultural factor predicting the seeking of treatment is socioeconomic status (SES; see Chapter 3) (Hall, Moreau, & Trussell, 2012). In fact, many conditions that may at first appear to be a function of ethnicity may actually be due to poverty. Early sociological studies describe a culture of poverty in which poverty over time influences the development of psychological traits and behaviors including the use of health services (Koos, 1954; Rundall & Wheeler, 1979). This lack of use is directly correlated with financial barriers to medical care as demonstrated by the increase in use of health care by low-income groups after the introduction of national insurance programs such as Medicaid and Medicare in the 1960s. SES may also influence the type of care sought. Kleinman (1980) showed that only upper-middle-class families treated all illnesses with Western biomedicine and only lower-class families treated all illnesses at home. Still, the opposite pattern was seen with wealthier Puerto Ricans in New York, who were more likely to consult spiritual healers than were poorer Puerto Ricans in New York (Garrison, 1977).

The Hospital Setting

Once people decide to use medical services, they might have to face the bureaucracies of a hospital (Griscti, Aston, Warner, Martin-Misener, & McLeod, 2017). There are both for-profit and nonprofit hospitals, and cities with many hospitals find each hospital competing for patients. Sometimes this can benefit the patient because hospitals offer discounts and special services to be more appealing. Many hospital administrators view health care primarily as a business (Knox, 1998). Unfortunately, this attitude can contribute to patient dissatisfaction with the process of getting treatment. Many millions of American citizens do not have health insurance of any form even after the Affordable Care Act passed, a factor that can prevent them from going to the hospital except for extreme situations. Most hospital visits begin with filling out forms and gathering information and are often accompanied by long waiting periods. For these reasons and a host of others, most people dread having to go to a hospital.

The majority of the tedium of going to a hospital is hard to avoid. Medical visits have to follow a certain pattern. A health-care professional, usually a physician's assistant or a nurse practitioner, first gathers basic information from the patient (e.g., medical history and main symptoms). Then a medical examination of the relevant areas of the body is conducted. Further medical tests are recommended or a diagnosis is made, followed by the prescription of a treatment regimen. The physician may only spend a very brief time with each patient, and this is often one of the major causes of dissatisfaction with the treatment-seeking process (Chung, Hamill, Kim, Walter, & Wilkins, 1999). A large body of research focuses on the quality of patient–physician communication (Haskard-Zolnierek & Williams, 2016). Doctors would like to spend more time with their patients (Probst, Greenhouse, & Selassie, 1997), but they cannot because most have a quota of patients that they need to see in a day (Waitzkin, 1985). Patient quotas are often set by the hospital as a result of the complex interplay of a health maintenance organization and insurance billing requirements.

▲ **Hospital Waiting Room.** Hospitals can be intimidating places, with constant activity, patient uncertainty, and unfamiliar equipment.

In clear recognition of the fact that hospitals are stressful for patients, more attention is being paid to ways that the physical environment of the hospital can be altered (Rashid & Zimring, 2008). In many cases, indoor environments may set in motion processes that cause stress by affecting individual and workplace dynamics. Ulrich (2004) reviewed more than 600 studies documenting the impact of a range of design features like improved lighting that can help reduce stress and pain and increase other outcomes. For example, lower noise levels were linked to less staff stress, increased workplace social support, and improved quality of care for patients (Blomkvist, Eriksen, Theorell, Ulrich, & Rasmanis, 2005). A conceptually similar study looked at the effects of the hospital environment on stress during blood donations. Ulrich, Simons, and Miles (2003) found that stress was lowest when there was no television playing in the rooms and when videotapes of nature scenes were playing. An important clinical implication of the findings is that the common practice of playing uncontrollable daytime television in health-care waiting areas where stress is a problem may actually have stressful, not stress-reducing, influences on many patients.

Staff Relations

Health psychologists have begun to pay attention to another level of interaction in hospitals. Going beyond the interaction between a doctor and a patient (discussed in more detail in the last section of this chapter), the diversity within hospital staff compels a look at staff relationships as well. Not only are patients culturally diverse, but hospital staffs are also diverse. In addition to European American staff, hospitals frequently have large numbers of doctors of Indian, Chinese, and Middle Eastern descent, and nurses from Mexico, the Philippines, and other non-White ethnicities (Galanti, 2014). Different cultures have different expectations of the roles played by the different levels of hospital staff. For example, some Indian male physicians tend to be sexist and are not respectful of female nurses (Gurung & Mehta, 2001). The doctor–nurse relationship can be strongly influenced by the culture of each person. Some cultures are more respectful of authority than others, and some have a greater desire to maintain harmony and avoid conflict. Nurses of Asian or Latino backgrounds are sometimes reticent to challenge questionable behavior by European American doctors (Galanti, 2014).

Ariel Skelley/ DigitalVision/ Getty Images

▲ **Staff Diversity.** Doctors and nurses often come from many different cultural backgrounds, backgrounds which affect their relationships with their patients and with one another.

Gender and culture also influence interdoctor and internurse relationships. Some Indian female physicians often feel intimidated by their male counterparts. Male nurses sometimes have discordant interactions with their female counterparts. Medicine is a hierarchical profession in which orders are followed by rank and not gender, but this hierarchy can often cause problems for men from male-dominant cultures. Medical staff members also face conflicts between their roles as health-care providers and their own religious beliefs. Galanti (2014) recounted a case study in which a nurse who was a Jehovah's Witness refused to aid in a blood transfer in an emergency room because blood transfusions were against her faith. In another case, a devout Catholic nurse refused to participate in an abortion.

ADHERENCE TO TREATMENT

Once the patient and practitioner interact and a diagnosis is made, the patient has to follow the doctor's prescription and recommendations. The extent to which a patient's behavior matches with his or her practitioner's advice is referred to as **adherence** (Kaplan & Simon, 1990). Adherence can vary in terms of the pattern displayed by the patient or in absolute terms measured by a quantitative assessment (Chambers & O'Carroll, 2016).

Nonadherence can cause morbidity and influence clinical diagnosis of treatment plans, the cost-effectiveness of health care, and the effectiveness of clinical trials (Shearer & Evans, 2001). The failure of a patient to adhere satisfactorily to a treatment costs the country between $100 billion to $300 billion a year (Dunbar-Jacobs et al., 2012). In the biomedical arena, adherence is focused more on medication compliance and refers to the degree or extent of conformity to the recommendations about day-to-day treatment by the provider with respect to the timing, dosage, and frequency (Cramer et al., 2008). Such medication compliance/adherence is especially critical for patients with acquired immunodeficiency syndrome (AIDS) for whom nonadherence can be fatal. Consequently, a large body of research focuses especially on increasing adherence among AIDS patients (e.g., Koenig et al., 2008).

> **Synthesize, Evaluate, Apply**
>
> - How do the different psychological processes interact to delay the seeking of treatment?
> - What recommendations do you have to make the hospital environment more patient friendly?
> - How can triggers be used to ensure all who need treatment get it?
> - When do you know when to go to a doctor? What are your triggers?

Adherence in general ranges from 15% to 93% (Haynes, McKibbon, & Kanani, 1996), prompting many to believe that finding ways to help patients follow medical treatments could have larger effects on health than any treatments specifically (Haynes, Ackloo, Sahota, McDonald, & Yao, 2008, p. 20). Poor adherence accounts for a 43% to 46% increased risk of failure in kidney transplants (Takemoto et al., 2007). Just having the physician pay closer attention to the patient after diagnosis (more monitoring and follow-ups) can increase treatment adherence (Llorca, 2008). Various psychosocial factors, including many cultural forces, influence the extent to which ill patients adhere to treatments.

There are many practical concerns that influence adherence. As you can guess, adherence rates vary according to the type of treatment prescribed and to the disease or illness a patient has. Rapoff (1999) showed that about 33% of patients do not adhere to prescriptions for acute illnesses, whereas around 55% of patients do not adhere to treatments for chronic illnesses (Erlen & Caruthers, 2007). Some treatments are easier to adhere to than others. You are much more likely to not do something that you dislike (it is easy to avoid eating brussels sprouts if you do not like them) than to stop doing something that you do like (avoid sweets). Some treatments are long term and complex, severely interfere with life, and affect desirable behaviors (Dunbar-Jacobs et al., 2012). Such treatments automatically are associated with low levels of adherence. Patients' intentions to adhere, their understanding of the treatment, and their satisfaction with their practitioners can also influence how likely they are to adhere. In fact, many of the health behavior change models, such as the Health Belief Model described in Chapter 7, also help predict which patients will adhere to their treatments.

There are imaginative ways to increase adherence. Brendryen and Kraft (2008) tested the effectiveness of a 54-week, fully automated digital multimedia smoking cessation intervention. The treatment group received 400 contacts by Internet and phone, resulting in improved adherence to free nicotine replacement therapy (NRT) and a higher level of postcessation self-efficacy. In similar support of the benefits of monitoring, Modi, Marciel, Slater, Drotar, and Quittner (2008) found that preadolescents and adolescents who spent more of their treatment time supervised by parents, particularly mothers, had better adherence. In fact, technology is playing a large role in monitoring adherence, such as electronic pill devices that record how many pills a patient takes (Chambers et al., 2016).

Nonadherence can take many different forms (Home, 2018). Ryan (1998) showed that villagers in Cameroon did not directly follow their doctor's advice, but they did still make an effort to do things that would improve their health. For example, they chose treatments that were less expensive and easier to perform than what the doctor ordered. Other individuals may go overboard. Reis (1993) found that patients with asthma used their sprays for relief more often than prescribed. Sometimes patients indirectly disobey their doctors' orders. Referred to as **creative nonadherence**, patients sometimes modify and supplement their treatment plans. For example, patients may save a dose for later or skip or discontinue a course of medicine if they are feeling well. Nonadherence and intentions to adhere are particularly important to watch for when patients start a new medication for a chronic illness (Clifford, Barber, & Home, 2008). In such cases, intentional nonadherers, compared with adherers, have lower perceptions of the necessity of their new medication and higher levels of concern about taking it. Conversely, unintentional nonadherers are not significantly different from adherers in terms of perceptions of medication necessity.

In addition to the psychological reasons that explain nonadherence, culture by itself can also be a major explanatory force. As described in Chapter 3, different cultural groups have different beliefs. People from different ethnic groups, racial groups, and different geographical regions, and even men and women—all may have beliefs that are barriers to adherence. For example, most European American women quickly go back to work after the births of their babies (Lobel & Mahaffey, 2019). In contrast, many Asian American women believe that a week or a month resting period (lying-in) is needed, during which the mother spends time in bed to recover. Different cultural groups also perceive their treatment differently, which can influence their adherence. For example, in a study of patients undergoing maintenance hemodialysis, Korean participants had higher emotional disturbance than their counterparts, whereas African American participants had higher negative perceptions of personal intervention or medical treatment controlling their disease (Kim, Evangelista, Phillips, Pavlish, & Kopple, 2012). Anderson (1993) suggested that the health-care system might be organized to favor the majority culture. Thus, social, political, and economic barriers can prevent minority group members from complying with their practitioner's prescriptions.

Hill Street Studios/ Corbis/ Getty Images

▲ **Nonadherence.** Complex treatments and having to take many medications often cause nonadherence.

One large area in which cultural beliefs interfere with adherence to treatment involves dietary practices (Vluggen, Hoving, Schaper, & de Vries, 2017). Many treatments involve either food restrictions or prescriptions to eat certain foods. These prescriptions may not fit with some cultural beliefs. For example, Muslims are forbidden to eat from sunrise to sunset during the month of Ramadan, an important Muslim festival. Orthodox Jews follow kosher dietary laws that forbid eating pork, shellfish, and nonkosher red meat and poultry, and also forbid mixing meat and dairy products. Hindus do not eat beef. Many Catholics do not eat meat on Fridays during the season of Lent. There are many documented cases in which hospital staffs unknowingly attempt to feed patients certain foods that are against the patients' cultural beliefs (Galanti, 2014).

The three main stages in the health–illness process (recognizing symptoms, seeking treatment, and adherence to treatment) are all related to patient–practitioner interactions.

PATIENT–PRACTITIONER INTERACTIONS

When a patient has recognized that he or she has symptoms of an illness and has sought treatment from a health-care professional, it is only the beginning of the journey toward recovery. Many things occur as the patient interacts with the health-care system: negotiating the paperwork of insurance and registration at the hospital to begin, and then actually seeing a doctor and getting a diagnosis. When you do see a doctor, the quality of your interaction with him or her can play a big role in how you feel and in the extent to which you adhere to the prescribed treatment (Rakel et al., 2011).

Patient–practitioner interactions can vary around some basic themes such as patient adherence (Williams, Haskard-Zolnierek, & DiMatteo, 2016) and patient satisfaction (Mosby et al., 2017). Szasz and Hollender (1956) describe three major models of patient–practitioner interaction. In the active-passive model, the doctor plays a pivotal role, making the majority of the decisions because the patient is unable to do so, often because of his or her medical condition. Here the patient has little to no say in what is done. In the guidance-cooperation model, the doctor still takes the primary role in diagnosis and treatment, but the patient plays a part by answering questions, although he or she does not take part in decision-making regarding treatment. In the mutual cooperation model, the doctor and patient work together at every stage, consulting each other on the planning of tests for diagnosis and in decisions regarding treatment. Obviously, the optimal model of interaction, the mutual cooperation model, is characterized by effective patient–practitioner communication and an open exchange of ideas and concerns. Good communication is perhaps one of the most critical ingredients in successful patient–practitioner interactions. Let's take a closer look at factors that influence these interactions.

Communication

Conversations between doctors and patients can range from being narrowly biomedical, in which the doctor uses a lot of medical jargon and limits conversation using closed-ended questions, to consumerist, in which the patient is primarily the one doing the talking and getting answers to questions. The extent to which doctors discuss psychological or social issues varies greatly, especially across cultures (Tsimtsiou, Benos, Garyfallos, & Hatzichristou, 2012). Many factors influence the quality of communication between doctors and patients (Clark et al., 2008) including both verbal and nonverbal behaviors (Gorawara-Bhat, Hafskjold, Gulbrandsen, & Eide, 2017).

Different cultures have different expectations for communication. It is clear that one type of communication will not fit all patients (Carrard, Schmid Mast, & Cousin, 2016). In the West, it is very common for people to use small talk, such as, "How are you doing?" It is rare that the speaker really wants to know the answers to rhetorical questions such as this. Non-Western cultures rarely engage in small talk to the same extent (Triandis, 1996). Sometimes it may seem like doctors and patients are from different planets, Mars and Venus (to borrow the analogy from a pop psychologist's flawed attempt to characterize male and female interactional patterns). It is not uncommon to see a patient looking confused at a doctor while the doctor is trying to explain a procedure or diagnosis using technical terms, with the patient understanding only a fraction of the conversation.

Psychologists have identified many key ways that communication can go wrong. One of the major cultural dimensions influencing patient–practitioner communication is individualism and collectivism. As described in Chapter 3, people in different cultures vary in the level to which they are self-focused or independent/individualistic or other/group-focused or

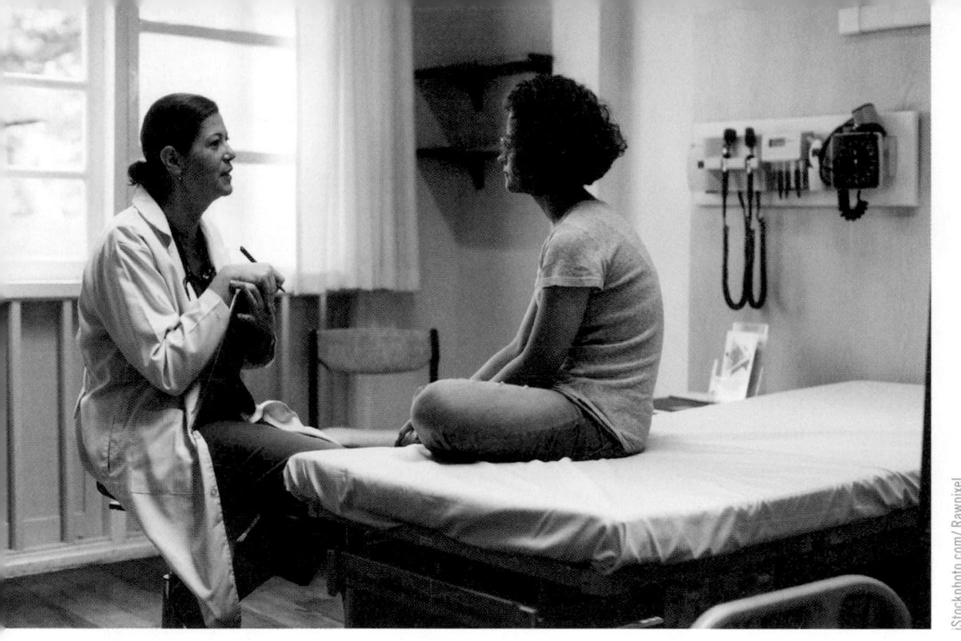

▲ **Patient/Practitioner Communication.** Good communication between doctor and patient is integral to patient adherence to a treatment plan. Unfortunately, many doctors are required to meet a certain number of patients in a day, necessitating quick patient/doctor interaction.

collectivistic. When it comes to communication between the doctor and patient, a patient's level of collectivism can be a key factor. Collectivists tend to communicate all but the most important piece of information, which the doctor is supposed to supply to make the whole message comprehensible (Triandis, 1996). This strategy has the advantage of allowing a collectivist to monitor another's feelings and avoid disrupting harmony (Armstrong & Swartzman, 2001). The individualist, on the other hand, who is not as concerned with maintaining social harmony, is more likely to get straight to the point. Combine an individualist doctor and a collectivistic patient and you have a recipe for frustration because the doctor wants the point and the patient is offended by the doctor's drive for the point.

Doctors have been found to do many things that inhibit communication. Some doctors may not listen to everything the patient says (Probst et al., 1997), often talking too much. A look at the statistics makes some doctors almost seem rude. Beckman and Frankel found in 1984 that on average, doctors cut off their patients after only 18 seconds. Happily, things have gotten better since this study (Roter & Hall, 2006). Still, in talking to patients, doctors may use too much medical jargon that the patient does not understand (Cormier, Cormier, & Weisser, 1984). Given the Latin roots of many disease classifications and the technical terms used to describe many procedures and even different parts of the body, it is not surprising that a layperson may be confused by medical jargon. Although providing a common language for doctors to communicate with each other and being valid ways to describe aspects of illness, the inappropriate use of medical terminology can confuse, frustrate, and even anger patients (Frankel, 1995). Phillips (1996) found that patients are particularly dissatisfied with treatment when doctors appear to deliberately use jargon even when it does not seem to be needed. Conversely, some doctors are said to dumb down the message or talk down to patients, assuming that they do not understand.

Patients contribute to communication problems with doctors as well. Patients are often very anxious when they go to a doctor (Graugaard & Finset, 2000). This anxiety may make them not describe all their symptoms or have difficulty concentrating on the doctor's questions. Sometimes patients from lower socioeconomic backgrounds or those who speak a different language may not understand what is being asked of them. Language problems can even occur between people who speak English. This author was raised in Mumbai, India, where the English spoken is British English (the queen's English). In India and Britain, a rubber is an eraser. In America, a rubber is a condom. In college, I quickly learned that difference (much to my embarrassment) after the first time I made a mistake on an exam and needed to erase it.

In a health-care setting, simple word usage can play a big role. One example is the word "positive." In most everyday contexts, positive connotes a good thing. In the context of an HIV test, however, having positive test results is not a good thing at all. To make matters worse, the same English word may mean different things in other languages. If someone told you that he or she got a stomachache from eating a *puto,* the language the person speaks makes a big difference. The word *puto* means rice cake in Filipino but male prostitute in Spanish.

Additionally, different symptoms may mean different things in different cultures, making some patients hesitant to describe a symptom that they believe relates to a very personal or private bodily function.

There is one more element of communication that stands apart from the previous discussion—communicating uncertainty. There is a growing trend toward shared decision making in medicine (Moumjid, Gafni, Brémond, & Carrère, 2007) that brings with it a need for patients to be able to interpret large amounts of medical information. Much of this information, such as outcomes, risks, and benefits, is often uncertain. Patients are faced with probabilities and relative risk formats (see research in Chapter 2) that are difficult to understand (Covey, 2007). This is particularly important when conveying information about the benefits and risks of different drugs (Schwartz, Woloshin, & Welch, 2007). This problem is compounded by cultural differences such as language mismatches.

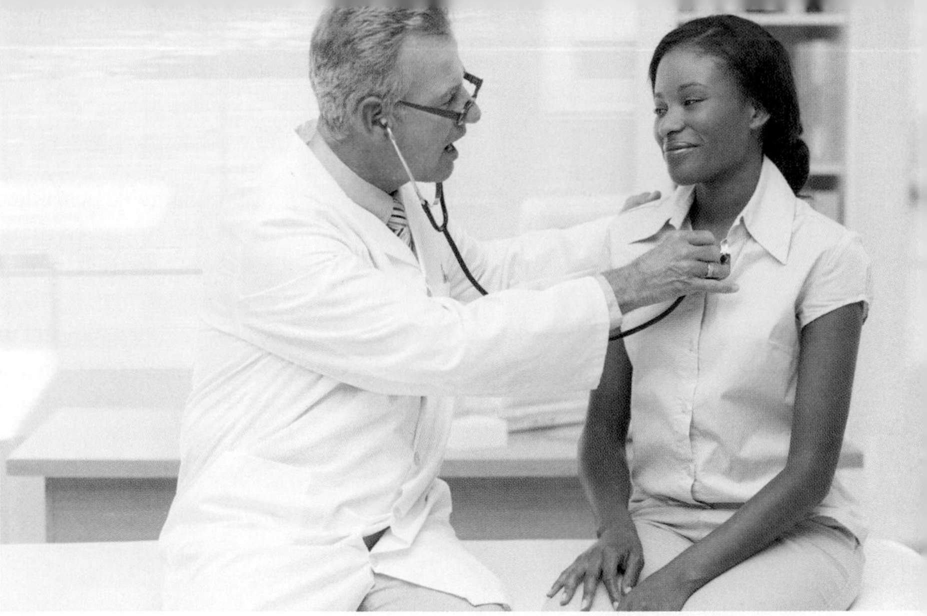

iStockphoto.com/ Wavebreakmedia

▲ **Gender Bias in Medicine.** It is important that doctors do not stereotype based on any cultural factor, including the gender of a patient. Research shows considerable sexism/gender biases in how patients are treated.

Gender and Cultural Stereotyping

We all hold various stereotypes. For example, you may believe that Asians are good at math, or women are bad at math. **Stereotypes** are widely held beliefs that people have certain characteristics because of their membership in a particular group. Many stereotypes may have a kernel of truth to them, but human beings treat stereotypes as if they are always accurate for all members of the group. Social psychologists have argued that we use stereotypes as a shortcut. When we do not have the cognitive time or energy to find out more about somebody, we fall back on what we have heard about the cultural group that he or she belongs to.

Stereotypes of doctors or patients based on their sex, ethnicity, or religion are one of the biggest factors influencing the quality of patient–practitioner communication and interactions. In the limited time that doctors and nurses have to interact with patients, their behavior may often be influenced by their stereotypes of their patients instead of realities. Many such stereotypes exist and play a role in the hospital setting. For example, Americans of Middle Eastern or Indian descent are often believed to be demanding and to express their pain freely and loudly (Galanti, 2014). Mexican Americans stereotypically have large families. Asian American men and women are stereotypically very quiet and stoic. If doctors see older patients or female patients, they may make assumptions about how the patients will behave or about their pain tolerance or behaviors based on ageist or sexist stereotypes (Hall, Epstein, DeCiantis, & McNeil, 1993).

It is important to remember, as discussed in Chapter 2, that even though there may be some individuals who fit a certain cultural stereotype, there is a lot of variance within cultures. Generalizations based on stereotypes can be inaccurate, may be offensive, and can sometimes result in malpractice claims. Sadly, there is empirical evidence showing that some cultural groups like African Americans, Latinos, or low SES individuals are given less information and are treated worse than other groups (Institute of Medicine [IOM], 2002). An extreme case of the problems with cultural stereotyping is discussed in the focus on clinical application section at the end of this chapter.

In addition to stereotyping of race and ethnicity, there is also evidence for differential treatment by sex. Women are treated differently from the way men are treated (Curtis et al., 2007).

For example, some forms of implantable heart devices are used two to three times more in men than in women with similar symptoms, even though heart disease is the leading cause of death among women. These devices are also used more in White men than in Black men. It gets worse for older women. When compared to men of the same age group, women older than 50 are less likely to be admitted to the hospital intensive care unit (ICU), have shorter stays in ICU if admitted, receive fewer emergency medical treatments, and are more at risk of dying in intensive care and in the hospital (Fowler et al., 2007). We also see this sex bias with knee surgery: Physicians

▼ FIGURE 9.4

Cultural Competency

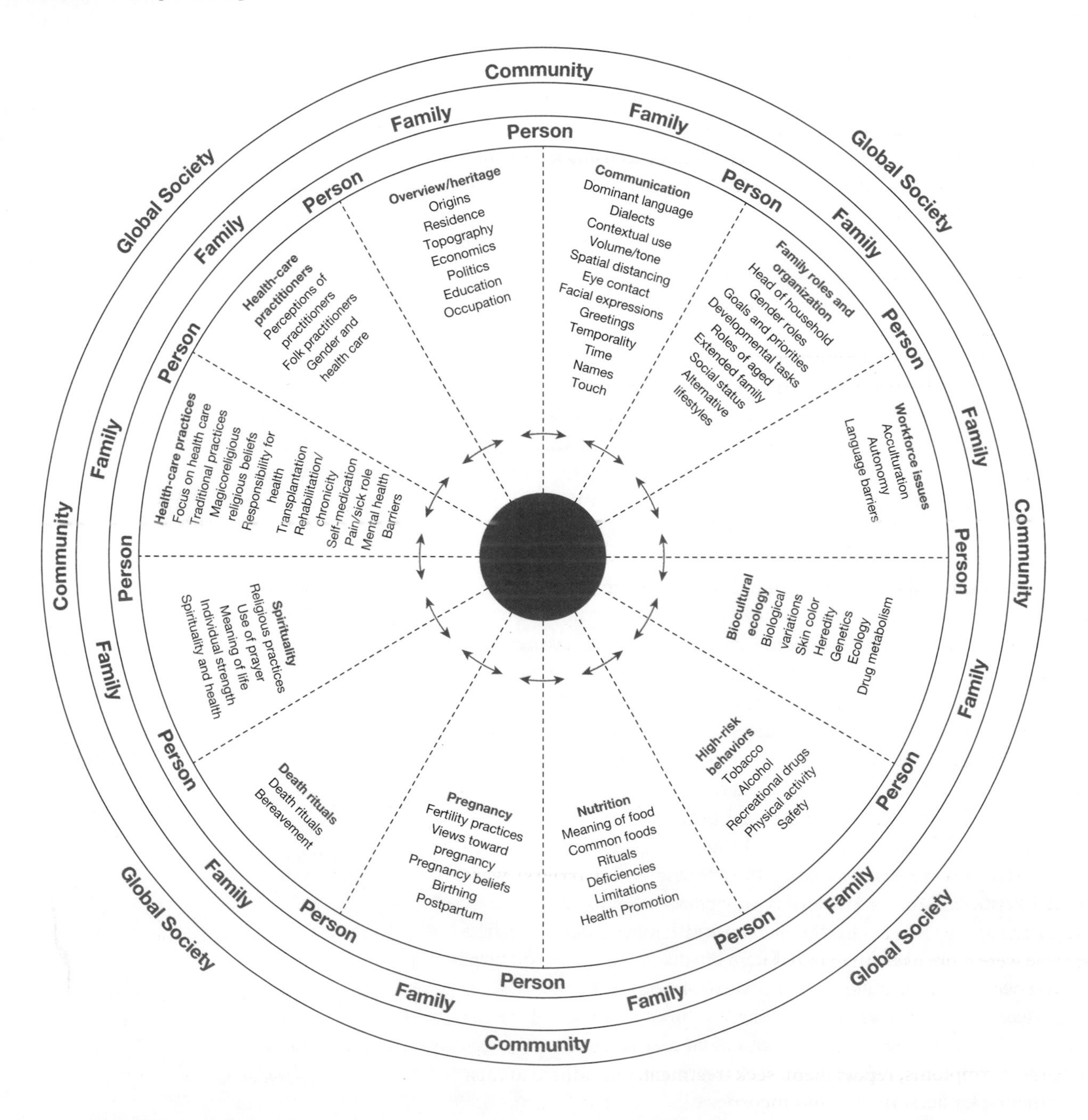

Source: Purnell (2005). Used with permission of the author.

are more likely to recommend knee surgery to a male patient than to a female patient. In one study, the odds of an orthopedic surgeon recommending total knee arthroplasty to a male patient was 22 times that for a female patient (Borkhoff et al., 2008).

Cultural Competency

Related to stereotyping is the concept of **cultural competency** (Purnell & Pontious, 2014, see Chapter 1 and 3) and the related terms **cultural awareness** and **cultural sensitivity.** To health-care providers working in culturally diverse areas, these terms have quite different meanings (Giger et al., 2007). Cultural awareness is an appreciation of the external or material signs of diversity, such as the arts, music, dress, food, religious activities, or physical characteristics. Cultural sensitivity reflects personal attitudes and includes not saying or doing things that might be offensive to someone from a different cultural or ethnic background than that of the health-care provider (Giger et al., 2007). Cultural competence incorporates but goes beyond cultural awareness and sensitivity; it is often defined as using a combination of culturally appropriate attitudes, knowledge, and skills that facilitate providing effective health care for diverse individuals, families, groups, and communities. One comprehensive model to guide the development of cultural competence is shown in Figure 9.4.

Eugenio Marongiu/ Cultura/ Getty Images

▲ **Woman wearing hijab.** Seeing someone in non-Western outfits can influence how they are stereotyped.

A health-care provider's understanding of patients' cultural characteristics, values, and traditions can contribute to the quality of treatment delivered. Poor cultural competency can negatively impact the communication between doctors and patients and consequently lead to poorer care (Hooper et al., 2017). Overreliance on stereotypes can lead to poor competency. Given the importance of this concept, researchers have developed measures of health-care provider cultural competence that nicely tap into patients' perceptions of their doctors and nurses. Lucas, Michalopoulou, Falzarano, Menon, and Cunningham (2008) developed the Healthcare Provider Cultural Competency measure, a theoretically grounded, generally applicable measure comprising patient judgments of their physician's cultural knowledge, awareness, and skill. Testing the scale with predominantly African American patients, the researchers showed perceptions of cultural competency correlated with measures of trust, satisfaction, and discrimination.

If health-care providers are not culturally competent and tend to stereotype, patients may feel discrimination. Perceived discrimination has also been studied in the relationship with health service use. Spencer and Chen (2004) found that discrimination played a role in informal help-seeking in a population of Chinese Americans. Sources of informal services for emotional problems could be considered as primarily help from friends and relatives (ethnic social support) or from traditional practitioners or physicians. In this study, subjects who reported experiencing language-based discrimination (poor treatment due to language barriers) were more likely to use informal support services for emotional problems. Additionally, there were significant gender differences. Females in the sample were more likely than males to seek informal services and help. As you can see, many different steps are involved in the process of getting treatment for and recovering from illness. Individual factors and cultural differences can influence the extent to which patients recognize their symptoms, report them, seek treatment, and adhere to their treatments. Understanding and incorporating these differences are critical to optimizing the success of a health-care system.

Synthesize, Evaluate, Apply

- What recommendations do you have to make the hospital environment more patient friendly?
- Given the time constraints faced by hospital staff, what can be done to improve patient treatment?
- Summarize how cultural differences create conflict between patients and practitioners and between staff members. What are key solutions?
- What can be done to prevent cultural stereotyping?

APPLICATION SHOWCASE

WHEN THE SPIRIT CATCHES YOU, CULTURES CLASH

BAAAM!!! When someone slams a door, you may jump back, startled at the sound. Your ears may ring and you may even direct a harsh stare in the direction of the person who did it. Would you worry about what the slamming could mean for your soul? Probably you would not, yet that is exactly what Foua Lee worried about when her elder daughter Yer Lee slammed the front door of the family apartment. Within seconds, Foua's youngest daughter and Yer's younger sister, Lia, fainted. The Lees had little doubt about what happened. The sound of the slamming door had been so alarming that little Lia Lee's soul had fled her body and become lost. What followed as the Lee family struggled to cure Lia is a tragic story of how the clash of two sets of cultural beliefs, in this case those of Western biomedicine and Hmong folk beliefs, can have fatal consequences. Cultural differences led to innumerable complications, deplorable patient–practitioner interactions, and delays in the recognition, reporting, and adequate treatment of Lia Lee's epilepsy or *quag dab peg,* literally translated from the Hmong language to mean "the spirit catches you and you fall down" (Fadiman, 1997).

The Hmong people originally lived in the hills of Laos in Southeast Asia. In 1975 Laos fell to Communist forces, and 150,000 Hmong fled to refugee camps in Thailand and then to America. In fact, the American government promised the Hmong asylum in exchange for their help in fighting the Vietnam War. Correspondingly, thousands of Hmong men, women, and children immigrated to America and settled primarily in California, Minnesota, and Wisconsin. Most of the Hmong immigrants did not speak English and held a belief system very different from that of Western culture. The Hmong believe that illness can be caused by a variety of different factors such as eating the wrong food, having sinful ancestors, being cursed, having one's blood sucked by a spirit or *dab,* touching a newborn mouse, and having bird dropping fall on one's head. The most common cause of illness is soul loss. When Lia Lee convulsed and collapsed, the family automatically thought that her soul was lost. And that's not all: paradoxically, the seizures were seen as a mixed blessing. To the Hmong, *quag dab peg* is a special illness and often the sign of a shaman. You can guess how that belief was received when they took Lia to the local hospital.

In the hospital, almost all of the issues described in this chapter became factors. Initially, none of the doctors or nurses could really understand what had happened to the little girl because none of the health practitioners spoke Hmong, the Lee family spoke very little English, and there were no interpreters on hand. Lia had stopped convulsing by the time she had reached the hospital so the only symptoms she showed were a cough and a congested chest. The resident on duty did what he could with the limited information, and Lia was sent home after her parents signed a paper acknowledging the receipt of instructions for care. However, the Lees could not read. The prescription was not followed. To accentuate the dangers of nonadherence, the Lee family decided to use their own treatment for the soul loss based on their own cultural beliefs. Lia Lee was soon back in the emergency room a second and then a third time. On the third arrival, the consulting physician deemed her to have meningitis and ordered a spinal tap, which Lia's parents initially resisted.

Lia had repeated seizures over the next few years, and there were problems with every step of her treatment. When she was checked into the hospital, her father and many other members of the family stayed with her, often ignoring the posted visiting hours and interfering with the treatment. At one time, the nurses had used restraints on Lia to prevent her from hurting herself when she had a seizure. Lia's father could not understand why this was being done to his daughter, and no one could speak Hmong to tell him. When the nurses were out of the room he untied Lia's restraints and placed her on the floor, much to the disapproval of the hospital staff who had to restrain her again. Most of the time the Lee parents were uncertain of what medicines to give Lia, and in another form of nonadherence, they just skipped giving her medications when the drug regimen became too complex, substituting folk remedies instead.

The Lee family sacrificed a cow, cut the heads off chickens, and attempted a number of different shamanistic remedies, but none worked. Still the family worked hard to keep Lia happy, even opting to keep her at home and take care of her instead of having her be in the hospital. Unfortunately, although many Hmong see epilepsy as a sign of divinity and are content to just care for the person with it without necessarily trying for a cure, this approach is not approved by Western society, and a family services agency removed Lia Lee from her loving parents and placed her in a foster home. The Lees got their daughter back, but it was not the end of Lia's problems. Sadly, after a further series of miscommunications between the Western doctors and this Hmong family, Lia Lee went into a coma and never regained consciousness. Lia Lee was 30 years old when she died in 2012.

What started out as a straightforward case of epilepsy spiraled out of control. Were the Lees to blame? Yes, in that they did not give Lia the medicines they were supposed to, but this nonadherence was a combination of their not understanding why the medicines were necessary and what they had to do, along with not wanting to do it because of their beliefs. Was the Western medical system to blame? Yes, in that many assumptions and guesses were made about Lia's illness, and often the Lees were stereotyped and mistreated because of it. The language barrier was also a large part of the problem and, as in many cases throughout our nation, the health practitioners did not have the time or the necessary cultural education to know better. Although this is an extreme case, the travesty of Lia's vegetative state resulting from the collision of these two cultures is, nonetheless, an important reminder of how cultural differences can impact the patient–practitioner interaction and the seeking and delivery of medical treatment.

CHAPTER REVIEW

SUMMARY ▶▶

- Illness behaviors are the varying ways individuals respond to physiological symptoms, monitor internal states, define and interpret symptoms, and essentially work toward getting better. The first step in coping with an illness is to identify the symptoms. Then individuals need to report their symptoms to a medical professional, and finally, adhere to treatment prescriptions. Delays can occur at each of these steps.
- Many psychological factors such as confirmation biases, personality styles, and attributional problems compounded by cultural differences interfere with accurate symptom recognition. Delays in appraising illness can lead to delays in seeking help and using health care. A number of different triggers increase the likelihood that people will seek treatment. SES is perhaps the largest cultural factor that predicts the seeking of treatment. People living in poverty are less likely to have sufficient health care or to use it effectively.
- The bureaucracies of the hospital setting sometimes make it difficult for patients to have their illnesses treated. A variety of factors influence staff relationships with patients. Staff often stereotype patients based on SES, sex, age, and ethnicity. In particular, stereotyping and prejudice, language barriers, use of jargon, and time pressure influence communication between patient and practitioners.
- Adherence to treatment varies based on the complexity of the treatment, the extent to which the treatment interferes with social functioning, and the duration and severity of the treatment. A large number of patients do not fully adhere to doctors' prescriptions. Nonadherence is compounded by different cultural factors.

TEST YOURSELF ▶▶

Check your understanding of the topics in this chapter by answering the following questions.

1. The varying ways that individuals respond to physiological symptoms, monitor internal states, recognize symptoms, and use health care are all considered
   a. health behaviors.
   b. illness behaviors.
   c. proactive coping.
   d. reactivity measures.
2. The first and most important step that the patient has to negotiate successfully in the transition from health to illness is the
   a. acceptance of sickness.
   b. recognition of symptoms.
   c. reporting of symptoms.
   d. preparation for sickness.
3. Research assessing the use of health care and services routinely finds that ___________do not use health care as much as others do.
   a. high SES individuals
   b. high self-esteem individuals
   c. women
   d. minority group members
4. Many social psychological processes help explain illness behaviors (or their absence). If you do not think you are sick, you are likely to ignore symptoms

of the sickness and only look for evidence that you are healthy. This is called

a. a self-fulfilling prophecy.
b. selective attention.
c. a confirmation bias.
d. impression management.

5. An example of how assigning meaning to a symptom can vary across cultures can be seen in how
   a. Mexican American children consider hearing voices to be a religious experience.
   b. Hmong Americans consider epilepsy to be purely a physical defect.
   c. American Indians consider cancer to be a White man's disease.
   d. Chinese Americans use acupuncture to re-align energy flow.

6. A patient's attitude to health care and the extent to which they want to be a part of their treatment is referred to as the level of
   a. self-control.
   b. self-efficacy.
   c. behavioral involvement.
   d. patient–practitioner coherence.

7. Which of the following is *not* a major reason why people do not seek treatment?
   a. People underestimate the significance of symptoms.
   b. People assume the symptoms will turn out to be nothing.
   c. People do not want to bother their doctors.
   d. People overestimate the significance of their symptoms.

8. There are many cultural reasons that explain why people do not recognize that they have symptoms of an illness. Often, a long time passes from a symptom occurrence to the recognition that it is a problem. This can be harmful and is referred to as
   a. appraisal delay.
   b. illness delay.
   c. use delay.
   d. cultural delay.

9. Which of the following is not one of the five triggers (Zola, 1964) that increase the likelihood of a person seeking treatment?
   a. The degree to which the symptoms frighten you
   b. The nature and quality of symptoms
   c. Whether you have experienced the symptom before
   d. If the symptoms interfere with work or personal relationships

10. The __________ form of patient–practitioner communication involves the patient doing the bulk of the talking and getting answers to their questions.
    a. mutual cooperative
    b. active-passive
    c. patient-focused
    d. consumerist

KEY TERMS, CONCEPTS, AND PEOPLE

adherence, **245**
appraisal delay, **241**
attributions, **237**
behavioral involvement, **239**
confirmation bias, **237**
creative nonadherence, **246**
cultural awareness, **251**
cultural competency, **251**
cultural sensitivity, **251**
hypochondriacs, **238**
illness behaviors, **233**
illness delay, **241**
illness representations, **235**
illusory correlation, **237**
informational involvement, **239**
lay-referral system, **242**
misattribute, **238**
private body consciousness, **239**
self-fulfilling prophecy, **238**
social sanctioning, **242**
stereotypes, **249**
triggers, **241**
use delays, **241**

ESSENTIAL READINGS ▶▶

Broadbent, E. (2019). Illness cognitions and beliefs. In T. A. Revenson & R. A. R. Gurung (Eds.), *Handbook of health psychology* (3e). New York, NY: Routledge.

Cameron, L. D., Durazo, A., & Rus, H. M. (2016). Illness representations. In Y. Benyamini, M. Johnston, & E. C. Karademas (Eds.), *Assessment in health psychology* (pp.45–59). Boston, MA: Hogrefe.

Galanti, G. (2014). *Caring for patients from different cultures: Case studies from American hospitals.* Philadelphia, PA: University of Pennsylvania Press.

Kleinman, A., Eisenberg, L., & Good, B. (1978). Culture, illness, and cure: Clinical lessons from anthropologic and cross-cultural research. *Annals of Internal Medicine, 88,* 250–258.

CHAPTER 10

DIVERSE APPROACHES TO PAIN

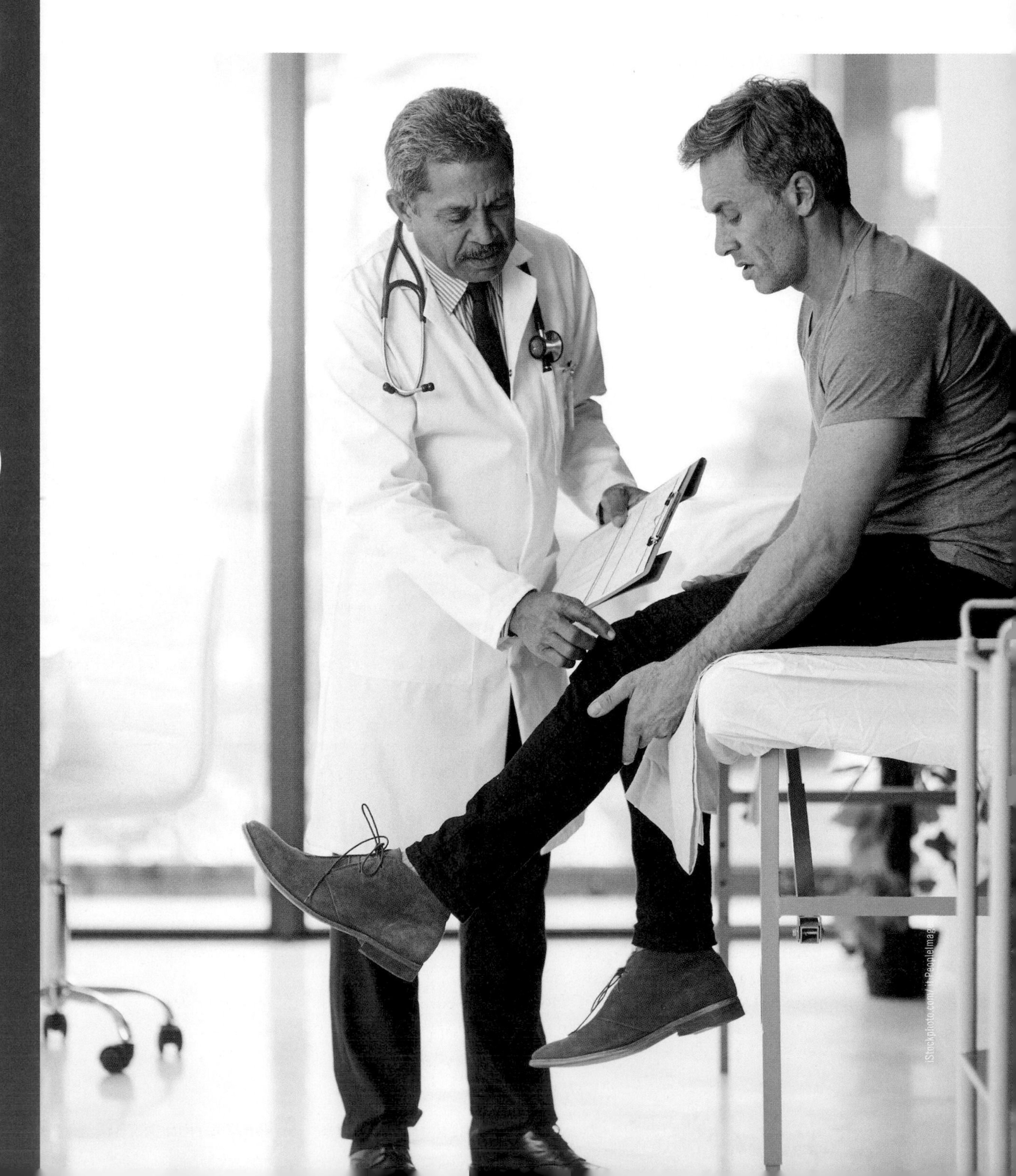

Chapter 10 Outline

MEASURING UP

HOW MUCH PAIN ARE YOU IN?

Instructions: Answer each of the following questions using the spaces below.

1. Did you have pain today?____no ____yes
2. Did you avoid or limit any of your activities or cancel plans today because of pain or changes in your pain?____no ____yes What activities?__________
3. Did you take all your pain medicine today according to instruction? ____no ____yes
4. Even though you took your pain medicine for persistent pain on schedule, were there times during the day that you experienced unrelieved breakthrough pain?____no ____yes
5. How many times did this happen today?__________

Source: Adapted from Native American Cancer Research Center (http://natamcancer.org/page202.html)

▼ Ponder This

What are the different things you try when you are in pain?

What are 10 different ways you could describe pain experiences you have had?

How do you think hospitals use psychological methods to reduce pain?

The world seems like such a different place when we are in pain. Whether it is a mild headache from a stressful day, the ache of a twisted ankle from a misstep, a stomach ache from spoiled food, or the skinned knee from a fall during basketball, pain is uncomfortable and is something we want to avoid. In the midst of a painful experience, we long for the time when the pain will be gone. We try anything we can to escape pain. For common pains such as headaches, we may reach for aspirin or may take a nap, hoping that the pain will be gone once the pill takes effect or when we wake up. There are many cultural differences in how we cope with pain, and many cultural explanations for why we feel pain.

What is pain? Why do we experience it? How is it caused? Maybe the most important question of all is, what are the ways to relieve it? In this chapter, we describe the phenomenon of pain and answer each of these questions. First, I discuss the different types of pain and look at how pain has been explained over the centuries. I then discuss some of the major ways we can cope with pain, making the distinction between short-term and long-term pain management. Lastly, I highlight some of the ways different cultures cope with pain.

KEY DEFINITIONS

What exactly is pain? The International Association for the Study of Pain (IASP) defines pain as "an unpleasant sensory and emotional experience associated with actual or potential tissue damage, or described in terms of such damage" (Merskey & Bogduk, 1994, p. 211). Notice that this definition incorporates the fact that pain is a subjective experience. In fact, in a demonstration of how subjective it can be, researchers had people play a virtual reality game. In it, the people were knights and either had their virtual arm protected by armor or not. All participants got a real electrical stimulation (i.e., on their actual arm and not in the game). Participants who had armor on *in the virtual world* reported less pain in response to the electrical shock (Weeth, Mühlberger, & Shiban, 2017).

At the most basic level, pain can be referred to as **nociception**, the activation of specialized nerve fibers and receptors (called nociceptors) in response to noxious or harmful stimuli such as heat, cold, pressure, or chemical stimuli. The nociceptors signal the occurrence of tissue damage, but this does not always lead to the experience of pain, which involves subjective psychological processing as well (Williams, 2010). When our bodies detect a noxious stimulus, the autonomic nervous system jumps into action and the heart beats faster, blood pressure rises, and the hypothalamic-pituitary-axis is activated.

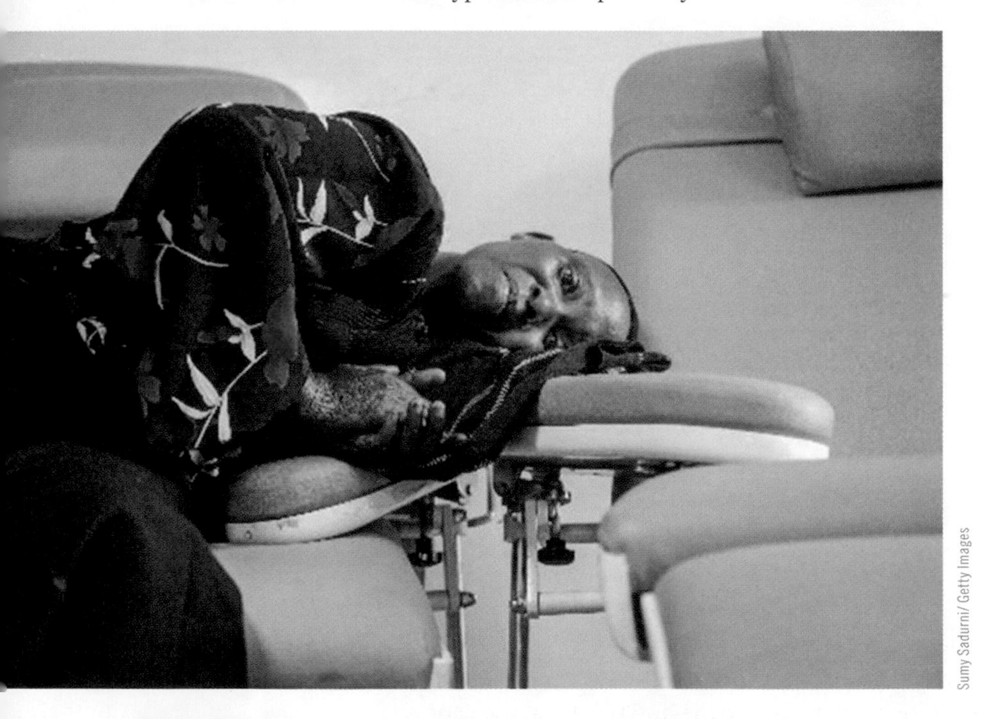

Sumy Sadurni/ Getty Images

▲ **Expressions and causes of pain vary significantly across cultures.** Women and African Americans report different levels of pain than men and European Americans.

Nociception is often accompanied by cognitive, behavioral, and affective states (Turk, Wilson, & Swanson, 2012). Your thoughts are influenced by pain, your behaviors change when you are in pain, and your feelings are influenced by pain. Of course, pain can also be purely emotional in nature, without nociception, and is often described as suffering. Pain is a phenomenon that clearly exemplifies how important taking a biopsychosocial approach can be. Whereas pain can have direct biological causes—for example, if you get punched on your arm you will more than likely feel pain—the experience of pain is strongly influenced by psychological and cultural factors.

As signified by the technical definition of nociception, pain is essential to survival. Some cultures interpret pain differently and may have different ways to cope with it, but in all cases pain serves the same purpose. Pain warns us of bodily danger and provides feedback of bodily functions. If you are hiking up a hill and you place your foot on a rock in the wrong way, your foot may hurt before you put all your weight on it. You automatically place it down in the right way. If you break your arm, the pain in the limb is a reminder to you to refrain from using it to give it time to heal. When you get too close to a fire, the pain from the heat reminds you to keep a safe distance from the fire. When you experience pain, you are more likely to go to a doctor. Unfortunately, the opposite is also true. Heart attack victims who did not experience too much pain delayed seeking care for their symptoms (Finnegan et al., 2000).

CULTURAL VARIATIONS IN THE EXPERIENCE OF PAIN

Many cultural factors influence the perception and experience of pain (Hruschak & Cochran, 2017), but two of these stand out: sex and ethnicity (Institute of Medicine [IOM], 2011; Ruau, Liu, Clark, Angst, & Butte, 2012). In large part, the cultural variations are due to differences in socialization and expectations across different cultural groups. Boys are socialized to not express themselves when experiencing pain and girls are socialized to express pain when they need to. If a man cries in pain, he is seen as less masculine, but it is perfectly acceptable for a woman to cry because of pain. There are also different expectations for pain tolerance across ethnicities and races. Middle Eastern women are more likely to scream during delivery than are Japanese women (Galanti, 2014).

Sex Differences

A growing body of research suggests that there are sex differences at every level—biological, psychological, and social—in the experience of persistent pain (Bernardes, Keogh, & Lima, 2008; Ruau et al., 2012). In a large study of 1,371 patients at a pain clinic, when men and women experienced the same level of pain severity, women reported higher pain acceptance, activity level, and social support, while men had more mood disturbances and lower activity levels (Rovner et al., 2017). A study of smokers showed that female smokers had significantly lower pain tolerance than male smokers (Bagot, Wu, Cavallo, & Krishnan-Sarin, 2017).

In perhaps one of the largest real-world data driven studies ever, Ruau et al. (2012) used more than 72,000 patients' pain ratings from a large hospital database. The authors found more than 160,000 pain scores in more than 250 primary diagnoses and analyzed differences in pain reported by men and women separated out by type of disease. Women reported significantly higher pain in most categories with the most significant differences in patients with disorders of the musculoskeletal, circulatory, respiratory, and digestive systems, followed by infectious diseases, and injury and poisoning.

In early studies of experimentally delivered stimuli to the body, women showed lower thresholds, greater ability to discriminate, higher pain ratings, and less tolerance of noxious stimuli than males (Berkley, 1997). Of note, these differences existed only for some forms of painful stimulations and varied based on situational factors such as the experimental setting. For internal pains, Berkley (1997) found that women report more multiple pains in more areas of the body than men do. A 10-year summary of laboratory research shows that the picture is not as clear cut as was once thought (Racine et al., 2012). Racine et al. (2012) suggest that females tolerate less thermal (heat, cold) and pressure pain than males, but that is not the case for tolerance to ischemic pain (pain related to blood stoppages), which is comparable in both sexes. The majority of the studies that measured pain intensity and unpleasantness showed no sex difference in many pain modalities.

Ethnic Differences

Members of different ethnic groups, similar to members of the two sexes, give very different meanings to the experience of pain. These differences take the form of when pain should be expressed, how the pain should be expressed (e.g., verbally or behaviorally), what the expression of the pain signifies about the individual, and how long the pain should be expressed (Bäärnhielm, 2012).

In a recent exploration of the racial and ethnic differences in experimental pain sensitivity, Kim et al. (2017) searched four databases (PubMed, EMBASE, the Cochrane Central Register of Controlled Trials, and PsycINFO) assessing a range of experimental pain studies. These included using heat, cold, pressure, electrical, and chemical stimuli. Researchers found that overall, African Americans, Asian Americans, and Hispanics had higher pain sensitivity compared with non-Hispanic European Americans, particularly lower pain tolerance, and higher pain ratings.

There are also significant ethnic disparities in the treatment of pain (IOM, 2011). Meghani, Byun, and Gallagher (2012) synthesized 20 years of accumulated evidence on ethnic disparities in treatment for pain in the United States. They examined the strength of the relationship between ethnicity and treatment, the groups at increased risk, and the effect of key moderators such as pain type and setting. Meghani et al. found that African Americans experienced both a higher number and higher magnitude of disparities than any other group. Treatment disparities were less for Latinos for traumatic/surgical pain but remained for nontraumatic/nonsurgical pain. Treatment disparities for African Americans remained consistent across the different settings and pain types. Perhaps the most alarming finding is that the treatment gap does not appear to be closing with time or existing policy initiatives.

The clinical literature on ethnicity and pain has been focused primarily on two ethnic groups, African Americans and European Americans (e.g., Umeda, Griffin, Cross, Heredia, & Okifuji, 2017), and the differences are clear. In a large meta-analysis of experimental pain, Rahim-Williams, Riley, Williams, and Fillingim (2012) found that African Americans had the lowest pain tolerance of all the ethnic groups studied. Riley et al. (2002) tested for ethnic differences in the processing of chronic pain in 1,557 European American and African American chronic pain patients. After researchers controlled for pain duration and education, African Americans reported significantly higher levels of pain unpleasantness, emotional response to pain, and pain behavior, but not pain intensity, than did European Americans. African Americans with chronic pain report significantly more pain and sleep disturbance as well as more symptoms consistent with post-traumatic stress disorder and depression than White Americans (Green, Baker, Sato, Washington, & Smith, 2003).

There is now a growing literature that includes Latin American populations (Barry, Glenn, Hoff, & Potenza, 2017; Sandberg et al., 2012). In one large community sample study, non-Latino African Americans and Latin Americans had higher risk for severe pain compared with non-Latino European Americans (Reyes-Gibby et al., 2007). Of note, some of these ethnic differences between African American, Latin American, and European Americans may be due to ethnic identity, which serves as a mediator (see Chapter 6) of the differences (Rahim-Williams et al., 2007).

Other ethnic groups show differences as well. A recent meta-analysis of studies of barriers to pain management showed that Asian patients' perceived barriers to managing cancer pain were significantly higher than those for Western patients, especially for concerns about disease progression, tolerance, and fatalism (Chen, Tang, & Chen, 2012).

Other cultural factors are important in the context of pain. Some ethnic groups may have language barriers that influence the success with which the patients convey their level of pain or understand the doctor's instructions. Many ethnic groups experience disproportional levels of stress due to acculturation or lower socioeconomic status. Prolonged experiences of stress could result from unemployment or family issues relating to changes in roles or the process of acculturating to a new dominant society. For example, Latinos are the fastest-growing ethnic group in North America but have experienced decreasing economic and educational levels and are underrepresented in those who have health insurance (Betancourt & Fuentes, 2001). All these factors represent significant psychological factors for Latinos and those in other cultural groups coping with chronic pain.

Before you assume that if someone is from a different culture he or she has to experience pain differently, remember that there are also big individual differences within cultures. In addition, a number of studies have failed to find significant cultural differences in pain perceptions (Flannery, Sos, & McGovern, 1981; Pfefferbaum, Adams, & Aceves, 1990). The different studies compared different ethnic groups *and* different measures of pain, making it tougher to understand the basic phenomenon. The samples are often not heterogeneous and are not always chosen by random sampling (Korol & Craig, 2001). Future health psychological research should aim to have bigger groups for comparison to produce a more thorough understanding of cultural differences. There is a particular need for a better understanding of some of the cultural healing techniques used for pain.

Sex and ethnic differences also interact, and this interaction changes as we grow older. One of the first meta-analyses on pain and aging changes what we thought about pain even 5 years ago. The new research suggests that as we age our pain thresholds increase, but tolerance of pain does not seem to change (Lautenbacher, Peters, Heesen, Scheel, & Kunz, 2017). Pain also tends to increase in frequency as we age (Mottram, Peat, Thomas, Wilkie, & Croft, 2008).

iStockphoto.com/ urf

▲ **Firewalking.** Members of some cultural groups seem to be able to endure firewalking without pain. Firewalking can also be explained by the laws of physics.

TYPOLOGIES AND BIOLOGY OF PAIN

Think about how you describe your sensations of pain. After running into a wall or a corner of the table, you may experience a numbing pain. A headache throbs. A tooth aches. A burn smarts. There are many different causes for the sensation we refer to as pain. In addition, many different words can be used to describe pain. Pain has been classified in many different ways (Dixon, 2016). Pain can be short term, referred to as **acute** pain, or experienced for a long period of time, termed **chronic** pain (Day, 2019). If the chronic pain is associated with a disease such as cancer, it is referred to as chronic malignant pain. If it is not associated with a malignant state, such as lower back pain, it is referred to as chronic noncancer pain (Turk, 2001a). Acute pain can last for minutes, hours, or even days or weeks. By definition it resolves within about 3 months of starting (Williams, 2010). Acute pain is also measured differently. For example, the ACTTION-APS-AAPM Acute Pain Taxonomy (AAAPT) is a multidimensional acute pain classification system designed to classify acute pain along the following dimensions: (1) core criteria, (2) common features, (3) modulating factors, (4) impact/functional consequences, and (5) disease state pain mechanisms (Kent et al., 2017).

Synthesize, Evaluate, Apply

- What cultural factors influence your experience of pain?
- How would people with different approaches to health (as described in Chapter 3) experience pain differently? Given what you know about different cultures, what other differences in the experience of pain would you think exist?

Chronic pain often persists for months or even years and is now considered a disease by some pain organizations such as the European Federation of IASP chapters (Williams, 2010). Pain can be limited to a small area, say your lower back, or spread out over a large area, for example your entire body when you have the flu.

In addition to terms based on the duration of the pain (e.g., acute and chronic), pain can be described based on its origins. For example, purely psychological pain without a physiological basis is referred to as **psychogenic pain**. Pure nociception without significant psychological pain is referred to as **neuropathic pain**. Similarly, physiological pain without specific tissue damage is referred to as **somatic pain** (Turk et al., 2012).

There are four distinct physiological processes critical to understanding pain: transduction, transmission, modulation, and perception (Torta, Legrain, Mouraux, & Valentini, 2017). **Transduction** takes place at the level of the receptors where chemical (e.g., caustic fumes), mechanical (e.g., a pinprick), or thermal (e.g., a flame) energy is converted in electrochemical nerve impulses.

RESEARCHER SPOTLIGHT

Kim Dixon received her PhD in clinical psychology and practices at the Tuscaloosa VA Medical Center. She is past president of the Society for Health Psychology. Want to know more about how to measure pain and pain behavior? Read her chapter mentioned in Essential Readings (Dixon, 2016).

This electrochemical energy is then transmitted or relayed from the sensory receptors to the central nervous system. Substance P is a neurotransmitter that plays a role in **transmission.** The sensory nerve fibers transmitting signals from the receptors to the spinal cord are called **afferent fibers** and are part of the peripheral nervous system. The spinal cord neurons that relay the signal up to the brain are part of the central nervous system and ascend to the brainstem. In the brain, neurons transmit impulses between the thalamus and the various parts of the cortex. **Modulation** refers to the neural activity leading to the control of pain transmissions between

▼ FIGURE 10.1

Four Basic Processes Involved in Recognizing Pain

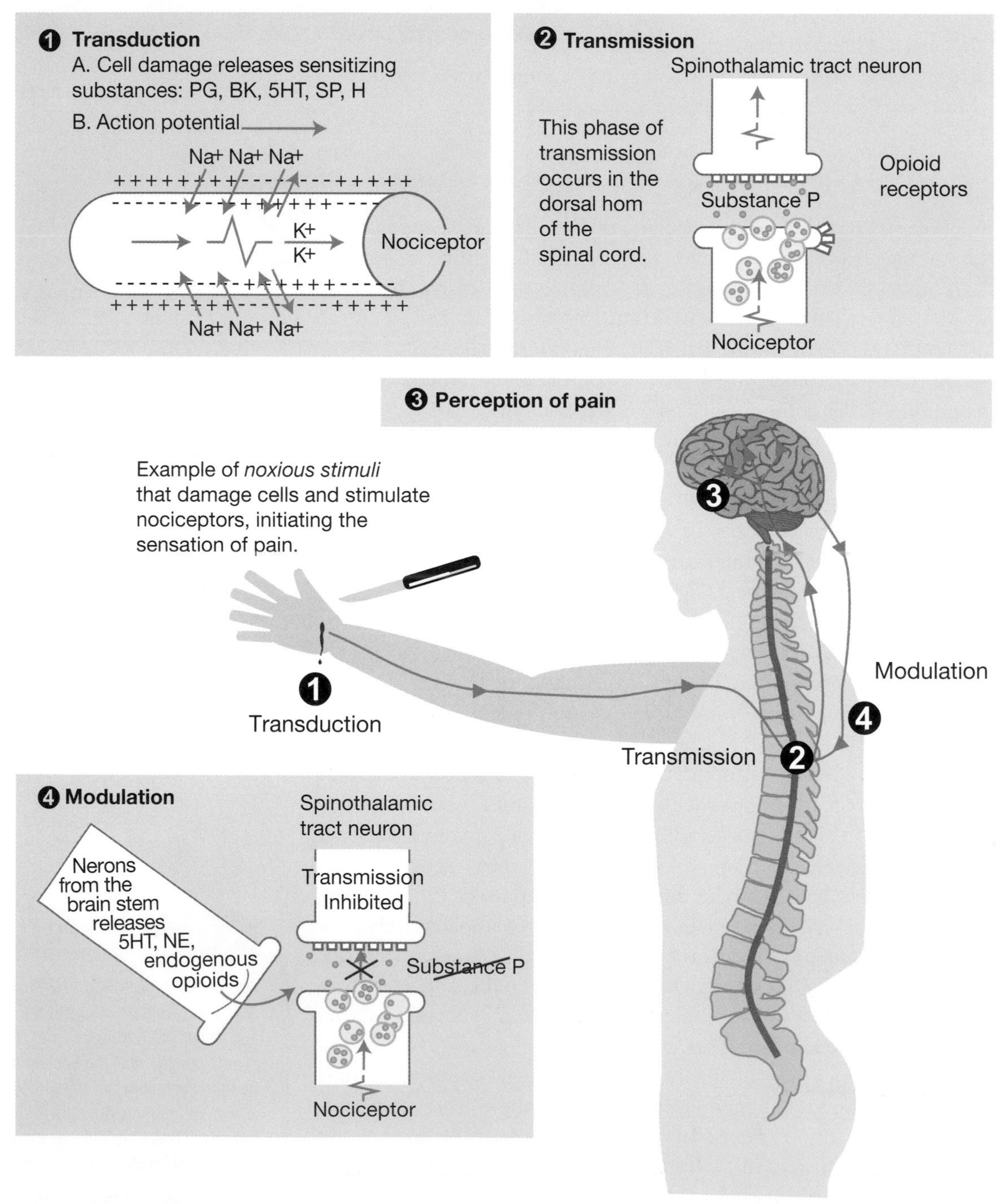

Source: From McCaffery and Pasero, *Pain: Clinical Manual*, p. 21. Copyright © 1999 Mosby, Inc. Adapted by permission of Elsevier.

the various parts of the brain. The main parts of the nervous system involved in modulation are the frontal cortex, hypothalamus, periaqueductal gray matter, reticular formation, and medulla in the brain and the areas of the spinal cord to be described shortly. The end result of these three processes is **perception** of pain when the neural activity of transmission and modulation results in a subjective experience (Figure 10.1).

MEASURING PAIN

Given the multifaceted nature of pain (e.g., intensity, pain behaviors), it is particularly difficult to measure (Dixon, 2016). Can we objectively measure tissue damage? Not very easily. Furthermore, the same physical problem may cause different amounts of pain to different people. A broken limb may hurt Nikhil much more than the same break may hurt Nathan. Given the number of words that one can use to describe pain, we also encounter major language issues when we try to ask someone if he or she is in pain or what sort of pain he or she is experiencing. These issues make measuring pain difficult.

The Initiative on Methods, Measurement, and Pain Assessment in Clinical Trials (IMMPACT) identified the main areas of pain to be assessed (Dworkin et al., 2008): pain intensity, physical functioning, emotional functioning, and overall well-being. Due to this work and the Institute of Medicine's (IOM's) report on the state of pain management in America (IOM, 2011), most hospitals in North America now consider pain to be a **vital sign**, one of five basic measures that doctors get from patients (Tompkins, Hobelmann, & Compton, 2017). Temperature, pulse, blood pressure, and respiration are the other four.

Given how many people are in pain, there are a number of major national efforts similar to IMMPACT to measure pain. A National Pain Strategy for population research uses mail surveys and health-care data of thousands of Americans to assess chronic pain (Von Korff et al., 2016).

Given that pain has to be measured right away, how do you do it if the patient does not speak English and no interpreter is available? How do you do it if the patient is a young child who cannot comprehend the question?

Basic Pain Measures

Hospitals have a variety of simple ways to assess pain that can be used across cultures. Regardless of the race, ethnicity, or age of the patient, illustrations of different levels of pain can help in pain assessment (Jensen & Karoly, 2011). A sample pictorial measure of pain is shown in Figure 10.2. The young patient is shown a series of 6 to 10 descriptive faces. At one end of the spectrum is a green smiling face (representing no or low pain). At the other end of the spectrum is a red frowning face (representing lots of pain). The patient indicates which face best represents how he or she is feeling. This measure is also used with patients from different cultural

▼ FIGURE 10.2

Visual Pain Scale

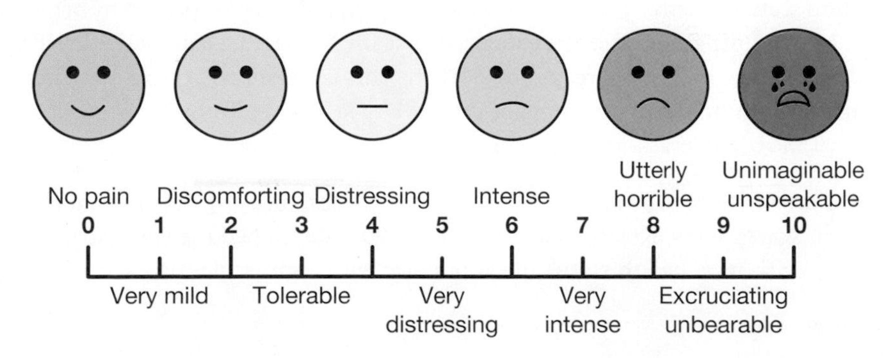

backgrounds with simple instructions printed in different languages beneath it (McGrath & Gillespie, 2001). For example, in many hospitals ranging from Green Bay, Wisconsin, to Los Angeles, California, color clipboards or posters with the scale shown in Figure 10.2 have instructions in Spanish.

Together with this simple pictorial measure, hospitals also use a continuous measure of pain intensity. Common measures include a numeric rating scale (NRS), a verbal rating scale (VRS), or the visual analog scale (VAS). With NRSs, patients are instructed to pick how much pain they are feeling on a scale of 0 to 10 (or 0–100) with 0 meaning no pain and 10 signifying extreme pain. The end points often have verbal descriptors such as "no pain" and "worst pain," which often prove problematic to older adults or some cultural groups that may not be able to conceptualize a subjective perception as a number (Dixon, 2016).

VRSs consist of a list of anywhere from 4 to 15 adjectives arranged in a row. The words represent growing levels of pain. The VAS is a straight line often 10 centimeters long with verbal descriptors at each end. Patients are asked to mark the spot on the line that represents their level of pain. Hospital staff then measure where the mark is on paper. In a study of doctors, 56% preferred NRSs, 20% preferred VRSs, and only 7% preferred VASs (Price, Bush, Long, & Harkins, 1994).

Even simple measures can reveal important procedural problems. Patients and physicians often disagree in their assessment of pain intensity. Staton et al. (2007) explored the impact of patient factors on underestimation of pain intensity. Physicians underestimated pain intensity relative to their patients 39% of the time. Forty-six percent agreed with their patients' pain perception, and 15% of physicians overestimated their patients' pain levels by more than 2 points. Racism raised its ugly head again: physicians were twice as likely to underestimate pain in African American patients compared to all other ethnicities combined.

The McGill Pain Questionnaire (MPQ) A number of validated pain questionnaires are used in addition to the preceding simple measures of pain. The MPQ is one of the earliest and most frequently used questionnaires and draws on the fact that we use words to describe pain (Melzack, 1975). It consists of 78 pain descriptors grouped into 20 categories that vary along three main dimensions: sensory, affective, and evaluative. Each dimension taps into different aspects of pain. The sensory aspect captures the frequency, location, and sensory quality of pain, such as spreading, burning, pulsing, or crushing. The affective aspect captures more emotional qualities like annoying, terrifying, exhausting, or sickening. The evaluative aspect captures the experience of pain (e.g., agonizing or excruciating). In addition, patients can indicate where exactly they feel pain on two outlines of the human body as shown in Figure 10.3.

The Multidimensional Pain Inventory (MPI) The MPI consists of 52 questions divided into three main sections (Kerns, Turk, & Rudy, 1985). Using a more biopsychosocial approach, the first section assesses the intensity of pain, the patient's view of his or her own functioning with pain and other aspects such as the extent to which pain interferes with the patient's life. The second section measures the patient's views of how those with close relationships respond to him or her. The third section assesses the extent to which the pain prevents the patient from taking part in daily life by measuring how often the patient partakes in 30 different daily activities. This form of measurement of the patient's perceptions and behaviors is seen in other pain measures as well. For example, the Multiaxial Assessment of Pain (MAP) (Turk & Rudy, 1986) measures both psychological and behavioral aspects of pain.

The Short Form with 36 Questions (SF-36) Some general measures of health include measures of pain. Ware, Snow, Kosinski, and Gandek (1993) developed the (pedestrian, but precisely named) SF-36, a health status questionnaire with eight scales assessing most of the

▼ FIGURE 10.3

A Hospital Measure of Pain

Notice the many different aspects of the phenomenon of pain that are assessed.

ST. VINCENT HOSPITAL GREEN BAY, WISCONSIN

www.stvincenthospital.org PAIN ASSESSMENT FORM

Date ________

Patient's Goal ________

Age ________

1. Current Intensity:

—10 Worst pain imaginable
—9
—8
—7
—6
—5
—4
—3
—2
—1
—0

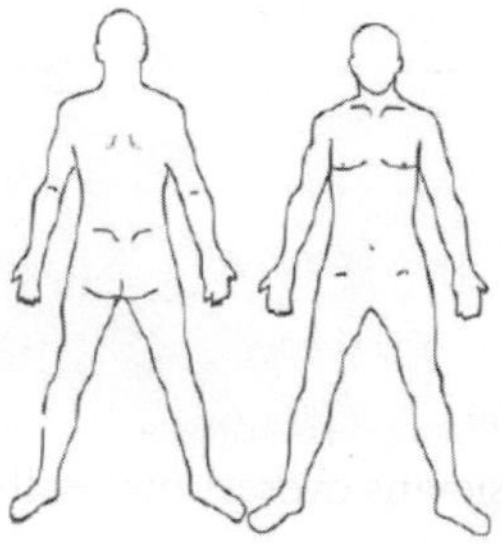

2. How and when did pain begin? Did something trigger your pain?

____

____

3. Where is the pain located? I = Internal, E = External. Use drawing.
4. Is pain:

   Continuous Intermittent

   Describe patterns/changes

   ____

   ____

   ____

   ____

5. Describe in your own words what your pain feels like. ________
6. What makes the pain better/what has helped in the past? ________
7. What makes the pain worse/what has not helped in the past? ________

   ____

8. What other symptoms accompany your pain? ________
9. How does pain affect your:

   Sleep ________

   Appetite ________

   Physical Activity ________

(Continued)

(Continued)

Concentration __________

Emotions (Anxiety Factor) __________

Social Relationships __________

What would you like to do that you are not able to now? __________

10. What do you think is causing your pain? __________
11. Current analgesics and nonpharmacologic regimes: __________
12. Plan/comments:

____

____

____

__________ Signature/Date __________

1. Medical History

Diabetes	Depression	Peptic Ulcer	Gout
Liver Disease	Renal Disease	Osteoarthritis	Cardiac Disease
Fibromyalgia	Rheumatoid Arthritis	Neuromuscular Disease	HTN
Migraines	Wounds	Spondylolisthesis	Other

2. Previous Treatments

Pain Clinic Injections	Chronic Pain Clinic	Spiritual Consult	Guided Imagery
Massage Therapy	Herbal Treatment	Psychotherapy	Body Mechanics
Vocational Rehab	Aquatic Therapy	Physical Therapy	Other
Occupational Therapy	Dietary Consult Relaxation		

3. Other Physician Consults:

Chiropractic	Neurosurgeon	Addictionologist
Rehab Physiatrist	Orthopod	Pain Physician
Rheumatologist	Neurologist	Other

4. Tobacco, Alcohol, Nonprescription meds. Explain __________
5. Allergies __________
6. Liver Function _____ AST _____ ALT _____ Alk. Phos.
7. Renal Function _____ Great. _____ BUN
8. Other medications __________

____

9. Side effects of analgesics/adjuvants:

Constipation Xerostomia Drowsiness Twitching Other

10. History of accidents __________

____

11. History of previous surgeries:

12. Results of scans, x-rays, cultures, etc.____

13. Other consultants and their recommendations____

14. Follow-up visits and recommendations:

Date Comments Signature

important dimensions of health status. Together with measuring aspects such as physical and social functioning, the SF-36 also has a measure of bodily pain. The Bodily Pain Scale has a range of 0 to 100 and has been suggested as a good tool for busy primary care clinicians because its use facilitates and focuses listening, and the result can be viewed as a vital sign (Wetzler, Lum, & Bush, 2000).

Ecological Momentary Assessment (EMA) The most recent measure of pain captures pain experiences in the routine of day to day life (Okifuji, Bradshaw, Donaldson, & Turk, 2011). In EMA, patients carry electronic diaries such as iPads and report on their pain during different parts of their day. This allows researchers to study pain in the patients' home and work environments and under normal conditions. EMA uses repeated and extensive data collection of real-time reports of patients' current pain (Williams, 2010). By adding together the reports made at the time the pain is experienced, researchers no longer have to rely on the patient remembering what their past pain levels were.

Other Measures Other psychological tests such as the Minnesota Multiphasic Personality Inventory (MMPI) and the Beck Depression Inventory (Beck, Ward, Mendelson, Mock, & Erbaugh, 1961) are also used to get a sense of a person's pain. For example, patients who are likely to experience chronic pain are also likely to score high on the MMPI subscales of hypochondriasis, depression, and hysteria (referred to as the neurotic triad) (Bradley & Van der Heide, 1984).

In addition to paper and pencil measures and interviews, you can also assess the extent to which people are in pain by just observing their behaviors (Caporaso, Pulkovski, Sprott, & Mannion, 2012). Even for something as mundane as sleeping in an odd way and getting a crick in your neck, your behaviors change. You walk with a slightly different step because of the pain in your neck, and you may grimace as you turn your head. For patients with chronic pain, the pain can impact many aspects of their lives. They may moan and groan in pain, walk with trouble, and even avoid doing things that they have to do, such as picking up a bag of groceries. Likewise, even if patients report not feeling a lot of pain, a doctor can get a sense of their pain levels by watching how they sit, stand, move, and talk (Fordyce, 1990). Some often used measures of pain behaviors include the Pain Behavior Checklist (Kerns et al., 1991) and the UAB Pain Behavior Scale (Richards, Nepomuceno, Riles, & Suer, 1982). Both these measures are brief and effectively and reliably measure pain behaviors (Dixon, 2016).

The use of objective pain measures is also important when treating patients who cannot speak (such as patients in intensive care units). Objective measures vary in applicability based on the types of patients they are used with (see Li, Puntillo, & Miaskowski, 2008, for a review). Although the physiological measures such as electroencephalography, electromyography (EMG), and skin conductance are often used to assess pain (Day, 2018), they have not always been found to be very helpful (Flor, 2001).

Finally, and as a testimony to health psychology's biopsychosocial approach, a set of measures assesses psychological factors that may influence the experience of pain. One major factor is catastrophizing, "an exaggerated negative mental set which comes to bear during actual or anticipated pain experience" (Sullivan et al., 2001, p. 53). People higher in catastrophizing report higher levels of pain, poorer overall functioning, and worse mood. Individuals who catastrophize perceive pain as unbearable, horrible, and worst imaginable. Catastrophizing can be measured using either the Coping Strategies Questionnaire (Tan, Jensen, Robinson-Whelen, Thornby, & Monga, 2001) or the Pain Catastrophizing Scale (Sullivan, Bishop, & Pivik, 1995).

THEORIES OF PAIN

Early Physiological and Psychological Approaches

So how did humankind explain pain in the first place? Healers, shamans, and physicians throughout history encountered people with pain and were driven to help them get rid of it. To treat pain, one must have a sense of how it is caused. There have been many explanations for pain over the past 4,000 or so years. Stone tablets dating to 2600 B.C. mention pain (Bonica, 1990). Egyptian papyrus dating to the 4th century B.C. documents the goddess Isis's recommendation of opium to treat the god Ra's headaches (Turk et al., 2012). Table 10.1 summarizes the main theories of pain. Going back as far as we can to the ancient Greeks, we find that pain was considered an experience subject to rational thinking just like any other experience or behavior. Centuries later, Descartes (1664) provided one of the first theories of how we experience pain. He argued that pain is the result of specific stimuli acting on the body: the stronger the stimuli, the stronger the pain. Descartes hypothesized the existence of long nerves that extended through the body from the brain to the sense organs. Sensations at the skin's surface—for example, the

▼ TABLE 10.1

Main Theories of Pain from a Historical Perspective

Approximate Date	Source or Explanation of Pain
3000 B.C.E.	Evil spirits
1000 B.C.E.	God's will
500 B.C.E.	Irrational thinking (Greeks)
1664	Specific stimuli (Descartes)
1886	Pattern theory (Goldschneider)
1894	Specificity theory (Von Frey)
1959	Pain-prone personality (Engel)
1965	Gate control theory (Melzack and Wall)
1974	Cognitive-behavioral model (Brewer)
1990	Diathesis-stress theory of pain (Turk et al.)
1999	Neuromatrix theory of pain (Melzack)

bite of a dog—would be relayed to the brain, which would then coordinate a response (pulling your hand away).

This unidimensional model of pain used a **specificity** concept, later made explicit by Von Frey (1894). Pain was thought to be a specific independent sensation such as heat or touch, with specialized receptors responding to specific stimuli. Specialized centers in the brain would then stimulate actions to avoid further harm. Concurrent with the formulation of the specificity theory, Goldschneider (1886) suggested that pain results from a combination of impulses from nerve endings. According to this **pattern theory**, different patterns of stimulations caused different types of pain. No separate pain system was needed and instead of the intensity of the stimulus, strong, mild, and medium levels of pain resulted in how impulses were integrated in the dorsal horn of the spinal cord.

Although prevalent for many years, neither model explained some basic observations. For example, patients with similar objectively determined injuries vary greatly in their reports of pain severity (Turk, 2001a). Similarly, patients experiencing the same reports of pain who are treated in similar ways do not experience similar relief. Furthermore, surgery designed to alleviate pain by severing the neurological pathways responsible for it often does not work (Day, 2018).

In contrast to both these physiological theories (neither of which had any place for psychological influences on pain), Engel (1959) proposed one of the first models to allow for the role of emotions and perceptions. Having a **pain-prone personality** was thought to predispose a person to experience persistent pain. Expanded on by Blumer and Heilbronn (1984), the pain-prone person tends to deny emotional and interpersonal problems, is unable to cope with anger and hostility, and has a family history of depression, alcoholism, and chronic pain. Not only was there little empirical support for this theory (Turk & Salovey, 1984), but it did not account for how pain itself can produce changes in personality. Nonetheless, there is something intuitively satisfying about individual differences in pain perception. In recognition of the fact that psychological factors can predispose one to pain, the American Psychiatric Association created two psychiatric diagnoses: pain associated with psychological factors either with or without a diagnosed medical condition (Turk, 2001b).

Biopsychological Theories of Pain

So far, the different theories we have discussed were primarily physiological or psychological in nature. In lieu of purely psychological predispositions to pain, many researchers attempted to link these two aspects (e.g., Pilowsky & Spence, 1975; Waddell, Main, Morris, DiPaola, & Gray, 1984).

Bettman/ Getty Images

▲ **Descartes' Theory of Nerves Transmitting Stimulus to the Brain.** According to Descartes, there was a specific system for pain that was responsible for the sensation of the stimulus and the experience of the pain. Here, the nerves transmit the stimulus of heat and pain to the brain, which controls the response of the retraction of the foot.

One of the earlier models, the cognitive-behavioral model (e.g., Brewer, 1974; Turk, Meichenbaum, & Genest, 1983), suggested that people get conditioned to experience pain on the basis of learned expectations (Xia, Mørch, Matre, & Andersen, 2017). For example, you hear that dentist office visits can be painful and you condition yourself to fear going to the dentist and then experience more pain when you do go. People with pain are thought to have negative expectations about their own ability to function normally without experiencing pain and believe they have limited ability to control pain.

Similar to the cognitive-behavioral model, and as a variation on the pain-prone personality idea, theorists proposed that some individuals may have physiological predispositions to pain that interact with psychological factors to cause pain (Peng, Fuchs, & Gatchel, 2006). Referred to as the **diathesis-stress model**, Flor, Birbaumer, and Turk (1990) proposed that predisposing factors, such as a reduced threshold of nociception, precipitating stimuli, such as an injury, and maintaining processes, such as the expectation that the pain will persist, are all important in explaining pain. Although this theory provides a compelling model for the etiology of many forms of pain, the most widely accepted theory of pain is one first published in 1965.

The Gate Control Theory of Pain

The most effective and most studied biopsychosocial theory of pain is **Melzack** and Wall's (1965) **gate control theory (GCT)** of pain. This model proposed that the bulk of the action takes place in the dorsal horn substantia gelatinosa of the spinal cord and is influenced by the brain. The diagram in Figure 10.4 shows the key components of this model.

Some basic features of the GCT are consistent with older theories of pain. For example, we start with pain receptors located throughout the body. Some are on the surface just under the skin. These receptors inform us when we are poked, scratched, cut, or scraped. Other receptors are deeper in the muscles and among the glands and organs, telling us about muscular strains and pulls and changes in normal functions. In partial support of specificity theory, some receptors only convey pain information. Others also report on general sensations such as contact and temperature. All of these receptors send nerve projections to the spinal cord to the aforementioned dorsal horn. Now here is where the GCT was innovative. Instead of these nerves from the receptors sending impulses directly to the brain, the GCT proposed that the neural impulses from the peripheral nervous system are modulated by a gate-like mechanism in the dorsal horn before they flow into the central nervous system up to the brain. What exactly is going on in the dorsal horn?

Three main types of nerve fibers are involved: A fibers, C fibers, and the gate interneurons (see Figure 10.4). Melzack and Wall (1965) found that the diameters of the fibers of the peripheral nervous system varied in size. A-beta fibers have a large diameter and are myelinated (insulated with a protein sheath), resulting in quick transmission of impulses. C fibers are smaller in diameter and are not myelinated, resulting in slower transmission of impulses. A-delta fibers, another form of A fiber, are also small in diameter and have a function similar to that of C fibers. Each of the different fibers (A-beta, A-delta, and C) synapse on both the interneuron and on to the central nervous system neurons going up to the brain (see Figure 10.4). The interneurons are hypothetical gates that are located in the spinal cord and do not allow pain sensations to be relayed up to the brain if they are stimulated by the A-beta fibers (meaning that they close the gate). If they are not stimulated or if they are inhibited by the action of the C fibers or A-delta fibers, they allow pain sensations to be sent up to the brain (i.e., the gate remains open). The interneuron is thus an inhibitory neuron. The status of the gate depends on the balance of activity between small diameter (A-delta and C) and large diameter (A-beta) fibers.

The theorized combination of large fiber, small fiber, interneuron, and descending neuron activity has many implications for when and how we experience pain. First, it nicely explains why some pains are short lived whereas others persist for long periods of time. Whenever we experience sharp pains for a short period of time (we step on a tack), the A-beta fibers are activated and (1) send a fast message up to the brain via the central nervous system and (2) activate the interneuron, shut the gate, and turn the pain experience off. This is why we only feel the pain for a short period. When we experience slow, aching, burning pains with greater motivational and affective components, the C or A-delta fibers have probably been stimulated. They not only pass on the impulse to the brain, but they also inhibit the firing of the interneuron closing the gate. Some chronic conditions may cause long-term pain by deactivating the A-beta fibers. Herniated discs, tumors, and some injuries may decrease the firing of large fibers, making even mild stimuli that are not typically painful cause severe pain for extended periods of time (Turk, 2001a).

▼ FIGURE 10.4

Key Components of the Gate Control Theory

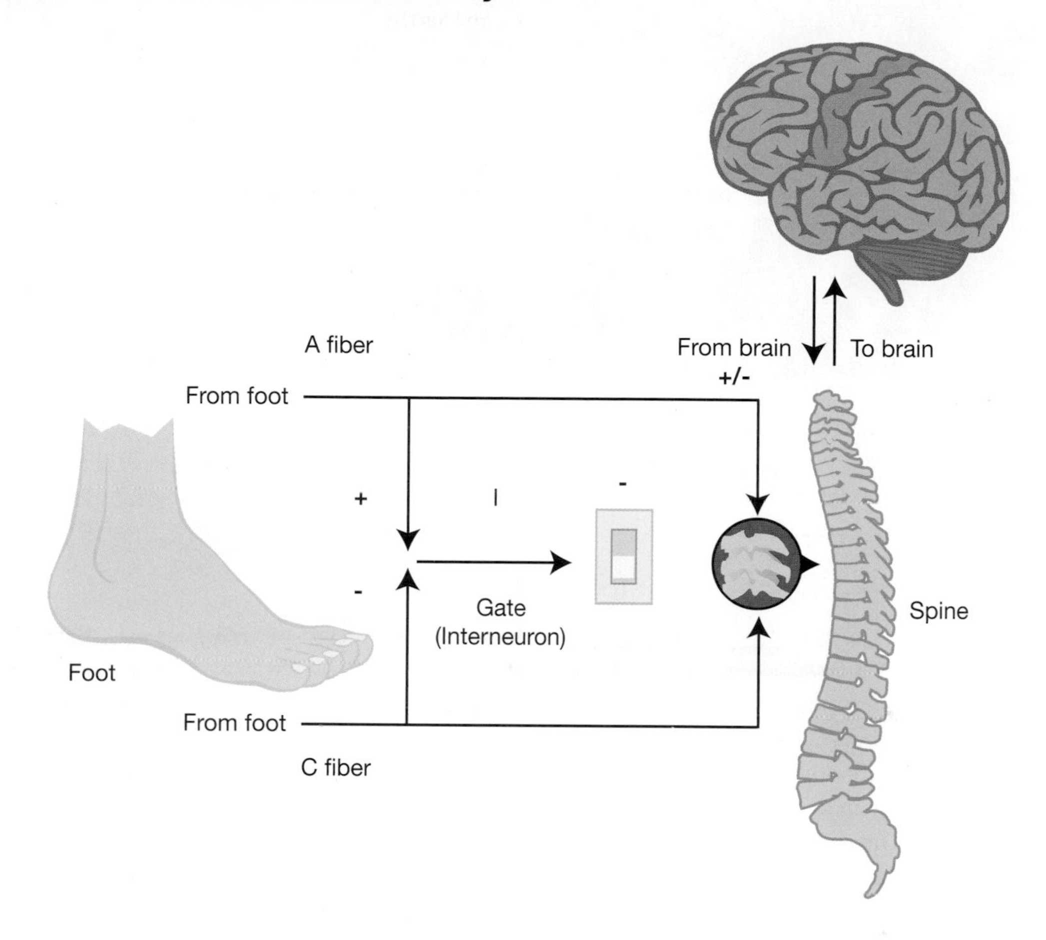

The GTC also explains some of the behaviors that we use to relieve pain. We often try to shut the gate ourselves. If we have a sharp pain in a certain spot, even something small like a bug bite, we often scratch around the pain or pinch ourselves close by to reduce the pain. This **counterirritation** serves to activate the large fibers that stimulate the interneuron, shutting the gate and providing temporary relief (Vo & Drummond, 2014). Counterirritation is sometimes achieved with the delivery of minute bursts of electricity to nerve endings right under the skin near the painful area or near the spinal cord near the painful area. This transcutaneous electrical nerve stimulation has been found to produce relief for a variety of diverse pains (Piché, Arsenault, Poitras, Rainville, & Bouin, 2010). Together with psychological ways to activate the descending **efferent pathways** and close the gate described above, researchers have found that electrically stimulating the brain can also reduce pain (Khedr, Sharkawy, Attia, Ibrahim Osman, & Sayed, 2017), a process referred to as **stimulation-produced analgesia**.

Although the physiological details of GCT have been challenged and revised (Nathan, 1976; Wall, 1989), the theory has held as scientific data accumulated. This theory is credited as a source of inspiration for diverse clinical applications to control and manage pain (Katz & Rosenbloom, 2015).

Synthesize, Evaluate, Apply

- Combine the different measures of pain to generate an optimal measure of pain.
- Compare and contrast the main theories of pain.
- Are there any types of pain that the gate control theory would not be able to explain?

▲ **Room with a view.** Based on the finding that a good view can help patients cope with pain, you can now buy curtains with scenic views on them. Now, even if a patient doesn't get a room with a view, or if the hospital is not in a scenic location, patients can still reap some benefits of seeing natural vistas.

THE PSYCHOLOGY OF PAIN

In one of the earliest studies of how psychological factors influence pain, Beecher (1955) compared World War II soldiers' experiences of pain on the battlefield with the pain experienced by civilians. He found that for injuries of similar severity, approximately 80% of the civilians requested painkillers whereas only 33% of the soldiers did. Even the self-reports were different. Whereas only 42% of the soldiers reported that their pain was in the severe to medium range, 75% of civilians reported their pain to be in this range. The stress of battle and possibly the realization that their injuries meant they were returning home seemed to lessen the soldiers' pain. Clearly, psychological factors influence pain.

Psychological Factors and Pain

There are two major categories of psychological factors influencing pain: psychiatric disorders and psychological characteristics (Williams, 2010). People who are depressed, anxious, or have personality disorders also tend to experience more pain. Depression occurs with pain 52% of the time in pain clinics, 27% of the time in primary care clinics, and 18% of the time in general population studies (Bair, Robinson, Katon, & Kroenke, 2003). Anxiety, depression, and pain occur together 23% of the time (Bair, Wu, Damush, Sutherland, & Kroenke, 2008). It is important to note that pain is often a separate issue and should be treated with its own intervention or treatment.

There are a number of psychological characteristics that influence pain. For example, locus of control and catastrophizing (discussed previously) are two key psychological factors that are important. If patients believe they have control over the pain (an internal locus of control) they are less likely to report physical and psychological symptoms (Büssing, Ostermann, Neugebauer, & Heusser, 2010). For example, chronic back pain patients with high external locus of control needed more treatment help (Oliveira et al., 2012).

Where does psychological control fit in with the biological models discussed above? Melzack and Wall (1965) also proposed that descending pathways from the brain also modulate activity at the level of the dorsal horn. In addition to the afferent transmissions to the spinal cord from the receptors in the periphery, efferent (from the brain via the spinal cord to the receptors) activity also influences pain sensations. Different psychological states such as anxiety or fear can increase the levels of pain experienced. In such scenarios, the descending pathway activates the C fibers that turn the interneuron off and increase the pain sensations making their way up to the brain. On the other hand, when someone is happy or optimistic, these positive affective states also influence the transmission of pain because the descending pathways now activate the interneurons and shut the gate, lessening the pain sensation. For this reason, a football player may not feel the pain of a violent tackle if it is in the middle of an important game, and he is excited or focused on winning. Similarly, if a person is bleeding from a cut but has not noticed she was hurt, she may not feel any pain.

A lot depends on how we appraise an event. Similar to Lazarus's cognitive appraisal theory of stress (see Chapter 5), if we appraise a wound or illness to be severe, descending pathways from the brain to the dorsal horn can accentuate the level of pain experienced. In fact, even appraising a painful event as a challenge (vs. a threat or harm) is associated with higher pain tolerance (Wang, Jackson, & Cai, 2016). Beliefs about pain can drive appraisals too. Forty percent of the variance in physical functioning and 30% of the variance in feelings of pain reports may be attributed to how people think about their pain (Romano, Jensen, & Turner, 2003).

Social learning can even influence pain. Bandura (1969; remember the Bobo doll study from Intro Psych?) first highlighted the role of observational or social learning in many areas of human life. If a young child sees her mother receive an injection without a reaction, the child will probably not react as much to receiving an injection herself. If the same child sees her mom scream and yell in pain when receiving an injection, this child may expect to feel a lot of pain as well. A number of studies have documented the role of social learning (e.g., Fan, Chen, & Cheng, 2016).

iStockphoto.com/ KatarzynaBialasiewicz

▲ **Virtual Reality (VR) and Pain.** New techniques developed by researchers use VR helmets to help alleviate pain. Here, a patient is led through an exercise.

Pain and pain behaviors can be modified by other basic learning and behaviorist theories as well (Egorova, Park, & Kong, 2017). Psychological pain can be operantly conditioned. For example, if complaining a lot when one is in pain results in getting a lot of attention, the pain behavior can be reinforced and strengthened. Chronic pain patients report more pain when they have spouses who are considerate and caring (Thieme, Spies, Sinha, Turk, & Flor, 2005).

Pain can also be classically conditioned. If every visit to the dentist's office is accompanied by pain, such as pain that occurs sometimes with a lot of drilling, one is likely to experience fear at just the thought of going to the dentist. This classically conditioned fear can predispose a person to experience more pain when he or she actually goes to the dentist. Even if you have not experienced pain at a dentist's office, just believing a visit can be painful can be enough to activate those descending pathways and increase your experience of pain. A large body of research documents the fact that patients' beliefs about pain, their attitudes, the context in which the pain is experienced, expectancies, and perceptions all affect their reports of pain (Jensen, Tomé-Pires, deGalán, Solé, & Miró, 2017; Turk, 2001a).

Synthesize, Evaluate, Apply

- What are other possible reasons to explain the results of Beecher's study with soldiers?
- What aspects of the hospital setting (described in Chapter 9) can negatively influence the experience of pain?
- How does the cognitive appraisal model of stress relate to pain perception?

▼ TABLE 10.2

Major Pain Management Techniques

Physiological		Physiological	
Chemical	Stimulation	Self-regulation	Other
Aspirin, acetaminophen, ibuprofen	Acupuncture	Biofeedback	Hypnosis
Morphine	Transcutaneous electrical nerve stimulation (surgical)	Relaxation	Distraction
	Stimulation-produced analgesia	Meditation	Long term self-management
		Guided imagery	

PAIN MANAGEMENT TECHNIQUES

There are three main categories of pain management techniques. The entire list is summarized in Table 10.2. The use of each of these will depend on the duration of the pain, the tolerance levels of individuals, and their pain thresholds. Some of us have high **thresholds** for pain. This means it takes a lot of painful stimuli for us to perceive something as being painful. Even if we have a low threshold for pain and perceive pain easily, we may still have a high **tolerance** level. Tolerance is the amount beyond which pain becomes unbearable, and we cannot accept any more. The main cultural differences that I discussed previously relate more to pain tolerance than to pain threshold. Men and women or members of different ethnicities tend to have different tolerance levels based on their expectations and cultural backgrounds.

We will examine some primarily physiological ways to reduce pain and also a wide variety of psychological techniques. Methods in each of these two categories can be used to cope with either acute or chronic pain although they are all used primarily for short-term treatment. The discussion of the third category of techniques will focus specifically on chronic pain and will include self-management programs. Our goal is to understand analgesia or pain relief.

Physiological Treatments

Chemical For most common pains, such as twisted ankles, headaches, bruises, and body aches from colds or flu, most individuals turn to over-the-counter medications. In most countries around the world, a number of tablets are available to alleviate pain. You have probably taken an aspirin, a Tylenol, or a Motrin at some point (or many) in your life. The use of these quick-shot pain relievers is so common that you can even buy pills with the active chemical ingredients (e.g., aspirin, acetaminophen, or ibuprofen) in bulk packages of 500 to 1,000 pills. These medications act locally, often at the site of the pain (Lampl, Voelker, & Steiner, 2012). There are three major categories of physiological pain relievers: non-opioids such as acetaminophen, opioids such as oxycodone and morphine, and adjuvants such as benzodiazepines (valium), corticosteroids, antidepressants, and local anesthetics (Szallasi, 2010).

For pain associated with surgery and for chronic pains, patients are often given stronger medications like narcotics such as morphine. Morphine binds to receptors in the periaqueductal gray area of the midbrain and produces pronounced analgesia and pleasant moods. Because of its effectiveness, there is a tendency for patients to want to use it regularly. This can lead to tolerance, drug dependence, and addiction (Katzman et al., 2014). Morphine is part of a class of chemicals referred to as opiates, drugs made from plants that regulate pain in the body by mimicking the effects of opioids, chemicals made by the body that regulate pain. First discovered by Akil, Mayer, and Liebeskind (1976), opioids (more technically, endogenous opioid peptides) can be divided into three main classes: beta-endorphins, proenkephalin, and prodynorphin. Each class exerts its pain-relieving effects in different parts of the body.

Opioid therapy for chronic noncancer pain is controversial due to concerns regarding its long-term effectiveness and the possibility of addiction (Knight et al., 2017). A systematic review of the clinical evidence on patients treated with opioids showed little evidence of addiction (Noble, Tregear, Treadwell, & Schoelles, 2008). Signs of opioid addiction were reported in only 0.05% (1/2,042) of patients and abuse in only 0.43% (3/685). The study did show that many patients withdrew from the clinical trials due to adverse effects or due to not getting sufficient pain relief. The controversy exists because there is also some evidence for addiction. Another study showed addiction in 50% of chronic nonmalignant pain patients and up to 7.7% for cancer patients (Hojsted & Sjogren, 2007).

Interestingly enough, there are some clear cultural differences in who is given opioids. Pletcher, Kertesz, Kohn, and Gonzales (2008) looked at pain-related visits to U.S. emergency departments using reason-for-visit and physician diagnosis codes from 13 years (1993–2005) of the National Hospital Ambulatory Medical Care Survey. The authors found that pain-related visits accounted for 42% of emergency department visits. Of note, European American patients with pain were more likely to receive an opioid (31%) than African American (23%), Latin American (24%), or Asian American patients (28%).

Our body sometimes releases opioids when we are stressed, a state that can be induced by motor activity such as physical activity. You have probably heard of a phenomenon known as the runner's high, referring to a positive mood state achieved by approximately 20 minutes of physical activity such as running (Whitehead, 2016). This is a form of **stress-induced analgesia (SIA)** and has also been documented in a variety of experimental settings (Gaab et al., 2017; Olango & Finn, 2014). For example, rats who are stressed by repeated immersions in cold water show SIA and higher pain tolerance when their tails are placed on a hot plate (no, this is not a pretty picture). Healthy young men who exercise also increase their pain tolerance (Vaegter et al., 2017).

Acupuncture This Chinese traditional medicine treatment, discussed in Chapter 3, is often used to relieve pain (Lee, Pittler, Shin, Kong, & Ernst, 2008). The acupuncturist inserts fine metal needles into the skin at predetermined points. These points, charted from the work of Chinese physicians over centuries, are thought to stimulate energy flow. Disruptions in energy flow can cause pain. Western biomedicine interprets the effectiveness of acupuncture as being due to the needles stimulating large fibers that close the gate. Acupuncture can produce such high levels of analgesia that even entire surgical procedures in China have been performed without the use of anesthetics. Not only has acupuncture been empirically shown to reduce pain, but also it does so without the side effects of many other medications (Tang, Yin, Rubini, & Illes, 2016).

There is considerable debate surrounding the effectiveness of acupuncture to reduce pain. Where some studies show acupuncture can be more effective than Western medicine (Lang, 2012), others fail to find a significant effect of acupuncture treatment (Lewis, Sim, & Barlas, 2017). Some studies suggest that acupuncture works because of a placebo effect (e.g., Müller et al., 2016; White et al., 2012), but it has been found to produce endorphins because the injection of naloxone, an endorphin blocker, also reduces the effectiveness of acupuncture. Furthermore, if the location of the needle is moved by even millimeters from where it is supposed to be, there is no analgesic effect, supporting a valid physiological basis for this treatment.

Another treatment from Chinese traditional medicine—*qi gong* (see Chapter 3)—is also showing promise in pain management (Vincent, Hill, Kruk, Cha, & Bauer, 2010). A review of 141 studies including randomized clinical trials (see Chapter 2) demonstrated greater pain reductions in the *qi gong* groups compared with control groups (Lee, Pittler, & Ernst, 2007). There was a significant effect of *qi gong* compared with general care for treating chronic pain.

Surgery Sometimes pain can be so intense that a person may just want to cut out that part of his or her body to get rid of the pain. Some version of this macabre scenario did take place hundreds of years ago when surgeons cut off infected limbs for which there was no cure, but this is not something considered today. Yet, given our understanding of the physiological pathways of pain, some treatments for pain do involve the severing of nerves that transmit pain or lesioning of sections of the brain responsible for pain perceptions. Unfortunately, although this method sounds great in theory, practical usage is limited because pain relief from surgery tends to be short lived as nerve pathways grow back and reconnect. Spinal surgery for back pain leaves 70–75% of patients still in pain (Day, 2018).

Other Physiology-Related Methods There are now medical devices that offer patients nonsurgical options for treating some pains such as chronic lower back pain. These methods involve computerized decompression systems that have been clinically tested to be effective (Macario, Richmond, Auster, & Pergolizzi, 2008).

There are also some physiological treatments that do not involve medication. Many hospitals use heat, cold, and vibrations to alleviate pain. Heat, for example, may be applied over or around the painful area or on the opposite side of the body from where the pain is (contralaterally), and it helps relieve the pain. Hot packs and rubber hot water bottles are most commonly used. Plastic bags with ice or ice water, ice packs, and cloths soaked in cold water are used to deliver cold. Some of the pains that benefit from cold include arthritis and other musculoskeletal pain, bleeding, episiotomy, skin damage, swelling, acute arthritis pain, and headaches (Triest-Robertson, 2011). Heat tends to decrease sensitivity to pain while cold numbs. Both help with muscle spasms. Neither is used for more than 20–30 minutes and is discontinued if there is skin irritation. Vibration (using handheld, cordless vibrators) and light massage are also used for muscle spasm pain, neck and back pain, tension headaches, and tooth pains.

JamesBrey/ E+/ Getty Images

▲ **Stress-Induced Analgesia.** Rats are immersed in cold water or made to exercise excessively to cause stress which then releases pain killers in their brains. Sure, treadmills are used but this looks more fun.

Psychological Treatments

A wide variety of psychological methods can be used to reduce pain. As discussed in the previous chapter and earlier in this chapter, our expectations of hospitals, injuries, or treatments can influence our experience of pain and discomfort. If you think a certain wound or procedure is going to be painful, you will probably experience more pain. You can use this same psychological angle to your advantage. If you expect a certain method of pain relief to work, it probably will. This power of expectation is often referred to as a placebo effect. Beyond expectations influencing pain, our psychology can influence our experience of pain in a variety of other ways.

Psychological States and Cognitive Styles Given those descending pathways from the brain, our moods can influence our pain. As discussed in the section on the GCT, if we are anxious, depressed, tense, fearful, or sad, we are likely to experience more pain. Often these negative mood states can lead to biased forms of thinking. These cognitive biases can accentuate the feelings of pain and need to be modified. For example, people often exaggerate the extent of an injury (catastrophize), believe the pain will last forever (stable attributional style), believe they have no control over the pain (external locus of control), or just give up and fail to try to alleviate their pain (learned helplessness). Other pain patients feel victimized by the situation and cannot get past the fact that the pain is happening to them. They often blame themselves and feel worthless, sometimes excessively dwelling on the pain. Changing these detrimental cognitions can aid pain relief.

Distraction Another way to vary psychological states to lessen pain is to distract the person from the pain (Marsdin, Noble, Reynard, & Turney, 2012). If you have a headache or a stomach ache and are not doing anything but sitting and thinking about how bad you are feeling, chances are you will not feel much better anytime soon. Instead, if you distract yourself from the pain by reading, watching television or a movie, or surfing on the Internet, you can alleviate some of the pain. Cognitive distraction can also take the form of guided imagery in which patients immerse themselves in an involving and pleasing scenario (Adeola et al., 2015) or listen to music (Johnson et al., 2017).

Hypnosis One method that combines distraction with relaxation and a self-fulfilling prophecy is hypnosis (from the Greek word for sleep). It was first popularized by the Austrian Mesmer who hypnotized patients (this treatment later became known as mesmerism) to effect cures in 18th century Europe and then later was practiced by the Scottish physician Braid who used it as anesthesia for surgery and then by Freud in his treatment of psychopathology. Under hypnosis, some patients have been able to withstand treatments that would otherwise cause considerable pain (Hosseinzadegan, Radfar, Shafiee-Kandjani, & Sheikh, 2017).

In hypnosis, a patient is induced into a relaxed state, often by being told to focus on an object or the calming voice of the doctor, and is then given a suggestion (e.g., the pain is fading) that is recalled when the patient comes out of the hypnotic trance (Hilgard, 1978). Although the exact mechanism by which hypnotism works is still unclear, hypnosis can influence both affective and sensory components of pain (Lang et al., 2000) and science is uncovering more of the neurochemistry behind its effects (Terhune & Kadosh, 2012).

General Cognitive Methods Other cognitive methods to treat pain are similar to those used to cope with stress. As described in Chapter 5 in the context of stress, biofeedback, relaxation, guided imagery, mindfulness, and meditation are all forms of cognitive therapy that can also alleviate pain (Smith & Norman, 2017; Su et al., 2016; Vago & Nakamura, 2011). Biofeedback allows a person to get more control over his or her autonomic activity and together with relaxation and meditation helps to reduce anxiety and muscle tension. This facilitates the redirection of blood flow away from the painful areas. Even meditation by itself has been found to be very effective for pain relief (Morone, Greco, & Weiner, 2008). Relaxation is also a significant treatment for pain (Lin, 2012). Like massages? That works too (Buttagat, Narktro, Onsrira, & Pobsamai, 2016).

It bears repeating that different health problems have different challenges for pain management. For example, one specific difficulty relating to effective pain control in patients with chronic kidney disease is that pain killers are underprescribed in patients on dialysis in end-stage kidney disease (Williams & Manias, 2008). Pain management also varies by who is being treated. In a review of 1,469 published articles on interventions for acute pain in hospitalized children, Stinson, Yamada, Dickson, Lamba, and Stevens (2008) found distraction and hypnosis to be the two leading treatment methods. Other methods may work better for other patients (see the section at the end of the chapter).

▲ **Animal Magnetism?** Franz Anton Mesmer (1734–1815) hypnotizing a patient.

What You See Matters Sometimes even a good view can reduce pain. In a fascinating example, patients recovering from gallbladder surgery whose windows faced greenery and trees requested significantly fewer painkillers than patients who did not have a view (Ulrich, 1984)! The difference having a good view can have on pain tolerance and health has spawned numerous studies investigating the link between environments and health (e.g., hospital design work; Lechtzin et al., 2010). More medical environments include computer generated nature scenes or art images projected on the walls of patients' hospital rooms, often combined with background music of the patient's choice. Tse, Ng, Chung, and Wong (2002) measured study participants' pain thresholds while wearing lightweight eyeglasses that projected an illusion of watching a 52-inch television screen at 6.5 feet in distance. One group watched a silent nature video. The control group watched a blank screen. Participants watching the nature scene tolerated more pain although it would have been more conclusive if the study had another condition where patients were distracted by something else (to show that nature, not just any distraction, did the trick). Even listening to sounds of nature can alleviate pain (Cutshall et al., 2011). Studies such as these suggest that even simulating natural environments is tied to increased pain control and decreased patient suffering (Malenbaum, Keefe, de C. Williams, Ulrich, & Somers, 2008).

Even virtual reality is coming into play. Immersive **virtual reality (VR)** has proved to be potentially valuable as a pain control technique (Jones, Moore, & Choo, 2016; Maani et al., 2011). In virtual reality environments, patients see realistic images without distractions. A common methodology involves patients wearing a high-tech VR helmet with a 60-degree field-of-view head-mounted display. The technology allows users to interact at many levels with the virtual environment, using many of their senses and encouraging them to completely enter the virtual world they are experiencing. The distraction from being in a virtual world apparently leads to lower experiences of pain and discomfort (Teeley et al., 2012). Wondering if playing video games also has the same effect on pain? Apparently, it does (Parry et al., 2012).

Synthesize, Evaluate, Apply

- What are the biopsychosocial bases of the different pain management techniques?
- What guidelines would you recommend for the use of morphine, a potentially addictive pain reliever?
- Describe a technique to use both classical and operant conditioning to alleviate pain.
- Evaluate the pros and cons of each of the different pain management techniques.

SELF-MANAGEMENT OF CHRONIC PAIN

Many of the methods discussed in the preceding section are used extensively to treat acute pain. Some of them, such as imagery and hypnosis, are used with chronic pain as well. Still, chronic pain is different and calls for unique strategies. One category of pain relief therapy differs from the straightforward medical model in terms of its goals for change and in terms of who is responsible for change. **Self-management** programs (e.g., Hadjistavropoulos, 2012; Hanson & Gerber, 1990) make the patient with chronic pain the one with the major responsibility for making the change rather than the doctor or the health professional staff. These programs have fewer side effects because psychological changes—ways of thinking and behaving—are emphasized over the use of medications. In most cases, physicians refer patients to such programs only after medications have been tried. Correspondingly, there is less use of physical procedures and medication and more use of cognitive-behavioral change.

These programs focus on many different elements of the pain experience: the emotional, cognitive, and sensory experiences of pain; the behaviors and actions influenced by pain; and the social consequences of pain, such as the balance of work and play, daily physical activity, and interactions with the social environment. The patient is trained to attend to and modify many of the cognitive processes that can influence pain perception as discussed earlier, for example: the focus of attention, memories of previous experiences with pain and events related to the pain condition, perceived coping alternatives, expectations regarding impact of chronic pain on well-being, and attitudes and beliefs regarding oneself and others. The main goals of such programs are to

1. provide skill training to divert attention away from pain;
2. improve physical condition (via physical reconditioning);
3. increase daily physical activity;

4. provide ways to cope more effectively with episodes of intense pain (without medication);
5. provide skills to manage depression, anger, and aggression; and
6. decrease tension, anxiety, stressful life demands, and interpersonal conflict.

After an intensive interview, staff evaluate pain and pain behaviors and take a medical history. The medical staff then assesses the patient's functional status, such as his or her actual physical, emotional, and mental status. The patient and staff together develop program goals, and the patient signs a contract agreeing to work toward the goals. The specific components include some medication but are primarily geared toward patient education. The patient gets skills training, learns relaxation, and learns how to change maladaptive cognitions and maladaptive behaviors (like poor nutritional habits). Finally, the program includes relapse prevention and follow up.

Pain is something that we all will experience at some point in our lives. There are a number of different ways that we can cope with pain, and our cultural backgrounds may favor some over others. Given the complexity and the potential severity of the pain experience, the more ways that you know about how to cope with pain, the better off you will be.

APPLICATION SHOWCASE

A HOSPITAL CASE STUDY

Pain assessment is a growing focus in hospitals around America (IOM, 2011). In this chapter we discussed many physiological and psychological ways that pain is managed, but what do patients actually use? This section will give you a view from the ground up and will discuss a clinical assessment of patient satisfaction with pain management and the varying preferences for different types of pain management.

Many hospitals pay close attention to how successful they are in helping patients cope with pain. In Green Bay, Wisconsin, there are three major nonprofit hospitals, and representatives from each hospital gather once a month to evaluate how pain is being treated. This Pain and Comfort Team (PACT) reviews the latest research on pain management and holds training sessions for health-care professionals to pass on new information. PACT also periodically assesses patient satisfaction with pain treatment (Triest-Robertson, 2011). This description of one of their studies provides a rich picture of what patients go through in a hospital (Triest-Robertson, Gurung, Brosig, Whitfield, & Pfutzenreuter, 2001).

Patients in short-term stay, postsurgery wards, and a cancer ward completed a short one-page questionnaire either before leaving the hospital or at home. Together 445 patients participated in the study. The questionnaire asked what patients' worst pain experience was, how often this pain was experienced, and which of a number of pain relief methods was used to cope with the pain. Patients were also asked how satisfied they were with the health-care professionals they interacted with.

The worst pain experienced by patients on a standard 10-point scale was 6.28. Of great pragmatic significance, location of completion of the questionnaires was a significant factor: satisfaction with pain management was

(Continued)

(Continued)

significantly higher when forms were completed in the hospital. Once patients went home, it is likely that their recollection of their experiences was not as fresh as when they were still in the hospital. Of course, the reason for the pain also made a difference. As you may expect, satisfaction with pain relief significantly differed by floor. Patients who were in short-term stay were the most satisfied with their pain management. The differences were significant even when controls were added for severity of pain (i.e., worst pain) and the number of times worst pain was experienced (both of these variables were significant factors).

So how do patients cope with pain? People use many different ways to cope with pain. The study found that although medication was the most commonly chosen pain relief method, with 50% of the respondents saying they used pills or morphine when they felt pain, a significant number of different methods were also used. Close to 20% of the patients also used prayer and relaxation, 14% used breathing techniques and other forms of distraction, and 8% used music. Which of these was the most effective? Although medications again came out a clear winner (8.9 on a 9-point scale with 9 being most relief), other forms of pain management were very effective as well. Relaxation and prayer were both rated 6.8, and breathing and distraction rated in the high 5s. Music was only rated a little more than 1.

The predictors of satisfaction with pain management also varied by floor. The most significant predictors of satisfaction were the number of times worst pain was experienced, how often patients were asked what their acceptable level of pain was, and how much control they perceived they had. Assessment studies such as this can provide hospitals with clear-cut ways to improve the services they provide and to decrease their patients' experiences of pain.

CHAPTER REVIEW

SUMMARY ▶▶

- Pain has physiological and psychological components and behavioral, cognitive, and affective states. Two of the largest cultural variations in pain are due to ethnicity and sex, both influenced by socialization. Females have lower thresholds and less tolerance for pain than males. When and how pain should be expressed varies among ethnic groups.
- Pain can be acute or chronic and can get worse with time or stay stable. It is measured by simple pictorial measures or by questionnaire. One of the most common questionnaire measures, the **McGill Pain Questionnaire,** assesses sensory, affective, and evaluative aspects of pain.
- Early theories of pain attributed causes to spiritual sources. Various models of pain have been formulated, ranging from the unidimensional specificity theory hypothesizing specialized receptors for pain to the heavily psychological pain-prone personality idea, which suggested that certain personality types were more likely to experience pain. The most commonly used theory is the gate control theory, which posits that pain can be modulated at the level of the spinal cord and can also be influenced by impulses coming from the brain.
- Four basic physiological processes critical to the experience of pain are transduction, transmission, modulation, and perception. Psychologically, classical conditioning, operant conditioning, and observational learning can influence pain.
- Some ways to relieve pain include counterirritation, transcutaneous electrical nerve stimulation, and stimulation-produced analgesia.
- A range of physiological and psychological treatments are available. Physiological treatments include the use of medication, acupuncture, and surgery. Psychological treatments include distraction, hypnosis, biofeedback, relaxation, guided imagery, and progressive muscle relaxation.
- The management of chronic pain often calls for additional techniques. The most common are self-management programs for pain in which patients are empowered to control their experiences to alleviate their pain.

TEST YOURSELF ▶▶

Check your understanding of the topics in this chapter by answering the following questions.

1. Pain or nociception can best be defined as
   a. the activation of nerve fibers signaling tissue damage.
   b. the activation of specific sensory areas of the brain.
   c. being hurt in body or spirit.
   d. experiencing severe physical or psychological discomfort.

2. There are many cultural variations in the experience of pain. These differences are primarily due to
   a. genetics.
   b. age.
   c. socialization.
   d. tolerance.

3. There is evidence for sex differences at ________ level of the experience of pain.
   a. the biological
   b. the psychological
   c. the social
   d. every

4. The bulk of the clinical research done on ethnic differences in pain has compared
   a. Asian Americans with African Americans.
   b. Asian Americans with European Americans.
   c. Latinos with European Americans.
   d. African Americans with European Americans.

5. As we grow older,
   a. our threshold for pain decreases.
   b. our threshold for pain increases.
   c. our tolerance increases.
   d. we report pain less.

6. Pain experienced with diseases such as cancer is classified as
   a. acute.
   b. chronic malignant.
   c. chronic sensory.
   d. acute malignant.

7. There are many distinct processes critical to the experience of pain. ________takes place at the level of the receptors where the nerve impulses are stimulated.
   a. Transmission
   b. Transduction
   c. Modulation
   d. Perception

8. One of the pain questionnaire measures is the
   a. Rosenberg Pain scale.
   b. Melzack and Wall self-diagnosis scale.
   c. Turk Pain Report.
   d. McGill Pain Questionnaire.

9. One of the novel features of gate control theory is the presence of a(n) ________ that modulates the experience of pain at the level of the spinal cord.
   a. neurochemical
   b. interneuron
   c. hormone
   d. trigger gland

10. Activities such as prolonged physical activity and even meditation have been shown to release ________into our system, which are accompanied by pain relief.
    a. opiates
    b. opioids
    c. oeretonin
    d. cortisol

KEY TERMS, CONCEPTS, AND PEOPLE ▶▶

acute, **261**
afferent fibers, **262**
chronic, **261**
counterirritation, **271**
diathesis-stress model, **269**
efferent pathways, **271**
gate control theory (GCT), **270**

ESSENTIAL READINGS

Audette, J. F., & Bailey, A. (Eds.) (2008). *Integrative pain medicine: The science and practice of complementary and alternative medicine in pain management*. Totowa, NJ: Humana Press.

Day, M. (2019). Chronic pain. In T. A. Revenson & R. A. R. Gurung (Eds.), *Handbook of health psychology* (3e). New York, NY: Routledge.

Dixon, K. E. (2016). Pain and pain behaviors. In Y. Benyamini, M. Johnston, & E. C. Karademas (Eds.), *Assessment in health psychology* (pp. 147–159). Boston, MA: Hogrefe.

Melzack, R., & Wall, P. D. (1965). Pain mechanisms: A new theory. *Science, 150*(3699), 971–979.

iStockphoto.com/ it:PeopleImages

CHAPTER 11

CHRONIC ILLNESS, TERMINAL ILLNESS, AND DEATH

Chapter 11 Outline

MEASURING UP

HOW SATISFIED ARE YOU WITH LIFE?

Below are five statements that you may agree or disagree with. Using the 1–7 scale below, indicate your agreement with each item by placing the appropriate number on the line preceding that item. Please be open and honest in your responding. See Diener et al. 1985, for an interpretation of your score.

- 7 - Strongly agree
- 6 - Agree
- 5 - Slightly agree
- 4 - Neither agree nor disagree
- 3 - Slightly disagree
- 2 - Disagree
- 1 - Strongly disagree

____ In most ways my life is close to my ideal.

____ The conditions of my life are excellent.

____ I am satisfied with my life.

____ So far I have gotten the important things I want in life.

____ If I could live my life over, I would change almost nothing.

Source: Diener, E., Emmons, R. A., Larsen, R. J., & Griffin, S. (1985). The satisfaction with life scale. *Journal of Personality Assessment, 49,* 71–75.

Colds, body aches, headaches, and fevers are temporary ailments that most of us suffer occasionally and none of us looks forward to. Unfortunately, not all illnesses are temporary or acute. A person can develop a chronic or long-term disease that persists for years. Some chronic diseases may even be terminal, such as cancer, diabetes, cardiovascular disease (CVD), and coronary heart disease (CHD). Most adults are affected by chronic illnesses and 70% die as a result of one (CDC, 2018).

The National Center for Chronic Disease Prevention and Health Promotion (2018) defines chronic diseases as those illnesses that are preventable and that pose a significant burden in mortality, morbidity, and cost. The term "disease" is defined here as an objective and definable

▼ Ponder This

> What do you think are the most common reasons people die?
>
> In what ways can your family and neighborhood influence the development of a chronic illness?
>
> How do you think religious beliefs and health interact?

process characterized by physiological symptoms (Sperry, 2006). The term "disease" is often used interchangeably with the term "illness," which is more commonly defined as the subjective experience of a disease state. Health psychology focuses on the treatment of **chronic illnesses** and subjective experiences of chronic diseases.

Acute diseases often have a single cause, are treatable with single or limited biological intervention, and are usually curable. Chronic diseases in their advanced states rarely have cures and may flare up and die down over time. Back pain may be acute or chronic; arthritis is usually chronic. Biopsychosocial interventions are commonly used to help adjustment to chronic illnesses (Hoyt & Stanton, 2019).

Some chronic illnesses occur early in life, such as asthma (see Chapter 4 for more on asthma), and last for a lifetime. Others, such as cancers, may strike at any age. Most chronic illnesses are accompanied by some physiological, psychological, and social changes for the individual, and culture influences the ways of coping with these illnesses (Cho & Lu, 2017; Cillessen, van de Van, & Karremans, 2017). There are differences in how men and women cope, in how the old and the young cope, and in how different ethnic and religious groups cope. In this chapter, we focus on some of the common topics surrounding chronic illnesses. How do you react when you find out you have a chronic illness? What does having a chronic illness do to your life? What can you do to cope? How do different people cope?

Though often referred to collectively, there is great variation within each type of chronic disease. For example, there are many different types of cancer, such as lung, breast, and prostate cancer, and the biological and psychological correlates of one type may not be the same for another. Chronic illnesses also vary in other ways. It may be a **progressive illness**—an illness that becomes worse with time—or a **remitting illness**—one that diminishes with time and ends. Treatments can vary in duration and invasiveness and the extent to which they interrupt daily life. Some treatments may require hospital admittance, while others may require only self-administered medications. Prognoses vary, and more and more chronic diseases previously incurable are now curable. The pain from a chronic disease and the side effects of treatment often vary tremendously from illness to illness and even from person to person (with the same illness). Consequently, the clinician needs to consider many different biopsychosocial factors when trying to understand how people cope with and adjust to chronic illnesses.

RunStudio/ Digital Vision/ Getty Images

▲ **Back Pain.** Back pain is one of the most commonly reported chronic pains.

PREVALENCE OF CHRONIC ILLNESSES

What are the most common chronic illnesses? Historically, some evidence suggests most people died relatively young. Archaeological evidence suggests the main causes of death were predation by animals and other hostile humans. There were few, if any, chronic illnesses. Most illnesses resulting from viruses or bacteria were short-lived simply because there were few cures for them—if you got sick, you died. During the Roman Empire (around A.D. 100), **life expectancy** was between 22 and 25 years. Recent estimates, shown in Table 11.1, suggest that Western women born in 2010 will live about 81 years and men will live about 76 years (*National Vital Statistics Reports,* 2016). This is a big change even when compared to only 100 years ago: women born in 1900 lived on average 48.3 years and men lived 46.3 years. This change in life expectancy is largely due to the immense improvements in medicine that can postpone death. However, we do not all have the same life expectancy: Table 11.1 shows dramatic ethnic differences in life expectancies both by sex and by ethnicity throughout the years. African American and European American men's and women's life expectancies changed over time, and both groups have different life expectancies today. There is also a significant sex difference—women live on average 5 years longer than men. Science has yet to explain this fact. The reasons may be that women give and receive more social support, may be biologically fitter, and engage in fewer risky behaviors.

Today, the major causes of death are heart disease, cancer, lower respiratory diseases, cerebrovascular diseases, and accidents (CDC, 2016). There are surprising statistics: more than 83 million Americans have a CVD (the total population of the United States is 327 million; U.S. Census, n.d.); 76 million Americans have high blood pressure; nearly 7 million Americans have had strokes (American Heart Association, 2018), and 12 million men and women have some type of cancer (Jemal et al., 2017). Diabetes, an illness that can hasten the onset of CVDs, is a common chronic illness with more than 18 million Americans estimated to have either type 1

▼ TABLE 11.1

Life Expectancy across Age, Race, and Sex, Selected Years Final 2009 and Preliminary 2010, United States

	All races[1]		White[2]		Black[2]	
Measure and sex	2010	2009	2010	2009	2010	2009
All deaths	2,465,936	2,437,163	2,112,458	2,086,355	286,800	286,623
Male	1,231,215	1,217,379	1,050,382	1,037,475	145,731	146,239
Female	1,234,721	1,219,784	1,062,076	1,048,880	141,068	140,384
Age-adjusted death rate[3,4]	746.2	749.6	741.0	742.8	897.7	912.7
Male	886.2	890.9	877.5	880.5	1,103.4	1,123.1
Female	634.3	636.8	630.1	631.3	752.0	763.3
Life expectancy at birth (years)[5]	78.7	78.6	79.0	78.8	75.1	74.7
Male	76.2	76.0	76.5	76.4	71.8	71.4
Female	81.1	80.9	81.3	81.2	78.0	77.7
All infant deaths	24,548	26,412	15,933	16,817	7,388	8,312
Infant morality rate[6]	6.14	6.39	5.19	5.30	11.61	12.64

[Data based on a continuous file of records received from the states. Figures for 2010 are based on weighted data rounded to the nearest individual, so categories may not add to totals]

1Includes races other than White and Black.
2Race categories are consistent with 1977 Office of Management and Budget (OMB) standards. Multiple-race data were reported for deaths by 37 states and the District of Columbia in 2010 and by 34 states and the District of Columbia in 2009, and were reported for births (used as the denominator in computing infant mortality rates by 38 states and the District of Columbia in 2010 and by 33 states and the District of Columbia in 2009. Multiple-race data for these reporting areas were bridged to single-race categories of the 1977 OMB standards for comparability with other reporting areas.
3Rates for 2009 are revised and may differ from rates previously published.
4Per 100,000 U.S. standard population, based on the year 2000 standard.
5Life expectancies for 2009 have been updated and may differ from those previously published.
6Deaths under age 1 year per 1,000 live births in specified group.

Source: Adapted from Table A page 3. http://www.cdc.gov/nchs/data/nvsr/nvsr60/nvsr60_04.pdf.

▼ FIGURE 11.1

Projected Levels of Major Chronic Diseases by the Year 2023

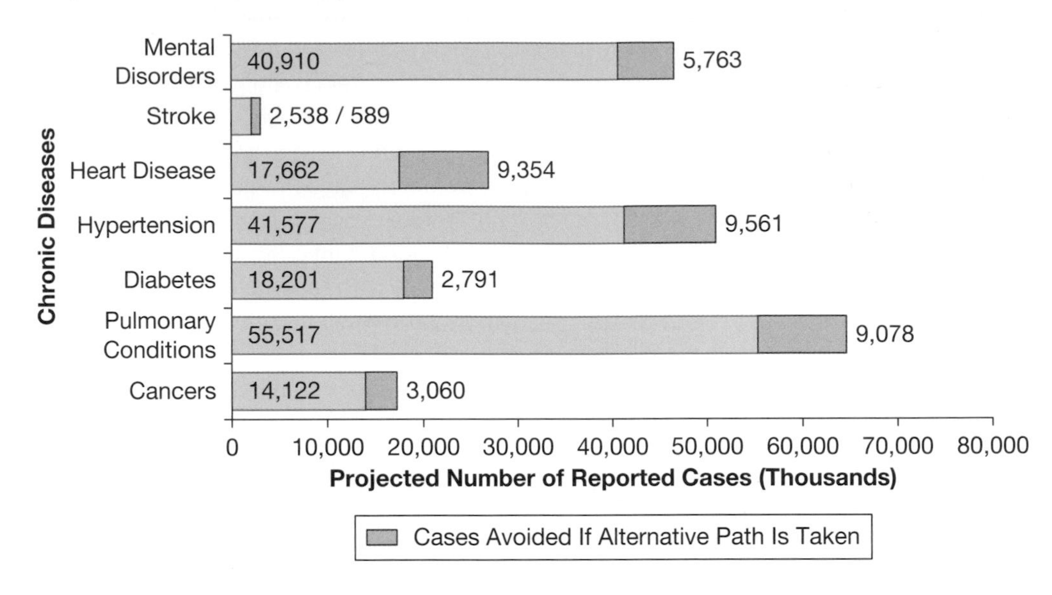

Source: Data retrieved from the Milken Institute.

> **Synthesize, Evaluate, Apply**
>
> - What are the most common chronic illnesses?
> - What sociocultural factors explain the most common causes of death and chronic illness?
> - How do chronic illnesses vary?

or type 2 diabetes (American Heart Association, 2018). In fact, heart disease and stroke account for approximately 65% of deaths due to diabetes (CDC, 2018). The prognosis is dim. Figure 11.1 shows the projected levels of major chronic diseases by the year 2023.

COPING WITH CHRONIC ILLNESSES

Improving one's diet, refraining from smoking, and consuming minimal alcoholic beverages (see Chapter 7) may help prevent chronic illnesses, but do not guarantee avoiding these illnesses.

Goals of Treatment

Before we discuss how one can cope with having a chronic illness, it is important to consider some goals for treatment. Science has made many advances in the treatment of cancer and HIV infection, and some research suggests that illnesses such as CHD and diabetes can be reversed (e.g., Campbell & Campbell, 2016; Ornish et al., 1998); however, we still cannot cure these illnesses. Therefore, helping people cope with having these illnesses becomes very important. Health psychologists have studied different forms of adjustment to chronic illness (Hoyt, 2019). Five major forms of adjustment are the successful performance of daily tasks, the absence of psychological disorders, low levels of negative affect and high levels of positive affect, good functional status, and the experience of satisfaction in different areas of life (Stanton, Collins, & Sworowski, 2001). Of all of these, the most common psychological outcome studied is the quality of life (Morgan & McGee, 2016).

Quality of Life

The most commonly used measure of how someone is coping with a chronic illness is a measure of his or her **quality of life** (QOL). Sometimes called health-related quality of life (HRQOL) or discussed as **well-being**, the past 40 years has seen an upsurge in research on QOL (Morgan & McGee, 2016). QOL features prominently in the study of how patients cope with diseases and is important for planning further treatment (Brodsky, Spritzer, Hays, & Hui, 2017). QOL was originally a measure made by the physician, purely by whether the disease was present or absent. If the disease presence was strong, it was assumed that QOL would be low. It is now clear that patients are the best judges of their own QOL. Asking patients how much pain they are experiencing and how they feel (e.g., assessing depression and anxiety) is a valuable way to determine how well they are coping (Morrow, Hayen, Quine, Scheinberg, & Craig, 2012). Assess your own QOL with one of the most common measures of QOL (Table 11.2).

Quality of life includes several components. Similar to measures of adjustment, QOL includes a measure of physical status and functioning, psychological status, social functioning, and the presence of the disease- or treatment-related symptoms. As you can guess, using a patient's subjective view can be relative and, therefore, problematic. For example, a patient may compare a treatment progress and corresponding quality of life to another patient's and become discouraged. Nonetheless, QOL is still the primary measure of adjustment to chronic illnesses.

A wide array of measures assesses QOL. Figure 11.2 lists some of the major assessment tools, ranging from the generic to the specific, and separated by disease- or patient-specific types. In the age of the Internet can you Google for some? Yes indeed. The good news is you can find a number of credible collections of measures with accompanying psychometric information (Morgan & McGee, 2016). These include the Patient Reported Outcomes and Quality of Life Instruments database (PROQOLID; Emery, Perrier, & Acquadro, 2005), the On-Line Guide to Quality-of-Life Assessment database (OLGA; http://www.olga-qol.com), and Optum (http://www.optum.com).

Let's take a look at the different biological, psychological, and sociocultural factors that can influence QOL and adjustment.

BIOPSYCHOSOCIAL COMPONENTS OF ADJUSTMENT

Many of us will contract a chronic illness at some point in our lives. However, it is clear that changing health behaviors can greatly reduce the chance of contracting some chronic illnesses (LaCaille & Hooker, 2019; Mermelstein & Brikmanis, 2019). Furthermore, psychological strategies can help one cope with chronic illness. For example, in a longitudinal study of patients with inflammatory bowel disease and arthritis, patients who displayed gratitude were less depressed later in the study (Sirois & Wood, 2017). In fact, feeling grateful was a significant predictor of lowered depression even after controlling for other psychological variables such as illness cognitions discussed in Chapter 10. Similarly, two other psychological variables, optimism and hope, are strong aids to helping patients cope with chronic diseases (Schiavon, Marchetti, Gurgel, Busnello, & Reppold, 2017).

Adjustment to chronic illnesses has many different components. Patients need to cope with not only their own affect, behaviors, and cognitions concerning the illness but also with revising their lifestyles to accommodate the treatment and coping with how others in their social networks respond to them because of their illness (Day, 2019; Hoyt & Stanton, 2019). They may experience many different feelings including anxiety, depression, and frustration, and may not be able to perform common functions such as going to work or even shopping for their own groceries. It is critical for patients to integrate the illness into their life. However, it is easy for patients to be stressed by the illness (Chawla & Kafescioglu, 2012). Daily tasks, changing symptoms, and fluctuating emotions can be overwhelming (Emery, 2019). There are numerous challenges to the process of integration; successful self-management with psychosocial, vocational, and existential

▼ TABLE 11.2

The World Health Organization Quality of Life Brief Measure

The following questions ask how you feel about your quality of life, health, or other areas of your life. I will read out each question to you, along with the response options. **Please choose the answer that is most appropriate.** If you are unsure about which response to give to a question, the first response you think of is often the best one. Please keep in mind your standards, hopes, pleasures, and concerns. We ask that you think about your life **in the last four weeks.**					
	Very poor	**Poor**	**Neither poor nor good**	**Good**	**Very good**
1. How would you rate your quality of life?	1	2	3	4	5
	Very dissatisfied	**Dissatisfied**	**Neither satisfied nor dissatisfied**	**Satisfied**	**Very satisfied**
2. How satisfied are you with your health?	1	2	3	4	5
The following questions ask about **how much** you have experienced certain things in the past four weeks.					
	Not at all	**A little**	**A moderate amount**	**Very much**	**An extreme amount**
3. To what extent do you feel that physical pain prevents you from doing what you need to do?	5	4	3	2	1
4. How much do you need any medical treatment to function in your daily life?	5	4	3	2	1
5. How much do you enjoy life?	1	2	3	4	5
6. To what extent do you feel your life to be meaningful?	1	2	3	4	5
The following questions ask about how much you have experienced certain things **in the** past **four weeks.**					
	Not at all	**A little**	**A moderate amount**	**Very much**	**Extremely**
7. How well are you able to concentrate?	1	2	3	4	5
8. How safe do you feel in your daily life?	1	2	3	4	5
9. How healthy is your physical environment?	1	2	3	4	5
The following questions ask about how completely you experienced or were able to do certain things in the past four weeks.					
	Not at all	**A little**	**Moderately**	**Mostly**	**Completely**
10. Do you have enough energy for everyday life?	1	2	3	4	5
11. Are you able to accept your bodily appearance?	1	2	3	4	5
12. Have you enough money to meet your needs?	1	2	3	4	5
13. How available to you is the information that you need in your day-to-day life?	1	2	3	4	5
14. To what extent do you have the opportunity for leisure activities?	1	2	3	4	5
	Very poor	**Poor**	**Neither poor nor good**	**Good**	**Very good**
15. How well are you able to get around?	1	2	3	4	5

	Very dissatisfied	Dissatisfied	Neither satisfied nor dissatisfied	Satisfied	Very satisfied
16. How satisfied are you with your sleep?	**1**	**2**	**3**	**4**	**5**
17. How satisfied are you with your ability to perform your daily living activities?	**1**	**2**	**3**	**4**	**5**
18. How satisfied are you with your capacity for work?	**1**	**2**	**3**	**4**	**5**
19. How satisfied are you with yourself?	**1**	**2**	**3**	**4**	**5**
20. How satisfied are you with your personal relationships?	**1**	**2**	**3**	**4**	**5**
21. How satisfied are you with your sex life?	**1**	**2**	**3**	**4**	**5**
22. How satisfied are you with the support you get from your friends?	**1**	**2**	**3**	**4**	**5**
The following questions ask about how completely you experienced or were able to do certain things in the past four weeks.					
	Very dissatisfied	**Dissatisfied**	**Neither satisfied nor dissatisfied**	**Satisfied**	**Very satisfied**
23. How satisfied are you with the conditions of your living place?	**1**	**2**	**3**	**4**	**5**
24. How satisfied are you with your access to health services?	**1**	**2**	**3**	**4**	**5**
25. How satisfied are you with your transport?	**1**	**2**	**3**	**4**	**5**
The following question refers to how often you have felt or experienced certain things in the past four weeks.					
	Never	**Seldom**	**Quite often**	**Very often**	**Always**
26. How often do you have negative feelings such as blue mood, despair, anxiety, depression?	**1**	**2**	**3**	**4**	**5**

	Raw score	Transformed scores* 4–20	Transformed scores* 0–100
Equations for computing domain scores	**Raw score**	**4–20**	**0–100**
27. Domain 1 (6-Q3) + (6-Q4) + Q10 + Q15 + Q16 + Q17 + Q18 ☐ + ☐ + ☐ + ☐ + ☐ + ☐ + ☐	**a=**	**b:**	c:
28. Domain 2 Q5 + Q6 + Q7 + Q11 + Q19 + (6-Q26) ☐ + ☐ + ☐ + ☐ + ☐ + ☐	**a=**	**b:**	c:
29. Domain 3 Q20 + Q21 + Q22 ☐ + ☐ + ☐	**a=**	**b:**	c:
30. Domain 4 Q8 + Q9 + Q12 + Q13 + Q14 + Q23 + Q24 + Q25 ☐ + ☐ + ☐ + ☐ + ☐ + ☐ + ☐+ ☐	**a=**	**b:**	c:

*See Procedures Manual, pages 13–15.

Source: WHOQOL-BREF (December 1996) WHOQOL-BREF Introduction, Administration, Scoring and Generic Version of the Assessment. Geneva: World Health Organization. Retrieved from http://www.who.int/mental_health/media/en/76.pdf.

▼ FIGURE 11.2

Major Measures of Quality of Life

Type	Focus	Examples of assessment tools
Generic	Patient or general population groups	36-Item Short-Form Health Survey (SF-36; McHorney, Ware, Lu, & Sherbourne, 1994; McHorney, Ware, & Raczek, 1993; Ware & Sherbourne, 1992) Nottingham Health Profile (Hunt, McEwen, & McKenna, 1985; Hunt et al., 1980) The World Health Organization Quality of Life (WHOQOL) measure (MHOQOL Group, 1995) Functional Limitations Profile (Charlton, Patrick, Matthews, & West, 1981; Patrick, Peach, & Gregg, 1982)
Disease- or patient-specific	Particular group/ diagnosis	HeartQoL (Oldridge et al., 2014a, 2014b) Minnesota Living with Heart Failure Questionnaire (Rector, Kubo, & Cohn, 1987) Seattle Angina Questionnaire (Spertus et al., 1995)
Dimension-specific	Particular component of QoL	Global Mood Scale (Denollet, 1993; Denollet & Brutsaert, 1995) Hospital Anxiety and Depression Scale (Zigmond & Snaith, 1983) The Beck Depression Inventory (BDI; Beck, Steer, Ball, & Ranieri, 1996; Beck, Ward, Mendelson, Mock, & Erbaugh, 1961)
Individual	Aspects of life determined by the individual	Schedule for the Evaluation of Individual Quality of Life (SEIQoL; Hickey et al., 1996; McGee, O'Boyle, Hickey, O'Malley, & Joyce, 1991; O'Boyle McGee, Hickey, O'Malley, & Joyce, 1992) Patient Generated Index (Ruta, Garratt, Leng, Russell, & MacDonald, 1994)
Utility	Hierarchy of preferences of a particular group	EuroQoL (EQ-SD; Dolan, 1997; Kind, 1996; Shaw, Johnson, & Coons, 2005) Health Utilities Index (Feeny et al., 2002; Horsman, Furlong, Feeny, & Torrance, 2003; Torrance et al., 1996)

support is critical. Next, I will discuss some of the different components of adjustment using the major approaches in health psychology.

Biological Issues

Biologically, different chronic illnesses will have different courses. For example, coronary heart disease (CHD) and cancer, the two leading causes of death for Americans, inflict significant changes in the body. Cancer causes cells to grow uncontrollably, harming surrounding tissue and limiting normal function. In CHD, the blood vessels around the heart are clogged with plaque and fat, changing blood flow and possibly leading to a heart attack. Other chronic illnesses such as diabetes and asthma similarly have physiological correlates, such as changes in insulin sensitivity and the blocking of breathing channels (Kalyva, Eiser, & Papathanasiou, 2016). The slow physiological changes limit functioning in many areas and are often accompanied by pain (Hoyt & Stanton, 2012). Consequently, physical rehabilitation is a big component of any treatment of chronic illnesses. The loss of function and increase in pain also have major consequences for how the patient views the world, and psychological issues need to be considered as well.

Psychological Issues

Psychological Aspects of Coping There has been growing interest in the role of psychological factors in adjustment to chronic illnesses (Samson & Siam, 2008). In a review of both theoretical and empirical literature on adjusting to chronic illnesses, Stanton et al. (2001) identified two key multidimensional psychological aspects. First, the individual has to go through an adjustment, which includes cognitive aspects such as intrusive thoughts and changing views of the self, emotional aspects such as depression and anxiety, and behavioral and physical aspects such as dealing with pain or not being able to perform daily activities. Second, the sick person must make interpersonal adjustments, negotiating personal relationships with friends and family as well as professional relationships with health-care providers. Positive adjustment includes the mastery of illness-related tasks, the absence of a psychological disorder and negative feelings, perceptions of high quality of life, and the maintenance of adequate functional status and social roles (Hoyt & Stanton, 2019).

Perhaps one of the most effective psychological resources that a person with a chronic illness has is his or her mental approach to the situation and **appraisals** (see Chapter 5, Lazarus & Folkman, 1984). Patients' primary and secondary appraisals of the illness can correspondingly influence how they fare. If the illness is seen as a challenge (primary appraisal) and they believe they have a lot of social support to cope with it (secondary appraisal), they will probably have a higher QOL (Gatchel & Oordt, 2003b). For example, in a study of colorectal cancer-specific concerns in a population-based sample of colorectal cancer survivors, patients' threat appraisals significantly predicted their quality of life up to 2 years after treatment (Steginga, Lynch, Hawkes, Dunn, & Aitken, 2009).

A number of health psychologists have modified cognitive appraisal theory from its original context (i.e., stress) and have adapted it to help explain coping with chronic illnesses such as arthrit, is breast cancer, prostate cancer, and AIDS (Merz et al., 2011; Schwartz & Rapkin, 2012). In fact, new work teases apart appraisals from personality factors. The Quality of Life Appraisal Profile–Version 2 (QOLAPv2) helps assess individual differences and is useful in explaining why people experiencing very different health states may report the same QOL (Rapkin, Garcia, Michael, Zhang, & Schwartz, 2017). First developed with 4,173 respondents, the QOLAPv2 is useful across populations and provides better predictions of QOL than measures of personality alone.

Psychological Responses to Chronic Illness There are some common psychological responses to chronic illnesses (Martire & Schulz, 2012). **Denial** is one of the psychological reactions first felt the moment a person is informed that he or she has a chronic illness. The person may feel unbalanced and consciously or unconsciously attempt to block out reality and the implications of the test. Denial may be beneficial for a very short period early in the process because it reduces anxiety, but it is harmful in the long term because it decreases adherence to treatment and is associated with delays in reporting and seeking treatment. You can measure denial in this context with the Illness Denial Questionnaire (IDQ; Ferrario et al., 2017). The IDQ is a 24-item true/false measuring three major subcomponents: denial of negative emotions, resistance to change, and conscious avoidance.

iStockphoto.com/ fstop123

▲ **Physical Therapy.** Physical therapy is an important part of coping with the biological aspects of chronic illnesses, but mobility can influence the psychosocial aspects as well.

Another common psychological reaction to a positive test result or even experiencing symptoms of a chronic illness is **anxiety**. Anxiety interferes with healthy functioning, causing a person to cope poorly and to delay the recognition and reporting of symptoms. Anxiety is often high when the patient is waiting for test results, receiving a diagnosis, and awaiting invasive medical procedures. Not knowing about the course of the illness or not having enough information about what the illness entails is especially anxiety provoking. Such lack of information-induced anxiety is more pronounced in populations of lower SES and in some ethnic groups.

The most common negative reaction to a chronic illness is **depression** (Giardini et al., 2017). Depression can be either biological or psychological in nature and often goes undiagnosed because its symptoms are shadowed by the symptoms of the chronic illness. Unlike anxiety, depression tends to be a long-term reaction and increases as pain and disability increase. When patients get depressed, they are less motivated to cope actively with the illness, tend to interpret any bodily change negatively, and sometimes even commit or attempt suicide.

The form of psychological reaction varies also depending on the illness and varies considerably across individuals with the same illness. Personality factors, the amount of social support one receives or perceives to have, and cultural beliefs surrounding the illness can all influence coping with the illness and can alleviate depression and anxiety. Chapter 6 included details about the ways different personalities influence coping. The same relationships that link stress and coping link chronic illnesses and coping.

The Big Five personality variables (conscientiousness, agreeableness, neuroticism, openness to experience, and extroversion; see Chapter 6) have been linked to coping in general (Smith, 2019) and coping with chronic illnesses in particular (Sirois, 2015). Similarly, being high in positive affect is also a good thing for those with chronic illnesses. Positive affect was significantly associated with having a lower risk of dying from any cause (i.e., all cause mortality) in people with diabetes (Moskowitz, Epel, & Acree, 2008). In a study of the role of religious involvement, spirituality, and physical/emotional functioning in a sample of African American men and women with cancer, positive affect was a key factor in predicting better adjustment (Holt et al., 2011).

Optimism is another powerful personality characteristic in coping with chronic illnesses (Giardini et al., 2017). Carver et al. (1993) first demonstrated convincingly the role of optimism in women coping with breast cancer. When measured before surgery, the optimistic women were those using more active coping and facing the disease, and those with less distress. This pattern held for three further assessments at 3, 6, and 12 months after surgery.

Optimism is also helpful in coping with diabetes mellitus, rheumatoid arthritis, and multiple sclerosis (Fournier, de Ridder, & Bensing, 2002), breast cancer (Sohl et al., 2012), coronary bypass surgery (Tindle et al., 2012), and HIV infection (Peterson, Miner, Brennan, & Rosser, 2012). Building optimism can go a long way. For example, falling, common in older chronically ill adults, predicts poorer physical health and greater negative emotions among the group (Ruthig, Chipperfield, Newall, Perry, & Hall, 2007). Falling also causes drops in optimism, which mediates the effects of falling on health and well-being. Recovery from falling can be enhanced by bolstering optimism (Ruthig et al., 2007). In general, different personality characteristics can greatly help coping (Smith, 2019).

Another important component of psychological coping is related to how patients compare themselves with others with the disease and how much meaning they derive from the illness. For example, studies on upward and downward social comparison show that people can sometimes compare themselves with those better off than they are ("Boy, my coworker has the same problem, and he is doing so much better than I am") or worse off than themselves ("Oh, at least I am doing better than my neighbor who has the same illness"). Women who cope better with breast cancer make comparisons with people who are inferior or less fortunate than they are to enhance their own self-esteem (Wood, Taylor, & Lichtman, 1985). Chinese women facing breast cancer were also found to make the best of it. The essences of Chinese women's experiences were that they faced the reality of the cancer diagnosis, took an active part in the cancer treatment, sustained an optimistic spirit, maintained physical activity, reflected, and then moved on (Fu, Xu, Liu, & Haber, 2008).

Finding meaning in your illness can often be beneficial, leading to lower mortality and morbidity (Hooker, Masters, & Park, 2018), but in some cases it can be detrimental to well-being as well. Originally, research documented that finding meaning in your experience can lead to positive well-being and better adjustment to the disease (Taylor, 1983). There are some important qualifications to this early finding. Tomich and Helgeson (2004) examined the consequences of finding meaning (they called it benefit finding) on QOL in 364 women diagnosed with stage I, II, or III breast cancer. Benefit finding and QOL were measured 4 months postdiagnosis (Tl), 3 months after Tl (T2), and 6 months after T2 (T3). Women with lower socioeconomic status, minority women, and those with more severe levels of the disease perceived more benefits at baseline. Benefit finding was associated with more negative affect at baseline and also interacted with the stage of disease, such that negative relationships to QOL across time were limited to those with more severe disease. Findings suggest that there are qualifiers as to whether finding something good in the bad is, in itself, good or bad (Yanez, Stanton, Hoyt, Tennen, & Lechner, 2011). We discuss this further in Chapter 13.

Synthesize, Evaluate, Apply

- Evaluate the main goals of treatment. Should there be more?
- Why is it important to have a valid and reliable measure of quality of life?
- How do the main biopsychosocial components of adjustment to chronic illness compare with the factors for adjustment to stress? Identify the similarities and differences.
- How do you think different personality characteristics (e.g., optimism) will change how one reacts to a chronic illness?

CULTURE AND CHRONIC ILLNESS

A person's sociocultural environment has many implications for how he or she copes with chronic illnesses. Jose, who lives with a large extended Mexican American family, is going to cope with a diagnosis of cancer differently from how Joshua copes, who lives alone and far away from his European American family. Jessica, a devout Catholic, may face breast cancer very differently from Carmel, an agnostic. Friends, family, and society can make a big difference in how one copes. If you get a chronic illness that is disdained in society, you are likely to be discriminated against for having the disease, and this discrimination can negatively influence your ability to cope with it.

Family and Neighborhoods

The environment in which you live can accentuate a disease or help control it (Gurung et al., 2004). Stressful events influence anxiety levels, thereby influencing adjustment to the disease (Lepore & Evans, 1996). In a major review of the ways that sociocultural factors can affect a patient, Taylor, Repetti, and Seeman (1997) traced the different ways that unhealthy environments—stressful work or family situations, living in a neighborhood with a high crime rate, being unemployed, or having multiple chronic burdens—can reduce social support and hurt adaptation to illness. As shown in Figure 11.3 each of these different elements plays a role in influencing perceptions and the availability of coping resources.

The importance of social factors such as the family and community structures increases when the person with the chronic illness is a child (Lyon et al., 2011). For example, the family dynamics can change significantly when a child is diagnosed with diabetes. Some families become more protective and controlling when an adolescent has diabetes (if you thought an early curfew was bad when you were young, imagine your parents wanting complete control over what you eat and drink). In such situations, families may get overtaxed and summon help from the extended family, neighbors, or the community. The neighborhood may be key as a supportive community is proven to be advantageous (Waverijn, Heijmans, & Groenewegen, 2017).

▼ FIGURE 11.3

Various Aspects of Our Environments Can Influence How We Cope with Chronic Illnesses

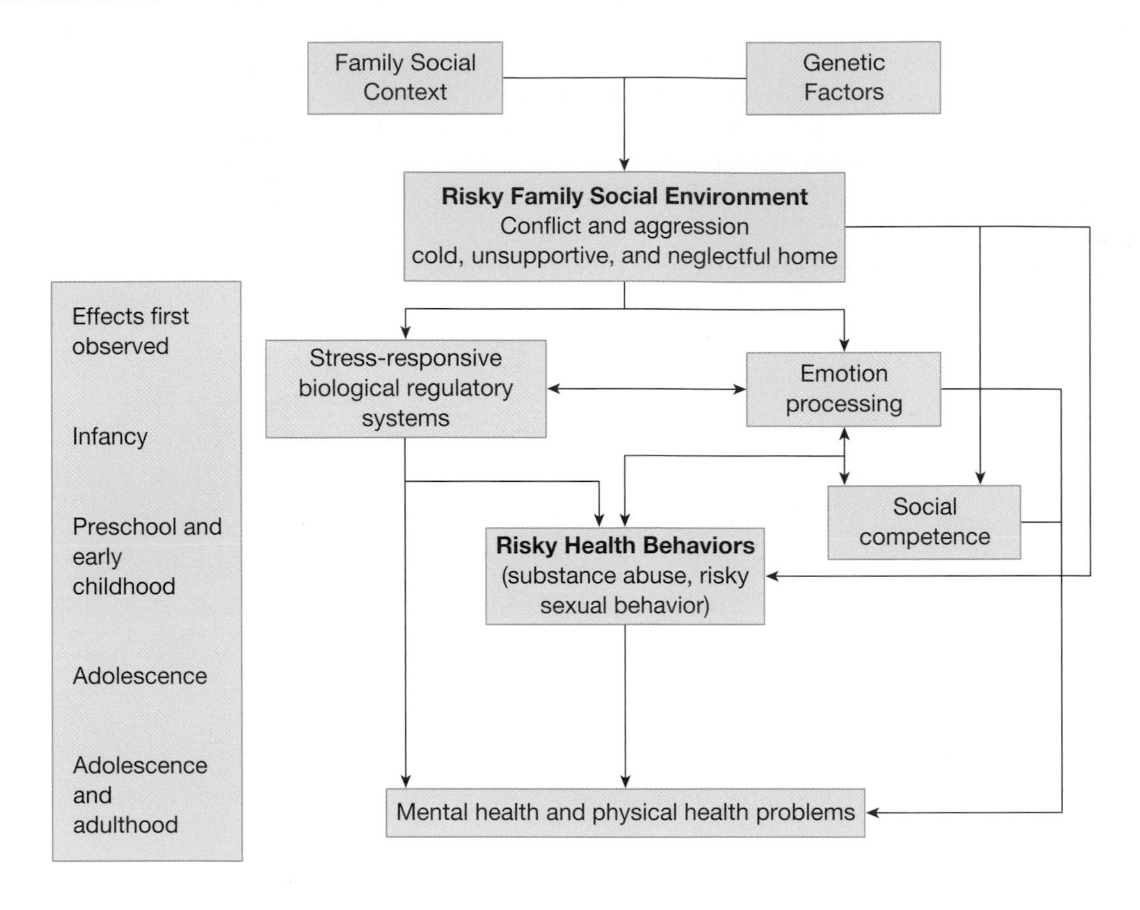

Statistics show that adolescents living in dangerous neighborhoods are more susceptible to engaging in risky behaviors, hence accentuating the course of their chronic illnesses (Obeidallah et al., 2001).

The composition of a family can vary. Each form of family described below relates to a different family environment and can influence family members' coping with chronic illnesses. The **nuclear family** usually consists of a female mother, a male father, and unmarried children. Nuclear families account for approximately 25% of the different types of families in North America. The **blended family** consists of two parents, either or both of whom may have been previously married, with their children. The **extended family** consists of a blended or nuclear family plus grandparents or grandchildren, aunts, uncles, and other relatives. Some ethnic groups are more likely to have extended families living together than others. For example, 31% of African American families are extended versus 20% of other ethnic groups. Some ethnic groups and some religions also include *fictive kin* in the basic family unit. Many Catholic Mexican Americans (and other Catholics) have godparents—close friends of the family who serve as the children's additional caregivers. You may also hear about a **broken family**, consisting of divorced parent living with kids.

Families that argue and in which relationships are cold, unsupportive, and neglectful are referred to as **risky families** (Repetti et al., 2002). Biology and social environments interact as negative family characteristics (such as abuse, aggression, or conflict) create vulnerabilities that interact with genetically based vulnerabilities and can negatively impact chronic illnesses. Specifically, someone growing up in a risky family can actually show differences in their genes.

In one recent longitudinal study of nearly 300 adolescents, researchers followed the participants for 5 years and mapped early negative family relationships onto later genes. Testing blood samples showed risky family processes related to more negative emotions and shorter telomeres in genes (Brody, Yu, & Shalev, 2017).

SES and ethnicity also play key roles. Families living below the poverty line are more likely to live in high-crime areas where the risks to children increase and the accessibility to health-care services decreases. The connection between these different variables can be seen in intergenerational links between mothers and children with PTSD (Linares & Cloitre, 2004). Some psychologists study whether one type of family is better than another. Particular attention has been paid to families with same-sex parents (two male or two female parents) and single-parent families. At present, no clear evidence suggests that either of these two types of families is unhealthy for children (Frost & Svensson, 2019).

Chronic Illness and Ethnicity

Your cultural environment is important as well. The experience and outcomes of an illness are shaped by cultural factors that influence how it is perceived, labeled, and explained, and how the experience is valued (Broadbent, 2019). For example, African Americans with chronic illness have poorer outcomes than European Americans in the United States (Lederer et al., 2008). Therefore, we actually learn ways of being ill that depend on our cultural backgrounds (see Chapter 3). Someone coming from a self-reliant farm family may be taught to downplay illness and put on a brave face and keep on working. Someone else who grew up in a city may be more likely to follow the complete bed rest prescriptions of a doctor.

Both the patients' and the providers' cultural approaches to the source of disease and illness affect patients' care-seeking behavior and treatment opinions, choices, and compliance (Turner, 1996). In the past few years, practitioners have been sensitized to the role of cultural factors, especially acculturation, in rates of life-threatening chronic illnesses. For example, when treating migrants, practitioners are now more aware of casual factors of illnesses such as having to deal with changing diets and stress from their new environment, stressors that often lead to certain diseases like obesity and prostate cancer (Jasso, Massey, Rosenzweig, & Smith, 2004). There is also extensive research on the role of linguistic competency (e.g., Ngo-Metzger et al., 2003) and ethnic match of patient and practitioner in coping with chronic illnesses (e.g., Tarn et al., 2005; see Chapter 9 for more on this topic).

Some cultural groups react to chronic illnesses differently from others (Galanti, 2014). Many collectivist groups see chronic illnesses as something that an entire family or community, not just the individual, has to cope with. In the last section of Chapter 9, we discussed how the Hmong family rallied around the sick child with epilepsy and endured personal hardships to take care of her. There are similar cultural patterns across different religious and ethnic groups. For example, many church groups have organized programs to take care of chronically ill worshippers.

Are there cultural differences in how ethnic groups cope with specific illnesses? Research in this area is growing. For example, Culver, Arena, Wimberly, Antoni, and Carver (2004) tested for differences in coping responses in middle-class African American, Latinas, and European American women with early stage breast cancer. They found only two differences in coping (controlling for medical variables, education, and distress). Compared with European American women, the other two groups both reported using humor-based coping less and religion-based coping more. There was one difference in how coping related to distress: Venting related more strongly to elevated distress among Latinas than among non-Latinas (Culver et al., 2004).

Religion (as seen in coping with breast cancer) plays a key role in understanding cultural differences in coping with chronic illnesses (Park & Carney, 2019). Spirituality in particular plays an especially strong role in the self-management of chronic illness among older women (Harvey, 2008). In a study directly testing the role of religion in coping with pain and psychological adjustment, Abraido-Lanza, Vasquez, and Echeverria (2004) found that Latinos with arthritis reported using high levels of religious coping. Further analysis indicated that religious coping was correlated with active but not passive coping and directly related to psychological well-being. Passive coping was associated with greater pain and worse adjustment. Findings such as this, together with similar work in other ethnic groups, such as African American (Holt et al., 2011), suggest that interventions and community-based outreach approaches should embrace an appreciation for expressions and experiences of spirituality for both patients and caregivers.

The cultural group's beliefs about health and illness are important as well (Arellano & Sosa, 2018). For many chronic medical problems, a patient's coping behaviors and adherence to treatment will depend on the quality of the patient–practitioner interaction (see Chapter 8). Some earlier studies suggest that patients whose beliefs favor folk medicine are healthier when they seek treatment from folk healers rather than biomedical doctors (Kleinman, Eisenberg, & Good, 1978; Mehl-Medrona, 1998; also see Chapter 3). This could be because of the corresponding belief systems as well as the relative closeness in social class between patient and practitioner. In other cases, it may be because the doctor's own cultural identity may influence how he or she treats a patient from a similar culture (Gurung & Mehta, 2001). In many folk and traditional medical systems, a greater emphasis is also placed on communication, which can increase patient satisfaction and adherence to treatment.

Prejudice and discrimination account for many negative outcomes for certain cultural groups. Lederer et al. (2008) conducted a retrospective cohort study of 280 non-Hispanic African American and 5,272 non-Hispanic European American adults age 40 years and older with chronic obstructive pulmonary disease (COPD). The patients were listed for lung transplantation in the United States between 1995 and 2004. After listing for lung transplantation, African American patients were less likely to undergo transplantation and more likely to die or to be removed from the list compared with the non-Hispanic European American patients. Unequal access to care may have contributed to these differences. African Americans in the study were more likely to have pulmonary hypertension, to be obese and diabetic, to lack private health insurance, and to live in poorer neighborhoods.

▲ **Hospital Chapel.** Many hospitals have chapels such as the one shown here. Caregivers can come and pray for their loved ones and even patients who are too sick to go to church can go say a prayer.

Social Support

The most research conducted in sociocultural factors of chronically ill patients is in social support (Knoll, Scholz, & Bitzen, 2019). Empirical studies and reviews show that people with more social support have more positive adjustment to chronic illnesses. Illnesses studied ranged from cancer (Rogers, Mitchell, Franta, Foster, & Shires, 2017) to rheumatic diseases (Shim et al., 2017). Having a socially supportive environment often makes the patient more actively cope with the illness and less likely to disengage and get worse (Rosland et al., 2012). In the case of a chronic illness such as coronary heart disease, social network size and having a stressed partner can influence morbidity and mortality by influencing whether patients attend rehabilitation (Molloy, Perkins-Porras, Strike, & Steptoe, 2008). Social networks also help maintain quality of life and are particularly important for low SES individuals (Barden, Barry, Khalifian, & Bates, 2016; Ruiz et al., 2019).

There are some important cultural differences in how social support is used (Taylor, Welch, Kim, Sherman, 2007; Wong & Lu, 2017). For example, a review of studies on culture and social support shows that Asians and Asian Americans are more reluctant to explicitly ask for support from others than are European Americans (Kim, Sherman, & Taylor, 2008). This is likely due to their concern about the potentially negative relational consequences of such behaviors. Asians and Asian Americans are more likely to use and benefit from forms of support that do not involve explicit disclosure of personal stressful events and feelings of distress. I will discuss more about the role of culture and social support in chronic illnesses later in this book.

Synthesize, Evaluate, Apply

- How would you apply the different biopsychosocial models to the design of an intervention to help people cope with chronic illnesses?
- Map out the relationship between different sociocultural factors and coping with a chronic illness.
- Using the broad discussion of culture described in Chapter 1, what cultural groups do you think would cope better with chronic illnesses and why?

INTERVENTIONS

Health psychologists are invaluable in providing important interventions and guidance to help primary care physicians with chronically ill patients (Jonkman, Schuurmans, Groenwold, Hoes, & Trappenburg, 2016). Interventions to help patients with chronic illnesses serve to alleviate the different biopsychosocial problems they may experience (Hoyt & Stanton, 2012). Many interventions train patients to set goals or modify how they make decisions (Kangovi et al., 2017). Interventions also target caregivers of chronically ill patients to reduce their psychological burden and increase their subjective well-being (Martire & Schulz, 2012). I will provide a brief overview of different treatments for chronic illnesses here. Each treatment will be covered in greater detail in Chapters 12 to 14.

Physicians prescribe treatment as each illness dictates. Illnesses such as CHD often require surgery of some form if the blockages to the arteries are too severe (Bishop, 2018). CVD patients are often given medications such as statins to reduce their cholesterol levels and slow down the clogging of their arteries. Illnesses such as cancer and HIV infection often require medications designed to slow down the growth of the cancerous cells or viral activity (Golub, 2019). In many cases, patients are also given pharmacological agents to help with psychological problems such as depression and anxiety or to reduce pain to increase motor activity.

Motivational interviewing (MI) is a type of counseling that helps patients to change coping behaviors (Rollnick, William, & Butler, 2008). Motivational interviewing is a directive, patient-centered counseling style for eliciting behavior change by helping patients to explore and resolve ambivalence. A well-validated approach used to work with people who are not ready to or who do not believe they can change their behaviors, MI builds on a patient's internal motivation to change without telling him or her what to do. MI is particularly useful for unhealthy behaviors such as smoking (Borrelli, Endrighi, Hammond, & Dunsiger, 2017). The approach uses a combination of empathic listening, exploring ambivalence, and eliciting and strengthening change talk. Psychological interventions such as MI are primarily designed to change health behaviors that influence the progression of disease or to help the patient cope with the stress and other negative affects related to the illness. Interventions may aim to reduce smoking behavior, to improve nutrition and dietary choices, or to increase physical activity. Psychological help may be provided in the form of individual or family therapy in which the patient or the patient's caregivers are provided with cognitive and behavioral skills to better cope with the illness.

A large number of interventions are designed to provide social support (Knoll et al., 2019). These can take the form of individually delivered support messages via health-care worker visits, the telephone, or the Internet, but more often are through support groups. Support group members discuss issues of mutual concern, which helps to satisfy unmet needs, and provides support in addition to that provided by friends and family members. Groups also provide a form of public commitment to adhere to and change behaviors to help cope with the illness.

Groups do not always work for everyone. Helgeson, Cohen, Schulz, and Yasko (2000) determined the extent to which individual difference variables moderated the effects of an information-based educational group and how an emotion-focused peer discussion group helped women with breast cancer. Women who needed outside support (e.g., did not have strong personal connections) benefited the most from the educational group, and peer discussion groups were helpful for women who lacked support from their partners or doctors. Surprisingly, however, too much support can be detrimental. Helgeson et al. (2000) found that the discussion groups were harmful for women who already had high levels of personal support.

A number of reviews provide important insights into interventions to help people cope with chronic illnesses. In one recent review, Martire and Helgeson (2017) suggest family members are the most important aid in children's and adults' illness management. Evidence suggests a dyadic approach to chronic illness management that targets the influence of close relationships may be the most helpful and sustainable method to effect patient behavior. Specifically, dyadic approaches aimed at helping patients and family members to find ways to set goals together may best benefit family members who are ill or are at risk because of poor health behaviors. In another review, Ghosh and Deb (2017) systematically reviewed positive psychology interventions in chronic physical illness and found writing is the most commonly used method for administration (see emotional expression in Chapter 6). Positive psychology interventions are considered feasible and acceptable by patients, but findings about their usefulness are inconclusive.

COPING WITH TERMINAL ILLNESS

The course of chronic illnesses can begin in childhood and can last a lifetime. Many chronic illnesses are treatable but not curable and some can be fatal. Some chronic illnesses, such as cancer, are often referred to as advancing or **terminal illnesses** because people with these diseases often die after a relatively short time (although this time can range from months to a few years). Not only is coping with a weakening body difficult, but also facing the reality of approaching death is an even bigger psychological challenge and can lead to many changes in outlook (Danel et al., 2017).

What can be done to make the end of life easier? Problems with communication and visiting hours and too many administrative details can be trying to the patient and family members. Care is highly fragmented in a hospital and multiple caregivers pass through a patient's room daily, monitoring the patient and performing different tests. In general, care should be taken to counter the effects of hospitalization (Buzgova, Sikorova, & Jarosova, 2016). Patients and their families arrive with anxiety, and emotions are high if death is imminent. Health-care practitioners need to be explicitly prepared to address these issues. In particular, informed consent procedures should be closely followed whereby patients are told of their condition and the treatments available, if any. Patients should also be helped to accept their situation and prepare for death. This normally means helping patients to use their remaining time well.

Psychological counseling should be made available for both the patient and his or her family. The patient may need help in facing death and in making sense of life. The family may need help to cope both with their grief and with the strain of caregiving. Both the patient and his or her family also may need help communicating with each other, in saying goodbye, and in dealing with sometimes conflicting needs (the patient fearing death and the family unable to imagine living without the patient). One of the alternatives to dying in a hospital is dying in a hospice; hospices are described in detail at the end of this chapter.

THE ROLE OF RELIGIOUS DIVERSITY

Religion has a long history of being included in studies of health (Koenig, 2015; Levin & Schiller, 1987). Research supports the link between religion and health (Park & Carney, 2019; Von Dras, 2017) although the bulk of the studies are correlational in nature. One of the most salient aspects of culture, religion is intrinsically tied to the other major elements of culture such as race and ethnicity. It is important to keep in mind the diversity of religious beliefs between and within groups of people. For instance, different races often have different religious beliefs. Also, even though North America is primarily Christian, there are still a significant number of North Americans who have non-Christian beliefs. Regardless of beliefs, turning to one's spirituality can be a form of coping and can even help with pain management. However, this link is also an example of the differences between a correlational study and an experiment. Simply because people who are religious are also usually people who cope better with illness, does not allow us to conclude that religion causes better health. Nonetheless, what is important is that religion can help, and in the context of chronic and terminal illnesses, health psychologists should use any tool that can make a difference.

One of the growing number of studies on different ethnic groups illustrates this point well (Tovar, 2017). Abraido-Lanza et al. (2004) tested for the link among religious, passive, and active coping, pain, and psychological adjustment in a sample of 200 Latinos with arthritis. The participants reported using high levels of religious coping that was correlated with active but not with passive coping. Religious coping was directly related to psychological well-being. Passive coping was associated with greater pain and worse adjustment (Abraido-Lanza et al., 2004). Traditional Latinos tend to be very religious, practicing Catholicism, *curanderismo,* or, more often, a blend of both (as discussed in Chapter 3). With the growing number of North Americans who are Latino, the findings of Abraido-Lanza et al. (2004) and other such studies suggest a greater focus on the role of ethnicity and religion on coping.

A person's religious beliefs often become more important as the end of life nears. Religious beliefs vary regarding the role of pain and of the role and significance of death. Different religions even have different ways to treat death and distinct ways to treat the lifeless human body. The deeper your faith, the more likely you are to turn to it if you or someone you love is dying (Boucher, 2017). The way death is treated within a culture can influence how well the patient copes (Corr & Corr, 2007; Doughty, 2017). For example, for devout Catholics, suffering is related to original sin and a Catholic has to face suffering like Christ did. Death is the freeing of the soul to the father who is in heaven. A righteous, well-lived life serves as preparation for death. As death draws near, the family and the terminally ill patient can draw solace from the visitation of a priest who will help the patient finalize his or her earthly affairs (Bussing & Poier, 2017). There is a final confession of sins, receiving of Holy Communion (a piece of bread or wafer that represents the body of Christ), an anointing, and a last blessing, known as the *last rites.* This scripted ritual goes a long way to help the terminally ill patient and family come to terms with the impending loss.

Muslims, or followers of Islam, see death as the termination of the soul's attachment to the body (Amer, 2017). Death is a blessing and a gift for the believer. To prepare, the person must do penance and be careful to not be under obligation to any other human being—the patient should make sure that he or she pays any dues or debts owed. Cleanliness at the time of death is more important than at any other time. Especially important is the edict that the seriously ill must die at home. To Hindus, suffering is part of *maya,* or illusion (Agnihotri & Agnihotri, 2017). The only way to transcend suffering is to be free from the cycle of birth and death and rebirth. The Hindu tries to work off bad karma from an early point in life and the place of your karmic cycle is indicated by your status in the world; for example, if you sinned in your past lives you will be reborn as an animal or, even worse, as a worm. This belief in predetermined fate helps reduce the anxiety of death. Other Eastern religions share some of these beliefs. Buddhists speak of and contemplate death often, in stark contrast to many non-Buddhists (Colgan et al., 2017). Pain is unavoidable, but attitudes and behavior influence suffering. According to Buddhists, the only way to avoid suffering is to free the self from desire, which is the cause of suffering. The Buddhist believes that as long as there is fear of death, life is not being lived to its fullest. Contemplating death can free us from fear, change the way we live and our attitude toward life, and help us face death healthily.

The sense that death can be joyous is also reflected in different religious traditions (Doughty, 2017). The Irish wake is often a rousing celebration of the recently departed's life and is accompanied by drinking and dancing. To the Sikhs of India, death is seen as a great opportunity to do something we put off all our lives. It is a chance to cleanse the soul of psychic fantasy, and life is an opportunity to practice dying, until one dies a death that will not have to be repeated. Death is not sad; friends chant and sing hymns near the dying to set a peaceful vibration and inspire the dying person to be in the best frame of mind. Hence, many religions downplay the sadness of death and emphasize the happiness coming from freedom and the unification with the creator.

DEATH

Different cultural groups face death differently, whether it is one's own death or the death of a close friend or family member (Corr & Corr, 2007; Noppe & Noppe, 2008). In addition, it matters how and when death arrives; the major causes of death vary across the life span. How and when death occurs automatically influences how survivors cope.

Death Across the Life Span

Focusing on how we develop is important in understanding why mortality and morbidity varies across age groups. The main causes of death are not the same at each point of the life cycle (see Table 11.3). Birth defects are the leading cause of infant deaths in the United States. Other major causes include complications from low birth weight (LBW), sudden infant death syndrome, and problems from labor, delivery, and other maternal complications (National Center for Health Statistics, 2017). The trauma of losing a child and the way parents cope can vary with the ethnic group and the expectations they have, and many other cultural variables can play a role. Many Mexican American mothers tend to have higher levels of stress during pregnancy. The idea that pregnancy is stressful is actually rooted in the culture: the Spanish word for labor is *dolor,* which also is the root for the words "sorrow" and "pain." Other cultural variables beyond ethnicity can be important too. Many poor families do not have the health insurance or facilities to receive good prenatal care. Poor expecting mothers who are not well fed automatically have an increased chance of complications during labor and delivery (Sinja et al., 2017).

Injury and accidents are the leading causes of death for children, adolescents, and young adults (National Center for Health Statistics, 2017). As we age, we succumb to more diseases that are related to unhealthy behaviors. The top three killers of adults (age 25 to 55) and older adults (age 55 and older) are coronary heart disease, cancer, and stroke (National Center for Health Statistics, 2017), each exacerbated by eating badly, smoking, and overindulging in alcohol.

Aging should not always be associated with illness and sickness either. In one particularly impressive longitudinal study, researchers (clearly not the same ones) observed 1,500 Californians over 80 years. The study showed that eating well, getting physical activity, and giving and receiving a lot of social support are some of the factors that can provide many happy years of life for older adults (Friedman & Martin, 2011). There were also some surprises: some of the people who worked the hardest, lived the longest, getting and staying married was not directly associated with longer lives for women, and the traits most associated with thriving were persistence and being prudent.

The physical deterioration of cells associated with aging is related to specific diseases in adulthood. For example, many elderly adults experience marked problems in thinking and remembering or **dementia**. The most common problem is one that you will have heard about: Alzheimer's disease, a degenerative disease of the brain that leads to dementia, makes even simple everyday tasks like grocery shopping difficult. Other major causes of dementia include Parkinson's disease and stroke.

These differences in causes of mortality indicate how different areas of health psychological research will be applied at different times of the life cycle. Prevention of injuries should be a major

▼ TABLE 11.3

Main Causes of Death across the Lifespan in the United States

Age Range	Top Three Leading Causes of Death in 2010
1–4 years	1. Accidents (unintentional injuries) 2. Congenital malformations, deformations, and chromosomal abnormalities 3. Assault (homicide)
5–14 years	1. Accidents (unintentional injuries) 2. Congenital malformations, deformations, and chromosomal abnormalities 3. Diseases of heart
15–24 years	1. Accidents (unintentional injuries) 2. Malignant neoplasms 3. Assault (homicide)
25–44 years	1. Accidents (unintentional injuries) 2. Malignant neoplasms 3. Diseases of heart
45–64 years	1. Malignant neoplasms 2. Diseases of heart 3. Accidents (unintentional injuries)
65 years and over	1. Malignant neoplasms 2. Diseases of heart 3. Chronic lower respiratory diseases

Adapted from Table 7. Deaths and death rates for the 10 leading causes of death in specified age groups: http://www.cdc.gov/nchs/data/nvsr/nvsr60/nvsr60_04.pdf Page 54.

goal when intervening with children, a decrease in unhealthy behaviors is a pertinent goal for children and young adults and help in coping with chronic and terminal disease is a critical goal for elderly persons.

The Path to Death

As the moment of death approaches, some explicit physiological changes accompany the different psychological stages. Dying patients often experience incontinence, losing control of their bladder and other bodily functions. In particular, patients may be unable to control their salivation and will not be able to feed themselves or even eat solid food as their digestive systems reduce functioning. With cancer or CHD, there is often an increase in pain and medical practitioners prescribe high doses of morphine, even putting the delivery of morphine under the patient's own control. In this way patients can self-administer medication to alleviate their pain and suffering. Patients may experience severe memory problems or have problems concentrating. Interactions with caregivers and hospital staff can become difficult, which can lead to misunderstandings and miscommunication. Friends and family often have trouble facing the patient in this state, and the patient may not want to be seen by anyone. Talking about death is taboo among many North American the last few days of a patient's life can be very difficult as visitors and even medical personnel do not always know how to approach the topic. Consequently, death education is an important area of research. Given the number of tragedies on college campuses,

RESEARCHER SPOTLIGHT

Dr. Illene Cupit earned a PhD from Temple University and currently teaches at the University of Wisconsin–Green Bay. She is past president of the Association for Death Education. She is a leading authority on death, dying, and loss and focuses on how different cultures cope with death.

there is a special emphasis on helping students cope with grief (Cox, Dean, & Kowalski, 2015; Cupit, Servaty-Seib, Tedrick Parikh, Walker, & Martin, 2016).

Facilitating Death

Should life be terminated if a patient is in tremendous pain and discomfort or is comatose? This is one of the most controversial ethical issues regarding health care. **Euthanasia**, **physician-assisted suicide**, and the withdrawing of life-sustaining treatment are some of the most difficult moral and ethical dilemmas we face today. Euthanasia is the termination of life by the injection of a lethal drug. Assisted suicide involves a physician supplying a lethal drug while not actually administering it himself or herself. When life-sustaining treatment is withdrawn, the underlying disease takes its own course. All are subjects of intense national debate (Bulmer, Böhnke, & Lewis, 2017).

One of the most famous scenarios involves Terri Schiavo. By 2005 Schiavo, a Florida woman, had been in a persistent vegetative state for 15 years. Her husband, Michael Schiavo, battled her parents over whether his wife should be allowed to die. He argued that because she was brain dead it would not be fair to keep her alive. Terri Schiavo suffered heart failure from a potassium imbalance in 1990. Her husband said his wife told him that she would not want to be kept alive artificially. Doctors who testified on behalf of Michael Schiavo said that his wife had no hope for recovery. She was fed through a tube but breathed on her own. Terri Schiavo's parents, Bob and Mary Schindler, maintained that their daughter could be helped with therapy. After years of litigation and appeals, Terri Schiavo's feeding tube was removed in October 2004, only to be reinserted 6 days later after the Florida legislature, in emergency session, passed a law that affected only Terri Schiavo. The legislation gave Governor Jeb Bush the power to intervene in the case, and he ordered the feeding tube reinserted. In early 2005 the tube was removed again and Terri Schiavo died on March 31, 2005, of starvation and dehydration. What should have been done here? Should she have been kept alive? Was Terri conscious of the world around her? Did she experience psychological pain by being kept alive? Her vegetative state made it difficult to answer any of these questions.

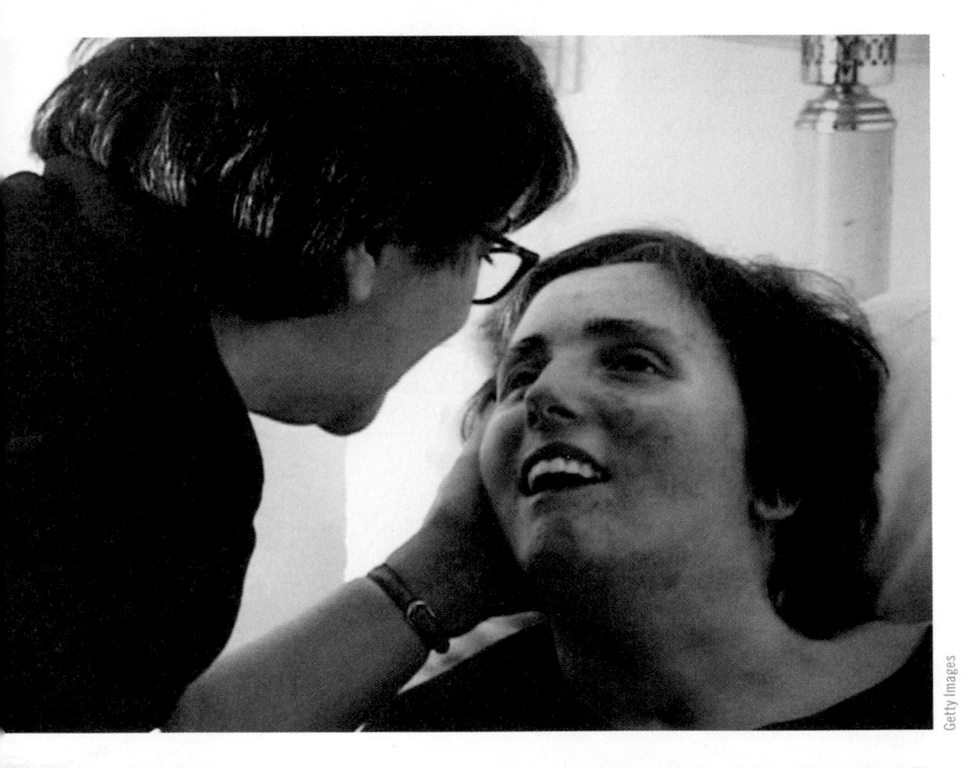
Getty Images

▲ **Terri Schiavo.** Terri Schiavo of Florida had been in a coma for 15 years. Her husband wanted to turn off life support but her family wanted to keep her alive. She died in March 2005. What information can help decide what should have been done?

Ripped from the headlines: "Nerve implant 'restores consciousness' to man in persistent vegetative state." Not ripped, the actual headline. And I'm not making it up. This is exactly what *The Guardian* reported in September 2017. Physicians fitted a man in a coma for 15 years (yes, same as Terri Schiavo when she died) with a neural implant that stimulated the vagus nerve. He started to track objects with his eyes and began to stay awake (Devlin, 2017). You can bet all future cases are going to be even tougher to decide.

Apart from this now classic case, the most publicized event that put these procedures into public consciousness was Dr. **Jack Kevorkian**'s assistance in 130 suicides since 1990. This Michigan doctor helped patients end their own lives even in the face of threats to his own life. Three juries refused to convict him despite a Michigan statute established for that purpose. The uproar surrounding his case led to intense political movements with advocates on both sides of the issue, and

Kevorkian was imprisoned. He served 8 years of a 10- to 25-year sentence for second-degree murder, was released in 2007 and even ran for Congress, but lost. He died of liver disease in 2011 without assistance. In 1994 Oregon became the first state to legalize forms of euthanasia.

There are interesting arguments on both sides. Be warned, how surveys are worded can influence attitudes toward assisting death (Magelssen, Supphellen, Nortvedt, & Materstvedt, 2016). One of the most important ethical principles in medicine is that the patient has autonomy (Angell, 1997). Terminally ill patients may spend months experiencing excruciating pain and discomfort in the process of dying. The extent of pain felt and the amount of cognition present are criteria that can be used to argue for allowing, or even mandating, a person to end his or her own life. It is still very hard to draw a line. Even if a person is in extreme pain, **palliative care** (a form of treatment aimed at alleviating symptoms without necessarily affecting the cause) could be used (Tanuseputro, Budhwani, Bai, & Wodchis, 2017). If a person is in a coma and has no measurable cognitive functioning, there is still no guarantee that cognition will not return or that the person is not thinking or feeling. Sometimes the decision to cut off life support is made easier by the patient having filled out a living will in which he or she clearly specifies the conditions under which life support should be terminated. My mother-in-law filled one out and it made a big difference for her family after she died. A sample of a living will is shown in Table 11.4.

Families also play a major role in this issue (Mayer et al., 2017). However, research shows that surrogate preferences can inaccurately reflect patients' treatment wishes (Haley et al., 2002). Families provide the majority of care for individuals with chronic illness for many reasons, including a sense of attachment, cultural expectations, and preferences for avoiding institutional care. Although it is optimal for the families, patients, and health-care providers to have ongoing discussions about goals of care, it is often only when the patient's condition worsens that decisions regarding end-of-life care take place. Research suggests that family members are often key decision makers for end-of-life issues regardless of patients' prior preferences concerning end-of-life care. Doctors tend to consult with family members even in the presence of written advance directives from their patients (Mowery, 2007).

In relation, should one extend the life of a conscious and aware terminally ill patient (in contrast to the case described above)? There is some debate about whether a simple and low-cost intervention, such as having a volunteer visit, can extend the life of terminally ill patients. One study suggests this (Herbst-Damm & Kulik, 2005); others suggest it is critical to look beyond effects on longevity and assess the influence on quality of life (Hanoch, 2007).

Are There Stages?

Many in the lay population have heard of the concept of stages of death and that people who are dying experience a series of emotions. Spoiler alert: It's not what you think. This somewhat inaccurate belief stems from work published by Elisabeth Kübler-Ross (1969). Kübler-Ross interviewed more than 200 dying patients and concluded that the process of dying involves five stages that vary in their emotional content and intensity. First comes denial, an initial reaction to the thought of death. This stage lasts around 2 days, can be a form of emotional coping (see Chapter 6), and can mask anxiety without necessarily removing it. Next comes **anger**, a stage in which patients are upset that death is happening to them. In many ways, the fact that they are dying violates a sense of the world being just. Most people believe that they do not deserve to die because they have been good or at least have not been bad enough to be punished with death. There is often misplaced resentment and a lot of irritability.

Bargaining comes next. Patients try to restore their belief in a just world and may promise to be good or live life better (e.g., give a lot to charity) in exchange for life. This trading for life then gives way to depression. The patient feels a lack of control and now grieves in expectation of his or her death, a process known as **anticipatory grief**. The depression is often driven by a realization that a person will be losing his or her past and will also be losing all that was possible in a future. Finally, the patient may reach a stage of **acceptance** in which he or she fully

▼ TABLE 11.4

A Simple Living Will: North Carolina Statutory Form, **G.S. 90-321**

NORTH CAROLINA COUNTY OF ______________________
DECLARATION OF A DESIRE FOR A NATURAL DEATH
I, ______________________, being of sound mind, desire that, as specified below, my life not be prolonged by extraordinary means or by artificial nutrition or hydration if my condition is determined to be terminal and incurable or if I am diagnosed as being in a persistent vegetative state. I am aware and understand that this writing authorizes a physician to withhold or discontinue extraordinary means or artificial nutrition or hydration, in accordance with my specifications set forth below (Initial any of the following, as desired):
_____ If my condition is determined to be terminal and incurable, I authorize the following:
_____ My physician may withhold or discontinue extraordinary means only.
_____ In addition to withholding or discontinuing extraordinary means if such means are necessary, my physician may withhold or discontinue either artificial nutrition or hydration, or both.
_____ If my physician determines that I am in a persistent vegetative state, I authorize the following:
_____ My physician may withhold or discontinue extraordinary means only.
_____ In addition to withholding or discontinuing extraordinary means if such means are necessary, my physician may withhold or discontinue either artificial nutrition or hydration, or both.
This the ________________ day of ________________
Signature: ______________________________
I hereby state that the declarant, ________________, being of sound mind signed the above declaration in my presence and that I am not related to the declarant by blood or marriage and that I do not know or have a reasonable expectation that I would be entitled to any portion of the estate of the declarant under any existing will or codicil of the declarant or as an heir under the Intestate Succession Act if the declarant died on this date without a will. I also state that I am not the declarant's attending physician or an employee of the declarant's attending physician, or an employee of a health facility in which the declarant is a patient or an employee of a nursing home or any group-care home where the declarant resides. I further state that I do not now have any claim against the declarant.
Witness: ______________________________
Witness: ______________________________
CERTIFICATE
I, ________________, Clerk (Assistant Clerk) of Superior Court or Notary Public (circle one as appropriate) for ________________ County hereby certify that ________________, the declarant, appeared before me and swore to me and to the witnesses in my presence that this instrument is his/her Declaration Of A Desire For A Natural Death, and that he/she had willingly and voluntarily made and executed it as his/her free act and deed for the purposes expressed in it.
I further certify that ________________ and ________________, witnesses, appeared before me and swore that they witnessed ________________, declarant, sign the attached declaration, believing him/her to be of sound mind; and also swore that at the time they witnessed the declaration (i) they were not related within the third degree to the declarant or to the declarant's spouse, and (ii) they did not know or have a reasonable expectation that they would be entitled to any portion of the estate of the declarant upon the declarant's death under any will of the declarant or codicil thereto then existing or under the Intestate Succession Act as it provides at that time, and (iii) they were not a physician attending the declarant or an employee of an attending physician or an employee of a health facility in which the declarant was a patient or an employee of a nursing home or any group-care home in which the declarant resided, and (iv) they did not have a claim against the declarant. I further certify that I am satisfied as to the genuineness and due execution of the declaration.

acknowledges that death cannot be avoided. At this point the patient is often very weak and faces death with a peaceful calm.

Although these stages sound appropriate, and you probably can nod your head and see how a dying person could go through them, there is little empirical evidence for these stages (Jurecic, 2017). There is research on each of these emotions (e.g., acceptance, Davis, Deane, Lyons, & Barclay, 2017), but not to prove stages exist. Kübler-Ross used only cross-sectional research and did not follow patients as they got closer to death. The fact is that people may experience these stages but not necessarily in the order just described. One constant feature in Kübler-Ross's stages of death is that most people will experience some depression just before death. How someone experiences death varies based on his or her culture, how much social support he or she has, the physiological progression of his or her disease, and other factors. Consequently, other researchers have attempted to explain the experience of dying (e.g., Pattison, 1977; Shneidman, 1980), although they only hypothesize variations on Kübler-Ross's five stages. The five emotions seem to represent the most relevant experiences of the dying patient.

CULTURAL VARIATIONS IN DEATH AND DYING

When the time of death draws closer and it is clear that little can be done for the dying patient, it is important to help the person and his or her family prepare for death. We have discussed already some of the traditional ways this has been done, such as psychological counseling. There is an important additional dimension to consider when you look beyond the biology and psychology surrounding dying: culture. From a psychological perspective, fear, depression, and even denial of death may be common for patients and their families, but the exact experiences vary significantly across cultural groups (Galanti, 2014; Irish, Lundquist, & Nelsen, 1993).

European American health practitioners are often unintentionally ethnocentric, and this ethnocentricity makes it difficult for them to fully comprehend the experiences of people from other cultures. With an emotionally charged situation such as dying, this issue becomes even more important. Cultural differences become more evident from even a basic level of definition of key terms. It may seem clear what being dead is, but do not take death for granted. In many cultures, people are considered officially dead when Western biomedicine would consider them still alive and vice versa (Rosenblatt, 1993). There are correspondingly some significant differences in the expression and experience of emotions such as grief and loss. In some cultures, it is normal for people to cut themselves or otherwise hurt themselves to express their loss. Some East Indians, for example, fast for weeks as a sign of grieving. There are also cultural differences in the fear of death. African Americans report higher levels of death anxiety than European Americans (Depaola, Griffin, Young, & Neimeyer, 2003).

Some of these cultural variations are seen in the rituals that accompany death. Making sure that the adequate ritual is conducted for the bereaved person is often critical to the health and coping of those left behind. Although they are not given any attention in the health psychological literature to date, cultural differences in dealing with the dead may have important implications for psychological adjustment. Many cultural beliefs may clash with the beliefs of Western biomedicine, and hospital policies may prohibit certain practices, but they are important practices nonetheless. For example, in the American Indian culture, the burning of sage and other herbs is part of many religious ceremonies and is also used to prepare the soul of the dying person for the afterlife. Hospitals have nonsmoking policies and lighting a fire may seem clearly out of the question. But if sage is not burned, it could jeopardize the happiness of the

ISSOUF SANOGO / AFP/ Getty Images

▲ **Cultural Rituals for Death and Dying.** Different cultures have very different rituals for death and dying. These caskets are part of the burial rituals of the people of Ghana who use different shapes of coffins for different individuals.

dying patient's soul and greatly hurt his or her family. Health-care professionals have to be aware of such cultural practices and negotiate a way to satisfy all concerned. For Muslims, there are also clear-cut practices that have to be followed at the time of death. As soon as a relative sees that the person is dead, he or she must turn the body to face Mecca (the site in the Middle East of the Kaaba, the Muslim's holiest space). They also have someone sitting close by read the Koran (the word of God as channeled through the prophet Mohammed), close the body's mouth and eyes and cover the face, and quickly bathe the body and cover it with white cotton (Gilanshah, 1993).

Health practitioners are more effective in helping individuals during the difficult time of coping with death when they are sensitive to different cultural traditions. Many of the specific considerations needed are difficult for members of different ethnic groups to mention themselves. In the middle of coping with loss, it may be too much to expect a member of a different cultural group to explain exactly what is needed. It is likewise difficult for health-care workers to know all the different cultural idiosyncrasies surrounding death, but both groups need to work toward ensuring an adaptive experience for all concerned. For some groups, this sharing and explaining of cultural routines may be especially difficult. For example, given the negative points in the history of African Americans and American Indians in North America (Washington, 2006), both these ethnic groups have particularly strained relationships with European Americans and the health-care institution in particular (Barrett, 1998). Consequently, the development of separate models to understand how different cultural groups understand death and dying has increased (Corr & Corr, 2007). Barrett (1995, 1998), for example, has derived a list of special considerations for caregivers working with African Americans who experience loss (Table 11.5). Although devised for African Americans, these models serve as good reminders for health professionals working with any cultural group.

Sex, Gender, and Death

In the context of culture, it is also important to look at sex differences relating to the experience of death. Scholarship in death studies suggests that the different perceptions and experiences of men and women must also (in addition to cultural differences) be taken into consideration to best help those dying as well as those caring for the dead and grieving (Noppe, 2004).

Martin and Doka (2000) remarked that the benchmark for grieving is normally set as how women handle loss. Women tend to show emotion, seek social support, talk about loss, and allow time to grieve openly, things not normally done by men (Cook, 1988). In a major review of gender differences in adjustment to bereavement, Stroebe, Stroebe, and Schut (2001) reported that

▼ TABLE 11.5

Critical Considerations for Helping African Americans Cope with Death and Dying

1.	Understand the sociocultural influences from both Western and African traditions that combine to influence the attitudes, beliefs, and values.
2.	Acknowledge and appreciate the uniqueness of the subgroups of African Americans (when in doubt, ask).
3.	Be sensitive to basic differences in quality of life and differences in death rates and causes for African Americans versus European Americans.
4.	Understand the impact of collective losses that African Americans often grieve for.
5.	Include a consideration of SES as well as religion and spirituality.
6.	Acknowledge the role of cultural mistrust regarding health.
7.	Be sensitive to the value placed by African Americans on expressions of condolence.
8.	Understand the role played by and expectations for the clergy and spiritual leaders (often higher expectations than for the medical community).

Source: Barret (1998). Reprinted with permission.

women express their emotions more than men, although they found little evidence for the hypothesis that working through grief helps them recover faster. Particularly interesting is the fact that men suffer relatively greater health consequences when grieving than women, possibly because widowers get less support than widows (Stroebe & Stroebe, 1983). Specifically, widowers are significantly more distressed and depressed than widows and also have a higher incidence of mental illnesses. Widows have been found to suffer from fewer physical health problems and illnesses than widowers and are less likely to die during the period of acute grief after the loss of a spouse (Stroebe et al., 2001). Keeping these ethnic and sex differences in mind is clearly important in understanding how different subgroups of people experience the certainty of death.

Synthesize, Evaluate, Apply

- How does religion play a role in chronic and terminal illnesses and coping with death?
- Are there biopsychosocial factors that could be used to justify when euthanasia is appropriate?
- How can cultural variations in death and dying be translated into better health care?

APPLICATION SHOWCASE

HOSPICE

When it is clear that your death is approaching, how would you like to die? This may be a morbid thought; however, thinking about it now rather than later could influence how much discomfort you experience at life's end. For most terminal illnesses, the physical and psychological signs that death is near are relatively obvious: loss of interest in eating and drinking, withdrawal from the outside world, more sleeping, hands and feet may become discolored and cool, breathing and blood pressure changes, or cognitive impairment. When the signs appear, patients are normally admitted into a hospital where they are monitored until they stop breathing. Sometimes hospitalized patients choose to be released from a hospital so that they and their family members can receive hospice care and the patient can die at home. Hospice care is very much focused on the patient and the patient's family, friends, and caregivers.

Hospice is a form of care that has its origins in medieval times. In the early 19th century, hospices were places where pilgrims, travelers, the homeless, and the destitute were offered lodging, usually by a religious group. In 1967, an English doctor, Cicely Saunders, felt that terminally ill persons needed better care and began a new movement. The word **"hospice"** is derived from the words for hospitality and guesthouse, and hospices are also referred to as nursing homes for the dying. The hospice movement spread to the United States over the next 10 years, and today there are hospices in every state and around the world (National Hospice and Palliative Care Organization [NHPCO], 2017).

Hospices tend to be small, residential institutions where the treatment is focused on the patient's QOL rather than on curing the illness (Noe & Smith, 2012). Though hospice care can be delivered in a hospice facility (i.e., not at home), most patients on hospice care die at home. There are only (as of 2016) 4,199 free-standing hospice facilities in the United States, so going on to hospice usually means you will continue to live where you are living and be cared for by a hospice team in that place, which is the patient's home. For 2009 NHPCO estimates that approximately 41.6% of all deaths in the United States were under the care of a hospice program.

Unlike in a hospital, hospices do not attempt to cure the patient or prolong life (Kastenbaum, 1999; NHPCO, 2010). The dying are comforted, and their pain and other symptoms are alleviated. Unlike hospitals, patients are urged to customize their surroundings and make them seem like home. Patients can wear their own clothes (no uncomfortable hospital gowns) and bring in pictures, paintings, or other personal effects. The patient and family are included in the care plan, and emotional, spiritual, and practical support is given based on the patient's wishes and

(Continued)

(Continued)

family's needs. Similar to church-affiliated hospitals, some hospices have been started by churches and religious groups (sometimes in connection with their hospitals), but hospices serve a broad community and do not require patients to adhere to any particular set of beliefs. Most hospice patients are cancer patients, but hospices accept anyone regardless of age or type of illness.

A patient can ask to be placed on hospice care at any time during a terminal illness, although it is usually the case that the patient's primary care physician has stated that the patient has 6 months or less to live. In America, the decision belongs to the patient although many people are not comfortable with the idea of stopping active efforts to beat the disease in the switch to palliative care. Hospice staff members are highly sensitive to this debate and facilitate discussions of the same with the patient and family. As you can guess, the decision-making process for hospice care has many components. In a study of patients with advanced cancer, Chen, Haley, Robinson, and Schonwetter (2003) found that patients receiving hospice care were significantly older, were less educated, and had more people in their households. Hospice patients had multiple health conditions and worse activities of daily living scores than non-hospice patients and were also more realistic about their disease course than their non-hospice counterparts.

The process commonly starts with the patient's physician, who tells the patient and/or family that no more treatment options are available and that it is time to consider hospice care. The patient then signs consent and insurance forms, similar to the forms patients sign when they enter a hospital, acknowledging that the care is palliative (aimed to provide pain relief and symptom control) rather than curative. A hospice team then prepares an individualized care plan addressing the amount of caregiving needed by the patient, and staff visit regularly and are always accessible. Unlike in a hospital, while in hospice care, family, friends, or paid caregivers deliver most of the care, but hospice agencies provide volunteers to assist the families and to provide the primary caregivers with support. Hospice patients are also cared for by a team of physicians, nurses, social workers, counselors, hospice-certified nursing assistants, clergy, therapists, and volunteers—and each provides assistance based on his or her own area of expertise. In addition, hospices provide medications, supplies, equipment, and hospital services related to the terminal illness.

There is considerable empirical evidence for the efficacy of hospices. The National Hospice Work Group and the NHPCO both conducted one of the most comprehensive assessments of hospice. The two groups spearheaded a detailed 2-year study of the efficacy of end-of-life care and studied more than 3,000 caregivers and patients. Some of the key results were that the majority of patients entering hospice in pain were made comfortable within days of admission, and caregivers' confidence in the care of their loved ones increased because of hospice services (Ryndes et al., 2001).

The hospice emphasis on palliative care can be seen in comparisons of pain relief (Azoulay et al., 2008). Hospice patients are twice as likely as non-hospice patients to receive regular treatment for daily pain (Miller, Mor, Wu, Gozalo, & Lapane, 2002). For example, Miceli and Mylod (2003) looked at how satisfied family members were with the end-of-life care their loved ones received. Family satisfaction with hospice care was generally quite high, although the timing of the referral was critical. It was critical to get patients into hospice care earlier rather than later. Families rated services lower almost across the board when the referral to hospice was deemed too late.

Experiments comparing hospices to hospitals are hard to do and unethical (randomly assigning a dying loved one to a condition is clearly unpalatable), but some studies have compared the experiences of patients in each setting. Compared with patients in hospitals, patients in hospices and their families report more peace of mind and greater satisfaction with care (Ganzini et al., 2002; Roscoe & Hyer, 2008). Note that in most cases there are few significant differences in pain symptoms and activities of daily living, although hospice patients report more overall psychological well-being (Gatchel & Oordt, 2003a).

Does hospice prolong life? Patients in hospices do not necessarily live longer (Kane, Klein, Bernstein, & Rothenberg, 1986), but evidence shows that life expectancy may be stretched. One study showed the mean survival was 29 days longer for hospice patients than for non-hospice patients (Connor, Pyenson, Fitch, Spence, & Iwasaki, 2007). In congestive heart failure patients, the mean survival period jumped from 321 days to 402 days. The mean survival period was also significantly longer for hospice patients with lung cancer (39 days) and pancreatic cancer (21 days), while marginally significant for colon cancer (33 days). Lung cancer patients receiving early palliative care lived 23.3% longer than those who delayed palliative treatment as is currently the standard (Ternel et al., 2010).

There are some significant cultural differences in hospice use as well. Colon and Lyke (2003) found that African Americans and Latinos both used hospice services at significantly lower rates than European Americans. In addition, African American use of hospices declined significantly during the study (1995 to 2001), whereas European American use increased. Similarly, Ngo-Metzger, Phillips, and McCarthy (2008) found that Asian Americans had lower rates of hospice use than European American patients. Japanese Americans had a shorter median length of stay (21 days), and Filipino Americans had a longer median length of stay (32 days) than European American patients (26 days). Perhaps it is not surprising that many North American doctors endorse hospice as the better option for patients at the end of life (Prochaska, Putman, Tak, Yoon, & Curlin, 2017).

CHAPTER REVIEW

SUMMARY ▶▶

- Chronic illnesses are illnesses that persist over a long period of time. The most common chronic illnesses are cancer, cardiovascular disease, AIDS, back pain, diabetes, and arthritis. Some of these, such as cardiovascular disease, are reversible, but most are terminal. Most chronic diseases show varying incidence rates across different cultural groups.
- To help patients and their families cope with the changes in lifestyle from chronic illnesses, health psychologists often focus on improving the quality of life (QOL) of the individual. Quality of life is measured by assessing physical and psychological status together with functioning.
- Patients' cognitive appraisals of their situation and their own personal goals are critical components of coping with chronic illnesses. Common responses to the diagnosis of a chronic illness are denial, anxiety, and depression. Optimism is a powerful tool in coping with illness.
- Sociocultural factors play a major role in coping with chronic illnesses. The quality of one's close relationships, interactions with family and friends, and even the neighborhood one lives in can all influence QOL. Patients with strong religious beliefs or from certain ethnic groups may have different coping responses.
- A majority of health psychological interventions are designed to provide chronically ill patients with social support. Although many interventions show success, not all group support interventions work for everyone.
- The proximity of death brings its own specific challenges. Together with physiological and psychological deterioration, patients often experience denial, anger, depression, acceptance, or anticipatory grief and sometimes bargain (not always in this order).
- Physician-assisted suicide, euthanasia, and the withdrawal of life support are controversial issues in terminal care. Patients are urged to complete living wills that specify what they would like to be done if they are nonresponsive, in a coma, or receiving life support. Palliative care and hospice care are both commonly used forms of care that do not include attempts to cure the illness and prolong life.
- Not all cultures define death in the same way. Based on varying cultural philosophies regarding the purpose of life and the nature of the afterlife, different cultures have different behaviors and procedures for coping with the impending death of a loved one.

TEST YOURSELF ▶▶

Check your understanding of the topics in this chapter by answering the following questions.

1. The current life expectancy estimate for American women born in 2006 is approximately ________ years.
   a. 65
   b. 72
   c. 78
   d. 82
2. The most prevalent chronic disease is also the nation's primary cause of death. That illness is
   a. coronary heart disease.
   b. cancer.
   c. diabetes.
   d. pneumonia.
3. From a health psychologist's perspective, one of the main treatment goals for those with a chronic illness is
   a. increasing the quality of life.
   b. preventing the spread of the disease.
   c. safeguarding other family members.
   d. curing the disease.
4. From a biological standpoint, chronic illnesses are difficult to cope with because they
   a. disrupt normal life functioning.
   b. are often contagious.
   c. always bring pain.
   d. fluctuate unpredictably.

5. One of the most effective psychological resources that people with chronic illness have is
   a. self-esteem.
   b. appraisals of situations.
   c. levels of extroversion.
   d. hardiness.
6. One of the first psychological reactions to discovering you have a chronic illness is
   a. denial.
   b. depression.
   c. anxiety.
   d. optimism.
7. One of the psychological reactions to a chronic illness that tends to be long term and increases as pain and disability increase is
   a. denial.
   b. depression.
   c. anxiety.
   d. fear.
8. Psychological interventions to help people cope with chronic illnesses are primarily designed to
   a. change health behaviors that influence disease progression.
   b. change personality traits to make the person more optimistic.
   c. physically rehabilitate the person to make them live life normally.
   d. help caregivers care for the patients.
9. Social support is good to help people cope, but Helgeson et al. (2000) warn that
   a. those who really do not need it benefit the most.
   b. support is only helpful if people believe it will help.
   c. getting more support if you already have enough can be harmful.
   d. not providing enough support can hurt more than providing none at all.
10. _______ is the termination of life by a lethal drug administered by a physician.
   a. Euthanasia
   b. Mercy killing
   c. Self-suicide
   d. Assisted suicide

KEY TERMS, CONCEPTS, AND PEOPLE

ESSENTIAL READINGS

Hoyt, M. (2019). Adjustment to chronic illness. In T. A. Revenson & R. A. R. Gurung (Eds.), *Handbook of health psychology* (3e). New York, NY: Routledge.

Morgan, K., & McGee, H. (2016). Quality of life. In Y. Benyamini, M. Johnston, & E. C. Karademas (Eds.), *Assessment in health psychology* (pp.189–200). Boston, MA: Hogrefe.

Park, C., & Carney, B. (2019). Religion/spirituality and health: Modeling potential pathways of influence. In T. A. Revenson & R. A. R. Gurung (Eds.), *Handbook of health psychology* (3e). New York, NY: Routledge.

MAJOR ILLNESS

CHAPTER 12

PSYCHONEUROIMMUNOLOGY AND HIV

Chapter 12 Outline

MEASURING UP

HOW STRONG IS YOUR IMMUNE SYSTEM?

Your immune system function may need help if you check two or more of the following (note that some numbered items are not included here, so numbers are not consecutive.)

____1. Three or more ear infections in one year
____2. Two or more sinus infections in one year
____3. Oral antibiotics use more than twice in one year
____4. Two or more episodes of pneumonia in one year
____6. Recurring deep skin or organ abscess
____10. Family history of immune deficiency
____11. Increase or susceptibility to infections
____12. Cancer
____15. Diarrhea/habitual constipation
____19. Diabetes
____20. Rheumatoid arthritis
____21. Systemic lupus erythematosus
____27. Eczema
____28. Stress
____35. Crave sugar or sweets
____36. Need for intravenous antibiotics to clear infections
____37. Lack of energy
____38. Illness more than twice a year
____39. Difficulty digesting certain foods
____40. Food allergies
____41. Recent or frequent use of antibiotics
____42. Sore or painful joints
____43. Difficulty maintaining ideal weight
____44. Slow recovery from illness
____45. Exposure to air pollution daily
____46. Poor resistance to disease
____47. Belching or gas after meals
____48. Feeling out of control
____49. Food/chemical sensitivities
____50. Recurrent yeast/fungal infections
____52. Asthma
____53. Depression
____55. Acne
____56. Migraines
____57. Anxiety
____58. Insomnia
____59. Hives

Source: https://oawhealth.com/2013/02/07/calculate-your-immune-system-function/

▼ Ponder This

What can you do to strengthen your own immune system?

What are the main ways different physiological systems interact to influence immunity?

How could yoga influence coping with immune diseases?

Open your mouth, breathe in, and chew. Chew? You have probably heard stories about how we are surrounded by millions and millions of bacteria. You may have seen those television specials that show you just how many living things are harbored by your mouth or on a patch of your skin or on the surface of your pillow or in the carpet. Well, these are more than just stories. A microscopic examination of the air we breathe, the water we drink, and the world around us reveals a teeming multitude of life. Bacteria, viruses, and germs of various sorts cohabitate our world. Many of these viruses and bacteria can cause us to get sick. The common cold and the flu are some examples of what happens to the body when we are infected by viruses. However, given the number of infectious agents to which our bodies are exposed regularly, we do not get sick that often. Why is this? The answer is that we have a specialized arrangement of cells, organs, and processes that is designed to ward off such threats and protect the body from infection: the immune system.

When our immune system is strong, we are less susceptible to illness. When we are stressed or otherwise psychologically challenged and our immune system is weakened, we are more susceptible to disease and illness. In addition, some diseases such as lupus and AIDS can debilitate our immune defenses and threaten our health and our lives regardless of our psychological makeup. In Chapter 4, you met the key components of the immune system. I discussed how the immune system works and recounted what happens when it fails or is compromised. In this chapter I will explore the role played by cultural factors and the many differences in immune-related diseases across cultural groups. In particular, you will learn how sex and ethnicity, two major cultural aspects, play large roles in the experience and incidence of HIV infection and AIDS.

PSYCHONEUROIMMUNOLOGY

Biopsychological science has discovered relatively recently that the immune system is strongly influenced by the nervous system and correspondingly by our minds and thinking (Ader, Felten, & Cohen, 1991; Segerstrom, 2012). The influence of psychological processes on immune functioning (the biopsycho connection) can be seen in many ways. At the physiological level, there is evidence for direct explicit connections between the endocrine and autonomic systems and the immune system (see Chapter 4). When we are stressed by physical (such as an infection) or psychological (such as living in a high-crime neighborhood) causes, the two systems act together (Robles et al., 2019). When we are well, the two are balanced. A disruption in the communication between the nervous and immune systems (caused by stress or illness) plays a major role in a wide range of disorders characterized by an over- or under-reactive immune system. For example, the activity of the immune system could be the connection linking psychological stress experienced by a pregnant mother and the health of her baby (Christian, 2012). Figure 12.1 summarizes the major autoimmune disorders.

Beyond the physiological link there is a clear psychological link (Nassau, Tien, & Fritz, 2008) hence the term "psychoneuroimmuno." For example, psychological interventions such as stress management are used to help gay and bisexual men infected with HIV (Adam, Hart, Mohr, Coleman, & Vernon, 2017). In a particularly vivid early demonstration (the one that got me hooked on this stuff), Futterman, Kemeny, Shapiro, and Fahey (1994) had an actor imagine that he was rejected for a part or had just won an acting award.

Even the faked feelings of intense sadness led to an increase in immune cells in the bloodstream whereas the happy act led to a decrease. Findings such as these are all encompassed by the fascinating area of psychoneuroimmunology.

RESEARCHER SPOTLIGHT

Margaret Kemeny, PhD, is professor of psychiatry and director of health psychology at the University of California, San Francisco. An expert in the immune system and health psychology, she is one of the leading scientists to advance the field of psychoneuroimmunology.

▼ FIGURE 12.1

Major Autoimmune Disorders

Disease	Symptoms and Tests of Diseases	
	Symptoms	Tests to determine if person has the disease
Hashimoto's thyroiditis (underactive thyroid)	• tiredness • depression • sensitivity to cold • weight gain • muscle weakness and cramps • dry hair • tough skin • constipation • sometimes there are no symptoms	• blood test for thyroid stimulating hormone (TSH)
Graves' disease (overactive thyroid)	• insomnia (not able to sleep) • irritability • weight loss without dieting • heat sensitivity • sweating • fine brittle hair • weakness in muscles • light menstrual periods • bulging eyes • shaky hands • sometimes there are no symptoms	• blood test for thyroid stimulating hormone (TSH)
Lupus	• swelling and damage to the joints, skin, kidneys, heart, lungs, blood vessels, and brain • "butterfly" rash across the nose and cheeks • rashes on other parts of the body • painful and swollen joints • sensitivity to the sun	• exam of lab tests (anti-nuclear antibody [ANA] test, blood tests, and urine tests)
Multiple sclerosis (MS)	• weakness and trouble with coordination, balance, speaking, and walking • paralysis • tremors • numbness and tingling feeling in arms, legs, hands, and feet	• exam of body • exam of brain, spinal cord, and nerves (neurological exam) • x-ray tests (magnetic resonance imaging [MRI] and magnetic resonance spectroscopy [MRS]) • other tests on the brain and spinal cord fluid to look for things linked to these diseases
Rheumatoid arthritis	• inflammation begins in the tissue lining your joints and then spreads to the whole joint (hand joints are the most common site, but it can affect most joints in the body) • muscle pain • deformed joints • weakness • fatigue • loss of appetite • weight loss • becoming confined to bed in severe cases	• blood tests may indicate anemia (when body does not have enough red blood cells) and an antibody called rheumatoid factor (RF). (Some people with RF never get this disease, and others with the disease never have RF.)

Source: U.S. Department of Health and Human Services (2008).

The field of **psychoneuroimmunology (PNI)** evolved out of the disciplines of biology and psychology and is dedicated to understanding the interplay between these disparate systems (Golub & Fikslin, 2019). PNI developed in response to research findings highlighting the fact that both

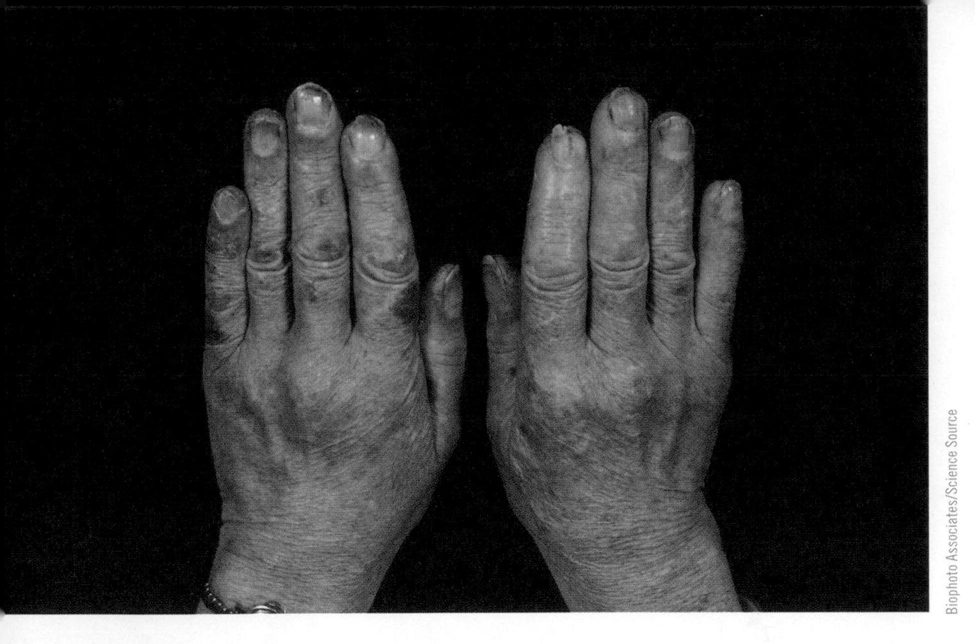

▲ **Lupus.** Hands of a patient with lupus, a chronic inflammatory disease that can affect the skin, as well as joints, kidneys, and other organs.

psychological and physical factors (especially stress) can affect the functioning of the immune system. As the name implies, PNI researchers study interactions between the nervous system, the endocrine system, the immune system, and psychological activity and behavior. This collaboration of researchers is needed because the cells of the immune, endocrine, and nervous systems each bear receptors that respond to the same neurotransmitters, neurohormones, and neuropeptides.

Behavioral Conditioning and Immunity

From a health psychological perspective, there are two main pillars of PNI research. The first pillar is the observation that alterations of immune function can be linked to a conditioned stimulus (CS), such that the CS becomes able to instigate immune changes similar to those instigated by the unconditioned stimulus (UCS) with which it has been paired (Wirth et al., 2011). Whereas the UCS would be some immunosuppressive drug, the CS could be a sound, a light, or, more commonly, flavored water. Thus, similar to how Pavlov conditioned a dog to salivate to the sound of a bell, researchers found that they could condition the body's immune system to also respond to a CS. Ader and Cohen (1975) conducted the classic study in this area when they demonstrated a conditioned immune response in rats. They paired a novel-tasting solution (sweet water, the CS) with an illness-inducing drug (cyclophosphamide, the UCS). The drug served to suppress the immune system.

After learning trials (pairing the CS and UCS), Ader and Cohen gave one group of animals the CS only, gave another group plain water, and gave a third group the UCS again. All animals were then immunized with sheep red blood cells and the immune responses were measured. As predicted, both the groups that got the UCS and the one that got the CS showed a suppressed immune system demonstrating that the body could be conditioned to react as if it received a drug. Similar studies have been conducted in humans as well. For example, Buske-Kirschbaum, Kirschbaum, Stierle, Lehnert, and Hellhammer (1992) gave college students sherbet (the CS) paired with epinephrine (the UCS). The UCS caused an unconditioned response of increasing the number of natural killer (NK) cells. When given sherbet a few days later (without the UCS), the students experienced a similar increase in NK cell activity. Conditioned immunosuppression has now amassed a sizeable body of support (Lückemann, Unteroberdörster, Kirchhof, Schedlowski, & Hadamitzky, 2017).

An active area of PNI research has fine-tuned conditioning processes (Ader et al., 1991), and research is now getting closer to giving us an understanding of the neural mechanisms that account for conditioned immune responses. We know that injections of chemical substances into specific areas of the brain that the nucleus acumbens may play an important role in conditioned immune modulations (Saurer et al., 2008). Unfortunately, even the titles of some of this research are hard to understand and require extensive knowledge of, and future study in, physiology. For example, look at this title: "TRIF contributes to epileptogenesis in temporal lobe epilepsy during TLR4 activation" (Wang et al., 2018).

Stress and Immunity

The second major pillar of PNI research is the association between the immune system and stress (Segerstrom, 2012). Knowledge of a stress–immune link can be traced back to the work of Hans Selye. Selye found that immune tissues such as the thymus atrophied in rats that were subjected to stress. Health psychologists have accumulated significant evidence that stressful life events and psychological distress predict biologically verified infectious illnesses by impacting the immune system (McCully, 2017). Upper respiratory infections such as the common cold have been the primary disease model used in the literature (Cohen et al., 1998). For example, Sheldon Cohen and colleagues have inoculated healthy individuals (volunteers for the study) with common cold or flu viruses after assessing for stress. The volunteers were kept in quarantine and monitored for the development of the illness. In one demonstration of the importance of strong family bonds, adults whose parents lived apart and never spoke during their childhood were more than three times as likely to develop a cold when exposed to the upper respiratory virus than adults from intact families (Murphy, Cohen, Janicki-Deverts, & Doyle, 2017).

Synthesize, Evaluate, Apply

- How can conditioning be used to create an immune response greater than that stimulated by a certain dose of a drug?
- What are the different ways in which stress and coping can influence the immune system's response?
- How are psychological factors linked with immunity?

Stress in general has been reliably associated with the functioning of the immune system (Anderson, 2018; Yrondi et al., 2017). Stress is inversely related to circulating lymphocytes such that the more stress we experience, the fewer lymphocytes are produced by our bodies (Golub & Fikslin, 2019). Stress is also accompanied by a redistribution of lymphocytes, and extended stress has been linked to the shrinking of the thymus (Sapolsky, 2017). Stress has been shown to kill T cells by a form of suicide killing, in which cortisol damages the DNA of the T cell, mutating it and causing it to eat itself up from the inside out (Compton & Cidlowski, 1986). Acute stressors such as final exams and sleep deprivation have been found to suppress immune function, causing an increase in illness (e.g., Kiecolt-Glaser et al., 1984; Kroll et al., 2017) and even slower wound healing (Kiecolt-Glaser, Page, Marucha, MacCallum, & Glaser, 1998; Meesters et al., 2017). Many life events are associated with immune system changes, such as job stress and unemployment (Boscolo et al., 2012), loss of a partner (Kemeny et al., 1995), separation (Kennedy, Kiecolt-Glaser, & Glaser, 1988), the strain of caregiving (Allen et al., 2017), and natural disasters (Felger, Haroon, & Miller, 2016). As can be expected, chronic illnesses negatively impact immunity as well (Georgopoulos et al., 2017) and stress reduces the immune system's ability to cope with chronic illnesses.

Note also, however, that acute stress may sometimes jump-start the **immune system**. In an inventive study, Schedlowski et al. (1993) wired 45 first-time parachutists and gathered measures of their stress chemicals and immune cells from one-half hour before their first jump, all the way through their jump, and then for some time after the jump. The numbers of both lymphocytes and NK cells significantly increased just after they jumped and then decreased greatly (to numbers below where they were before the whole process) one hour later. Thus, our immune responses are heavily tied to the context and chronicity of the stress. Why does chronic stress suppress the immune system? The best answer is that suppression prevents over-activity and consequently autoimmune diseases. Remember that one of the functions of the immune system is to distinguish self from non-self. If this process fails, problems ensue. Sometimes it does fail. With multiple sclerosis, for example, part of the nervous system is attacked by the body's own immune cells. In lupus, the cartilage around joints is attacked by the body's immune cells.

HIV AND AIDS

One of the most fatal autoimmune diseases is AIDS. Figures 12.2 and 12.3 show key global statistics on HIV/AIDS. These are two short acronyms, but each is associated with large amounts of pain, fear, death, and sadness. **Acquired immunodeficiency syndrome (AIDS)** is one of the most well-known of all the illnesses that cause death from complications with the immune system. AIDS is also a classic example of why it is important to focus on both psychological and biological processes (Golub & Fikslin, 2019). Figure 12.3 shows the number of people with AIDS worldwide.

Since the beginning of the AIDS epidemic in the late 1970s, it is estimated that more than one-half million people have died of AIDS in the United States, and many millions have died

▼ FIGURE 12.2

Number of New HIV Infections in 2016 and Change Since 2010

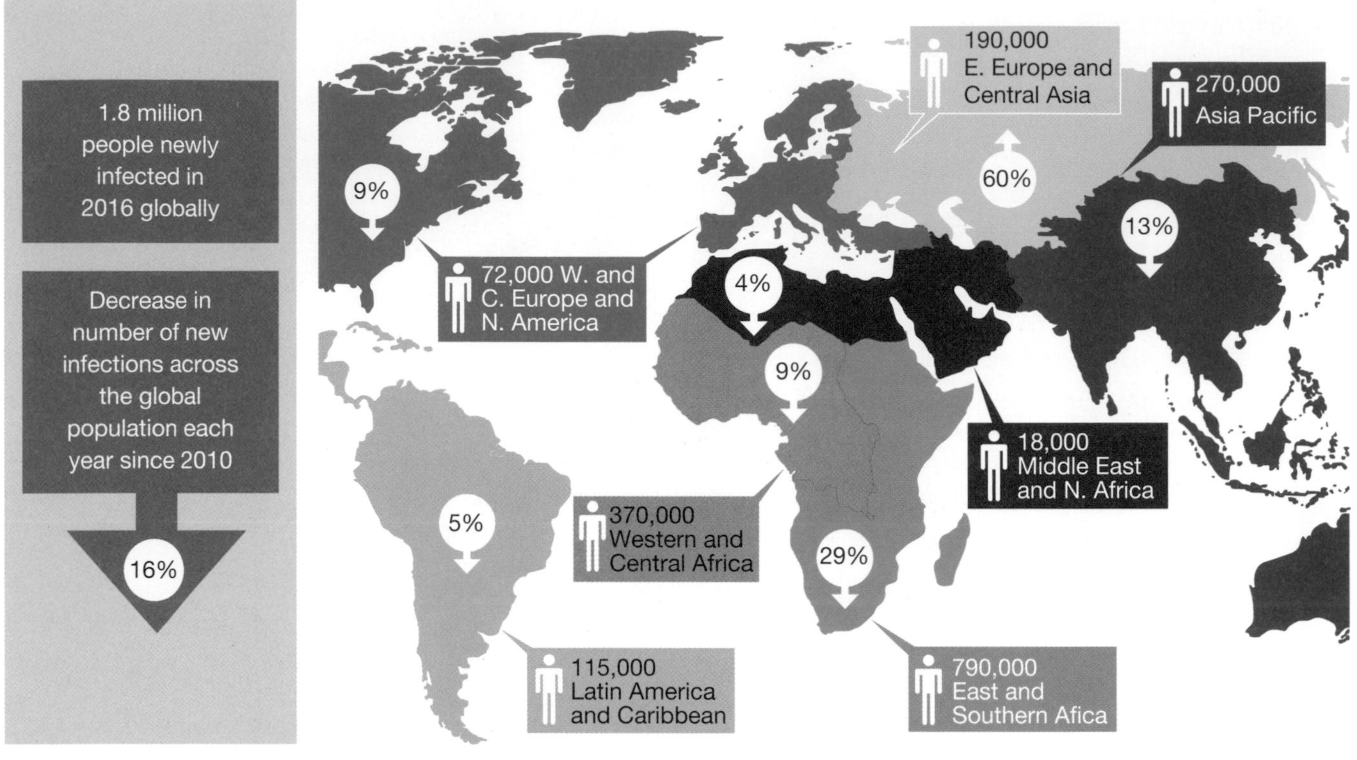

Source: Republished by permission of Avert, www.avert.org.

▼ FIGURE 12.3

People Living with HIV Worldwide

- In 2016, there were 36.7 million [30.8 million–42.9 million] people living with HIV.
    - 34.5 million [28.8 million–40.2 million] adults
    - 17.8 million [15.4 million–20.3 million] women (15+ years)
    - 2.1 million [1.7 million–2.6 million] children (<15 years)

Source: http://www.unaids.org/en/resources/fact-sheet

worldwide (CDC, 2018; World Health Organization [WHO], 2004). In this disorder, the immune system is gradually weakened and finally disabled by the **human immunodeficiency virus (HIV)**. HIV infection is now clearly a world pandemic, and although great strides are being made in understanding the epidemiology of the disease, the number of infected people worldwide continues to grow at an alarming rate, as shown in Figure 12.2 (WHO, 2017). More than 1.8 million people became newly infected with HIV in 2016 and 37 million people are currently living with HIV (UNAIDS, 2017). Some areas of the world have much higher rates than others. For example, Africa is more heavily affected by HIV and AIDS than any other region of the world. An estimated 22.9 million people were living with HIV at the end of 2016 and approximately 1.9 million additional people were infected with HIV during that year (UNAIDS, 2017). There are cultural differences among these diseases. Infection rates among African Americans are significantly higher than for European Americans (43% vs. 26%) and Latino Americans (26%) (CDC, 2018).

The History of AIDS

The CDC coined the term "AIDS" in 1982; HIV was discovered and named in 1984. Like most new diseases, the medical community first noticed similarities among the symptoms, such as fever, and pneumonia. In 1978 gay men in the United States and Sweden and heterosexuals in Tanzania and Haiti began showing symptoms of what would later come to be known as AIDS.

SAJJAD HUSSAIN / AFP / Getty Images

▲ **Those Impacted by AIDS.** Not just a "gay man's disease," AIDS has killed men, women, and children, and everyone has been influenced by it.

The epidemic became evident in the year 1981. In June of that year, the CDC reported that five young men, all active homosexuals, were treated for a special type of pneumonia (caused by *Pneumocystis carinii*) at three different hospitals in Los Angeles. At the same time, reports of 26 cases of a unique form of cancer (Kaposi's sarcoma) were also reported among gay men. Kaposi's sarcoma had been previously only a rare form of relatively benign cancer that tended to occur in older people. Because there was so little known about the transmission of what seemed to be a new disease, there was concern about contagion and whether the disease could be passed on by people who had no apparent signs or symptoms. For a long time, people believed that AIDS was just a disease seen in gay men and something that would not harm heterosexuals or women. AIDS was often referred to as a gay disease, and gay men were subjected to even more societal wrath. Men who were infected with HIV and at risk for AIDS were often shunned. Hollywood star Tom Hanks illustrated the prejudice and discrimination experienced by gay men, both in the workplace and in everyday life, in his Oscar-winning performance in the movie *Philadelphia* (1993). You see how his character's coworkers and even some of his character's friends start to treat him differently once his symptoms start showing. Matthew McConaughey won an Oscar for his performance playing Ron Woodroof, an AIDS patient diagnosed with HIV, in *Dallas Buyers Club* (2013).

The medical journal *Lancet* even called it the gay compromise syndrome, whereas at least one newspaper referred to it as GRID (gay-related immune deficiency). They were wrong. When it began turning up in children, since it can be transmitted from mother to child, and in transfusion recipients, public perceptions began to change. Until then it was entirely an epidemic seen in gay men, and it was easy for the average person to think it would not happen to him or her. The number of people who could become infected widened again at the beginning of 1983, when it was reported that the disease could be passed on heterosexually from men to women.

Business Wire/ Getty Images

▲ **Many Children Are Impacted By AIDS.** Campaigns are directed to help children who have lost parents to AIDS.

Worldwide, researchers searched frantically to identify the cause. At the CDC researchers had been continuing to investigate the cause of AIDS through a study of the sexual contacts of homosexual men in Los Angeles and New York. They identified a man as the link between a number of different cases, and they named him Patient O, for "Out of California" (some who read the published article on him misread the "O" as a "0" and referred to him as Patient Zero). He was a Canadian flight attendant named Gaëtan Dugas, whose job and sexual habits caused him to spread the virus. A large number of individuals infected early in the epidemic had some sort of contact with Dugas. Between 1983 and 1984, researchers at the Pasteur Institute in France and at the CDC and National Cancer Institute managed to crack the mystery and identified two viruses they believed caused AIDS: lymphadenopathy virus (LAV) and human T-lymphotropic virus type III (HTLV-III). In 1985 it was clear that both viruses were the same and were referred to as HIV. For an account of the history of AIDS, read *And the Band Played On* (Shilts, 2000).

From where did this virus come in the first place? During the early years of the epidemic, it was assumed that HIV made the transition from animals to humans at some time during the 1970s. It was not until 1999 that research suggested HIV had crossed over into the human population from a particular species of chimpanzee, probably through blood contact that occurred during hunting and field dressing of the animals (Gao et al., 1999).

HIV is transmitted primarily through the exchange of bodily fluids, and not by sitting on toilet seats that have been used by HIV carriers, as was once believed. Blood contains the highest concentration of the virus, followed by semen, followed by vaginal fluids, followed by breast milk. The most common ways of passing on HIV are by unprotected sexual contact, particularly vaginal or anal intercourse, and direct blood contact including injection drug needles, blood transfusions, accidents in health-care settings, or certain blood products. This is why blood donation centers are very careful about how they collect blood and why every needle is only used once and then discarded. For many years, people did not give blood because they feared HIV infection.

In 2008 the CDC introduced a new way to measure the incidence of HIV. New technology called the Serological Testing Algorithm for Recent HIV Seroconversion (STARHS) helps identify which HIV infections are new (CDC, 2018). STARHS determines which positive HIV tests represent new HIV infections (those that occurred within approximately the past 5 months). Before, HIV diagnosis data could only provide the best indication of recent trends in key populations. The problem was that diagnosis data only indicated when a person was diagnosed with HIV, not when an individual was actually infected, which can occur many years before a diagnosis. In 2008, using the new intricate statistics, data from 22 states (with specific HIV reporting systems) were extrapolated to the general population to provide the first national estimates of HIV incidence based on direct measurement. The method led to new estimates for national HIV (Hall et al., 2008).

The Difference between HIV and AIDS

Remember that HIV is the virus that causes AIDS and that HIV and AIDS are not synonymous. The Centers for Disease Control and Prevention defines someone as having AIDS if he or she is HIV positive and meets one or both of these conditions: has had at least one of 21 AIDS-defining opportunistic infections and/or has had a CD4 cell count (T cell count) of 200 cells or less (a normal CD4 count varies by laboratory, but usually is in the 600 to 1,500 range; CDC, 2018). A person can be HIV positive for a long time before developing AIDS. Currently, the average time between HIV infection and the appearance of signs that could lead to an AIDS diagnosis is 8 to 11 years. This time varies greatly from person to person and can depend on many factors including a person's health status and behaviors. Primary HIV infection is the first stage of HIV disease, when the virus first establishes itself in the body. Some researchers use the term *acute HIV infection* to describe the period of time between when a person is first infected with HIV and when antibodies against the virus are produced by the body (usually 6 to 12 weeks). Today, medical treatments that can slow down the rate at which HIV infection weakens the immune system are available. You may have heard about protein cocktails, combinations of medications that slow down the progression of the disease. Considered to be one of the best treatments available, the cocktail or **highly active antiretroviral therapy (HAART)** involves a variety of anti-HIV drugs that keep the virus from replicating. The utility of a combination of drugs is that if one certain combination does not work, another combination may. One of the most commonly used components of HAART is zidovudine (AZT). Other treatments can prevent or cure some of the illnesses associated with AIDS. As with other diseases, early detection offers more options for treatment and preventive health care.

AIDS research is actively working toward a cure and much is known about slowing down the disease. New drugs such as maraviroc, vicriviroc, and enfuvirtide increase the immune system's suppression of the virus and increase CD4 counts compared with a placebo (Pichenot, Deuffic-Burban, Cuzin, & Yazdanpanah, 2012). New data and considerations support initiating therapy before CD4 cell count declines to less than 350/microL (Hammer et al., 2008). The International AIDS Society–USA panel recommends that for patients with 350 CD4 cells/microL or more, the decision to begin therapy should be individualized based on the presence of other illness diagnoses, risk factors for progression to AIDS and non-AIDS diseases, and patient readiness for treatment. In addition to the prior recommendation that a high plasma viral load and rapidly declining CD4 cell count should prompt the start of treatment, developing illnesses such as heart disease or other serious conditions should prompt earlier therapy (Hammer et al., 2008).

PHYSIOLOGICAL CORRELATES OF HIV/AIDS

HIV is a retrovirus, an RNA virus that secretes an enzyme that injects its own RNA into DNA inside the cells that it infects (Segerstrom, 2012). DNA is where our genetic code is stored. When the HIV RNA manipulates the DNA of the host cell, the host cell functions improperly. HIV infects the cells of the immune system, specifically TH. About 60% of TH cells have a receptor known as CD4 whereas some TH (Helper T) cells have CD8 receptors (each has specific activation and suppression functions in the system). Two of the main physiological symptoms of AIDS are low numbers of CD4 T cells and higher than average numbers of CD8 cells. If you are healthy you probably have about 1,000 CD4 T cells per milliliter of blood. The sickest AIDS patient will have an average of less than 50 of these cells. The lack of these cells corresponds to the AIDS patient being unable to mount an effective immune defense. This invasion of HIV into the system proceeds through four main stages as shown in Figure 12.4.

Some people newly infected with HIV experience some flu-like symptoms (CDC, 2018). These symptoms, which usually last no more than a few days, might include fevers, chills, night

▼ FIGURE 12.4

Stages of HIV Infection

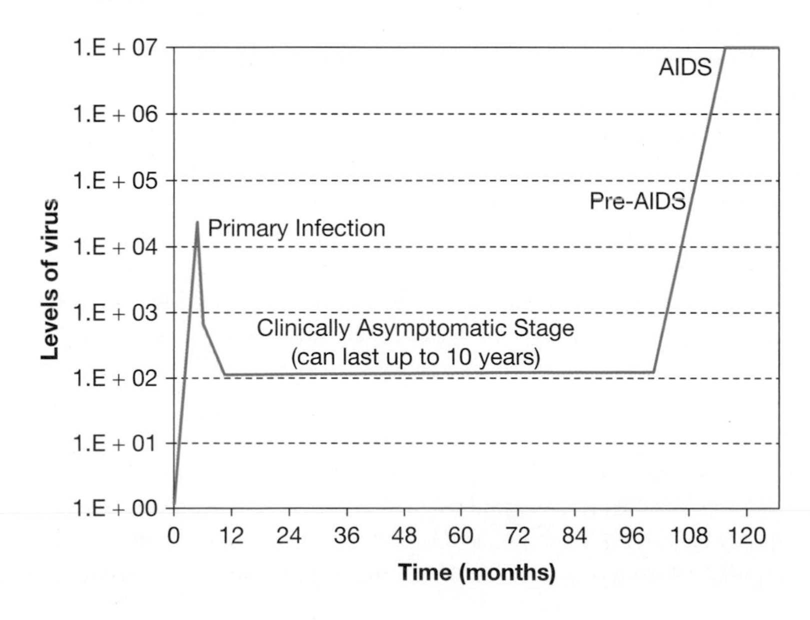

sweats, and rashes (not cold-like symptoms). Other people either do not experience acute infection or have symptoms so mild that they may not notice them. Given the general character of the symptoms of acute infection, they can easily have causes *other* than HIV, such as a flu infection. For example, if a person had some risk for HIV a few days ago and is now experiencing flu-like symptoms, it might be possible that HIV is responsible for the symptoms, but it is *also* possible that he or she has some other viral infection. Often some people with HIV have no symptoms, and studies of the effects of HIV normally include additional analyses to control for illness severity. HIV-positive patients can be either asymptomatic or symptomatic with or without an AIDS diagnosis. Classification as HIV/symptomatic requires the presence of at least one of the following symptoms in the past 6 months: diarrhea (one to six times per week or more), night sweats (one to six times per week or more), fevers (one to six times per week or more), yeast infections (two or more), weight loss of more than 10 pounds, thrush, or hairy leukoplakia, a precancerous condition that is seen as small thickened white patches, usually inside the mouth or vulva (CDC, 2018).

There are no common symptoms for individuals who have AIDS. Classification as having AIDS requires the presence of fewer than 200 CD4 T cells and/or an AIDS-defining condition (e.g., toxoplasmosis or cryptococcosis). When immune system damage is more severe, people may experience **opportunistic infections** (called opportunistic because they are caused by organisms that cannot induce disease in people with normal immune systems but take the opportunity to flourish in people with HIV infection). Most of these more severe infections, diseases, and symptoms fall under the CDC's definition of full-blown AIDS. Again, the median time to receive an AIDS diagnosis among those infected with HIV is 7 to 10 years.

PSYCHOLOGICAL CORRELATES OF HIV/AIDS

The utility of the biopsychosocial approach of health psychology is especially clear when one experiences an illness such as AIDS because both severe physiological and psychological problems are seen with the development of full-blown AIDS (Brandt, Jardin, Sharp, Lemaire, & Zvolensky, 2017). Psychological factors can influence the acquisition of HIV, the development of HIV infection into AIDS, and the progression of AIDS. As with other chronic illnesses, HIV/AIDS is influenced by a variety of psychological factors. Some psychological factors help a person cope with HIV infection and AIDS whereas others can shorten the time one lives with AIDS. AIDS patients often experience severe depression and poor quality of life. Patients without depression had significantly healthier immune systems (e.g., lower plasma neopterin concentrations, higher CD4(+) cell counts and hemoglobin concentrations) and better QOL scores than depressive patients (Yang, Thai, & Choi, 2016). In particular, optimism, social support, and coping styles are important psychosocial resources that have been consistently associated with good psychological and physical outcomes and that have been directly associated with lower emotional distress in patients with HIV infection (Furlotte & Schwartz, 2017; Zimmerman & Kirschbaum, 2017).

Optimism refers to generalized outcome expectancies that good things, rather than bad things, will happen and is associated with boosts in immune systems in the presence of HIV infection, higher NK cell cytotoxicity during stress and in some patients, protection against HIV exposure by decreasing intentions to engage in unsafe sex (Kalichman & Ramachandran, 1999; Levy et al., 2017). Optimists tend to cope better with stress, experience less negative mood effects, and may practice better health behaviors (Ironson & Hayward, 2008). Optimists, in general, show better psychological well-being (Kleiman et al., 2017), suggesting that optimism may be an important moderator of the likelihood of depression in response to a stressor such as HIV infection.

As discussed previously in Chapter 6, the presence of social support has been found to be health promoting and health restoring and is associated also with a decrease in mortality risk and progression of AIDS (Golub & Fikslin, 2019). Studies of populations with HIV infection suggest that social support from peers is critical for emotional well-being (Galvan, Davis, Banks, &

Bing, 2008) and, in periods of crisis, family support may become an especially important determinant of emotional well-being (Crystal & Kersting, 1998). In a 5-year study of HIV-positive patients, Theorell et al. (1995) found that participants who had more emotional support and reported better social networks showed significantly lesser declines in their T cell counts over the course of the study. Social support can even be useful delivered over the Internet (Kalichman et al., 2003).

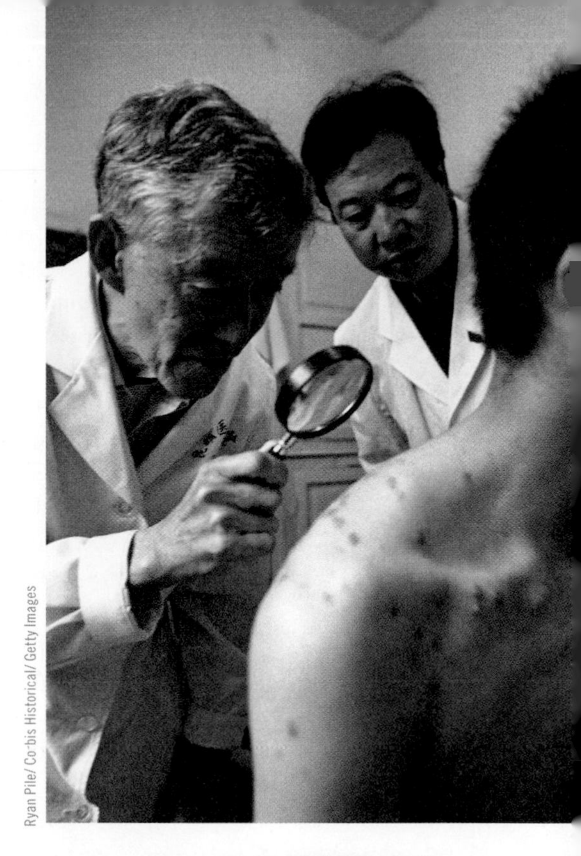

Ryan Pile/ Corbis Historical/ Getty Images

▲ **Providing Treatment.** Here, renowned Kunming dermatologist Dr. Want Zhengwen leads a grassroots outreach program to train doctors at the frontlines of southwest China's AIDS epidemic.

The amount of social support one has can also influence the transition from being HIV positive to actually developing AIDS (Leserman et al., 2000). Paradoxically, social support is one thing that persons with HIV infection or AIDS find harder to get because the label of being HIV positive or having AIDS often becomes stigmatizing, and people tend to avoid the patient (sometimes from the misplaced fear that HIV infection can be transmitted in the air or through casual contact).

Coping strategies, as described in Chapter 6, refer to the specific efforts, both behavioral and psychological, that people use to master, tolerate, reduce, or minimize stressful events (Lazarus & Launier, 1978). Among the coping strategies believed to relate to coping with HIV infection, different types stand out (Temoshok, Wald, Synowski, & Garzino-Demo, 2008). Problem-solving strategies include planning to confront the stressor and taking action; avoidance strategies include efforts to distract oneself from, ignore, or forget the stressor; and social support-seeking strategies include attempts to obtain emotional and information support. The first two categories map directly onto two major types of coping as analyzed in the literature—approach and avoidant coping (Lazarus & Folkman, 1991). An individual can approach a stressor and make active efforts to resolve it or he or she could try to avoid the problem (Moos & Schaefer, 1993). The third category emphasizes and incorporates the need for and importance of social support in the coping process (e.g., Sarason, Sarason, & Gurung, 2001). Turning to religion is a form of coping that is rising in use as well (Rzeszutek, Oniszczenko, & Firląg-Burkacka, 2017).

In general, patients with HIV infection who rely more on approach coping and who seek support tend to have a higher quality of life and experience less negative affect than those who make use of avoidant coping (Deichert et al., 2008). Despite the differences in health and health risk factors between minority and nonminority populations (Sikkema, Wagner, & Bogart, 2000), very few studies test for differences in psychosocial factors among ethnic groups. Some studies show that different ethnic groups vary in how social support is provided and used (e.g., Simoni, Demas, Mason, Drossman, & Davis, 2000), others show that different ethnic groups vary in coping styles in response to HIV infection (Heckman et al., 2000). Culture can play a key role as ethnic minority women living with HIV who more strongly identified with their cultural groups experienced more positive effects of social support as well (Lopez, Antoni, Fekete, & Penedo, 2012).

Psychological Factors Influencing Progression

Understanding psychological factors and core elements of personality also provides insight into AIDS progression (Ironson & Hayward, 2008). Ironson, O'Cleirigh, Weiss, Schneiderman, and Costa (2008) examined the role of the Big Five personality domains (neuroticism, extroversion, openness, agreeableness, conscientiousness) on change in CD4 cells and other indicators of immune health. The researchers used an ethnically diverse sample of HIV-seropositive patients who completed a personality assessment (NEO-PI-R) and underwent comprehensive psychological assessment and blood sampling every 6 months for 4 years. AIDS indicators and personality were strongly associated. Personality factors that were significantly associated with slower disease progression over 4 years included openness, extroversion, and conscientiousness.

Specific personality characteristics significantly related to slower disease progression were assertiveness, positive emotions, and gregariousness (extroversion); ideas, esthetics (openness); achievement striving, and order (conscientiousness). Personality styles that helped patients remain engaged (e.g., creative interactors, upbeat optimists, welcomers, and go getters) had slower disease progression, whereas the homebody profile (low extroversion–low openness) was significantly associated with faster disease progression (Ironson et al., 2008).

Understandably, when a person first finds out he or she may be HIV positive, they often experience intense anxiety and maybe even some denial, which is often followed by depression (Sherr, Clucas, Harding, Sibley, & Catalan, 2011). AIDS patients who deny the reality of their being HIV positive often experience a more rapid development of symptoms (Ironson, Schneiderman, Kumar, & Antoni, 1994). There are some curious exceptions. Reed, Kemeny, Taylor, Wang, and Visscher (1994) found that HIV-positive men who denied their diagnosis actually survived longer than those who accepted their fate. Conflicting evidence such as this clearly demonstrates the need to better understand the ways different psychological constructs interact to influence coping.

One psychological outcome of HIV infection and AIDS is unequivocally dangerous: depression. Depression is a critical psychosocial risk factor for individuals with compromised immune systems (Greeson et al., 2008). It is a common experience of AIDS patients (Sherr et al., 2011) and is related to physical symptomatology, number of days spent in bed, and progression of HIV infection (e.g., Cole & Kemeny, 1997). Anxiety and depression also have physiological consequences (Leserman, 2008). For example, Greeson et al. (2008) found a significant relationship between higher distress levels and greater disease severity. This relationship was mediated by diminished natural killer (NK) cell count and cytotoxic function, as well as increased cytotoxic (CD8[+]) T cell activation. As a testimony to the usefulness of a biopsychosocial approach, Greeson et al. (2008) found that a psychoimmune model accounted for 67% of the variation in HIV disease severity.

Next, I will use the example of depression to highlight some important cultural differences in the experience of HIV infection and AIDS, especially focusing on the cultural components of sex and ethnicity.

Synthesize, Evaluate, Apply

- What factors in the history and nature of AIDS are most responsible for the worldwide health epidemic of this disease today?
- Compare and contrast coping with AIDS with coping with stress. What techniques would be more beneficial in this context?
- In what ways does the delivery of social support have to be modified in the context of AIDS?

CULTURAL VARIATIONS IN HIV/AIDS

Women and HIV/AIDS

Depression is more prevalent among women than men with HIV infection, and many studies have focused on depressed women at risk for and with HIV (Fasce, 2008). This is a change from even 5 years ago when much of what was known about the psychosocial concomitants of AIDS was provided by studies of gay men (Mays & Cochran, 1987). Gay men infected with HIV tend to be more economically advantaged, better educated, likely to be European American, and often have no dependents, relative to women infected with HIV (Siegel, Karus, Ravies, & Hagan, 1998). Women account for an increasing percentage of new cases of HIV infection (CDC, 2018), and low-income women of color are especially at risk (Gurung et al., 2004).

Differences between ethnic groups change with time. Some years ago, Latina women were seven times more likely to get AIDS than European American women (Klevens, Diaz, Fleming, Mays, & Frey, 1999). Ten years later, Latina women were four times more likely to contract AIDS than European American women (CDC, 2018). In 2009, Latinos accounted for 20% of new HIV infections in the United States while representing approximately 16% of the total U.S. population (CDC, 2018). Women account for 50% of all estimated HIV infections worldwide, and the proportion of women infected is rapidly increasing in every geographical area (UNAIDS, 2018).

Some key physiological differences between men and women increase women's likelihood to be infected. Women are more likely than men to be infected with HIV via heterosexual sex, and male to female transmission of HIV is eight times more likely than female to male transmission (Padian, Shiboski, Glass, & Vittinghoff, 1997). Whereas vaginal fluids can be easily washed off the male anatomy after sex, seminal fluids can reside within the female vagina for a long period, increasing the chance of infection. Furthermore, the tissue lining the walls of the vagina is fragile and prone to injury and related infection. Psychological power differentials are important as well (Thorburn, Harvey, & Ryan, 2005). It is also harder for women to raise the issue of condom use than it is for men, given the traditional power differentials in the sexes, the possibility of abuse, or cultures in which women are not supposed to admit to sexual knowledge (Abel & Chambers, 2004).

Women with HIV infection and chronic depressive symptoms are up to 2.4 times more likely to die even after controls were added for other clinical features known to be associated with morbidity and mortality (Ickovics et al., 2001). Such differences in incidence and in the responses (e.g., depression) compel a closer look at this group of individuals.

Ethnicity and HIV/AIDS

Together with gender, ethnicity may also be a critical variable in the relationship between depression, HIV status, and health (Mays, Maas, Ricks, & Cochran, 2012). There are some clear-cut differences in mortality patterns, health status, and health risk factors between ethnic minorities compared with each other and with the European American population (Sikkema et al., 2000; Sue, 2000). For example, African American and Latina women account for approximately 73% of AIDS cases diagnosed among women in the United States (CDC, 2018). African Americans and Latino Americans have been disproportionately affected by HIV infection, as is demonstrated by HIV seroprevalence and in the numbers of reported cases of AIDS (CDC, 2018). Among women, as of 2016, African American women had the highest incidence rate of AIDS (57%), compared with European American women (21%; CDC, 2018). Figure 12.5 shows the differences in prevalence of HIV across ethnicities.

Ethnic and sex differences in HIV infection and AIDS also interact (Tedaldi, Absalon, Thomas, Shlay, & van den Berg-Wolf, 2008). Are psychological problems such as depression a greater risk factor for ethnic minority HIV-positive women? Additional knowledge on the concomitants of depression in women with HIV infection across different ethnic groups is sorely needed (Sikkema et al., 2000). To fill this need, Gurung et al. (2004) studied an ethnically diverse sample of low-income women at risk for AIDS. The prospective design followed 350 African American, Latina, and European American women over a 6-month period to assess the relationship of HIV status, SES, and chronic burden to depression and examine the moderation of these effects by psychosocial resources (social support, optimism, and coping style). HIV status and ethnicity were significantly associated with depressed mood at each point, but not with changes over time.

Gurung et al. (2004) paint a graphic picture of how ethnicity, SES, and sex can influence coping with HIV infection. Being seropositive for HIV was a significant stressor associated with depression, but it was also associated with a substantially greater number of chronic burdens affecting all aspects of life, including money, housing, work, vulnerability to crime, and relationships. The fact that these differences were found

▼ FIGURE 12.5

New HIV Diagnoses and U.S. Population by Race/ Ethnicity, 2015

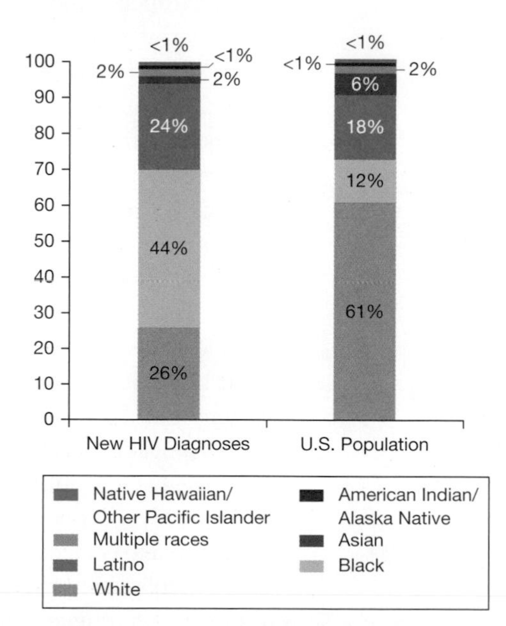

Source: The Kaiser Family Foundation's State Health Facts. Data Source: CDC, HIV Surveillance Report, Diagnosis of HIV Infection in the United States and Dependent Areas, November 2017.

between the HIV-seropositive and HIV-seronegative women after controlling for SES suggests that seropositivity confers risk for these additional burdens and highlights how biology and the social world directly interact. HIV infection thus increases vulnerability to depression both in its own right and secondarily by expanding the range of chronic burdens to which low-income seropositive women are vulnerable. Moreover, although HIV-positive women were significantly more depressed than HIV-negative women, changes in depression over the 6-month period of the investigation were more strongly predicted by changes in the chronic burdens the women faced that are frequently associated with low SES.

Studies have begun to take a close look at the ethnicity by sex interaction. Tillerson (2008) examined key HIV risk factors (risky sex, drug use, inconsistent disclosure of same-sex behavior by male partners, and sexually transmitted diseases) to explain the higher incidence of HIV infection among African American women. A review of studies published between 1985 and 2006 showed that African American women are no more likely to have unprotected sex, have multiple sexual partners, or use drugs than women of other ethnic groups. Some studies did suggest that African American women are more likely to have risky sex partners and STDs and African American men are less likely to disclose their same-sex behavior to female partners (Tillerson, 2008).

There is also an interaction between ethnicity and health behaviors. By itself, poor health behaviors aggravate HIV by reducing immune functioning (e.g., cigarette smoking; Robinson, Moody-Thomas, & Gruber, 2012; Shuter, Bernstein, & Moadel, 2012). Different ethnic groups perform health behaviors to different extents, which further muddies the water. Take the case of drug use (sharing needles is a major cause of the spread of HIV). Between 1992 and 2004, the proportion of patients admitted to hospitals reporting using injections declined 44% among African Americans but only 14% for European Americans (Broz & Ouellet, 2008). Similarly, the peak age for heroin users in treatment increased 10 years for African Americans while declining over 10 years for European Americans.

These studies and others on other cultural variables (e.g., socioeconomic status; Werth, Borges, McNally, Maguire, & Britton, 2008) provide clear examples of why a biopsychosocial approach to understanding chronic illnesses such as HIV infection is critical.

Other Cultural Issues

Race, ethnicity, and nationality also influence the extent to which **sexual mixing** takes place (Wong et al., 2008). Sexual mixing, which has been found to have a central influence on HIV transmission rates (Tornesello et al., 2008), is defined as the extent to which people engage in sexual activities with sexual partners from other sexual networks (dissortative mating) versus partners from their own network (assortative mixing). Heavy mixers form an important link in the spread of HIV infection. Laumann, Gagnon, Michael, and Michaels (1994) examined sexual mixing in a national sample of heterosexual adults aged 18 to 49. Their data indicated that for respondents with multiple sexual partners, women are more likely than men to be heavy mixers (14% vs. 11%) and that Latino males (59% vs. 17% African American and 5% Caucasian) and females (33% vs. 4% African American and 15% Caucasian) are more likely than other males and females to be heavy mixers with African American males and Caucasian females reporting moderate levels of mixing. Developmental state is important, and these patterns vary by age group. Young adult Latino males and females report the heaviest mixing.

Advances in genetic research and the ability to hone in on specific parts of genes are providing new insights into cultural differences in diseases such as HIV infection and AIDS (Dogan et al., 2015; Klimas, Koneru, & Fletcher, 2008). For example, Mays et al. (2002) suggested that one useful area to consider in identifying ethnic differences in HIV infection is in the distribution of human leukocyte antigen (HLA). HLA molecules serve to initiate the immune response by how they present antigens to T cells, which, as described above, then clear the virus from the body. Ethnic variations in the genes encoding HLA molecules can affect antigen presentation and, correspondingly, how the host responds (Pérez et al., 2008). Variations in aspects of HLA molecules (the specific details of which are technically beyond the scope of this text) have been found across racial groups. Some aspects of HLA were four times more likely to be found in African Americans than in European Americans (Dunston, Henry, Christian, Ofosu, & Callendar, 1989). Osborne and Mason (1993) have also found aspects of HLA unique to the Latino population. The new discoveries are paving the way for the design of new genetic therapies targeting specific gene variations among individuals (McNicholl & Smith, 1997).

There are also important differences in social network use across cultural groups. Aitken, Higgs, and Bowden (2008) compared the social networks of Vietnamese Australian injecting drug users (IDUs) with those of other ethnicities. Results showed that the Vietnamese IDUs were more highly connected, intricate, and dense networks. The Vietnamese Australians were at greater risk for blood-borne infection (and had relatively high HIV prevalence; Aitken et al., 2008). Similarly, Ferreira (2008) explored how a South African community coped with living with HIV/AIDS. The study found that community members coped with HIV/AIDS by relying on culture and family, faith in God, religion, and prayer. Inner strength, hope, optimism, and expectancy appeared to be key resources for informal settlement residents (Ferreira, 2008).

The great ethnic discrepancies in incidence and prevalence of HIV and AIDS compel more cross-cultural research, but this has been slow in developing. Much research continues to be conducted using European American men (Mays et al., 2002) although researchers such as Wyatt et al. (2002) and Sikkema, Hansen, Kochman, Tate, and Difranciesco (2004) focus on mixed ethnic samples of women. African Americans, who make up 34% of all AIDS cases (Fahey & Flemming, 1997), previously made up only 7% of National Institutes of Health HIV studies (Ready, 1988). Similarly, Latinos represent 17% of AIDS cases but were only represented by 9% of research participants (Mays et al., 2002).

HEALTH PSYCHOLOGICAL MODELS RELATING TO HIV/AIDS

Given that one of the major ways of contracting HIV infection is via unprotected or risky sexual activity, you may think that one easy way to curtail the spread of AIDS is to get people to have safe sex. Of course, that is easier said than done. For years, researchers have been trying to get men and women to have safe sex. These efforts range from educating individuals on the proper use of condoms to changing behavioral intentions. In a general sense, practicing safe sex is analogous to any other health behavior and consequently most of the research designed to change health behaviors (discussed in Chapter 7) applies here as well. For example, researchers have used the Health Belief Model and the Theory of Planned Behavior to influence beliefs and intentions in regard to condom use and safe sex (Rendina, Whitfield, Grov, Starks, & Parsons, 2017). Indeed, most HIV interventions are adapted from existing theories and models such as the Transtheoretical model (Tung, Hu, Efird, Su, & Yu, 2013) and other evidence-based interventions (EBIs) to save time and money. Wingood and DiClemente (2008) developed a framework for adapting HIV-related EBIs, known as the ADAPT-ITT model. The ADAPT-ITT model consists of eight sequential phases that inform HIV prevention providers and researchers of a prescriptive method for adapting EBIs.

There are also models designed specifically for HIV patients. For example, the Information-Motivation-Behavioral Skills (Starace, Massa, Amico, & Fisher, 2006) model of health behavior provides a framework for guiding HIV risk reduction interventions and has been modified for many different subgroups (e.g., for men who have sex with men at high-risk for HIV infection; Kalichman, Picciano, & Roffman, 2008). In another example, Catania, Kegeles, and Coates (1990b) proposed the AIDS Risk Reduction Model (ARRM), which states that people must first understand the threat of HIV infection and recognize that their behaviors put them at risk for infection with the virus and consequently developing the disease. In a recent demonstration of

Per-Anders Pettersson/ Getty Images News

▲ **Public Service Ads Designed to Inform about HIV/AIDS.** Here is an example of a public service ad from South Africa.

the efficacy of the model, Champion and Collins (2012) designed an intervention specifically for Mexican and African American adolescent women with a history of abuse and sexually transmitted infection and showed it was effective for prevention of infection.

Attitudes toward the protective behavior matter too. Using condoms can significantly reduce the risk of contracting a sexually transmitted disease, but many people believe that condoms reduce sexual pleasure, and this belief decreases condom use (Albarracin et al., 2000). Others may not be confident in their ability to properly use condoms (Rosario, Nahler, Hunter, & Gwadz, 1999). As suggested by the social norms component of the Theory of Planned Behavior, people's attitudes toward condom use will also be influenced by what they think the norms are and what they believe their friends and partners think about it (Fischer, Fisher, & Rye, 1995). Other factors influencing condom use include concurrent alcohol or drug use, level of commitment between the people having sex, level of sexual arousal—more arousal leads to less use of condoms—and the type of relationship—women are more likely to practice safer sex in casual sexual relationships (Gordon, Carey, & Carey, 1997; Katz, Fortenberry, Zimet, Blythe, & Orr, 2000).

Richard Levine / Corbis News/ Getty Images

▲ **Public Service Ads Designed to Inform about HIV/AIDS.** Here is an example of a public service ad from the United States.

The first line of attack is most often education. If you can increase a person's knowledge about an illness, automatically their beliefs about their own susceptibility or vulnerability to it as well as their sense of the severity of the disease (factors from the Health Belief Model) will change. There are many misperceptions about HIV infection and who is most likely to get it. I already mentioned that people tend to believe that it is something just homosexuals get. In general, studies have found that although some segments of the population are well informed about AIDS (e.g., gay men), others such as adolescents are not (LeBlanc, 1993). Similarly, Murphy, Mann, O'Keefe, and Rotheram-Borus (1998) found that single, inner-city women often have little knowledge of AIDS or what behaviors place them at risk. Methods for providing education vary. General interventions that provide counseling about HIV infection seem to be effective to curtail the activity of those already infected with HIV but are not as effective for those who are not (Weinhardt, Carey, Johnson, & Bickman, 1999). Instead, more targeted interventions (e.g., those aimed at very specific populations) have proved to be more effective (Hardré, Garcia, Apamo, Mutheu, & Ndege, 2012).

Jeff Greenberg / Universal Images Group/ Getty Images

▲ **Public Service Ads Designed to Inform about HIV/AIDS.** Here is an example of a public service ad from Australia.

Beyond education about AIDS, health psychological interventions have also targeted sexual activity (Chin et al., 2012). For most health behaviors, the best predictor of future behavior is past behavior. Old habits die hard. If a person has used condoms and practiced safe sex before, he or she is more likely to do it in the future. Modifying sexual behavior becomes especially difficult because it is linked to ideas of freedom and spontaneity. For many young men and women, being independent translates into not having to do anything (e.g., particularly have sex) in any specific way (even safely). Modification of sexual behavior has been found to be a threat to identity (McKusick, Horstman, & Coates, 1985). Consequently, many interventions are designed to vary different aspects of the process of indulging in sexual behavior. Some teach people how to exercise self-control and not rush into sex, which is more often unsafe (Miller, Bettencourt, DeBro, & Hoffman, 1993). Other interventions model skills to avoid high-risk behaviors (Van der Velde & Van der Pligt, 1991).

In general, group-based interventions designed to reduce risky sexual behavior work better than interventions to reduce sexual activity (i.e., increase abstinence; Chin et al., 2012). Correspondingly, most interventions focus on sexual risk behavior (Gerressu & Stephenson, 2008). Noar (2008) examined 18 meta-analyses (9,423 participants, essentially a meta-meta-analysis) and found that all meta-analyses examining interventions aimed to increase condom use and reduce general sexual risk were statistically significant (Odds ratio = 1.34 and .78, respectively). A majority of the meta-analyses (9 of 11) showed interventions for reducing unprotected sex were significant (odds ratio = .76). Interventions for reducing numbers of sexual partners (odds ratio = .87) and reducing STDs (odds ratio = .74) were also effective.

You may be surprised at what works. Albarracin, Leeper, Earl, and Durantini (2008) found that even having people read educational brochures increased the likelihood they would watch an educational video, which in turn increased participation in a counseling session designed to educate about reducing risky sexual behavior. People expecting the counseling to be useful were more likely to attend the session after watching the video (i.e., expectation was a mediator).

Being HIV positive does not signify the end of sexual activity. Safe sex does not mean no sex either. More than 70% of people infected with HIV continue to be sexually active (Kline & VanLandingham, 1994), and a large number of interventions seek to increase disclosure of status. Such interventions empower those with HIV infection to disclose their status to friends and family. Not only does this disclosure provide the patient with more opportunities for social support, but it also allows their sexual partners to make informed decisions about sexual activity with them. In addition, men who disclose their HIV status are more likely to practice safe sex (DeRosa & Marks, 1998).

The changing demographics of America and the ethnic differences in HIV incidence have led a number of researchers to focus on specific ethnic groups when designing interventions. In one meta-analysis, Albarracin, Albarracin, and Durantini (2008) examined data from studies (more than 110,000 participants) assessing the efficacy of HIV-prevention interventions across samples with higher and lower concentrations of Latinos. Groups with higher percents of Latinos did not benefit from the interventions as much as groups with lower percents of Latinos (e.g., did not increase condom use). Interestingly, groups with more Latinos only benefited from intervention strategies that included threat-inducing arguments. Groups with greater percents of Latinos/ Latin Americans benefited from interventions conducted by a lay community member,

Jonas Gratzer / LightRocket/ Getty Images

▲ **Yoga for Health.** More and more groups offer yoga classes specifically designed for people with HIV/AIDS. Inside the Yash Foundation, a nongovernmental organization based in Nashik, India, HIV-positive women practice yoga to strengthen their bodies. The postures and movements serve to relieve many of the physical symptoms, ease anxiety, and help with coping.

whereas groups with lower percents of these groups increased condom use the most in response to experts. Supporting the subtext of this book, there were important differences by sex, acculturation, and nationality.

In a similar meta-analysis focused on an ethnic group, Darbes, Crepaz, Lyles, Kennedy, and Rutherford (2008) reviewed HIV interventions for heterosexual African Americans to determine the overall efficacy in reducing HIV-risk sex behaviors and incident sexually transmitted diseases and identify intervention characteristics associated with efficacy. They found 38 randomized controlled trials (1988 to 2005) that showed that interventions significantly reduced unprotected sex (odds ratio = 0.75) and marginally decreased incidents of sexually transmitted diseases (odds ratio = 0.88; Darbes et al., 2008). Successful intervention components included cultural tailoring, aiming to influence social norms in promoting safe sex behavior, using peer education, providing skills training on correct use of condoms and communication skills needed for negotiating safer sex, and multiple sessions and opportunities to practice learned skills (refer to Chapter 6 for intervention best practices and Chapter 1 for odds ratios).

To tackle health disparities head on is critical to ensure that interventions reflect cultural competence. For example, Latino Americans have unique cultural and social characteristics and norms that place them at risk for HIV exposure (Weidel, Provencio-Vasquez, Watson, & Gonzalez-Guarda, 2008). Correspondingly, there is now a group intervention designed for Latino patients living with HIV/AIDS in New York City (Acevedo, 2008). The intervention attempts to compensate for cultural influences on adherence, social isolation, stigma, disclosure, safer sex practices, and patient–provider communication. Similarly, Sister-to-Sister is a skill-building HTV7STD risk-reduction intervention for African American women that had significant effects in reducing self-reported sexual risk behavior and biologically confirmed STD incidence (O'Leary, Jemmott, & Jemmott, 2008). In analyses of mediating variables, O'Leary et al. (2008) found that self-efficacy for condom carrying was the critical factor. Apparently, the skill-building sexual risk-reduction interventions on women's use of condoms worked to improve the women's belief that they would be successful using condoms. In fact, self-efficacy was more important than characteristics of male partners (e.g., their reactions to the woman wanting to use a condom).

Psychological Interventions for Those with HIV/AIDS

Focusing on psychological states is key. A review of psychological interventions for HIV-positive persons showed intervening can improve psychological adjustment and consequently positively affect neuroendocrine regulation and immune status (Carrico & Antoni, 2008). Psychological interventions are particularly effective in reducing the depression experienced by those with HIV (Sherr et al., 2011) and increasing coping skills (Harding, Liu, Catalan, & Sherr, 2011). It is possible that a large part of the effect is due to the intervention groups providing social support and a key research agenda item is a fine-tuned examination of the effects of individual components of complex psychological interventions.

Given that stress can also negatively impact the immune system (as discussed previously), stress management becomes even more important for people with HIV. Some interventions aimed at reducing the ill effects of HIV infection and AIDS have used physical activity and cognitive-behavioral approaches (Sherr et al., 2011). For example, aerobic exercise training was found to lessen the drop in immune functioning that normally accompanies being informed of a positive HIV test (La Perriere et al., 1991). Cognitive-behavioral stress management interventions have similar effects (Antoni et al., 1991, 2001; Cruess et al., 2000), although not all such attempts are successful (Coates, McKusick, Kuno, & Stites, 1989).

There has been a lot of recent research designed to compare the role of stress management interventions in enhancing immune function. McCain et al. (2008) conducted a randomized clinical trial to test effects of three 10-week stress management approaches—cognitive-behavioral relaxation training, tai chi training, and spiritual growth groups. Compared to the control group, both the relaxation and tai chi groups used less emotion-focused coping. Furthermore, all intervention groups showed better immune cell functioning. Scott-Sheldon, Kalichman, Carey, and Fielder (2008) evaluated interventions to reduce stress as a means to improve health among persons living with HIV. Their meta-analytic review integrated the results of 35 randomized controlled trials examining the efficacy of 46 separate stress management interventions for 3,077 HIV positive adults. Compared to control group participants, Scott-Sheldon et al. (2008) found that stress-management interventions reduce anxiety, depression, distress, and fatigue and improve quality of life, a finding supported by Clucas, Sibley, Harding, Liu, Catalan, and Sherr (2011). In contrast, stress-management interventions did not appear to improve CD4+ counts or viral load compared with controls. Clearly, this conclusion about the absence of effect on immune functioning is inconsistent with McCain et al. (2008). Why? The studies reviewed by Scott-Sheldon et al. (2008) had shorter assessment periods (measured typically within one-week of the interventions) and participants were in more advanced stages of HIV (HIV-positive for an average of 5 years). Furthermore, the sample was predominately male and European American.

Synthesize, Evaluate, Apply

- How do cultural factors influence the behaviors that put someone at risk for HIV infection and for its spread?
- Given the fatal course of HIV infection, what psychological factors could explain why people would still continue to engage in unsafe sexual practices/drug use?
- Compare and contrast interventions for HIV/AIDS with interventions to improve health behaviors such as mammogram screenings.

APPLICATION SHOWCASE

YOGA AND COPING WITH ILLNESSES SUCH AS HIV/AIDS

Scientists are working hard to find the cures for chronic and terminal illnesses such as cancer and AIDS, and although advancements are being made, there are no absolute cures as yet. A large focus then is on how best to help the patient cope with the pain and discomfort of the illness. Health psychologists are very useful in this regard. Many cognitive and behavioral approaches are used, but a majority of techniques involve some form of relaxation training, such as guided imagery or meditation. One particular technique that has become popular with the North American general public and one that is growing in utility in the treatment of chronic illnesses as well is yoga (Agarwal, Kumar, & Lewis, 2015). Approximately 6% of Americans use yoga for health purposes (NCCAM, 2017).

Up to a few years ago (and maybe in the minds of some of you today as well) yoga conjured up images of people bent into twisted, uncomfortable shapes and was a lifestyle

(Continued)

(Continued)

associated with hippies, flower children, and pacifism. There are many stereotypes about yoga, and this is a good time to look at the facts. Practices such as yoga are likely to become more accepted in public consciousness as the utility of using the mind to calm and relax the body gets even stronger empirical validation. To the millions of practitioners of yoga, the benefits are clear, and many people practice yoga daily. Given that a complete yoga lifestyle does include the practicing of many healthy behaviors like not smoking, limiting drinking alcohol, physical activity, relaxation and meditation, good eating, and getting enough sleep, the practice of yoga shows a potential for enhancing the quality of life of those with chronic illnesses.

Yoga originated in India approximately 4,000 years ago, and the word is derived from Sanskrit (an ancient Indian language), meaning to unite. There are many different aspects in the practice of yoga. The physical postures are just one aspect. Derived from Hinduism and Buddhism, the practice of yoga has as its basic goal the transformation of the self and diminished cravings. Yoga is a part of the Ayurvedic approach to health. Traditionally practitioners believed that a universal spirit pervades everything and used yoga to clear the mind and release this spirit. A stressed mind was compared with a turbid lake and yoga calmed the waters. There are four main types of yoga. Hatha yoga stresses purification, postures, relaxation, and diet. Hatha yoga and variations of it are the most common forms of yoga in North America. The most common variation is Iyengar yoga, which is characterized by precise poses often with the aid of various props, such as cushions, benches, wood blocks, straps, and even sand bags. Other variations are Astanga yoga (involving synchronizing of breath with a progressive series of postures) and Bhikram yoga (in which postures are done in a 100°F heated room). Other forms of yoga include Jnana yoga (yoga of wisdom involving a study of literature and striving for attainment of right views), Bhakti yoga (yoga of devotion, finding inner change through prayer or religious ecstasy), and Karma yoga (yoga of action and the pursuit of a higher social purpose).

Yoga involves a lot more than just striking poses. Traditional yoga has eight parts (angas or limbs). There are four practices and four experiences for which one should strive. The practices involve (1) attitude toward the world (abstinence, truthfulness, and chastity), (2) attitude toward self (purification and contentment), (3) posture (or asana, which is what you probably have heard of), and (4) breath regulation (*pranayama*). The four experiences are (1) withdrawal of senses (*pratyaha*), (2) fixed attention (*dhyana*), (3) contemplation (*dharana*), and (4) absolute concentration (superconsciousness/*samadhi*). A true yoga practitioner would not only do the physical components but also strive to live life in accordance with the moral and psychological components. Only a small number of the many Americans who practice yoga strive for (or even know about) the complete scope of the practice.

The use of yoga for the treatment of chronic illnesses is increasing, and empirical studies of its effectiveness for a range of illnesses have slowly begun to be reported (Littman et al., 2012). For example, patients with multiple sclerosis in a yoga class showed significant improvement in measures of fatigue compared with a control group of patients with similar levels of the disease (Oken et al., 2004). Similar successes have been found with cardiovascular functioning (Harinath et al., 2004) and diabetes (Alexander et al., 2012). Yoga has been implemented in a number of different health-care programs. For example, the Stanford Cancer Supportive Care Program (SCSCP) at the Center for Integrative Medicine at Stanford Hospitals offers yoga to both cancer patients and their families. A recent assessment showed that more than 90% of the patients using the SCSCP felt there was benefit to the program, and yoga was one of the classes with the highest number of participants (Rosenbaum et al., 2004).

In the context of HIV infection and AIDS, a number of AIDS patients use yoga to ease their pain and negative feelings (Bonadies, 2004) or reduce their high blood pressure and risk for cardiovascular disease (Cade et al., 2010). In a study of complementary and alternative medicine (CAM) use in a British Columbia HIV treatment center, 36% said they used yoga (Dhalla, Chan, Montaner, & Hogg, 2006). AIDS patient Steve McCeney (quoted in the *Yoga Journal,* 2001) provides a glimpse of what it is like. He said, "Sometimes I don't know what it's like to feel normal anymore, but I do know that after an hour of restorative poses, I feel like a new person mentally, spiritually, and physically." An international group of yoga therapists provides a variety of special resources and information for AIDS patients, and studies of the effects of yoga on HIV infection are being conducted.

Some yoga postures are thought to activate the hormonal system of the body, the ductless glands of the body, to start to balance their activities. For example, I talked earlier about the role of the thymus gland in the immune system. Open-chested poses such as Supta Baddha Konasana (reclining bound angle pose) or Setu Bandha over bolsters or a bench (bridge pose) stimulate the thymus gland (Kout, 1992). Yoga also can be a psychological booster, helping patients to strengthen their minds and build their resolve. In the words of another AIDS patient:

> Yoga is the main thing that makes me feel good, besides emotional things I can do with a partner or being in love. I really feel it if I don't have it every week. It is a big security blanket. Yoga does more for me than anything else I do. It makes so much sense, especially now that I am studying massage and learning about the organs. I'm feeling more in touch with my body than I thought I ever could. It helps me to slow down and look at life week by week, day by day; using what I have, not always wanting more; learning to live in the moment. (Kout, 1992)

CHAPTER REVIEW

SUMMARY

- Psychoneuroimmunology is a field that focuses on how psychological factors influence immune functioning. Research in PNI includes that done on behavioral conditioning of the immune response and the association between the immune system and stress. Stress has been reliably associated with the functioning of the immune system, mostly having a negative effect (e.g., in the long run) but sometimes activating it as well (in the short run).
- Acquired immunodeficiency syndrome (AIDS) and the human immunodeficiency virus (HIV), first noticed in the early 1980s, are a worldwide threat to health. Although a cure is yet to be found, health psychologists can be influential in helping change behaviors that can cause the spread of this disease. Originally thought to be a disease affecting only homosexual men, AIDS is now known to strike both heterosexuals and homosexuals alike. Low socioeconomic status individuals and those from some minority groups have a disproportionate risk for contracting this disease.
- Many psychological factors such as optimism and social support can be useful in helping a person with AIDS live a longer life. Similarly, problem-solving, avoidance, and support-seeking strategies all relate to coping with HIV infection.
- Specific health behavior change models such as the AIDS Risk Reduction Model (ARRM) have been designed to help combat the spread of AIDS, and research is now addressing understudied cultural populations such as women and minority groups.

TEST YOURSELF

Check your understanding of the topics in this chapter by answering the following questions.

1. A clear example of the connection between the mind and body, especially between psychology and immune functioning, is that
   a. real emotional experience is related to immune changes.
   b. any emotional experience, even faked, leads to immune changes.
   c. only faked emotional experiences lead to immune changes.
   d. thinking about increased immune activity can create it.

2. A girl with lupus was given a shot of a strong drug. At the same time, she was exposed to the scent of rose perfume and the taste of cod liver oil. After a few pairings of these three (drug, oil, scent) her body had a physiological response to the rose scent even without the full dose of the strong drug. This is an example of
   a. conditioned immunity.
   b. operant conditioning.
   c. psychoneuroimmunological reactivity.
   d. compensatory responding.

3. Why does chronic stress suppress the immune system?
   a. It conserves body resources.
   b. It serves as a warning.
   c. It prevents the organism from being too active.
   d. It prevents over activation.

4. Which of the following statements is true?
   a. AIDS and HIV are synonyms.
   b. A person can have AIDS without being HIV positive.
   c. A person who is HIV negative develops AIDS.
   d. A person can be HIV positive without having AIDS.

5. AIDS was first discovered and named in the
   a. 1950s.
   b. 1960s.
   c. 1970s.
   d. 1980s.

6. Currently, the average time between HIV infection and the appearance of the first signs of AIDS is
   a. 5–10 months.
   b. 1–2 years.
   c. 3–5 years.
   d. 8–11 years.

7. The most common cultural group to have HIV is
    a. African Americans.
    b. Latino Americans.
    c. minority women.
    d. low SES men.
8. The extent to which people engage in sexual activities with sexual partners from other sexual networks is known as ____________ and is a central influence on AIDS transmission.
    a. miscegenation
    b. the contact hypothesis
    c. sexual mixing
    d. transgroup sexuality
9. People newly infected with HIV report
    a. depression.
    b. hyperactivity.
    c. flu-like symptoms.
    d. cold-like symptoms.
10. One alternative medical treatment borrowed from a non-Western culture is increasing in popularity among AIDS patients and works on a biopsychosocial level. This is
    a. sweat lodges.
    b. acupressure.
    c. tai chi.
    d. yoga.

KEY TERMS, CONCEPTS, AND PEOPLE ▶▶

acquired immunodeficiency syndrome (AIDS), **319**

highly active antiretroviral therapy (HAART), **322**

human immunodeficiency virus (HIV), **320**

immune system, **319**

opportunistic infections, **324**

psychoneuroimmunology (PNI), **317**

sexual mixing, **328**

ESSENTIAL READINGS ▶▶

Ader, R., Felten, D. L., & Cohen, N. (2001). *Psychoneuroimmunology.* San Diego, CA: Academic Press.

Golub, S., & Fikslin, R. (2019). HIV/AIDS. In T. A. Revenson & R. A. R. Gurung (Eds.), *Handbook of health psychology* (3e). New York, NY: Routledge.

Segerstrom, S. (2012). *The Oxford handbook of psychoneuroimmunology*. Boston, MA: Oxford University Press.

Simon Jarratt/Corbis/VCG/ Getty Images

CHAPTER 13

CANCER

Fundamentals and Cultural Variations

iStockphoto.com/ KatarzynaBialasiewicz

Chapter 13 Outline

MEASURING UP

ARE YOU AT RISK FOR CANCER?

If you answer no to any of the questions, your risk for developing various kinds of cancer may be elevated.

Answer the following questions:	*Making Changes*
1. Do you protect your skin from overexposure to the sun? ________ 2. Do you abstain from smoking or using tobacco in any form? ________ 3. If you're over 40 or if family members have had colon cancer, do you get routine digital rectal exams? ________ 4. Do you eat a balanced diet that includes the RDA for vitamins A, B, and C? ________ 5. If you're a woman, do you have regular Pap tests and pelvic exams? ________ 6. If you're a man over 40, do you get regular prostate exams? ________ 7. If you have burn scars or a history of chronic skin infections, do you get regular checkups? ________	**Cutting Your Cancer Risk** You may not be able to control every risk factor in your life or environment, but you can protect yourself from the obvious ones. • *Avoid excessive exposure to ultraviolet light.* If you spend a lot of time outside, you can protect your skin by using sunscreen and wearing long-sleeved shirts and a hat. Also, wear sunglasses to protect your eyes. Don't purposely put yourself at risk by binge sunbathing or by using sunlamps. • *Avoid obvious cancer risks.* Besides ultraviolet light, other environmental factors that have been linked with cancer include tobacco, asbestos, and radiation.

(Continued)

(Continued)

Answer the following questions:	*Making Changes*
8. Do you avoid smoked, salted, pickled, and high-nitrate foods? ________ 9. If your job exposes you to asbestos, radiation, cadmium, or other environmental hazards, do you get regular check-ups? ________ 10. Do you limit your consumption of alcohol? ________ 11. Do you avoid using tanning salons or home sunlamps? ________ 12. If you're a woman, do you examine your breasts every month for lumps? ________ 13. Do you eat plenty of vegetables and other sources of fiber? ________ 14. If you're a man, do you perform regular testicular self-exams? ________ 15. Do you wear protective sunglasses in sunlight? ________ 16. Do you follow a low-fat diet? ________ 17. Do you know the cancer warning signs? ________	• *Keep yourself as healthy as possible.* The healthier you are, the better able your body is to ward off diseases that can predispose you to cancer. Get regular exercise; eat a balanced, high-fiber, low-fat diet; and avoid excessive alcohol use. • *Be alert to changes in your body.* You know your body rhythms and appearance better than anyone else, and only you will know if certain things aren't right. Changes in bowel habits, skin changes, or unusual lumps or discharges—anything out of the ordinary—may be clues that require further medical investigation. • *Don't put off seeing your doctor if you detect any changes.* Procrastination can't hurt anyone but you.

Source: Hales (2000).

▼ Ponder This

Which of your behaviors will most likely put you at risk for cancer?

What are the different psychological and physiological causes for cancer?

What psychological theories discussed previously can be used to increase cancer screening?

If you are reading this in a public place, observe the people around you. If you are reading this alone, think of the faces of your colleagues, students, or coworkers. Want to know some sobering facts? A high percentage of the people you see or the people you are thinking of have had a close encounter with cancer. They either know someone who was diagnosed with it or may have been diagnosed with it themselves. Statistics say close to half of us will develop some form of cancer in our lifetimes. More than 1.6 million new cases of cancer are diagnosed every year, and cancer is the second leading cause of death in the United States (after heart disease; American Cancer Society [ACS], 2018). In 2017 more than 600,000 people will probably die from cancer in the United States alone.

You might know someone with cancer yourself—your mother, father, uncle, aunt, brother, or sister. You probably know of many who have cancer: Cyclist Lance Armstrong, golfer Arnold Palmer, master chef Julia Child; actresses Shirley Temple, Suzanne Somers, and Edie Falco; anchorman Peter Jennings, New York Yankee's manager Joe Torre, former first ladies Betty Ford and Nancy Reagan, the writer Gloria Steinem; and politicians Bob Dole, Colin Powell, John Kerry, and Rudy Giuliani. The author of *Jurassic Park,* Michael Crichton, and Apple's Steve Jobs also had cancer.

Even saying the word "cancer" conjures up images of sadness or dread. The fear of cancer has been so pervasive that finding a cure for it is often seen as the pinnacle of achievement, the truly ambitious child's dream. People jest about how the epitome of an impressive resume would be "found a cure for cancer" rating equally with "brokered world peace." The good news is that health psychology is demonstrating how preventive measures can greatly reduce the incidence of cancer. What you do (and how much attention you paid to Chapters 7 and 8 on health behaviors) can predict your likelihood of getting cancer. Want to hear some even better news? Health psychological research designed to improve cancer **screening** and increase early detection is helping more people survive what was once a terminal disease (Stanton, 2019). Today there are more than 15.5 million cancer survivors (ACS, 2017). Nearly 67% of adult cancer patients and 83% of child cancer patients can expect to live 5 years or longer after diagnosis (ACS, 2017). Most breast cancers, for example, are diagnosed at an early stage and up to 99% of those with localized disease survive 5 years (ACS, 2017).

What exactly is this dreadful disease? How do you get it? Who gets it? How is it treated? How can one survive it? These are just some of the questions we will answer in this chapter. We will also examine how cancer varies across cultural lines and is influenced by psychological factors.

RESEARCHER SPOTLIGHT

Annette Stanton is the chair of the Health Psychology department at the University of California, Los Angeles. She earned a PhD in clinical psychology from the University of Connecticut. Stanton is a prolific scholar with interests in testing theories of stress and coping and related conceptual models in individuals and couples confronting cancer, reproductive problems, and other stressors. Check out her chapter in Essential Readings (Stanton, 2019).

PREVALENCE OF CANCER

Cancer has been around for centuries and has been called the emperor of all maladies (Mukherjee, 2010). As mentioned, unfortunately the chances of our developing some form of cancer in our lifetime are pretty high, and the chances get higher as we get older, dropping again after age 85 (Harding, Pompei, & Wilson, 2012). For people between the ages of 60 and 70, there is a one in three chance (if you are male) or one in four chance (if you are female) of getting cancer. This incidence drops to a 1 in 12 and 1 in 11 chance for men and women between the ages of 40 and 59, respectively, and a 1 in 52 chance for men between the ages of 1 and 39 (1 in 73 for women in the same category). Culture is again very important. Prevalence rates vary across many levels of culture—by sex, ethnicity, and geography. Differences in rates by sex are shown in Figure 13.1.

We are making strides in the fight against cancer (Stanton, 2019). New results on the incidence of cancer show that it is not as common as it was before, although the good news favors European American populations. Jemal et al. (2008) collected cancer morbidity and mortality data from several government organizations such as the Centers for Disease Control and Prevention, evaluated trends in cancer incidence and death rates, and compared survival rates over time and across racial/ethnic populations. The good news is that incidence rates for all cancers combined decreased from 1990 through 2004. Overall cancer death rates in 2004 compared with 1990 in men and 1991 in women decreased by 18.4% and 10.5%, respectively (Jemal et al., 2008). The bad news from a cultural perspective is that cancer-specific survival rates are lower and the risk of dying from cancer once it is diagnosed is higher in most minority populations compared with the European American population, as shown in Table 13.1 (Jemal et al., 2008). The relative risk of death from cancer (all types combined) compared with that for European American men and women was higher for both Latino men (1.16) and American Indian men (1.69).

Amanda Edwards/ WireImage/ Getty Images

▲ **Survivor.** Michael C. Hall, American actor known for his role in *Dexter*, is a survivor of Hodgkin's Lymphoma.

WHAT IS CANCER?

Similar to *stress* and *pain*, the word *cancer* has many different forms and meanings. *Cancer* is derived from *carcinos* and *carcinoma*, terms first used by the Greek Hippocrates to describe

▼ FIGURE 13.1

Prevalence of Cancer in the United States

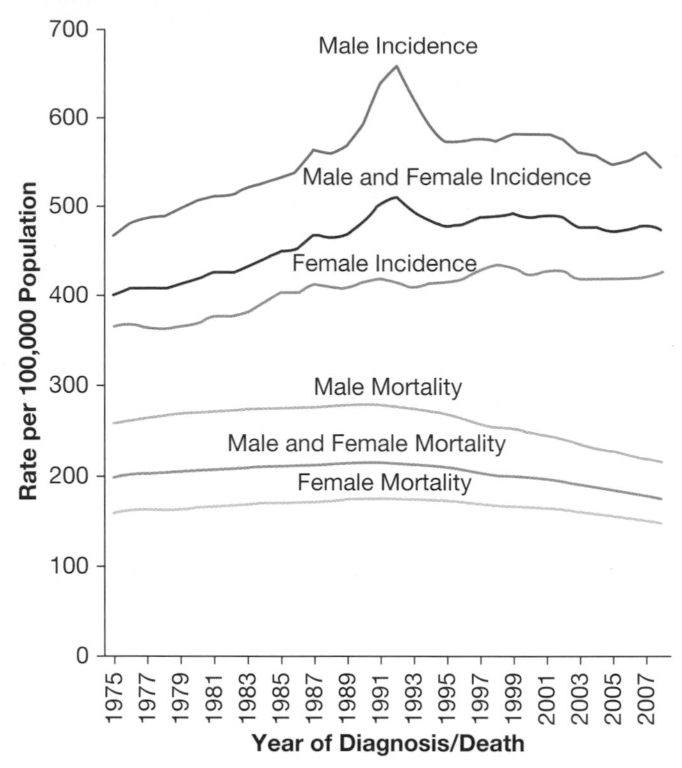

Source: CA: A Cancer Journal for Clinicians, Siegel, R., Naishadham, D., Jemal, A., v.62.1, January/February 2012. © 2012 by Wiley, Inc. Reproduced by permission of Wiley, Inc.

▼ TABLE 13.1

Overall and Breast Cancer Incidence and Death Rates across Ethnic Groups in the United States

All Cancers		
Racial/Ethnic Group	**Incidence Rate**	**Death Rate**
All	470.1	192.7
African American/Black	504.1	238.8
Asian/Pacific Islander	314.9	115.5
Hispanic/Latino	356.0	129.1
American Indian/Alaska Native	297.6	160.4
White	477.5	190.7
Breast Cancer		
Racial/Ethnic Group	**Incidence Rate**	**Death Rate**
All	127.8	25.5
African American/Black	118.3	33.8
Asian/Pacific Islander	89.0	12.6
Hispanic/Latino	89.3	16.1
American Indian/Alaska Native	69.8	16.1
White	132.5	25.0

Source: Cancer Health Disparities was originally published by the National Cancer Institute, http://www.cancer.gov/cancertopics/factsheet/disparities/cancer-health-disparities, non-ulcer-forming and ulcer-forming tumors. The shape of a spreading cancer cell resembles the outstretching legs of a crab to which these words refer (in Greek the word for crab is *cancer*, think of the zodiac sign). Although typically discussed as one illness, cancer is a group of diseases that vary in terms of incidence and mortality rates, epidemiology, risk factors and causes, and treatments. Also, understanding cancer and its effects through a cultural approach is an important area of health psychology because a comprehensive understanding of cancer requires a consideration of sex, gender, ethnicity, geographical location, sexual orientation, and all the other aspects of what makes up culture.

First, let's look at basic biology and some terminology. Cancer is the name given to the illness or condition caused by the presence of a malignant tumor. A malignant tumor or cancerous cell is identified as one showing uncontrollable cell growth that destroys healthy tissue. Cells that show abnormal growth are also referred to as **neoplasms**. Normally our cells grow, divide, and die in an orderly fashion, and cell growth is more pronounced when we are young. As we grow older, cells in most parts of the body divide only to replace worn-out or dying cells and to repair injuries. Because cancer cells continue to grow and divide, they are different from normal cells. Instead of dying, they outlive normal cells and continue to form new abnormal cells.

When a normal cell turns cancerous, it is often the result of a mutation in the cell's DNA that alters it and makes it grow uncontrollably, disrupting surrounding tissue and often spreading to organs all around the body (Pecorino, 2016). Most of the time when DNA becomes damaged, the body is able to repair it. In cancer cells, the damaged DNA cannot be repaired. Such genetic mutations can also be inherited, which accounts for why risk for cancer increases if someone in a person's family has had cancer. Many times, though, a person's cancerous cell mutations occur because of exposure to environmental toxins such as cigarette smoke or other **carcinogens** (cancer-causing substances). The branch of medicine that concerns the study and treatment of cancer is referred to as oncology, and this is the term used more frequently in hospitals.

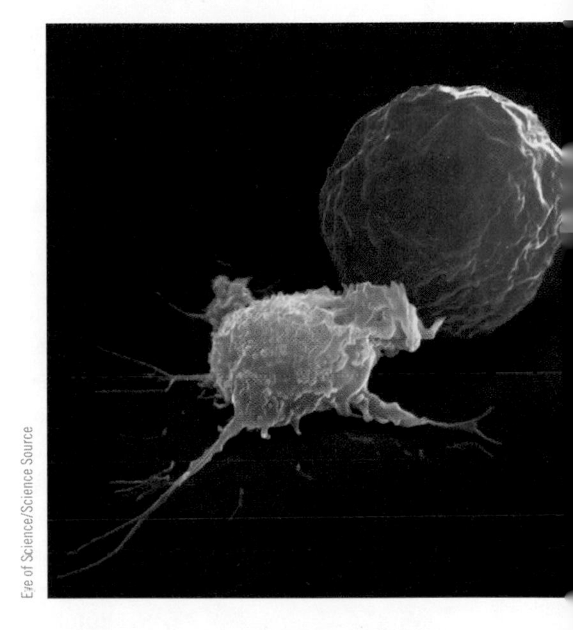
Eye of Science/Science Source

▲ **A Cancer Cell Being Attacked by Immune System Killer T Cells.** A Colored Scanning Electron Micrograph (SEM) image shows a human Natural Killer (NK) cell attacking a cancer cell. The yellow NK cell has numerous long fluid-projections, which are beginning to flow around the large orange cancer cell. Natural killer cells are a type of white blood cell known as T- lymphocytes. These have the ability to destroy virus-infected cells and tumor cells. On contact with the surface of a tumor cell, the NK cell recognizes certain proteins called antigens, which activate its cell-killing mechanism. The NK cell then binds to and destroys the cancer cell using toxins.

Types of Cancer

There are more than 100 different types of cancer, and even tumors within each type show a lot of variability. However, note that not all tumors are cancerous or **malignant**. **Benign** or noncancerous tumors do not **metastasize** or spread to other parts of the body and, with very rare exceptions, are not life threatening. Some cancers, such as leukemia, do not form tumors. Instead, these cancer cells involve the blood and blood-forming organs and circulate through other tissues where they grow (King & Robins, 2006). The course of the disease and the likelihood of survival vary greatly with each type of cancer. Therefore, if someone just says he or she has cancer, you should not make any generalizations about his or her experiences until you have more details. Some cancers show very little deviation in patterns of disease course, and psychosocial influences on coping and treatment are minimal (Henderson & Baum, 2002). That said, psychosocial factors do relate to differences in disease progression (Macciò et al., 2012).

The key variables that influence the interaction between biological, psychological, and social factors and the role each plays in cancer mortality or morbidity are cancer site, type, and severity. The most common sites for cancer are the lungs, breasts, prostate gland, colon, and rectum (the latter two are often affected together, which is referred to as colorectal cancer). The top 10 cancer sites by sex and related incidence and mortality statistics for each are shown in Figures 13.2 and 13.3.

There are four main types of cancer. The most common are **carcinomas** that start in the surface layers of the body or epithelial cells. This form of cancer accounts for the bulk of cancer cases and is seen in the most common sites. **Sarcomas** are cancers of the muscles, bones, and cartilage. **Lymphomas** are cancers of the lymphatic system and are referred to as Hodgkin's

▼ FIGURE 13.2

Estimated New U.S. Cancer Cases by Sex, 2018

Estimated New Cases

Males		
Prostate	164,690	19%
Lung & bronchus	121,680	14%
Colon & rectum	75,160	9%
Urinary bladder	62,380	7%
Melanoma of the skin	55,150	6%
Kidney & renal pelvis	42,680	5%
Non-Hodgkin lymphoma	41,730	5%
Oral cavity & pharynx	37,160	4%
Leukemia	35,030	4%
Liver & intrahepatic bile duct	30,610	3%
All Sites	**856,370**	**100%**

Females		
Breast	266,120	30%
Lung & bronchus	112,350	13%
Colon & rectum	64,640	7%
Uterine corpus	63,230	7%
Thyroid	40,900	5%
Melanoma of the skin	36,120	4%
Non-Hodgkin lymphoma	32,950	4%
Pancreas	26,240	3%
Leukemia	25,270	3%
Kindney & renal pelvis	22,660	3%
All Sites	**878,980**	**100%**

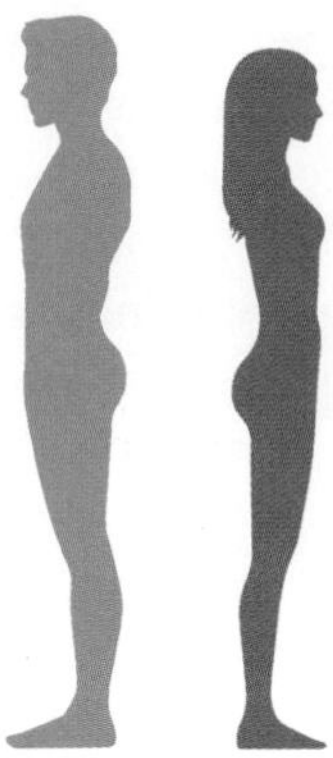

Source: American Cancer Society. Cancer Facts and Figures 2018. Atlanta: American Cancer Society, Inc.

disease if the cancer spreads from a single lymph node (non-Hodgkin lymphomas are found at several sites). **Leukemias** are cancers that are found in the blood and bone marrow. In leukemia, white blood cells proliferate to displace red blood cells, which causes anemia (a shortage of red blood cells), bleeding, and other immune system problems (ACS, 2017).

The severity of cancer is determined by a multifactor assessment of stage. The **TNM system** is the most common method used to stage cancer (ACS, 2017). It provides three main pieces of information. The T describes the size of the tumor and whether cancer has spread to nearby tissues and organs. The N describes how far the cancer has spread to nearby lymph nodes. Given that the lymph nodes are critical components of the body's immune system, they are often heavily involved in fighting cancer cells. The M indicates the extent to which the cancer has metastasized. Letters or numbers after the T, N, and M give more details about each of these factors. For example, a tumor classified as Tl, NO, M0 is a tumor that is very small, has not spread to the lymph nodes, and has not spread to distant organs of the body. Once TNM descriptions have been established, they can be grouped together into a simpler set of stages, stages 0 through IV. In general, the lower the number, the less the cancer has spread. A higher number, such as stage IV, indicates a more serious, widespread cancer (ACS, 2017).

CULTURAL VARIATIONS IN THE INCIDENCE OF CANCER

Similar to the ethnic differences in incidence of HIV infection described in the previous chapter, there are large differences in the cultural makeup of people who have cancer both across nations and across ethnic and racial groups (ACS, 2017; Kim & Lwing, 2017; Song et al., 2014; Vahabi et al., 2017). In fact, there is a growing body of research clarifying the link between cancer and membership in certain ethnic groups (Chen et al., 2011). Before looking at possible biological reasons why one ethnicity may be more at risk than another, let's first look at the different patterns of cancer across diverse ethnic groups.

There are two main statistics to bear in mind when studying the prevalence of cancer. The first is **incidence** or rates of newly diagnosed cases of the disease. The second is actual mortality. Keeping the two numbers separate is important because there are many people who are diagnosed with cancer who live (remember there was good news), and the number of survivors varies across cultural groups. So even if there are two cultural groups who both have the same incidence levels for a certain type of cancer, they may not show the same mortality rates. Figure 13.3 shows the incidence and mortality rates for the main types of cancer broken down by two main cultural variables, sex and ethnicity.

As you can see, different ethnic groups and the two sexes do not get cancer or die from it in the same ways (ACS, 2017; Dornelas, 2018a). African Americans have the highest general cancer incidence rates and mortality rates of any population in the United States, with this difference being driven more by higher rates of cancer among African American men. Illustrating the difference between incidence and mortality, American Indians have greater mortality rates relative to their incidence rates, suggesting that if they have cancer they are more likely to die of it. Separating total cases of cancer from individual types of cancer is important too. Although Asian Americans show much lower rates of cancer than European Americans in general, their rates of colorectal cancer diagnoses are about the same. In contrast to some other ethnic differences, European American women are more likely to have lung cancer than are African American women (ACS, 2017).

In addition to these ethnic differences, there are significant sex differences in cancer incidence as well. Men experience higher incidences of cancer in general (ACS, 2017). The most common sites for male cancer are the prostate gland, the lungs, the colon, and the rectum (ACS, 2017). Testicular cancer is relatively uncommon among men in general, but it is one of the most common forms of cancer in younger men aged 15 to 35. For some time, male cancers did not receive as much research attention as female cancers, and we know less about the etiology of most male cancers and men's psychological and social experiences with cancer (Dornelas, 2018a). No-Shave November is a recent phenomenon (did you know it started to raise awareness about male prostate cancer?).

The most common sites for female cancer for women of most ethnic groups are the breasts, lungs, colon, and rectum. In case you were wondering, men do get breast cancer although the rates are infinitesimal. Breast cancer incidence rates are somewhat counter to normal ethnic

▼ FIGURE 13.3

Estimated U.S. Cancer Deaths by Sex, 2018

Estimated Deaths

Males			Females		
Lung & bronchus	83,550	26%	Lung & bronchus	70,500	25%
Prostate	29,430	9%	Breast	40,920	14%
Colon & rectum	27,390	8%	Colon & rectum	23,240	8%
Pancreas	23,020	7%	Pancreas	21,310	7%
Liver & intrahepatic bile duct	20,540	6%	Ovary	14,070	5%
Leukemia	14,270	4%	Ulterine corpus	11,350	4%
Esophagus	12,850	4%	Leukemia	10,100	4%
Urinary bladder	12,520	4%	Liver & intrahepatic bile duct	9,660	3%
Non-Hodgkin lymphoma	11,510	4%	Non-Hodgkin lymphoma	8,400	4%
Kidney & renal pelvis	10,010	3%	Brain & other nervous system	7,340	4%
All Sites	**323,630**	**100%**	**All Sites**	**286,010**	**100%**

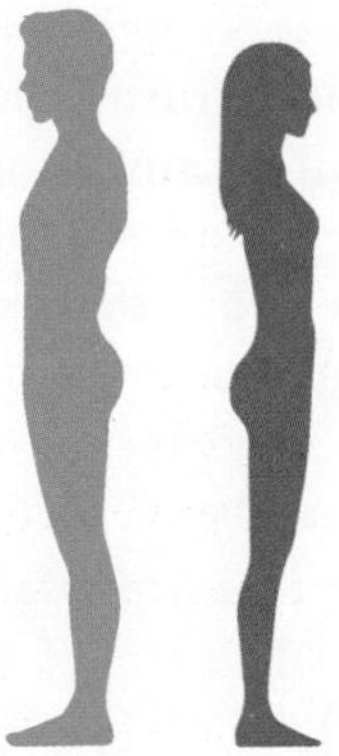

Estimates are rounded to the nearest 10, and cases exclude basal cell and squamous cell skin cancers and in situ carcinoma except urinary bladder, Ranking is based on modeled projections and may differ from the most recent oberrved date.

Source: American Cancer Society. Cancer Facts and Figures 2018. Atlanta: American Cancer Society, Inc.

difference patterns: A higher incidence of breast cancer has been reported both in European American women and women of higher socioeconomic status (SES) compared to women of other ethnicities and lower SES (Vainshtein, 2008). Other common cancers tend to vary by ethnicity but usually include cancers of the reproductive organs (e.g., the uterus, cervix, and ovaries) and may be due to some ethnic groups such as Asian American and Latina women not getting screened for the cancers (Suchday et al., 2019).

Cultural Differences in Beliefs and Knowledge about Cancer

Some of the cultural differences in cancer incidence are explained by cultural differences pertaining to beliefs held about cancer, people's attitudes toward cancer, and knowledge of cancer (Licqurish et al., 2017). Many studies have shown that low socioeconomic groups are less knowledgeable about cancer regardless of their sex, ethnicity, or religion (e.g., Wu et al., 2012). Ethnically diverse groups exhibit different levels of knowledge as well. African Americans (Ogunsanya et al., 2017), Arab Americans (Abboud et al., 2017), Latinos (Szalacha, Kue, & Menon, 2017), Chinese Americans (Robison et al., 2014), and Korean Americans (Sin, Ha, & Taylor, 2016) have all been found to have lower levels of knowledge about risk factors and cancer symptoms than European American groups.

Sometimes these cultural differences are linked to cultural beliefs and misconceptions about disease in general (Banerjee et al., 2011). Many religious individuals may believe that cancer is just punishment for sins or that cancer has spiritual meaning (Koffman, Morgan, Edmonds, Speck, & Higginson, 2008). The misperceived causes of cancer may also be more tangible. Vietnamese, Chinese, and Latino Americans Luque, Castañeda, Tyson, Vargas, Proctor, & Meade, 2010) reported poor hygiene or dirt as a cause for breast and cervical cancer. Another common cultural cancer belief is **fatalism**, the belief that a person with cancer cannot live a normal life and will die (Duberstein et al., 2017). High levels of fatalism have been found in African Americans (Bustillo et al., 2017), Korean and Chinese Americans (Gonzalez et al., 2016), and Latinos (Ramirez, 2014).

A vivid example of how culture influences perceptions is seen in the views of American Indians. Many American Indians see cancer as a White man's disease and something that is a punishment for one's actions or the actions of a family member (Yost et al., 2017). Some of them see cancer as a natural part of life's pathway and as providing a lesson from which to learn. Many also see cancer as penance and a person with cancer must wear the pain to protect other members of the community (Burhansstipanov, 2000). A diagnosis of cancer is equivalent to a doctor shooting a hole through the spirit and thus results in depression and fear of the doctor instead of trust. Beliefs about how you can get cancer may seem outlandish to the ethnocentric non-Indians. Some American Indians believe cancer can result from a curse or from violating tribal mores like stepping on a frog or urinating on a spider. Others believe that it is contagious and that it can be caught from a mammography machine or from the child of someone who has cancer (Burhansstipanov, 2000). Some American Indians do not want to even talk about cancer for fear of catching the cancer spirit. Regardless of the extent to which you think these beliefs are far-fetched, they have to be respected and anticipated to optimize helping the American Indians who do hold them.

DEVELOPMENTAL ISSUES IN CANCER

You are more likely to get cancer as you get older (Emery et al., 2019). The rates for cancer increase dramatically over the life span. Incidence rates range from less than 15 per 100,000 for those younger than 15 years of age to more than 2,000 per 100,000 for those older than 75 (National Cancer Institute, 2017). Age is a cultural variable as well, and one that also needs to be attended to in understanding cancer.

We consider cancer a developmental disease (Meyerowitz, Bull, & Perez, 2000). Why is this? Although cancer is primarily diagnosed in older adults, cancers actually develop when people are younger. Because there typically is a large gap between when a tumor starts to grow and when it is large enough to be diagnosed, exposure to many of the risk factors for cancer (described below) at a young age necessarily predicts the occurrence of cancer at an older age. Significant risks for cancer are also associated with the different developmental milestones (as described in Chapter 4). There is a risk associated with girls starting to menstruate early (Colditz & Frazier, 1995; Merviel et al., 2011) and dietary problems during the reproductive years link to the development of oral and other cancers in older women years later (Bravi et al., 2012). Risks also associate with menopause and the ways that women cope with it. The biggest risk factor for cancer—smoking (Gram et al., 2012)—has a strong developmental link: smoking almost always begins in the teenage years; few adults initiate a regular smoking habit (Park, McCoy, Erausquin, & Bartlett, 2018).

Synthesize, Evaluate, Apply

- What are the benefits and problems with celebrities speaking publicly about their cancers?
- What can be done to demystify cancer?
- How can coming from a different cultural background influence your risk of getting cancer?
- How are different cultural beliefs and knowledge levels about cancer related to broader sociocultural differences such as cross-cultural approaches to health?
- Do you think there is more or less stigma associated with having cancer than with having HIV/AIDS? Why?

Developmental age also influences how people, especially children, will cope with a cancer diagnosis. For example, Barrera et al. (2003) recruited preschool, school age, and adolescent patients and measured their psychological adjustment and quality of life (QOL) 3, 9, and 15 months after cancer was diagnosed. The children's age at diagnosis significantly affected both their adjustment and QOL. At 3 months after diagnosis, preschoolers had more externalizing behavior problems than did adolescents. Preschoolers had better QOL than adolescents did at all three assessments, suggesting that preschoolers with cancer are at risk for behavior problems and adolescents are at risk for poor QOL. Studies such as these are gentle reminders that the psychological reactions to cancer experienced by adults may be very different from those of children (Anderzén et al., 2008). A developmental approach also helps us understand how family interactions change when one family member has cancer (Jones et al., 2008).

PHYSIOLOGICAL CORRELATES OF CANCER

The physiological symptoms of cancer depend on the size, location, and stage of cancer (Weinberg, 2013). If a cancer has reached a later stage and metastasizes, then symptoms may occur at different locations in the body. As the mutant cells divide, they exert pressure on the surrounding organs, blood vessels, and nerves that is consciously felt by the individual (Pecorino, 2016). Some cancers, such as pancreatic cancer, are not felt until the cell has reached an advanced stage of development. Some of the general symptoms of cancer are fever, fatigue, pain, changes in the skin, and weight loss. Remember that having these symptoms does not necessarily mean a person has cancer but suggests that something is not right (there are many other reasons for these same symptoms). Sometimes, cancer cells release substances into the bloodstream that cause symptoms not generally thought to result from cancers (Pecorino, 2016). For example, some cancers of the pancreas can release substances that cause blood clots to develop in veins of the legs. Some lung cancers produce hormone-like substances that change blood calcium levels, affecting nerves and muscles and causing weakness and dizziness.

Together with general symptoms, some symptoms are more specifically indicative of cancer. Any changes in your excretory functions could signify cancer of the colon (such as constant diarrhea) or bladder/prostate gland (such as painful urination or blood in the urine). Sores that do not heal, especially in the mouth or on sexual organs, are signs of skin cancers. As a rule, the appearance of blood in fluids in which you do not normally see it like in the saliva, urine, stool, nonmenstrual vaginal fluids, or breast fluid should be reported to a doctor immediately. The appearance of lumps in the breast, testicles, or lymph nodes may also be a sign of cancer. In general, it is clear that the better you know your body, the more aware you will be of changes that may signify problems with it.

PSYCHOLOGICAL CORRELATES OF CANCER

You can divide the reality of cancer into three main phases: the period leading up to a diagnosis, the diagnosis and reactions to it, and the period following it. Psychological factors may play a role in all three, although the research evidence on how psychology influences progression is clearer than that on its role in the development of cancer.

Psychological Factors in Cancer Incidence

There is presently little unequivocal proof that psychological factors cause cancer (e.g., Stanton, 2018), except for the case of stress. We discuss this in more detail later. There are at least three general pathways through which psychological factors may influence the development of cancer: (1) direct effects of psychological processes on bodily systems, (2) healthy and unhealthy behaviors, and (3) responses to perceived or actual illness, such as screening behaviors or adherence to treatment recommendations (Henderson & Baum, 2002). The main psychological processes studied have been personality, social support, depression, stress, and health behaviors. Stress and health behaviors are perhaps the most pervasive and will be discussed later in the chapter.

▲ **Coping with Cancer.** Side-effects of chemotherapy include change in appearance; these changes have significant psychological coping implications.

Although receiving a lot of attention in the mid-1980s, the role of *personality* in cancer has been somewhat exaggerated. Morris, Greer, Pettingale, and Watson (1981) first found an association between breast cancer and anger suppression, leading to the hypothesis of a cancer-prone or **Type C personality** (Zozulya, Gabaeva, Sokolov, Surkina, & Kost, 2008). A Type C person was described as cooperative, appeasing, unassertive, and compliant and as someone who did not express negative emotions (Temoshok, 1987). Some later reviews supported these early findings, but some contradictory findings suggest that personality plays only a small role in cancer etiology (McKenna, Zevon, Corn, & Rounds, 1999).

Let's take a closer look at the role personality does or does not play with cancer. Nabi et al. (2008) looked at the responses of 14,445 participants age 39 to 54 who first completed measures of personality in 1993 (e.g., the Personality Stress Inventory that assesses cancer-prone, coronary heart disease [CHD]-prone, ambivalent, healthy, rational, and anti-social personality types). About 13 years later, the researchers followed up with the participants and found that mortality *was* predicted by hostility and CHD-prone, ambivalent, antisocial, and healthy personality types, but *not* by Type C personalities. Given the data, personality only plays a limited role in the progression of cancer.

If personality can have a limited effect, what about one's social environment? Social support appears not to have a strong protective effect against cancer development (Fox, 1998) although it does play a significant role in coping with cancer (as discussed in the next section). To be fair, social support research is hampered by the fact that there are many different types of social support (as described in Chapter 6), and because it is operationally defined in different ways, study comparisons are difficult (Knoll, 2018). If your intuition says that social support must influence incidences of cancer, you are right (although don't let intuition get in the way of empirical evidence to the contrary). For instance, socially isolated women were found to have a higher cancer incidence, although this relationship was not found in men (Reynolds & Kaplan, 1990).

There is slightly more evidence for the role of depression in cancer incidence than that for social support (Chen & Lin, 2011). Two literature reviews have shown depression to be a marginally significant risk factor for cancer (McKenna et al., 1999), and at least two prospective studies strengthen this conclusion (Gallo, Armenian, Ford, Eaton, & Khachaturian, 2000; Penninx et al., 1998). Gallo et al. (2000) used a large population-based sample in Baltimore, following approximately 2,000 individuals for 13 years. Although there was no link between cancer and depression across the board, there was a significant association between depression and cancer for women. In conjunction with similar sex differences for social support, it is clear that the link between psychological factors and cancer may be very different for men and women. This difference may be linked to biological pathways or may be indicative of greater cultural differences between the sexes that have biopsychosocial components (e.g., Taylor, Kemeny, Reed, Bower, & Gruenewald, 2000).

Psychological Responses to Cancer Diagnosis

Even being screened for a potential cancer can be a fearful experience (Wardle & Pope, 1992). A positive diagnosis (i.e., that cells are cancerous) can be devastating and has been referred to as causing an existential plight (Weisman & Worden, 1972), resulting in higher levels of depression in the 6 months following diagnosis (Boyes, Girgis, D'Este, & Zucca, 2011). In addition to anxiety, denial, and depression—the major responses to learning you have a chronic illness, as covered in Chapter 10—a cancer diagnosis and its treatment result in stress and a lowered QOL (Dornelus, 2018b). The high emotions experienced right after diagnoses do lessen with time, and emotions actually improve as recovery begins after the end of treatment. Two other highly psychologically disturbing times occur during treatment, whether it is surgery or radiotherapy (Dornelus, 2018b).

In general, depression is more common in those patients undergoing active treatment and those experiencing pain or with a history of stressors or low social support, rather than those in follow-up treatment (Johansen, Dalton, & Bidstrup, 2011). Approximately half of cancer patients meet the American Psychiatric Association's criteria for having a psychological disorder, the majority of them being related to emotional and/or behavioral problems resulting from having to adjust to cancer (Tope, Ahles, & Silberfarb, 1993). More than half of those treated for cancer experience fear, pain, insomnia, and related anxiety disorders (Derogatis et al., 1983).

Psychological Factors in Cancer Progression and Coping

Similar to HIV infection and other chronic illnesses, some psychological characteristics help one cope better with cancer and also influence the course of the disease. Similar to the factors associated with incidence, a person's personality, social support, depression, stress, and health behaviors again figure prominently (Smith, 2018; Stanton, 2018).

Personality We have already discussed how personality relates to cancer *incidence*—meaning whether personality has any influence over whether someone will *get* cancer (its influence is very limited). In the late 1970s, the first positive links between personality and cancer *progression* were seen. How people coped with cancer seemed to be one of the most important factors. Patients who denied they had cancer had higher disease recurrence rates (Greer, Morris, & Pettingale, 1979). Other studies followed and have established that avoidant, repressive, or unexpressive personalities or coping styles are associated with poorer disease courses (Epping-Jordan, Compas, & Howell, 1994). Other personality characteristics are important, too. For example, optimism is strongly and positively correlated with active coping and emotional regulation coping strategies and strongly negatively correlated with avoidant coping strategies (Scheier, Weintraub, & Carver, 1986). Optimists, in general, show better psychological well-being (Armor & Taylor, 1998). In the context of cancer, a number of studies show that optimism predicts better adjustment for a variety of cancers (early-stage breast cancer, Carver et al., 1994; Kurtz, Kurtz, Given, & Given, 2008; breast/ovarian or colorectal cancer, Geirdal & Dahl, 2008).

Social Support The case for a positive correlation between social support and survival of cancer patients is very strong (Imm et al., 2017; LeBarre & Riding-Malon, 2017). Of course, some of the best studies to look at are prospective in nature. For example, Garssen and Goodkin (1999) reviewed 38 prospective studies assessing the role of psychological factors in cancer progression and found that low levels of social support consistently promoted cancer progression. In terms of specific aspects of social support, having a high number of confidants with which to discuss personal problems (Maunsell, Brisson, & Deschenes, 1995), having a high number of social connections (Reynolds & Kaplan, 1990), having more contact with friends and supportive others (Waxler-Morrison, Hislop, Mears, & Kan, 1991), and believing that you have a lot of emotional support (Ell, Nishomoto, Mediansky, Mantell, & Hamovitch, 1992) all link to slower progression of cancer and higher rates of survival. A growing body of work suggests that spiritual sources, such as belief in a God and prayer, also provide social support, aiding adjustment and slowing cancer progression (Chaturvedi & Venkateswaran, 2008), although women who were not spiritual before cancer diagnosis but turned to God after diagnosis show lower levels of well-being than women who were always religious (Schreiber & Brockopp, 2012).

Depression has also been linked to cancer progression (Fann et al., 2008) with a number of studies suggesting that depression and lower quality of life in general have adverse effects on survival (Butow, Coates, & Dunn, 1999). We discuss further the role of social support and depression in the section about interventions later in this chapter.

Finding Meaning One of the active areas of psychosocial research in coping with cancer revolves around the notion of finding meaning or **benefit finding**. Taylor (1983) first reported that 53% of women in whom breast cancer was diagnosed reported that they experienced positive changes in their lives since their diagnosis, a finding often replicated (Ching, Martinson, & Wong, 2012; Cordova, Cunningham, Carlson, & Andrykowski, 2001). Most of the research that followed linked benefit finding to positive outcomes (e.g., Davis, Nolen-Hoeksema, & Larson, 1998). Additional research suggests that there are many forms of benefit finding such as social relationship and personal growth benefit finding (Weaver, Llabre, Lechner, Penedo, & Antoni, 2008). There are even effective therapies designed to help people find benefits in cancer (Lechner, Stoelb, & Antoni, 2008).

Now here's a twist. Some longitudinal studies of benefit finding (much of the previously cited work was cross-sectional) suggest that benefit finding may not always be good. Tomich and Helgeson (2004) followed 364 women for a 6-month period and found that benefit finding was associated with more negative emotions although the negative associations with QOL were limited to those women with more severe disease. Some interesting cultural variations were found as well (Simon & Wardle, 2008). Lower socioeconomic status (SES) women and African American and Latina women (independent of SES) were more likely to find benefit in their cancer than European American women (Tomich & Helgeson, 2004). If it is useful to be optimistic, shouldn't finding benefit be good too? Research is under way to unravel this contradiction because nothing in the data collected offered a definite resolution (Tomich & Helgeson, 2004).

Although we have discussed the role of psychological factors in cancer progression, we would be remiss if we did not mention the effect cancer has on social relationships. The caregivers—spouses, friends, relatives—of cancer patients often experience negative outcomes as well (Coyne,

Wollin, & Creedy, 2012). For example, psychological interventions have been designed to help the spouses of women with breast cancer that reduce the spouse's anxiety and depression (Kadmon, Ganz, Rom, & Woloski-Wruble, 2008; Lewis et al., 2008). If one spouse has cancer, the other spouses' quality of life suffers unless both partners have a high-quality marital relationship (Bergelt, Koch, & Petersen, 2008).

Synthesize, Evaluate, Apply

- Why should cancer be conceptualized as a developmental disease? How can this concept change how it is studied and the treatments for it?
- What personality characteristics interact with health behaviors to influence risk of cancer? How do personality characteristics affect progression of cancer?
- Evaluate the benefits and problems with benefit finding. At what stage do you think this process can be most helpful? When can it hurt and why?

CANCER, STRESS, AND IMMUNITY

Stress has been shown to influence both the incidence of cancer and its progression, although again, the link for the latter is stronger. There is no equivocation: stress-related psychosocial factors influence cancer. Chida, Hammer, Wardle, and Steptoe (2008) conducted a meta-analysis of 165 studies and found that stress-related psychosocial factors were associated with higher cancer incidence in initially healthy populations, poorer survival in patients with diagnosed cancer, and higher cancer mortality. In another study, women who experienced four to six major life stressors were more than five times at higher risk for breast cancer (Kruk, 2012). A cancer diagnosis sets up a negative cycle of experiences between stress and illness (see Chapters 12 and 14 for other examples). The diagnosis and treatment cause stress that in turn influences the course of the disease by affecting the immune system (Nelson et al., 2008).

Stress has a direct effect on the activity of natural killer (NK) cells, which themselves are critical in the body's fight against cancer (Weinberg, 2013). Patients with a variety of cancers have lowered NK cell activity in the blood to begin with (Whiteside & Herberman, 1994). Low NK cell activity in cancer patients is significantly associated with the spread of cancer and in patients treated for metastases, the survival time without metastasis correlates with NK cell activity. Correspondingly, the experience of any additional stress can have direct effects on the development of the cancer, complementing and antagonizing the low NK cell levels. Stress can also increase unhealthy behaviors that can accelerate illness progression (Carlson, Speca, Faris, & Patel, 2007). The patient may increase drug, tobacco, or alcohol use, get less sleep or physical activity, or eat badly, all behaviors that may further affect immunity (Friedman, Klein, & Specter, 1991).

It may be no surprise that cancer can stress you, but can stress actually give you cancer? We discussed the negative impact stress can have on our minds and bodies in Chapter 5, so this is clearly a possibility. In fact, this question has been actively debated (Reiche, Nunes, Morimoto, 2004; Tez & Tez, 2008). Retrospective studies of stress and the onset of cancer have shown mixed results and are heavily criticized (Delahanty & Baum, 2001), but prospective studies show that, in general, patients with a subsequent diagnosis of cancer reported more severe stressful events than control groups (Geyer, 1993). Stress has been shown to damage DNA, and this has been suggested as a general pathway through which stress can influence the development of cancer (Forlenza & Baum, 2000). In a meta-analysis of 46 studies, McKenna et al. (1999) found that the relationship between stressful life events and cancer was only modest (see also Nielsen et al., 2008).

HEALTH BEHAVIORS AND CANCER

As mentioned in the introduction to this chapter, many of your health behaviors predict your likelihood of getting cancer and the course cancer takes (Anand et al., 2008; Beesley, Eakin, Janda, & Battistutta, 2008; Stanton, 2018). The Measuring Up opener lists some of the main health behaviors that put you at risk for getting cancer. Take a moment to see how you fare. To some extent the results may surprise you. ("You mean doing *that* puts me at risk for cancer?" Yes, it may.) The usual unhealthy behaviors turn up again (see Chapter 7) and, not surprisingly, cultural differences in the practice of some of these behaviors are significant in explaining cultural differences in cancer.

Tobacco Use

Do you want an easy way to decrease your risk of getting cancer? Make sure you do not smoke. Probably the most clear-cut cause of cancer is tobacco use (ACS, 2017; Mermelstein, 2018). Smokers have nine times the risk of getting lung cancer compared with nonsmokers (Lubin, Richter, & Blot, 1984); only 10% of lung cancer patients have never smoked (Subramanian & Govindan, 2007). Note that this risk is nine times—not double, not triple—but nine times. Talk about really playing with fire! Cigarette smoking accounts for at least 30% of all cancer deaths. As shown in Table 13.2, smoking is a major cause of cancers of the lung, larynx (voice box), oral cavity, pharynx (throat), and esophagus and is a contributing cause in the development of cancers of the bladder, pancreas, liver, uterine cervix, kidney, stomach, colon and rectum, and some leukemias (Stanton, 2019).

The link between smoking and cancer is best illustrated when we look at populations that increased tobacco use. Smoking rates among women rose dramatically between the 1960s and the 1990s, and deaths due to lung cancer in women increased correspondingly (CDC, 2017). Shopland (1996) showed that the risk of contracting lung cancer for women who smoke is

▼ TABLE 13.2

Mortality and Excess Mortality, According to Sex and Smoking Status*

	Women			Men		
	Never Smoked	Current Smoker	% of Excess Mortality†	Never Smoked	Current Smoker	% of Excess Mortality†
Cause of Death	deaths/1000 person-yr‡			deaths/1000 person-yr‡		
All causes	1035.5	2541.8	—	1528.0	3921.9	—
Diseases established as caused by smoking§	474.7	1729.0	83.3	802.4	2806.6	83.8
Additional diseases associated with smoking						
All infection, A00–B99	19.7	43.5	1.6	28.4	64.6	1.5
Breast cancer, C50	62.7	79.8	1.1	—	—	—
Prostate cancer, C61	—	—	—	65.7	85.6	0.8
Rare cancers‖	42.0	41.8	0.0	25.5	35.0	0.4
Cancers of unknown site	28.1	71.2	2.8	40.5	110.5	2.9
Hypertensive heart disease, I11	7.7	13.3	0.4	12.1	33.1	0.9
Essential hypertension and hypertensive renal disease, I10 and I15	7.9	17.0	0.6	10.4	23.8	0.6
All other respiratory diseases**	14.3	21.7	0.5	22.9	41.2	0.8
Ischemic disorders of the intestines, K55	2.8	14.6	0.8	2.8	13.9	0.5
Liver cirrhosis, K70 and K74	6.9	20.8	0.9	10.5	47.9	1.6

Cause of Death	Women			Men		
	Never Smoked	Current Smoker	% of Excess Mortality†	Never Smoked	Current Smoker	% of Excess Mortality†
	deaths/1000 person-yr‡			deaths/1000 person-yr‡		
All other digestive diseases††	20.0	35.3	1.0	23.7	55.9	1.3
Renal failure, N17–N19	16.1	25.6	0.6	25.0	41.2	0.7
Additional rare causes combined‡‡	51.7	93.4	2.8	38.6	64.1	1.1
Unknown causes	33.0	90.9	3.8	53.4	104.9	2.2
Excess risk explained by additional outcomes			16.9			15.3

* Data are from 2000 to 2011 from a pooled contemporary cohort comprising the Cancer Prevention Study II Nutriton Cohort, the Nurses' Health Study I cohort, the Health Professionals Follow-up Study cohort, the Women's Health Initiative cohort, and National Institutes of Health-AARP Diet and Health Study cohort. Each listed cause is followed by the *International Classification of Diseases, 10th Revision* (ICD-10) code associated with that disease.
† We calculated excess mortality by dividing the disease-specific excess mortality among current smokers (as compared with persons who never smoked) by the all-cause excess mortality. Totals may not add to 100% because of rounding and nonsignificant associations in outcomes that are not shown.
‡ Mortality was age-standardized to the 2000 U.S. population distribution.
§ Included are the diseases that have been established by the U.S. Surgeon General as caused by smoking.
¶ Tuberculosis is not included in this category.
| Included are all cancer sites other than the 12 that have been established as causal by the Surgeon General and cancers of the breast, prostate, and brain; other leukemias; melanoma; and non-Hodgkin's lymphoma (individual data for which are provided in Tables S2 and S3 in the Supplementary Appendix).
** Included are ICD-10 codes J00-J99 other than pneumonia and influenza, COPD, and pulmonary fibrosis (individual data for which are provided in Tables S2 and S3 in the supplementary Appendix).
†† Included are ICD-10 codes K00-K93 other than ischemic disorders of the intestines, liver cirrhosis, and other liver diseases (individual data for which are provided in Tables S2 ans S3 in the supplementary Appendix).
‡‡ Included are causes that are not shown separately in Tables S2 and S3 in the Supplementary Appendix: ICD-10 codes H00-H95, L00-L99, M00-M99, O00-U89, and Z00-Z99.
Source: New England Journal of Medicine.

1,200% greater than that for women who do not smoke, and one-quarter of all cancer deaths among women can be attributed to smoking. In men, almost 85% of lung cancers are related to cigarette smoking (CDC, 2017). The fact that men smoke more than women accounts for approximately 90% of the sex differences in lung cancer mortality (Mellström & Svanborg, 1987) and other carcinomas as well (Hassan et al., 2008). As men's and women's smoking rates become similar, their lung cancer rates also become similar. Figure 13.4 shows how smoking rates have changed in the United States since 1900.

Differences in tobacco use also highlight many of the cultural differences in cancer rates. Different ethnic groups have had different historical relationships with tobacco, serving to either increase or decrease their exposure to it. African Americans, for example, had heavy exposure to tobacco from the early 1600s when Africans were forced into slavery on southern tobacco-growing plantations and in tobacco manufacturing during the colonial period (Gately, 2003). Tobacco was used in South America and Latin America even before the European colonization, and the *curanderismos* (see Chapter 3) often used tobacco in religious and healing practices. Even today, cigarette smoking is considered a social activity for Latinos, consistent with cultural values of *personalismo* (importance of personal relations) (Marin, Marin, Perez-Stable, Sabogal, & Otero-Sabogal, 1990). Not surprisingly, many Latin American countries show high rates of smoking (Müller & Wehbe, 2008). Many Asian groups also have had a long history of smoking. In China, tobacco was mixed with opium and smoked and was used also medicinally. In India, the end of a hard day in the fields was often marked by the smoking of a *hookah*, a contraption that bubbles tobacco through water. Use of a hookah to smoke also has become a trendy habit in many North American cities. Statistics prove that even exposure to secondhand smoke is associated with cancer incidence (Miller et al., 2007).

Diet

For the majority of Americans who do not smoke, eating a nutritionally balanced diet and being physically active are the most important ways to reduce cancer risk (LaCaille, 2019; Mermelstein, 2019; Song, 2019). Evidence suggests that one-third of the 550,000 cancer deaths that occur in the United States each year are due to unhealthy diet and insufficient physical activity (Greger, 2015). Different cultural groups have different eating habits (see Chapter 8), which

▼ FIGURE 13.4

U.S. Cigarette Consumption over Time

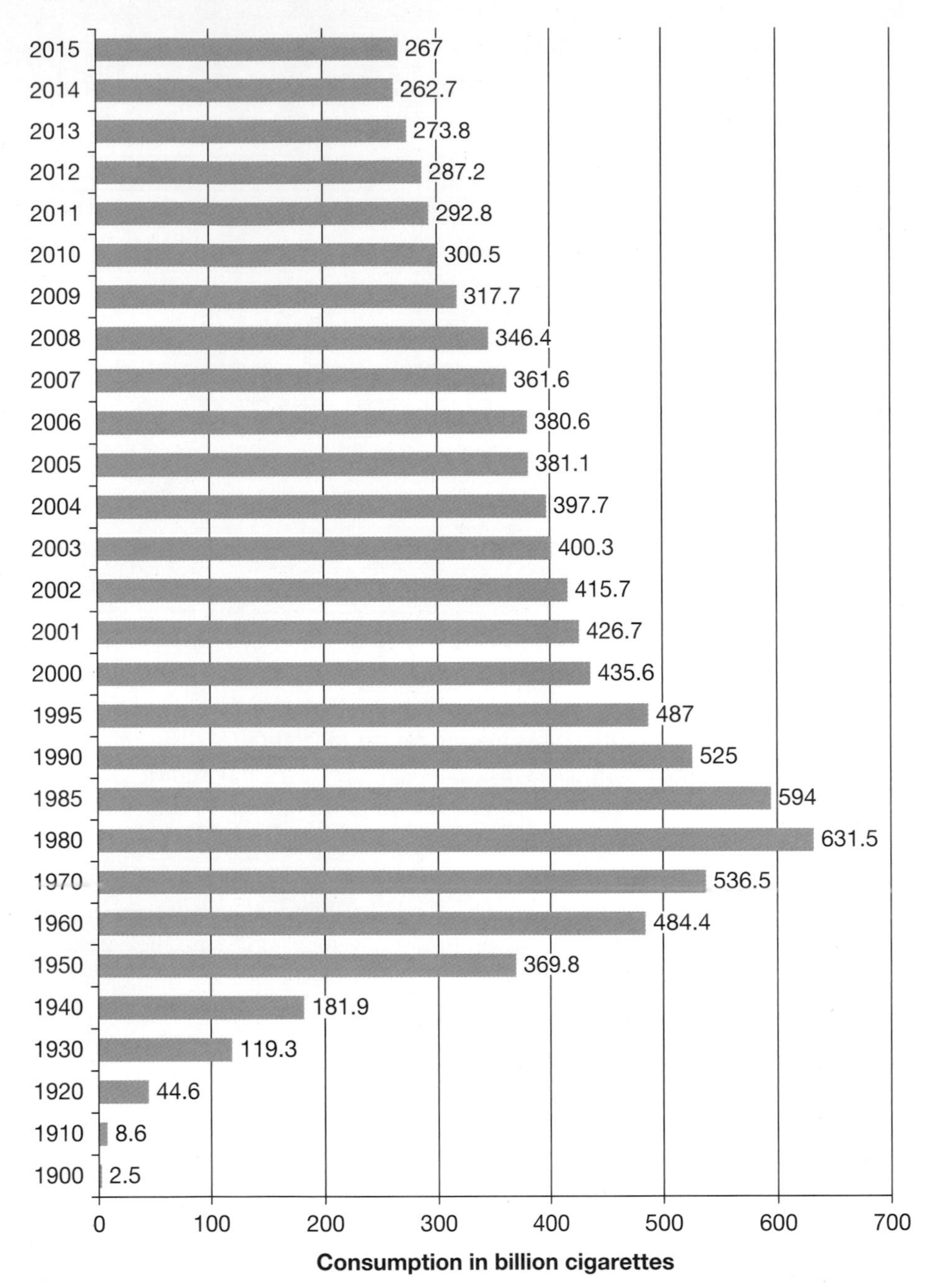

Source: Based on data from the U.S. Census Bureau.

can accentuate their risk for cancer. There are a number of dietary features that are linked to an increased risk for cancer (Singletary & Milner, 2008; Willett & Trichopoulos, 1996). For example, eating too much fat and not getting enough fiber have been associated with increased cancer incidence (Steinmaus, Nunez, & Smith, 2000; Wynder et al., 1997). On the other hand, diets with high consumption of fruits and vegetables are associated with a lower risk for several types of cancer (Potter & Steinmetz, 1996). In Hawaii, native Hawaiians have the shortest life expectancy of any ethnic group because of their diets, including high consumption of cholesterol-containing foods and red meat, animal fat, eggs, milk, and cheese (the traditional roast pig at a luau is an example).

The data for some cancers are stronger than those for others. Eating a lot of animal fat has been linked to breast cancer (Freedman, Kipnis, Schatzkin, & Potischman, 2008) and to colon cancer (Biasi, Mascia, & Poli, 2008), though not to prostate cancer (Crowe et al., 2008). There are some fats such as omega-3 polyunsaturated fat (found in salmon) that may actually prevent cancer and are associated with lower rates of breast cancer and colorectal cancer (Simopoulos, 2008), but evidence supporting this finding is still mixed.

The diet-cancer link is probably mediated by obesity. Bad diets and eating too much make people overweight and obese. Obesity may promote breast cancer because of the effects of adipose tissue on epithelial cell growth (Guthrie & Carroll, 1999) or on the production and functioning of hormones such as estrogen (Mezzetti et al., 1998). Obesity has also been linked to a higher incidence of colon, endometrial, pancreatic, and gallbladder cancers (Stolzenberg-Solomon et al., 2008).

A wide variety of foods are supposed to help prevent cancer and also to cure it. Only a small percentage of the foods touted as curative have stood the test of scientific research (Table 13.3). Be warned that there are a lot of television and Internet reports of so-called cancer-busting foods for which there is no scientific basis. For example, eating grapes is supposed to be good, but the effects have not been proven. That said, eating a diet with high amounts of fruits and vegetables, especially those containing antioxidants, does seem to increase the cancer-fighting capacity of the body (Cao, Booth, Sadowski, & Prior, 1998). Also, eating soy products and broccoli actually does seem to help prevent some cancers (Moyad, 1999), and vegetarianism similarly has been linked to lower incidence of cancer (Hebert et al., 1998).

As far as popular diets like South Beach and Atkins go, the Mediterranean diet, which is rich in nuts, grains, and olive oil, has shown the most promise for keeping cancer at bay (Benetou

▼ TABLE 13.3

Foods Supposed to Help Prevent and Treat Cancer

Component	Food	Cancer Link
Fiber	Carrots, beets, onions, potatoes	Prevents colon, stomach
Folate and folic acid	Leafy vegetables, grains, legumes	Prevents breast
Antioxidants	Fruits, vegetables, nuts, grains	Potential
Beta-carotene	Carrots, cantaloupe, other orange foods	Potential
Vitamin E	Nuts, broccoli, corn oil	Potential
Vitamin A	Liver, egg yolks, milk, cabbage	No clear link
Vitamin C	Citrus fruits, leafy vegetables	No clear link
Selenium	Meat, bread	No clear link
Vitamin B	Brussels sprouts	No clear link
Flavones/Indoles	Broccoli, artichokes, celery	No clear link
Phytochemicals	Soy products	Potential
Omega-3 fatty acids	Fish oils, salmon	No clear link
Aspartame	Artificial sweetener	No clear link
High-fat diets		Increased risk of breast, colon, rectum, prostate, endometrium

et al., 2008). For the rest of the things you may hear about, for example, vitamin A or C, the mineral selenium, and flavonoids (effective antioxidants that you'll hear more about in the next chapter), there is enough research to suggest that each is a potential cancer fighter (Knekt et al., 1997), but we are far from having a guaranteed perfect anticancer diet. However, we are getting closer, as more and more nutrients prove to be viable cancer fighters (Freeman et al., 2000). As always, you should be a critical consumer of what claims you hear or read about.

Given that some foods may have the potential to reduce the risk for cancer, it follows that cultural differences in dietary patterns correspondingly explain cultural differences in cancer incidence and progression. For example, there is a lower incidence of breast cancer among Latinas than among non-Latino European American women. Can diet explain this? Murtaugh et al. (2008) examined the associations of dietary patterns (e.g., Western, Native Mexican, Mediterranean) with risk for breast cancer in Latinas (757 cases, 867 controls) and non-Latino European American women (1,524 cases, 1,598 controls) from the Four-Corners Breast Cancer Study. They found that it was the dietary pattern followed and not just the ethnicity that was important. The Western dietary pattern was associated with greater risk, and the Native Mexican and Mediterranean dietary patterns were associated with lower risk of breast cancer.

Physical Activity

The reasons for staying in shape (or getting in shape) continue to increase (LaCaille, 2018). A large body of evidence suggests that physical activity, especially during our younger years, can reduce the risk of breast (Awatef et al., 2011) and endometrial cancer (Patel et al., 2008) in women, and colon cancer in men (Coups, Hay, & Ford, 2008). Getting regular physical activity also lowers the risk for breast cancer for both pre- and postmenopausal women (Gilliland, Li, Baumgartner, Crumley, & Samet, 2001). Being active is good for men too. Physical activity reduces the rate of prostate cancer in men (Thorsen, Courneya, Stevinson, & Fosså, 2008) and could protect both men and women from colon cancer (Batty & Thune, 2000). However, the relationship between physical activity and testicular cancer is a little inconsistent: some studies suggest there is no risk (Thune & Lund, 1994), others suggest physical activity is a risk factor *for* testicular cancer (Srivastava & Kreiger, 2000). For lung cancer, a relationship has yet to be fully established (Kubík et al., 2007).

Sun Exposure

Few people lying on the beach soaking in the sun's rays are thinking about the fact that they have almost tripled their chances of getting squamous cell skin cancer (ACS, 2017). Did you know that 45% of Americans who live to 65 years of age get skin cancer at least once? Prevention is again the key: 78% of skin cancers reported could have been prevented if people younger than age 18 had put on sunscreen.

Even tanning booths are carcinogenic. A 15- to 20-minute session is equivalent in **ultraviolet (UV) ray** exposure to one full day at the beach. Although tanning salons often advertise that sun bed tanning is safer than sunbathing outside, the intensity of light in tanning beds is actually much greater. The customer not only has light rays above his or her body but also below it. Many of the older tanning beds emit short-wave UV rays, which burn the outer layers of the skin. The majority of the tanning beds used today, however, emit long-wave UV rays, which actually penetrate deeper and weaken the skin's inner connective tissue. Tanning salon rays also increase the damage that is done by the sunlight, because the UV light from the tanning beds thins the skin, making it less able to heal. Both the sun and tanning beds produce a tan from UV rays. UV rays cause the skin to protect itself from burning by producing additional pigmentation and coloring. Overexposure to these UV rays can lead to eye injury, premature wrinkling, light-induced skin rashes, and increased chances of skin cancer. To get that nice tanned look without the risk, consumers are now flocking to risk-free tanning booths that use sprays.

So, should you stay out of the sun altogether? No, that's not right, either. Although overexposure to sunlight can be very detrimental to one's health, we still need some amount of exposure to sunlight for both physical and psychological reasons. A lack of sunlight is associated with poor mood, as well as with a condition called seasonal affective disorder. Sunlight is also a major source of vitamin D in humans, because it produces vitamin D in the skin after exposure to UV radiation (Weinrich, Ellison, Weinrich, Ross, & Reis-Starr, 2001). Without vitamin D, diseases such as rickets occur. In direct relationship to this chapter, sunlight exposure has also been found to reduce the risk of advanced breast cancer among women with light skin pigmentation (John, Schwartz, Koo, Wang, & Ingles, 2007).

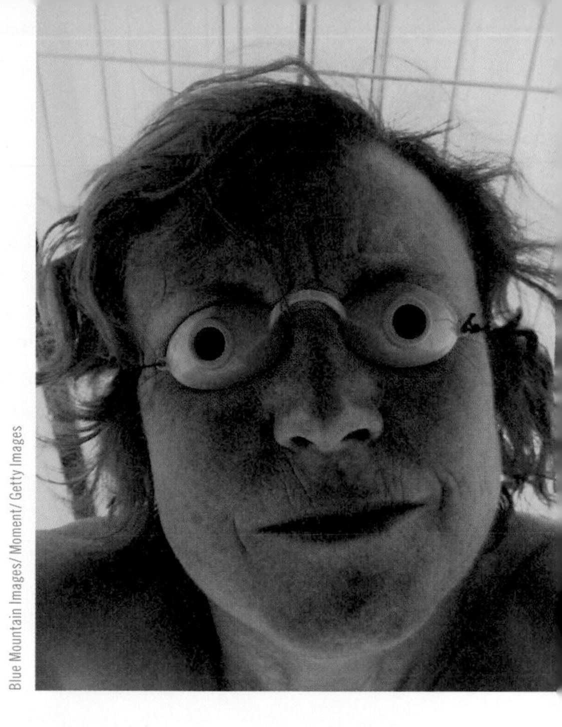
Blue Mountain Images/ Moment/ Getty Images

▲ **Tanning.** Visiting a tanning booth, even once, can expose you to carcinogenic ultraviolet rays. A safer alternative for a tanned look is a spray-on tan.

TREATMENT OPTIONS

Cancer need no longer be a death sentence, although many people still believe it is. Although earlier cancer detection increases its chances of being completely treated, even some cancers in their later stages can be successfully treated. Because cancer is essentially cells that are out of control, the main goal of treatment is to get the cells out of the body. There are three major ways to treat cancer.

Surgery

The oldest and most straightforward way to treat cancer is *surgery*, during which the surgeon can remove the tumor. Surgery is most successful when the cancer has not spread because this provides the best chance of removing all the mutant cells. Surgery also has other uses in cancer (ACS, 2017). **Preventive surgery** is performed to remove tissue that is not malignant as yet but has a high chance of turning malignant. This happens in the case of women with a family history of breast cancer who also have a mutant breast cancer gene (*BRCA1* or *BRCA2*). Preventive surgery may also be used to remove parts of the colon if polyps, small stalk-shaped growths (not the little marine animals), are found.

Diagnostic surgery is the process of removing a small amount of tissue to either identify a cancer or to make a diagnosis (ACS, 2017). If the patient does receive a positive diagnosis of cancer, sometimes **staging surgery** is needed to ascertain what stage of development the cancer is in. This form of surgery helps determine how far the cancer has spread and provides a *clinical stage* for the growth. If the cancer has been localized to a small area, **curative surgery** can be used to remove the growth. This is the primary form of treatment for cancer and is often used in conjunction with the other treatments. If it is not possible to remove the entire tumor without damaging the surrounding tissues, **debulking surgery** reduces the tumor mass. Finally, **palliative surgery** is used to treat complications of advanced disease (not as a cure), and **restorative surgery** is used to modify a person's appearance after curative surgery (e.g., breast reconstructive surgery after a **mastectomy** or breast removal).

Chemotherapy

The second major form of treatment for cancer involves taking medications with the aim of disabling the cancer growth, a process referred to as **chemotherapy** (ACS, 2017). The medications are either given in pill form, in the form of an injection, or in the form of an intravenous injection (medication delivered through a catheter right into a vein). The type of cancer and its severity determine the frequency of chemotherapy, and it can range from daily to monthly medication. This form of treatment can have very strong side effects but often results in successful outcomes. Patients who undergo chemotherapy (or chemo for short) may lose all their hair (not just the hair on their head as is commonly believed), experience severe nausea, and have a dry mouth and skin.

Chemotherapy also has biopsychosocial effects (Schlatter & Cameron, 2010). Biologically, the treatment lowers both red and white blood cell counts. Fewer red blood cells make a person anemic and feel weak and tired. A reduced number of white blood cells makes a person more prone to infection, and a person undergoing chemotherapy needs to take special care to not be exposed to germs or sources of contamination. Psychologically, the fatigue can lead to low moods and also a loss of sexual desire and low sociability. Social interactions become strained as well. The patient often feels embarrassed by not having any hair and may not want to be seen by other people or may be too tired to interact. Simultaneously, many visitors and friends feel uncomfortable at the sight of the hairless, fatigued patient. As with most chronic illnesses it is important for the patient's support networks to be prepared for and compensate for the effects of treatment.

Radiation Therapy

The third major form of treatment for cancer involves the use of radioactive particles aimed at the DNA of the cancer cells, a process referred to as **radiation therapy** (ACS, 2017). Radiation used for cancer treatment is called ionizing radiation because it forms ions as it passes through tissues and dislodges electrons from atoms. The ionization causes cell death or a genetic change in the cancerous cells (King & Robins, 2006). There are many different types of radiation treatments (e.g., electron beams, high-energy photons, protons, and neutrons), each sounding like something out of a science fiction movie and varying in intensity and energy. The process for getting radiation therapy is a little more complex than that for chemotherapy and surgery, although the preliminary stages are the same. Medical personnel first need to identify the location and size of the tumor and then pick the correct level of radiation. The key is to be able to do the most damage to the cancerous cells without damaging the normal cells. This is hard to do because the radiation stream cannot differentiate between types of cells, and normal cells often end up being affected as part of the process, resulting in side effects of treatment. The total dose of radiation, a rad, is often broken down into fractions, and delivered over several weeks. Radiation therapy is perhaps the most involved type of therapy, with treatments usually being given daily, 5 days a week, for 5 to 7 weeks (ACS, 2017). The main side effects are fatigue and irritation of the body areas close to the radiation site, often accompanied by some disruption of functioning. For example, radiation to the mouth and throat area can cause loss of salivary function, difficulty in swallowing, and a redness of the neck and surrounding areas.

Other Treatments

In addition to these three main forms of treatment, there are also a variety of other possible ways to treat cancer. For example, **immunotherapy** involves the activation of the body's own immune system to fight the cancer (King & Robins, 2006). There are also a number of alternative and complementary therapies that help people cope with cancer (some of which are believed to keep cancer at bay as well). These include aromatherapy, music therapy, yoga, massage therapy, meditation to reduce stress, special diets like taking peppermint tea for nausea, and acupuncture. There is growing public interest, especially among those living with cancer and/or the relatives of people with cancer, in obtaining information about complementary and alternative medicine (CAM) as discussed in Chapter 3 and methods of treatment. This interest is even more prevalent among individuals from different cultural groups who may have approaches and beliefs about cancer and its treatment that vary greatly from the view held by Western biomedicine. Very often cancer patients do not tell their doctors that they are also trying other treatments. Although there may be many treatments for cancer used by other cultures that are actually beneficial, very few methods have been tested by Western science and correspondingly North American health practitioners recommend very few alternative methods.

The stance of Western biomedicine is reflected particularly well in how the ACS refers to complementary and alternative medicine. The ACS (2018) defines alternative methods as "unproved or disproved methods, rather than evidence-based or proven methods to prevent, diagnose, and treat cancer" and complementary methods as "those supportive methods used to complement evidence-based treatment." The American Cancer Society acknowledges that more research is needed to determine the safety and effectiveness of many of these methods and advocates for peer-reviewed scientific evidence of the safety and efficacy of these methods. Health-care practitioners recognize the need to balance access to alternative and complementary therapies while protecting patients against methods that might be harmful to them. For example, the American Cancer Society supports patients having access to CAM but strongly encourages more oversight and accountability by governmental, public, and private entities to protect the public from harm. Part of the problem arises from the fact that harmful drug interactions may occur and must be recognized. In addition, sometimes use of the other treatments causes delays in starting standard therapies and is detrimental to the success of cancer treatment.

Chris Hondros/ Getty Images News/ Getty Images

▲ **Radiation Therapy.** A cancer patient has his head immobilized before targeted laser-guided radiation treatment.

When treatments succeed in keeping cancer at bay, the health psychologist's job is not done. There is evidence that breast cancer survivors are at risk for developing secondary tumors (Dörffel, Riepenhausen, Lüders, Brämswig, & Schellong, 2015). Similarly problematic, low levels of posttraumatic stress disorder (PTSD) and other stress-related problems have been seen in child cancer survivors (Schrag, McKeown, Jackson, Cuffe, & Neuberg, 2008). Many cancer survivors begin to (or continue to) use many complementary and alternative treatments. For example, Gansler, Kaw, Crammer, and Smith (2008) studied more than 4,000 survivors and found the most frequently reported treatments were prayer/spiritual practice (61.4%), relaxation (44.3%), faith/spiritual healing (42.4%), nutritional supplements/vitamins (40.1%), meditation (15%), religious counseling (11.3%), massage (11.2%), and support groups (9.7%). Such treatments may provide the survivors with psychological benefits and prevent relapse, though this possibility has not been tested.

BEHAVIORAL INTERVENTIONS

The main way to reduce the death rates from cancer is to increase the practice of healthy behaviors and decrease other behavioral contributions to cancer risk (Lovely & Fowler, 2018). The general approaches to improving common behaviors—reduce tobacco use, eat a nutritionally balanced meal, and get physical activity—have been covered in some detail in Chapters 7 and 8. Although challenging, interventions to get people to change old habits, such as what they eat, are beginning to be successful (Kumanyika et al., 2000) and health psychologists have focused on a range of psychosocial interventions for patients with cancer (Faul & Jacobsen, 2012; Stanton, 2019). Another major health behavior not covered in as much detail before is getting routine screenings.

Aiding Prevention: Increasing Screening Behaviors

One of the strongest contributions of health psychological research has been to illustrate how we can increase health behaviors that will ensure the early detection of cancer. The most direct early detection behavior is screening, and a number of interventions attempt to increase cancer screenings especially for breast, cervical, and colorectal cancer (del Junco et al., 2008). Early detection ensures that the cancer can be treated in an early stage, almost literally being nipped in the bud. Screening can take two main forms: screening by professionals and medical

▼ TABLE 13.4

Screening Guidelines for the Early Detection of Breast Cancer, American Cancer Society, 2018

• Yearly mammograms are recommended starting at age 40 and continuing for as long as a woman is in good health.
• A clinical breast examination should be part of a periodic health examination, about every 3 years for women in their 20s and 30s and every year for women 40 and older.
• Women should know how their breasts normally feel and report any breast changes promptly to their health-care providers. Breast self-examination is an option for women starting in their 20s.
• Women at increased risk (e.g., family history, genetic tendency, and past breast cancer) should talk with their doctors about the benefits and limitations of starting mammography screening earlier, having additional tests (i.e., breast ultrasound and MRI), or having more frequent examinations.

equipment such as mammograms, and screening that you can do at home such as testicular or breast self-examinations. The American Cancer Society has a clear set of recommendations for when and how often a person should be screened/should check for cancer (Table 13.4 shows recommendations for breast cancer screenings). The big question here is: Even if you know how often you should get screened, will you do it?

The **Health Belief Model (HBM)** described in Chapter 7 (Rosenstock, 1974) is the model used most often to guide interventions to increase screening behavior (Capik & Gözüm, 2011). According to this model, the extent to which you see yourself as being susceptible to cancer, the extent to which you believe cancer to have severe consequences, the perceived barriers keeping you from getting screened, and the perceived benefits to getting screened all combine to predict your screening behavior. A number of interventions have included components especially designed to influence different parts of the HBM (e.g., Farmer, Reddick, D'Agostino, & Jackson, 2007). The Application Showcase section at the end of this chapter gives you a concrete example of an intervention aimed at increasing screening.

The model works well. Even increasing people's knowledge about cancer severity and the benefits of screening increases the likelihood that people will get screened (DiPlacido, Zauber, & Redd, 1998). Factors that influence perceptions of susceptibility or risk are important as well (Cole, Bryant, McDermott, Sorrell, & Flynn, 1997). People with a family history of breast cancer and those who had breast problems are more likely to get screened (McCaul, Branstetter, Schroeder, & Glasgow, 1996). Susceptibility is not as predictive of self-examinations (Miller, Shoda, & Hurley, 1996). Having strong perceived barriers to screening are some of the strongest predictors of self-examinations (Wyper, 1990). Other significant barriers to getting screened are the costs of tests, the lack of health insurance, the lack of time, and an inconvenient test location (Maxwell, Bastani, & Warda, 1998).

▲ **Ad Campaign to Increase Screening for Colorectal Cancer.** Colorectal cancer is another cancer that can be successfully treated if it is detected early enough. This is one of the posters in a national campaign to increase screenings.

Paradoxically, believing yourself to be extremely susceptible to cancer (e.g., taking a genetic test showing you have a mutated gene) or having a strong knowledge of severity and the fact that the disease could be fatal sometimes keeps people from getting screened (Sutton, Bickler, Sancho-Aldridge, & Saidi, 1994). The fear of actually finding something can keep people from even getting the test (Bastani, Marcus, & Hollatz-Brown, 1991). This problem is amplified in some cultural groups. Fatalism, discussed previously, among older, low-income

▼ TABLE 13.5

Cultural Differences in Screening (Percent of Sample)

Screening Test	Asian Americans	Latino	European American
Clinical breast examination	60	89	98
Mammogram	61	80	93
Pap test	56	16	99
Mammogram or Pap test in past 2 years	46	50	56
Pap test in past 3 years	66	74	16

Source: Hiatt, R. A., Pasick, R. J., Perez-Stable, E. J., McPhee, S. J., Engelstad, L., Lee, M. et al. (1996). Pathways to early cancer detection in the multiethnic population of San Francisco Bay area. *Health Education Quarterly, 23* (Suppl.), S10–S27.

Mexican American women is associated with lower Pap smear rates (a test for uterine cancer) (Suarez, Rouche, Nichols, & Simpson, 1997).

Cultural Differences in Screening

Cultural differences arise once more in the use of preventive measures for cancer. Low SES women are less likely to get mammograms (Ruiz et al., 2019). Non-European American groups do not use routine screening tests as frequently as European American groups (Lee et al., 2011) and, consequently, have more severe cancer at diagnosis (Gotay et al., 2001). Hiatt et al. (1996) collected some of the best detailed information on ethnic differences in screening from a study of 4,228 individuals in the San Francisco Bay area. Illustrative data from Hiatt et al. (1996) and from the National Center for Health Statistics at the CDC collected around the same time are shown in Table 13.5.

As you can see, there are significant differences between African Americans, Latinos, European Americans, and Asian Americans. In terms of ever having a screening test for both breast and cervical cancer, Asian Americans reported significantly lower rates. Similar patterns can be seen for adherence to recommendations to get screening tests. Why is this? The main barriers to getting screened, described above, particularly affect low SES men and women across all ethnic groups (Hoffman-Goetz, Breen, & Meissner, 1998). For some cultural groups the embarrassment of having the test keeps them away. Asian American and Latina women, for example, are embarrassed when undergoing breast and cervical cancer screenings (Lee et al., 2011; Maxwell et al., 1998). Cultural beliefs about modesty and who is allowed to see the naked body also have an influence. For members of many cultures it is inappropriate for an unknown member of the opposite sex, such as a doctor or nurse, to see the person's body (Gurung, 2014). Such issues are seen in the preferences of Vietnamese, Chinese, and Latina women to request service from a female physician (Galanti, 2014).

The previously mentioned paradox between fear and screening (more fear of having cancer leads to avoiding the screening) is evidenced in both Latina and African American women (Friedman et al., 1995; Lobell, Bay, Rhoads, & Keske, 1998). In fact, the fear that the radiation from a mammogram is dangerous is higher among Asian and Latina women than among European American women (Dibble, Vanomi, & Miaskowski, 1997). African American and Latina women also report more fear of the pain associated with mammograms (Stein, Fox, & Murata, 1991). Finally, non-European American ethnic groups also report higher levels of incorrect knowledge about screening and cancer in general (Yi, 1998). Some of this could be due to recent immigration-related issues, including a combination of inadequate English proficiency, acculturation problems, and potentially male-dominated family structures, which prevent some women from receiving community-based public health information (Wismer et al., 1998).

Inhibiting Progression and Helping Patients Cope

Going beyond the prevention of cancer, another category of interventions has been designed to prolong life after diagnosis and to reduce patients' treatment anxiety (Yang, Brothers, & Andersen, 2008). Social support again figures prominently (Helgeson et al., 1999). In the classic demonstration of the effectiveness of social support, Spiegel, Bloom, Kraemer, and Gottheil (1989) had women with breast cancer attend weekly supportive group therapy meetings. This group lived on average 36.6 months after the start of the intervention. In contrast, survival of the control patients who only received standard cancer care averaged 18.9 months. More recently, Fawzy et al. (1993) used a structured social support group to reduce distress and enhance the immune functioning in patients with newly diagnosed cancer. The group involved health education, illness-related problem solving, and relaxation, and members met weekly for 6 weeks. By 6 months, the intervention group showed lower levels of emotional distress, depression, confusion, and fatigue than the control group. Even their immune activity was higher. In general, such support groups are designed to promote the development of supportive relationships among group members and encourage expression of patients' feelings or disease-related anxieties (Henderson & Baum, 2002).

Some interventions focus directly on cancer pain. Ward et al. (2008) developed an intervention to decrease cancer pain (RIDcancerPain) and tested it using a classic randomized control trial. The main variables of interest, pain severity, pain interference with life, and overall quality of life and coping style were measured three times (baseline, 1, and 2 months later). Participants in the intervention group who experienced pain related to metastatic cancer showed greater decreases in pain severity than those in control (Ward et al., 2008).

Other potentially useful psychological interventions involve relaxation training or hypnosis (Carlson, Speca, Patel, & Goodey, 2003) although neither method has received solid empirical support. For example, although relaxation is often recommended for cancer-related pain (Millard, 1993) and has been found to be a useful tool in pain management in general (see Chapter 10), a recent review found only two studies that used a controlled randomized design to directly examine the effectiveness of relaxation training (Redd & Jacobsen, 2001). Sloman, Brown, Aldana, and Chee (1994) used both progressive muscle relaxation and mental imagery to reduce patients' pain. Randomly assigned hospital patients were trained to relax by either a nurse or with the use of an audiotape. The intervention group reported significantly less pain and requested less pain medication. A similar study by Syrjala, Donaldson, Davis, Kippes, and Carr (1995) compared relaxation training with cognitive-behavioral coping training and found that both methods worked.

Keeping cultural differences in beliefs about cancer in mind, some interventions build on cultural values to change health behaviors that could cause cancer. For example, Lichtenstein and Lopez (1999) developed a program to reduce smoking in American Indian tribes in the Northwest by using American Indian staff to ensure the target population that the intervention was at least partly Indian-owned. Distinctions were made between social uses of tobacco and ritualistic uses and tribal representatives were closely involved in the process of developing American Indian-specific materials on smoking cessation.

In general, a number of psychosocial interventions have shown promise for alleviating the pain and discomfort of cancer. When used in conjunction with medications, these interventions can help make life bearable and even enjoyable for the patient with cancer.

Synthesize, Evaluate, Apply

- Health behaviors play a large role in putting someone at risk for cancer. How does each behavior interact with the others?
- What factors should go into the choice of a treatment?
- How would you design an intervention to reduce risks for cancer?
- Pick a health behavior change model and use it to increase screening behaviors.
- What can be done to reduce the delay between identification of cancer symptoms and going in to a doctor?

INCREASING CANCER SCREENING

A number of adages support the importance of early intervention for cancer. There is truth to the adages, "A stitch in time saves nine," "An ounce of prevention is worth a pound of cure," and so on. Many chronic illnesses take a long time to develop and are not always detectable in their early stages. That said, as described earlier in this chapter, cancer is a disease that can be cured if it is caught early enough. Consequently, one of the most common clinical applications of health psychological theory is in the design of interventions to increase health screening behaviors (Aiken, Gerend, & Jackson, 2001). Interventions provide a wonderful window to look at theory in action. Let's take a close look at one intervention in particular to give you a better sense of the problem and a feel for how interventions are done.

A prototypical example of a screening intervention is one conducted by Leona Aiken and colleagues (Aiken et al., 1994). Although there are more recent interventions as discussed previously, this one served as a model for later research and bears close scrutiny. Their main goal was to increase mammography screening rates in accordance with American Cancer Society guidelines that suggest women should have a baseline mammogram between 35 and 39 years of age and then have a mammogram every year or two up to age 50 and yearly after age 50. There have been a lot of very public debates about these recommendations and about the effectiveness of screening in general. Health experts agree that women in their 50s should get mammograms. The debate centers on whether the tests reduce the risk of breast cancer for women in their 40s. Another factor is that mammograms can sometimes be inaccurate: nearly one in four women who regularly have a mammogram will have at least one false-positive result (Christiansen et al., 2000), but the benefits do seem to outweigh the costs.

Breast cancer receives some of the highest levels of funding of all cancer research, and, consequently, the majority of cancer research in the field of health psychology involves studies on the incidence and progression of this disease. Breast cancer is a malignant tumor that starts from cells of the breast. The breast itself is made up of lobules, ducts, fatty and connective tissue, blood vessels, and lymph vessels. When breast cancer cells reach the underarm lymph nodes and continue to grow, they cause the nodes to swell. Once cancer cells have reached these nodes they are more likely to spread to other organs of the body as well. There are several types of breast tumors. Most are abnormal benign growths. Some lumps are not really tumors at all. These lumps are often caused by the formation of scar tissue and are also benign. To detect the growth of cancers as early as possible, women in their 20s and 30s should have a clinical breast examination (CBE) as part of a regular physical examination by a health expert preferably every 3 years (American Cancer Society, 2018). Women are also urged to conduct regular breast self-examinations (BSE) to also detect abnormalities in changes. Unfortunately, growths have to be relatively large to be felt by BSEs or even CBEs. Mammograms, on the other hand, can detect extremely small particles in the breast and, consequently, it is important for women to go get screened.

The theory used by Aiken et al. (1994) was the Health Behavior Model (HBM). They designed an intervention that targeted each of the four components of the HBM: perceived susceptibility, severity, benefits, and barriers.

The sample comprised 295 primarily middle-class European American women. The authors sent out letters of invitation to 253 female support groups around the state of Arizona asking them if they would like to participate in a study. Forty-four groups replied. Each volunteer was given a pretest (before the intervention) and an assessment right after the intervention. She was then contacted 3 months later during the time when actual compliance was measured. At each assessment, the women's intention to get a screening and questions based on the model were used: What prevents you from getting a mammogram (barriers)? How susceptible do you think you are to getting breast cancer (vulnerability)?

There were three experimental groups. One group received an educational program. This group was given information about prevalence rates of breast cancer and its risk factors to increase perceived susceptibility. The pathological course of the disease and survival rates were described to increase severity and the advantages of early screening were described to increase perceived benefits. To decrease barriers, the authors stressed the minimal nature of the risks (women feared the radiation from the mammography machine could be dangerous) and low costs and presented a slide show of the procedure so it was clear what exactly was done.

The second experimental group received the educational program plus psychological training. The women were presented with counterarguments against mammography, actors modeled the process with a role-play, provided action steps for women to take (gave them the addresses and phone numbers of where to go to get a mammogram), made the women commit to calling and making an appointment by signing a form, and then mailed the women copies of the signed form and action steps 2 weeks later. The control group only completed the preintervention questionnaire.

What was the result? Not surprisingly, two to three times more women in the intervention groups went to get screened than women in the control group. In

(Continued)

(Continued)

assessing the exact reasons behind the increase in compliance, Aiken et al. (1994) conducted a mediational analysis, which is a statistical procedure that illustrates links between chains of variables and tests for mediation as we discussed in Chapter 5. Essentially, they asked whether the HBM variables such as susceptibility, severity, benefits, and barriers served to mediate the connection between the intervention and the change in behavior (West & Aiken, 1997). In keeping with the predictions of the HBM model, strong mediational pathways were found between perceived susceptibility and perceived benefits to intentions, and there was a strong link between intentions to get screened and actually going in for a screening. Aiken et al. (1994) also found that perceived susceptibility played a substantial role in predicting behavior. In fact, the authors found that perceived susceptibility played both an indirect role in influencing behavior (intervention → susceptibility → benefits → intentions) and a direct role as well (intervention → susceptibility → intentions).

Such psychological interventions nicely demonstrate the effectiveness of health psychological research and the role it plays in health behavior change and the prevention of illness.

CHAPTER REVIEW

SUMMARY

- Cancer is the second leading cause of death in the United States, and the chances of being diagnosed with cancer increase with age. Cancer is the name given to a category of illnesses in which the main problem is the presence of a malignant tumor. Cancer cells form because of cell mutations in DNA caused by exposure to environmental toxins and unhealthy behaviors such as smoking.
- Tumors vary in where they are found, can be malignant or benign, and can vary in severity. The four main types of cancer are carcinomas (starting in surface layers of the body), sarcomas (in muscles, bones, or cartilage), lymphomas (in the lymphatic system), and leukemias (in the blood or bone marrow).
- There are large differences in the cultural makeup of people who have cancer. Both incidence rates and mortality rates vary across cultures. African Americans have the highest general cancer rates. Men experience higher incidences of cancer than women. These cultural differences also extend to beliefs and knowledge about cancer.
- Cancer can be considered a developmental disease because the chances of getting it increase as you age, and health behaviors at different stages of development may put one more at risk for having cancer.
- Psychological factors play a part in both the incidence of cancer and in responding to diagnosis although the effects are stronger for the latter. Personality traits such as optimism, the presence of social support, and finding meaning in the illness are all associated with coping with cancer and its progression.
- The key health behaviors associated with a higher incidence of cancer are tobacco use, poor diets, and a lack of physical activity. Sun exposure and the use of tanning beds also are associated with cancer incidence.
- The main treatments for cancer are surgery, chemotherapy, radiation therapy, and immunotherapy. A number of alternative and complementary therapies such as yoga, massage, meditation, and acupuncture are also used to help patients cope with cancer.
- Health psychologists aid in the prevention of cancer by designing behavioral interventions to increase screening behaviors. There are a number of cultural differences in screening behaviors with low SES individuals being the most likely to not get screened consistent with guidelines. There are also significant differences in screening behaviors among African Americans, Latinos, European Americans, and Asian Americans.
- Some interventions are designed to inhibit the progression of cancer and help patients cope.

TEST YOURSELF

Check your understanding of the topics in this chapter by answering the following questions.

1. Cancer is the __________ cause of death in America.
   a. leading
   b. second-leading

c. third-leading
d. fourth-leading

2. Cancer is best defined as
   a. an illness caused by the presence of a malignant tumor.
   b. a mutated cell.
   c. a cell with retarded growth.
   d. a cell with accelerated growth.

3. Not all cells with abnormal cell growth are cancerous. The type that destroys healthy tissue is referred to as
   a. neoplasmic.
   b. malignant.
   c. benign.
   d. mutant.

4. Cancer-causing substances are referred to as
   a. carcinogens.
   b. malignancies.
   c. teratogens.
   d. neoplasmas.

5. The most common site for cancer for men is the
   a. lungs.
   b. prostate gland.
   c. colon.
   d. pancreas.

6. Cancers that start at the surface layers of the body are called
   a. lymphomas.
   b. carcinomas.
   c. sarcomas.
   d. leukemias.

7. _______ have the highest general cancer incidence rates in America.
   a. Asian Americans
   b. African Americans
   c. European Americans
   d. Latinos

8. _______ believe that cancer is punishment for one's actions or that of a family member and that one must bear the pain to protect other members of one's communities.
   a. African Americans
   b. Laotians
   c. American Indians
   d. Latinos

9. The single most dangerous health behavior in context of cancer is
   a. smoking.
   b. drinking alcohol.
   c. not exercising.
   d. eating badly.

10. The health psychological model that is most commonly used to get people to get screened for cancer when they should is
    a. the Health Belief Model.
    b. the Theory of Planned Behavior.
    c. the Transtheoretical Model.
    d. Social Norm Marketing.

KEY TERMS, CONCEPTS, AND PEOPLE

benefit finding, **350**
benign, **343**
carcinogens, **343**
carcinomas, **343**
chemotherapy, **357**
curative surgery, **357**
debulking surgery, **357**
diagnostic surgery, **357**
fatalism, **346**
Health Belief Model (HBM), **360**
immunotherapy, **358**
incidence, **344**
leukemias, **344**
lymphomas, **343**
malignant, **343**
mastectomy, **357**
metastasize, **343**
neoplasms, **343**
palliative surgery, **357**
preventive surgery, **357**
radiation therapy, **358**
restorative surgery, **357**
sarcomas, **343**
screening, **341**
staging surgery, **357**
TNM system, **344**
Type C personality, **348**
ultraviolet (UV) ray, **356**

ESSENTIAL READINGS ▶▶

Anderson, B. L., Kiecolt-Glaser, J., & Glaser, R. (1994). A biobehavioral model of cancer stress and disease course. *American Psychologist, 49,* 389–404.

Mukherjee, S. (2010). *The emperor of maladies: A biography of cancer.* New York, NY: Scribner.

Stanton, A. (2019). Cancer. In T. A. Revenson & R. A. R. Gurung (Eds.), *Handbook of health psychology* (3e). New York, NY: Routledge.

CHAPTER 14

CARDIOVASCULAR DISEASE

Fundamentals and Cultural Variations

Steve Debenport/E+/Getty Images

Chapter 14 Outline

MEASURING UP

HOW WELL DO YOU KNOW RISK FACTORS FOR CARDIOVASCULAR DISEASE?

On a scale of 0 to 4 (with 0 = *not at all*, 1 = *little*, 2 = *somewhat*, 3 = *a lot*, and 4 = *extremely*), to what extent do you think each of these contribute to the development of heart disease? (Follow the source link for answers.)

1. genetics and family history
2. aging
3. gender
4. smoke and toxic substances
5. polluted water and air
6. dust
7. war
8. secondhand smoke
9. tobacco and hookah smoking
10. drug abuse
11. drinking
12. malnutrition
13. physical inactivity
14. physical work pressure
15. psychological stress
16. anger and rage
17. emotions such as fear or joy
18. sadness and grief
19. depression
20. marital discord and misbehavior
21. discomfort due to financial problems and lack of money
22. high cholesterol
23. hypertension
24. diabetes
25. obesity and overweight

Source: https://www.ncbi.nlm.nih.gov/pmc/articles/PMC5290683/

▼ Ponder This

What are some stereotypes of who gets heart disease and why?

Which health behaviors do you think most predict heart attacks?

Can you actually reverse the course of heart disease?

"Quick! Call 911! I think Pat is having a heart attack!" You have probably seen enough movies to imagine what this scenario must look like: a person writhing in pain on the floor, chest clutched between sweaty fingers. Perhaps this is in a crowded restaurant and worried onlookers are debating the best course of action. As you picture this scene, as yourself this question: What does Pat look like? You most likely picture Pat as an old or middle-aged Caucasian man, probably someone's grandfather or uncle named Patrick. Heart problems are often expected of older men, but this stereotype is not accurate. In fact, heart-related diseases are common in older women as well and Pat in this scene could very well be Patricia. There is a marked lack of awareness of the high risk for heart attack among women. In addition, did you know that heart-related diseases are the third most common cause of death for children younger than age 15? Therefore, Pat could be a young boy or an older woman having a heart problem. But that's not all. Heart attacks are not always as dramatic as the scenario described here either.

▼ FIGURE 14.1

Prevalence of the Most Common Cardiovascular Diseases in the U.S.

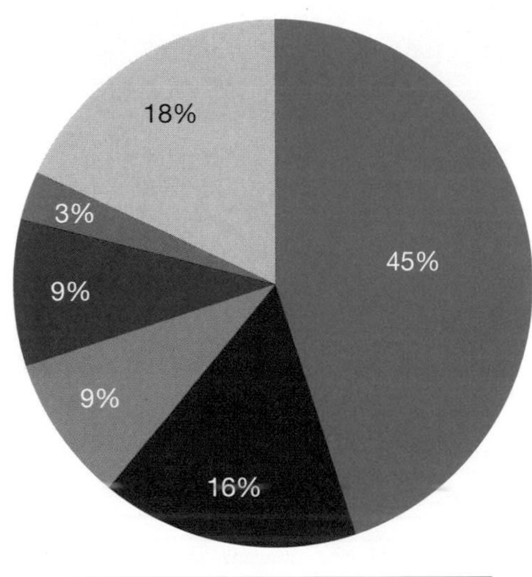

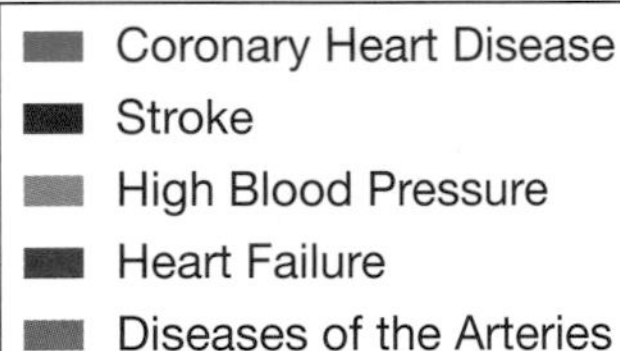

Source: Data from the American Heart Association (2017).

This chapter describes the class of diseases that affect the heart and circulatory system and reviews the main biopsychosocial determinants and the factors that alleviate the illness. The core causes of most of the cardiovascular diseases (CVDs) are very similar. We focus on the most common: coronary heart disease, stroke, and hypertension. Figure 14.1 shows the prevalence of each in relation to the other. I will also highlight the many cultural factors that influence the effects and progression of heart diseases.

PREVALENCE OF CARDIOVASCULAR DISEASES

By 2030 almost 23.6 million people will die from CVDs worldwide (World Health Organization [WHO], 2017). Although that is still a lot of people, the good news is that heart disease death rates have been dropping. In the United States rates dropped 25.8% between 1999 and 2005, and a further 10% from 2006 to 2010 (CDC, 2011; National Center for Health Statistics, 2008). Stroke deaths dropped 24.4%, from 61 to 47 deaths per 100,000 people. Deaths from cardiovascular disease have dropped also in some European countries (WHO, 2017). Yet heart problems and those related to the circulatory system are still the leading causes of death globally (WHO, 2011; Figure 14.2) and problems due to heart disease vary from country to country. Fatality due to heart disease is affected also by differences in health behaviors among countries. Some of these varying major risk factors are blood pressure, blood cholesterol, smoking, physical activity, and diet. One-fifth of all deaths in developing countries such as India and Mexico and two-fifths of all deaths in developed countries such as the United States, Britain, and Canada are attributable to heart diseases (Murray & Lopez, 1997). The number of deaths from cardiovascular disease by sex and age is shown in Figure 14.3.

Much of our understanding of heart disease comes from a large-scope longitudinal study begun more than 50 years ago. In the late 1940s, the U.S. Public Health Service selected the town of Framingham, Massachusetts, to be the site of a large-scale study to understand why

▼ FIGURE 14.2

Global Deaths from Coronary Heart Disease

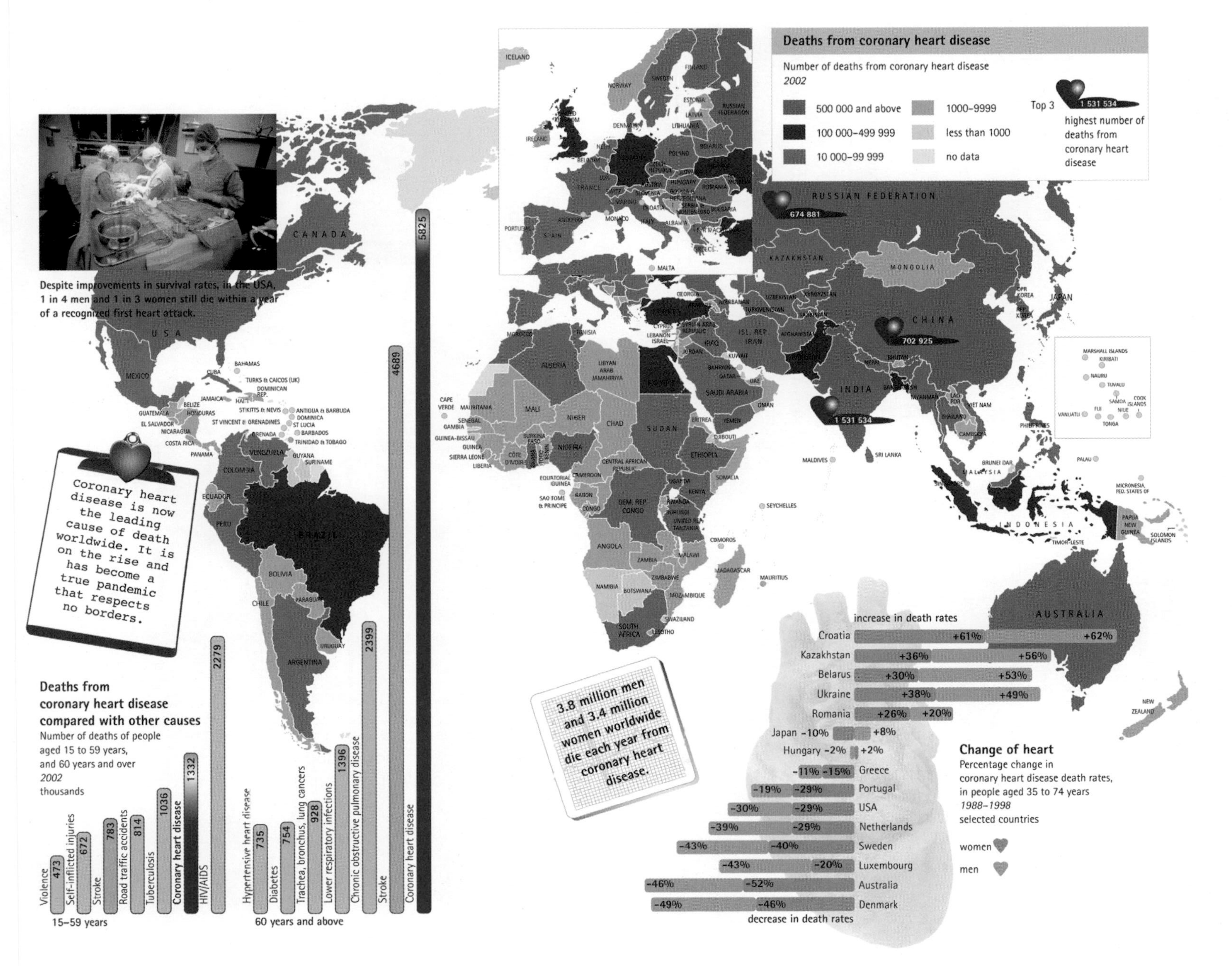

Source: Roth, G. A., et al., 2017.

heart disease had become North America's number one killer. A total of more than 5,000 healthy male and female residents between ages 30 and 60 were enrolled as the first cohort of participants. Every 2 to 4 years, study participants are given extensive medical examinations including a medical history, blood tests, and other tests of current health status. The **Framingham heart study** was the first to establish a relationship between levels of cholesterol and high blood pressure and their effect on heart disease risk (Apel, Klein, McDermott, & Westhoff, 1997). The researchers found that a lifestyle with a bad diet, sedentary living, smoking, and unrestrained weight gain accelerated the occurrence of cardiovascular problems. Even today, new information about heart disease is based on the latest assessments made with Framingham participants (Ramsay et al., 2011). The children and grandchildren of the original cohort participate today and are referred to as the offspring or third-generation cohorts (Ai et al., 2011). Let's take a closer look at these often-fatal diseases.

WHAT IS CARDIOVASCULAR DISEASE?

Diseases resulting from problems with the heart and the circulatory system are all gathered under the general heading of **cardiovascular disease (CVD)**. The most common are coronary heart disease (CHD) and heart failure (both commonly referred to as heart attacks), strokes, and hypertension or high blood pressure (medically referred to as essential hypertension). Others include abnormal heart rhythms, congenital heart disease, heart valve failure, electrical conduction disorder, heart muscle disease (cardiomyopathy), rheumatic fever, pulmonary heart disease, cerebrovascular disease, and diseases of the veins, arteries, and lymph nodes (the last three collectively are called vascular diseases). Many other medical conditions put you at risk for CVD. Major risk factors include high blood pressure, diabetes, kidney disease, arthritis, and obesity (Xu, Stokes, & Meredith, 2016). To get a better feel for how CVDs develop, this is a good time to refresh yourself on the circulatory system (described in Chapter 4).

▼ FIGURE 14.3

Death Rates for Diseases of the Heart by Age and Sex, United States, 2015

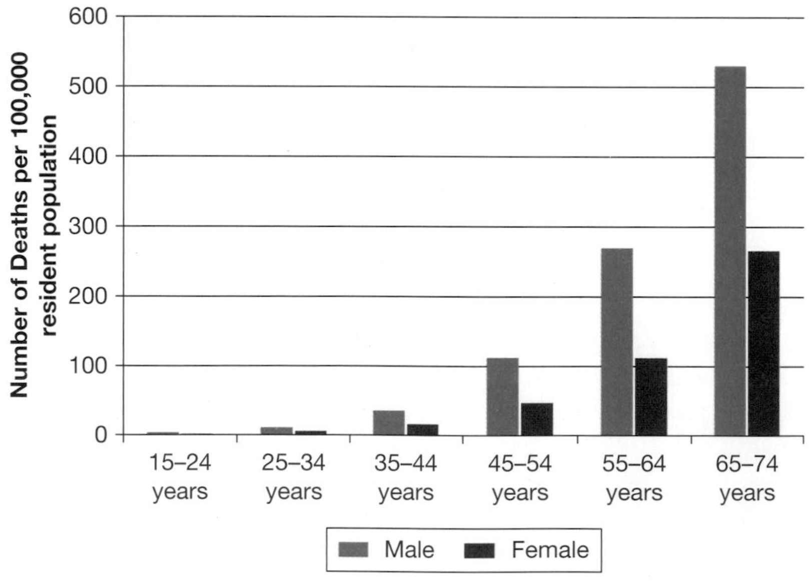

Source: https://www.cdc.gov/nchs/data/hus/hus16.pdf

National Center for Health Statistics. Health, United States, 2016: With Chartbook on Long-term Trends in Health. Hyattsville, MD. 2017.

Coronary heart disease (CHD) is a condition in which the small blood vessels that supply blood and oxygen to the heart narrow due the accumulation of fat or scar tissue. It is also called coronary artery disease. As the coronary arteries narrow, blood flow to the heart can slow down or even stop, causing chest pain, shortness of breath, or a heart attack. Coronary heart disease is the leading cause of death in America.

iStockphoto.com/ Henk Badenhorst

▲ **Blood Pressure.** High blood pressure is one of the easiest ways to detect a risk for heart problems and is associated with obesity, bad diets, and not enough physical activity.

Hypertension or high blood pressure is a condition in which the blood pressure remains chronically elevated. Blood pressure that stays between 120 and 139/80 and 89 mm Hg is considered prehypertension and blood pressure above this level (140/90 mm Hg or higher) is considered hypertension. Hypertension increases the risk for heart attack and stroke.

Stroke is the third-leading cause of death in the United States behind CHD and cancer and is the leading cause of disability among adults. Approximately 550,000 people have strokes each year, with approximately 150,000 of them fatal. Stroke is a type of CVD that affects the arteries leading to and within the brain. A stroke occurs when a blood vessel to the brain is either blocked by a clot or bursts. When that happens, part of the brain cannot get the blood and oxygen it needs and it begins to die (American Stroke Association, 2018). We will discuss more of the physiological and psychological aspects of CVDs later in the chapter.

CULTURAL VARIATIONS IN THE INCIDENCE OF CARDIOVASCULAR DISEASE

As with other chronic illnesses, there are some significant cultural differences in the incidence of CVDs (Chand, Wu, Qiu, & Hajjar, 2017). As shown in Figure 14.4, Asian or Pacific Islanders show the lowest numbers of deaths due to heart disease followed by American Indians and Latinos and then by African Americans and White Americans who do not show large differences. Men experience more strokes than women, and Black and Latino men experience more strokes than White men (see Table 14.1).

The incidence variations are often due to differences in the levels of knowledge about the disease, differences in health behaviors, and risk factors among different cultural groups (Hertz, McDonald, Unger, & Lustik, 2007). For example, Hamner and Wilder (2008) used the Coronary Heart Disease Knowledge Test to measure knowledge of CVD in rural Alabama women. The average on the test was 8.50 (out of 20). The participants were at significant risk for CVD. The women recognized that smoking and obesity were issues, but were less aware of factors such as personality, oral contraceptive use, hypertension, diabetes, and family history. How you would fare on the test? You should do pretty well once you get to the end of this chapter.

There are many cultural differences that could account for higher CVD incidence. The higher risk for heart attack shown by South Asians is attributed, in part, to a higher prevalence of diabetes (Patel et al., 2008) and other risk factors (e.g., Bathula, Francis, Hughes, & Chaturvedi, 2008) in some South Asian populations. Higher rates can also be due to the psychological experiences of different groups that relate to CVD (Baker, Richter, & Anand, 2001). For example, hostility, anger, and social support, each of which play a key role in the development of CVD, also vary across cultures and map onto larger cultural dimensions (see Chapter 3).

▼ FIGURE 14.4

Death Rates for Diseases of the Heart by Ethnicity and Sex, United States, 2015

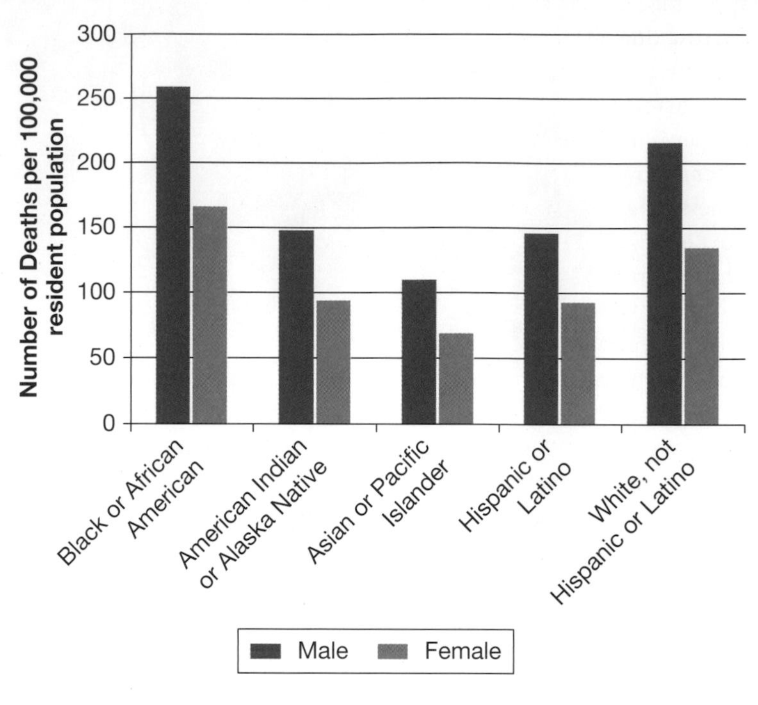

Source: https://www.cdc.gov/nchs/data/hus/hus16.pdf

▼ TABLE 14.1

Stroke

Population Group	Prevalence, 2014: Age ≥ 20 y	New and Recurrent Attacks, All Ages	Mortality, 2014: All Ages
Both sexes	7,200,000 (2.7%)	795,000	133,103
Males	3,100,000 (2.4%)	370,000 (46.5%)†	55,471 (41.7%)
Females	4,100,000 (2.9%)	425,000 (53.5%)†	77,632 (58.3%)
White males	2.2%	325,000‡	41,410
White females	2.8%	365,000‡	60,916
Black males	3.9%	45,000‡	7,650
Black females	4.0%	60,000‡	9,233
Hispanic males	2.0%	. . .	4,092
Hispanic females	2.6%	. . .	4,621
Asian males	1.0%	. . .	1,890
Asian females	2.5%		2,382
American Indian or Alaska Native	3.0%	. . .	616

Ellipses (. . .) indicate data not available.

*Mortality for Hispanic, American Indian or Alaska Native, and Asian and Pacific Islander people should be Interpreted with caution **because** of inconsistencies in reporting Hispanic origin or race or the death certificate compared with censuses, surveys, and birth certificates. Studies have shown underreporting on death certificates of American Indian **or Alaska Native, Asian and Pacific Islander, and Hispanic decedents, as well as undercounts** of these groups in censuses.

Hypertension, a CVD, also shows strong cultural differences and is found at a higher rate in African Americans (Bokhour et al., 2016). Some evidence suggests an intriguing sociobiological reason. High blood pressure is positively correlated to dark skin color, which could induce more discrimination (i.e., because of being darker skinned) (Ilali & Taraghi, 2010).

Anger and other components of the Type A personality such as competitiveness and time urgency are closely tied to the individualistic/collectivistic dimension of culture. People in individualistic cultures are more competitive, which is viewed as a desirable trait. Those in collectivistic cultures are more cooperative, and competition against members of one's group is often discouraged. Social support, similarly, is seen more in collectivistic cultures (Moscardino, Scrimin, Capello, & Altoè, 2010; Shavitt et al., 2016). Time orientation varies with another cultural dimension: **fluid time versus fixed time**. In most cultures in North America, time is fixed: when you say you will meet someone at 10:00 a.m., you mean exactly that. In fluid-time cultures, such as those in India and among certain groups such as the Maori in New Zealand and American Indians, meeting someone at 10:00 a.m. really means you will show up anywhere between 10:15 a.m. and 10:30 a.m. This is understood and expected, and no one is frustrated when someone is late. In fact, in many East Indian American communities, people set appointments and specify whether they mean an exact time or Indian Style Time. Accelerated blood pressure due to time constraints is generally less common in such cultures, and the stress of being late accordingly is different as well.

There is some indication that increased risk of CHD in some ethnic populations may be due to basic differences in the epidemiology of **atherosclerosis**, the accumulation of fatty substances in the blood vessels. Some racial and ethnic populations are also inadequately prescribed antiplatelet therapy—daily aspirin doses—despite their higher risk (Saunders & Ofili, 2008). As discussed in Chapter 9, there are cultural differences in health care–seeking behavior and patient–practitioner interactions. For example, South Asians do not use ambulances as often when experiencing heart emergencies (reflecting cultural differences or possibly geographical proximity to hospitals; Ben-Shlomo, Naqvi, & Baker, 2008). There is also evidence of differences in how doctors manage patients with chest pain according to their cultural backgrounds. Doctors may have a lower threshold for giving thrombolytic therapy (treatment that breaks up blood clots) to South Asian men with chest pain because they are aware of the increased risk of CHD in this population (Ben-Shlomo et al., 2008).

New areas of research investigate biological markers of CHD that may vary by culture. For example, **C-reactive protein (CRP)** concentrations are associated with risk of CHD (Heffner, Waring, Roberts, Eaton, & Gramling, 2011). Kelley-Hedgepeth et al. (2008) conducted a cross-sectional study of 3,154 women enrolled in the Study of Women's Health across the Nation (SWAN), a culturally diverse prospective study. The study population was 47% European American, 28% African American, 17% Chinese American and Japanese American, and 9% Latino. The African American women had the highest median CRP concentrations, followed by Latinas, European American, and then Asian American women.

In another detailed study of the links among culture, biology, and CHD, Nasir et al. (2008) assessed nearly 7,000 individuals in the Multi-Ethnic Study of Atherosclerosis (MESA). The researchers focused on different types of calcifications that correspond to atherosclerosis and CHD. Clear ethnic differences emerged. The highest prevalence of calcifications was observed in European Americans, followed by Latinos and African Americans, with the lowest levels of calcification among Chinese Americans. It is still not clear how these underlying differences map onto the differential incidence of CHD (Manolio et al., 2008). Calcification, although related to long-term distress (Seldenrijk, Hamer, Lahiri, Penninx, & Steptoe, 2012), is surprisingly inversely correlated to perceived racism among African Americans (Everage, Gjelsvik, McGarvey, Linkletter, & Loucks, 2012).

Two other cultural dimensions beyond ethnicity can also influence CVD. In the **control versus constraint** dimension (Trompenaars, 1997), control cultures believe that they have absolute control of their outcomes (similar to having an internal locus of control). Contrastingly, people in constraint cultures believe everything is in the hands of God or fate. Those in control cultures may have higher levels of anxiety and stress and correspondingly have more risk for heart problems (Baker et al., 2001). Similarly, the level of emotionality may make a difference as well. **Neutral cultures**, such as that of Japan, do not sanction the open display of emotions. In contrast, **affect cultures**, such as that of Italy, place a premium on the display of emotions. Not expressing and processing emotions could also lead to higher levels of CVD (Cristea et al., 2011).

Sex differences, another element of culture, appear in not just the incidence of CVD (Bishop, 2019) but also in patient–practitioner interactions.

Adams et al. (2008) tested for the sources of uncertainty and sex bias in doctors' diagnoses and decision-making relating to CVD. They randomly selected male and female doctors in England and the United States and showed them video clips of actors portraying patients with CVD. They had patients of different ages, both sexes, and different ethnicities and socioeconomic status. The doctors were interviewed about their decision making. Adams et al. found differences in male and female doctors' responses to different types of patient information. The female doctors remembered information differently than did the men (e.g., more patient cues). All doctors paid more attention to male patients' age and considered more age-related disease possibilities for men than women.

George Bishop received his PhD in psychology from Yale University and served at the Walter Reed Army Institute of Research. He is now with Yale–National University of Singapore and is an expert on the role of anger in coronary heart disease. See Bishop (2019) in Essential Readings.

DEVELOPMENTAL ISSUES IN CARDIOVASCULAR DISEASE

A number of developmental issues connect to CVD. For example, low birth weight is now known to be associated with increased rates of CVD (Alhusen et al., 2014). Suboptimal growth in infancy and rapid childhood weight gain exacerbate the effects of impaired prenatal growth. As we age we have a greater risk for developing CVDs. A large part of this risk is due to wear and tear on our arteries and the accumulation of plaque that increases with time, but this risk also has psychosocial correlates. People go through different stages of physical, social, and cognitive development.

Erikson, for example, hypothesized that we progress through eight different life stages, each with its own challenges and milestones. The life changes that accompany social development can serve as stressors that, in turn, can lead to higher risks for CVDs. Some milestones include puberty, graduation from high school or college, a first job, and perhaps losing a first job. Even relationships, dating, and marriage can be important correlates of CVDs (see the upcoming section on stress for more on the impact of transitions). Satisfying relationships can provide social support, and acrimonious relationships or divorces could raise blood pressure and otherwise negatively impact health. Important negative life events corresponding to developmental stages increase in frequency in the months before a heart attack (Welin et al., 1992). Although heart disease has been studied more extensively in men, studies of women also show that heart disease patients experience a significantly larger number of negative life changes, many of them related to family life (Vaccarino & Bremner, 2017).

Beyond developmentally related life events, it is also important to factor in development and take a life span approach to CVD because one of the main psychosocial correlates of CVD—social support—changes over time and social isolation is tied to higher rates of CVD (Heffner et al., 2011). Younger women with poor social networks have higher levels of heart problems (Carroll, Diez Roux, Fitzpatrick, & Seeman, 2013). Surprisingly, older retired women with more extensive social networks also had a higher incidence of cardiac problems.

The additional networks for older women could have come with more mental burdens. To understand conflicting data such as these, it is important to look at how social support changes over the life span (see Chapter 6 and Eslami et al., 2017).

PHYSIOLOGICAL CORRELATES OF CARDIOVASCULAR DISEASE

The primary physiological antecedent for the incidence of CVDs is atherosclerosis (American Heart Association, 2018). Microscopic accumulations of fats within artery walls progress to visible fatty streaks as early as childhood (Strong et al., 1999). This accumulation of fat, often in the form of plaque, reduces and sometimes blocks the arteries supplying blood to the heart. The plaque build-up can get so great as to tear the artery, creating a snag in which a blood clot can form to block the artery. Lesions are sometimes observed in adolescents and become increasingly common with age. This interference in blood flow to the heart is what causes heart attacks. A related condition is the hardening of the arteries, or **arteriosclerosis**, in which the arteries lose their elasticity and are more susceptible to blockages from clots or plaques (McEniery & Cockcroft, 2007).

> **Synthesize, Evaluate, Apply**
>
> - Evaluate the pros and cons of basing a lot of information on studies such as the Framingham heart study. What concerns with the study do you have?
> - Each culture has factors that make people less likely or more likely to get CVD. Can you think of some examples from your own culture?
> - Trace the connections between different health behaviors and different heart diseases.
> - How can the different cultural variations that you have been exposed to in other chapters also explain differences in the incidence and progression of cardiovascular diseases?

Some of the main physiological risk factors cannot be changed: age, sex, and family history. As mentioned, the risk for having a CVD increases as a person gets older, and men younger than 50 are more likely to develop a problem. At around 50 years of age, corresponding to when women reach menopause, women have a greater risk for CVDs than men (Mattar et al., 2008). It is also clear that having a parent or relative with a CVD greatly increases the incidence rates of CVDs (Yamada, Ichihara, & Nishida, 2008). Genetic linkage analyses of families and sibling pairs have implicated several loci and candidate genes in predisposition to CVD, and genes that contribute to genetic susceptibility to these conditions are beginning to be identified (Qureshi et al., 2015).

Other physiological factors predicting the incidences of CVDs are high blood pressure, diabetes, high cholesterol level, inactivity, and being overweight or obese (Bishop, 2019). Men with diabetes, for example, are twice as likely to develop CVD whereas women with diabetes are up to seven times as likely to develop CVD (American Diabetes Association, 2018). In fact, coronary heart disease is the most common cause of death among diabetic patients. The increased risk of CHD in type 2 diabetes is due, in part, to irregularities with fat storage and metabolism. Diabetic dyslipidemia, for example, is characterized by elevated triglycerides, low high-density lipoprotein cholesterol (HDL) and increased low-density lipoprotein cholesterol (LDL) particles (Karalis, 2008). As you can see, this second group of physiological factors can all be modified depending on a person's health behaviors (more on this later).

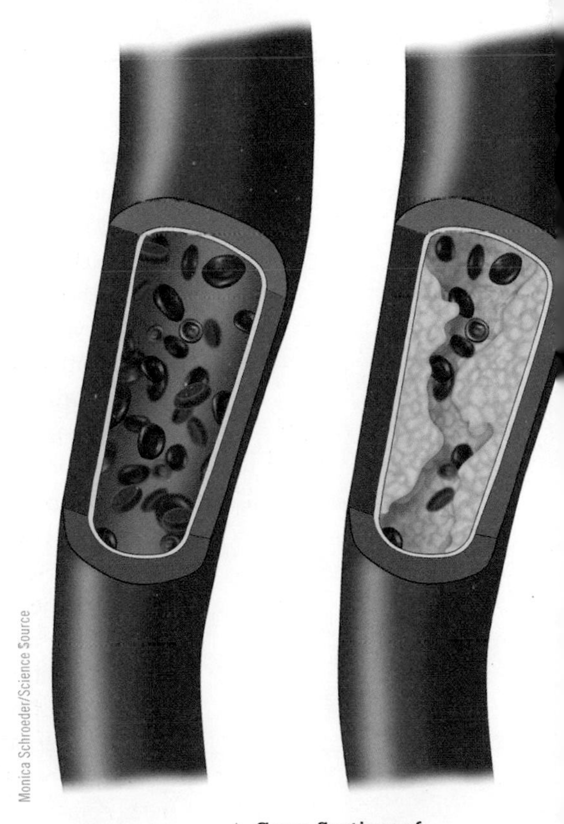

▲ **Cross-Sections of Human Arteries.** The artery on the left is normal (clear wide opening). The artery on the right has a much smaller bore due to the accumulation of plaque (atherosclerosis).

Another important issue in the modifiable physiological risk factors is the fact that different cultural groups vary in their genetic predispositions. Some ethnic groups are more prone to high blood pressure (Minor, Wofford, & Jones, 2008). Some groups are more prone to be overweight. These underlying differences in risk factors could explain cultural differences in CVD. Hypertension is significantly higher in African Americans than European Americans and minority status is significantly associated with diabetes (Kurian &

Cardarelli, 2007). For example, laboratory studies measuring participants' **cardiovascular reactivity** to different stressors have found that African Americans show higher blood pressure and epinephrine responses to tasks compared with European American participants (Mills, Berry, Dimsdale, & Nelesen, 1993) though the effects are sometimes only psychological (e.g., blame) versus physiological (Neumann et al., 2011).

Salomon and Jagusztyn (2008) looked at the relationship between discrimination and cardiovascular responses to interpersonal incivility among African American, Latino, and European Americans. Participants completed a measure of past discrimination which was related to higher resting systolic blood pressure (SBP) among Latino participants and lower resting SBP among European American participants. Reporting being discriminated against was related to attenuated SBP and heart reactivity among Latino participants. Discrimination was not related to resting levels or reactivity among African American participants. Their findings suggest that the relationship between discrimination and cardiovascular risk differs by ethnicity. As testified to by this empirical evidence, cardiovascular reactivity—changes in heart rate and blood pressure in response to stress—varies greatly between individuals. This reactivity is a key physiological risk factor for the development of CVD (Holt-Lunstad, Smith, & Uchino, 2008).

As discussed in Chapter 8, there are also significant ethnic and geographical differences in obesity, tobacco use, diet, and activity levels—all key health behaviors related to CHD (discussed in detail below).

PSYCHOLOGICAL CORRELATES OF CARDIOVASCULAR DISEASE

There is strong evidence for a link between psychological characteristics and the development of CVDs (Nabi et al., 2008), making this set of diseases a prime candidate for use of the biopsychosocial approach of health psychology. Of all the chronic diseases, CVDs are perhaps most illustrative of the importance of focusing on psychological factors together with biological factors (Betensky, Contrada, & Glass, 2012). Psychological factors, such as personality traits (e.g., hostility), anger, depression, social support, and stress, and health behaviors, such as dietary habits and physical activity, have all been intrinsically tied to the incidence and progression of CVDs (Suchday, Tucker, & Krantz, 2002).

Perhaps the best-known controversy regarding the psychological causes of heart attacks revolves around a constellation of personality characteristics called the Type A personality (see Chapter 6). Friedman and Rosenman (1974) noted that heart patients who showed a sense of time urgency (always doing more than one thing at the same time), competitiveness, and hostility in their interactions with other people were found to have a higher risk for CHD. In contrast, the Type B personality is relaxed, patient, and easygoing. The original finding that was greeted with enthusiasm did not bear further examination (Shekelle et al., 1985). However, a number of people still believe that having a Type A personality, in general, is not necessarily a positive attribute. What seems more accurate is that being *hostile* is the problem (Boyle, Jackson, & Suarez, 2007). Hostility and anger are negative emotions that can trigger a heart attack and even sudden death among individuals who are at risk (Lampert, 2010). A study of 1,000 men over a 30-year follow-up period found that high scores on a measure of trait anger were associated with a three- to six-fold increase in CHD (Chang, Ford, Meoni, Want, & Klag, 2002). Hostility can also lessen the benefits of receiving social support (Holt-Lunstad et al., 2008). The role of hostility is so critical that for every dollar spent on anger-management treatments or hostility therapy, there is an approximate savings of two dollars in hospitalization costs in the following 6 months (Davidson, Gidron, Mostofsky, & Trudeau, 2007). How's that for a good deal?

The relationship between two variables is rarely straightforward. Research has begun to look for the factors that may mediate the relationship between hostility and the increased risk of CHD (see Chapter 6 for more on mediation). One such variable is carotenoid, a substance in most plants that is known to have antioxidant properties. Antioxidants, in turn, may be mediators for atherosclerosis. Ohira et al. (2008) found that high hostility predicted future low levels of some serum carotenoids, which may help to explain the association of hostility and cardiovascular risk observed in epidemiologic studies.

Other negative emotions play a role in cardiac arrest too (Betensky, Contrada, & Glass, 2012). Feeling sad and depressed may also increase your likelihood of heart problems and the progression of CVD (Bishop, 2019). Meta-analyses have found that the presence of clinically significant depression can increase the risk of CHD by 30% to 90% among otherwise healthy individuals (Carney & Freedland, 2017). Anda et al. (1993) studied the relationship of both depressed affect and hopelessness to CHD incidence using data from a large cohort of 2,832 North American adults. The participants had no history of CHD or serious illness at baseline. Anda et al. (1993) found that people who were depressed were significantly more likely to have a fatal heart attack (relative risk 1.5). Depression was also associated with an increased risk of nonfatal heart attacks.

In other studies of survivors of heart attacks, depression was related to increased mortality in the 6-month period after the first heart attack (Blumenthal, 2008). Similarly, feeling hopeless, an emotion often accompanying depression, can independently predict the incidence of CVD as well (Gidron, Levy, & Cwikel, 2007). A variety of different types of social supports also relate to CVD (Seeman & Syme, 1987), and social support is often a moderating factor (Orth-Gomer et al., 1993). Social support could influence the development of CVD by buffering the person from the effects of stress (the moderator role), consequently safeguarding the person from the deleterious effects that stress has on the circulatory system (Krantz & Lundgren, 1998).

Supportive networks also ensure that a person is more likely to get help and to comply with doctor's orders. If a man is at risk for a heart attack and he is not supposed to eat fatty foods, smoke, or drink too much, a supportive partner and good friends are likely to make sure that he does not. In support of this link, studies of unmarried patients without close confidants showed them to be more likely to die over a 5-year period (Case, Moss, Case, McDermott, & Eberly, 1992). Patients with large social networks are also more likely to cope better (such as attend rehab) after a cardiac incident (Molloy, Perkins-Porras, Strike, & Steptoe, 2008).

Not having healthy social networks, another measure of social support, is also related to the incidence of CVD, but some studies show this relationship is not always significant when demographic differences such as income level or marital status are accounted for (Morris, Wannamethee, Lennon, Thomas, & Whincup, 2008). In a sizable study on the power of social support, Sundquist, Lindstrom, Malmstrom, Johansson, and Sundquist (2004) examined whether low social participation predicted incidence rates of CHD. They followed 6,861 Swedish women and men for nearly 10 years and found that persons with low social participation (as measured by an interview) had the highest risk of CHD. They were more than twice as likely (relative risk 2.15) to have another heart attack than those with high social participation. This increased risk remained even after controls were added for education and smoking habits (Sundquist et al., 2004).

In another large study, Ikeda et al. (2008) examined prospectively the association between social support and risk of coronary heart disease and stroke incidence and mortality within a cohort of 44,152 Japanese men and women. Low social support was associated with higher risk of stroke mortality in men.

Sometimes not getting social support can be fatal. Depressed patients in the Enhancing Recovery in Coronary Heart Disease (ENRICHD) trial and those with lower perceived social support (even without elevated depressive symptoms) were at increased risk for death (Lett et al., 2007). Such findings have prompted a call for a form of special social support screening for depressed CVD patients (Thombs, 2008). Not having enough social support is often related to not having enough resources in general and is strongly linked to socioeconomic status (SES). Especially in developing countries, SES is negatively correlated with the risk of CVD (Kaplan & Keil, 1993; Karamanou, Protogerou, Tsoucalas, Androutsos, & Poulakou-Rebelakou, 2016).

In a study of the relationship between SES and CVD, Marmot et al. (1991) studied British civil servants in the Whitehall part of London (the Whitehall studies). They showed that higher rates of CVD were seen in men of lower employment grade. At every rung of the bureaucratic ladder, men in the lower positions were worse off. There are other possible mediators. In a study of an ethnically diverse population, participants with more emotional social support showed higher high-density lipoprotein (HDL) cholesterol levels. The mediators? Physical activity and wine intake. These are but two health behaviors influenced by social support that may have the result of reducing cardiovascular disease risk (Fischer Aggarwal, Liao, & Mosca, 2008).

Stress

You may have heard of the television show and movies of the same title, *Sex and the City*, but have you considered that a show could be called *Stress and the City*? In fact, city living marks the brain (Abbott, 2011). Studies in different cultures have shown that the stress from living in an urban environment can make you nine times more likely to develop CVD compared with living in a rural area (Gupta, Gupta, Jakovcic, & Zak, 1996).

A little stress can go a long way. Not only does being stressed influence your health behaviors (as described in Chapter 8), but it also increases your likelihood of developing a number of diseases. In Chapter 5, we described how our body's reactions to short-term physical stressors are thought to have evolved to get us out of danger. You should also remember that these same responses, when activated for a long period of time (chronic stress), can begin to break down the body's systems (e.g., allostatic load). Cardiovascular problems are some of the most common ways that the body breaks down.

Superficially, the relationship is pretty intuitive. What happens when we get stressed? At the physiological core of the response, the catecholamines and cortisol pumped into the bloodstream increase blood flow, thus raising blood pressure. The heart is pumping faster, and blood is shunting around the body faster. There are also changes in how we metabolize food for energy (details in Chapter 5). This constellation of factors that accompany the experience and process of stress take a toll on the circulatory system and aid in the incidence of CVD (Janssen et al., 2012). A sizeable body of research documents how various stressors, particularly those at work, accentuate CVD via effects on blood pressure (Chandola et al., 2008). Together with the work front, environmental stress (especially that caused by low SES) and stress from interpersonal relationships at home have also been associated with the incidence of CVD.

Even watching sports can be stressful and lead to a heart attack! Wilbert-Lampen et al. (2008) examined the link between emotional stress and the incidence of heart attacks during the 2006 World Cup soccer games played in Germany. They found that watching a stressful soccer match more than doubles the risk of an acute cardiovascular event. On days of matches involving the German team, the incidence of cardiac emergencies was 2.66 times that during the control period. So, take it easy during March Madness and the Super Bowl!

Acute stress (e.g., a person's being the victim of an assault or having to deliver a very difficult presentation) can also trigger heart problems if the individual already is at risk because of atherosclerosis (Gottdiener et al., 1994). Early work showed that catastrophic events such as earthquakes and the death of a spouse could also initiate a heart attack (Meisel et al., 1991). After the big Northridge earthquake outside Los Angeles, California, in 1994, a significant increase in heart attacks was seen compared with the incidence in the previous week (Kloner, Leor, Poole, & Perritt, 1997).

The work-stress and CVD relationship has garnered the most research attention (Karasek, Collins, Clays, Bortkiewicz, & Ferrario, 2010). We can all acknowledge the fact that working can be stressful. Even if you enjoy your job, having to work can still challenge the body. The stress from work can be even more dangerous if you are overworked, have too many roles to fulfill, are not clear what your job role is, are bored with your job, or do not have support at work. No matter what the exact cause, work stress can accentuate the chances of developing CVD. Even job status is important. For example, Wamala, Mittleman, Horsten, Schenck-Gustafsson, and Orth-Gomer (2000) used data from the Stockholm Female Coronary Risk Study, a population-based case-control study comprising 292 women with CHD aged 65 years or younger and 292 age-matched healthy women, and found that unskilled women had four times the risk for CHD compared with the executive/professional women. Simultaneous adjustment for traditional risk factors and job stress lowered this risk to 2.45. Similar findings are found for men (Schnall et al., 1994).

There are also some interesting cultural differences in the work-stress relationship. Higher job strain was a major explanation for why Lithuanian men had four times the risk for CVD than Swedish men (Kristensen et al., 1998). In Japan, there is even a term for death from overwork: *karoshi* (Nishiyama & Johnson, 1997).

Researchers have only recently begun to look at the interaction of work stress and home stress. Orth-Gomer et al. (2000) followed women for an average of 5 years after hospitalization in one of the first studies to look at the longitudinal effects of marital stress and work stress in women patients. They found that stressful experiences from marital relationships may seriously affect prognosis in women with CHD, whereas living alone without a partner had no effect.

Recent work on stress and heart disease aims to examine how stress can increase negative health behaviors such as smoking (Byrne & Mazanov, 2016) and a concept called vital exhaustion. Vital exhaustion is marked by feeling low, extreme fatigue, and increased irritability. People with CVD who show vital exhaustion are twice as likely to have recurring heart attacks (Frestad & Prescott, 2017).

Synthesize, Evaluate, Apply

- What psychosocial factors explain why heart diseases are one of the biggest health issues in the 21st century?
- Using what you know of the causes and types of stress (Chapter 5), which forms of stress do you think best explain CVD and which theory of stress would be most useful for this?

HEALTH BEHAVIORS AND CARDIOVASCULAR DISEASE

Tobacco Use

The number one behavior to avoid if you want to minimize your risk for cardiovascular diseases is smoking (Mermelstein, 2019). You can see why we have spent so much time on this topic (see Chapter 8). Together with being an important risk factor for other chronic diseases such as cancer (see Chapter 13), cigarette smoking has also been identified as an important factor in the development of CVD (Bishop, 2019).

In one of the clearest demonstrations of this link, Doll, Peto, Boreham, and Sutherland (2004) followed approximately 35,000 British doctors from 1951 to 2001 and found that the dangers of smoking varied with cohorts. Men born in 1900 through 1930 who smoked only cigarettes and continued smoking died on average about 10 years sooner than lifelong nonsmokers. Quitting was beneficial regardless of the age at which it was attempted. Men who quit when 60, 50, 40, or 30 years of age gained, respectively, about 3, 6, 9, or 10 years of life expectancy (Doll et al., 2004). Another large study of 563,144 participants (82% of whom were Asian) showed evidence that smoking aggravated blood pressure and together these two factors substantially increased the risk of CVD (Nakamura et al., 2008). The risk of CVD is almost three times as high for smokers as it is for nonsmokers, and the risk for smokers is higher if they are younger (Baker et al., 2001).

What effects do smoking bans or governmental regulations to curb smoking have? Consider the following case. In 1993, the state of Massachusetts introduced the Massachusetts Tobacco Control Program (MTCP). This reduced how many people smoked in the state by 29%. That's not all. There was a 31% decline in death rates due to CVD (from 1993 to 2003, 425 fewer CVD deaths; Kabir, Connolly, Clancy, Koh, & Capewell, 2008). C-reactive protein (CRP) levels (predictors of CVD as discussed earlier) also drop when a smoker quits the habit (Hastie, Haw, & Pell, 2008).

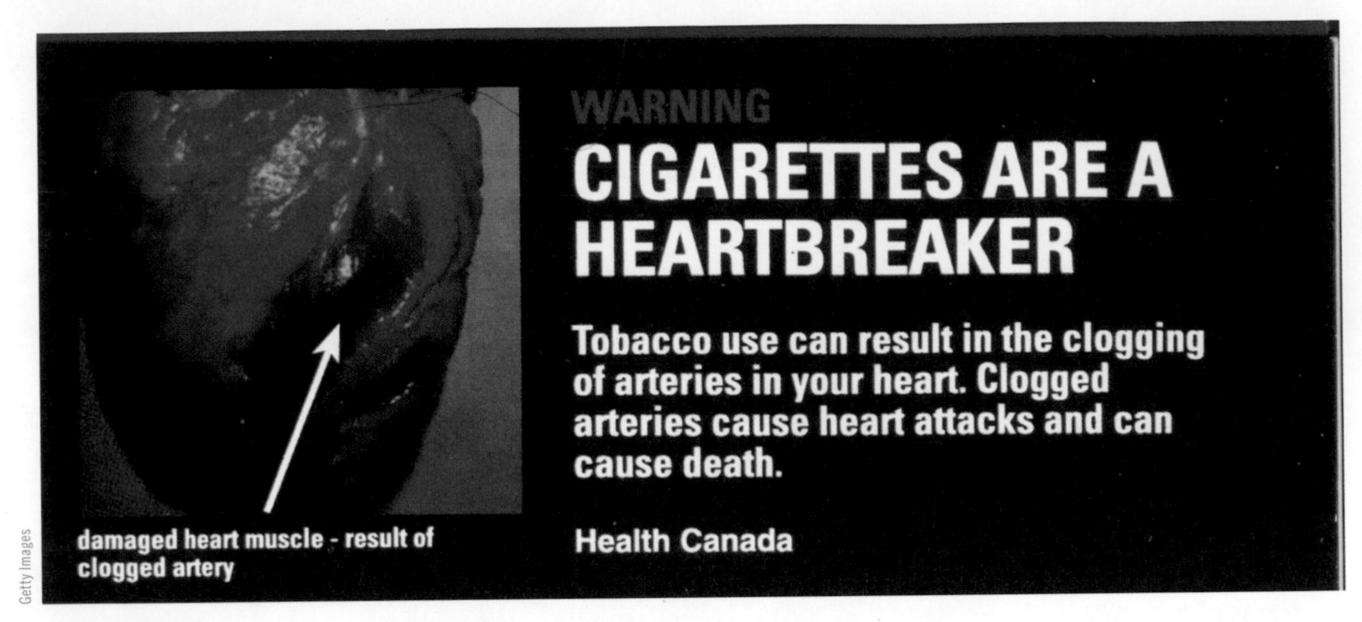

▲ **Smoking and Cardiovascular Disease.** A warning on a Canadian cigarette packet. Those who can quit smoking significantly reduce their risk for contracting a cardiovascular disease.

People around the world smoke. Smoking is more common in some cultures than in others, and the link between CVD and smoking is not the same across cultures. For example, although there are relatively high rates of smoking in countries such as Japan and China, CVD mortality and morbidity are not proportionally as high (WHO, 2012). In other countries, high levels of other unhealthy behaviors also accompany high smoking rates. Europeans tend to smoke more than Americans do in general and also consume diets higher in saturated fats (Baker et al., 2001). Recent attention has turned to the presence of risk factors that accentuate the effect of smoking, and some of the most important are dietary factors and cholesterol.

Diet

Your food choices play a large role in your overall health and well-being. What you eat determines the levels of nutrients available for your cells and ensures the smooth and healthy functioning of your bodily symptoms (Greger, 2015). There are many dietary factors that influence the incidence and progression of CVD (Figure 14.5), and diet is a factor that affects the interaction between culture, psychology, and behavior (Van Horn et al., 2008). Your diet can influence your cholesterol level, your blood pressure, your tolerance for glucose (and consequently your risk for diabetes), your likelihood to be overweight, and even how your blood coagulates. Each of these factors is associated with the development of CVD (Brunner et al., 2008; Fung et al., 2008).

The two most common risk factors for hypertension beyond age and family history are too much salt in the diet and obesity. The specific role diet plays with hypertension can be seen in a study of the Dietary Approaches to Stop Hypertension (DASH) diet (Fung et al., 2008). The diet of 88,517 female nurses was assessed seven times during 1980–2004. Researchers then calculated a DASH score based on eight food and nutrient components (fruits, vegetables, whole grains, nuts and legumes, low-fat dairy, red and processed meats, sweetened beverages, and sodium). There was a direct negative correlation between DASH scores and heart disease; the better the score the less likely a heart attack. The DASH score was also significantly associated with lower risk of stroke and lower levels of C-reactive protein.

In a similar analysis, Brunner et al. (2008) compared four dietary patterns: unhealthy (white bread, processed meat, fries, and full-cream milk); sweet (white bread, biscuits, cakes, processed meat, and high-fat dairy products); Mediterranean-like (fruit, vegetables, rice, pasta, and wine); and healthy (fruit, vegetables, whole-meal bread, low-fat dairy, and little alcohol) in nearly 8,000 participants. Compared with the unhealthy pattern, the healthy pattern reduced the risk of CVD and diabetes.

▼ FIGURE 14.5

Dietary Recommendations to Minimize Cardiovascular Disease

- Eat a variety of fruits and vegetables. Choose five or more servings per day.
- Eat a variety of grain products, including whole grains. Choose six or more servings per day.
- Include fat-free and low-fat milk products, fish, legumes (beans), skinless poultry, and lean meats.
- Choose fats and oils with 2 grams or less saturated fat per tablespoon, such as liquid and tub margarines, canola oil, and olive oil.
- Balance the number of calories you eat with the number you use each day. (To find that number multiply the number of pounds you weigh now by 15 calories. This represents the average number of calories used in one day if you're moderately active. If you get very little exercise, multiply your weight by 13 instead of 15. Less-active people burn fewer calories.)
- Maintain a level of physical activity that keeps you fit and matches the number of calories you eat. Walk or do other activities for at least 30 minutes on most days. To lose weight, do enough activity to use up more calories than you eat every day.
- Limit your intake of foods high in calories or low in nutrition, including foods like soft drinks and candy that have a lot of sugars.
- Limit foods high in saturated fat, trans fat, and/or cholesterol, such as full-fat milk products, fatty meats, tropical oils, partially hydrogenated vegetable oils, and egg yolks. Instead choose foods low in saturated fat, trans fat, and cholesterol from the first four points above.
- Eat less than 6 grams of salt (sodium chloride) per day (2,400 milligrams of sodium).
- Have no more than one alcoholic drink per day if you're a woman and no more than two if you're a man. One drink means it has no more than half an ounce of pure alcohol. Examples of one drink are 12 ounces of beer, 4 ounces of wine, 1.5 ounces of 80-proof spirits, or 1 ounce of 100-proof spirits.

Source: American Heart Association (2012).

Similar to CHD, a lower risk of stroke has been related to the intake of fruits and vegetables. In an analysis of data from the Physicians' Health Study, a study of 22,071 U.S. male physicians, Hak et al. (2004) found that men who were in the bottom fifth for intake of antioxidants (such as alpha-carotene, beta-carotene, and lycopene) had the highest risk of stroke.

One of the most important risk factors for CVD is cholesterol level. Cholesterol is found in most animal products and is an important component of cell walls and membranes. It is also a main component of plaque. As discussed in Chapter 8, we have high-density lipoprotein (HDL) and low-density lipoprotein (LDL) cholesterol, and if you want to prevent heart disease, you need to keep your total cholesterol level below 200 milligrams per deciliter (American Heart Association, 2018). As the level of cholesterol in the blood increases, the risk of CVD increases as well (Ballantyne, 2004). LDLs seem to be the primary factor, and a number of treatments (e.g., statins) aim to reduce the LDL levels in the bloodstream (Goldstein et al., 2008). A high cholesterol level is even more likely to cause CVD in people with other health issues such as diabetes (Tanasescu, Cho, Manson, & Hu, 2004). One other major risk factor may be a diet high in saturated fat, though this lipid hypothesis is being heavily contested (He, Xu, & Van Horn, 2007; Ravnskov, 2008).

Diets including fish (Streppel, Ocké, Boshuizen, Kok, & Kromhout, 2008; Whelton, He, Whelton, & Munter, 2004) and high levels of whole grains and fiber (Singh et al., 2002) are particularly good for you. Many believe fish oil helps with cholesterol issues (Leaf, Kang, & Xiao, 2008). In an illustrative intervention, Singh et al. recruited 1,000 patients with **angina pectoris** and **myocardial infarctions** and had half of them eat a diet rich in whole grains, fruits, vegetables, walnuts, and almonds (referred to as an **Indo-Mediterranean diet**). The control group ate a diet suggested by the National Cholesterol Education Program (NCEP). Interestingly, the intervention group had fewer heart problems, including heart attacks (both fatal and nonfatal), and showed lower cholesterol levels than the control group. The Indo-Mediterranean diet is one of the protective factors of culture: people in and from the southern part of Europe who follow it show lower incidence of CVD (Knoops et al., 2004).

A related cultural diet component is alcohol. For example, the French have relatively low levels of CVD even though French food is known to be rich in saturated fats. This French paradox (see Chapter 8) has been linked to moderate consumption of alcohol. One or two glasses of wine per day seem to reduce the incidence of CVD (Rimm & Ellison, 1995; Saremi & Arora, 2008). Too much alcohol (e.g., binge drinking) does not lessen your CVD risk (Bagnardi, Zatonski, Scotti, La Vecchia, & Corrao, 2008). Research suggests a J-shaped association between alcohol consumption and CVD. Low levels of drinking relate to lower rates of CVD than abstaining (Ronksley, Brien, Turner, Mukamal, & Ghali, 2011). Do not be mistaken: this is not a reason for underage drinking, and binge drinking is still not a good thing.

Physical Activity

In terms of physical activity, not only is exercising useful in reducing the risks of CVD but being physically inactive actually increases the risks (Varghese et al., 2016). In this respect, standing still actually makes you slide backward on the continuum of health. In a global look at physical activity, the INTERHEART study, leisure-time as well as mild to moderate occupational physical activity resulted in lower rates of CVD. Owners of cars and televisions tended to lead to more sedentary behavior and showed an increased risk of CVD (Held et al., 2012).

A key component of treatment and many behavioral interventions to reduce CVD hence includes some form of physical activity. Taylor, Lerner, Sage, Lehman, and Seeman (2004) presented a review of the effectiveness of exercise-based cardiac rehabilitation in patients with CHD. Their study included 48 trials with a total of 8,940 patients and found that compared with control subjects, exercise was associated both with fewer deaths from all causes and fewer deaths from heart attacks. Patients who exercised also showed greater reductions in total cholesterol level, systolic blood pressure, and smoking. In a specific example, Blumenthal et al. (2004) examined the link between physical exercise and CVD mortality and morbidity among 2,078 heart attack patients who were participating in the Enhancing Recovery in Coronary Heart Disease (ENRICHD) multicenter clinical trial. Patients reporting regular exercise had less than half the heart attacks of those patients who reported no regular exercise.

The most commonly recommended form of exercise is cardiovascular training, especially walking and increasing movement (ACS, 2018). A recent world-wide study involving more than 15,000 participants examined the relationship between self-reported physical activity and both cardiovascular and all-cause mortality. In this study individuals reporting the highest levels of physical activity showed significantly reduced all-cause mortality as well as significantly reduced cardiovascular mortality (Steward et al., 2017).

TREATMENT OPTIONS

The specific treatment for CVD is determined by the severity of the symptoms, the size and quantity of areas with **ischemias** (reduced blood flow), how well the left ventricle of the heart is pumping, and other medical factors such as severity of chest pain (American Heart Association, 2018). As you can tell from the previous sections, unhealthy lifestyles (e.g., bad eating habits and not getting enough physical activity) are key determinants of whether you will develop a CVD. Correspondingly, changing health behaviors is one of the most critical treatment options to prevent the development of symptoms, relieve the symptoms, and lower the risk of heart attack and death. The primary goal will be to change unhealthy behaviors.

The patient is normally admitted to a **cardiac rehabilitation program**. Rehabilitation programs educate patients on the best way to change their lifestyles and use a combination of physical activity and social support to improve their overall functioning and prevent death (Vossen et al., 2008). If the person smokes, a smoking cessation program will be prescribed. He or she will also receive consultations on how to change diet, reduce salt intake, and eat more nutritionally balanced meals. If excessive drinking or not enough physical activity is the issue, it is critical to tackle each of these problems. Patients may even be told to start taking aspirin. Aspirin, you say?

That's right, not just any headache or pain killer, but aspirin. Many studies have shown that aspirin reduces the risk of heart attack in people with known CHD (Hayden, Pignone, Phillips, & Mulrow, 2002; Sofi, Marcucci, Gori, Abbate, & Gensini, 2008). In fact, for people at increased risk for CHD, studies have shown that aspirin therapy reduced the risk by 28%, although there are some risks associated with taking aspirin (Hayden et al., 2002). Major risks of aspirin therapy include bleeding inside the brain or gastrointestinal tract, and this treatment is not recommended for individuals with a low risk for CVD (Kondavallv Seshasai et al., 2012) or those with migraines (Kurth, Diener, & Buring, 2011). It may be necessary to help restore the blood flow to the affected parts of the heart if the ischemias are serious or the disease continues to worsen despite measures to slow it down (sometimes because the person continues the unhealthy behaviors). In patients with critical conditions, surgery is often needed.

A review of CR practices world-wide found that programs lasted for a median of 20 sessions and were generally delivered by physicians, nurses, and physiotherapists (Pesah, Supervia, Turk-Adawi, & Grace, 2017). Rehabilitation not only leads to increases in healthy behaviors and decreases in unhealthy behaviors, but it also saves money. A clinical trial of a community-based CR program in the Netherlands showed significant improvement in risk factors such as lack of exercise, smoking, and being overweight (Minneboo et al., 2017).

Surgery

There are two main forms of invasive surgery to deal with blockages: angioplasty and cardiac bypass surgery (American Heart Association, 2018). **Angioplasty** is a procedure done to open a partially blocked blood vessel so that blood can flow through it more easily (Figure 14.6). It is most often done on arteries that deliver blood to the heart (coronary arteries) when they are narrowed by atherosclerosis. The procedure involves the insertion of a thin, flexible tube (catheter) through an artery in the groin or arm, which is carefully guided into the artery that is narrowed. This is not a comfortable procedure. Once the tube reaches the narrowed artery, a small balloon at the end of the tube is inflated. The balloon may remain inflated from 20 seconds to 3 minutes. The pressure from the inflated balloon pushes the plaque against the wall of the artery opening up the passageway to improve blood flow. Once the fat and calcium build-up is compressed, a small, expandable wire tube called a stent is sometimes inserted into the artery to keep it open.

▼ FIGURE 14.6

Balloon Angioplasty

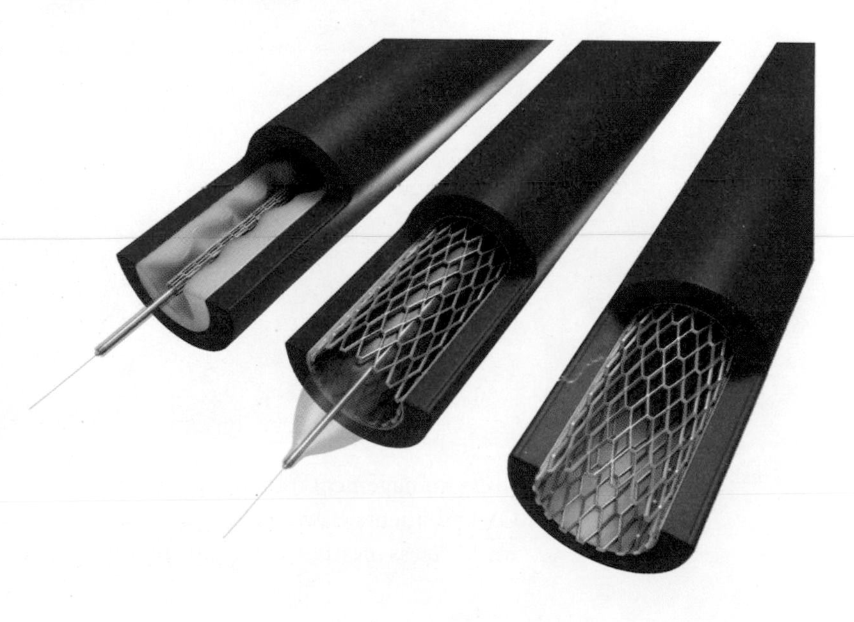

Another way to deal with the blockage is to just go around it. If you are driving to work, and you hear that there is a traffic jam ahead, you may take an alternative route. In the circulatory system there are few alternative routes for blood to take, so medical personnel create one. **Cardiac bypass surgery** involves taking a blood vessel from elsewhere in the body (usually the chest or leg) and using it to redirect blood flow around a severely blocked artery. Blood is redirected through the new blood vessel, bypassing the blocked artery and restoring blood flow to the affected portion of the heart muscle.

Behavioral Interventions

Most health psychological behavioral interventions for CVD take the form of cardiac rehabilitation programs (e.g., Weidner & Kendel, 2010). These programs are hard to assess because they have many different components. If there is a change in risk, a decrease in mortality, or an increase in quality of life, any one of the components could have caused it (or even an interaction of several components). That said, meta-analytical studies have shown that rehabilitation programs in general have accounted for reductions in mortality compared with that for control groups (Bishop, 2019). Programs building physical activity have been particularly effective (Khare et al., 2012).

Given the number of psychological factors involved in CVD, a number of interventions to reduce stress and negative emotions have also been tried, and the news is good (Koertge et al., 2008). Linden et al. (1996) reviewed studies that collectively evaluated 2,024 patients who received psychosocial treatment versus 1,156 control subjects and found that the psychosocially treated patients showed greater reductions in psychological distress, systolic blood pressure, heart rate, and cholesterol level. Patients who did not receive psychosocial treatment were more likely to die earlier and had heart attacks reoccur during the first 2 years of follow up. The most common interventions attempted to modify personal characteristics such as hostility, stress, and social support.

One of the earliest and most ambitious interventions was conducted by Friedman et al. (1986). They observed 1,013 heart patients for 4.5 years to determine whether their Type A behaviors could be altered. There were three experimental groups: a control section of 270 patients received group cardiac counseling, an experimental section of 592 patients received both group cardiac counseling and Type A behavioral counseling, and 151 patients served as a comparison group. The results were startling. At the end of the study, 35.1% of participants given cardiac and Type A behavior counseling reduced their Type A behavior compared with 9.8% of participants given only cardiac counseling, and the heart attack recurrence rate was only 12.9%. The recurrence rate in the control group was 21.2%, and the comparison group fared worse (recurrence rate of 28.2%). There was also a significant difference in the number of cardiac deaths between the experimental and control participants, clearly showing that altering Type A behavior reduces cardiac morbidity and mortality (Friedman et al., 1986). Given that the critical component of Type A behavior is hostility, you should expect that interventions designed specifically to reduce hostility should work even better (Friedman et al., 1996).

Hero Images/ Getty Images

▲ **Fresh Vegetables.** Diets low in carbohydrates have been shown to reduce CVD risk factors.

Interventions to improve stress management and increase social support also reduce the effects of CVD (Cowan et al., 2008; Koertge et al., 2008). Blumenthal et al. (2002) examined the effects of exercise and stress management training over a 5-year follow-up period in 94 male patients with established CVD. Patients either exercised (three times per week) or partook in a one and one-half-hour weekly class on stress management. Blumenthal et al. (2002) found that stress management was associated with a significant reduction in heart attack episodes over each of the first 2 years of follow up and after 5 years. The stress management was even significantly cheaper than the exercise program.

Given the positive role played by a healthy diet (discussed previously), it is not surprising that many interventions focus on changing diets. The OmniHeart Trial compared three diets designed to reduce CVD risk (de Souza, Swain, Appel, & Sacks, 2008). One diet was high in carbohydrates. Two diets replaced carbohydrates with either unsaturated fat or protein. The lower carbohydrate diets improved the CVD risk factors.

Synthesize, Evaluate, Apply

- How would you make people more aware of the risks of smoking, bad eating, and not exercising in relation to CVD?
- Use the Health Belief Model and the transtheoretical model to design an intervention to reduce risks for CVD.

APPLICATION SHOWCASE

THE LIFESTYLE HEART TRIAL

For many years, the first twangs of heart pains—evidence of atherosclerosis—and the eventual heart attack, signified the end of life. The prognosis was bad, and life would never be the same for the many thousand men and women who discovered that they had heart disease. Medical research had come up with ways to ease the pain and prolong life, but CHD was mostly seen to be a dead-end street—you venture down it and you will not be returning. Health psychologists helped engineer a number of interventions to help, for example, the Ischemic Heart Disease Life Stress Monitoring Program (Frasure-Smith & Prince, 1987) and the Recurrent Coronary Prevention Program (Friedman et al., 1986), but these were primarily designed to increase social support and decrease the stress of patients with CHD. Alleviation of suffering is a good thing, but could CHD actually be reversed? **Dean Ornish** surprised the health community by showing that it could.

Ornish et al. (1998) conducted one of the first multiple component interventions designed to change peoples' behaviors to reverse heart disease. Patients with CHD are especially susceptible to the effects of bad eating and insufficient exercise. If you can get people who have CHD to change these behaviors, will the physiological disease change as well? To test this, Ornish et al. randomly sampled 48 patients with moderate to severe CHD and randomly assigned them to one of two groups.

The 24 patients in the experimental group, an intensive lifestyle change group, were given special prescriptions of how to change their behaviors. As the name of the group implies, membership in this group was no walk in the park (although walks in the park were involved). This experimental group was told to severely restrict how much meat they ate and to switch to an essentially vegetarian diet. They were not to eat more than 10% fat (in contrast to the Atkins diet you may have heard a lot about that was discussed in Chapter 7). The rest of the diet was divided into 12% to 20% proteins and 70% to 75% carbohydrates, predominantly complex (meaning carbohydrates most often found in nuts and whole grains). All caffeine-containing beverages were eliminated, and alcohol consumption was discouraged. No animal products were allowed in the vegetarian diet except an egg white and one cup per day of nonfat milk or yogurt. Patients were also told to stop smoking (if they were smokers) and were helped with smoking cessation. Physical activity also had to be increased, and they were given a program of moderate levels of aerobic exercise to do. Each patient was told to exercise at least five times per week for a total of 5 hours. They could either walk or jog.

Together with these important health behaviors (nonsmoking, eating well, and getting physical activity), the Ornish program also aimed to reduce stress levels. We have discussed how emotional stress plays an important

(Continued)

(Continued)

role in just about all illnesses. In CHD, stress makes arteries constrict and increases blood clot speed, both of which cause heart attacks. To make matters worse, stressed people are more likely to smoke, overeat, drink too much, and overwork. The Lifestyle trial included yoga exercises (primarily stretching), relaxation techniques involving breathing, meditation and mental imagery training, and social support groups. Patients in the control group were not asked to make lifestyle changes other than those recommended by their cardiologists (often similar though not in magnitude and not backed up by trained professionals with follow ups).

The results were astounding. After 1 year, patients in the experimental group showed a significant overall reduction of coronary atherosclerosis as measured by X-rays of heart blood vessels injected with radioactive chemicals (coronary angiography). The arteries went from being 40.0% blocked (stenosis) to 37.8% in the experimental group, but blockages increased from 42.7% to 46.1% in the control group. Overall, 82% of experimental patients experienced reduced blockages. The experimental group was able to make and maintain the lifestyle changes and also showed a 37% reduction in low-density lipoprotein level and a 91% reduction in cardiac problems. The control group showed a 165% increase in cardiac problems. Given that the control group was not doing as well, you would be right in wondering if it was ethical for the experiment to continue. The researchers did not explicitly address this, but one can assume that time period was a critical component in the intervention.

Was this a fluke? As good scientists should, Ornish et al. extended the study to confirm the findings and see if they persisted. One concern was that the lifestyle change was too drastic and would be difficult to maintain. Skip ahead 4 years. When assessing the health and behaviors of the original sample 5 years from the start of the original study, Ornish et al. (1998) found there was even more reduction and continued improvement. In the experimental group, the average percent diameter stenosis was 7.9% relative improvement after 5 years. In contrast, the average percent diameter stenosis in the control group was 27.7% relative worsening after 5 years. Twenty-five cardiac events occurred in the experimental group versus 45 events in the control group during the 5-year follow up. Even better, the people in the lifestyle change group showed better results than the people in the control group who were taking fat-lowering medications (none of the experimental group was taking any).

Similar positive effects of lifestyle change have also been shown in the Illinois WISEWOMAN study (Khare et al., 2012) and the large Nurses' Health Study that followed 85,941 healthy women from 1980 to 1994 (Stampfer et al., 2000). The women who did not smoke, were a healthy weight, ate well, and got sufficient physical activity had an 83% less risk of a heart attack (Stampfer et al., 2000). Other studies also varied dietary intake or increased exercise with similar results.

It is undoubtedly difficult to live a healthy life, and it definitely takes a lot of willpower and help to keep to a healthy regimen such as the one prescribed by the **Lifestyle Heart Trial,** but the results are clear. Not only can healthy behaviors keep heart disease from worsening, they can actually reverse it as well. Given that some people may not be able to tolerate lipid-lowering drugs, the fact that participants in this study showed improvement without the drugs is extremely important. It may be that the extremely rigorous levels of change are not needed, but why take a chance on your health? Be well aware of your behaviors and don't forget how many different benefits eating well, not smoking, and being physically active can have.

This is a wonderful example of how health behaviors can be changed to reverse heart disease, but there are a few caveats. It can be argued that these findings cannot easily be generalized to the population at large because the participants of Ornish et al. were highly motivated and compliant, both important attributes for a demanding intervention. Nevertheless, the point they make is clear: What you do with your lifestyle will determine how long you will live.

CHAPTER REVIEW

SUMMARY ▶▶

- Cardiovascular diseases result from problems with the heart and the circulatory system. The most common are coronary heart disease or cardiovascular disease (CVD), heart failure, strokes, and high blood pressure or hypertension. Others include abnormal heart rhythms, pulmonary heart disease, and diseases of veins, arteries, and lymph nodes.
- American Indians show the lowest instances of deaths due to coronary heart disease followed by Asian Americans and Latinos. In contrast, all non-European ethnic groups have a higher risk for strokes. Anger, competitiveness, and time urgency are some of the main psychological differences among ethnic groups that could account for the differences in CVD.

- The accumulation of wear and tear on the circulatory system as we age accounts for significant developmental differences in the incidence of CVD. Social support networks also change as we age although the exact relationship is still unclear.
- The accumulation of fatty substances in the blood vessels and the thickening of the arteries are the most common precursors to CVD. The main physiological risk factors are age, sex, family history, obesity, diabetes, hypertension, high cholesterol levels, and inactivity. The main psychological predictors of CVD are stress, hostility, negative emotions, depression, and low social support.
- Changing unhealthy lifestyles is critical to preventing and treating CVD. Patients normally join cardiac rehabilitation programs to reduce stress and improve health behaviors such as quitting smoking, increasing physical activity, and eating better. Patients with severe CVD may need surgery, ranging from angioplasty to open blocked blood vessels to cardiac bypass surgery in which blood flow is redirected around blocked areas.
- Behavioral interventions such as the program of Dean Ornish and colleagues and those conducted by Friedman and colleagues demonstrate that CVD is reversible.

TEST YOURSELF ▶▶

Check your understanding of the topics in this chapter by answering the following questions.

1. The largest percent of deaths from cardiovascular disease is due to
   a. coronary heart disease.
   b. stroke.
   c. congestive heart failure.
   d. high blood pressure.
2. One major source of information on the course and development of heart disease is the
   a. Alameda County study.
   b. Berkeley study.
   c. Framingham study.
   d. MacArthur study.
3. Heart-related diseases are more common in
   a. older men.
   b. older women.
   c. young adults.
   d. infants.
4. The ethnic group with the lowest number of deaths due to coronary heart disease is
   a. European Americans.
   b. Asian Americans.
   c. American Indians.
   d. Latinos.
5. A culture that is high in _______ is more likely to have stress-related heart problems.
   a. collectivism
   b. individualism
   c. fluid time
   d. constraint
6. Having high levels of _______ is one of the most important personality risk factors for CVD.
   a. optimism
   b. time urgency
   c. hostility
   d. neuroticism
7. The primary physiological precursor of CVD is
   a. stress.
   b. phagocytosis.
   c. angina pectoris.
   d. atherosclerosis.
8. Certain cultural groups have greater genetic predispositions for CVD than others. ________, for example, show higher blood pressure reactivity to stressful tasks.
   a. European Americans
   b. American Indians
   c. African Americans
   d. Asian Americans
9. The number one behavior to avoid in order to minimize the risks for cardiovascular disease is
   a. bad eating.
   b. smoking.
   c. excessive drinking.
   d. insufficient sleep.
10. The best diet to keep CVD at bay appears to be the
    a. Atkins diet.
    b. South Beach diet.
    c. Indo-Mediterranean diet.
    d. Zone diet.

KEY TERMS, CONCEPTS, AND PEOPLE ▶▶

affect cultures, **376**
angina pectoris, **383**
angioplasty, **385**
arteriosclerosis, **377**
atherosclerosis, **375**
C-reactive protein (CRP), **375**
cardiac rehabilitation program, **384**
cardiovascular disease (CVD), **372**
cardiovascular reactivity, **378**
control versus constraint, **376**
coronary heart disease (CHD), **373**
fluid time versus fixed time, **375**
Framingham heart study, **372**
hypertension, **373**
Indo-Mediterranean diet, **383**
ischemias, **384**
Lifestyle Heart Trial, **388**
myocardial infarctions, **383**
neutral cultures, **376**
Ornish, Dean, **387**
stroke, **373**

ESSENTIAL READINGS ▶▶

Baker, B., Richter, A., & Anand, S. S. (2001). From the heartland: Culture, psychological factors, and coronary heart disease. In S. S. Kazarian & D. R. Evans (Eds.), *Handbook of cultural health psychology* (pp. 141–162). San Diego, CA: Academic Press.

Bishop, G. (2019). Cardiovascular disease. In T. A. Revenson & R. A. R. Gurung (Eds.), *Handbook of health psychology* (3e). New York, NY: Routledge.

Ornish, D., Scherwitz, L. W., Billings, J. H., Gould, K. L., Merritt, T. A., Sparler, S., . . . Brand, R. J. (1998). Intensive lifestyle changes for reversal of coronary heart disease. *Journal of the American Medical Association, 280*(23), 2001–2007.

CHAPTER 15

CONTROVERSIES AND THE FUTURE OF HEALTH PSYCHOLOGY

iStockphoto.com/CasarsaGuru

Chapter 15 Outline

You may have heard people say, "Don't miss the forest for the trees," referring to how we often miss the big picture when we focus too much on the small details. Hopefully by this point of the book, you have a very good sense of the many species of trees there are in the forest that is health psychology. This is a good time to step back and look at some of the bigger issues. We can actually take the forest analogy a long way. The field of health psychology is so vibrant, exciting, and sometimes wild (there are areas that still need a lot of cultivation), an invitation to learn more about it is akin to saying "Welcome to the jungle." Like a forest, some areas of health psychology, such as stress and coping, are the old oaks that have been studied for many years. Other areas such as psychoneuroimmunology are the young saplings, newer and still growing. Different parts of the forest can be used for many different purposes: the basic research in health psychology can be applied in many different ways and translated into interventions and programs that can be life saving as well as increase the quality of life. There are also areas of the forest that are enjoyable to be in, such as joining a team studying **positive psychology**—research findings that help us understand complex psychosocial issues and alleviate the pain and suffering of those with chronic illnesses. Some parts of the forest are dark and uninviting, the areas of health psychology that are rife with ethical concerns and difficult implications such as genetic testing and the design of some interventions or suggestions for policy change that may be perceived as compromising individual freedoms. There are also many areas of the forest yet to be discovered.

Health psychology is rising in awareness in U.S. schools and colleges. Near 70% of U.S. psychology departments offer a course in Health Psychology (Norcross et al., 2016). Health psychology also features predominantly in recent introductory psychology textbooks (e.g., Griggs, 2014). In fact, health psychology is rated as one of the most important and interesting topics covered in introductory psychology (McCann, Immel, Kadah-Ammeter, & Adelson, 2016), a course taken by approximately 1.5 million students a year (Gurung et al., 2016). What's next for the field of health psychology? What are the opportunities available for you as a burgeoning health psychologist? Perhaps dealing with ongoing and current controversies is a good place to start (Gurung & Bruns, 2012).

ONGOING AND CURRENT CONTROVERSIES

How Important Are Health Behaviors Really?

I hope that by this point of the book you are convinced that improving your health behaviors can help you cope with stress, keep illness at bay, and help you recover from illness. Surprisingly, not all parts of the scientific community saluted the importance of health behaviors, a controversy in the field of health psychology referred to as the "great debate" (Kaplan & Davidson, 2010, p. 3).

Prominent health psychologists debated this topic at the request of the Psychosomatic Society (Relman & Angell, 2002; Williams, Schneiderman, Relman, & Angell, 2002). The debaters evaluated 23 articles on the benefits of psychosocial interventions that aimed to change health behaviors, and Relman and Angell (2002) concluded that none showed meaningful effects. This conclusion was criticized as overly relying on methodological flaws and relying on too few studies (i.e., 23).

A recent review of many more studies showed the evidence heavily favors the effectiveness of psychosocial interventions designed to change health behaviors (Glanz, Rimer, & Viswanath, 2015). Yes indeed, poor eating, smoking, and drinking should be curtailed (see Chapter 8).

Who Can Be Called a Medical Psychologist?

Act 251, a law passed in Louisiana in 2009 defined the term "medical psychologist" as a psychologist who is trained in psychopharmacology and who used medical methods to treat mental health conditions. This definition, a reversal from previous ways of defining it, created significant confusion for the public with regard to what the term medical psychologist actually meant (Gurung & Bruns, 2012).

Act 251 creates two classes of paraprofessionals, which are medical psychology assistants and psychometrists. Standards for training and scope of practice for these paraprofessionals are not defined by Act 251, but instead are referred to the prescribing psychologist to decide. In contrast, licensed clinical psychologists are not authorized to hire such paraprofessionals. Similarly, Act 251 allows prescribing psychologists to order medical tests, such as MRIs or blood work, while clinical psychologists cannot. The Interdivisional Healthcare Committee (2010) was concerned that Act 251 disenfranchised licensed clinical psychologists who worked in medical settings. This was because under Act 251, licensed clinical psychologists working in medical settings were now *not* licensed as medical psychologists, and this could have a negative impact on their practice. Conversely, by gaining the title of licensed medical psychologist, prescribing psychologists could appear to have expertise in health psychology, rehabilitation psychology, or neuropsychology, even though they had no specific training in these specialties (Interdivisional Healthcare Committee, 2010).

The Issue of Professional Status

In 2009, the American Medical Association Resolution 303 sought legislation so that only MDs could be called doctor. The AMA resolved that the title *doctor* only be used in a medical setting and can only be applied to physicians licensed to practice medicine (Illinois Delegation, 2008). Similarly, the terms *physician* and *psychologist* are legally reserved in most states. They are specific, and this restriction is appropriate. In contrast, although the term *doctor* is general, its Latin root has nothing to do with either medicine or psychology, but rather means teacher. Even so, it remains legally possible for physicians to gain ownership of the term *physician* or other terms. To do so, all that is required is to convince the majority of a state's legislators to restrict the use of a term. Had the AMA been successful in this endeavor, health psychologists would be greatly affected, as the loss of the honorific term doctor would result in a loss of status in health-care settings.

Moving beyond controversies outside the field, there are many avenues for improvement and advancement within the field.

LOOKING TO THE FUTURE

Health psychology has come a long way. In Chapter 1, I sketched the history of health psychology and the different organizations that cater to people using the health psychological approach. The Division of Health Psychology (**Division 38**) of the American Psychological Association (APA) changed its name to the **Society for Health Psychology**. The Society for Behavioral Medicine and the American Psychosomatic Society are even older (founded in 1978 and 1942, respectively). Times are changing, and the awareness of the role of psychology in health and well-being is now explicit and prominent. For example, the APA has using focusing on using psychology to improve health and life in general as part of its mission (Belar, 2016).

As we contemplate the approaching third decade of the millennium, let's take a look at where health psychology is going (and may need to go).

NicolasMcComber/ istockphoto

▲ **Health Varies across Cultural Groups.** These two women, who may lead very similar lives, could have very dissimilar health needs based simply on their differing ethnicities.

A Greater Focus on Sociocultural Issues

This book was written with the explicit goal of increasing awareness of sociocultural issues. In looking back over the different chapters, you notice that some chapters included a lot more culture in them than others. You may think I swayed off course in the chapters without too much culture, but that's not so. The shortage of information on culture in some areas mirrors a sad lack of information of cultural differences in some areas of health psychology. Many faculty complain that topics related to health disparities and diversity do not receive enough attention in textbooks (Panjwani et al., 2017). Clearly more classes need to be using this book. The good news is that there is an increase in works focusing on culture. In 2014 I edited a two-volume set titled *Multicultural Approaches to Health and Wellness in America* (Gurung, 2014). There are now books focused exclusively on Latino health (Tovar, 2017) and Mexican American health (Aceticia & Avula, 2018).

Stella Kalinina/ Blend Images/ Getty Images

▲ **Gerontology.** As the large generation known as the baby boomers moves into their senior citizen years, it becomes even more important for us to understand the health impacts of living a longer life. Some of the best job opportunities are going to be in gerontology researching and working with older adults.

A Focus on Developmental Issues and the Life Span

Older adults are the largest consumers of health care, and the number of older adults is increasing every year. As the population grows older and life expectancy increases, it becomes even more important to identify and change the behaviors that increase the incidence of chronic illnesses of middle and later adulthood (Siegler, Elias, & Bosworth, 2012). Increased longevity affects men and women differently. Women tend to live longer, and this has its own unique implications. For example, there will be a large number of older women living with chronic but not life-threatening illnesses (e.g., arthritis). Ways to manage pain and stress are going to be especially important (Keefe et al., 2002; Spiro, 2007). A developmental context is critical for a thorough understanding of chronic diseases (Berg, Smith, Henry, & Pearce, 2007).

Fine-Tuning the Biopsychosocial Model

By now you should be comfortable with the main health psychological approach, the biopsychosocial model (Matarazzo, 1980; Suls, Luger, & Martin, 2010). Since its inception in the late 1970s, the biopsychosocial model has served as a guiding principle and has fueled dramatic advances in health psychological research (Boyer, 2008; Suls & Rothman, 2004). Clearly a useful and accurate model, it has been supported by a variety of research (Revenson & Gurung, 2019). However, there is still a way to go.

To fully capitalize on the strengths of a **multidimensional approach**, it is critical for health psychologists to pay more attention to the links between the different subsystems and improve the data collected to assess each subsystem. This may mean collecting physiological, self-report, and sociological data, possibly over a long period of time. There is a clear need to work toward greater applications of the biopsychosocial model and move it from the theoretical realm into a more practical one, while also ensuring that practice informs research and both (practice and research) inform policy changes (Keefe et al., 2002).

Still, there has been some development toward using a biopsychosocial approach on a large scale. Three new evidence-based medical treatment guidelines, the Colorado Guidelines (Colorado Division of Workers' Compensation, 2007), the ODG (Official Disability Guidelines; Work Loss Data Institute, 2009), and the American College of Occupational and Environmental Medicine Guidelines (ACOEM, 2008) adopt a biopsychosocial treatment model and recommend (and in many cases even *require*) psychological evaluation and treatment for patients who need spinal surgery, or who have chronic pain. Remarkably, some states legalized these guidelines as medical regulations for workers compensation, and other states are considering doing so. Referred to as biopsychosocial laws (Bruns, Mueller, & Warren, 2010), these are the first instances where biopsychosocial medical treatment guidelines were reviewed by multiple medical societies, developed with adherence to evidence-based medicine principles, and enacted into law. If health psychologists believe in the biopsychosocial model, do we need to merge medical law with mental health law? One implication is that existing federal and state privacy laws typically regard psychological records as more confidential than medical records. In contrast, medical records can be accessed by all treating professionals.

TECHNOLOGICAL INNOVATIONS

Tools for the Delivery of Health Care

Telehealth, or more broadly eHealth, is no longer a new term or a novel way to deliver health care (PausJenssen, Spooner, Wilson, & Wilson, 2008). **Behavioral telehealth** has been used in one form or another for more than 40 years, but current technological developments such as high-speed Internet and wireless capabilities are making this form of service delivery even more common. Recognizing the growing use of ICT, the Federal Communication Commission initiated the Rural Healthcare Pilot Program Broadband Initiative in 2007 to provide funds for deployment of broadband networks to rural areas. Not surprisingly, organizations receiving the funds still have problems with program deployment highlighting the need to pay attention to the rolling out of telehealth (Whitten, Holtz, Krupinski, & Alverson, 2010). However, it is clear that the development, adoption, and implementation of a broad range of new eHealth applications (e.g., online health information websites, interactive electronic health records) holds tremendous promise (Kreps & Neuhauser, 2010). Stand back and make way for the growing area of digital health psychology (Yardley, Bradbury, Nadarzynski, & Hunter, 2019).

Technology and Health Information

An associated issue for health psychologists to be aware of is people's use of the Internet to get health information (Dart, 2008). If someone experiences a certain symptom or seems to be developing a certain illness, he or she can log onto the Internet and using sites such as WebMD, get a good idea of what he or she may (or may not) have (see Figure 15.1). Parents are especially likely to also reach out to the Internet when their kids show signs of sickness (Khoo, Bolt, Babl, Jury, & Goldman, 2008). There are some important cultural differences here too. Research shows that Latinos do not use the Internet for health information as much as non-Latino European Americans (Peña-Purcell, 2008). Furthermore, Latinos have been found to view the Internet as damaging to physician-patient relationships. Internet use has also been suggested as a plausible mediator of the relationship between SES and subjective health (Wangberg et al., 2008).

The Internet can also greatly expand research opportunities and increase accessibility to personal medical information. Researchers can now conduct major surveys online with very little associated time or money, and large databases can be made available to research collaborations (more on this later). Even patients are going to have more control over their health information. The Health Insurance Portability and Accountability Act (HIPAA) that took effect in 2003 includes regulations that allow patients to examine their computerized medical records to correct mistakes and seek action against misuse of their records.

BSIP/ Universal Images Group/ Getty Images

▲ **Teleconsultation.** Some doctors now give colleagues and patients health information via online health websites, chat rooms, or even personalized emails.

ENHANCED TRAINING

Training in the areas of cultural competency and awareness of life span issues will also have to be enhanced (Purnell & Pontious, 2014). Health psychologists often graduate ill prepared for their role within a culturally diverse society and could consequently do great harm. To keep up with the increasing diversification of the United States, health psychologists must be informed and aware of not only life span development issues (due to the aging population) but also culturally appropriate research methods (Smith & Suls, 2004). Present training programs give trainees very limited exposure to these two very important areas but, as with this book, the awareness and inclusion of these areas are growing.

Division 38 (Health Psychology) of the American Psychological Association took explicit steps to enhance the training of health psychologists and developed a list of competencies for both clinical and nonclinical health psychologists (Masters, France, & Thorne, 2009). Table 15.1 lists the suggested competencies that are taught in many programs in health psychology without reference to clinical training.

The Current Procedural Terminology (CPT) manual was updated with new billing codes designed to capture behavioral services provided to patients to address physical health problems. The health and behavior assessment and intervention, or H&B CPT codes, apply to psychological services that address behavioral, social, and psychophysiological conditions in the treatment or management of patients diagnosed with physical health problems (APA, 2008). As more and more behavioral and psychological treatments are reimbursed (e.g., smoking cessation), the financial barriers to prevention will be eliminated.

The existence and use of H&B CPT codes highlights a practical element of health psychology. A significant number of health psychologists have their doctorates in clinical psychology and are practicing clinical psychologists (more on careers in the section at chapter's end). Reading the research cited in this book does not allow for much insight into the practice-side of health psychology, a realm where the use (or

▼ FIGURE 15.1

Looking for Answers

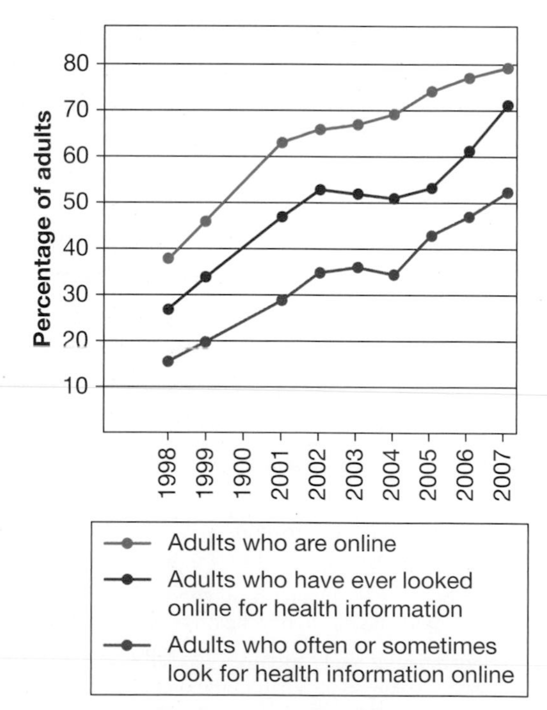

Source: Based on "Cyberchondriacs" on the Rise? *The Harris Poll*, 2010.

▼ TABLE 15.1

Competencies for Non-Clinical Health Psychologists

A. Knowledge base: The entry-level health psychologist researcher should have knowledge of:
• The historical relationship of health psychology to the basic sciences, public health, and clinical investigation.
• Scientific foundations and methods of psychology and exposure to allied health disciplines (e.g. epidemiology, physiology, genomics, bioinformatics)
• Biobehavioral, social-environmental, and psychological factors associated with health behaviors, illness, and disease.
• Mechanistic and mediational pathways between contextual, psychosocial, and biological phenomena as they relate to disease progression, health promotion, and illness prevention.
• Biological, psychological, behavioral and sociocultural tools (e.g., psychophysiological assessment, interview techniques, assessment development, observational coding, focus groups, web-based informatics tools) relevant to individuals and systems.
• Dynamic interactions between populations and contextual variations (age, gender, ethnicity, culture, religion, etc.) on health behavior and health outcomes.
• Pathophysiology of disease and the implications for development of biopsychosocial treatments.
• Appropriate methods and procedures to develop a program of research.
• Strengths and potential pitfalls of role relationships that characterize interdisciplinary collaborative research.
• Regulatory and ethics competence in relation to interdisciplinary research.
B. Applications: The entry-level health psychologist should be able to:
• Evaluate biopsychosocial findings related to physical health or illness/injury/disability.
• Assess biopsychosocial and behavioral risk factors for the development of physical illness, injury, or disability.
• Assist in assessment of new and emerging health technologies.
• Develop health psychology research protocols and evaluate their effectiveness and quality.
• Evaluate biopsychosocial and cognitive assessment tools appropriate to understanding physical illness, injury, or disability.
• Design and evaluate empirically supported health promotion, prevention, and other interventions appropriate to target populations in the context of an interdisciplinary team.
• Apply diverse methodologies to address contextual, psychosocial, and biological processes as they relate to disease progression, health promotion, and illness prevention.
• Select, apply, and interpret data analytic strategies that are best suited to the diverse research questions and levels of analysis characteristic of health psychology.
• Work toward translation of research findings to applied settings.
• Translate issues presented by professionals from other disciplines into research questions and appropriate methods for investigation.
• Integrate the talents and skills of professionals from different disciplines and different levels of training (e.g., masters, doctoral) to optimize research.
• Integrate within and lead in the formulation of interdisciplinary research teams.
• Accurately and efficiently communicate research findings in a manner that is consistent with the highest standards within the profession in ways that can be understood by fellow psychologists, professionals from other disciplines, and lay audiences alike.
• Write a research proposal of a quality sufficient to be submitted to a granting agency.
• Publish in peer reviewed journals in the area of health psychology.
• Understands the bounds/limits of one's research competence.
• Obtain proficiency in a traditional area of psychology such as psychophysiology, psychometrics, statistics, affect and cognition, or social psychology.
• Obtain knowledge, exposure, and competence outside of an area of traditional psychology (e.g., epidemiology, genetics, neural imaging, body imaging, assaying biomarkers, nutrition, exercise, sleep).
• Demonstrate adequate training and evidence of skill as a teacher, and have the requisite knowledge to develop and implement an undergraduate health psychology course.
• Understand the role and responsibilities of an effective mentor, and have the ability to promote the development of research and teaching competencies in graduate and undergraduate students.

Source: Division 38(Health Psychology), 2012

lack) of H&B codes has been problematic. Taking a glance into the politics may be useful, and the dynamics of code use also help highlight another side of the biopsychosocial nature of the field. First some details.

Battles rage around these CPT (Current Procedural Terminology) codes, because they are how all health professionals bill for their services and earn their income (Gurung & Bruns, 2012). There is some turf battling: the American Medical Association literally owns the codes for all professions, meaning they wield enormous power. If the AMA decides to suddenly delete H&B or other codes with a wave of the hand, certain areas of clinical health psychology practice would be devastated.

If health psychologists want to have a more direct impact on the health of patients, you can guess that being able to treat (and bill) patients (and get paid) is critical. Correspondingly, there is a lot of activity within APA to give clinical health psychologists a broader ability to bill their patients for services they have provided. But change is not easy. Making changes to billing codes is incredibly difficult. The H&B codes took 6 to 7 years to push through. A subsequent tweaking of the H&B language took another 3 years or so. Psychology has only a handful of codes in a massive document, and the AMA has historically blocked the APA from any direct involvement in creating it. APA has faced resistance on many fronts, with psychiatry (and other groups) lobbying intensively against it.

BIOPSYCHOCULTURAL HEALTH PSYCHOLOGY

Taken as a whole, health psychologists have made gigantic strides in the prevention of illness and in aiding those of us who do get sick. Research has honed in on key topics such as sleep (Zhou, Bakker, & Johnson, 2019) and veterans (Trivedi, 2019). Biological methodologies and techniques have led to a new area, health neuroscience (Zoccola, Woody, & Bryant, 2019). There is still more to be done, but the utility of a taking a biopsychosocial approach has already paid dividends. Now all we need is to expand our focus across the life span and to better incorporate diverse cultural backgrounds (Purnell et al., 2011). The fact is that there really is not enough of a social focus in the biopsychosocial approach (Keefe et al., 2002). Indeed, what we do and why we do it are shaped by a variety of factors, and our health and well-being are no exceptions. A **biopsychocultural** approach might provide health psychology with stronger direction that not only incorporates the social nature of our interactions but also explicitly acknowledges the role that culture plays in our lives.

Synthesize, Evaluate, Apply

- How would you summarize the state of the field of health psychology?
- How would you prioritize the different future directions described above?
- Generate your own description of health psychology, synthesizing what you have learned in this book.
- Are there other areas of culture, development, and health that have not been discussed in this book?

CHAPTER REVIEW

SUMMARY ▶▶

- Health psychology as a separate field has now been in existence for approximately 35 years, although its roots go back much farther. It has many areas of specialization and organizations that cater to individuals from different fields.
- There are significant controversies around the field of health psychology relating to the issue of labels, diagnostic criteria, professional status, and evidence-based practices.
- There is a great need for health psychology to focus more on cultural issues. There are significant cultural differences in health behaviors and health in general. Health psychologists have only recently begun to focus explicitly on differences in cultural groups. This focus

calls for more training and cultural awareness. With the increasing diversity in North America, there is an urgent need for more cross-cultural health psychology research.

- Although it is clear that health issues vary as we age and that the causes of death vary for different age groups, health psychologists have yet to focus on developmental issues and the life span. Disparate literature studies reporting on developmental issues should be initiated for studies of health as we age.
- Additional work needs to be done on refining the biopsychosocial model. Still used more in the theoretical realm, the biopsychosocial model needs to be put into practice more often.
- The need for more cultural and developmental research in health psychology is going to require more multilevel and interdisciplinary collaborations. These collaborations will foster the design of more powerful interventions.
- Technology is changing rapidly. Research designs and interventions need to keep abreast of novel ways to collect data and monitor individuals. The greater use of portable computers, the Internet, and even multifunction cellular phones gives the health psychologist a wealth of new ways to get trained as we reach people and change behavior.
- Interventions need to better account for the time course of diseases, different levels of analysis, cultural differences, and a focus on health threats across the life span.
- Training programs in health psychology need to be revised to keep up with the changing nature of the field and the increasing need for cultural competency.
- Health psychologists need to pay more attention to the use and utility of complementary and alternative medicine (CAM). The uses of CAM are growing, and they may prove to be effective aids to conventional treatments in addition to providing psychological buffers to illness.

TEST YOURSELF ▶▶

Check your understanding of the topics in this chapter by answering the following questions.

1. Although a relatively new area of psychology, Health Psychology, as a division of the American Psychological Association, has been around for more than
   a. 10 years.
   b. 15 years.
   c. 30 years.
   d. 50 years.

2. In many health psychological studies ethnicity is treated as a ________ variable, thereby downplaying its importance.
   a. moderator
   b. mediator
   c. independent
   d. control

3. Who are the largest consumers of health care?
   a. Latinos
   b. Older adults
   c. Infants and adolescents
   d. Asian Americans

4. Although the biopsychosocial model is well used, some aspects of it are favored over others. One component of it that is not studied as much is the ________ component.
   a. cultural
   b. biological
   c. psychological
   d. social

5. Given the specific training needed to be well versed with the different components of the biopsychosocial model, the future of health psychology will rely on
   a. better funding.
   b. international collaborations.
   c. multidimensional collaborations.
   d. new graduate departments.

6. A new innovation in health psychology is the use of new forms of delivery of services. One such area is
   a. rural outreach.
   b. behavioral telehealth.
   c. intercultural consultation.
   d. multimodal contact.

7. A challenge for health psychologists to face is the increasing role of ________ in health education.
   a. movies
   b. television
   c. the Internet
   d. peers

8. An advance in medical science that has direct implications for health psychologists is the increasing use of

a. living organ and tissue transplants.
b. cloning.
c. subcutaneous micropumps.
d. computerized diagnosis mechanisms.

9. The division of the American Psychological Association dedication to health psychology is
 a. 2.
 b. 8.
 c. 38.
 d. 45.

10. The use of empirical proven research to guide treatment is referred to as
 a. Empirical Behavioral Medicine.
 b. Evidence-Based Medicine.
 c. Pragmatic Science.
 d. Biobehavioral Treatments.

KEY TERMS, CONCEPTS, AND PEOPLE

behavioral telehealth, **396**
biopsychocultural, **399**
Current Procedural Terminology (CPT), **397**
Division 38, **394**
multidimensional approach, **396**
positive psychology, **393**
Society for Health Psychology, **394**

ESSENTIAL READINGS

Trivedi, R. (2019). Psychiatric illness among military veterans in the United States. In T. A. Revenson & R. A. R. Gurung (Eds.), *Handbook of health psychology* (3e). New York, NY: Routledge.

Zhou, E., Bakker, J. P., & Johnson, D. A. (2019). Sleep. In T. A. Revenson & R. A. R. Gurung (Eds.), *Handbook of health psychology* (3e). New York, NY: Routledge.

Zoccola, P., Woody, A., & Bryant, A. M. (2019). Health neuroscience. In T. A. Revenson & R. A. R. Gurung (Eds.), *Handbook of health psychology* (3e). New York, NY: Routledge.

iStockphoto.com/ CasarsaGuru

GLOSSARY

Acquired immunodeficiency syndrome (AIDS): Illness resulting in a deficiency within the immune system, with a number of manifestations, rather than a single disease. Caused by HIV.

Action: Stage in the Transtheorerical Model where subjects are actually changing their behavior. The change has to have taken place over the past 6 months and should involve active efforts to change the behavior.

Acupuncture: One of the most scientifically validated forms of alternative medicine; involves the use of fine needles inserted into specific points on the body. Acupuncture is theorized to keep the balance between yin and yang, thus allowing for the normal flow of qi throughout the body and restoring health to the mind and body.

ADAPT-ITT: Theoretical model consists of eight sequential phases that inform HIV prevention providers and researchers of a prescriptive method for adapting evidence-based interventions.

Addiction: State in which the body relies on a substance for normal functioning.

Adherence: Extent to which a patient's behavior matches with his or her practitioner's advice.

Affect cultures: Cultures such as the culture in Italy that place a premium on the display of emotions.

Afferent fibers: Sensory nerve fibers transmitting signals from the receptors to the spinal cord.

Alcohol abuse: Characterized by one or more of the following as a result of alcohol use: (1) failure to fulfill major role obligations; (2) recurrent physically hazardous use; (3) recurrent alcohol-related legal problems, or (4) continued use despite persistent alcohol-related social or interpersonal problems.

Allopathy: Conventional or Western medicine that treats disease by the use of remedies to produce effects different from those produced by the disease under treatment.

Allostasis: The ability to achieve stability through change.

Analgesia: Pain relief or the inability to feel pain.

Analyses of variance (ANOVAs): Statistical rest that examines if group means vary from each other. It uses an F-ratio test.

Angina pectoris: Medical term for heart attacks or myocardial infarctions (or cardiac arrest). Chest pain is a common symptom.

Angioplasty: Treatment for cardiovascular disease involving a procedure done to open a partially blocked blood vessel so that blood can flow through it more easily.

Anorexia nervosa: Disorder defined by the following criteria: refusing to maintain body weight at or above a minimally normal weight for age and height; having an intense fear of gaining weight or becoming fat, even though underweight; having a disturbed view of the way in which one's body weight or shape is experienced, undue influence of body weight or shape on self-evaluation, or denial of the seriousness of the current low body weight; and experiencing amenorrhea (the absence of at least three consecutive menstrual cycles).

Anticipatory grief: Process in which a dying patient feels a lack of control and now grieves in expectation of his or her death.

Antigens: Specific immune cells that are earmarked for specific germs or antigens. Also known as antibody generators.

Appraisal delay: Time taken to recognize one has symptoms after they first appear.

Appraisals: Way a potentially stressful event is interpreted. A significant component of Lazarus' psychological explanation of why we get stressed.

Approach coping: Form of coping where you actively attempt to solve the problem or address the stressor.

Assessment: Obtaining information according to a goal.

Atherosclerosis: Disease caused by the accumulation of fatty substances in the blood vessels.

Attribution: Cognitive process of assigning meaning to a symptom or behavior.

Avoidant coping: Form of coping where you focus more on emotions resulting from the stressor and ignore or avoid the stressful experience itself. It involves mental or behavioral methods to deal with the feelings resulting from the stress.

Ayurveda: Ancient system of medicine that focuses on the body, the sense organs, the mind, and the soul. It originated in India approximately 4,000 years ago.

Bargaining: Stage of death in which patients try to restore their belief in a just world and may promise to be good or live life better in exchange for life.

Bariatric surgery: Weight loss surgery. There are many forms such as lap band surgery and gastric bypass surgery.

Behavioral cueing: Certain events, situations, people, or locations that act as stimuli that result in behaviors conditioned to be associated with them. When a smoker always smokes in his or her car, the car is a signal to the smoker's body that nicotine is coming and makes smoking more likely.

Behavioral involvement: A patient's attitude toward self-care, specifically an active involvement in treatment.

Behavioral medicine: Interdisciplinary field of medicine that includes psychological, sociological, and biological views on health and illness. Behavioral telehealth health care delivered over the telephone or through other technical means such as the Internet.

Benefit finding: Finding meaning in a chronic illness and growing.

Benign: Noncancerous tumors.

Binge drinkers: Men who have consumed five or more and women who have consumed four or more drinks in a row at least once during the previous 2 weeks.

Biofeedback: Procedure where a computer or other monitoring device measures heart rate and systolic and diastolic blood pressure in real time, allowing one to modify one's behavior and thinking to see resulting changes in cardiovascular reactions. A form of relaxation.

Biomedical approach: An approach that sees health primarily as the state in which disease is absent.

Biopsychocultural approach: An approach to studying human behavior that incorporates biological, psychological, and cultural factors.

Biopsychosocial approach: An approach that focuses on the biology or physiology underlying health, the psychology or thoughts, feelings, and behaviors influencing health, and the ways that society and culture influence health.

Blended family: Family consisting of two parents, either or both of whom may have been previously married, with their children.

Body mass index (BMI): Standard measure of weight calculated by multiplying weight by 703 and dividing by the square of height measured in inches [BMI 5 (Wt 3 703)/(H t 3 Ht)].

Broken families: Families consisting of divorced and/or single parents living with their kids.

Bulimia nervosa: Disorder characterized by the following criteria: recurrent episodes of binge eating; recurrent use of inappropriate compensatory behaviors in order to prevent weight gain; engaging in binge eating and inappropriate compensatory behaviors, on average, at least two times per week for 3 months; and having a self-evaluation that is unduly influenced by body shape and weight.

Carcinogens: Cancer-causing substances.

Carcinomas: Cancers that start in the surface layers of the body or epithelial cells. This form of cancer accounts for the bulk of cancer cases and is seen in the most common sites.

Cardiac rehabilitation program: Programs educate patients on the best way to change their lifestyles and use a combination of physical activity and social support to improve their overall functioning and prevent death.

Cardiovascular disease: General category of diseases resulting from problems with the heart and the circulatory system. Includes coronary heart disease (CHD) (also referred to as coronary artery disease [CAD]) and heart failure (both commonly referred to as heart attacks), strokes, and hypertension or high blood pressure.

Cardiovascular reactivity: Changes in heart rate and blood pressure in response to stress.

Cell-mediated immunity: Form of immune reaction that takes place at the level of the cell. Cell-mediated immunity involves the action of T cells although the first stages are similar to the process for humoral-mediated immunity.

Chemotherapy: Treatment involving taking medications with the aim of disabling cancer growth.

Chronic illnesses: Illnesses that persist over long periods of time.

Cognitive appraisal model: Richard Lazarus's theory of why we get stressed and defined as the imbalance between the demands placed on the individual and that individual's resources to cope.

Complementary and alternative medicine [CAM]: Any non-Western approach to health and wellness. Most common CAMs include acupuncture and reiki.

Conditioned immune response: When the reaction of the body's immune system comes about via classical conditioning and not by direct stimulation of a drug or other factor.

Confirmation bias: Phenomenon by which, when we believe something is true, we change the way we interpret new information and the way we look at the world because of it. We tend to try to confirm our belief and have a bias in how we process information.

Constraint cultures: Cultures where people believe everything is in the hands of God or is fate.

Contemplation: Stage in the Transtheoretical Model where people recognize they may be doing something unhealthy.

Control cultures: Cultures where people believe that they have absolute control of their outcomes (similar to having an internal locus of control).

Coping: Process of making efforts to manage distressing problems and emotions that affect the physical and psychological outcomes of stress.

Coronary artery disease: Disease developing due to the build-up of a combination of fat, salts, and scar tissue or plaque in the arteries that supply the heart with blood. The build-up can lead to heart failure or heart attack.

Correlation coefficient: Statistical measure of the association between two or more variables. It is represented by the letter r and can range from $+1.00$ to -1.00. Values closer to 1 (regardless of sign) signify stronger associations.

Counterirritation: Process by which we may try to reduce pain by itching or poking a point on our skin around where the pain is felt.

Creative nonadherence: When patients indirectly disobey their doctors' orders often by modifying and supplementing their treatment plans.

Cultural competency: Health-care provider's understanding of patients' cultural characteristics, values, and traditions.

Culture: Dynamic, yet stable, set of goals, beliefs, and attitudes shared by a group of people. Culture can also include similar physical characteristics (e.g., skin color), psychological characteristics (e.g., levels of hostility), and common superficial features (e.g., hairstyle and clothing).

***Curanderismo*:** Holistic system of healing practiced by many Latin Americans and blending spirituality and Western approaches to health and healing.

Curative surgery: Treatment for cancer used to remove the growth.

Current procedural terminology (CPT) manual: The American Medical Association's policy specifying billing codes designed to capture behavioral services provided to patients to address physical health problems.

Cytotoxicity: The degree to which something is toxic to living cells and a measure of the strength of immune cells.

da Vinci, Leonardo: A Florentine artist, painter, sculptor, architect, engineer, and scientist who lived from 1452 to 1519. Leonardo studied the structure of the body using dissection and created elaborate anatomical drawings of humans and animals that aided medical research of the same.

Debulking surgery: Treatment to reduce the tumor mass in cancer.

Dementia: A term to describe a group of symptoms such as problems in thinking and remembering, often experienced by older adults.

Denial: One of the first psychological reactions felt the moment a person is informed that he or she has a chronic illness or realizes he or she is dying.

Diabetes mellitus: Severe, chronic form of diabetes caused by insufficient production of insulin and resulting in disruption in the breaking down and storage of carbohydrates, fats, and proteins. This disease often appears in childhood and is characterized by increased sugar levels in the blood and urine and excessive thirst.

Diagnostic surgery: Process of removing a small amount of tissue either to identify a cancer or to make a diagnosis.

Diathesis-stress model: Idea that some individuals may have physiological predispositions to certain factors such as depression, stress, or pain that interacts with psychological factors to cause those outcomes.

Differentiation: Process by which a less specialized cell becomes a more specialized cell. The extent to which differentiation occurs is an indicator of the strength of one's immune system.

Eating disorders: Severe disturbance in eating behaviors. Diagnostic criteria are currently provided for two eating disorders, anorexia nervosa and bulimia nervosa, and a third general category, eating disorder not otherwise specified.

Ecological theory: A way of examining behavior developed by Bronfrenbrenner, and that identifies different levels or systems in which the individual acts rather than just focusing on the individual.

Effect size: An objective and standardized measure of the significance and magnitude of a result of a statistical test.

Efferent pathways: Sensory nerve fibers transmitting signals from the spinal cord to receptors in the skin and tissues.

Epidemiology: Branch of medicine that studies the frequency, distribution, and causes of different diseases with an emphasis on the role of the physical and social environment.

Etiology: The origin and causes of diseases.

Euthanasia: The termination of life by the injection of a lethal drug.

Evidence-based treatments: Treatments that are dependent on critically evaluated research and are essentially empirically tested.

Exercise: Activity planned with the goal of improving one or more aspects of physical fitness.

Experiment: Form of research design that helps us determine causality. In experiments, the researcher manipulates one variable, the independent variable, and measures how changes in this variable influence another variable, the dependent variable.

Extended family: Family consisting of a blended or nuclear family plus grandparents or grandchildren, aunts, uncles, and other relatives.

Familialism: Cultural value that emphasizes close family relationships, bonds, and ties.

Fatalism: The belief that a person with cancer cannot live a normal life and will die.

Fight-or-flight theory: Walter Cannon's theory of stress hypothesizing that organism's respond to stressful events with a nervous system activation that prepares them to actively engage the stressor. The body essentially is energized to either fight the stressor or flee.

Fixed time: Cultural orientation toward time where individuals are exact with regard to time and expect to be somewhere or start events at exactly the time specified.

Fluid time: Cultural orientation toward time where individuals are flexible with regard to time and do not expect to be someplace or start engagements or events at exactly the time specified.

Food preferences: Biologically programmed inclinations toward certain foods. Can be modified by experiences.

Framingham study: Large-scale longitudinal study following more than 5,000 residents of Framingham, Massachusetts, that has contributed to our understanding of heart disease.

French paradox: The fact that most people in France have a diet that is high in fat but still have lower rates of heart disease.

Galen: Physician of the Emperor Marcus Aurelius in Rome. Galen lived from 129 to 216. One of the most influential of the Greek physicians, he published a wide body of work that shaped Western biomedicine.

Gate control theory: Model of pain proposing that key processes in the experience of pain take place in the dorsal horn substantia gelatinosa of the spinal cord and are influenced by the brain.

General adaptation syndrome: Hans Selye's theory of stress suggesting that organisms have a general way of responding to all stressors. When faced with a stressor, the body first goes into a state of alarm, then attempts to cope during a period of resistance, and finally breaks down in a state of exhaustion.

Grouping variables: Variables such as race or ethnicity often statistically controlled for in analyses where culture is not the focus of the study. Hardiness personality trait characterized by the ability to bounce back into action after facing a stressor.

Harvey, William: British physician who lived from 1578 to 1657. His 1628 paper, "An Anatomical Study of the Motion of the Heart and of the Blood in Animals," first explained how blood was pumped from the heart throughout the body, then returned to the heart.

Hazard ratio: A measure of relative risk of a treatment or intervention referring to the probability of seeing a certain event in a treatment group versus a control group.

Health: State of complete physical, mental, and social well-being. The health belief model is a major theory of health behavior that suggests that our beliefs relating to the effectiveness, ease, and consequences of doing (or nor doing) a certain behavior will determine whether we do (or not do) that behavior.

Health disparities: Differences in health that are not only unnecessary and avoidable but, in addition, are considered unfair and unjust.

Health education: Term for the collection of efforts to teach people to limit behaviors detrimental to their health and increase behaviors that are conducive to health. Health educators pay attention to a range of factors including the individual, interpersonal relationships, institutions, community, and public policy.

Health psychology: The area of psychology that focuses on how biological, psychological, and society factors can influence how we stay healthy, why we get sick, and how we cope best and recover from illness.

Healthy behaviors: Any specific behaviors that maintain and enhance health.

Healthy People 2020: A science-based, 10-year national program designed to promote health and prevent disease.

Highly active antiretroviral therapy (HAART): Most commonly used treatment for AIDS that involves many different anti-HIV drugs that keep the virus from replicating.

Hippocrates: A Greek physician often referred to as the father of medicine, who lived from 460 to 370 B.C. He based his medical practice on observations and on the study of the human body. He held the belief that illness had a physical and a rational explanation.

Homeostasis: An optimal level or ideal level of bodily functions. This varies for each individual and relates to blood glucose level, body temperature, rate of circulation, and breathing.

Hospice: Nursing homes where the dying are comforted and their pain and other symptoms are alleviated.

Human immunodeficiency virus (HIV): The virus responsible for causing AIDS.

Humoral-mediated immunity: Form of immune reaction that takes place at the level of the tissue and involving immune cells circulating in the blood. Humoral-mediated immunity involves the action of B cells although the first stages are similar to the process for cell-mediated immunity.

Hypertension: Medical term for high blood pressure, a condition in which the blood pressure remains chronically elevated.

Hypochondriac: A psychological disorder characterized by excessive preoccupation with one's health and constant worry about developing physical illnesses.

Illness behaviors: Varying ways individuals respond to physiological symptoms, monitor internal states, define and interpret symptoms, make attributions, take remedial actions, and use various forms of informal and formal care.

Illness delay: Time between the recognition that one is ill to the decision to seek care.

Illusory correlation: Belief that our expectations have been correct more times than they actually have been.

Immununotherapy: Treatment involving the activation of the body's own immune system to fight cancer or other diseases.

Indo-Mediterranean diet: Diet rich in whole grains, fruits, vegetables, walnuts, and almonds.

Incidence rates: Frequency of new cases of a disease during a year.

Information-motivation-behavioral skills: Theoretical model of health behavior change devised primarily for reducing unhealthy practices associated with AIDS and which provides a framework for guiding HIV risk-reduction interventions.

Informational involvement: Measure of how much the patient wants to know about his or her illness and specific details of its treatment.

Insulin: Major endocrine hormone secreted by the islet cells of the pancreas. It facilitates the use of glucose by the body's cells and plays a major role in the metabolism of food.

Intention: A person's subjective probability that he or she will perform the behavior in question.

Interventions: Specific programs designed to assess levels of behaviors, introduce ways to change them, measure whether change has occurred, and assess the impact of the change.

Ischemia: Condition in which the blood flow is restricted to a part of the body. For example, cardiac ischemia occurs when blood flow and oxygen to the heart muscle is disrupted. Ischemias often lead to heart attacks.

Lay-referral system: Nonprofessionals such as family, friends, and neighbors who patients rely on to help cope with illness symptoms instead of seeking biomedical treatment.

Leading health indicators: The major health concerns in the United States at the beginning of the 21st century as reflected by the Healthy People 2020 program.

Leukemias: Cancers that are found in the blood and bone marrow.

Life expectancy: The age at which a person would be expected to die given biopsychosocial factors existing in society at that time.

Living will: A legal document in which a person clearly specifies medical treatments in conditions when he or she is unable to express consent such as when life support should be terminated.

Logistic regression: Statistical analysis that predicts the probability of the occurrence of an event.

Lymphomas: Cancers of the lymphatic system.

Maintenance: Stage in the Transtheoretical Model where people try to not fall back into performing their unhealthy behaviors or relapsing. They may still be changing their behaviors and performing new behaviors, but they are not doing them as often as someone in the action stage.

Malignant: Cancerous tumors.

Mastectomy: Breast removal.

Mastery: The extent to which one regards one's life chances as being under one's own control.

Mediation: Intervening process (variable) through which an antecedent variable influences an outcome variable. Mediation can be described as a relationship where an independent variable changes a mediating variable, which then changes a dependent variable.

Melatonin: A hormone produced in the brain by the pineal gland. The production and release of melatonin is stimulated by darkness and suppressed by light.

Menopause: Stage when the female ovaries stop producing eggs. It occurs around the age of 50 and is accompanied by a drop in hormone levels.

Metastasize: Spreading to other parts of the body.

Moderator: Variable that changes the magnitude (and sometimes the direction) of the relationship between an antecedent variable and an outcome variable.

Modulation: The neural activity leading to the control of pain transmissions between the various parts of the brain.

Morbidity: Number of cases of a disease that exist at a given point in time.

Mortality: Number of deaths related to a specific cause.

Multidimensional approaches: Research that includes a consideration of biological, psychological, and societal processes incorporating different levels of measurement, different research methods, and different statistical analyses.

Multivariate analyses of variance (MANOVAs): A statistical test that examines if group means on a number of related variables vary from each other.

Myocardial infarctions: Also known as angina pectoris or cardiac arrest. Chest pain is a common symptom.

MyPlate: A schematic guide that offers personalized eating plans and interactive tools to help plan and assess food choices, and advice to find a balance between food and physical activity, and to get the most nutrition out of calories consumed.

National Electronic Clinical Trials and Research (NECTAR): Electronic network that makes the results of clinical trials easy to find and use.

National Institutes of Health (NIH) Roadmap: Government funded and organized plan that sketches out 28 cross-institutional projects especially designed to tackle multifaceted issues such as obesity that result from a variety of different biopsychosocial factors.

Neoplasms: Cells that show abnormal growth.

Neuropathic pain: Pure nociception without significant psychological pain.

Neutral cultures: Cultures such as that of Japan that do not sanction the open display of emotions.

Nociception: Technical name for pain, the activation of specialized nerve fibers that signal the occurrence of tissue damage.

Nonimmunologic defenses: Body defenses and barriers that do not rely on the cells of the immune system and are referred to as nonimmunologic defenses. Examples include the skin, mucus, and the process of coughing.

Nonspecific immunity: Internal immune processes that do not differentiate between different types of germs or disease threats. These nonspecific immune defenses work on a wide variety of disease-causing microorganisms.

Normative beliefs: What a person thinks others think about the behavior in question.

Nuclear family: Family consisting usually of two parents and unmarried children.

Obesity: Having a body mass index (BMI) of 30 or greater.

Odds ratio: Ratio of the odds of an event occurring in one group to the odds of it occurring in another group. An odds ratio of 1 suggests the phenomenon is equally likely in both groups. An odds ratio greater than 1 suggests the phenomenon is more likely to occur in the first group.

Opiates: Drugs, such as morphine or codeine, containing or derived from opium and tending to induce sleep and alleviate pain.

Opioids: Substances produced in the body that have effects similar to opiates (such as morphine). Mainly associated with the relief of pain.

Opportunistic infections: Infections caused by organisms that cannot induce disease in people with normal immune systems but take the opportunity to flourish in people with HIV infection.

Optimism: Personality trait where a person has a general tendency to expect that good things, rather than bad things, will happen.

Pain-prone personality: Personality type that predisposes a person to experience persistent pain.

Palliative care: Form of treatment aimed at alleviating symptoms without necessarily affecting the cause.

Palliative surgery: Treatment used to treat complications of advanced disease (not as a cure).

Pattern theory: Idea that pain results from a combination of impulses from nerve endings. Different patterns of stimulations caused different types of pain.

Personality: An individual's unique set of consistent behavioral traits, where traits are durable dispositions to behave in a particular way in a variety of situations.

Phagocytosis: Process by which immune cells (e.g., macrophages) destroy germs or viruses by engulfing them and breaking them down.

Physical activity: Any bodily movement produced by contract ion of the skeletal muscles that results in energy expenditure.

Physician-assisted suicide: Euthanasia involving a physician who supplies the actual drug although not actually administering it himself or herself.

Placebo: An inactive substance that appears similar to the experimental drug.

Positive Psychology: The area of psychology that involves the scientific study of the strengths and virtues that enable individuals and communities to thrive. Major foci are emotions and individual traits.

Pre-term birth: A baby born before 37 weeks of pregnancy.

Precontemplation: Stage in the Transtheoretical Model when people are not aware that they are practicing a behavior that is unhealthy or do not intend to take any action to change a behavior (especially not in the next 6 months).

Preparation: Stage in the Transtheoretical Model where people are ready to take action to change the behavior. They generate a plan and have specific ideas of how to change.

Prevalence rates: Proportion of the population that has a particular disease at a particular time (commonly reported as cases per 1,000 or 100,000 people).

Preventive surgery: Treatment to remove tissue that is not yet malignant but that has a high chance of turning malignant.

Primary appraisal: First stage in Lazarus's cognitive appraisal model of stress where we determine the nature of an event, whether harmful, damaging, or challenging.

Private body consciousness: Degree to which one is sensitive to one's health states resulting in increased vigilance over the body.

Progressive illness: Chronic illnesses that get worse with time.

Proliferation: Extent to which the immune cells multiply and produce more cells. Proliferation is mostly seen as a sign of a strong immune system.

Psychogenic pain: Purely psychological pain without a physiological basis.

Psychoneuroimmunology: A field of study that evolved out of the disciplines of biology and psychology and is dedicated to understanding the interplay between these disparate systems.

Qi: Chinese word to describe the natural energy of the universe. The main goal of Traditional Chinese Medicine is to balance the qi of the body and to increase qi if needed when one is ill. It also translates to life force or air.

Quality of life: A measure of physical status and functioning, psychological status, social functioning, and the presence of the disease- or treatment-related symptoms.

Radiation therapy: Treatment involving the use of radioactive particles aimed at the DNA of the cancer cells in order to disable them.

Randomized clinical trials (RCTs): Commonly used experimental method in health psychology research in which one group gets an experimental drug or intervention treatment and a second group unknowingly gets a placebo or nothing (the control group).

Reductionist: Process of explaining something by breaking it down to its smallest part.

Regression analysis: Statistical test in which an outcome is predicted from a set of variables.

Religiosity: Measure of how religious a person is, commonly assessed by counting the frequency of temple/church/mosque/synagogue attendance, the average frequency of prayer, and the commitment to religious rituals.

Remitting illness: An illness that eases with time and ends.

Replication crisis: The issue in contemporary science where the findings from past research cannot be found again in identically designed studies.

Risky families: Families in which a lot of arguing occurs between family members and in which relationships are cold, unsupportive, and neglectful.

Role ambiguity: Degree to which required information regarding role expectations is available, clear, and communicated to the individual playing the role (e.g., an employee).

Role conflict: Incompatibility of expectations for a given role and between different roles.

Role theory: A role is the set of behaviors to be performed and is determined by one's own perceptions and the expectations of others. As an individual accumulates roles, the quantity and incompatibility of role demands increase. An individual experiences role strain that results in increased role conflict and ambiguity.

Sarcomas: Cancers of the muscles, bones, and cartilage.

Screening: Process of checking for cancer.

Secondary appraisal: Second stage in Lazarus's cognitive appraisal model of stress where we determine whether we have the resources to manage an even an event. Relates to primarily appraisal.

Secondhand smoke: Tobacco smoke inhaled by nonsmokers who are in the presence of smokers.

Self-efficacy: Conviction that one can successfully execute the behavior required to produce the outcome.

Self-fulfilling prophecy: Belief that if one thinks something is going to happen, it is more likely to happen. Social psychologists suggest a person's expectancy of an outcome or behavior can subconsciously or consciously change her behavior to make the outcome more likely.

Self-management programs: Treatments for pain relief that make the patient with chronic pain the one with the major responsibility for making the change rather than the doctor or the health professional staff.

Sensory specific satiety: When only one type of food is available at a meal, people eat a moderate amount of it. If a second food is then introduced, the amount of the new food eaten will be more than if it was presented by itself.

Serological testing algorithm for recent HIV seroconversion: New technology developed by the CDC that determines which positive HIV tests represent new HIV infections (those that occurred within approximately the past 5 months).

Sex: An innate, biological characteristic. Men have an XY sex chromosome. Women have an XX sex chromosome.

Sexual mixing: The extent to which people engage in sexual activities with sexual partners from other sexual networks (dissortative mating) versus partners from their own network (assortative mixing).

Shaman: Although a general term used for the practitioners of folk medicine, the word *shaman* originated in Eastern Europe and means she or he who knows. Shamans are also referred to as medicine men and use a range of herbs and rituals to cure.

Social convoy model: Theory suggesting that people are motivated to maintain their social network sizes as they themselves age, despite changes in the composition of the networks. Individuals construct and maintain social relationships while becoming increasingly aware of specific strengths and weaknesses of particular members.

Social support: Feeling of being loved, esteemed, and cared for. Also, emotional, informational, or instrumental assistance from others.

Socioeconomic status (SES): Measure of an individual, family, or group's relative economic and social level most commonly measured by income and education level.

Socioemotional selectivity theory: Theory of social support change that proposes that people prune their social networks to maintain a desired emotional state depending on the extent to which time is perceived as limited. Basic functions of social interaction, such as maintaining a good mood, differ in respect to their relative importance for determining social preferences across the life span.

Somatic pain: Physiological pain without specific tissue damage.

Specificity: Idea that pain was a specific independent sensation such as heat or touch, with specialized receptors responding to specific stimuli.

Spillover: Transmission of stress from one domain of an individual's life into other domains of life.

Staging surgery: Treatment to ascertain in which stage of development the cancer is. This form of surgery helps determine how far the cancer has spread and provides a clinical stage for the growth.

Standard drink: A 12-ounce serving of beer (a standard bottle or can), a 5-ounce glass of wine, or a 1.5-ounce of gin, vodka, rum, or scotch is a standard serving.

Statistically significant: When the probability of the results being found by chance are very small, often less than 5 in 100.

Stereotypes: Widely held beliefs that people have certain characteristics because of their membership in a particular group.

Stimulation-produced analgesia: Process by which electrically stimulating the brain can reduce pain.

Stress: Defined in a variety of ways but most simply as an upsetting of homeostasis. A state caused when the perceived demands on the organism exceeded the resources to meet those demands.

Stress contagion effect: When two or more domains or areas of a person's life are connected, stress from one area can spill over into the other area. If work and home are interconnected, stress from one area can influence the ocher.

Stress-induced analgesia: Pain relief produced when our body releases opioids when we are stressed, a state that can also be induced by motor activity such as physical activity.

Stroke: A type of cardiovascular disease that affects the arteries leading to and within the brain. A stroke occurs when a blood vessel to the brain is blocked either by a clot or bursts. When that happens, part of the brain cannot get the blood (and oxygen) it needs, so it starts to die.

Structural equation modeling: A statistical analysis that tests for how well a theorized set of relationships between variables matches data collected.

Synergistic effect: A phenomenon where two or more factors (e.g., smoking and drinking) act together to create an effect greater than that predicted by knowing only the separate effects of the individual factors.

Systematic desensitization: A form of classical conditioning in which stressful thoughts or events are paired with relaxation.

Tao: A major Chinese philosophical approach to life and the universe. Based on the *Tao Te Ching* written by Lao Tzu approximately 2,000 years ago, the tao is translated to mean way of life or order of the universe and can be also seen as a state of being.

Tend-and-befriend: Shelley Taylor's and colleagues' theory of how women, when faced with a stressor, may either tend to infants or others and befriend other females and cultivate female bonds as opposed to fighting or fleeing.

Terminal illnesses: Chronic illnesses such as cancer or AIDS are often referred to as advancing or terminal because people with these diseases often die after a relatively short time ranging from months to a few years.

Termination: Stage in the Transtheoretical Model where a person is no longer tempted by the unhealthy behavior she has changed.

Threshold: Level of stimuli needed to experience something such as pain or stress.

TNM system: Most common method used to stage cancer. The T describes the size of the tumor and whether cancer has spread to nearby tissues and organs. The N describes how far the cancer has spread to nearby lymph nodes. The M indicates the extent to which the cancer has metastasized.

Tolerance level: Amount beyond which pain becomes unbearable and intolerable.

Traditional Chinese Medicine (TCM): Holistic system of medicine and approach to health and healing originating in China approximately 4,000 years ago. Major treatments include acupuncture and the use of herbs.

Transduction: Process occurring at the level of the receptors where chemical, mechanical, or thermal energy is converted in electrochemical nerve impulses.

Transtheoretical Model: Major theory of health behavior change that identifies different stages we process through as we think about, attempt to, and finally change any specific behavior.

Triggers: Factors that increase the likelihood that a person will seek treatment.

Type C personality: Cancer-prone personality where the person is cooperative, appeasing, unassertive, and compliant and someone who does not express negative emotions.

Ultraviolet (UV) rays: Electromagnetic radiation present in sunlight and associated with skin cancer.

Use: Time delay between the decision to seek care and the actual behaviors to obtain medical health care.

Vesalius, Andreas: A Flemish anatomist and doctor, who lived from 1514 to 1564. His dissections of the human body helped to correct misconceptions dating from ancient times.

Vital signs: Five basic measures that doctors get from patients (temperature, pulse, blood pressure, pain level, and respiration).

Yin and yang: Two opposing forces that, according to traditional Chinese Medicine, combine to create everything in the universe. Yin and yang are mutually interdependent, constantly interactive, and potentially interchangeable forces.

REFERENCES

Abbott, A. (2011). City living marks the brain. *Nature, 474*(7352), 429. doi:10.1038/474429a

Abboud, S., De Penning, E., Brawner, B. M., Menon, U., Glanz, K., & Sommers, M. S. (2017). Cervical cancer screening among Arab women in the United States: An integrative review. *Oncology Nursing Forum, 44*(1), E20–E33. doi:10.1188/17.ONF.E20–E33

Abel, E., & Chambers, K. B. (2004). Factors that influence vulnerability to STDs and HIV/AIDS among Hispanic women. *Health Care for Women International, 25*, 761–780.

Abradio-Lanza, A. F., Mendoza, S., & Armbrister, A. N. (2019). Latino health. In T. Revenson & R. A. R. Gurung (Eds.), *Handbook of health psychology* (3e). New York, NY: Routledge.

Abraido-Lanza, A. F., Vasquez, E., & Echeverria, S. E. (2004). En las manos de Dios [in God's hands]: Religious and other forms of coping among Latinos with arthritis. *Journal of Consulting and Clinical Psychology, 72*, 91–102.

Abrams, D. B., Herzog, T. A., Emmons, K. M., & Linnan, L. (2000). Stages of change versus addiction: A replication and extension. *Nicotine and Tobacco Research, 2*, 223–229.

Acevedo, V. (2008). Cultural competence in a group intervention designed for Latino patients living with HIV/AIDS. *Health and Social Work, 33*(2), 111–120.

Adam, B. D., Hart, T. A., Mohr, J., Coleman, T., & Vernon, J. (2017). HIV-related syndemic pathways and risk subjectivities among gay and bisexual men: A qualitative investigation. *Culture, Health & Sexuality, 19*(11), 1254–1267. doi:10.1080/13691058.2017.1309461

Adamo, S. A. (2016). The stress response and immune system share, borrow, and reconfigure their physiological network elements: Evidence from the insects. *Hormones and Behavior, 88*, 25–30. doi:10.1016/j.yhbeh.2016.10.003

Adams, A., Buckingham, C., Lindenmeyer, A., McKinlay, J., Link, C., Marceau, L., & Arber, S. (2008). The influence of patient and doctor gender on diagnosing coronary heart disease. *Sociology of Health and Illness, 30*(1), 1–18.

Adams, J., & White, M. (2007). Are the stages of change socioeconomically distributed? A scoping review. *American Journal of Health Promotion, 21*, 237–247.

Adams, K. F., Schatzkin, A., Harris, T. B., Kipnis, V., Mouw, T., Ballard-Barbash, R. . . . Leitzmann, M. F. (2006). Overweight, obesity, and mortality in a large prospective cohort of persons 50 to 71 years old. *New England Journal of Medicine, 355*, 763–778.

Adams, P. F., Hendershot, G. E., & Marano, M. A. (1999). Current estimates from the National Health Interview Survey, 1996. National Center for Health Statistics. *Vital Health Statistics, 10*, 1–203.

Adeola, M., Baird, C. L., Sands, L. P., Longoria, N., Henry, U., Nielsen, J., & Shields, C. G. (2015). Active despite pain: Patient experiences with guided imagery with relaxation compared to planned rest. *Clinical Journal of Oncology Nursing, 19*(6), 649–652. doi:10.1188/15.CJON.649-652

Ader, R., & Cohen, N. (1975). Behaviorally conditioned immunosuppression. *Psychosomatic Medicine, 37*, 333–340.

Ader, R., Felten, D. L., & Cohen, N. (1991). *Psychoneuroimmunology* (2nd ed.). San Diego, CA: Academic Press.

Adler, E., Hoon, M. A., Mueller, K. L., Chandrasekar, J., Ryba, N. J. P., & Zuker, C. S. (2000). A novel family of mammalian taste receptors. *Cell, 100*, 693–702.

Adler, N. E., & Ostrove, J. M. (1999). Socioeconomic status and health: What we know and what we don't. In N. E. Adler & M. Marmot (Eds.), *Socioeconomic status and health in industrial nations: Social, psychological, and biological pathways* (pp. 3–15). New York, NY: New York Academy of Sciences.

Adler, N. E., & Rehkopf, D. H. (2008). U.S. Disparities in health: Descriptions, causes, and mechanisms. *Annual Review of Public Health, 29*, 235–252.

Adler, N. E., Boyce, T., Chesney, M. A., Cohen, S., Folkman, S., Kahn, R. L., & Syme, S. L. (1994). Socioeconomic status and health: The challenge of the gradient. *American Psychologist, 49*(1), 15–24. doi.10.1037/0003 066X.49.1.15

Adler, N. E., Singh-Manoux, A., Schwartz, J., Stewart, J., Matthews, K., & Marmot, M. G. (2008). Social status and health: A comparison of British civil servants in Whitehall II with European and African Americans in CARDIA. *Social Science and Medicine, 66*, 1034–1045.

Aekplakorn, W., Hogan, M. C., Tiptaradol, S., Wibulpolprasert, S., Punyaratabandhu, P., & Lim, S. S. (2008). Tobacco and hazardous or harmful alcohol use in Thailand: Joint prevalence and associations with socioeconomic factors. *Addictive Behaviors, 33*, 503–514.

Affleck, G., Tennen, H., & Apter, A. (2001). Optimism, pessimism, and daily life with chronic illness. In E. C. Chang (Ed.), *Optimism & pessimism: Implications for theory, research, and practice* (pp. 147–168). Washington, DC: American Psychological Association.

Affleck, G., Tennen, H., Urrows, S., Higgins, P., Abeles, M., Hall, C., Karoly, P., & Newton, C. (1998). Fibromyalgia and women's pursuit of personal goals: A daily process analysis. *Health Psychology, 17*, 40–77.

Agarwal, D. P., & Seitz, H. K. (2001). *Alcohol in health and disease.* New York, NY: Marcel Dekker.

Agarwal, P. K., Shi, L., Daniel, L. M., Yang, P. H., Khoo, P. C., Quek, B. H., . . . Rajadurai, V. S. (2017). Prospective evaluation of the ages and stages questionnaire 3rd edition in very-low-birthweight infants. *Developmental Medicine & Child Neurology, 59*(5), 484–489. doi:10.1111/dmcn.13307

Agarwal, R. P., Kumar, A., & Lewis, J. E. (2015). A pilot feasibility and acceptability study of yoga/meditation on the quality of life and markers of stress in persons living with HIV who also use crack cocaine. *Journal of Alternative and Complementary Medicine, 21*(3), 152–158. doi:10.1089/acm.2014.0112

Agnihotri, V., & Agnihotri V. (2017). Hinduism, Jainism, and Sikhism. In D. Von Dras (Ed.), *Better Health through Spiritual Practices* (pp. 29–42). Santa Barbara, CA: Praeger.

Ahmadi, F. (2006). *Culture, religion and spirituality in coping: The example of cancer patients in Sweden.* Uppsala, Sweden: Uppsala University Press.

Ahmed, N., Bestall, J. C., Ahmedzai, S. H., Payne, S. A., Clark, D., & Noble, B. (2007). Systematic review of the problems and issues of accessing specialist palliative care by patients, careers and health and social care professionals. *Palliative Medicine, 18*, 525–542.

Ai, A. L., Peterson, C., & Huang, B. (2003). The effect of religious-spiritual coping on positive attitudes of adult Muslim refugees from Kosovo and Bosnia. *International Journal for the Psychology of Religion, 13*, 29–47.

Ai, M., Otokozawa, S., Asztalos, B. F., White, C. C., Cupples, L., Nakajima, K., . . . Schaefer, E. J. (2011). Adiponectin: An independent risk factor for coronary heart disease in men in the Framingham Offspring Study. *Atherosclerosis, 217*(2), 543–548. doi:10.1016/j.atherosclerosis.2011.05.035

Aiken, L. G., West, S. G., Woodward, C. K., Reno, R. R., & Reynolds, K. D. (1994). Increasing screening mammography in asymptomatic women: Evaluation of a second-generation, theory-based program. *Health Psychology, 13*, 526–538.

Aiken, L. S., Gerend, M. A., & Jackson, K. M. (2001). Subjective risk and health protective behavior: Cancer screening and cancer prevention. In A. Baum, T. A. Revenson, & J. E. Singer (Eds.), *Handbook of health psychology* (1e, pp. 727–746). Mahwah, NJ: Erlbaum.

Aiken, L. S., Gerend, M. A., Jackson, K. M., & Ranby, K. W. (2012). Subjective risk and health-protective behavior: Prevention and early detection. In A. Baum, T. A. Revenson, & J. Singer (Eds.), *Handbook of health psychology* (2e, pp. 113–145). New York, NY: Taylor & Francis.

Aiken, L. S., West, S. G. (1991). *Multiple regression: Testing and interpreting interactions*. Newbury Park, CA: SAGE.

Ainsworth, M. D. S., Blehar, M. C., Water, E., & Wall, S. (1978). *Patterns of attachment: A psychological study of the strange situation*. Oxford, UK: Erlbaum.

Aisenberg, E. (2001). The effects of exposure to community violence upon Latina mothers and preschool children. *Hispanic Journal of Behavioral Sciences, 23*, 378–398.

Aitken, C., Higgs, P., Bowden, S. (2008). Differences in the social networks of ethnic Vietnamese and non-Vietnamese injecting drug users and their implications for blood-borne virus transmission. *Epidemiology and Infection, 136*(3), 410–416.

Ajzen, I. (1988). *Attitudes, personality, and behavior*. Homewood, IL: Dorsey Press.

Ajzen, I., & Madden, T. J. (1986). Prediction of goal-directed behavior: Attitudes, intentions, and perceived behavioral control. *Journal of Experimental Social Psychology, 22*, 453–474.

Akil, H., Mayer, D. J., & Liebeskind, J. C. (1976). Antagonism of stimulation-produced analgesia by naloxone, a narcotic antagonist. *Science, 191*, 961–962.

Akins, S., Smith, C. L., & Mosher, C. (2010). Pathways to adult alcohol abuse across racial/ethnic groups: An application of general strain and social learning theories. *Journal of Drug Issues, 40*(2), 321–351.

Alarcón, G., Cservenka, A., & Nagel, B. J. (2017). Adolescent neural response to reward is related to participant sex and task motivation. *Brain and Cognition, 111*, 51–62. doi:10.1016/j.bandc.2016.10.003

Alban, M. W., & Pocknell, V. (2017). Cognitive factors affecting freeze-like behavior in humans. *Journal of General Psychology, 144*(2), 140–156. doi:10.1080/00221309.2016.1276046

Albarracín, D., Leeper, J., Earl, A., & Durantini, M. (2008). From brochures to videos to counseling: exposure to HIV-prevention programs. *AIDS and Behavior, 12*(3), 354–362.

Albarracin, J., Albarracin, D., & Durantini, M. (2008). Effects of HIV-prevention interventions for samples with higher and lower percents of Latinos and Latin Americans: A meta-analysis of change in condom use and knowledge. *AIDS and Behavior, 12*(4), 521–543.

Albarrcin, D., McNatt, P. S., Williams, W. R., Hoxworth, T., Zenilman, J., Ho, R. M., . . . Iatesta, M. (2000). Structure of outcome beliefs in condom use. *Health Psychology, 19*, 458–468.

Albert, C. M., Manson, J. E., Cook, N. R., Ajani, U. A., Gaziano, J. M., & Hennekens, C. E. (1999). Moderate alcohol consumption and the risk of sudden cardiac death among U.S. male physicians. *Circulation, 100*, 944–950.

Alcántara, C., Abelson, J. L., & Gone, J. P. (2012). Beyond anxious predisposition: *Padecer de Nervios* and *Ataque de Nervios* add incremental validity to predictions of current distress among Mexican mothers? *Depression & Anxiety 29*(1), 23–31. doi:10.1002/da.20855

Aldwin, C. (2019). Coping. In T. A. Revenson & R. A. R. Gurung (Eds.), *Handbook of health psychology* (3e). New York, NY: Routledge.

Aldwin, C. M. (1994). *Stress, coping, and development: An integrative perspective*. New York, NY: Guilford Press.

Aldwin, C. M., & Revenson, T. A. (1987). Does coping help? A reexamination of the relation between coping and mental health. *Journal of Personality and Social Psychology, 53*, 337–348.

Aldwin, C. M., Sutton, K. J., & Lachman, M. (1996). The development of coping resources in adulthood. *Journal of Personality, 64*, 837–871.

Aldwin, C., Folkman, S., Schaefer C., Coyne, J. C., & Lazarus, R. S. (1980, August). Ways of coping: A process measure. Paper presented at the meeting of the American Psychological Association, Montreal, PQ, Canada.

Alexander, E. (1950). *Psychosomatic medicine*. New York, NY: Norton.

Alexander, G., Innes, K. E., Bourguignon, C., Bovbjerg, V. E., Kulbok, P., & Taylor, A. (2012). Patterns of yoga practice and physical activity following a yoga intervention for adults with or at risk for type 2 diabetes. *Journal of Physical Activity & Health, 9*(1), 53–61.

Alexander, R. W. (2010). President's address: Common mechanisms of multiple disease: Why vegetables and exercise are good for you. *Transactions of the American Clinical and Climatological Association, 121*, 1–20.

Alexander, V., Tripp, S., & Zak, P. J. (2015). Preliminary evidence for the neurophysiologic effects of online coupons: Changes in oxytocin, stress, and mood. *Psychology & Marketing, 32*(9), 977–986. doi:10.1002/mar.20831

Alhusen, J. L., Bullock, L., Sharps, P., Schminkey, D., Comstock, E., & Campbell, J. (2014). Intimate partner violence during pregnancy and adverse neonatal outcomes in low-income women. *Journal of Women's Health, 23*(11), 920–926. doi:10.1089/jwh.2014.4862

Ali, N., Nitschke, J. P., Cooperman, C., & Pruessner, J. C. (2017). Suppressing the endocrine and autonomic stress systems does not impact the emotional stress experience after psychosocial stress. *Psychoneuroendocrinology, 78*, 125–130. doi:10.1016/j.psyneuen.2017.01.015

Allen, A. P., Curran, E. A., Duggan, Á., Cryan, J. F., Chorcoráin, A. N., Dinan, T. G., . . . Clarke, G. (2017). A systematic review of the psychobiological burden of informal caregiving for patients with dementia: Focus on cognitive and biological markers of chronic stress. *Neuroscience and Biobehavioral Reviews, 73*, 123–164. doi:10.1016/j.neubiorev.2016.12.006

Allport, G. W. (1961). *Patterns and growth in personality*. New York, NY: Holt.

Al-Saffar, S., Borga, P., Edman, G., & Hallstrom, T. (2003). The etiology of post-traumatic stress disorder in four ethnic groups in outpatient psychiatry. *Social Psychiatry and Psychiatric Epidemiology, 38,* 456–462.

Altabe, M. N. (2001). Issues in the assessment and treatment of body image disturbance in culturally diverse populations. In J. K. Thompson (Ed.), *Body image, eating disorders, and obesity: An integrative guide for assessment and treatment* (pp. 129–147). Washington, DC: American Psychological Association.

Alvord, L. A., & Van Pelt, E. C. (2000). *The scalpel and the silver bear: The first Navajo woman surgeon combines Western medicine and traditional healing.* New York, NY: Bantam Books.

Amer, M. M. (2017). Islam and health. In D. Von Dras (Ed.), *Better health through spiritual practices* (pp. 183–204). Santa Barbara, CA: Praeger.

American Cancer Society. (2005). Incidence and mortality rates by site, race, and ethnicity, U.S., 1997–2001. Author, Atlanta, GA.

American Cancer Society. (2017a). American Cancer Society recommendations for the early detection of breast cancer. Author, Atlanta, GA. Retrieved from https://www.cancer.org/cancer/breast-cancer/screening-tests-and-early-detection/american-cancer-society-recommendations-for-the-early-detection-of-breast-cancer.html

American Cancer Society. (2017b). Cancer facts & figures 2017. Author, Atlanta, GA. Retrieved from https://www.cancer.org/content/dam/cancer-org/research/cancer-facts-and-statistics/annual-cancer-facts-and-figures/2017/cancer-facts-and-figures-2017.pdf

American Cancer Society. (2017c). How is chemotherapy used to treat cancer? Author, Atlanta, GA. Retrieved from https://www.cancer.org/treatment/treatments-and-side-effects/treatment-types/chemotherapy/how-is-chemotherapy-used-to-treat-cancer.html

American Cancer Society. (2017d). How surgery is used for cancer. Author, Atlanta, GA. Retrieved from https://www.cancer.org/treatment/treatments-and-side-effects/treatment-types/surgery/how-surgery-is-used-for-cancer.html

American Cancer Society. (2017e). Radiation therapy basics. Author, Atlanta, GA. Retrieved from https://www.cancer.org/treatment/treatments-and-side-effects/treatment-types/radiation/basics.html

American Cancer Society. (2017f). What kinds of cancer treatment are there? Author, Atlanta, GA. Retrieved from https://www.cancer.org/treatment/treatments-and-side-effects/complementary-and-alternative-medicine/complementary-and-alternative-methods-and-cancer/kinds-of-treatment.html

American Cancer Society. (2018). Cancer A–Z. Author, Atlanta, GA. Retrieved from www.cancer.org

American College of Occupational and Environmental Medicine. (2008). Occupational medicine practice guidelines. Retrieved from https://www.acoem.org/practiceguidelines.aspx

American College of Occupational and Environmental Medicine. (2008). Chronic pain treatment guidelines. In K. Hegmann (Ed.), *Occupational medicine practice guidelines* (2nd ed.). Beverly Farms, MA: OEM Press.

American Diabetes Association. (2000). Type 2 diabetes in children and adolescents. *Pediatrics, 105,* 671–680.

American Diabetes Association. (2018). Are you at risk? Retrieved from http://www.diabetes.org/

American Heart Association. (2004, December). African Americans and cardiovascular disease statistics. Author, Dallas, TX. Retrieved from http://www.americanheart.org/presenter.jhtml?identifier=1200000

American Heart Association. (2012). Executive summary: heart disease and stroke statistics 2012 update: A report from the American Heart Association. *Circulation 125,* 188–197. doi:10.1161/CIR.0b013e3182456d46

American Heart Association. (2018). What is cardiovascular disease? Retrieved from http://www.heart.org/HEARTORG/Conditions/What-is-Cardiovascular-Disease_UCM_301852_Article.jsp#.Wtynf9Pwai4

American Medical Association. (2012). Eliminating health disparities. Author, Chicago, IL. Retrieved from https://www.ama-assn.org/delivering-care/reducing-disparities-health-care

American Psychiatric Association. (1994). *Diagnostic and statistical manual of mental disorders: DSM-IV* (4th ed.). Washington, DC: Author.

American Psychiatric Association. (2000). *Diagnostic and statistical manual of mental disorders: DSM-IVR* (4e, rev.). Washington, DC: Author.

American Psychiatric Association. (2011). *DSM 5 development.* Washington, DC: Author.

American Psychological Association. (2012). Stress in America: Our health at risk. Author, Washington, DC. Retrieved from http://www.apa.org/news/press/releases/stress/2011/health-risk.pdf

American Psychological Association. (2017). Stress in America: The state of our nation. Author, Washington, D.C. Retrieved from http://www.apa.org/news/press/releases/stress/index.aspx

American Psychosomatic Society. (2018). Mission statement. Author, McLean, VA. Retrieved from http://www.psychosomatic.org/about/index.cfm

American Stroke Association. (2004). Reducing risk. Author, Washington, DC. Retrieved from http://www.strokeassociation.org/presenter.jhtml?identifier.jhtml?identifier=1200037. December 2004.

American Stroke Association. (2018). About stroke. Author, Washington, DC. Retrieved from http://www.strokeassociation.org/STROKEORG/AboutStroke/About-Stroke_UCM_308529_SubHomePage.jsp

Amirkhan, J. H. (1990). A factor analytically derived measure of coping: The coping strategy indicator. *Journal of Personality and Social Psychology, 59,* 1066–1074.

Anacker, A. M. J., & Beery, A. K. (2013). Life in groups: The roles of oxytocin in mammalian sociality. *Frontiers in Behavioral Neuroscience, 7,* 10. doi:10.3389/fnbeh.2013.00185

Anand, K. J. S., & Craig, K. D. (1996). Editorial: New perspectives on the definition of pain. *Pain, 67,* 3–6.

Anand, P., Kunnumakara, A. B., Sundaram, C., Harikumar, K. B., Tharakan, S. T., Lai, O. S., . . . Aggarwal, B. (2008). Cancer is a preventable disease that requires major lifestyle changes. *Pharmaceutical Research, 25*(9), 2097–2116.

Anand, S., & Yusuf, S. (1998). Risk stratification for sympathetic atherosclerosis. In J. S. Ginsberg (Ed.), *Critical decisions in thrombosis and hemostasis* (pp. 179–189). Hamilton, ON, Canada: BC Decker.

Anda, R., Williamson, D., Jones, D., Macera, C., Eaker, E., Glassman, A., & Marks, J. (1993). Depressed affect, hopelessness, and the risk of ischemic heart disease in a cohort of U.S. adults. *Epidemiology, 4,* 285–294.

Andersen, J. L., Schjerling, P., & Saltin, B. (2000). Muscle, genes and athletic performance. *Scientific American, 283*(3), 48.

Andersen, R. M., Rice, T. H., & Kominski, G. F. (Eds.). (2007). *Changing the U.S. health care system: Key issues in health services policy and management* (3e). San Francisco, CA: Jossey-Bass.

Andersen, R., Lewis, S. Z., Giachello, A. L., Aday, L. A., & Chiu, G. (1981). Access to medical care among the Hispanic population of the southwestern United States. *Journal of Health and Social Behavior, 22,* 78–89.

Anderson, B. L. (1992). Psychological interventions for cancer patients to enhance the quality of life. *Journal of Consulting and Clinical Psychology, 60*, 552–568.

Anderson, B. L. (2002). Behavioral outcomes following psychological interventions for cancer patients. *Journal of Consulting and Clinical Psychology, 70*, 590–610.

Anderson, B. L., & Tewfik, H. H. (1985). Psychological reactions to radiation therapy: Reconsideration of the adaptive aspects of anxiety. *Journal of Personality and Social Psychology, 48*, 1024–1032.

Anderson, B. L., Farrar, W. B., Golden-Kreutz, D., Kutz, L. A., MacCallum, R., Courtney, M. E., & Glaser, R. (1998). Stress and immune responses following surgical treatment for regional breast cancer. *Journal of the National Cancer Institute, 90*, 30–36.

Anderson, B. L., Kiecolt-Glaser, J. K., & Glaser, R. (1994). A biobehavioral model of cancer stress and disease course. *American Psychologist, 49*, 389–404.

Anderson, C. A., Shibuya, A., Ihori, N., Swing, E. L., Bushman, B. J., Sakamoto, A., . . . Saleem, M. (2010). Violent video game effects on aggression, empathy, and prosocial behavior in eastern and western countries: A meta-analytic review. *Psychological Bulletin, 136*, 151–173. doi:10.1037/a0018251

Anderson, G. (2018). Linking the biological underpinnings of depression: Role of mitochondria interactions with melatonin, inflammation, sirtuins, tryptophan catabolites, DNA repair and oxidative and nitrosative stress, with consequences for classification and cognition. *Progress in Neuro-Psychopharmacology & Biological Psychiatry, 80*, 255–266. doi:10.1016/j.pnpbp.2017.04.022

Anderson, J. M. (1993). Ethnocultural communities as partners in research. In R. Masie, L. L. Menseh, & K. A. McLeod (Eds.), *Health and cultures: Exploring the relationships* (vol. *1*, pp. 319–328). Oakville, ON, Canada: Mosaic Press.

Anderson, K. F., & Finch, J. K. (2017). The role of racial microaggressions, stress, and acculturation in understanding Latino health outcomes in the USA. *Race and Social Problems, 9*, 218–233. doi:10.1007/s12552-017-9212-2

Anderson, M. R., Akeeb, A., Lavela, J., Chen, Y., & Mellman, T. A. (2017). Period 3 gene polymorphism and sleep adaptation to stressful urban environments. *Journal of Sleep Research, 26*(1), 115–118. doi:10.1111/jsr.12451

Anderson, N. B. (1995). Behavioral and sociocultural perspectives in ethnicity and health: Introduction to the special issue. *Health Psychology, 14*, 589–591.

Anderson, N. H. (1990). *Contributions to information integration theory* (Vol. 1). Hillsdale, NJ: Erlbaum.

Anderson, R. T., Hogan, P., Appel, L., Rosen, R., & Shumaker, S. A. (1997). Baseline correlates with quality of life among men and women with medication-controlled hypertension. *Journal of the American Geriatrics Society, 45*, 1080–1085.

Anderson, S. F., & Maxwell, S. E. (2017). Addressing the "replication crisis": Using original studies to design replication studies with appropriate statistical power. *Multivariate Behavioral Research, 52*(3), 305–324. doi:10.1080/00273171.2017.1289361

Anderson, T. C. (2017). Complementary and alternative medicine for managing stress. In Wadhwa S. (Ed.), *Optimism and stress* (pp. 313–327). Santa Barbara, CA: Greenwood Press.

Anderson-Fye, E. P., & Becker, A. E. (2004). Sociocultural aspects of eating disorders. In J. K. Thompson (Ed.), *Handbook of eating disorders and obesity* (pp. 565–589). Hoboken, NJ: John Wiley.

Anderzén Carlsson, A., Sørlie, V., Gustafsson, K., Olsson, M., & Kihlgren, M. (2008). Fear in children with cancer: Observations at an outpatient visit. *Journal of Child Health Care: For Professionals Working with Children in the Hospital and Community, 12*(3), 191–208.

Andrews, G. J. (2002). Towards a more place-sensitive nursing research: An invitation to medical and health geography. *Nursing Inquiry, 9*, 221–238.

Angell, M. (1985). Disease as a reflection of the psyche. *New England Journal of Medicine, 312*(24), 1570–1572.

Angell, M. (1997). The Supreme Court and physician-assisted suicide: The ultimate right. *New England Journal of Medicine, 336*, 50–53.

Antoni, M. H., & Carrico, A. W. (2012). Psychological and biobehavioral processes in HIV diseases. In A. Baum, T. A. Revenson, & J. Singer (Eds.), *Handbook of health psychology* (2e, pp. 755–770). New York, NY: Guilford.

Antoni, M. H., & Lutgendorf, S. (2007). Psychosocial factors and disease progression in cancer. *Current Directions in Psychological Science, 16*(1), 42–46.

Antoni, M. H., Baggett, L., Ironson, G., LaPerriere, A., August, S., Klimas, N., . . . Fletcher, M. A. (1991). Cognitive-behavioral stress management intervention buffers distress responses and immunologic changes following notification of HIV-1 seropositivity. *Journal of Consulting and Clinical Psychology, 59*, 906–915.

Antoni, M. H., Cruess, D. G., Cruess, S., Lutgendorf, S., Kumar, M., Ironson, G., . . . Schneiderman, N. (2001). Cognitive-behavioral stress management intervention effects on anxiety, 24-hr urinary norepinephrine output, and T-cytotoxic/suppressor cells over time among symptomatic HIV-infected gay men. *Journal of Consulting and Clinical Psychology, 68*, 31–35.

Antoni, M. H., Lehman, J. M., Kilbourn, K. M., Boyers, A. E., Culver, J. L., Alferi, S. M., . . . Carver, C. S. (2001). Cognitive-behavioral stress management intervention decreases the prevalence of depression and enhances benefit finding among women under treatment for early-stage breast cancer. *Health Psychology, 20*, 20–32.

Antonucci, T. C. (1991). Attachment, social support, and doping with negative life events in mature adulthood. In E. M. Cummings, A. L. Greene, & K. H. Karraker, (Eds.), *Life-span developmental psychology: Perspectives on stress and coping* (pp. 261–276). Hillsdale, NJ: Erlbaum.

Antonucci, T. C., & Akiyama, H. (1987). An examination of sex differences in social support among older men and women. *Sex Roles, 17*, 737–749.

Antonucci, T. C., & Akiyama, H. (1995). Convoys of social relations: Family and friendships within a life span context. In R. Blieszner & V. H. Bedford (Eds.), *Handbook of aging and the family* (pp. 355–371). Westport, CT: Greenwood Press/Greenwood Publishing Group.

Antonucci, T. C., Ajrouch, K. J., & Birditt, K. S. (2014). The convoy model: Explaining social relations from a multidisciplinary perspective. *Gerontologist, 54*(1), 82–92. doi:10.1093/geront/gnt118

Apel, M., Klein, K., McDermott, R. J., & Westhoff, W. W. (1997). Restricting smoking at the University of Koln, Germany: A case study. *Journal of American College Health, 45*, 219–223.

Apullan, F., Bourassa, M., Tardif, J., Fortier, A., Gayda, M., Nigam, A. (2008). Usefulness of self-reported leisure-time physical activity to predict long-term survival in patients with coronary heart disease. *American Journal of Cardiology, 102*(4), 375–379.

Arcaya, M. C., & Figueroa, J. F. (2017). Emerging trends could exacerbate health inequities in the United States. *Health Affairs, 36*(6), 992–998. doi:10.1377/hlthaff.2017.0011

Arcaya, M. C., Lowe, S. R., Asad, A. L., Subramanian, S. V., Waters, M. C., & Rhodes, J. (2017). Association of posttraumatic stress disorder symptoms with migraine and headache after a natural disaster. *Health Psychology, 36*(5), 411–418. doi:10.1037/hea0000433

Arellano-Morales, L., & Sosa, E. T. (2018). *Latina/o American health and mental health: Practices and challenges.* Santa Barbara, CA: Praeger.

Arias, D. C. (2004). Alternative medicines' popularity prompts concern. *Nation's Health, 34,* 6.

Armor, D. A., & Taylor, S. E. (1998). Situated optimism: Specific outcome expectancies and self regulation. In M. P. Zanna (Ed.), *Advances in experimental social psychology* (pp. 309–379). New York, NY: Academic Press.

Armor, D. A., & Taylor, S. E. (1998). When predictions fail: The dilemma of unrealistic optimism. In T. Gilovich, D. Griffin, & D. Kahneman (Eds.), *Heuristics and biases: The psychology of intuitive judgment* (pp. 334–347). New York, NY: Cambridge University Press.

Armstrong, K. (2015). *Fields of blood: Religion and the history of violence.* New York, NY: Random House.

Armstrong, T. L., & Swartzman, L. C. (2001). Cross-cultural differences in illness models and expectations for the health care provider-client/patient interaction. In S. S. Kazarian & D. R. Evans (Eds.), *Handbook of cultural health psychology* (pp. 63–84). San Diego, CA: Academic Press.

Arnetz, B. B., Wasserman, J., Pertrii, B., Brenner, S. O., Levi, L., Eneroth, P., . . . Petterson, I. L. (1987). Immune function in unemployed women. *Psychosomatic Medicine, 49,* 3–12.

Arntz, A., & de Jong, P. F. (1993). Anxiety, attention and pain. *Journal of Psychosomatic Research, 37,* 423–431.

Arslantaş, H., Adana, F., Ergin, F., Gey, N., Biçer, N., & Kıranşal, N. (2012). Domestic violence during pregnancy in an eastern city of Turkey: A field study. *Journal of Interpersonal Violence, 27*(7), 1293–1313. doi:10.1177/0886260511425248

Ashing-Giwa, K., & Ganz, P. A. (1997). Understanding the breast cancer experience of African-American women. *Journal of Psychosocial Oncology, 15,* 19–35.

Asiodu, I. V., Waters, C. M., Dailey, D. E., & Lyndon, A. (2017). Infant feeding decision-making and the influences of social support persons among first-time African American mothers. *Maternal and Child Health Journal, 21*(4), 863–872. doi:10.1007/s10995-016-2167-x

Aspinwall, L. G., & Taylor, S. E. (1992). Modeling cognitive adaptation: A longitudinal investigation of the impact of individual differences and coping on college adjustment and performance. *Journal of Personality and Social Psychology, 63,* 989–1003.

Aspinwall, L. G., & Taylor, S. E. (1997). A stitch in time: Self-regulation and proactive coping. *Psychological Bulletin, 121,* 417–436.

Aspinwall, L. G., Kemeny, M. E., Taylor, S. E., Schneider, S. G., & Dudley, E. T. (1991). Psychosocial predictors of gay men's AIDS risk-reduction behavior. *Health Psychology, 10,* 432–444.

Aspinwall, L., & Tedeschi, R. (2010). The value of positive psychology for health psychology: progress and pitfalls in examining the relation of positive phenomena to health. *Annals of Behavioral Medicine: A Publication of the Society of Behavioral Medicine, 39*(1), 4–15.

Assari, S., & Lankarani, M. M. (2017). Reciprocal associations between depressive symptoms and mastery among older adults; black-white differences. *Frontiers in Aging Neuroscience, 8*(9). doi:10.3389/fnagi.2016.00279

Association of State and Provincial Psychology Boards. (2010). ASPPB model act for licensure and registration of psychologists. Author, Tyrone, GA. Retrieved from http://www.asppb.net/files/Final_Approved_MLRA_November_2010.pdf

Astin, J. A., Marie, A., Pelletier, K. R., Hansen, E., & Haskell, W. L. (1998). A review of the incorporation of complementary and alternative medicine by mainstream physicians. *Archives of Internal Medicine, 158,* 2303–2310.

Atkinson, J. S., Schönnesson, L. N., Williams, M. L., & Timpson, S. C. (2008). Associations among correlates of schedule adherence to antiretroviral therapy (ART): A path analysis of a sample of crack cocaine using sexually active African-Americans with HIV infection. *AIDS Care, 20,* 260–269.

Auerbach, S. M. (1989). Stress management and coping research in the health care setting: An overview and methodological commentary. *Journal of Consulting and Clinical Psychology, 57,* 388–395.

Auerbach, S. M. (2000). Should patients have control over their own health care? Empirical evidence and research issues. *Annals of Behavioral Medicine, 22,* 246–259.

Ault, N., Evans, C., Burton, J., & Sheppard, Z. (Eds.). (2012). *Advanced clinical practice in HIV care: A handbook for nurses, midwives and other healthcare practitioners.* London, UK: Routledge.

Avila, E., Parker, J. (2000). *Woman who glows in the dark: Curandera reveals traditional Aztec secrets of physical and spiritual health.* New York, NY: Tarcher Penguin.

Awatef, M., Olfa, G., Rim, C., Asma, K., Kacem, M., Makram, H., & . . . Slim, B. (2011). Physical activity reduces breast cancer risk: A case-control study in Tunisia. *Cancer Epidemiology, 35*(6), 540–544.

Ax, A. F. (1953). The physiological differentiation between fear and anger in humans. *Psychosomatic Medicine, 15,* 433–442.

Ayantunde, A., Welch, N., & Parsons, S. (2007, March). A survey of patient satisfaction and use of the Internet for health information. *International Journal of Clinical Practice, 61*(3), 458–462.

Ayyanar, M., Sankarasivaraman, K., & Ignacimuthu, S. (2008). Traditional healing potential of Paliyars in Southern India. *Ethnobotanical Leaflets, 12,* 311–317.

Azoulay, D., Hammerman-Rozenberg, R., Cialic, R., Ein Mor, E., Jacobs, J., & Stessman, J. (2008). Increasing opioid therapy and survival in a hospice. *Journal of the American Geriatrics Society, 56*(2), 360–361.

Bäärnhielm, S. (2012). The meaning of pain: A cultural formulation of a Syrian woman in Sweden. *Transcultural Psychiatry, 49*(1), 105–120. doi:10.1177/1363461511427781

Baba, V. V., Jamal, M., & Tourigny, L. (1998). Work and mental health: A decade in Canadian research. *Canadian Psychology, 39,* 94–107.

Baban, A., & Craciun, C. (2007). Changing health-risk behaviors: Areview of theory and evidence-based interventions in health psychology. *Journal of Cognitive and Behavioral Psychotherapies, 7*(1), 45–67.

Babyak, M., Blumenthal, J. A., Herman, S., Khatri, P., Doraiswamy, M., Moore, K., . . . Krishnan, K. R. (2000). Exercise treatment for major depression: Maintenance of therapeutic benefit at 10 months. *Psychosomatic Medicine, 62,* 633–638.

Bachen, E. A., Marsland, A. L., Manuck, S. B., & Cohen, S. (1998). Immunomodulation: Psychological stress and immune competence. In T. F. Kresina (Ed.), *Handbook of immune modulating agents* (pp. 145–159). New York, NY: Marcel Dekker.

Baer, J. S., Stacy, A., & Larimer, M. (1991). Biases in the perception of drinking norms among college students. *Journal of Studies on Alcohol, 52,* 580–586.

Baer, R. A. (2003). Mindfulness training as a clinical intervention: A conceptual and empirical review. *Clinical Psychology: Science and Practice, 10*, 125–143.

Bagla, P. (2011). Piercing the Veil of Ayurveda. *Science, 334*(6062), 1491.

Bagnardi, V., Zatonski, W., Scotti, L., La Vecchia, C., & Corrao, G. (2008). Does drinking pattern modify the effect of alcohol on the risk of coronary heart disease? Evidence from a meta-analysis. *Journal of Epidemiology and Community Health, 62*(7), 615–619.

Bagot, K. S., Wu, R., Cavallo, D., & Krishnan-Sarin, S. (2017). Assessment of pain in adolescents: Influence of gender, smoking status and tobacco abstinence. *Addictive Behaviors, 67*, 79–85. doi:10.1016/j.addbeh.2016.12.010

Bai, Y., Wunderlich, S., & Fly, A. (2011). Predicting intentions to continue exclusive breastfeeding for 6 months: A comparison among racial/ethnic groups. *Maternal & Child Health Journal, 15*(8), 1257–1264. doi:10.1007/s10995-010-0703-7

Bailey, F. J., & Dua, J. (1999). Individualism-collectivism, coping styles, and stress in international and Anglo-Australian students: A comparative study. *Australian Psychologist, 34*, 177–182.

Bair, M. J., Robinson, R. L., Katon, W., & Kroenke, K. (2003). Depression and pain comorbidity: A literature review. *Archives of Internal Medicine, 163*(20), 2433.

Bair, M., Wu, J., Damush, T., Sutherland, J., & Kroenke, K. (2008). Association of depression and anxiety alone and in combination with chronic musculoskeletal pain in primary care patients. *Psychosomatic Medicine, 70*(8), 890–897.

Baker, B., Richter, A., & Anand, S. S. (2001). From the heartland: Culture, psychological factors, and coronary heart disease. In S. S. Kazarian & D. R. Evans (Eds.), *Handbook of cultural health psychology* (pp. 141–162). San Diego, CA: Academic Press.

Baker, M. K., Kennedy, D. J., Bohle, P. L., Campbell, D. S., Knapman, L., Grady, J., . . . Fiatarone Singh, M. A., (2007). Efficacy and feasibility of a novel tri-modal robust exercise prescription in a retirement community: Arandomized, controlled trial. *Journal of the American Geriatrics Society, 55*, 1–10.

Ball, D. M., & Murray, R. M. (1994). Genetics of alcohol misuse. *British Medical Bulletin, 50*, 18–35.

Ball, K., Berch, D. B., Helmers, K. F., Jobe, J. B., Leveck, M. D., Marsiske, M., . . . Willis, S. L. (2002). Effects of cognitive training interventions with older adults: A randomized controlled trial. *Journal of the American Medical Association, 288*, 2271–2281.

Ballantyne, C. M. (2004). Achieving greater reductions in cardiovascular risk: Lessons from statin therapy on risk measures and risk reduction. *American Heart Journal, 148*, S3–S8.

Ballard, T. J., Saltzman, L. E., Gazmararian, J. A., Spitz, A. M., Lazorick, S., & Marks, J. S. (1998). Violence during pregnancy: Measurement issues. *American Journal of Public Health, 88*, 274–276.

Ballard-Reisch, D. S. (1990). A model of participative decision making for physician/patient interaction. *Health Communication, 2*, 91–104.

Balls Organista, P., Organista, K., & Kurasaki, K. (2002). The relationship between acculturation and ethnic minority health. In K. M. Chun, P. Balls Organista, G. Marin, & S. Sue (Eds.), *Acculturation: Advances in theory, measurement, and applied research* (pp. 139–161). Washington, DC: American Psychological Association.

Balodhi, J. P. (1999). Traditional Indian system of medicine as applicable to treatment of mental illness. In A. Sahni (Ed.), *Mental health care in India* (pp. 132–138). Bangalore, India: Indian Society of Health Administrators.

Band, P. R., Le, N. D., Fang, R., & Deschamps, M. (2002). Carcinogenic and endocrine disrupting effects of cigarette smoke and risk of breast cancer. *The Lancet, 360*, 1044–1050.

Bandura, A. (1969). Social learning of moral judgments. *Journal of Personality & Social Psychology, 11*, 275–279.

Bandura, A. (1977). *Social learning theory*. Englewood Cliffs, NJ: Prentice Hall.

Bandura, A. (1986). *Social foundations of thought and action: A social cognitive theory*. Englewood Cliffs, NJ: Prentice-Hall.

Bandura, A. (1998). Health promotion from the perspective of Social Cognitive Theory. *Psychology and Health, 13*, 623–649.

Bandura, A. (2000). Cultivate self-efficacy for personal and organizational effectiveness. In E. A. Locke (Ed.), *The Blackwell handbook of principles of organizational behavior*. New York, NY: Cambridge University Press.

Banerjee, A., Watt, L., Gulati, S., Sung, L., Dix, D., Klassen, R., & Klassen, A. (2011). Cultural beliefs and coping strategies related to childhood cancer: The perceptions of South Asian immigrant parents in Canada. *Journal of Pediatric Oncology Nursing, 28*(3), 169–178.

Bantha, R., Moskowitz, J. T., Acree, M., & Folkman, S. (2007). Socioeconomic differences in the effects of prayer on physical symptoms and quality of life. *Journal of Health Psychology, 12*, 249–260.

Barber, L. K., & Santuzzi, A. M. (2017). Telepressure and college student employment: The costs of staying connected across social contexts. *Stress and Health, 33*(1), 14–23. doi:10.1002/smi.2668

Barber, S. J., Opitz, P. C., Martins, B., Sakaki, M., & Mather, M. (2016). Thinking about a limited future enhances the positivity of younger and older adults' recall: Support for socioemotional selectivity theory. *Memory & Cognition, 44*(6), 869–882. doi:10.3758/s13421-016-0612-0

Barden, E. P., Barry, R. A., Khalifian, C. E., & Bates, J. M. (2016). Sociocultural influences on positive affect: Social support adequacy from one's spouse and the intersections of race and SES. *Journal of Social and Clinical Psychology, 35*(6), 455–470. doi:10.1521/jscp.2016.35.6.455

Barha, C. K., Davis, J. C., Falck, R. S., Nagamatsu, L. S., & Liu-Ambrose, T. (2017). Sex differences in exercise efficacy to improve cognition: A systematic review and meta-analysis of randomized controlled trials in older humans. *Frontiers in Neuroendocrinology, 46*, 71–85. doi:10.1016/j.yfrne.2017.04.002

Barker, D. (2008). Human growth and cardiovascular disease. *Paediatric Programme, 61*, 21–38.

Barnato, A., Llewellyn-Thomas, H., Peters, E., Siminoff, L., Collins, E., & Barry, M. (2007). Communication and decision making in cancer care: Setting research priorities for decision support/patients' decision aids. *Medical Decision Making, 27*(5), 626–634.

Barner, J. C., Bohman, T. M., Brown, C. M., & Richards, K. M. (2010). Use of complementary and alternative medicine for treatment among African-Americans: A multivariate analysis. *Research in Social and Administrative Pharmacy, 6*(3), 196–208.

Barnes, P. M., Adams, P. F., Powell-Griner, E. (2005). *Health characteristics of the American Indian and Alaskan Native adult population: United States, 1999–2003*. Centers for Disease Control and Prevention, Atlanta, GA.

Barnes, P. M., Powell-Griner, E., McFann, K., & Nahin, R. L. (2004). Complementary and alternative medicine use among adults: United States, 2002. *Advance Data, 343*, 1–19.

Barnes, P., Bloom, B., & Nahin, R. (2008). Complementary and alternative medicine use among adults and children: United States 2007. *National Health Statistics Reports*, (12), 1–23.

Barr, P. (2017). Compassion fatigue and compassion satisfaction in neonatal intensive care unit nurses: Relationships with work stress and perceived social support. *Traumatology, 23*(2), 214–222. doi:10.1037/trm0000115

Barr-Anderson, D., van den Berg, P., Neumark-Sztainer, D., & Story, M. (2008). Characteristics associated with older adolescents who have a television in their bedrooms. *Pediatrics, 121*, 718–724.

Barrera, M., Strycker, L. A., MacKinnon, D. P., & Toobert, D. J. (2008). Social-ecological resources as mediators of two-year diet and physical activity outcomes in type 2 diabetes patients. *Health Psychology, 27*, S118–S125.

Barrera, M., Wayland, L., D'Agostino, N. M., Gibson, J., Weksberg, R., & Malkin, D. (2003). Developmental differences in psychological adjustment and health-related quality of life in pediatric cancer patients. *Children's Health Care, 32*, 215–232.

Barrett, B. (1995). Ethnomedical interactions: Health and identity on Nicaragua's Atlantic coast. *Social Science and Medicine, 40*, 1611–1621.

Barrett, B. (1998). When should there be liability for negligently causing psychiatric illness? *Work and Stress, 12*, 101–111.

Barrett, R. K. (1998). Sociocultural considerations for working Blacks experiencing loss and grief. In K. Doka (Ed.), *Living with grief: How we are—how we grieve* (pp. 83–96). Washington, DC: Taylor & Francis.

Barry, D. T., Glenn, C. P., Hoff, R. A., & Potenza, M. N. (2017). Group differences in pain interference, psychiatric disorders, and general medical conditions among Hispanics and whites in the U.S. general population. *Psychiatry Research, 258*, 337–343. doi:10.1016/j.psychres.2017.08.049

Barsky, A. J. (1988). *Worried sick: Our troubled quest for wellness*. New York, NY: Little, Brown.

Barsky, A. J., Ahern, D. K., Bailey, E. D., Saintfort, F., Liu, E. B., & Peekna, H. M. (2001). Hypochondriacal patients' appraisal of health and physical risks. *American Journal of Psychiatry, 158*, 783–787.

Bartone, P. T., Johnsen, B. H., Eid, J., Hystad, S. W., & Laberg, J. C. (2016). Hardiness, avoidance coping, and alcohol consumption in war veterans: A moderated mediation study. *Stress and Health, 33*(5), 498–507. doi:10.1002/smi.2734

Bartoshuk, L. M. (1988). Taste. In R. C. Atkinson, R. J. Herrnstein, G. Lindzey, & R. D. Luce (Eds.), *Stevens' handbook of experimental psychology: Perception and motivation* (Vol. 1). New York, NY: John Wiley.

Bartoshuk, L. M. (1993). The biological basis of food perception and acceptance. *Food Quality and Preference, 4*, 21–32.

Bartoshuk, L. M., Rifkin, B., Marks, L. E., & Hooper, J. E. (1988). Bitterness of KCI and benzoate: Related to genetic status for sensitivity to PTC/PROP. *Chemical Senses, 13*, 517–528.

Bastani, R., Marcus, A., & Hollatz-Brown, A. (1991). Screening mammography rates and barriers to use: A Los Angeles County survey. *Preventive Medicine, 20*, 350–363.

Bates, L. M., Acevedo-Garcia, D., Alegría, M., & Krieger, N. (2008). Immigration and generational trends in body mass index and obesity in the United States: Results of the National Latino and Asian American Survey, 2002–2003. *American Journal of Public Health, 98*,70–77.

Bates, M. S., Edwards, W. T., & Anderson, K. O. (1993). Ethnocultural influences on variation in chronic pain perception. *Pain, 52*, 101–112.

Bates, M. S., Rankin-Hill, L., & Sanchez-Ayendez, M. (1997). The effects of the cultural context of health care on treatment of and response to chronic pain and illness. *Social Science & Medicine, 45*, 1433–1447.

Bathula, R., Francis, D., Hughes, A., & Chaturvedi, N. (2008). Ethnic differences in heart rate: can these be explained by conventional cardiovascular risk factors? *Clinical Autonomic Research, 18*(2), 90–95.

Battié, M. C., Jones, C., Schopflocher, D. P., & Hu, R. W. (2012). Health-related quality of life and comorbidities associated with lumbar spinal stenosis. *Spine Journal, 12*(3), 189–195. doi:10.1016/j.spinee.2011.11.009

Batty, D., & Thune, I. (2000). Does physical activity prevent cancer? Evidence suggests protection against colon cancer and probably breast cancer. *British Medical Journal, 321*, 1424–1425.

Bau, P. F. D., Bau, C. H. D., Rosito, G. A., Manfroi, W. C., & Fuchs, F. D. (2007). Alcohol consumption, cardiovascular health, and endothelial function markers. *Alcohol, 41*, 479–488.

Baum, A., & Dougall, A. L. (2002). Terrorism and behavioral medicine. *Current Opinion in Psychiatry, 15*, 617–621.

Baum, A., O'Keefe, M. K., & Davidson, L. M. (1990). Acute stressors and chronic response: The case of traumatic stress. *Journal of Applied Social Psychology, 20*, 1643–1654.

Baumrind, D. (1991). Effective parenting during the early adolescent transition. In P. A. Cowan & M. Hetherington (Eds.), *Family transitions*. Hillsdale, NJ: Erlbaum.

Bausell, R. B. (2007). *Snake oil science: The truth about complementary and alternative medicine*. Cambridge, MA: Oxford Press.

Beals, J., Novins, D. K., Whitesell, N. R., Spicer, P., Mitchell, C. M., & Manson, S. M. (2005). Prevalence of mental disorders and utilization of mental health services in two American Indian reservation populations. *American Journal of Psychiatry, 162*, 1723–1732.

Bearison, D. J., Minian, N., & Granowetter, L. (2002). Medical management of asthma and folk medicine in a Hispanic community. *Journal of Pediatric Psychology, 27*, 385–392.

Beaton, E., & Simon, T. (2011). How might stress contribute to increased risk for schizophrenia in children with chromosome 22q11.2 deletion syndrome? *Journal of Neurodevelopmental Disorders, 3*(1), 68–75.

Beauchamp, K., Baker, S., McDaniel, C., Moser, W., Zalman, D. C., Balinghoff, J., Cheung, A. T., & Stecker, M. (2001). Reliability of nurses' neurological assessments in the cardiothoracic surgical intensive care unit. *American Journal of Critical Care, 10*, 298–305.

Beck, A. T. (1976). *Cognitive therapy and the emotional disorders*. Oxford, UK: International Universities Press.

Beck, A. T., Ward, C. H., Mendelson, M., Mock, J., & Erbaugh, J. (1961). An inventory for measuring depression. *Archives of General Psychology, 4*, 561–571.

Becker, A. E., Burwell, R. A., Gilman, S. E., Herzog, D. B., & Hamburg, P. (2002). Eating behaviors and attitudes following prolonged exposure to television among ethnic Fijian adolescent girls. *British Journal of Psychiatry, 180*(6), 509–514.

Becker, A. E., Fay, K., Agnew-Blais, J., Guarnaccia, P. M., Striegel-Moore, R. H., & Gilman, S. E. (2010). Development of a measure of "acculturation" for ethnic Fijians: Methodologic and conceptual considerations for application to eating disorders research. *Transcultural Psychiatry, 47*(5), 754–788. doi:10.1177/1363461510382153

Becker, M. H. (Ed.). (1974). The health belief model and personal health behavior. *Health Education Monographs, 2*, entire issue.

Beckman, H. B., & Frankel, R. M. (1984). The effect of physician behavior on the collection of data. *Annals of Internal Medicine, 101*, 692–696.

Bedford, F. (2012). A perception theory in mind-body medicine: Guided imagery and mindful meditation as cross-modal adaptation. *Psychonomic Bulletin & Review, 19*(1), 24–45. doi:10.3758/s13423-011-0166-x

Bediako, S. M., Lavender, A. R., & Yasin, Z. (2007). Racial centrality and health care use among African American adults with sickle cell disease. *Journal of Black Psychology, 33*, 422–438.

Beebe, M., Dalton, J. A., & Espronceda, M. (2008). *Current procedural terminology, professional ed.* Washington, DC: American Medical Association.

Beecher, H. K. (1955). The powerful placebo. *Journal of the American Medical Association, 159*, 1602–1606.

Beeken, R., Simon, A., von Wagner, C., Whitaker, K., & Wardle, J. (2011). Cancer fatalism: Deterring early presentation and increasing social inequalities? *Cancer Epidemiology, Biomarkers & Prevention, 20*(10), 2127–2131.

Beesley, V., Eakin, E., Janda, M., & Battistutta, D. (2008). Gynecological cancer survivors' health behaviors and their associations with quality of life. *Cancer Causes and Control, 19*(7), 775–782.

Belar, C. D. (2008). Clinical health psychology: A health care specialty in professional psychology. *Professional Psychology: Research and Practice, 39*, 229–233.

Belar, C. D., & Deardorff, W. W. (2009). *Clinical health psychology in medical settings: A practitioner's guidebook.* Washington, DC: American Psychological Association.

Belar, C. D., McIntyre, T. M., & Matarazzo, J. D. (2003). Health psychology. In D. K. Freedheim (Ed.), *Handbook of psychology: History of psychology*, (pp. 451–464). New York, NY: John Wiley.

Belcher, B. R., Berrigan, D., Dodd, K. W., Emken, B., Chih-Ping, C., & Spruijt-Metz, D. (2010). Physical activity in U.S. youth: Effect of race/ethnicity, age, gender, and weight status. *Medicine & Science in Sports & Exercise, 42*(12), 2211–2221. doi:10.1249/MSS.0b013e3181e1fba9

Belle, D. (1989). *Children's social networks and social supports.* Oxford, UK: John Wiley.

Benetou, V., Trichopoulou, A., Orfanos, P., Naska, A., Lagiou, P., Boffetta, P., & Trichopoulos, D. (2008). Conformity to traditional Mediterranean diet and cancer incidence: The Greek EPIC cohort. *British Journal of Cancer, 99*(1), 191–195.

Benotsch, E. G., Lutgendorf, S. K., Watson, D., Fick, L. J., & Lang, E. V. (2000). Rapid anxiety assessment in medical patients: Evidence for the validity of verbal anxiety ratings. *Annals of Behavioral Medicine, 22*, 199–203.

Ben-Shlomo, Y., Naqvi, H., & Baker, I. (2008). Ethnic differences in healthcare-seeking behaviour and management for acute chest pain: Secondary analysis of the MINAP dataset 2002–2003. *Heart* (British Cardiac Society), *94*(3), 354–359.

Benyamini, Y. (2016). Self-rated health. In Y. Benyamini, M. Johnston, & E. C. Karademas (Eds.), *Assessment in health psychology* (pp. 118–130). Boston, MA: Hogrefe.

Benyamini, Y., & Johnson, M. (2016). Introduction. In Y. Benyamini, M. Johnson, & E. C. Karademas (Eds.), *Assessment in health psychology* (pp. 3–18). Boston, MA: Hogrefe.

Ben-Zur, H. (2002). Coping, affect and aging: The roles of mastery and self-esteem. *Personality and Individual Differences, 32*, 357–372.

Berg, C. J., Haardörfer, R., McBride, C. M., Kilaru, V., Ressler, K. J., Wingo, A. P., . . . Smith, A. (2017). Resilience and biomarkers of health risk in black smokers and nonsmokers. *Health Psychology, 36*(11), 1047–1058. doi:10.1037/hea0000540

Berg, C., Smith, T., Henry, N., & Pearce, G. (2007). A developmental approach to psychosocial risk factors and successful aging. In *Handbook of health psychology and aging* (pp. 30–53). New York, NY: Guilford Press.

Bergelt, C., Koch, U., & Petersen, C. (2008). Quality of life in partners of patients with cancer. *Quality of Life Research, 17*(5), 653–663.

Berger, J., Heinrichs, M., von Dawans, B., Way, B. M., & Chen, F. S. (2016). Cortisol modulates men's affiliative responses to acute social stress. *Psychoneuroendocrinology, 63*, 1–9. doi:10.1016/j.psyneuen.2015.09.004

Berkanovic, E., & Telesky, C. (1985). Mexican-American, Black-American and White-American differences in reporting illnesses, disability and physician visits for illnesses. *Social Science and Medicine, 20*, 567–577.

Berkley, K. J. (1997). Sex differences in pain. *Behavioral and Brain Sciences, 20*, 371–380.

Berkman, L. F. (1985). The relationship of social networks and social support to morbidity and mortality. In S. Cohen & S. L. Syme (Eds.), *Social support and health* (pp. 241–262). San Diego, CA: Academic Press.

Berkman, L. F. (1995). The role of social relations in health promotion. *Psychosomatic Medicine, 57*, 245–254.

Berkman, L. F., & Syme, S. L. (1979). Social networks, host resistance, and mortality: A nine-year follow-up study of almeda county residents. *American Journal of Epidemiology, 109*(2), 186–204.

Berkman, L. F., & Syme, S. L. (1994). Social networks, host resistance, and mortality: A nine year follow-up study of Alameda County residents. In A. Steptoe & J. Wardle (Eds.), *Psychosocial processes and health: A reader* (pp. 43–67). New York, NY: Cambridge University Press.

Berkman, L. F., Vaccarino, V., & Seeman, T. (1993). Gender differences in cardiovascular morbidity and mortality: The contribution of social networks and support. *Annals of Behavioral Medicine, 15*, 112–118.

Berkman, L., & Syme, S. L. (1979). Social networks, host resistance, and mortality: A nine-year follow-up study of Alameda County residents. *American Journal of Epidemiology, 109*, 186–204.

Berlin, J. A., & Colditz, G. A. (1990). A meta-analysis of physical activity in the prevention of coronary heart disease. *American Journal of Epidemiology, 132*, 612–628.

Berman, B. A., & Gritz, E. R. (1991). Women and smoking: Current trends and issues for the 1990s. *Journal of Substance Abuse, 3*, 221–238.

Bernabei, R., Gambassi, G., Lapane, K., Landi, F., Gatsonis, C., Dunlop, R., (1998). Management of pain in elderly patients with cancer. *Journal of the American Medical Association, 279*, 1877–1882.

Bernardes, S. F., Keogh, E., Lima, M. L. (2008). Bridging the gap between pain and gender research: A selective literature review. *European Journal of Pain, 12*, 427–440.

Bernstein, L., Henderson, B. E., Hanisch, R., Sullivan-Halley, J., & Ross, R. K. (1994). Physical exercise and reduced risk of breast cancer in young women. *Journal of the National Cancer Institute, 86*, 1403–1408.

Berrol, S. C. (1995). *Growing up American: Immigrant children in America then and now.* New York, NY: Twayne.

Berry, J. W., Trimble, J. E., Olmedo, E. L. (1986). Assessment of acculturation. In W. J. Lonner & J. W. Berry (Eds.), *Field methods in cross-cultural research* (pp. 291–324). Thousand Oaks, CA: SAGE.

Bersamira, C. S., Lin, Y. A., Park, K., & Marsh, J. C. (2017). Drug use among Asian Americans: Differentiating use by acculturation status and gender. *Journal of Substance Abuse Treatment, 79*, 76–81.

Berthoud, H., & Morrison, C. (2008). The brain, appetite, and obesity. *Annual Review of Psychology, 59*, 55–92.

Bestehorn, K., Wegscheider, K., & Völler, H. (2008). Contemporary trends in cardiac rehabilitation in Germany: atient characteristics, drug treatment, and risk-factor management from 2000 to 2005. *European Journal of Cardiovascular Prevention and Rehabilitation, 15*(3), 312–318.

Betencourt, H., & Fuentes, J. L. (2001). Culture and Latino issues in health psychology. In S. S. Kazarian & D. R. Evans (Eds.), *Handbook of cultural health psychology* (pp. 305–321). San Diego, CA: Academic Press.

Betensky, J. D., Contrada, R. J., & Glass, D. C. (2012). Psychosocial factors in cardiovascular disease: Emotional states, conditions, and attributes. In A. Baum, T. A. Revenson, & J. Singer (Eds.), *Handbook of health psychology* (2e, pp. 637–662). New York, NY: Guilford.

Bevans, M., & Sternberg, E. (2012). Caregiving burden, stress, and health effects among family caregivers of adult cancer patients. *Journal of the American Medical Association, 307*(4), 398–403.

Bexton, W. H., Heron, W., & Scott, T. H. (1954). Effects of decreased variation in the sensory environment. *Canadian Journal of Psychology, 8*, 70–76.

Bhui, K., & Fletcher, A. (2000). Common mood and anxiety states: Gender differences in the protective effect of physical activity. *Social Psychiatry and Psychiatric Epidemiology, 35*, 28–35.

Bian, Z., Lu, B., Moher, D., Wu, T., Li, Y., Shang, H., & Cheng, C. (2011). Consolidated standards of reporting trials (CONSORT) for traditional Chinese medicine: Current situation and future development. *Frontiers of Medicine, 5*(2), 171–177. doi:10.1007/s11684-011-0132-z

Biasi, F., Mascia, C., & Poli, G. (2008). The contribution of animal fat oxidation products to colon carcinogenesis, through modulation of TGF-beta1 signaling. *Carcinogenesis, 29*(5), 890–894.

Bijur, P. E., Kurzon, M., Overpeck, M. D., & Scheidt, P. C. (1992). Parental alcohol use, problem drinking, and children's injuries. *Journal of the American Medical Association, 267*, 3166–3171.

Billings, A. G., & Moos, R. H. (1984). Coping, stress, and social resources among adults with unipolar depression. *Journal of Personality and Social Psychology, 46*, 877–891.

Bishnoi, D., & Kaur, T. (2010). Predictor of cardiovascular disease with respect to BMI, WHR and lipid profile in females of three population groups. *Biology & Medicine, 2*(2), 32–41.

Bishop, G. (2019). Cardiovascular disease. In T. A. Revenson & R. A. R. Gurung (Eds.), *Handbook of health psychology* (3e). New York, NY: Routledge.

Bjelakovic, G., Nikolova, D., Gluud, L. L., Simonetti, R. G., & Gluud, C. (2008). Antioxidant supplements for prevention of mortality in healthy participants and patients with various diseases. *Cochrane Database of Systematic Reviews*, 2, Art. No.: CD007176. doi:10.1002/14651858.CD007176.

Black, K., & Lobo, M. (2008). A conceptual review of family resilience factors. *Journal of Family Nursing, 14*, 33–55.

Blair, S. N., Kohl, H. W., Gordon, N. F., & Paffenbarger, R. S. (1992). How much physical activity is good for health? *Annual Review of Public Health, 13*, 99–126.

Blaisdell, R. K. (1998). Culture and cancer in Kanaka Maoli (Native Hawaiians). *Asian American and Pacific Islander Journal of Health, 6*, 400.

Blanchard, C. G., Albrecht, T. L., Ruckdeschel, J. C., & Grant, C. H. (1995). The role of social support in adaptation to cancer and to survival. *Journal of Psychosocial Oncology, 13*, 75–95.

Blanchard, E. B., & Andrasik, F. (1985). Management of chronic headaches: A psychological approach. *Psychology practitioner guidebooks*. Elmsford, NY: Pergamon Press.

Blanchrd, E. B., Lackner, J. M., Jaccard, J., Rowell, D., Carosella, A. M., & Powell, C., . . . Kuhn, E., (2008). The role of stress in symptom exacerbation among IBS patients. *Journal of Psychosomatic Research, 64*, 119–128.

Blashill, A. J., Perry, N., & Safren, S. A. (2011). Mental health: A focus on stress, coping, and mental illness as it relates to treatment retention, adherence, and other health outcomes. *Current HIV/AIDS Reports, 8*(4), 215–222. doi:10.1007/s11904-011-0089-1

Bleichhardt, G., Timmer, B., & Rief, W. (2005). Hypochondriasis among patients with multiple somatoform symptoms: Psychopathology and outcome of a cognitive-behavioral therapy. *Journal of Contemporary Psychotherapy, 35*, 239–249.

Bleiker, E., Hendriks, J., Otten, J., Verbeek, A., & van der Ploeg, H. (2008). Personality factors and breast cancer risk: A 13-year follow-up. *Journal of the National Cancer Institute, 100*(3), 213–218.

Bleuler, M. (1963). Conception of schizophrenia within the last fifty years and today. *Proceedings of the Royal Society of Medicine, 56*, 945–952.

Blomkvist, V., Eriksen, C. A., Theorell, T., Ulrich, R., & Rasmanis, G. (2005). Acoustics and psychosocial environment in intensive coronary care. *Occupational and Environmental Medicine, 62*, e1. doi:10.1136/OEM2004.017632

Blondel, B. (1998). Social and medical support during pregnancy: An overview of the randomized controlled trials. *Prenatal Neonatal Medicine, 3*, 141–144.

Blow, A. J., Bowles, R. P., Farero, A., Subramaniam, S., Lappan, S., Nichols, E., . . . Guty, D. (2017). Couples coping through deployment: Findings from a sample of National Guard families. *Journal of Clinical Psychology, 73*(12), 1753–1767. doi:10.1002/jclp.22487

Blum, K., Noble, E. P., Sheridan, P. J., Montgomery, A., Ritchie, T., Jagadeeswaran, P., . . . Cohn, J. B. (1990). Allelic association of human dopamine D2 receptor gene in alcoholism. *Journal of the American Medical Association, 263*, 2055–2060.

Blumenthal, J. (2008). Depression and coronary heart disease: association and implications for treatment. *Cleveland Clinic Journal of Medicine, 75*, S48–53.

Blumenthal, J. A., Babyak, M. A., Carney, R. M., Huber, M., Saab, P. G., Burg, M. M., . . . Kaufmann, P. G. (2004). Exercise, depression, and mortality after myocardial infarction in the ENRICHD trial. *Medicine and Science in Sports and Exercise, 36*, 746–755.

Blumenthal, J. A., Babyak, M., Wei, J., O'Connor, C., Waugh, R., Eisenstein, E., . . . Reed, G. (2002a). Usefulness of psychosocial treatment of mental stress-induced myocardial ischemia in men. *American Journal of Cardiology, 89*, 164–168.

Blumenthal, J. A., Sherwood, A., Gullette, E. C. D., Georgiades, A., & Tweedy, D. (2002b). Biobehavioral approaches to the treatment of essential hypertension. *Journal of Consulting and Clinical Psychology, 70*, 569–589.

Blumer, D., & Heilbronn, M. (1984). Chronic pain as a variant of depressive disease: A rejoinder. *Journal of Nervous and Mental Disease, 172*, 405–407.

Boehm, J. K., & Kubzansky, L. D. (2012). The heart's content: The association between positive psychological well-being and cardiovascular health. *Psychological Bulletin, 138*(4), 655–669. doi:10.1037/a0027448

Bogg, T., & Roberts, B. W. (2004). Conscientiousness and health-related behaviors: A meta-analysis of the leading behavioral contributors to mortality. *Psychological Bulletin, 130*, 887–919.

Bokhour, B. G., Fix, G. M., Gordon, H. S., Long, J. A., DeLaughter, K., Orner, M. B., . . . Houston, T. K. (2016). Can stories influence African-American patients' intentions to change hypertension management behaviors? A randomized control trial. *Patient Education and Counseling, 99*(9), 1482–1488. doi:10.1016/j.pec.2016.06.024

Boland, R. (1997). HIV and depression. *American Journal of Psychiatry, 154*, 1632–1633.

Bolger, N. (1990). Coping as a personality process: A prospective study. *Journal of Personality and Social Psychology, 59*, 525–537.

Bolger, N., DeLongis, A., Kessler, R., & Wethington, E. (1989). The contagion of stress across multiple roles. *Journal of Marriage and Family, 51*, 175–183.

Bolger, N., Stadler, G., Paprocki, C., & DeLongis, A. (2010). Grounding social psychology in behavior in daily life: The case of conflict and distress in couples. In C. R. Agnew, D. E. Carlston, W. G. Graziano, J. R. Kelly, C. R. Agnew, D. E. Carlston, . . . J. R. Kelly (Eds.), *Then a miracle occurs: Focusing on behavior in social psychological theory and research* (pp. 368–390). New York, NY: Oxford University Press.

Boll, T. J., Johnson, S. B., Perry, N. W., & Rozensky, R. H. (Eds.). (2002). *Handbook of clinical health psychology*, Vol. 1, *Medical disorders and behavioral applications*. Washington, DC: American Psychological Association.

Bomyea, J., Amir, N., & Lang, A. J. (2012). The relationship between cognitive control and posttraumatic stress symptoms. *Journal of Behavior Therapy & Experimental Psychiatry, 43*(2), 844–848. doi:10.1016/j.jbtep.2011.12.001

Bonadies, V. (2004). A yoga therapy program for AIDS-related pain and anxiety: implications for therapeutic recreation. *Therapeutic Recreation Journal, 38*(2), 148–166.

Bond, B., Hirota, L., Fortin, J., & Col, N. (2002). Women like me: Reflections on health and hormones from women treated for breast cancer. *Journal of Psychosocial Oncology, 20*, 39–56.

Bond, D. S., Lyle, R. M., Tappe, M. K., Seehafer, R. S., & D'Zurilla, T. J. (2002). Moderate aerobic exercise, T'ai Chi, and social problem-solving ability in relation to psychological stress. *International Journal of Stress Management, 9*, 329–343.

Bonica, J. J. (1990). History of pain concepts and theories. In J. J. Bonica, J. D. Loeser, C. R. Chapman, & W. E. Fordyce (Eds.), *The management of pain* (pp. 2–17). Philadelphia, PA: Lea & Febiger.

Bonneville-Roussy, A., Evans, P., Verner-Filion, J., Vallerand, R. J., & Bouffard, T. (2017). Motivation and coping with the stress of assessment: Gender differences in outcomes for university students. *Contemporary Educational Psychology, 48*, 28–42. doi:10.1016/j.cedpsych.2016.08.003

Borkhoff, C. M., Hawker, G. A., Kreder, H. J., Glazier, R. H., Mahomed, N. N., & Wright, J. G. (2008). The effect of patients' sex on physicians' recommendations for total knee arthroplasty. *Canadian Medical Association Journal, 178*, 681–687.

Borrelli, B., Endrighi, R., Hammond, S. K., & Dunsiger, S. (2017). Smokers who are unmotivated to quit and have a child with asthma are more likely to quit with intensive motivational interviewing and repeated biomarker feedback. *Journal of Consulting and Clinical Psychology, 85*(11), 1019–1028. doi:10.1037/ccp0000238

Bortsov, A., Liese, A., Bell, R., Dabelea, D., D'Agostino, R., Hamman, R., . . . Mayer-Davis, E. (2011). Sugar-sweetened and diet beverage consumption is associated with cardiovascular risk factor profile in youth with type 1 diabetes. *Acta Diabetologica, 48*(4), 275–282. doi:10.1007/s00592-010-0246-9

Borzekowski, D. L. G., Robinson, T. N., & Killen, J. D. (2000). Does the camera add 10 pounds? Media use, perceived importance of appearance, and weight concerns among teenage girls. *Journal of Adolescent Health, 26*, 36–41.

Boscolo, P., Forcella, L., Reale, M., Vianale, G., Battisti, U., Bonfiglioli, R., . . . & Salerno, S. (2012). Job strain in different types of employment affects the immune response. *Work* (Reading, MA), *41*(0), 2950–2954.

Bouchard, C. (1995). Genetics and the metabolic syndrome. *International Journal of Obesity, 19*, S52–S59.

Bouchard, C. (2001). Physical activity and health: Introduction to the dose-response symposium. *Medicine and Science in Sports and Exercise, 33*, S347–S350.

Bouchard, C., Tremblay, A., Despres, J. P., Nadeau, A., Lupien, P., Theriault, G., . . . Fournier, G. (1990). The response to long-term overfeeding in identical twins. *New England Journal of Medicine, 322*, 1477–1482.

Boucher, N. A. (2017). Faith, family, filiality, and fate. *Journal of Applied Gerontology, 36*(3), 351–372. doi:10.1177/0733464815627958

Bourg Carter, S. (2011). *High octane women: How superachievers can avoid burnout*. Amherst, NY: Prometheus. doi:10.1177/0095798410396087

Bova, C., Burwick, T. N., Quinones, M. (2008). Improving women's adjustment to HIV infection: Results of the Positive Life Skills workshop project. *Journal of the Association of Nurses in AIDS Care, 19*, 58–65.

Bowie, J. V., Bell, C. N., Ewing, A., Kinlock, B., Ezema, A., Thorpe, R. J. Jr., & LaVeist, T. A. (2017). Religious coping and types and sources of information used in making prostate cancer treatment decisions. *American Journal of Men's Health, 11*(4), 1237–1246. doi:10.1177/1557988317690977

Bowlby, J. (1958). The nature of the child's tie to his mother. *International Journal of Psychoanalysis, 39*, 350–373.

Bowling, N. A., Khazon, S., Alarcon, G. M., Blackmore, C. E., Bragg, C. B., Hoepf, M. R., . . . Li, H. (2017). Building better measures of role ambiguity and role conflict: The validation of new role stressor scales. *Work & Stress, 31*(1), 1–23. doi:10.1080/02678373.2017.1292563

Boyer, B. (2008). Theoretical models of health psychology and the model for integrating medicine and psychology. In *Comprehensive handbook of clinical health psychology* (pp. 3–30). Hoboken, NJ: John Wiley.

Boyes, A. W., Girgis, A., D'Este, C., & Zucca, A. C. (2011). Flourishing or floundering? Prevalence and correlates of anxiety and depression among a population-based sample of adult cancer survivors 6 months after diagnosis. *Journal of Affective Disorders, 135*(1–3), 184–192. doi:10.1016/j.jad.2011.07.016

Boykin-McElhaney, K., & Allen, J. P. (2001). Autonomy and social functioning: The moderating effect of risk. *Child Development, 72*, 220–235.

Boyle, S., Jackson, W., & Suarez, E. (2007). Hostility, anger, and depression predict increases in C3 over a 10-year period. *Brain, Behavior, and Immunity, 21*(6), 816–823.

Bozorgzadeh, S., Bahadorani, N., & Sadoghi, M. (2017). Sufism and optimal health. In D. Von Dras (Ed.), *Better health through spiritual practices* (pp. 205–227). Santa Barbara, CA: Praeger.

Brabers, A. E. M., van Dijk, L., Groenewegen, P. P., & de Jong, J. D. (2016). Do social norms play a role in explaining involvement in medical decision-making? *European Journal of Public Health, 26*(6), 901–905. doi:10.1093/eurpub/ckw069

Brack, A., Kesitilwe, K., & Ware, M. E. (2010). Taking the pulse of undergraduate health psychology: A nationwide survey. *Teaching of Psychology, 37*, 271–275. doi:10.1080/00986283.2010.510962

Bradfield, J., Taal, H., Timpson, N., Scherag, A., Lecoeur, C., Warrington, N., . . . & Evans, D. (2012). A genome-wide association meta-analysis identifies new childhood obesity loci. *Nature Genetics, 44*(5), 526–531. doi:10.1038/ng.2247

Bradford, D. (2005). *African herbalism and spiritual divination.* London, UK: New Press.

Bradley, L. A., & Van der Heide, L. H. (1984). Pain-related correlates of MMPI profile subgroups among back pain patients. *Health Psychology, 3*, 157–174.

Bradley, R. H., & Corwyn, R. F. (2002). Socioeconomic status and child development. *Annual Review of Psychology, 53*, 371–399.

Bradshaw, M., Kent, B. V., Henderson, W. M., & Setar, A. C. (2017). Subjective social status, life course SES, and BMI in young adulthood. *Health Psychology, 36*(7), 682–694. doi:10.1037/hea0000487

Braet, C., Van Vlierberghe, L., Vandevivere, E., Theuwis, L., & Bosmans, G. (2013). Depression in early, middle and late adolescence: Differential evidence for the cognitive diathesis–stress model. *Clinical Psychology & Psychotherapy, 20*(5), 369–383.

Braithewaite, R. L., Bianchi, C., & Taylor, S. E. (1994). Ethnographic approach to community organization and health empowerment. *Health Education Quarterly, 21*, 407–419.

Brandt, C. P., Jardin, C., Sharp, C., Lemaire, C., & Zvolensky, M. J. (2017). Main and interactive effects of emotion dysregulation and HIV symptom severity on quality of life among persons living with HIV/AIDS. *AIDS Care, 29*(4), 498–506. doi:10.1080/09540121.2016.1220484

Brannon & Feist. (2007). *Health psychology: An introduction to behavior and health.* San Francisco, CA: Wadsworth.

Brassington, G. S., Hekler, E. B., Cohen, Z., & King, A. C. (2012). Health-enhancing physical activity. In A. Baum, T. A. Revenson, & J. Singer (Eds.), *Handbook of health psychology* (2e, pp. 353–374). New York, NY: Taylor & Francis.

Braveman, P. (2006). Health disparities and health equity: Concepts and measurement. *Annual Review of Public Health, 27*, 167–94.

Bravi, F. F., Edefonti, V. V., Randi, G. G., Garavello, W. W., La Vecchia, C. C., Ferraroni, M. M., & . . . Decarli, A. A. (2012). Dietary patterns and the risk of esophageal cancer. *Annals of Oncology, 23*(3), 765–770.

Bravo, D. Y., Derlan, C. L., Umaña-Taylor, A. J., Updegraff, K. A., & Jahromi, L. B. (2017). Processes underlying Mexican-origin adolescent mothers' BMI. *Cultural Diversity and Ethnic Minority Psychology, 24*(2), 284–293. doi:10.1037/cdp0000181

Brendryen, H., & Kraft, P. (2008). Happy ending: A randomized controlled trial of a digital multi-media smoking cessation intervention. *Addiction, 103*, 478–484.

Breslau, N., & Rasmussen, B. K. (2001). The impact of migraine: Epidemiology, risk factors, and co-morbidities. *Neurology. Special Headache-Related Disability in the Management of Migraine, 56*, S4–S12.

Breslow, R. A., Sorkin, J. D., Frey, C. M., & Kessler, L. G. (1997). Americans' knowledge of cancer risk and survival. *Preventive Medicine, 26*, 170–177.

Brett, J. F., Brief, A. P., Burke, M. J., George, J. M., Webster, J. (1990). Negative affectivity and the reporting of stressful life events. *Health Psychology, 9*, 57–68.

Brewer, W. (1974). There is no convincing evidence for operant or classical conditioning in adult humans. In W. Weimer & D. Palermo (Eds.), *Cognition and the symbolic processes* (pp. 115–138). Hillsdale, NJ: Erlbaum.

Brissette, I., Scheier, M. F., & Carver, C. S. (2002). The role of optimism in social network development, coping, and psychological adjustment during a life transition. *Journal of Personality and Social Psychology, 82*, 102–111.

Brisson, C., Laflamme, N., Moisan, J., Milot, A., Masse, B., & Vezina, M. (1999). Effects of family responsibilities and job strain on ambulatory blood pressure among white-collar woman. *Psychosomatic Medicine, 61*, 205–213.

Broad, W. J. (2012). *The science of yoga: The risks and the rewards.* New York, NY: Simon & Schuster.

Broadbent, E. (2019). Illness cognitions and beliefs. In T. A. Revenson & R. A. R. Gurung (Eds.), *Handbook of health psychology* (3e). New York, NY: Routledge.

Broadbent, E., Kahokehr, A., Booth, R., Thomas, J., Windsor, J., Buchanan, C., & . . . Hill, A. (2012). A brief relaxation intervention reduces stress and improves surgical wound healing response: A randomised trial. *Brain, Behavior, and Immunity, 26*(2), 212–217.

Broadbent, E., Petrie, K. J., Main, J., & Weinman, J. (2006). The brief illness perception questionnaire. *Journal of Psychosomatic Research, 60*(6), 631–637.

Brodsky, M., Spritzer, K., Hays, R. D., & Hui, K. (2017). Change in health-related quality-of-life at group and individual levels over time in patients treated for chronic myofascial neck pain. *Journal of Evidence-Based Complementary & Alternative Medicine, 22*(3), 365–368. doi:10.1177/2156587216662779

Brody, G. H., Yu, T., & Shalev, I. (2017). Risky family processes prospectively forecast shorter telomere length mediated through negative emotions. *Health Psychology, 36*(5), 438–444. doi:10.1037/hea0000443

Brondolo, E., Lackey, S., & Love, E. (2012). Race and health: Racial disparities in hypertension and links between racism and health. In A. Baum, T. A. Revenson, & J. Singer (Eds.), *Handbook of health psychology* (2e, pp. 569–594). New York, NY: Taylor & Francis.

Bronfrenbrenner, U. (1977). Toward an experimental ecology of human development. *American Psychologist, 32*, 513–531.

Bronzaft, A. L., & McCarthy, D. P. (1975). The effect of elevated train noise on reading ability. *Environment and Behavior, 7*, 517–527.

Brooks-Gunn, J., & Duncan, G. J. (1997). The effects of poverty on children. *Future of Children, 7*, 55–71.

Brown, D. L. (2008). African American resiliency: Examining racial socialization and social support as protective factors. *Journal of Black Psychology, 34*, 32–48.

Brown, D. R. (1992). Physical activity, aging, and psychological well-being: An overview of the research. *Canadian Journal of Sport Sciences, 17*, 185–193.

Brown, G. W., & Harris, T. (1978). Social origins of depression: A reply. *Psychological Medicine, 8*, 577–588.

Brown, J. D. (1991). Staying fit and staying well: Physical fitness as a moderator of life stress. *Journal of Personality and Social Psychology, 60*, 555–561.

Brown, J. L., Vanable, P. A., Carey, M. P., & Elin, L. (2011). Computerized stress management training for HIV+ women: A pilot intervention study. *AIDS Care, 23*(12), 1525–1532. doi:10.1080/09540121.2011.569699

Brown, K. W., & Moskowitz, D. S. (1997). Does unhappiness make you sick? The role of affect and neuroticism in the experience of common physical symptoms. *Journal of Personality and Social Psychology, 72*, 907–917.

Brown, R. T., Wiener, L., & Kupst, M. J. (2008). Single parents of children with chronic illness: An understudied phenomenon. *Journal of Pediatric Psychology, 33*, 408–421.

Brownson, R. C., Chang, J. C., Davis, J. R., & Smith, C. A. (1991). Physical activity on the job and cancer in Missouri. *American Journal of Public Health, 81*, 639–643.

Brownson, R. C., Eyler, A. A., King, A. C., Brown, D. R., Shyu, Y., & Sallis, J. F. (2000). Patterns and correlates of physical activity among U.S. women 40 years older. *American Journal of Public Health, 90*, 264–270.

Broz, D., Ouellet, L. (2008). Racial and ethnic changes in heroin injection in the United States: Implications for the HIV/AIDS epidemic. *Drug and Alcohol Dependence, 94*(1–3), 221–233.

Bruchac, J. (1993). *The Native American sweat lodge: History and legends*. Freedom, CA: Crossing Press.

Brumberg, J. J. (1997). *The body project: An intimate history of American girls.* New York, NY: Vintage.

Brummett, B. H., Helms, M. J., Dahlstrom, W. G., & Siegler, I. C. (2006). Prediction of all-cause mortality by the Minnesota Multiphasic Personality Inventory Optimisim-pessimism Scale scores: Study of a college sample during a 40-year follow-up period. *Mayo Clinical Proceedings, 81*, 1541–1544.

Brunkard, J., Namulanda, G. & Ratard, R. (2008). Hurricane Katrina deaths, Louisiana, 2005. *Disaster Medicine and Public Health Preparedness, 2*, 215–223. doi:10.1097/DMP.0b013e31818aaf55

Brunner, E. J., Mosdol, A., Witte, D. R., Martikainen, P., Stafford, M., Shipley, M. J., & Marmot, M. G. (2008). Dietary patterns and 15-y risks of major coronary events, diabetes, and mortality. *American Journal of Clinical Nutrition, 87*(5), 1414–1421.

Bruns, D., & Disorbio, J. M. (2009). Assessment of biopsychosocial risk factors for medical treatment: A collaborative approach. *Journal of Clinical Psychology in Medical Settings, 16*(2), 127–147.

Bruns, D., Mueller, K., & Warren, P. A. (2010). A review of evidence-based biopsychosocial laws governing the treatment of pain and injury. *Psychological Injury and Law, 3*(3), 169–181.

Bruss, M. B., Applegate, B., Quitugua, J., Palacios, R. T., & Morris, J. R. (2007). Ethnicity and diet of children: Development of culturally sensitive measures. *Health Education and Behavior, 34*, 735–747.

Bryk, A. S., & Raudenbush, S. W. (1992). *Hierarchical linear models: Applications and data analysis methods.* Newbury Park, CA: SAGE.

Buchanan, T. W., & Tranel, D. (2008). Stress and emotional memory retrieval: Effects of sex and cortisol response. *Neurobiology of Learning and Memory, 89*, 134–141.

Budescu, M., Taylor, R. D., & McGill, R. (2011). Stress and African American women's smoking/drinking to cope: Moderating effects of kin social support. *Journal of Black Psychology, 37*(4), 452–484.

Bulmer, M., Böhnke, J. R., & Lewis, G. J. (2017). Predicting moral sentiment towards physician-assisted suicide: The role of religion, conservatism, authoritarianism, and big five personality. *Personality and Individual Differences, 105*, 244–251. doi:10.1016/j.paid.2016.09.034

Burhansstipnov, L. (2000). Urban Native American health issues. *Cancer, 888*, 987–993.

Burke, A., Upchurch, D. M., Dye, C., & Chyu, L. (2006). Acupuncture use in the United States: Findings from the National Health Interview Survey. *Journal of Alternative and Complementary Medicine, 12*, 639–648.

Burke, G. L., Bertoni, A. G., Shea, S., Tracy, R., Watson, K. E., Blumenthal, R. S., & Carnethon, M. R. (2008). The impact of obesity on cardiovascular disease risk factors and subclinical vascular disease: The multi-ethnic study of atherosclerosis. *Archives of Internal Medicine, 168*, 928–935.

Burleson, B. R., & Mortenson, S. R. (2003). Explaining cultural differences in evaluations of emotional support behaviors: Exploring the mediating influences of value systems and interaction goals. *Communication Research, 30*, 113–146.

Burns, A. B., Brown, J. S., Sachs-Ericsson, N., Plant, E. A., Curtis, J. T., Fredrickson, B. L., Joiner, T. E. (2008). Upward spirals of positive emotion and coping: Replication, extension, and initial exploration of neurochemical substrates. *Personality and Individual Differences, 44*, 360–370.

Burns, V. E., Drayson, M., Ring, C., & Carroll, D. (2002). Perceived stress and psychological well-being are associated with antibody status after meningitis C conjugate vaccination. *Psychosomatic Medicine, 64*, 963–970.

Bush, A. L., Jameson, J. P., Barrera, T., Phillips, L. L., Lachner, N., Evans, G., & . . . Stanley, M. A. (2012). An evaluation of the brief multidimensional measure of religiousness/spirituality in older patients with prior depression or anxiety. *Mental Health, Religion & Culture, 15*(2), 191–203. doi:10.1080/13674676.2011.566263

Buske-Kirschbaum, A., Kirschbaum, C., Stierle, H., Lehnert, H., & Hellhammer, D. (1992). Conditioned increase of natural killer cell activity (NKCA) in humans. *Psychosomatic Medicine, 54*, 123–132.

Büssing, A., & Poier, D. (2017). Christianity: Catholic and seventh-day adventist examples. In D. Von Dras (Ed.), *Better health through spiritual practices: A guide to religious behaviors and perspectives that benefit mind and body* (pp. 151–182). Santa Barbara, CA: Praeger.

Büssing, A., Ostermann, T., Neugebauer, E., & Heusser, P. (2010). Adaptive coping strategies in patients with chronic pain conditions and their interpretation of disease. *BMC Public Health, 10*, 507. doi:10.1186/1471-2458-10-507

Bustillo, N. E., McGinty, H. L., Dahn, J. R., Yanez, B., Antoni, M. H., Kava, B. R., & Penedo, F. J. (2017). Fatalism, medical mistrust, and pretreatment health-related quality of life in ethnically diverse prostate cancer patients. *Psycho-Oncology, 26*(3), 323–329. doi:10.1002/pon.4030

Butler, K. M., Rayens, M., Hahn, E. J., Adkins, S. M., & Staten, R. R. (2012). Smoke-free policy and alcohol use among undergraduate college students. *Public Health Nursing, 29*(3), 256–265. doi:10.1111/j.1525-1446.2011.01000.x

Butler, S. M., Black, D. R., Blue, C. L., Gretebeck, RJ. (2004). Change in diet, physical activity, and body weight in female college freshman. *American Journal of Health Behavior, 28*, 24–32.

Butow, P. N., Coates, A. S., & Dunn, S. M. (1999). Psychosocial predictors of survival in metastatic melanoma. *Journal of Clinical Oncology, 17*, 2256–2263.

Buttagat, V., Narktro, T., Onsrira, K., & Pobsamai, C. (2016). Short-term effects of traditional Thai massage on electromyogram, muscle tension and pain among patients with upper back pain associated with myofascial trigger points. *Complementary Therapies in Medicine, 28*, 8–12. doi:10.1016/j.ctim.2016.07.004

Buzgova, R., Sikorova, L., & Jarosova, D. (2016). Assessing patients' palliative care needs in the final stages of illness during hospitalization. *American Journal of Hospice & Palliative Medicine, 33*(2), 184–193. doi:10.1177/1049909114556528

Byers, T., & Doyle, C. (2004). Diet, physical activity, and cancer . . . what's the connection? Retrieved from https://www.cancer.org/cancer/cancer-causes/diet-physical-activity/diet-and-physical-activity.html

Bynum, W. (2008). *The history of medicine (A very short introduction).* Boston, MA: Oxford University Press.

Byrd, T. L., Mullen, P. D., Selwyn, B. J., & Lorimor, R. (1996). Initiation of prenatal care by low-income Hispanic women in Houston. *Public Health Reports, 111*, 536–540.

Byrd-Bredbenner, C., Lagiou, P., & Trichopoulou, A. (2000). A comparison of household food availability in 11 countries. *Journal of Human Nutrition & Dietetics, 13*, 197–204.

Byrd-Williams, C., Kelly, L. A., Davis, J. N., Spruijt-Metz, D., Goran, M. I. (2007). Influence of gender, BMI and Hispanic ethnicity on physical activity in children. *International Journal of Pediatric Obesity, 2*, 159–166.

Byrne, D., & Mazanov, J. (2016). Smoking and cardiovascular risk: Role of stress in the genesis of smoking behavior. In M. Alvarenga & D. Byrne, *Handbook of psychocardiology* (pp. 79–97). New York, NY: Springer.

Byrne, M. L., Horne, S., O'Brien-Simpson, N. M., Walsh, K. A., Reynolds, E. C., Schwartz, O. S., . . . Allen, N. B. (2017). Associations between observed parenting behavior and adolescent inflammation two and a half years later in a community sample. *Health Psychology, 36*(7), 641–651. doi:10.1037/hea0000502

Byrne-Davis, L., & Vedhara, K. (2008). Psychoneuroimmunology. *Social and Personality Psychology Compass, 2*(2), 751–764.

Caballero, A. R., Sunday, S. R., & Halmi, K. A. (2004). A comparison of cognitive and behavioral symptoms between Mexican and American eating disorder patients. *International Journal of Eating Disorders, 34*, 136–141.

Cade, W. T., Reeds, D. N., Mondy, K. E., Overton, E. T., Grassino, J. J., Tucker, S. S., & . . . Yarasheski, K. E. (2010). Yoga lifestyle intervention reduces blood pressure in HIV-infected adults with cardiovascular disease risk factors. *HIV Medicine, 11*(6), 379–388. doi:10.1111/j.1468-1293.2009.00801.x

Cahill, L., Prins, B., Weber, M., & McGaugh, J. L. (1994). Beta-adrenergic activation and memory for emotional events. *Nature, 371*, 702–704.

Cairney, J., Kwan, M. Y. W., Veldhuizen, S., & Faulkner, G. E. J. (2014). Who uses exercise as a coping strategy for stress? Results from a national survey of Canadians. *Journal of Physical Activity & Health, 11*(5), 908–916. doi:10.1123/jpah.2012-0107

Calandri, E., Graziano, F., Borghi, M., & Bonino, S. (2016). Depression, positive and negative affect, optimism and health-related quality of life in recently diagnosed multiple sclerosis patients: The role of identity, sense of coherence, and self-efficacy. *Journal of Happiness Studies, 19*(1), 277–295. doi:10.1007/s10902-016-9818-x

Calhoun, G., & Alforque, M. (1996). Prenatal substance afflicted children: An overview and review of the literature. *Education, 117*, 30–39.

Callister, L. C. (2003). Cultural influences on pain perceptions and behaviors. *Home Health Care Management and Practice, 15*, 207–211.

Calvo, M. G., Szabo, A., & Capafons, J. (1996). Anxiety and heart rate under psychological stress: The effects of exercise-training. *Anxiety, Stress and Coping, 9*, 321–337.

Cameron, L. D., Durazo, A., & Rus, H. M. (2016). Illness representations. In Y. Benyamini, M. Johnston, & E. C. Karademas (Eds.), *Assessment in health psychology* (pp. 45–59). Boston, MA: Hogrefe.

Campaign for Tobacco-free Kids. (2017). What we do. Author, Washington, DC. Retrieved from www.tobaccofreekids.org

Campbell, C. M., France, C. R., Robinson, M. E., Logan, H. L., Geffken, G. R., & Fillingim, R. B. (2008). Ethnic differences in the nociceptive flexion reflex (NFR). *Pain, 134*, 91–96.

Campbell, M. K., Hudson, M. A., Resnicow, K., Blakeney, N., Paxton, A., & Baskin, M. (2007). Church-based health promotion interventions: Evidence and lessons learned. *Annual Review of Public Health, 28*, 213–234.

Campbell, R., Greeson, M. R., Bybee, D., & Raja, S. (2008). The cooccurrence of childhood sexual abuse, adult sexual assault, intimate partner violence, and sexual harassment: A mediational model of post-traumatic stress disorder and physical health outcomes. *Journal of Consulting and Clinical Psychology, 76*, 194–207.

Campbell, T. A., Auerbach, S. M., & Kiesler, D. J. (2007). Relationship of interpersonal behaviors and health-related control appraisals to patient satisfaction and compliance in a university health center. *Journal of American College Health, 55*, 333–340.

Campbell, T. C., & Campbell, T. M. (2016). *The China study: The most comprehensive study of nutrition ever conducted.* Dallas, TX: BenBella Books.

Campfield, L. A., Smith, F. J., & Burn, P. (1996). The OB protein (leptin) pathway—A link between adipose tissue mass and central neural networks. *Hormone and Metabolic Research, 28*, 619–632.

Campos, B., & Kim, H. S. (2017). Incorporating the cultural diversity of family and close relationships into the study of health. *American Psychologist, 72*(6), 543–554. doi:10.1037/amp0000122

Campos, B., Schetter, C. D., Abdou, C. M., Hobel, C. J., Glynn, L. M., & Sandman, C. A. (2008). Familialism, social support, and stress: Positive implications for pregnant Latinas. *Cultural Diversity and Ethnic Minority Psychology, 14*,155–162.

Cannon, W. B. (1914). The interrelations of emotions as suggested by recent physiological researches. *American Journal of Physiology, 25*, 256–282.

Cannon, W. B. (1929). *Bodily changes in pain, hunger, fear and rage.* Oxford, UK: Appleton.

Cannon, W. B. (1932). *The wisdom of the body*. New York, NY: Norton.

Cantor, M. H. (1979). Neighbors and friends: An overlooked resource in the informal support system. *Research on Aging, 1*, 434–463.

Cao, G., Booth, S. L., Sadowski, J. A., & Prior, R. (1998). Increases in human plasma antioxidant capacity after consumption of controlled diets high in fruits and vegetables. *American Journal of Clinical Nutrition, 68*, 1081–1087.

Cao, H., Liu, Z., Steinmann, P., Mu, Y., Luo, H., & Liu, J. (2012). Chinese herbal medicines for treatment of hand, foot, and mouth disease: A systematic review of randomized clinical trials. *European Journal of Integrative Medicine, 4*(1), e85–e111. doi:10.10.16/J.EUJIM.2011.11.004

Capik, C., & Gözüm, S. (2011). Development and validation of health beliefs model scale for prostate cancer screenings (HBM-PCS): Evidence from exploratory and confirmatory factor analyses. *European Journal of Oncology Nursing, 15*(5), 478–485.

Caplan, G. (1964). *Principles of preventive psychiatry*. Oxford, UK: Basic Books.

Caporaso, F., Pulkovski, N., Sprott, H., & Mannion, A. (2012). How well do observed functional limitations explain the variance in Roland Morris scores in patients with chronic non-specific low back pain undergoing physiotherapy? *European Spine Journal, 21* Suppl 2187–195.

Cappell, H., & Greeley, J. (1987). Alcohol and tension reduction: An update on research and theory. In H. T. Blane & K. E. Leonard (Eds.), *Psychological theories of drinking and alcoholism* (pp. 15–50). New York, NY: Guilford Press.

Cardoso, A. L., Guedes, J. R., Pereira de Almeida, L., & Pedroso de Lima, M. C. (2012). miR-155 modulates microglia-mediated immune response by down-regulating SOCS-1 and promoting cytokine and nitric oxide production. *Immunology, 135*(1), 73–88. doi:10.1111/j.1365-2567.2011.03514.x

Cardoso, C., Valkanas, H., Serravalle, L., & Ellenbogen, M. A. (2016). Oxytocin and social context moderate social support seeking in women during negative memory recall. *Psychoneuroendocrinology, 70*, 63–69. doi:10.1016/j.psyneuen.2016.05.001

Carey, B. (2008). Psychiatrists revise the book of human troubles. *New York Times*, December, 17. Retrieved from https://www.nytimes.com/2008/12/18/health/18psych.html

Carlson, L. E., Speca, M., Patel, K. D., & Goodey, E. (2003). Mindfulness-based stress reduction in relation to quality of life, mood, symptoms of stress, and immune parameters in breast and prostate cancer outpatients. *Psychosomatic Medicine, 65*, 571–581.

Carlson, L., Speca, M., Faris, P., & Patel, K. (2007). One year pre-post intervention follow-up of psychological, immune, endocrine and blood pressure outcomes of mindfulness-based stress reduction (MBSR) in breast and prostate cancer outpatients. *Brain, Behavior, and Immunity, 21*(8), 1038–1049.

Carmichael Olson, H., Streissguth, A.P., Sampson, P. D., Barr, H. M., Bookstein, F. L., & Thiede, K. (1997). Association of prenatal alcohol exposure with behavioral and learning problems in early adolescence. *Journal of the American Academy of Child & Adolescent Psychiatry, 36*(9), 1187–1194.

Carnagey, N. L., Anderson, C. A., & Bushman, B. J. (2007). The effect of video game violence on physiological desensitization to real life violence. *Journal of Experimental Social Psychology, 43*, 489–496.

Carney, D. R., Cuddy, A. J. C., & Yap, A. J. (2010). Power posing: Brief nonverbal displays affect neuroendocrine levels and risk tolerance. *Psychological Science, 21*(10), 1363–1368. doi:10.1177/0956797610383437

Carney, D. R., Cuddy, A. J. C., & Yap, A. J. (2015). Review and summary of research on the embodied effects of expansive (vs. contractive) nonverbal displays. *Psychological Science, 26*, 657–663. doi:10.1177/0956797614566855

Carney, R. M., & Freedland, K. E. (2017). Depression and coronary heart disease. *Nature Reviews Cardiology, 14*(3), 145–155. doi:10.1038/nrcardio.2016.181

Carpenter, M. J., Strange, C., Jones, Y., Dickson, M. R., Carter, C. Moseley, M. A., & Gilbert, G. E. (2007). Does genetic testing result in behavioral health change? Changes in smoking behavior following testing for alpha-1 antitrypsin deficiency. *Annals of Behavioral Medicine, 33*, 22–28.

Carrard, V., Schmid Mast, M., & Cousin, G. (2016). Beyond "one size fits all": Physician nonverbal adaptability to patients' need for paternalism and its positive consultation outcomes. *Health Communication, 31*(11), 1327–1333. doi:10.1080/10410236.2015.1052871

Carrico, A., & Antoni, M. (2008). Effects of psychological interventions on neuroendocrine hormone regulation and immune status in HIV-positive persons: A review of randomized controlled trials. *Psychosomatic Medicine, 70*(5), 575–584.

Carroll, J. E., Diez Roux, A. V., Fitzpatrick, A. L., & Seeman, T. (2013). Low social support is associated with shorter leukocyte telomere length in late life: Multi-ethnic study of atherosclerosis. *Psychosomatic Medicine, 75*(2), 171–177. doi:10.1097/PSY.0b013e31828233bf

Carstensen, L. L. (1987). Age-related changes in social activity. In L. L. Carstensen & B. A. Edelstein (Eds.), *Handbook of clinical gerontology* (pp. 222–237). Elmsford, NY: Pergamon Press.

Carstensen, L. L., & Fisher, J. E. (1991). Treatment application for psychological and behavioral problems of the elderly in nursing homes. In P. A. Wisocki (Ed.), *Handbook of clinical behavior therapy with the elderly client. Applied clinical psychology* (pp. 337–362). New York, NY: Plenum Press.

Carstensen, L. L., Isaacowitz, D. M., & Charles, S. T. (1999). Taking time seriously: A theory of socioemotional selectivity. *American Psychologist, 54*, 165–181.

Carter, C. S. (1998). Neuroendocrine perspectives on social attachment and love. *Psychoneuroendocrinology, 23*, 779–818.

Carter, R. T., Muchow, C., & Pieterse, A. L. (2017). Construct, predictive validity, and measurement equivalence of the race-based traumatic stress symptom scale for black Americans. *Traumatology, 24*(1), 8–16. doi:10.1037/trm0000128

Carvajal, S. C., Garner, R. L., & Evans, R. I. (1998). Dispositional optimism as a protective factor in resisting HIV exposure in sexually active inner-city minority adolescents. *Journal of Applied Social Psychology, 28*, 2196–2211.

Carver, C. S., & Scheier, M. F. (1994). Situational coping and coping dispositions in a stressful transaction. *Journal of Social and Personality Psychology, 56*, 267–283.

Carver, C. S., & Scheier, M. F. (1999). Stress, coping, and self-regulatory processes. In L. A. Pervin & O. P. John (Eds.), *Handbook of personality: Theory and research* (2nd ed.) (pp. 553–575). New York, NY: Guilford Press.

Carver, C. S., & Vargas, S. (2011). Coping and health. In A. Steptoe, K. Freedland, J. R. Jennings, M. M. Llabre, S. B. Manuck, & E. J. Susman (Eds.), *Handbook of behavioral medicine: Methods and applications* (pp. 197–208). New York, NY: Springer.

Carver, C. S., Pozo, C., Harris, S. D., Noriega, V., Scheier, M. F., Robinson, D. S., . . . Clark, K. C. (1993). How coping mediates the effect of optimism on distress: A study of women with early stage breast cancer. *Journal of Social and Personality Psychology, 65*, 375–390.

Carver, C. S., Pozo-Kaderman, C., Harris, S. D., Noriega, V., Scheier, M. F., Robinson, D. S., Clark, K. C. (1994). Optimism versus pessimism predicts the quality of women's adjustments to early stage breast cancer. *Cancer, 73*, 1213–1220.

Carver, C. S., Scheier, M. F., & Weintraub, J. K. (1989). Assessing coping strategies: A theoretically based approach. *Journal of Personality and Social Psychology, 56*, 267–283.

Case, R. B., Moss, A. J., Case, N., McDermott, M., & Eberly, S. (1992). Living alone after myocardial infarction: Impact on prognosis. *Journal of the American Medical Association, 267*, 515–524.

Caspersen, C. J., Powell, K. E., & Christenson, G. M. (1985). Physical activity, exercise, and physical fitness: Definitions and distinctions for health related research. *Public Health Reports, 100*, 126–131.

Caspi, A., Begg, D., Dickson, N., Harrington, H., Langley, J., Moffitt, T. E., & Silva, P. A. (1997). Personality differences predict health-risk behaviors in young adulthood: Evidence from a longitudinal study. *Journal of Personality and Social Psychology, 73*, 1052–1063.

Caspi, A., Hariri, A. R., Holmes, A., Uher, R., & Moffitt, T. E., (2010). Genetic sensitivity to the environment: The case of the serotonin transporter gene and its implications for studying complex diseases and traits. *American Journal of Psychiatry, 167*(5), 509–527.

Cassel, J. (1976). The contribution of the social environment to host resistance. *American Journal of Epidemiology, 104*, 107–123.

Cassetta, J. A., Boden-Albala, B., Sciacca, R. R., & Giardina, E. V. (2007). Association of education and race/ethnicity with physical activity in insured urban women. *Journal of Women's Health, 16*, 902–908.

Cassidy, J., & Shaver, P. R. (1999). *Handbook of attachment: Theory, research, and clinical applications.* New York, NY: Guilford Press.

Catania, J. A., Binson, D., Dolcini, M. M., Moskowitz, J. T., & van der Straten, A. (2002). Frontiers in the behavioral epidemiology of HIV/STDs. In A. Baum, T. A. Revenson, & J. E. Singer (Eds.), *Handbook of health psychology* (pp. 777–800). Mahwah, NJ: Erlbaum.

Catania, J. A., Kegeles, S. M., & Coates, T. J. (1990a). Psychosocial predictors of people who fail to return for their HIV test results. *AIDS, 4*, 261–262.

Catania, J. A., Kegeles, S. M., & Coates, T. J. (1990b). Towards an understanding of risk behavior: An AIDS risk reduction model (ARRM). *Health Education Quarterly, 17*, 381–399.

Cattell, R. B. (1966). *The scientific analysis of personality*. Chicago, IL: Aldine.

Cauce, A. M., Felner, R. D., & Primavera, J. (1982). Social support in high-risk adolescents: Structural components and adaptive impact. *American Journal of Community Psychology, 10*, 417–428.

Cederbaum, J. A., Rice, E., Craddock, J., Pimentel, V., & Beaver, P. (2017). Social networks of HIV-positive women and their association with social support and depression symptoms. *Women & Health, 57*(2), 268–282. doi:10.1080/03630242.2016.1157126

Centers for Disease Control and Prevention (CDC). (2003). Deaths, final data for 2001, National vital statistics reports, 52. Author, Atlanta, GA. Retrieved from http://www.cdc.gov/nchs/data/nvsr/nvsr52/nvsr52_03.pdf

Centers for Disease Control and Prevention (CDC). (2004). Deaths, final data for 2002, National vital statistics reports, 53. Author, Atlanta, GA. Retrieved from http://www.cdc.gov/nchs/fastats/infmort.htm

Centers for Disease Control and Prevention (CDC). (2005). Measuring healthy days: Population assessment of health-related quality of life. Author, Atlanta, GA. Retrieved from https://www.cdc.gov/hrqol/

Centers for Disease Control and Prevention (CDC). (2015). Health disparities. National Center for Health Statistics. Multiple Cause of Death 1999–2015. Author, Atlanta, GA. Retrieved from http://wonder.cdc.gov/mcd-icd10.html.

Centers for Disease Control and Prevention (CDC). (2016). Cigarette smoking among adults—United States, 2005–2015. *Morbidity and Mortality Weekly Report 65*(44), 1205–1211.

Centers for Disease Control and Prevention (CDC). (2018). Resources for researchers. Retrieved from https://www.cdc.gov/nchs/nchs_for_you/researchers.htm

Centers for Disease Control. (2018). Chronic Disease Prevention and Health Promotion. Atlanta, GA. Retrieved from https://www.cdc.gov/chronicdisease/index.htm

Cerin, E., Vandelanotte, C., Leslie, E., & Merom, D. (2008). Recreational facilities and leisure-time physical activity: An analysis of moderators and self-efficacy as a mediator. *Health Psychology, 27*, S126–S135.

Cervone, D., Shadel, W. G., Smith, R. E., & Fiori, M. (2006). Self-regulation: Reminders and suggestions from personality science. *Applied Psychology: An International Review, 55*(3), 333–385.

Cesario, J., Jonas, K. J., & Carney, D. R. (2017). CRSP special issue on power poses: What was the point and what did we learn? *Comprehensive Results in Social Psychology, 2*(1), 1–5.

Chafin, S., Christenfeld, N., & Gerin, W. (2008). Improving cardiovascular recovery from stress with brief post-stress exercise. *Health Psychology, 27*, S64–S72.

Chambers, J. A., & O'Carroll, R. E. (2016). Adherence to medical advice. In Y. Benyamini, M. Johnston, & E. C. Karademas (Eds.), *Assessment in health psychology* (pp. 86–102). Boston, MA: Hogrefe.

Champion, J., & Collins, J. L. (2012). Comparison of a theory-based (AIDS Risk Reduction Model) cognitive behavioral intervention versus enhanced counseling for abused ethnic minority adolescent women on infection with sexually transmitted infection: Results of a randomized controlled trial. *International Journal of Nursing Studies, 49*(2), 138–150. doi:10.1016/j.ijnurstu.2011.08.010

Champion, V. L. (1999). Revised susceptibility, benefits, and barriers scale for mammography screening. *Research in Nursing and Health, 22*, 341–348.

Champion, V. L., Ray, D. W., Heilman, D. K., & Springston, J. K. (2000). A tailored intervention for mammography among low-income African-American women. *Journal of Psychosocial Oncology, 18*, 1–13.

Champion, V., & Menon, U. (1997). Predicting mammography and breast self-examination in African American women. *Cancer Nursing, 20*, 315–322.

Chan, C.W. and Chang, J.K. (1976). The role of Chinese medicine in New York City's Chinatown. *American Journal of Chinese Medicine, 4*(1), 31–45.

Chan, S. (2012). Early adolescent depressive mood: Direct and indirect effects of attributional styles and coping. *Child Psychiatry & Human Development, 43*(3), 455–470. doi:10.1007/s10578-011-0275-9

Chand, G. B., Wu, J., Qiu, D., & Hajjar, I. (2017). Racial differences in insular connectivity and thickness and related cognitive impairment in hypertension. *Frontiers in Aging Neuroscience*, 9. doi:10.3389/fnagi.2017.00177

Chandarana, P., & Pellizzari, J. R. (2001). Health psychology: South Asian perspectives. In S. S. Kazarian & D. R. Evans (Eds.), *Handbook of cultural health psychology* (pp. 411–444). San Diego, CA: Academic Press.

Chandola, T., Britton, A., Brunner, E., Hemingway, H., Malik, M., Kumari, M., . . . Marmot, M. (2008). Work stress and coronary heart disease: What are the mechanisms? *European Heart Journal, 29*(5), 640–648.

Chang, D. M., Chang, W. Y., Kuo, S. Y., & Chang, M. L. (1997). The effects of traditional antirheumatic herbal medicines on immune response cells. *Journal of Rheumatology, 24*, 436–441.

Chang, E. C. (1998). Dispositional optimism and primary and secondary appraisal of a stressor: Controlling for confounding influences and relations to coping and psychological and physical adjustment. *Journal of Personality and Social Psychology, 74*, 1109–1120.

Chang, J., & Wittert, G. (2009). Effects of bariatric surgery on morbidity and mortality in severe obesity. *International Journal of Evidence-Based Healthcare, 7*(1), 43–48. doi:10.1111/j.1744-1609.2009.00123.x

Chang, P. P., Ford, D. E., Meoni, L. A., Wang, N.,, & Klag, M. J. (2002). Anger in young men and subsequent premature cardiovascular disease: The precursors study. *Archives of Internal Medicine, 162*(8), 901–906. doi:10.1001/archinte.162.8.901

Chassin, L., Rogosch, F., & Barrera, M. (1991). Substance use and symptomatology among adolescent children of alcoholics. *Journal of Abnormal Psychology, 100*, 449–463.

Chaturvedi, S., & Venkateswaran, C. (2008, March). New research in psychooncology. *Current Opinion in Psychiatry, 21*(2), 206–210

Chawla, N., & Kafescioglu, N. (2012). Evidence-based couple therapy for chronic illnesses: enriching the emotional quality of relationships with emotionally focused therapy. *Journal of Family Psychotherapy, 23*(1), 42–53. doi:10.1080/08975353.2012.654080

Chen, B., Zhou, Y., Yang, P., Liu, L., Qin, X., & Wu, X. (2011). CDH1 −160C>A gene polymorphism is an ethnicity-dependent risk factor for gastric cancer. *Cytokine, 55*(2), 266–273. doi:10.1016/j.cyto.2011.04.008

Chen, C., Tang, S., & Chen, C. (2012). Meta-analysis of cultural differences in Western and Asian patient-perceived barriers to managing cancer pain. *Palliative Medicine, 26*(3), 206–221. doi:10.1177/0269216311402711

Chen, E. (2004). Why socioeconomic status affects the health of children. *Current Directions in Psychological Science, 13*, 112–115.

Chen, E., Brody, G. H., & Miller, G. E. (2017). Childhood close family relationships and health. *American Psychologist, 72*(6), 555–566. 10.1037/amp0000067

Chen, H., Haley, W. E., Robinson, B. E., & Schonwetter, R. S. (2003). Decisions for hospice care in patients with advanced cancer. *Journal of the American Geriatrics Society, 51*, 789–797.

Chen, S., Tsai, J., & Lee, W. (2009). The impact of illness perception on adherence to therapeutic regimens of patients with hypertension in Taiwan. *Journal of Clinical Nursing, 18*(15), 2234–2244. doi:10.1111/j.1365-2702.2008.02706.x

Chen, Y., & Lin, H. (2011). Increased risk of cancer subsequent to severe depression—A nationwide population-based study. *Journal of Affective Disorders, 131*(1–3), 200–206. doi:10.1016/j.jad.2010.12.006

Chen, Z., Klimentidis, Y. C., Bea, J. W., Ernst, K. C., Hu, C., Jackson, R., & Thomson, C. A. (2017). Body mass index, waist circumference, and mortality in a large multiethnic postmenopausal cohort—Results from the women's health initiative. *Journal of the American Geriatrics Society, 65*(9), 1907–1915. doi:10.1111/jgs.14790

Cherr, G., Zimmerman, P., Wang, J., & Dosluoglu, H. (2008). Patients with depression are at increased risk for secondary cardiovascular events after lower extremity revascularization. *Journal of General Internal Medicine, 23*(5), 629–634.

Cherry, K. E., Sampson, L., Galea, S., Marks, L. D., Nezat, P. F., Baudoin, K. H., & Lyon, B. A. (2017). Optimism and hope after multiple disasters: Relationships to health-related quality of life. *Journal of Loss and Trauma, 22*(1), 61–76. doi:10.1080/15325024.2016.1187047

Chesney, M. A., & Antoni, M. H. (2002). Innovative approaches to health psychology: Prevention and treatment lessons from AIDS. *Application and practice in health psychology*. Washington, DC: American Psychological Association.

Chesney, M. A., & Ozer, E. M. (1995). Women and health: in search of a paradigm. *Women's Health: Research on Gender, Behavior and Policy, 1*, 3–26.

Chesney, M., & Darbes, L. (1998). Social support and heart disease in women: Implications for intervention. In K. Orth-Gomer & M. Chesney (Eds.), *Women, stress, and heart disease* (pp. 165–182). Mahwah, NJ: Erlbaum.

Chida, Y., & Steptoe, A. (2009). The association of anger and hostility with future coronary heart disease: A meta-analytic review of prospective evidence. *Journal of the American College of Cardiology, 53*(11), 936–946.

Chida, Y., Hamer, M., Wardle, J., & Steptoe, A. (2008). Do stress-related psychosocial factors contribute to cancer incidence and survival? *Nature Clinical Practice. Oncology, 5*(8), 466–475.

Child and Adolescent Health Measurement Initiative. (2016). Who we are. Author, Baltimore, MD. Retrieved from http://www.cahmi.org/

Chilman, C. S. (1993). Hispanic families in the United States. In H. P. McAdoo (Ed.), *Family ethnicity: Strength in diversity* (pp. 141–163). Newbury Park, CA: SAGE.

Chin, H. B., Sipe, T., Elder, R., Mercer, S. L., Chattopadhyay, S. K., Jacob, V., & . . . Santelli, J. (2012). The effectiveness of group-based comprehensive risk-reduction and abstinence education interventions to prevent or reduce the risk of adolescent pregnancy, human immunodeficiency virus, and sexually transmitted infections. *American Journal of Preventive Medicine, 42*(3), 272–294. doi:10.1016/j.amepre.2011.11.006

Ching, S. Y., Martinson, I. M., & Wong, T. S. (2012). Meaning making: Psychological adjustment to breast cancer by Chinese women. *Qualitative Health Research, 22*(2), 250–262. doi:10.1177/1049732311421679

Cho, D., & Lu, Q. (2017). The association between fear of cancer recurrence and quality of life among Chinese cancer survivors: Main effect hypothesis and buffering hypothesis. *Quality of Life Research, 26*(9), 2375–2385. doi:10.1007/s11136-017-1585-6

Choi, H. K., & Curhan, G. (2008). Soft drinks, fructose consumption, and the risk of gout in men: Prospective cohort study. *British Medical Journal, 336*, 309–312.

Choi, H., Meininger, J. C., Roberts, R. E. (2006). Ethnic differences in adolescents' mental distress, social stress, and resources. *Adolescence, 41*, 263–283.

Choi, S., Rankin, S., Stewart, A., & Oka, R. (2008). Effects of acculturation on smoking behavior in Asian Americans: A meta-analysis. *Journal of Cardiovascular Nursing, 23*, 67–73.

Choi, T., Lee, M., Kim, T., Zaslawski, C., & Ernst, E. (2012). Acupuncture for the treatment of cancer pain: A systematic review of randomised clinical trials. *Supportive Care in Cancer, 20*(6), 1147–1158. doi:10.1007/s00520-012-1432-9

Chopra, A., & Doiphode, V. (2002). Ayurvedic medicine: Core concept, therapeutic principles, and current relevance. *Medical Clinics of North America, 86*, 75–89.

Chopra, A., Saluja, M., Tillu, G., Venugopalan, A., Narsimulu, G., Handa, R., & . . . Patwardhan, B. (2012). Comparable efficacy of standardized Ayurveda formulation and hydroxychloroquine sulfate (HCQS) in the treatment of rheumatoid arthritis (RA): A randomized investigator-blind controlled study. *Clinical Rheumatology, 31*(2), 259–269. doi:10.1007/s10067-011-1809-z

Chou, K. (2012). Perceived discrimination and depression among new migrants to Hong Kong: The moderating role of social support and neighborhood collective efficacy. *Journal of Affective Disorders, 138*(1/2), 63–70. doi:10.1016/j.jad.2011.12.029

Chowdhury, R. I., Islam, M. A., Gulshan, J., & Chakraborty, N. (2007). Delivery complications and healthcare-seeking behaviour: The Bangladesh Demographic Health Survey, 1999–2000. *Health and Social Care in the Community, 15*, 254–264.

Chrisler, J. C. (2018). Teaching health psychology from a size-acceptance perspective. *Fat Studies, 7*(1), 33–43, doi:10.1080/21604851.2017.1360668

Christensen, A. J., Smith, T. W., Turner, C. W., Holman, J. M., & Gregory, M. C. (1990). Type of hemodialysis and preference for behavioral involvement: Interactive effects on adherence in end-stage renal disease. *Health Psychology, 9*, 225–236.

Christian, L. (2012). Psychoneuroimmunology in pregnancy: immune pathways linking stress with maternal health, adverse birth outcomes, and fetal development. *Neuroscience and Biobehavioral Reviews, 36*(1), 350–361.

Christiansen, C. L., Wang, F., Barton, M. B., Kreuter, W., Elmore, J. G., Gelfand, A. E., & Fletcher, S. W. (2000). Predicting the cumulative risk of false-positive mammograms. *Journal of the National Cancer Institute, 92*, 1657–1666.

Chun, C., Moos, R. H., & Cronkite, R. C. (2006). Culture: A fundamental context for the stress and coping paradigm. In P. T. P. Wong & L. C. J. Wong (Eds.), *Handbook of multicultural perspectives on stress and coping* (pp. 29–53). Dallas, TX: Spring.

Chung, H., & Breslau, N. (2008). The latent structure of post-traumatic stress disorder: Tests of invariance by gender and trauma type. *Psychological Medicine, 38*, 563–573.

Chung, K. C., Hamill, J. B., Kim, H. M., Walter, M. R., & Wilkins, E. G. (1999). Predictors of patients satisfaction in an outpatient plastic surgery clinic. *Annals of Plastic Surgery, 42*, 56–60.

Chung, R. C., & Lin, K. (1994). Help-seeking behavior among Southeast Asian refugees. *Journal of Community Psychology, 22*, 109–120.

Ciechanowski, P. S., Walker, E. A., Katon, W. J., & Russo, J. E. (2002). Attachment theory: A model for health care utilization and somatization. *Psychosomatic Medicine, 64*, 660–667.

Cillessen, L., van de Van, M. O., & Karremans, J. C. (2017). The role of trait mindfulness in quality of life and asthma control among adolescents with asthma. *Journal of Psychosomatic Research, 99*, 143–148. doi:10.1016/j.jpsychores.2017.06.014

Clancy, S. M., & Dollinger, S. J. (1993). Photographic description of the self: Gender and age differences in social connectedness. *Sex Roles, 29*, 477–495.

Clark, D. O. (1995). Racial and educational differences in physical activity among older adults. *Gerontologist, 35*, 472–480.

Clark, M. (1959). *Health in the Mexican American culture.* Berkeley, CA: University of California Press.

Clark, N. M., Cabana, M. D., Nan, B., Gong, Z. M., Slish, K. K., Birk, N. A., & Kaciroti, N. (2008). The clinician-patient partnership paradigm: Outcomes associated with physician communication behavior. *Clinical Pediatrics, 47*, 49–57.

Clark, P. I., Scarisbrick-Hauser, A., Gautam, S. P., & Wirk, S. J. (1999). Anti-tobacco socialization in homes of African-American and White parents, and smoking and nonsmoking parents. *Journal of Adolescent Health, 24*, 329–339.

Clauss-Ehlers, C. S. (2008). Sociocultural factors, resilience, and coping: Support for a culturally sensitive measure of resilience. *Journal of Applied Developmental Psychology, 29*, 197–212.

Clifford, S., Barber, N., & Horne, R. (2008). Understanding different beliefs held by adherers, unintentional nonadherers, and intentional nonadherers: Application of the Necessity-Concerns Framework. *Journal of Psychosomatic Research, 64*, 41–46.

Clucas, C., Sibley, E., Harding, R., Liu, L., Catalan, J., & Sherr, L. (2011). A systematic review of interventions for anxiety in people with HIV. *Psychology, Health & Medicine, 16*(5), 528–547. doi:10.1080/13548506.2011.579989

Coates, T. J., McKusick, L., Kuno, R., & Stites, D. (1989). Stress management training reduces number of sexual partners but does not enhance immune function in men infected with HIV. *American Journal of Public Health, 79*, 885–887.

Cobb, C. L., Xie, D., & Sanders, G. L. (2016). Coping styles and depression among undocumented hispanic immigrants. *Journal of Immigrant and Minority Health, 18*(4), 864–870. doi.10.1007/s10903-015-0270-5

Cobb, S. (1976). Social support as a moderator of life stress. *Psychosomatic Medicine, 38*, 300–314.

Cockerham, W. C. (1997). Lifestyles, social class, demographic characteristics, and health behavior. In D. S. Gochman (Ed.), *Handbook of health behavior research. 1: Personal and social determinants* (pp. 253–265). New York, NY: Plenum Press.

Coddington, R. D. (1972). The significance of life events as etiologic factors in the diseases of children. I. A survey of professional workers. *Journal of Psychosomatic Research, 16*, 7–18.

Coe, C. L. (2010). All roads lead to psychoneuroimmunology. In J. M. Suls, K. W. Davidson, & R. M. Kaplan (Eds.), *Handbook of health psychology and behavioral medicine* (pp. 182–202). New York, NY: Guilford.

Cohen Silver, R., Holman, E. A., McIntosh, D. N., Poulin, M., & Gil-Rivas, V. (2002). Nationwide longitudinal study of psychological responses to September 11. *Journal of the American Medical Association, 288*, 1235–1244.

Cohen, K. (2003). *Honoring the medicine: The essential guide to Native American healing.* New York, NY: Ballantine Books.

Cohen, S., & Herbert, T. B. (1996). Health psychology: Psychological factors and physical disease from the perspective of human psychoneuroimmunology. *Annual Review of Psychology, 47*, 113–142.

Cohen, S., & Wills, T. A. (1985). Stress, social support, and the buffering hypothesis. *Psychological Bulletin, 98*, 310–357.

Cohen, S., Alper, C., Doyle, W., Adler, N., Treanor, J., & Turner, R. (2008). Objective and subjective socioeconomic status and susceptibility to the common cold. *Health Psychology, 27*(2), 268–274.

Cohen, S., Evans, G. W., Krantz, D. S., & Stokols, D. (1980). Physiological, motivational, and cognitive effects of aircraft noise on children: Moving from the laboratory to the field. *American Psychologist, 35*, 231–243.

Cohen, S., Frank, E., Doyle, W. J., Skoner, D. P., Rabin, B. S., & Gwaltney, J. M. Jr. (1998). Types of stressors that increase susceptibility to the common cold in healthy adults. *Health Psychology, 17*, 214–223.

Cohen, S., Glass, D. C., & Singer, J. E. (1973). Apartment noise, auditory discrimination, and reading ability in children. *Journal of Experimental Social Psychology, 9*, 407–422.

Cohen, S., Kamarck, T., & Mermelstein, R. (1983). A global measure of perceived stress. *Journal of Health and Social Behavior, 24*, 385–396.

Cokley, K. (2007). Critical issues in the measurement of ethnic and racial identity: Areferendum on the state of the field. *Journal of Counseling Psychology, 54*, 224–234.

Col, N., Ngo, L., Fortin, J., Goldberg, R., & O'Connor, A. (2007). Can computerized decision support help patients make complex treatment decisions? A randomized controlled trial of an individualized menopause decision aid. *Medical Decision Making, 27*(5), 585–598.

Colditz, G. A., & Frazier, A. L. (1995). Models of breast cancer show that risk is set by early events in life: Prevention efforts must shift focus. *Cancer Epidemiology, Biomarkers and Prevention, 4*, 567–571.

Cole, S. R., Bryant, C. A., McDermott, R. J., Sorrell, C., & Flynn, M. (1997). Beliefs and mammography screening. *American Journal of Preventive Medicine, 13*, 439–443.

Cole, S. W., & Kemeny, M. E. (1997). Psychobiology of HIV infection. *Critical Reviews in Neurobiology, 11*, 289–321.

Cole, T.B. (2006). Rape at U.S. colleges often fueled by alcohol. *Journal of the American Medical Association, 296*, 504–505.

Coleman, K., Koffman, J., & Daniels, C. (2007). Why is this happening to me? Illness beliefs held by haredi Jewish breast cancer patients: An exploratory study. *Spirituality and Health International, 8*, 121–134.

Coleman-Cowger, V., Schauer, G. L., & Peters, E. N. (2017). Marijuana and tobacco co-use among a nationally representative sample of U.S. pregnant and non-pregnant women: 2005–2014 national survey on drug use and health findings. *Drug and Alcohol Dependence, 177*, 130–135. doi:10.1016/j.drugalcdep.2017.03.025

Colgan, D. D., Hidalgo, N. J., & Priester, P. E. (2017). The middle path to health: The relationship between Buddhist practices and beliefs, and health outcomes. In D. Von Dras (Ed.), *Better health through spiritual practices* (pp. 43–72). Santa Barbara, CA: Praeger.

Colgan, D. D., Hidalgo, N. J., & Priester, P. E. (2017). The middle path to health: The relationship between Buddhist practices and beliefs, and health outcomes. In D. Von Dras (Ed.), *Better health through spiritual practices* (pp. 43–72). Santa Barbara, CA: Praeger.

Colin, J. & Paperwalla, G. (2012). People of Haitian heritage. In L. Purnell, *Transcultural health care: A culturally competent approach* (chap. 15). Philadelphia, PA: F.A. Davis.

Collins, F. C. (2007) *The language of God: Scientist presents evidence for belief.* New York, NY: Free Press.

Collins, F. S., & McKusick, V. A. (2001). Implications of the Human Genome Project for medical science. *Journal of the American Medical Association, 285*, 540–544.

Collins, R. L., Martino, S. C., Kovalchik, S. A., D'Amico, E. J., Shadel, W. G., Becker, K. M., & Tolpadi, A. (2017). Exposure to alcohol advertising and adolescents' drinking beliefs: Role of message interpretation. *Health Psychology, 36*(9), 890–897. doi:10.1037/hea0000521

Colon, M., & Lyke, J. (2003). Comparison of hospice use and demographics among European Americans, African Americans, and Latinos. *American Journal of Hospice and Palliative Care, 20*, 182–190.

Colorado Division of Workers' Compensation. (2007). Rule 17, Exhibit 9: Chronic pain disorder medical treatment Guidelines. Author, Denver, CO. Retrieved from https://www.colorado.gov/pacific/sites/default/files/Rule_17_Exhibit_9_Chronic_Pain_Disorder.pdf

Colquhoun, D., & Novella, S. P. (2013). Acupuncture is theatrical placebo. *Anesthesia and Analgesia, 116*, 1360–1363.

Commerford, M. C., Gular, E., Orr, D. A., Reznikoff, M., & O'Dowd, M. A. (1994). Coping and psychological distress in women with HIV/AIDS. *Journal of Community Psychology, 22*, 224–230.

Compas, B. E., Connor-Smith, J. K., Saltzman, H., Thomsen, A. H., & Wadsworth, M. E. (2001). Coping with stress during childhood and adolescence: Problems, progress, and potential in theory and research. *Psychological Bulletin, 127*, 87–127.

Compton, M. M., & Cidlowski, J. A. (1986). Rapid in vivo effects of glucocorticoids on the integrity of rat lymphocyte genomic DNA. *Endocrinology, 118*, 38.

Connor, S. R., Pyenson, B., Fitch, K., Spence, C., & Iwasaki, K. (2007). Comparing hospice and nonhospice patient survival among patients who die within a three year window. *Journal of Pain Symptom Management, 33*, 238–246.

Conroy, D. E., Hedeker, D., McFadden, H. G., Pellegrini, C. A., Pfammatter, A. F., Phillips, S. M., . . . Spring, B. (2017). Lifestyle intervention effects on the frequency and duration of daily moderate–vigorous physical activity and leisure screen time. *Health Psychology, 36*(4), 299–308. doi:10.1037/hea0000418

Constans, J. I., Vasterling, J. J., Deitch, E., Han, X., Teten Tharp, A. L., Davis, T. D., & Sullivan, G. (2012). Pre-Katrina mental illness, postdisaster negative cognitions, and PTSD symptoms in male veterans following Hurricane Katrina. *Psychological Trauma: Theory, Research, Practice, and Policy, 4*(6), 568–577. doi:10.1037/a0027487

Contrada, R. J., & Guyll, M. (2001). On who gets sick and why: The role of personality, stress, and disease. In A. Baum, T. A. Revenson, & J. E. Singer (Eds.), *Handbook of health psychology* (pp. 59–81). Mahwah, NJ: Erlbaum.

Contrada, R. J., Ashmore, R. D., Gary, M. L., Coups, E., Egeth, J. D., Sewell, A., . . . Chasse, V. (2000). Ethnicity-related sources of stress and their effects on well-being. *Current Directions in Psychological Science, 9*, 136–139.

Conway, T. L., Vickers, R. R., Weid, H. W., & Rahe, R. (1981). Occupational stress and variation in cigarette, coffee, and alcohol consumption. *Journal of Health and Social Behavior, 22*, 155–165.

Cook, J. J. (1988). Dad's double binds. Rethinking fathers' bereavement from a men's studies perspective. *Journal of Contemporary Ethnography, 17*, 285–308.

Cooke, L. (2007). The importance of exposure for healthy eating in childhood: Review. *Journal of Human Nutrition and Dietetics, 20*, 294–301.

Cooper, C. L., Cooper, R. F., & Faragher, E. B. (1989). Incidence and perception of psychosocial stress: The relationship with breast cancer. *Psychological Medicine, 19*, 415–422.

Copeland, E. P., & Hess, R. S. (1995). Differences in young adolescents' coping strategies based on gender and ethnicity. *Journal of Early Adolescence, 15*, 203–219.

Cordova, M. J., Cunningham, L. L. C., Carlson, C. R., & Andrykowski, M. A. (2001). Posttraumatic growth following breast cancer: A controlled comparison study. *Health Psychology, 20*, 176–185.

Cormier, L. S., Cormier, W. H., & Weisser, R. J. (1984). *Interviewing and helping skills for health professionals*. Belmont, CA: Wadsworth.

Corr, C. A., Corr, D. M. (2007). Culture, socialization, and dying. In D. Balk, C. Wogrin, G. Thornton, & D. Meagher (Eds.), *Handbook of thanatology: The essential body of knowledge for the student of death, dying, and bereavement* (3–10). Northbrook, IL: Association for Death Education and Counseling.

Corrao, G., Bagnardi, V., Vittadini, G., & Favilli, S. (2000). Capture-recapture methods to size alcohol related problems in a population. *Journal of Epidemiology and Community Health, 54*, 603–610.

Corrao, G., Rubbiati, L., Bagnardi, V., Zambon, A., & Poikolainen, K. (2000). Alcohol and coronary heart disease: A meta-analysis. *Addiction, 95*, 1505–1524.

Corsica, J., Hood, M., Azarbad, L., & Ivan, I. (2012). Revisiting the revised master questionnaire for the psychological evaluation of bariatric surgery candidates. *Obesity Surgery, 22*(3), 381–388.

Cosway, R., Endler, N. S., Sadler, A. J., & Deary, I. J. (2000). The coping inventory for stressful situations: Factorial structure and associations with personality traits and psychological health. *Journal of Applied Biobehavioral Research, 5*, 121–143.

Cottington, E. M., Matthews, K. A., Talbott, E., & Kuller, L. H. (1986). Occupational stress, suppressed anger, and hypertension. *Psychosomatic Medicine, 48*, 249–260.

Coughlin, S. (2008). Surviving cancer or other serious illness: A review of individual and community resources. *Cancer Journal for Clinicians, 58*(1), 60–64.

Coups, E., Hay, J., & Ford, J. (2008). Awareness of the role of physical activity in colon cancer prevention. *Patient Education and Counseling, 72*(2), 246–251.

Covey, J. (2007). A meta-analysis of the effects of presenting treatment benefits in different formats. *Medical Decision Making, 27*, 638–654.

Covey, L. A., & Feltz, D. L. (1991). Physical activity and adolescent female psychological development. *Journal of Youth and Adolescence, 20*, 463–474.

Cowan, M. J., Freedland, K. E., Burg, M. M., Saab, P. G., Youngblood, M. E., Cornell, C. E . . . Czajkowski, S. M. (2008). Predictors of treatment response for depression and inadequate social support—the ENRICHD randomized clinical trial. *Psychotherapy and Psychosomatics, 77*(1), 27–37.

Cowley, G. (1998). Can you eat to beat malignancy? A controversial diet book is just one sign of the revolutionary new thinking about food and health. *Newsweek, 132*, 60–67.

Cox, B. E., Dean, J. G., & Kowalski, R. (2015). Hidden trauma, quiet drama: The prominence and consequence of complicated grief among college students. *Journal of College Student Development, 56*(3), 280–285.

Cox, D. J., & Gonder-Frederick, L. (1992). Major developments in behavioral diabetes research. *Journal of Consulting and Clinical Psychology, 60*, 628–638.

Cox, T. (1978). *Stress*. London, UK: Macmillan Press.

Cox, T., & Ferguson, E. (1991). Individual differences, stress and coping. In C. L. Cooper & R. Payne (Eds.), *Personality and stress: Individual differences in the stress process* (pp. 7–30). Oxford, UK: John Wiley.

Coyne, E., Wollin, J., & Creedy, D. (2012). Exploration of the family's role and strengths after a young woman is diagnosed with breast cancer: Views of women and their families. *European Journal of Oncology Nursing, 16*(2), 124–130.

Coyne, J. C., & Gottlieb, B. H. (1996). The mismeasure of coping by checklist. *Journal of Personality, 64*, 959–991.

Coyne, J. C., & Racioppo, M. W. (2000). Never the twain shall meet? Closing the gap between coping research and clinical intervention research. *American Psychologist, 55*, 655–664.

CPA Task Force on Prescriptive Authority for Psychologists in Canada. (2010). *Report to the Canadian Psychological Association Board of Directors*. Ottowa, ON, Canada: Canadian Psychological Association.

Crabb, D. W. (1993). The liver. In M. Galanter (Ed.), *Recent developments in alcoholism*, Vol. 11, *Ten years of progress* (pp. 207–230). New York, NY: Plenum Press.

Craig, K. D. (1998). The facial display of pain. In G. A. Finley & P. J. McGrath (Eds.), *Measurement of pain in infants and children* (pp. 103–122). Seattle, WA: IASP Press.

Cramer, J. A., Roy, A., Burrell, A., Fairchild, C. J., Fuldeore, M. J., Ollendorf, D. A., & Wong, P. K. (2008). Medication compliance and persistence: Terminology and definitions. *Value in Health, 11*, 44–47.

Crandell, T. L., Crandell, C., & Vander Zanden, J. W. (2011). *Human development*. New York, NY: McGraw-Hill.

Crane, R. S., Brewer, J., Feldman, C., Kabat-Zinn, J., Santorelli, S., Williams, J. M. G., & Kuyken, W. (2017). What defines mindfulness-based programs? The warp and the weft. *Psychological Medicine, 47*(6), 990–999. doi:10.1017/S0033291716003317

Cristea, I. A., Sucala, M., Stefan, S., Igna, R., David, D., & Szentagotai Tatar, A. (2011). Positive and negative emotions in cardiac patients: The contributions of trait optimism, expectancies and hopes. *Cognition, Brain, Behavior, 15*(3), 317–329.

Cross, S. E., & Madson, L. (1997). Models of the self: Self-construals and gender. *Psychological Bulletin, 122*, 5–37.

Crow, T. M. (2001) *Native plants, native healing: Traditional Muskogee way*. Summertown, TN: Native Voices.

Crowe, F. L., Key, T. J., Appleby, P. N., Travis, R. C., Overvad, K., Jakobsen, M. U., . . . Riboli, E. (2008). Dietary fat intake and risk of prostate cancer in the European Prospective Investigation into Cancer and Nutrition. *American Journal of Clinical Nutrition, 87*(5), 1405–1413.

Croyle, R. T., & Barger, S. T. (1993). Illness cognition. In S. Maes, H. Leventhal, & M. Johnston (Eds.), *International review of health psychology* (pp. 29–49). Chichester, UK: John Wiley.

Cruess, D. G., Antoni, M. H., Schneiderman, N., Ironson, G., McCabe, P., Fernandez, J. B., . . . Kumar, M. (2000). Cognitive-behavioral stress management increases free testosterone and decreases psychological distress in HIV-seropositive men. *Health Psychology, 19*, 12–20.

Crum, A. J., Akinola, M., Martin, A., & Fath, S. (2017). The role of stress mindset in shaping cognitive, emotional, and physiological responses to challenging and threatening stress. *Anxiety, Stress & Coping, 30*(4), 379–395. doi:10.1080/10615806.2016.1275585

Crystal, S., & Kersting, R. C. (1998). Stress, social support, and distress in a statewide population of persons with AIDS in New Jersey. *Social Work in Health Care, 28*, 41–60.

Culver, J. L., Arena, P. L., Wimberly, S. R., Antoni, M. H., & Carver, C. S. (2004). Coping among African-American, Hispanic, and non-Hispanic White women recently treated for early stage breast cancer. *Psychology and Health, 19*, 157–166.

Cundiff, J. M., Boylan, J. M., Pardini, D. A., & Matthews, K. A. (2017). Moving up matters: Socioeconomic mobility prospectively predicts better physical health. *Health Psychology, 36*(6), 609–617. doi:10.1037/hea0000473

Cunradi, C. B., Moore, R. S., & Ames, G. (2008). Contribution of occupational factors to current smoking among active-duty U.S. Navy careerists. *Nicotine and Tobacco Research, 10*, 429–437.

Cupit, I. N., Servaty-Seib, H., Tedrick Parikh, S., Walker, A. C., & Martin, R. (2016). College and the grieving student: A mixed-methods analysis. *Death Studies, 40*(8), 494–506. doi:10.1080/07481187.2016.1181687

Curbow, B., Somerfield, M. R., Baker, F., Wingard, J. R., & Legro, M. W. (1993). Personal changes, dispositional optimism, and psychological adjustment to bone marrow transplantation. *Journal of Behavioral Medicine, 16*, 423–443.

Curran, P. J., Stice, E., & Chassin, L. (1997). The relation between adolescent alcohol use and peer alcohol use: A longitudinal random coefficients model. *Journal of Consulting and Clinical Psychology, 65*, 130–140.

Curtis, L. H., Al-Khatib, S. M., Shea, A. M., Hammill, B. G., Hernandez, A. F., & Schulman, K. A. (2007). Sex differences in the use of implantable cardioverter-defibrillators for primary and secondary prevention of sudden cardiac death. *Journal of the American Medical Association, 298*, 1517–1524.

Cusumano, D. L., & Thompson, J. K. (2001). Media influence and body image in 8–11-year-old boys and girls: A preliminary report on Multidimensional Media Influence Scale. *International Journal of Eating Disorders, 29*, 37–44.

Cutrona, C. E. (1990). Stress and social support: In search of optimal matching. *Journal of Social and Clinical Psychology, 9*, 3–14.

Cutshall, S. M., Anderson, P. G., Prinsen, S. K., Wentworth, L. J., Olney, T. L., Messner, P. K., & . . . Bauer, B. A. (2011). Effect of the combination of music and nature sounds on pain and anxiety in cardiac surgical patients: A randomized study. *Alternative Therapies in Health & Medicine, 17*(4), 16–21.

Cuttler, C., Spradlin, A., Nusbaum, A. T., Whitney, P., Hinson, J. M., & McLaughlin, R. J. (2017). Blunted stress reactivity in chronic cannabis users. *Psychopharmacology, 234*(15), 2299–2309. doi:10.1007/s00213-017-4648-z

Czajkowski, S. M., Powell, L. H., Adler, N., Naar-King, S., Reynolds, K. D., Hunter, C. M., . . . Charlson, M. E. (2015). From ideas to efficacy: The ORBIT model for developing behavioral treatments for chronic diseases. *Health Psychology, 34*, 971–982. doi:10.1037/hea0000161

Dafoe, W., & Huston, P. (1997). Current trends in cardiac rehabilitation. *Canadian Medical Association Journal, 156*, 527–533.

Dalton, M. A., Ahrens, M. B., Sargent, J. D., Mott, L. A., Beach, M. L., Tickle, J. J., & Heatherton, T. F. (2002). Relation between parental restrictions on movies and adolescent use of tobacco and alcohol. *Effective Clinical Practice, 5*, 1–10.

Dalton, R., Scheeringa, M.S., & Zeanah, C.H. (2008). Did the prevalence of PTSD following Hurricane Katrina match a rapid needs assessment prediction? A template for future public planning after large-scale disasters. *Psychiatric Annals, 38*, 134–144.

Daly, C. M., Foote, S. J., & Wadsworth, D. D. (2017). Physical activity, sedentary behavior, fruit and vegetable consumption and access: What influences obesity in rural children? *Journal of Community Health, 42*(5), 968–973. doi:10.1007/s10900-017-0343-6

Damschroder, L. J., Zikmund-Fisher, B. J., & Ubel, P. A. (2008). Considering adaptation in preference elicitations. *Health Psychology, 27*, 394–399.

Danel, D. P., Siennicka, A. E., Fedurek, P., Frackowiak, T., Sorokowski, P., Jankowska, E. A., & Pawlowski, B. (2017). Men with a terminal illness relax their criteria for facial attractiveness. *American Journal of Men's Health, 11*(4), 1247–1254. doi:10.1177/1557988317692504

Daoud, A. I., Geissler, G. J., Wang, F., Saretsky, J., Daoud, Y. A., & Lieberman, D. E. (2012). Foot strike and injury rates in endurance runners: A retrospective study. *Medical Science Sports and Exercise, 3*, 1325–1334.

Darbes, L., Crepaz, N., Lyles, C., Kennedy, G., & Rutherford, G. (2008). The efficacy of behavioral interventions in reducing HIV risk behaviors and incident sexually transmitted diseases in heterosexual African Americans. *AIDS* (London, UK), *22*(10), 1177–1194.

Dart, J. (2008). The Internet as a source of health information in three disparate communities. *Australian Health Review: A Publication of the Australian Hospital Association, 32*(3), 559–569.

Dasgupta, D., & Ray, S. (2017). Is menopausal status related to women's attitudes toward menopause and aging? *Women & Health, 57*(3), 311–328. doi:10.1080/03630242.2016.1160965

Dash, B., Junius, A. M. M., & Dash, V. B. (1997). *Handbook of Ayurveda*. New Delhi, India: Loftus Press.

Daubenmier, J. J., Weidner, G., Sumner, M. D., Mendell, N., Merritt-Worden, T., Studley, J., Ornish, D. (2007). The contribution of changes in diet, exercise, and stress management to changes in coronary risk in women and men in the multisite cardiac lifestyle intervention program. *Annals of Behavioral Medicine, 33*, 57–68.

David, J. P., & Suls, J. (1999). Coping efforts in daily life: Role of Big Five traits and problem appraisals. *Journal of Personality, 67*, 265–294.

David, P., & Johnson, M. A. (1998). The role or self in third-person effects about body image. *Journal of Communication, 48*, 37–58.

David, R. J., & Collins, J. W. (1997). Differing birth weight among infants of U.S.-born Blacks, African-born Blacks and U.S.-born Whites. *New England Journal of Medicine, 337*, 1209–1233.

Davidson, K., & Prkachin, K. (1997). Optimism and unrealistic optimism have an interacting impact on health-promoting behavior and knowledge changes. *Personality and Social Psychology Bulletin, 23*, 617–625.

Davidson, K., Gidron, Y., Mostofsky, E., & Trudeau, K. (2007). Hospitalization cost offset of a hostility intervention for coronary heart disease patients. *Journal of Consulting and Clinical Psychology, 75*(4), 657–662.

Davidson, K., Trudeau, K., & Smith, T. (2006). Introducing the new health psychology series evidence-based treatment reviews: Progress not perfection. *Health Psychology, 25*(1), 1–2.

Davidson, R. J., Kabat-Zinn, J., Schumacher, J., Rozenkranz, M., Muller, D., Santorelli, S. F., . . . Sheridan, J. F. (2003). Alterations in brain and immune function produced by mindfulness meditation. *Psychosomatic Medicine, 65*, 564–570.

Davis, C. (2017). A commentary on the associations among "food addiction," binge eating disorder, and obesity: Overlapping conditions with idiosyncratic clinical features. *Appetite, 115*, 3–8. doi:10.1016/j.appet.2016.11.001

Davis, C. G., Nolen-Hoeksema, S., & Larson, J. (1998). Making sense of loss and benefiting from the experience: Two construals of meaning. *Journal of Personality and Social Psychology, 75*, 561–574.

Davis, E. L., Deane, F. P., Lyons, G. C. B., & Barclay, G. D. (2017). Is higher acceptance associated with less anticipatory grief among patients in palliative care? *Journal of Pain and Symptom Management, 54*(1), 120–125. doi:10.1016/j.jpainsymman.2017.03.012

Davis, R. E., Peterson, K. E., Rothschild, S. K., & Resinicow, K. (2011) Pushing the envelope for cultural appropriateness: Does evidence support cultural tailoring in type 2 diabetes interventions for Mexican American adults? *Diabetes Education, 37*(2), 227–238. doi:10.1177/0145721710395329

Day, M. (2019). Chronic pain. In T. A. Revenson & R. A. R. Gurung (Eds.), *Handbook of health psychology* (3e). New York, NY: Routledge.

de Bloom, J., Sianoja, M., Korpela, K., Tuomisto, M., Lilja, A., Geurts, S., & Kinnunen, U. (2017). Effects of park walks and relaxation exercises during lunch breaks on recovery from job stress: Two randomized controlled trials. *Journal of Environmental Psychology, 51*, 14–30. doi:10.1016/j.jenvp.2017.03.006

De Boer, J. B., Sprangers, M. A. B., Aaronson, N. K., Lange, J. M. A., & van Dam, F. S. (1996). A study of the reliability, validity and responsiveness of the HIV Overview of Problems Evaluation System (HOPES) in assessing the quality of life of patients with AIDS and symptomatic HIV infection. *Quality of Life Research, 5*, 339–347.

de Haan, A. M., Boon, A. E., Vermeiren, R. M., & de Jong, J. T. (2012). Ethnic differences in utilization of youth mental health care. *Ethnicity & Health, 17*(1/2), 105–110. doi:10.1080/13557858.2011.645150

de Jong, J. T. V. M. (2005). Commentary: Deconstructing critiques on the internationalization of PTSD. *Culture, Medicine, and Psychiatry, 29*, 361–370.

de Lapparent, M. (2008). Willingness to use safety belt and levels of injury in car accidents. *Accident Analysis and Prevention, 40*, 1023–1032.

De Lira-Garcia, C., Bacardí-Gascón, M., & Jimrnez-Cruz, A. (2012). Preferences of healthy and unhealthy foods among 3 to 4 year old children in Mexico. *Asia Pacific Journal of Clinical Nutrition, 21*(1), 57–63.

de Souza, R., Swain, J., Appel, L., & Sacks, F. (2008). Alternatives for macronutrient intake and chronic disease: Comparison of the Omni-Heart diets with popular diets and with dietary recommendations. *The American Journal of Clinical Nutrition, 88*(1), 1–11.

De Vellis, B. M. (1995). The psychological impact of arthritis: Prevalence of depression. *Arthritis Care and Research, 8*, 284–289.

De Vellis, B. M., Revenson, T. A., & Blalock, S. J. (1997). Rheumatic disease and women's health. In S. J. Gallant, G. P. Keita, & R. Royak-Shaler (Eds.), *Health care for women: Psychological, social, and behavioral influences* (pp. 333–347). Washington, DC: American Psychological Association.

Dean, B. B., Borenstein, J. E., Henning, J. M., Knight, K., & Merz, C. N. (2004). Can change in high-density lipoprotein cholesterol levels reduce cardiovascular risk? *American Heart Journal, 147*, 966–976.

Deapen, D., Lui, L., Perkins, C., Bernstein, L., & Ross, R. K. (2002). Rapidly rising breast cancer incidence rates among Asian-American women. *International Journal of Cancer, 99*, 747–750.

Deater-Deckard, K., Dodge, K. A., Bates, J. E., & Pettit, G. S. (1996). Physical discipline among African Americans and European American mothers: Links to children's externalizing behaviors. *Developmental Psychology, 32*, 1065–1072.

DeBellonia, R. R., Marcus, S., Shih, R., Kashani, J., Rella, J.G., & Ruck B. (2008). Curanderismo: Consequences of folk medicine. *Pediatric Emergency Care, 24*, 228–229.

DeBernardo, R. L., Aldinger, C. E., Dawood, O. R., Hanson, R. E., Lee, S., & Rinaldi, S. R. (1999). An e-mail assessment of undergraduate's attitudes toward smoking. *Journal of American College Health, 48*, 61–66.

Decker, C. (2007). Social support and adolescent cancer survivors: A review of the literature. *Psycho-Oncology, 16*(1), 1–11.

DeFrain, J., Millspaugh, E., & Xiaolin, X. (1996). The psychosocial effects of miscarriage: Implications for health professionals. *Families, Systems and Health, 14*, 331–347.

DeFronzo, R., Panzarella, C., & Butler, A. C. (2001). Attachment, support seeking, and adaptive inferential feedback: Implications for psychological health. *Cognitive and Behavioral Practive, 8*, 48–52.

DeGarmo, D. S., Patras, J., & Eap, S. (2008). Social support for divorced fathers' parenting: Testing a stress-buffering model. *Family Relations, 57*, 35–48.

Dehghan, M., Mente, A., Zhang, X., Swaminathan, S., Li, W., Viswanathan, M., . . . Mapanga, R. (2017). Associations of fats and carbohydrate intake with cardiovascular disease and mortality in 18 countries from five continents (PURE): A prospective cohort study. *The Lancet, 390*(10107), 2050–2062. doi:10.1016/S0140-6736(17)32252-3

Deibert, C., Maliski, S., Kwan, L., Fink, A., Connor, S., & Litwin, M. (2007). Prostate cancer knowledge among low-income minority men. *Journal of Urology, 177*(5), 1851–1855.

Deichert, N., Fekete, E., Boarts, J., Druley, J., & Delahanty, D. (2008). Emotional support and affect: Associations with health behaviors and active coping efforts in men living with HIV. *AIDS and Behavior, 12*(1), 139–145.

del Junco, D. J., Vernon, S. W., Coan, S. P., Tiro, J. A., Bastian, L. A., Savas, L. S., . . . Rakowski, W. (2008). Promoting regular mammography screening I. A systematic assessment of validity in a randomized trial. *Journal of The National Cancer Institute, 100*(5), 333–346.

Delahanty, D. L., & Baum, A. (2001). Stress and breast cancer. In A. Baum, T. A. Revenson, & J. E. Singer (Eds.), *Handbook of health psychology* (1e, pp. 747–756). Mahwah, NJ: Erlbaum.

Dellifraine, J., & Dansky, K. (2008). Home-based telehealth: A review and meta-analysis. *Journal of Telemedicine and Telecare, 14*(2), 62–66.

DeLongis, A., Folkman, S., & Lazarus, R. S. (1988). The impact of daily stress on health and mood: Psychological and social resources as mediators. *Journal of Personality and Social Psychology, 54*(3), 486–495.

Delva, J., Johnston, L. D., & O'Malley, P. M. (2007). The epidemiology of overweight and related lifestyle behaviors: Racial/ethnic and socioeconomic status differences among American youth. *American Journal of Preventive Medicine, 33*, S178–S186.

Demark-Wahnefried, W., Rimer, B. K., & Wimer, E. P. (1997). Weight gain in women diagnosed with breast cancer. *Journal of the American Dietetic Association, 97*, 519–529.

Dembrowski, T. M., MacDougall, J. M., Williams, R. B., Haney, T. L., & Blumenthal, J. A. (1985). Components of Type A, hostility, and anger in relationship to angiographic findings. *Psychosomatic Medicine, 47*, 219–233.

Dempster, M., McCorry, N. K., Brennan, E., Donnelly, M., Murray, L., & Johnston, B. T. (2012). Psychological distress among survivors of esophageal cancer: The role of illness cognitions and coping. *Diseases of the Esophagus, 25*(3), 222–227. doi:10.1111/j.1442-2050.2011.01233.x

den Boer, J. J., Oostendorp, R. A., Beems, T., Munneke, M., Oerlemans, M., & Evers, A. W. (2006). A systematic review of bio-psychosocial risk factors for an unfavourable outcome after lumbar disc surgery. *European Spine Journal, 15*(5), 527–536.

Dendana, M., Messaoudi, S., Hizem, S., Jazia, K., Almawi, W., Gris, J., & Mahjoub, T. (2012). Endothelial protein C receptor 1651C/G polymorphism and soluble endothelial protein C receptor levels in women with idiopathic recurrent miscarriage. *Blood Coagulation & Fibrinolysis, 23*(1), 30–34.

Dennerstein, L. (1996). Well-being, symptoms and the menopausal transition. *Maturitas, 23*, 147–157.

Dennett, D. C. (2017). *From bacteria to Bach and back: The evolution of minds*. New York, NY: Norton.

Depaola, S. J., Griffin, M., Young, J. R., & Neimeyer, R. A. (2003). Death anxiety and attitudes toward the elderly among adults: The role of gender and ethnicity. *Death Studies, 27*, 335–354.

Department of Justice (2015). National Crime Victimization Survey. Bureau of Justice Statistics. Retrieved from https://www.bjs.gov/

Derogatis, L. R., Morrow, G. R., Fetting, J., Penman, D., Piasetsky, S., Schmale, A. M., . . . Carnicke, C. L., Jr. (1983). The prevalence of psychiatric disorders among cancer patients. *Journal of the American Medical Association, 249*, 953–957.

DeRosa, C. J., & Marks, G. (1998). Preventive counseling in HIV-positive men and self-disclosure of serostatus to sex partners: New opportunities for prevention. *Health Psychology, 17*, 224–331.

Derryberry, M. (1960). Health education: Its objectives and methods. *Health Education Monographs, 8*, 5–11.

Descartes, R. (1664). *Treatise of Man*. Amherst, NY: Prometheus.

DeSpelder, L. A., & Strickland, A. (2007). Culture, socialization, and death education. In D. Balk, C., Wogrin, G. Thornton, & D. Meagher (Eds.), *Handbook of thanatology: The essential body of knowledge for the student of death, dying, and bereavement* (303–314). Northbrook, IL: Association for Death Education and Counseling.

DeStefano, A. M. (2001) *Latino folk medicine: Healing herbal remedies from ancient traditions*. New York, NY: Ballantine Books.

Deuster, P. A., Su Jong, K., Remaley, A. T., & Poth, M. (2011). Allostatic Load and Health Status of African Americans and Whites. *American Journal of Health Behavior, 35*(6), 641–653.

Devlin, H (September, 2017). Nerve implant "restores consciousness" to man in persistent vegetative state. *The Guardian*. Retrieved from https://www.theguardian.com/science/2017/sep/25/nerve-implant-restores-consciousness-to-man-in-vegetative-state

DeVol, R., Bedroussian, A., Charuworn, A., Chatterjee, A., Kim, I. K., Kim, S., & Klowden, K. (2007). *An unhealthy America: The economic burden of chronic disease—charting a new course to save lives and increase productivity and economic growth*. Retrieved from http://www.milkeninstitute.org/publications/view/321

Dhalla, S., Chan, K., Montaner, J., & Hogg, R. (2006). Complementary and alternative medicine use in British Columbia—A survey of HIV positive people on antiretroviral therapy. *Complementary Therapies in Clinical Practice, 12*(4), 242–248.

Dhalla, S., Poole, G., Singer, J., Patrick, D. M., & Kerr, T. (2012). Cognitive factors and willingness to participate in an HIV vaccine trial among HIV-positive injection drug users. *Psychology, Health & Medicine, 17*(2), 223–234. doi:10.1080/13548506.2011.608803

Di Iorio, C. R., Carey, C. E., Michalski, L. J., Corral-Frias, N., Conley, E. D., Hariri, A. R., & Bogdan, R. (2017). Hypothalamic-pituitary-adrenal axis genetic variation and early stress moderates amygdala function. *Psychoneuroendocrinology, 80*, 170–178. doi:10.1016/j.psyneuen.2017.03.016

Diamond, J. (2011). *Collapse: How societies choose to fail or succeed*. New York, NY: Penguin.

Diamond, J. M. (1999). *Guns, germs, and steel: The fates of human societies*. New York, NY: Norton.

Diaz, R. M., Ayala, G., Bein, E., Henne, J., Marin, B. V. (2001). The impact of homophobia, poverty, and racism on the mental health of gay and bisexual Latino men: Findings from 3 U.S. cities. *American Journal of Public Health, 91*, 927–932.

Dibble, S. L., Vanoni, J. M., & Miaskowski, C. (1997). Woman's attitudes toward breast cancer screening procedures: Differences by ethnicity. *Women's Health Issues, 7*, 47–54.

Dickerson, S. S., & Kemeny, M. E. (2004). Acute stressors and cortisol responses: A theoretical integration and synthesis of laboratory research. *Psychological Bulletin, 130*, 355–391.

DiClemente, C. C., & Prochaska, J. O. (1982). Self-change and therapy change of smoking behavior: A comparison of processes of change in cessation and maintenance. *Addictive Behaviors, 7*, 133–142.

Diefenbach, M. A., Mohamed, N. E., Turner, G., & Diefenbach, C. S. (2010). Psychosocial interventions for patients with cancer. In J. M. Suls, K. W. Davidson, & R. M. Kaplan (Eds.), *Handbook of health psychology and behavioral medicine* (pp. 462–475). New York, NY: Guilford.

Dietz, W. H. (1998). Health consequences of obesity in youth: Childhood predictors of adult disease. *Pediatrics, 101*, 518–525.

Diez Roux, A. V., Merkin, S. S., Arnett, D., Chambless, L., Massing, M., Nieto, F. J., . . . Watson, R. L. (2001). Neighborhood of residence and incidence of coronary heart disease. *New England Journal of Medicine, 345*, 99–107.

Dignan, M., Sharp, P., Blinson, K., Michielutte, R., Konen, J., Bell, R., & Lane, C. (1995). Development of a cervical cancer education program for Native American women in North Carolina. *Journal of Cancer Education, 9*, 235–242.

DiMatteo, M. R. (1991). *The psychology of health, illness, and medical care: An individual perspective.* Belmont, CA: Brooks/Cole.

DiMatteo, M. R. (2004a). Variations in patients' adherence to medical recommendations: A quantitative review of 50 years of research. *Medical Care, 32*, 200–209.

DiMatteo, M. R. (2004b). Social support and patient adherence to medical treatment: A meta-analysis. *Health Psychology, 23*, 207–218.

Ding, X., & Staudinger, J. L. (2005). Induction of drug metabolism by forskolin: The role of the pregnane X receptor and the protein kinase A signal transduction pathway. *Journal of Pharmacology and Experimental Therapeutics, 312*, 849–856.

DiPietro, J. A., Costigan, K. A., Hilton, S. C., & Pressman, E. K. (1999). Effects of socioeconomic status and psychosocial stress on the development of the fetus. *Annals of the New York Academy of Sciences, 896*, 356–358.

DiPlacido, J., Zauber, A., & Redd, W. H. (1998). Psychosocial issues in cancer screening. In J. Holland, W. Breitbart, M. Massie, M. Lederberg, M. Loscalzo, & R. McCorkle (Eds.), *Psycho-oncology* (pp. 161–176). New York, NY: Oxford University Press.

Discovering statistics using IBM SPSS Statistics. Thousand Oaks, CA: SAGE.

Dise-Lewis, J. E. (1988). The Life Events and Coping Inventory: An assessment of stress in children. *Psychosomatic Medicine, 50*, 484–499.

Distefan, J. M., Gilpin, E. A., Sargent, J. D., & Pierce, J. P. (1999). Do movie stars encourage adolescents to start smoking? Evidence from California. *Preventive Medicine, 28*, 1–11.

Ditzen, B., Schmidt, S., Strauss, B., Nater, U. M., Ehlert, U., & Heinrichs, M. (2008). Adult attachment and social support interact to reduce psychological but not cortisol responses to stress. *Journal of Psychosomatic Research, 64*, 479–486.

Dixon, H., Niven, P., Scully, M., & Wakefield, M. (2017). Food marketing with movie character toys: Effects on young children's preferences for unhealthy and healthier fast food meals. *Appetite, 117*, 342–350. doi:10.1016/j.appet.2017.07.014

Dixon, K. E. (2016). Pain and pain behaviors. In Y. Benyamini, M. Johnston, & E. C. Karademas (Eds.), *Assessment in health psychology* (pp.147–159). Boston, MA: Hogrefe.

Dogan, M. V., Xiang, J., Beach, S. R. H., Cutrona, C., Gibbons, F. X., Simons, R. L., . . . Philibert, R. A. (2015). Ethnicity and smoking-associated DNA methylation changes at HIV co-receptor GPR15. *Frontiers in Psychiatry, 6*, 132. doi:10.3389/FPSYT.201500132

Dohrenwend, B. S., & Dohrenwend, B. P. (1974). *Stressful life events: Their nature and effects.* Oxford, UK: John Wiley.

Doll, R., Peto, R., Boreham, J., & Sutherland, I. (2004). Morality in relation to smoking: 50 years' observations on male British doctors. *British Medical Journal, 328*(7455), 1519. doi:10.1136/BMJ38142.554479

Dominus, S. (2017). When the revolution came for Amy Cuddy. *New York Times* magazine, October 18. Retrieved from https://www.nytimes.com/2017/10/18/magazine/when-the-revolution-came-for-amy-cuddy.html

Dong, G., Ren, W., Wang, D., Yang, Z., Zhang, P., Zhao, Y., & He, Q. (2011). Exposure to secondhand tobacco smoke enhances respiratory symptoms and responses to animals in 8,819 children in kindergarten: Results from 25 districts in northeast China. *Respiration, 81*(3), 179–185. doi:10.1159/000321222

Dooley, L. N., Slavich, G. M., Moreno, P. I., & Bower, J. E. (2017). Strength through adversity: Moderate lifetime stress exposure is associated with psychological resilience in breast cancer survivors. *Stress and Health, 33*(5), 549–557. doi:10.1002/smi.2739

Doom, J. R., Doyle, C. M., & Gunnar, M. R. (2017). Social stress buffering by friends in childhood and adolescence: Effects on HPA and oxytocin activity. *Social Neuroscience, 12*(1), 8–21. doi:10.1080/17470919.2016.1149095

Dörffel, W., Riepenhausen, M., Lüders, H., Brämswig, J., & Schellong, G. (2015). Secondary malignancies following treatment for Hodgkin's lymphoma in childhood and adolescence: A cohort study with more than 30 years' follow-up. *Deutsches Ärzteblatt International, 112*(18), 320–327.

Dornelas, E. A. (2018). *Psychological treatment of patients with cancer.* Washington, DC: American Psychological Association. doi.10.1037/0000054-012

Dorsel, T. N., & Baum, A. (1989). Undergraduate health psychology: Another challenge for an ambitious field. *Psychology & Health, 3*(2), 87–92. doi:10.1080/08870448908400368

Dougall, A. L., & Baum, A. (2002). Stress, health, and illness. In A. Baum, T. A. Revenson, & J. E. Singer (Eds.), *Handbook of health psychology* (1e, pp. 321–338). Mahwah, NJ: Erlbaum.

Doughty, C. (2017). *From here to eternity: Travelling the world to find the good death.* New York, NY: Norton.

Doumas, D. M., Margolin, G., & John, R. S. (2003). The relationship between daily marital interaction, work, and health-promoting behaviors in dual-earner couples: An extension of the work-family spillover model. *Journal of Family Issues, 24*, 3–20.

Drapeau, M., Blake, E., Dobson, K. S., & Körner, A. (2017). Coping strategies in major depression and over the course of cognitive therapy for depression. *Canadian Journal of Counselling & Psychotherapy / Revue Canadienne de Counseling et de Psychothérapie, 51*(1), 18–39. Retrieved from http://cjc-rcc.ucalgary.ca/cjc/index.php/rcc/article/view/2838

Duan, N., Fox, S. A., Derose, K. P., & Carson, S. (2000). Maintaining mammography adherence through telephone counseling in a church-based trial. *American Journal of Public Health, 90*, 1468–1471.

Dube, M. F., & Green, C. R. (1982). Methods of collection of smoke for analytical purposes. *Recent Advances in Tobacco Science, 8*, 42–102.

Duberstein, P. R., Chen, M., Chapman, B. P., Hoerger, M., Saeed, F., Guancial, E., & Mack, J. W. (2017). Fatalism and educational disparities in beliefs about the curability of advanced cancer. *Patient Education and Counseling, 101*(1), 113–118. doi:10.1016/j.pec.2017.07.007

Duff, D. C., Levine, T. R., Beatty, M. J., Woolbright, J., & Park, H. S. (2007). Testing public anxiety treatments against a credible placebo control. *Communication Education, 56*, 72–88.

Dunbar-Jacobs, J., Schlenk, E., & McCall, M. (2012). Patient adherence to treatment regimen. In A. Baum, T. A. Revenson, & J. Singer (Eds.), *Handbook of health psychology* (2e, pp. 271–292). New York, NY: Guilford Press.

Duncan, C., Jones, K., & Moon, G. (1999). Smoking and deprivation: Are there neighbourhood effects? *Social Science and Medicine, 48*, 497–505.

Dunkel-Schetter, C., & Bennett, T. L. (1990). Differentiating the cognitive and behavioral aspects of social support. In B. R. Sarason & I. G. Sarason (Eds.), *Social support: An interactional view* (pp. 267–296). Oxford, UK: John Wiley.

Dunkel-Schetter, C., Feinstein, L. G., Taylor, S. E., & Falke, R. L. (1992). Patterns of coping with cancer. *Health Psychology, 11*, 79–87.

Dunkel-Schetter, C., Gurung, R. A. R., Lobel, M., & Wadhwa, P. (2001). Psychosocial processes in pregnancy: Stress as a central organizing concept. In A. Baum, J. Singer, & T. Revenson (Eds.), *Handbook of health psychology* (1e, pp. 495–518). New York, NY: John Wiley.

Dunkel-Schetter, C., Sagrestano, L. M., Feldman, P., & Killingsworth, C. (1996). Social support and pregnancy: A comprehensive review focusing on ethnicity and culture. In G. R. Pierce, B. *Handbook of social support and the family* (pp. 375–412). New York, NY: Plenum.

Dunn, A. (1989). Psychoneuroimmunology for the psychoneuroendocrinologist: A review of animal studies of nervous system-immune system interactions. *Psychoneuroendocrinology, 14*, 251–272.

Dunn, A. L., Trivedi, M. H., & O'Neal, H. A. (2001). Physical activity dose-response effects on outcomes of depression and anxiety. *Medicine and Science in Sports and Exercise, 33*, S587–S597.

Dunston, G. M, Henry, L. W., Christian, J., Ofosu, M. D., & Callendar, C. O. (1989). HLA-DR3, DQ heterogeneity in American Blacks is associated with susceptibility and resistance to insulin dependent diabetes mellitus. *Transplantation Proceedings, 21*, 653–655.

Durkheim, É (1951). *Suicide*. New York, NY: Free Press.

Durvasula, R., Regan, P., Ureño, O., & Howell, L. (2008). Predictors of cervical cancer screening in Asian and Latina university students. *College Student Journal, 42*(2), 243–253.

Dusseldorp, E., van Elderen, T., Maes, S., Meulman, J., & Kraaij, V. (1999). A meta-analysis of psychoeducational programs for coronary heart disease patients. *Health Psychology, 18*, 506–519.

Dweck, C. S., & Sorich, L. (1999). Mastery-oriented thinking. In C. R. Snyder (Ed.), *Coping*. New York, NY: Oxford University Press.

Dworetzky, B. A., Townsend, M. K., Pennell, P. B., & Kang, J. H. (2012). Female reproductive factors and risk of seizure or epilepsy: Data from the Nurses' Health Study II. *Epilepsia (Series 4), 53*(1), e1–e4. doi:10.1111/j.1528-1167.2011.03308.x

Dworkin, R. H., Turk, D. C., Wyrwich, K. W., Beaton, D., Cleeland, C. S., Farrar, J. T . . . Zavisic, S. (2008) Interpreting the clinical importance of treatment outcomes in chronic pain clinical trials: IMMPACT recommendations. *Journal of Pain 9*(2), 105–121.

Dwyer, C. M. (2008). Individual variation in the expression of maternal behaviour: A review of the neuroendocrine mechanisms in the sheep. *Journal of Neuroendocrinology, 20*(4), 526–534. doi:10.1111/j.1365-2826.2008.01657.x

Eagleman, D. (2011). *Incognito: The secret lives of the brain*. New York, NY: Vintage Press.

Eagleman, D., & Downar, J. (2015). *Brain and behavior: A cognitive neuroscience perspective*. Oxford, UK: Oxford University Press.

Eccleston, C. (1995). Chronic pain and distraction: An experimental investigation into the role of sustained and shifting attention in the processing of chronic persistent pain. *Behavior Research and Therapy, 33*, 391–405.

Eden, K. B., Orleans, C. T., Mulrow, C. D., Pender, N. J., & Teutsch, S. M. (2002). Advice from primary care providers about physical activity: A recommendation from the U.S. Preventive Services Task Force. *Annals of Internal Medicine, 137*, 40–41.

Edgar, L., Rosberger, Z., & Nowlis, D. (1992). Coping with cancer during the first year after diagnosis: Assessment and intervention. *Cancer, 69*, 817–828.

Edman, J. L., & Yates, A. (2004). Eating disorder symptoms among Pacific Island and Caucasian women: The impact of self-dissatisfaction and anger discomfort. *Journal of Mental Health, 13*, 143–150.

Edut, O. (1998). *Adios, Barbie: Young women write about body image and identity*. New York, NY: Seal Press.

Edwards, C. L., Sollers, J., Collins-McNeil, J., Miller, J., Jones, B., Baker, C. S., . . . Whitfield, K. (2019). African American health. In T. A. Revenson, & R. A. R. Gurung (Eds.), *Handbook of health psychology* (3e). New York, NY: Routledge.

Edwards, C. P. (1993). Behavioral sex differences in children of diverse cultures: The case of nurturance to infants. In M. E. Pereira & L. A. Fairbanks (Eds.), *Juvenile primates: Life history, development, and behavior* (pp. 327–338). New York, NY: Oxford University Press.

Edwards, J. R., & Rothbard, N. P. (2000). Mechanisms linking work and family: Clarifying the relationship between work and family constructs. *Academy of Management Review, 25*, 179–199.

Egberts, M. R., van de Schoot, R., Geenen, R., & Van Loey, N. E. E. (2017). Parents' posttraumatic stress after burns in their school-aged child: A prospective study. *Health Psychology, 36*(5), 419–428. doi:10.1037/hea0000448

Egorova, N., Park, J., & Kong, J. (2017). In the face of pain: The choice of visual cues in pain conditioning matters. *European Journal of Pain, 21*(7), 1243–1251. doi:10.1002/ejp.1024

Eisler, I., Dare, C., Russell, G. F. M., Szmukler, G., le Grange. D., & Dodge, E. (1997). Family and individual therapy in anorexia nervosa: A 5-year follow up. *Archives of General Psychiatry, 54*, 1025–1030.

Eldred, C., & Sykes, C. (2008). Psychosocial interventions for carers of survivors of stroke: A systematic review of interventions based on psychological principles and theoretical frameworks. *British Journal of Health Psychology, 13*(3), 563–581.

Eliade, M. (1964) *Shamanism: Archaic techniques of ecstasy*. Princeton, NJ: Princeton University Press.

Elkin, I. (1994). The NIMH Treatment of Depression Collaborative Research Program: Where we began and where we are. In A. E. Bergin & S. Garfield (Eds.), *Handbook of psychotherapy and behavior change* (4e, pp. 114–139). Oxford, UK: John Wiley.

Ell, K., & Dunkel-Schetter, C. (1994). Social support and adjustment to myocardial infarction, angioplasty, and coronary artery bypass surgery. In S. A. Shumaker & S. M. Czajkowski (Eds.), *Social support and cardiovascular disease. Plenum series in behavioral psychophysiology and medicine* (pp. 301–332). New York, NY: Plenum Press.

Ell, K., Nishomoto, R., Mediansky, L., Mantell, J., & Hamovitch, M. (1992). Social relations, social support and survival among patients with cancer. *Journal of Psychosomatic Research, 36*, 531–541.

Ellenberger, H. (1981). *The discovery of the unconscious*. New York, NY: Basic Books.

Ellis, A. (1987). The impossibility of achieving consistently good mental health. *American Psychologist, 42*, 364–375.

Elmore, J. G., Moceri, V. M., Carter, D., & Larson, E. B. (1998). Breast carcinoma tumor characteristics in Black and White women. *Cancer, 83*, 2509–2515.

Emery, C. F., Landers, J. D., & Shoemake, J. D. (2019). Aging and health. In T. A. Revenson & R. A. R. Gurung (Eds.), *Handbook of health psychology* (3e). New York, NY: Routledge.

Emery, M.-P., Perrier, L.-L., & Acquadro, C. (2005). Patient-Reported Outcome and Quality of Life Instruments Database (PROQOLID): Frequently asked questions. *Health and Quality of Life Outcomes, 3*, 12. http://doi.org/10.1186/1477-7525-3-12

Emery, S., Kim, Y., Choi, Y., Szczypka, G., Wakefield, M., & Chaloupka, F. J. (2012). The effects of smoking-related television advertising on smoking and intentions to quit among adults in the United States: 1999–2007. *American Journal of Public Health, 102*(4), 751–757. doi:10.2105/AJPH.2011.300443

Engel, L. (1959). *New trends in the care and treatment of the mentally ill.* Oxford, UK: National Association for Mental Health.

Epping-Jordan, J. E., Compas, B. E., & Howell, D. C. (1994). Predictors of cancer progression in young adult men and women: Avoidance, intrusive thoughts, and psychological symptoms. *Health Psychology, 13*, 539–547.

Erblich, J. (2019). Alcohol. In T. A. Revenson & R. A. R. Gurung (Eds.), *Handbook of health psychology* (3e). New York, NY: Routledge.

Erickson, E. H. (1968) *Identity, youth and crisis*. New York, NY: W. W. Norton Company

Erickson, S., Gerstle, M., & Montague, E. (2008). Repressive adaptive style and self-reported psychological functioning in adolescent cancer survivors. *Child Psychiatry and Human Development, 39*(3), 247–260.

Erlen, J. A., Caruthers, D. (2007). Adherence to medical regimens. In P. Kennedy, *Psychological management of physical disabilities: A practitioner's guide* (pp. 203–232). New York, NY: Routledge/Taylor & Francis.

Ernst, S. A., Brand, T., Reeske, A., Spallek, J., Petersen, K., & Zeeb, H. (2017). Care-related and maternal risk factors associated with the antenatal nondetection of intrauterine growth restriction: A case-control study from Bremen, Germany. *BioMed Research International*. doi:10.1155/2017/1746146

Eschleman, K. J., Alarcon, G. M., Lyons, J. B., Stokes, C. K., & Schneider, T. (2012). The dynamic nature of the stress appraisal process and the infusion of affect. *Anxiety, Stress & Coping, 25*(3), 309–327. doi:10.1080/10615806.2011.601299

Escobar, A. (1999). Are all food pyramids created equal? *Family Economics and Nutrition Review, 12*, 75–78.

Escobar, J. I., Randolph, E. T., & Hill, M. (1986). Symptoms of schizophrenia in Hispanic and Anglo veterans. *Culture, Medicine and Psychiatry, 10*, 259–276.

Eshun, S., & Gurung, R. A. R. (Eds.). (2009). *Culture and mental health: Sociocultural influences on mental health*. Malden, MA: Blackwell.

Eslami, B., Di Rosa, M., Barros, H., Stankunas, M., Torres-Gonzalez, F., Ioannidi-Kapolou, E., . . . Melchiorre, M. G. (2017). Lifetime abuse and perceived social support among the elderly: A study from seven European countries. *European Journal of Public Health, 27*(4), 686–692. doi:10.1093/eurpub/ckx047

Espino, D. V., & Maldonado, D. (1990). Hypertension and acculturation in elderly Mexican Americans: Results from 1982–84 Hispanic HANES. *Journal of Gerontology, 45*, M209–M213.

Everage, N. J., Gjelsvik, A., McGarvey, S. T., Linkletter, C. D., & Loucks, E. B. (2012). Inverse associations between perceived racism and coronary artery calcification. *Annals of Epidemiology, 22*(3), 183–190. doi:10.1016/j.annepidem.2012.01.005

Everly, G. S., & Girdano, D. A. (1980). *The stress mess solution*. Bowie, MD: Robert J. Brady.

Evers, A. W. M., Kraaimaat, F. W., Geenen, R., & Bijlsma, J. W. J. (1997). Determinants of psychological distress and its course in the first year after diagnosis in rheumatoid arthritis patients. *Journal of Behavioral Medicine, 20*, 489–504.

Everson, S. A., Goldberg, D. E., Kaplan, G. A., & Cohen, R. D. (1996). Hopelessness and risk of mortality and incidence of myocardial infarction and cancer. *Psychosomatic Medicine, 58*, 113–121.

Exline, J. J., Hall, T. W., Pargament, K. I., & Harriott, V. A. (2017). Predictors of growth from spiritual struggle among Christian undergraduates: Religious coping and perceptions of helpful action by God are both important. *Journal of Positive Psychology, 12*(5), 501–508. doi:10.1080/17439760.2016.1228007

Exline, J. J., Yali, A. M., & Lobel, M. (1999). When God disappoints: Difficulty forgiving God and its role in negative emotion. *Journal of Health Psychology, 4*, 365–379.

Fadiman, A. (1997). *The spirit catches you and you fall down: A Hmong child, her American doctors, and the collision of two cultures.* New York, NY: Farrar, Straus and Giroux.

Fagot-Campagna, A., Pettitt, D. J., Engelgau, M. M., Burrows, N. R., Geiss, L. S., Valdez, R., . . . Narayan, K. M. (2000). Type 2 diabetes among North American children and adolescents: An epidemiologic review and a public health perspective. *Journal of Pediatrics, 136*, 664–672.

Fahey, J. L., & Flemming, D. S. (Eds.). (1997). *AIDS/HIV reference guide for medical professionals* (4e). Baltimore, MD: Williams & Wilkins.

Fahey, J. W., Zhang, Y., & Talalay, P. (1997). Broccoli sprouts: An exceptionally rich source of inducers of enzymes that protect against chemical carcinogens. *Proceeding of the National Academy of Sciences, USA, 94*, 10367–10372.

Faith, M. S., Fontaine, K. R., Baskin, M. L., & Allison, D. (2007). Toward the reduction of population obesity: Macrolevel environmental approaches to the problems of food, eating, and obesity. *Psychological Bulletin, 133*, 205–226.

Falagas, M., Zarkadoulia, E., Ioannidou, E., Peppas, G., Christodoulou, C., & Rafailidis, P. (2007). The effect of psychosocial factors on breast cancer outcome: Asystematic review. *Breast Cancer Research, 9*(4), R44–R44.

Falzon, L., Davidson, K. W., & Bruns, D. (2010). Evidence searching for evidence-based psychology practice. *Professional Psychology: Research and Practice, 41*(6), 550–557. doi:10.1037/a0021352

Fan, Y., Chen, C., & Cheng, Y. (2016). The neural mechanisms of social learning from fleeting experience with pain. *Frontiers in Behavioral Neuroscience, 10*, 9. doi:10.3389/fnbeh.2016.00011

Fan, Y., Yuan, J., Wang, R., Gao, Y., & Yu, M. (2008). Alcohol, tobacco, and diet in relation to esophageal cancer: The Shanghai Cohort Study. *Nutrition and Cancer, 60*(3), 354–363.

Fang, C. Y., Miller, S. M., Bovbjerg, D. H., Bergman, C., Edelson, M. I., Rosenblum, N. G., . . . Douglas, S. D. (2008). Perceived stress is associated with impaired T-cell response to HPV16 in women with cervical dysplasia. *Annals of Behavioral Medicine, 35*(1), 87–96.

Fann, J. R., Thomas-Rich, A. M., Katon, W. J., Cowley, D., Pepping, M., McGregor, B. A., & Gralow, J. (2008). Major depression after breast cancer: A review of epidemiology and treatment. *General Hospital Psychiatry, 30*(2), 112–126.

Farmer, D., Reddick, B., D'Agostino, R., & Jackson, S. (2007). Psychosocial correlates of mammography screening in older African American women. *Oncology Nursing Forum, 34*(1), 117–123.

Farmer, D., Reddick, B., D'Agostino, R., & Jackson, S. (2007, January). Psychosocial correlates of mammography screening in older African American women. *Oncology Nursing Forum, 34*(1), 117–123.

Farmer, M. E., Locke, B. Z., Moscicki, E. K., Dannenberg, A. L., Larson, D. B., & Radloff, L. S. (1988). Physical activity and depressive symptoms: The NHANES I epidemiologic follow-up study. *American Journal of Epidemiology, 128*, 1340–1351.

Farooqi, Y.N. (2006). Traditional healing practices sought by Muslim psychiatric patients in Lahore, Pakistan. *International Journal of Disability, Development and Education, 53*, 401–415.

Farquharson, B., Johnston, M., & Bugge, C. (2011). How people present symptoms to health services: A theory-based content analysis. *Journal of the Royal College of General Practitioners, 61*(585), 267–273.

Farran, C. J., Paun, O., & Elliot, M. H. (2003). Spirituality in multicultural caregivers of persons with dementia. *Dementia, 2*, 353–377.

Fasce, N. (2008). Depression and social support among men and women living with HIV. *Journal of Applied Biobehavioral Research, 12*(3), 221–236.

Faucett, J., Gordon, N., & Levine, J. (1994). Differences in postoperative pain among four ethnic groups. *Journal of Pain and Symptom Management, 9*, 383–389.

Faul, L. A., & Jacobsen, P. B. (2012). Psychosocial interventions for people with cancer. In A. Baum, T. A. Revenson, & J. Singer (Eds.), *Handbook of health psychology 2e* (pp. 697–716). New York, NY: Guilford.

Fawzy, F. I., Fawzy, N., Hyun, C. S., Guthrie, D., Fahey, J. L., & Morton, D. (1993). Malignant melanoma: Effects of an early structured psychiatric intervention, coping, and effective state on recurrence and survival six years later. *Archives of General Psychiatry, 50*, 681–689.

Federal Trade Commission. (2016). Cigarette report for 2016. Retrieved from https://www.ftc.gov/system/files/documents/reports/federal-trade-commission-cigarette-report-2016-federal-trade-commission-smokeless-tobacco-report/ftc_cigarette_report_for_2016_0.pdf

Feeney, J. A., & Ryan, S. M. (1994). Attachment style and affect regulation: Relationships with health behavior and family experiences of illness in a student sample. *Health Psychology, 13*, 334–345.

Feifel, H., & Strack, S. (1989). Coping with conflict situations: Middle-aged and elderly men. *Psychology & Aging, 4*, 26–33.

Feldman Barrett, L. (2017). *How emotions are made: The secret life of the brain.* New York, NY: Houghton Mifflin Harcout.

Feldman, P. J., Cohen S., Gwaltney, J. M., Jr., Doyle, W. J., & Skoner, D. P. (1999). The impact of personality on the reporting of unfounded symptoms and illness. *Journal of Personality and Social Psychology, 77*, 370–378.

Feldman, R., Weller, A., Zagoory-Sharon, O., & Levine, A. Evidence for a neuroendocrinological foundation of human affiliation: Plasma oxytocin levels across pregnancy and the postpartum period predict mother-infant bonding. *Psychological Science, 18*(11), 965–970.

Felger, J. C., Haroon, E., & Miller, A. H. (2016). Inflammation and immune function in PTSD: Mechanisms, consequences, and translational implications. In I. Liberzon & K. J. Ressler (Eds.), *Neurobiology of PTSD: From brain to mind; neurobiology of PTSD: From brain to mind* (pp. 239–263). New York, NY: Oxford University Press.

Ferguson, C. J., San Miguel, C., Garza, A., & Jerabeck, J. M. (2012). A longitudinal test of video game violence influences on dating and aggression: A 3-year longitudinal study of adolescents. *Journal of Psychiatric Research, 46*(2), 141–146. doi:10.1016/j.jpsychires.2011.10.014

Ferguson, E. (2000). Hypochondriacal concerns and the Five Factor Model of Personality. *Journal of Personality, 68*(4), 705–724.

Ferguson, E., Matthews, G., & Cox, T. (2010) The appraisal of life events (ALE) scale: Reliability and validity. *British Journal of Health Psychology, 4*(2), 97–116

Ferrando, S., & Freyberg, Z. (2008). Treatment of depression in HIV positive individuals: A critical review. *International Review of Psychiatry* (Abingdon, UK), *20*(1), 61–71.

Ferrario, S. R., Giorgi, I., Baiardi, P., Giuntoli, L., Balestroni, G., Cerutti, P., . . . Vidotto, G. (2017). Illness denial questionnaire for patients and caregivers. *Neuropsychiatric Disease and Treatment, 13*(8), 909–916. doi:10.2147/NDT.S128622

Ferreira, R. (2008, March). Culture at the heart of coping with HIV/AIDS. *Journal of Psychology in Africa, 18*(1), 97–104.

Field, A. (2018). Field, D. (1999). A cross-cultural perspective on continuity and change in social relations in old age: Introduction to a special issue. *International Journal of Aging and Human Development, 48*, 257–261.

Field, T. M. (1998). Massage therapy effects. *American Psychologist, 53*, 1270–1281.

Field, T. M. (2002). Infants' need for touch. *Human Development, 45*, 100–103.

Fields, H. F. (1987). *Pain.* New York, NY: McGraw-Hill.

Figueroa, W. S., & Zoccola, P. M. (2015). Individual differences of risk and resiliency in sexual minority health: The roles of stigma consciousness and psychological hardiness. *Psychology of Sexual Orientation and Gender Diversity, 2*(3), 329–338. doi:10.1037/sgd0000114

Fillingim, R. B. (2003). Sex-related influences on pain: A review of mechanisms and clinical implications. *Rehabilitation Psychology, 48*, 165–174.

Finch, B.K., Kolody, B., & Vega, W.A. (2000). Perceived discrimination and depression among Mexican-origin adults in California, *Journal of Health and Social Behavior, 41*, 295–313.

Finckh, U. (2001). The dopamine D2 receptor gene and alcoholism: Association studies. In D. P. Agarwal & H. K. Seitz (Eds.), *Alcohol in health and disease* (pp. 151–176). New York, NY: Marcel Dekker.

Finkelstein, E. A., Brown, D. S., & Evans, W. D. (2008). Do obese persons comprehend their personal health risks? *American Journal of Health Behavior, 32*, 508–516.

Finlayson, G., King, N., & Blundell, J. (2008). The role of implicit wanting in relation to explicit liking and wanting for food: Implications for appetite control. *Appetite, 50*, 120–127.

Finn, M., & Robinson, E. R. (2012). Personality and Drinking Behavior in Alcohol Dependence: A Survival Analysis. *Alcoholism Treatment Quarterly, 30*(2), 146–162. doi:10.1080/07347324.2012.663300

Finnegan, J. R. Jr., Meischke, H., Zapka, J. G., Leviton, L., Meshack, A., Benjamin-Garner, R., . . . Stone E. (2000). Patient delay in seeking care for heart attack symptoms: Findings from focus groups conducted in five U.S. regions. *Preventive Medicine, 31*(3):205–213.

Fiori, M. C., Jorenby, D. E., Wetter, D. W., Kenford, S. L., Smith, S. S., & Baker, T. B. (1993). Prevalence of daily and experimental smoking among UW-Madison undergraduates, 1989–1993. *Wisconsin Medical Journal, 92*, 605–608.

Fischer Aggarwal, B., Liao, M., & Mosca, L. (2008). Physical activity as a potential mechanism through which social support may reduce cardiovascular disease risk. *Journal of Cardiovascular Nursing, 23*(2), 90–96.

Fischer, W. A., Fisher, J. D., & Rye, B. J. (1995). Understanding and promoting AIDS-preventive behavior: Insights from the theory of reasoned action. *Health Psychology, 14*, 255–264.

Fishbein, M., & Ajzen, I. (1975). *Belief, attitude, intention and behavior: An introduction to theory and research.* Boston, MA: Addison-Wesley.

Fisher, J. D., & Fisher, W. A. (1992). Changing AIDS-risk behavior. *Psychological Bulletin, 111*, 455–474.

Fisher, J. D., Bell, P. A., & Baum, A. (1984). *Environmental psychology* (2nd ed.). New York, NY: Holt, Rinehart & Winston.

Fisher, T. L., Burnet, D. L., Huang, E. S., Chin, M. H., & Cagney, K. A. (2007). Cultural leverage: Interventions using culture to narrow racial disparities in health care. *Medical Care Research and Review, 64*, 243S–282S.

Fiske, S. T. (1998) Stereotyping, prejudice, and discrimination. In D. T. Gilbert, S. T. Fiske, & G. Lindzey (Eds.), *The handbook of social psychology* (pp. 357–411). New York, NY: McGraw-Hill.

Fiske, S. T. (2004). *Social beings: A core motives approach to social psychology.* New York, NY: John Wiley.

Fitchett, G., Rybarczyk, B. D., DeMarco, G. A., & Nicholas, J. J. (1999). The role of religion in medical rehabilitation outcomes: A longitudinal study. *Rehabilitation Psychology, 44*, 333–353.

Fitzsimmons, E. E., & Bardone-Cone, A. M. (2011). Coping and social support as potential moderators of the relation between anxiety and eating disorder symptomatology. *Eating Behaviors, 12*(1), 21–28. doi:10./j.eatbeh.2010.09.002

Flaherty, J., & Richman, J. A. (1989). Gender differences in the perception and utilization of social support: Theoretical perspectives and an empirical test. *Social Science & Medicine, 28*, 1221–1228.

Flannery, R. B., Sos, J., & McGovern, P. (1981). Ethnicity as a factor in the expression of pain. *Psychosomatics, 22*, 39–50.

Flegal, K. M., Carroll, M. D., Kit, B. K., & Ogden, C. L. (2012). Prevalence of obesity and trends in the distribution of body mass index among U.S. adults, 1999–2010. *Journal of the American Medical Association, 307*(5), 491–497. doi:10.1001/jama.2012.39

Flegal, K. M., Carroll, M. D., Kuczmarski, R. J., & Johnson, C. L. (1998). Overweight and obesity in the United States: Prevalence and trends, 1960–1994. *International Journal of Obesity, 22*, 39–48.

Fleishman, J. A., & Fogel, B. (1994). Coping and depressive symptoms among young people with AIDS. *Health Psychology, 13*, 156–169.

Fleming, R., Baum, A., Gisriel, M. M., & Gatchel, R. J. (1982). Mediating influences of social support on stress at Three Mile Island. *Journal of Human Stress, 8*, 14–22.

Flensborg-Madsen, T., Johansen, C., Grønbæk, M., & Mortensen, E. (2011). A prospective association between quality of life and risk for cancer. *European Journal of Cancer, 47*(16), 2446–2452. doi:10.1016/j.ejca.2011.06.005

Fletcher, G. F. (1996). The antiatherosclerotic effect of exercise and development of an exercise prescription. *Cardiology Clinics, 14*, 85–96.

Flor, H. (2001). Psycho physiological assessment of the patient with chronic pain. In D. C. Turk & R. Melzack (Eds.), *Handbook of pain assessment* (2nd ed., pp. 76–96). New York, NY: Guilford Press.

Flor, H., Birbaumer, N., & Turk, D. C. (1990). The psychobiology of chronic pain. *Advances in Behavior Research & Therapy, 12*, 47–84.

Flor, H., Kerns, R. D., & Turk, D. C. (1987). The role of spouse reinforcement, perceived pain, and activity levels of chronic pain patients. *Journal of Psychosomatic Research, 31*, 251–259.

Flum, D. R. Salem, L. Elrod, J. B. Dellinger, E. P. Cheadle, A. Chan, L. (2005). Early mortality among Medicare beneficiaries undergoing bariatric surgical procedures. *Journal of the American Medical Association, 294*, 1903–1908.

Foley, K. M. (1997). Competent care for the dying instead of physician-assisted suicide. *New England Journal of Medicine*, 54–58.

Folkman, S., & Lazarus, R. S. (1985). If it changes it must be a process: Study of emotion and coping during three stages of a college examination. *Journal of Personality and Social Psychology, 48*(1), 150–170. doi.10.1037/0022-3514.48.1.150

Folkman, S., & Lazarus, R. S. (1988). *Ways of coping questionnaire.* Palo Alto, CA: Mind Garden.

Folkman, S., & Moskowitz, J. T. (2000). Positive affect and the other side of coping. *American Psychologist, 55*, 647–654.

Folkman, S., Lazarus, R. S., Dunkel-Schetter, C., DeLongis, A., & Gruen, R. J. (1986). Dynamics of a stressful encounter: Cognitive appraisal, coping, and encounter outcomes. *Journal of Personality and Social Psychology, 50*(5), 992–1003. doi.10.1037/0022-3514.50.5.992

Folkman, S., Lazarus, R. S., Gruen, R. J., & DeLongis, A. (1986). Appraisal, coping, health status, and psychological symptoms. *Journal of Personality and Social Psychology, 50*, 571–579.

Folsom, D. P., Gilmer, T., Barrio, C., Moore, D. J., Bucardo, J., Lindamer, L. A., . . . Jeste, D. V. (2007). A longitudinal study of the use of mental health services by persons with serious mental illness: Do Spanish-speaking Latinos differ from English-speaking Latinos and Caucasians? *American Journal of Psychiatry, 164*, 1173–1180.

Fontane, P. E. (1996). Exercise, fitness, feeling well: Aging well in contemporary society. II. Choices and processes. *American Behavioral Scientist, 39*, 288–305.

Forcier, K., Stroud, L. R., Papandonatos, G. D., Hitsman, B., Reiches, M., Krishnamoorthy, J., & Niaura, R. (2006). Links between physical fitness and cardiovascular reactivity and recovery to psychological stressors: Ameta-Analysis. *Health Psychology, 25*, 723–739.

Ford, E. S. (1999). Body mass index and colon cancer in a national sample of adult U.S. men. *American Journal of Epidemiology, 150*, 390–398.

Fordyce, W. E. (1976). *Behavioral methods for chronic pain and illness.*St. Louis, MO: C.V. Mosby.

Fordyce, W. E. (1988). Pain and suffering: A reappraisal. *American Psychologist, 43*, 276–282.

Fordyce, W. E. (1990). Environmental and interoceptive influences on chronic low back pain behavior: Response. *Pain, 43*, 133–134.

Forlenza, M. J., & Baum, A. (2000). Psychosocial influences on cancer progression: Alternative cellular and molecular mechanisms. *Current Opinion in Psychiatry, 13*, 639–645.

Fors, E. A., Sexton, H., & Gotestam, G. (2002). The effect of guided imagery and amitriptyline on daily fibromyalgia pain: A prospective, randomized, controlled trial. *Journal of Psychiatric Research, 36*, 179–187.

Forsythe, L., Thorn, B., Day, M., & Shelby, G. (2011). Race and sex differences in primary appraisals, catastrophizing, and experimental pain outcomes. *Journal of Pain, 12*(5), 563–572. doi:10.1016/j.jpain.2010.11.003

Foster, J. M., Sanderman, R., van der Molen, T., Mueller, T., & van Sonderen, E. (2008). Personality influences the reporting of side effects of inhaled corticosteroids in asthma patients. *Journal of Asthma, 45*(8), 664–669. doi:10.1080/02770900802127022

Fournier, M., d'Arripe-Longueville, F., Rovere, C., Easthope, C. S., Schwabe, L., El Methni, J., & Radel, R. (2017). Effects of circadian cortisol on the development of a health habit. *Health Psychology, 36*(11), 1059–1064. doi:10.1037/hea0000510

Fournier, M., de Ridder, D., & Bensing, J. (2002a). How optimism contributes to the adaptation of chronic illness: A prospective study into the enduring effects of optimism on adaptation moderated by the controllability of chronic illness. *Personality and Individual Differences, 33*, 1163–1183.

Fournier, M., de Ridder, D., & Bensing, J. (2002b). Optimism and adaptation to chronic disease: The role of optimism in relation to self-care options of Type I diabetes mellitus, rheumatoid arthritis and multiple sclerosis. *British Journal of Health Psychology, 7*, 409–432.

Fournier, M., de Ridder, D., & Bensing, J. (2003). Is optimism sensitive to the stressors of chronic disease? The impact of Type 1 diabetes mellitus and multiple sclerosis on optimistic beliefs. *Psychology and Health, 18*, 277–294.

Fowler, R. A., Sabur, N., Li, P., Juurlink, D. N., Pinto, R., Hladunewich, M. A., . . . (2007). Sex-and age-based differences in the delivery and outcomes of critical care. *Canadian Medical Association Journal, 177*(12), doi:10.1503/cmaj. 071112.

Fox, B. H. (1998). A hypothesis about Spiegel et al.'s 1989 paper on psychosocial intervention and breast cancer survival. *Psycho-Oncology, 7*, 361–370.

Fox, C., Pencina, M., Wilson, P., Paynter, N., Vasan, R., & D'Agostino, R. (2008). Lifetime risk of cardiovascular disease among individuals with and without diabetes stratified by obesity status in the Framingham heart study. *Diabetes Care, 31*(8), 1582–1584.

Francis, M. E., & Pennebaker, J. W. (1992). Putting stress into words: Writing about personal upheavals and health. *American Journal of Health Promotion, 6*, 280–287.

Frankel, R. M. (1995). Emotion and the physician-patient relationship. *Motivation and Emotion, 19*, 163–173.

Frankenhaeuser, M., Lundenberg, U., Fredrikson, M., Melin, B., Tuomisto, M., & Myrsten, A-L. (1989). Stress on and off the job as related to sex and occupational status in white- collar workers. *Journal of Organizational Behavior, 10*, 321–346.

Frankl, V. (1963). *Man's search for meaning*. Boston, MA: Beacon.

Franko, D. L., Thompson, D., Affenito, S. G., Barton, B. A., & Striegel-Moore, R. H. (2008). What mediates the relationship between family meals and adolescent health issues. *Health Psychology, 27*, S109–S117.

Frasure-Smith, N., & Prince, R. H. (1987). The ischemic heart disease life stress monitoring program: Possible therapeutic mechanisms. *Psychology and Health, 1*, 273–285.

Frasure-Smith, N., Lesperance, F., & Talajic, M. (1995). The impact of negative emotions on prognosis following myocardial infarction: Is it more than depression? *Health Psychology, 14*, 388–398.

Freburg, L. A. (2016). *Discovering behavioral neuroscience: An introduction to biological psychology*. Boston, MA: Cengage.

Fredrickson, B. L., Tugade, M. M., Waugh, C. E., & Larkin, G. R. (2003). What good are positive emotions in crisis? A prospective study of resilience and emotions following the terrorist attacks on the United States on September 11th, 2001. *Journal of Personality and Social Psychology, 84*, 365–376.

Freedland, K. E. (2017). A new era for health psychology. *Health Psychology, 36*(1), 1–4. doi:10.1037/hea0000463

Freedman, J. L. (1975). *Crowding and behavior*. San Francisco, CA: W. H. Freeman.

Freedman, K. S., Nelson, N. M., & Feldman, L. L. (2012). Smoking initiation among young adults in the United States and Canada, 1998–2010: A systematic review. *Preventing Chronic Disease, 9*, 110037. doi:10.5888/pcd9.110037

Freedman, L., Kipnis, V., Schatzkin, A., Potischman, N. (2008). Methods of epidemiology: Evaluating the fat-breast cancer hypothesis–comparing dietary instruments and other developments. *Cancer Journal* (Sudbury, MA), *14*(2), 69–74.

Freeman, M. A., Hennessy, E. V., & Marzullo, D. M. (2001). Defensive evaluation of antismoking messages among college-age smokers: The role of possible selves. *Health Psychology, 20*, 424–33.

Freeman, V. L., Meydani, M., Yong, S., Pyle, J., Wan, Y., Arvizu-Durazo, R., & Liao, Y. (2000). Prostatic levels of tocopherols, carotenoids, and retinol in relation to plasma levels and self-reported usual dietary intake. *American Journal of Epidemiology, 151*, 109–118.

Frestad, D., & Prescott, E. (2017) Vital exhaustion and depression: A reply to Bianchi and colleagues. *Psychosomatic Medicine, 79*(7), 836–837. doi:10.1097/PSY.0000000000000501

Freud, S. (1940/1964). New introductory lectures on psychoanalysis. In J. Strachey (Ed.), *The standard edition of the complete psychological works of Sigmund Freud* (Vol. 22). London, UK: Hogarth.

Friedman, G. D., Armstrong, M. A., Kipp, H., & Klatsky, A. L. (2003). Wine, liquor, beer, and mortality. *American Journal of Epidemiology, 158*, 585–595.

Friedman, H. (2008, July 18). The multiple linkages of personality and disease. *Brain, Behavior, and Immunity, 22*(5), 668–675.

Friedman, H. S. (2000). Long-term relations of personality and health: Dynamisms, mechanisms, tropism. *Journal of Personality, 68*, 1089–2008.

Friedman, H. S., & Adler, N. E. (2011). The intellectual roots of health psychology. In H. F. Friedman (Ed.), *The Oxford handbook of health psychology* (pp. 3–14). New York, NY: Oxford University Press.

Friedman, H. S., & Booth-Kewley, S. (1987). The "disease-prone personality." A meta-analytic view of the construct. *American Psychologist, 42*, 539–555.

Friedman, H. S., & Martin, L. R. (2011). *The longevity project: Surprising discoveries for health and long life from the landmark eight-decade study*. New York, NY: Hudson Street Press.

Friedman, H. S., Hall, J. A., & Harris, M. J. (1995). Type A behavior, nonverbal expressive style, and health. *Journal of Personality and Social Psychology, 48*, 1299–1315.

Friedman, H., & Silver, R. (Eds.). 2007. *Foundations of health psychology*. New York, NY: Oxford University Press.

Friedman, H., Klein, T., & Specter, S. (1991). Immunosuppression by marijuana and components. In R. Ader & D. L. Felton (Eds.), *Psychoneuroimmunology* (pp. 931–953). San Diego, CA: Academic Press.

Friedman, L. C., Webb, J. A., Weinberg, A. D., Lane, M., Cooper, H. P., & Woodruff, A. (1995). Breast cancer screening: Racial/ethnic differences in behaviors and beliefs. *Journal of Cancer Education, 10*, 213–216.

Friedman, M., & Rosenman, R. H. (1959). Association of specific overt behavior pattern with blood and cardiovascular findings:

Blood cholesterol level, blood clotting time, incidence of arcus senilis, and clinical coronary artery disease. *Journal of the American Medical Association, 169*, 1286–1296.

Friedman, M., & Rosenman, R. H. (1974). *Type A behavior and your heart.* New York, NY: Knopf.

Friedman, M., Breall, W. S., Goodwin, M. L., Sparagon, B. J., Ghandour, G., & Fleischmann, N. (1996). Effect of Type A behavioral counseling on frequency of silent myocardial ischemia in coronary patients. *American Heart Journal, 132*, 933–940.

Friedman, M., Thoresen, C. E., Gill, J. J., Ulmer, D., Powell, L. H., Price, V. A., . . . Dixon, T. (1986). Alteration of Type A behavior and its effect on cardiac recurrences in post myocardial infarction patients: Summary results of the recurrent coronary prevention project. *American Heart Journal, 112*, 653–665.

Friedman-Wheeler, D. G., Pederson, J. E., Rizzo-Busack, H. M., & Haaga, D. A. F. (2016). Measuring outcome expectancies for specific coping behaviors: The Coping Expectancies Scale (CES). *Journal of Psychopathology and Behavioral Assessment, 38*(3), 421–432. doi:10.1007/s10862-016-9539-9

Friedrich, J. (1996). Assessing students' perceptions of psychology as a science: Validation of a self-report measure. *Teaching of Psychology, 23*, 6–13.

Frone, M. R., Russell, M., & Cooper, M. L. (1995). Relationship of work and family stressors to psychological distress: The independent moderating influence of social support, mastery, active coping, and self-focused attention. In R. Crandall & P. L. Perrewé (Eds.), *Occupational stress: A handbook* (pp. 129–150). Philadelphia, PA: Taylor & Francis.

Frost, D. M., & Svensson, M. E. D. (2019). Sexual minority health. In T. A. Revenson & R. A. R. Gurung (Eds.), *Handbook of health psychology* (3e). New York, NY: Routledge.

Fu, M. R., Xu, B., Liu, Y., & Haber, J. (2008). "Making the best of it": Chinese women's experiences of adjusting to breast cancer diagnosis and treatment. *Journal of Advanced Nursing, 63*, 155–165.

Fuchs, F. D., & Chambless, L. E. (2007). Is the cardioprotective effect of alcohol real? *Alcohol, 41*, 399–402.

Fudin, R., & Lembessis, E. (2004). The Mozart effect: Questions about the seminal findings of Rauscher, Shaw and colleagues. *Perceptual & Motor Skills, 98*, 389–406.

Fuentes, M., Hart-Johnson, T., & Green, C. R. (2007). The association among neighborhood socioeconomic status, race, and chronic pain in Black and White older adults. *Journal of the National Medical Association, 99*, 1160–1169.

Fujimoto, W. Y. (1992). The growing prevalence of non-insulin-dependent diabetes in migrant Asian populations and its implications for Asia. *Diabetes Research and Clinical Practice, 15*, 167–183.

Fukushima, Y., Ohmura, H., Mokuno, H., Kajimoto, K., Kasai, T., Hirayama, S., & . . . Daida, H. (2012). Non-high-density lipoprotein cholesterol is a practical predictor of long-term cardiac death after coronary artery bypass grafting. *Atherosclerosis (00219150), 221*(1), 206–211. doi:10.1016/j.atherosclerosis.2011.12.012

Fuller, T. D., Edwards, J. N., Sermsri, S., & Vorakitphokatron, S. (1993). Gender and health: Some Asian evidence. *Journal of Health and Social Behavior, 34*, 252–271.

Fulton, J. P., Rakowski, W., & Jones, A. C. (1995). Determinants of breast cancer screening among inner-city Hispanic women in comparison with other inner-city women. *Public Health Reports, 110*, 476–482.

Fung, T., Chiuve, S., McCullough, M., Rexrode, K., Logroscino, G. Hu, F. (2008). Adherence to a DASH-style diet and risk of coronary heart disease and stroke in women. *Archives of Internal Medicine, 168*(7), 713–720.

Furlotte, C., & Schwartz, K. (2017). Mental health experiences of older adults living with HIV: Uncertainty, stigma, and approaches to resilience. *Canadian Journal on Aging, 36*(2), 125–140. doi:10.1017/S0714980817000022

Futterman, A. D., Kemeny, M. E., Shapiro, D., & Fahey, J. L. (1994). Immunological and physiological changes associated with induced positive and negative mood. *Psychosomatic Medicine, 56*, 499–511.

Gaab, J., Jiménez, J., Voneschen, L., Oschwald, D., Meyer, A. H., Nater, U. M., & Krummenacher, P. (2017). Psychosocial stress-induced analgesia: An examination of effects on heat pain threshold and tolerance and of neuroendocrine mediation. *Neuropsychobiology, 74*(2), 87–95. doi:10.1159/000454986

Gabbiadini, A., Cristini, F., Scacchi, L., & Monaci, M. G. (2017). Testing the model of goal-directed behavior for predicting binge drinking among young people.*Substance Use & Misuse, 52*(4), 493–506. doi.10.1080/10826084.2016.1245335

Gaines, S. O., Jr. (1997). *Culture, ethnicity, and personal relationship processes.* New York, NY: Routledge.

Galanti, G. (2014). *Caring for patients from different cultures.* Philadelphia, PA: University of Pennsylvania Press.

Galantino, M., Galbavy, R., Quinn, L. (2008). Therapeutic effects of yoga for children: A systematic review of the literature. *Pediatric Physical Therapy, 20*(1), 66–80.

Galdas, P. M., Johnson, J. L., Percy, M. E., & Ratner, P. A. (2010). Help seeking for cardiac symptoms: Beyond the masculine–feminine binary. *Social Science & Medicine, 71*(1), 18–24. doi:10.1016/j.socscimed.2010.03.006

Galea, S., Brewin, C. R., Jones, R. T., King, D. W., King, L. A., McNally, R. J., . . . Kessler, R. C. (2007). Exposure to hurricane-related stressors and mental illness after hurricane Katrina. *Archives of General Psychiatry, 64*, 1427–1434.

Gall, T. L., & Cornblat, M. W. (2002). Breast cancer survivors give voice: A qualitative analysis of spiritual factors in long-term adjustment. *Psycho-Oncology, 11*, 524–535.

Gall, T. L., & Evans, D. R. (1987). The dimensionality of cognitive appraisal and its relationship to physical and psychological well-being. *Journal of Psychology, 121*(6), 539–546.

Gallagher, S., Phillips, A. C., Ferraro, A. J., Drayson, M. T., & Carroll, D. (2008). Social support is positively associated with the immunoglobulin M response to vaccination with pneumococcal polysaccharides. *Biological Psychology, 78*, 211–215.

Gallicchio, L., Hoffman, S. C., & Helzlsouer, K. J. (2007). The relationship between gender, social support, and health-related quality of life in a community-based study in Washington County, Maryland. *Quality of Life Research, 16*, 777–786.

Galligan, R. F., & Terry, D. J. (1993). Romantic ideals, fear of negative implications, and the practice of safe sex. *Journal of Applied Social Psychology, 23*, 1685–1711.

Gallo, J. J., Armenian, H. K., Ford, D. E., Eaton, W. W., & Khachaturian, A. S. (2000). Major depression and cancer: The 13-year follow-up of the Baltimore epidemiologic catchment area sample (United States). *Cancer Causes and Control, 11*, 751–758.

Galvan, F., Davis, E., Banks, D., Bing, E. (2008, May). HIV stigma and social support among African Americans. *AIDS Patient Care and Standards, 22*(5), 423–436.

Gansler, T., Kaw, C., Crammer, C., & Smith, T. (2008). A population-based study of prevalence of complementary methods use by cancer survivors: are port from the American Cancer Society's studies of cancer survivors. *Cancer, 113*(5), 1048–1057.

Gant, L. M., & Ostrow, D. G. (1995). Perceptions of social support and psychological adaptation to sexually acquired HIV among White and African American men. *Social Work, 40*, 215–224.

Ganzini, L., Harvath, T. A., Jackson, A., Goy, E. R., Miller, L. L., & Delorit, M. A. (2002). Experiences of Oregon nurses and social workers with hospice patients who requested assistance with suicide. *New England Journal of Medicine, 347*, 582–588.

Gao, F., Bailes, E., Robertson, D. L., Chen, Y., Rodenburg, C. M., Michael, S. F., . . . Hahn, B. H. (1999). Origin of HIV-1 in the chimpanzee *Pan troglodytes troglodytes. Nature, 397*, 436–441.

Garcia, H. B., & Lee, P. C. Y. (1989). Knowledge about cancer and use of health care services among Hispanic- and Asian-American older adults. *Journal of Psychosocial Oncology, 6*, 157–177.

Garcia, K., & Mann, T. (2003). From "I wish" to "I will": Social-cognitive predictors of behavioral intentions. *Journal of Health Psychology, 8*, 347–360.

Garcia-Palacios, A., Hoffman, H. G., Richards, T. R., Seibel, E. J., & Sharar, S. R. (2007). Use of virtual reality distraction to reduce claustrophobia symptoms during a mock magnetic resonance imaging brain scan: A case report. *Cyber Psychology and Behavior, 10*, 485–488.

Garnett, G. P., & Anderson, R. M. (1993). Contact tracing and the estimation of sexual mixing patterns: The epidemiology of gonococcal infections. *Sexually Transmitted Diseases, 20*, 181–190.

Garrett, D. D., Kovacevic, N., McIntosh, A. R., & Grady, C. L. (2011) The importance of being variable. *Journal of Neuroscience, 31*(12), 4496–4503. doi:10.1523/JNEUROSCI.5641-10.2011

Garrido, S., Eerola, T., & McFerran, K. (2017). Group rumination: Social interactions around music in people with depression. *Frontiers in Psychology, 8*, 10. doi:10.3389/FPSYG.2017.00490

Garrison, V. (1977). Doctor, espirista, or psychiatrist: Health seeking behavior in a Puerto Rican neighborhood of New York City. *Medical Anthropologist, 1*, 165–191.

Garssen, B., & Goodkin, K. (1999). On the role of immunological factors as mediators between psychosocial factors and cancer progression. *Psychiatry Research, 85*, 51–61.

Gartland, N., O'Connor, D. B., & Lawton, R. (2012) The effects of conscientiousness on the appraisals of daily stressors. *Stress Health (28)*1, 80–86. doi:10.1002/smi.1404

Gatchel, R. J. (2005). *Clinical essentials of pain management.* Washington, DC: American Psychological Association.

Gatchel, R. J., & Oordt, M. S. (2003a). *Clinical health psychology and primary care: Practical advice and clinical guidance for successful collaboration.* Washington, DC: American Psychological Association.

Gatchel, R. J., & Oordt, M. S. (2003b). Coping with chronic or terminal illness. In R. J. Gatchel & M. S. Oordt (Eds.), *Clinical health psychology and primary care: Practical advice and clinical guidance for successful collaboration* (pp. 213–233). Washington, DC: American Psychological Association.

Gately, I. (2003). *Tobacco: Cultural history of how an exotic plant seduced civilization.* New York, NY: Grove Press.

Gaussoin, S. A., Espeland, M. A., Absher, J., Howard, B. V., Jones, B. M., & Rapp, S. R. (2012). Ascertaining dementia-related outcomes for deceased or proxy-dependent participants: An overview of the Women's Health Initiative Memory Study supplemental case ascertainment protocol. *International Journal of Geriatric Psychiatry, 27*(2), 205–214. doi:10.1002/gps.2714

Gayda, M., Brun, C., Juneau, M., Levesque, S., & Nigam, A. (2008). Long-term cardiac rehabilitation and exercise training programs improve metabolic parameters in metabolic syndrome patients with and without coronary heart disease. *Nutrition, Metabolism, and Cardiovascular Diseases, 18*(2), 142–151.

Gazmararian, J. A., Adams, M. M., & Pamuk, E. R. (1996). Associations between measures of socioeconomic status and maternal health behavior. *American Journal of Preventive Medicine, 12*, 108–115.

Geertsen, R., Kane, R. L., Klauber, M. R., Rindflesh, M., & Gray, R. (1975). A re-examination of Suchman's views on social factors in health care utilization. *Journal of Health and Social Behavior, 16*, 226–37.

Geirdal, A., & Dahl, A. (2008). The relationship between psychological distress and personality in women from families with familial breast/ ovarian or hereditary non-polyposis colorectal cancer in the absence of demonstrated mutations. *Journal of Genetic Counseling, 17*(4), 384–393.

Gelernter, J., Goldman, D., & Risch, N. (1992). The A1 allele at the D2 dopamine receptor gene and alcoholism: A reappraisal. *Journal of the American Medical Association, 269*, 1673–1677.

George, L. K. (1989). Stress, social support, and depression over the life-course. In K. S. Markides & C. L. Cooper (Eds.), *Aging, stress and health* (pp. 241–267). Oxford, UK: John Wiley.

George, M. C., Wongmek, A., Kaku, M., Nmashie, A., & Robinson-Papp, J. (2017). A mixed-methods pilot study of mindfulness-based stress reduction for HIV-associated chronic pain. *Behavioral Medicine, 43*(2), 108–119. doi:10.1080/08964289.2015.1107525

Georgopoulos, A. P., James, L. M., Carpenter, A. F., Engdahl, B. E., Leuthold, A. C., & Lewis, S. M. (2017). Gulf war illness (GWI) as a neuroimmune disease. *Experimental Brain Research, 235*(10), 3217–3225. doi:10.1007/s00221-017-5050-0

Gerlach, L. B., Kavanagh, J., Watkins, D., Chiang, C., Kim, H. M., & Kales, H. C. (2017). With a little help from my friends?: Racial and gender differences in the role of social support in later-life depression medication adherence. *International Psychogeriatrics, 29*(9), 1485–1493, doi:10.1017/S104161021700076X

Gerressu, M., & Stephenson, J. (2008). Sexual behaviour in young people. *Current Opinion in Infectious Diseases, 21*(1), 37–41.

Gerstein, D. R., & Green, L. W. (1993). *Preventing drug abuse: What do we know?* Washington, DC: National Academy Press.

Gesell, A. (1928). *Infancy and human growth.* Oxford, UK: Macmillan.

Geyer, S. J. (1993). Urinalysis and urinary sediment in patients with renal disease. *Clinical Laboratory Medicine, 13*, 13–20.

Ghasemipour, Y., & Ghorbani, N. (2010). Mindfulness and basic psychological needs among patients with coronary heart disease. *Iranian Journal of Psychiatry and Clinical Psychology, 16*(2), 154–162.

Ghosh, A., & Deb, A. (2017). Positive psychology interventions for chronic physical illnesses: A systematic review. *Psychological Studies, 62*, 213–232. doi:10.1007/s12646-017-0421-y

Giannoglou, G., Chatzizisis, Y., Zamboulis, C., Parcharidis, G., Mikhailidis, D., & Louridas, G. (2008). Elevated heart rate and atherosclerosis: An overview of the pathogenetic mechanisms. *International Journal of Cardiology, 126*(3), 302–312.

Giardini, A., Pierobon, A., Callegari, S., Caporotondi, A., Stabile, M., Avvenuti, G., & Majani, G. (2017). Optimism may protect chronic heart failure patients from depressive symptoms: Relationships between depression, anxiety, optimism, pessimism and illness perception. *Psicoterapia Cognitiva e Comportamentale, 23*(1), 27–39.

Giblin, P. T., Poland, M. L., & Ager, J. W. (1990). Effects of social supports on attitudes, health behaviors and obtaining prenatal care. *Journal of Community Health, 15*, 357–368.

Gidron, Y., Levy, A., & Cwikel, J. (2007). Psychosocial and reported inflammatory disease correlates of self-reported heart disease in women from south of Israel. *Women and Health, 44*(4), 25–40.

Giger, J., Davidhizar, R., Purnell, L., Taylor-Harden, J., Phillips, J., & Strickland, O. (2007). American Academy of Nursing Expert Panel Report: Developing cultural competence to eliminate health disparities in ethnic minorities and other vulnerable populations. *Journal of Transcultural Nursing, 18*(2), 95–102.

Gil, S., & Weinberg, M. (2015). Coping strategies and internal resources of dispositional optimism and mastery as predictors of traumatic exposure and of PTSD symptoms: A prospective study. *Psychological Trauma: Theory, Research, Practice, and Policy, 7*(4), 405–411. doi:10.1037/tra0000032

Gilanshah, F. (1993). Islamic customs regarding death. In D. P. Irish, K. F. Lundquist, & V. J. Nelsen (Eds.), *Ethnic variations in dying, death, and grief: Diversity in universality* (pp. 137–145). Philadelphia, PA: Taylor and Francis.

Gilbert, S. C. (2003). Eating disorders in women of color. *Clinical Psychology: Science and Practice, 10*, 444–455.

Gillespie, S. L., Christian, L. M., Alston, A. D., & Salsberry, P. J. (2017). Childhood stress and birth timing among African American women: Cortisol as biological mediator. *Psychoneuroendocrinology, 84*, 32–41. doi:10.1016/j.psyneuen.2017.06.009

Gilligan, R. (2008). Promoting resilience in young people in long-term care: The relevance of roles and relationships in the domains of recreation and work. *Journal of Social Work Practice, 22*, 37–50.

Gilliland, F. D., Li, Y., Baumgartner, K. B., Crumley, D., & Samet, J. (2001). Physical activity and breast cancer risk in Hispanic and non-Hispanic White women. *American Journal of Epidemiology, 154*, 442–450.

Gilliland, S. S., Carter, J. S., Perez, G. E., Two Feathers, J., Kenui, C. K., & Mau, M. K. (1998). Recommendations for development and adaptation of culturally competent community health interventions in minority populations with Type 2 diabetes mellitus. *Diabetes Spectrum, 11*, 166–174.

Giolas, M. H., & Sanders, B. (1992). Pain and suffering as a function of dissociation level and instructional set. *Dissociation, 5*, 205–209.

Girvan, C., & Savage, T. (2010). Identifying an appropriate pedagogy for virtual worlds: A communal constructivism case study. *Computers & Education, 55*(1), 342–349. doi:10.1016/j.compedu.2010.01.020.

Given, C. (2003). Introduction: The state of the knowledge of intervention research in cancer care. In *Evidence-based cancer care and prevention: Behavioral interventions* (pp. 1–16). New York, NY: Springer.

Glantz, S., Slade, J., Bero, L. A., Hanauer, P., & Barnes, D. E. (1998). *The Cigarette Papers*. Berkeley, CA: University of California Press.

Glanz, K., & Kegler, M. (2012). Processes of health behavior change. In A. Baum, T. A. Revenson, & J. Singer (Eds.), *Handbook of health psychology* (2e, pp. 99–112). New York, NY: Taylor & Francis.

Glanz, K., Halpern, A. C., Saraiya, M. (2006). Behavioral and community interventions to prevent skin cancer: What works? *Archives of Dermatology, 142*, 356–60.

Glanz, K., Rimer, B. K., & Marcus-Lewis, F. M. (2002). Theory, research, and practice in health behavior and education. In K. Glanz, B. K. Rimer, & F. M. Lewis (Eds.), *Health behavior and health education: Theory, research, and practice* (pp. 22–43). San Francisco, CA: Jossey-Bass.

Glanz, K., Rimer, B. K., Viswanath, K. (Eds.). (2015). *Health behavior and health education: Theory, research, and practice* (5e). San Francisco: Jossey-Bass.

Glass, D. C., & Singer, J. E. (1972). *Urban stress: Experiments on noise and social stressors*. New York, NY: Academic Press.

Gleiberman, L., Harburg, E., Frone, M.R., Russell, M., & Cooper, M.L. (1995). Skin colour, measures of socioeconomic status, and blood pressure among blacks in Erie County, NY. *Annals of Human Biology, 22*, 69–73.

Gluck, M. E., & Geliebter, A. (2002). Racial/ethnic differences in body image and eating behaviors. *Eating Behaviors, 3*, 143–151.

Goessl, V. C., Curtiss, J. E., & Hofmann, S. G. (2017). The effect of heart rate variability biofeedback training on stress and anxiety: A meta-analysis. *Psychological Medicine, 47*(15), 2578–2586. doi:10.1017/S0033291717001003

Gogos, C. A., Ginopoulos, P., Salsa, B., Apostolidou, E., Zoumbos, N. C., & Kalfarentzos, F. (1998). Dietary omega-3 polyunsaturated fatty acids plus vitamin-E restore immunodeficiency and prolong survival for severely ill patients with generalized malignancy. *Cancer, 82*, 395–402.

Goldberg, M. G., DePue, J., Kazura, A., & Niaura, R. (1998). Models for provider-patient interaction: Applications to health behavior change. In S. A. Shumaker, E. B. Schron, J. K. Okene, & W. L. McBee (Eds.), *The handbook of health behavior change* (2nd ed., pp. 283–304). New York, NY: Springer.

Goldenberg, I., Jonas, M., Tenenbaum, A., Boyko, V., Matetzky, S., Shotan, A., . . . Reicher-Reiss, H. (2003). Current smoking, smoking cessation, and the risk of sudden cardiac death in patients with coronary artery disease. *Archives of Internal Medicine, 163*, 2301–2306.

Goldman, L. K., & Glantz, S. A. (1998). Evaluation of antismoking advertising campaigns. *Journal of the American Medical Association, 279*, 772–777.

Goldman, M. S., DelBoca, F. K., & Darkes, J. (1999). Alcohol expectancy theory: The application of cognitive neuroscience. In K. E. Leonard & H. T. Blane (Eds.), *Psychological theories of drinking and alcoholism* (pp. 203–246). New York, NY: Guilford Press.

Goldman, R. H., Stason, W. B., Park, S. K., Kim, R., Schnyer, R. N., Davis, R. B., Legedza, A. T. R., & Kaptchuk, Ted J. (2008). Acupuncture for treatment of persistent arm pain due to repetitive use: A randomized controlled clinical trial. *Clinical Journal of Pain, 24*, 211–218.

Goldmann, E., Aiello, A., Uddin, M., Delva, J., Koenen, K., Gant, L., & Galea, S. (2011). Pervasive exposure to violence and posttraumatic stress disorder in a predominantly African American Urban Community: The Detroit Neighborhood Health Study. *Journal of Traumatic Stress, 24*(6), 747–751. doi:10.1002/jts.20705

Goldscheider, A. (1894). Ueber den schmerz im physiologischer und klinischer hinsicht. Berlin, Germany: Hirschwald.

Goldstein, A. O., Sobel, R. A., & Newman, G. R. (1999). Tobacco and alcohol use in G-rated children's animated films. *Journal of the American Medical Association, 281*, 1131–1137.

Goldstein, L. B., Amarenco, P., LaMonte, M., Gilbert, S., Messig, M., Callahan, A., Welch, M. A. (2008). Relative effects of statin therapy on stroke and cardiovascular events in men and women: Secondary analysis of the Stroke Prevention by Aggressive Reduction in Cholesterol Levels (SPARCL) Study. *Stroke, 39*(9), 2444–2448.

Goldston, K., & Baillie, A. (2008). Depression and coronary heart disease: Are view of the epidemiological evidence, explanatory mechanisms and management approaches. *Clinical Psychology Review, 28*(2), 288–306.

Golub, S., & Fikslin, R. (2019). HIV/AIDS. In T. A. Revenson & R. A. R. Gurung (Eds.), *Handbook of health psychology* (3e). New York, NY: Routledge.

Gomes, A. R., Faria, S., & Lopes, H. (2016). Stress and psychological health: Testing the mediating role of cognitive appraisal. *Western Journal of Nursing Research, 38*(11), 1448–1468. doi:10.1177/0193945916654666

Gondwe, K. W., White-Traut, R., Brandon, D., Pan, W., & Holditch-Davis, D. (2017). The role of sociodemographic factors in maternal psychological distress and mother-preterm infant interactions. *Research in Nursing & Health, 40*(6), 528–540. doi:10.1002/nur.21816

González, J., Jover, L., Cobo, E., & Muñoz, P. (2010). A web-based learning tool improves student performance in statistics: A randomized masked trial. *Computers & Education, 55*(2), 704–713. doi:10.1016/j.compedu.2010.03.003.

Gonzalez, P., Nuñez, A., Wang-Letzkus, M., Lim, J., Flores, K. F., & Nápoles, A. M. (2016). Coping with breast cancer: Reflections from Chinese American, Korean American, and Mexican American women. *Health Psychology, 35*(1), 19–28. doi:10.1037/hea0000263

Goodall, C., Sabo, J., Cline, R., & Egbert, N. (2012). Threat, efficacy, and uncertainty in the first 5 months of national print and electronic news coverage of the H1N1 virus. *Journal of Health Communication, 17*(3), 338–355. doi:10.1080/10810730.2011.626499

Goodkin, K., Feaster, D. J., Tuttle, R., Blaney, N. T., Kumar, M., Baum, M. K., . . . Fletcher, M. A. (1996). Bereavement is associated with time-dependent decrements in cellular immune function in asymptomatic human immunodeficiency virus type 1-seropositive homosexual men. *Clinical and Diagnostic Laboratory Immunology, 3*, 109–113.

Goodman, E. (1999). The role of socioeconomic status gradients in explaining differences in U.S. adolescents' health. *American Journal of Public Health, 89*, 1522–1528.

Goodman, E., Huang, B., Schafer-Kalkhoff, T., & Adler, N. E. (2007). Perceived socioeconomic status: A new type of identity which influences adolescents' self-rated health. *Journal of Adolescent Health, 41*, 479–487.

Goodmon, L. B., Middleditch, A. M., Childs, B., & Pietrasiuk, S. E. (2016). Positive psychology course and its relationship to well-being, depression, and stress. *Teaching of Psychology, 43*(3), 232–237. doi:10.1177/0098628316649482

Goodwin, I. (2003). The relevance of attachment theory to the philosophy, organization, and practice of adult mental health care. *Clinical Psychology Review, 23*, 35–56.

Goodwin, R., & Giles, S. (2003). Social support provision and cultural values in Indonesia and Britain. *Journal of Cross-Cultural Psychology, 34*, 240–245.

Gorawara-Bhat, R., Hafskjold, L., Gulbrandsen, P., & Eide, H. (2017). Exploring physicians' verbal and nonverbal responses to cues/concerns: Learning from incongruent communication. *Patient Education and Counseling, 100*(11), 1979–1989. doi:10.1016/j.pec.2017.06.027

Gordon, C. M., Carey, M. E., & Carey, K. B. (1997). Effects of a drinking event on behavioral skills and condom attitudes in men: Implications for HIV risk from a controlled experiment. *Health Psychology, 16*, 490–495.

Gordon, D. F., & Cerami, T. (2000). Cancers common in men. In R. M. Eisler & M. Hersen (Eds.), *Handbook of gender, culture, and health* (pp. 179–195). Mahwah, NJ: Erlbaum.

Gortmaker, S. L. (1985). Demography of chronic childhood diseases. In N. Hobbs & J. M. Perrin (Eds.), *Issues in the care of children with chronic illness: A sourcebook on problems, services, and policies* (pp. 135–154). San Francisco, CA: Jossey-Bass.

Gotay, C. C., Muraoka, M. Y., & Holup, J. (2001). Cultural aspects of cancer prevention and control. In S. S. Kazarian & D. R. Evans (Eds.), *Handbook of cultural health psychology* (pp. 163–193). San Diego, CA: Academic Press.

Gottdiener, J. S., Krantz, D. S., Howell, R. H., Hecht, G. M., Klein, J., Falconer, J. J., & Rozanski, A. (1994). Induction of silent myocardial ischemia with mental stress testing: Relation to the triggers of ischemia during daily life activities and to ischemic functional severity. *Journal of the American College of Cardiology, 24*, 1645–1651.

Gottesman, D., & Lewis, M. (1982). Differences in crisis reactions among cancer and surgery patients. *Journal of Consulting and Clinical Psychology, 50*, 381–388.

Gottfredson, D. C., & Koper, C. S. (1996). Race and sex differences in the prediction of drug use. *Journal of Consulting and Clinical Psychology, 64*, 305–313.

Gottfried, A. W., Gottfried, A. E., Bathurst, K., Guerin, D. W., & Parramore, M. M. (2003). Socioeconomic status in children's development and family environment: Infancy through adolescence. In M. H. Bornstein & R. H. Bradley (Eds.), *Socioeconomic status, parenting and child development. Monographs in parenting series* (pp. 189–207). Mahwah, NJ: Erlbaum.

Gottlieb, B. (2016). Coping. In Y. Benyamini, M. Johnston, & E. C. Karademas (Eds.), *Assessment in health psychology* (pp. 118–130). Boston, MA: Hogrefe.

Gourdine, M. A. (2011). *Reclaiming our health: A guide to African American wellness*. New Haven, CT: Yale University Press.

Graef, J. E., Rief, W., Nestoriuc, Y., & Weise, C. (2017). The more vivid the imagination the better: The role of the vividness of imagination in vasoconstriction training and vasodilatation training. *Applied Psychophysiology and Biofeedback, 42*(4), 283–298. doi:10.1007/s10484-017-9373-1

Gram, I., Lukanova, A., Brill, I., Braaten, T., Lund, E., Lundin, E., & . . . . Kaaks, R. (2012). Cigarette smoking and risk of histological subtypes of epithelial ovarian cancer in the EPIC cohort study. *International Journal of Cancer. Journal International Du Cancer, 130*(9), 2204–2210. doi:10.1002/ijc.26235

Grant, B. F., Harford, T. C., Chou, P., Pickering, R., Dawson, D. A., Stinson, F. S., & Noble, J. (1991). Prevalence of *DSM-III-R* alcohol abuse and dependence, United States, 1988. *Alcohol, Health, and Research World, 15*, 91–96.

Grant, B. F., Hartford, T. C., Dawson, D. A., Chou, P., Dufor, M., & Pickering, R. (1994). Prevalence of *DSM-IV* alcohol abuse and dependence, United States, 1992. *Alcohol, Health, and Research World, 18*, 243–248.

Grant, R. L., & Hood, R. (2017). Complex systems, explanation and policy: Implications of the crisis of replication for public health research. *Critical Public Health, 27*(5), 525–532. doi:10.1080/09581596.2017.1282603

Graugaard, P. K., & Finset, A. (2000). Trait anxiety and reactions to patient-centered and doctor-centered styles of communication: An experimental study. *Psychosomatic Medicine, 62*, 33–39.

Graustella, A. J., & MacLeod, C. (2012). A critical review of the influence of oxytocin nasal spray on social cognition in humans: Evidence and future directions. *Hormones & Behavior, 61*(3), 410–418. doi:10.1016/j.yhbeh.2012.01.002

Green, C. R., Baker, T. A., Sato, Y., Washington, T. L., & Smith, E. M. (2003). Race and chronic pain: A comparative study of young Black and White Americans presenting for management. *Journal of Pain, 4*, 176–183.

Green, L. W., Kreuter, M. W., Partridge, K. B., & Deeds, S. G. (1980). *Health education planning: A diagnostic approach*. Mountain View, CA: Mayfield.

Greenberg, J. A., & Pollack, B. (1981). Motivating students to not smoke. *Journal of Drug Education, 11*, 341–359.

Greenberg, M. A., & Stone, A. A. (1992). Emotional disclosure about trauma and its relation to health: Effects of previous disclosure and trauma severity. *Journal of Personality and Social Psychology, 63*, 75–84.

Greendale, G. A., Barrett-Conner, E., Edelstein, S., Ingles, S., & Halle, R. (1995). Lifetime leisure exercise and osteoporosis: The Rancho Bernardo study. *American Journal of Epidemiology, 141*, 951–959.

Greenhough, B. (2011). Citizenship, care and companionship: Approaching geographies of health and bioscience. *Progress in Human Geography, 35*(2), 153–171. doi:10.1177/0309132510376258

Greenland, K., & Taulke-Johnson, R. (2017). Gay men's identity work and the social construction of discrimination. *Psychology & Sexuality, 8*(1–2), 81–95. doi:10.1080/19419899.2017.1311934

Greenspan, J. D., Craft, R. M., LeResche, L., Arendt-Nielsen, L., Berkley, K. J., Fillingim, R. B., . . . Traub, R. J. (2007). Studying sex and gender differences in pain and analgesia: A consensus report. *Pain, 132*, S26–S45.

Greenwald, P., Clifford, C., Pilch, S., Heimendinger, J., & Kelloff, G. (1995). New directions in dietary studies in cancer: The National Cancer Institute. In J. B. Longnecker (Ed.), *Nutrition and biotechnology in heart disease and cancer* (pp. 229–239). New York, NY: Plenum Press.

Greer, S., Morris, T., & Pettingale, K. W. (1979). Psychological responses to breast cancer: Effect on outcome. *The Lancet*, 785–787.

Greeson, J., Hurwitz, B., Llabre, M., Schneiderman, N., Penedo, F., & Klimas, N. (2008, August 5). Psychological distress, killer lymphocytes and disease severity in HIV/AIDS. *Brain, Behavior, and Immunity, 22*(6), 901–911.

Greger, M. (2015). *How not to die: Discover the foods scientifically proven to prevent and reverse disease.* New York, NY: Flatiron Books.

Griffin, K., Rabkin, J. G., Remien, R. H., & Williams, J. B. (1998). Disease severity, physical limitations and depression in HIV-infected men. *Journal of Psychosomatic Research, 44*, 219–227.

Griffith, D. M., Mason, M. A., Rodela, M., Matthews, D. D., Tran, A., Royster, M., . . . Eng, E. (2007). A structural approach to examining prostate cancer risk for rural southern African American men. *Journal of Health Care for the Poor and Underserved, 18*(4 Suppl), 73–101.

Griffiths, S., Murray, S. B., Bentley, C., Gratwick-Sarll, K., Harrison, C., & Mond, J. M. (2017). Sex differences in quality of life impairment associated with body dissatisfaction in adolescents. *Journal of Adolescent Health, 61*(1), 77–82. doi:10.1016/j.jadohealth.2017.01.016

Griffiths, W. (1972). Health education definitions, problems, and philosophies. *Health Education Monographs, 31*, 12–14.

Griggs, R. A. (2014). Topical coverage in introductory textbooks from the 1980s through the 2000s. *Teaching of Psychology, 41*(1), 5–10.

Grinstein-Cohen, O., Katz, A., & Sarid, O. (2016). Religiosity: Its impact on coping styles among women undergoing fertility treatment. *Journal of Religion and Health, 56*(3), 1032–1041. doi:10.1007/s10943-016-0344-2

Griscti, O., Aston, M., Warner, G., Martin-Misener, R., & McLeod, D. (2017). Power and resistance within the hospital's hierarchical system: The experiences of chronically ill patients. *Journal of Clinical Nursing, 26*(1–2), 238–247. doi:10.1111/jocn.13382

Gronbaek, M., Deis, A., Sorensen, T. I. A., Becker, U., Schnohr, P., & Jensen, G. (1995). Mortality associated with moderate intake of wine, beer, or spirits. *British Medical Journal, 310*, 1165–1169.

Grossman, K., Grossman, K. E., Spangler, S., Suess, G., & Unzner, L. (1985). Maternal sensitivity and newborn orientation responses as related to quality of attachment in northern Germany. In I. Bretherton & E. Waters (Eds.), *Growing points of attachment theory: Monographs of the Society for Research for Child Development, 50*(1–2, Serial No. 209).

Grube, J. W., & Wallack, L. (1994). Television beer advertising and drinking knowledge, beliefs, and intentions among schoolchildren. *American Journal of Public Health, 84*, 254–259.

Grube, J. W., McGree, S. T., & Morgan, M. (1986). Beliefs related to cigarette smoking among Irish college students. *International Journal of the Addictions, 21*, 701–706.

Gruenewald, T. L., Taylor, S. E., Klein, L. C., & Seeman, T. E. (1999). Gender disparities in acute stress research [Abstract]. Proceedings of the Society of Behavioral Medicine's 20th Annual Meeting. *Annals of Behavioral Medicine, 21*, S141.

Gruenwald, T. (2019). Stress processes. In T. A. Revenson & R. A. R. Gurung (Eds.), *Handbook of health psychology* (3e). New York, NY: Routledge.

Grunberg, N. E., & Klein, L. C. (1998). Biological obstacles to adoption and maintenance of health-promoting behaviors. In S. A. Shumaker, E. Schron, J. Ockene, & W. L. McBee (Eds.), *The handbook of health behavior changes* (2nd ed., pp. 269–282). New York, NY: Springer.

Grunberg, N. E., Berger, S. S., & Starosciak, A. K. (2012). Tobacco use: Psychology, neurobiology, and clinical implications. In A. Baum, T. A. Revenson, & J. Singer (Eds.), *Handbook of health psychology* (2e, pp. 311–332). New York, NY: Taylor & Francis.

Grunberg, N. E., Brown, K. J., & Klein, L. C. (1997). Tobacco smoking. In A. Baum, S. Newman, J. Weinman, R. West, & C. McManus (Eds.), *Cambridge handbook of psychology, health, and medicine* (pp. 606–611). New York, NY: Cambridge University Press.

Grunberg, N. E., Faraday, M. M., & Rahman, M. A. (2002). The psychobiology of nicotine self-administration. In A Baum, T. A. Revenson, & J. E. Singer (Eds.), *Handbook of health psychology* (1e, pp. 249–262). Mahwah, NJ: Erlbaum.

Guenole, N., Chernyshenko, S., Stark, S., McGregor, K., & Ganesh, S. (2008). Measuring stress reaction style: A construct validity investigation. *Personality and Individual Differences, 44*, 250–262.

Guérin, E., Goldfield, G., & Prud'homme, D. (2017). Trajectories of mood and stress and relationships with protective factors during the transition to menopause: Results using latent class growth modeling in a canadian cohort. *Archives of Women's Mental Health, 20*(6), 733–745. doi:10.1007/s00737-017-0755-4

Gump, B. B., & Matthews, K. A. (2000). Are vacations good for your health? The 9-year mortality experience after the multiple risk factor intervention trial. *Psychosomatic Medicine, 62*, 608–612.

Guo, Q., Johnson, C. A., Unger, J. B., Lee, L., Xie, B., Chou, C., . . . Pentz, M. (2007). Utility of the theory of reasoned action and theory of planned behavior for predicting Chinese adolescent smoking. *Addictive Behaviors, 32*, 1066–1081.

Gupta, M. P., Gupta, M., Jakovcic, S., & Zak, R. (1996). Catecholamines and cardiac growth. *Molecular and Cellular Biochemistry, 163/164*, 203–213.

Gurung, R. A. R. (2012). A multicultural approach to health psychology. *American Journal of Lifestyle Medicine, 7*(1), 4–12. doi:10.1177/1559827612444548

Gurung, R. A. R. (Ed.). (2014). *Multicultural approaches to health and wellness in America: Major issues and cultural groups.* Westport, CT: Praeger.

Gurung, R. A. R., & Abhold, J. (2004). A report on the "You Know You Want To" campaign: Changing social norms to reduce college smoking. Unpublished technical report, University of Wisconsin-Oshkosh, Oshkosh, WI.

Gurung, R. A. R., & Bruns, D. (2013). Health psychology and policy: When politics infiltrates the science. In D. S. Dunn, R. A. R., Gurung, K. Z. Naufel, & J. H. Wilson (Eds.), *Controversy in the psychology classroom: Using hot topics to foster critical thinking* (pp. 255–242). Washington, DC: American Psychological Association.

Gurung, R. A. R., & Mehta, V. (2001). Relating ethnic identity, acculturation, and attitudes toward treating minority clients. *Cultural Diversity and Ethnic Minority Psychology, 7*, 139–151.

Gurung, R. A. R., & Prieto, L. (Eds.). (2009). *Getting culture: Incorporating diversity across the curriculum*. Sterling, VA: Stylus.

Gurung, R. A. R., Dunkel-Schetter, C., Collins, N., Rini, C., & Hobel, C. (2005). Psychosocial predictors of perceived prenatal stress. *Journal of Social and Clinical Psychology, 24*, 497–519.

Gurung, R. A. R., Hackathorn, J., Enns, C., Frantz, S., Cacioppo, J. T., Loop, T., & Freeman, J. E. (2016). Strengthening introductory psychology: A new model for teaching the introductory course. *American Psychologist, 71*(2), 112–124.

Gurung, R. A. R., & Roethel, A. (2009). Stress culture. In S. Eshun, & R. A. R. Gurung (Eds.), *Sociocultural influences on mental health*. Malden, MA: Blackwell.

Gurung, R. A. R., Taylor, S. E., & Seeman, T. (2003). Accounting for changes in social support among married older adults: Insights from the MacArthur Studies of Successful Aging. *Psychology and Aging, 18*, 487–496.

Gurung, R. A. R., Taylor, S. E., Kemeny, M., & Myers, H. (2004). "HIV is not my biggest problem": The impact of HIV and chronic burden on depression in women at risk for AIDS. *Journal of Social and Clinical Psychology, 23*, 490–511.

Gurung, R. A. R., Von Dras, D. (2007). Social support and aging. In L. O. Randal (Ed.), *Aging and the elderly: Psychology, sociology, and health*. New York, NY: Nova Science.

Guthrie, N., & Carroll, K. K. (1999). Specific versus non-specific effects of dietary fat on carcinogenesis. *Progress in Lipid Research, 38*, 261–271.

Guthrie, R. (2003). *Even the rat was white*. New York, NY: Harper and Row.

Guyton, A. C. (1977). *Basic human physiology: Normal function and mechanisms of disease*. Philadelphia, PA: Saunders.

Hadjistavropoulos, T. (2012). Self-management of pain in older persons: Helping people help themselves. *Pain Medicine, 13*, S67–S71. doi:10.1111/j.1526-4637.2011.01272.x

Hage, F. G., Adegunsoye, A., Mundkur, M., & Nanda, N. C. (2012). The role of echocardiography in the evaluation and management of aortic stenosis in the older adult. *International Journal of Cardiology, 155*(1), 39–48. doi:10.1016/j.ijcard.2011.01.080

Hagger M. S., Chatzisarantis N. L., Alberts H. A., Anggono C. O., Batailler C. B., Birt A. R., . . . Zwienenberg, M. (2016). A multilab preregistered replication of the ego-depletion effect. *Perspectives on Psychological Science, 11*, 546–573. doi:10.1177/1745691616652873

Hagger, M. S., Koch, S., Chatzisarantis, N. L. D., & Orbell, S. (2017). The common sense model of self-regulation: Meta-analysis and test of a process model. *Psychological Bulletin, 143*(11), 1117–1154. doi:10.1037/bul0000118

Hagger, M. S., Lonsdale, A. J., Hein, V., Koka, A., Lintunen, T., Pasi, H., & . . . Chatzisarantis, N. D. (2012). Predicting alcohol consumption and binge drinking in company employees: An application of planned behaviour and self-determination theories. *British Journal of Health Psychology, 17*(2), 379–407. doi:10.1111/j.2044-8287.2011.02043.x

Hagger, M. S., Wood, C., Stiff, C., & Chatzisarantis, N. L. D. (2010). Ego depletion and the strength model of self-control: A meta-analysis. *Psychological Bulletin, 136*(4), 495–525. doi:10.1037/a0019486

Hagger-Johnson, G. E., & Whiteman, M. C. (2007). Conscientiousness facets and health behaviors: A latent variable modeling approach. *Personality and Individual Differences, 43*, 1235–1245.

Haghighi, M., Taghdisi, M. H., Nadrian, H., Moghaddam, H. R., Mahmoodi, H., & Alimohammadi, I. (2017). Safety culture promotion intervention program (SCPIP) in an oil refinery factory: An integrated application of Geller and health belief models. *Safety Science, 93*, 76–85. doi:10.1016/j.ssci.2016.11.019

Haines, M. P. (1996). *A social norms approach to preventing binge drinking at colleges and universities*. Newton, MA: Higher Education Center for Alcohol and Drug Prevention.

Hajdu, Z., & Hohmann, J. (2012) An ethnopharmacological survey of the traditional medicine utilized in the community of Porvenir, Bajo Paraguá Indian Reservation. *Bolivia Journal of Ethnopharmacology, 139*(3), 838–857. doi:10.1016/j.jep.2011.12.029

Hak, A. E., Ma, J., Powell, C. B., Campos, H., Gaziano, J. M., Willet, W. C., & Stampfer, M. J. (2004). Prospective study of plasma carotenoids and tocopherols in relation to risk of ischemic stroke. *Stroke, 35*, 1584–1588.

Hak, E., Wei, F., Nordin, J., Mullooly, J., Poblete, S., & Nichol, K. L. (2004). Development and validation of a clinical prediction rule for hospitalization due to pneumonia or influenza or death during influenza epidemics among community-dwelling elderly persons. *Journal of Infectious Diseases, 189*, 450–459.

Hales, D. (2015). *An invitation to health*, 16e. Belmont, CA: Cengage.

Haley, W. E., Allen, R. S., Reynolds, S., Chen, H., Burton, A., & Gallagher-Thompson, D. (2002). Family issues in end-of-life decision making and end-of-life care. *American Behavioral Scientist, 46*, 284–298.

Haley, W. E., Turner, J. A., & Romano, J. M. (1985). Depression in chronic pain patients: Relation to pain, activity, and sex differences. *Pain, 23*, 337–343.

Hall, C., Hall, J., Pfriemer, J., Wimberley, P., & Jones, C. (2007). Effects of a culturally sensitive education program on the breast cancer knowledge and beliefs of Hispanic women. *Oncology Nursing Forum, 34*(6), 1195–1202.

Hall, H. I., Song R., Rhodes P., Prejean J., An, Q., Lee, L. M., . . . Janssen, R. S. (2008). Estimation of HIV incidence in the United States. *Journal of the American Medical Association, 300*(5), 520–529.

Hall, J. A., Epstein, A. M., DeCiantis, M. L., & McNeil, B. J. (1993). Physicians' liking for their patients: More evidence for the role of affect in medical care. *Health Psychology, 12*, 140–146.

Hall, J. D., Ashley, D. M., Bramlett, R. K., Dielmann, K. B., Murphy, J. J. (2005). ADHD assessment: A comparison of negative versus positive symptom formats. *Journal of Applied School Psychology, 21*, 163–173.

Hall, K., Moreau, C., & Trussell, J. (2012). Determinants of and disparities in reproductive health service use among adolescent and young adult women in the United States, 2002–2008. *American Journal of Public Health, 102*(2), 359–367. doi:10.2105/AJPH.2011.300380

Hamaideh, S. H. (2012). Occupational stress, social support, and quality of life among Jordanian mental health nurses. *Issues in Mental Health Nursing, 33*(1), 15–23. doi:10.3109/01612840.2011.605211

Hamburg, N. M., Keyes, M. J., Larson, M. G., Vasan, R. S., Schnabel, R., Pryde, M. M., . . . Benjamin, E. J. (2008). Cross-sectional relations of digital vascular function to cardiovascular risk factors in the Framingham Heart Study. *Circulation, 117*(19), 2467–2474.

Hammen, C. (2003). Interpersonal stress and depression in women. *Journal of Affective Disorders, 74*, 49–57.

Hammer, S. M., Eron, J. J. Jr., Reiss, P., Schooley, R. T., Thompson, M. A., Walmsley, S., . . . Volberding, P. A. (2008). Antiretroviral treatment of adult HIV infection: 2008 recommendations of the International AIDS Society-USA panel. *Journal of the American Medical Association, 300*(5), 555–570.

Hamner, J., & Wilder, B. (2008). Knowledge and risk of cardiovascular disease in rural Alabama women. *Journal of the American Academy of Nurse Practitioners, 20*(6), 333–338.

Hampson, S. E., Goldberg, L. R., Vogt, T. M., & Dubanoski, J. P. (2007). Mechanisms by which childhood personality traits influence adult health status: Educational attainment and healthy behaviors. *Health Psychology, 26*, 121–125.

Han, G. S. (2011). *The rise of Western medicine and revival of traditional medicine in Korea: A brief history*. Honululu, HI: University of Hawai'i Press.

Hanahan, D., & Weinberg, R. A. (2000). The hallmarks of cancer. *Cell, 100*, 57–70.

Hance, M., Carney, R. M., Freedland, K. E., & Skala, J. (1996). Depression in patients with coronary heart disease: A 12-month follow-up. *General Hospital Psychiatry, 18*, 61–65.

Hancock, L. (2000). *Tobacco use reduction guide for colleges and universities: Spring, 2000*. Richmond, VA: Office of Health Promotion, Virginia Commonwealth University.

Handschin, C., & Spiegelman, B. M. (2008). The role of exercise and PGC1α in inflammation and chronic disease. *Nature, 454*(7203), 463–469. doi:10.1038/nature07206

Hanoch, Y. (2007). Terminally ill patients and volunteer support: Is it the right intervention? *Health Psychology, 26*, 537–538.

Hansen, G. (2011). Eating disorders and self-harm in Japanese culture and cultural expressions. *Journal of the German Institute for Japanese Studies, Tokyo, 23*(1), 49–69. doi:10.1515/cj.2011.004

Hansen, W. B. (1993). School-based alcohol prevention programs. *Alcohol Health and Research World, 17*, 54–60.

Hanson, M. D., & Chen, E. (2007). Socioeconomic status and health behaviors in adolescence: A review of the literature. *Journal of Behavioral Medicine, 30*, 263–285.

Hanson, R. W., & Gerber, K. E. (1990). *Coping with chronic pain: A guide to patient self-management*. New York, NY: Guilford Press.

Harburg, E., Gleiberman, L., Russell, M., & Cooper, M. L. (1991). Anger-coping styles and blood pressure in Black and White males: Buffalo, New York. *Psychosomatic Medicine, 53*, 153–164.

Harding, C., Pompei, F., & Wilson, R. (2012). Peak and decline in cancer incidence, mortality, and prevalence at old ages. *Cancer (0008543X), 118*(5), 1371–1386. doi:10.1002/cncr.26376

Harding, R., Liu, L., Catalan, J., & Sherr, L. (2011). What is the evidence for effectiveness of interventions to enhance coping among people living with HIV disease? A systematic review. *Psychology, Health & Medicine, 16*(5), 564–587. doi:10.1080/13548506.2011.580352

Hardré, P. L., Garcia, F., Apamo, P., Mutheu, L., & Ndege, M. (2012). Information, affect and action: Motivating reduction of risk behaviors for HIV/AIDS in Kenya and Tanzania. *Sex Education, 12*(1), 1–24. doi:10.1080/14681811.2011.601143

Harinath, K., Malhotra, A. S., Pal, K., Prasad, R., Kumar, R., Kain, T. C., . . . Sawhney, R. C. (2004). Effects of Hatha Yoga and Omkar meditation on cardiorespiratory performance, psychologic profile, and melatonin secretion. *Journal of Alternative and Complementary Medicine, 10*, 261–269.

Harkness, K. L., Bruce, A. E., Lumley, M. N. (2006). The role of childhood abuse and neglect in the sensitization to stressful life events in adolescent depression. *Journal of Abnormal Psychology, 115*, 730–741.

Harmon, M. P., Castro, F. G., & Coe, K. (1996). Acculturation and cervical cancer: Knowledge, beliefs, and behaviors of Hispanic women. *Women and Health, 24*, 37–57.

Harris, J. B., Schwartz, S. M., & Thompson, B. (2008). Characteristics associated with self-identification as a regular smoker and desire to quit among college students who smoke cigarettes. *Nicotine and Tobacco Research, 10*, 69–76.

Harris, K. A. (2017). The spirituality of the eastern Cherokee and Ani-Yun-Wiya shamanistic medicine. In D. Von Dras (Ed.), *Better health through spiritual practices* (pp. 287–307). Santa Barbara, CA: Praeger.

Harris, K. M, Edlund, M. J., & Larson, S. (2005). Racial and ethnic differences in the mental health problems and use of mental health care, *Medical Care, 43*, 775–784.

Harrison, K. (2000). Television viewing, fat stereotyping, body shape standards, and eating disorder symptomatology in grade school children. *Communication Research, 27*, 617–640.

Harrison, K., & Bond, B. J. (2007). Gaming magazines and the drive for muscularity in preadolescent boys: A longitudinal examination. *Body Image, 4*, 269–277.

Harrison, K., Taylor, L. D., & Marske, A. L. (2006). Women's and men's eating behavior following exposure to ideal-body images and text. *Communication Research, 33*, 507–529.

Harte, J. L., Eifert, G. H., & Smith, R. (1995). The effects of running and meditation on beta-endorphin, corticotrophin-releasing hormone and cortisol in plasma, and on mood. *Biological Psychology, 40*, 251–265.

Harvey, A. G., & Tang, N. Y. (2012). (Mis)perception of sleep in insomnia: A puzzle and a resolution. *Psychological Bulletin, 138*(1), 77–101. doi:10.1037/a0025730

Harvey, I. S. (2008). Assessing self-management and spirituality practices among older women. *American Journal of Health Behavior, 32*, 157–168.

Harvey, M. R., & Tummala-Narra, P. (2007). Sources and expression of resilience in trauma survivors: Ecological theory, multicultural perspectives. *Journal of Aggression, Maltreatment and Trauma, 14*, 1–7.

Haskell, W. L., Lee, I. M., Pate, R. R., Powell, K. E., Blair, S. N., Franklin, B. A., . . . Bauman, A. (2007). Physical activity and public health: Updated recommendation for adults from the American College of Sports Medicine and the American Heart Association. *Medical Science Sports Exercise, 39*, 1423–1434.

Hassan, M. M., Spitz, M. R., Thomas, M. B., El-Deeb, A. S., Glover, K. Y., Nguyen, N. T., . . . Li, D. (2008). Effect of different types of smoking and synergism with hepatitis C virus on risk of hepatocellular carcinoma in American men and women: case-control study. *International Journal of Cancer, 123*(8), 1883–1891.

Hastie, C., Haw, S., & Pell, J. (2008). Impact of smoking cessation and lifetime exposure on C-reactive protein. *Nicotine and Tobacco Research, 10*(4), 637–642.

Haug, M. R., & Ory, M. G. (1987). Issues in elderly patient/provider interactions. *Research on Aging, 9*, 3–44.

Haugen, T., Säfvenbom, R., & Ommundsen, Y. (2011). Physical activity and global self-worth: The role of physical self-esteem indices and gender. *Mental Health and Physical Activity, 4*(2), 49–56. doi:10.1016/j.mhpa.2011.07.001

Haven, J., Burns, A., Britten, P., & Davis, C. (2006). Developing the consumer interface for the MyPyramid food guidance system. *Journal of Nutrition and Educational Behavior, 38*, S124–S135.

Hawkes, C. (2007). Regulating food marketing to young people worldwide: Trends and policy drivers. *American Journal of Public Health, 97*, 1962–1973.
Hawkins, C., & Miaskowski, C. (1996). Testicular cancer: A review. *Oncology Nursing Forum, 23*, 1203–1213.
Hayden, M., Pignone, M., Phillips, C., & Mulrow, C. (2002). Aspirin for the primary prevention of cardiovascular events: A summary of the evidence for the U.S. Preventive Services Task Force. *Annals of Internal Medicine, 136*, 161–173.
Haynes, R. Ackloo, E. Sahota, N., McDonald, H. P., & Yao, X. (2008). Interventions for enhancing medication adherence. *Cochrane Database of Systematic Reviews, 16*(2), CD000011. doi:10.1002/14651858.CD000011.pub3
Haynes, R. B., McKibbon, K. A., & Kanani, R. (1996). Systematic review of randomized controlled trials of the effects of patient adherence and outcomes of interventions to assist patients to follow prescriptions for medications. *Cochrane Library, 2*, 1–26.
Hays, R. B., Turner, H., & Coates, T. J. (1992). Social support, AIDS-related symptoms, and depression among gay men. *Journal of Consulting and Clinical Psychology, 60*, 463–469.
Hazan, C., & Shaver, P. (1987). Romantic love conceptualized as an attachment process. *Journal of Personality and Social Psychology, 52*, 511–524.
Hazuda, H. P., Haffner, S. M., Stern, M. P., & Eifler, C. W. (1988). Effects of acculturation and socioeconomic status on obesity and diabetes in Mexican Americans. *American Journal of Epidemiology, 128*, 1289–1301.
He, J., Vupputuri, S., Allen, K., Prerost, M. R., Hughes, J., & Whelton, P. K. (1999). Passive smoking and the risk of coronary heart disease—A meta-analysis of epidemiologic studies. *New England Journal of Medicine, 340*, 920–926.
He, K., Xu, Y., & Van Horn, L. (2007). The puzzle of dietary fat intake and risk of ischemic stroke: A brief review of epidemiologic data. *Journal of the American Dietetic Association, 107*(2), 287–295.
He, W., Sengupta, M., Velkoff, V. A., & DeBarros, K. A. (2005). 65+ in the United States: 2005. U.S. Department of Health and Human Services, Washington, DC. http://www.census.gov/prod/2006pubs/p23-209.pdf
Healthy People. (2010). Healthy people. Retrieved from https://healthypeople.gov/2010/.
HealthyPeople.gov. n.d. Healthy People 2020 topics and objectives: Objectives A–Z. Retrieved from https://www.healthypeople.gov/2020/topics-objectives
Healy, K. M. (2000). Cultural perspectives. Concepts of alternative healing systems: An overview of Mexican curanderismo. *Perspective on Physician Assistant Education, 11*, 51–55.
Heaney, C. A., & Viswanath, K. (2015). Introduction to models of interpersonal influences on health behavior. In K. Glanz, B. K. Rimer, & K. Viswanath (Eds.), *Health behavior: Theory, research, and practice* (5e, pp. 151–181). San Fransisco, CA: Jossey-Bass.
Heaven, R., & Booth, T. (2003). *Vodou shaman: The Haitian way of healing and power*. New York, NY: Destiny Press.
Hebert, J. R., Hurley, T. G., Olendzki, B. C., Teas, J., Ma, Y., & Hampl, J. S. (1998). Nutritional and socioeconomic factors in relation to prostate cancer mortality: A cross-national study. *Journal of the National Cancer Institute, 90*, 1637–1647.
Hecht, E. E., Robins, D. L., Gautam, P., & King, T. Z. (2017). Intranasal oxytocin reduces social perception in women: Neural activation and individual variation. *NeuroImage, 147*, 314–329. doi:10.1016/j.neuroimage.2016.12.046
Heckman, T. J., Kockman, A., Sikkema, K. J., Kalichman, S. C., Masten, J., & Goodkin, K. (2000). Late middle-aged and older men living with HIV/AIDS: Race differences in coping, social support, and psychological distress. *Journal of the National Medical Association, 92*, 436–444.
Heffner, K. L., Waring, M. E., Roberts, M. B., Eaton, C. B., & Gramling, R. (2011). Social isolation, C-reactive protein, and coronary heart disease mortality among community-dwelling adults. *Social Science & Medicine, 72*(9), 1482–1488. doi:10.1016/j.socscimed.2011.03.016
Heinberg, L. J., & Thompson, J. K. (1995). Body image and televised images of thinness and attractiveness: A controlled laboratory investigation. *Journal of Social and Clinical Psychology, 14*, 325–338.
Heiss, G., Wallace, R., Anderson, G. L., Aragaki, A., Beresford, S. A., Brzyski, R., . . . Stefanick, M. L. (2008). Health risks and benefits 3 years after stopping randomized treatment with estrogen and progestin. *Journal of the American Medical Association, 299*, 1036–1045.
Heitkamp, H. C., Schulz, H., Rocker, K., & Dickhuth, H. H. (1998). Endurance training in females: Changes in beta-endorphin and ACTH. *International Journal of Sports Medicine, 19*, 260–264.
Held, C., Iqbal, R., Lear, S. A., Rosengren, A., Islam, S., Mathew, J., & Yusuf, S. (2012). Physical activity levels, ownership of goods promoting sedentary behaviour and risk of myocardial infarction: Results of the INTERHEART study. *European Heart Journal, 33*, 452–466.
Helgeson, V. S. (2012). Gender and health: A social psychological perspective. In A. Baum, T. A. Revenson, & J. Singer (Eds.), *Handbook of health psychology* (2e, pp. 519–538). New York, NY: Taylor & Francis.
Helgeson, V. S., & Cohen, S. (1996). Social support and adjustment to cancer: Reconciling descriptive, correlational, and intervention research. *Health Psychology, 15*, 135–148.
Helgeson, V. S., & Fritz, H. L. (2000). The implications of unmitigated agency and unmitigated communion for domains of problem behavior. *Journal of Personality, 68*, 1031–1057.
Helgeson, V. S., Cohen, S., Schultz, R., & Yasko, J. (1999). Education and peer discussion group interventions and adjustment to breast cancer. *Archives of General Psychiatry, 56*, 340–347.
Helgeson, V. S., Cohen, S., Schulz, R., & Yasko, J. (2000). Group support interventions for women with breast cancer: Who benefits from what? *Health Psychology, 19*, 107–114.
Helgeson, V. S., Snyder, P., & Steltman, H. (2004). Psychological and physical adjustment to breast cancer over 4 years: Identifying distinct trajectories of change. *Health Psychology, 23*, 3–15.
Helmstetter, F. J., & Bellgowan, P. S. (1994). Hypoalgesia in response to sensitization during acute noise stress. *Behavioral Neuroscience, 108*, 177–185.
Helsley, J. D. (2008). Post-traumatic stress disorder. In J. R. Vanin & J. D. Helsley (Eds.), *Anxiety disorders: A pocket guide for primary care. Current clinical practice* (pp. 175–181). Totowa, NJ: Humana Press.
Helweg, W. A., & Helweg, M. U. (1990). *An immigrant success story: East Indians in America*. London, UK: Hurst.
Hemenover, S. H., & Dienstbier, R. A. (1996). Prediction of stress appraisals from mastery, extraversion, neuroticism, and general appraisal tendencies. *Motivation and Emotion, 20*, 299–317.
Henderson, B. N., & Baum, A. (2002). Neoplasms. In T. J. Boll & S. B. Johnson (Eds.), *Handbook of clinical health psychology* (pp. 37–64). Washington, DC: American Psychological Association.
Henderson, G., & Springer-Littles, D. (1996). *A practitioner's guide to understanding indigenous and foreign cultures: An analysis of relationships between ethnicity, social class, and therapeutic intervention strategies*. Springfield, IL: Charles C Thomas.
Henderson-King, D., Henderson-King, E., & Hoffman, L. (2001). Media images and women's self evaluations: Social context and

importance of attractiveness as moderators. *Personality and Social Psychology Bulletin, 27*, 1407–1416.
Henriksen, L., Feighery, E. C., Schleicher, N. C., & Fortmann, S. P. (2008). Receptivity to alcohol marketing predicts initiation of alcohol use. *Journal of Adolescent Health, 42*, 28–35.
Herbert, T. B., & Cohen, S. (1993). Stress and immunity in humans: A meta-analytic review. *Psychosomatic Medicine, 55*, 364–379.
Herbst-Damm, K. L., & Kulik, J. A. (2005). Volunteer support, marital status, and the survival time of terminal ill patients. *Health Psychology, 24*(2), 225–229. doi:10.1037/0278-6133.24.2.225
Herman-Stahl, M., & Petersen, A. C. (1996). The protective role of coping and social resources for depressive symptoms among young adolescents. *Journal of Youth and Adolescence, 25*, 733–753.
Hernández-Martínez, C., Arija Val, V., Escribano Subías, J., & Canals Sans, J. (2012). A longitudinal study on the effects of maternal smoking and secondhand smoke exposure during pregnancy on neonatal neurobehavior. *Early Human Development, 88*(6), 403–408. doi:10.1016/j.earlhumdev.2011.10.004
Herring, D., Britten, P., Davis, C., & Tuepker, K. (2000). Serving sizes in the food guide pyramid and on the nutrition facts label: What's different and why? *Nutrition Insights*, 22. Retrieved from https://www.cnpp.usda.gov/sites/default/files/nutrition_insights_uploads/Insight22.pdf
Herts, K., Khaled, M., & Stanton, A. (2017). Correlates of self-efficacy for disease management in adolescent/young adult cancer survivors: A systematic review. *Health Psychology, 36*(3), 192–205. doi.10.1037/hea0000446
Hertz, R., McDonald, M., Unger, A., & Lustik, M. (2007). Racial and ethnic disparities in the prevalence and management of cardiovascular risk factors in the United States workforce. *Journal of Occupational and Environmental Medicine, 49*(10), 1165–1175.
Hetherington, M. M., & Rolls, B. J. (1996). Sensory-specific satiety: Theoretical frameworks and central characteristics. In E. D. Capaldi (Ed.), *Why we eat what we eat: The psychology of eating* (pp. 267–290). Washington, DC: American Psychological Association.
Hiatt, R. A., & Rimer, B. K. (1999). A new strategy for cancer control research. *Cancer Epidemiology, Biomarkers, and Prevention, 8*, 957–964.
Hiatt, R. A., Pasick, R. J., Pérez-Stable, E. J., McPhee, S. J., Engelstad, L., Lee, M., . . . Stewart, S. (1996). Pathways to early cancer detection in the multiethnic population of San Francisco Bay area. *Health Education Quarterly, 23*, S10–S27.
Higginbotham, J. C., Trevino, F. M., & Ray, L. A. (1990). Utilization of curanderos by Mexican Americans: Prevalence and predictors. Findings from HHANES 1982–84. *American Journal of Public Health, 80*, 32–35.
Hightower, M. (1997). Effects of exercise participation on menstrual pain and symptoms. *Women Health, 26*, 15227.
Hilgard, E. R. (1978). Covert pain in hypnotic analgesia: Its reality as tested by the real-simulator design. *Journal of Abnormal Psychology, 87*, 655–663.
Hill, A. (1993). The use of pain coping strategies by patients with phantom limb pain. *Pain, 55*, 347–353.
Hill, E. J., Hawkins, A. J., Ferris, M., & Weitzman, M. (2001). Finding an extra day a week: The positive influence of perceived job flexibility on work and family life balance. *Family Relations, 50*, 513–524.
Hill, E. M., & Gick, M. L. (2011). The big five and cervical screening barriers: Evidence for the influence of conscientiousness, extraversion and openness. *Personality & Individual Differences, 50*(5), 662–667. doi:10.1016/j.paid.2010.12.013
Hill, P. C., & Pargament, K. I. (2003). Advances in the conceptualization and measurement of religion and spirituality: Implications for physical and mental health research. *American Psychologist, 58*, 64–74.
Hill, R. (1949). *Families under stress*. New York, NY: Harper & Row.
Hill, S. E., Bell, C., Bowie, J. V., Kelley, E., Furr-Holden, D., LaVeist, T. A., & Thorpe, R. J. Jr. (2017). Differences in obesity among men of diverse racial and ethnic background. *American Journal of Men's Health, 11*(4), 984–989. doi:10.1177/1557988315580348
Hilliard, M. E., Monaghan, M. M., Cogen, F. R., & Streisand, R. R. (2011). Parent stress and child behaviour among young children with type 1 diabetes. *Child: Care, Health & Development, 37*(2), 224–232. doi:10.1111/j.1365-2214.2010.01162.x
Hillman, C. H., Erickson, K. I., & Kramer, A. F. (2008). Be smart, exercise your heart: Exercise effects on brain and cognition. *Nature Reviews Neuroscience, 9*, 58–65.
Hilts, P. J. (1996). *Smoke screen: The truth behind the tobacco industry cover-up*. Reading, MA: Addison-Wesley
Hines, A. M., & Caetano, R. (1998). Alcohol and AIDS-related sexual behavior among Hispanics: Acculturation and gender differences. *AIDS Education and Prevention, 10*, 533–547.
Hines, A. M., Snowden, L. R., & Graves, K. L. (1998). Acculturation, alcohol consumption and AIDS-related risky sexual behavior among African American women. *Women and Health, 27*, 17–35.
Hobfoll, S. E. (1989). Conservation of resources. *American Psychologist, 44*, 513–524.
Hobfoll, S. E. (2011). Conservation of resource caravans and engaged settings. *Journal of Occupational and Organizational Psychology 84*(1), 116–122. doi:10.1111/j.2044-8325.2010.02016.x
Hochbaum, G. M. (1958). *Public participation in medical screening programs: A sociopsychological study* (PHS Publication No. 572). Washington, DC: Government Publishing Office.
Hodge, C. N., Jackson, L. A., & Sullivan, L. A. (1993) The freshman 15—facts and fantasies about weight gain in college women. *Psychology of Women Quarterly, 17*, 119–126.
Hoffman, B. M., Papas, R. K., Chatkoff, D. K., & Kerns, R. D. (2007). Meta-analysis of psychological interventions for chronic low back pain. *Health Psychology, 26*, 1–9.
Hoffman, H. G., Patterson, D. R., Carrougher, G. J., & Sharar, S. R. (2001). Effectiveness of virtual reality-based pain control with multiple treatments. *Clinical Journal of Pain, 17*, 229–235.
Hoffman, H. G., Patterson, D. R., Seibel, E., Soltani, M., Jewett-Leahy, L., & Sharar, S. R. (2008). Virtual reality pain control during burn wound debridement in the hydrotank. *Clinical Journal of Pain, 24*, 299–304.
Hoffman-Goetz, L., & Friedman, D. (2006). A systematic review of culturally sensitive cancer prevention resources for ethnic minorities. *Ethnicity and Disease, 16*(4), 971–977.
Hoffman-Goetz, L., Breen, N. L., & Meissner, H. (1998). The impact of social class on the use of cancer screening within three racial/ethnic groups in the United States. *Ethnicity and Disease, 8*, 43–51.
Hojsted, J. & Sjogren, P. (2007). Addiction to opioids in chronic pain patients: A literature review. *European Journal of Pain, 11*, 490–518.
Holahan, C. J., Moos, R. H., & Schaefer, J. A. (1996). Coping, stress resistance, and growth: Conceptualizing adaptive functioning. In M. Zeidner & N. S. Endler (Eds.), *Handbook of coping: Theory, research, applications* (pp. 24–43). Oxford, UK: John Wiley.
Holahan, C. J., Moos, R. H., Holahan, C. K., & Brennan, P. L. (1997). Psychosocial adjustment in patients reporting cardiac illness. *Psychology and Health, 12*, 345–359.
Holder-Perkins, V., & Wise, T. N. (2001). Somatization disorder. In K. A. Phillips (Ed.), *Somatoform and factitious disorders: Review*

of psychiatry, 1–26. Washington, DC: American Psychiatric Association.

Holland, J. C. (1989). Anxiety and cancer: The patient and the family. *Journal of Clinical Psychiatry*, *50*, 20–25.

Holman, E. A, Silver R. C., Poulin, M., Andersen, J., Gil-Rivas, V., & McIntosh, D. N. (2008). Terrorism, acute stress, and cardiovascular health: A 3-year national study following the September 11th attacks. *Archives of General Psychiatry*, *65*(1), 73–80. doi:10.1001/archgenpsychiatry.2007.6

Holm-Denoma, J. M., Joiner, T. E., Vohs, K. D., & Heatherton, T. F. (2008). The "freshman fifteen" (the "freshman five" actually): Predictors and possible explanations. *Health Psychology*, *27*, S3–S9.

Holmes, T. H., & Rahe, R. H. (1967). The Social Readjustment Rating Scale. *Journal of Psychosomatic Research*, *11*, 213–218.

Holt, C., Wang, M., Caplan, L., Schulz, E., Blake, V., & Southward, V. (2011). Role of religious involvement and spirituality in functioning among African Americans with cancer: Testing a mediational model. *Journal of Behavioral Medicine*, *34*(6), 437–448. doi:10.1007/s10865-010-9310-8

Holt-Lunstad, J., Smith, T., & Uchino, B. (2008). Can hostility interfere with the health benefits of giving and receiving social support? The impact of cynical hostility on cardiovascular reactivity during social support interactions among friends. *Annals of Behavioral Medicine: A Publication of the Society of Behavioral Medicine*, *35*(3), 319–330.

Holzapfel, C., Grallert, H., Baumert, J., Thorand, B., Döring, A., Wichmann, H., & . . . Mielck, A. (2011). First investigation of two obesity-related loci (TMEM18, FTO) concerning their association with educational level as well as income: The MONICA/KORA study. *Journal of Epidemiology and Community Health*, *65*(2), 174–176.

Hon, K. L. E., Leung, T. F., Ng, P. C., Lam, M. C. A., Kam, W. Y. C., Wong, K. Y., . . . Leung, P. C. (2007). Efficacy and tolerability of a Chinese herbal medicine concoction for treatment of a topic dermatitis: A randomized, double-blind, placebo-controlled study. *British Journal of Dermatology*, *157*, 357–363.

Hooker, S. A., Masters, K. S., & Park, C. L. (2018). A meaningful life is a healthy life: A conceptual model linking meaning and meaning salience to health. *Review of General Psychology*, *22*(1), 11–24. doi:10.1037/gpr0000115

Hooper, E. M., Comstock, L. M., Goodwin, J. M., & Goodwin, J. S. (1982). Patient characteristics that influence physician behavior. *Medical Care*, *20*, 630–638.

Hooper, L. M., Huffman, L. E., Higginbotham, J. C., Mugoya, G. C. T., Smith, A. K., & Dumas, T. N. (2017). Associations among depressive symptoms, wellness, patient involvement, provider cultural competency, and treatment nonadherence: A pilot study among community patients seen at a university medical center. *Community Mental Health Journal*, *54*(2), 138–148. doi:10.1007/s10597-017-0133-8

Hoover, S. M. (2002). The culturalist turn in scholarship on media and religion. *Journal of Media and Religion*, *1*, 25–36.

Horne, R., Chan, A., & Wileman, V. (2019). Adherence to treatment. In T. A. Revenson & R. A. R. Gurung (Eds.), *Handbook of health psychology* (3e). New York, NY: Routledge.

Horwitz, S. M., Morgenstern, H., DiPietro, L., & Morrison, C. L. (1998). Determinants of pediatric injuries. *American Journal of Diseases in Children*, *142*, 605–611.

Hosler, A. S., Nayak, S. G., & Radigan, A. M. (2011). Stressful events, smoking exposure and other maternal risk factors associated with gestational diabetes mellitus. *Paediatric & Perinatal Epidemiology*, *25*(6), 566–574. doi:10.1111/j.1365-3016.2011.01221.x

Hosseinzadegan, F., Radfar, M., Shafiee-Kandjani, A., & Sheikh, N. (2017). Efficacy of self-hypnosis in pain management in female patients with multiple sclerosis. *International Journal of Clinical and Experimental Hypnosis*, *65*(1), 86–97. doi:10.1080/00207144.2017.1246878

House, J. S., Umberson, D., & Landis, K. R. (1988). Structures and processes of social support. *Annual Review of Sociology*, *14*, 293–318.

Hovelius, B. (1998). Kvinnors underordning inom halso-och sjukvarden. [Women hold a subordinate position in the medical and health care system]. *Socialmedicinsk Tidskrift*, *75*, 1–2, 4–7.

Hovell, M. F., Mewborn, C. R., Randle, Y., & Fowler-Johnson, S. (1985). Risk of excess weight gain in university women: A three-year community controlled analysis. *Addictive Behavior*, *10*, 15–28.

Howard, G., Wagenknecht, L. E., Burke, G. L., Diez-Roux, A., Evans, G. W., McGovern, P., . . . Tell, G. S. (1998). Cigarette smoking and progression of atherosclerosis: The Antherosclerosis Risk in Communities (ARIC) study. *Journal of the American Medical Society*, *279*, 119–124.

Howard, J. H., Willie, L. (1984). *Oklahoma Seminoles: Medicine, magic, and religion*. Norman, OK: Oklahoma University Press.

Hoyt, M. (2019). Adjustment to chronic illness. In T. A. Revenson & R. A. R. Gurung (Eds.), *Handbook of health psychology* (3e). New York, NY: Routledge.

Hoyt, M. A., & Stanton, A. L. (2012). Adjustment to chronic illness. In A. Baum, T. A. Revenson, & J. Singer (Eds.), *Handbook of health psychology* (2e, pp. 219–246). New York, NY: Guilford.

Hoyt, M. A., & Stanton, A. L. (2019). Adjustment to chronic illness. In T. A. Revenson & R. A. R. Gurung (Eds.), *Handbook of health psychology* (3e). New York, NY: Routledge.

Hruschak, V., & Cochran, G. (2017). Psychosocial and environmental factors in the prognosis of individuals with chronic pain and comorbid mental health. *Social Work in Health Care*, *56*(7), 573–587. doi:10.1080/00981389.2017.1326074

Hsiao, A., Wong, M. D., Goldstein, M. S., Becerra, L. D., Cheng, E. M., & Wenger, N. S. (2006). Complementary and alternative medicine use among Asian-American subgroups: Prevalence, predictors, and lack of relationship to acculturation and access to conventional health care. *Journal of Alternative and Complementary Medicine*, *12*, 1003–1010.

Hsu, E. (Ed.). (2010). *Innovation in Chinese medicine*. Cambridge, UK: Cambridge University Press.

Hu, F. B., Leitzmann, M. F., Stampfer, M. J., Colditz, G. A., Willett, W. C., & Rimm, E. B. (2001). Physical activity and television watching in relation to risk for Type 2 diabetes mellitus in men. *Archives of Internal Medicine*, *161*, 1542–1549.

Hu, F. B., Manson, J. E., Stampfer, M.J., Colditz, G., Liu, S., Solomon, C. G., & Willett, W. C. (2001). Diet, lifestyle, and the risk of type 2 diabetes mellitus in women. *New England Journal of Medicine*, *345*, 790–797.

Huang, J. Z., & Joseph, J. G. (1999, May). Does small area income inequality influence the hospitalization of children? A disease-specific analysis. Paper presented at the meeting of the New York Academy of Sciences, Bethesda, MD.

Hubbell, F. A., Chavez, L. R., Mishra, S. I., & Valdez, R. B. (1996). Differing beliefs about breast cancer among Latinas and Anglo women. *Western Journal of Medicine*, *164*, 405–409.

Huffman, J. W. (1981). Endometriosis in young teen-age girls. *Pediatric Annals*, *10*, 44–49.

Husson, O., Denollet, J., Ezendam, N. P. M., & Mols, F. (2017). Personality, health behaviors, and quality of life among colorectal cancer survivors: Results from the PROFILES registry. *Journal* of Psychosocial Oncology, 35(1), 61–76. doi:10.1080/07347332.2016.1226227

Hwang, K., & Cragun, R. T. (2017). Agnostic, atheistic, and nonreligious orientations. In D. Von Dras (Ed.), *Better health through spiritual practices* (pp. 309–333). Santa Barbara, CA: Praeger.

Hyun, O. L., Wanjeong, Y. A., Bok-Hee, Y., Miller, B. C., Schvaneveldt, J., & Lau, S. (2002). Social support for two generations of new mothers in selected populations in Korea, Hong Kong, and the United States. *Journal of Comparative Family Studies, 33*, 57–70.

Ickovics, J. R., Hamburger, M. E., Vlahov, D., Schoenbaum, E. E., Schuman, P., Boland, R. J., & Moore, J. (2001). Mortality, CD4 cell count decline, and depressive symptoms among HIV-seropositive women: Longitudinal analysis from the HIV Epidemiology Research Study. *Journal of the American Medical Association, 285*, 1466–1474.

Ickovics, J. R., Thayaparan, B., & Ethier, K. A. (2002). Women and AIDS: A contextual analysis. In A. Baum, T. A. Revenson, & J. E. Singer (Eds.), *Handbook of health psychology* (1e, pp. 817–841). Mahwah, NJ: Erlbaum.

Ikeda, A., Iso, H., Kawachi, I., Yamagishi, K., Inoue, M., & Tsugane, S. (2008). Social support and stroke and coronary heart disease: The JPHC study cohorts II. *Stroke, 39*(3), 768–775.

Ilali, E. E., & Taraghi, Z. Z. (2010). Comparison of risk factors of CHD in the men and women with MI. *Pakistan Journal of Biological Sciences, 13*(7), 344–347.

Illinois Delegation. (2008). *American Medical Association House of Delagates Resolution: 303 (A-08)*. American Medical Association, Chicago, IL.

Imm, K. R., Williams, F., Housten, A. J., Colditz, G. A., Drake, B. F., Gilbert, K. L., & Yang, L. (2017). African American prostate cancer survivorship: Exploring the role of social support in quality of life after radical prostatectomy. *Journal of Psychosocial Oncology, 35*(4), 409–423. doi:10.1080/07347332.2017.1294641

Institute of Medicine (IOM). (2010). *Redesigning continuing education in the health professions*. Washington, DC: National Academy Press.

Institute of Medicine Committee on Advancing Pain Research, Care, and Education. (2011). *Relieving pain in America: A blueprint for transforming prevention, care, education, and research*. Washington, DC: Author.

Interdivisional Healthcare Committee. (2010, November 1). IHC concerns regarding medical psychology: Follow-up summary and analysis. Author, Washington, DC. Retrieved from http://www.healthpsych.com/ihc/medpsych.pdf

Irby-Shasanmi, A., & Leech, T. G. J. (2017). "Because I don't know": Uncertainty and ambiguity in closed-ended reports of perceived discrimination in U.S. health care. *Ethnicity & Health, 22*(5), 458–479. doi:10.1080/13557858.2016.1244659

Irish, D. P., Lundquist, K. F., & Nelson, V. J. (Eds.). (1993). *Ethnic variations in dying, death, and grief: Diversity in universality*. Philadelphia, PA: Taylor & Francis.

Ironson, G., & Hayward, H. (2008, June). Do positive psychosocial factors predict disease progression in HIV-1? A review of the evidence. *Psychosomatic Medicine, 70*(5), 546–554.

Ironson, G., O'Cleirigh, C., Weiss, A., Schneiderman, N., & Costa, P. (2008). Personality and HIV disease progression: Role of NEO-PI-R openness, extraversion, and profiles of engagement. *Psychosomatic Medicine, 70*(2), 245–253.

Ironson, G., Schneiderman, H., Kumar, M., & Antoni, M. H. (1994). Psychosocial stress, endocrine and immune response in HIV-1 disease. *Homeostasis in Health and Disease, 35*, 137–148.

Irwin, C. E., Cataldo, M. F., Matheny, A. P., & Peterson, L. (1992). Health consequences of behaviors: Injury as a model. *Pediatrics, 90*, 798–807.

Irwin, M. (2008). Human psychoneuroimmunology: 20 years of discovery. *Brain, Behavior, and Immunity, 22*(2), 129–139.

Isaac, M., & Rief, W. (2017). Behavioural interventions for life style diseases: Where are we now? *Current Opinion in Psychiatry, 30*(5), 323–325. doi:10.1097/YCO.0000000000000353

IsHak, W., Kahloon, M., & Fakhry, H. (2011). Oxytocin role in enhancing well-being: A literature review. *Journal of Affective Disorders, 130*(1/2), 1–9. doi:10.1016/j.jad.2010.06.001

Israel-Cohen, Y., & Kaplan, O. (2016). Traumatic stress during population-wide exposure to trauma in Israel: Gender as a moderator of the effects of marital status and social support. *Stress and Health, 32*(5), 636–640. doi:10.1002/smi.2647

Iturralde, E., Weissberg-Benchell, J., & Hood, K. (2017). Avoidant coping and diabetes-related distress: Pathways to adolescents type 1 diabetes outcomes. *Health Psychology, 36*(3), 236–244. doi:10.1037/hea0000445

Iverson, G. L, Stampfer, H. G., & Gaetz, M. (2002). Reliability of circadian heart pattern analysis in psychiatry. *Psychiatric Quarterly, 73*, 195–203.

Izzo, A. A., Hoon-Kim, S., Radhakrishnan, R., and Williamson, E. M. (2016). A critical approach to evaluating clinical efficacy, adverse events and drug interactions of herbal remedies. *Phytotherapy Research, 30*, 691–700. doi:10.1002/ptr.5591

Jackson, R. W., Treiber, F. A., Turner, J. R., Davis, H., & Strong, W. B. (1999). Effects of race, sex, and socioeconomic status upon cardiovascular stress responsively and recovery in youth. *International Journal of Psychophysiology, 31*, 111–119.

Jacoby, S. F., Tach, L., Guerra, T., Wiebe, D. J., & Richmond, T. S. (2017). The health status and well-being of low-resource, housing-unstable, single-parent families living in violent neighborhoods in Philadelphia, Pennsylvania. *Health & Social Care in the Community, 25*(2), 578–589. doi:10.1111/hsc.12345

Jadalla, A., & Lee, J. (2012). The relationship between acculturation and general health of Arab Americans. *Journal of Transcultural Nursing, 23*(2), 159–165.

Jafarkarimi, H., Saadatdoost, R., Sim, A. T. H., & Hee, J. M. (2016). Behavioral intention in social networking sites ethical dilemmas: An extended model based on theory of planned behavior. *Computers in Human Behavior, 62*, 545–561. doi:10.1016/j.chb.2016.04.024

Jain, R., & Jain, S. (2011). Traditional medicinal plants as anticancer agents from Chhattishgarh, India: An overview. *International Journal of Phytomedicine, 2*(3). doi:10.5138/ijpm.v2i3.108

James, A., Leone, L., Katz, M., McNeill, L., & Campbell, M. (2008). Multiple health behaviors among overweight, class I obese, and class II obese persons. *Ethnicity and Disease, 18*(2), 157–162.

James, D. S., Pobee, J. W., Oxidine, D., Brown, L., & Joshi, G. (2012). Using the health belief model to develop culturally appropriate weight-management materials for African-American women. *Journal of The Academy of Nutrition & Dietetics, 112*(5), 664–670. doi:10.1016/j.jand.2012.02.003

James, W. (1902). *Varieties of religious experience*. Cambridge, MA: Harvard University Press.

Jamner, L. D., Alberts, J., Leigh, H., & Klein, L. C. (1998). Affiliative need and endogenous opioids. Paper presented at the annual meetings of the Society of Behavioral Medicine, New Orleans, LA.

Janeway, C. A., & Travers, P. (1996). *Immuno biology: The immune system in health and disease*. New York, NY: Garland Publishing.

Jang, Y., Park, N. S., Chiriboga, D. A., & Kim, M. T. (2017). Latent profiles of acculturation and their implications for health: A study with Asian Americans in central Texas. *Asian American Journal of Psychology, 8*(3), 200–208. doi:10.1037/aap0000080

Janssen, I., Powell, L., Jasielec, M., Matthews, K., Hollenberg, S., Sutton-Tyrrell, K., & Everson-Rose, S. (2012). Progression of coronary artery calcification in black and white women: Do the stresses and rewards of multiple roles matter? *Annals of Behavioral Medicine, 43*(1), 39–49. doi:10.1007/s12160-011-9307-8

Janz, N. K., & Becker, M. H. (1984). The Health Belief Model: A decade later. *Health Education Quarterly, 11*, 1–47.

Janz, N., Champion, V. L., & Strecher, V. J. (2002). The Health Belief Model. In K. Glanz, B. K. Rimer, & F. M. Lewis (Eds.), *Health behavior and health education: Theory, research, and practice* (pp. 45–66). San Francisco, CA: Jossey-Bass.

Jaser, S. S., Patel, N., Xu, M., Tamborlane, W. V., & Grey, M. (2017). Stress and coping predicts adjustment and glycemic control in adolescents with type 1 diabetes. *Annals of Behavioral Medicine, 51*(1), 30–38. doi:10.1007/s12160-016-9825-5

Jasinska, A. J., Chua, H., Ho, S., Polk, T. A., Rozek, L. S., & Strecher, V. J. (2012). Amygdala response to smoking-cessation messages mediates the effects of serotonin transporter gene variation on quitting. *Neuroimage, 60*(1), 766–773. doi:10.1016/j.neuroimage.2011.12.064

Jasso, G., Massey, D. S., Rosenzweig, M. R., & Smith, J. P. (2004). *Immigrant health: Selectivity and acculturation.* Working paper 04/23, Institute for Fiscal Studies, London, UK.

Jeffery, R. W., French, S. A., Raether, C., & Baxter, J. E. (1994). An environment intervention to increase fruit and salad purchases in a cafeteria. *Preventive Medicine, 23*, 788–792.

Jemal, A., Bray, F., Center, M. M., Ferlay, J., Ward, E., & Forman, D. (2011). Global cancer statistics. *CA: A Cancer Journal for Clinicians, 61*, 69–90. doi:10.3322/caac.20107

Jemal, A., Clegg, L. X., Ward, E., Ries, L. A. G., Wu, X., Jamison, P. M., . . . Edwards, B. K. (2004). Annual report to the nation on the status of cancer, 1975–2001, with a special feature regarding survival. *Cancer, 101*, 3–27.

Jemal, A., Siegel, R., Ward, E., Hao, Y., Xu, J., Murray, T., & Thun, M. J. (2008). Cancer statistics, 2008. *CA: A Cancer Journal for Clinicians, 58*(2), 71–96.

Jemal, A., Tiwari, R. C., Murray, T., Ghafoor, A., Samuels, A., Ward, E., . . . Thun, M. J. (2004). Cancer statistics, 2004. *CA: A Cancer Journal for Clinicians, 54*(1), 8–29.

Jemal, A., Ward, E. M., Johnson, C. J., Cronin, K. A., Ma, J. Ryerson, A. B., . . . Weir, H. K. (2017). Annual report to the nation on the status of cancer, 1975–2014, featuring survival. *Journal of the National Cancer Institute, 109*(9). doi:10.1093/jnci/djx030

Jemmott, J. B., Jemmott, L. S., & Fong, G. T. (1992). Reductions in HIV risk–associated sexual behaviors among Black male adolescents: Effects of an AIDS prevention intervention. *American Journal of Public Health, 82*, 372–377.

Jemmott, J. B., Jemmott, L. S., & Hacker, C. I. (1992). Predicting intentions to use condoms among African-American adolescents: The risk-associated behavior. *Ethnicity Discussions, 2*, 371–380.

Jennings, K. M. (1997). Getting a Pap smear: Focus group responses of African American and Latina women. *Oncology Nursing Forum, 24*, 827–835.

Jensen, M. P., & Karoly, P. (2001). Self-report scales and procedures for assessing pain in adults. In D. C. Turk & R. Melzack (Eds.), *Handbook of pain assessment* (2nd ed., pp. 15–34). New York, NY: Guilford Press.

Jensen, M. P., Tomé-Pires, C., de, l. V., Galán, S., Solé, E., & Miró, J. (2017). What determines whether a pain is rated as mild, moderate, or severe? The importance of pain beliefs and pain interference. *Clinical Journal of Pain, 33*(5), 414–421. doi:10.1097/AJP.0000000000000429

Jensen, M. P., Turner, J. A., & Romano, J. M. (1994). What is the maximum number of levels needed in pain intensity measurement? *Pain, 58*, 387–392.

Jensen, M. R. (1987). Psychobiological factors predicting the course of breast cancer. *Journal of Personality. Special Personality and Physical Health, 55*, 317–342.

Jensen-Doss, A. (2011). Practice involves more than treatment: How can evidence-based assessment catch up to evidence-based treatment? *Clinical Psychology: Science and Practice, 18*(2), 173–177. doi:10.1111/j.1468-2850.2011.01248.x

Jerome, L. W., DeLeon, P. H., James, L. C., Folen, R., Earles, J., & Gedney, J. J. (2000). The coming of age of telecommunication in psychological research and practice. *American Psychologist, 55*, 407–421.

Jerram, K. L., & Coleman, P. G. (1999). The Big Five personality traits and reporting of health problems and health behaviour in old age. *British Journal of Health Psychology, 4*, 181–192.

Jessor, R., Turbin, M. S., & Costa, F. M. (1998). Protective factors in adolescent health behavior. *Journal of Personality and Social Psychology, 75*, 788–800.

Jianfrei, G. S., Tregonning, S., & Keenan, L. (2008). Social interaction and participation: Formative evaluation of online CME modules. *Journal of Continuing Education in the Health Professional, 28*, 3, 172–179.

Jillson-Boostrom, I. (1992). The impact of HIV on minority populations. In P. I. Ahmed & N. Ahmed (Eds.), *Living and dying with AIDS* (pp. 235–254). New York, NY: Plenum.

Jin, H., Folsom, D., Sasaki, A., Mudaliar, S., Henry, R., Torres, M., & . . . Jeste, D. (2011). Increased Framingham 10-year risk of coronary heart disease in middle-aged and older patients with psychotic symptoms. *Schizophrenia Research, 125*(2/3), 295–299. doi:10.1016/j.schres.2010.10.029

Jo, A., Maxwell, A., Wong, W., & Bastani, R. (2008). Colorectal cancer screening among underserved Korean Americans in Los Angeles County. *Journal of Immigrant and Minority Health/Center for Minority Public Health, 10*(2), 119–126.

Johansen, C., Dalton, S., & Bidstrup, P. (2011). Depression and cancer: The role of culture and social disparities. In D. W. Kissane, M. Maj, N. Sartorius, D. W. Kissane, M. Maj, N. Sartorius (Eds.), *Depression and cancer* (pp. 207–223). Oxford, UK: Wiley-Blackwell.

Johansson, M., Hassmén, P., & Jouper, J. (2008). Acute effects of qigong exercise on mood and anxiety. *International Journal of Stress Management, 15*, 199–207.

John, E., Schwartz, G., Koo, J., Wang, W., & Ingles, S. (2007). Sun exposure, vitamin D receptor gene polymorphisms, and breast cancer risk in a multiethnic population. *American Journal of Epidemiology, 166*(12), 1409–1419.

John, O. P., & Srivastava, S. (1999). The Big Five Trait taxonomy: History, measurement, and theoretical perspectives. In L. A. Pervin & O. P. Oliver (Eds.), *Handbook of personality: Theory and research* (2nd ed., pp. 102–138). New York, NY: Guilford Press.

Johnson, A. J., Kekecs, Z., Roberts, R. L., Gavin, R., Brown, K., & Elkins, G. R. (2017). Feasibility of music and hypnotic suggestion to manage chronic pain. *International Journal of Clinical and Experimental Hypnosis, 65*(4), 452–465. doi:10.1080/00207144.2017.1348858

Johnson, L. S. (1997). Developmental strategies for counseling the child whose parent or sibling has cancer. *Journal of Counseling and Development, 75*, 417–427.

Johnson, M., Benyamini, Y., & Karademas, E.C. (2016). Measurement issues in health psychology. In Y. Benyamini, M. Johnson, & E. C. Karademas (Eds.), *Assessment in health psychology* (pp. 320–334). Boston, MA: Hogrefe.

Johnson, P. J., Ward, A., Knutson, L., & Sendelbach, S. (2012). Personal use of complementary and alternative medicine (CAM) by U.S. health care workers. *Health Services Research, 47*(1 Pt 1), 211–227. doi:10.1111/j.1475-6773.2011.01304.x.

Johnson, S. K. (2008). Biology of medically unexplained illness. In S. K. Johnson (Ed.), *Medically unexplained illness: Gender and biopsychosocial implications* (pp. 49–60). Washington, DC: American Psychological Association.

Johnson-Greene, D., & Denning, J. (2008). Neuropsychology of alcoholism. In A. M. Horton & D. Wedding (Eds.), *The neuropsychology handbook* (3e, pp. 729–752). New York, NY: Springer.

Johnston, D. W., Tuomisto, M. T., & Patching, G. R. (2008). The relationship between cardiac reactivity in the laboratory and in real life. *Health Psychology, 27*, 34–42.

Johnston, L. D., O'Malley, P. M., & Bachman, J. G. (2001). *Monitoring the future: National survey results on drug use, 1975–2000*, vol. 2, *College students and adults ages 19–40* (NIH Publication No. 01–4925). Bethesda, MD: National Institute on Drug Abuse.

Jones, C. H. (2005). The spectrum of therapeutic influences and integrative health care: Classifying health care practices by mode of therapeutic action. *Journal of Alternative and Complementary Medicine, 11*, 937–944.

Jones, E. E., Kannouse, D. E., Kelley, H. H., Nisbett, R. E., Valins, S., & Weiner, B. (Eds.). (1972). *Attribution: Perceiving the causes of behavior*. Morristown, NJ: General Learning Press.

Jones, F., & Fletcher, B. C. (1993). An empirical study of occupational stress transmission in working couples. *Human Relations, 46*, 881–903.

Jones, G. C., Crews, J. E., & Danielson, M. L. (2010). Health risk profile for older adults with blindness: An application of the international classification of functioning, *Disability, and Health Framework. Ophthalmic Epidemiology, 17*, 400–410. doi:10.3109/09286586.2010.528137

Jones, R. A., Taylor, A. G., Bourguignon, C., Steeves, R., Fraser, G., Lippert, M., . . . Kilbridge, K. L. (2008). Family interactions among African American prostate cancer survivors. *Family and Community Health, 31*(3), 213–220.

Jones, S. M. W., Weitlauf, J., Danhauer, S. C., Qi, L., Zaslavsky, O., Wassertheil-Smoller, S., . . . LaCroix, A. Z. (2017). Prospective data from the Women's health initiative on depressive symptoms, stress, and inflammation. *Journal of Health Psychology, 22*(4), 457–464. doi:10.1177/1359105315603701

Jones, T., Moore, T., & Choo, J. (2016). The impact of virtual reality on chronic pain. *PLoS One, 11*(12). doi:10.1371/journal.pone.0167523

Jonkman, N. H., Schuurmans, M. J., Groenwold, R. H. H., Hoes, A. W., & Trappenburg, J. C. A. (2016). Identifying components of self-management interventions that improve health-related quality of life in chronically ill patients: Systematic review and meta-regression analysis. *Patient Education and Counseling, 99*(7), 1087–1098. doi:10.1016/j.pec.2016.01.022

Joseph, A. M., Hecht, S. S., Murphy, S. E., Lando, H., Carmella, S. G., Gross, M., . . . Hatsukami, D. K. (2008). Smoking reduction fails to improve clinical and biological markers of cardiac disease: A randomized controlled trial. *Nicotine and Tobacco Research, 10*, 471–481.

Joseph, C., Saltzgaber, J., Havstad, S., Johnson, C., Johnson, D., Peterson, E., & . . . Ownby, D. (2011). Comparison of early-, late-, and non-participants in a school-based asthma management program for urban high school students. *Trials, 12*, 141.

Julien, R. M. (2001). *A primer of drug action*. New York, NY: Worth.

Jurecic, A. (2017). Cautioning health-care professionals: Bereaved persons are misguided through the stages of grief. *Omega: Journal of Death and Dying, 75*(1), 92–93. doi:10.1177/0030222817701499

Just, J., Louie, L., Abrams, E., Nicholas, S. W., Wara, D., Stein, Z., & King, M. C. (1992). Genetic risk factors for perinatally acquired HIV-1 infection. *Pediatric and Perinatal Epidemiology, 6*, 215–224.

Juvrud, J., & Rennels, J. L. (2017). "I don't need help": Gender differences in how gender stereotypes predict help-seeking. *Sex Roles, 76*(1–2), 27–39. doi:10.1007/s11199-016-0653-7

Kabat, G. C., Kim, M. Y., Jean-Wactawski-Wende, Bea, J. W., Edlefsen, K. L., Adams-Campbell, L. L., & . . . Rohan, T. E. (2012). Anthropometric factors, physical activity, and risk of Non-Hodgkin's lymphoma in the Women's Health Initiative. *Cancer Epidemiology, 36*(1), 52–59. doi:10.1016/j.canep.2011.05.014

Kabat-Zinn, J. (2003). Mindfulness-based interventions in context: Past, present, and future. *Clinical Psychology: Science and Practice, 10*, 144–156.

Kabir, Z., Connolly, G., Clancy, L., Koh, H., Capewell, S. (2008). Coronary heart disease deaths and decreased smoking prevalence in Massachusetts, 1993–2003. *American Journal of Public Health, 98*(8), 1468–1469.

Kadmon, I., Ganz, F., Rom, M., & Woloski-Wruble, A. (2008). Social, marital, and sexual adjustment of Israeli men whose wives were diagnosed with breast cancer. *Oncology Nursing Forum, 35*(1), 131–135.

Kahleova, H., Lloren, J. I., Mashchak, A., Hill, M., & Fraser, G. E. (2017). Meal frequency and timing are associated with changes in body mass index in Adventist health study 2. *Journal of Nutrition, 147*(9), 1722–1728. doi:10.3945/jn.116.244749

Kahn, B. E., & Wansink, B. (2004) The influence of assortment structure on perceived variety and consumption quantities. *Journal of Consumer Research, 30*(4), 519–533.

Kahn, E. (1963). On crises. *Psychiatric Quarterly, 37*, 297–305.

Kahn, R. L., & Antonucci, T. C. (1984). *Social supports of the elderly: Family/friends/professionals*. Final Report to the National Institute on Aging (No. AG01632). Bethesda,. MD: National Institute on Aging.

Kahn, R. L., Wolfe, D. M., Quinn, R. P., Snoek, J. D., & Rosenthal, R. A. (1964). *Organizational stress: Studies in role conflict and ambiguity*. Oxford, UK: John Wiley.

Kalichman, S. C., & Ramachandran, B. (1999). Mental health implications of new HIV treatments. In D. G. Ostrow & S. C. Kalichman (Eds.), *AIDS prevention and mental health* (pp. 137–150). Dordrecht, Netherlands: Springer.

Kalichman, S. C., Benotsch, E. G., Weinhardt, L., Austin, J., Luke, W., & Cherry, C. (2003). Health-related Internet use, coping, social support, and health indicators in people living with HIV/AIDS: Preliminary results from a community survey. *Health Psychology, 22*(1), 111–116. doi:10.1037/0278-6133.22.1.111

Kalichman, S. C., Carey, M. P., & Johnson, B. T. (1996). Prevention of sexually transmitted HIV infection: A meta-analytic review of the behavioral outcome literature. *Annals of Behavioral Medicine, 18*, 6–15.

Kalichman, S. C., Heckman, T., Kochman, A., Sikkema, K., & Bergholte, J. (2000). Depression and thoughts of suicide among middle-aged and older persons living with HIV-AIDS. *Psychiatric Services, 51*, 903–907.

Kalichman, S., Picciano, J., & Roffman, R. (2008). Motivation to reduce HIV risk behaviors in the context of the information, motivation and behavioral skills (IMB) model of HIV prevention. *Journal of Health Psychology, 13*(5), 680–689.

Kalil, K. M., Gruber, J. E., Conley, J., & Sytniac, M. (1993). Social and family pressures on anxiety and stress during pregnancy. *Journal of Prenatal and Perinatal Psychology and Health, 8*, 113–118.

Kallianpur, A. R., Lee, S., Gao, Y., Lu, W., Zheng, Y., Ruan, Z., . . . Zheng, W. (2008). Dietary animal-derived iron and fat intake and breast cancer risk in the Shanghai Breast Cancer Study. *Breast Cancer Research and Treatment, 107*(1), 123–132.

Kalyva, E., Eiser, C., & Papathanasiou, A. (2016). Health-related quality of life of children with asthma: Self and parental perceptions. *International Journal of Behavioral Medicine, 23*(6), 730–737. doi:10.1007/s12529-016-9558-7

Kam, L., Knott, V. E., Wilson, C., & Chambers, S. K. (2012). Using the theory of planned behavior to understand health professionals' attitudes and intentions to refer cancer patients for psychosocial support. *Psycho-Oncology, 21*(3), 316–323. doi:10.1002/pon.1897

Kane, R. L., Klein, S. J., Bernstein, L., & Rothenberg, R. (1986). The role of hospice in reducing the impact of bereavement. *Journal of Chronic Diseases, 39*, 735–742.

Kangovi, S., Mitra, N., Smith, R. A., Kulkarni, R., Turr, L., Huo, H., . . . Long, J. A. (2017). Decision-making and goal-setting in chronic disease management: Baseline findings of a randomized controlled trial. *Patient Education and Counseling, 100*(3), 449–455. doi:10.1016/j.pec.2016.09.019

Kannel, W., Evans, J., Piper, S., & Murabito, J. (2008). Angina pectoris is a stronger indicator of diffuse vascular atherosclerosis than intermittent claudication: Framingham study. *Journal of Clinical Epidemiology, 61*(9), 951–957.

Kannel, W., Vasan, R., Keyes, M., Sullivan, L., & Robins, S. (2008). Usefulness of the triglyceride-high-density lipoprotein versus the cholesterol-high-density lipoprotein ratio for predicting insulin resistance and cardiometabolic risk (from the Framingham Offspring Cohort). *American Journal of Cardiology, 101*(4), 497–501.

Kanner, A. D., Coyne, J. C., Schaefer, C., & Lazarus, R. S. (1981). Comparison of two modes of stress measurement: Daily hassles and uplifts versus major life events. *Journal of Behavioral Medicine, 4*, 1–39.

Kaplan, C. M., Saha, D., Molina, J. L., Hockeimer, W. D., Postell, E. M., Apud, J. A., . . . Tan, H. Y. (2016). Estimating changing contexts in schizophrenia. *Brain, 139*(7), 2082–2095. doi:10.1093/brain/aww095

Kaplan, G. A., & Keil, J. E. (1993). Socioeconomic factors and cardiovascular disease: A review of the literature. *Circulation, 88*, 1973–1998.

Kaplan, H. B. (Ed.). (1983). *Psychosocial stress: Trends in theory and research*. New York, NY: Academic Press.

Kaplan, M., Marks, G., & Mertens, S. (1997). Distress and coping among women with HIV infection: Preliminary findings from a multiethnic sample. *American Journal of Orthopsychiatry, 6*, 47–53.

Kaplan, R. M., & Davidson, K. W. (2010). The great debate on the contribution of behavioral interventions. In J. M. Suls, K. W. Davidson, & R. M. Kaplan, (Eds.), *Handbook of health psychology and behavioral medicine* (pp. 3–14). New York, NY: Guilford.

Kaplan, R. M., & Groessl, E. J. (2002). Applications of the cost-effectiveness methodologies in behavioral medicine. *Journal of Consulting and Clinical Psychology, 70*, 482–493.

Kaplan, R. M., & Simon, H. J. (1990). Compliance in medical care: Reconsideration of self-predictions. *Annals of Behavioral Medicine, 12*, 66–71.

Kaplow, J. B., Gipson, P. Y., Horwitz, A. G., Burch, B. N., & King, C. A. (2014). Emotional suppression mediates the relation between adverse life events and adolescent suicide: Implications for prevention. *Prevention Science, 15*(2), 177–185. doi:10.1007/s11121-013-0367-9

Kaptchuk, T. J. (2000). *The web that has no weaver: Understanding Chinese medicine*. Chicago, IL: Contemporary Books.

Kapur, N. K., (2007). Rosuvastatin: A highly potent statin for the prevention and management of coronary artery disease. *Expert Review of Cardiovascular Therapy, 5*, 161–175.

Kapur, R.L. (1979). The role of traditional healers in mental health care in rural India. *Social Sciences and Medicine, 13B*, 27–31.

Karademas, E. C., Benyamini, Y., & Johnston, M. (2016) Introduction. In Y. Benyamini, M. Johnston, & E. C. Karademas (Eds.), *Assessment in health psychology* (pp. 3–19). Boston, MA: Hogrefe.

Karademas, E. C., Kynigopoulou, E., Aghathangelou, E., & Anestis, D. (2011). The relation of illness representations to the 'end-stage' appraisal of outcomes through health status, and the moderating role of optimism. *Psychology & Health, 26*(5), 567–583. doi:10.1080/08870441003653488

Karalis, D. (2008). The role of lipid-lowering therapy in preventing coronary heart disease in patients with type 2 diabetes. *Clinical Cardiology, 31*(6), 241–248.

Karamanou, M., Protogerou, A., Tsoucalas, G., Androutsos, G., & Poulakou-Rebelakou, E. (2016). Milestones in the history of diabetes mellitus: The main contributors. *World Journal of Diabetes, 7*(1), 1–7. http://doi.org/10.4239/wjd.v7.i1.1

Karasek, D., Ahern, J., & Galea, S. (2012). Social norms, collective efficacy, and smoking cessation in urban neighborhoods. *American Journal of Public Health, 102*(2), 343–351.

Karasek, R., Collins, S., Clays, E., Bortkiewicz, A., & Ferrario, M. (2010). Description of a large-scale study design to assess work-stress-disease associations for cardiovascular disease. *International Journal of Occupational Medicine & Environmental Health (Instytut Medycyny Pracy Im. Jerzego Nofera), 23*(3), 293–312.

Karatzias, T., Jowett, S., Yan, E., Raeside, R., & Howard, R. (2017). Depression and resilience mediate the relationship between traumatic life events and ill physical health: Results from a population study. *Psychology, Health & Medicine, 22*(9), 1021–1031. doi:10.1080/13548506.2016.1257814

Karim, K., Bailey, M., & Tunna, K. (2000). Nonwhite ethnicity and the provision of specialist palliative care services: Factors affecting doctors' referral patterns. *Palliative Medicine, 14*, 471–478.

Karim, S., Saeed, K., Rana, M. H., Mubbashar, M. H., & Jenkins, R. (2004). Pakistan mental health country profile. *International Review of Psychiatry, 16*, 83–92.

Karon, J. M., Rosenberg, P. S., McQuillan, G., Khare, M., Gwinn, M., & Petersen, L. R. (1996). Prevalence of HIV infection in the United States, 1984 to 1992. *Journal of the American Medical Association, 276*, 126–131.

Kashanian, M., Javadi, F., & Haghighi, M. (2010). Effect of continuous support during labor on duration of labor and rate of cesarean delivery. *International Journal of Gynecology & Obstetrics, 109*(3), 198–200. doi:10.1016/j.ijgo.2009.11.028

Kashima, Y., Yamaguchi, S., Kim, U., Choi, S.-C., Gelfand, M. J., & Yuki, M. (1995). Culture, gender, and self: A perspective from individualism-collectivism research. *Journal of Personality and Social Psychology, 69*, 925–938.

Kastenbaum, R. (1999). Dying and bereavement. In J. C. Cavanaugh & S. K. Whitbourne (Eds.), *Gerontology: An interdisciplinary perspective* (pp. 155–185). New York, NY: Oxford University Press.

Katz, B. P., Fortenberry, J. D., Zimet, G. D., Blythe, M. J., & Orr, D. P. (2000). Partner-specific relationship characteristics and condom use among adolescents with sexually transmitted infections. *Journal of Sex Research, 37*, 69–75

Katz, E. R., Kellerman, J., & Siegel, S. E. (1980). Behavioral distress in children with cancer undergoing medical procedures: Developmental considerations. *Journal Consulting and Clinical Psychology, 48*, 356–365.

Katz, J., & Rosenbloom, B. N. (2015). The golden anniversary of Melzack and Wall's gate control theory of pain: Celebrating 50 years of pain research and management. *Pain Research & Management, 20*(6), 285–286. doi:10.1155/2015/865487

Katzman, J. G., Comerci, G. D., Landen, M., Loring, L., Jenkusky, S. M., Arora, S., . . . Geppert, C. M. A. (2014). Rules and values: A coordinated regulatory and educational approach to the public health crises of chronic pain and addiction. *American Journal of Public Health, 104*(8), 1356–1362. doi:10.2105/AJPH.2014.301881

Katzman, M. A., Hermans, K. M. E., Van Hoeken, D., & Hoek, H. W. (2004). Not your "typical island woman": Anorexia nervosa is reported only in subcultures in Curacao. *Culture, Medicine, and Psychiatry, 28*(4), 463–492.

Katzmarzyk, P. T. (2001). Obesity in Canadian children. *Canadian Medical Association Journal, 164*, 1563–1564.

Kavasch, E. B., & Baar, K. (1999). *American Indian healing arts: Herbs, rituals, and remedies for every season of life.* New York, NY: Bantam Books.

Kawachi, I., Colditz, G. A., Speizer, F. E., Manson, J. E., Stampfer, M. J., Willett, W. C., & Hennekens, C. H. (1997). A prospective study of passive smoking and coronary heart disease. *Circulation, 95*, 2374–2379.

Kazak, A. E., Bosch, J., & Klonoff, E. A. (2012). *Health Psychology* special series on health disparities. *Health Psychology, 31*(1), 1–4. doi:10.1037/a0026507

Kazarian, S. S., & Evans, D. R. (2001). *Handbook of cultural health psychology.* New York, NY: Academic Press.

Kazdin, A. (2008). Evidence-based treatment and practice: New opportunities to bridge clinical research and practice, enhance the knowledge base, and improve patient care. *American Psychologist, 63*(3), 146–159.

Keats, D. M. (2000). Cross-cultural studies in child development in Asian contexts. *Cross-Cultural Research: Journal of Comparative Social Science, 34*, 339–350.

Kebelo, K., & Rao, T. (2012). Role stressors as predictors of psychological strain among academic officers of Ethiopian higher education institutions. *Journal of The Indian Academy of Applied Psychology, 38*(2), 367–373.

Keefe, F. J., Buffington, A. L. H., Studts, J. L., & Rumble, M. E. (2002). Behavioral medicine: 2002 and beyond. *Journal of Consulting and Clinical Psychology, 70*, 852–857.

Keefe, F. J., Smith, S. J., Buffington, A. L. H., Gibson, J., Studts, J. L., & Caldwell, D. S. (2002). Recent advances and future directions in the biopsychosocial assessment and treatment of arthritis. *Journal of Consulting and Clinical Psychology, 70*, 640–656.

Keefe, S. E., Padilla, A. M., & Carlos, M. L. (1979). The Mexican-American extended family as an emotional support system. *Human Organization, 38*, 144–152.

Keel, P. K., & Klump, K. L. (2003). Are eating disorders culture-bound syndromes? Implications for conceptualizing their etiology. *Psychological Bulletin, 129*(5), 747–769.

Keinan, G. (1997). Social support, stress, and personality: Do all women benefit from their husband's presence during childbirth? in G. R. Pierce, B. Lakey, I. G. Sarason, & B. R. Sarason (Eds.), *Sourcebook of social support and personality* (pp. 409–427). New York, NY: Plenum Press.

Kelley, E. A., Bowie, J. V., Griffith, D. M., Bruce, M., Hill, S., & Thorpe, R. J. Jr. (2016). Geography, race/ethnicity, and obesity among men in the United States. *American Journal of Men's Health, 10*(3), 228–236. doi:10.1177/1557988314565811

Kelley, M. L., & Tseng, H. (1992). Cultural differences in child rearing: A comparison of immigrant Chinese and Caucasian American mothers. *Journal of Cross-Cultural Psychology, 23*, 444–455.

Kelley, M. L., Milletich, R. J., Hollis, B. F., Veprinsky, A., Robbins, A. T., & Snell, A. K. (2017). Social support and relationship satisfaction as moderators of the stress-mood-alcohol link association in U.S. Navy members. *Journal of Nervous and Mental Disease, 205*(2), 99–105.

Kelley-Hedgepeth, A., Lloyd-Jones, D. M., Colvin, A., Matthews, K. A., Johnston, J., Sowers, M. R . . . Chae, C. U. (2008). Ethnic differences in C-reactive protein concentrations. *Clinical Chemistry, 54*(6), 1027–1037.

Kelly, C., Ricciardelli, L. A., & Clarke, J. D. (1999). Problem eating attitudes and behaviors in young children. *International Journal of Eating Disorders, 25*, 281–286.

Kelty, M. F., Hoffman, R. R., III, Ory, M. G., & Harden, J. T. (2000). Behavioral and sociocultural aspects of aging. In R. M. Eisler & M. Hersen (Eds.), *Handbook of gender, culture, and health* (pp. 139–160). Mahwah, NJ: Erlbaum.

Kemeny, M. E. (2003). An interdisciplinary research model to investigate psychosocial cofactors in disease: Application to HIV-1 pathogenesis. *Brain, Behavior, & Immunity, 17*, S62–S72.

Kemeny, M. E., Weiner, H., Duran, R., Taylor, S. E., Visscher, B., & Fahey, J. L. (1995). Immune system changes after the death of a partner in HIV-positive gay men. *Psychosomatic Medicine, 57*, 547–554.

Kendall, P. C. (1999). Clinical significance. *Journal of Consulting and Clinical Psychology, 67*, 283–284.

Kendrick, K. M., Da Costa, A. P., Broad, K. D., Ohkura, S., Guevara, R., Levy, F., & Keverne, E. B. (1997). Neural control of maternal behavior and olfactory recognition of offspring. *Brain Research Bulletin, 44*, 383–395.

Kennedy, S., Kiecolt-Glaser, J. K., & Glaser, R. (1988). Immunological consequences of acute and chronic stressors: Mediating role of interpersonal relationships. *British Journal of Medical Psychology, 61*, 77–85.

Kent, M. L., Tighe, P. J., Belfer, I., Brennan, T. J., Bruehl, S., Brummett, C. M., . . . Terman, G. (2017). The ACTTION–APS–AAPM pain taxonomy (AAAPT) multidimensional approach to classifying acute pain conditions. *Journal of Pain, 18*(5), 479–489. doi:10.1016/j.jpain.2017.02.421

Kepes, S., Bushman, B. J., & Anderson, C. A. (2017). Violent video game effects remain a societal concern: Reply to Hilgard, Engelhardt, and Rouder (2017). *Psychological Bulletin, 143*(7), 775–782. doi:10.1037/bul0000112

Kern, M. L., & Friedman, H. S. (2011). Personality and pathways of influence on physical health. *Social & Personality Psychology Compass, 5*(1), 76–87. doi:10.1111/j.1751-9004.2010.00331.x

Kern, S., & Ziemssen, T. (2008). Brain-immune communication psychoneuroimmunology of multiple sclerosis. *Multiple Sclerosis* (Houndmills, Basingstoke, UK), *14*(1), 6–21.

Kerns, R. D., Haythornthwaite, J., Rosenberg, R. Southwick, S., Giller, E. L., & Jacob, M. C. (1991). The Pain Behavior Check List (PBCL): Factor structure and psychometric properties. *Journal of Behavioral Medicine, 14*, 155–167.

Kerns, R. D., Turk, J. A., & Rudy, T. E. (1985). The West Haven-Yale Multidimensional Pain Inventory (WHYMPI). *Pain, 23*, 345–356.

Kerr, J. H., & Kuk, G. (2001). The effects of low and high intensity exercise on emotions, stress, and effort. *Psychology of Sport and Exercise, 2*, 173–186.

Kessing, Lars V., Harhoff, M., & Andersen, P. K. (2008). Increased rate of treatment with antidepressants in patients with multiple sclerosis. *International Clinical Psychopharmacology, 23*, 54–59.

Kessler, R. C., Crum, R. M., Warner, L. A., Nelson, C. B., Schulenberg, J., & Antony, J. C. (1997). Lifetime co-occurrence of *DSM-III-R* alcohol abuse and dependence with other psychiatric disorders in the national comorbidity survey. *Archives of General Psychiatry, 54*, 313–321.

Kessler, R.C., Mickelson, K.D., & Williams, D.R. (1999). The prevalence, distribution, and mental health correlates of perceived discrimination in the United States. *Journal of Health and Social Behavior, 40*, 208–230.

Kesteloot, H., Sasaki, S., Xie, J., & Joossens, J. V. (1994). Secular trends in cerebrovascular mortality. *Journal of Human Hypertension, 8*, 401–408.

Khaleque, A. (2017). Perceived parental hostility and aggression, and children's psychological maladjustment, and negative personality dispositions: A meta-analysis. *Journal of Child and Family Studies, 26*(4), 977–988. doi:10.1007/s10826-016-0637-9

Khare, M. M., Carpenter, R., Huber, R., Bates, N. J., Cursio, J. F., Balmer, P. W., & . . . Loo, R. K. (2012). Lifestyle intervention and cardiovascular risk reduction in the Illinois WISEWOMAN Program. *Journal of Women's Health (15409996), 21*(3), 294–301. doi:10.1089/jwh.2011.2926

Khedr, E. M., Sharkawy, E. S. A., Attia, A. M. A., Ibrahim Osman, N. M., & Sayed, Z. M. (2017). Role of transcranial direct current stimulation on reduction of postsurgical opioid consumption and pain in total knee arthroplasty: Double randomized clinical trial. *European Journal of Pain, 21*(8), 1355–1365. doi:10.1002/ejp.1034

Khoo, K., Bolt, P., Babl, F., Jury, S., & Goldman, R. (2008). Health information seeking by parents in the Internet age. *Journal of Paediatrics and Child Health, 44*(7–8), 419–423.

Kiecolt-Glaser, J. K., & Glaser, R. (1991). Stress and immune function in humans. In R. Ader, D. L. Felten, & N. Cohen (Eds.), *Psychoneuroimmunology* (2nd ed., pp. 849–867). New York, NY: Academic Press.

Kiecolt-Glaser, J. K., Bane, C., Glaser, R., Malarkey, W. B. (2003). Love, marriage, and divorce: Newlyweds' stress hormones foreshadow relationship changes. *Journal of Consulting and Clinical Psychology, 71*, 176–188.

Kiecolt-Glaser, J. K., Garner, W., Speicher, C., Penn, G. M., Holliday, J., & Glaser, R. (1984). Psychosocial modifiers of immunocompetence in medical students. *Psychosomatic Medicine, 46*, 7–14.

Kiecolt-Glaser, J. K., Glaser, R., Cacioppo, J. T., & Malarkey, W. B. (1998). Marital stress: Immunologic, neuroendocrine, and autonomic correlates. *Annals of the New York Academy of Sciences, 840*, 656–663. doi.10.1111/j.1749-6632.1998.tb09604.x

Kiecolt-Glaser, J. K., Glaser, R., Dyer, C., Shuttleworth, E., Ogrocki, P., & Speicher, C. E. (1987). Chronic stress and immunity in family caregivers of Alzheimer's disease victims. *Psychosomatic Medicine, 49*, 523–535.

Kiecolt-Glaser, J. K., Page, G. G., Marucha, P. T., MacCallum, R. C., & Glaser, R. (1998). Psychological influences on surgical recovery: Perspectives from psychoneuroimmunology. *American Psycologist, 53*, 11209–11218.

Kiecolt-Glaser, J., & Wilson, S. J. (2017). Lovesick: How couples' relationships influence health. *Annual Review of Clinical Psychology, 13*, 421–443. doi:10.1146/annurev-clinpsy-032816-045111

Kiesler, D. J., & Auerbach, S. M. (2006). Optimal matches of patient preferences for information, decision-making and interpersonal behavior: Evidence, models and interventions. *Patient Education and Counseling, 61*, 319–341.

Kilbourne, B., Cummings, S. M., & Levine, R. (2012). Alcohol diagnoses among older Tennessee Medicare beneficiaries: race and gender differences. *International Journal of Geriatric Psychiatry, 27*(5), 483–490. doi:10.1002/gps.2740

Kilmer, R. P., Cowen, E. L., & Wyman, P. A. (2001). A micro-level analysis of developmental, parenting, and family milieu variables that differentiate stress-resilient and stress-affected children. *Journal of Community Psychology, 29*, 391–416.

Kilpatrick, D. C., Hague, R. A., Yap, P. L., & Mok, J. L. (1991). HLA antigen frequencies in children born to HIV-infected mothers. *Disease Markers, 9*, 21–26.

Kim, E., Han, J., Moon, T., Shaw, B., Shah, D. V., McTavish, F. M., & Gustafson, D. H. (2012). The process and effect of supportive message expression and reception in online breast cancer support groups. *Psycho-Oncology, 21*(5), 531–540. doi:10.1002/pon.1942

Kim, E., Lee, J., Sung, Y., & Choi, S. M. (2016). Predicting selfie-posting behavior on social networking sites: An extension of theory of planned behavior. *Computers in Human Behavior, 62*, 116–123. doi:10.1016/j.chb.2016.03.078

Kim, H. J., Yang, G. S., Greenspan, J. D., Downton, K. D., Griffith, K. A., Renn, C. L., . . . Dorsey, S. G. (2017). Racial and ethnic differences in experimental pain sensitivity: Systematic review and meta-analysis. *Pain, 158*(2), 194–211. doi:10.1097/j.pain.0000000000000731

Kim, H. K., & Lwing, M. O. (2017). Cultural effects on cancer prevention behaviors: Fatalistic cancer beliefs and risk optimism among asians in singapore. *Health Communication, 32*(10), 1201–1209. doi:10.1080/10410236.2016.1214224

Kim, H. S., Sherman, D. K., Mojaverian, T., Sasaki, J. Y., Park, J., Suh, E. M., & Taylor, S. E. (2011). Gene–culture interaction: Oxytocin receptor polymorphism (OXTR) and emotion regulation. *Social Psychological and Personality Science, 2*(6), 665–672. doi:10.1177/1948550611405854

Kim, H. S., Sherman, D. K., Sasaki, J. V., Jun, X., Chu, T. Q., Chorong, R., & . . . Taylor, S. E. (2010). Culture, distress, and oxytocin receptor polymorphism (OXTR) interact to influence emotional support seeking. *Proceedings of The National Academy of Sciences of the United States of America, 107*(36), 15717–15721.

Kim, H. S., Sherman, D. K., & Taylor, S. E. (2008). Culture and social support. *American Psychologist, 63*(6), 518–526. doi:10.1037/0003-0666x

Kim, J. E., & Zane, N. (2016). Help-seeking intentions among Asian American and White American students in psychological distress: Application of the Health Belief Model. *Cultural Diversity and Ethnic Minority Psychology, 22*(3), 311 321. http://dx.doi.org/10.1037/cdp0000056

Kim, J. M., Chang, E., & Downey, C. (2012). Integrating positive psychology and developmental viewpoints into the study of mental health across diverse groups. In E. C. Chang & C. A. Downey (Eds.), *Handbook of race and development in mental health* (pp. 1–10). New York, NY: Springer Science + Business Media. doi:10.1007/978-1-4614-0424-8_1

Kim, J., & Dellon, A. L. (2001). Pain at the site of tarsal tunnel incision due to neuroma of the posterior branch of the saphenous nerve. *Journal of the American Podiatric Medical Association, 91*, 109–113.

Kim, K., Yu, E. S., Chen, E. H., Kim, J., & Brintnall, R. A. (1998). Colorectal cancer screening: Knowledge and practices among Korean Americans. *Cancer Practice, 6*, 167–175.

Kim, Y., Evangelista, L. S., Phillips, L. R., Pavlish, C., & Kopple, J. D. (2012). Racial/ethnic differences in illness perceptions in minority patients undergoing maintenance hemodialysis. *Nephrology Nursing Journal, 39*(1), 39–49.

Kimbro, R. (2009). Acculturation in context: Gender, age at migration, neighborhood ethnicity, and health behaviors. *Social Science Quarterly* (Blackwell Publishing Limited), *90*, 1145.

King, J. (2017). North American indigenous spiritualities. In D. Von Dras (Ed.), *Better health through spiritual practices* (pp. 263–286). Santa Barbara, CA: Praeger.

King, R. J. B., & Robins, M. W. (2006). *Cancer biology*. New York, NY: Benjamin Cummings.

Kirscht, J. P. (1971). Social and psychological problems of surveys on health and illness. *Social Science and Medicine, 5*, 519–526.

Kister, I., Munger, K., Herbert, J., & Ascherio, A. (2012). Increased risk of multiple sclerosis among women with migraine in the Nurses' Health Study II. *Multiple Sclerosis (13524585), 18*(1), 90–97. doi:10.1177/1352458511416487

Kiviniemi, M. T., Orom, H., & Giovino, G. A. (2011). Psychological distress and smoking behavior: The nature of the relation differs by race/ethnicity. *Nicotine & Tobacco Research, 13*(2), 113–119. doi:10.1093/ntr/ntq218

Klass, D. (2007). Religion, spirituality in loss, grief, and mourning. In D. Balk, C. Wogrin, G. Thornton, & D. Meagher (Eds.), *Handbook of thanatology: The essential body of knowledge for the student of death, dying, and bereavement* (pp. 121–131). Northbrook, IL: Association for Death Education and Counseling.

Klayman, D. L. (1985). Qinghaosu (Artemisinin): An antimalarial drug from China. *Science, 228*, 1049–1055.

Kleiman, E. M., Chiara, A. M., Liu, R. T., Jager-Hyman, S., Choi, J. Y., & Alloy, L. B. (2017). Optimism and well-being: A prospective multi-method and multi-dimensional examination of optimism as a resilience factor following the occurrence of stressful life events. *Cognition and Emotion, 31*(2), 269–283. doi:10.1080/02699931.2015.1108284

Kleinman, A. (1980). *Patients and healers in context of cultures*. Berkeley, CA: University of California Press.

Kleinman, A., Eisenberg, L., & Good, B. (1978). Culture, illness, and care: Clinical lessons from anthropological and cross-cultural research. *Annals of Internal Medicine, 88*, 251–258.

Klevens, R. M., Diaz, T., Fleming, P. L., Mays, M. A., & Frey, R. (1999). Trends in AIDS among Hispanics in the United States, 1991–1996. *American Journal of Public Health, 89*, 1104–1106.

Klimas, N., Koneru, A. O., & Fletcher, M. A. (2008). Overview of HIV. *Psychosomatic Medicine, 70*(5), 523–530. doi:10.1097/PSY.0b013e31817ae69f

Kline, A., & VanLandingham, M. (1994). HIV-infected women and sexual risk reduction: The relevance of existing models of change. *AIDS Education and Prevention, 6*, 390–402.

Kline, K. A., Fekete, E. M., Sears, C. M. (2008). Hostility, emotional expression, and hemodynamic responses to laboratory stressors: Reactivity attenuating effects of a tendency to express emotion interpersonally. *International Journal of Psychophysiology, 68*, 177–185.

Kloner, R. A., Leor, J., Poole, W. K., & Perritt, R. (1997). Population-based analysis of the effect of the Northridge earthquake on cardiac death in Los Angeles, California. *Journal of the American College of Cardiology, 31*, 1174–1180.

Klonoff, E. A., & Landrine, H. (2001). Depressive symptoms and smoking among U.S. Black adults: Absence of a relationship. *Journal of Health Psychology, 6*, 645–649

Knekt, P., Järvinen, R., Seppänen, R., Hellövaara, M., Teppo, L., Pukkala, R., & Aromaa, A. (1997). Dietary flavonoids and the risk of lung cancer and other malignant neoplasms. *American Journal of Epidemiology, 146*, 223–230.

Knight, G. P., Bernal, M. E., Garza, C. A., Cota, M. K., & Ocampo, K. A. (1993). Family socialization and the ethnic identity of Mexican-American children. *Journal of Cross-Cultural Psychology, 24*, 99–114.

Knight, K. R., Kushel, M., Chang, J. S., Zamora, K., Ceasar, R., Hurstak, E., & Miaskowski, C. (2017). Opioid pharmacovigilance: A clinical-social history of the changes in opioid prescribing for patients with co-occurring chronic non-cancer pain and substance use. *Social Science & Medicine, 186*, 87–95. doi:10.1016/j.socscimed.2017.05.043

Knoll, N., Scholz, U., & Bitzen, B. (2019). Social support and family processes. In T. A. Revenson & R. A. R. Gurung (Eds.), *Handbook of health psychology* (3e). New York, NY: Routledge.

Knoops, K. T. B., de Groot, L. C. P. G. M., Kromhout, D., Perrin, A., Moreiras-Varela, O., Menotti, A., & van Staveren, W. A. (2004). Mediterranean diet, lifestyle factors, and 10-year mortality in elderly European men and women: The HALE project. *Journal of the American Medical Association, 292*(12), 1433–1439. doi:10.1001/jama.292.12.1433

Knouse, S. B. (1991). Social support for Hispanics in the military. *International Journal of Intercultural Relations, 15*, 427–444.

Knox, P. (1998). *The business of healthcare*. Green Bay, WI: Bellin.

Kobasa, S. C., Maddi, S. R., & Kahn, S. (1982). Hardiness and health: A prospective study. *Journal of Personality and Social Psychology, 42*, 168–177.

Koenig, H. G. (2015). Religion, spirituality, and health: A review and update. *Advances in Mind–Body Medicine, 29*, 19–26.

Koenig, H. G., Pargament, K. I., & Nielsen, J. (1998). Religious coping and health status in medically ill hospitalized older adults. *Journal of Nervous and Mental Disease, 186*, 513–521.

Koenig, L. J., Pals, S. L., Bush, T., Pratt Palmore, M., Stratford, D., & Ellerbrock, T. V. (2008). Randomized controlled trial of an intervention to prevent adherence failure among HIV-infected patients initiating antiretroviral therapy. *Health Psychology, 27*, 159–169.

Koertge, J., Janszky, I., Sundin, O., Blom, M., Georgiades, A., László, K. D . . . Ahnve, S. (2008). Effects of a stress management program on vital exhaustion and depression in women with coronary heart disease: A randomized controlled intervention study. *Journal of Internal Medicine, 263*(3), 281–293.

Koffman, J., Morgan, M., Edmonds, P., Speck, P., & Higginson, I. J. (2008). "I know he controls cancer": The meanings of religion among Black Caribbean and White British patients with advanced cancer. *Social Science and Medicine, 67*(5), 780–789. doi:10.1016/J.SOCSCIMED.2008.05.004

Kohl, H. W. III. (2001). Physical activity and cardiovascular disease: Evidence for a dose response. *Medicine and Science in Sports and Exercise, 33*, S472–S483.

Komiyama, O., Kawara, M., & De Laat, A. (2007). Ethnic differences regarding tactile and pain thresholds in the trigeminal region. *Journal of Pain, 8*, 363–369.

Kompier, M. A., & DiMartino, V. (1995). Review of bus drivers' occupational stress and stress prevention. *Stress Medicine, 11*, 253–262.

Kondavallv Seshasai, S., Wijesuriya, S., Sivakumaran, R., Nethercott, S., Erqou, S., Sattar, N., & Ray, K. K. (2012). Effect of aspirin on vascular and nonvascular outcomes: Meta-analysis of randomized controlled trials. *Archives of Internal Medicine, 172*(3), 209–216. doi:101001/archinternmed.2011.628

Konijn, E. A., Nije Bijvank, M., & Bushman, B. J. (2007). I wish I were a warrior: The role of wishful identification in effects of violent video games on aggression in adolescent boys. *Developmental Psychology, 43*, 1038–1044.

Konik, J., & Smith, C. A. (2015). Medicalizing women's weight: Bariatric surgery and weight-loss drugs. In M. C. McHugh & J. C. Chrisler (Eds.), *The wrong prescription for women: How medicine and media create a "need" for treatments, drugs, and surgery* (pp. 203–219). Santa Barbara, CA: Praeger.

Koordeman, R., Anschutz, D., & Engels, R. (2012). The effect of alcohol advertising on immediate alcohol consumption in college students: An experimental study. *Alcoholism, Clinical and Experimental Research, 36*(5), 874–880. doi:10.1111/j.1530-0277.2011.01655.x

Koos, E. L. (1954). *The health of Regionville: What the people thought and did about it.* New York, NY: Columbia University Press.

Korbman, M., Appel, M., & Rosmarin, D. H. (2017). Judaism and health. In D. Von Dras (Ed.), *Better health through spiritual practices* (pp. 119–150). Santa Barbara, CA: Praeger.

Korhonen, T., Goodwin, A., Miesmaa, P., Dupuis, E. A., & Kinnunen, T. (2011). Smoking cessation program with exercise improves cardiovascular disease biomarkers in sedentary women. *Journal of Women's Health (15409996), 20*(7), 1051–1064. doi:10.1089/jwh.2010.2075

Korin, M. R., Kaplan, R. M., & Davidson, K. W. (2010). The evidence-based movement in health psychology. In J. M. Suls, K. W. Davidson, & R. M. Kaplan (Eds.), *Handbook of health psychology and behavioral medicine* (pp. 303–314). New York, NY: Guilford.

Korol, C. T., & Craig, K. D. (2001). Pain from the perspectives of health psychology and culture. In S. S. Kazarian & D. R. Evans (Eds.), *Handbook of cultural health psychology* (pp. 241–265). San Diego, CA: Academic Press.

Korte, S. M., Koolhaas, J. M., Wingfield, J. C., & McEwen, B. S. (2005). The Darwinian concept of stress: Benefits of allostasis and costs of allostatic load and the trade-offs in health and disease. *Neuroscience and Biobehavioral Reviews, 29*, 3–38.

Kothe, E. J., Mullan, B. A., & Butow, P. P. (2012). Promoting fruit and vegetable consumption. Testing an intervention based on the theory of planned behaviour. *Appetite, 58*(3), 997–1004. doi:10.1016/j.appet.2012.02.012

Kout, P. (1992). Yoga and AIDS. *Journal of International Association of Yoga Therapists, 3*, 18–24.

Kraaij, V., Garnefski, N., Schroevers, M., van der Veek, S., Witlox, R., & Maes, S. (2008). Cognitive coping, goal self-efficacy and personal growth in HIV-infected men who have sex with men. *Patient Education and Counseling, 72*(2), 301–304.

Kraemer, H. C., Kiernan, M., Essex, M., & Kupfer, D. J. (2008). How and why criteria defining moderators and mediators differ between the Baron & Kenny and MacArthur approaches. *Health Psychology, 27*, S101–S109.

Kraemer, R. R., Dzewaltowski, D. A., Blair, M. S., Rinehardt, K. F., & Castracane, V. D. (1990). Mood alteration from treadmill running and its relationship to beta-endorphin, corticotropin, and growth hormone. *Journal of Sports Medicine and Physical Fitness, 30*, 241–246.

Krantz, D. S. (1995). Editorial: Health psychology: 1995–1999. *Health Psychology, 14*, 3.

Krantz, D. S., & Lundgren, N. R. (1998).Cardiovascular disorders. In A. S. Bellack & M. Hersen (Eds.), *Comprehensive clinical psychology* (pp. 189–216). New York, NY: Pergamon Press.

Krantz, D. S., & Manuck, S. B. (1984). Acute psychophysiologic reactivity and risk of cardiovascular disease: A review and methodologic critique. *Psychological Bulletin, 96*, 435–464.

Krantz, D. S., Helmers, K. F., Nebel, L. E., Gottdiener, J. S., & Rozanski, A. (1991). Mental stress and myocardial ischemia in patients with coronary disease: Current status and future direction. In A. P. Shapiro & A. Baum (Eds.), *Behavioral aspects of cardiovascular disease: Perspectives in behavioral medicine* (pp. 11–27). Mahwah: NJ: Erlbaum.

Krause, N. (1998). Neighborhood deterioration, religious coping, and changes in health during late life. *Gerontologist, 38*, 653–664.

Kreimer, A. R., Alberg, A. J., Daniel, R., Gravitt, P. E., Viscidi, R., Garrett, E. S., . . . Gillison, M. L. (2004). Oral human papillomavirus infection in adults is associated with sexual behavior and HIV serostatus. *Journal of Infectious Diseases, 189*, 686–699.

Kreps, G., & Neuhauser, L. (2010). New directions in eHealth communication: Opportunities and challenges. *Patient Education and Counseling, 78*(3), 329–336. doi:10.1016/j.pec.2010.01.013.

Kreuter, M., Strecher, V. J., & Glassman, B. (1999). One size does not fit all: The case for tailoring print materials. *Annals of Behavioral Medicine, 21*, 276–283.

Kreuzer, M., Krauss, M., Kreienbrock, L., Jockel, K. H., & Wichmann, H. E. (2000). Environmental tobacco smoke and lung cancer: A case-control study in Germany. *American Journal of Epidemiology, 151*, 241–250.

Kriska, A. (2000). Ethnic and cultural issues in assessing physical activity. *Research Quarterly for Exercise and Sport, 71*, 47–54.

Kristensen, M., Kucinskiene, Z., Bergdahl, B., Calkauskas, H., Urmonas, V., & Orth-Gomer, K. (1998). Increased psychosocial strain in Lithuanian versus Swedish men: The LiVicordia study. *Psychosomatic Medicine, 60*, 277–282.

Kroenke, K., Bair, M., Damush, T., Hoke, S., Nicholas, G., Kempf, C., . . . Sutherland, J. (2007). Stepped Care for Affective Disorders and Musculoskeletal Pain (SCAMP) study: Design and practical implications of an intervention for comorbid pain and depression. *General Hospital Psychiatry, 29*, 506–517.

Krohne, H. W. (1993). Vigilance and cognitive avoidance as concepts in coping research. In H. W. Krohne (Ed.), *Attention and avoidance: Strategies in coping with aversiveness* (pp. 19–50). Ashland, OH: Hogrefe & Huber.

Kroll, J. L., Werchan, C. A., Reeves, A. G., Bruemmer, K. J., Lippert, A. R., & Ritz, T. (2017). Sensitivity of salivary hydrogen sulfide to psychological stress and its association with exhaled nitric oxide and affect. *Physiology & Behavior, 179*, 99–104. doi:10.1016/j.physbeh.2017.05.023

Krueger, P., Saint Onge, J., & Chang, V. (2011). Race/ethnic differences in adult mortality: The role of perceived stress and health behaviors. *Social Science & Medicine (1982), 73*(9), 1312–1322.

Kruk, J. (2012). Self-reported psychological stress and the risk of breast cancer: A case-control study. *Stress: The International Journal on the Biology of Stress, 15*(2), 162–171. doi:10.3109/10253890.2011.606340

Krystal, J. H., D'Souza, D. C., Petrakis, I. L., Belger, A., Berman, R. M., Charney, D. S., . . . Madonick, S. (1999). NMDA agonists and antagonists as probes of glutamatergic dysfunction and pharmacotherapies in neuropsychiatric disorders. *Harvard Review of Psychiatry, 7*, 125–144.

Kuba, S. A., Harris-Wilson, D. J., & O'Toole, S. K. (2012). Understanding the role of gender and ethnic oppression when treating Mexican American women for eating disorders. *Women & Therapy, 35*(1/2), 19–30. doi:10.1080/02703149.2012.634715

Kubík, A., Zatloukal, P., Tomásek, L., Pauk, N., Havel, L., Dolezal, J., & Pleski, I. (2007). Interactions between smoking and other exposures associated with lung cancer risk in women: Diet and physical activity. *Neoplasma, 54*(1), 83–88.

Kubler-Ross, E. (1969). *On death and dying*. New York, NY: MacMillan Company.
Kübler-Ross, E. (1970). The care of the dying: Whose job is it? *Psychiatry in Medicine, 1*, 103–107.
Kumanyika, S. K., Van Horn, L., Bowen, D., Perri, M. G., Rolls, B. J., Czajkowski, S. M., & Schron, E. (2000). Maintenance of dietary behavior change. *Health Psychology, 19*, 42–56.
Kumar, S., Jawaid, T., & Dubey, S. D. (2011) Therapeutic plants of Ayurveda: A review on anticancer. *Pharmacognosy Journal, 3*(23), 1–11. doi:10.5530/pj.2011.23.1
Kuo, B. C. H., Soucie, K. M., Huang, S., & Laith, R. (2017). The mediating role of cultural coping behaviours on the relationships between academic stress and positive psychosocial well-being outcomes. *International Journal of Psychology*. doi:10.1002/ijop.12421
Kurian, A., & Cardarelli, K. (2007). Racial and ethnic differences in cardiovascular disease risk factors: A systematic review. *Ethnicity and Disease, 17*(1), 143–152.
Kurth, T., Diener, H., & Buring, J. E. (2011). Migraine and cardiovascular disease in women and the role of aspirin: Subgroup analyses in the Women's Health Study. *Cephalalgia, 31*(10), 1106–1115. doi:10.1177/0333102411412628
Kurtz, M., Kurtz, J., Given, C., & Given, B. (2008). Patient optimism and mastery-do they play a role in cancer patients' management of pain and fatigue? *Journal of Pain and Symptom Management, 36*(1), 1–10.
Kushi, L., Doyle, C., McCullough, M., Rock, C., Demark-Wahnefried, W., Bandera, E., & . . . Gansler, T. (2012). American Cancer Society Guidelines on nutrition and physical activity for cancer prevention: Reducing the risk of cancer with healthy food choices and physical activity. *CA:A Cancer Journal for Clinicians, 62*(1), 30–67. doi:10.3322/caac.20140
Kusnecov, A. W. (2002). Behavioral conditioning of the immune system. In A. Baum, T. A. Revenson, & J. E. Singer (Eds.), *Handbook of health psychology* (1e, pp. 105–116). Mahwah, NJ: Erlbaum.
La Perriere, A. R., Fletcher, M. A., Antoni, M. H., Ironson, G., Klimas, N., & Schneiderman, N. (1991). Aerobic exercise training in an AIDS risk group. *International Journal of Sports Medicine, 12*, S53–S57.
La, I. S., & Yun, E. K. (2017). Effects of stress appraisal on the quality of life of adult patients with multiple myeloma and their primary family caregivers in Korea. *Psycho-Oncology, 26*, 1640–1646. doi:10.1002/pon.4348
Laban, C. J., Gernaat, H. B. P. E., Komproe, I. H., van der Tweel, I. & de Jong, J. T. V. M. (2005). Post-migration living problems and common psychiatric disorders in Iraqi asylum seekers in the Netherlands. *Journal of Nervous and Mental Disease, 193*, 825–832.
Laborde, S., Guillén, F., Watson, M., & Allen, M. S. (2017). The light quartet: Positive personality traits and approaches to coping in sport coaches. *Psychology of Sport and Exercise, 32*, 67–73. doi:10.1016/j.psychsport.2017.06.005
LaCaille, R. A., & Hooker, S. A. (2019). Physical activity. In T. A. Revenson & R. A. R. Gurung (Eds.), *Handbook of health psychology* (3e). New York, NY: Routledge.
LaChausse, R. G. (2012). My student body: Effects of an Internet-based prevention program to decrease obesity among college students. *Journal of American College Health, 60*(4), 324–330. doi: 10.1080/07448481.2011.623333
Lafferty, C. K., Heaney, C. A., & Chen, M. S., Jr. (1999). Assessing decisional balance for smoking cessation among Southeast Asian males in the U.S. *Health Education Research, 14*, 139–146.
Lagos, V. I., Perez, M. A., Ricker, C. N., Blazer, K. R., Santiago, N. M, Feldman, N., . . . Weitzel, J. N. (2008). Social-cognitive aspects of underserved Latinas preparing to undergo genetic cancer risk assessment for hereditary breast and ovarian cancer. *Psycho-Oncology, 17*(8), 774–782.
Laidsaar-Powell, R., Butow, P., Bu, S., Fisher, A., & Juraskova, I. (2017). Oncologists' and oncology nurses' attitudes and practices towards family involvement in cancer consultations. *European Journal of Cancer Care, 26*(1). doi:10.1111/ecc.12470
Lairson, D. R., DiCarlo, M., Myers, R. E., Wolf, T., Cocroft, J., Sifri, R., . . . Wender, R. (2008). Cost-effectiveness of targeted and tailored interventions on colorectal cancer screening use. *Cancer, 112*(4), 779–788.
Lam, C. N., & Lim, S. (2014). Traditional Chinese medicine: A healing approach from the past to the future. In R. A. R. Gurung (Ed.), *Multicultural approaches to health and wellness in America* (pp. 198–225). Santa Barbara, CA: Praeger.
Lam, W. Y., & Fresco, P. (2015). Medication adherence measures: An overview. *BioMed Research International*, e217047. doi:10.1155/2015/217047
Lamb, T. (2004). Yoga and asthma. Interational Association of Yoga Therapists, Little Rock, AR. Retrieved from https://yogastudies.org/wp-content/uploads/asthma.pdf.
Lampert, R. (2010). Anger and ventricular arrhythmias. *Current Opinion in Cardiology, 25*(1), 46–52.
Lampl, C., Voelker, M., & Steiner, T. J. (2012). Aspirin is first-line treatment for migraine and episodic tension-type headache regardless of headache intensity. *Journal of Head & Face Pain, 52*(1), 48–56. doi:10.1111/j.1526-4610.2011.01974.x
Lampl, M., Frongillo, E. F., & Johnson, M. L. (1997). Stasis without saltation? *Annals of Human Biology, 24*, 65–68.
Landrine, H., & Klonoff, E. A. (1992). Culture and health-related schemes: A review and proposal for interdisciplinary integration. *Health Psychology, 11*, 267–276.
Landrine, H., & Klonoff, E. A. (2001). Cultural diversity and health psychology. In A. Baum, T. A. Revenson, & J. E. Singer (Eds.), *Handbook of health psychology* (1e, pp. 851–891). Mahwah, NJ: Erlbaum.
Landry, S. H., Denson, S. E., & Swank, P. R. (1997). Effects of medical risk and socioeconomic status on the rate of change in cognitive and social development for low birth weight children. *Journal of Clinical and Experimental Neuropsychology, 19*, 261–274.
Landsbergis, P. A., Schnall, P. L, Warren, K., & Pickering, T. G. (1994). Association between ambulatory blood pressure and alternative formulations of job strain. *Scandinavian Journal of Work, Environment and Health, 20*, 349–363.
Lang, C., Feldmeth, A. K., Brand, S., Holsboer-Trachsler, E., Pühse, U., & Gerber, M. (2017). Effects of a physical education-based coping training on adolescents' coping skills, stress perceptions and quality of sleep. *Physical Education and Sport Pedagogy, 22*(3), 213–230. doi:10.1080/17408989.2016.1176130
Lang, D. (2012). Acupuncture for cancer pain in adults. *International Journal of Evidence-Based Healthcare, 10*(1), 86. doi:10.1111/j.1744-1609.2012.00257.x
Lang, E. V., Benotsch, E. G., Fick, L. J., Lutgendorf, S., Berbaum, M. L., Berbaum, K. S., & Spiegel, D. (2000). Adjunctive non-pharmacological analgesia for invasive medical procedures: A randomised trial. *Lancet, 355*(9214),1486–1490.
Lang, F. R., & Carstensen, L. L. (1994). Close emotional relationships in late life: Further support for proactive aging in the social domain. *Psychology and Aging, 9*, 315–324.
Lang, F. R., Staudinger, U. M., & Carstensen, L. L. (1998). Perspectives on socioemotional selectivity in late life: How

personality and social context do (and do not) make a difference. *Journals of Gerontology, 53B*, P21–P30.
Langens, T. A., & Schûler, J. (2007) Effects of written emotional expression: The role of positive expectancies. *Health Psychology 26*(2), 174–182. doi:10.1037/0278-6133.26.2.174
Langer, E. J., & Rodin, J. (1976). The effects of choice and enhanced personal responsibility for the aged: A field experiment in an institutional setting. *Journal of Personality and Social Psychology, 34*, 191–198.
Lansford, J. E., Sherman, A. M., & Antonucci, T. C. (1998). Satisfaction with social networks: An examination of socioemotional selectivity theory across cohorts. *Psychology and Aging, 13*, 544–552.
Larson, R., & Asmussen, L. (1991). Anger, worry, and hurt in early adolescence: An enlarging world of negative emotions. In M. E. Colten & S. Gore (Eds.), *Adolescent stress: Causes and consequences—social institutions and social change* (pp. 21–41). Hawthorne, NY: Aldine de Gruyter.
Larsson, M. L., Frisk, L., Hallstrom, J., Kiviloog, J., & Lundback, B. (2001). Environmental tobacco smoke exposure during childhood is associated with increased prevalence of asthma in adults. *Chest, 120*, 711–718.
Lathia, N., Sandstrom, G. M., Mascolo, C., & Rentfrow, P. J. (2017). Happier people live more active lives: Using smartphones to link happiness and physical activity. *PLoS One, 12*(1), 13. doi:10.1371/journal.pone.0160589
Lauby-Secretan, B., Scoccianti, C., Loomis, D., Grosse, Y., Bianchini, F., & Straif, K. (2016). Body fatness and cancer: Viewpoint of the IARC working group. *New England Journal of Medicine, 375*(8), 794–798.
Laumann, E. O., Gagnon, J. H., Michael, R. T., & Michaels, S. (1994). *The social organization of sexuality: Sexual practices in the United States*. Chicago, IL: University of Chicago Press.
Laursen, B. (1996). Closeness and conflict in adolescent peer relationships: Interdependence with friends and romantic partners. In W. M. Bukowski, A. F. Newcomb, & W. W. Hartup (Eds.), *The company they keep: Friendship in childhood and adolescence. Cambridge studies in social and emotional development* (pp. 186–210). New York, NY: Cambridge University Press.
Lautenbacher, S., & Strian, F. (1991). Sex differences in pain and thermal sensitivity. *Perception and Psychophysics, 50*, 179–183.
Lautenbacher, S., Peters, J. H., Heesen, M., Scheel, J., & Kunz, M. (2017). Age changes in pain perception: A systematic-review and meta-analysis of age effects on pain and tolerance thresholds. *Neuroscience and Biobehavioral Reviews, 75*, 104–113. doi:10.1016/j.neubiorev.2017.01.039
Lauver, L. S. (2008). Parenting foster children with chronic illness and complex medical needs. *Journal of Family Nursing, 14*, 74–96.
Lawlis, G. F., Achterberg, J., Kenner, L., & Kopetz, K. (1984). Ethnic and sex differences in response to clinical and induced pain in chronic spinal pain patients. *Spine, 9*, 751–754.
Lawrence, E. M., Rogers, R. G., & Wadsworth, T. (2015). Happiness and longevity in the United States. *Social Science & Medicine, 145*, 115–119. doi:10.1016/j.socscimed.2015.09.020
Lazarus, R. S. (1966). *Psychological stress and the coping process*. New York, NY: McGraw-Hill.
Lazarus, R. S. (1991). Progress on a cognitive-motivational-relational theory of emotion. *American Psychologist, 46*, 819–834.
Lazarus, R. S. (2000). Toward better research on stress and coping. *American Psychologist, 55*, 665–673.
Lazarus, R. S., & Folkman, S. (1984). *Stress, appraisal, and coping*. New York, NY: Springer.
Lazarus, R. S., & Folkman, S. (1991). *Stress and coping*. New York, NY: Columbia University Press.
Lazarus, R. S., & Launier, R. (1978). Stress-related transactions between person and environment. In L. A. Pervin & M. Lewis (Eds.), *Perspectives in interactional psychology* (pp. 287–322). New York, NY: Plenum.
Leach, J. (1995). Psychological first-aid: A practical aide-memoire. *Aviation, Space, and Environmental Medicine, 66*, 668–674.
Leaf, A., Kang, J., & Xiao, Y. (2008). Fish oil fatty acids as cardiovascular drugs. *Current Vascular Pharmacology, 6*(1), 1–12.
Leandro, M. (2012). Young drivers and speed selection: A model guided by the Theory of Planned Behavior. *Transportation Research: Part F, 15*(3), 219–232. doi:10.1016/j.trf.2011.12.011
LeBarre, S., & Riding-Malon, R. (2017). Posttraumatic growth in breast cancer survivors: Sources of support in rural and non-rural areas. *Journal of Rural Mental Health, 41*(1), 54–65. doi:10.1037/rmh0000069
LeBlanc, A. J. (1993). Examining HIV-related knowledge among adults in the U.S. *Journal of Health and Social Behavior, 34*, 23–36.
Lechi, A. (2017). The obesity paradox: Is it really a paradox? Hypertension. *Eating and Weight Disorders, 22*(1), 43–48. doi:10.1007/s40519-016-0330-4
Lechner, S., Stoelb, B., & Antoni, M. (2008). Group-based therapies for benefit finding in cancer. In *Trauma, recovery, and growth: Positive psychological perspectives on post-traumatic stress* (pp. 207–231). Hoboken, NJ: John Wiley.
Lechtzin, N., Busse, A. M., Smith, M. T., Grossman, S., Nesbit, S., & Diette, G. B. (2010). A randomized trial of nature scenery and sounds versus urban scenery and sounds to reduce pain in adults undergoing bone marrow aspirate and biopsy. *Journal of Alternative & Complementary Medicine, 16*(9), 965–972. doi:10.1089/acm.2009.0531
Ledbetter, D., & Faucett, W. (2008). Issues in genetic testing for ultra-rare diseases: Background and introduction. *Genetics in Medicine, 10*(5), 309–313.
Lederer, D. J., Benn, E. K., Barr, R.G., Wilt, J. S., Reilly, G., Sonett, J. R., . . . Kawat, S. M. (2008). Racial differences in waiting list outcomes in chronic obstructive pulmonary disease. *American Journal of Respiratory and Critical Care Medicine, 177*, 450–454.
Lee, D. B., Kim, E. S., & Neblett, E. W. Jr. (2017). The link between discrimination and telomere length in African American adults. *Health Psychology, 36*(5), 458–467. doi:10.1037/hea0000450
Lee, E., Tripp-Reimer, T., Miller, A., Sadler, G., & Lee, S. (2007). Korean American women's beliefs about breast and cervical cancer and associated symbolic meanings. *Oncology Nursing Forum, 34*(3), 713–720.
Lee, H., Lundquist, M., Ju, E., Luo, X., & Townsend, A. (2011). Colorectal cancer screening disparities in Asian Americans and Pacific Islanders: Which groups are most vulnerable? *Ethnicity & Health, 16*(6), 501–518. doi:10.1080/13557858.2011.575219
Lee, I. M., & Skerrett, P. J. (2001). Physical activity and all-cause mortality: What is the dose-response relation? *Medicine and Science in Sports and Exercise, 33*, S459–S471.
Lee, I. M., Paffenbarger, R. S., & Hsieh, C. C. (1992). Physical activity and risk of prostatic cancer among college alumni. *American Journal of Epidemiology, 135*, 169–179.
Lee, M. C. (2000). Knowledge barriers, and motivators related to cervical cancer screening among Korean-American women: A focus group approach. *Cancer Nursing, 23*, 168–175.
Lee, M. S., Pittler, M. H., & Ernst, E. (2007). External qigong for pain conditions: A systematic review of randomized clinical trials. *Journal of Pain, 8*, 827–831.

Lee, M. S., Pittler, M. H., Shin, B., Kong, J. C., & Ernst, E. (2008). Bee venom acupuncture for musculoskeletal pain: A review. *Journal of Pain, 9*, 289–297.

Lee, S. M. (2005). Physical activity among minority populations: What health promotion practitioners should know—a commentary. *Health Promotion Practice, 6*, 447–452.

Lee, Y., & Styne, D. (2013). Influences on the onset and tempo of puberty in human beings and implications for adolescent psychological development. *Hormones and Behavior, 64*(2), 250–261. doi:10.1016/j.yhbeh.2013.03.014

Lee-Lin, F., Menon, U., Pett, M., Nail, L., Lee, S., & Mooney, K. (2007). Breast cancer beliefs and mammography screening practices among Chinese American immigrants. *Journal of Obstetric, Gynecologic, and Neonatal Nursing, 36*(3), 212–221.

Lee-Lin, F., Pett, M., Menon, U., Lee, S., Nail, L., Mooney, K., & Itano, J. (2007). Cervical cancer beliefs and pap test screening practices among Chinese American immigrants. *Oncology Nursing Forum, 34*(6), 1203–1209.

Leigh, B. C., & Stall, R. (1993). Substance use and risky sexual behavior for exposure to HIV: Issues in methodology, interpretation, and prevention. *American Psychologist, 48*, 1035–1045.

Leigh, B. C., Schafer, J., & Temple, M. T. (1995). Alcohol use and contraception in first sexual experiences. *Journal of Behavioral Medicine, 18*, 81–95.

Lemos-Giraldez, S., & Fidalgo-Aliste, A. M. (1997). Personality dispositions and health-related habits and attitudes: A cross-sectional study. *European Journal of Personality, 11*, 197–209.

Leng, G. (1999). A year of acupuncture in palliative care. *Palliative Medicine, 13*, 163–164.

Lepore, S. J. (1997). Measurement of chronic stressors. In S. Cohen, R. C. Kessler, & L. U. Gordon (Eds.), *Measuring stress: A guide for health and social scientists* (pp. 102–120). London, UK: Oxford University Press.

Lepore, S. J., & Evans, G. W. (1996). Coping with multiple stressors in the environment. In M. Zeidner & N. S. Endler (Eds.), *Handbook of coping: Theory, research, applications* (pp. 350–377). Oxford, UK: John Wiley.

Lerman, C., Caporaso, N. E., Audrain, J., Main., D., Bowman, E. D., Lockshin, B., . . . Shields, P. G. (1999). Evidence suggesting the role of specific genetic factors in cigarette smoking. *Health Psychology, 18*, 14–20.

Leserman, J. (2008). Role of depression, stress, and trauma in HIV disease progression. *Psychosomatic Medicine, 70*(5), 539–545.

Leserman, J., Petitto, J. M., Golden, R. N., Gaynes, B. N., Gu, H., Perkins, D. O., . . . Evans, D. L. (2000). Impact of stressful life events, depression, social support, coping, and cortisol on progression of AIDS. *American Journal of Psychiatry, 157*, 1221–1228.

Lester, B. M., Boukydis, C. F., & Twomey, J. E. (2000). Maternal substance abuse and child outcome. In C. H. Zeahnah (Ed.), *Handbook of infant mental health* (2nd ed., pp. 161–175). New York, NY: Guilford Press.

Lett, H. S., Blumenthal, J. A., Babyak, M. A., Catellier, D. J., Carney, R. M., Berkman, L. F., . . . Schneiderman, N. (2007). Social support and prognosis in patients at increased psychosocial risk recovering from myocardial infarction. *Health Psychology, 26*, 418–427.

Levenson, J. L. (2007). Psychiatric issues in gastrointestinal disorders. *Primary Psychiatry, 14*, 35–38.

Leventhal, E. A., Hansell, S., Diefenbach, M., Leventhal, H., & Glass, D. C. (1996). Negative affect and self-report of physical symptoms: Two longitudinal studies of older adults. *Health Psychology, 15*, 193–199.

Leventhal, H. (1970). Findings and theory in the study of fear communications. In L. Berkowitz (Ed.), *Advances in Experimental Social Psychology* (pp. 111–186). New York, NY: Academic Press.

Leventhal, H., Bodnar-Deren, S., Breland, J. Y., Hash-Concerse, J., Phillips, L. A., Leventhal, E. A., & Cameron, L. D. (2012). Modeling health and illness behavior: The approach of the Commonsense Model. In A. Baum, T. A. Revenson, & J. Singer (Eds.), *Handbook of health psychology* (2e, pp. 3–35). New York, NY: Guilford Press.

Leventhal, H., Diefenbach, M., & Leventhal, E. A. (1992). Illness cognition: Using common sense to understand treatment adherence and affect cognition interactions. *Cognitive Therapy and Research, 16*, 143–163.

Leventhal, H., Musumeci, T. J., & Contrada, R. J. (2007). Current issues and new directions in psychology and health: Theory, translation, and evidence-based practice. *Psychology and Health, 22*(4), 381–386.

Leventhal, H., Weinman, J., Leventhal, E., & Phillips, L. (2008). Health psychology: The search for pathways between behavior and health. *Annual Review of Psychology, 59*(1), 477–505.

Levin, J. S., & Schiller, P. L. (1987). Is there a religious factor in health? *Journal of Religion and Health, 26*, 9–36.

Levitsky, D. A., Halbmaier, C. A., & Mrdjenovic, G. (2004) The freshman weight gain: A model for the study of the epidemic of obesity. *International Journal of Obesity Related Metabolic Disorders, 28*, 1435–1442.

Levitsky, L. L. (2000). Type 2 diabetes in children and adolescents. *Pediatrics, 105*, 671–680.

Levitsky, L. L. (2002). Type 2 diabetes: The new epidemic of childhood. Presented at the American Academy of Pediatrics Annual Meeting, Boston, MA.

Levitt, S., Kempen, P. M., Mor, V., Bernabei, R., Lapane, K. L., & Gambassi, G. (1999). Managing pain in elderly patients. *Journal of the American Medical Association, 281*, 605–606.

Levy, M. E., Phillips, G., Magnus, M., Kuo, I., Beauchamp, G., Emel, L., . . . Mayer, K. (2017). A longitudinal analysis of treatment optimism and HIV acquisition and transmission risk behaviors among black men who have sex with men in HPTN 061. *AIDS and Behavior, 21*(10), 2958–2972. doi:10.1007/s10461-017-1756-z

Levy, R. I. (1996). Essential contrasts: Differences in parental ideas about learners and teaching in Tahiti and Nepal. In S. Harkness & C. M. Super (Eds.), *Parents' cultural belief systems: Their origins, expressions, and consequences* (pp. 123–142). New York, NY: Guilford Press.

Lewinsohn, P. M., Joiner, T. E., & Rohde, P. (2001). Evaluation of cognitive diathesis-stress models in predicting major depressive disorder in adolescents. *Journal of Abnormal Psychology, 110*, 203–215.

Lewis, F. M., Cochrane, B. B., Fletcher, K. A., Zahlis, E. H., Shands, M. E., Gralow, J. R., . . . Schmitz, K. (2008). Helping her heal: A pilot study of an educational counseling intervention for spouses of women with breast cancer. *Psycho-Oncology, 17*(2), 131–137.

Lewis, J., Sim, J., & Barlas, P. (2017). Acupuncture and electro-acupuncture for people diagnosed with subacromial pain syndrome: A multicentre randomized trial. *European Journal of Pain, 21*(6), 1007–1019. doi:10.1002/ejp.1001

Lewis, T. H. (1990). *The medicine men: Oglala Sioux ceremony and healing*. Lincoln, NE: Nebraska Press.

Lewy, A. J., Lefler, B. J., Emens, J. S., & Bauer, V. K. (2006). The circadian basis of winter depression. *Proceedings of the National Academy of Sciences, 103*, 7414–7419.

Li, C., Zhou, L., Lin, G., & Zuo, Z. (2009). Contents of major bioactive flavones in proprietary traditional Chinese medicine products and reference herb of Radix Scutellariae. *Journal of Pharmaceutical & Biomedical Analysis, 50*(3), 298–306. doi:10.1016/j.jpba.2009.04.028

Li, D., Puntillo, K., & Miaskowski, C. (2008). A review of objective pain measures for use with critical care adult patients unable to self-report. *Journal of Pain, 9*, 2–10.

Liabsuetrakul, T., & Oumudee, N. (2011). Effect of health insurance on delivery care utilization and perceived delays and barriers among southern Thai women. *BMC Public Health, 11*, 510. doi:10.1186/1471-2458-11-510

Liang, W., Wang, J. H., Chen, M. Y., Feng, S., Lee, M., Schwartz, M. D., . . . Mandelblatt, J. S. (2008). Developing and validating a measure of Chinese cultural views of health and cancer. *Health Education and Behavior, 35*(3), 361–375.

Liao, Y. (2011). *Traditional Chinese medicine*. Boston, MA: Cambridge University Press.

Licciardone, J. C. (2003). Perceptions of drinking and related findings from the Nationwide Campuses Study. *Journal of American College Health, 51*, 238–246.

Lichstein, K. L., Riedel, B. W., Wilson, N. M., Lester, K. W., & Aguillard, R. N. (2001). Relaxation and sleep compression for late-life insomnia. *Journal of Consulting and Clinical Psychology, 69*, 227–239.

Lichtenstein, A. H., Rasmussen, H., Yu, W. W., Epstein, S. R., Russell, R. M. (2008). Modified MyPyramid for older adults. *Journal of Nutrition, 138*, 5–11.

Lichtenstein, E., & Lopez, K. (1999). Enhancing tobacco control policies in Northwest Indian tribes. In National Cancer Institute (Ed.), *Native outreach: A report to American Indian, Alaska Native, and Native Hawaiian communities* (pp. 57–65). Washington, DC: National Institutes of Health.

Lichtman, S. W., Pisarska, K., Berman, E. R., Pestone, M., Dowling, H., Offenbacher, E . . . Heymsfield, S. B. (1992). Discrepancy between self-reported and actual caloric intake and exercise in obese subjects. *New England Journal of Medicine, 327*, 1893–1898.

Licqurish, S., Phillipson, L., Chiang, P., Walker, J., Walter, F., & Emery, J. (2017). Cancer beliefs in ethnic minority populations: A review and meta-synthesis of qualitative studies. *European Journal of Cancer Care, 26*(1). doi:10.1111/ecc.12556

Liddell, A., & Locker, D. (1997). Gender and age differences in attitudes to dental pain and dental control. *Community Dental and Oral Epidemiology, 25*, 314–318.

Lieber, J. (1994). Conflict and its resolution in preschoolers with and without disabilities. *Early Education and Development, 5*, 5–17.

Liebeskind, J. C., Lewis, J. W., Shavit, Y., & Terman, G. W. (1983). Our natural capacities for pain suppression. *Advances in Pain Research and Therapy, 1*, 8–11.

Liedl, A., Müller, J., Morina, N., Karl, A., Denke, C., & Knaevelsrud, C. (2011). Physical activity within a CBT intervention improves coping with pain in traumatized refugees: Results of a randomized controlled design. *Pain Medicine* (Malden, MA), *12*(2), 234–245. doi:10.1111/j.1526-4637.2010.01040.x

Liewer, L., Mains, D., Lykens, K., & René, A. (2008). Barriers to women's cardiovascular risk knowledge. *Health Care for Women International, 29*(1), 23–38.

Light, E., & Lebowitz, B. (1989). *Alzheimer's disease treatment and family stress: Directions for research*. Rockville, MD: National Institute of Mental Health.

Lilienfeld, S. (2010). Is it unethical to conduct nonevidence-based practice? Paper presented at the annual meeting of the American Psychological Association convention, San Diego, CA.

Lilienfeld, S. O. (2012). Public skepticism of psychology: Why many people perceive the study of human behavior as unscientific. *American Psychologist, 67*(2), 111–129. doi:10.1037/a0023963

Lilienfeld, S. O. (2017). Psychology's replication crisis and the grant culture: Righting the ship. *Perspectives on Psychological Science, 12*(4), 660–664. doi:10.1177/1745691616687745

Lin, F., Shaw, L. J., Berman, D. S., Callister, T. Q., Weinsaft, J. W., Wong, F. J., . . . Min, J. K. (2008). Multidetector computed tomography coronary artery plaque predictors of stress-induced myocardial ischemia by SPECT. *Atherosclerosis, 197*(2), 700–709.

Lin, P. (2012). An evaluation of the effectiveness of relaxation therapy for patients receiving joint replacement surgery. *Journal of Clinical Nursing, 21*(5/6), 601–608. doi:10.1111/j.1365-2702.2010.03406.x

Lin, T., & Lin, M. C. (1978). Service delivery issues in Asian-North American communities. *American Journal of Psychiatry, 135*, 454–456.

Linares, L. O., & Cloitre, M. (2004). Intergenerational links between mothers and children with PTSD spectrum illness. In R. R. Silva (Ed.), *Posttraumatic stress disorders in children and adolescents: Handbook; posttraumatic stress disorders in children and adolescents: Handbook* (pp. 177–201). New York, NY: W. W. Norton.

Lindemann, B. (2001). Receptors and transduction in taste. *Nature, 413*(6852), 219–225. doi.10.1038/35093032

Lindemann, E. (1944). Symptomatology and management of acute grief. *American Journal of Psychiatry, 101*, 141–148.

Linden, W., Lenz, J. W., & Stossel, C. (1996). Alexithymia, defensiveness and cardiovascular reactivity to stress. *Journal of Psychosomatic Research, 41*, 575–583.

Linden, W., Stossel, C., & Maurice, J. (1996). Psychosocial interventions for patients with coronary artery disease: A meta-analysis. *Archives of Internal Medicine, 156*, 745–752.

Linn, S., & Novosat, C. L. (2008). Calories for sale: Food marketing to children in the twenty-first century. *Annals of the American Academy of Political and Social Science, 615*, 133–155.

Lipkus, I. M. (2007). Numeric, verbal, and visual formats of conveying health risks: Suggested best practices and future recommendations. *Medical Decision Making, 27*, 696–713.

Lipton, J. A., & Marbach, J. J. (1984). Ethnicity and the pain experience. *Social Science & Medicine, 19*, 1279–1298.

Littman, A., Bertram, L., Ceballos, R., Ulrich, C., Ramaprasad, J., McGregor, B., & McTiernan, A. (2012). Randomized controlled pilot trial of yoga in overweight and obese breast cancer survivors: Effects on quality of life and anthropometric measures. *Supportive Care in Cancer, 20*(2), 267–277. doi:10.1007/s00520-010-1066-8

Littrell, J. (1996). How psychological states affect the immune system: Implications for interventions in the context of HIV. *Health and Social Work, 21*, 287–295.

Littrell, J. (2008). The mind-body connection: Not just a theory anymore. *Social Work in Health Care, 46*(4), 17–37.

Litwak, E. (1985). *Helping the elderly: The complementary roles of informal networks and formal systems*. New York, NY: Guilford Press.

Liu, C., & Li, H. (2018). Stressors and stressor appraisals: The moderating effect of task efficacy. *Journal of Business and Psychology, 33*(1), 141–154. doi:10.1007/s10869-016-9483-4

Liu, J. J., McErlean, R. A., & Dadds, M. R. (2012). Are we there yet? The clinical potential of intranasal oxytocin in psychiatry. *Current Psychiatry Reviews, 8*(1), 37–48.

Liu, L., Duan, J., Tang, Y., Guo, J., Yang, N., Ma, H., & Shi, X. (2012). Taoren–Honghua herb pair and its main components promoting blood circulation through influencing on hemorheology, plasma coagulation and platelet aggregation. *Journal of Ethnopharmacology, 139*(2), 381–387. doi:10.1016/j.jep.2011.11.016

Liu, X., Gao, H., Li, B., Cheng, M., Ma, Y., Zhang, Z., . . . Wang, Min. (2007). Pulse wave velocity as a marker of arteriosclerosis and its comorbidities in Chinese patients. *Hypertension Research* [Japan], *30*(3), 237–242.

Livingston, E. H. (2007). Obesity, mortality, and bariatric surgery death rates. *Journal of the American Medical Association, 298*, 2406–2408.

Llabre, M. M., Klein, B. R., Saab, P. G., McCalla, J. B., & Schneiderman, N. (1998). Classification of individual differences in cardiovascualr responsivity: The contribution of reactor type controlling for race and gender. *International Journal of Behavioral Medicine, 5*, 213–229.

Llorca, P. (2008). Monitoring patients to improve physical health and treatment outcome. *European Neuropsychopharmacology, 18*, S140–S145.

Lobel, M., & Mahaffey, B. L. (2019). Mental health and emotional distress during pregnancy. In T. A. Revenson & R. A. R. Gurung (Eds.), *Handbook of health psychology* (3e). New York, NY: Routledge.

Lobell, M., Bay, R. C., Rhoads, K. V., & Keske, B. (1998). Barriers to cancer screening in Mexican-American women. *Mayo Clinic Proceedings, 73*, 301–308.

Lobell, M., Yali, A. M., Zhu, W., & DeVincent, C. (1998). Emotional reactions to the stress of high-risk pregnancy: The role of optimism and coping [Abstract]. *Annals of Behavioral Medicine, 20*, 29.

Locker, D., Shapiro, D., & Liddell, A. (1997). Overlap between dental anxiety and blood-injury fears: Psychological characteristics and response to dental treatment. *Behavior Research and Therapy, 35*, 585–590.

Loken, E., & Gelman, A. (2017). Measurement error and the replication crisis. *Science, 355*(6325), 584–585. doi:10.1126/science.aal3618

Lolak, S., Connors, G. L., Sheridan, M. J., & Wise, T. N. (2008). Effects of progressive muscle relaxation training on anxiety and depression in patients enrolled in an outpatient pulmonary rehabilitation program. *Psychotherapy and Psychosomatics, 77*, 119–125.

Long, E., Ponder, M., & Bernard, S. (2017). Knowledge, attitudes, and beliefs related to hypertension and hyperlipidemia self-management among African-American men living in the southeastern United States. *Patient Education and Counseling, 100*(5), 1000–1006. doi:10.1016/j.pec.2016.12.011

Longnecker, M. P., Gerhardsson de Verdier, M., Frumkin, H., & Carpenter, C. (1995). A case-control study of physical activity in relation to risk of cancer of the right colon and rectum in men. *International Journal of Epidemiology, 24*, 42–50.

Looks for Buffalo Hand, F. (1998). *Learning journey on the Red Road.* Toronto, ON: Learning Journey Communications.

Lopez, C., Antoni, M., Fekete, E., & Penedo, F. (2012). Ethnic Identity and Perceived Stress in HIV+ Minority Women: The Role of Coping Self-Efficacy and Social Support. *International Journal of Behavioral Medicine, 19*(1), 23–28. doi:10.1007/s12529-010-9121-x

Lopez, R. A. (2005). Use of alternative folk medicine by Mexican American women. *Journal of Immigrant Health, 7*, 23–31.

López-Roig, S., & Pastor, M. (2016). Cultural adaptation of measures. In Y. Benyamini, M. Johnston, & E. C. Karademas (Eds.), *Assessment in health psychology; assessment in health psychology* (pp. 265–277). Boston, MA: Hogrefe.

Loprinzi, P. D., Cardinal, B. J., Winters-Stone, K., Smit, E., & Loprinzi, C. L. (2012). Physical activity and the risk of breast cancer recurrence: A literature review. *Oncology Nursing Forum, 39*(3), 269–274.

Lorenz, K. (1935). The companion in the bird's world: The fellow-member of the species as releasing factor of social behavior. *Journal für Ornithologie Beiblatt, 83*, 137–213.

Loue, S., Lane, S. D., Lloyd, L. S., & Loh, L. (1999). Integrating Buddhism and HIV prevention in U.S. Southeast Asian communities. *Journal of Health Care for the Poor and Underserved, 10*, 100–121.

Lovejoy, T., & Fowler, D. (2019). Designing and evaluating health psychology interventions. In T. A. Revenson & R. A. R. Gurung (Eds.), *Handbook of health psychology* (3e). New York, NY: Routledge.

Lowe, S. R., Quinn, J. W., Richards, C. A., Pothen, J., Rundle, A., Galea, S., . . . Bradley, B. (2016). Childhood trauma and neighborhood-level crime interact in predicting adult posttraumatic stress and major depression symptoms. *Child Abuse & Neglect, 51*, 212–222. doi:10.1016/j.chiabu.2015.10.007

Lubin, J. H., Richter, B. S., & Blot, W. J. (1984). Lung cancer risk with cigar and pipe use. *Journal of the National Cancer Institute, 73*, 377–381.

Lucas, T., Michalopoulou, G., Falzarano, P., Menon, S., & Cunningham, W. (2008). Health-care provider cultural competency: Development and initial validation of a patient report measure. *Health Psychology, 27*, 185–193.

Lückemann, L., Unteroberdörster, M., Kirchhof, J., Schedlowski, M., & Hadamitzky, M. (2017). Applications and limitations of behaviorally conditioned immunopharmacological responses. *Neurobiology of Learning and Memory, 142*, 91–98. doi:10.1016/j.nlm.2017.02.012

Luckow, A., Reifman, A., & McIntosh, D. N. (1998). Gender differences in coping: A meta-analysis. Poster session presented at the 106th Annual Convention of the American Psychological Association, San Francisco, CA.

Luo, Y., Xu, J., Granberg, E., & Wentworth, W. M. (2012). A Longitudinal study of social status, perceived discrimination, and physical and emotional health among older adults. *Research on Aging, 34*(3), 275–301. doi:10.1177/0164027511426151

Luque, J. S., Castañeda, H., Tyson, D., Vargas, N., Proctor, S., & Meade, C. D. (2010). HPV awareness among Latina immigrants and Anglo-American women in the southern United States: Cultural models of cervical cancer risk factors and beliefs. *NAPA Bulletin, 34*(1), 84–104. doi:10.1111/j.1556-

Lurquin J. H., Michaelson L. E., Barker J. E., Gustavson D. E., von Bastian C. C., Carruth N. P., & Miyake, A. (2016). No evidence of the ego-depletion effect across task characteristics and individual differences: A pre-registered study. *PLoS One, 11*, e0147770. doi:10.1371/journal.pone.0147770

Lurquin, J. H., & Miyake, A. (2017). Challenges to ego-depletion research go beyond the replication crisis: A need for tackling the conceptual crisis. *Frontiers in Psychology, 8*, 568. doi:10.3389/FPSYG.2017.00568

Luszczynska, A., & Hagger, M. (2016). Health behavior. In Y. Benyamini, M. Johnston, & E. C. Karademas (Eds.), *Assessment in health psychology* (pp. 60–72). Boston, MA: Hogrefe.

Luszczynska, A., Kruk, M., & Boberska, M. (2019). Measurement in health psychology research. In T. A. Revenson & R. A. R. Gurung (Eds.), *Handbook of health psychology* (3e). New York, NY: Routledge.

Lutgendorf, S., Klimas, N. G., Antoni, M., Brickman, A., & Fletcher, M. A. (1995). Relationships of cognitive difficulties to immune measures, depression and illness burden in chronic fatigue syndrome. *Journal of Chronic Fatigue Syndrome, 1*, 23–41.

Lutz, D. J., & Sternberg, R. J. (1999). Cognitive development. In M. H. Bornstein & M. E. Lamb (Eds.), *Developmental psychology: An advanced textbook* (4e, pp. 275–311). Mahwah, NJ: Erlbaum.

Lynch, A. M., Kashikar-Zuck, S., Goldschneider, K. R., & Jones, B. A. (2007). Sex and age differences in coping styles among children with chronic pain. *Journal of Pain and Symptom Management, 33*, 208–216.

Lynn, J. (2001). Serving patients who may die soon and their families: The role of hospice and other services. *Journal of the American Medical Association, 285*, 925–932.

Lyon, M. E., Garvie, P. A., Kao, E., Briggs, L., He, J., Malow, R., & . . . McCarter, R. (2011). Spirituality in HIV-infected adolescents and their families: FAmily CEntered (FACE) advance care planning and medication adherence. *Journal of Adolescent Health, 48*(6), 633–636. doi:10.1016/j.jadohealth.2010.09.006

Lyssenko, V. (2004). The human body composition in statics and dynamics: Ayurveda and the philosophical schools of Vaisesika and Samkhya. *Journal of Indian Philosophy, 32*, 31–56.

Maack, D. J., Buchanan, E., & Young, J. (2015). Development and psychometric investigation of an inventory to assess fight, flight, freeze tendencies: The fight, flight, freeze questionnaire. *Cognitive Behaviour Therapy, 44*(2), 117–127. doi:10.1080/16506073.2014.972443

Maani, C., Hoffman, H., Morrow, M., Maiers, A., Gaylord, K., McGhee, L., & DeSocio, P. (2011). Virtual reality pain control during burn wound debridement of combat-related burn injuries using robot-like arm mounted VR goggles. *Journal of Trauma, 71*(1 Suppl), S125–S130.

Macario, A., Richmond, C., Auster, M., & Pergolizzi, J. V. (2008). Treatment of 94 outpatients with chronic discogenic low back pain with the DRX9000: A retrospective chart review. *Pain Practice, 8*, 11–17.

Macciò, A., Madeddu, C., Gramignano, G., Mulas, C., Floris, C., Sanna, E., & . . . Mantovani, G. (2012). A randomized phase III clinical trial of a combined treatment for cachexia in patients with gynecological cancers: Evaluating the impact on metabolic and inflammatory profiles and quality of life. *Gynecologic Oncology, 124*(3), 417–425. doi:10.1016/j.ygyno.2011.12.435

MacDonald, R. A., Mitchell, L. A., Dillon, T., Serpell, M. G., Davies, J. B., & Ashley, E. A. (2003). An empirical investigations of the anxiolytic and pain reducing effects of music. *Psychology of Music, 31*, 187–203.

Macintyre, S. (1997). The Black report and beyond: What are the issues? *Social Science and Medicine, 44*, 723–745.

Macintyre, S., Hunt, K., & Sweeting, H. (1996). Gender differences in health: Are things really as simple as they seem? *Social Science and Medicine, 42*, 617–624.

Mackay, C., Cox, T., Burrows, G., & Lazzerini, T. (1978). An inventory for the measurement of self-reported stress and arousal. *British Journal of Social and Clinical Psychology, 17*(3), 283–284.

Mackenzie, C. S., Reynolds, K., Cairney, J., Streiner, D. L., & Sareen, J. (2012). Disorder-specific mental health service use for mood and anxiety disorders: Associations with age, sex, and psychiatric comorbidity. *Depression & Anxiety (1091-4269), 29*(3), 234–242. doi:10.1002/da.20911

MacKenzie, M. J., Kotch, J. B., Lee, L., Augsberger, A., & Hutto, N. (2011). A cumulative ecological–transactional risk model of child maltreatment and behavioral outcomes: Reconceptualizing early maltreatment report as risk factor. *Children & Youth Services Review, 33*(11), 2392–2398. doi:10.1016/j.childyouth.2011.08.030

MacKinnon, D. P. (2008). *Introduction to statistical mediation analysis*. Mahwah, NJ: Erlbaum.

MacKinnon, D. P., & Luecken, L. J. (2008). How and for whom? Mediation and moderation in health psychology. *Health Psychology, 27*, S99–S100.

Maddi, S. R. (2012). Resilience and consumer behavior for higher quality of life. In D. Mick, S. Pettigrew, C. Pechmann, J. L. Ozanne, D. Mick, S. Pettigrew, . . . J. L. Ozanne (Eds.), *Transformative consumer research for personal and collective well-being* (pp. 647–662). New York, NY: Routledge/Taylor & Francis Group.

Maddi, S. R., & Kobasa, S. C. (1991). The development of hardiness. In A. Monat & R. S. Lazarus (Eds.), *Stress and coping: An anthology* (3e, pp. 245–257). New York, NY: Columbia University Press.

Madon, S., Guyll, M., Buller, A. A., Scherr, K. C., Willard, J., & Spoth, R. (2008). *Journal of Personality and Social Psychology, 95*(2), 369–384. doi:10.1037/0022-3514.95.2.369

Madrigal, L., Gill, D. L, & Willse, J. T. (2017). Gender and the relationships among mental toughness, hardiness, optimism and coping in collegiate athletics: A structural equation modeling approach. *Journal of Sports Behavior, 40*(1), 68–86.

Madsen, W. (1955). Shamanism in Mexico. *Southwestern Journal of Anthropology, 3*, 48–57.

Maes, S., Leventhal, H., & de Ridder, D. T. D. (1996). Coping with chronic diseases. In M. Zeidner & N. S. Endler (Eds.). *Handbook of coping: Theory, research, applications* (pp. 221–251). Oxford, UK: John Wiley.

Magelssen, M., Supphellen, M., Nortvedt, P., & Materstvedt, L. J. (2016). Attitudes towards assisted dying are influenced by question wording and order: A survey experiment. *BMC Medical Ethics, 17*: 24. doi:10.1186/s12910-016-0107-3

Magill, L. (2001). The use of music therapy to address the suffering in advanced cancer pain. *Journal of Palliative Care, 17*, 167–172.

Magnano, P., Paolillo, A., Platania, S., & Santisi, G. (2017). Courage as a potential mediator between personality and coping. *Personality and Individual Differences, 111*, 13–18. doi:10.1016/j.paid.2017.01.047

Magnus, M. (2004). Prostate cancer knowledge among multiethnic black men. *Journal of the National Medical Association, 96*(5), 650–656.

Mah, B. L. (2016). Oxytocin, postnatal depression, and parenting: A systematic review. *Harvard Review of Psychiatry, 24*(1), 1–13. doi:10.1097/HRP.0000000000000093

Mahbub-E-Sobhani, Haque, N., Salma, U., & Ahmed, A. (2011). Immune modulation in response to stress and relaxation. *Pakistan Journal of Biological Sciences, 14*(6), 363–374.

Mahler, H. I., & Kulik, J. A. (1991). Health care involvement preferences and social-emotional recovery of male coronary-artery-bypass patients. *Health Psychology, 10*, 399–408.

Mailis-Gagnon, A., Yegneswaran, B., Nicholson, K., Lakha, S., Papagapiou, M., Steiman, A. J . . . Zurowski, M. (2007). Ethnocultural and sex characteristics of patients attending a tertiary care pain clinic in Toronto, ON, Canada. *Pain Research and Management, 12*, 100–106.

Maisto, S. A., Carey, K. B., & Bradizza, C. M. (1999). Social learning theory. In K. E. Leonard & H. T. Blane (Eds.), *Psychological theories of drinking and alcoholism. The Guilford substance abuse series* (2nd ed., pp. 106–163). New York, NY: Guilford Press.

Majuri, J., Joutsa, J., Johansson, J., Voon, V., Alakurtti, K., Parkkola, R., . . . Kaasinen, V. (2017). Dopamine and opioid neurotransmission in behavioral addictions: A comparative PET study in pathological gambling and binge eating. *Neuropsychopharmacology, 42*(5), 1169–1177. doi:10.1038/npp.2016.265

Makoae, L. N., Greeff, M., Phetlhu, R. D., Uys, L. R., Naidoo, J. R., Kohi, T. W., . . . Holzemer, W. L. (2008). Coping with HIV-related stigma in five African countries. *Journal of the Association of Nurses in AIDS Care, 19*(2), 137–146.

Malenbaum, S., Keefe, F. J., de C. Williams, A. C., Ulrich, R., & Somers, T. J. (2008). Pain in its environmental context: Implications for designing environments to enhance pain control. *Pain, 134*, 241–244.

Malinen, K., Rönkä, A., Sevón, E., & Schoebi, D. (2017). The difficulty of being a professional, a parent, and a spouse on the same day: Daily spillover of workplace interactions on parenting, and the role of spousal support. *Journal of Prevention & Intervention in the Community, 45*(3), 156–167. doi:10.1080/10852352.2016.1198121

Manatū Hauora (Ministry of Health, New Zealand). (2012). Tatau Kura Tangata: Health of older Māori chart book 2011: Overview Spinning Wheel. http://www.health.govt.nz/publication/tatau-kura-tangata-health-older-maori-chart-book-2011-overview-spinning-wheel

Mandel, R., & Nicol, C. J. (2017). Re-direction of maternal behavior in dairy cows. *Applied Animal Behaviour Science*, doi:10.1016/j.applanim.2017.06.001

Mann, T. (2015). *Secrets from the eating lab: The science of weight loss, the myth of willpower, and why you should never diet again.* New York, NY: Harper Collins.

Mann, T., Nolen-Hoeksema, S., Huang, K., Burgard, D., Wright, A., & Hanson, K. (1997). Are two interventions worse than none? Joint primary and secondary prevention of eating disorders in college females. *Health Psychology, 16*, 215–225.

Mann, T., Tomiyama, A.J., Westling, E., Lew, A., Samuels, B., & Chatman, J. (2007). Medicare's search for effective obesity treatments: Diets are not the answer. *American Psychologist, 62*, 220–233.

Manne, S., & Badr, H. (2010). Intimacy processes and psychological distress among couples coping with head and neck or lung cancers. *Psycho-Oncology, 19*(9), 941–954. doi:10.1002/pon.1645

Manolio, T. A., Arnold, A. A., Post, W., Bertoni, A. G., Schreiner, P. J., Sacco, R. L., . . . Szklo, M. (2008). Ethnic differences in the relationship of carotid atherosclerosis to coronary calcification: The Multi-Ethnic Study of Atherosclerosis. *Atherosclerosis, 197*(1), 132–138.

Manson, J. E., Hsia, J., Johnson, K. C., Rossouw, J. E., Assaf, A. R., Lasser, N. L . . . Cushman, M. D. (2003). Estrogen plus progestin and the risk of coronary heart disease. *New England Journal of Medicine, 349*, 523–534.

Manson, J. E., Willett, W. C., Stampfer, M. J., Colditz, G. A., Hunter, D. J., Hankinson, S. E., . . . Speizer, F. E. (1995). Body weight and mortality among women. *New England Journal of Medicine, 333*, 677–685.

Manson, S. M., Shore, J. H., Baron, A. E., Ackerson, L., & Neligh, G. (1992). Alcohol abuse and dependence among American Indians. In J. E. Helzer & G. J. Canino (Eds.), *Alcoholism in North America, Europe, and Asia* (pp. 113–130). London, UK: Oxford University Press.

Manyam, B. V. (2004). Diabetes mellitus, ayurveda, and yoga. *Journal of Alternative and Complementary Medicine, 10*, 223–225.

Marcus, A. (2008). Proposed guidelines for workers' comp patients roil pain specialists. ACOEM recommendations blasted as "dogmatic," Pandering to insurance companies. *Pain Medicine News, 6*(1).

Marcus, B. H. (1993). Binge eating in obesity. In C. G. Fairburn & G. T. Wilson (Eds.), *Binge eating: Nature, asssessment, and treatment* (pp. 77–96). New York, NY: Guilford Press.

Marcus, B. H., Dubbert, P. M., Forsyth, L. H., McKenzie, T. L., Stone, E. K., Dunn, A. L., & Blair, S. N. (2000). Physical activity behavior change: Issues in adoption and maintenance. *Health Psychology, 19(Suppl 1)*, 32–41.

Marcus, D. A., Nash, J. M., & Turk, D. C. (1994). Diagnosing recurring headaches: HIS criteria and beyond. *Headache, 34*, 329–336.

Margolin, A., Avants, S. K., Kleber, H. D. (1998). Investigating alternative medicine therapies in randomized controlled trials. *Journal of the American Medical Association, 280*, 1626–1628.

Margolin, A., Kleber, H. D., Avants, S. K., Konefal, J., Gawin, F., Stark, E., . . . Vaughan, R. (2002). Acupuncture for the treatment of cocaine addiction: A randomized controlled trial. *Journal of the American Medical Association, 287*, 55–63.

Marin, G., Marin, B. V., Perez-Stable, E. J., Sabogal, F., & Otero-Sabogal, R. (1990). Changes in information as a function of a culturally appropriate smoking cessation community intervention for Hispanics. *American Journal of Community Psychology, 17*, 847–864.

Marinelli, R. D., & Plummer, O. K. (1999). Healthy aging: Beyond exercise. *Activities, Adaptation and Aging, 23*, 1–11.

Marini, S., Morotti, A., Ayres, A. M., Crawford, K., Kourkoulis, C. E., Lena, U. K., . . . Anderson, C. D. (2017). Sex differences in intracerebral hemorrhage expansion and mortality. *Journal of the Neurological Sciences, 379*, 112–116. doi:10.1016/j.jns.2017.05.057

Markel, H. (2015, March). In 1850, Ignaz Semmelweis saved lives with three words: Wash your hands. PBS. Retrieved from https://www.pbs.org/newshour/health/ignaz-semmelweis-doctor-prescribed-hand-washing

Markey, C. N. (2004). Culture and the development of eating disorders: A tripartite model. *Eating Disorders: Journal of Treatment & Prevention, 12*, 139–156.

Markey, C. N., Ericksen, A. J., Markey, P. M., & Tinsley, B. J. (2001). Personality and family determinants of preadolescents' participation in health-compromising and health-promoting behaviors. *Adolescent and Family Health, 2*, 83–90.

Markey, C. N., Markey, P. M., Ericksen, A. J., & Tinsley, B. J. (2006). Children's behavioral patterns, the Five-Factor model of personality, and risk behaviors. *Personality and Individual Differences, 41*, 1503–1513.

Markey, M. A., Vander Wal, J. S., Gibbons, J. L. (2009). Culture and eating disorders. In S. Eshun R. A. R. Gurung (Eds.), *Sociocultural factors influencing mental health.* Malden, MA: Blackwell-Wiley.

Marks, D. F. (1996). Health psychology in context. *Journal of Health Psychology, 1*, 7–21.

Marks, D. F. (1998). Addiction, smoking and health: Developing policy-based interventions. *Psychology, Health and Medicine, 3*, 97–111.

Markus, H. R., & Kitayama, S. (1991). Culture and the self: Implications for cognition, emotion, and motivation. *Psychological Review, 98*, 224–253.

Marlatt, G. A., & George, W. H. (1990). Relapse prevention and the maintenance of optimal health. In S. A. Shumaker, E. B. Schron, & J. K. Ockene (Eds.), *The handbook of health behavior change* (pp. 44–63). New York, NY: Springer.

Marlon, P. M. (2012). Alcohol-induced memory blackouts as an indicator of injury risk among college drinkers. *Injury Prevention, 18*(1), 44–49.

Marmot, M. (1994). Work and other factors influencing coronary health and sickness absence. *Work and Stress, 8*, 191–201.

Marmot, M. G., Stansfeld, S. Stansfeld, S., Patel, C., North, F., Head, J., . . . Davey Smith, G. (1991). Health inequalities among British civil servants: The Whitehall II study. *The Lancet, 337*, 1387–1393.

Marsdin, E., Noble, J. G., Reynard, J. M., & Turney, B. W. (2012). Audiovisual distraction reduces pain perception during shockwave lithotripsy. *Journal of Endourology, 26*(5), 531–534. doi:10.1089/end.2011.0430

Marsella, A. J., & Christopher, M. A. (2004). Ethnocultural considerations in disasters: An overview of research, issues, and directions. *Psychiatric Clinics of North America, 27*, 521–539.

Marshall, G., Agarwal, S., Lloyd, C., Cohen, L., Henninger, E., & Morris, G. (1998). Cytokine dysregulation associated with exam stress in healthy medical students. *Brain Behavior and Immunology, 12*, 297–307.

Marshall, R. D., Bryant, R. A., Amsel, L., Suh, E. J., Cook, J. M., Neria, Y. (2007). The psychology of ongoing threat: Relative risk appraisal, the September 11 attacks, and terrorism-related fears. *American Psychologist, 62*, 304–316.

Marsland, A. L., Bachen, E. A., & Cohen, S. (2012). Stress, immunity, and susceptibility to upper respiratory infectious disease. In A. Baum, T. A. Revenson, & J. Singer (Eds.), *Handbook of health psychology* (2e, pp. 717–738). New York, NY: Guilford.

Martel, F. L., Nevison, C. M., Rayment, F. D., Simpson, M. J. A., & Keverne, E. B. (1993). Opioid receptor blockade reduces maternal affect and social grooming in rhesus monkeys. *Psychoneuroimmunology, 18*, 307–321.

Martin, M. P., Dean, M., Smith, M. W., Winkler, C., Gerrard, B., Michael, N. L., . . . Carrington, M. (1998). Genetic acceleration of AIDS progression by a promoter variant of CCR5. *Science, 282*, 1907–1911.

Martin, N., & Montagne, R. (2017, May, 12). U.S. has the worst rate of maternal deaths in the developed world. National Public Radio, Washington, DC. Retrieved from https://www.npr.org/2017/05/12/528098789/u-s-has-the-worst-rate-of-maternal-deaths-in-the-developed-world

Martin, S., Young, S., Billings, D., & Bross, C. (2007). Health care-based interventions for women who have experienced sexual violence: A review of the literature. *Trauma, Violence and Abuse, 8*(1), 3–18.

Martin, T. L., & Doka, K. J. (2000). *Men don't cry . . . women do: Transcending gender stereotypes of grief.* Oxford, UK: John Wiley.

Martinent, G., & Nicolas, M. (2016). A latent profile transition analysis of coping within competitive situations. *Sport, Exercise, and Performance Psychology, 5*(3), 218–231. doi.10.1037/spy0000062

Martinez, R. G., Chavez, L. R., & Hubbell, F. A. (1997). Purity and passion: Risk and morality in Latina immigrants' and physicians' beliefs about cervical cancer. *Medical Anthropology, 17*, 337–362.

Martinez, R., Taylor, M. J., Calvert, W. J., Hirsch, J. L., & Webster, C. K. (2014). Sanreria as a culturally responsive healing practice. In R. A. R. Gurung (Ed.), *Multicultural Approaches to Health and Wellness in America* (pp. 330–348). Santa Barbara, CA: Praeger.

Martínez-Hernáez, A., Carceller-Maicas, N., DiGiacomo, S. M., & Ariste, S. (2016). Social support and gender differences in coping with depression among emerging adults: A mixed-methods study. *Child and Adolescent Psychiatry and Mental Health, 10*(2). doi:10.1186/s13034-015-0088-x

Martire, L. M., & Helgeson, V. S. (2017). Close relationships and the management of chronic illness: Associations and interventions. *American Psychologist, 72*(6), 601–612. doi:10.1037/amp0000066

Martire, L. M., Schulz, R. (2012). Caregiving and care receiving in later life: Health effects and promising interventions. In A. Baum, T. A. Revenson, & J. Singer (Eds.), *Handbook of health psychology* (2e, pp. 293–307). New York, NY: Guilford.

Mason, J. W. (1971). A re-evaluation of the concept of "non-specificity" in stress theory. *Journal of Psychiatric Research, 8*, 323–333.

Mason, V. L., Skevington, S. M., & Osborn, M. (2008). The quality of life of people in chronic pain: Developing a pain and discomfort module for use with the WHOQOL. *Psychology and Health, 23*, 135–154.

Masters, K. S., France, C. R., & Thorn, B. E. (2009). Enhancing preparation among entry-level clinical health psychologists: Recommendations for "best practices" from the first meeting of the Council of Clinical Health Psychology Training Programs (CCHPTP). *Training and Education in Professional Psychology, 3*(4), 193–201. doi:10.1037/a0016049.

Matarazzo, J. D. (1980). Behavioral health and behavioral medicine: Frontiers for a new health psychology. *American Psychologist, 35*(9), 807–817.

Matarrazo, J., Weiss, S. M., Herd, J. A., Miller, N. E., & Weiss, S. M. (1984). *Behavioral health: A handbook of health enhancement and disease prevention.* New York, NY: Wiley-Interscience.

Maton, K. I. (1989). The stress-buffering role of spiritual support: Cross-sectional and prospective investigations. *Journal for the Scientific Study of Religion, 28*, 310–323.

Matsumoto, D., & Juang, L. (2017). *Culture and psychology* (6e). Belmont, CA: Cengage

Mattar, C., Harharah, L., Su, L., Agarwal, A., Wong, P., & Choolani, M. (2008). Menopause, hormone therapy and cardiovascular and cerebrovascular disease. *Annals of the Academy of Medicine, Singapore, 37*(1), 54–62.

Matterne, U., Diepgen, T. L., & Weisshaar, E. (2011). A longitudinal application of three health behaviour models in the context of skin protection behaviour in individuals with occupational skin disease. *Psychology & Health, 26*(9), 1188–1207. doi:10.1080/08870446.2010.546859

Matthews, K. A. (1992). Myths and realities of the menopause. *Psychosomatic Medicine, 54*, 1–9.

Matthews, K. A., Boylan, J. M., Jakubowski, K. P., Cundiff, J. M., Lee, L., Pardini, D. A., & Jennings, J. R. (2017). Socioeconomic status and parenting during adolescence in relation to ideal cardiovascular health in black and white men. *Health Psychology, 36*(7), 673–681. 10.1037/hea0000491

Matthews, K. A., Raikkonen, K., Sutton-Tyrrell, K., & Kuller, L. H. (2004). Optimistic attitudes protect against progression of carotid atherosclerosis in healthy middle-aged women. *Psychosomatic Medicine, 66*(5), 640–644. doi:10.1097/01.psy.0000139999.99756.a5

Matthews, K. A., Shumaker, S. A., Bowen, D. J., Langer, R. D., Hunt, J. R., Kaplan, R. M., . . . Ritenbaugh, C. (1997). Women's Health Initiative: Why now? What is it? What's new? *American Psychologist, 52*, 101–116.

Mattlin, J. A., Wethington, E., & Kessler, R. C. (1990). Situational determinants of coping and coping effectiveness. *Journal of Health and Social Behavior, 31*, 103–122.

Mau, M. K., Glanz, K., Severino, R., Grove, J. S., Johnson, B., Curb, J. D. (2001). Mediators of lifestyle behavior change in native Hawaiians: Initial findings from the Native Hawaiian Diabetes Intervention program. *Diabetes Care, 24*, 1770–1775.

Maunsell, E., Brisson, J., & Deschenes, L. (1995). Social support and survival among women with breast cancer. *Cancer, 76*, 631–637.

Mauriello, L. M., Ciavatta, M. H., Paiva, A. L., Sherman, K. J., Castle, P. H., Johnson, J. L., & Prochaska, J. M. (2010). Results of a multi-media multiple behavior obesity prevention program for adolescents. *Preventive Medicine, 51*(6), 451–456. doi:10.1016/j.ypmed.2010.08.004

Mauriello, L. M., Gökbayrak, N., Van Marter, D. F., Paiva, A. L., & Prochaska, J. M. (2012). An internet-based computer-tailored intervention to promote responsible drinking: Findings from a pilot test with employed adults. *Alcoholism Treatment Quarterly, 30*(1), 91–108. doi:10.1080/07347324.2012.635528

Mausbach, B. T., von Känel, R., Patterson, T. L., Dimsdale, J. E., Depp, C. A., Aschbacher, K., . . . Grant, I. (l2008). *Health Psychology, 27*, S172–S179.

Maxwell, A. E., Bastani, R., & Warda, U.S. (1998). Mammography utilization and related attitudes among Filipino-American women. *Cancer Epidemiological Biomarkers and Prevention, 6*, 719–726.

Maxwell, S. E., Lau, M. Y., & Howard, G. S. (2015). Is psychology suffering from a replication crisis? What does "failure to replicate" really mean? *American Psychologist, 70*(6), 487–498. doi:10.1037/a0039400

Mayer, P. A., Esplin, B., Burant, C. J., Wilson, B. M., Krall, M. L., Daly, B. J., & Gatliff, J. (2017). In my best interest: Characteristics of completed comprehensive advance directives at a Veterans Affairs medical center. *American Journal of Hospice & Palliative Medicine, 34*(2), 160–165.

Mayer, S. E., & Jencks, C. (1989). Growing up in poor neighborhoods: How much does it matter? *Science 243*, 1441–1445.

Mayes, V. O., & Lacy, B. B. (1989). *Nanise: A Navajo herbal–one hundred plants from the Navajo Reservation*. Tsaile, AZ: Navajo Community College Press.

Mays, V. M., & Cochran, S. D. (1987). Acquired immunodeficiency syndrome and Black Americans: Special psychosocial issues. *Public Health Reports, 102*, 224–231.

Mays, V. M., Cochran, S. D., & Barnes, N. W. (2007). Race, race-based discrimination, and health outcomes among African Americans. *Annual Reviews of Psychology, 58*, 201–225.

Mays, V. M., Maas, R. M., Ricks, J., & Cochran, S. D. (2012). HIV and African American women in the U.S. South: A social determinants approach to population level HIV prevention and intervention efforts. In A. Baum, T. A. Revenson, & J. Singer (Eds.), *Handbook of health psychology* (2e, pp. 771–802). New York, NY: Guilford.

Mays, V. M., So, B. T., Cochran, S. D., Detels, R., Benjamin, R., Allen, E., & Kwon, S. (2002). HIV disease in ethnic minorities: Implications of racial/ethnic differences in disease susceptibility and drug dosage response for HIV infection and treatment. In A. Baum, T. A. Revenson, & J. E. Singer (Eds.), *Handbook of health psychology* (1e, pp. 801–816). Mahwah, NJ: Erlbaum.

Mazure, C. M. (1998). Life stressors as risk factors in depression. *Clinical Psychology: Science and Practice, 5*, 291–313.

McCabe, M. P., & Ricciardelli, L. A. (2003). Sociocultural influences on body image and body changes among adolescent boys and girls. *Journal of Social Psychology, 193*, 5–26.

McCaffery, K., Irwig, L., & Bossuyt, P. (2007). Patient decision aids to support clinical decision making: Evaluating the decision or the outcomes of decision. *Medical Decision Making, 27*, 619–625.

McCain, N. L., Gray, D. P., Elswick, R. K., Robins, J. W., Tuck, I., Walter, J. M., . . . Ketchum, J. M. (2008). A randomized clinical trial of alternative stress management interventions in persons with HIV infection. *Journal of Consulting and Clinical Psychology, 76*(3), 431–441.

McCann, L. I., Immel, K. R., Kadah-Ammeter, T. L., & Adelson, S. K. (2016). The importance and interest of introductory psychology textbook topics: Student opinions at technical college, 2-, and 4-year institutions. *Teaching of Psychology, 43*(3), 215–220. doi.10.1177/0098628316649477

McCaul, K. D., Branstetter, A., Schroeder, D. M., & Glasgow, R. E. (1996). What is the relationship between breast cancer risk and mammography screening? A meta-analytic review. *Health Psychology, 15*, 423–429.

McCauley, J., Kern, D. E., Kolodner, K., Dill, L., & Schroeder, A. F. (1997). Clinical characteristics of women with a history of childhood abuse: Unhealed wounds. *Journal of the American Medical Association, 277*, 1362–1368.

McClintock, M. K. (1998). Whither menstrual synchrony? *Annual Review of Sex Research, 9*, 77–98.

McClure, F. H., Chavez, D. V., Agars, M. D., Peacock, M. J., Matosian, A. (2008). Resilience in sexually abused women: Risk and protective factors. *Journal of Family Violence, 23*, 81–88.

McCormick, M. C. (1985). The contribution of low birth weight to infant mortality and childhood morbidity. *New England Journal of Medicine, 312*, 82–89.

McCormick, M. C., Brooks-Gunn, J., Shorter, T., Holmes, J. H., Wallace, C. Y., & Heagarty, M. C. (1990). Factors associated with smoking in low-income pregnant women: Relationship to birth weight, stressful life events, social support, health behaviors and mental distress. *Journal of Clinical Epidemiology, 43*, 441–448.

McCormick, R. A., Dowd, E. T., Quirk, S., & Zegarra, J. H. (1998). The relationship of NEO-PI performance to coping styles, patterns of use, and triggers for use among substance abusers. *Addictive Behaviors, 23*, 497–507.

McCrae, R. R. (1984). Situational determinants of coping responses: Loss, threat, and challenge. *Journal of Personality and Social Psychology, 46*, 919–928.

McCrae, R. R., & Costa, P. T. (1987). Validation of the five-factor model of personality across instruments and observers. *Journal of Personality and Social Psychology, 52*, 81–90.

McCubbin, H. I., & Patterson, J. M. (1983). The family stress process: The double ABCX model of adjustment and adaptation. *Marriage and Family Review, 6*, 7–37.

McCully, K. S. (2017). Hyperhomocysteinemia, suppressed immunity, and altered oxidative metabolism caused by pathogenic microbes in atherosclerosis and dementia. *Frontiers in Aging Neuroscience, 9*(12). doi:10.3389/fnagi.2017.00324

McDonald, L. M., & Korabik, K. (1991). Sources of stress and ways of coping among male and female managers. *Journal of Social Behavior and Personality. Special Handbook on Job Stress, 6*, 185–198.

McEniery, C., & Cockcroft, J. (2007). Does arterial stiffness predict atherosclerotic coronary events? *Advances in Cardiology, 44*, 160–172.

McEwen, B. S. (1998). Protective and damaging effects of stress mediators. *New England Journal of Medicine, 338*, 171–179.

McEwen, B. S., & Wingfield, J. C. (2003). The concept of allostasis in biology and biomedicine. *Hormones and Behavior, 43*, 2–15.

McEwen, B. S., Biron, C. A., Brunson, K. W., Bulloch, K., Chambers, W. H., Dhabhar, F. S., . . . Weiss, J. M. (1997). The role of adrenocorticoids as modulators of immune function in health and disease: Neural, endocrine, and immune interactions. *Brain Research Reviews, 23*, 79.

McEwen, B., & Lasley, E. (2007). Allostatic load: When protection gives way to damage. In A. Monat, R. S. Lazarus, G. Reevy, A. Monat, R. S. Lazarus, G. Reevy (Eds.), *The Praeger handbook on stress and coping* (pp. 99–109). Westport, CT: Praeger.

McFarland, B., Bigelow, D., Zani, B., Newsom, J., & Kaplan, M. (2002). Complementary and alternative medicine use in Canada and the United States. *American Journal of Public Health, 92*, 1616–1618.

McFarlane, J., Parker, B., & Soeken, K. (1996a). Abuse during pregnancy: Associations with maternal health and infant birth weight. *Nursing Research, 45*, 37–42.

McFarlane, J., Parker, B., & Soeken, K. (1996b). Physical abuse, smoking, and substance use during pregnancy: Prevalence, interrelationships, and effects on birth weight. *Journal of Obstetric, Gynecologic, and Neonatal Nursing, 25*, 313–320.

McGee, R., Williams, S., & Elwood, M. (1994). Depression and the development of cancer: A meta-analysis. *Social Science and Medicine, 38*, 187–192.

McGinnis, J. M., & Foege, W. H. (1993). Actual causes of death in the United States. *Journal of the American Medical Association, 270*, 2207–2213.

McGonigal, J. (2015). *SuperBetter: The power of living gamefully*. New York, NY: Penguin.

McGrath, J. E. (1970). *Social and psychological factors in stress*. Oxford, UK: Holt, Rinehart, & Winston.

McGrath, P. A., & Gillespie, J. (2001). Pain assessment in children and adolescents. In D. C. Turk & R. Melzack (Eds.), *Handbook of pain assessment* (2nd ed.) (pp. 97–118). New York, NY: Guilford.

McGue, M. (1999). Behavioral genetic models of alcoholism and drinking. In K. E. Leonard & H. T. Blane (Eds.), *Psychological theories of drinking and alcoholism* (2nd ed., pp. 372–421). New York, NY: Guilford Press.

McKenna, M. C., Zevon, M. A., Corn, B., & Rounds, J. (1999). Psychosocial factors and the development of breast cancer: A meta-analysis. *Health Psychology, 18*, 520–531.

McKusick, L., Horstman, W., & Coates, T. J. (1985). AIDS and sexual behavior reported by gay men in San Francisco. *American Journal of Public Health, 75*, 493–496.

McLaughlin, K. A., Berglund, P., Gruber, M. J., Kessler, R. C., Sampson, N. A., & Zaslavsky, A. M. (2011). Recovery from PTSD following Hurricane Katrina. *Depression & Anxiety (1091–4269), 28*(6), 439–446. doi:10.1002/da.20790

McLoyd, V. C. (1990). The impact of economic hardship on Black families and children: Psychological distress, parenting, and socioeconomic development. *Child Development, 61*, 311–346.

McNally, R. J. (1997). Implicit and explicit memory for trauma-related information in PTSD. *Annals of the New York Academy of Sciences, 821*, 219–224.

McNicholl, J., & Smith, D. (1997). Host genes and HIV: The role of the chemokine receptor gene CCR5 and its allele (32 CCR5). *Emerging Infectious Diseases, 3*, 261–272.

McPhee, S. J., Bird, J. A., Davis, T., Ha, N. T., Jenkins, C. N. H., & Le, B. (1997). Barriers to breast and cervical cancer screening among Vietnamese American women. *American Journal of Preventive Medicine, 13*, 205–213.

McPhee, S. J., Bird, J. A., Ha, N. T., Jenkins, C. N. H., Fordham, D., & Le, B. (1996). Pathways to early cancer detection for Vietnamese women: Suc khoe la vang! (Health is gold!). *Health Education Quarterly, 23*, S60–S75.

McWhirter, J. E., & Hoffman-Goetz, L. (2016). Application of the health belief model to U.S. magazine text and image coverage of skin cancer and recreational tanning (2000–2012). *Journal of Health Communication, 21*(4), 424–438. doi:10.1080/10810730.2015.1095819

McWilliams, L. A., Cox, B. J., & Enns, M. W. (2003). Use of the Coping Inventory for Stressful Situations in a clinically depressed sample: Factor structure, personality correlates, and prediction of distress. *Journal of Clinical Psychology, 59*, 423–437.

Meagher, M. W., Arnau, R. C., & Rhudy, J. L. (2001). Pain and emotion: Effects of affective picture modulation. *Psychosomatic Medicine, 63*, 79–90.

Meaney, M. J. (2001). Nature, nurture, and the disunity of knowledge. *Annals of the New York Academy of Sciences, 935*, 50–61.

Mechanic, D. (1995). Sociological dimensions of illness behavior. *Social Sciences and Medicine, 41*, 1207–1216.

Meesters, A., Bosch-Meevissen, Y. M. C., Weijzen, C. A. H., Buurman, W. A., Losen, M., Schepers, J., . . . Peters, M. L. (2017). The effect of mindfulness-based stress reduction on wound healing: A preliminary study. *Journal of Behavioral Medicine*. doi:10.1007/s10865-017-9901-8

Meghani, S. H., Byun, E., & Gallagher, R. M. (2012). Time to take stock: A meta-analysis and systematic review of analgesic treatment disparities for pain in the United States. *Pain Medicine, 13*(2), 150–174. doi:10.1111/j.1526-4637.2011.01310.x

Mehl-Medrona, L. (1998). *Coyote medicine: Lessons from Native American healing*. New York, NY: Simon and Schuster.

Mehrotra, N., Gaur, S., & Petrova, A. (2012). Health care practices of the foreign born Asian Indians in the United States. A community based survey. *Journal of Community Health, 37*(2), 328–334. doi:10.1007/s10900-011-9449-4

Mehta, K. M., Fung, K. Z., Kistler, C. E., Chang, A., & Walter, L. (2017). Impact of cognitive impairment on screening mammography use in older U.S. women. *American Journal of Public Health, 100*(10), 1917–1923.

Meichenbaum, D., & Cameron, R. (1983). Stress inoculation training: Toward a general paradigm for training coping skills. In D. Meichenbaum & M. E. Jaremko (Eds.), *Stress reduction and prevention* (pp. 115–154). New York, NY: Plenum Press.

Meier, N. F., & Welch, A. S. (2016). Walking versus biofeedback: A comparison of acute interventions for stressed students. *Anxiety, Stress, & Coping, 29*(5), 463–478. doi:10.1080/10615806.2015.1085514

Meisel, S. R., Kutz, I., Dayan, K. I., Pauzer, H., Chetboun, I., Arbel, Y., & David, D. (1991). Effect of Iraqi missile war on incidence of acute myocardiac infarction and sudden death in Israeli civilians. *The Lancet, 338*, 660–661.

Mellman, T. A. (1997). Psychobiology of sleep disturbances in posttraumatic stress disorder. *Annals of the New York Academy of Sciences, 821*, 142–149.

Mellström, D., & Svanborg, A. (1987). Tobacco smoking—a major cause of sex differences in health. *Comprehensive Gerontology. Section A, Clinical and Laboratory Sciences, 1*(1), 34–39.

Melzack, R. (1975). The McGill Pain Questionnaire: Major properties and scoring methods. *Pain, 1*, 277–299.

Melzack, R. (1999). Pain and stress: A new perspective. In R. J. Gatchel & D. C. Turk (Eds.), *Psychosocial factors in pain: Critical perspectives* (pp. 89–106). New York, NY: Guilford Press.

Melzack, R., & Casey, K. L. (1968). Sensory, motivational, and central control determinants of pain: A new conceptual model. In D. Kenschalo (Ed.), *The skin senses* (pp. 423–443). Springfield, IL: Charles C Thomas.

Melzack, R., & Wall, P. D. (1965). Pain mechanisms: A new theory. *Science, 150*, 971–979.

Meng, X., & D'Arcy, C. (2016). Coping strategies and distress reduction in psychological well-being? A structural equation modelling analysis using a national population sample. *Epidemiology and Psychiatric Sciences, 25*(4), 370–383. doi:10.1017/S2045796015000505

Menozzi, D., Sogari, G., Veneziani, M., Simoni, E., & Mora, C. (2017). Eating novel foods: An application of the theory of planned behaviour to predict the consumption of an insect-based product. *Food Quality and Preference, 59*, 27–34. doi:10.1016/j.foodqual.2017.02.001

Mercer, S. H., Zeigler-Hil, V., Wallace, M., & Hayes, D. M. (2011). Development and initial validation of the Inventory of Microaggressions Against Black Individuals. *Journal of Counseling Psychology, 58*(4), 457–469. doi:10.1037/a0024937

Meredith, H. V. (1973). Somatological development. In B. B. Wolman (Ed.), *Handbook of general psychology*. Englewood Cliffs, NJ: Prentice Hall.

Merikangas, K. R. (1990). The genetic epidemiology of alcoholism. *Psychological Medicine, 20*, 11–22.

Merluzzi, T. V., Philip, E. J., Yang, M., & Heitzmann, C. A. (2016). Matching of received social support with need for support in adjusting to cancer and cancer survivorship. *Psycho-Oncology, 25*(6), 684–690. doi:10.1002/pon.3896

Mermelstein, R. (2019). Weight loss and obesity. In T. A. Revenson & R. A. R. Gurung (Eds.), *Handbook of health psychology* (3e). New York, NY: Routledge.

Mermelstein, R., & Brikmanis, K. (2019). Weight loss and obesity. In T. A. Revenson, & R. A. R. Gurung (Eds.), *Handbook of health psychology* (3e). New York, NY: Routledge.

Merskey, H. M. & Boduk, N. (1994) *Classifications of Chronic Pain*, 2e. Seattle, WA: IASP Press.

Merton, R. K. (2010) The self-fulfilling prophecy. *Antioch Review, 68*(1), 173–190.

Merviel, P., Jovance, O., Naepels, P., Fauvet, R., Cabry-Goubet, R., Gagneur, O., & Gondry, J. (2011). Existe-t-il encore de facteurs de risque de survenue d'un cancer du sein? [Do there still exist risk factors for breast cancer?]. *Gynécologie, Obstétrique & Fertilité, 39*(9), 486–490.

Merz, E. L., Malcarne, V. L., Ko, C. M., Sadler, M., Kwack, L., Varni, J. W., & Sadler, G. (2011). Dyadic concordance among prostate cancer patients and their partners and health-related quality of life: Does it matter? *Psychology & Health, 26*(6), 651–666. doi:10.1080/08870441003721251

Metts, S., Manns, H., & Kuzic, L. (1996). Social support structures and predictors of depression in persons who are seropositive. *Journal of Health Psychology, 1*, 367–382.

Meyer, I. H. (2003). Prejudice, social stress, and mental health in lesbian, gay, and bisexual populations: Conceptual issues and research evidence, *Psychological Bulletin, 129*, 674–697.

Meyer, T. J., & Mark, M. M. (1995). Effects of psychosocial interventions with adult cancer patients: A meta-analysis of randomized experiments. *Health Psychology, 14*, 101–108.

Meyerowitz, B. E., Bull, A. A., & Perez, M. A. (2000). Cancers common in women. In R. M. Eisler & M. Herson (Eds.), *Handbook of gender, culture and health* (pp. 197–225). Mahwah, NJ: Erlbaum.

Meyerowitz, B. E., Richardson, J., Hudson, S., & Leedham, B. (1998). Ethnicity and cancer outcomes: Behavioral and psychosocial considerations. *Psychological Bulletin, 123*, 47–71.

Meyers, L. B., & Vetere, A. (2002). Adult romantic attachment styles and health-related measures. *Psychology, Health, and Medicine, 7*, 175–180.

Meyler, D., Stimpson, J. P., & Peek, M. K. (2007). Health concordance within couples: Asystematic review. *Social Science and Medicine, 64*, 2297–2310.

Mezzetti, M., La Vecchia, C., Decarli, A., Boyle, P., Talamini, R., & Franceschi, S. (1998). Population attributable risk for breast cancer: Diet, nutrition, and physical exercise. *Journal of the National Cancer Institute, 90*, 389–394.

Mian, M., Lauzon, N., Stämpfli, M., Mossman, K., & Ashkar, A. (2008). Impairment of human NK cell cytotoxic activity and cytokine release by cigarette smoke. *Journal of Leukocyte Biology, 83*(3), 774–784.

Miceli, P. J., & Mylod, D. E. (2003). Satisfaction of families using end-of-life care: Current successes and challenges in the hospice industry. *American Journal of Hospice & Palliative Care, 20*, 360–370.

Michel, G. (2007). Daily patterns of symptom reporting in families with adolescent children. *British Journal of Health Psychology, 12*, 245–260.

Michie, S. (2019). Theories of health behavior change. In T. A. Revenson & R. A. R. Gurung (Eds.), *Handbook of health psychology* (3e). New York, NY: Routledge.

Michie, S., Hardeman, W., Fanshawe, T., Prevost, A. T., Taylor, L., & Kinmonth, A. L. (2008). Investigating theoretical explanations for behaviour change: The case study of ProActive. *Psychology and Health, 23*, 25–39.

Michie, S., Marques, M. M., Norris, E., & Johnston, M. (2019). Theories of health behavior change. In T. A. Revenson & R. A. R. Gurung (Eds.), *Handbook of health psychology* (3e). New York, NY: Routledge.

Michie, S., Rothman, A. J., & Sheeran, P. (2007). Current issues and new direction in psychology and health: Advancing the science of behavior change. *Psychology and Health, 22*, 249–253.

Millard, R. W. (1993). Behavioral assessment of pain and behavioral pain management. In R. B. Patt (Ed.), *Cancer Pain* (pp. 85–97). Philadelphia, PA: Lippincott.

Miller, A. M., & Champion, V. L. (1997). Attitudes about breast cancer and mammography: Racial, income, and educational differences. *Women's Health, 26*, 41–63.

Miller, G. E., & Chen, E. (2010). Harsh family climate in early life presages the emergence of a proinflammatory phenotype in adolescence. *Psychological Science (SAGE), 21*(6), 848–856. doi:10.1177/0956797610370161

Miller, G. M., & Cole, S. W. (1998). Social relationships and the progression of human immunodeficiency virus infection: A review of evidence and possible underlying mechanisms. *Annals of Behavioral Medicine, 20*, 181–189.

Miller, J. H. (2010). Evidence-based practice and the future of counseling: The debate revisited. *Counselling Psychology Quarterly, 23*(4), 425–428. doi:10.1080/09515070.2010.526814

Miller, J., Safranski, M., & Heuer, L. (2004). Mexican American use of folk medicine for the treatment of diabetes. *Rural Clinical Quarterly, 1*(3).

Miller, L. C., Bettencourt, B. A., DeBro, S. C., & Hoffman, V. (1993). Negotiating safer sex: Interpersonal dynamics. In J. B. Pryor & G. D. Reeder (Eds.), *The social psychology of HIV infection* (pp. 85–123). Hillsdale, NJ: Erlbaum.

Miller, M. C. (1992). Winnicott unbound: The fiction of Philip Roth and the sharing of potential space. *International Review of Psycho-Analysis, 19*, 445–456.

Miller, M., Marty, M. D., Broadwin, R., Johnson, K. C., Salmon, A. G., Winder, B., & Steinmaus, C. (2007). The association between exposure to environmental tobacco smoke and breast cancer: A view by the California Environmental Protection Agency. *Preventive Medicine, 44*(2), 93–106.

Miller, S. C., Mor, V., Wu, N., Gozalo, P., & Lapane, K. (2002). Does receipt of hospice care in nursing homes improve the management of pain at the end of life? *Journal of the American Geriatrics Society, 50*, 507–515.

Miller, S. M. (1987). Monitoring and blunting: Validation of a questionnaire to assess styles of information seeking under threat. *Journal of Personality and Social Psychology, 52*, 345–353.

Miller, S. M., & Diefenbach, M. A. (1998). The Cognitive-Social Health Information-Processing (C-SHIP) model: A theoretical framework for research in behavioral oncology. In D. S. Krantz & A. Baum (Eds.), *Technology and methods in behavioral medicine* (pp. 219–244). Mahwah, NJ: Erlbaum.

Miller, S. M., Shoda, Y., & Hurley, K. (1996). Applying cognitive-social theory to health-protective behavior: Breast self-examination in cancer screening. *Psychological Bulletin, 119,* 70–94.

Miller, W. R., & Thoresen, C. E. (2003). Spirituality, religion, and health: An emerging research field. *American Psychology, 58,* 24–35.

Millington, B. (2012). Use it or lose it: Ageing and the politics of brain training. *Leisure Studies, 31*(4), 429–446. doi:10.1080/02614367.2011.589865

Mills, P. J., Berry, C. C., Dimsdale, J. E., & Nelesen, R. A. (1993). Temporal stability of task-induced cardiovascular, adrenergic, and psychological responses: The effects of race and hypertension. *Psychophysiology, 30,* 187–204.

Milne, S., Orbell, S., & Sheeran, P. (2002) Combining motivational and volitional interventions to promote exercise participation: Protection motivation theory and implementation intentions. *British Journal of Healthy Psychology* 7(pt 2), 163–184.

Minger, D. (2013). *Death by food pyramid: How shoddy science, sketchy politics, and shady special interests ruined your health . . . and how to reclaim it!.* Malibu, CA: Primal Blueprint.

Minneboo, J., Lachman, S., Snaterse, M., Jorstad, H., ter Riet, G., Boekholdt, M., . . . Peters, R. (2017). Community-based lifestyle intervention in patients with coronary arter disease: The RESPONSE-2 trial. *Journal of the American College of Cardiology, 70,* 318–327.

Minor, D., Wofford, M., & Jones, D. (2008). Racial and ethnic differences in hypertension. *Current Atherosclerosis Reports, 10*(2), 121–127.

Mischel, W. (1984). Convergences and challenges in the search for consistency. *American Psychologist, 39,* 351–364.

Mishra, S. I., Luce-Aoelua, P., & Hubbell, F. A. (1998). Identifying the cancer control needs of American Samoans. *Asian American and Pacific Islander Journal of Health, 6,* 277–285.

Missoni, E., Kern, J., & Missoni, I. (2012). Physical inactivity changes in Croatia: The CroHort study. *Collegium Antropologicum, 36 Suppl,* 1257–259.

Mitchison, D., Hay, P., Griffiths, S., Murray, S. B., Bentley, C., Gratwick-Sarll, K., . . . Mond, J. (2017). Disentangling body image: The relative associations of overvaluation, dissatisfaction, and preoccupation with psychological distress and eating disorder behaviors in male and female adolescents. *International Journal of Eating Disorders, 50*(2), 118–126. doi:10.1002/eat.22592

Mittleman, M. A., Maclure, M., Sherwood, J. B., Mulry, R. P., Tofler, G. H., Jacobs, S. C., . . . Muller, J. E. (1995). Triggering of acute myocardial infarction onset by episodes of anger. *Circulation, 92,* 1720–1725.

Mo, B. (1992). Modesty, sexuality, and breast health in Chinese-American women. *Western Journal of Medicine, 157*(3), 260–264.

Mo, P., & Coulson, N. (2008). Exploring the communication of social support within virtual communities: A content analysis of messages posted to an online HIV/AIDS support groups. *Cyberpsychology & Behavior, 11*(3), 371–374.

Modi, A. C., Marciel, K. K., Slater, S. K., Drotar, D., & Quittner, A. L. (2008). The influence of parental supervision on medical adherence in adolescents with cystic fibrosis: Developmental shifts from pre to late adolescence. *Children's Health Care, 37,* 78–82.

Mokdad, A. H., Marks, J. S., Stroup, D. F., & Gerberding, J. L. (2005). Correction: Actual causes of death in the United States. *Journal of the American Medical Association, 293,* 293–294.

Mokdad, A. H., Marks, J. S., Stroup, D. F., & Gerberding, J. L. (2004). Actual causes of death in the United States, 2000. *Journal of American Medical Association. 291*(10): 1238–1245.

Moljord, I., Eriksen, L., Moksnes, U., & Espneg, G. (2011). Stress and happiness among adolescents with varying frequency of physical activity. *Perceptual & Motor Skills, 113*(2), 631–646. doi:10.2466/02.06.10.13.PMS.113.5.631-646

Molloy, G. J. Perkins-Porras, L. Strike, P. C., & Steptoe, A. (2008). Social networks and partner stress as predictors of adherence to medication, rehabilitation attendance, and quality of life following acute coronary syndrome. *Health Psychology, 27,* 52–58.

Molloy, G., Perkins-Porras, L., Strike, P., & Steptoe, A. (2008). Social networks and partner stress as predictors of adherence to medication, rehabilitation attendance, and quality of life following acute coronary syndrome. *Health Psychology, 27*(1), 52–58.

Monroe, S. M., & Harkness, K. L. (2005). Life stress, the "kindling" hypothesis, and the recurrence of depression: Considerations from a life stress perspective. *Psychological Review, 112,* 417–445.

Monroe, S. M., & Simons, A. D. (1991). Diathesis-stress theories in the context of life stress research: Implications for the depressive disorders, *Psychological Bulletin, 110,* 406–425.

Montano, D. E., & Kasprzyk, D. (2015). Theory of reasoned action, theory of planned behavior, and the integrated behavioral model. In K. Glanz, B. K. Rimer, & K. Viswanath (Eds.), *Health behavior: Theory, research, and practice* (5e, pp. 95–124). San Fransisco, CA: Jossey-Bass.

Montano, D., Kasprzyk, D., von Haeften, I., & Fishbein, M. (2001). Toward an understanding of condom use behaviours: A theoretical and methodological overview of Project SAFER. *Psychology, Health and Medicine, 6,* 139–150.

Monte, T. (1993). *World medicine: The east west guide to healing your body.* New York, NY: Penguin Putnam.

Monteleone, P., Tortorella, A., Castaldo, E., Di Filippo, C., & Maj, M. (2007). The Leu 72Met polymorphism of the ghrelin gene is significantly associated with binge eating disorder. *Psychiatric Genetics, 17,* 13–16.

Moon, P. (2011). *New Zealand in the twentieth century: The nation, the people.* Auckland, NZ: Harper Collins.

Moore, J., Schuman, P., Schoenbaum, E., Boland, B., Solomon, L., & Smith, D. (1999). Severe adverse life events and depressive symptoms among women with, or at risk for, HIV infection in four cities in the United States of America. *AIDS, 13,* 2459–2468.

Moos, R. H. (2008). Active ingredients of substance use-focused self-help groups. *Addiction, 103,* 387–396.

Moos, R. H., & Schaefer, J. A. (1993). Coping resources and processes: Current concepts and measures. In L. Goldberger & S. Breznitz (Eds.), *Handbook of stress: Theoretical and clinical aspects* (2nd ed., pp. 234–257). New York, NY: Free Press.

Moradi, B., & Risco, C. (2006). Perceived discrimination experiences and mental health of Latina/o American persons. *Journal of Counseling Psychology, 53,* 411–421.

Moran, K., Quan, L., Bennett, E., & Franklin, R. (2011). Where the evidence and expert opinion meet: Guidelines to prevent open water recreational drowning. *International Journal of Aquatic Research and Education, 5*(3), 224–238.

Morgan, K., & McGee, H. (2016). Quality of life. In Y. Benyamini, M. Johnston, & E. C. Karademas (Eds.), *Assessment in health psychology* (pp.189–200). Boston, MA: Hogrefe.

Morgan, W. P. (1997). Methodological considerations. In W. P. Morgan (Ed.), *Physical activity and mental health* (pp. 3–32). Washington, DC: Taylor & Francis.

Moritz, S., Pfuhl, G., Lüdtke, T., Menon, M., Balzan, R. P., & Andreou, C. (2017). A two-stage cognitive theory of the positive symptoms of psychosis. Highlighting the role of lowered decision thresholds. *Journal of Behavior Therapy and Experimental Psychiatry, 56*, 12–20. doi:10.1016/j.jbtep.2016.07.004

Morone, N. E., Greco, C. M., & Weiner, D. K. (2008). Mindfulness meditation for the treatment of chronic low back pain in older adults: A randomized controlled pilot study. *Pain, 134*, 310–319.

Morrill, A. C., Ickovics, J. R., Golubchikov, V., Beren, S. E., & Rodin, J. (1996). Safer sex: Predictors of behavioral maintenance and chance for heterosexual women. *Journal of Consulting and Clinical Psychology, 64*, 819–828.

Morris, J. N., Heady, J. A., Raffle, P. A. B., Roberts, C. G., & Parks, J. W. (1953). Coronary heart disease and physical activity of work. *The Lancet, 2*, 1053–1057.

Morris, R., Wannamethee, G., Lennon, L., Thomas, M., & Whincup, P. (2008). Do socioeconomic characteristics of neighbourhood of residence independently influence incidence of coronary heart disease and all-cause mortality in older British men? *European Journal of Cardiovascular Prevention and Rehabilitation, 15*(1), 19–25.

Morris, T., Greer, S., Pettingale, K. W., & Watson, M. (1981). Patterns of expression of anger and their psychological correlates in women with breast cancer. *Journal of Psychosomatic Research, 25*, 111–117.

Morrow, A. M., Hayen, A. A., Quine, S. S., Scheinberg, A. A., & Craig, J. C. (2012). A comparison of doctors', parents' and children's reports of health states and health-related quality of life in children with chronic conditions. *Child: Care, Health & Development, 38*(2), 186–195. doi:10.1111/j.1365-2214.2011.01240.x

Morrow, M. L., Heesch, K. C., Dinger, M. K., Hull, H.R., Kneehans, A. W., & Fields, D. A. (2006). Freshman 15: Fact or fiction? *Obesity, 14*, 1438–1443.

Mortensen, E. L., Jensen, H. H., Sanders, S. A., & Reinisch, J. M. (2001). Better psychological functioning and higher social status may largely explain the apparent health benefits of wine: A study of wine and beer drinking in young Danish adults. *Archives of Internal Medicine, 161*, 1844–1849.

Mosby, D. L., Manierre, M. J., Martin, S. S., Kolm, P., Abuzaid, A. S., Jurkovitz, C. T., . . . Weintraub, W. S. (2017). Patient satisfaction with care after coronary revascularization. *The Patient: Patient-Centered Outcomes Research, 11*(2), 217–223. doi:10.1007/s40271-017-0274-4

Moscardino, U., Scrimin, S., Capello, F., & Altoè, G. (2010). Social support, sense of community, collectivistic values, and depressive symptoms in adolescent survivors of the 2004 Beslan terrorist attack. *Social Science & Medicine, 70*(1), 27–34. doi:10.1016/j.socscimed.2009.09.035

Moseley, K. L., Freed, G. L., Bullard, C. M. & Goold, S. D. (2007). Measuring African-American parents' cultural mistrust while in a health-care setting: A pilot study. *Journal of the National Medical Association, 99*, 15–21.

Moskowitz, J. T., Epel, E. S., & Acree, M. (2008). Positive affect uniquely predicts lower risk of mortality in people with diabetes. *Health Psychology, 27*, S73–S82.

Moss-Morris, R., Weinman, J., Petrie, K. J., Horne, R., Cameron, L. D., & Buick, D. (2002) The revised illness perception questionnaire (IPQ-R). *Psychology and Health, 17*(1), 1–16.

Mottram, S., Peat, G., Thomas, E., Wilkie, R., & Croft, P. (2008). Patterns of pain and mobility limitation in older people: Cross-sectional findings from a population survey of 18,497 adults aged 50 years and over. *Quality of Life Research, 17*, 529–539.

Mõttus, R., McNeill, G., Jia, X., Craig, L. C. A., Starr, J. M., & Deary, I. J. (2013). The associations between personality, diet and body mass index in older people. *Health Psychology, 32*(4), 353–360. doi:10.1037/a0025537

Moumjid, N., Gafni, A., Brémond, A., & Carrère, M. (2007). Shared decision making in the medical encounter: Are we all talking about the same thing? *Medical Decision Making, 27*, 539–546.

Mowery, R. L. (2007). The family, larger systems, and end-of-life decision making. In D. Balk, C. Wogrin, G. Thornton, D. Meagher (Eds.), *Handbook of thanatology: The essential body of knowledge for the student of death, dying, and bereavement* (pp. 93–102). Northbrook, IL: Association for Death Education and Counseling.

Moyad, M. A. (1999). Soy, disease prevention, and prostate cancer. *Seminars in Urologic Oncology, 17*, 97–102.

Mo-Yeol K., & Yun-Chul, H. (2017). Crossover effect of spouse weekly working hours on estimated 10-years risk of cardiovascular disease. *PLoS One, 12*(8) doi:10.1371/journal.pone.0182010

Mrazek, D. A., Klinnert, M., Mrazek, P. J., Brower, A., McCormick, D., Rubin, B . . . Jones, J. (1999). Prediction of early-onset asthma in genetically at-risk children. *Pediatric Pulmonology, 27*, 85–94.

Muellersdorf, M., & Soederback, I. (2000). The actual state of the effects, treatments, and incidence of disabling pain in a gender perspective: A Swedish study. *Disabilities and Rehabilitation, 22*, 840–854.

Mukherjee, S. (2010). *The emperor of maladies: A biography of cancer*. New York, NY: Scribner.

Mukherjee, S. (2016). *The gene: An intimate history*. New York, NY: Scribner.

Mulder, C., de Vroome, E., van Griensven, G., Antoni, M. H., & Sandfort, T. (1999). Distraction as a predictor of the virological course of HIV-1 infection over a 7-year period in gay men. *Health Psychology, 18*, 1072113.

Mullen, P. D., Hersey, J. C., & Iverson, D. C. (1987). Health behavior models compared. *Social Science and Medicine, 24*, 973–981.

Müller, B., Nordt, C., Lauber, C., & Rössler, W. (2007). Changes in social network diversity and perceived social support after psychiatric hospitalization: Results from a longitudinal study. *International Journal of Social Psychiatry, 53*, 564–575.

Müller, F., & Wehbe, L. (2008). Smoking and smoking cessation in Latin America: A review of the current situation and available treatments. *International Journal of Chronic Obstructive Pulmonary Disease, 3*(2), 285–293.

Muller, J. E. (1999). Circadian variation and triggering of acute coronary events. *American Heart Journal, 137*, S1–S8.

Muller, J. E., Tofler, G. H., & Stone, P. H. (1989). Circadian variation and triggers of onset of acute cardiovascular disease. *Circulation, 79*, 733–743.

Müller, M., Kamping, S., Benrath, J., Skowronek, H., Schmitz, J., Klinger, R., & Flor, H. (2016). Treatment history and placebo responses to experimental and clinical pain in chronic pain patients. *European Journal of Pain, 20*(9), 1530–1541. doi:10.1002/ejp.877

Muñoz, M., Bayona, J., Sanchez, E., Arevalo, J., Sebastian, J., Arteaga, F., & . . . Shin, S. (2011). Matching social support to individual needs: A community-based intervention to improve HIV treatment adherence in a resource-poor setting. *AIDS and Behavior, 15*(7), 1454–1464. doi:10.1007/s10461-010-9697-9

Murberg, T. A., Bru, E., & Stephens, P. (2002). Personality and coping among congestive heart failure patients. *Personality and Individual Differences, 32*, 775–784.

Murdoch, D., Pihl, R. O., & Ross, D. (1990). Alcohol and crimes of violence: Present issues. *International Journal of the Addictions, 25*, 149–157.

Murphy, D., Mann, T., O'Keefe, Z., & Rotheram-Borus, M. J. (1998). Number of pregnancies, outcome expectancies, and social norms among HIV-infected young women. *Health Psychology, 17*, 470–475.

Murphy, M. L. M., Cohen, S., Janicki-Deverts, D., & Doyle, W. J. (2017). Offspring of parents who were separated and not speaking to one another have reduced resistance to the common cold as adults. *PNAS Proceedings of the National Academy of Sciences of the United States of America, 114*(25), 6515–6520. doi:10.1073/pnas.1700610114

Murphy, S. L., Xu, J. Q., & Kochanek, K. D. (2012). Deaths: Preliminary data for 2010. *National Vital Statistics Reports, 60*(4). Hyattsville, MD: National Center for Health Statistics.

Murphy, S. L., Xu, J., & Kochanek, K. D. (2012). Deaths: Preliminary data for 2012. *National Vital Statistics Reports, 60*(4).

Murray, C. J., & Lopez, A. D. (1997). Mortality by cause for eight regions of the world: Global burden of disease study. *The Lancet, 349*, 1269–1276.

Murray, E. J., & Segal, D. L. (1994). Emotional processing in vocal and written expression of feelings about traumatic experiences. *Journal of Traumatic Stress, 7*, 391–405.

Murray, V. (1992). Sexual career paths of Black adolescent females: A study of socioeconomic status and other life experiences. *Journal of Adolescent Research, 7*, 4–27.

Murtaugh, M. A., Sweeney, C., Giuliano, A. R., Herrick, J. S,, Hines, L., Byers, T., . . . Slattery, M. L. (2008). Diet patterns and breast cancer risk in Hispanic and non-Hispanic white women: The Four-Corners Breast Cancer Study. *American Journal of Clinical Nutrition, 87*(4), 978–984.

Muscat, J. E., Richie, J. P., Thompson, S., & Wynder, E. L. (1996). Gender differences in smoking and risk for oral cancer. *Cancer Research, 56*, 5192–5197.

Mussolino, A. E., Looker, A. C., & Orwoll, E. S. (2001). Jogging and bone mineral density in men: Results from NHANES III. *American Journal of Public Health, 91*, 1056–1059.

Mutambudzi, M., Meyer, J. D., Reisine, S., & Warren, N. (2017). A review of recent literature on materialist and psychosocial models for racial and ethnic disparities in birth outcomes in the U.S., 2000–2014. *Ethnicity & Health, 22*(3), 311–332. doi:10.1080/13557858.2016.1247150

Myers, H. F., & Rodriguez, N. (2002). Acculturation and physical health in racial and ethnic minorities. In K. M. Chun, P. B. Organista, & G. Marin (Eds.), *Acculturation: Advances in theory, measurement, and applied research*. Washington, DC: American Psychological Association.

Myers, L. B., & Midence, K. (Eds.). (1998). *The handbook of health behavior change* (2nd ed.). New York, NY: Springer.

Myers, L. B., & Vetere, A. (2002). Adult romantic attachment styles and health-related measures. *Psychology, Health and Medicine, 7*, 175–180.

Naar-King, S., Rongkavilit, C., Wang, B., Wright, K., Chuenyam, T., Lam, P., & Phanuphak, P. (2008). Transtheoretical model and risky sexual behaviour in HIV + youth in Thailand. *AIDS Care, 20*(2), 205–211.

Nabi, H., Kivimäki, M., Zins, M., Elovainio, M., Consoli, S., Cordier, S., . . . Singh-Manoux, A. (2008). Does personality predict mortality? Results from the GAZEL French prospective cohort study. *International Journal of Epidemiology, 37*(2), 386–396.

Nabi, R. L., & Horner, J. R. (2001). Victims with voices: How abused women conceptualize the problem of spousal abuse and implications for intervention and prevention. *Journal of Family Violence, 16*, 237–253.

Nahin, R. L., & Straus, S. E. (2001). Research into complementary and alternative medicine: Problems and potential. *British Medical Journal, 20, 322*(7279), 161–164.

Naimi, T. S., Brewer, R. D., Mokdad, A., Clark, D., Serdula, M. K., & Marks, J. S. (2003). *Binge Drinking among U.S. Adults, 289*(1), 70–75.

Nakamura, K., Barzi, F., Lam, T. H., Huxley, R., Feigin, V. L., Ueshima, H., . . . Woodward, M. (2008). Cigarette smoking, systolic blood pressure, and cardiovascular diseases in the Asia-Pacific region. *Stroke, 39*(6), 1694–1702.

Nashold, B., Somjen, G., & Friedman, H. (1972). Paresthesias and EEG potentials evoked by stimulation of the dorsal funiculi in man. *Experimental Neurology, 36*, 273–287.

Nasir, K., Katz, R., Takasu, J., Shavelle, D. M., Detrano, R., Lima, J. A., . . . Budoff, M. J. (2008). Ethnic differences between extra-coronary measures on cardiac computed tomography: Multi-ethnic study of atherosclerosis (MESA). *Atherosclerosis, 198*(1), 104–114.

Nassau, J., Tien, K., & Fritz, G. (2008). Review of the literature: Integrating psychoneuroimmunology into pediatric chronic illness interventions. *Journal of Pediatric Psychology, 33*(2), 195–207.

Nathan, P. W. (1976). The gate control theory of pain: A critical review. *Brain, 99*, 123–158.

Nathanson, C. A. (1977). Sex roles as variables in preventive health behavior. *Journal of Community Health, 3*, 142–55.

National Cancer Institute. (2011). Survellience Epidemiology and End Results (SEER). Retrieved from http://seer.cancer.gov/csr/1975_2008/browse_csr.php?section=2&page=sect_02_table.07.html

National Cancer Institute. (2012). Declines in Smoking and Lung Cancer Mortality in the U.S.: 1975–2000. *Journal of the National Cancer Institute, 104*(7), NP.

National Cancer Institute. (2017). About cancer. Author, Atlanta, GA. Retrieved from https://www.cancer.gov/about-cancer

National Cancer Institute. (2017). Cancer health disparities. Author, Atlanta, GA. Retrieved from http://www.cancer.gov/cancertopics/factsheet/disparities/cancer-health-disparities

National Center for Complementary and Integrative Health. (2017). Uses of complementary approaches in the U.S. Author, Bethesda, MD. Retrieved from https://nccih.nih.gov/research/statistics/NHIS/2012

National Center for Health Statistics. (2004). *Vital and health statistics, 13*, 149. Hyattsville, MD: U.S. Public Health Service.

National Center for Health Statistics. (2006). *Chartbook on trends in the health of Americans. Health, United States, 2006*. Hyattsville, MD: Public Health Service.

National Center for Health Statistics. (2017). Multiple cause of death 1999–2016, on CDC WONDER Online Database. Retrieved from http://wonder.cdc.gov/mcd-icd10.html

National Diabetes Information Clearinghouse. (2018). Diabetes. Author, Washington, DC. Retrieved from https://www.niddk.nih.gov/health-information/diabetes

National Highway Traffic Safety Administration (NHTSA). (2017). Seat belt use in 2016- Use rates in the states and territories. Author, Washington, DC. Retrieved from https://www.nhtsa.gov/sites/nhtsa.dot.gov/files/documents/812417seatbeltuse2016.pdf

National Hospice and Palliative Care Organization. (2017). *NHPCO facts and figures: Hospice care in America*. Alexandria, VA: Author.

National Institutes of Health. (NIH). (2009). *Opportunities and challenges in digestive diseases research: Recommendations of the national commission on digestive diseases.* NIH Publication 08–6514. Bethesda, MD: National Institutes of Health.

National Research Council. (2004). *Eliminating health disparities: Measurement and data needs.* Washington, DC: The National Academies Press.

National Vital Statistics Reports. (2012). Author, Hyattsville, MD. Retrieved from https://www.cdc.gov/nchs/products/nvsr.htm

Nealey-Moore, J., Smith, T., Uchino, B., Hawkins, M., & Olson-Cerny, C. (2007). Cardiovascular reactivity during positive and negative marital interactions. *Journal of Behavioral Medicine, 30*(6), 505–519.

Nees, F., Tzschoppe, J., Patrick, C., Vollstädt-Klein, S., Steiner, S., Poustka, L., & . . . Rietschel, M. (2012). Determinants of early alcohol use in healthy adolescents: The differential contribution of neuroimaging and psychological factors. *Neuropsychopharmacology, 37*(4), 986–995. doi:10.1038/npp.2011.282

Negoianu, D., & Goldfarb, S. (2008). Just add water. *Journal of the American Society of Nephrology, 19*, 1041–1043.

Nelson, D. E., Bland, S., Powell-Griner, E., Klein, R., Wells, H. E., Hogelin, G., & Marks, J. S. (2002). State trends in health risk factors and receipt of clinical preventive services among U.S. adults during the 1990s. *Journal of the American Medical Association, 287*, 2659–2668.

Nelson, E. L., Wenzel, L. B., Osann, K., Dogan-Ates, A., Chantana, N., Reina-Patton, A., . . . Monk, B. J. (2008). Stress, immunity, and cervical cancer: Biobehavioral outcomes of a randomized clinical trail. *Clinical Cancer Research, 14*, 2111–2118.

Nelson, J. (2009, September 1). LAMP bill passes: Prescriptive authority repealed, MPs transferred to medical. *Psychology Times*, 3.

Nelson, J. (2010, October 1). "Psychologist" defined: MPs who supervise must retain psych license. *Psychology Times, 1–3.*

Nelson, S., McCoy, G., Stetter, M., & Vanderwagen, W. C. (1992). An overview of mental health services for American Indians and Alaska Natives in the 1990s. *Hospital and Community Psychiatry, 43*, 257–261.

Nelson-Becker, H., Atwell, L., & Russo, S. (2017). Lesser known spiritualities: Baha'i, Zoroastrianism and Rastafarianism. In D. Vondras (Ed.), *Better health through spiritual practices: A guide to religious behaviors and practices that benefit mind and body* (pp. 229–262). Santa Barbara, CA: Praeger.

Neumann, S. A., Maier, K. J., Brown, J. P., Giggey, P. P., Cooper, D. C., Synowski, S. J., & . . . Waldstein, S. R. (2011). Cardiovascular and psychological reactivity and recovery from harassment in a biracial sample of high and low hostile men and women. *International Journal of Behavioral Medicine, 18*(1), 52–64. doi:10.1007/s12529-010-9110-0

Neumark-Sztainer, D., Wall, M. M., Story, M., & Perry, C. L. (2003). Correlates of unhealthy weight-control behaviors among adolescents: Implications for prevention programs. *Health Psychology, 22*, 88–98.

Newnham, J. (1998). Consequences of fetal growth restriction. *Current Opinion in Obstetrics and Gynecology, 10*, 145–149.

Newsom, J. T., Huguet, N., McCarthy, M. J., Ramage-Morin, P., Kaplan, M. S., Bernier, J., & . . . Oderkirk, J. (2012). Health behavior change following chronic illness in middle and later life. *Journals of Gerontology Series B: Psychological Sciences & Social Sciences, 67B*(3), 279–288.

Ng, M. (2007). New perspectives on Mars and Venus: Unravelling the role of androgens in gender differences in cardiovascular biology and disease. *Heart, Lung and Circulation, 16*(3), 185–192.

Ng-Mak, D. S. (1999). A further analysis of race differences in the National Longitudinal Mortality Study. *American Journal of Public Health, 89*, 1748–1752.

Ngo-Metzger, Q., Massagli, M. P., Clarridge, B. R., Manocchia, M., Davis, R. B., Iezzoni, L. I., & Phillips, R. S. (2003). Linguistic and cultural barriers to care: Perspectives of Chinese and Vietnamese immigrants. Linguistic and cultural barriers to care. *Journal of Internal Medicine, 18*, 44–52.

Ngo-Metzger, Q., Phillips, R., & McCarthy, E. (2008). Ethnic disparities in hospice use among Asian-American and Pacific Islander patients dying with cancer. *Journal of the American Geriatrics Society, 56*(1), 139–144.

Niaura, R., & Abrams, D. B. (2002). Smoking cessation: Progress, priorities, and prospectus. *Journal of Consulting and Clinical Psychology, 70*, 494–509.

Nicassio, P. M., Meyerowitz, B. E., & Kerns, R. D. (2004). The future of health psychology interventions. *Health Psychology, 23*, 132–137.

Nicholas, D. R., & Stern, M. (2011). Counseling psychology in clinical health psychology: The impact of specialty perspective. *Professional Psychology: Research and Practice, 42*(4), 331–337. doi:10.1037/a0024197

Nicolosi, R. J., & Schaefer, E. J. (1992). Pathobiology of hypercholesterolemia and atherosclerosis: Genetic and environment determinants of elevated lipoprotein levels. In I. S. Ockene & J. K. Ockene (Eds.), *Prevention of coronary heart disease* (pp. 69–102). Boston, MA: Little, Brown.

Nicolson, P., Kopp, Z., Chapple, C. R., & Kelleher, C. (2008). It's just the worry about not being able to control it! A qualitative study of living with overactive bladder. *British Journal of Health Psychology, 13*, 343–359.

NIDA Research Report. (2000). Anabolic steroid abuse (DHHS Publication No. 00–3721). Department of Health and Human Services, Washington, DC.

Nidich, S., Rainforth, M., Haaga, D., Hagelin, J., Salerno, J., Travis, F., & . . . Schneider, R. (2009). A randomized controlled trial on effects of the Transcendental Meditation program on blood pressure, psychological distress, and coping in young adults. *American Journal of Hypertension, 22*(12), 1326–1331.

Niedenthal, P. M., & Beike, D. R. (1997). Interrelated and isolated self-concepts. *Personality and Social Psychology Review, 1*, 106–128.

Niederhoffer, K. G., & Pennebaker, J. W. (2002). Sharing one's story: On the benefits of writing or talking about emotional experience. In C. R. Snyder & S. J. Lopez (Eds.), *Handbook of positive psychology* (pp. 573–583). London, UK: Oxford University Press.

Nielsen, N., Kristensen, T., Strandberg-Larsen, K., Zhang, Z., Schnohr, P., & Grønbaek, M. (2008). Perceived stress and risk of colorectal cancer in men and women: A prospective cohort study. *Journal of Internal Medicine, 263*(2), 192–202.

Nielsen, N., Strandberg-Larsen, K., Grønbaek, M., Kristensen, T., Schnohr, P., & Zhang, Z. (2007). Self-reported stress and risk of endometrial cancer: A prospective cohort study. *Psychosomatic Medicine, 69*(4), 383–389.

Niklason, L. E., & Langer, R. (2001). Prospects for organ and tissue replacement. *Journal of the American Medical Association, 285*, 573–576.

Nishiyama, K., & Johnson, J. V. (1997). Karoshi—Death from overwork: Occupational health consequences of Japanese production management. *International Journal of Health Services: Planning, Administration, Evaluation, 27*, 625–641.

Nkansah-Amankra, S., Luchok, K. J., Hussey, J., Watkins, K., & Xiaofeng, L. (2010). Effects of maternal stress on low birth weight and preterm birth outcomes across neighborhoods of South Carolina, 2000–2003. *Maternal & Child Health Journal, 14*(2), 215–226. doi:10.1007/s10995-009-0447-4

Noar, S. (2008). Behavioral interventions to reduce HIV-related sexual risk behavior: Review and synthesis of meta-analytic evidence. *AIDS and Behavior, 12*(3), 335–353.

Noar, S. M. (2005). A health educator's guide to theories of health behavior. *International Quarterly of Community Health Education, 24*, 75–92.

Noar, S. M. (2006). A10-year retrospective of research in health mass media campaigns: Where do we go from here? *Journal of Health Communication, 11*(1), 21–42.

Noar, S. M., & Zimmerman, R. S. (2005). Health Behavior Theory and cumulative knowledge regarding health behaviors: Are we moving in the right direction? *Health Education Research, 20*, 275–290.

Noar, S. M., Benac, C. N., Harris, M. S. (2007). Does tailoring matter? Meta-analytic review of tailored print health behavior change interventions. *Psychological Bulletin, 133*, 673–693.

Noble, M., Tregear, S. J., Treadwell, J. R., & Schoelles, K. (2008). Long-term opioid therapy for chronic noncancer pain: A systematic review and meta-analysis of efficacy and safety. *Journal of Pain and Symptom Management, 35*, 214–228.

Noda, H., Iso, H., Toyoshima, H., Date, C., Yamamoto, A., Kikuchi, S., . . . Tamakoshi, A. (2008). Smoking status, sports participation and mortality from coronary heart disease. *Heart (British Cardiac Society), 94*(4), 471–475.

Noc, K., & Smith, P. (2012). Quality measures for the U.S. hospice system. *Ageing International, 37*(2), 165–180. doi:10.1007/s12126-010-9100-1

Noël, L. (2010). An ethnic/racial comparison of causal beliefs and treatment preferences for the symptoms of depression among patients with diabetes. *Diabetes Educator, 36*(5), 816–827.

Noh, S., & Kaspar, B. (2003). Perceived discrimination and depression: Moderating effects of coping, acculturation, and ethnic support. *American Journal of Public Health, 93*, 232–238.

Noh, S., Beiser, M., Kaspar, V., Hou, F., & Rummens, J. (1999). Perceived racial discrimination, depression, and coping: A study of Southeast Asian refugees in Canada. *Journal of Health and Social Behavior, 40*, 193–207.

Nolte, S., Elsworth, G. R., Sinclair, A. J., Osborne, R. H. (2007). The extent and breadth of benefits from participating in chronic disease self-management courses: A national patient-reported outcomes survey. *Patient Education and Counseling, 65*, 351–360.

Noonan, A. S., Velasco-Mondragon, H. E., & Wagner, F. A. (2016). Improving the health of African Americans in the UDA: An overdue opportunity for social justice. *Public Health Reviews, 37*(12). doi 10.1186/s40985-016-0025-4

Noppe, I. C. (2004). Gender and death: Parallel and intersecting pathways. In J. Berzoff & P. R. Silverman (Eds.), *Living with dying: A handbook for end-of-life healthcare practitioners*. New York, NY: Columbia University Press.

Noppe, I. C., & Noppe, L. D. (2008). When a friend dies. In K. J. Doka & A. S. Tucci (Eds.), *Living with grief: Children and adolescents* (pp.175–192). Washington, DC: Hospice Foundation of America.

Norbeck, J. S., & Anderson, N. J. (1989). Psychosocial predictors of pregnancy outcomes in low-income Black, Hispanic, and White women. *Nursing Research, 38*, 204–209.

Norcross, J. C., Hailstorks, R., Aiken, L. S., Pfund, R. A., Stamm, K. E., & Christidis, P. (2016). Undergraduate study in psychology: Curriculum and assessment. *American Psychologist, 71*(2), 89–101.

Norlander, T., Bood, S. A., & Archer, T. (2002). Performance during stress: Affective personality, age, and regularity of physical exercise. *Social Behavior and Personality, 30*, 495–508.

Norris, F. H., Murphy, A. D., Kaniasty, K., Perilla, J. L., & Ortis, D. C. (2001). Postdisaster social support in the United States and Mexico: Conceptual and contextual considerations. *Hispanic Journal of Behavioral Sciences, 23*, 469–497.

Norris, F. H., Perilla, J. L., Ibanez, G. E., & Murphy, A. D. (2001). Sex differences in symptoms of posttraumatic stress: Does culture play a role? *Journal of Traumatic Stress, 14*, 7–28.

Norris, F., Byrne, C. M., & Diaz, E. (2002). *The range, magnitude, and duration of effects of natural and human-caused disasters: A review of the empirical literature*. Washington, DC: National Center for PTSD.

Norrish, A. E., Jackson, R. T., Sharpe, S. J., & Skeaff, C. M. (2000). Prostate cancer and dietary carotenoids. *American Journal of Epidemiology, 151*, 119–23.

Norton, S., Sacker, A., Young, A., & Done, J. (2011). Distinct psychological distress trajectories in rheumatoid arthritis: Findings from an inception cohort. *Journal of Psychosomatic Research, 71*(5), 290–295. doi:10.1016/j.jpsychores.2011.05.006

Nurses' Health Study. (2008). Nurses' Health Study. Author, Cambridge, MA: Harvard University Press. Retrieved from http://www.channing.harvard.edu/nhs/index.html

Nyamathi, A. M., Stein, J. A., & Brecht, M. L. (1995). Psychosocial predictors of AIDS risk behavior and drug use behavior in homeless and drug addicted women of color. *Health Psychology, 14*, 265–273.

Nyswander, D. B. (1966). Education for health: Some principles and their application. *Health Education Monographs, 14*, 65–70.

O'Brien, E. M., Atchison, J. W., Gremillion, H. A., Waxenberg, L. B., & Robinson, M. E. (2008). Somatic focus/awareness: Relationship to negative affect and pain in chronic pain patients. *European Journal of Pain, 12*, 104–115.

O'Connell, J. M., Wilson, C., Manson, S. M., & Acton, K. J. (2012). The costs of treating American Indian adults with diabetes within the Indian Health Service. *American Journal of Public Health, 102*(2), 301–308. doi:10.2105/AJPH.2011.300332

O'Conner, G. T., Buring, J. E., Yusuf, S., Goldhaber, S. Z., Olmstead, E. M., Paffenbarger, R. S. Jr., & Hennekens, C. H. (1989). An overview of randomized trials of rehabilitation with exercise after myocardial infarction. *Circulation, 80*, 234–244.

O'Connor, A. M., Bennett, C., Stacey, D., Barry, M. J., Col, N. F., Eden, K. B., . . . Rovner, D. R. (2007). Do patient decision aids meet effectiveness criteria of the international patient decision aid standards collaboration? A systematic review and meta-analysis. *Medical Decision Making, 27*(5), 554–574.

O'Connor, D. B., & Ferguson, E. (2016). Stress and stressors. In Y. Benyamini, M. Johnston, & E. C. Karademas (Eds.), *Assessment in health psychology* (pp.103–117). Boston, MA: Hogrefe.

O'Connor, D. B., Jones, F., Conner, M., McMillan, B., & Ferguson, E. (2008). Effects of daily hassles and eating style on eating behavior. *Health Psychology, 27*, S20–S31.

O'Connor, D. B., Wilson, A. E., & Lawton, R. (2017). Interactive effects of trait self-control and stress appraisals on blood pressure responses to a laboratory stressor. *International Journal of Behavioral Medicine, 24*(4), 602–612. doi:10.1007/s12529-017-9632-9

O'Donovan, A., & Hughes, B. M. (2008). Factors that moderate the effect of laboratory-based social support on cardiovascular reactivity to stress. *International Journal of Psychology and Psychological Therapy, 8*, 85–102.

O'Driscoll, M., Byrne, S., . . . McGillicuddy, A., Lambert, S., & Sahm, L. J. (2017). The effects of mindfulness-based interventions for health and social care undergraduate students—A systematic review of the literature. *Psychology, Health & Medicine, 22*(7), 851–865. doi:10.1080/13548506.2017.1280178

O'Kane, A. A., Park, S. Y., Mentis, H., Blandford, A., & Chen, Y. (2016). Turning to peers: Integrating understanding of the self, the condition, and others' experiences in making sense of complex chronic conditions. *Computer Supported Cooperative Work (CSCW), 25*(6), 477–501. doi:10.1007/s10606-016-9260-y

O'Leary, A., Jemmott, L., & Jemmott, J. (2008). Mediation analysis of an effective sexual risk-reduction intervention for women: The importance of self-efficacy. *Health Psychology, 27*(2 Suppl), S180–4.

Obeidallah, D. A., Brennan, R. T., Brooks-Gunn, J., Kindlon, D., & Earls, F. (2000). Socioeconomic status, race, and girls' pubertal maturation: Results from the Project on Human Development in Chicago neighborhoods. *Journal of Research on Adolescence 10*, 443–464.

Obeidallah, D. A., Hauser, S. T., & Jacobson, A. M. (1999). The long branch of phase-environment fit: Concurrent and longitudinal implications of match and mismatch among diabetic and nondiabetic youth. *Journal of Adolescent Research, 14*, 95–121.

Ockene, J., Kristeller, J. L., Goldberg. R., & Ockene, I. (1992). Smoking cessation and severity of disease: The coronary artery smoking intervention study. *Health Psychology, 11*, 119–126.

Office of Disease Prevention and Health Promotion. (2014). HealthyPeople 2020: Disparities. Author, Washington, DC. Retrieved from https://www.healthypeople.gov/2020/about/foundation-health-measures/Disparities

Offit, P. A. (2013). *Do you believe in magic? The sense and nonsense of alternative medicine.* New York, NY: Harper.

Ogden, C. L., Carroll, M. D., Curtin, L.R., McDowell, M. A., Tabak C. J., & Flegal, K. M. (2006). Prevalence of overweight and obesity in the United States, 1999–2004. *Journal of the American Medical Association, 295*, 1549–1555.

Ogden, C. L., Carroll, M. D., & Flegal, K. M. (2008). High body mass index for age among U.S. children and adolescents, 2003–2006. *Journal of the American Medical Association, 299*, 2401–2405.

Ogden, C. L., Carroll, M. D., Kit, B. K., & Flegal, K. M. (2012). Prevalence of obesity and trends in body mass index among U.S. children and adolescents, 1999–2010. *Journal of the American Medical Association, 307*(5), 483–490. doi:10.1001/jama.2012.40

Ogden, J. (2003). Some problems with social cognition models: A pragmatic and conceptual analysis. *Health Psychology, 22*, 424–428.

Ogunsanya, M. E., Brown, C. M., Odedina, F. T., Barner, J. C., Adedipe, T. B., & Corbell, B. (2017). Knowledge of prostate cancer and screening among young multiethnic black men. *American Journal of Men's Health, 11*(4), 1008–1018. doi:10.1177/1557988316689497

Ogus, E. D., Greenglass, E. R., & Burke, R. J. (1990). Gender-role differences, work stress and depersonalization. *Journal of Social Behavior and Personality, 5*, 387–398.

Ohira, T., Hozawa, A., Iribarren, C., Daviglus, M. L., Matthews, K. A., Gross, M. D., & Jacobs, D. R. Jr. (2008). Longitudinal association of serum carotenoids and tocopherols with hostility: The CARDIA study. *American Journal of Epidemiology, 167*(1), 42–50.

Oken, B. S., Kishiyama, S., Zajdel, D., Bourdette, D., Carlsen, J., Haas, M., . . . Mass, M. (2004). Randomized controlled trial of yoga and exercise in multiple sclerosis. *Neurology, 62*, 2058–2064.

Okifuji, A., Bradshaw, D., Donaldson, G., & Turk, D. (2011). Sequential analyses of daily symptoms in women with fibromyalgia syndrome. *Journal of Pain, 12*(1), 84–93.

Olango, W. M., & Finn, D. P. (2014). Neurobiology of stress-induced hyperalgesia. In B. K. Taylor & D. P. Finn (Eds.), *Behavioral neurobiology of chronic pain; behavioral neurobiology of chronic pain* (pp. 251–280). New York, NY: Springer-Verlag. doi:10.1007/7854_2014_302

Olbrisch, M. E., Benedict, S. M., Ashe, K., & Levenson, J. L. (2002). Psychological assessment and care of organ transplant patients. *Journal of Consulting and Clinical Psychology, 70*, 771–783.

Oliveira, T. H., Oliveira, V. C., Melo, R. C., Melo, R. M., Freitas, A. E., & Ferreira, P. H. (2012). Patients in treatment for chronic low back pain have higher externalised beliefs: A cross-sectional study. *Brazilian Journal of Physical Therapy / Revista Brasileira De Fisioterapia, 16*(1), 35–39.

Olson, C. (2017). Ways of healing and the roles of harmony, purity, and violent rhetoric in Japanese Shinto and shamanism. In D. Vondras (Ed.), *Better health through spiritual practices: A guide to religious behaviors and practices that benefit mind and body* (pp. 97–119). Santa Barbara, CA: Praeger.

Olson, H. C., Streissguth, A. P., Sampson, P. D. Barr, H. M., Bookstein, F. L., & Thiede, K. (1997). Association of prenatal alcohol exposure with behavioral and learning problems in early adolescence. *Journal of the American Academy of Child and Adolescent Psychiatry, 36*, 1187–1194.

Olson, J. M., Roese, N. J., & Zanna, M. P. (1996). Expectancies. In E. T. Higgins & A. W. Kruglanski (Eds.), *Social psychology: Handbook of basic principles* (pp. 211–239). New York, NY: Guilford Press.

Omran, A. R. (2005). The epidemiologic transition: A theory of the epidemiology of population change. *Milbank Quarterly, 83*(4), 731–757. doi:10.1111/j.1468-0009.2005.00398.x

Ondeck, D. M. (2003). Impact of culture on pain. *Home Health Care Management & Practice, 15*, 255–257.

Ong, L. M. L., DeHaes, J. C. J. M., Hoos, A. M., & Lammes, F. B. (1995). Doctor-patient communication: A review of the literature. *Social Science and Medicine, 40*, 903–918.

Oomen, J. S., Owen, L. J., & Suggs, L. S. (1999). Culture counts: Why current treatment models fail Hispanic women with Type 2 diabetes. *Diabetes Educator, 25*, 220–225.

Open Science Collaboration. (2015). Estimating the reproducibility of psychological science. *Science, 349*(6251), aac4716. doi:10.1126/science.aac4716

Orbell, S., & Henderson, C. J. (2016). Automatic effects of illness schema activation on behavioral manifestations of illness. *Health Psychology, 35*(10), 1144–1153. doi:10.1037/hea0000375

Ornish, D., Brown, S. E., Scherwitz, L. W., Billings, J. H., Armstrong, W. T., Ports, T. A., McLanahan, S. M., Kirkeeide, R. L., Brand, R. J., & Gould, K. L. (1990). Can lifestyle changes reverse coronary heart disease? The lifestyle heart trial. *The Lancet, 336*, 129–133.

Ornish, D., Scherwitz, L. W., Billings, J. H., Gould, K. L., Merritt, T. A., Sparler, S., . . . Brand, R. J. (1998). Intensive lifestyle changes for reversal of coronary heart disease. *Journal of the American Medical Association, 280*, 2001–2007.

Ortega, S., Beauchemin, A., & Kaniskan, R. B. (2008). Building resiliency in families with young children exposed to violence: The safe start initiative pilot study. *Best Practices in Mental Health, 4*, 48–64.

Orth-Gomer, K., & Johnson, J. V. (1987). Social network interaction and mortality: A six year follow-up study of a random sample of the Swedish population. *Journal of Chronic Diseases, 40*, 949–957.

Orth-Gomer, K., Chesney, M., & Wenger, N. K. (1998). *Women, stress, and heart disease.* Mahwah, NJ: Erlbaum.

Orth-Gomer, K., Rosengren, A., & Wilhelmsen, L. (1993). Lack of social support and incidence of coronary heart disease in middle-aged Swedish men. *Psychosomatic Medicine, 55*, 37–43.

Orth-Gomer, K., Wamala, S. P., Horsten, M., Schenck-Gustafsson, K., Schneiderman, N., & Mittleman, M. A. (2000). Marital stress worsens prognosis in women with coronary heart disease: The Stockholm female coronary risk study. *Journal of the American Medical Association, 284*, 3008–3014.

Ortiz, I. E., & Torres, E. C. (2007). Curanderismo and the treatment of alcoholism: findings from a focus group of Mexican curanderos . . . folk healers. *Alcoholism Treatment Quarterly, 25*,79–90.

Osborne, L., & Mason, J. (1993). HLA A/B haplotype frequencies among U.S. Hispanic and African American populations. *Human Genetics, 91*, 326–332.

Ostafin, B., & Brooks, J. (2011). Drinking for relief: Negative affect increases automatic alcohol motivation in coping-motivated drinkers. *Motivation & Emotion, 35*(3), 285–295. doi:10.1007/s11031-010-9194-5

Oxlad, M., & Wade, T. D. (2008). Longitudinal risk factors for adverse psychological functioning six months after coronary artery bypass graft surgery. *Journal of Health Psychology, 13*, 79–92.

Oze, I., Matsuo, K., Ito, H., Wakai, K., Nagata, C., Mizoue, T., & . . . Tsugane, S. (2012). Cigarette smoking and esophageal cancer risk: An evaluation based on a systematic review of epidemiologic evidence among the Japanese population. *Japanese Journal of Clinical Oncology, 42*(1), 63–73.

Ozer, E. J., Best, S. R., Lipsey, T. L., & Weiss, D. S. (2003) Predictors of posttraumatic stress disorder and symptoms in adults: A meta-analysis. *Psychological Bulletin, 129*(1), 52–73.

Pacquiao, D. (2007). The relationship between cultural competence education and increasing diversity in nursing schools and practice settings. *Journal of Transcultural Nursing, 18*, 28S–37S.

Padian, N. S., Shiboski, S., Glass, S., & Vittinghoff, E. (1997). Heterosexual transmission of HIV in northern California: Results from a 10 year study. *American Journal of Epidemiology, 146*, 350–357.

Padilla, A. M., & Ruiz, R. A. (1973). *Latino mental health: A review of literature.* Washington, DC: U.S. Government Publishing Office.

Paez, K. A., Allen, J. K., Carson, K. A., & Cooper, L. A. (2008). Provider and clinic cultural competence in a primary care setting. *Social Science and Medicine, 66*, 1204–1216.

Paffenbarger, R. S., Hyde, R. T., Wing, A. L., & Hsieh, C. (1986). Physical activity, all-cause mortality, and longevity of college alumni. *New England Journal of Medicine, 314*, 605–613.

Paffenbarger, R. S., Lee, I., & Leung, R. (1994). Physical activity and personal characteristics associated with depression and suicide in American college men. *Acta Psychiatrica Scandinavica, 89*, 16–22.

Painter, J. E., Borba, C. C., Hynes, M., Mays, D., & Glanz, K. (2008). The use of theory in health behavior research from 2000 to 2005: A systematic review. *Annals of Behavioral Medicine, 35*(3), 358–362. doi:10.1007/s12160-008-9042-y

Pakenham, K. I., Dadds, M. R., & Terry, D. J. (1994). Relationship between adjustment to HIV and both social support and coping. *Journal of Consulting & Clinical Psychology, 62*, 1194–1203.

Panagiotakos, D., Pitsavos, C., Chrysohoou, C., Skoumas, I., & Stefanadis, C. (2008). Five-year incidence of cardiovascular disease and its predictors in Greece: The ATTICA study. *Vascular Medicine* (London, UK), *13*(2), 113–121.

Panjwani, A. A., Gurung, R. A. R., & Revenson, T. A. (2017). The teaching of undergraduate health psychology: A national survey. *Teaching of Psychology, 44*(3), 268–273. doi:10.1177/0098628317712786

Parenteau, S. C. (2017). Religious coping and substance use: The moderating role of sex. *Journal of Religion and Health, 56*(2), 380–387. doi:10.1007/s10943-015-0166-7

Pargament, K. I. (1997). *The psychology of religion and coping: Theory, research, practice.* New York, NY: Guilford Press.

Pargament, K. I. (2002). The bitter and the sweet: An evaluation of the costs and benefits of religiousness. *Psychological Inquiry, 13*, 168–181.

Pargament, K. I., Koenig, H. G., & Perez, L. M. (2000). The many methods of religious coping: Development and initial validation of the RCOPE. *Journal of Clinical Psychology, 56*, 519–543.

Pargament, K. I., Smith, B. W., Koenig, H. G., & Perez, L. (1998). Patterns of positive and negative religious coping with major life stressors. *Journal for the Scientific Study of Religion, 37*, 710–724.

Parhan, T. A., & Helms, J. E. (1985). Attitudes of racial identity and self-esteem: An exploratory investigation. *Journal of College Student Personnel, 26*, 143–151.

Parikh, N., Hwang, S., Larson, M., Levy, D., & Fox, C. (2008). Chronic kidney disease as a predictor of cardiovascular disease (from the Framingham Heart Study). *American Journal of Cardiology, 102*(1), 47–53.

Park, C. L., & Folkman, S. (1997). The role of meaning in the context of stress and coping. *General Review of Psychology, 2*, 115–144.

Park, C. L., & Gaffey, A. E. (2007). Relationships between psychosocial factors and health behavior change in cancer survivors: An integrative review. *Annals of Behavioral Medicine, 34*, 115–134.

Park, C. L., Cohen, L. H., & Murch, R. L. (1996). Assessment and prediction of stress-related growth. *Journal of Personality, 64*, 71–105.

Park, C. L., Holt, C. L., Le, D., Christie, J., & Williams, B. R. (2017). Positive and negative religious coping styles as prospective predictors of well-being in African Americans. *Psychology of Religion and Spirituality,10*(1), 55–62. doi:10.1037/rel0000124

Park, C., & Carney, B. (2019). Religion/spirituality and health: Modeling potential pathways of influence. In T. A. Revenson & R. A. R. Gurung (Eds.), *Handbook of health psychology* (3e). New York, NY: Routledge.

Park, C., & Gaffey, A. (2007). Relationships between psychosocial factors and health behavior change in cancer survivors: An integrative review. *Annals of Behavioral Medicine: A Publication of the Society of Behavioral Medicine, 34*(2), 115–134.

Park, E., McCoy, T. P., Erausquin, J. T., & Bartlett, R. (2018). Trajectories of risk behaviors across adolescence and young adulthood: The role of race and ethnicity. *Addictive Behaviors, 76*, 1–7. doi:10.1016/j.addbeh.2017.07.014

Park, J. H., & DeFrank, R. S. (2018). The role of proactive personality in the Stressor–Strain model. *International Journal of Stress Management, 25*(1), 44–59 doi:10.1037/str0000048

Parker, B., McFarlane, J., & Soeken, K. (1994). Abuse during pregnancy: Effects on maternal complications and birth weight in adult and teenage women. *Obstetrics and Gynecology, 84*, 323–328.

Parker, S., Tong, T., Bolden, S., & Wingo, P. (1997). Cancer statistics, 1997. *Cancer Journal for Clinicians, 47*, 5–27.

Parkes, C. M., Stevenson-Hinde, J., & Marris, P. (1991). *Attachment across the life cycle.* New York, NY: Tavistock/Routledge.

Parry, I. S., Bagley, A., Kawada, J., Sen, S., Greenhalgh, D. G., & Palmieri, T. L. (2012). Commercially available interactive video games in burn rehabilitation: therapeutic potential. *Burns (03054179), 38*(4), 493–500. doi:10.1016/j.burns.2012.02.010

Parry, J., & Ryan, A. (1995). *A cross cultural look at death, dying and religion.* Stamford, CT: Wadsworth.

Parsons, O. A. (1994). Determinants of cognitive deficits in alcoholics: The search continues. *Clinical Neuropsychologist, 8*, 39–58.

Pasick, R., & Burke, N. (2008). A critical review of theory in breast cancer screening promotion across cultures. *Annual Review of Public Health, 29*, 351–368.

Pate, R. H. (1995). Certification of specialities: Not if, but how. *Journal of Counseling & Development, 74*, 181–184.

Pate, R. R., Pratt, M., Blair, S. N., Haskell, W. L., Macera, C. A., Bouchard, C . . . Wilmore, J. H. (1995). Physical activity and public health: A recommendation from the Centers for Disease Control and Prevention and the American College of Sports Medicine. *Journal of American Medical Association, 273*, 402–407.

Patel, A. V., Feigelson, H. S., Talbot, J. T., McCullough, M. L., Rodriguez, C., Patel, R. C., . . . Calle, E. E. (2008). The role of body weight in the relationship between physical activity and endometrial cancer: Results from a large cohort of U.S. women. *International Journal of Cancer, 123*(8), 1877–1882.

Patel, J. V., Lim, H. S., Gunarathne, A., Tracey, I., Durrington, P. N., Hughes, E. A. & Lip, G. Y. (2008). Ethnic differences in myocardial infarction in patients with hypertension: Effects of diabetes mellitus. *Monthly Journal of the Association of Physicians, 101*(3), 231–236.

Patterson, C. J., Fulcher, M., & Wainright, J. (2002). Children of lesbian and gay parents: Research, law, and policy. In B. L. Bottoms, M. Bull Kovera, B. D. McAuliff (Eds.), *Children, social science and the law* (pp. 176–199). New York, NY: Cambridge University Press.

Patterson, D. R., Adcock, R. J., & Bombardier, C. H. (1997). Factors predicting hypnotic analgesia in clinical burn pain. *International Journal of Clinical and Experimental Hypnosis, 45*, 377–395.

Patterson, J. (2002). Integrating family resilience and family stress theory. *Journal of Marriage and Family, 64*, 349–360.

Patterson, J. M. (2002). Understanding family, resilience. *Journal of Clinical Psychology, 58*, 233–247.

Patterson, J. M., & Garwick, A. W. (1994). Levels of meaning in family stress theory. *Family Process, 33*, 287–304.

Patterson, J. M., & McCubbin, H. I. (1987). Adolescent coping style and behaviors: Conceptualization and measurement. *Journal of Adolescence, 10*, 163–186.

Pattison, E. M. (1977). Ten years of change in alcoholism treatment and delivery systems. *American Journal of Psychiatry, 134*, 261–266.

Paus, T. (1999). Imaging the brain before, during, and after trans-cranial magnetic stimulation. *Neuropsychologia, 37*, 219–224.

PausJenssen, A., Spooner, B., Wilson, M., & Wilson, T. (2008). Cardiovascular risk reduction via tele-health: A feasibility study. *Canadian Journal of Cardiology, 24*(1), 57–60.

Payman, V., George, K., & Ryburn, B. (2008). Religiosity of depressed elderly inpatients. *International Journal of Geriatric Psychiatry, 23*, 16–21.

Peacock, E. J., & Wong, P. T. P. (1990). The Stress Appraisal Measure (SAM): A multidimensional approach to cognitive appraisal. *Stress Medicine, 6*, 227–236.

Pearlin, L. I., & Schooler, C. (1978). The structure of coping. *Journal of Health and Social Behavior, 19*, 2–21.

Pearlin, L. I., & Skaff, M. M. (1995). Stressors and adaptation in late life. In M. Gatz (Ed.), *Emerging issues in mental health and aging* (pp. 97–123). Washington, DC: American Psychological Association.

Pecorino, L. (2016). *Molecular biology of cancer: Mechanism, targets, and therapeutics 4e.* Oxford, UK: Oxford University Press.

Peña-Purcell, N. (2008). Hispanics' use of Internet health information: An exploratory study. *Journal of the Medical Library Association, 96*(2), 101–107.

Pendleton, J., Hopkins, C., Anai, S., Nakamura, K., Chang, M., Grissett, A., & Rosser, C. J. (2008). Prostate cancer knowledge and screening attitudes of inner-city men. *Journal of Cancer Education, 23*(3), 172–179.

Peng, A., Riolli, L. T., Schaubroeck, J., & Spain, E. P. (2012). A moderated mediation test of personality, coping, and health among deployed soldiers. *Journal of Organizational Behavior, 33*(4), 512–530. doi:10.1002/job.766

Peng, Y. B., Fuchs, P. N., & Gatchel, R. J. (2006). Chronic pain: The diathesis-stress model. In B. B. Arnetz & R. Ekman (Eds.), *Stress in health and disease* (pp. 333–341). Weinheim, Germany: Wiley-VCH Veriag GmbH & Co KGaA. doi:10.1002/3527609156.ch20

Penley, J. A., & Tomaka, J. (2002). Associations among the Big Five, emotional responses and coping with acute stress. *Personality and Individual Differences, 32*, 1215–1128.

Penn, N. E., Kramer, J., Skinner, J. F., Velasquez, R. J., Yee, B. W. K., Arellano, L. M., & Williams, J. P. (2000). Health practices and health-care systems among cultural groups. In R. M. Eisler & M. Hersen (Eds.), *Handbook of gender, culture, and health* (pp. 105–138). Mahwah, NJ: Erlbaum.

Pennebaker, J. W., & Beall, S. K. (1986). Confronting a traumatic event: Toward an understanding of inhibition and disease. *Journal of Abnormal Psychology, 95*, 274–281.

Pennebaker, J. W., & Graybeal, A. (2001). Patterns of natural language use: Disclosure, personality, and social integration. *Current Directions in Psychological Science, 10*, 90–93.

Pennebaker, J. W., & Susman, J. (1988) Disclosure of trauma and psychosomatic processes. *Social Science and Medicine, 26*, 327–332.

Pennebaker, J.W. (1991). Self-expressive writing: Implications for health, education, and welfare. In S.I. Fontaine, P. Elbow, & P. Belanoff (Eds.), *Nothing begins with N: New investigations of freewriting* (pp. 157–172). Carbondale, IL: Southern Illinois Press.

Penninx, B. W. J. H., Guralnik, J. M., Havlik, R. J., Pahor, M., Ferrucci, L., Cerhan, J. R., & Wallace, R. B. (1998). Chronically depressed mood and cancer risk in older persons. *Journal of the National Cancer Institute, 90*, 1888–1896.

Pereira, M. A., Kriska, A. M., Collins, V. R., Dowse, G. K., Tuomilehto, J., Alberti, K. G. (1998). Occupational status and cardiovascular disease risk factors in the rapidly developing, high-risk population of Mauritius. *American Journal of Epidemiology, 148*, 148–159.

Pérez, C., L. Larsen, M. V., Gustafsson, R., Norström, M. M., Atlas, A., Nixon, D. F., . . . Karlsson, A. C. (2008). Broadly immunogenic HLA class I super-type-restricted elite CTL epitopes recognized in a diverse population infected with different HIV-1 subtypes. *Journal of Immunology, 180*(7), 5092–5100.

Perez-Stable, E. J., Sabogal F., Otero-Sabogal R., Hiatt R. A., & McPhee S. J. (1992). Misconceptions about cancer among Latinos and Anglos. *Journal of the American Medical Association, 268*, 3219–3223.

Perkins, H. W. (Ed.). (2003). *The social norms approach to preventing school and college age substance abuse: A handbook for educators, counselors, and clinicians.* San Francisco, CA: Jossey-Bass.

Perkins, H. W., Meilman, P., Leichliter, J., Cashin, J., & Presley, C. (1999). Misperceptions of the norms for the frequency of alcohol and other drug use on college campuses. *Journal of American College Health, 47*, 253–258.

Perkins, P., Cooksley, C. D., & Cox, P. D. (1996). Breast cancer: Is ethnicity an independent prognostic factor for survival? *Cancer, 78*, 1241–1247.

Perlman, B., & McCann, L. I. (1999). The most frequently listed courses in the undergraduate psychology curriculum. *Teaching of Psychology, 26*(3), 177.

Perloff, R. M., Bonder, B., Ray, G. B., Ray, E. B. & Siminoff, L. A. (2006). Doctor-patient communication, cultural competence and minority health: Theoretical and empirical perspectives. *American Behavioral Scientist, 49*, 835–852.

Perna, L., Mielck, A., Lacruz, M., Emeny, R., Holle, R., Breitfelder, A., & Ladwig, K. (2012). Socioeconomic position, resilience, and health behaviour among elderly people. *International Journal of Public Health, 57*(2), 341–349.

Perry-Jenkins, M., Repetti, R. L., & Crouter, A. C. (2002). Work and family in the 1990s. *Journal of Marriage and the Family, 62*, 981–998.

Persky, V., Kempthorne-Rawson, J., & Shekelle, R. (1987). Personality and risk of cancer: 20-year follow-up of the Western Electric study. *Psychosomatic Medicine, 49*, 435–449.

Pesah, E., Supervia, M., Turk-Adawi, K., & Grace, S. (2017). A review of cardiac rehabilitation delivery around the world. *Progress in Cardiovascular Diseases, 60*, 267–280.

Pesek, T.J., Helton, L.R., & Nair, M. (2006). Healing across cultures: Learning from traditions. *Eco-Health, 3*, 114–118.

Peters, W. M. K., Green, J. M., & Gauthier, P. E. (2014). Native American medicine: The implications of history and the embodiment of culture. In R. A. R. Gurung (Ed.), *Multicultural approaches to health* (pp. 171–196). Santa Barbara, CA: Praeger.

Peterson, J. L., Miner, M. H., Brennan, D. J., & Rosser, B. (2012). HIV treatment optimism and sexual risk behaviors among HIV positive African American men who have sex with men. *AIDS Education & Prevention, 24*(2), 91–101. doi:10.1521/aeap.2012.24.2.91

Petridou, E., Zavitsanos, X., Dessypris, N., Frangakis, C., Mandyla, M., Doziadis, S., & Trichopoulous, D. (1997). Adolescents in high-risk trajectory: Clustering of risky behavior and the origins of socioeconomic health differentials. *Preventive Medicine, 26*, 215–219.

Petrie, H. J., Stover, E. A., & Horswill, C. A. (2004) Nutritional concerns for the child and adolescent competitor. *Nutrition, 20*(7–8), 620–631.

Petrie, K. J., Booth, R., Pennebaker, J. W., Davidson, K. P., & Thomas, M. (1995). Disclosure of trauma and immune response to Hepatitis B vaccination program. *Journal of Consulting and Clinical Psychology, 63*, 787–792.

Pettingale, K. W. (1985). Towards a psychobiological model of cancer: Biological considerations. *Social Science and Medicine, 20*, 779–787.

Pew Research Center. (2017). American say religious aspects of Christmas are declining in public life. Author, Washington, DC. Retrieved from http://www.pewforum.org/2017/12/12/americans-say-religious-aspects-of-christmas-are-declining-in-public-life/

Pew Research Center. (2008). U.S. Religious landscape survey: Religious affiliation Author, Washington, DC. Retrieved from http://www.pewforum.org/2008/02/01/u-s-religious-landscape-survey-religious-affiliation/

Pfefferbaum, B., Adams, J., & Aceves, J. (1990). The influence of culture on pain in Anglo and Hispanic children with cancer. *ournal of the American Academy of Child and Adolescent Psychiatry, 29*, 642–647.

Pham, C. T., & McPhee, S. J. (1992). Knowledge, attitudes, and practices of breast and cervical cancer screening among Vietnamese women. *Journal of Cancer Education, 7*, 305–310.

Phares, T., Stohlman, S., Hwang, M., Min, B., Hinton, D., & Bergmann, C. (2012). CD4 T cells promote CD8 T cell immunity at the priming and effector site during viral encephalitis. *Journal of Virology, 86*(5), 2416–2427.

Phelps, C., Bennett, P., Jones, H., Hood, K., Brain, K., & Murray, A. (2010). The development of a cancer genetic-specific measure of coping: The GRACE. *Psycho-Oncology, 19*(8), 847–854. doi:10.1002/pon.1629

Phillips, B. (2012). Towards evidence based medicine for paediatricians. *Archives of Disease in Childhood, 97*(2), 172. doi:10.1136/archdischild-2011-301382

Phillips, D. (1996). Medical professional dominance and client dissatisfactions: A study of doctor-patient interaction and reported dissatisfaction with medical care among female patients at four hospitals in Trinidad and Tobago. *Social Science and Medicine, 42*, 1419–1425.

Phillips, D. P., Liu, G. C., Kwok, K., Jarvinen, J. R., Zhang, W., & Abramson, I. A. (2001). The *Hound of the Baskervilles* effect: Natural experiment on the influence of psychological stress on timing of death. *British Medical Journal, 323*(7327), 1443–1446.

Phillips, W. T., Kiernan, M., & King, A. C. (2002). The effects of physical activity on physical and psychological health. In A. Baum, T. A. Revenson, & J. E. Singer (Eds.), *Handbook of health psychology* (1e, pp. 627–659). Mahwah, NJ: Erlbaum.

Phinney, J. S. (1996). When we talk about American ethnic groups, what do we mean? *American Psychologist, 51*, 918–927.

Phinney, J., & Rosenthal, D. (1992). Ethnic identity formation in adolescence: Process, context, and outcome. In G. Adams, T. Gulotta, & R. Montemayor (Eds.), *Identity formation during adolescence* (pp. 145–172). Newbury Park, CA: SAGE.

Piché, M., Arsenault, M., Poitras, P., Rainville, P., & Bouin, M. (2010). Widespread hypersensitivity is related to altered pain inhibition processes in irritable bowel syndrome. *Pain, 148*(1), 49–58. doi:10.1016/j.pain.2009.10.005

Pichenot, M., Deuffic-Burban, S., Cuzin, L., & Yazdanpanah, Y. (2012). Efficacy of new antiretroviral drugs in treatment-experienced HIV-infected patients: A systematic review and meta-analysis of recent randomized controlled trials. *HIV Medicine, 13*(3), 148–155. doi:10.1111/j.1468-1293.2011.00953.x

Pickin, C., & St. Leger, S. (1993). *Assessing health need using the life cycle framework*. Buckingham, UK: Open University Press.

Pierce, G. R., Lakey, B., Sarason, I. G., & Sarason, B. R. (1997). Sourcebook of social support and personality. In G. R. Pierce, B. Lakey, I. G. Sarason, & B. R. Sarason (Eds.), *The Plenum series in social/clinical psychology*. New York, NY: Plenum Press.

Pietschnig, J., Voracek, M., & Formann, A. K. (2010). Mozart effect–Shmozart effect: A meta-analysis. *Intelligence, 38*(3), 314–323. doi:10.1016/j.intell.2010.03.001

Pilatti, A., Cupani, M., & Pautassi, R. M. (2015). Personality and alcohol expectancies discriminate alcohol consumption patterns in female college students. *Alcohol and Alcoholism, 50*(4), 385–392. doi:10.1093/alcalc/agv025

Pillai, J. A., Hall, C. B., Dickson, D. W., Buschke, H., Lipton, R. B., & Verghese, J. (2011). Association of crossword puzzle participation with memory decline in persons who develop dementia. *Journal of The International Neuropsychological Society, 17*(6), 1006–1013. doi:10.1017/S1355617711001111

Pilowsky, I., & Spence, N. D. (1975). Patterns of illness behavior in patients with intractable pain. *Journal of Psychosomatic Research, 19*, 279–287.

Pinckney, R. (2003). *Blue roots: African American folk magic of the Gullah people*. Orangeburg, SC: Sandlapper Publishing CO.

Pineles, B. L., Park, E., & Samet, J. M. (2014). Systematic review and meta-analysis of miscarriage and maternal exposure to tobacco smoke during pregnancy. *American Journal of Epidemiology, 179*(7), 807–823. doi:10.1093/aje/kwt334

Pines, A. M., Ben-Ari, A., Utaso, A., & Larson, D. (2002). A cross-cultural investigation of social support and burnout. *European Psychologist, 7*, 256–264.

Piper, L. (2011). The ethical leadership challenge: Creating a culture of patient- and family-centered care in the hospital setting. *Health Care Manager, 30*(2), 125–132.

Pi-Sunyer, X. (1998). A clinical view of the obesity problem. *Science, 299*, 859–861.

Pivik, R. T., Tennal, K. B., Chapman, S. D., & Gu, Y. (2012). Eating breakfast enhances the efficiency of neural networks engaged during mental arithmetic in school-aged children. *Physiology & Behavior, 106*(4), 548–555. doi:10.1016/j.physbeh.2012.03.034

Planalp, S., & Trost, M. (2008). Communication issues at the end of life: Reports from Hospice Volunteers. *Health Communication, 23*(3), 222–233.

Pleis, J.R., & Lethbridge-Çejku, M. (2007). Summary health statistics for U.S. adults: National Health Interview Survey, 2006. *National Center for Health Statistics. Vital Health Statistics, 10*(235).

Pletcher, M. J., Kertesz, S. G., Kohn, M. A., & Gonzales, R. (2008). Trends in opioid prescribing by race/ethnicity for patients seeking care in us emergency departments. *Journal of the American Medical Association, 299*, 70–78.

Polich, J., Pollock, V. E., & Bloom, F. E. (1994). Meta-analysis of P300 amplitude from males at risk for alcoholism. *Psychological Bulletin, 115*, 55–73.

Politi, M. C., Han, P. K. J., & Col, N. F. (2007). Communicating the uncertainty of harms and benefits of medical interventions. *Medical Decision Making, 27*, 681–695.

Pollan, M. (2008). *In Defense of Food: An eater's manifesto*. London, UK: Penguin.

Pollock, S. E. (1986). Human responses to chronic illness: Physiologic and psychosocial adaptation. *Nursing Research, 35*, 90–95.

Polyakova, S. A., & Pacquiao, D. F. (2006). Psychological and mental illness among elder immigrants from the former Soviet Union. *Journal of Transcultural Nursing, 17*, 40–49.

Pomerleau, O. F., & Kardia, S. L. R. (1999). Introduction to the featured section: Genetic research on smoking. *Health Psychology, 18*, 3–6.

Pope, L., & Wolf, R. L. (2012). The influence of labeling the vegetable content of snack food on children's taste preferences: A pilot study. *Journal of Nutrition Education & Behavior, 44*(2), 178–182. doi:10.1016/j.jneb.2010.02.006

Popkin, B. M., & Udry, J. R. (1998). Adolescent obesity increases significantly in second- and third-generation U.S. immigrants: The National Longitudinal Study of Adolescent Health. *Journal of Nutrition, 128*, 701–706.

Porter, J. R., & Washington, R. E. (1993). Minority identity and self-esteem. *Annual Review of Sociology, 19*, 139–161.

Porter, N. (2003). *Report of focus group findings for messages development related to CDC/ACSM physical activity guidelines*. Contract No.: GS-23F0231N. Centers for Disease Control and Prevention, Washington, DC.

Porter, R. (2002). *Blood and guts: A short history of medicine*. New Delhi, India: Penguin.

Potter, J. D., & Steinmetz, K. (1996). Vegetables, fruit, and phytoestrogens as preventative agents. *IARC Science Publications, 139*, 61–90.

Powell, L. H., Shahabi, L., & Thoresen, C. E. (2003). Religion and spirituality: Linkages to physical health. *American Psychologist, 58*, 36–52.

Prasadarao, P. S. D. V. (2014). Understanding international perspectives: Implications for U.S. health and wellness. In R. A. R. Gurung (Ed.), *Multicultural approaches to health and wellness in America* (pp. 1–34). Santa Barbara, CA: Praeger.

Prasadarao, P. S. D. V., & Sudhir, P.M. (2001). Clinical psychology in India. *Journal of Clinical Psychology in Medical Settings, 8*, 31–38.

Praschak-Rieder, N., Willeit, M., Sitte, H. H., Meyer, J. H., & Kasper, S. (2011). FC29-05 - Season, sunlight, and brain serotonin function. *European Psychiatry, 261981, 26*(1), 1981. doi:10.1016/S0924-9338(11)73684-7

Prati, G., Pietrantoni, L., & Zani, B. (2012). The prediction of intention to consume genetically modified food: Test of an integrated psychosocial model. *Food Quality & Preference, 25*(2), 163–170. doi:10.1016/j.foodqual.2012.02.011

Pratt, L. A., & Brody, D. J. (2008). Depression in the United States household population, 2005–2006. Data Brief 7, National Center for Health Services, Washington, DC. http://www.cdc.gov/nchs/data/databriefs/db07.pdf

Prestage, G., Down, I., Bradley, J., McCann, P., Brown, G., Jin, F., & Hurley, M. (2012). Is optimism enough? Gay men's beliefs about HIV and their perspectives on risk and pleasure. *Sexually Transmitted Diseases, 39*(3), 167–172.

Price, D., Bush, F., Long, S., & Harkins, S. (1994). A comparison of pain measurement characteristics of mechanical visual analogue and simple numerical rating scales. *Pain, 56*(2), 217–226.

Primack, B. A., Longacre, M. R., Beach, M. L., Adachi-Mejia, A. M., Titus, L. J., & Dalton, M. A. (2012). Association of established smoking among adolescents with timing of exposure to smoking depicted in movies. *Journal of The National Cancer Institute, 104*(7), 549–555.

Probst, J. C., Greenhouse, D. L., & Selassie, A. W. (1997). Patient and physician satisfaction with an outpatient care visit. *Journal of Family Practice, 45*, 418–425.

Prochaska, J. O., & DiClemente, C. C. (1983). Stages and processes of self-change in smoking: Towards an integrative model of change. *Journal of Consulting and Clinical Psychology, 51*, 390–395.

Prochaska, J. O., Redding, C. A. & Evers, K. E. (2015). The transtheoretical model and stages of change. In K. Glanz, B. K. Rimer, & K. Viswanath (Eds.), *Health behavior: Theory, research, and practice* (5e, pp. 125–148). San Fransisco, CA: Jossey-Bass.

Prochaska, J. O., Redding, C. A., & Evers, K. E. (2002). The transtheoretical model and stages of change. In K. Glanz, B. K. Rimer, & F. M. Lewis (Eds.), *Health behavior and health education: Theory, research, and practice* (pp. 99–120). San Francisco, CA: Jossey-Bass.

Prochaska, M. T., Putman, M. S., Tak, H. J., Yoon, J. D., & Curlin, F. A. (2017). U.S. physicians overwhelmingly endorse hospice as the better option for most patients at the end of life. *American Journal of Hospice & Palliative Medicine, 34*(6), 556–558. doi:10.1177/1049909116636344

Protheroe, J., Bower, P., Chew-Graham, C., Peters, T., & Fahey, T. (2007). Effectiveness of a computerized decision aid in primary care on decision making and quality of life in menorrhagia: results of the MENTIP randomized controlled trial. *Medical Decision Making, 27*(5), 575–584.

Pruessner, M., Cullen, A. E., Aas, M., & Walker, E. F. (2017). The neural diathesis-stress model of schizophrenia revisited: An update on recent findings considering illness stage and neurobiological and methodological complexities. *Neuroscience and Biobehavioral Reviews, 73*, 191–218. doi:10.1016/j.neubiorev.2016.12.013

Prus, A. (2018). *Drugs and the neuroscience of behavior: An introduction to psychopharmacology.* Los Angeles, CA: SAGE.

Pryzdoga, J., & Chrisler, J. C. (2000). Definitions of gender and sex: The subtleties of meaning. *Sex Roles, 43*, 553–569.

Ptacek, J. T., Smith, R. E., & Zanas, J. (1992). Gender, appraisal, and coping: A longitudinal analysis. *Journal of Personality, 60*, 747–771.

Puig-Perez, S., Hackett, R. A., Salvador, A., & Steptoe, A. (2017). Optimism moderates psychophysiological responses to stress in older people with type 2 diabetes. *Psychophysiology, 54*(4), 536–543. doi:10.1111/psyp.12806

Purnell, L. (2009). *Guide to culturally competent health care*. Philadelphia, PA: F. A. Davis.

Purnell, L. (2013). *Transcultural health care: A culturally competent approach* (4ed). Philadelphia, PA: Davis.

Purnell, L., & Pontious, S. (2014). In R. A. R. Gurung (Ed.), *Multicultural approaches to health and wellness in America: Major issues and cultural groups* (pp. 1–28). Santa Barbara, CA: Praeger.

Purnell, L., Davidhizar, R. E., Giger, J., Strickland, O. L., Fishman, D., & Allison, D. M. (2011). A guide to developing a culturally competent organization. *Journal of Transcultural Nursing, 22*(1), 7–14. doi:10.1177/1043659610387147

Puvanachandra, P., Hoe, C., El-Sayed, H., Saad, R., Al-Gasseer, N., Bakr, M., & Hyder, A. (2012). Road traffic injuries and data systems in Egypt: Addressing the challenges. *Traffic Injury Prevention, 13*, Suppl, 144–156.

Qi, L., Parast, L., Cai, T., Powers, C., Gervino, E. V., Hauser, T. H., & . . . Doria, A. (2011). Genetic susceptibility to coronary heart disease in type 2 diabetes: 3 independent studies. *Journal of the American College of Cardiology, 58*(25), 2675–2682. doi:10.1016/j.jacc.2011.08.054

Qureshi, N., Kai, J., Middlemass, J., Dhiman, P., Cross-Bardell, L., Acharya, J., . . . Standen, P. J. (2015). Comparison of coronary heart disease genetic assessment with conventional cardiovascular risk assessment in primary care: Reflections on a feasibility study. *Primary Health Care Research and Development, 16*(6), 607–617. doi:10.1017/S1463423615000122

Racette, S. B., Deusinger, S. S., Strube, M. J., Highstein, G. R., & Deusinger, R. H. (2005) Weight changes, exercise, and dietary patterns during freshman and sophomore years of college. *Journal of American College Health, 53*, 245–251.

Racine, M., Tousignant-Laflamme, Y., Kloda, L. A., Dion, D., Dupuis, G., & Choinière, M. (2012). A systematic literature review of 10 years of research on sex/gender and experimental pain perception – Part 1: Are there really differences between women and men? *Pain (03043959), 153*(3), 602–618. doi:10.1016/j.pain.2011.11.025

Raglin, J. S. (1997). Anxiolytic effects of physical activity. In W. P. Morgan (Ed.), *Physical activity and mental health. Series in health psychology and behavioral medicine* (pp. 107–126). Philadelphia, PA: Taylor & Francis.

Rahe, R. H. (1972). Subjects' recent life changes and their near future illness reports. *Annals of Clinical Research, 4*, 250–265.

Rahim-Williams, B., Riley, J., Williams, A., & Fillingim, R. (2012). A quantitative review of ethnic group differences in experimental pain response: Do biology, psychology, and culture matter? *Pain Medicine* (Malden, MA), *13*(4), 522–540. doi:10.1111/j.1526-4637.2012.01336.x

Rahim-Williams, F. B., Riley, J. L., Herrera, D., Campbell, C. M., Hastie, B. A., & Fillingim, R. B. (2007). Ethnic identity predicts experimental pain sensitivity in African Americans and Hispanics. *Pain, 129*, 177–184.

Rainville, P., Carrier, B., Hofbauer, R. K., Bushnell, M. C., & Duncan, G. H. (1999). Dissociation of sensory and affective dimensions in pain using hypnotic modulation. *Pain, 82*, 159–171.

Rakel, D., Barrett, B., Zhang, Z., Hoeft, T., Chewning, B., Marchand, L., & Scheder, J. (2011). Perception of empathy in the therapeutic encounter: Effects on the common cold. *Patient Education & Counseling, 85*(3), 390–397. doi:10.1016/j.pec.2011.01.009

Ramakrishna, J., & Weiss, M. G. (1992, September). Health, illness, and immigration: East Indians in the United States. *Western Journal of Medicine, 157*(3), 265–271.

Ramsay, S., Morris, R., Whincup, P., Papacosta, A., Thomas, M., & Wannamethee, S. (2011). Prediction of coronary heart disease risk by Framingham and SCORE risk assessments varies by socioeconomic position: Results from a study in British men. *European Journal of Cardiovascular Prevention and Rehabilitation, 18*(2), 186–193.

Ranby, K. (2019). Major research designs in health psychology. In T. A. Revenson & R. A. R. Gurung (Eds.), *Handbook of health psychology* (3e). New York, NY: Routledge.

Rand, C. S., & Weeks, K. (1998). Measuring adherence with medication regimens in clinical care and research. In S. A. Shumaker, E. B. Schron, J. K. Ockene, & W. L. McBee (Eds.), *The handbook of health behavior change* (2nd ed., pp. 114–132). New York, NY: Springer.

Randall, A. (2012). Why Black women are fat. *New York Times*, May 6. http://www.nytimes.com/2012/05/06/opinion/sunday/why-black-women-are-fat.html?_r=1&partner=rss&emc=rss

Ranehill, E., Dreber, A., Johannesson, M., Leiberg, S., Sul, S., & Weber, R. A. (2015). Assessing the robustness of power posing: No effect on hormones and risk tolerance in a large sample of men and women. *Psychological Science, 26*(5), 653–656. doi:10.1177/0956797614553946

Rapkin, B. D., Garcia, I., Michael, W., Zhang, J., & Schwartz, C. E. (2017). Distinguishing appraisal and personality influences on quality of life in chronic illness: Introducing the quality-of-life appraisal profile version 2. *Quality of Life Research, 26*, 2815–2829. doi:10.1007/s11136-017-1600-y

Rapoff, M. A. (1999). *Adherence to pediatric medical regimens*. New York, NY: Kluwer Academic/Plenum Publishers.

Rashid, M., & Zimring, C. (2008). review of the empirical literature on the relationship between indoor environment and stress in health care and office settings: Problems and prospects of sharing evidence. *Environment and Behavior, 40*, 151–190.

Rauschenbach, C., & Hertel, G. (2011). Age differences in strain and emotional reactivity to stressors in professional careers. *Stress & Health, 27*(2), e48–e60. doi:10.1002/smi.1335

Rauscher, F. H., Shaw, G. L., & Ky, K. N. (1995). Listening to Mozart enhances spatial-temporal reasoning: Towards a neurophysiological basis. *Neuroscience Letters, 185*, 44–47.

Ravnskov, U. (2008). The fallacies of the lipid hypothesis. *Scandinavian Cardiovascular Journal: SCJ, 42*(4), 236–239.

Ravussin, E., & Rising, R. (1992). Daily energy expenditure in humans: Measurements in a respiratory chamber and by doubly labeled water. In J. M. Kinney & H. N. Tucker (Eds.), *Energy metabolism: Tissue determinants and cellular corollaries* (pp. 81–96). New York, NY: Raven Press.

Ravussin, E., Valencia, M. E., Esparza, J., Bennett, P. H., & Schulz, L. O. (1994). Effects of a traditional lifestyle on obesity in Pima Indians. *Diabetes Care, 17*, 1067–1074.

Rawl, S. M., Champion, V. L., Menon, U., & Foster, J. L. (2000). The impact of age and race on mammography practices. *Health Care for Women International, 21*, 583–597.

Ray, C., Jefferies, S., & Weir, W. R. (1995). Life-events and the course of chronic fatigue syndrome. *British Journal of Medical Psychology, 68*, 323–331.

Read, J., & Gorman, B. (2007). Racial/ethnic differences in hypertension and depression among U.S. adult women. *Ethnicity and Disease, 17*(2), 389–396.

Ready, T. (1988). Too few minorities in AIDS tests, critics say, scientists "ignoring" Blacks, Hispanics, women. *Washington Watch*, 1.

Reaven, P. D., Barrett-Conner, E., & Edelstein, S. (1991). Relation between leisure-time physical activity and blood pressure in older women. *Circulation, 83*, 559–565.

Redd, W. H., & Jacobsen, P. (2001). Behavioral intervention in comprehensive cancer care. In A. Baum, T. A. Revenson, & J. E. Singer (Eds.), *Handbook of health psychology* (1e, pp. 757–776). Mahwah, NJ: Erlbaum.

Redding, C. A., Brown-Peterside, P., Noar, S. M., Rossi, J. S., & Koblin, B. A. (2011). One session of TTM-tailored condom use feedback: A pilot study among at-risk women in the Bronx. *AIDS Care, 23*(1), 10–15. doi:10.1080/09540121.2010.498858

Reed, G. M., Kemeny, M. E., Taylor, S. E., & Visscher, B. R. (1999). Negative HIV-specific expectations and AIDS-related bereavement as predictors of symptom onset in asymptomatic HIV- positive gay men. *Health Psychology, 18*, 354–363.

Reed, G. M., Kemeny, M. E., Taylor, S. E., Wang, H. Y., & Visscher, B. R. (1994). Realistic acceptance as a predictor of decreased survival time in gay men with AIDS. *Health Psychology, 13*, 299–307.

Reedy, J., Mitrou, P. N., Krebs-Smith, S. M., Wirfält, E., Flood, A., Kipnis, V., . . . Subar, A. F. (2008). Index-based dietary patterns and risk of colorectal cancer: The NIH-AARP Diet and Health Study. *American Journal of Epidemiology, 168*(1), 38–48.

Reich, M., Lesur, A., & Perdrizet-Chevallier, C. (2008). Depression, quality of life and breast cancer: A review of the literature. *Breast Cancer Research and Treatment, 110*(1), 9–17.

Reiche, E. M. V., Nunes, S., & Morimoto, H. (2004). Stress, depression, the immune system, and cancer. *The Lancet Oncology, 5*, 617–625.

Reid, D. P. (1989). *The tao of health, sex, and longevity: A modern practical guide to the ancient way*. New York, NY: Simon & Schuster.

Reis, A. L. (1993). Adherence in the patient with pulmonary disease. In J. E. Hodgkin, G. L. Conners, & C. W. Bell (Eds.), *Pulmonary rehabilitation* (2nd ed., pp. 86–101). Philadelphia, PA: Lippincott.

Relman, A. S., & Angell, M. (2002). Resolved: Psychosocial interventions can improve clinical outcomes in organic disease (Con). *Psychosomatic Medicine, 64*(4), 558–563.

Renahy, E., Parizot, I., & Chauvin, P. (2008). Health information seeking on the Internet: Adouble divide? Results from a representative survey in the Paris metropolitan area, France, 2005–2006. *BMC Public Health, 8*, 69–69.

Renaud, S. C., Gueguen, R., Siest, G., & Salamon, R. (1999). Wine, beer, and mortality in middle-aged men from eastern France. *Archives of Internal Medicine, 159*, 1865–1870.

Rendina, H. J., Whitfield, T. H. F., Grov, C., Starks, T. J., & Parsons, J. T. (2017). Distinguishing hypothetical willingness from behavioral intentions to initiate HIV pre-exposure prophylaxis (PrEP): Findings from a large cohort of gay and bisexual men in the U.S. *Social Science & Medicine, 172*, 115–123. doi:10.1016/j.socscimed.2016.10.030

Repetti, R. L. (1998). The promise of a multiple roles paradigm for women's health research. *Women's Health: Research on Gender, Behavior, and Policy, 4*, 273–80.

Repetti, R. L., & Wood, J. (1997). Effects of daily stress at work on mothers' interactions with preschoolers. *Journal of Family Psychology, 11*, 90–108.

Repetti, R. L., Taylor, S. E., & Seeman, T. E. (2002). Risky families: Family social environment and the mental and physical health of offspring. *Psychological Bulletin, 128*, 330–366.

Repetti, R., & Wang, S. (2017). Effects of job stress on family relationships. *Current Opinion in Psychology, 13*, 15–18. doi:10.1016/j.copsyc.2016.03.010

Revenson, T. A., & Lepore, S. J. (2012). Coping in social context. In A. Baum, T. A. Revenson, & J. Singer (Eds.), *Handbook of health psychology* (2e, pp. 193–218). New York, NY: Taylor & Francis.

Reyes-Gibby, C. C., Aday, L. A., Todd, K. H., Cleeland, C., Anderson, K. O. (2007). Pain in aging community-dwelling adults in the United States: Non-Hispanic Whites, Non-Hispanic Blacks, and Hispanics. *Journal of Pain, 8*, 75–84.

Reynolds, D. V. (1969). Surgery in the rat during electrical analgesia induced by focal brain stimulation. *Science, 164*, 444–445.

Reynolds, P., & Kaplan, G. A. (1990). Social connections and risk for cancer: Prospective evidence from the Alameda County Study. *Behavioral Medicine, 16*, 101–110.

Ricciardelli, L. A., & McCabe, M. P. (2001). Dietary restraint and negative effect as mediators of body dissatisfaction and bulimic behavior in adolescent girls and boys. *Behavior Research and Therapy, 39*, 1317–1329.

Richards, J. M., Pennebaker, J. W., & Beall, W. E. (1995). The effects of criminal offense and disclosure in prison inmates. Paper presented at the Midwest Psychological Association, Chicago.

Richards, J. S., Nepomuceno, C., Riles, M., & Suer, Z. (1982). Assessing pain behavior: The UAB pain behavior scale. *Pain, 14*(4), 393–398. doi:10.1016/0304-3959(82)90147-6

Richards, R., & Smith, C. (2007). Environmental, parental, and personal influences on food choice, access, and overweight status among homeless children. *Social Science and Medicine, 65*, 1572–1583.

Richardson, P. J., Wodak, A. D., Atkinson, L., Saunders, J. B., & Jewitt, D. E. (1986). Relationship between alcohol intake, myocardial enzyme activity, and myocardial function in dilated cardiomyopathy: Evidence for the concept of alcohol induced heart muscle disease. *British Heart Journal, 56*, 165–170.

Richman, L. S., Kohn-Wood, L. P., & Williams, D. R. (2007). The role of discrimination and racial identity for mental health service utilization. *Journal of Social and Clinical Psychology, 26*, 960–981.

Richmond, M. (2004). *Practice organization action alert*. APAPO Government Relations Office. Washington, DC.

Ries, L. A. G. (1996). Cancer rates. In A. Harras, B. K. Edwards, W. J. Blot, & L. A. G. Ries (Eds.), *Cancer rates and risks* (pp. 9–54). NIH Publication No. 96–961). Bethesda, MD: National Cancer Institute.

Rigotti, N. A., Lee, J. E., & Wechsler, H. (2000). U.S. college students' use of tobacco products: Results of a national survey. *Journal of the American Medical Association, 264*, 699–705.

Riley, J. L., Wade, J. B., Myers, C. D., Sheffield, D., Papas, R. K., & Price, D. D. (2002). Racial/ethnic differences in the experience of chronic pain. *Pain, 100*, 291–298.

Rime, B. (1995). Mental rumination, social sharing, and the recovery from emotional exposure. In J. W. Pennebaker (Ed.), *Emotion, disclosure, & health* (pp. 271–291). Washington, DC: American Psychological Association.

Rimer, B. K. (1994). Mammography use in the U.S.: Trends and the impact of interventions. *Annals of Behavioral Medicine, 16*, 317–326.

Rimer, B. K. (2002). Perspectives on intrapersonal theories of health behavior. In K. Glanz, B. K. Rimer, & F. M. Lewis (Eds.), *Health behavior and health education: Theory, research, and practice* (pp. 144–164). San Francisco, CA: Jossey-Bass.

Rimer, B. K., & Kreuter, M. W. (2006). Advancing tailored health communication: A persuasion and message effects perspective. *Journal of Communication*, 56S184-S201. doi:10.1111/j.1460-2466.2006.00289.x

Rimm, E. B., & Ellison, R. C. (1995). Alcohol in the Mediterranean diet. *American Journal of Clinical Nutrition*, *61*, 1378S–1382S.

Risberg, G. (1994). Sexual violence as a health problem: Caregivers' reluctance to ask questions makes rehabilitation of women more difficult. *Lakartidningen*, *91*, 4770–4771.

Rittenberg, V., Sobaleva, S., Ahmad, A., Oteng-Ntim, E., Bolton, V., Khalaf, Y., & . . . El-Toukhy, T. (2011). Influence of BMI on risk of miscarriage after single blastocyst transfer. *Human Reproduction* (Oxford, UK), *26*(10), 2642–2650.

Roach, M. (2006). *Spook: Science tackles the afterlife*. New York, NY: Norton.

Robert, S. A. (1999). Socioeconomic risk factors for breast cancer: Distinguishing individual- and community-level effects. *Epidemiology*, *15*, 4422450

Roberts, S., & Nuru-Jeter, A. (2011). Universal alcohol/drug screening in prenatal care: A strategy for reducing racial disparities? Questioning the assumptions. *Maternal & Child Health Journal*, *15*(8), 1127–1134. doi:10.1007/s10995-010-0720-6

Robins, L. N., Locke, B. Z., & Regier, D. A. (1991). An overview of psychiatric disorders in America. In L. N. Robins & D. A. Regier (Eds.), *Psychiatric disorders in America: The epidemiologic catchment areas study* (pp. 328–366). New York, NY: Free Press.

Robinson, H., Ravikulan, A., Nater, U. M., Skoluda, N., Jarrett, P., & Broadbent, E. (2017). The role of social closeness during tape stripping to facilitate skin barrier recovery: Preliminary findings. *Health Psychology*, *36*(7), 619–629. doi:10.1037/hea0000492

Robinson, T. N., Patrick, K., Eng, T. R., & Gustafson, D. (1998). An evidence-based approach to interactive health communication: A challenge to medicine in the information age. *Journal of Psychosomatic Research*, *47*, 439–447.

Robinson, W., Moody-Thomas, S., & Gruber, D. (2012). Patient perspectives on tobacco cessation services for persons living with HIV/AIDS. *AIDS Care*, *24*(1), 71–76. doi:10.1080/09540121.2011.582078

Robison, K., Clark, L., Eng, W., Wu, L., Raker, C., Clark, M., . . . Dizon, D. S. (2014). Cervical cancer prevention: Asian-American women's knowledge and participation in screening practices. *Women's Health Issues*, *24*(2), e231–e236. doi:10.1016/j.whi.2013.12.005

Robles, T., Mercado, E., Nooteboom, P., Price, J., & Romney, C. (2019). Biological processes of health. In T. A. Revenson & R. A. R. Gurung (Eds.), *Handbook of health psychology* (3e). New York, NY: Routledge.

Roethel, A., & Gurung, R. A. R. (2007, August). *Managing stress: Which techniques are the most effective?* Poster presented at the annual meeting of the American Psychological Association: San Francisco, CA.

Rogers, A. T. (2010). Exploring health beliefs and care-seeking behaviors of older USA-dwelling Mexicans and Mexican-Americans. *Ethnicity & Health*, *15*, 581–599.

Rogers, C. R., Mitchell, J. A., Franta, G. J., Foster, M. J., & Shires, D. (2017). Masculinity, racism, social support, and colorectal cancer screening uptake among African American men: A systematic review. *American Journal of Men's Health*, *11*(5), 1486–1500. doi:10.1177/1557988315611227

Rogers, E. M. (1983). *Diffusion of innovations*. New York, NY: Free Press.

Rogers, H. L., Siminoff, L. A., Longo, D. R., & Thomson, M. D. (2017). Coping with prediagnosis symptoms of colorectal cancer: A study of 244 individuals with recent diagnosis. *Cancer Nursing*, *40*(2), 145–151. doi:10.1097/NCC.0000000000000361

Rogers, S. J., Parcel, T. L., & Menaghan, E. G. (1991). The effects of maternal working conditions and mastery on child behavior problems: Studying the intergenerational transmission of social control. *Journal of Health and Social Behavior*, *32*, 145–164.

Rogers, V. L., Griffin, M., Wykle, M. L., & Fitzpatrick, J. J. (2009). Internet versus face-to-face therapy: Emotional self-disclosure issues for young adults. *Issues in Mental Health Nursing*, *30*(10).

Roizen, J. (1997). Epidemiological issues in alcohol-related violence. In M. Galanter (Ed.), *Recent developments in alcoholism* (pp. 7–40). New York, NY: Plenum.

Roland, A. (1991). *In search of self in India and Japan: Toward a cross-cultural psychology*. Princeton, NJ: Princeton University Press.

Rollman, G. B. (2003). Sex makes a difference: Experimental and clinical pain responses. *Clinical Journal of Pain*, *19*, 204–207.

Rollnick, S., William, W. R., & Butler, C.C. (2008). *Motivational interviewing in health care: Helping patients change behavior*. New York, NY: Guilford Press.

Rolls, B. J., & Shide, D. J. (1992). Moth naturalistic and laboratory-based studies contribute to the understanding of human eating behavior. *Appetite*, *19*, 76–77.

Romano, J. M., Jensen, M. P., & Turner, J. A. (2003). The chronic pain coping inventory-42: Reliability and validity. *Pain (03043959)*, *104*(1/2), 65. doi:10.1016/S0304-3959(02)00466-9

Ronksley, P. E., Brien, S. E., Turner, B. J., Mukamal, K. J., & Ghali, W. A. (2011). Association of alcohol consumption with selected cardiovascular disease outcomes: A systematic review and meta-analysis. *BMJ*, *342*, d671. doi:10.1136/BMJ.D671

Roohafza, H., Talaei, M., Pourmoghaddas, Z., Rajabi, F., & Sadeghi, M. (2012). Association of social support and coping strategies with acute coronary syndrome: A case-control study. *Journal of Cardiology*, *59*(2), 154–159.

Rook, K. S., & Schuster, T. L. (1996). Compensatory processes in the social networks of older adults. In G. R. Pierce, B. R. Sarason, & I. G. Sarason (Eds.), *Handbook of social support and the family. Plenum series on stress and coping* (pp. 219–248). New York, NY: Plenum Press.

Roos, L. E., Giuliano, R. J., Beauchamp, K. G., Gunnar, M., Amidon, B., & Fisher, P. A. (2017). Validation of autonomic and endocrine reactivity to a laboratory stressor in young children. *Psychoneuroendocrinology*, *77*, 51–55. doi:10.1016/j.psyneuen.2016.11.023

Rosario, M., Nahler, K., Hunter, J., & Gwadz, M. (1999). Understanding the unprotected sexual behaviors of gay, lesbian, and bisexual youths: An empirical test of the cognitive-environmental model. *Health Psychology*, *18*, 272–80.

Roscoe, L., & Hyer, K. (2008). Quality of life at the end of life for nursing home residents: Perceptions of hospice and nursing home staff members. *Journal of Pain and Symptom Management*, *35*(1), 1–9.

Rose, T., Barker, M., Maria Jacob, C., Morrison, L., Lawrence, W., Strömmer, S., . . . Baird, J. (2017). A systematic review of digital interventions for improving the diet and physical activity behaviors of adolescents. *Journal of Adolescent Health*, *61*(6), 669–677. doi:10.1016/j.jadohealth.2017.05.024

Rosen, D., Spencer, M. S., Tolman, R. M., Williams, D. R., Jackson, J. S. (2003). Psychiatric disorders and substance dependence among unmarried low-income mothers. *Health and Social Work*, *28*, 157–65.

Rosenbaum, E., Gautier, H., Fobair, P., Neri, E., Festa, B., Hawn, M., . . . Spiegel, D. (2004). Cancer supportive care, improving the quality of life for cancer patients: A program evaluation report. *Supportive Care in Cancer*, *12*, 293–301.

Rosenberg, M. (1965). *Society and the adolescent self image.* Princeton, NJ: Princeton University Press.

Rosenberg, P. S., & Biggar, R. J. (1998). Trends in HIV incidence among young adults in the United States. *Journal of the American Medical Association, 279,* 1894–1899.

Rosenberger, P. H., Jokl, P., & Ickovics, J. (2006). Psychosocial factors and surgical outcomes: An evidence-based literature review. *Journal of the American Academy of Orthopedic Surgery, 14*(7), 397–405.

Rosenblatt, P. C. (1993). Cross-cultural variation in the experience, expression, and understanding of grief. In D. P. Irish, K. F. Lund-quist, & V. J. Nelsen (Eds.), *Ethnic variations in death, dying, and grief.* Washington, DC: Taylor & Francis.

Rosenblatt, P. C. (2007). Culture, socialization, and loss, grief and mourning. In D. Balk, C. Wogrin, G. Thornton, D. Meagher (Eds.), *Handbook of thanatology: The essential body of knowledge for the student of death, dying, and bereavement* (pp. 115–120). Northbrook, IL: Association for Death Education and Counseling.

Rosenhan, D. L., & Seligman, M. E. P. (1989). *Abnormal psychology* (2nd ed.). New York, NY: Norton.

Rosenman, R. H., & Friedman, M. (1974). Neurogenic factors in pathogenesis of coronary heart disease. *Medical Clinics of North America, 58,* 269–279.

Rosenstock, I. M. (1960). What research in motivation suggests for public health. *American Journal of Public Health, 50,* 295–301.

Rosenstock, I. M. (1974). Historical origins of the health belief model. In M. H. Becker (Ed.), *The health belief model and personal health behavior* (pp. 1–8). Thorofare, NJ: Slack.

Rosenstock, I. M., Strecher, V. J., & Becker, M. H. (1988). The health belief model and HIV risk behavior change. In J. Peterson & R. DiClemente (Eds.), *Preventing AIDS: Theory and practice of behavior interventions* (pp. 5–24). New York, NY: Plenum Press.

Rosenthal, D. (1970). *Genetic theory and abnormal behavior.* New York, NY: McGraw-Hill.

Rosenthal, L., & Gronich, B. S. (2019). Gender and health. In T. A. Revenson & R. A. R. Gurung (Eds.), *Handbook of health psychology* (3e). New York, NY: Routledge.

Rosland, A., Heisler, M., & Piette, J. (2012). The impact of family behaviors and communication patterns on chronic illness outcomes: A systematic review. *Journal of Behavioral Medicine, 35*(2), 221–239. doi:10.1007/s10865-011-9354-4

Ross, C. E., & Mirowsky, J. (1979). A comparison of life-event-weighting schemes: Change, undesirability, and effect-proportional indices. *Journal of Health and Social Behavior, 20,* 166–177.

Ross, N., Maupin, J., & Timura, C. A. (2011) Knowledge organization, categories, and ad hoc groups: Folk medical models among Mexican migrants in Nashville. *Journal of the Society for Psychological Anthropology, 39*(2), 165–188. doi:10.1111/j.1548-1352.2011.01183.x

Rossouw, J. E., Anderson, G. L., Prentice, R. L., LaCroix, A. Z., Kooperberg, C., Stefanick, M. L., . . . Ockene, J. (2002). Risks and benefits of estrogen plus progestin in healthy postmenopausal women: Principal results from the Women's Health Initiative randomized controlled trial. *Journal of the American Medical Association, 288,* 321–333.

Roter, D. L., Stewart, M., Putnam, S. M., Lipkin, M., Jr., Stiles, W., & Inui, T. S. (1997). Communication patterns of primary care physicians. *Journal of the American Medical Association, 277,* 350–356.

Roter, D., & Hall, J. A. (2006). *Doctors talking with patients/patients talking with doctors* (2e). Westport, CT: Greenwood Publishing Press.

Rotheram-Borus, M. J., & Duan, N. (2003). Next generation of preventive interventions. *Journal of the American Academy of Child and Adolescent Psychiatry, 42*(5), 518–526.

Rotheram-Borus, M. J., Song, J., Gwadz, M., Lee, M., Van Rossem, R., & Koopman, C. (2003). Reductions in HIV risk among runaway youth. *Preventive Science, 4,* 173–187.

Rothman, A. J., Hertel, A. W., Baldwin, A. S., & Bartels, R. D. (2008). Understanding the determinants of health behavior change: Integrating theory and practice. In J. Y. Shah, W. L. Gardner, J. Y. Shah, W. L. Gardner (Eds.), *Handbook of motivation science* (pp. 494–507). New York, NY: Guilford Press.

Rothschild, S., Martin, M., Swider, S., Lynas, C., Avery, E., Janssen, I., & Powell, L. (2012). The Mexican-American Trial of Community Health workers (MATCH): Design and baseline characteristics of a randomized controlled trial testing a culturally tailored community diabetes self-management intervention. *Contemporary Clinical Trials, 33*(2), 369–377.

Rovner, G. S., Sunnerhagen, K. S., Björkdahl, A., Gerdle, B., Börsbo, B., Johansson, F., & Gillanders, D. (2017). Chronic pain and sex-differences; women accept and move, while men feel blue. *PLoS One, 12*(4). doi:10.1371/journal.pone.0175737

Rowan-Robinson, K. (2017). Sun protection for preventing basal cell and squamous cell skin cancers. *Public Health Nursing, 34*(3), 312–313. doi:10.1111/phn.12312

Rowlands, I., & Lee, C. (2010). 'The silence was deafening': Social and health service support after miscarriage. *Journal of Reproductive and Infant Psychology, 28*(3), 274–286. doi:10.1080/02646831003587346

Roy, M. P., Steptoe, A., & Kirschbaum, C. (1998). Life events and social support as moderators of individual differences in cardiovascular and cortisol reactivity. *Journal of Personality and Social Psychology, 75,* 1273–1281.

Royce, R. A., Sena, A., Cates, W., Jr., & Cohen, M. S. (1997). Sexual transmission of HIV. *New England Journal of Medicine, 336,* 1072–1078.

Rozanski, A., Bairey, C. N., Krantz, D. S., Friedman, J., Resser, K. J., Morell, M., . . . Berman, D. S. (1994). Mental stress and the induction of silent myocardial ischemia in patients with coronary artery disease. In A. Steptoe & J. Wardle (Eds.), *Psychosocial processes and health: A reader* (pp. 147–165). New York, NY: Cambridge University Press.

Rozanski, A., Blumenthal, J. A., & Kaplan, J. (1999). Impact of psychological factors on the pathogenesis of cardiovascular disease and implications for therapy. *Circulation, 99,* 2192–2217.

Rozin, P. (1990). Development in the food domain. *Developmental Psychology, 26,* 555–563.

Ruau, D., Liu, L., Clark, J., Angst, M., & Butte, A. (2012). Sex differences in reported pain across 11,000 patients captured in electronic medical records. *Journal of Pain, 13*(3), 228–234.

Rüdell, K., & Diefenbach, M. (2008). Current issues and new directions in psychology and health: Culture and health psychology. Why health psychologists should care about culture. *Psychology and Health, 23*(4), 387–390.

Rudolph, K. D., & Hammen, C. (1999). Age and gender as determinants of stress exposure, generation, and reactions in youngsters: A transactional perspective. *Child Development, 70,* 660–677.

Rueger, S. Y., Malecki, C. K., Pyun, Y., Aycock, C., & Coyle, S. (2016). A meta-analytic review of the association between perceived social support and depression in childhood and adolescence. *Psychological Bulletin, 142*(10), 1017–1067. doi:10.1037/bul0000058

Ruiz, J., Steffen, P., Doyle, C. Y., Flores, M. A., & Price, S. N. (2019). Socioeconomic status and health. In T. A. Revenson &

R. A. R. Gurung (Eds.), *Handbook of health psychology* (3e). New York, NY: Routledge.

Rundall, T. G., & Wheeler, J. R. (1979). The effect of income on use of preventive care: An evaluation of alternative explanations. *Journal of Health and Social Behavior, 20*, 397–406.

Running, A., Girard, D., & Tolle, L. (2008). When there is nothing left to do, there is everything left to do. *American Journal of Hospice and Palliative Medicine, 24*(6), 451–454.

Russel, M., Cooper, M. L., Frone, M. R., & Welte, J. W. (1991). Alcohol drinking patterns and blood pressure. *American Journal of Public Health, 81*, 452–457.

Russell, M. (1990). The influence of sociodemorgraphic characteristics on familial alcohol problems: Data from a community sample. *Alcohol Clinical Experimental Research, 14*, 221–226.

Ruthig, J. C., Chipperfield, J. G., Newall, N. E., Perry, R. P., Hall, N. C. (2007). Detrimental effects of falling on health and well-being in later life: The mediating roles of perceived control and optimism. *Journal of Health Psychology, 12*, 231–248.

Ryan, G. W. (1998). What do sequential behavioral patterns suggest about the medical decision-making process? Modelling home case management of acute illnesses in a rural Cameroonian village. *Social Science and Medicine, 46*, 209–225.

Ryff, C. D., & Singer, B. (2003a). Thriving in the face of challenge: The integrative science of human resilience. In F. Kessel, P. L. Rosenfield, & N. Anderson (Eds.), *Expanding the boundaries of health and social science: Case studies in interdisciplinary innovation* (pp. 181–205). London, UK: Oxford University Press.

Ryff, C. D., & Singer, B. (2003b). Flourishing under fire: Resilience as a prototype of challenged thriving. In C. L. M. Keyes & J. Haidt (Eds.), *Flourishing: Positive psychology and the life well-lived* (pp. 15–36). Washington, DC: American Psychological Association.

Ryndes, T., Connor, S., Cody, C., Merriman, M., Bruno, S., Fine, P., & Dennis, J. (2001). Report on the alpha and beta pilots of end result outcome measures constructed by the outcomes forum, a joint effort of the National Hospice and Palliative Care Organization and the National Hospice Work Group. Retrieved from www.nhpco.org

Rzeszutek, M., Oniszczenko, W., & Firląg-Burkacka, E. (2017). Social support, stress coping strategies, resilience and posttraumatic growth in a polish sample of HIV-infected individuals: Results of a 1 year longitudinal study. *Journal of Behavioral Medicine, 40*(6), 942–954. doi:10.1007/s10865-017-9861-z

Saab, P. G., McCalla, J. R., Coons, H. L., Christensen, A. J., Kaplan, R., Johnson, S. B., . . . Melamed, B. (2004). Technological and medical advances: Implications for health psychology. *Health Psychology, 23*(2), 142–146. doi:10.1037/0278-6133.23.2.142

Saal, W., & Kagee, A. (2012). The applicability of the Theory of Planned Behaviour in predicting adherence to ART among a South African sample. *Journal of Health Psychology, 17*(4), 362–370. doi:10.1177/1359105311416875

Sable, M. R., Stockbauer, J. W., Schramm, W. F., & Land, G. H. (1990). Differentiating the barriers to adequate prenatal care in Missouri, 1987–88. *Public Health Report, 105*, 9–555.

Sagrestano, L. M., Feldman, P., Rini, K. C., Woo, G., & Dunkel-Schetter, C. (1999). Ethnicity and social support during pregnancy. *American Journal of Community Psychology, 27*, 869–898.

Saguy, A. C., & Almeling, R. (2008). Fat in the fire? Science, the news media, and the "obesity epidemic." *Sociaological Forum, 23*, 53–83.

Sallis, J. F. & Owen, N.. (2015). Ecological models of health behavior. In K. Glanz, B. K. Rimer, & K. Viswanath (Eds.), *Health behavior: Theory, research, and practice* (5e, pp. 43–64). San Fransisco, CA: Jossey-Bass.

Salmon, P. (2001). Effects of physical exercise on anxiety, depression, and sensitivity to stress: A unifying theory. *Clinical Psychology Review, 21*, 33–61.

Salomon, K., & Jagusztyn, N. (2008). Resting cardiovascular levels and reactivity to interpersonal incivility among Black, Latina/o, and White individuals: The moderating role of ethnic discrimination. *Health Psychology, 27*(4), 473–481.

Salovey, P., Rothman, A. J., & Rodin, J. (1998). Health behavior. In D. T. Gilbert, S. T. Fiske, & G. Lindzey (Eds.), *The handbook of social psychology* (vol. 2, 4e, pp. 633–683). New York, NY: McGraw-Hill.

Sam, D. L., & Berry, J. W. (2016). *The Cambridge handbook of acculturation psychology* (2e). Cambridge, UK: Cambridge University Press.

Sampson, R. J., Morenoff, J. D., & Gannon-Rowley, T. (2002). Assessing "neighborhood effects": Social processes and new directions in research. *Annual Review of Sociology, 28*, 443–478.

Samson, A., & Siam H. (2008). Adapting to major chronic illness: A proposal for a comprehensive task-model approach. *Patient Education and Counseling, 70*, 426–429.

Sánchez, L., Lana, A., Hidalgo, A., Rodríguez, J., Del Valle, M., Cueto, A., . . . López, M. L. (2008). Risk factors for second primary tumours in breast cancer survivors. *European Journal of Cancer Prevention, 17*(5), 406–413.

Sandberg, J., Grzywacz, J., Talton, J., Quandt, S., Chen, H., Chatterjee, A., & Arcury, T. (2012). A cross-sectional exploration of excessive daytime sleepiness, depression, and musculoskeletal pain among migrant farmworkers. *Journal of Agromedicine, 17*(1), 70–80.

Sandborn, K. M. (2000). Predicting depressive symptoms after miscarriage: A path analysis based on the Lazarus paradigm. *Journal of Women's Health and Gender-Based Medicine, 9*, 191–207.

Sanders, S. H., Brena, S. F., Spier, C. J., Beltrutti, D., McConnell, H., & Quintero, O. (1992). Chronic low back pain patients around the world: Cross-cultural similarities and differences. *Clinical Journal of Pain, 8*, 317–23.

Sandlund, E. S., & Norlander, T. (2000). The effects of Tai Chi Chuan relaxation and exercise on stress responses and well- being: An overview of research. *International Journal of Stress Management, 7*, 139–149.

Santee, R. (2017). Health, spirituality, and Chinese thought. In D. Von Dras (Ed.), *Better health through spiritual practices* (pp. 73–96). Santa Barbara, CA: Praeger.

Santhanam, P., Coles, C. D., Li, Z., Li, L., Lynch, M., & Hu, X. (2011). Default mode network dysfunction in adults with prenatal alcohol exposure. *Psychiatry Research: Neuroimaging Section, 194*(3), 354–362. doi:10.1016/j.pscychresns.2011.05.004

Santiago, C., Etter, E., Wadsworth, M. E., & Raviv, T. (2012). Predictors of responses to stress among families coping with poverty-related stress. *Anxiety, Stress & Coping, 25*(3), 239–258. doi:10.1080/10615806.2011.583347

Santry, H. P., Gillen, D. L., & Lauderdale, D. S. (2005). Trends in bariatric surgical procedures. *Journal of the American Medical Association, 294*, 1909–1917.

Saper, R. B., Eisenberg, D. M., Davis, R. B., Culpepper, L., & Phillips, R. S. (2004). Prevalence and patterns of adult yoga use in the United States: Results of a National Survey. *Alternative Therapies and Health Medicine, 10*, 44–49.

Sapolsky, R. M. (1991). Poverty remains. *The Sciences* (September–October), 8.

Sapolsky, R. M. (2002). *A primate's memoir.* New York, NY: Touchstone Books.
Sapolsky, R. M. (2004/1994). *Why zebras don't get ulcers: An updated guide to stress, stress-related disease and coping* (3e). New York, NY: Freeman.
Sapolsky, R. M. (2017). *Behave: The biology of humans at our best and worst.* New York, NY: Penguin.
Sarabdjitsingh, R. A., Joëls, M. M., & de Kloet, E. R. (2012). Glucocorticoid pulsatility and rapid corticosteroid actions in the central stress response. *Physiology & Behavior, 106*(1), 73–80. doi:10.1016/j.physbeh.2011.09.017
Sarafino, E. P. (2001). *Behavior modification: Principles of behavior change* (2nd ed.). Mountain View, CA: Mayfield.
Saran, P. (1985). *Asian Indian experience in the United States.* Cambridge, MA: Schenkman.
Sarason, B. R., Sarason, I. G., & Gurung, R. A. R. (2001). Close personal relationships and health outcomes: A key to the role of social support. In B. R. Sarason & S. Duck (Eds.), *Personal relationships: Implications for clinical and community psychology* (pp. 15–41). Chichester, UK: John Wiley.
Sarason, I. G., Johnson, J. H., & Siegel, J. M. (1978). Assessing the impact of life changes: Development of the life experiences survey. *Journal of Consulting and Clinical Psychology, 46,* 932–946.
Saremi, A., & Arora, R. (2008). The cardiovascular implications of alcohol and red wine. *American Journal of Therapeutics, 15*(3), 265–277.
Sargent, J. D., Dalton, M. A., Beach M. L., Mott, L. A., Tickle, J. J., Ahrens, M. B., & Heatherton, T. F. (2002). Viewing tobacco use in movies: Does it shape attitudes that mediate adolescent smoking? *American Journal of Preventive Medicine, 22,* 137–145.
Sargent, J. D., Dalton, M. A., Heatherton, T., & Beach, M. (2003). Modifying exposure to smoking depicted in movies: A novel approach to preventing adolescent smoking. *Archives of Pediatrics and Adolescent Medicine, 157,* 643–648.
Saunders, E., & Ofili, E. (2008). Epidemiology of atherothrombotic disease and the effectiveness and risks of antiplatelet therapy: Race and ethnicity considerations. *Cardiology in Review, 16*(2), 82–88.
Saurer, T., Ijames, S., Carrigan, K., & Lysle, D. (2008). Neuroimmune mechanisms of opioid-mediated conditioned immunomodulation. *Brain, Behavior, and Immunity, 22*(1), 89–97.
Scarinci, I. C., Bandura, L., Hidalgo, B., & Cherrington, A. (2012). Development of a theory-based (PEN-3 and Health Belief Model), Culturally relevant intervention on cervical cancer prevention among Latina immigrants using intervention mapping. *Health Promotion Practice, 13*(1), 29–40. doi:10.1177/1524839910366416
Schaal, B., Tremblay, R. E., Soussignan, R., & Susman, E. J. (1996). Male testosterone linked to high social dominance but low physical aggression in early adolescence. *Journal of the American Academy of Child and Adolescent Psychiatry, 35,* 1322–1330.
Schachter, S. (1959). *The psychology of affiliation: Experimental studies of the sources of gregariousness.* Oxford, UK: Stanford University Press.
Schachter, S. (1980). Nonpsychological explanations of behavior. In L. Festinger (Ed.), *Retrospective on social psychology* (pp. 131–157). New York, NY: Oxford University Press.
Schachter, S., & Singer, J. E. (1962). Cognitive, social, and physiological determinants of emotional state. *Psychological Review, 69,* 379–399.
Schaefer, C. A., & Gorsuch, R. L. (1991). Psychological adjustment and religiousness: The multivariate belief-motivation theory of religiousness. *Journal for the Scientific Study of Religion, 30,* 448–461.
Schaie, K. W. (1993). The Seattle Longitudinal Study: A thirty-five-year inquiry of adult intellectual development. *Zeitschrift für Gerontologie, 26,* 129–137.
Schaller, T. K., & Malhotra, N. K. (2015). Affective and cognitive components of attitudes in high-stakes decisions: An application of the theory of planned behavior to hormone replacement therapy use. *Psychology & Marketing, 32*(6), 678–695. doi:10.1002/mar.20809
Schedlowski, M., Jacobs, R., Stratmann, G., Richter, S., Hädicke, A., Tewes, U., . . . Schmidt, R. E. (1993). Changes of natural killer cells during acute psychological stress. *Journal of Clinical Immunology, 13,* 119–126.
Scheier, M. F., & Bridges, M. W. (1995). Person variables and health: Personality predispositions and acute psychological states as shared determinants for disease. *Psychosomatic Medicine, 57,* 255–268.
Scheier, M. F., Matthews, K. A., Owens, J. F., Magovern, G. J. Sr., Lefebvre, R. C., Abbott, R. A., & Carver, C. S. (2003). Dispositional optimism and recovery from coronary artery bypass surgery: The beneficial effects of physical and psychological well-being. In P. Salovey & A. J. Rothman (Eds.), *Social psychology of health: Key readings in social psychology* (pp. 342–361). New York, NY: Psychology Press.
Scheier, M. F., Weintraub, J. K., & Carver, C. S. (1986). Coping with stress: Divergent strategies of optimists and pessimists. *Journal of Personality and Social Psychology, 51,* 1257–1264.
Scherck, K. A. (1997). Recognizing a heart attack: The process of determining illness. *American Journal of Critical Care, 6,* 267–273.
Scherwitz, L., Graham, L. E., & Ornish, D. (1985). Self-involvement and the risk factors for coronary heart disease. *Advances, 2,* 6–18.
Schiavon, C. C., Marchetti, E., Gurgel, L., Busnello, F. M., & Reppold, C. T. (2017). Optimism and hope in chronic disease: A systematic review. *Frontiers in Psychology, 7,* 10. doi:10.3389/fpsyg.2016.02022
Schlatter, M., & Cameron, L. (2010). Emotional suppression tendencies as predictors of symptoms, mood, and coping appraisals during AC chemotherapy for breast cancer treatment. *Annals of Behavioral Medicine: A Publication of The Society of Behavioral Medicine, 40*(1), 15–29.
Schnall, P. L., Landsbergis, P. A., & Baker, D. (1994). Job strain and cardiovascular disease. *Annual Review of Public Health, 15,* 381–411.
Schneider (2008). Evaluations of stressful transactions: What's in an appraisal? *Stress and Health, 24*(2), 151–158. https://doi.org/10.1002/smi.1176
Schooler, T. Y. & Baum, A. (2000). Neuroendocrine influence on the health of diverse populations. R. M. Eisler & M. Hersen (Ed.), *Handbook of gender, culture, and health* (pp. 3–18). Mahweh, NJ: Erlbaum.
Schrag, N., McKeown, R., Jackson, K., Cuffe, S., & Neuberg, R. (2008). Stress-related mental disorders in childhood cancer survivors. *Pediatric Blood and Cancer, 50*(1), 98–103.
Schreiber, J., & Brockopp, D. (2012). Twenty-five years later-what do we know about religion/spirituality and psychological well-being among breast cancer survivors? A systematic review. *Journal of Cancer Survivorship: Research and Practice, 6*(1), 82–94.
Schreurs, K. M., & de Ridder, D. T. D. (1997). Integration of coping and social support perspectives: Implications for the study of adaptation to chronic diseases. *Clinical Psychology Review, 17,* 89–112.

Schroecksnadel, K., Sarcletti, M., Winkler, C., Mumelter, B., Weiss, G., Fuchs, D., . . . Zangerle, R. (2008). Quality of life and immune activation in patients with HIV-infection. *Brain, Behavior, and Immunity*, *22*(6), 881–889.

Schroeder, D. H., & Costa, P. T. (1984). Influence of life event stress on physical illness: Substantive effects or methodological flaws? *Journal of Personality and Social Psychology*, *46*, 853–863.

Schuckit, M. A., Tapert, S., Matthews, S. C., Paulus, M. P., Tolentino, N. J., Smith, T. L., & . . . Simmons, A. (2012). fMRI differences between subjects with low and high responses to alcohol during a stop signal task. *Alcoholism: Clinical & Experimental Research*, *36*(1), 130–140. doi:10.1111/j.1530-0277.2011.01590.x

Schucklit, M. A. (1994). Low level of response to alcohol as a predictor of future alcoholism. *American Journal of Psychiatry*, *151*, 184–189.

Schultz, P., Nolan, J. M., Cialdini, R. B., Goldstein, N. J., & Griskevicius, V. (2007). The constructive, destructive, and reconstructive power of social norms. *Psychological Science* (Wiley-Blackwell), *18*(5), 429–434. doi:10.1111/j.1467-9280.2007.01917.x

Schulz, P., Schlotz, W., & Becker, P. (2011). *The Trier Inventory of Chronic Stress (TICS) - manual.* (W. Schlotz, trans.). Gottingen, Germany: Hogrefe.

Schure, M. B., Christopher, J., & Christopher, S. (2008). Mind-body medicine and the art of self-care: Teaching mindfulness to counseling students through yoga, meditation, and Qigong. *Journal of Counseling and Development*, *86*, 47–56.

Schutte, J. W., Valerio, J. K., & Carrillo, V. (1996). Optimism and socioeconomic status: A cross-cultural study. *Social Behavior and Personality*, *24*, 9–18.

Schuurman, D. (2008). Grief groups for grieving children and adolescents. In K. J. Doka & A. S. Tucci (Eds.), *Living with grief: Children and adolescents* (pp. 255–268). Washington, DC: Hospice Foundation of America.

Schwartz, C., & Rapkin, B. (2012). Understanding appraisal processes underlying the thentest: A mixed methods investigation. *Quality of Life Research*, *21*(3), 381–388. doi:10.1007/s11136-011-0023-4

Schwartz, L. M., Woloshin, S., & Welch, H. G. (2007). The drug facts box: Providing consumers with simple tabular data on drug benefit and harm. *Medical Decision Making*, *27*, 655–662.

Schwarzer, R. (1992). *Self-efficacy: Thought control of action.* Washington, DC: Hemisphere.

Schwarzer, R. (2008). Modeling health behavior change: How to predict and modify the adoption and maintenance of health behaviors. *Applied Psychology: An International Review*, *57*, 1–29.

Schwarzer, R., & Schwarzer, C. (1996). A critical survey of coping instruments. In M. Zeidnes & N. S. Endler (Eds.), *Handbook of coping: Theory, research, applications* (pp. 107–132). Oxford, UK: John Wiley.

Schwarzer, R., Dunkel-Schetter, C., & Kemeny, M. (1994). The multidimensional nature of received social support in gay men at risk of HIV infection and AIDS. *American Journal of Community Psychology*, *22*, 319–339.

Scollan-Koliopoulos, M., Walker, E., & Rapp, K. (2011). Self-regulation theory and the multigenerational legacy of diabetes. *Diabetes Educator*, *37*(5), 669–679.

Scott-Sheldon, L. A. J., Kalichman, S. C., Carey, M. P., & Fielder, R. L. (2008). Stress management interventions for HIV+ adults: A meta-analysis of randomized controlled trials, 1989 to 2006. *Health Psychology*, *27*, 129–139.

Seeman, T. E., & Syme, S. L. (1987). Social networks and coronary artery disease: A comparison of the structure and function of social relations as predictors of disease. *Psychosomatic Medicine*, *49*, 341–354.

Seeman, T. E., Singer, B. H., Horwitz, R. I., & McEwen, B. S. (1997).Price of adaptation: Allostatic load and its health consequences— MacArthur studies of successful aging. *Archives of Internal Medicine*, *157*, 2259–2268.

Segal, L. M., Rayburn, J., & Beck, S. E. (2017). The state of obesity: Better policies for a healthier America. Trust for America's health. Retrieved from https://stateofobesity.org/files/stateofobesity2017.pdf

Segerstrom, S. (2012). *The Oxford handbook of psychoneuroimmunology*. Boston, MA: Oxford University Press.

Segerstrom, S. C. (2007). Stress, energy, and immunity: An ecological view. *Current Directions in Psychological Science*, *16*, 326–330.

Segerstrom, S. C., & Miller, G. E. (2004). Psychological stress and the human immune system: A meta-analytic study of thirty years of inquiry. *Psychological Bulletin*, *130*, 601–630.

Segerstrom, S. C., Out, D., Granger, D. A., & Smith, T. (2016). Biological and physiological measures in health psychology. In Y. Benyamini, M. Johnston, & E. C. Karademas (Eds.), *Assessment in health psychology* (pp. 227–238). Boston, MA: Hogrefe.

Segerstrom, S. C., Taylor, S. E., Kemeny, M. E., & Fahey, J. L. (1998). Optimism is associated with mood, coping and immune change in response to stress. *Journal of Personality and Social Psychology*, *74*, 1646–1655.

Segrin, C. (1999). Social skills, stressful life events, and the development of psychosocial problems. *Journal of Social and Clinical Psychology*, *19*, 14–34.

Seldenrijk, A., Hamer, M., Lahiri, A., Penninx, B. H., & Steptoe, A. (2012). Psychological distress, cortisol stress response and subclinical coronary calcification. *Psychoneuroendocrinology*, *37*(1), 48–55. doi:10.1016/j.psyneuen.2011.05.001

Seligman, M. E. P., & Csikszentmihalyi, M. (2000). Positive psychology: An introduction. *American Psychologist*, *55*, 5–14.

Sellick, S. M., & Zaza, C. (1998). Critical review of 5 nonpharmacologic strategies for managing cancer pain. *Cancer Prevention and Control*, *2*, 7–14.

Selye, H. (1956). *The stress of life*. New York, NY: McGraw-Hill.

Seo, D., Macy, J. T., Torabi, M. R., & Middlestadt, S. E. (2011). The effect of a smoke-free campus policy on college students' smoking behaviors and attitudes. *Preventive Medicine*, *53*(4/5), 347–352. doi:10.1016/j.ypmed.2011.07.015

Serlachius, A., Northam, E., Frydenberg, E., & Cameron, F. (2012). Adapting a generic coping skills programme for adolescents with type 1 diabetes: A qualitative study. *Journal of Health Psychology*, *17*(3), 313–323.

Shafer, T. J., Wagner, D., Chessare, J., Schall, M. W., McBride, V., Zampiello, F. A., . . . Lin, M. J. (2008). U.S. organ donation breakthrough collaborative increases organ donation. *Critical Care Nursing Quarterly*, *31*(3), 190–210.

Shah, S., Ayash, C., Pharaon, N., & Gany, F. (2008). Arab American immigrants in New York, NY: Health care and cancer knowledge, attitudes, and beliefs. *Journal of Immigrant and Minority Health/Center for Minority Public Health*, *10*(5), 429–436.

Shavitt, S., Cho, Y. I., Johnson, T. P., Jiang, D., Holbrook, A., & Stavrakantonaki, M. (2016). Culture moderates the relation between perceived stress, social support, and mental and physical health. *Journal of Cross-Cultural Psychology*, *47*(7), 956–980. doi:10.1177/0022022116656132

Shavitt, S., Sanbonmatsu, D. M., Smittipatana, S., & Posavac, S. S. (1999). Broadening the conditions for illusory correlation formation: Implications for judging minority groups. *Basic and Applied Social Psychology*, *21*, 263–279.

Shearer, H. M., & Evans, D. R. (2001). Adherence to health care. In S. S. Kazarian & D. R. Evans (Eds.), *Handbook of cultural health psychology* (pp. 113–138). San Diego, CA: Academic Press.

Sheeran, P. (2002). Intention-behavior relations: A conceptual and empirical review. *European Review of Social Psychology, 12*,1–36.

Sheikh, A. A. (Ed.). (2003). *Healing images: The role of imagination in health.* Amityville, NY: Baywood Publishing.

Shekelle, R. B., Hulley, S. B., Neaton, J. D., Billings, J. H., Borhani, N. O., Gerace, T. A., . . . Stamler, J. (1985). The MRFIT behavior pattern study II: Type A behavior and incidence of coronary heart disease. *American Journal of Epidemiology, 122*, 559–570.

Sher, K. J. (1991). *Children of alcoholics: A critical appraisal of theory and research.* Chicago, IL: University of Chicago Press.

Sher, K. J., & Trull, T. J. (1994). Personality and disinhibitory psycopathology: Alcoholism and antisocial personality disorder. *Journal of Abnormal Psychology, 103*, 92–102.

Sherr, L., Clucas, C., Harding, R., Sibley, E., & Catalan, J. (2011). HIV and Depression - a systematic review of interventions. *Psychology, Health & Medicine, 16*(5), 493–527. doi:10.1080/13548506.2011.579990

Shields, C. A., Spink, K. S., Chad, K., Muhajarine, N., Humbert, L., & Odnokon, P. (2008). Youth and adolescent physical activity lapsers: Examining self-efficacy as a mediator of the relationship between family social influence and physical activity. *Journal of Health Psychology, 13*, 121–130.

Shilts, M., Horowitz, M., & Townsend, M. S. (2009). Guided goal setting: Effectiveness in a dietary and physical activity intervention with low-income adolescents. *International Journal of Adolescent Medicine and Health, 21*(1), 111–122. doi:10.1515/IJAMH.2009.21.1.111

Shilts, R. (2000). *And the band played on: Politics, people, and the AIDS epidemic.* New York, NY: Stonewall Inn.

Shim, E., Song, Y. W., Park, S., Lee, K., Go, D. J., & Hahm, B. (2017). Examining the relationship between pain catastrophizing and suicide risk in patients with rheumatic disease: The mediating role of depression, perceived social support, and perceived burdensomeness. *International Journal of Behavioral Medicine, 24*(4), 501–512. doi:10.1007/s12529-017-9648-1

Shlomi Polachek, I., Manor, A., Baumfeld, Y., Bagadia, A., Polachek, A., Strous, R. D., & Dolev, Z. (2017). Sex differences in psychiatric hospitalizations of individuals with psychotic disorders. *Journal of Nervous and Mental Disease, 205*(4), 313–317. doi:10.1097/NMD.0000000000000645

Shneidman, E. S. (1980). A possible classification of suicidal acts based on Murray's need system. *Suicide and Life-Threatening Behavior, 10*, 175–181.

Shojaeizadeh, D., Sadeghi, R., Tarrahi, M., Asadi, M., Safari, H., & Lashgarara, B. (2012). The effect of educational intervention on prevention of osteoporosis through Health Belief Model (HBM) in volunteers of Khorramabad city's Health Centers in 2010–2011. *Annals of Biological Research, 3*(1), 300–307.

Shopland, D. R. (1996). U.S. cigar consumption. *Journal of the National Cancer Institute, 89*, 999.

Shopland, D. R., Eyre, H. J., & Pechacek, T. F. (1991). Smoking-attributable cancer mortality in 1991: Is lung cancer now the leading cause of death among smokers in the United States? *Journal of the National Cancer Institute, 83*, 1142–1148.

Shorris, E. (1992). *Latinos: A biography of the people.* New York, NY: Norton.

Shumaker, S. A., & Hill, D. R. (1991). Gender differences in social support and physical health. *Health Psychology. Special Gender and Health, 10*, 102–111.

Shumaker, S., & Czajkowski, S. M. (Eds.). (1994). *Social support and cardiovascular disease.* Plenum series in behavioral psychophysiology and medicine. New York, NY: Plenum Press.

Shuter, J., Bernstein, S. L., & Moadel, A. B. (2012). Cigarette smoking behaviors and beliefs in persons living with HIV/AIDS. *American Journal of Health Behavior, 36*(1), 75–85.

Siafaka, V., Hyphantis, T. N., Alamanos, I., Fountzilas, G., Skarlos, D., Pectasides, D., . . . Pavlidis, N. (2008). Personality factors associated with psychological distress in testicular cancer survivors. *Journal of Personality Assessment, 90*(4), 348–355.

Siegel, K., Karus, D., Raveis, V. H., & Hagan, D. (1998). Psychological adjustment of women with HIV/AIDS: Racial and ethnic comparisons. *Journal of Community Psychology, 26*, 439–455.

Siegeler, K., Sachser, N., & Kaiser, S. (2011). The social environment during pregnancy and lactation shapes the behavioral and hormonal profile of male offspring in wild cavies. *Developmental Psychobiology, 53*(6), 575–584. doi:10.1002/dev.20585

Siegler, I. C., Bastian, L. A., Steffens, D. C., Bosworth, H. B., & Costa, P. T. (2002). Behavioral medicine and aging. *Journal of Consulting and Clinical Psychology, 70*, 843–851.

Siegler, I. C., Elias, M. F., & Bosworth, H. B. (2012). Aging and health. In A. Baum, T. A. Revenson, & J. Singer (Eds.), *Handbook of health psychology* (2e, pp. 617–636). New York, NY: Guilford.

Siegler, I. C., Hooker, K., Bosworth, H. B., Elias, M. F., & Spiro, A. (2010). Adult development, aging, and gerontology. In J. M. Suls, K. W. Davidson, & R. M. Kaplan (Eds.), *Handbook of health psychology and behavioral medicine* (pp. 147–162). New York, NY: Guilford.

Siegrist, J., & Marmot, M. (2004). Health inequalities and the psychosocial environment: Two scientific challenges. *Social Science and Medicine, 58*, 1463–1473.

Sikkema, K. J., Hansen, N. B., Kochman, A., Tate, D. C., & Difranciesco, W. (2004). Outcomes from a randomized controlled trial of a group intervention for HIV positive men and women coping with AIDS-related loss and bereavement. *Death Studies, 28*, 187–209.

Sikkema, K. J., Wagner, L. I., & Bogart, L. M. (2000). Gender and cultural factors in prevention of HIV infection among women. In R. M. Eisler & M. Hersen (Eds.), *Handbook of gender, culture, and health* (pp. 299–319). Mahwah, NJ: Erlbaum.

Simmons, D. (2011). The role of ethnography in STI and HIV/AIDS education and promotion with traditional healers in Zimbabwe. *Health Promotion International, 26*(4), 476–483.

Simon, A., & Wardle, J. (2008). Socioeconomic disparities in psychosocial well-being in cancer patients. *European Journal of Cancer, 44*(4), 572–578.

Simonds, J. F. (1976). Psychiatric status of diabetic youth in good and poor control. *International Journal of Psychiatry in Medicine, 7*, 133–151.

Simoni, J. M., Demas, P., Mason, H. R. C., Drossman, J. A., & Davis, M. L. (2000). HIV disclosure among women of African descent: Associations with coping, social support, and psychological adaptation. *AIDS and Behavior, 4*(2), 147–158. doi:10.1023/A:1009508406855

Simons, D. J., Boot, W. R., Charness, N., Gathercole, S. E., Chabris, C. F., Hambrick, D. Z., & Stine-Morrow, E. (2016). Do "brain-training" programs work? *Psychological Science in the Public Interest, 17*(3), 103–186. doi:10.1177/1529100616661983

Simopoulos, A. (2008). The importance of the omega-6/omega-3 fatty acid ratio in cardiovascular disease and other chronic diseases. *Experimental Biology and Medicine* (Maywood, NJ), *233*(6), 674–688.

Sims, E. R. (1987). Relaxation therapy as a technique for helping patients cope with the experience of cancer: A selected review of the literature. *Journal of Advanced Nursing, 12*, 583–591.

Sin, M., Ha, A., & Taylor, V. (2016). Sociocultural barriers to lung cancer screening among korean immigrant men. *Journal of Community Health, 41*(4), 790–797. doi:10.1007/s10900-016-0154-1

Singh, A. (2007). Action and reason in the theory of Ayurveda. *AI & Society, 21*, 27–46.

Singh, R. B., Dubnov, G., Niaz, M. A., Ghosh, S., Singh. R., Rastogi, S. S., . . . Berry, E. M. (2002).Effect of an Indo-Mediterranean diet on progression of coronary artery disease in high risk patients (Indo-Mediterranean Diet Heart Study): A randomized single-blind trial. *The Lancet, 360*, 1455–1462.

Singletary, K., & Milner, J. (2008, July). Diet, autophagy, and cancer: A review. *Cancer Epidemiology, Biomarkers and Prevention, 17*(7), 1596–1610.

Sirois, F. M. (2015). Who looks forward to better health? Personality factors and future self-rated health in the context of chronic illness. *International Journal of Behavioral Medicine, 22*(5), 569–579. doi:10.1007/s12529-015-9460-8

Sirois, F. M., & Wood, A. M. (2017). Gratitude uniquely predicts lower depression in chronic illness populations: A longitudinal study of inflammatory bowel disease and arthritis. *Health Psychology, 36*(2), 122–132. doi:10.1037/hea0000436

Skaff, M. M., Pearlin, L. I., & Mullan, J. T. (1996). Transition in the caregiving career: Effects on sense of mastery. *Psychology and Aging, 11*, 247–257.

Skevington, S. M. (1995). *Psychology of pain*. Oxford, UK: John Wiley.

Skinner, B. F. (1938). *The behavior of organisms*. Englewood Cliffs, NJ: Appleton-Century-Crofts.

Skinner, C. S., Tiro, J., & Champion, V. L. (2015). The health belief model. In K. Glanz, B. K. Rimer, & K. Viswanath (Eds.), *Health behavior: Theory, research, and practice* (5e, pp. 75–94). San Fransisco, CA: Jossey-Bass.

Skinner, E. A., Edge, K., Altman, J., & Sherwood, H. (2003). Searching for the structure of coping: A review and critique of category systems for classifying ways of coping. *Psychological Bulletin, 129*, 216–269. doi:10.1037/0033-2909.129.2.216

Sladek, M. R., Doane, L. D., Jewell, S. L., & Luecken, L. J. (2017). Social support coping style predicts women's cortisol in the laboratory and daily life: The moderating role of social attentional biases. *Anxiety, Stress & Coping, 30*(1), 66–81. doi:10.1080/10615806.2016.1181754

Slater, M. A., Hall, H. F., Atkinson, J. H., & Garfin, S. R. (1991). Pain and impairment beliefs in chronic low back pain: Validation of the Pain and Impairment Relationship Scale (PAIRS). *Pain, 44*, 51–56.

Slavin, L. A., Rainer, K. L., McCreary, M. L., & Gowda, K. K. (1991). Toward a multicultural model of the stress process. *Journal of Counseling & Development: Special Multiculturalism as a Fourth Force in Counseling, 70*, 156–163.

Slezackova, A., & Sobotkova, I. (2017). Family resilience: Positive psychology approach to healthy family functioning. In U. Kumar (Ed.), *The Routledge international handbook of psychosocial resilience* (pp. 379–390). New York, NY: Routledge.

Sloman, R., Brown, P., Aldana, E., & Chee, E. (1994). The use of relaxation for the promotion of comfort and pain relief in persons with advanced cancer. *Contemporary Nursing, 3*, 333–339.

Smedley, B. D., & Syme, S. L. (Eds.). (2000). *Promoting health: Intervention strategies from social and behavioral research*. Washington, DC: National Academy Press.

Smilkstein, G., Helsper-Lucas, A., Ashworth, C., Montano, D., & Pagel, M. (1984). Prediction of pregnancy complications: An application of the biopsychosocial model. *Social Science and Medicine, 18*, 315–321.

Smith, B. W., Pargament, K. I., Brant, C., & Oliver, J. M. (2000). Noah revisited: Religious coping by church members and the impact of the 1993 Midwest flood. *Journal of Community Psychology, 28*, 169–186.

Smith, C. A., Wallston, K. A., & Dwyer, K. A. (1995). On babies and bathwater: Disease impact and negative affectivity in the self-reports of persons with rheumatoid arthritis. *Health Psychology, 14*, 64–73.

Smith, G. T., Goldman, M. S., Greenbaum, P. E., & Christiansen, B. A. (1995). Expectancy for social facilitation from drinking: The diveregent paths of high-expectancy and low-expectancy adolescents. *Journal of Abnormal Psychology, 104*, 32–40.

Smith, K. E., & Norman, G. J. (2017). Brief relaxation training is not sufficient to alter tolerance to experimental pain in novices. *PLoS One, 12*(5). doi:10.1371/journal.pone.0177228

Smith, M. S., & Wallston, K. A. (1992). How to measure the value of health. *Health Education Research, 7*, 129–135.

Smith, M., Patterson, E., Wahed, A., Belle, S., Berk, P., Courcoulas, A., & . . . Wolfe, B. (2011). Thirty-day mortality after bariatric surgery: Independently adjudicated causes of death in the longitudinal assessment of bariatric surgery. *Obesity Surgery, 21*(11), 1687–1692.

Smith, M., Seplaki, C., Biagtan, M., Dupreez, A., & Cleary, J. (2008). Characterizing Hospice Services in the United States. *Gerontologist, 48*(1), 25–31.

Smith, T. (2019). Personality and health. In T. A. Revenson & R. A. R. Gurung (Eds.), *Handbook of health psychology* (3e). New York, NY: Routledge.

Smith, T. W., & Ruiz, J. M. (2002). Psychosocial influences on the development and course of coronary heart disease: Current status and implications for research and practice. *Journal of Consulting & Clinical Psychology, 70*, 548–568.

Smith, T. W., & Suls, J. (2004). Introduction to the special section on the future of health psychology. *Health Psychology, 23*, 115–118.

Smith, T. W., Gallo, L. C., Shivpuri, S., & Brewer, A. L. (2012). Personality and health: Current issues and emerging perspectives. In A. Baum, T. A. Revenson, & J. Singer (Eds.), *Handbook of health psychology* (2e, pp. 375–404). New York, NY: Taylor & Francis.

Smith, T. W., Kendall, P. C., & Keefe, F. J. (2002). Behavioral medicine and clinical health psychology: Introduction to the special issue, a view from the decade of behavior. *Journal of Consulting and Clinical Psychology, 70*, 459–462.

Smith, T. W., Orleans, C. T., & Jenkins, C. D. (2004). Prevention and health promotion: Decades of progress, new challenges, and an emerging agenda. *Health Psychology, 23*, 126–131.

Smith, W. A., Hung, M., & Franklin, J. D. (2011). Racial Battle Fatigue and the MisEducation of Black Men: Racial Microaggressions, Societal Problems, and Environmental Stress. *Journal of Negro Education, 80*(1), 63–82.

Smith-Jackson, T., & Reel, J. J. (2012). Freshmen women and the "freshman 15": Perspectives on prevalence and causes of college weight gain. *Journal of American College Health, 60*(1), 14–20. doi:10.1080/07448481.2011.555931

Smyth, J. M., & Pennebaker, J. W. (2001). What are the health effects of disclosure? In A. Baum, T. A. Revenson, & J. E. Singer (Eds.), *Handbook of health psychology* (1e, pp. 339–348). Mahwah, NJ: Erlbaum.

Snell, J. E. (1967). Hypnosis in the treatment of the "hexed" patient. *American Journal of Psychiatry, 124*, 311–316.

Snell, J. L., & Buck, E. L. (1996). Increasing cancer screening: A meta-analysis. *Preventive Medicine, 25*, 702–707.

Snow, M. G., Prochaska, J. O., & Rossi, J. S. (1992). Stages of change for smoking cessation among former problem drinkers: A cross-sectional analysis. *Journal of Substance Abuse, 4*, 107–116.

Society of Behavioral Medicine. (2018). Mission statement. Author, Washington, DC. Retrieved from http://www.sbm.org/about/

Society of Behavioral Medicine. (n.d.a). Finding and applying to grad school. Author, Washington, DC. Retrieved from http://www.apa.org/education/grad/index.aspx

Society of Behavioral Medicine. (n.d.b). Training. Author, Washington, DC. Retrieved from http://www.sbm.org/training

Sofi, F., Capalbo, A., Cesari, F., Abbate, R., & Gensini, G. (2008). Physical activity during leisure time and primary prevention of coronary heart disease: An updated meta-analysis of cohort studies. *European Journal of Cardiovascular Prevention and Rehabilitation, 15*(3), 247–257.

Sofi, F., Marcucci, R., Gori, A., Abbate, R., & Gensini, G. (2008). Residual platelet reactivity on aspirin therapy and recurrent cardiovascular events—a meta-analysis. *International Journal of Cardiology, 128*(2), 166–171.

Sohl, S. J., Schnur, J. B., Sucala, M., David, D., Winkel, G., & Montgomery, G. H. (2012). Distress and emotional well-being in breast cancer patients prior to radiotherapy: An expectancy-based model. *Psychology & Health, 27*(3), 347–361. doi:10.1080/08870446.2011.569714

Solomon, G. F., Segerstrom, S. C., Grohr, P., Kemeny, M., & Fahey, J. (1997). Shaking up immunity: Psychological and immunologic changes after a natural disaster. *Psychosomatic Medicine, 59*, 114–127.

Somerfield, M. R., & McCrae, R. R. (2000). Stress and coping research: Methodological challenges, theoretical advances, and clinical applications. *American Psychologist, 55*, 620–625.

Song, A. (2019). Weight loss and obesity. In T. A. Revenson & R. A. R. Gurung (Eds.), *Handbook of health psychology* (3e). New York, NY: Routledge.

Song, L., Weaver, M. A., Chen, R. C., Bensen, J. T., Fontham, E., Mohler, J. L., . . . Sleath, B. (2014). Associations between patient–provider communication and socio-cultural factors in prostate cancer patients: A cross-sectional evaluation of racial differences. *Patient Education and Counseling, 97*(3), 339–346. doi:10.1016/j.pec.2014.08.019

Sonstoem, R. J. (1997). Physical activity and self-esteem. In W. P. Morgan (Ed.), *Physical activity and mental health* (pp. 127–143). Washington, DC: Taylor & Francis.

Sorokowska, A., Pellegrino, R., Butovskaya, M., Marczak, M., Niemczyk, A., Huanca, T., & Sorokowski, P. (2017). Dietary customs and food availability shape the preferences for basic tastes: A cross-cultural study among Polish, Tsimane' and Hadza societies. *Appetite, 116*, 291–296. doi:10.1016/j.appet.2017.05.015

Soskolne, V., Marie, S., & Manor, O. (2007). Beliefs, recommendations and intentions are important explanatory factors of mammography screening behavior among Muslim Arab women in Israel. *Health Education Research, 22*(5), 665–676.

Soudijn, K. A., Hutschemaekers, G. J. M., & Van de Vijver, F. J. R. (1990). Culture conceptualizations. In F. J. R. Van de Vijver & G. J. M. Hutschemaeker (Eds.), *The investigation of culture: Current issues in cultural psychology* (pp. 19–39). Tilburg, Netherlands: Tilburg University Press.

Spaulding, R., Davis, K., & Patterson, J. (2008). A comparison of telehealth and face-to-face presentation for school professionals supporting students with chronic illness. *Journal of Telemedicine and Telecare, 14*(4), 211–214. doi:10.1258/jtt.2008.071003.

Spencer, M. S., & Chen J. (2004) Effect of discrimination on mental health service utilization among Chinese Americans. *American Journal of Public Health, 94*(5), 809–814.

Spera, S. P., Buhrfeind, E. D., & Pennebaker, J. W. (1994). Expressive writing and coping with job loss. *Academy of ManagementJournal, 37*(3), 722–733. doi:10.2307/256708

Sperry, L. (2006). *Psychological treatment of chronic illness: The biopsychosocial therapy approach.* Washington, DC: American Psychological Association.

Spiegel, D. (1996). Cancer and depression. *British Journal of Psychiatry, 168*, 109–116.

Spiegel, D., Bloom, J. R., Kraemer, H. C., & Gottheil, E. (1989, October 14). Effects of psychosocial treatment on survival of patients with metastatic breast cancer. *The Lancet*, 888–891.

Spiro, A. (2007). The relevance of a lifespan developmental approach to health. In *Handbook of health psychology and aging* (pp. 75–93). New York, NY: Guilford Press.

Sprangers, M. A. (1996). Response-shift bias: A challenge to the assessment of patients' quality of life in cancer clinical trials. *Cancer Treatment Review, 22*, 55–62.

Spruance, S. L., Reid, J. E., Grace, M., & Samore, M. (2004). Hazard ratio in clinical trials. *Antimicrobial Agents Chemotherapy, 48*(8), 2787–2792. doi:10.1128/AAC.48.8.2787-2792.2004

Srivastava, A., & Kreiger, N. (2000). Relation of physical activity to risk of testicular cancer. *American Journal of Epidemiology, 151*(1), 78–87.

Stack, C. B., & Burton, L. M. (1993). Kinscripts. *Journal of Comparative Family Studies, 24*, 157–170.

Stack, S. (2003). Media coverage as a risk factor in suicide. *Journal of Epidemiology and Community Health, 57*, 238–240.

Stafford, H., Saltzstein, S., Shimasaki, S., Sanders, C., Downs, T., & Robins Sadler, G. (2008). Racial/ethnic and gender disparities in renal cell carcinoma incidence and survival. *Journal of Urology, 179*(5), 1704–1708.

Stampfer, M. J., Hu, F. B., Manson, J. E., Rimm, E. B., & Willett, W. C. (2000). Primary prevention of coronary heart disease in women through diet and lifestyle. *New England Journal of Medicine, 343*, 16–22.

Stanfeld, S. A., Rael, E. G., Head, J., Shipley, M., & Marmot, M. (1997). Social support and psychiatric sickness absence: A prospective study of British civil servants. *Psychological Medicine, 27*, 35–48.

Stanton, A. (2019). Cancer. In T. A. Revenson & R. A. R. Gurung (Eds.), *Handbook of health psychology* (3e). New York, NY: Routledge.

Stanton, A. L., & Revenson, T. A. (2011). Adjustment to chronic disease: Progress and promise in research. In H. Friedman (Ed.), *The Oxford handbook of health psychology* (pp. 244–272). New York, NY: Oxford University Press.

Stanton, A. L., & Snider, P. R. (1993). Coping with a breast cancer diagnosis: A prospective study. *Health Psychology, 12*, 16–23.

Stanton, A. L., Collins, C. A., & Sworowski, L. (2001). Adjustment to chronic illness: Theory and research. In A. Baum, T. A. Revenson, & J. E. Singer (Eds.), *Handbook of health psychology* (1e, pp. 387–404). Mahwah, NJ: Erlbaum.

Starace, F., Massa, A., Amico, K., & Fisher, J. (2006). Adherence to antiretroviral therapy: An empirical test of the information-motivation-behavioral skills model. *Health Psychology, 25*(2), 153–162.

Stare, J., & Maucort-Boulch, D. (2016). Odds ratio, hazard ratio, and relative risk. *Metodoloski zvezki, 13*, 59–67.

Starr, C., & McMillan, B. (2016) *Human biology* (11e) Boston, MA: Cengage Learning.

Starrs, C. J., Abela, J. R. Z., Zuroff, D. C., Amsel, R., Shih, J. H., Yao, S., . . . Hong, W. (2017). Predictors of stress generation in adolescents in mainland China. *Journal of Abnormal Child Psychology, 45*(6), 1207–1219. doi:10.1007/s10802-016-0239-4

Staton, L. J., Panda, M., Chen, I., Genao, I., Kurz, J., Pasanen, M., . . . Cykert, S. (2007). When race matters: Disagreement in pain perception between patients and their physicians in primary care. *Journal of the National Medical Association, 99*, 532–537.

Statsiewicz, P. R., & Lisman, S. A. (1989). Effects of infant cries on alcohol consumption in college males at risk for child abuse. *Child Abuse and Neglect, 13*, 463–470.

Steginga, S. K., Lynch, B. M., Hawkes, A., Dunn, J., & Aitken, J. (2009). Antecedents of domain-specific quality of life after colorectal cancer. *Psycho-Oncology, 18*(2), 216–220. doi:10.1002/pon.1388

Stein, J. A., Fox, S. A., & Murata, P. J. (1991). The influence of ethnicity, socioeconomic status, and psychological barriers on use of mammography. *Journal of Health and Social Behavior, 32*, 101–113.

Steinberg, W., & Tenner, S. (1994). Acute pancreatitis. *New England Journal of Medicine, 330*, 1198–1210.

Steinmaus, C., Nunez, S., & Smith, A. H. (2000). Diet and bladder cancer: A meta-analysis of six dietary variables. *American Journal of Epidemiology, 151*, 693–702.

Stekelenburg, J., Jager, B. E., Kolk, P. R., Westen, E. H. M. N., van der Kwaak, A., & Wolffers, I. N. (2005). Health care seeking behaviour and utilization of traditional healers in Kalabo, Zambia. *Health Policy, 71*, 67–81.

Stern, D. (1995). *The Motherhood Constellation: A unified view of parent-infant psychotherapy.* New York, NY: Basic Books.

Stevenson, J. C., Hodis, H. N., Pickar, J. H., & Lobo, R. A. (2011). HRT and breast cancer risk: A realistic perspective. *Climacteric, 14*(6), 633–636. doi:10.3109/13697137.2011.590618

Stevenson, R. G. (2008). Helping students cope with grief. In K. J. Doka & A. S. Tucci (Eds.), *Living with grief: Children and adolescents* (pp. 317–334). Washington, DC: Hospice Foundation of America.

Steward, R., Held, C., Hadziosmanovic, N., Armstrong, P., Cannon, C., Granger, C., . . . White, H. (2017). Physical activity and mortality in patients with stable coronary heart disease. *Journal of the American College of Cardiology, 70*, 1689–1700.

Stewart, D. E., Abbey, S. E., Shnek, Z. M., Irvine, J., & Grace, S. L. (2004). Gender differences in health information needs and decisional preferences in patients recovering from an acute ischemic coronary event. *Psychosomatic Medicine 66*, 42–48.

Stice, E. (2002). Risk and maintenance factors for eating pathology: A meta-analytic review. *Psychological Bulletin, 128*, 825–848.

Stice, E., Shaw, H., & Marti, C. N. (2006). A meta-analytic review of obesity prevention programs for children and adolescents: The skinny on interventions that work. *Psychological Bulletin, 132*, 667–691.

Stice, E., Shaw, H., & Nemeroff, C. (1998). Dual pathway model of bulimia nervosa: Longitudinal support for dietary restraint and affect-regulation mechanisms. *Journal of Social and Clinical Psychology, 17*, 129–149.

Stickel, F., Egerer, G., & Seitz, H. K. (2002). Hepatotoxicity of botanicals. *Public Health Nutrition, 3*, 113–124.

Stinson, D. A., Logel, C., Zanna, M. P., Holmes, J. G., Cameron, J. J., Wood, J. V., & Spencer, S. J. (2008). The cost of lower self-esteem: Testing a self-and social-bonds model of health. *Journal of Personality and Social Psychology, 94*, 412–428.

Stinson, J., Yamada, J., Dickson, A., Lamba, J., & Stevens, B. (2008). Review of systematic reviews on acute procedural pain in children in the hospital setting. *Pain Research and Management, 13*, 51–57.

St-Laurent, J., De Wals, P., Moutquin, J., Niyonsenga, T., Noiseux, M., & Czernis, L. (2008). Biopsychosocial determinants of pregnancy length and fetal growth. *Paediatric & Perinatal Epidemiology, 22*(3), 240–248. doi:10.1111/j.1365-3016.2008.00926.x

Stoloff, M., McCarthy, M., Keller, L., Varfolomeeva, V., Lynch, J., Makara, K., & . . . Smiley, W. (2010). The undergraduate psychology major: An examination of structure and sequence. *Teaching of Psychology, 37*(1), 4–15. doi:10.1080/00986280903426274

Stolzenberg-Solomon, R. Z., Adams, K., Leitzmann, M., Schairer, C., Michaud, D. S., Hollenbeck, A., . . . Silverman, D. T. (2008). Adiposity, physical activity, and pancreatic cancer in the National Institutes of Health-AARP Diet and Health Cohort. *American Journal of Epidemiology, 167*(5), 586–597.

Stone, A. A., Bovbjerg, D. H., Neale, J. M., Napoli, A., Valdimarsdottir, H., Cox, D., . . . Gwaltney, J. M. Jr. (1992). Development of common cold symptoms following experimental rhinovirus infection is related to prior stressful life events. *Behavioral Medicine, 18*, 115–120.

Stoppelbein, L., McRae, E., & Greening, L. (2017). A longitudinal study of hardiness as a buffer for posttraumatic stress symptoms in mothers of children with cancer. *Clinical Practice in Pediatric Psychology, 5*(2), 149–160. doi:10.1037/cpp0000168

Strawbridge, W. J., Shema, S. J., Cohen, R. D., Roberts, R. E., & Kaplan, G. A. (1998). Religiosity buffers effects of some stressors on depression but exacerbates others. *Journals of Gerontology: Series B: Psychological Sciences and Social Sciences, 53B*, S118–S126.

Streblow, D., Dumortier, J., Moses, A., Orloff, S., & Nelson, J. (2008). Mechanisms of cytomegalovirus-accelerated vascular disease: induction of paracrine factors that promote angiogenesis and wound healing. *Current Topics in Microbiology and Immunology, 325*, 397–415.

Streissguth, A. P., Sampson, P. D., Olson, H. C., Bookstein, F. L., Barr, H. M., Scott, M., . . . Mirsky, A. F. (1994). Maternal drinking during pregnancy: Attention and short-term memory in 14-year old offspring—A longitudinal prospective study. *Alcohol: Clinical and Experimental Research, 19*, 202–218.

Streppel, M., Ocké, M., Boshuizen, H., Kok, F., & Kromhout, D. (2008). Long-term fish consumption and n-3fatty acid intake in relation to (sudden) coronary heart disease death: The Zutphen study. *European Heart Journal, 29*(16), 2024–2030.

Strickhouser, J. E., Zell, E., & Krizan, Z. (2017). Does personality predict health and well-being? A metasynthesis. *Health Psychology, 36*(8), 797–810. doi:10.1037/hea0000475

Strodl, E., Kenardy, J., & Aroney, C. (2003). Perceived stress as a predictor of the self-reported new diagnosis of symptomatic CHD in older women. *International Journal of Behavioral Medicine, 10*, 205–220.

Stroebe, M. S., & Stroebe, W. (1983). Who suffers more? Sex differences in health risks of the widowed. *Psychological Bulletin, 93*, 279–301.

Stroebe, M. S., Hansson, R. O., Stroebe, W., & Schut, H. (Eds.). (2001). *Handbook of bereavement research: Consequences, coping, and care.* Washington, DC: American Psychological Association.

Stroebe, M., Stroebe, W., & Schut, H. (2001). Gender differences in adjustment to bereavement: An empirical and theoretical review. *Review of General Psychology, 5*, 62–83.

Stroebe, W. (2008). *Dieting, overweight, and obesity: Self-regulation in a food-rich environment*. Washington, DC: American Psychological Association.

Strong, J. P., Malcom, G. T., McMahan, C. A., Tracy, R. E., Newman, W. P. 3rd, Herderick, E. E., & Cornhill, J. F. (1999). Prevalence and extent of atherosclerosis in adolescents and young adults: Implications for prevention from the pathobiological determinants of atherosclerosis in youth study. *Journal of the American Medical Association, 281*, 727–735.

Su, D., Li, L., & Pagán, J. A. (2008). Acculturation and the use of complementary and alternative medicine. *Social Science and Medicine, 66*, 439–453.

Su, I., Wu, F., Liang, K., Cheng, K., Hsieh, S., Sun, W., & Chou, T. (2016). Pain perception can be modulated by mindfulness training: A resting-state fMRI study. *Frontiers in Human Neuroscience*, 10. doi:10.3389/fnhum.2016.00570

Su, Y., Kao, C., Hsu, C., Pan, L., Cheng, S., & Huang, Y. (2017). How does Mozart's music affect children's reading? The evidence from learning anxiety and reading rates with e-books. *Journal of Educational Technology & Society, 20*(2), 101–112.

Suarez, L., Rouche, R. A., Nichols, D., & Simpson, D. M. (1997). Knowledge, behavior, and fears concerning breast and cervical cancer among older low-income Mexican-American women. *American Journal of Preventive Medicine, 13*, 137–142.

Subramanian, J., & Govindan, R. (2007). Lung cancer in never smokers: A review. *Journal of Clinical Oncology, 25*(5), 561–570.

Suchday, S., Feher, Z. M., & Grujicic, N. (2019). Asian American health. In T. A. Revenson & R. A. R. Gurung (Eds.), *Handbook of health psychology* (3e). New York, NY: Routledge.

Suchday, S., Ramanayake, N. P., Benkhoukha, A., Santoro, A. F., Marquez, C., & Nakao, G. (2014). Ayurveda: An alternative in the Unites States. In R. A. R. Gurung (Ed.), *Multicultural approaches to health and wellness in America* (pp. 152–169). Santa Barbara, CA: Praeger.

Suchday, S., Tucker, D. L., & Krantz, D. S. (2002). Diseases of the circulatory system. In T. J. Boll, S. B. Johnson, N. W. Perry, & R. H. Rozensky, *Handbook of clinical health psychology*, Vol. *1, Medical disorders and behavioral applications* (pp. 203–238). Washington, DC: American Psychological Association.

Suchman, E. A. (1965). Social patterns of illness and medical care. *Journal of Health and Human Behavior, 6*, 2–16.

Sue, D. (2000). Health risk factors in diverse cultural groups. In R. M. Eisler & M. Hersen (Eds.), *Handbook of gender, culture, and health* (pp. 85–104). Mahwah, NJ: Erlbaum.

Sue, D. W. (2010). Microagressions, marginality, and oppression: An introduction. In D. W. Sue (Ed.), *Microaggressions and marginality: Manifestation, dynamics, and impact* (pp. 3–22). Hoboken, NJ: John Wiley.

Sue, S. (2006). Cultural competency: From philosophy to research and practice. *Journal of Community Psychology, 34*, 237–245.

Sue, S., Nakamura, C. Y., Chung, R., & Yee-Bradbury, C. (1994). Mental health research on Asian Americans. *Journal of Community Psychology, 22*, 181–187.

Suleiman, A. B. (2001). The untapped potential of telehealth. *International Journal of Medical Informatics, 61*, 103–112.

Sullivan, M. J. L., Bishop, S. R., & Pivik, J. (1995). The pain catastrophizing scale: Development and validation. *Psychological Assessment, 7*(4), 524–532. doi:10.1037/1040-3590.7.4.524

Sullivan, M. J. L., Thorn, B., Haythornthwaite, J. A., Keefe, F., Martin, M., Bradley, L. A., & Lefebvre, J. C. (2001). Theoretical perspectives on the relation between catastrophizing and pain. *Clinical Journal of Pain, 17*(1), 52–64. doi:10.1097/00002508-200103000-00008

Suls, J. M., Luger, T., & Martin, R. (2010). The biopsychosocial model and the use of theory in health psychology. In J. M. Suls, K. W. Davidson, R. M. Kaplan, J. M. Suls, K. W. Davidson, R. M. Kaplan (Eds.), *Handbook of health psychology and behavioral medicine* (pp. 15–27). New York, NY: Guilford Press.

Suls, J., & Rothman, A. (2004). Evolution of the biopsychosocial model: Prospects and challenges for health psychology. *Health Psychology, 23*, 119–126.

Suls, J., Davidson, K., & Kaplan, R. (Eds.). (2010). *Handbook of health psychology and behavioral medicine*. New York, NY: Guilford Press.

Sundquist, K., Lindstrom, M., Malmstrom, M., Johansson, S. E., & Sundquist, J. (2004). Social participation and coronary heart disease: A follow-up study of 6900 women and men in Sweden. *Social Science and Medicine, 58*, 615–622.

Hyun, S. H., & Wansoo, P. (2008). Clinical characteristics of alcohol drinking and acculturation issues faced by Korean immigrants in the United States. *Journal of Social Work Practice in the Addictions, 8*, 3–20. doi:10.1080/15332560802108597

Sung, J. F., Blumenthal, D. S., Coates, R. J., & Alema-Mensah, E. (1997). Knowledge, beliefs, attitudes, and cancer screening among inner-city African-American women. *Journal of the National Medical Association, 89*, 405–411.

Suominen-Taipale, A. L., Martelin, T., Koskinen, S., Holmen, J., & Johnsen, R. (2006). Gender differences in health care use among the elderly population in areas of Norway and Finland. Across-sectional analysis based on the HUNT study and the FINRISK Senior Survey. *BMC Health Services Research, 6*, 110, doi:10.1186/1472-6963-6-110

Sussman S., Dent C. W., Severson H. H., Burton D., & Flay B. R. (1998). Self-initiated quitting among adolescent smokers. *Preventive Medicine, 27*, A19–A28.

Sutter, N., & Paulson, S. (2016). Predicting college students' intention to graduate: A test of the theory of planned behavior. *College Student Journal, 50*(3), 409–421.

Sutton S., Bickler G., Sancho-Aldridge J., & Saidi G. (1994). Prospective study of predictors of attendance for breast screening in inner London. *Journal of Epidemiology and Community Health, 48*, 65–73.

Sutton, S. (2005). Stage theories of health behavior. In M. Conner & P. Norman (Eds.), *Predicting health behavior: Research and practice with social cognition models* (2nd ed.). Buckingham, UK: Open University Press.

Svoboda, R. E. (2004). *Ayurveda: Life, health, and longevity*. New Delhi, India: Penguin.

Swanson, K. M. (2000). Predicting depressive symptoms after miscarriage: A path analysis based on the Lazarus paradigm. *Journal of Women's Health and Gender-Based Medicine, 9*, 191–206.

Swanson, R. F. (2016). *Ethnic identity and its relationship to the academic achievement of African American male adolescent students* (doctoral dissertation, Mercer University). Retrieved from http://www.worldcat.org/title/ethnic-identity-and-its-relationship-to-academic-achievement-of-african-american-male-adolescent-students/oclc/930139071

Swaroop, S. R., DeLoach, C. D., & Sheikh, F. (2014). Islamic healing approaches, beliefs and health-related practices. In R. A. R. Gurung (Ed.), *Multicultural approaches to health and wellness in America* (pp. 167–193). Santa Barbara, CA: Praeger.

Swartz, A., Strath, S., Parker, S., Miller, N., & Cieslik, L. (2007). Ambulatory activity and body mass index in White and non-White older adults. *Journal of Physical Activity and Health, 4*, 294–304.

Sylvia, L. G., Ametrano, R. M., & Nierenberg, A. A. (2010). Exercise treatment for bipolar disorder: Potential mechanisms of action mediated through increased neurogenesis and decreased allostatic load. *Psychotherapy and Psychosomatics, 79*(2), 87–96. doi:10.1159/000270916

Syman, S. (2010). *The subtle body: The story of yoga in America*. New York, NY: Farrar, Strauss, & Giroux.

Syrjala, K. L., Donaldson, G. W., Davis, M. W., Kippes, M. E., & Carr, J. E. (1995). Relaxation and imagery and cognitive-behavioral training reduce pain during cancer treatment: A controlled clinical trial. *Pain, 63*, 189–198.

Szabo, L. (2017). Too many older patients get cancer screenings. *New York Times*, December 19. Retrieved from https://www.nytimes.com/2017/12/19/well/live/cancer-screening-tests-seniors-older-patients-harms-overdiagnosis-overtreatment.html

Szalacha, L. A., Kue, J., & Menon, U. (2017). Knowledge and beliefs regarding breast and cervical cancer screening among Mexican-heritage Latinas. *Cancer Nursing, 40*(5), 420–427. doi:10.1097/NCC.0000000000000423

Szallasi, A. (Ed.). (2010). *Analgesia: Methods and protocols*. Boston, MA: Humana.

Szasz, T. S., & Hollender, M. H. (1956). A contribution to the philosophy of medicine: The basic models of the doctor-patient relationship. *Archives of Internal Medicine, 97*, 585–592.

Szymanska, M., Schneider, M., Chateau-Smith, C., Nezelof, S., & Vulliez-Coady, L. (2017). Psychophysiological effects of oxytocin on parent–child interactions: A literature review on oxytocin and parent–child interactions. *Psychiatry and Clinical Neurosciences, 71*(10), 690–705. doi:10.1111/pcn.12544

Tackett, J. L., Herzhoff, K., Smack, A. J., Reardon, K. W., & Adam, E. K. (2017). Does socioeconomic status mediate racial differences in the cortisol response in middle childhood? *Health Psychology, 36*(7), 662–672. doi:10.1037/hea0000480

Takahashi, K. (1986). Examining the strange-situation procedure with Japanese mothers and 12-month-old infants. *Developmental Psychology, 22*, 265–270.

Takemoto, S. K., Pinksy, B. W., Schnitzler, M. A., Lentine, K. L., Willoughby, L. M., Burrough, & Bunnapradist, S. (2007). A retrospective analysis of immunosuppression compliance, dose reduction and discontinuation in kidney transplant recipients. *American Journal of Transplantation* 7(12), 2704–2711. doi:10.1111/j.1600-6143.2007.01966.x

Talebi, M., Matheson, K., & Anisman, H. (2016). The stigma of seeking help for mental health issues: Mediating roles of support and coping and the moderating role of symptom profile. *Journal of Applied Social Psychology, 46*(8), 470–482. doi:10.1111/jasp.12376

Tamimi, R. M., Hankinson, S. E., Campos, H., Spiegelman, D., Zhang, S., Colditz, G. A., & Hunter, D. J. (2005). Plasma carotenoids, retinol, and tocopherols and risk of breast cancer. *American Journal of Epidemiology, 161*, 153–160.

Tan, G., Jensen, M. P., Robinson-Whelen, S., Thornby, J. I., & Monga, T. N. (2001). Coping with chronic pain: A comparison of two measures. *Pain, 90*(1–2), 127–133. doi:10.1016/S0304-3959(00)00395-X

Tanasescu, M., Cho, E., Manson, J. E., & Hu, F. B. (2004). Dietary fat and cholesterol and the risk of cardiovascular disease among women with Type 2 diabetes. *American Journal of Clinical Nutrition, 79*, 999–1005.

Tang, D. W., Hello, B., Mroziewicz, M., Fellows, L. K., Tyndale, R. F., & Dagher, A. (2012). Genetic variation in CYP2A6 predicts neural reactivity to smoking cues as measured using fMRI. *Neuroimage, 60*(4), 2136–2143. doi:10.1016/j.neuroimage.2012.01.119

Tang, T. S., Solomon, L. J., McCracken, L. M. (2000). Cultural barriers to mammography, clinical breast exam, and breast self-exam among Chinese women 60 and older. *Preventive Medicine, 31*, 575–583.

Tang, Y., Yin, H., Rubini, P., & Illes, P. (2016). Acupuncture-induced analgesia: A neurobiological basis in purinergic signaling. *Neuroscientist, 22*(6), 563–578. doi:10.1177/1073858416654453

Tanuseputro, P., Budhwani, S., Bai, Y. Q., & Wodchis, W. P. (2017). Palliative care delivery across health sectors: A population-level observational study. *Palliative Medicine, 31*(3), 247–257. doi:10.1177/0269216316653524

Tarn, D. M., Meredith, L.S., Kagawa-Singer, M., Matsumura, S., Bito, S., Oye, R. K., . . . Wenger, N. S. (2005). Trust in one's physician: The role of ethnic match, autonomy, acculturation, and religiosity among Japanese and Japanese Americans. *Annals of Family Medicine, 3*, 339–347.

Taubes, G. (2011). *Why we get fat*. New York, NY: Random House.

Taubes, G. (2017). *The case against sugar*. New York, NY: Knoff.

Tausch, C., Marks, L. D., Brown, J., Cherry, K. E., Frias, T., McWilliams, Z., & . . . Sasser, D. D. (2011). Religion and coping with trauma: Qualitative examples from Hurricanes Katrina and Rita. *Journal of Religion, Spirituality & Aging, 23*(3), 236–253. doi:10.1080/15528030.2011.563203

Taylor, A. H., Doust, J., & Webborn, N. (1998). Randomised controlled trial to examine the effects of a GP exercise referral programme in Hailsham, East Sussex, on modifiable coronary heart disease risk factors. *Journal of Epidemiology and Community Health, 52*, 595–601.

Taylor, R. M., Gibson, F., Franck, L. S. (2008). A concept analysis of health-related quality of life in young people with chronic illness. *Journal of Clinical Nursing, 17*, 1823–1833.

Taylor, R. S., Brown, A., Ebrahim, S., Jolliffe, J., Noorani, H., Rees, K., Skidmore, B., . . . Oldridge, N. (2004). Exercise-based rehabilitation for patients with coronary heart disease: Systematic review and meta-analysis of randomized controlled trials. *American Journal of Medicine, 116*, 682–692.

Taylor, S. (2011). The future of social-health psychology: Prospects and predictions. *Social and personality compass, 5*(5), 275–284. doi:10.1111/j.1751.9004.2011.00360.x

Taylor, S. E. (1983). Adjustment to threatening events: A theory of cognitive adaptation. *American Psychologist, 38*, 1161–1173.

Taylor, S. E. (1990). Health psychology. *American Psychologist, 45*(1), 40–50.

Taylor, S. E. (2010). Health psychology. In R. F. Baumeister, E. J. Finkel (Eds.), *Advanced social psychology: The state of the science* (pp. 697–731). New York, NY: Oxford University Press.

Taylor, S. E. (2012). Tend and befriend theory. In P. M. Van Lange, A. W. Kruglanski, & E. Higgins (Eds.), *Handbook of theories of social psychology* (Vol. 1, pp. 32–49). Thousand Oaks, CA: SAGE.

Taylor, S. E., & Master, S. L. (2011). Social responses to stress: The tend-and-befriend model. In R. J. Contrada, A. Baum (Eds.), *The handbook of stress science: Biology, psychology, and health* (pp. 101–109). New York, NY: Springer.

Taylor, S. E., Kemeny, M. E., Apsinwall, L. G., Schneider, S. G., Rodriguez, R., & Herbert, M. (1992). Optimism, coping, psychological distress, and high-risk sexual behavior among men at risk for acquired immunodeficiency syndrome (AIDS). *Journal of Personality and Social Psychology, 63*, 460–473.

Taylor, S. E., Kemeny, M. E., Reed, G. M., Bower, J. E., & Gruenewald, T. L. (2000). Psychological resources, positive illusions, and health. *American Psychologist, 55*, 99–109.

Taylor, S. E., Klein, L. C., Lewis, B. P., Gruenewald, T. L., Gurung, R. A. R., & Updegraff, J. A. (2000). Biobehavioral responses to stress in females: Tend-and-befriend, not fight-or-flight. *Psychological Review, 107*, 411–429.

Taylor, S. E., Lerner, J. S., Sage, R. M., Lehman, B. J., & Seeman, T. E. (2004). Early environment, emotions, responses to stress, and health. *Journal of Personality, 72*, 1365–1393.

Taylor, S. E., Lewis, B. P., Gruenewald, T. L., Gurung, R. A. R., Updegraff, J. A., & Klein, L. C. (2002). Sex differences in biobehavioral responses to threat: Reply to Geary and Flinn. *Psychological Review, 109*, 751–753.

Taylor, S. E., Lichtman, R. R., & Wood, J. V. (1984). Attributions, beliefs about control, and adjustment to breast cancer. *Journal of Personality and Social Psychology, 46*, 489–502.

Taylor, S. E., Repetti, R. L., & Seeman, T. (1997). Health psychology: What is an unhealthy environment and how does it get under the skin? *Annual Review of Psychology, 48*, 411–447.

Taylor, S. E., Sherman, D. K., Kim, H. S., Jarcho, J., Takagi, K., & Dunagan, M. S. (2004). Culture and social support: Who seeks it and why? *Journal of Personality and Social Psychology, 87*, 354–362.

Taylor, S. E., Welch, W., Kim, H. S., & Sherman, D. K. (2007). Cultural differences in the impact of social support on psychological and biological stress responses. *Psychological Science, 18*, 831–837.

Tedaldi, E. M., Absalon, J., Thomas, A. J., Shlay, J. C, & van den Berg-Wolf, M. (2008). Ethnicity, race, and gender. Differences in serious adverse events among participants in an antiretroviral initiation trial: Results of CPCRA 058 (FIRST Study). *Journal of Acquired Immune Deficiency Syndromes, 47*(4), 441–448. doi:10.1097/QAI.0B013E3181609DA8

Teeley, A., Soltani, M., Wiechman, S., Jensen, M., Sharar, S., & Patterson, D. (2012). Virtual reality hypnosis pain control in the treatment of multiple fractures: A case series. *American Journal of Clinical Hypnosis, 54*(3), 184–194.

Temoshok, L. (1987). Personality, coping style, emotion and cancer: Toward an integrative model. *Cancer Surveys, 6*, 837–857.

Temoshok, L., Wald, R., Synowski, S., & Garzino-Demo, A. (2008). Coping as a multisystem construct associated with pathways mediating HIV-relevant immune function and disease progression. *Psychosomatic Medicine, 70*(5), 555–561.

Temple, J. L., Giacomelli, A. M., Roemmich, J. N., & Epstein, L. H. (2008). Habituation and within-session changes in motivated responding for food in children. *Appetite, 50*(2/3), 390–396. doi:10.1016/j.appet.2007.09.005.

Tennen, H., Affleck, G., Armeli, S., & Carney, M. A. (2000). A daily process approach to coping: Linking theory, research, and practice. *American Psychologist, 55*, 626–636.

Terhune, D., & Kadosh, R. (2012). The emerging neuroscience of hypnosis. *Cortex, 48*(3), 382–386. doi:10.1016/j.cortex.2011.08.007

Ternel, J. S., Greer, J. A., Muzikansky, A., Gallagher, E. R., Admane, S., Jackson, V. A . . . Lynch, T. J. (2010). Early palliative care for patients with metastatic non-small-cell lung cancer. *New England Journal Medicine, 363*, 733–742.

Tez, M., & Tez, S. (2008). Is cancer an adaptation mechanism to stress? *Cell Biology International, 32*(6), 713–713.

Thadhani, R., Camargo, C. A., Stampfer, M. J., Curhan, G. C., Willett, W. C., & Rimm, E. B. (2002). Prospective study of moderate alcohol consumption and risk of hypertension in young women. *Archives of Internal Medicine, 162*, 569–576.

Thakur, E. R., Sansgiry, S., Petersen, N. J., Stanley, M., Kunik, M. E., Naik, A. D., & Cully, J. A. (2017). Cognitive and perceptual factors, not disease severity, are linked with anxiety in COPD: Results from a cross-sectional study. *International Journal of Behavioral Medicine, 25*(1), 74–84. doi:10.1007/s12529-017-9663-2

Theakston, J. A., Stewart, S. H., Dawson, M. Y., Knowlden-Loewen, S. A. B., & Lehman, D. R. (2004). Big Five personality domains predict drinking motives. *Personality & Individual Differences, 37*, 971–984.

Theeke, L. A., Goins, R., Moore, J., & Campbell, H. (2012). Loneliness, depression, social support, and quality of life in older chronically ill Appalachians. *Journal of Psychology, 146*(1/2), 155–171. doi:10.1080/00223980.2011.609571

Theorell, T., & Harenstam, A. (2000). Influence of gender on cardiovascular disease. In R. M. Eisler & M. Herson (Eds.), *Handbook of gender, culture, and health* (pp. 161–177). Mahwah, NJ: Erlbaum.

Theorell, T., Blomkvist, V., Jonsson, H., Schulman, S., Berntorp, E., & Stigenendal, L. (1995). Social support and the development of immune function in HIV infection. *Psychosomatic Medicine, 57*, 32–36.

Thiara, G., Cigliobianco, M., Muravsky, A., Paoli, R. A., Mansur, R., Hawa, R., . . . Sockalingam, S. (2017). Evidence for neurocognitive improvement after bariatric surgery: A systematic review. *Psychosomatics: Journal of Consultation and Liaison Psychiatry, 58*(3), 217–227. doi:10.1016/j.psym.2017.02.004

Thieden, E. (2008). Sun exposure behaviour among subgroups of the Danish population. Based on personal electronic UVR dosimetry and corresponding exposure diaries. *Danish Medical Bulletin, 55*(1), 47–68.

Thieme, K., Spies, C., Sinha, P., Turk, D. C., & Flor, H. (2005). Predictors of pain behaviors in fibromyalgia syndrome. *Arthritis & Rheumatism, 53*(3), 343–350. doi:10.1002/art.21158

Thoits, P. A. (1983). Multiple identities and psychological well-being: A reformulation and the test of the social isolation hypothesis. *American Sociological Review 48*, 174–187.

Thomas, R. M. (1999). *Human development theories: Windows on culture.* Thousand Oaks, CA: SAGE.

Thombs, B. (2008). Perceived social support predicts outcomes following myocardial infarction: A call for screening? *Health Psychology, 27*(1), 1–1.

Thompson, B., Coronado, G., Chen, L., Thompson, L. A., Halperin, A., Jaffe, R., . . . Zbikowiski, S. M. (2007). Prevalence and characteristics of smokers at 30 Pacific Northwest colleges and universities. *Nicotine and Tobacco Research, 9*, 429–438.

Thorburn, S., Harvey, S. M., & Ryan, E. A. (2005). HIV prevention heuristics and condom use among African-Americans at risk for HIV. *AIDS Care, 17*, 335–344.

Thorn, B., Cross, T., & Walker, B. (2007). Meta-analyses and systematic reviews of psychological treatments for chronic pain: Relevance to an evidence-based practice. *Health Psychology, 26*(1), 10–12.

Thornicroft, G., Rose, D., & Kassam, A. (2007). Discrimination in health care against people with mental illness. *International Review of Psychiatry, 19*, 113–122.

Thorogood, M., Simera, I., Dowler, E., Summerbell, C., & Brunner, E. (2007). A systematic review of population and community dietary interventions to prevent cancer, *Nutrition Research Reviews, 20*, 74–88.

Thorpe, R., Koster, A., Bosma, H., Harris, T., Simonsick, E., Eijk, J., & . . . Kritchevsky, S. (2012). Racial differences in mortality in older adults: Factors beyond socioeconomic status. *Annals of*

Behavioral Medicine, 43(1), 29–38. doi:10.1007/s12160-011-9335-4

Thorsen, L., Courneya, K., Stevinson, C., & Fosså, S. (2008). A systematic review of physical activity in prostate cancer survivors: Outcomes, prevalence, and determinants. *Supportive Care in Cancer, 16*(9), 987–997.

Throne, L. C., Bartholomew, J. B., Craig, J., & Farrar, R. P. (2000). Stress reactivity in fire fighters: An exercise intervention. *International Journal of Stress Management, 7*, 235–246.

Thune, I., & Furberg, A. S. (2001). Physical activity and cancer risk: Dose-response and cancer, all sites and site-specific. *Medicine and Science in Sports and Exercise, 33*, S530–S550.

Thune, I., & Lund, E. (1994). Physical activity and the risk of prostate and testicular cancer: A cohort study of 53,000 Norwegian men. *Cancer Causes & Control, 5*(6), 549–556.

Tian, Y., & Robinson, J. D. (2017). Predictors of cell phone use in distracted driving: Extending the Theory of Planned Behavior. *Health Communication, 32*(9), 1066–1075. doi:10.1080/10410236.2016.1196639

Tiegel, I. M. (2017). Diathesis-stress model for understanding physiological and psychological and psychological effects of stress. In S. Wadhwa (Ed.), *Stress in the modern world: Understanding science and society* (pp.35–44). Santa Barbara, CA: Greenwood.

Tillerson, K. (2008). Explaining racial disparities in HIV/AIDS incidence among women in the U.S.: A systematic review. *Statistics in Medicine, 27*(20), 4132–4143.

Tindle, H., Belnap, B., Houck, P. R., Mazumadar, S., Scheier, M. F., Matthews, K. A., & . . . Rollman, B. L. (2012). Optimism, response to treatment of depression, and rehospitalization after coronary artery bypass graft surgery. *Psychosomatic Medicine, 74*(2), 200–207. doi:10.1097/PSY.0b013e318244903f

Tobin, A. J., & Dusheck, J. (2001). *Asking about life*. Pacific Grove, CA: Brooks/Cole.

Tod, A. M., Craven, J., & Allmark, P. (2008). Diagnostic delay in lung cancer: A qualitative study. *Journal of Advanced Nursing, 61*, 336–343.

Tom, N. C., & Assinder, S. J. (2010). Oxytocin: Recent developments. *Biomolecular Concepts, 1*(5/6), 367–380. doi:10.1515/BMC.2010.036

Tomich, P. L., & Helgeson, V. S. (2004). Is finding something good in the bad always good? Benefit finding among women with breast cancer. *Health Psychology, 23*, 16–23.

Tomono, T. (2010). The relationships among interpersonal intolerance of ambiguity, dispositional interpersonal stress coping, and mental health. *Japanese Journal of Social Psychology, 25*(3), 221–226.

Tompkins, D. A., Hobelmann, J. G., & Compton, P. (2017). Providing chronic pain management in the "Fifth vital sign" era: Historical and treatment perspectives on a modern-day medical dilemma. *Drug and Alcohol Dependence, 173*, S11–S21. doi:10.1016/j.drugalcdep.2016.12.002

Tope, D. A., Ahles, T. A., & Silberfarb, P. M. (1993). Psycho-oncology: Psychological well-being as one component of quality of life. *Psychotherapy and Psychosomatics, 60*, 129–147.

Tornesello, M., L. Duraturo, M. L., Giorgi-Rossi, P., Sansone, M., Piccoli, R., Buonaguro, L., & Buonaguro, F. M. (2008). Human papillomavirus (HPV) genotypes and HPV16 variants in human immunodeficiency virus-positive Italian women. *Journal of General Virology, 89*(Pt 6), 1380–1389.

Torres, E., Sawyer, T. L. (2005). *Curandero: Life in Mexican folk healing*. Albuquerque, NM: University of New Mexico Press.

Torres, L., Driscoll, M., & Voell, M. (2012). Discrimination, acculturation, acculturative stress, and Latino psychological distress: A moderated mediational model. *Cultural Diversity & Ethnic Minority Psychology, 18*(1), 17–25.

Torrey, E. F. (1969). The case for the indigenous therapist. *Archives of General Psychiatry, 20*, 365–373.

Torta, D. M., Legrain, V., Mouraux, A., & Valentini, E. (2017). Attention to pain! A neurocognitive perspective on attentional modulation of pain in neuroimaging studies. *Cortex, 89*, 120–134. doi:10.1016/j.cortex.2017.01.010

Tovar, M. A. (2017). *Mexican American psychology: Social, cultural, and clinical perspectives*. Santa Barbara, CA: Praeger.

Tovian, S. M. (2004). Health services and health care economics: The health psychology marketplace. *Health Psychology, 23*, 119–125.

Tracey, D. J., Walker, J. S., & Carmody, J. J. (2000). Chronic pain: Neural basis and interactions with stress. In D. T. Kenny & J. G. Carison (Eds.), *Stress and health: Research and clinical applications* (pp. 105–125). Amsterdam, Netherlands: Harwood Academic Publishers.

Treat, T. A., Viken, R. J., Kruschke, J. K., & McFall, R. M. (2010). Role of attention, memory, and covariation-detection processes in clinically significant eating-disorder symptoms. *Journal of Mathematical Psychology, 54*(1), 184–195. doi:10.1016/j.jmp.2008.11.003

Tremblay, P. F., Graham, K., & Wells, S. (2008). Severity of physical aggression reported by university students: A test of the interaction between trait aggression and alcohol consumption. *Personality and Individual Differences, 45*, 3–9.

Tremlett, H. H., Fu, P. P., Yoshida, E. E., & Hashimoto, S. S. (2011). Symptomatic liver injury (hepatotoxicity) associated with administration of complementary and alternative products (Ayurveda-AP-Mag Capsules). *European Journal of Neurology, 18*(7), e78–e79. doi:10.1111/j.1468-1331.2011.03373.x

Triandis, H. C. (1996). The psychological measurement of cultural syndromes. *American Psychologist, 51*, 407–415.

Trichopoulou, A., & Lagiou, P. (1997). Healthy traditional Mediterranean diet: An expression of culture, history, and lifestyle. *Nutrition Reviews, 55*, 383–390.

Triest-Robertson, S. (2011, April). Pain management: A multidisciplinary approach. Presentation given at the University of Wisconsin, Green Bay, WI.

Triest-Robertson, S., Gurung, R. A. R., Brosig, C., Whitfield, N., & Pfutzenreuter, M. (2001, March). Assessing satisfaction with hospital pain management. Paper presented at the meeting of the Society for Behavioral Medicine, Seattle, WA.

Triscari, M. T., Faraci, P., Catalisano, D., D'Angelo, V., & Urso, V. (2015). Effectiveness of cognitive behavioral therapy integrated with systematic desensitization, cognitive behavioral therapy combined with eye movement desensitization and reprocessing therapy, and cognitive behavioral therapy combined with virtual reality exposure therapy methods in the treatment of flight anxiety: A randomized trial. *Neuropsychiatric Disease and Treatment, 11*, 2591–2598. doi:10.2147/NDT.S93401

Trivedi, R. (2019). Psychiatric illness among military veterans in the United States. In T. A. Revenson & R. A. R. Gurung (Eds.), *Handbook of health psychology* (3e). New York, NY: Routledge.

Trogdon, J., Finkelstein, E., Feagan, C., & Cohen, J. (2012). State- and payer-specific estimates of annual medical expenditures attributable to obesity. *Obesity* (Silver Spring, MD), *20*(1), 214–220. doi:10.1038/oby.2011.169

Troiano, R. P., Flegal, K. M., Kuczmarski, R. J., Campbell, S. M., & Johnson, C. L. (1995). Overweight prevalence and trends for children and adolescents. The National Health and Nutrition Examination Surveys, 1963 to 1991. *Archives of Pediatrics and Adolescent Medicine, 149*, 1085–1091.

Trompenaars, F. (1997). *Riding the waves of culture: Understanding cultural diversity in business.* London, UK: Nicholas Brealey.
Trotter, R. T. (2001). Curanderismo: A picture of Mexican-American folk healing. *Journal of Alternative and Complementary Medicine, 7,* 129–131.
Trotter, R. T., & Chavira, J. A. (1997). *Curanderismo: Mexican American folk healing.* Athens, GA: University of Georgia Press.
Trudeau, L., Lillehoj, C., Spoth, R., & Redmond, C. (2003). The role of assertiveness and decision making in early adolescent substance initiation: Mediating processes. *Journal of Research on Adolescence, 13,* 304–328.
Truffer, C. J., Keehan, S., Smith, S., Cylus, J., Sisko, A., Poisal, J. A., . . . Clemens, M. K. (2010). Health spending projections through 2019: The recession's impact continues. *Health Affairs, 29*(3), 522–529.
Tse, M. M. Y., Ng, J. K. F., Chung, J. W. Y., Wong, T. K. S. (2002). The effect of visual stimulation via the eyeglass display and the perception of pain. *Cyber Psychology and Behavior, 5,* 65–75.
Tsenkova, V. K. Love, G. D. Singer, B. H., & Ryff, C. D. (2008). Coping and positive affect predict longitudinal change in glycosylated hemoglobin. *Health Psychology, 27,* S163–S171.
Tsimtsiou, Z., Benos, A., Garyfallos, A. A., & Hatzichristou, D. (2012). Predictors of physicians' attitudes toward sharing information with patients and addressing psychosocial needs: A cross-sectional study in Greece. *Health Communication, 27*(3), 257–263. doi:10.1080/10410236.2011.578333
Tucker, J. S., Orlando, M., & Ellickson, P. L. (2003). Patterns and correlates of binge drinking trajectories from early adolescence to young adulthood. *Health Psychology, 22,* 79–87.
Tugade, M. M., Fredrickson, B. L., & Barrett, L. F. (2004). Psychological resilience and positive emotional granularity: Examining the benefits of positive emotions on coping and health. *Journal of Personality, 72,* 1161–1190.
Tullmann, D. F., Haugh, K. H., Dracup, K. A., & Bourguignon, C. (2007). A randomized controlled trial to reduce delay in older adults seeking help for symptoms of acute myocardial infarction. *Research in Nursing and Health, 30,* 485–497.
Tummala-Narra, P., Alegria, M., & Chen, C. (2012). Perceived discrimination, acculturative stress, and depression among South Asians: Mixed findings. *Asian American Journal of Psychology, 3*(1), 3–16. doi:10.1037/a0024661
Tung, W., Hu, J., Efird, J. T., Su, W., & Yu, L. (2013). HIV knowledge and condom intention among sexually abstinent chinese students. *International Nursing Review, 60*(3), 366–373. doi:10.1111/inr.12039
Turbin, M. S., Jessor, R., & Costa, F. M. (2000). Adolescent cigarette smoking: Health-related behavior of normative transgression? *Prevention Science, 1,* 115–124.
Turchik, J. A., & Gidycz, C. A. (2012). Exploring the Intention-Behavior Relationship in the Prediction of Sexual Risk Behaviors: Can It Be Strengthened? *Journal of Sex Research, 49*(1), 50–60. doi:10.1080/00224499.2011.578220
Turk, C. S., Gatz, M., Kato, K., & Pedersen, N. (2008). Physical health 25 years later: The predictive ability of neuroticism. *Health Psychology, 27*(3), 369–378.
Turk, D. C. (2001a). Combining somatic and psychosocial treatment for chronic pain patients: Perhaps 1 1 1 does 5 3. *Clinical Journal of Pain, 17,* 281–283.
Turk, D. C. (2001b). Treatment of chronic pain: Clinical outcomes, cost-effectiveness, and cost benefits. *Drug Benefit Trends, 13,* 36–38.
Turk, D. C. (2002a). A diathesis-stress model of chronic pain and disability following traumatic injury. *Pain Research & Management, 7,* 9–20.
Turk, D. C. (2002b). Clinical effectiveness and cost-effectiveness of treatments for patients with chronic pain. *Clinical Journal of Pain, 18,* 355–365.
Turk, D. C. (2002c). Cognitive-behavioral techniques and cost-effectiveness of treatments for patients with chronic pain. *Catalog of Selected Documents in Psychology, 10,* 17.
Turk, D. C. (2002d). Suffering and dysfunction in fibromyalgia syndrome. *Journal of Musculoskeletal Pains, 10,* 85–96.
Turk, D. C., & Melzack, R. (Eds.). (2001). *Handbook of pain assessment* (2nd ed., pp. 97–118). New York, NY: Guilford Press.
Turk, D. C., & Nash, J. M. (1996). Psychological issues, in chronic pain. In R. K. Portenoy, K. Foley, & R. Kanner (Eds.), *Contemporary neurology* (pp. 245–260). Philadelphia, PA: Davis.
Turk, D. C., & Okifuji, A. (2002). Psychological factors in chronic pain: Evolution and revolution. *Journal of Consulting and Clinical Psychology, 70,* 678–690.
Turk, D. C., & Rudy, T. E. (1986). MAP-ping out the terrain. *Journal of Pain and Symptom Management, 1,* 235–237.
Turk, D. C., & Salovey, P. (1984). Chronic pain as a variant of depressive disease: A critical reappraisal. *Journal of Nervous and Mental Disease, 172,* 398–404.
Turk, D. C., Meichenbaum, D., & Genest, M. (1983). *Pain and behavioral medicine: A cognitive-behavioral perspective.* New York, NY: Guilford.
Turk, D. C., Wilson, H. D., & Swanson, K. S. (2012). Psychological and physiological bases of chronic pain. In A. Baum, T. A. Revenson, & J. Singer (Eds.), *Handbook of health psychology* (2e, pp. 149–174). New York, NY: Guilford Press.
Turner, D. C. (1996). The role of culture in chronic illness. *American Behavioral Scientist, 39,* 717–728.
Turner, D. C., Cobb, J. M., & Steptoe, A. (1996). Psychosocial stress and susceptibility to upper respiratory tract illness in an adult population sample. *Psychosomatic Medicine, 58,* 404–412.
Turner, R. J., & Avison, W. R. (1992). Innovations in the measurement of life stress: Crisis theory and the significance of event resolution. *Journal of Health and Social Behavior, 33,* 36–50.
Turnwald, B. P., Jurafsky, D., Conner, A., & Crum, A. J. (2017). Reading between the menu lines: Are restaurants' descriptions of "healthy" foods unappealing? *Health Psychology, 36*(11), 1034–1037. doi:10.1037/hea0000501
Tuzcu, E. M., Kapadia, S. R., Tutar, E., Ziada, K. M., Hobbs, R. E., McCarthy, P. M., . . . Nissen, S. E. (2001). High prevalence of coronary atherosclerosis in asymptomatic teenagers and young adults: Evidence from intravascular ultrasound. *Circulation, 103,* 2705–2710.
U.S. Census Bureau. (2012). State and county quickfacts. Author, Washington, DC. Retrieved from https://www.census.gov/quickfacts/fact/table/US/HSG010216
U.S. Census Bureau. (2017). Population clock. Author, Washington, DC. Retrieved from https://www.census.gov/
U.S. Census Bureau. (n.d.). Data. Author, Washington, DC. Retrieved from https://www.census.gov/data.html
U.S. Department of Agriculture (USDA). n.d. A brief history of USDA food guides. Author, Washington, DC. Retrieved from www.choosemyplate.gov/brief-history-usda-food-guides
U.S. Department of Health and Human Services (DHHS). (2000a). Best practices for comprehensive tobacco control programs. Author, Washington, DC. Retrieved from http://www.hsca.com/membersonly/USDHHSlink.htm.
U.S. Department of Health and Human Services (DHHS). (1988). Surgeon general's report on nutrition and health. Author, Atlanta, GA. Retrieved from https://profiles.nlm.nih.gov/nn/b/c/q/g/

U.S. Department of Health and Human Services (DHHS). (1996). Surgeon general's report on physical acitivity and health. Author, Atlanta, GA. Retrieved from https://wonder.cdc.gov/wonder/prevguid/m0042984/m0042984.asp

U.S. Department of Health and Human Services (DHHS). (1996). Surgeon general's report on physical acitivity and health. Author: Atlanta, GA.

U.S. Department of Health and Human Services (DHHS). (2000b, 12 January). Healthy people 2010 fact sheet. Office of Disease Prevention and Health Promotion. Author, Washington, DC.

U.S. Department of Health and Human Services (DHHS). (2001). *Mental health: Culture, race, and ethnicity—A supplement to mental health: A report of the surgeon general.* Rockville, MD: U.S. Department of Health and Human Services, Substance Abuse and Mental Health Services Administration, Center for Mental Health Services.

U.S. Department of Health and Human Services (DHHS). (2003). Racial and ethnic disparities in infant mortality rates: 60 Largest U.S. Cities, 1995–1998. *Morbidity and Mortality Weekly Report,* 51. Retrieved from https://www.cdc.gov/mmwr/preview/mmwrhtml/mm5115a4.htm

U.S. Department of Health and Human Services (DHHS). (2007). *Health, United States 2007.* Author, Washington, DC.

U.S. Department of Health and Human Services (DHHS). (2008). *Healthy People 2010.* Author, Washington, DC. Retrieved October 21, 2008, from https://healthypeople.gov/2010/

U.S. Department of Health and Human Services (DHHS). (2010). *Heart disease and African Americans.* Author, Washington, DC. Retrieved from https://minorityhealth.hhs.gov/omh/browse.aspx?lvl=4&lvlid=19

U.S. Department of Health and Human Services (DHHS). (2011). *2012 HHS poverty guidelines.* Author, Washington, DC. Retrieved from http://aspe.hhs.gov/poverty/12poverty.shtml

U.S. Department of Health and Human Services (DHHS). 1988. Publication No. 8840210. Author, Washington, DC.

U.S. Department of Justice. (2006). *2006 National Crime Victimization Survey.* Author, Washington, DC.

U.S. Department of Justice. (2015). *National Crime Victimization Survey, 2010–2014.* Office of Justice Programs, Bureau of Justice Statistics. Author, Washington, DC.

U.S. Department of Labor. (2003). *Occupational stress: Counts and rates.* Retrieved from https://www.bls.gov/opub/mlr/cwc/occupational-stress-counts-and-rates.pdf

U.S. National Library of Medicine. (2012). *Miscarriage.* Author, Washington, DC. Retrieved from http://www.nlm.nih.gov/medlineplus/ency/article/001488.htm

Uchino, B. N. (2009). Understanding the links between social support and physical health: A life-span perspective with emphasis on the separability of perceived and received support. *Perspectives on Psychological Science, 4*(3), 236–255. doi:10.1111/j.1745-6924.2009.01122.x

Uchino, B. N., Cacioppo, J. T., & Kiecolt-Glaser, J. K. (1996). The relationship between social support and physiological processes: A review with emphasis on underlying mechanisms and implications for health. *Psychological Bulletin, 119,* 488–531.

Uchino, B., Bowen, K., Carlisle, M., & Birmingham, W. (2012). Psychological pathways linking social support to health outcomes: A visit with the "ghosts" of research past, present, and future. *Social Science & Medicine, 74*(7), 949–957. doi:10.1016/j.socscimed.2011.11.023

Udwadia, F. E. (2000). *Man and medicine: A history.* New Delhi, India: Oxford University Press.

Ukraintseva, S., & Yashin, A. I. (2003). Individual aging and cancer risk: How are they related? *Demographic Research, 9,* 164–196.

Ulbrich, P. M., & Bradsher, J. E. (1993). Perceived support, help seeking, and adaptation to stress among older Black and White women living alone. *Journal of Aging and Health, 5,* 365–386.

Ullrich, P. A., & Lutgendorf, S. L. (2002). Journaling about stressful events: Effects of cognitive processing and emotional expression. *Annals of Behavioral Medicine, 24,* 244–250.

Ulrich, R. (2004). The role of the physical environment in the hospital of the 21st century: A once-in-a-life-time opportunity. Report to the Center for Health Design for the Designing the 21st Century Hospital Project. Retrived from https://www.healthdesign.org/system/files/Ulrich_Role%20of%20Physical_2004.pdf

Ulrich, R. S. (1984). View through a window may influence recovery from surgery. *Science, 224,* 420–421.

Ulrich, R. S., Simons, R. F., & Miles, M. A. (2003). Effects of environmental simulations and television on blood donor stress. *Journal of Architectural and Planning Research, 20,* 38–47.

Umeda, M., Griffin, C., Cross, A., Heredia, C., & Okifuji, A. (2017). Conditioned pain modulation among young, healthy, and physically active African American and non-Hispanic white adults. *Journal of Psychosomatic Research, 98,* 64–70. doi:10.1016/j.jpsychores.2017.05.012

UNAIDS. (2017). About. Author, Geneva, Switzerland. Retrieved from http://www.unaids.org/en

Unger, J. B., McAvay, G., Bruce, M. L., Berkman, L., & Seeman, T. (1999). Variation in the impact of social network characteristics on physical functioning in elderly persons: MacArthur Studies of Successful Aging. *Journals of Gerontology: Series B: Psychological Sciences & Social Sciences, 54B,* S245–S251.

Upchurch, D. M., Chyu, L., Greendale, G.A., Utts, J., Bair, Y. A., Zhang, G., & Gold, E. B. (2007). Complementary and alternative medicine use among American women: Findings from the National Health Interview Survey, 2002. *Journal of Women's Health, 16*(1), 102–113.

Utsey, S. O., Payne, Y. A., Jackson, E. S., & Jones, A. M. (2002). Race-related stress, quality of life indicators, and life satisfaction among elderly African Americans. *Cultural Diversity and Ethnic Minority Psychology, 8,* 224–233.

Uvnas-Moberg, K. (1996). Neuroendocrinology of the mother–child interaction. *Trends in Endocrinology and Metabolism, 7,* 126–131.

Uvnäs-Moberg, K., Handlin, L., & Petersson, M. (2015). Self-soothing behaviors with particular reference to oxytocin release induced by non-noxious sensory stimulation. *Frontiers in Psychology, 5,* 1529. doi:10.3389/FPSYG.2014.01529

Uy, J. P., & Galván, A. (2017). Acute stress increases risky decisions and dampens prefrontal activation among adolescent boys. *NeuroImage, 146,* 679–689. doi:10.1016/j.neuroimage.2016.08.067

Vaccarino, V., & Bremner, J. D. (2017). Behavioral, emotional and neurobiological determinants of coronary heart disease risk in women. *Neuroscience and Biobehavioral Reviews, 74,* 297–309. doi:10.1016/j.neubiorev.2016.04.023

Vachon, M. (2008). Meaning, spirituality, and wellness in cancer survivors. *Seminars in Oncology Nursing, 24*(3), 218–225.

Vaegter, H. B., Hoeger Bement, M., Madsen, A. B., Fridriksson, J., Dasa, M., & Graven-Nielsen, T. (2017). Exercise increases pressure pain tolerance but not pressure and heat pain thresholds in healthy young men. *European Journal of Pain, 21*(1), 73–81. doi:10.1002/ejp.901

Vago, D., & Nakamura, Y. (2011). Selective attentional bias towards pain-related threat in fibromyalgia: Preliminary evidence for effects of mindfulness meditation training. *Cognitive Therapy & Research, 35*(6), 581–594. doi:10.1007/s10608-011-9391-x

Vahabi, M., Lofters, A., Kim, E., Wong, J. P., Ellison, L., Graves, E., & Glazier, R. H. (2017). Breast cancer screening utilization among women from muslim majority countries in Ontario, Canada. *Preventive Medicine, 105*, 176–183. doi:10.1016/j.ypmed.2017.09.008

Vaidya, D., Becker, D. M., Bittner, V., Mathias, R. A., & Ouyang, P. (2011). Ageing, menopause, and ischaemic heart disease mortality in England, Wales, and the United States: Modelling study of national mortality data. *BMJ, 343*(7822), d5170. doi:10.1136/bmj.d5170

Vainshtein, J. (2008). Disparities in breast cancer incidence across racial/ethnic strata and socioeconomic status: A systematic review. *Journal of the National Medical Association, 100*(7), 833–839.

Valdez, J., N. (2014). Curanderismo: A complementary and alternative approach to Mexican American health psychology. In R. A. R. Gurung (Ed.), *Multicultural approaches to health and wellness in America* (pp. 227–257). Santa Barbara, CA: Praeger.

Van De Ven, M. M., & Engels, R. E. (2011). Quality of life of adolescents with asthma: The role of personality, coping strategies, and symptom reporting. *Journal of Psychosomatic Research, 71*(3), 166–173. doi:10.1016/j.jpsychores.2011.03.002

van der Velde, F. W., & van der Pligt, J. (1991). AIDS-related health behavior: Coping, protection motivation, and previous behavior. *Journal of Behavioral Medecine, 14*, 429–451.

Van Dyke, M. E., Vaccarino, V., Dunbar, S. B., Pemu, P., Gibbons, G. H., Quyyumi, A. A., & Lewis, T. T. (2017). Socioeconomic status discrimination and C-reactive protein in African- American and white adults. *Psychoneuroendocrinology, 82*, 9–16. doi:10.1016/j.psyneuen.2017.04.009

van Erp, S. J. H., Brakenhoff, L. K. M. P., Vollmann, M., van, d. H., Veenendaal, R. A., Fidder, H. H., . . . Scharloo, M. (2017). Illness perceptions and outcomes in patients with inflammatory bowel disease: Is coping a mediator? *International Journal of Behavioral Medicine, 24*(2), 205–214. doi:10.1007/s12529-016-9599-y

Van Horn, L., McCoin, M., Kris-Etherton, P. M., Burke, F, Carson, J. A., Champagne, C. M . . . Sikand, G. (2008). The evidence for dietary prevention and treatment of cardiovascular disease. *Journal of the American Dietetic Association, 108*(2), 287–331.

van Ingen, E., Utz, S., & Toepoel, V. (2016). Online coping after negative life events: Measurement, prevalence, and relation with Internet activities and well-being. *Social Science Computer Review, 34*(5), 511–529. doi:10.1177/0894439315600322

Van Itallie, T. B. (1985). Health implications of overweight and obesity in the United States. *Annals of Internal Medicine, 103*, 983–989.

van Servellen, G., Sarna, L., Nyamathi, A., Padilla, G. V., Brecht, M. L., & Jablonski, K. J. (1998). Emotional distress in women with symptomatic HIV disease. *Issues in Mental Health Nursing, 19*, 173–188.

van Uffelen, J. Z., Wong, J., Chau, J. Y., van der Ploeg, H. P., Riphagen, I., Gilson, N. D., & . . . Brown, W. J. (2010). Occupational sitting and health risks: A systematic review. *American Journal of Preventive Medicine, 39*(4), 379–388. doi:10.1016/j.amepre.2010.05.024

Van Velden, D. P., Kotze, M. J., Blackhurst, D. M., Marnewick, J. L., & Kidd, M. M. (2011). Health claims on the benefits of moderate alcohol consumption in relation to genetic profiles. *Journal of Wine Research, 22*(2), 123–129. doi:10.1080/09571264.2011.603221

van Venrooij, J., Fluitman, S., Lijmer, J., Kavelaars, A., Heijnen, C., Westenberg, H., & . . . Gispen-de Wied, C. (2012). Impaired neuroendocrine and immune response to acute stress in medication-naive patients with a first episode of psychosis. *Schizophrenia Bulletin, 38*(2), 272–279.

Van't Spijker, A., Trijsburg, R. W., & Duivenvoorden, H. J. (1997). Psychological sequelae of cancer diagnosis: A meta-analytical review of 58 studies after 1980. *Psychosomatic Medicine, 59*, 280–293.

Varela-Lema, L., Taioli, E., Ruano-Ravina, A., Barros-Dios, J. M., Anantharaman, D., Benhamou, S., . . . Ragin, C. C. (2008). Meta-analysis and pooled analysis of GSTM1 and CYP1A1 polymorphisms and oral and pharyngeal cancers: A HuGE-GSEC review. *Genetics in Medicine, 10*(6), 369–384.

Varghese, T., Schultz, W. M., McCue, A. A., Lambert, C. T., Sandesara, P. B., Eapen, D. J., . . . Sperling, L. S. (2016). Physical activity in the prevention of coronary heart disease: Implications for the clinician. *Heart, 102*, 904–909.

Vasquez, E., Gonzalez-Guarda, R., & De Santis, J. (2011). Acculturation, depression, self-esteem, and substance abuse among Hispanic men. *Issues in Mental Health Nursing, 32*(2), 90–97.

Vassillière, C. T., Holahan, C. J., & Holahan, C. K. (2016). Race, perceived discrimination, and emotion-focused coping. *Journal of Community Psychology, 44*(4), 524–530. doi:10.1002/jcop.21776

Vega, W. A., Sribney, W. M., Aguilar-Gaxiola, S., & Kolody, B. (2004). 12-Month prevalence of *DSM-III-R* psychiatric disorders among Mexican Americans: Nativity, social assimilation, and age determinants. *Journal of Nervous and Mental Disease, 192*(8), 532–541. doi:10.1097/01.nmd.0000135477.57357.b2

Vega, W. A., Kolody, B., Aguilar-Gaxiola, S., Alderete, E., Catalano, R., & Caraveo-Anduaga, J. (1998). Lifetime prevalence of *DSM-III-R* psychiatric disorders among urban and rural Mexican Americans in California. *Archives of General Psychiatry, 55*, 771–782.

Velez, J. A., Greitemeyer, T., Whitaker, J. L., Ewoldsen, D. R., & Bushman, B. J. (2016). Violent video games and reciprocity: The attenuating effects of cooperative game play on subsequent aggression. *Communication Research, 43*(4), 447–467. doi:10.1177/0093650214552519

Vella, E. J., Kamarck, T. W., & Shiffman, S. (2008). Hostility moderates the effects of social support and intimacy on blood pressure in daily social interactions. *Health Psychology, 27*, S155–S162.

Ventura, J., Nuechterlein, K. H., Lukoff, D., & Hardesty, J. P. (1989). Aprospective study of stressful life events and schizophrenic relapse. *Journal of Abnormal Psychology, 4*, 407–411.

Verbrugge, L. M. (1985). Triggers of symptoms and health care. *Social Science and Medicine, 20*, 855–876.

Veroff, J., Kulka, R., & Douvan, E. (1981). *Mental health in America: Patterns of help-seeking from 1957 to 1976*. New York, NY: Basic Books.

Vessey, M., Painter, R., & Yeates, D. (2003). Mortality in relation to oral contraceptive use and cigarette smoking. *The Lancet, 362*, 185–191.

Vickers, A., Ohlsson, A., Lacy, J. B., & Horsley, A. (2002). Massage for promoting growth and development of preterm and/or low birth-weight infants. *Cochrane Database System Review, 2*, CD000390.

Victor, M. (1993). Persistent altered mentation due to ethanol. *Neurology Clinic, 11*, 639–661.

Vincent, A., Hill, J., Kruk, K. M., Cha, S. S., & Bauer, B. A. (2010). External Qigong for Chronic Pain. *American Journal of Chinese Medicine, 38*(4), 695–703.

Viney, L. L., Walker, B. M., Robertson, T., Lilley, B., & Evan, C. (1994). Dying in palliative care units and in hospital: A comparison of the quality of life of terminal cancer patients. *Journal of Consulting and Clinical Psychology, 62*, 157–166.

Vinson, M. A. (1989). Acute transient memory loss. *American Family Physician, 39*, 249–254.

Vitaliano, P. P., Russo, J., Carr, J. E., Maiuro, R. D., & Becker, J. (1985). The ways of coping checklist: Revision and psychometric properties. *Multivariate Behavioral Research, 20*(1), 3–26. doi:10.1207/s15327906mbr2001_1

Vluggen, S., Hoving, C., Schaper, N. C., & de Vries, H. (2017). Exploring beliefs on diabetes treatment adherence among Dutch type 2 diabetes patients and healthcare providers. *Patient Education and Counseling, 101*(1), 92–98. doi:10.1016/j.pec.2017.07.009

Vo, L., & Drummond, P. D. (2014). Coexistence of ipsilateral pain-inhibitory and facilitatory processes after high-frequency electrical stimulation. *European Journal of Pain, 18*(3), 376–385. doi:10.1002/j.1532-2149.2013.00370.x

Volicer, B. J., Isenberg, M. A., & Burns, M. W. (1977). Medical-surgical differences in hospital stress factors. *Journal of Human Stress, 3*, 3–13.

Volkow, N., Wang, G., Fowler, J., & Tomasi, D. (2012). Addiction circuitry in the human brain. *Annual Review of Pharmacology and Toxicology, 52*, 321–336.

Von Dras, D. D. (Ed.). (2017). *Better health through spiritual practices: A guide to religious behaviors and perspectives that benefit mind and body.* Santa Barbara, CA: Praeger.

von Knorring, L., Oreland, L., & von Knorring, A. (1987). Personality traits and platelet MAO activity in alcohol and drug abusing teenage boys. *Acta Psychiatica Scandinavica, 75*, 307–314.

Von Korff, M., Dublin, S., Walker, R. L., Parchman, M., Shortreed, S. M., Hansen, R. N., & Saunders, K. (2016). The impact of opioid risk reduction initiatives on high-dose opioid prescribing for patients on chronic opioid therapy. *Journal of Pain 17*, 101–110. doi:10.1016/j.jpain.2015.10.002

Vossen, C., Hoffmann, M., Hahmann, H., Wüsten, B., Rothenbacher, D., & Brenner, H. (2008). Effect of APOE genotype on lipid levels in patients with coronary heart disease during a 3-week inpatient rehabilitation program. *Clinical Pharmacology and Therapeutics, 84*(2), 222–227.

Voydanoff, P. (2002). Linkages between the work-family interface and work, family, and individual outcomes: An integrative model. *Journal of Family Issues, 23*, 138–164.

Wachholtz, A. B., Pearce, M. J., & Koenig, H. (2007). Exploring the relationship between spirituality, coping, and pain. *Journal of Behavioral Medicine, 30*, 311–318.

Waddell, G., Main, C. J., Morris, E. W., DiPaola, M., & Gray, I. C. (1984). Chronic low-back pain, distress and illness behavior. *Spine, 9*, 209–213.

Wadhwa, P. D., Dunkel-Schetter, C., Chicz-DeMet, A., Porto, M., & Sandman, C. A. (1996). Prenatal psychosocial factors and the neuroendocrine axis in human pregnancy. *Psychosomatic Medicine, 58*, 432–446.

Wadhwa, P. D., Sandman, C. A., Porto, M., Dunkel-Schetter, C., & Garite, T. J. (1993). The association between prenatal stress and infant birth weight and gestational age at birth: A prospective investigation. *American Journal of Obstetrics and Gynecology, 69*, 858–865.

Waitzkin, H. (1985). Information giving in medical care. *Journal of Health and Social Behavior, 26*, 81–101.

Wakefield, A. B., Carlisle, A. G., Hall, A. G., Attree, M. J. (2008). The expectations and experiences of blended learning approaches to patient safety education. *Nurse Education in Practice, 8*, 54–61.

Wakefield, M., Flay, B., Nichter, M., & Giovino, G. (2003). Role of the media in influencing trajectories of youth smoking. *Addiction, 98*, 79–103.

Waldron, I. (1991). Effects of labor force participation on sex differences in mortality and morbidity. In M. Frankenhaeuser, U. Lund-berg, & M. Chesney (Eds.), *Women, work, and health: Stress and opportunities* (pp. 17–38). New York, NY: Plenum Press.

Waldron, I. (1995). Contributions of changing gender differentials in behaviour to changing gender differences in mortality. In D. Sabo & D. Gordon (Eds.), *Men's health and illness: Gender, power and the body*. London, UK: SAGE.

Walfish, S. (2010). Psychological correlates of laparoscopic adjustable gastric band and gastric bypass patients. [Comparative Study]. *Obesity Surgery, 20*(4), 423–425.

Walker, J. S., & Carmody, J. J. (1998). Experimental pain in healthy human subjects: Gender differences in nociception and in response to ibuprofen. *Anesthesia and Analgesia, 86*, 1257–1262.

Wall, P. D. (1989). The dorsal horn. In P.D. Wall & R. Melzack (Eds.), *Textbook of pain* (2nd ed., pp. 102–111). New York, NY: Churchill-Livingstone.

Wallace, L. M., Priestman, S. G., Dunn, J. A., & Priestman, T. J. (1993). The quality of life of early breast cancer patients treated by two different radiotherapy regimens. *Clinical Oncology, 5*, 228–233.

Wallin, P., & Clark, A. L. (1964). Religiosity, sexual gratification, and marital satisfaction in the middle years of marriage. *Social Forces, 42*, 303–309.

Wallston, K. A. (1992). Hocus-pocus, the focus isn't strictly on locus: Rotter's social learning theory modified for health. *Cognitive Therapy and Research. Special Cognitive Perspectives in Health Psychology, 16*, 183–199.

Walsemann, K. M., Goosby, B. J., & Farr, D. (2016). Life course SES and cardiovascular risk: Heterogeneity across race/ethnicity and gender. *Social Science & Medicine, 152*, 147–155. doi:10.1016/j.socscimed.2016.01.038

Walsh, R., & Shapiro, S. L. (2006). The meeting of meditative disciplines and Western psychology: A mutually enriching dialogue. *American Psychologist, 61*, 227–239.

Wamala, S. P., Mittleman, M. A., Horsten, M., Schenck-Gustafsson, K., & Orth-Gomer, K. (2000). Job stress and the occupational gradient in coronary heart disease risk in women. The Stockholm Female Coronary Risk Study. *Social Science and Medicine, 51*, 481–489.

Wan, T. H., & Soifer, S. J. (1974). Determinants of physician utilization: A causal analysis. *Journal of Health and Social Behavior, 15*, 100–108.

Wandner, L., Scipio, C., Hirsh, A., Torres, C., & Robinson, M. (2012). The perception of pain in others: how gender, race, and age influence pain expectations. *Journal of Pain, 13*(3), 220–227.

Wang, D., & Audette, J. F. (2008). Acupuncture in pain management. In J. F. Audette & A. Bailey (Eds.), Integrative pain medicine: The science and practice of complementary and alternative medicine in pain management. *Contemporary pain medicine* (pp. 379–416). Totowa, NJ: Humana Press.

Wang, F. X., Yang, X. L., Ma, Y. S., Wei, Y. J., Yang, M. H., Chen, X., . . . Liu, S. (2017). TRIF contributes to epileptogenesis in temporal lobe epilepsy during TLR4 activation. *Brain, Behavior, and Immunity, 67*, 65–76. doi:10.1016/j.bbi.2017.07.157

Wang, H. X., Leineweber, C., Kirkeeid`e, R., Svane, B., Schenck-Gustafsson, K., Theorell, T., & Orth-Gomér, K. (2007).

Psychosocial stress and atherosclerosis: family and work stress accelerate progression of coronary disease in women. The Stockholm Female Coronary Angiography Study. *Journal of Internal Medicine, 261*, 245–254.

Wang, M. P., Ho, S.Y., Lo, W. S., & Lam, T. H. (2012). Smoking family, secondhand smoke exposure at home, and nicotine addiction among adolescent smokers. *Addictive Behaviors, 37*(60), 743–746. doi:10.1016/j.addbeh.2012.02.016

Wang, M., Lightsey, O. R., Pietruszka, T., Uruk, A. C., & Wells, A. G. (2007). Purpose in life and reasons for living as mediators of the relationship between stress, coping, and suicidal behavior. *Journal of Positive Psychology, 2*, 195–204.

Wang, S., & Lau, A. S. (2015). Mutual and non-mutual social support: Cultural differences in the psychological, behavioral, and biological effects of support seeking. *Journal of Cross-Cultural Psychology, 46*(7), 916–929. doi:10.1177/0022022115592967

Wang, S., Repetti, R., & Campos, B. (2011). Job stress and family social behavior: The moderating role of neuroticism. *Journal of Occupational Health Psychology, 16*(4), 441–456.

Wang, Y., Jackson, T., & Cai, L. (2016). Causal effects of threat and challenge appraisals on coping and pain perception. *European Journal of Pain, 20*(7), 1111–1120. doi:10.1002/ejp.835

Wangberg, S., Andreassen, H., Prokosch, H., Santana, S., Sørensen, T., & Chronaki, C. (2008). Relations between Internet use, socioeconomic status (SES), social support and subjective health. *Health Promotion International, 23*(1), 70–77.

Wankel, L. M., & Berger, B. G. (1990). The psychological and social benefits of sport and physical activity. *Journal of Leisure Research, 22*, 167–182.

Wannamethee, S. G., & Shaper, A. G. (1992). Blood lipids: The relationship with alcohol intake, smoking, and body weight. *Journal of Epidemiology and Community Health, 46*, 197–202.

Wannamethee, S. G., & Shaper, A. G. (1999). Type of alcoholic drink and risk of major coronary heart disease events and all-cause mortality. *American Journal of Public Health, 89*, 685–690.

Wannamethee, S. G., Shaper, A. G., & Alberti, G. M. M. (2000). Physical activity protects against diabetes and heart disease. *Geriatics, 35*, 78.

Wansink, B., & Sobal, J. (2007). Mindless eating: The 200 daily food decisions we overlook. *Environment and Behavior, 39*, 106–123.

Wansink, B., van Ittersum, K., & Painter, J. E. (2006). Ice cream illusions: Bowls, spoons, and self-served portion sizes. *American Journal of Preventive Medicine, 31*, 240–243.

Ward, M. M., Mefford, I. N., Parker, S. D., Chesney, M. A., Taylor, C. B., Keegan, D. L., & Barchas, J. D. (1983). Epinephrine and norepinephrine responses in continuously collected human plasma to a series of stressors. *Psychosomatic Medicine, 45*, 471–86.

Ward, S., Donovan, H., Gunnarsdottir, S., Serlin, R. C., Shapiro, G. R., & Hughes, S. (2008). A randomized trial of a representational intervention to decrease cancer pain (RID-CancerPain). *Health Psychology, 27*, 59–67.

Wardle, J., & Pope, R. (1992). The psychological costs of screening for cancer. *Journal of Psychosomatic Research, 36*, 609–624.

Ware, J. E. Jr., Snow, K. K., Kosinski, M., & Gandek, B. (1993). *SF-36 health survey. Manual and interpretation guide*. Boston, MA: Health Institute, New England Medical Center.

Warren, J., Fernández, M., Harper, G., Hidalgo, M., Jamil, O., Torres, R. (2008). Predictors of unprotected sex among young sexually active African American, Hispanic, and White MSM: The importance of ethnicity and culture. *AIDS and Behavior, 12*(3), 459–468.

Washington, H. A. (2006). *Medical apartheid: The dark history of medical experimentation on black Americans from colonial times to the present*. New York, NY: Harlem Moon.

Wasylkiw, L., & Fekken, G. C. (2002). Personality and self-reported health: Matching predictors and criteria. *Personality and Individual Differences, 33*, 607–620.

Waszczuk, M. A., Li, X., Bromet, E. J., Gonzalez, A., Zvolensky, M. J., Ruggero, C., . . . Kotov, R. (2017). Pathway from PTSD to respiratory health: Longitudinal evidence from a psychosocial intervention. *Health Psychology, 36*(5), 429–437. doi:10.1037/hea0000472

Waters, E., Merrick, S., Treboux, D., Crowell, J., & Albersheim, L. (2000). Attachment security in infancy and early adulthood: A twenty-year longitudinal study. *Child Development, 71*, 684–689.

Watkins-Hayes, C., Pittman-Gay, L., & Beaman, J. (2012). 'Dying from' to 'living with': Framing institutions and the coping processes of African American women living with HIV/AIDS. *Social Science & Medicine, 74*(12), 2028–2036. doi:10.1016/j.socscimed.2012.02.001

Watson, D., & Hubbard, B. (1996). Adaptational style and dispositional structure: Coping in the context of the five-factor model. *Journal of Personality, 64*, 737–774.

Watson, M., & Homewood, J. (2008) Mental adjustment to cancer scale: Psychometric properties in a large cancer cohort. *Psychooncology, 17*(11), 1146–1151. doi:10.1002/pon.1345

Waverijn, G., Heijmans, M., & Groenewegen, P. P. (2017). Neighbourly support of people with chronic illness; Is it related to neighbourhood social capital? *Social Science & Medicine, 173*, 110–117. doi:10.1016/j.socscimed.2016.12.004

Waxler-Morrison, N., Hislop, T. G., Mears, B., & Kan, L. (1991). Effects of social relationships on survival for women with breast cancer: A prospective study. *Social Science & Medicine, 33*, 177–183.

Way, B. M., & Taylor, S. E. (2011). A polymorphism in the serotonin transporter gene moderates cardiovascular reactivity to psychosocial stress. *Psychosomatic Medicine, 73*(4), 310–317. doi:10.1097/PSY.0b013e31821195ed

Way, E. L., & Chen, C. F. (1999). Modern clinical applications related to Chinese traditional theories of drug interactions. *Perspectives in Biology and Medicine, 42*, 512–525.

Weaver, K., Llabre, M., Lechner, S., Penedo, F., & Antoni, M. (2008). Comparing unidimensional and multidimensional models of benefit finding in breast and prostate cancer. *Quality of Life Research, 17*(5), 771–781.

Webb, M. S., & Carey, M. P. (2008). Tobacco smoking among low-income black women: Demographic and psychosocial correlates in a community sample. *Nicotine and Tobacco Research, 10*, 219–229.

Webster, L. R., & Fine, P. G. (2010). Approaches to improve pain relief while minimizing opioid abuse liability. *Journal of Pain, 11*(7), 602–611. doi:10.1016/j.jpain.2010.02.008

Wechler, H., Moeykens, B., Davenport, A., Castillo, S., & Hansen, J. (2000). The adverse impact of heavy episodic drinkers on other college students. *Journal of Studies on Alcohol, 56*, 628–634.

Wechsler, H., Kelley, K., Seibring, M., Kuo, M., & Rigotti, N. A. (2001). College smoking policies and smoking cessation programs: Results of a survey of college health center directors. *Journal of American College Health, 49*, 205–212.

Weeth, A., Mühlberger, A., & Shiban, Y. (2017). Was it less painful for knights? Influence of appearance on pain perception. *European Journal of Pain, 21*(10), 1756–1762. doi:10.1002/ejp.1087

Wei, M., Liao, K., Heppner, P., Chao, R., & Ku, T. (2012). Forbearance coping, identification with heritage culture, acculturative stress, and psychological distress among Chinese international students. *Journal of Counseling Psychology, 59*(1), 97–106.

Weidel, J., Provencio-Vasquez, E., Watson, S., & Gonzalez-Guarda, R. (2008). Cultural considerations for intimate partner violence and HIV risk in Hispanics. *Journal of the Association of Nurses in AIDS Care, 19*(4), 247–251.

Weidner, G., & Kendel, F. (2010). Prevention of coronary heart disease. In J. M. Suls, K. W. Davidson, & R. M. Kaplan (Eds.), *Handbook of health psychology and behavioral medicine* (pp. 354–369). New York, NY: Guilford.

Weihs, K., & Reiss, D. (1996). Family reorganization in response to cancer: A developmental perspective. In L. Baider, C. L. Cooper, & A. Kaplan De-Nour (Eds.), *Cancer and the family* (pp. 3–29). Oxford, UK: John Wiley.

Weinberg, R. A. (2013). *Biology of cancer* (2e). New York, NY: Garland Science.

Weinberger, M., Hiner, S. L., & Tierney, W. M. (1987). In support of hassles as a measure of stress in predicting health outcomes. *Journal of Behavioral Medicine, 10*, 19–31.

Weinhardt, L. S., Carey, M. P., Johnson, B. T., & Bickman, N. L. (1999). Effects of HIV counseling and testing on sexual risk behavior: A meta-analytic review of published research, 1985–1987. *American Journal of Public Health, 89*, 1397–1405.

Weinraub, M., Horvath, D. L., & Gringles, M. B. (2002). Single parenthood. In M. H. Bornstein (Ed.), *Handbook of parenting: Vol. 3: Being and becoming a parent* (2nd ed., pp. 109–140). Mahwah, NJ: Erlbaum.

Weinrich, S., Ellison, G., Weinrich, M., Ross, K. S., & Reis-Starr, C. (2001). Low sun exposure and elevated serum prostate specific antigen in African American and Caucasian men. *American Journal of Health Studies, 17*, 148–156.

Weinstein, N. D. (1993) Testing four competing theories of health-protective behavior. *Healthy Psychology, 12*(4), 324–333.

Weinstein, N. D. (2007). Misleading tests of health behavior theories. *Annals of Behavioral Medicine, 33*, 1–10.

Weinstein, N. D., & Sandman, P. M. (1992). A model of the precaution adoption process: Evidence from home radon testing. *Health Psychology, 11*, 170–180.

Weisman, A. D., & Worden, J. W. (1972). Risk-rescue rating in suicide assessment. *Archives of General Psychiatry, 26*, 553–560.

Welin, L., Larsson, B., Svardsudd, K., Tibblin, B., & Tibblin, G. (1992).Social network and activities in relation to mortality from cardiovascular diseases, cancer and other causes: A 12 year follow up of the study of men born in 1913 and 1923. *Journal of Epidemiology and Community Health, 46*, 127–132.

Welsh, S., Davis, C., & Shaw, A. (1993). *USDA's Food Guide: Background and Development* (Miscellaneous Publication No. 1514). Washington, DC: U.S. Government Publishing Office.

Wendorf, A. R., Brouwer, A. M., & Mosack, K., E. (2014). Stress and culture. In R. A. R. Gurung (Ed.), *Multicultural approaches to health and wellness in America* (pp. 89–114). Santa Barbara, CA: Praeger.

Wendorf, B., & Bellegrade-Smith, P. (2014). Vodou in North America: Healing one person, healing the universe. In R. A. R. Gurung (Ed.), *Multicultural approaches to health and wellness in America* (pp. 309–327). Santa Barbara, CA: Praeger.

Werner, J., Frost, M., Macnee, C. L., McCabe, S., & Rice, V. (2012). Major and minor life stressors, measures, and health outcomes. In V. Rice (Eds.), *Handbook of stress, coping, and health: Implications for nursing research, theory, and practice* (2nd ed.) (pp. 126–154). Thousand Oaks, CA: SAGE.

Werth, J. L., Borges, N. J., McNally, C. J., Maguire, C. P., & Britton, P. J. (2008). The intersections of work, health, diversity, and social justice: Helping people living with HIV disease. *Counseling Psychologist, 36*, 16–41.

West, S. G., & Aiken, L. S. (1997). Towards understanding individual effects in multiple component prevention programs: Design and analysis strategies. In K. Bryant, M. Windle, & S. West (Eds.), *The science of prevention: Methodological advances from alcohol and substance abuse research* (pp. 167–209). Washington, D. C.: American Psychological Association.

Westbrook, M. T., & Viney, L. L. (1983). Age and sex differences in patients' reactions to illness. *Journal of Health and Social Behavior, 24*, 313–324.

Westman, M. (2001). Stress and strain crossover. *Human Relations, 54*, 717–752.

Westman, M., & Etizon, D. (1995). Crossover of stress, strain, and resources from one spouse to another. *Journal of Organizational Behavior, 16*, 169–181.

Westman, M., & Vinokur, A. D. (1998). Unraveling the relationship of distress levels within couples: Common stressors, empathic reactions, or crossover via social interaction? *Human Relations, 51*, 137–156.

Wethington, E. (2000). Expecting stress: Americans and the "midlife crisis." *Motivation and Emotion: Special Integrating Quantitative and Qualitative Approaches, 24*, 85–103.

Wethington, E., McLeod, J. D., & Kessler, R. C. (1987). The importance of life events for explaining sex differences in psychological distress. In R. C. Barnett, L. Biener, & G. K. Baruch (Eds.), *Gender and stress* (pp. 144–156). New York, NY: Free Press.

Wetzler, H. P., Lum, D. L., & Bush, D. M. (2000). Using the SF-36 survey in primary care. In M. E. Maruish (Ed.), *Handbook of psychological assessment in primary care settings* (pp. 583–621). Mahwah, NJ: Erlbaum.

Wheeler, K., Wagaman, A., & McCord, D. (2012). Personality traits as predictors of adherence in adolescents with type I diabetes. *Journal of Child & Adolescent Psychiatric Nursing, 25*(2), 66–74. doi:10.1111/j.1744-6171.2012.00329.x

Whelton, S. P., He, J., Whelton, P. K., & Muntner, P. A. (2004). Meta-analysis of observational studies on fish intake and coronary heart disease. *American Journal of Cardiology, 93*, 1119–1123.

Whitbeck, L. B., McMorris, B. J., Hoyt, D. R., Stubben, J. D., LaFramboise, T. (2002). Perceived discrimination, traditional practices, and depressive symptoms among American Indians in the Upper Midwest. *Journal of Health and Social Behavior, 43*, 400–418.

White, A. R., & Ernst, E. (1999). A systematic review of randomized controlled trials of acupuncture for neck pain. *Rheumatology, 38*, 143–147.

White, P., Bishop, F. L., Prescott, P., Scott, C., Little, P., & Lewith, G. (2012). Practice, practitioner, or placebo? A multifactorial, mixed-methods randomized controlled trial of acupuncture. *Pain, 153*(2), 455–462. doi:10.1016/j.pain.2011.11.007

Whitehead, M. (1992). The concepts and principles of equity and health. *International Journal of Health Services, 22*, 429–45.

Whitehead, P. M. (2016). The runner's high revisited: A phenomenological analysis. *Journal of Phenomenological Psychology, 47*(2), 183–198. doi:10.1163/15691624-12341313

Whiteside, T. L., & Herberman, R. B. (1994). Role of human natural killer cells in health and disease. *Clinical and Diagnostic Laboratory Immunology, 1*, 125–133.

Whitfield, K. E., Weidner, G., Clark, R., & Anderson, N. B. (2002). Sociodemographic diversity and behavioral medicine. *Journal of Consulting and Clinical Psychology, 70*, 463–481.

Whiting, B., & Whiting, J. (1975). *Children of six cultures*. Cambridge, MA: Harvard University Press.

Whittemore, R., & Dixon, J. (2008). Chronic illness: The process of integration. *Journal of Clinical Nursing, 17*, 177–187.

Whitten, P., Holtz, B., Krupinski, E., & Alverson, D. (2010). Challenges of the rural healthcare pilot program broadband initiative. *Telemedicine and e-Health, 16*(3), 370–372. doi:10.1089/tmj.2009.0134.

Whitten, P., Kingsley, C., Cook, D., Swirczynski, D., & Doolittle, G. (2001). School-based telehealth: An empirical analysis of teacher, nurse, and administrator perceptions. *Journal of School Health, 71*, 173–180.

Wicherts, J. M., Veldkamp, C. L. S., Augusteijn, H. E. M., Bakker, M., van Aert, Robbie C. M., & van Assen, Marcel A. L. M. (2016). Degrees of freedom in planning, running, analyzing, and reporting psychological studies: A checklist to avoid p-hacking. *Frontiers in Psychology, 7*, 12.

Wiederhold, M. D., & Wiederhold, B. K. (2007). Virtual reality and interactive simulation for pain distraction. *Pain Medicine, 8*, S182–S188.

Wiggert, N., Wilhelm, F. H., Nakajima, M., & al'Absi, M. (2016). Chronic smoking, trait anxiety, and the physiological response to stress. *Substance use & Misuse, 51*(12), 1619–1628. doi:10.1080/10826084.2016.1191511

Wiggins, J. S., & Trapnell, P. D. (1997). Personality structure: The return of the Big Five. In R. Hogan, J. A. Johnson, & S. Briggs (Eds.), *Handbook of personality psychology* (pp. 737–765). San Diego, CA: Academic Press.

Wight, R., LeBlanc, A., de Vries, B., & Detels, R. (2012). Stress and mental health among midlife and older gay-identified men. *American Journal of Public Health, 102*(3), 503–510.

Wilbert-Lampen, U., Leistner, D., Greven, S., Pohl, T., Sper, S., Völker, C., . . . Steinbeck, G. (2008). Cardiovascular events during World Cup soccer. *New England Journal of Medicine, 358*(5), 475–483.

Wilcox, S., & King, A. (1999). Health behaviors and aging. In W. R. Hazzard, J. P. Blass, W. H. Ettinger, J. B. Halter, & J. G. Ouslander (Eds.), *Principles of geriatric medicine and gerontology* (pp. 287–302). New York, NY: McGraw-Hill.

Wilfley, D., Tibbs, T., Van Buren, D., Reach, K., Walker, M., Epstein, L. (2007). Lifestyle interventions in the treatment of childhood overweight: A meta-analytic review of randomized controlled trials. *Health Psychology, 26*(5), 521–532.

Willett, J. B., & Singer, J. D. (1995). It's déjà vu all over again: Using multiple-spell discrete-time survival analysis. *Journal of Educational and Behavioral Statistics, 20*, 41–67.

Willett, W. C., & Trichopoulos, D. (1996). Nutrition and cancer: A summary of the evidence. *Cancer Causes and Control, 7*, 178–180.

Willi, C., Bodenmann, P., Ghali, W. A., Faris, P. D., & Cornuz, J. (2007). Active smoking and the risk of type 2 diabetes: A systematic review and meta-analysis. *Journal of the American Medical Association, 298*, 2654–2664.

Williams, A., & Manias, E. (2008). A structured literature review of pain assessment and management of patients with chronic kidney disease. *Journal of Clinical Nursing, 17*, 69–81.

Williams, D. A. (2010). Pain and painful syndromes (including rheumatoid arthritis and fibromyalgia). In J. M. Suls, K. W. Davidson, & R. M. Kaplan (Eds.), *Handbook of health psychology and behavioral medicine* (pp. 476–493). New York, NY: Guilford.

Williams, D. R. (1995). The concept of race in health services research: 1966–1990. *Hospital Services Research, 30*, 261–274.

Williams, D. R., & Collins, C. (1995). U.S. socioeconomic and racial differences in health: Patterns and explanations. *Annual Review of Sociology, 21*, 349–377.

Williams, D. R., Haile, R., Neighbors, H., Gonzalez, H. M., Baser, R., & Jackson, J. S. (2007). The mental health of Black Caribbean immigrants: Results from the National Survey of American Life. *American Journal of Public Health, 97*(1), 52–59. doi:10.2105/AJPH.2006.088211

Williams, G. D., Stinson, F. S., Sanchez, L. L., & Dufour, M. C. (1998, December). *Apparent per capita alcohol consumption: National, state, and regional trends, 1977–1996* (NIAAA Surveillance Report No. 47). Washington, DC: U.S. Government Publishing Office.

Williams, L., O'Connor, R. C., Howard, S., Hughes, B. M., Johnston, D. W., Hay, J. L., . . . O'Carroll, R. E. (2008). Type-D personality mechanisms of effect: The role of health-related behavior and social support. *Journal of Psychosomatic Research, 64*, 63–69.

Williams, P. G., Holmbeck, G. N., & Greenley, R. N. (2002). Adolescent health psychology. *Journal of Consulting and Clinical Psychology, 70*, 828–842.

Williams, R. B. (1987). Refining the Type A hypothesis: Emergence of the hostility complex. *The American Journal of Cardiology, 60*, 27J–32J.

Williams, R., Schneiderman, N., Relman, A.S., & Angell, M. (2002). Resolved: Psychosocial interventions can improve clinical outcomes in organic disease-rebuttals and closing arguments. *Psychosomatic Medicine, 64*(4), 564–567.

Williams, S. L., Haskard-Zolnierek, K., & DiMatteo, M. R. (2016). Improving adherence to health regimens. In J. C. Norcross, G. R. VandenBos, D. K. Freedheim, & N. Pole (Eds.), *APA handbook of clinical psychology: Psychopathology and health (vol. 4); APA handbook of clinical psychology: Psychopathology and health* (pp. 551–565). Washington, DC: American Psychological Association. doi.10.1037/14862-026

Williamson, A. A., Fox, B., J., Creswell, P. D., Kuang, X., Ceglarek, S. L., Brower, A. M., & Remington, P. L. (2011). An observational study of the secondary effects of a local smoke-free ordinance. *Preventing Chronic Disease, 8*(4), A83. Retrieved from http://www.cdc.gov/pcd/issues/2011/jul/10_0123.htm

Williamson, D. A., Martin, C. K., Anton, S. D., York-Crowe, E., Han, H., Redman, L., & Ravussin, E. (2008). Is caloric restriction associated with development of eating-disorder symptoms? Results from the CALERIE trial. *Health Psychology, 27*, S32–S42.

Willich, S. N. (1995). Circadian influences and possible triggers of sudden cardiac death. *Sport Science Review, 4*, 31–45.

Wills, T. A., & Ainette, M. G. (2012). Social networks and social support. In A. Baum, T. A. Revenson, & J. Singer (Eds.), *Handbook of health psychology* (2e, pp. 465–492). New York, NY: Taylor & Francis.

Wills, T. A., & Cleary, S. D. (1999). Peer and adolescent substance use among 6th–9th graders: Latent growth analysis of influence versus selection mechanisms. *Health Psychology, 18*, 453–463.

Wills, T. A., Bantam, E. O., & Ainette, M. G. (2016). Social support. In Y. Benyamini, M. Johnston & E. C. Karademas (Eds.), *Assessment in health psychology; assessment in health psychology* (pp. 131–146). Boston, MA: Hogrefe.

Wilson, D. K. (2008). Commentary for health psychology special issue: Theoretical advances in diet and physical activity interventions. *Health Psychology, 27*, S1–S2.

Wilson, R. S., Schneider, J. A., Boyle, P. A., Arnold, S. E., Tang, Y., & Bennett, D. A. (2007). Chronic distress and incidence of mild cognitive impairment. *Neurology, 68*, 2085–2092.

Windich-Biermeier, A., Sjoberg, I., Dale, J. C., Eshelman, D., Guzzetta, C. E. (2007). Effects of distraction on pain, fear, and distress during venous port access and venipuncture in children and adolescents with cancer. *Journal of Pediatric Oncology Nursing, 24*, 8–19.

Wing, R. R., & Phelan, S. (2012). Obesity. In A. Baum, T. A. Revenson, & J. Singer (Eds.), *Handbook of health psychology* (2e, pp. 333–352). New York, NY: Guilford Press.

Wing, R. R., & Polley, B. A. (2002). Obesity. In A. Baum, T. A. Revenson, & J. E. Singer (Eds.), *Handbook of health psychology* (1e, pp. 263–279). Mahwah, NJ: Erlbaum.

Wingood, G., & DiClemente, R. (2008). The ADAPT-ITT model: A novel method of adapting evidence-based HIV Interventions. *Journal of Acquired Immune Deficiency Syndromes (1999), 47*, Suppl 1, S40–6.

Winnicott, D. W. (1965). *The maturational processes and the facilitating environment: Studies in the theory of emotional development.* Oxford, UK: International Universities Press.

Winslow, R. W., Franzini, L. R., & Hwang, J. (1992). Perceived peer norms, casual sex, and AIDS risk prevention. *Journal of Applied Social Psychology, 22*, 1809–1827.

Wirth, T., Ober, K., Prager, G., Vogelsang, M., Benson, S., Witzke, O., & . . . Schedlowski, M. (2011). Repeated recall of learned immunosuppression: Evidence from rats and men. *Brain, Behavior & Immunity, 25*(7), 1444–1451. doi:10.1016/j.bbi.2011.05.011

Wismer, B. A., Moskowitz, J. M., Chen, A. M., Kang, S. H., Novotny, T. E., Min, K., & Tager, I. B. (1998). Mammography and clinical breast examination among Korean American women in two California counties. *Preventive Medicine, 27*, 144–151.

Wisner, B. L., Jones, B., & Gwin, D. (2010). School-based meditation practices for adolescents: A resource for strengthening self-regulation, emotional coping, and self-esteem. *Children & Schools, 32*(3), 150–159. doi:10.1093/cs/32.3.150

Wolf, A. M., Gortmaker, S. L., Cheung, L., Gray, H. M., Herzog, D. B., & Colditz, G. A. (1993) Activity, inactivity, and obesity: Racial, ethnic, and age differences among schoolgirls. *American Journal of Public Health, 83*(11), 1625–1627.

Wolfe, J., & Proctor, S. P. (1996). The Persian Gulf War: New findings on traumatic exposure and stress. *PTSD Research Quarterly, 7*, 1–8.

Wollman, N., Yoder, B. L., Brumbaugh-Smith, J. P., & Haynes, C. (2007). Last decade sees closing poverty gap between minorities and whites, young and old, women and men. Large income gap between poor and rich persists. Retrieved from http://www.manchester.edu/links/ViolenceIndex/NewsReleases/PovertyGap2007.pdf

Womack, V. Y., & Sloan, L. R. (2017). The association of mindfulness and racial socialization messages on approach-oriented coping strategies among African Americans. *Journal of Black Studies, 48*(4), 408–426. doi:10.1177/0021934717696789

Wong, C. C. Y., & Lu, Q. (2017). Match between culture and social support: Acculturation moderates the relationship between social support and well-being of Chinese American breast cancer survivors. *Quality of Life Research, 26*(1), 73–84. doi:10.1007/s11136-016-1362-y

Wong, F. Y., Huang, Z. J., He, N., Smith, B. D., Ding, Y., Fu, C., & Young D. (2008). HIV risks among gay-and non-gay-identified migrant money boys in Shanghai, China. *AIDS Care, 20*(2), 170–180.

Wong, J. Y., Fong, D. Y., Choi, A. W., Tiwari, A., Chan, K. L., & Logan, T. K. (2016). Problem-focused coping mediates the impact of intimate partner violence on mental health among Chinese women. *Psychology of Violence, 6*(2), 313–322. doi:10.1037/a0039496

Wong, M. S., Showell, N. N., Bleich, S. N., Gudzune, K. A., & Chan, K. S. (2017). The association between parent-reported provider communication quality and child obesity status: Variation by parent obesity and child race/ethnicity. *Patient Education and Counseling, 100*(8), 1588–1597. doi:10.1016/j.pec.2017.03.015

Wood, J. V., Taylor, S. E., & Lichtman, R. R. (1985). Social comparison in adjustment to breast cancer. *Journal of Personality and Social Psychology, 49*, 1169–1183.

Wood, M. D., Vinson, D. C., & Sher, K. J. (2002). Alcohol use and misuse. In A. Baum, T. A. Revenson, & J. E. Singer (Eds.), *Handbook of health psychology* (1e, pp. 280–318). Mahwah, NJ: Erlbaum.

Woodward, M., Oliphant, J., Lowe, G., & Tunstall-Pedoe, H. (2003). Contribution of contemporaneous risk factors to social inequality in coronary heart disease and all causes mortality. *Preventive Medicine, 36*, 561–568.

Work Loss Data Institute. (2009). *Official disability guidelines.* Encinitas, CA: Work Loss Data Institute.

World Health Organization (WHO). (1996). WHOQOL-BREF: Introduction, administration, scoring and generic version of the assessment. Author, Geneva, Switzerland. Retrieved from http://www.who.int/mental_health/media/en/76.pdf

World Health Organization (WHO). (2012). Preamble to the Constitution of the World Health Organization as adopted by the International Health Conference, New York, 19 June - 22 July 1946; signed on 22 July 1946 by the representatives of 61 States (Official Records of the World Health Organization, no. 2, p. 100) and entered into force on 7 April 1948. Author, Geneva, Switzerland. Retrieved from http://www.who.int/governance/eb/who_constitution_en.pdf

World Health Organization (WHO). (2018). Physical activity. Author, Geneva, Switzerland. Retrieved from http://www.who.int/about/en/

Wortley, P. M., & Fleming, P. L. (1997). AIDS in women in the United States. *Journal of the American Medical Association, 278*, 911–916.

Wright, C. C., Barlow, J. H., Turner, A. P., & Bancroft, G. V. (2003). Self-management training for people with chronic disease: An exploratory study. *British Journal of Health Psychology, 8*, 456–476.

Wu, D. Y., Munoz, M., Espiritu, B., Zeladita, J., Sanchez, E., Callacna, M . . . Shin, S. (2008). Burden of depression among impoverished HIV-positive women in Peru. *Journal of Acquired Immune Deficiency Syndromes, 48*(4), 500–504. doi:10.1097/QAI.0B013E31817DC3E9

Wu, L., Lin, L., Chen, S., Hsu, S., Loh, C., Wu, C., & Lin, J. (2012). Knowledge and attitudes regarding cervical cancer screening among women with physical disabilities living in the community. *Research in Developmental Disabilities, 33*(2), 376–381. doi:10.1016/j.ridd.2011.08.005

Wu, Y., Wei, Y., Tai, Y., Chen, K., & Li, H. (2012). Clinical outcomes of traditional Chinese medicine compound formula in treating sleep-disordered breathing patients. *American Journal of Chinese Medicine, 40*(1), 11–24.

Wyatt, G. E. (1994). The sociocultural relevance of sex research: Challenges for the 1990s and beyond. *American Psychologist, 49*, 748–754.

Wyatt, G. E., Myers, H. F, Williams, J. K., Kitchen, C. R., Loeb, T., Carmona, J. V., . . . Presley, N. (2002). Does history of trauma contribute to HIV risk for women of color? Implications for prevention and policy. *American Journal of Public Health, 92*, 660–666.

Wyllie, A. H. (1980). Glucocorticoid-induced thymocyte apoptosis is associated with endogenous endonuclease activation. *Nature, 284*, 555–556.

Wynder, E. L., Cohen, L. A., Muscat, J. E., Winters, B., Dwyer, J. T., & Blackburn, G. (1997). Breast cancer: Weighing the evidence for a promoting role of dietary fat. *Journal of the National Cancer Institute, 89*, 766–775.

Wyper, M. A. (1990). Breast self-examination and the Health Belief Model: Variations on a theme. *Research in Nursing and Health, 13*, 421–428.

Xia, W., Mørch, C. D., Matre, D., & Andersen, O. K. (2017). Exploration of conditioned pain modulation effect on long-term potentiation-like pain amplification in humans. *European Journal of Pain, 21*(4), 645–657. doi:10.1002/ejp.968

Xiaoxing, Z. H., & Baker, D. W. (2007). Differences in leisure-time, household, and work-related physical activity by race, ethnicity, and education. *Journal of General Internal Medicine, 20*, 259–266.

Xu, B., Stokes, M., & Meredith, I. (2016). Fundamentals of cardiology for the non-cardiologist. In M. E. Alvarenga & D. Byrne, *Handbook of psychocardiology* (pp. 21–44). New York, NY: Springer.

Xu, Y. (2007). Adaptation strategies of Asian nurses working in Western countries. *Home Health Care Management & Practice, 19*, 146–148.

Yahav, R., & Cohen, M. (2008). Evaluation of a cognitive-behavioral intervention for adolescents. *International Journal of Stress Management, 15*, 173–188.

Yali, A. M., & Revenson, T. A. (2004). How changes in population demographics will impact health psychology: Incorporating a broader notion of cultural competence into the field. *Health Psychology, 23*, 147–155.

Yamada, Y., Ichihara, S., & Nishida, T. (2008). Molecular genetics of myocardial infarction. *Genomic Medicine, 2*(1–2), 7–22.

Yanez, B. R., Stanton, A. L., Hoyt, M. A., Tennen, H., & Lechner, S. (2011). Understanding perceptions of benefit following adversity: How do distinct assessments of growth relate to coping and adjustment to stressful events? *Journal of Social & Clinical Psychology, 30*(7), 699–721. doi:10.1521/jscp.2011.30.7.699

Yang, H., Brothers, B., & Andersen, B. (2008). Stress and quality of life in breast cancer recurrence: Moderation or mediation of coping? *Annals of Behavioral Medicine, 35*(2), 188–197.

Yang, L., Wellman, L., Ambrozewicz, M., & Sanford, L. (2011). Effects of stressor predictability and controllability on sleep, temperature, and fear behavior in mice. *Sleep, 34*(6), 759–771.

Yang, Y., Thai, S., & Choi, J. (2016). An evaluation of quality of life among cambodian adults living with HIV/AIDS and using antiretroviral therapy: A short report. *AIDS Care, 28*(12), 1546–1550. doi:10.1080/09540121.2016.1192100

Yao, L., & Robert, S. A. (2011). Examining the racial crossover in mortality between African American and White older adults: A multilevel survival analysis of race, individual socioeconomic status, and neighborhood socioeconomic context. *Journal of Aging Research*, Article ID 132073. doi:10.4061/2011/132073

Yardley, L., Bradbury, K., Nadarzynski, & Hunter, C. (2019). Digital health psychology. In T. A. Revenson & R. A. R. Gurung (Eds.). *Handbook of health psychology* (3e). New York, NY: Routledge.

Yeager, K. K., Anda, R. F., Macera, C. A., Donehoo, R. S., & Eaker, E. D. (1995). Sedentary lifestyle and state variation in coronary heart disease. *Public Health Reports, 110*, 100–102.

Yeh, C. J., Inman, A. C., Kim, A. B., & Okubo, Y. (2006). Asian American families' collectivistic coping strategies in response to 9/11. *Cultural Diversity & Ethnic Minority Psychology, 12*, 134–148. doi:10.1037/1099-9809.12.1.134

Yeoman, P. D., & Forman, E. M. (2009). Cultural factors in traumatic stress. In S. Eshun & R. A. R. Gurung (Eds.), *Sociocultural issues in mental health.* Malden, MA: Wiley-Blackwell.

Yi, H., Stinson, F. S., Williams, G. D., & Bertolucci, D. (1998, December). *Trends in alcohol-related fatal traffic crashes, United States: 1975–1996* (Surveillance Report No. 46, National Institute on Alcohol Abuse and Alcoholism). Washington, DC: U.S. Department of Health and Human Services.

Yi, J. K. (1994). Breast cancer screening practices by Vietnamese women. *Journal of Women's Health, 3*, 205–213.

Yi, K. (1998). Diet, lifestyle, and colorectal cancer: Is hyperinsulinemia the missing link? *Nutritional Review, 56*, 275–279.

Ying, Y. W. (1995). Cultural orientation and psychological well-being in Chinese Americans. *American Journal of Community Psychology, 23*, 893–911.

Yoon, E., Adams, K., Clawson, A., Chang, H., Surya, S., & Jérémie-Brink, G. (2017). East Asian adolescents' ethnic identity development and cultural integration: A qualitative investigation. *Journal of Counseling Psychology, 64*(1), 65–79. doi:10.1037/cou0000181

Yost, K. J., Bauer, M. C., Buki, L. P., Austin-Garrison, M., Garcia, L. V., Hughes, C. A., & Patten, C. A. (2017). Adapting a cancer literacy measure for use among Navajo women. *Journal of Transcultural Nursing, 28*(3), 278–285. doi:10.1177/1043659616628964

Young, A. J., & Lowe, G. M. (2001). Antioxidant and prooxidant properties of carotenoids. *Archives of Biochemistry and Biophysiology, 385*, 20–27.

Young, D., & Limbers, C. A. (2017). Avoidant coping moderates the relationship between stress and depressive emotional eating in adolescents. *Eating and Weight Disorders, 22*(4), 683–691. doi:10.1007/s40519-017-0396-7

Yrondi, A., Sporer, M., Péran, P., Schmitt, L., Arbus, C., & Sauvaget, A. (2017). Electroconvulsive therapy, depression, the immune system and inflammation: A systematic review. *Brain Stimulation, 11*(1), 29–51. doi:10.1016/j.brs.2017.10.013

Yuh, J., Neiderhiser, J. M., Spotts, E. L., Pedersen, N. L. Lichtenstein, P., Hansson, K., . . . Reiss, D. (2008). The role of temperament and social support in depressive symptoms: A twin study of mid-aged women. *Journal of Affective Disorders, 106*, 99–105.

Zafar, A., Belard, J. L., Gilani, S., Murad, F., Khan, M., & Merrell, R. C. (2008). The impact of curriculum on a national telehealth program. *Telemedicine Journal and e-Health, 14*(2), 195–198. doi:10.1089/tmj.2007.0029.

Zagorsky, J. L., & Smith, P. K. (2011). The freshman 15: A critical time for obesity intervention or media myth? *Social Science Quarterly* (Blackwell), *92*(5), 1389–1407. doi:10.1111/j.1540-6237.2011.00823.x

Zak, P. J., Kurzban, R., & Matzner, W. T. (2005). Oxytocin is associated with human trustworthiness. *Hormones and Behavior, 48*(5), 522–527. doi:10.1016/j.yhbeh.2005.07.009

Zakowski, S. G., Ramati, A., Morton, C., Johnson, P., & Flanigan, R. (2004). Written emotional disclosure buffers the effects of social constraints on distress among cancer patients. *Health Psychology, 23*, 555–563.

Zampollo, F., Kniffin, K., Wansink, B., & Shimizu, M. (2012). Food plating preferences of children: The importance of presentation on desire for diversity. *Acta Paediatrica, 101*(1), 61–66. doi:10.1111/j.1651-2227.2011.02409.x

Zampollo, F., Wansink, B., Kniffin, K. M., Shimizu, M., & Omori, A. (2012). Looks good enough to eat: How food plating preferences differ across cultures and continents. *Cross-Cultural Research, 46*(1), 31–49. doi:10.1177/1069397111418428

Zaza, C., Sellick, S. M., Willian, A., Reyno, L., & Browman, G. P. (1999). Health care professionals' familiarity with non-pharmacological strategies for managing cancer pain. *Psycho-Oncology, 8*, 99–111.

Zeidner, M., & Hammer, A. L. (1992). Coping with missile attack: Resources, strategies, and outcomes. *Journal of Personality, 60*, 709–746.

Zeidner, M., Matthews, G., & Shemesh, D. O. (2016). Cognitive-social sources of wellbeing: Differentiating the roles of coping style, social support and emotional intelligence. *Journal of Happiness Studies, 17*(6), 2481–2501. doi:10.1007/s10902-015-9703-z

Zhang, H., Liang, M. J., & Ye, H. L. (1995). Clinical study on the effects of Bu Yang Huan Wu decoction on coronary heart disease. *Chinese Journal of Integrated Traditional and Western Medicine, 15*, 213–215.

Zhang, Q., Huang, W., Lv, X., & Yang, Y. (2011). The association of ghrelin polymorphisms with coronary artery disease and ischemic chronic heart failure in an elderly Chinese population. *Clinical Biochemistry, 44*(5/6), 386–390. doi:10.1016/j.clinbiochem.2010.12.013

Zhao, G., Ford, E., Li, C., & Mokdad, A. (2008). Are United States adults with coronary heart disease meeting physical activity recommendations? *American Journal of Cardiology, 101*(5), 557–561.

Zhou, E., Bakker, J. P., & Johnson, D. A. (2019). Sleep. In T. A. Revenson & R. A. R. Gurung (Eds.), *Handbook of health psychology* (3e). New York, NY: Routledge.

Zhou, H., Peng, J., Wang, D., Kou, L., Chen, F., Ye, M., . . . Liao, S. (2017). Mediating effect of coping styles on the association between psychological capital and psychological distress among Chinese nurses: A cross-sectional study. *Journal of Psychiatric and Mental Health Nursing, 24*(2–3), 114–122. doi:10.1111/jpm.12350

Zhou, Z. H., Hu, Y. H., & Pi, D. H. (1991). Clinical and experimental observations of treatment of peptic ulcer with Wie Yan An (easing peptic ulcer) capsule. *Journal of Traditional Chinese Medicine, 2*, 34–39.

Zhu, L., Pickle, L. W., Ghosh, K., Naishadham, D., Portier, K., Chen, H., & . . . Jemal, A. (2012). Predicting U.S.- and state-level cancer counts for the current calendar year. *Cancer (0008543X), 118*(4), 1100–1109. doi:10.1002/cncr.27405

Zimmer, M. H., & Zimmer, M. (1998). Socioeconomic determinants of smoking behavior during pregnancy. *Social Science Journal, 35*, 133–142.

Zimmerman, R. S., & Kirschbaum, A. L. (2017). News of biomedical advances in HIV: Relationship to treatment optimism and expected risk behavior in U.S. MSM. *AIDS and Behavior, 22*(2), 367–378. doi:10.1007/s10461-017-1744-3

Zissimopoulos, J. M., Barthold, D., Brinton, R. D., & Joyce, G. (2017). Sex and race differences in the association between statin use and the incidence of Alzheimer disease. *JAMA Neurology, 74*(2), 225–232. doi:10.1001/jamaneurol.2016.3783

Zoccola, P., Woody, A., & Bryant, A. M. (2019). Health neuroscience. In T. A. Revenson & R. A. R. Gurung (Eds.), *Handbook of health psychology* (3e). New York, NY: Routledge.

Zola, I. K. (1964). Illness behavior of the working class: Implications and recommendations. In A. Shostak & W. Gomberg (Eds.), *Blue collar world: Study of the American worker* (pp. 350–362). Englewood Cliffs, NJ: Prentice Hall.

Zozulya, A. A., Gabaeva, M.V., Sokolov, O. Y., Surkina, I. D., & Kost, N. V. (2008). Personality, coping style, and constitutional neuroimmunology. *Journal of Immunotoxicology, 5*, 221–225.

Zucker, A. (2007). Ethical and legal issues and end-of-life decision making. In D. Balk, C. Wogrin, G. Thornton, D. Meagher (Eds.), *Handbook of thanatology: The essential body of knowledge for the student of death, dying, and bereavement* (pp. 103–112). Northbrook, IL: Association for Death Education and Counseling.

Zuniga, M. E. (1992). Families with Latino roots. In E. W. Lynch & M. J. Hanson (Eds.), *Developing cross-cultural competence: A guide for working with young children and their families* (pp. 151–179). Baltimore, MD: Paul H. Brookes.

NAME INDEX

SUBJECT INDEX